THE BIBLE IN ENGLISH

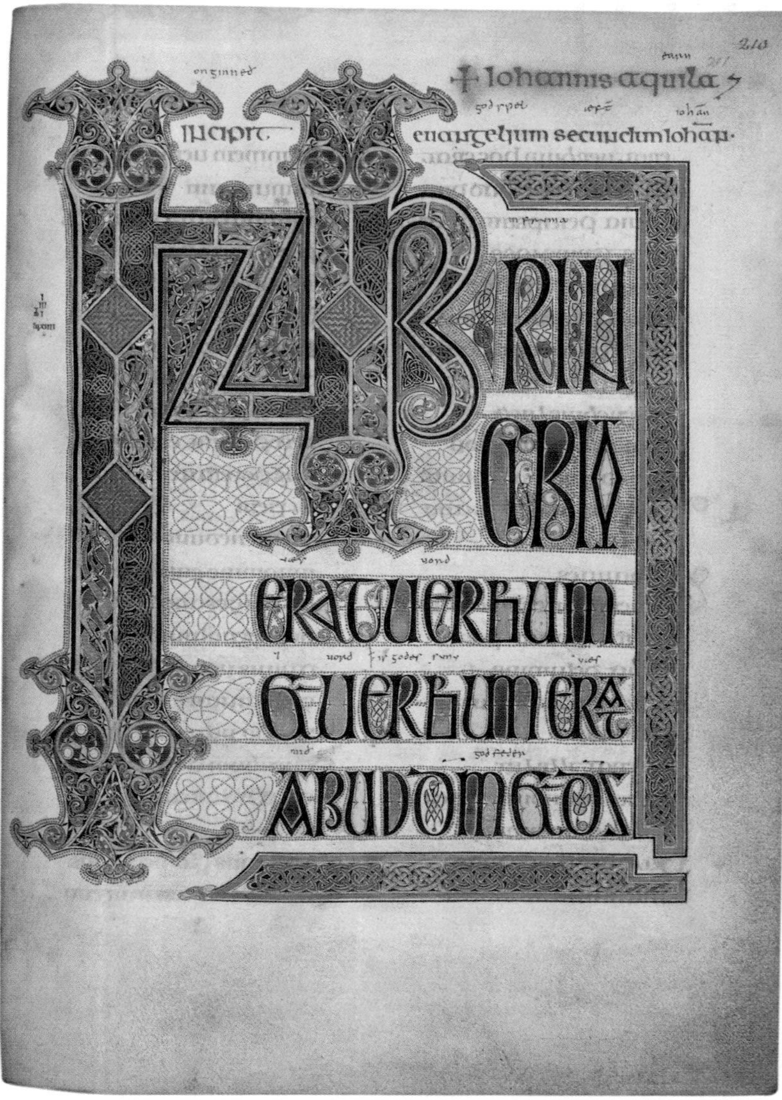
Iohannis aquila
incipit
evangelium secundum iohan

THE BIBLE IN ENGLISH

ITS HISTORY AND INFLUENCE

David Daniell

Yale University Press
New Haven & London

Designed by Gillian Malpass

Printed and bound in the USA

Library of Congress Cataloging-in-Publication Data

Daniell, David.
The Bible in English / by David Daniell.
p.   cm.
Includes bibliographical references and index.
ISBN 0-300-09930-4 (alk. paper)
1. Bible. English—Versions—History.   I. Title.
BS455 .D27 2003
220.5′2′009—dc21

2002153177

A catalogue record for this book is available from
The British Library

Frontispiece
An opening of the Lindisfarne Gospels, made in AD 698 or soon after,
showing the first verses of St John's Gospel in Latin,
and the interlinear handwritten gloss in Old English
made by Aldred between AD 946 and 968, which is the earliest
surviving translation of the Gospels into any form of the English language.
(MS BL Cotton Nero D. iv; reproduced by permission of the British Library).

To the memory of William Tyndale, ?1494–1536,
translator of genius, martyred for giving English readers
the Bible from the original languages.

Contents

Acknowledgements

CORNELIUS NARY WAS A LEARNED Paris-trained Roman Catholic priest in Dublin who in 1719 courageously attacked the Rheims Catholic New Testament of 1582 for being linguistically over a hundred years out of date, and too bulky and expensive for his parishioners. In that year, he published a new translation of his own, in a handy octavo, the first new English version ever to be made in Ireland. It had a remarkable Preface. Here is the second paragraph.

> I am not insensible of my insufficiency for so great an undertaking, nor of the many censures and reprehensions to which my weakness shall render my work obnoxious. I have always before my eyes the answer which the learned Genebrard made to Henry III of France, who being desirous to have a good French translation of the Bible, asked Genebrard, how much time would the finishing of such a work take up, and what would be the expense thereof? This great man, who had thoroughly understood the matter, and was very well apprized of the difficulty of such an undertaking, answered. That it would take up to thirty years, that there should be thirty divines well read in the oriental languages employed in the work, that no less than two hundred thousand crowns would defray the charges, and that after all he would not promise his Majesty that the work should be free from all manner of imperfections.

The enterprise is a different one, but the content of this book has been in my mind for a long time, though I have been far from doing nothing else. Excellent help has been given me, though not from thirty divines well read in the oriental languages. From several institutions I have received generous support, but, sadly, the two hundred thousand crowns failed to arrive. I have, however, very special sympathy with the good doctor's first sentence and last words. The imperfections in this book are my own. They would be almost infinitely greater had I not received so much help. It is a privilege to acknowledge here first of all my thanks to the Leverhulme Trust for a two-year Emeritus Fellowship, without which most of the research assistance would have been impossible. I thank also the British Academy for a small Humanities grant. I am grateful to the President and Fellows of Magdalen College, Oxford, for awarding me a Visiting Fellowship and for permission to reproduce in chapters 14, 18 and 20 material from my Waynflete Lectures, delivered in Trinity Term, 1996, and also to the Fellows' Librarian at Magdalen and her staff. To the Principal and Fellows of Hertford College, Oxford, and to the Master and Fellows of St Catherine's College, Oxford, I express my appreciation of the honour of being elected to life-time Honorary Fellowships there. To the Chairman and Governors of the Henry E. Huntingdon Library, San Marino, California, I am most grateful for the award of the Mayers Fellowship for March 1998.

To ten people I owe thanks for special assistance with research: Christopher Daniell, Lucy Davies, Meraud Grant Ferguson, Liana Lupas, Juliette Marsh, Ruth Mayers, Greg Patton, Gillian Stickings, James Stickings and Victoria Thompson: their dedication, sometimes over a long period, and the quality of their resulting work, were, as well of great value, an inspiration. Errors and infelicities that remain are mine.

I acknowledge help given by David Alexander, Peter Auksi, Michael Billington, Ruth Bottigheimer, Joan Bridgman, Tom Buhler, Mary Clow, W. R. Cooper, Hilary Day, Martin Holt Dotterweich, Richard Duerden, Susan Felch, Jonathan Finch, John Goldfinch, Paul Gutjahr, Andrew Hadfield, Ralph Hanna, Marylin Hollinshead, Andrew Hope, Robert Ireland, Gordon Jackson, Kate Jones, John King, Guido Latre, Simon McKeown, Jeanette Mitterhofer, Anne O'Donnell, Michael Parsons, Andrew Pettegree, Anne Richardson, Michel Roquebert, Alec Ryrie, Herbert Samworth, Michael Schmidt, A. J. Slavin, Michael Smythe, Steve Sohmer, Carsten Peter Thiede, Peter Thuesen, Grace Tiffany, Nicholas Watson, Ralph Werrell and Michael Wood. For particular help in San Marino and Pasadena I am grateful to Alan Jutzi, Tom Lange and David Zeidberg. Joe Johnson and his family in Paxton, Florida, held up my arms (as in Exodus 17:12) at a crucial stage.

I owe special thanks to the Trustees, officers and members of the Tyndale Society for their special support and forbearance while their chairman so obviously had his mind elsewhere. For skilled help with matters of computing I thank Andrew Daniell, Christopher Daniell and Deborah Pollard. For excellent typing I am grateful to Elizabeth Noone.

Parts of this book were given in earlier forms as the Hertford Tyndale Lecture, University of Oxford; the A. G. Dickens Lecture, Robinson College, Cambridge; the Beatrice Ward Lecture, London; the Lambeth Tyndale Lecture, Lambeth Palace; the Staley lectures at William Tyndale College, Michigan; the Forum Lecture at Brigham Young University, Utah;

the Hertford Lecture at Hartford University, Connecticut; at conferences at the Catholic University of America, the Huntington Library, the Károli Gáspár Reformed University and Pázmany Péter University, Budapest and Piliscsaba, Hungary; the International Tyndale Conferences at Oxford, Geneva and San Diego; the International Shakespeare Conference 2000, Stratford-upon-Avon; the annual lecture of the Dissenting Deputies; the Christadelphian Fellowship, Bristol; the British Library; and as lectures at University College, London, the University of St Andrews, Peterborough, Wells and Gloucester Cathedrals, the University of Mainz, the Catholic University of Leuven, Roehampton Institute, the University of Bristol, the University of Kent at Canterbury, the Theological Society, Nottingham, the Literary and Philosophical Society, Leicester, the British Council, Brussels, the University of California at Los Angeles and Tyndale College, Toronto.

I owe special thanks to the unfailing skills and help of the librarians of the British Library, the Bodleian Library, the London Library, Lambeth Palace Library, Dr Williams's Library, the Bible Society (Cambridge), the American Bible Society (New York), the Huntington Library, and the Humanities Library of California Institute of Technology.

Out of all the books on which I have relied, I make here special mention of four. The first two are the essential tools in the craft of writing English Bible history: T. H. Darlow and H. F. Moule, whose two-volume (four-book) catalogue of 1903–11 was revised and expanded by A. S. Herbert as *Historical Catalogue of the Printed Editions of the English Bible, 1525–1961* (1968); and Margaret T. Hills, *The English Bible in America [. . .] 1777–1957* (New York, 1962). I am among many who have valued David Norton's breadth of knowledge, wisdom of judgement and generosity of spirit, and therefore single out his *History of the Bible as Literature*, in both its two-volume (Cambridge, 1993) and condensed one-volume (2000) versions. I also join many people who are firmly kept on the right lines with dates and discernments in *A Traveller's History of England* (Adlestrop, 1991, rev. 1996) by my elder son, Christopher Daniell, who has for that, as for much else, my special gratitude.

Ruth Thackeray copy-edited the text and Meg Davies compiled the index. It has been, as always, a privilege to work with my editor, Gillian Malpass at Yale University Press. She has my special, and warmest, appreciation.

My greatest debt is to my family. For the patience, understanding, love and support of my wife Dorothy and our sons Chris and Andy, over a long time, I can only express here a fraction of my thanks.

Preface

This book is about how important the Bible in English has been in the life of Britain and North America.

To many people, thoughtful and thoughtless alike, that is something that hardly needs saying. 'Everyone knows' that 'the world's bestseller' has been significant. As attention is directed elsewhere, however, into overwhelming immediacies of ephemera, what 'everyone knows' slips the mind. The English Bible has tended to disappear. Of course that is not true for hundreds of thousands of believing Christians, for some of whom a Bible in English is a part of daily life. But for well over a billion English speakers in the second Christian millennium, when the global English language is as alive as it has ever been, the Bible, if known of at all, is no more than a distant oddity. Even among the culturally knowing, like teachers of western history, awareness of the content of the Bible seems to have vanished altogether – often from ignorance, but sometimes from hostility. The aim of this book is to begin in a small way to put English Bibles back into the picture, and challenge some assumptions.

LARGE NUMBERS

English is the most translated-into language in the world. It is, for example, Homer's second language; while there have been little more than a dozen translations of the *Iliad* and *Odyssey* into French, English has had several hundred. So it is with the Bible, only many, many times more. Since Tyndale's first printed Bible translations into English from the original languages of Greek and Hebrew, in the 1520s and 1530s, there have been published in English over 350 new translations of the complete Bible, and some thousands including new translations of the New Testament alone, and some separate books like the Psalms. It is part of the point of this book to comment on the chief of these.

Trying to put the English Bible back into discussions of events and experiences in British and American history where it was important is an activity of some variety. For Wyclif's time in the 1380s and after, as from

Tyndale's in the 1520s, we need to be thinking of sheer numbers: more Wycliffite Bible manuscripts, about 230, have survived than of any other kind in English – the nearest rival is Chaucer with over sixty – and that survival was in spite of 130 years of the most long-lasting repression ever seen in the life of Britain, that beginning with the Act of 1401, *De heretico comburendo* (that heretics should be burned), but made fully effective by Arundel's Constitutions in 1409, still in force in the 1530s. In the English Reformation, hundreds of thousands of printed Bibles were bought: during the reign of Elizabeth, in a population of under six million, easily half a million copies; and before 1640 a clear million.[1]

CONTEXTS

In a different cultural procedure, room must be found for the English Bible in considering English writing. Scholars of the great Elizabethan and Jacobean literature have been happy to find many modern matters of state and power adumbrated there, and to rejoice in the extraordinary depth of reading and thought shown by Spenser, Shakespeare, Donne or Jonson. That a lot of this was directly biblical in origin, indeed could hardly be otherwise, is now regarded as a matter for the briefest footnote, if that. The pious work, begun in Victoria's reign, of locating Shakespearean words and phrases in their biblical sources is now, surely, complete.[2] But to stand and suggest to a young Shakespeare scholar that a detailed knowledge of the New Testament is an essential companion to Shakespearean study is to find one's hearer looking across the room for someone more interesting.

Again, the English Bible was involved in – indeed, made – public affairs. It came to many in the mid-1990s as a surprise that ideas put about in the English Civil War came not so much from the struggles for power by a few driven men, or from economics, but from the Bible: not just from a specific English Bible, the Geneva Version, but from its even more specific marginal notes.[3] That its rival, the originally much-disliked 1611 'Authorised Version', the King James Version (KJV), by then known in extraordinary detail, was after 1660 an instrument of government control, and foremost in the consciousness of Royalists and Parliamentarians alike, even if not – as it so often was – explicitly quoted, has now to be restated.

LIGHTING

Some of the work in this book has to be the switching-off of special lighting, to reveal an illusion for what it is. The sudden elevation of that

1611 'AV' (KJV) to near-divine status in 1769, and, for many people, for ever after, so that 'Avolatry' went hand in hand with the mindless adoration of Shakespeare ('Bardolatry') for two hundred years and more, is a strange phenomenon, especially as it went with the radical alteration of both texts. Stranger still is a twentieth-century insistence in large parts of the United States of America that this version, imagined to be the personal work of King James the First, and known often as the 'Saint James Version', is the 'inerrant Word of God', unchallengeable even to its merest dot and comma.

In the later twentieth-century work of translating the Bible into English from Greek and Hebrew, mundane lighting became the fashion. From the 1980s, the trend to issue the English Bible in 'the language we use today' went a long way further into reducing the Bible's magnificence, and magnificent variety, to a uniform dreariness.

MYTHS

Not long ago, in a room in the Metropolitan Museum of Art in New York, I found myself in front of a Raphael *Madonna and Child*, and by chance alongside a group of older teenagers. Their scholarly instructor pointed out the painting's strong perspective, and that it is led into by, on the left, St Peter, 'who, as you see, has keys on his belt, because he was the first pope', and on the right, St Paul, 'who has a sword on his belt, because he had been a soldier'. Both statements are plain wrong. Even defenders of the popes agree that St Peter was not the first.[4] St Paul was never a soldier: he has a sword because he is, prominently, holding the open Scriptures, 'the sword of the Spirit'. Jesus told Peter that he would give him 'the keys of the kingdom of heaven' because of his statement of faith (Matthew 16:19), with no mention of popes. Paul included in 'the whole armour of God [. . .] the sword of the Spirit, which is the word of God' (Ephesians 6:13–17). What Raphael's picture tells the observer was, in that recent moment, twisted into one-line 'facts' which simply wiped out both faith and the Bible.

DISPROPORTIONATE ATTENTION

An odd partitioning must be revealed. From the 1970s, serious writers have shown a marked 'Bible-blindness', even while the new theorising about everything biblical was energising high intellectual excitements. One more specific blindness, or at least astigmatism, needs comment. Where the Bible *is* in our contemporary picture, when critics and commentators are dealing with historical effects or theories of literature, the New Testament does not receive the attention it should. To take a clear example: a milestone in the intellectual revivification of the Bible and its books was the publication in 1987 of *The Literary Guide to the Bible* edited by Robert Alter and Frank Kermode. This drew together nearly twenty years of new interpretative work, and it was illuminating for many academics and common readers. These large pages, 666 in total (perhaps a coincidence to the famous number in Revelation 13:18), devote attention to all the books of the Bible, with introductions to each Testament, and seven general essays at the end. The Old Testament occupies 375 pages, the New Testament 170, with a mere twenty-four pages given to all Paul's epistles, the same number as to 1 and 2 Samuel. The impression given, which may well be accurate for the late twentieth century, is that for the editors of that book, Hebrew narrative is more interesting and important than the bedrock of Christian theology. Five of the seven general essays are strongly Hebrew in interest. True, there are, in the Western Christian Bible, thirty-nine books in the Old Testament as against only twenty-seven in the New. True again, the New Testament absorbed much of the Old: the presence of the Old Testament in the New is not mere literary effect – theologically the Jewish Scriptures are vital both to Jesus and to Paul. True yet again, all the essays are stimulating. For a very serious book for use in largely, and officially, Christian societies, however, and in countries whose histories are overwhelmingly Christian, in which over many centuries the Christian writings of Paul have had greatest effect, the proportions feel wrong. One notices this effect elsewhere: in David Lyle Jeffrey's big *Dictionary of Biblical Tradition in English Literature* (1992)[5] the work of Jewish scholars on the Old Testament far outweighs that of Christians on the New Testament, quite disproportionately for the literature considered. Why is this? There has not been so much less recent Christian intellectual activity.

By chance or Providence, it happens that the present writer's stronger interest is in the New Testament. A lifetime with the Greek New Testament, a study begun as a schoolboy under the encouragement of my father, will be seen to have made its mark. When undergraduate Hebrew (as an extra, voluntary, subject) had slipped away almost to nothing, there was surely the hand of Providence during vital years in the writing of this book in the presence for me of an unmatchable guide into Hebrew matters, the late (and still greatly lamented) Dr Michael Weitzman, to whose brilliance, clarity, energy, generosity with time and knowledge, and above all, friendship, I here pay tribute.

'KJV'

I gave time to considering what name to use for the great 1611 English Bible. To give it its older name, 'Authorised Version', or 'AV', would have had two disadvantages: first, it was the name hallowed across the British Empire – but that version has had its greatest influence outside that part of world history, particularly in North America. Secondly, as a title it is simply not true – the 'Authorised Version' was never authorised. The 'King James Bible', or 'King James Version', 'KJB' or 'KJV', or simply 'King James', are customary in North America, though they still feel strange to older British Christians. Again, the words are simply not true, as King James's involvement was little more than receiving the sugary dedication to him.

One solution would have been simply to call it 'the 1611': but that would have reduced the world's most important written text to the form of an entry in a railway timetable. Wishing that there were some other title, like 'Miles Smith's Version' (he was the modest, clever, academically skilful general editor, and a fine English stylist), I settled for 'KJV' as being most widely understood.

PURITANS – WHO TAUGHT THE ENJOYMENT OF SEX

I have tried to avoid using the weasel word 'puritan'. It was adopted in the 1570s by Roman Catholic writers as a vaguely insulting term for their reforming enemies, and gained prominence in the literary controversies of the 1580s and after.[6] It was first used by 'Puritans' about themselves in 1605.[7] It has since then carried the most awkward freight. Thomas Fuller in 1655 wanted to banish it because of its imprecision.[8] For one thing, from the beginning, the word was loose enough to mean different things. For another, it must always be pointed out that in general usage the word 'Puritan' means something different on either side of the Atlantic, a difference that is confusingly invisible. In common speech in America, the 'Puritans' are largely historical, reverentially held as Founding Fathers, views of their emotional rigidity being drawn from high-school reading of *The Scarlet Letter*. In Britain their distinction is more usually theological. One meaning, can, however, surely be found to be constant: it has been a truth universally acknowledged that the Christian God's strong disapproval of pleasure of any kind, and especially sexual pleasure, even within marriage, is a doctrine that came from 'the Puritans'. Thus the philosopher A. C. Grayling wrote:

It was in particular Christian Puritanism after the Reformation that added the final touch to western attitudes to sex. Puritanism regards sex as an evil attendant on the expulsion from Eden. At its extreme, it teaches that husbands and wives sin if they enjoy their conjugal duty to reproduce. The generalisation of this miasma of prudery spread in Europe from the 17th century until its apogee in the 19th.[9]

Evidence is not given in support of these remarks, made in spite of the fact that it has been the teaching of the Roman Catholic Church that God's highest calling for a man or woman was to be celibate – more, to be separated from the life of the world, especially sexual life, as a monk or nun. What undoubtedly has, however, large evidence is the mainstream Puritan understanding which taught exactly the opposite.

> The Puritan's rejection of the monastic life, of celibacy as a require-ment for ministerial office, and of the notion that marriage was a lower form of spiritual life than the life of the voluntary virgin who devoted him- or herself to God – all of this meant that the Puritans, in a very central area of life, upheld a life-affirming, life-accepting attitude: within the confines of the marriage bed, sexuality and sexual pleasure were not only permitted, but seen as good things. Sex was not simply for pro-creation or to avoid fornication but was good in itself to the degree that it gave pleasure and comfort to both husband and wife.[10]

This pleasure is strongly visible in the writings of, for example, Daniel Rogers (1642); Thomas Gataker (1620, who quotes Proverbs 5:15, 18–19, ending 'let her breasts satisfy thee at all times, and delight in her love continually' (Geneva); and Richard Baxter (1678, exhorting 'Keep up your Conjugal Love in a constant heat and vigour').[11] The Puritans 'called for an emotional intimacy between men and women and a physical intimacy which required erotic delight on both sides'.[12]

Sexuality was celebrated not only in mainstream Puritan teaching. A glance at the writings of opponents shows what disturbing fantasies a perceived 'licence' could cause. Now, to try to construct a picture of 'Puritanism' from the satirical publications of its enemies is like trying to study Soviet missile strength in the 1950s using only information supplied by the Pentagon. Nevertheless, Kristen Poole's deductions from studies of pamphlets, sermons, poetry and plays show 'Puritans' as examples of 'cor-poreal transgressions (such as over-eating, drunkenness, promiscuous sexual behavior, and nakedness)'.[13] Much-publicised satirical attacks were made on radical sects that were minute in numbers, their invisibility leaving room for fervid inventions. Seventeenth-century curiosity and excitement were high in Europe about the promiscuity within the gatherings of the extreme 'Puritan' sect 'The Family of Love', which probably never existed. Certainly the parallel 'Adamites', who worshipped not only naked but in arousal, were invented.[14] In Shakespeare's *Twelfth Night*, Maria calling Malvolio 'a kind of puritan' may not be because he seems to her to be a repressive killjoy.[15] The word's meaning, in the sixteenth and seventeenth, and in the twentieth and twenty-first, centuries, was and is impossibly wide; and invariably, however used, it carried strong feelings.[16] What is, perhaps, common to all the usages is disturbance from something felt to be let loose, sometimes shown in reaction in repressive restriction, but as much (newly in the sixteenth century for the clergy) in joyful married sexuality as in anything else.

In the book that follows, when I do use the word, I shall try to restrict it to its ecclesiastical meaning, which is reasonably precise for British life in the sixteenth and seventeenth centuries. Early in the modern debate about the term, in 1965, Basil Hall pointed out that in the period 1570–1640 the word 'Puritan' would have been applied to the 'restlessly critical and occasionally rebellious members of the Church of England who desired some modifications in Church government and worship, but not to those who deliberately removed themselves from that Church'.[17] The latter was a later, and altogether looser, application.

A TRUE REVOLUTION

Earlier chapters in this book describe the arrival in England of Latin Bible texts; translations of parts of the Bible into Anglo-Saxon and Middle English; and the great work of the followers of John Wyclif in the 1380s in translating the whole Bible into English, from the Latin, and circulating many hand-written copies.

It needs to be stressed, however, that in what is properly called the Reformation, the arrival in the 1520s and 1530s of the whole Bible, translated into English from the original Greek and Hebrew texts, and printed for the widest distribution, was a true revolution in the history of the West.

For the medieval Church, the Bible certainly had authority, but it was alongside the greater authority of the practices and traditions which had grown over the centuries, including the 'unwritten verities.' In the teaching and preaching of the Church, the Bible, in Latin, was a sacred text from which verses, or illustrative incidents, could be extracted and used to underpin the common people's proper attention to the liturgies. The whole Bible was not in the picture.

Eamon Duffy puts this well:

He [Cardinal Pole in 1553] abhorred religious argument and the spirit of self-sufficiency which he believed indiscriminate Bible-reading by lay people was likely to encourage. Better for the people to absorb the faith through the liturgy, to find in attentive and receptive participation in the ceremonies and sacraments of the Church the grace and instruction on which to found the Christian life. This was the true Catholic way, the spirit of the *parvuli*, the 'little ones' of Christ, for whom penitence, not knowledge, was the true and only way to salvation. The object of preaching and teaching was not to impart knowledge, but to cause the people to lament their sins, seek the healing of the sacraments, and amend their lives.[18]

An opponent of John Wyclif in the early fifteenth century wrote of his horror that Wyclif was giving 'the pearl of the Gospel' to lay men and women, to be 'trodden underfoot by swine' – the Gospel, he wrote, 'that Christ gave to the doctors and clergy of the Church.'[19]

It is said, furthermore, that the ordinary English Christian had no need of an English Bible, as his or her faith was strengthened by biblical wall paintings or stained glass in the churches, or by biblical plays, or Caxton's *Golden Legend* (see below, pp. 107–8). Yet such paintings or glass, of Adam and Eve, Noah's ark or the Crucifixion, could represent only the smallest fragment of the Bible. True, the great fifteenth-century Mystery Play cycles in York or Coventry or Chester or elsewhere did dramatise more Bible stories: but few ordinary people could cross England to see them. And Caxton's *Golden Legend*, as well as being wildly beyond the reach of the milk-maid or ploughboy, turns out on investigation of its many forms to contain little of the Bible at all.

Access to the whole Bible in a vernacular opens up rich continents of new, and different, understanding of New Testament faith. At John 5:39, Christ exhorted his followers to 'Search the scriptures'. They found barriers in the way. Some of Christ's fiercest words are against the Pharisees because they 'shut up the kingdom of heaven against men' and the lawyers who 'have taken away the key of knowledge' (Matt. 23:13, Luke 11:52). The first makers of the printed Bible in English, a document that in various forms has swept the world for almost five hundred years, understood those words well. The Bible in Latin had been locked away from the common people. William Tyndale, early in his Preface to his 1534 New Testament, commenting on the locking out described in those passages, referred to 'the kingdom of heaven, which is the scripture and word of God.'[20]

Chapter 1

INTRODUCTION

THE IMPORTANCE OF THE BIBLE in the culture of the world should not need to be spelled out. The Jewish and Christian Scriptures, flowing together as they do, have for two thousand years flooded into all levels of Western living, a permeation greater even than the classical inheritance from Greece and Rome. The Bible has been high, often supreme, in its influence. At the start of the twenty-first century, to many educated Western minds, the Bible is a ridiculous irrelevance. Since the eighteenth century, university syllabuses have been made by men hostile to the word of God.[1] Yet, if by some hideous accident at the divine computer key-board the 'delete' key were pressed for the Bible, much of the content of Western culture would disappear and it would shrivel like a deflating balloon.

Spelling out, however, is just what is needed. In 1997, a great British university press issued the King James Bible, the 'Authorised Version', in a famous paperback series. The advertising of this special event was handled by a public relations firm. Early in the printed handout were these words: 'The Bible will stand alongside other conical [*sic*] classics such as Jane Austen's *Pride and Prejudice*, Zola's *Germinal* and Louisa May Alcott's *Little Women*.'

Bible stories, poems, proverbs, prophecies and teaching have the author-ity of great literature, shaping cultures. The Bible has been, and still is, the spiritual handbook of the faithful, studied and cherished as a companion of daily religious life. It is always both familiar and strange. Men and women who have never opened the covers are aware of it as something odd and special. Bible students of the greatest learning, working over a lifetime with the original languages, still find themselves surprised by new revelations of God within the familiar phrases.

WHAT THE BIBLE IS

To Christians, the Bible is the Word of God. The New Testament, written in the workaday Greek of the eastern Mediterranean in the middle of the first century AD, and shortly after, has four accounts of the life and work of Jesus ('Gospels'), followed by a narrative ('Acts') of the founding of some of the earliest congregations, across the Mediterranean as far as Rome, and letters ('Epistles') to those congregations. The New Testament has twenty-seven books, some short. What is in the New Testament has been for most of its life fixed at those twenty-seven books, though one African branch of Christianity, the Ethiopic church, has from the beginning included eight extra writings.

Placed before the New Testament, the first part of the Christian Bible is the Jewish Scriptures, known to Christians as the Old Testament, because to Christians these writings show an earlier understanding of God, pointing to the coming of Jesus. The Jewish Scriptures divide into three: the Law, probably better called 'The Teachings' (especially the Pentateuch, the five books beginning with Genesis), the Prophets (for example Jeremiah) and the Writings (including the Psalms) making a total of thirty-nine books, many of them long. All the Old Testament, with a small exception, was written in Hebrew, the ancient language found only in those Scriptures, and in the non-biblical literature found in the caves of Qumran.[2]

Thus the whole Bible has sixty-six 'books', giving it as a name the Latin word for books, *biblia*. Christians in the West are divided about fourteen additional books, found only in a pre-Christian Greek translation of the Hebrew, not in the original, often printed in English Bibles between the Testaments as the 'Apocrypha', but in Roman Catholic Bibles placed at various points in the Old Testament. They bring the total to eighty.

For Christians the root, core or heart of the Bible is the forgiving, regenerating and redeeming work of Jesus, the 'Word made flesh'. This is what the New Testament is about, and Christians understand the three sections of the Old Testament as pointing forward to Jesus as the expected Messiah, which means the anointed one of God (in Greek 'the Christ'). The teachings of Jesus are unique: attentive reading shows them to be startlingly more than an injunction to be nice to people. Jesus' work of healing describes also his restoration of human beings to the condition in which they were made by God. Christians focus particularly on the death of Jesus as a sacrifice made for all believers, and his resurrection. Soon after that event, his followers were unexpectedly activated by a new Spirit from God, a force which changed them from being frightened, timid and grieving people hiding in Jerusalem to adventurers carrying the good news of the releasing power of Christ far and wide.

Jesus taught his followers that God was his, and everyone's, Father. Christian theologians in later centuries, defending the New Testament revelation against other alluring speculations, formulated God as Father, Son and Holy Spirit, developing a thought first expressed by Jesus in Matthew 28:19, and by Paul in 2 Corinthians 13:14. One way to see the work of Jesus in the Gospels is as the only part of the story of God that can be told, that we can understand. 'The story behind the story' in fact cannot be told because God is God.[3] What we get is only a fragment of what God as Father means: but enough, as many generations of sons and daughters have found.

THE TRANSMISSION OF THE TEXTS

Hebrew is a language built on roots of three consonants. Because the Hebrew Scriptures have always been used in daily worship, survival of the manuscripts has been good. Problems arose with the pronunciation and interpretation of the consonants and 'vowel letters'; then a system of signs ('points') below and between the consonants was added in the early eighth century.[4] Because the text was sacred, special attention had to be given to the additions, with continual interpretation and disputation. The documents discovered from 1947 at Qumran, 'The Dead Sea Scrolls', have generally supported traditional readings. Problems continue to arise because Hebrew is a language which appears only in the Scriptures. Thus when there is a word occurring once which is difficult to understand, as in the accounts of the furnishings of the Tabernacle in the later chapters of Exodus, or Solomon's temple in 1 Kings 6 & 7 and in 2 Chronicles 3 & 4, it is not possible to appeal for help from other records (as one can, for example, with Greek writings). For Jews in Alexandria in Egypt in the second century BC, the Hebrew Scriptures were translated into Greek, on the whole well. This version circulated widely in the Mediterranean area, and it was the version known to, and quoted by, the earliest Christians when they wrote to each other. From a legend about the supposed miraculous making of identical copies by seventy-two isolated scholars, it is known as the Septuagint, or LXX. Further problems come from differences between that Septuagint and the Hebrew.

The New Testament was written in the ordinary Greek of everyday literature, biographies, historical writings or fictions: in other words, the contemporary 'hellenistic' Greek. Only the first four verses of St Luke's Gospel are in the stylised 'classical' Greek of historiography, though the prologues to some of the Epistles follow classical Greek styles. The Greek New Testament is the best-attested document in the world, surviving in about five thousand manuscripts. Since the sixteenth century, more, and earlier, Greek manuscripts have steadily been found: and the discovery of papyri of very early date indeed has added to knowledge. Leather manuscripts –

as at Qumran – or parchment scrolls were on treated animal hides: texts written on papyrus, made from the stem pith of the papyrus plant, were found preserved in the arid Egyptian soil, and among the Dead Sea Scrolls, and at a few other places, including Herculaneum. Caves in Qumran have yielded, as well as Hebrew, valuable Greek texts. The modern technical study of the relationships of the oldest texts has produced a reasonably stable Greek New Testament, though there remain disputes about some verses, and about the authority of certain families of ancient documents.

This book is about translation, and though we can be happy that the base texts of Greek and Hebrew are sufficiently secure, there are still problems. To illustrate the nature of disagreement, without stepping into the minefield of half a dozen disputed phrases which tend to raise strong feelings, I take a word in Paul's first letter to the Corinthians. Here, at 1 Corinthians 13:3, Paul is arguing that whatever grand actions are performed, if their basis is not love, then they are without profit. It is understood that his famous list is aimed especially at the Corinthian church. What then does he mean by his phrase 'Though I bestow all my goods to feed the poor, and though I give my body to be burned'? The first part is easy; the second very difficult on two grounds: first that martyrdom by burning was largely unknown there and at that time, and in any case 'give my body' is a peculiar phrase for it ('my body being taken' would be more logical). Second, the Greek word for 'to be burned', καυθήσωμαι (*kauthēsōmai*), differs by only one Greek letter from the word at that place in many manuscripts, καυχήσωμαι (*kauxēsōmai*), which means to exalt, or to boast. To dispose of the difficulty about burning by going over to this alternative reading is simply to raise a new problem – what can it mean? Certainly Paul seems to have some kind of self-sacrifice in mind, but handing over one's body to boasting is a peculiar idea. A solution may be in the nature of his own ministry as explained to the Corinthians elsewhere (2 Cor. 11:23–9 and 12:10), in which his consciousness of all kinds of sufferings in his body in the name of Christ might produce a 'boast', as if he were saying: 'This is what I have been through in bringing you the Gospel.' Yet if even this is done without love, he would then be saying in the controversial verse (1 Cor. 13:3), it will still 'profit me nothing'.

Such problems are, mercifully, not frequent: but the complexity of Paul's rhetorical skills means that they tend to arise with him rather than in the Gospels, something recognised in New Testament times (see 2 Peter 3:16). In only a very few cases, fragmentary in the whole New Testament, do such variants have more than a minor effect. More troublesome has been the larger question of manuscript authority. The general principle is always that the earlier is the better, on the grounds that fewer copyists' errors will have crept in. Scientific work at the end of the nineteenth century, extended in the twentieth, challenged the grounds of many readings from late and even incomplete manuscripts which, in a Greek New Testament printed in the sixteenth century, had later been made to set hard, as it were. From an incidental remark by a printer it became known as the 'Received Text', the *Textus Receptus*, as if it had exceptional authority: because it was the basis of KJV, some twenty-first century people will brook no criticism of it.

Modern chapter divisions in the whole (Latin) Bible are said to have been made by Stephen Langton, Archbishop of Canterbury between 1206 and 1228. Verse divisions did not appear in the New Testament until 1551, in a Greek and Latin edition made in Geneva. Before those times, quite elaborate systems of division were often made.

OBJECTIONS

People read the Bible for many different reasons. A hungry soul seeks and finds spiritual food. Some read it for daily insight into the goodness of God, or an immensity of experience described. Clever people dispute small or large sections. Others deny any possibility of truth when reported events seem wrong historically, or, as the alternative, they bend a historical record to fit. Some parts of the Bible, particularly of the Old Testament, produce revulsion and dismay, as in tales of slaughter in the books of Joshua and Judges, all apparently at the command of God; or in details of tribal laws. In the New Testament, some deride what they read as the appalling gender politics of Paul, without regard to whatever else he said. Even sympathetic readers find long stretches of Leviticus or Numbers troublingly tedious, or passages of some of the Prophets incomprehensible. Paul at his most theological is not an easy read. At the very end of the New Testament, the book of Revelation can be read merely as accounts of hallucinations, or as foretelling imminent catastrophes. Even devout Christians can sympathise with the Scottish minister who finished his reading with the words: 'If it hadna been the Lord's will, that verse had been better left out.'[5]

A religion is a revelation of God or it is nothing. Thomas Jefferson was one of many later eighteenth- and nineteenth-century thinkers who took scissors to cut up and paste the Gospels to reveal the remarkable system of ethics in the teaching of Jesus. Jefferson, like others at the time, threw away the 'superstitious nonsense' which was all the rest. He was awed by the ethical originality of what he found in the teaching of Jesus. What he put in his paste-up book in 1804 he found admirable, but it was quite

untrue to the original. The revelation of God as Father in any of the four
Gospels is in the whole experience, 'superstitious nonsense' and all. If
enlightened Jefferson found the accounts of the birth, death and resurrection of Jesus, his healings and other miracles offensive, then that should
be no surprise. Philosophical systems of ethics do not embrace the raising
of the dead.

So challenging is the whole Bible that it has always been tempting to
make of it a magic book. The unscrupulous can try to make a few words
– taken out of context, especially from the Old Testament – to act like a
fairy-tale potion. Down the ages, people have tried to make ancient ritual
commands into modern dogma: John Wyclif tackled the matter in Latin
at the University of Oxford in the 1370s (see p. 71 below). The problem
has got worse. For example, a certain prominent American broadcaster regularly attacks homosexuals because the third book of the Old Testament,
Leviticus, states that their acts are 'abomination' (18:22). In September
2000, a listener posted on the internet a letter in reply, which illuminates
the problem in terms obviously not intended to be flippant.

Dear Dr Laura,
When I burn a bull on the altar as a sacrifice I know it creates a
pleasing odour for the Lord (Lev. 1:9). The problem is that my neighbours complain that the odour is not pleasing to them. Should I smite
them?

I would like to sell my daughter into slavery, as sanctioned in Exodus
21:7. In this day and age, what do you think would be a fair price for
her?

Lev. 25:44 states that I may indeed possess slaves, both male and
female, provided they are purchased from neighbouring nations. A friend
of mine says this applies to Mexicans but not Canadians. Can you
clarify? Why can't I own Canadians?

I have a neighbour who insists on working on the Sabbath. Exodus
31:15 clearly states he should be put to death. Am I morally obligated
to kill him myself? [. . .]

My uncle has a farm. He violates Lev. 19:19 by planting two different crops in the same field, as does his wife by wearing garments
made of two different kinds of thread (cotton/polyester blend). He also
tends to blaspheme a lot. Is it really necessary that we go to all the
trouble of getting the whole town together to stone them? (Lev.
24:10–16). Couldn't we just burn them to death at a private family affair
like we do with people who sleep with our in-laws?

Thankyou again for reminding us that God's word is eternal and
unchanging.[6]

The Hebrew book of Leviticus, which those questions mock, was intended as part of a seamless single composition, the five-book Pentateuch, from the opening of Genesis to the end of Deuteronomy, written for a special hierarchy of Jerusalem priests working in the later Temple and thus exceptionally conservative. Leviticus gives the rules for proper procedures of ritual, and for purity. Both systems were aiming towards an ideal of Holiness for particular priests and occasionally for lay people as well. These ritual ordinances, here and in Exodus especially, have, as David Damrosch observed, 'warmed the hearts of few'.[7] (One can hear growls of sympathy from the Scottish minister.) Understanding the intention of such passages, an ideal of Holiness in a particularly limited circumstance, may help: as may taking to heart Jesus' words at Matthew 23:23, that too much attention to detailed literalness of the Law can lead to neglect of the weightier matters—judgement, mercy and faith. Otherwise in such passages one is reduced to echoing the words of another sturdy Scottish churchman, this time objecting to a different issue altogether, that of the union of Scottish churches: 'It is unconstitutional. It is impractical. It is illogical and absolutely idiotic. But I hae nae doot it is God's will.'[8]

THE BIBLE AND THE PEOPLE

Like Jews and Muslims, Christians are people of a book. It was made by the earliest believers. All these early Christian communities, for which the Greek word is mainly ἐκκλησία (*ekklēsia*) or συναγωγή (*synagōgē*), literally 'community' or 'congregation', are more individual and independent than is suggested by the word 'churches'. The picture of some of the earliest of them, as for example in 1 Corinthians 12–14, shows little if anything of any organised authoritarian structure, something which the word 'church' tends to suggest today. Each congregation would have leaders called either 'elders' or 'deacons', and sometimes 'overseers' (the literal form of the Greek word usually translated 'bishops') for a wider region. Two things united them all. First was the regular – weekly, possibly even daily – act of taking the bread and wine which symbolised the body and blood of Christ. For two thousand years this simple meal has been one of the two central facts of Christianity wherever it is found. The other was the then growing collection of writings that we call the Christian Scriptures.

Christians worshipping together since the very foundation of the faith have used the Psalms with special affection. In worship together, or in private reading at home, Psalms that begin 'The Lord is my shepherd' or 'The earth is the Lord's' or 'Unto thee, oh Lord, do I lift up my soul' have been cherished: to know the whole psalter by heart, as many Christians have done, is to have an endless spring of strength and humbleness before God in daily life. Further, when Jesus said 'Search the Scriptures' (John 5:39) he, like Paul, would have had the Prophets very much in mind. Christians from the beginning have found there the signs of the coming of the Messiah (or 'Christ'), and all the earliest Christian writings, Gospels and Epistles, are full of references to Old Testament prophecy. Paul, like all the early Christians, interpreted the prophecies of the Old Testament as showing that the work of Christ fulfilled the work of God in the world.

Jewish biblical commentary was, and still largely is, of many kinds. The most significant have been the *midrashim*, which are comments on the Hebrew, sometimes of great length, and always offering fluctuating interpretations from the moment, on a text which is fixed. Only from the Masoretes in the eighth to tenth centuries were the Hebrew Scriptures seen as not containing error; as harmonious, as unalterable even in the tiniest detail; yet at the same time capable of many meanings. Such free commentaries, though made according to strict rules, were central to the work of the rabbis; and we can see Jesus himself as a rabbinical teacher routinely answering questions about the Law. To him, however, and to his followers, the Law (originally, the first five books of the Bible, the 'Torah', but at the time of Jesus commonly the whole Hebrew Bible or 'Tanakh') was not a separate entity, but was to be seen and understood together with the Prophets and the insight provided by their writings into the present and future. Thus Jesus says in the synagogue, commenting on a passage in the Prophet Isaiah, 'Today this scripture has been fulfilled in your hearing' (Luke 4:21). The books of the Bible are interconnected. The New Testament writers often note that an event or saying 'fulfils' the Old. Take the Old Testament out and the New Testament diminishes. Study the Old Testament without the New, and the Christian revelation fades away. Take out of Christian life intimate personal knowledge of the work and words of Jesus, of the letters of Paul, and that religion becomes something different – which is what happened.

Christians are people of a book, like Jews and Muslims: but unlike them, Christians almost from the beginning knew their book only in translation, and even then, for over half the life of the Faith, had their book taken away from them. Jews, from long before Jesus until today, have had at the heart of their religion intense daily reading and full discussion by everyone of their open Scriptures – those very books which, as Christianity was founded and first developed, were freely quoted and expounded as the centre of the new faith, by Jesus himself as well the first Apostles and Fathers. The circulation in Greek of the Hebrew Scriptures and the New Testament, in the first centuries, was to allow the widest and most open Christian readership, and for the widest groups of hearers. From quite early, translation of the whole Bible into Latin was for the same purpose, as the Faith extended. But then, in the growing hierarchy of power that had become the Roman Church, it began to be felt by senior clergy in Rome (though not in the East, dominated by Constantinople), that ordinary people were not capable of understanding a book as complicated as the Bible. Though Jesus was so clearly a teacher and healer of the poor, the weak and the outcast, the Roman Church said that God had intended his whole Bible to be only for the priests and those doctors who were specially trained. Though Jesus was a liberator, giving freedom to women as well as men and to all 'outsiders', both Old and New Testaments were locked away from the people, the Bible considered too sacred to be touched by any but the most learned. It remained inaccessible in Latin for a thousand years, and the 'common version' of it, the Vulgate, came to be regarded as the true original. To translate it for the people became heresy, punishable by a solitary lingering death as a heretic; or, as had happened to the Cathars in southern France, or the Hussites in Bohemia and Lollards in England, official and bloody attempts to exterminate the species.

In the history of the world, the fact that reading the Word of God, either alone or in company, can dramatically change lives is overwhelmingly attested. For this to happen, the Word has to be understandable. The history of the Bible is a story of translation. The Hebrew Scriptures as they spread from Jerusalem needed translation into Greek to reach across the Mediterranean, and then both Testaments were translated at various times and in various ways into Latin, to be read throughout the Roman Empire. The necessary next stage, the translation from the originals into the many spoken languages of the known world, was blocked by the increasing power of the Bishop of Rome. He claimed supreme authority over the whole Church as pope (an authority always denied by the Orthodox churches to the East), and decreed that the Bible could exist only in the assembly of Latin translations made by Jerome about 400. Though Jerome unusually translated the Old Testament from the Hebrew, giving his work new standing, it was unfortunate that this translation, eventually known as the Vulgate, became fixed by the pope as the only permissible Bible in the whole Christian church. The Old and New Testaments did not just take second place to the pope's personal authority: as far as the ordinary faithful man and woman were concerned, they largely disappeared. Some stories remained universal in Christian minds, like those of Adam and Eve or Noah's ark, and the death of Christ on the Cross and the Resurrection: but all the detail of almost all the Bible, particularly the full theology of Paul, was unknown.

THE BIBLE IN ENGLISH

The fire that spread across Europe in the early sixteenth century, the Reformation, burned away a great deal that was superstitious as the Bible was rediscovered. Though that reform obviously had political and economic causes and effects, the new insights came in every northern European country from Christians at last being able to read the whole of both Testaments in their own languages. The thirteen letters of Paul are often difficult, reporting from the edges of a theological universe. These letters, however, especially the prime epistle to the congregation at Rome, when rediscovered by ordinary people across Europe in the early sixteenth century, turned nations upside down. A neat definition of the Reformation is 'People reading Paul'; and part of what they were reading was about justification by faith, not works. Justification is understanding of God's forgiveness and offer of union with Him, and as the New Testament makes clear, though works are obviously of great value, forgiveness is dependent only on a willingness to meet God. This revelation, unique in the religious literature of the world, has made the New Testament the instrument of change among people of every kind since the first century.

The English Bible is everywhere. If one has ever made light of something, shown the patience of Job, noticed the signs of the times, called someone the salt of the earth or full of good works, resolved to fight the good fight, been where two or three are gathered together, found that the spirit is willing but the flesh is weak, gathered filthy lucre, and, in spite of the powers that be, decided to eat, drink and be merry, then one has quoted the English Bible in phrases etched into our daily language for over four hundred years.

Not only the language. That Eve tempted Adam with an apple; that Noah built an ark; that Jacob saw a ladder, and served for Rachel seven years; that Samson pulled down the temple; that David slew Goliath; that Solomon 'in all his glory' captivated the Queen of Sheba and knew the languages of animals; that Jonah was swallowed by a whale; that Christ was born in Bethlehem and the angels appeared to shepherds in the fields, and later three wise men brought gifts; that Jesus preached and healed and was betrayed, and suffered and was crucified, and rose again the third day; that Saul had a blinding conversion on the Damascus road and became Paul – these are part of the English-speaking thought-processes, even if they are not exact. Someone says of an over-confident businessman that he thinks he can walk on water, and the speaker is unlikely to locate the idea in Matthew 14 or Mark 6, nor even as in the Gospels, nor even as in the New Testament and quite probably not even as in the Bible.

In the fifteenth and sixteenth centuries, Britain was slow to develop printing, and to have a printed vernacular Bible, in both cases because of political repression dating from the beginning of the fifteenth century, a severity ultimately caused by the success of the manuscript Bible translations made in English around 1380 under the influence of John Wyclif. When the first printed Bibles arrived in England, especially those made from Greek and Hebrew by William Tyndale in the 1520s and 1530s (for which he was burned), they were, however, of such outstanding quality that in the sixteenth century the Bibles in English were unique – in scholarship and use of language, in the numbers of fine translations made (ten separate versions made from Tyndale's first in 1526 to the famous 1611 KJV), and in influence on national life and culture. Luther's German translations were magnificent and influential, and made the first 'bestsellers'. Several versions in French and Dutch were interesting and influential. But it was from the familiar Bibles in English, the Geneva Bibles of 1560, 1576 and 1599, and from KJV after 1769, that so much of world influence grew.

It is important to emphasise the variety. Just as for nearly five hundred years the number of Bible translations into English has been far greater than into any other language, so, in the sixteenth century, England was unique in the number of different vernacular translations on offer. Instead of those ten separate English versions up to 1611, for example, Germany had two. Between Martin Luther's first New Testament in 1522 and 1600 there were many new issues of his work: about two hundred each of the whole Bible and the New Testament. (In the seventeenth century, the pattern was repeated, with fewer numbers.) The only other German translator was Hieronymus Emser, who printed his Roman Catholic revision of Luther's New Testament first in Dresden in 1527: it was several times reissued. Similarly, in French the New Testament translations of Lefèvre in 1524 and Olivétan in 1545 were the only versions: they were reprinted less frequently than the German Scriptures.[9]

Almost wholly out of sight in the modern, technical, world is the part played by the Bible in the making of natural science and especially the role of the Protestant approaches to texts in interpretations of the English Bible. 'It is commonly supposed that when in the early modern period individuals began to look at the world in a different way, they could no longer believe what they read in the Bible. [But . . .] the reverse is the case.'[10] Not only did the banishing of allegory by the new literalness break the ancient chains of never-ending, enclosed reference, so that proper 'scientific' observation could begin, which it swiftly did: 'By 1623 . . . the 600 plants described by the ancients had grown tenfold to 6,000'.[11] But also, the very Protestant quest for a pure and complete text of Scripture, shorn

of ancient institutional corruptions of all kinds, and now observed in the
original languages, was itself a motor that drove the clearer vision of the
world around. Even the Catholic scholar William Lindanus (born 1529)
wrote of 'the errors, vices, corruptions, additions, detractions, mutations,
uncertainties, obscurities, pollutions, barbarisms and solecisms of the vulgar
Latin translation'.[12] That the resulting 'pure' text contained its own difficulties was seized by Catholic polemicists to argue the need for Church
authority over it: but it was too late – the genie, as one might put it in
pagan terms, was out of the bottle. Learning, scientific knowledge, now
followed modern observation of the world, not ancient doctrinally motivated texts. Aristotle, however, was not thrown out: a version of his thought
had even been what theology was in Tyndale's Oxford years. In the section
of his *Obedience of a Christian Man* dealing with the foolish quibbles of
the Oxford schoolmen, Tyndale refers to Aristotle's *De coelo, De generatione
et corruptore* and the *Nichomachean Ethics*.[13] Peter Harrison writes:

> The Reformation was an attempt to reconstruct Christian religion from
> its origins, and those origins were to be discovered in the New Testa-
> ment. Because the authority of Christianity was now to be located, not
> in the total history of the Church, but in that short period in which
> the apostles lived, taught, and wrote, historical criticism of the biblical
> texts took on an unprecedented importance. The enterprise of natural
> history, during its constructive phase at least, was similarly the recon-
> struction or restoration of a past discipline which had been created by
> Aristotle, Theophrastus, Dioscorides, and to a lesser extent, Pliny. The
> reformers thus shared the historical sense of those humanist scholars
> who sought to correct errors in the Aristotelian encyclopaedia by
> returning to the original sources and original languages.[14]

FOUR GLORIES

The chapters that follow are to be read as a celebration of four things.
Firstly, of the range and power and versatility of the English language.
There are emerging three Englishes: the older literary language, which is
the vehicle of many remarkable Bible translations; those vigorous creoles
and dialects across the world which are still English, and sometimes have
parts of the Bible expressed in them – a subject outside the scope of this
book; and the efficient, limited, basic means of communication worldwide.
English is particularly friendly to neighbouring tongues. The English
language welcomes change, new words and new games with grammar,
making nouns of verbs and verbs of nouns. Recently the useful 'to
credential' has been seen, and the American 'to critique' has been used

for some time: those who horror at this as an American trick might remember that Shakespeare worked like that all the time.[15] This organic growth is why retranslation is so often essential, and why no English Bible was ever seen as definitive (or not until the 'King James Only' campaigns of late twentieth-century America). As Miles Coverdale wrote in 1538, he believed that the Holy Ghost is 'the author of his Scripture as well in the Hebrew, Greek, French, Dutch [the name includes German] and in English, as in Latin'.[16]

There have never been more translations into English available than there are now. Even the list of recommended versions, from one mainstream theological position, lists fifteen published versions of the entire Bible for study, and ten of them, all significantly different, appeared after the end of the Second World War. Study of the Bible means encountering both simplicity and complication, both of which the English language can handle well. The language of Christianity, and of the Bible, is both extremely simple, as in 'God is love', and technically difficult. It has regularly been insisted that both the Bible itself, and the experiences of worship, have needed simplifying, so that at Christmas some congregations sing, instead of the theology of an older carol, as it might be 'Word of the Father / Now in flesh appearing' the words 'Happy birthday to Jesus'. Technical difficulty has its very proper place. It is striking to observers of universities that the disciplines with difficult, specialist vocabularies, like medicine or law, remain most popular for applicants.

In any case, what is simplification? I give here an extract from a version of the New Testament made in 1996.

When you come before God, don't turn it into a theatrical production. All these people making a regular show of their prayers, hoping for stardom! Do you think God sits in a box seat? Here's what I want you to do: Find a quiet, secluded place so you won't be tempted to role-play before God. Just sit there as simply and honestly as you can manage. The world is full of so-called prayer-warriors who are prayer-ignorant. They're full of formulas and programs and advice, peddling techniques for getting what you want from God. Don't fall for that nonsense. This is your Father you're dealing with, and he knows better than you what you need. With a god like this loving you, you can pray very simply. Like this:

> Our father in heaven
> Reveal who you are.
> Set the world right:
> Do what's best —
> As above, so below.
> Keep us alive with three square meals,

> Keep us forgiven with you and forgiving others,
> Keep us safe from ourselves and the Devil.
> You're in charge!
> You can do anything you want!
> You're ablaze in beauty!
> Yes. Yes. Yes.[17]

Here is the same passage, the words of Jesus (as recorded in Matthew 6:5–13), in the translation made by William Tyndale in 1534:

And when thou prayest, thou shalt not be as the hypocrites are. For they love to stand and pray in the synagogues, and in the corners of the streets, because they would be seen of men. Verily I say unto you, they have their reward. But when thou prayest, enter into thy chamber, and shut the door to thee, and pray to thy father which is in secret: and thy father which seeth in secret shall regard thee openly.

And when ye pray, babble not much, as the heathen do: for they think that they shall be heard for their much babbling's sake. Be ye not like them therefore. For your father knoweth whereof ye have need, before ye ask of him. After this manner therefore pray ye.

O our father which art in heaven, hallowed be thy name. Let thy kingdom come. Thy will be fulfilled, as well in earth, as it is in heaven. Give us this day our daily bread. And forgive us our trespasses, even as we forgive our trespasses. And lead us not into temptation: but deliver us from evil. For thine is the kingdom and the power, and the glory for ever. Amen.[18]

Tyndale's English, with its 'thou', 'thy', 'ye', 'prayest', 'verily', 'hallowed' and so on, belongs to an older time. It is, however, faithful to its Greek original, and the archaisms do not hinder the sense. The punchy modern manner of the first passage produces disturbing complications and difficulties, like the running idea of theatre, or the muddled ideas of 'so-called prayer-warriors who are prayer-ignorant'. Prayer to 'keep us safe from ourselves' is not praying 'very simply': the Greek has nothing like that, and it is not at all clear what it is supposed to mean.

The English language has, as well as flexibility, an ancient strength which is thrown away at real cost; strength to carry the most difficult theological truths with ease. God's Word, while so often balm to the bruised spirit, is not intended, in the modern shallow phrase, 'to make me feel good about myself': a second's thought should show that by his very nature God is different from humanity, and his expressed word is usually unexpected. Moreover, the beauty of which the English language is capable is important here: what one receives from the Psalms or the Gospels, for example, in a fine translation (though one not made, it is to be hoped, for purely literary effect) is a sense of the goodness of God, the welcoming Father. Since the first English translations, by Tyndale and in the hundred years after him, were made to be read aloud, good sounds were important. (English is especially rich in onomatopoeic words – when given proper weight they tell their own story: 'splash', 'astonish', 'disgusting', 'warmth', 'trotting', 'thunder and lightning'.)

It is hoped that this book will show, as one glory, that of English. Secondly, this book is a celebration of the extraordinary story of the development of the English Bible, sometimes against terrible barriers: from the first Anglo-Saxon handwriting between the lines of eighth-century Latin Gospels to a modern catalogue offering hundreds of different Bibles in English. Thirdly, the English Bible is unique in that in its multiplicity of English versions it has been unlike any other book in any other country. Finally, the English Bible is open to everyone who can read it, held in the hand, studied in a group, or heard by a large congregation: what Tyndale opened has never been shut up.

Part 1

BEFORE PRINTING

Chapter 2

THE BIBLE IN BRITAIN FROM THE EARLIEST TIMES TO AD 850

A VISITOR TO THE BRITISH LIBRARY at St Pancras who skirts the fine entrance hall and goes through a door to the left, enters, up a few steps, the John Ritblat Gallery, the 'Treasures' room. It is a cool, spacious, low-ceilinged cave of wonders, and displays to the public some of the library's rarest possessions.

Across the floor in the first horizontal case is an object beyond price, the British Library's manuscript Cotton Nero D iv, written in double columns on vellum. This, the volume known as the Lindisfarne Gospels, is a masterpiece of early medieval book making, one of the few early Gospel books to have survived complete. The beauty of the big, fully decorated pages takes the breath.[1] A long time is needed to absorb the lines, shapes and colours even of a single opening of the 258 folios, as it might be the first words of St John's Gospel – 'In principio erat verbum' – opposite a decorative carpet page, in this place unusually elaborate (see frontispiece).

Unusually, the manuscript is dated by a surviving tenth-century colophon. That is an inscription at the end of a book naming the scribe or author, from a Greek word for 'finishing touch'. Here it tells us that it was made in AD 698, or soon after, by a scribe, Eadfrith, on Lindisfarne, the small, low 'Holy Island' off the north-east coast of England. Lindisfarne had been a missionary centre and monastic school since its foundation by the Irish monk Aidan, brought there in 625 at the request of Edwin, the powerful King of Northumbria. Eadfrith became Bishop of Lindisfarne in 698. He was responsible for the whole manuscript, both text and decoration, apart from a very few minor details. Though these Gospels are indeed special, artefacts as massive in concept and original in detail as a later English Gothic Cathedral, the specialness needs identifying carefully. In the words of Deirdre O'Sullivan, 'The writing of Scripture was a sacred act: one wonders what Aidan, Cuthbert or indeed Eadfrith himself would have thought to hear the Lindisfarne Gospels described as a "luxury".[2] As she earlier notes, 'the practice of writing was the most important activity of the devout monk within the western monastic tradition'.[3] Because the Rule of Benedict gave high importance to reading, privately as well as communally, the demand for texts was similarly high, so that 'monasteries would have needed at least as many texts as monks'; at Lindisfarne, 'a recent estimate gives a minimum number of nine scribes operating [. . .] in the mid eighth century'.[4] Moreover, 'the preparation of an elaborate manuscript may have been seen as an act of personal devotion, an individual's *opus dei*'.[5]

The Gospels must have been completed before Eadfrith's death in 721. It is more likely that it was finished to be part of the celebration of St Cuthbert, the greatest of the northern saints, who had earlier been bishop of Lindisfarne and had been buried there. The exhumation and elevation of his remains happened in about 698. Three centuries later, his shrine was established in Durham Cathedral, where a part of it can still be seen.

The book had a lively history. It went with the body of St Cuthbert on its seven years of travels over northern England, carried by the monks who had been driven out of Lindisfarne by the invading Vikings in 875. Symeon, the twelfth-century historian of Durham, tells a story: the harassed monks tried to embark at Whithorn on the Solway Firth to sail to Ireland. This was against St Cuthbert's express wishes, as he had no intention of accepting exile. They had hardly put to sea when a terrible storm blew up. Three huge waves swamped the boat and the water turned to blood. The terrified monks turned back, but not before the treasured copy of the Gospels had fallen overboard. Being holy, it did not sink. Some time later, following guidance given to one of the monks by Cuthbert in a dream, the volume was found lying on the strand about three miles out during an unusually low tide, quite undamaged by its immersion in salt water.[6] After further travels over the centuries, and having disappeared at the Dissolution of the monasteries in 1536, it emerged and was bought by Sir Robert Cotton a century later, going from his collection in 1700 into what became the British Museum in 1753, and thence to the British Library.

Though the text, and the four portraits of the Evangelists, are Mediterranean in influence, the Gospels are triumphantly 'insular' in conception and decoration (that is, a particular northern European fusion). In the making, vellum and ink of the highest quality were used. No fewer than forty different pigments have been identified. Some are local vegetable dyes. It is said that the lapis lazuli came from the Himalayas. After Eadfrith's death, the book was bound by Aethilwald, who succeeded him as bishop. The binding ornaments of gems and precious metals were added by Billfrith the Anchorite (that is, recluse), probably later in the 700s. The sequence of makers – the Bishop-and-scribe Eadfrith, the Bishop-and-bookbinder Aethilwald, the Anchorite-and-jeweller Billfrith – ends with a Aldred, a priest who was later provost of Chester-le-Street, where St Cuthbert's relics had been given sanctuary in 882.

It is with Aldred in Chester-le-Street that the story of the Bible in English can begin.

ALDRED

In the years between 946 and 968 Aldred added in his own handwriting, above the large Latin words, a running translation into Old English.[7] Thus, the beginning of the first chapter of John reads:

> *On fruman wæs word and ðhaet word wæs mid Gode*
> IN PRINCIPIO ERAT VERBUM ET VERBUM ERAT APUD DEUM
>
> *and Gode wæs ðhaet word. ðhaet wæs fruman mid Gode.*
> ET DEUS ERAT VERBUM. HOC ERAT IN PRINCIPIO APUD DEUM.

Literally translated, the Old English, in the Northumbrian dialect, says: 'In beginning was word and that word was with God and God was that word. That was in beginning with God.' This handwritten gloss is the earliest surviving translation of the Gospels into any form of the English language. The important point is that the glossing is of the Gospels. There had been Bible glossing into English before. The richly decorated Vespasian Psalter, also in the British Library (though not usually on display) contains the first fifty Psalms, central to worship in monasteries, glossed between the lines in Mercian dialect a hundred years before Aldred.[8] The Book of Cerne, a private prayer book with some Gospel extracts, Psalms and other devotional matter, made between 818 and 830, has an introduction in Old English giving instructions for its use. (The translation was not of course made for people at large, but to be heard as part of the worship and teaching of a monastery or collegiate church.) Aldred's running gloss to the Lindisfarne book, however, which is to the whole of each of the four Gospels, is unique – in length (the four books of the Gospels make almost exactly half the New Testament), in letting us know who made it, and in being the heart of the Christian message. As a book, the Lindisfarne Gospels is indeed exquisite to look at. That there is a translation into Old English is important. Yet best of all is that what is translated into the vernacular are the four Gospels, complete.

In the later Middle Ages, a large volume named 'the Bible' usually contained stories of later saints and their miracles, fanciful allegories, dense commentaries on a few verses, summaries of certain books, and sometimes only a word or two from the Bible itself, probably from parts not central to the Christian message; and all of it in Latin. Later, there were some vernacular translations of the Bible in manuscript in Europe: in England, especially in the 1380s, the 'Lollard' Bibles made under Wyclif were widespread. In the 1520s, the Christian world changed for ever when large numbers of men, women and children right across Europe began to read the whole New Testament, as it had been originally written, printed in their own language. Yet six hundred years before the Reformation, around 950, the whole of the Gospels, all the teaching of Jesus as well as the events in his life, could be read and heard: but only within the monastery, not generally by people outside the walls.

OLD ENGLISH

Old English was the language of most of England for seven centuries, from about 450, when the Anglo-Saxons arrived, until the twelfth century. A Germanic tongue of the invading Angles and Saxons, it had three main dialects: in Wessex, the south and west; in Mercia, middle England; and in Northumbria (the land north of the Humber, up to the Forth, first so named by Bede). After about 1150 it merged fully with the Norman French brought by William the Conqueror's invaders in 1066 to become a different, enriched, language, in modern times named 'Middle English'. Recognisable Modern English emerged about 1450. While the Northumbrian that Aldred used about 950 can seem difficult, it is not impenetrable. Aldred's Anglo-Saxon word order of subject-verb-object ('dog bites man') is the basic modern English word order, unlike the subject-object-verb ('dog man bites') preferred by Latin or later German, for example. That Saxon order is a significant inheritance in English. Vocabulary, too, can be familiar: Aldred's 'Gode' is the English 'God' and not the Latin *Deus* or French *Dieu*; his 'word' is 'word', not the Latin *verbum* or French *mot*: his 'and' is 'and', not the Latin or French *et*. Even so, a passage in Aldred's Old English can seem formidably alien. Here are his first two verses of Mark 4, the beginning of the Parable of the Sower:

> *& eftersona ongann læra to sæ*
> ET ITERUM COEPIT DOCERE AD MARE
>
> *& gesomnad wæs to him ðreat menigo*
> ET CONGREGATA EST AD EUM TURBA MULTA
>
> *sua þætte in scipp astag gesætt on sæ*
> ITA UT IN NAVEM ASCENDENS SEDERET IN MARI

& all ðreat ymb sæ ofer eorðo wæs
ET OMNIS TURBA CIRCA MARE SUPER TERRAM ERAT

& lærde hia in bispellum menigo &
ET DOCEBAT ILLOS IN PARABOLIS MULTA ET

cuoeð to him on lar his
DICEBAT ILLIS IN DOCTRINA SUA.[9]

It will be seen that Aldred is translating word for word. Here is the same passage in a respected twentieth-century version, NRSV (1989):

> And he began to teach beside the sea. Such a very large crowd gathered around him that he got into a boat on the sea and sat there, while the whole crowd was beside the sea on the land. He began to teach them many things in parables, and in his teaching he said to them [. . .]

The Old English gloss in the Lindisfarne Gospels is the first extensive written Old English that has survived: the manuscript of the epic poem *Beowulf*, for example, probably dates from about AD 1000, though there is no certainty. The later Anglo-Saxons had a rich literature, in prose and poetry. The prose was often Christian in slant, in sermons, homilies and saints' lives, and even in parts of the chronicles of national life. Almost all the thirty thousand lines of poetry in Old English that have survived are explicitly Christian: a great deal is based on the Bible, and some of the poems are imaginative extensions of parts of the Bible. The very first poem in English, written in the late 600s, Caedmon's hymn of Creation, is a Bible poem, as will be seen.

There was, however, no complete translation of the Bible. Britons, like Pelagius or Alcuin, living outside the islands, as well as resident historians like Gildas, Nennius and Bede, and even the poet-bishop Aldhelm, wrote Latin. The serious Viking threats to life in England began around 850, though raids began earlier: Lindisfarne was sacked in 793. Until the time of the full Viking invasions, apart from the Lindisfarne glosses, and the glossed Old English fragments of Psalms mentioned above, for more than five hundred years, the Bible in England was always and entirely in Latin.

What kind of Latin, however, is another story.

THE LATIN BIBLE COMES TO ENGLAND

Christianity at first spread in Greek, a language more than adequate for Christian life and theology. Educated Romans knew Greek. Their slaves and freedmen in Rome were mostly Greek in origin; they found Latin foreign. Among the people the Romans ruled, across the vast Greek Empire, the soldiers and administrators of their empire had communicated in a common Greek dialect, the *koiné*.[10] Christian converts knew Greek: it was still in use in Christian correspondence from Rome as late as AD 250. Jewish communities away from Jerusalem, for their Scriptures (to Christians the Old Testament), used the Greek Bible, the translation from Hebrew known as the Septuagint (usually abbreviated to LXX) begun in the third century BC. In about AD 240 the Septuagint was effectively clarified for Christians by the scholar and theologian Origen in a comparative version in six columns (one Hebrew and five different Greek texts), his *Hexapla*. That the New Testament was written in Greek, most of it in the first century AD, is a mark of the range of that language at the time.

In the Empire, Christian congregations quickly developed far from Rome, and could not count on metropolitan sophistication of language. The Roman province of North Africa, where the common language was Latin, became more and more important as a region of Christian thought. From about AD 200, Latin for theology as well as religious correspondence gradually took over from Greek. As the New Testament canon – what books, and in what order – became established (it was finally confirmed in Africa, at a council in Carthage in AD 397), so a New Testament in Latin grew. No complete Latin Bible from this time is known. Fragments of the Old Testament in Latin have survived, in the form known as Old Latin (or *Vetus Latina*: both names are used; and it should always be in mind that these Old Latin versions of the Old Testament were from the Greek Septuagint, never from the Hebrew – unlike Jerome's 'Vulgate'). They sometimes contained whole books. Of the New Testament more copies in Old Latin have survived, especially of the Gospels, but again even single books are often incomplete. What seems to be the oldest of these Latin manuscripts is a codex (bound leaves, not a scroll) of the Gospels, probably dating from before AD 371: it may have been written by Eusebius, the great historian of the early churches, who was martyred in that year.

More teasing even than the fitful survival of these earliest Old Latin Bible texts, however, is the erratic relation between them. Wide disagreements suggest that they have come from different originals. Some surprising agreements suggest a common first translator: agreements in the Old Testament are always from the Septuagint. More probable is the effect of a congregation borrowing a needed book or passage in Latin from a neighbouring church for a scribe to copy, and then passing the new copy on again for other people. In that process, scribes would make mistakes, and correct other scribes' errors, and sometimes adjust the Latin again to the Greek. Eccentricities not only multiplied, but did so in families of copies, so that scholars now recognise in the first three centuries of the faith two chief clans of Old Latin Bible texts, African and European. It is still not known how Africa was evangelised – from Rome or from the East. Thus we do not know the sources of the first recognisable Old Latin text, which is African in origin and dates from some time in the second century.

These Old Latin versions (fragments would be a better word), from wherever they came, were not only legion and all different: they were often peculiarly wrong and in strange Latin. Nevertheless, they influenced the vocabulary of the emerging Romance languages (Italian, Spanish, French and others) more than did the 'Vulgate', prepared by Jerome.[11]

JEROME

By the end of the fourth century, Rome was increasingly affirming itself as the centre of Christian power worldwide. In AD 382, the reforming Pope Damasus asked his secretary, the scholar Jerome, to make an official revision which would be from Rome, and definitive.[12] Widely travelled in Gaul and Syria, highly educated, and with his own large library, Jerome was a natural choice. By the following year, 383, he had issued the four Gospels in his new Latin version, which rapidly became standard. These were immediately followed by his first Psalter, known until the sixteenth century as the 'Roman Psalter'. Damasus died at the end of 384. Jerome had had hopes of succeeding him as pope, but was passed over. Late in 386, he settled at Bethlehem, where he lived an ascetic and scholarly life until his death in 420.

Jerome's Roman Psalter, heavily used in Italian churches, had in a few years been corrupted – no doubt unintentionally – by much copying. Jerome made another version, this time correcting his own readings through access to Origen's *Hexapla*: its popularity in Gaul gave it the name 'Gallican Psalter'. This is the version of the Psalms which has survived into the modern Vulgate, the Latin 'common version' which came to dominate the Christian world, though it was not called the *vulgata editio* until the thirteenth century. As a young hermit in Syria, Jerome had begun to learn Hebrew, and he now set about making his new Latin version of the whole Old Testament from Hebrew, a task which he finished in 405. His reverence for the Hebrew text made him give a place only to the books he found there. He set aside the fourteen or so books found only in the Septuagint, like Ecclesiasticus or the Wisdom of Solomon, even though most of them were already accepted by the Roman Church and absorbed in various places in Old Latin Bibles. Eleven hundred years later, the sixteenth-century reformers translated those books from the original languages as an Old Testament Apocrypha, a section firmly separated from the canonical Jewish Scriptures.

Jerome translated other works and wrote many biblical commentaries. A passionate man, usually engaged in controversy, what he left is not always straightforward. The Latin New Testament that he gave to the Church, which became the Vulgate, is itself a problem. There is no evidence that Jerome translated more than the Gospels. The rest of the New Testament in the Vulgate is probably taken from Old Latin sources unrevised by him. It is striking that his own commentaries on Paul's epistles do not show knowledge of any revision of the Old Latin texts.

AFTER JEROME

Jerome had enemies, eager to blacken his work. Just as in the sixteenth century priests and monks preached against the 'new languages of Greek and Hebrew', by which the Devil was taking church-goers away from the 'true' Latin Bible, so Jerome's Old Testament based on the Hebrew was attacked as too Jewish, unlike the 'true' Greek Septuagint in common use. Congregations across the Christian world disliked and rejected Jerome's new modern translation, because changes had been made to the versions they knew as children, which their parents and grandparents had loved. Such a story is familiar from most ages of the Bible. Augustine mentions in a letter to Jerome in 403 that a bishop in Tripoli had nearly lost his flock in the disturbance following his reading a lesson from Jonah in Jerome's new version.[13] Moreover, it was noticed that only the Gospels and Psalms had any papal status. In Bethlehem, Jerome had worked on the rest of the Bible on his own initiative.

By about AD 600 in the Old Latin versions there were already chapter divisions, of unequal length, with an explanatory preface either at the head of each, or assembled at the beginning of the manuscript. Old Latin prefaces began to be taken over into the Vulgate, and mixed with Jerome's prefaces. Jerome's 'Vulgate' came to dominate only gradually. Around this time, Pope Gregory said that both translations, an Old Latin version and Jerome's 'Vulgate', were in use in the Roman Church (that is, in the West), though he added that he himself preferred the new one. As might be expected, all the versions began to merge. More significantly, for one reason or another – sentiment, or memory, or the desire to 'correct' – scribes often preferred the older reading.

Thus the Latin Bible which first came to England was not fixed. Even texts ascribed to Jerome may have had only a distant relation to what he had prepared. What was read depended on the route by which it came.

CHRISTIAN ENGLAND

The Romans occupied the province of Britannia for four hundred years, which is one-fifth of English recorded history. They left quite a lot of names (Winchester, Colchester); some towns and villas; five thousand miles of long-distance roads, many still in use; alphabetical writing; and Christianity.

The Apostle Paul visited Christian communities widely, moving steadily west after his life-changing encounter with the living Christ on the Damascus road (Acts 9) until by the middle of the first century he had established the new faith in Rome, the seat of the Emperor. This is clear from the New Testament.

Luke's Gospel recounts the humble birth of Jesus, the babe laid in a manger, an outcast even from a common inn. He is telling 'most excellent Theophilus . . . the certainty of those things' in the life, miracles, teaching, death and resurrection of Jesus. Luke's second book, the Acts of the Apostles, recounts how Christ's disciples, following the visitation of the Holy Spirit, journeyed widely, preaching Christianity. It is a great sweep of narrative mostly following Paul across the eastern Mediterranean to Rome. Luke's point is the power of God in Jesus, from a birth in a barn at the edge of the Roman world to the heart of the Empire's power.

This, as Luke constantly makes clear, is not just history happening: it is all, most significantly, fulfilling the Scriptures, especially the Prophets. All the early Christians interpreted the prophecies of the Old Testament as showing that the work of Christ fulfilled the power of God to go 'unto the ends of the earth'. What came into play with the resurrection of Jesus was God's intention for the whole world.

It is clear that Paul did not mean to stop at Rome, significant as that arrival was. Ahead of his coming, he wrote his most important letter to the Christians already there, and to interested Jews. This is the Epistle to the Romans, which is largely the statement that above all others expresses the heart of Christian theology. At the end of this letter, he gives day-to-day information saying how much he has longed to see those people at Rome, and he will make that visit on his way to Spain (Romans 15:24). He seems to think of Rome as a base for even wider evangelising. From Spain, journeys could more easily be made northwards, by sea:

Cornwall could be reached from northern Spain in under a week.[14] A map of the world at that time would show, from a centre in Jerusalem, 'the ends of the earth', extending to remote islands to the north and west. Early Mediterranean Christians, including Paul, probably knew of the new Roman province of Britannia, including Ireland; no doubt they planned to evangelise there.

There are records of Christians in the islands from not long after Christ. Indeed, it is possible that some of the Mediterranean traders who came to the Roman province of Britannia – for West Country tin, for example – were Christians. It is not wholly impossible that the first Christians arrived soon after the invasion of AD 43 with additions to the Roman army, a date only ten years after the Resurrection, though this has to be romantic speculation. Paul's letter to the Romans is usually dated about the mid-50s.

There is a later legend that Joseph of Arimathaea – the 'rich man' (Matthew 27:57), 'counsellor' (Luke 23:50), 'disciple of Jesus' (John 19:38), who asked Pilate for the body of Jesus, and laid it in his sepulchre – not only came to England after the Resurrection, but brought with him the 'Holy Grail' (the cup used at the Last Supper). He is said to have built Britannia's first church, at Glastonbury, in Somerset. This story, though retold today, dates only from the twelfth century. It appears in a later, and anonymous, revision of a history of Glastonbury Abbey first made by William of Malmesbury in about 1135. Joseph of Arimathaea appears there as associated with Glastonbury alongside St Patrick and King Arthur. A separate legend tells how Joseph's staff took root and became the Glastonbury Thorn, an object of some veneration even now. None of the extensive archaeological excavations at Glastonbury and adjacent sites has yet produced any evidence for Roman Christianity there: the first Christian phase at Glastonbury seems to have been a sixth-century monastery.[15]

Harder evidence of Christianity in Britannia, however, does not begin until the second century, and even that is not especially solid. Tertullian, 'the Father of Latin Theology', writing from Carthage around AD 200, made the point that Christianity was by then established in the remoter fringes of the Roman Empire including even *Britannorum inaccessa Romanis loca* ('places of the British not approached by the Romans'). In Alexandria at about the same time, Origen celebrated the fact that Christianity was by then firmly found at the very ends of the world, *quae mundi limites tenent*, regions which include *Britannia* or *terra Britanniae*.[16]

Christianity in Roman Britain was not dominant, nor even strong. In all the rich artefacts surviving from the Roman occupation, archaeological evidence for Christianity is flimsy.[17] Objects give only circumstantial evidence: a late Roman tablet found in Bath in 1979, inscribed with the first recorded use of the word *Christianus* in Roman Britain;[18] and the celebrated word-square, or acrostic, first found in 1868 scratched on the wall of a Roman house at Cirencester (others are known, including one at Manchester). This nonsense phrase, ROTAS OPERA TENET AREPO SATOR (formerly thought to mean only, and mysteriously, 'the sower Arepo holds the wheels carefully') was deciphered in 1926 to show a cross made of PATER NOSTER twice, joined at the single N, and with A and O (Alpha and Omega: as in Revelation 1, 21, and 22) at either end (fig. 2).[19]

Archaeology of Roman sites in most of the period of the occupation shows an amalgam of beliefs, with pagan and sometimes Christian motifs side by side. Mithraism and Isis-worship were popular with the army and fortress towns. It is not known when Alban, the first Christian martyr in Britannia, died, but the likeliest dates are early or late in the third century. His story was often told in medieval hagiographies,[20] where he is described as a Roman officer in the city of Verulamium, the modern St Albans in Hertfordshire. Christians were being persecuted, usually for their insistent monotheism. In his house Alban hid a priest, whose Christian qualities impressed him. The priest was seized. While his execution was being prepared, Alban defended him, and died in his stead. His shrine is still venerated in St Albans Abbey as the place of his death or burial. That shrine was in place in 429, when it was specially visited by Bishop Germanus of Auxerre.

Constantine, who Christianised the Empire, had been proclaimed emperor in 306 in York, the military headquarters of the Romans in the islands of Britannia. Christianity in Britannia in 314 was strong enough for three bishops, from London, York and Colchester, to be sent to the Council of Arles in the south of France, which had been summoned by Constantine to deal with a schism in the African church.

All these events were before Jerome began his revisions, so that what biblical texts there were in Roman Britannia could only have been variants of Old Latin versions. It is impossible to say which they were. Among Christians in Northern Europe, the texts presumably belonged to a European group: but movements of texts across the Mediterranean were so frequent that descendants of African Old Latin texts are also likely. Lacking any remaining evidence, we simply do not know.

For the period immediately after the Romans, a key figure in the debate about what Bibles were in Britain is St Patrick. He was born into an upper-class provincial Roman-British family, and died in Ireland. His dates are unknown; they usually appear as 'probably *c.* 390–460'. That birth date is seven years after Jerome's first revision of the Gospels in Rome. How soon did that arrive in Britain? Was Patrick brought up to know it, or was he entirely dependent on the Old Latin Scriptures? A neat Irishism emerges. By studying Patrick's later use of Scripture, more accurate dates for his life might be established.[21] But also by studying Patrick's later use of Scripture, the positions of Old Latin and Jerome versions in Britain might be established. Each variable demolishes the other. The slightly later historian Gildas, educated possibly around 500, might seem to offer a surer base. Yet the best that can be said is that he might have known parts of the Jerome Old Testament, but he quotes the book of Job, for example, in its severely cut Old Latin version (lacking between seven hundred and eight hundred lines) as it existed even before Origen's *Hexapla* of about AD 200. For the New Testament, he used Old Latin and Jerome versions: but in any case he tended to quote from memory.[22]

Care is needed, moreover, not to misunderstand what is meant by 'Bible'. For many centuries, copies of any Latin Bible in Europe that were complete (known as 'pandects', from the Roman word for complete bodies of laws) were so rare as to be remarkable. A more usual reference is that given by Gregory of Tours in his *Historia Francorum* of about 576, noting of a Bible that 'three volumes had been placed upon the altar', then specifying that these were the Prophets, the Epistles and the Gospels.[23] In another place, the books are the Psalms, Samuel and Kings, and the Gospels.[24] A list of the eleven surviving Bible manuscripts from Anglo-Saxon England, up to the end of the ninth century, includes one which is merely a single leaf of Maccabees, one which has a few verses of Judges, one which is a leaf of Leviticus, one which is a leaf of Daniel, one which is a leaf of Numbers and three of Deuteronomy; a leaf of the Minor Prophets; one which has Wisdom and Ecclesiasticus and one, the 'Egerton Codex', with Proverbs, Ecclesiastes, Song of Songs, Wisdom and Ecclesiasticus.[25] These are, of course, only what have survived: but it seems likely, on the model of the Gospel books (see below), that Bible manuscripts circulated in groups, as it might be the Pentateuch or the Wisdom books. Of the rest of the eleven in the list above, one is a complete New Testament, and only two relate to original complete Bibles, one being the Codex Amiatinus (see also below) and one (of which only the Gospels and part of Acts have survived) probably from Canterbury.[26]

MISSION FROM ROME

When the Romans left south-east England, Christianity also drained away. Even now, little light from documents can be shed on the period long called the British Dark Ages. The conflicts with the earlier invading Germanic tribes, and then the arrival of Angles, Saxons and Jutes, are almost completely hidden. Stories like those about King Arthur were first told hundreds of years after the events, and elaborated more recently still.[27] Seen from Rome, England in the sixth century was pagan and barbaric: Pope Gregory I, noting 'the English, placed in a corner of the world [. . .] without faith, worshipping stocks and stones', determined to send missionaries.[28] He was stimulated, according to Bede, by the beauty of fair-headed English slaves in the market-place at Rome – told they were 'Angles', Gregory dubbed them 'Angels'. He sent Augustine (not, of course, the great African theologian, Augustine of Hippo), who, with his forty-strong mission, found at first that he could not cross the Channel, being so 'paralysed with terror' at having to face such a 'barbarous, fierce and unbelieving nation'.[29]

Safely arrived, in 597, in Kent, Augustine, rightly understanding the power of Anglo-Saxon kings, first converted the royal household there, without difficulty: King Aethelbert's Frankish wife, herself a Christian, had prepared the way. Within a year, Pope Gregory could report, ten thousand English had been baptised.[30] Augustine intended to set up an archbishopric at York, and, disobeying Pope Gregory, in Kent at Canterbury, the seat of Aethelbert and his Christian wife, and a royal centre. (Gregory had intended control to be from the two major Roman cities, from London as the greater in the south, and the lesser Roman provinces controlled from York.) Christianity in lowland Britain was being established again. An offshoot of the Kentish mission was an enterprise by Paulinus in York: he converted the King of Northumbria, and thus more thousands.

All did not go smoothly. It is estimated that in the years between the Romans and the Normans, England had over two hundred kings.[31] Rivalries between local royal houses broke the continuity of faith. By the mid-seventh century, two systems of Christianity were clashing in Britain. Augustine's mission from Rome had arrived from the south; but another branch of Christianity, ultimately Irish from the north and west, had evangelised as far south as East Anglia and Sussex (and far into Europe), and that from Rome. At the Synod of Whitby in 664, the Northumbrian church, influenced by the 'powerful, proud and energetic ecclesiastic' Wilfrid, Bishop of Hexham, sided with the practices and ethos of Rome. Though the result was important in the making of different links with the faith on the Continent and in the Mediterranean world, 'the simpler ascetic Christianity of the Irish tradition lost its influence on mainstream English, or at least Northumbrian, devotional life'.[32]

It may be instructive to speculate at this point. Though the differences were not absolute, and the sides had common ground, and the power of Rome in Europe was great, had the Synod of Whitby decided the other way, making the Celtic way the norm, British Christianity could have been markedly different. It would, for example, have avoided the severe repres-sions later imposed by Rome; not only the persistent martyrdoms of so many 'heretics', climaxing in the 1550s after nearly nine hundred years, but periods of intense censorship of thought, as for example that established in 1409 by Archbishop Thomas Arundel, lasting well over a century.

> The Roman Church reverenced the authoritative St Peter, the Celtic Church the sensitive St John [. . .]. 'The Celtic Church gave love, the Roman Church gave law': the epigram is as true as most epigrams, though doubtless both churches gave both. Authority was necessary to wean turbulent folk from their tribal quarrels; yet the Columban Church stood for a passionate religion which did not all die.[33]

Speculating more wildly still, and noting that there was no great Celtic urge to vernacular Scripture, one wonders whether the Roman abhorrence of Scripture in anything but Latin would have been avoided, and translators like Wyclif and Tyndale would have appeared earlier, unbranded as heretics.

Just as, however, later Britain had a cosmopolitan language, with Saxon, Norman French and Latin mingling to make a subtle and responsive tongue, so now Britain had a cosmopolitan Christianity, with some Irish, and, dominantly, Roman influences together.

The Church in England was influenced by the journeys of influential figures. One, the Archbishop of Canterbury from 669 to 690, Theodore of Tarsus, had come to England via Antioch, Constantinople and Rome. A man of outstanding learning, he made a school at Canterbury which attracted Irish pupils. His assistant, Hadrian, was African.[34] Journeys to Rome by English churchmen were common. That turbulent Wilfrid in Northumberland, Abbot of Ripon and finally Bishop of Hexham, who ensured at Whitby that the British Church was for nearly a thousand years dominated, if not yet controlled, by Rome, had travelled to Italy several times. The wealthy Benedict Biscop went to Italy five times. He was the founder in Northumbria (with endowments from the Northumbrian king, Ecgfrith) of the monasteries at Monkwearmouth in 674 and Jarrow in 681, those great centres of learning (and Bible copying) which nurtured the Venerable Bede (see below, pp. 37–9). Benedict, as did others, carried back to Northumbria from Italy, with great caravans of porters, large numbers of books and paintings of biblical subjects. He went to Gaul a number of times to bring back craftsmen for his monasteries.[35] Benedict and his successor Ceolfrith, in Rome together, learned the ways of chanting the liturgy at St Peter's, particularly so that the Psalms could be heard and thus understood – though in Latin, of course – to introduce them at Monkwearmouth and Jarrow for the devotions there, worship shared by

Bede. Like so many others, Bede and Ceolfrith learned the Psalter by heart: Ceolfrith at Jarrow recited his psalter twice daily in addition to the Offices, and on his last journey to Rome he 'daily chanted the psalter of David' (that is, probably most of Psalms 3–72) 'in order three times over'.[36]

The first known works of literature by a Briton were the theological writings of a Welshman named Morgan, who lived in Rome under the name of Pelagius. His famous heresy (which states, roughly, that we *can* pull ourselves up by our own bootstraps, and thus have no need of external grace), was dangerous to all the Church. St Germanus, Bishop of Auxerre, was sent to Rome to deal with it. As a home-grown heresy, Pelagianism seems to have been strong in Britain: Germanus engaged in public debate, apparently at Verulamium, with men of influence, 'conspicuous for their riches, brilliant in dress, and surrounded by a fawning multitude'.[37]

The inflow of books to Britain from the south up to the early eighth century is vividly illustrated by a story, told four hundred years later, by the twelfth-century chronicler William of Malmesbury. It is about the scholar Aldhelm (who had been a pupil of Theodore's school at Canterbury) shortly after he had been made Bishop of Sherborne.

> [He] was walking by the shore near Dover when he encountered some sailors who had apparently arrived from Gaul with a complete copy of the Old and New Testaments [presumably a pandect] for sale. Their price, however, was as high as their manners were insolent and they would not lower it for Aldhelm. Instead they put out to sea again with the Bible. However, retribution came at once in the form of a violent storm, putting them in great peril. They shouted to Aldhelm to help them, and he did so by making the sign of the cross, at which the storm died away and the ship was blown safely back to the shore. The sailors were now only too willing to sell Aldhelm the Bible at a fair price. According to William (who died about 1143), it was still to be seen at Malmesbury in his own day, but no trace of it now remains.[38]

CELTIC MISSIONS

On the western fringes of the British islands, Christianity had survived despite a probable Roman resurgence of paganism before those conquerors left: from the late fourth century, Anglo-Saxon invaders in the south and east had also arrived with their gods Woden and Thonor. Following the conversion of Constantine some time before AD 324, Christian monas-

teries spread rapidly in Europe. These places of seclusion from the world
for contemplation and work under the direction of an abbot (a father,
from the Aramaic *abba*) were developed under various rules, that of Benedict becoming dominant in the West. Monks in Ireland, established in
monasteries from Gaul, were vigorous as scholars, artists, warriors and missionaries. From them came those Celtic saints so attractively described by
Bede, and works of high art like the decorated Gospel books. From those
monks came, above all, over time the great movements of evangelising the
west and north of Britain – and far beyond (see map, fig. 3). Patrick evangelised Ireland (and drove out the snakes), Ninian converted the Picts of
south-west Scotland, and Kentigern evangelised Strathclyde. From Wales,
Illtud and David sent missionaries to darkest continental Europe. From
Ireland in 565 the powerful Donegal man Columba – warrior, statesman,
hermit and missionary, who died in 597 – founded, on the small, low
Hebridean island of Iona on the fringes of western Scotland, that collection of beehive huts which made the monastery there. It is a site still held
dear by many Christians. (Samuel Johnson famously wrote of his visit in
1773: 'That man is little to be envied, whose patriotism would not gain
force upon the plain of *Marathon*, or whose piety would not grow warmer
among the ruins of *Iona*.'[39] For England's greatest mind at the time,
Marathon and Iona were equal. Today the Iona Community is a force in
Christian Britain.)

From Iona the Celtic north and west were evangelised – and educated.
From Iona, Aidan founded in 635 his monastery on Lindisfarne, a site
chosen in obvious imitation of Iona. From Lindisfarne over north-east
England the evangelism was energetic. The Lindisfarne Gospels text is, as
it happens, a purer form of the Vulgate, probably taken from a text from
southern Italy. That is striking, as by then the Latin Bible had usually
become a mixture of Old Latin from many sources, with Jerome added,
miscopied, 'corrected' or 'improved', and sometimes, as often happened
when scribes wrote, with marginal notes absorbed into the text. The Irish
Latin Bible, spread through western Scotland and northern England,
was apparently an ancient, even pre-Jerome, mixture, in contrast to the
Lindisfarne Gospels. The variation perhaps did not greatly matter. If the
monks' burnside preachings did include readings from the Bible, they
would probably have been from small, portable collections of Bible texts
(usually still in Latin, of course). The volume 'The Bible', made as glorious as it could be, was far too precious to be taken wandering through
bog and heather in drenching rain. Its glory was as a sacred object to be
shown on special occasions to impress.

Sculpture, sharing some pictorial effects with the Gospel books, was less
concealed. While decorated pillars or slabs, different in each Celtic region

from Cornwall to Shetland, grew to show more New Testament iconography (the Crucifixion, for example – there are many Pictish cross-slabs), the Picts occupying most of Scotland still enjoyed the Old Testament David rending the jaws of the lion, Jonah and the whale or Daniel in the lions' den, as well as incidents from saints' lives.[40]

GOSPEL BOOKS

The Lindisfarne Gospels were not alone, though they are unique in having Old English glosses. We know of similar early books: for example, the Book of Armagh, the earliest New Testament made in Ireland, which dates from around 800. This has little decoration but contains lives of St Martin and St Patrick (twice) and 'St Patrick's Confession'. Elaborate, with initial letters so decorated as to be riddling, and intended for display, these books can be great works of art, among the richest treasures that these islands possess.

The earliest surviving fragments of such a Bible, dating from the middle of the seventh century, are a dozen leaves from a Gospel book, an Irish Old Latin text, made and decorated by an Irish scribe, and now in Durham Cathedral Library. Only slightly later, perhaps made about 675, is the beautiful Book of Durrow, the name of the Irish monastery in County Meath where it was later kept (now in Trinity College, Dublin): it is a Vulgate, and may have been made in Northumbria, or on Iona. The Otho-Corpus Gospels, now in the British Library in London and Corpus Christi College, Cambridge, are badly damaged: they may have been made in Lindisfarne, and perhaps were originally splendid. The Echternach Gospels, now in the Bibliothèque Nationale, Paris, are less fine. Whereas the great surviving Gospel books, like Lindisfarne, are written in a script characteristic of Northumbria, ultimately from Rome – large, clear rather monumental capitals called uncials (because the letters are said to be an inch high), the Echternach volume is in a small running script, 'cursive minuscule', more like modern rapid handwriting.[41] The Gospels from Lichfield and elsewhere are all rich with colour in interlaced designs and many symbolic images, sometimes drawn from the Bible, for example the beasts in the Book of Revelation.

The most richly decorated and complex is the Book of Kells; every page is different, but each belongs to the whole. It is not known when, between 750 and 825, or where in the islands, it was made, or by whom. One tradition suggests that it was at least begun on Iona. For centuries associated with Ireland, it is today in the Old Library of Trinity College, Dublin.

A complete Bible in England is noted just before 700: the Codex Grandior of Cassiodorus, brought by the Abbot Ceolfrith from Italy to Northumbria. It is, at least in the Old Testament, an Old Latin version. Ceolfrith set out to imitate it in making, at his scriptoria at Jarrow and Monkwearmouth, three great copies of the whole Bible now from the Jerome version. Two were to be placed in the churches of his monasteries for 'anyone' to read – that is, any residing monk or visitor who had Latin. One later disappeared totally. Another apparently arrived at the cathedral priory at Worcester: it was broken up, perhaps at the Reformation; some leaves are in the British Library.

The third has, however, wonderfully, survived. It was made at the monastery at Jarrow before 716 as a gift from Ceolfrith to St Peter's at Rome. Ceolfrith died in Langres in Burgundy. His book may have reached Rome, but it was for a long time at the monastery of Monte Amiata in central Italy. It is therefore known as the Codex Amiatinus, and is now in the Biblioteca Medicea-Laurenziana, Florence.[42] This massive book, 250 mm thick, the 1,030 leaves measuring 505 by 340 mm, and all weighing almost 75 pounds (the average weight of the breed of large dog called the Great Dane), is the oldest surviving copy of a complete Vulgate found anywhere: it has for its version of the Psalms Jerome's third revision, made from the original Hebrew, known as the *iuxta Hebraeos* or *Hebraicum*. The fact that it was made in Northumbria says a great deal about the state of Christian scholarship in northern England in the early eighth century.[43] Like everything else about it, the text is conspicuously Italian. Moreover, great care went into its creation: it is likely that Bede himself worked on it. So excellent is the Codex Amiatinus that it has stood as a base text for all later recensions of the Vulgate.

Codex Amiatinus contains three fine painted miniatures. One, preceding the New Testament, shows Christ in Majesty. One is a two-page depiction of the Tabernacle. The third, the famous 'Ezra miniature' in the preliminary leaves, shows a scholar, pen in hand, at work on an open volume. Behind him on shelves is a Bible in nine volumes (fig. 4). So at the start of a beautifully copied Bible is a picture of a scribe carefully copying a Bible. He is labelled Ezra, who during the Babylonian captivity preserved the Scriptures and thus the Jewish nation (see Ezra 7:10 and Nehemiah 8:1–8). His picture was probably copied from Cassiodorus's Codex Grandior, in which he may not have been labelled Ezra.[44]

Probably in the ninth century, the first surviving Bible from Southumbria (probably Kent), the very different Codex Aureus, was made. This sumptuous volume has purple pages with gold, silver and white script. Its history seems appropriately colourful, though all we know for certain is that it was redeemed from Viking plunderers by a couple who gave it to

Christ Church, Canterbury. Since the end of the seventeenth century it has been in the Royal Library of Stockholm.

From the correspondence of the Anglo-Saxon missionary and martyr Boniface (*c.* 675–*c.* 750) we know also of further Bible manuscript production in the south.[45] Glorious Gospels have survived. There must have been many much more ordinary copies of the Psalms and Gospels, and lectionaries of Old Testament readings, as well as everyday service books made, perhaps in England, for the more than two hundred religious foundations estimated to be in the land by the beginning of the ninth century: twenty-nine Gospel books and fifteen fragments have been identified as being in Anglo-Saxon England through the eighth century. The Stonyhurst Gospel, also from Monkwearmouth-Jarrow, is a pocket book (the Codex Amiatinus needed two men to carry it). To those Gospel books and fragments must be added a large number of intentional part-Bibles.[46]

Though complete Bibles were rarely made in the period, we know of other Christian literature, patristic commentaries or biblical studies, circulating in Britain and Ireland,[47] giving welcome evidence of Christian activity there at the time. Books of commentary carry with them the danger of everlasting wanderings in fancifully interpretative By-Path Meadows, further and further from the wellspring of Scripture; and that itself was, as already noted, not only usually fragmentary, but always remote from the ordinary people of the land.

BEDE

The Venerable Bede is our authority for almost all the history of these times. In his *History of the English Church and People*, written in Jarrow around 731, he tried to make complicated matters coherent. His concentration on the invasions of Angles, Saxons and Jutes and their conflicts, though persistent ever since, is over-simplified. Modern archaeology and place-name studies show that after the Romans left there were throughout the land some strong settlements – all pagan – from elsewhere in northern Europe;[48] and by the time of Augustine's mission in 597 these 'warring' invaders were already unitedly calling themselves 'English'. By 600, an Irish colony, Dalriada, had been established in western Scotland.

Yet Bede's importance as a source is very great. As a historian who absorbed the earlier, and wilder, writer, the Welsh Gildas, he was thorough: as acknowledged in his Preface, he received information from scholars abroad, checked his sources, verified his facts where he could, and wrote an attractive Latin. To Bede we owe the picture of the loss and chaos, after the Romans left, transformed into a unified British

Christianity from the work of such saints as Patrick, David, Augustine, Ninian and Columba, and especially through enrichment from the civilisation and culture of Rome. His writing of history, unmatched in England for four hundred years, and original, was influenced by the fourth-century Eusebius of Caesaraea and by Gregory of Tours.[49] He maintained that the Roman Church did well to enforce that union of the spiritual and temporal powers on Britain which led to stability through strong local administration. He wrote about his saints to make examples of what, and what not, to do; but, interested in people, he also gave pen-pictures of, for example, Aidan, Cuthbert and Oswald, and sketches of life in his time. Here is his famous story of the speech by one of King Edwin of Northumbria's chief advisers, at the council to decide whether the new religion brought by Bishop Paulinus should be accepted:

> O king, the present life of men on earth, in comparison with the time that is unknown to us, appears to me to be as if, when you are sitting at supper with your ealdormen and thegns in winter time, and a fire is lighted in the midst and the hall warmed, but everywhere outside the storms of wintry rain and snow are raging, a sparrow should come and fly rapidly through the hall, coming in at one door, and immediately out at the other. Whilst it is inside, it is not touched by the storm of winter, but yet, that tiny space of calm gone in a moment, from winter at once returning to winter, it is lost to your sight. Thus this life of men appears for a little while; but of what is to follow, or of what went before, we are entirely ignorant. Hence, if this new teaching brings greater certainty, it seems fit to be followed.[50]

Bede's aim as a historian was to encourage the conversion of the English people, and what he saw as its best future as subject to Rome and the pope. Like his lives of English and Irish saints, his Christian story of all England was intended to contrast with secular and more local sagas, though he wrote from a monastery (Monkwearmouth) that he hardly left. His scrupulousness allows him to be properly named 'The Father of English History', and his influence was deep. His interests, moreover, were wide. His scientific treatises were ahead of their time; particularly on the calculation of dates and time – he was the first to promote systematic use of *anno domini* dating – in which continental work came to him, by a natural route of learning, from Ireland.[51] He wrote on the nature of things, *De natura rerum*. He wrote books of instruction on metrics, rhetoric and spelling. He was an important exegete of the Bible, and knew Greek as well as Latin and, it is sometimes said, some Hebrew, though the evidence for any Hebrew in Northumbria at the time is scant.[52] He wrote biblical commentaries which were eagerly sought on the Continent, and hymns and homilies.

Before he died in 735 he began to translate the Gospel of John into Anglo-Saxon, 'into our mother tongue, to the great profit of the Church': he got no further than John 6:9, and what he made has not survived.[53]

Our loss of Bede's Anglo-Saxon Gospel is great; yet it is a little made up for by his account of Caedmon – according to him, Britain's first Anglo-Saxon poet, whose poems were biblical. Bede's account is in Latin: later Anglo-Saxon versions of the story may be from translations made by King Alfred.

CAEDMON

Bede relates in Book 4 of his *History* that Caedmon was an uneducated herdsman at the Abbey of Whitby when Hild was abbess there (657–80). What follows is Bede translated from the Latin by C. L. Wrenn:

[He] had not at any time learned anything of poems. Hence it was that sometimes when at a party, when it was decided for joyful entertainment that all in turn must recite verse to the harp's accompaniment, he when he saw the harp getting near to himself would arise from the midst of the feast and go out and walk back to his house. [Here the Alfredian version adds that it was from a feeling of shame, *for scome*, that he did so.] When on a certain occasion he had done this, and leaving the house where the party was held had gone out to the cattle-pens, as their care had been assigned to him for that night, and when there he had at the normal time given his limbs to sleep, a certain man was standing by him in a dream and, greeting him and calling him by his name, said: 'Caedmon, sing me something.' But he in answering said: 'I do not know how to sing: for it was just for this reason that I came away from the feast and departed hither, because I could not sing.' Again he who was talking with him said: 'Yet you *can* sing to me.' 'What', said Caedmon, 'must I sing?' Then the other said: 'Sing of the beginning of created things.' Now when Caedmon had received this answer, immediately he began to sing verses in praise of God the creator which he had never heard, of which this is the sense. 'Now we must praise the Author of the Kingdom of Heaven, the might of the Creator and the thoughts of His mind – the deeds of the Father of glory. [We must sing] how he who is eternal God, the Author of all marvellous things, was manifest: he who first created heaven as a roof-covering for the sons of men, and then as almighty guardian of mankind made the earth.' This is the sense but not the actual order of the words of what Caedmon had sung while sleeping. For poems, however excellently composed, cannot be translated word for word from one language into another

without damage to elegance and dignity. Now when he had risen from
his sleep, he retained in his memory everything which he had sung
while sleeping. And to these verses he quickly added more in the same
rhythm and meter in words of a poem worthy of God.

When morning had come, he went to the steward who was his chief
and shewed him what sort of gift he had received. He was then conducted to the Abbess and commanded to show what he had dreamed
in the presence of many learned men and to recite the poem: so that
by the judgement of everyone it might be tested of what kind or from
whence had come what he had related. And it seemed to them all that
it was a grace from heaven and granted by God. Then they expounded
to him a discourse of sacred history or doctrine, and commanded him,
if he could, to render this into the melody of poetry. So he, when he
had finished these matters, went away: and in the morning he came
back and produced it composed as he had been ordered in the most
excellent poetry. Wherefore the Abbess, immediately embracing the
grace of God in the man, instructed him with a proposal that he should
abandon the secular habit and take that of a monk. So she added him,
with his goods, after receiving him into the monastery, to the company
of the brethren: and she commanded that he should be taught the
whole sequence of sacred Scripture. Now he, taking all that he could
learn by hearing, retaining it in his mind, and turning it over like a
clean beast ruminating, converted it into the sweetest poetry. Indeed,
by the sweetness of its melody he made his teachers in their turn
become his listeners.[54]

The West Saxon version of Caedmon's hymn, which is all that has survived in Anglo-Saxon, made late in the ninth century, possibly translated
by Alfred, gives what we may take as being close to Caedmon's original
words:

> Nu sculon herigean   heofonrices weard,
> metodes meahte   and his modge þanc,
> weorc wuldorf æder,   swa he wundra gehwæs,
> ece drihten,   or onstealde.
> He ærest sceop   eorþan bearnum
> horfron to hrofe,   halif scyppend;
> þa middangeard   moncynnes weard,
> ece drihten,   æfter teode
> firum foldan,   frea ælmihtig.

> (Now must we praise   of heaven's kingdom the Keeper
> Of the Lord the power   and his Wisdom

The work of the Glory-Father,　　as he of marvels each,
The eternal Lord,　　　the beginning established.
He first created　　　of earth for the sons
Heaven as a roof,　　　the holy Creator.
Then the middle-enclosure　　　of mankind the Protector
The eternal Lord,　　　thereafter made
For men, earth　　　the Lord almighty.[55])

Bede's account is important for several reasons. It suggests what was, as it were, in the air. Here is, already, that genre of elaborate paraphrase of Bible subjects which will be a mark of Anglo-Saxon biblical poetry. Indeed, the three long poems *Genesis, Exodus* and *Daniel*, surviving only in the manuscript Junius II in the Bodleian Library, Oxford, a manuscript which dates from about 1000, were much later ascribed to Caedmon; scholarship now finds that extremely unlikely. Secondly, at a time when very few in Britain could read or write, much less be familiar with documents in church Latin, the formidable Hild must have recognised the value of Caedmon's gift in teaching about the Christian faith. Thirdly, in seventh-century Northumbria people connected with an abbey, though they could not read, could and did learn songs, play an instrument and perform when asked. They took for granted a living tradition of oral poetry, which seems to have contained Bible stories.

BIBLE KNOWLEDGE IN ANGLO-SAXON TIMES

Among the learned, there could be moderately wide knowledge of the Bible. Thus the *Life of Gregory the Great* written at Whitby between 690 and 704 has quotations from the Psalms and seven Old Testament books: in the New Testament, Matthew is the writer's favourite Gospel, and 1 Corinthians is his or her favourite Epistle; all is from the Vulgate. A *Life of St Guthlac* written in East Anglia between 730 and 740 by a monk, Felix, has thirty-five direct quotations from Scripture, twenty-five from the Vulgate. Bede's own *Life of St Cuthbert*, rich with biblical reference, uses the Vulgate with variations, and other textual Bible sources. And so on. Bede's knowledge of the Bible throughout his writings was wide and deep. He interpreted the biblical books that were the favourites of the Fathers, like Genesis or Luke's Gospel, and also those they ignored, like Ezra-Nehemiah and the Epistles of James, Peter, Jude and John (named 'the Catholic Epistles' as they were addressed to congregations generally).

Bede did not think of the Bible as a reference tool. His commentaries were intended to reveal the riches of biblical books to pastoral workers:

monks primarily, and all preachers and teachers concerned with the cure
of souls. The library he could use was well stocked, and the workers in
the scriptoria were busy making copies. There is evidence of much export
of manuscripts to Europe.[56] Above all, Bede had access not only to part-
Bibles, thanks to the acquisitions of the abbot Benedict and his successor
Ceolfrith, but also, remarkably, as already noted, to the complete Bible of
Cassiodorus, copied at Monkwearmouth three times, work which included
the Codex Amiatinus: England's greatest exegete lived and worked at the
place where was made England's greatest medieval Bible.

Bede died in 735. He did not see the great change that came over
Britain with the raids and invasions of the Vikings. By the time of his
death, every English king – and there were many – was at least nominally
Christian. 'The Bible', though present as object of veneration, was often
only small parts of Scripture with other material added, and was anyway
in a foreign tongue, known to few. What biblical exegesis there was, always
in Latin, came already in the form in which it would still be found
throughout Christendom eight hundred years later, and far beyond, 'the
dialectical use made by the later schoolmen of truncated texts, wrenched
from their contexts'.[57]

THE GOTHIC BIBLE

Before about AD 850 and the change brought by the serious arrival of the
Vikings, the countries to the south and east of England, lacked a scholar
of the calibre of Bede; scriptoria such as were found in Northumbria; and
with very rare exceptions, any attempts at translating even small parts of
the Bible into any vernacular.

One of the exceptions, however, is considerable. Made about 350 in the
vast 'Balkan' empire stretching from the Danube to the Don, in the land
of the Goths, a quite remarkable translation of the Latin into Gothic was
made by Bishop Ulfilas, also known as Wulflas, some of which has survived. The lavish Codex Argenteus, written on purple parchment in silver
and gold ink, contains the Gospels, with some large gaps. Seven other
surviving manuscripts give fragments of Gospels and Epistles in outline,
and one has three Old Testament chapters, Nehemiah 5–7.[58] These Gospels
are the oldest surviving text in any Germanic language. Ulfilas invented
an alphabetical script for them. Though an early form of a Low German
language, Gothic is a long way from the Anglo-Saxon of six hundred years
later – the distance of Chaucer from us. Since modern English is basically
Germanic, it is not surprising that occasionally phrases leap out even to
the modern eye, like the *Wha ist namo þein?* of Luke 8:30, in Anglo-Saxon

Hwaet ist ðin nama?; but there can have been no influence whatsoever on English versions.

Ulfilas translated the New Testament from the original Greek, and his Old Testament passages are from the Greek of the Septuagint. He is said to have not included Old Testament history, because the Goths were already warlike enough. His aim as a translator was to render every word in the Greek text by a corresponding word in the Gothic, even to the Greek particles μεν (*men*) and ἀν (*an*), though the result of that could be clumsy or meaningless. He kept to the Greek word order. This rigidity was out of respect for the sacred text. It included on the whole a word-for-word absoluteness, scorning more elegant variation, though this does not hold for all the Gospels. Codex Argenteus and its relatives, including a bilingual Gothic-Latin version, are not only wonderful in themselves – especially considering their early dates and that they are the only Gothic texts to have survived – they also allow useful study of the development of the Greek, and Latin, texts on which they were based.[59]

Of Bible texts in the common languages of the people of Europe before 850, that is all that has survived: it probably roughly indicates all that there was. Some tiny fragments of Matthew in the Bavarian dialect and three versions of the Lord's Prayer have survived.[60] Germanic dialects are the language of elaborate long poems, based on the Bible, written just before 850: a genre, taken up in England and France, which is a large topic in the following chapter.

The richness of the Bible in the British islands up to 850 must still be remarked. Continental and North African Latin Bibles (almost always parts of the whole) circulated, in various textual forms.[61] Yet that known succession of large and magnificent copies from dedicated Northumbrian and Irish scriptoria is unique.

There is also a hint of the making of more workaday small volumes: in noting this, it might be recalled that what Bede is said at the end of his life to have begun to translate into Anglo-Saxon, of all Scripture, was St John's Gospel. In AD 687, St Cuthbert died. In 1104, his coffin, on its way to Durham where it is enshrined, was opened. It was found to contain a remarkable small book. Now on display in the British Library, it is the earliest surviving European book with the binding – red leather laid over card in an interlace pattern – still attached. The small volume, with a beautiful script, in Latin, is St John's Gospel.

Chapter 3

THE ANGLO-SAXON BIBLE, 850–1066

THOUGH THERE WAS GREAT INTEREST in the Bible (in Latin), and a good
deal of translating, no complete versions in English were made in the
Anglo-Saxon period.

The Gospels, Psalms and other parts of the Old Testament were several
times translated: most often only as Old English glosses between the lines
of the Latin, keeping the Latin word order rather than writing fluent
English. Old English prose – for the language, the phrases 'Old English'
and 'Anglo-Saxon' are usually interchangeable – is capable of stylistic
excellence, even nobility; but the glory of Anglo-Saxon literature is in its
poetry, of which thirty thousand lines have survived. Most of the poetry
has some Christian basis, and much of it is directly biblical in origin,
as will be seen: no account of the Bible in England should neglect this
body of superb poetry. Hidden in an unfamiliar language, those magnificent visionary poems, and the Bible translations of Ælfric (pronounced
'Alfrich'), the Abbot of Eynsham, who built on the inspiration of King
Alfred a century before, are still somewhere in the DNA of our great
printed translations. As William Tyndale recollected in 1528:

> except my memory fail me and that I have forgotten what I read when
> I was a child thou shalt find in the English chronicle how that king
> Adelstone [Athelstan, 924–939] caused the holy scripture to be trans-
> lated into the tongue that then was in England and how the prelates
> exhorted him thereto.[1]

ALFRED

Alfred, King of Wessex from 871 to 899, inherited the throne at a time
of great difficulty for a country suffering under the Viking raids. Modern
understanding sees those westward Norse attacks as a result of their desire
for territory and treasure: Alfred understood them in Old Testament terms.
He saw himself – as did later English monarchs, particularly Henry VIII
and Edward VI – as an Old Testament king. To Alfred, the Viking attacks

were caused by English sinfulness. Two parts of this national degeneracy were the decline of English learning and the decay of the Church. Repairing the latter, by means of the church reforms under Alfred and Edward the Confessor, the foundation of the Benedictine monastic reform had to wait until some decades after Alfred's death, under Athelstan, the first king of all England, who reigned from 924 to 939. Alfred, however, set himself to rectify the first part, the lack of learning. He instituted a programme of translation into English of the books 'most needful for men to know', as he put it in the Preface to his translation of Pope Gregory I's sixth-century *Pastoral Care*. This was the first extended prose ever written in English. In the same place he expressed surprise that no previous generation of scholars should have thought to translate their books into English. He gave the example of the law being passed from Hebrew into Greek and then into Latin.

As well as Gregory's *Pastoral Care*, Alfred translated Boethius's *Consolation of Philosophy* and St Augustine's *Soliloquies*, and oversaw translation of Bede's *Ecclesiastical History*, Oriosus's *History against the Pagans*. He was almost certainly involved in the creation of the *Anglo-Saxon Chronicle*. Alfred was devout as well as learned. According to a contemporary biographer, Asser, he learned the canonical Office and kept it personally, and also had a personal liturgical anthology containing extracts from the Bible, passages of patristic exegesis and liturgical texts.[2] The first fifty Psalms in the Paris Psalter, which are prose translations, may be his (see below).

In the remaking of England, new law codes were needed. King Alfred and his eight successors down to Cnut, who reigned from 1016 to 1035, issued new codes, each dependent on its predecessor, in a tradition that went back to Ethelbert of Kent, around 600. Alfred's law codes, however, were most explicitly based on the Bible, which he studied for general principles of law-giving. He began his code with the Ten Commandments in Exodus 20, and in his introduction he drew heavily on the three Exodus chapters of social and domestic law that follow, translating passages as he needed. (Though short, this is the oldest passage of continuous prose translation from the Bible into English that we have, written some fifty years before the long Lindisfarne glosses to all the Gospels.)

As well as translating the five books mentioned above, Alfred was, in making these laws in English, stating a claim for the English as a part of universal Christian history. His laws were identified with Moses' laws. The English were identified with the Israelites. These were not imaginative games, such as Elizabethan or Victorian poets and painters played with the Arthurian legends. Old Testament history was God at work with nations. His streams were continuous. Using Moses and the Israelites put the English into the arterial system of divine purpose.

Alfred's work and authority gave the English language high status, something which lasted for a long time. It meant that Ælfric, for example, a hundred years later, was able to write his learned and exegetical homilies in English. That use of the vernacular was unique. Some of Ælfric's sources were in English: all similar work on the Continent was in Latin.

ANGLO-SAXON GLOSSES

Other English Bible translations have survived from Anglo-Saxon times, particularly in glosses. Glossing was a teaching method: in schools attached to monasteries, the teacher would read Latin phrases aloud, from a part-Bible, and expound them. The pupils, partly as a means of learning by heart, would copy the Latin and then gloss the words into their vernacular. Glossing was also, at a higher level, a means of interpreting Scripture.

The Lindisfarne Gospels were glossed in the mid-tenth century by Aldred. The Rushworth Gospels were glossed in the late tenth century by Farman (Matthew and the beginning of Mark in Mercian dialect) and Owun (who glossed the rest in Northumbrian dialect). A tenth-century translation of the Gospels into West Saxon, of which six manuscripts survive, is probably that said by Tyndale, as noted above, to have been made at the command of Athelstan. Grandson of Alfred, he was, as also noted above, the first true king of all England. Although no direct evidence has survived, his sponsorship is not unlikely.[3]

The Psalms have always been important liturgically. From this period, fourteen manuscripts survive of glossed Psalters. Eight are of Roman Psalms, and six Gallican (see chapter 2 above). Sometimes (as in Salisbury) the English gloss is based on a Roman text but written between the lines of a Gallican Psalter. Even when text and gloss correspond, the glosses are often copies from elsewhere. The largely original ones are the Lambeth (Lambeth Palace), Royal and Vespasian Psalters – the last, now in the British Library, being famous, not only because it is very early, dating from the ninth century, but also because it is in Mercian rather than West Saxon. The Paris Psalter has the Latin and English texts in parallel columns and thus is a translation, not a gloss. Furthermore, in this Paris manuscript, with fine marginal illustrations, each Psalm is preceded by an introduction in Anglo-Saxon, explaining and contextualising it. The first fifty Psalms are in prose and may be the work of Alfred. The remainder are in alliterative verse. Here is the beginning of Psalm 23 (Psalm 22, *Dominus regit*, in the Latin); as he often did, the translator has added his own occasional expansions, shown in parentheses. To help to illuminate, first is the same passage, also from the Latin, in later Middle English, the later Wyclif version from around 1380:

> The Lord gouerneth me, and no thing schal fail to me; in the place of pasture there he hath set me. He nurschide me on the watir of refreis-chyng; he convertide my soule. He ledde me forth on the pathis of riytfulness; for his name. Forwhi thouy Y schal go in the myddis of schadewe of deeth; Y shall not dreed yvels, for thou art with me. Thi yerde and thi staf; tho han coumfortid me.[4]
>
> Drihten me ræt; ne byð me nanes godes wan. And he me geset on swyðe good feoh-land: and fedde me be wætera staðum. And myn mod gehwyrfde (of unrotnesse on gefean); he me gelædde ofer þa wegas rihtwisnesse for his naman. þeah ic nu gange on midde þa sceade deaðes, ne ondræde ic me nan yfel: for þam þu byst mid me, Drihten; þin gyrd and þin stæf me afrefredon (þæt is þin þreaung and eft þin frefrung).

The first addition expands the meaning by adding 'from sorrow to joy'; the second equates the *gyrd* (rod) with *þreaung* (punishment) and the *stæf* (staff) with *frefung* (comfort). These comments probably depend on a commentary on the Psalms written by the Benedictine Ambrosius Autpertus, who died in 778.[5] Outside the Psalms, some of the first seven books of the Old Testament, Genesis to Judges, was either translated or adapted into English prose by the foremost Anglo-Saxon scholar Aelfric, of whom more will be said. Two books of the Bible which are not now thought to be of the highest importance were popular in Anglo-Saxon England: Proverbs and, from the Apocrypha, Ecclesiasticus (also known as 'The Wisdom of Jesus the Son of Sirach'), which resembles Proverbs. Both were glossed into Old English, but whether for monks and priests with poor Latin, or for the general public, is not known.

Short Latin quotations from the Bible with Saxon translations are found in the lives of saints, in sermons and in devotional texts as well as in law codes. There has been as yet no comprehensive catalogue or assessment of all the biblical quotations translated into Anglo-Saxon. What version of the Old Latin Bible or Jerome was the Latin source in use cannot now usually be determined. Anglo-Saxon authors took their Latin Bible quotations from secondary sources, often written on the Continent many centuries before. That a translation was from Old Latin may mean little more than that the patristic source quoted the Old Latin, not that the full text was available in England. There are too few surviving Latin manuscripts from England quoting the Bible in this period for a proper objective account of the availability of one, or other, of the Latin texts.

AELFRIC

Abbot of Cerne in Dorset, and later of Eynsham near Oxford, in the late
tenth and early eleventh centuries, Aelfric was the foremost figure among
Anglo-Saxon scholars. He wrote homilies, saints' lives, a Latin grammar,
pastoral letters and some biblical translations. His chief concern was teaching. He wanted to make sound doctrine in 'an authoritative body' available to those who could not read Latin.[6] He was a highly self-conscious
thinker and writer, setting out to make a large and integrated exposition
of the whole of Christian doctrine for English readers, in the two traditional realms of the *Temporale* (in the world) and *Sanctorale* (holy). He
succeeded. He went on being read and copied until the thirteenth century,
by which time Old English was no longer readily understood. He is
central to the understanding of the English Bible at this period.

Aelfric's work was summed up in 1959 in an elegant conceit.

> That it was a plan, consistently pursued, we can be certain from the
> way the parts take their place within the whole and because there is
> so little repetition. Moreover, in spite of repeated misgivings, unlike
> many another literary enterprise the scheme was in all essentials carried
> to completion. Its controlling idea was universal history with Christ's
> redemption of man at its centre. The conception which moulded
> Aelfric's writings was in fact that which moulded the Gothic cathedral
> later. His main structure, as it were, consisted of two series of homilies
> comprising Temporale and Sanctorale, later extended and completed
> with more Temporale homilies. *De Temporibus Anni*, the *Grammar* and
> *Colloquy*, and his letters for Wulfsige and Wulfstan and to the monks of
> Eynsham buttressed this edifice; *Lives* and Old Testament narratives
> enriched it with stained glass windows; 'occasional' pieces such as the
> *Letter to Sigeweard* gave it the synthesis of sculpture on the West Front.[7]

The homilies were first composed about 990 for Aelfric's own use as a
mass-priest at Cerne, and then issued in two series to make sure that the
clergy had enough orthodox preaching material in English. The first series
is designed for particular days in the Christian year, and the second for
saints' days. Most of the homilies are expositions of the passages (not by
any means all from the Bible) selected for reading day by day in church:
biblical saints' lives expound a passage of the Bible. The audience for which
he wrote was made up of monks, secular clerks and the laity, in monastic churches, collegiate churches, in cathedrals and also possibly in the
parish churches which were beginning to be founded. The homilies are
thus aimed at both the Latin-learned and the ignorant. Aelfric's distinctive prose makes them palatable by devices borrowed from vernacular

poetry – patterns of alliteration and rhythmic stress. Distinctive also is his material. There had been earlier collections of Latin and vernacular homilies made in England which were much more sensational in tone, full of warnings about the end of time. Aelfric by contrast gives a wide, balanced Christology: and he wrote in English.

The opening homily in the First Series deals with the Creation and the Fall. Lines 125–42 cover Genesis 3:1–7. Aelfric sets the Temptation and the character of the serpent in the context of a long earlier passage about the Creation and Fall of the Angels (lines 22–61), making it explicit that the serpent is *se deofol* [. . .] *on næddran hiwe*, envious and angry that Adam and Eve should enjoy what he has forfeited: he plotted to destroy them, *smeadon hu he hi fordon mihte*. He tells them that by eating the fruit they will become like angels, who had not been created blind but with such purity and innocence, *swa bilewite*, that they knew no evil thing, neither in sight nor in speech nor in deed. At the moment that they eat, they both become mortal, *ða wæron hi butu deadlice*, as well as knowing good and evil. Lines 177–202 of this opening homily cover the story of Noah and the Flood. After the Flood, God says to Noah *Ic wylle settan min wed betux me & eow*, and *þonne beo ic gemyndig mines weddes*. (*Wedd* is the stem of the modern word *wedding* and can mean a pledge or a covenant, or a dowry.[8])

The complete list of the titles of the homilies in the Second Series gives not only an overview of Aelfric's plan, but a clear picture of how much is based on the Bible. Of the first eight, six are on events early in the Gospels. Of the whole forty, half are directly biblical, and mostly New Testament; the only Old Testament subject is number 30, *Quando Legitur Iob*, 'When Job is to be read'. Most significant for a book about the Bible in English is Aelfric's habit, at the beginning of the relevant homily, of translating the day's reading from the New Testament, and, in the few cases, from the Old (only from Exodus, Joshua, Numbers and Job).

Ælfric's biblical translations

Ælfric's main Old Testament translation is commonly known as 'Aelfric's *Heptateuch*' (or *Hexateuch*, depending on which manuscript is considered), though not all of it is by him. In response to a request from his friend the ealdorman Ethelweard, he translated Genesis, at first reluctantly, as he was anxious that the private lives of the Patriarchs should not set a bad example, so that *sum dysig man* ('some foolish man') might think he could have several wives. He was also worried about incest in the Old Testament. As he explained in his Preface, he was concerned about those not sufficiently learned to be able to distinguish between *þære ealdan æ &*

þære niwan, the old and the new dispensations. Should any man live now
as they did under Moses' law, he is no Christian nor fit for any Christian to eat with. Priests with insufficient Latin are a particular worry as
they are incapable of understanding the symbolic meaning, *gastlicum adgite*,
of the Bible. So he added occasional phrases of exegesis to his translation.
In Genesis 22, in the narrative of Abraham's intended sacrifice of Isaac, he
twice adds the phrase *in þa ealdan wisan* ('in the old fashion') to make it
clear that such sacrifices were no longer appropriate.

As Ælfric went on, he found that his original stresses could be relaxed.
The apparently irreconcilable urges to be true to the original and to add
passages of analysis and interpretation, lest the original be misunderstood,
gave way to a freedom to interpolate and interpret, even to the extent
of shifting the emphasis of the original narrative. In his translations of
Maccabees and of Esther he is concerned not to glorify violence or to
validate vengeance.

WULFSTAN

After Aelfric, the other great Anglo-Saxon preacher was Wulfstan, Archbishop of York, who was also a great legislator under King Ethelred (reg.
978–1016) and King Cnut (reg. 1016–35). His sermons are quite different
from Aelfric's expansions of the daily readings, being about the Last
Things, all the fundamentals of the faith, the role of the Church, and contemporary morality. His most famous sermon is by 'the Wolf', the *Sermo
Lupi ad Anglos*, in which he anticipates an imminent Judgement. He
understands the travails from the Viking armies that the nation is enduring under Ethelred as a foretaste of Doomsday. He refers chiefly to
Genesis, the Gospels and Revelation. His law codes are heavily ecclesiastical. In those under Ethelred in 1008, out of thirty-five clauses only seven
are purely secular. The Laws of Cnut, promulgated around 1020, contain
an extensive passage on the minimum requirements for salvation, part of
which is:

> And we teach that each Christian person should learn so that at least
> he can understand correctly true belief and learn the Pater Noster and
> the Creed. [. . .] Christ himself sang the Pater Noster first and taught
> that prayer to his disciples.[9]

Thirty years before, in his homily *Passio Beati Stephani Protomartiris*, Aelfric
had the statement *Ealle we sind gedbroðra þe on god gelyfað; & we ealle cweðað.
pater noster qui es in celis. þæt is fæder þe eart in heofenum* ('We are all broth-

ers who live in God; and we all say *pater noster qui es in celis*, that is, Our Father which art in heaven').

ANGLO-SAXON BIBLICAL POETRY

Almost all surviving Old English poems are explicitly Christian. Many are based on (though not close translations of) parts of the Bible or Apocrypha, or saints' lives. Complete Latin Bibles were very few in England in the Anglo-Saxon period, as was seen in the previous chapter. The biblical sources of the poems would have been part-Bibles (the Pentateuch, the Gospels, the Prophets); liturgical documents with biblical material, including Psalters or Gospels for use in the Mass; and possibly private manuscripts designed to help biblical study.

Old English poetry is alliterative, not rhyming; a line typically consists of two two-stressed halves bound by alliteration. A line from early in 'The Dream of the Rood', for example, reads:

> *Syllic wæs se sigebeam*   *and ic synnum fah*
> ('Beautiful was the victory-tree   and I with sins stained')

Apart from the few lines of the early 'Caedmon' poem, quoted in Bede's *Ecclesiastical History* (see p. 40 above), most Old English poetry that survives is in four manuscripts, written or compiled in the late tenth to early eleventh centuries: Cotton Vitellius A.xv in the British Library; the Exeter Book in Exeter Cathedral Library; Junius 11 in the Bodleian Library, Oxford; and the Vercelli Book, in the Cathedral Library at Vercelli, near Milan. Only the poems in which the Bible is especially significant are discussed below. There is a great deal of poetry, pagan lines touched by Christianity, like the riddles of the Exeter Book, which have to lie outside the scope of this chapter.

Cotton Vitellius A.xv

Though its edges are charred, the manuscript Cotton Vitellius A.xv in the British Library survived a fire in the collection in 1731. These codices contain the only copy in existence, made around 1000, of the epic poem *Beowulf*. This is not a Christian work: but the unknown poet, setting his story in the sixth century, views his pagans through a Christian lens. There are shadowy biblical references. As the monster Grendel (like his mother, part of a race of semi-human outcasts descended from Cain after Abel's murder) aproaches the royal hall, it is a happy place, in which the king's bard is singing a song in praise of the Days of Creation. In his sermon, the old king, Hrothgar, uses imagery reminiscent of both Job 30:23 (faith in God's power at death) and Ephesians 6:16 (the shield of faith quenching 'all the fiery darts of the wicked', KJV).

Also in this manuscript is the poem 'Judith', which narrates the central events in the Book of Judith (in the Apocrypha) between chapters 12 and 15, with other echoes. The powerful story of this book (which comes to us in Greek) is itself possibly an elaboration of the story in Judges 4 of how a determined woman, Jael, assassinated in her tent the enemy commander Sisera. In Judith, names, dates and geography are often absurd, but the story is compelling. The widow Judith secured the confidence of Holofernes, an Assyrian commander besieging her city. She crept into his tent in the field at night, while he was drunkenly incapable, and with his own scimitar cut off his head. She took it back to her own city and saved the distressed Israelites. The standard patristic commentaries interpret Judith as a type of the Church and Holofernes as a type of the Devil. The Anglo-Saxon poem has much more about battle than the original, and it may be that the poem's Hebrews and Assyrians are intended as an allegory of the contemporary English battle against the Vikings. (Similarly Aelfric, in his *Treatise on the Old and New Testaments*, refers to a homily on Judith as intended to inspire his hearers to protect their land against an attacking army.)

The Exeter Book

The Exeter Book manuscript contains over twenty important poems, and nearly one hundred riddles. Of the three 'Christ' poems, 'Christ A' is a mosaic of genres, including twelve lyric poems, related to the church services for Advent, especially aimed at fulfilling Old Testament prophecies. The seventh lyric describes Joseph doubting Mary, derived from Matthew 1:18–21, and is in dialogue, perhaps looking forward to liturgical drama. 'Christ B', partly relating the Ascension with intermediate sources from Gregory and Bede, is ultimately biblical, particularly from Psalm 23, the ends of the Synoptic Gospels and the opening of Acts. Lines 600–685 of this poem stress the blessings, both earthly and heavenly, showered on to humanity by God, and our obligation of gratitude, both for Creation and for Redemption. It is the work of Cynewulf, an otherwise unknown poet who incorporates his signature in runes, the ancient Germanic alphabet largely used for carved inscriptions. Though his poems are transmitted in West Saxon, it is likely that he wrote in the Mercian of Middle England, or even Northumbrian. 'Christ C' is a poem on the Last Judgement, drawing chiefly on Revelation, and the Gospels' parallel apocalypses in

Matthew 24, Mark 13 and Luke 21. The subject was very common in Anglo-Saxon times. The poet draws on some of the vast patristic literature. That the world is old and nearing the Last Judgement; the transience of earthly experience; *contemptus mundi;* and the eternity of God and his kingdom dominate two fine poems in the Exeter Book, 'The Wanderer' and 'The Seafarer'. The lordless and landless exile is used in both as a metaphor for the human condition.

Junius II

The mansucript Junius II contains nothing but four poems, all important. Though all are Christian, they are not translations or even paraphrases of the Bible, but

> free reworkings, designed with greater or lesser thoroughness to inti-
> mate the significance of those events in terms of a Christian synthesis
> of Old and New Testament revelations of God's purpose for man and
> of man's duty in view of that purpose.[10]

They have been linked with the liturgy of Lent and Holy Week. They may have been a series of vernacular readings appropriate for use at these times in a religious community. 'Genesis A and B' is a composite poem based on the first twenty-two chapters of the book of Genesis, from Creation to Abraham and Isaac. The first 111 lines of 'Genesis A', however, covering only the first verse of the biblical Genesis, give a long account of the Fall of the angels, not in Genesis but understood by patristic writers to be assumed in that first biblical verse. This vivid narration was clearly known to John Milton as a source for *Paradise Lost*. The next hundred-odd lines paraphrase the Days of Creation. At that point, 'Genesis B' comes in as a long interpolation (lines 235–851 of the whole) on the Fall and its aftermath. The first seven verses of the biblical Genesis chapter 3 are expanded to over four hundred lines of verse, 442–851, including long passages of dialogue between Adam and Eve and the Devil. Though they are similar to fragments of a parallel Old Saxon poem in a manuscript in the Vatican Library, these lines are puzzlingly interesting, and have never been satisfactorily explained. No source even distantly corresponds to their deviations from the orthodox accounts (themselves usually some distance from the Hebrew narrative). Here in 'Genesis B', the forbidden tree is explicitly the tree of death, growing next to the tree of life. A subordinate devil does the tempting, claiming to be God's envoy and going for Adam first. The serpent is also seen as an angel of God, and Eve believes she is doing God's bidding: after eating the apple she has a vision of God enthroned, surrounded by a multitude of angels. The poet gives a Miltonic picture of Satan as an unconquerable angel thrust out of heaven into the darkness of hell and from there striving everlastingly with God, trying to destroy the newly created, and therefore newly loved, race of men and women. From line 852, 'Genesis A' resumes, continuing the elaborate paraphrase in over two thousand lines.

The second complete poem in Junius 11, 'Daniel', is a free paraphrase of the first five chapters of the biblical book, showing Daniel as a symbol of fearless Christian testimony in the face of the heathen, and as proof of divine providence and intervention. "Christ and Satan' is pseudo-biblical. 'Exodus' fairly wildly paraphrases chapters 11 to 14 of that book, the passage from Egypt and the crossing of the Red Sea, with many problematic patristic ideas, and interpolations of the stories of Noah and the Flood and the Sacrifice of Isaac. The pillars of fire and smoke are seen as a foreshadowing of Redemption on the Cross.

The Vercelli Book

The Vercelli Book contains, as well as vernacular homilies, three poems, all Christian and all with oblique relation to the Bible. 'Andreas' is an account of the ministry of the Apostle Andrew, derived from a lost Latin version of the Greek *Acts of St Andrew and St Matthew* (not in the New Testament). Cynewulf's 'The Fates of the Apostles' is a poem about deriving comfort from the deaths of the Apostles. Far above these in importance is the anonymous 150-line 'The Dream of the Rood'. This is a meditation on Christ's Cross of haunting beauty and power, narrated partly by the Dreamer and partly by the Cross itself. It is a vision that is biblical in the strong sense that its obvious source is the Crucifixion narratives in the Gospels, particlarly Matthew 27. Uniquely, the poem has a related version carved in runes on the sides of the eighth-century Ruthwell Cross (in what is now Dumfriesshire) (fig. 5). Veneration of the Cross may have increased in England after Pope Marinus gave a fragment of the true Cross, as he claimed it to be, to Alfred in 885.

To untrained modern eyes and ears, the language of this Christian dream-poem is difficult, but it is worth great attention. The Cross acts as a subject for meditation on our Redemption and its costs. The dreamer sees 'a gallows tree, but not of shame', decked with gold and jewels. As he looks, it streams with blood, and begins to speak, telling of the dreadful day when the skies were darkened and the rocks rent as the King of Heaven was uplifted in mortal agony. The poem parallels the Tudor and Stuart meditational lyrics of Donne or Herbert, Vaughan or Crashaw. Once grammar and vocabulary are grasped, it takes little time to accommodate the poetic form, and then to begin to see its force. It surely removes for ever any lingering notions of Anglo-Saxon creativity being 'primitive'. This moving, simple, sophisticated devotional experience, rooted in the Gospels, is a high point of English religious writing.

Chapter 4

ROMANCE AND PIETY, 1066–1350

AT THE BATTLE OF HASTINGS IN 1066, the Anglo-Saxons were defeated. They failed to stop the cross-Channel invasion of the Normans under William, Duke of Normandy, 'the Conqueror', whose aristocratic friends rapidly, and sometimes bloodily, occupied the whole of England. At all the levels of control throughout the country, after a decade or so the Anglo-Saxon language began to be driven out by French. For the following three centuries the language of government and culture in England was French. The language of the rituals of the Church was Latin. Only the wealthy French-speaking class could afford books. The English-speaking population was almost entirely illiterate. The Normans, keeping to themselves, were aiming to transplant their culture to English soil: they demolished the Anglo-Saxon cathedrals, and rebuilt them in the new Romanesque style. If it had not been for shifts in European power some centuries later, the English language, spoken as well as written, might possibly have become extinct.

A few Anglo-Saxon manuscripts, legal and biblical, were copied, with increasing ignorance about what they contained. After 1066 there is no record of new attempts to translate the Bible into English for two and a half centuries. The Bible in England was in either Latin or, occasionally, parts of it in Norman French. In spite of the strength of the earlier work, the ordinary English people became again deprived of access to much of the Bible apart from stories celebrated in the Church's year, a few Latin phrases from the Mass, and what seems to have been a persistent oral tradition. Stone parish churches were being built; but in the realm of the whole Word in the vernacular, the Conquest set the religious life of England back into the night. Two centuries before, Alfred saw the darkness of ignorance in the villages of the land and set his mind to bring light. William's conquest of those villages re-imposed biblical darkness.

It is true that the imported highest church dignitaries – Lanfranc and Anselm especially – were scholarly Archbishops of Canterbury with international reputations. It is true that the long poem *The Ormulum*, written about 1180, elaborated the Gospels and Acts. It is also true that the link with France brought a sort of richness: great impetus to monastic Latin writing, and the lifting of the horizons of romance through the twelfth- and thirteenth-century Latin chroniclers of England (particularly Matthew Paris), and especially through the cultural shocks brought by the Crusades. From what the Crusaders encountered, Latinate and French (aristocratic) England could take in exoticisms like mystic interpretations of the Church, the freedoms of the *fabliaux*, and new oriental stories of magic and wizardry, all internationally established, and building on the more locally grown chivalry. It is further true that in Oxford the link with Paris encouraged important thirteenth-century schoolmen: a scientist-philosopher-theologian like Roger Bacon, far ahead of his time, and the 'realist' Duns Scotus, the *Doctor Subtilis*, for whom there was a real exis- tence of 'universals'. He was opposed to Aquinas, as was his opponent, the 'Invincible Doctor', the 'nominalist' William of Occam, whose great prin- ciple, that entities must not be unnecessarily multiplied, became 'Occam's razor'.[1] But none of all this Latin, least of all the theology, had much to do with the Bible.[2]

England, generally from 1066 to 1204, tending to share a common ruler, whether king or duke, was a part of Normandy. The conquerors, the Norman aristocrats, were given the land to own, and it has ever since been a reason for claims of family superiority in England to say 'we came over with the Conqueror'. The Anglo-Norman upper classes had some Bible translations: the text of the Apocalypse (Revelation) appears in their Anglo-Norman language in the course of a commentary of which more than eighty manuscripts are known. There is even a hint of a whole Bible in Anglo-Norman French before 1360; but the manuscript vanished long ago.[3] For not far short of three hundred years, Bible translating in Britain belongs to the story of French literature, not English.

By 1400, however, change in the language had begun to be consoli- dated. A form that was recognisably English was displacing Anglo-Norman French. The mixture of Anglo-Saxon and Norman French, the English language from about 1200 until about 1450, has been clumsily, but permanently, labelled 'Middle English' (divided into Early and Late) as if it were something significant only because it stood between Old English and Modern English, the latter usually taken very roughly to begin around 1450.

It is important for the later story to see what went into the making of this quite new English language. Judgements in these matters can never be absolute. Just as legend has it that Hollywood's Cecil B. de Mille scripted a character in a major motion picture epic to cry, 'Men of the Middle Ages: let us go forward into the Renaissance'; so we must not imagine that everyone in the British Isles woke up one morning and found that they were all now speaking Middle English – or even in similar dialects. What the men and women of Britain spoke would depend entirely on where in the land they were, either geographically (London, or the Midlands' Little Puddlecombe-in-the-Marsh, or Sutton Perceval in the north – all mutually unintelligible dilalects – or, not speaking any form of English at all, over the borders of Wales or Scotland); or socially, or in terms of wealth, or education or travel. It would all still have had recognisable Saxon elements. Risking the absurdity of flinging the same blanket over the whole country, however, I make a few observations about Middle English.

MIDDLE ENGLISH

Anglo-Saxon, as its name implies, was a Germanic language from north-west Europe. Using the Rhine as a border, we can make a useful rough distinction. To the east of that river the Germanic languages shared similar vocabulary and were inflected, so that for the grammatical sense of nouns and pronouns, for example, there were variable markers attached to the words. To the west of the Rhine the family of Romance languages, today largely represented by Flemish, French, Spanish, Portuguese and Italian, shared a related, ultimately Low Latin, vocabulary, quite different from the Germanic. They shared also a different way with grammatical sense. Inflection-markers had largely disappeared, and position was everything, as in the difference mentioned above between 'dog bites man' and 'man bites dog'.

The earlier Germanic settlers in Britain gave us in their Anglo-Saxon language a vocabulary of the everyday – 'sheep', 'grass', 'rest', 'holy'. The Norman invaders, coming not from the east but from the south and south-west, brought their Romance, west-of-the-Rhine language. Their first, and chief, linguistic effect was on vocabulary. Now the words are French – 'mutton', 'herb', 'repose', 'sacred': the social difference is clear at once. Sheep are what the humble shepherd tends in the cold fields: mutton is what his lord and master eats at his comfortable table. What grew as the common grass is now the sophisticated herb. Repose is what the lady of the manor goes to take. Though later Anglo-Saxon sentences could be elaborate, the Saxon gift was the power of a clean, clear syntax, controlled by the basic subject-verb-object order. In Saxon writing, late Latinate sentences which, being full of what act as dependencies, were, for much of the time, if not always, long and, wherever possible, ornate, with the verb, which, as it were, drives the meaning, placed, as one could, at the end, were not attractively considered. Romance prose syntax, while not usually quite as ridiculous as that last sentence, does like to wander.

There grew in Britain a quite new, enriched, language. Norman French was the language of a conquering government and of the senior churchmen. Over a long time, the newer and older streams began to merge. We must notice three important effects. First – and it is a matter of the greatest significance – deep in the origins of the English language is a tendency to have two words for the same thing, like 'rest' and 'repose', 'holy' and 'sacred'. (A third word often came to join them later, with the Renaissance rediscovery of Latin and Greek texts, so that from that time we had 'holy', 'sacred', 'sanctified', 'hallowed' and 'hagio-'.) This multiple vocabulary was never stationary – English in any form has always been a fluid, changing language, open to influence, accessible to new words and ideas. So the doublet (or later, triplet) variants would drift slightly apart, to make the words 'holy' and 'sacred' say not quite the same thing: in the Church's parlance, one says 'Holy Ghost' not 'Sacred Ghost'. This capacity for subtle difference of senses in an almost doubled vocabulary is one main root of the richness of meaning in High Renaissance poetry in English, where an inventiveness, a daring, a fineness of observation, remained unmatched in Europe: there was only one Shakespeare, and he was English.

Second, more complex inflection systems broke down, to leave modern English with very few (the grammatical difference between 'he' and 'him', or 'who' and 'whom', and not too many others). This increased the fluidity, expanded what it was possible to say, allowed a common place for dialects, gave simple men and women an honourable voice, and removed (at least until the later eighteenth century) a need to strain to be 'correct'.

Third, the capacity to read Anglo-Saxon had been quite lost. Translators of any part of the Bible into English had to start again.

The Old English versions of the Bible were rediscovered and published in the second half of the sixteenth century for antiquarian, linked with nationalist, reasons by Elizabeth's first Archbishop of Canterbury, Matthew Parker: before the 'Norman Yoke', the sturdy English yeoman had no truck with papist practices. Just before that, the greatest Bible translators, aiming at the ordinary man and woman, particularly Tyndale and Coverdale, to whom the old written Anglo-Saxon Bible versions were known only by hearsay, connected – easily, it feels – with living Saxon forms in the spoken language. Tyndale's Jesus says 'I will, be thou clean' (Luke 5:13), words which can immediately be put back into Anglo-Saxon. The old stream, though for a while underground, had always been flowing. Making some fashionable counterfactual speculation – had the Angevin Empire, built by the Angevin occupier of the English throne, Henry II, not crumbled early in the thirteenth century under his youngest son, John; had John's son Henry III not lost Normandy, Anjou and Poitou; had the vagaries of the Hundred Years War not loosened the hegemony of all things French; and had a few more of the 'ifs' of history been different – then perhaps English, spoken and written by relatively few compared with continental languages, would, like the old Greek language known from its script as Linear B, have become extinct, though too Germanic to become, like Linear B, indecipherable. Bearing down from above for century upon century, French might have suffocated it. Those international things happened, however: France, seen from the English throne and peerage, was lost. Total loss of English was unlikely, but it is significant that it can even be considered. French was spoken at the English court until towards the end of the fourteenth century.

Glimpses of written English, from fairly early, suggest what was happening. Here are the four lines of the 'Canute Song' from about 1167, recorded by a monk of Ely:

> Merie sungen muneches binnen Ely,
> Tha Cnut chyning reu ther by;
> Roweth, cnihtes, noer the land,
> And here we thes muneches sang.[4]

This, with no claim to high art, shows some new Frenchified attempts at rhyme and assonance and a regular rhythm: in vocabulary and grammar it is Saxon. Though slight, it was written down and has survived because it was connected with a monastery. Sources of evidence for the continuance of oral Anglo-Saxon language are meagre. Yet as a straightforward ideal of common-or-garden expression, Saxon English, only slightly modified, obviously remained. What was popular everywhere in songs and games in strongly Saxon English would have been known by heart, never written. Perhaps 'absorbed by heart' is nearer the truth; young children in a playground still learn games and the words attached to them seemingly without effort. That there were long and elaborate stories which were not written is shown by the early life of the tales of the Midlands' Robin Hood, and the persistence in most parts of England, Wales and Scotland, of the legends of the ancient and fabulous King Arthur, and other, wilder, fancies, before Geoffrey of Monmouth imaginatively filled in the blanks of earlier history in Latin in the mid-twelfth century.

The vitality of mid-sixteenth-century prose, in particular Tyndale's writing for the common reader, can be adduced to determine the continued vitality of Saxon speech. It was never lost, and no more than coloured by French. It was, indeed, during the mid-sixteenth century that the older Saxon roots of language pushed up strong, fresh, shoots through the leaf-mould of the forest floor.

EARLY MIDDLE ENGLISH LITERATURE

Some English writing is found at the more formal end of the culture, and it is particularly interesting for what it shows is happening. Layamon (who worked, like Langland a century later, and the young Tyndale three centuries later, by the River Severn) wrote his *Brut* in the thirteenth century. He faces both ways. The poet tells the story of Britain from its eponymous founder, Brutus of Troy, to 689. He can write in the Old English epic tradition, with alliteration and syllabic freedom and movement, and in the new French way of syllabic strictness, rhyme and assonance. One of his chief sources is French, in octosyllabic couplets which clearly pull him along.

French models and forms dominate the cheerful *The Owl and the Nightingale*, a long Middle English poem from the beginning of the thirteenth century debating the values of the cloister (the owl) and the world (the nightingale). It is in skilful octosyllabic couplets, thoroughly French. There emerge three general 'matters' for later French-English Romance poems for aristocratic summer-house reading (rather than heard recited at night in the mead-hall): 'the matter of France' (Charlemagne and his knights); 'the matter of Britain' (Arthur and his knights); and 'the matter of Rome the great' – anything from antiquity, but especially Ovid. Not, we should notice, Old Testament 'matters' – of Creation, of Abraham or Moses, of the Exodus, or even of valiant kings like David: nor of the New Testament Passion. Middle English was finding suppleness of manner and a fluency of narrative (though native English romances could be dire, as Chaucer's Sir Thopas demonstrates deliciously). But it was mostly secular with, freshly, magic and mystery coming in from the East, and all decorative: even the elaborate rituals of courtly love, adulterous fantasy, which produced alluring literature throughout Europe, did not make a moral problem in daily life, only in boudoir reading. Of Middle English poetry, it is not remotely possible to say what was said of Old English poetry, that most of it is in some way Christian, and often biblical.

England was assuredly gripped by such romances, which appear in great variety. Two hundred years later, Tyndale wrote that even the Church, opposed to Scripture, was promoting tales of Robin Hood or Bevis of Hampton rather than the Bible. That is a reminder that for Tyndale, the idea of disseminating the Word of God was uphill work, though to him utterly essential for the souls' health of all people. The accessibility of the

Bible is generally taken so much for granted that it takes effort to grasp that in 1526 the New Testament could have been seen at first as a strange, even alien, intruder into popular minds full of Robin Hood, Bevis of Hampton, Hercules, Hector and Troilus (as Tyndale wrote) or 'hey troly loly' (as Coverdale wrote).[5]

MIDDLE ENGLISH BIBLE VERSIONS

The twenty-thousand-line *Ormulum*, a poetical English version by the monk Orm of the Gospels and the Acts of the Apostles, with a commentary, was written at the end of the twelfth century, as noted above. It survives in one manuscript in the Bodleian. Around 1250 there was written in rhyming couplets a long metrical version of the narrative parts of the Pentateuch, Genesis to Deuteronomy, named *Genesis and Exodus*. After a brief prologue, the four-thousand-line poem begins with Creation:

> In firme begining of mogt
> Was hevene and erðe samen wroght.
> þo bad God wurðen stund and stede,
> þis middes-werld ðor-inne he dede.
> Al was ðat firme ðhrosing in nigt,
> Til he wit hise word made ligt.

In literal translation this reads:

> In first beginning of nought
> Was heaven and earth together wrought.
> Then bade God to exist time and place,
> This middle-world therein he put.
> All was that first chaos in night,
> Till he with his word made light.[6]

The unknown author is dependent on far more than the Bible, filling out details and whole narratives from Peter Comestor's *Historia scholastica*, and from Josephus's *Antiquities of the Jews*. He adds romantic, indeed charming, stories. After the Fall, the once universally tame animals change: lions and bears, and nasty small flies, attack Adam. The daughter of Pharaoh, here called Teremuth, has magical experiences with the child Moses. As a handsome adult, Moses, while besieging the city of Sheba for the Egyptians, finds that it is yielded when the Princess Tarbis, daughter of the Ethiopian king, falls in love with him. Moses is able to leave her later with a clear conscience because he has made for her a magic ring, which makes her forget her love. Nothing of this is in the Bible, of course. The novelties owe much to the Grail poem by the French twelfth-century poet, Chrétien de Troyes. The story of Balaam (in Numbers 22 and following) has a new ending. Instead of the biblical brief blessing of Israel and departure, Balaam makes a suggestion to Balak, King of the Moabites.

> Take your young women, fair to see and soft to touch, those that are bright of hue and glad in speech, and have them march out to meet these men; so that when they come they will brew heart-burn with wine and beauty and seductive bodies, with soft and lovely words, to turn them from fear of God to the gods of thy land.[7]

This expands Numbers 25, which tells of Israel's 'whoredom' with the daughters of Moab, who worship Moabite gods – making sensual the word 'whoredom', which is used not primarily for sexual acts but for heathen worship.

At this time small parts of the book of Job were translated for devotional use, and anthologies contained some of the apocryphal Wisdom of Solomon, or the story of Adam and Eve elaborated to include legends of the Cross. A huge, dull, later fourteenth-century Middle English metrical paraphrase of extensive parts of the Old Testament has occasional flashes of imported colour – young David did not know his future wife Michal, but she shouted a warning, says the poet, which is why Saul's javelin missed him (1 Samuel 18:11–12). The feeling is that Scripture has lost out to secular romances. Monastic writers show themselves alarmed about it. In his *Bible in Early English Literature* David Fowler quotes two 'clerical authors': he gives first the title of a religious tract, and second, the Prologue to a Passion narrative:

> A little treatise of divinity to turn man from romances and jests [= gests, tales of heroic achievement in war], wherein he loses much of his time . . . , and to give him instead a thing that is profitable both to life and to soul. . . .

> Hear now a little tale that I will tell you, as we find it written in the gospel. It is not of Charlemagne nor of the Twelve Peers, but of Christ's Passion that he suffered here.[8]

Secular literature was the province of the professional minstrels, across Europe: but they did sometimes turn to the Bible for material. Two minstrel poems were *Jacob and Joseph*, composed soon after 1250 – the Genesis narrative, cut and elaborated purely for entertainment, as a good story[9] – and *Susannah*, composed about 1400, which is much more ornate, and develops 'Susan' as victim, as the Accused Queen like Constance in Chaucer's 'The Man of Law's Tale'.

In the middle of the fourteenth century there appeared three versions of the Psalms in Middle English. One is the anonymous West Midland Psalter. Here the Vulgate Latin verses (with some interpolations) alternate with the English. An older tradition ascribed them to one William of Shoreham: the oldest manuscript, (British Library, Add. MS 17376) has been dated from about 1340:[10] two later manuscripts are known. The other is a celebrated verse by verse translation, parallel to the Latin, preceding a commentary by Peter Lombard, made by the mystical writer Richard Rolle of Hampole around 1340. Thirty manuscripts of this are known, sometimes with a different commentary. The first known manuscript is in a north-country dialect (University College, Oxford, MS 64).[11] Rolle wrote many scriptural commentaries.

The fourteenth-century writers until recently grouped together as 'the mystics' (probably with an intention of dismissal from the canon of 'proper' literature) are from the late twentieth century beginning to be read afresh. Between 1340 and 1350, the popular Anglo-Norman Apocalypse (Revelation) appeared in an English translation, which has survived in sixteen manuscripts. Legendaries and Passion narratives, though indicators of piety, often stray far from the biblical text. There is some translation: a manuscript collection includes the beginning of Matthew, some of Acts and most of the Epistles.[12] Other manuscripts include harmonies of the Gospels, commentaries on the Ten Commandments, and other things. One British Library manuscript, Cotton Nero A x, is remarkable for containing unique copies of four anonymous fourteenth-century poems generally known as *Patience*, *Cleanness* and – masterpieces – *Pearl* and *Sir Gawain and the Green Knight*. Fascinating, indeed beautiful, as these are; interesting in their forms (revived alliteration, as well as some stanzas), in their piety and moral power; and though *Pearl*, a vision of the heavenly Jerusalem and probably commemorating a mourned daughter, has faint Gospel echoes (and strong ones from Revelation), and *Patience* is a versified account of Jonah, they are not, sadly, part of the story of the English Bible.

In all this Middle English literature roughly to 1350, there is vivid life, and variety, and a love of story and romance, and, occasionally, things brought in from the Bible. The most biblically influenced Middle English work is undoubtedly the encyclopedic *Cursor mundi* ('The Course of the World'), written about 1300.[13] This, in almost thirty thousand lines of rhyming couplets, tells parts of the biblical narrative in a framework of legends and romances, in English, French and Latin. *Cursor Mundi* is divided into seven parts according to the seven ages of man. Sometimes very close, as in the First Age, describing the temptation and the Fall, and sometimes wholly occupied with other things, as in the Seventh Age, the Bible is at least for some of the time a presence. When it is, it provides the basis for a great deal of elaboration, attached to the central Bible stories as the traditions had grown about them.

Chapter 5

THE WYCLIF ('LOLLARD') BIBLES

Something new, with a mysterious element to it, began to appear in England, in English, in the 1380s. Much-copied manuscripts appeared of the same large and demanding text – the Bible, even the whole Bible, and only that – translated into English from the Latin Vulgate, and said to be linked with, though not mentioning, the name of the Oxford scholar John Wyclif.

The phenomenon had four characteristics.

First, the content: the manuscripts were not of romantic or philosophical expansions of some Bible stories mixed with legends, saints' lives, tall tales from the East and a bit of fanciful British history. They were of the Bible itself, and could be of the complete Bible, or the complete New Testament; but even if less than complete, always only the Bible text, usually in canonical order, translated into English from the Latin with obvious care, written on vellum to last. They were generally free from additional matter; if there were glosses they were attempts at elucidation rather than aggression. They were the earliest complete Bibles, or New Testaments, in English. From their arrival, people in Britain could have had access for the first time to the whole of Scripture in their own language.[1] That the manuscripts were so often copied shows the great interest. They were used intensively for 150 years, until the arrival of Tyndale's first printed New Testament in 1526, and Coverdale's first printed complete Bible in 1535 – and even after.

Second, these manuscripts appear in large numbers. The whole Bible with the Apocrypha is a text of great size, disguised by modern techniques of paper making and printing. About twenty surviving manuscripts of the 1380s are of the whole Bible, almost ninety of the whole New Testament. Over 250 manuscripts survive, a larger number of copies than for any other medieval English text. It is impossible to calculate how many perished, but persecution of Lollards, and the burning of books, was systematic and fairly thorough. The nearest rival, the famous essay on the Prick of Conscience (the *Agenbyt of Inwit*, 'the again-bite of inward thought'), survives in 117 copies, less than half that number. Chaucer's *Canterbury*

Tales survive in sixty-four copies.[2] In spite of their destruction, Wyclif manuscripts of the New Testament were being read in the sixteenth century. In 1430, Nicholas Belward of Earsham in Norfolk bought a copy of the New Testament in London (for £12 6s 8d). In 1526, John Tyball from Steeple Bumpstead declared that he had in London bought Tyndale's New Testament, and that he already had most of the Wyclif New Testament.[3]

Third, though many of these manuscripts give the names of their owners after late Tudor times, there is nothing to identify the translator, the place of origin or date. Though it could be argued that this was not unusual, as at that time even original works were not always credited to their author, yet for texts of such importance 'the execution of such a novel and gigantic task',[4] the silence is noteworthy. The names of both Rolle and Trevisa appear on their translations of Bible material (Rolle's in his Psalms of about 1340; for Trevisa, see pp. 91–5 below). The translator's name of such a widely copied text might be expected, especially if he was such a prominent scholar as Wyclif.

Fourth, the manuscripts produced violent opposition, excessively expressed, directed at the supposed source. That was also new. Since the earliest Anglo-Saxon times, in England as in Europe generally, there had been no objection to Bible versions. The reasons for the closing down of work on the Bible in English had been linguistic and cultural, as from 1066, and not ecclesiastical. The pleasing later Middle English novelistic expansions of Joseph and his brothers or of Susannah bathing could raise only an objection of slight moral unease at unseriousness or titillation. In 1411, however, the English Archbishop of Canterbury, Thomas Arundel, wrote to Pope John XXIII:

> This pestilent and wretched John Wyclif, of cursed memory, that son of the old serpent [. . .] endeavoured by every means to attack the very faith and sacred doctrine of Holy Church, devising – to fill up the measure of his malice – the expedient of a new translation of the Scriptures into the mother tongue.[5]

The continuator of Henry Knighton's *Chronicle*, writing probably a little later, is more direct:

> This Master John Wyclif translated from Latin into English – the Angle not the angel speech – the Gospel that Christ gave to the doctors and clergy of the Church [. . .] so that by his means it has become vulgar and more open to lay men and women who can read than it usually is to quite learned clergy of good intelligence. And so the pearl of the Gospel is scattered abroad and trodden underfoot by swine.[6]

The latter quotation could hardly make more explicit the Church's determination to keep from the people what it maintained that 'Christ gave to the doctors and clergy of the Church'. It should not need saying that any open reading of the New Testament at all shows that Christ did no such thing. He taught, and died for, all humanity. We are here within the Church's comfortable doctrine that hearing the Latin services without understanding had sacramental value. Saints' lives were more orthodox than Scripture. The Bible was good only when it was not understood. A certain Father Caxton, a doctor of divinity no less, wrote that 'Holy Scripture was a false heresy'.[7]

Two questions emerge. First, were the enemies of these manuscripts correct in attributing them to Wyclif? Second, did the sudden hostility to Scripture in the vernacular have a particular cause? To take the latter question first, while noticing that the vehement hostility was powerful for well over a hundred years, and if anything, increasing; that it was peculiarly English; and that it was the cause of many terrible and lingering deaths. Before 1401, no one in Britain died for reading or hearing the Bible in Old or Middle English. In that year the English statute *De heretico comburendo* introduced for English heretics the penalty of death by burning alive. Heresy was soon to include reading – not just owning – even a scrap of Scripture not in Latin. This was new in the British Isles, and it was not like that in the rest of Europe. Why did it happen?

The hostility of the English Church to vernacular translations of its Latin Bible was based first of all on the belief that, as the chronicler wrote, Scripture was given only to, and could only be understood by, either the extremely learned, 'the doctors', or the clergy (at this time in Britain almost no one is likely to have known that the Latin was a late and imperfect version of the original Greek and Hebrew). A priest, by virtue of the grace of his priesthood, was given, it was believed, power to understand – not so much the words of the Bible as the patristic four-fold interpretations of them. All this had to be beyond lay people; not only was it too difficult for them; the Church declared (surely blasphemously), that it was not Christ's intention.

> In any case, the earthly hierarchy should be a model of the heavenly one, in that grace should be mediated from the higher ranks to the lower, from upper clergy to lower, and from lower clergy to laymen. Private Bible-reading by lay-people or by priests not intellectually equipped to follow the Vulgate themselves was liable to lead to heresy.[8]

Further, not only was accuracy of translation technically impossible, calling for unavailable subtlety: the divine clothes of the Latin of Scripture could not be turned into the meagre rags of vernacular English. And who would supervise the copying? The Vulgate was a university product, its reproduction overseen: but anyone could reproduce an English Bible without supervision. Further, again, by 1400, the Church was sanctioning beliefs and practices that were unbiblical: only trouble could follow that discovery by ordinary people.

Surprisingly, it is said that

> despite such general objections, no universal and absolute prohibition of the translation of the Scriptures into the vernacular nor of the use of such translations by clergy or laity was ever issued by any council of the Church or by any pope.[9]

This is impressive. It has the disadvantage, however, of giving not absolutely the right impression. The ninth-century Slav Bible was disowned by the pope (see below, p. 659). Pope Paul III in 1538 commanded the burning of English Bibles. In 1844, Pope Gregory XVI warned against Bibles in the vulgar tongue (see below, p. 705). Pope Innocent III in 1199 condemned the uses of Waldensian translations, as part of the ruthless persecution of those earliest southern European reformers. At the local level, however, campaigns to remove heresy and heretics seem to have worked on the principle that possession of vernacular Scripture meant heresy. In England that must have begun to happen only some time after the later manuscripts were written of Rolle's Psalter, say 1370–80. These, though they were the Scriptures in English, seem to have excited no hostility.

The cause of the sudden opposition was either the plaguing name of Wyclif, infecting the English Bible translations; or the evil of the translations themselves spilling on to Wyclif, who might have had little to do with them. Archbishop Arundel and the anonymous chronicler had no doubt that Wyclif was the cause. Arundel accused him of 'devising . . . the expedient of a new translation', which does not quite mean that he sat pen in hand. The chronicler wrote that he 'translated'. His Bohemian sympathiser Jan Hus, who had previously visited Wyclif in Oxford, wrote, while Wyclif's disciples were with him in Prague: 'By the English it is said that Wyclif translated the whole Bible from Latin into English.'[10] These statements seem firm enough; but they are not. The Hus remark is carefully qualified, 'By the English it is said . . .'. The two hostile statements were made over a quarter of a century after Wyclif's death. They could belong to that kind of vilification later found, for example, in attacks on Tyndale: on no evidence, his enemies (particularly More) said that he had been with Luther in Wittenberg. (As discussed below, it is unlikely that

Tyndale and Luther ever met:[11] the idea of Luther-and-Wittenberg was used as the source of evil heresy in Europe, so Tyndale had to be said to have been there.) Accusing Wyclif of the heretical translations would damn a hated scholar.

Evaluating Wyclif's part in translating the Vulgate into English – how much of it, if any at all, was with his own pen in his own hand – is not easy. We may come to it by way of a view of his life and beliefs.[12]

JOHN WYCLIF

The 'Morning Star' of the Reformation (the phrase is John Bale's in 1548[13]) was born near Richmond in Yorkshire in 1324. He became a fellow of Merton College, Oxford, and in 1361, at thirty-seven, Master of Balliol, until probably 1366. He studied and taught logic and metaphysics, and was, as even the bare facts of his Oxford career demonstrate, outstanding as a scholastic philosopher.[14] As Anthony Kenny has remarked:

> if Wyclif was the Morning Star of the Reformation, he was also the Evening Star of Scholasticism . . . , [that] synthesis of Christian and Aristotelian ideas which is perhaps the greatest intellectual legacy of the Middle Ages. Wyclif was the last of the great Oxford schoolmen . . . ; those who were interested in his kind of philosophy disowned him as a heretic, and those who hailed him as a forerunner regarded scholastic philosophy as one of the corruptions from which the Reformation offered liberation.[15]

After twenty years of scholarly life at Oxford, having in 1372 received from Oxford his doctorate in theology, he became chaplain to Edward III in 1374. By then he had written, among other matters, on logic, Aristotelian but with examples from Scripture, and above all his *Summa de ente*, his major philosophical work. He attacked the fashionable nominalism of Duns Scotus and Occam.

The writing of the 'heretic' Wyclif was systematically destroyed by the Church in England some time after his death; scholars have had to go to Protestant Bohemia for copies. In the 1870s, the senior Catholic scholar who was offered the position of editing Wyclif's Latin Works for the Wyclif Society was told that a translation into the vernacular would be forbidden.[16] In spite of the editing enterprise of that society from 1883 to 1922, the *Summa* has still not been published as a whole. An account of Wyclif has to include mention of his large Latin philosophical and theological output, on which the later charge of heresy was founded; and of the fact that since the charge of heresy he has been almost completely unread.[17]

The Church throughout Europe was harmed by the two simultaneous popes, in Rome and Avignon, 'two worthless priests [. . .] cursing and reviling each other', as Macaulay put it.[18] When the Schism broke out, Wyclif was working on *On the Truth of Sacred Scripture*, 'a defence of the authority and inerrancy of the Bible; one of the writings which earned Wyclif the soubriquet "Evangelical Doctor" '.[19] His defence is orthodox, though he has, as elsewhere, no truck with papal claims of the force of the 'unwritten verities'. He tackles at length 'the question how far the ceremonial laws of the Old Testament are obligatory in the New'.[20] In passing, in other minor works, he anticipates Erasmus's plea for the Scriptures in the vernacular: he does not in this book address the question of whether, as the laity are to read the Bible, every farmhand will have to learn Latin. He gives us no clue about whether he himself did such work.[21] He turned from the schoolmen to political writing about the nature of the Church, probably beginning his *On Civil Dominion* ('dominion' means property), quite early. In 1374, no doubt chosen because of his high standing in Oxford as the most eminent theologian of the time, and his political interests, he was part of a delegation to Bruges to negotiate the growing dispute between King Edward and Pope Gregory XI over papal appointments in England and the English payment (or non-payment for forty years) of papal tribute. Perhaps as a reward for this service, and though he held other livings, in April 1374 he was presented by the Crown to the rectory of Lutterworth in Leicestershire, for ever after associated with his name. Disillusioned by his experience of the futility of discussions with papal negotiators, he strengthened his denials of the validity of the pope's claims to permanent endowments. Pope and bishops tried to silence him, but he was able to continue teaching and writing because he had a powerful patron in John of Gaunt, Duke of Lancaster, the effective ruler of England (Edward III, in his great age, lost control of the court and Richard II succeeded him as a child). Successive popes, at Avignon, were under the control of the French kings, still England's ancient enemies: soon in the 'Great Schism' there would be for nearly forty years two popes, one in Rome and one in France, each supported by rival European powers.

In England, it was a time of increasing disturbance, and growing challenge to the papal assumption of the highest political power in the land. Gaunt protected Wyclif from attacks on his unorthodox doctrines: he, and the court, gained in return a learned propagandist. Wyclif, 150 years before Tyndale in his *Obedience of a Christian Man* (1528), began to think through the whole question of civil authority. He found no New Testament basis for the Church's feudal power. From the Bible he drew his doctrine of 'dominion by grace', whereby each man was immediately and directly responsible to God, to obey God's law, which meant not canon law but the Bible, which was the codification, in both Testaments, of the law of God. His theory of dominion meant that the Bible as a whole was applicable to the whole of human life. Wyclif was a scholarly commentator on the Bible, and a powerful preacher, 'of intense moral urgency'.[22]

In 1377, Wyclif was summoned to appear before the Bishop of London at St Paul's Cathedral to answer charges of heresy, found in *On Civil Dominion*. John of Gaunt and other nobility accompanied him, and would have supported his defence, but the assembly ended in riot when, it is said, the people of London thought the duke was insulting their bishop. In the following year, the bishops brought Wyclif before them at Lambeth: he was to be investigated for heresy, of which Pope Gregory XI accused him in bulls. This time an intervention by Joan of Kent (the widow of the Black Prince and Richard II's mother) prevented him from being formally accused of heresy. Later in 1378, the government was glad to use Wyclif's skills to defend them in a scandal of violated sanctuary: the king's men had pursued an escaped prisoner into Westminster Abbey and killed him. Wyclif, who elaborated his defence in two Latin treatises, found (in spite of the government's weak position) that his understanding of the corruption of the Church was deepened, especially when from that year there were two warring popes. Wyclif's solution to what he saw as the scandal of papal claims of temporal power and material possessions was to return to the purity of the Apostles, his 'communism', stripping the Church of its property.[23]

Wyclif's theological attacks included writing against prayers to saints and pilgrimages. Not all his ideas broke wholly new ground. The Bishop of Armagh from 1348 to 1360, Richard Fitzralph, had written against the papal privileges and possessions of the friars; he, similarly, depended on earlier work still. Yet these were defending the primary rights of the popes against subsidiaries like the friars. Wyclif's radical thinking saw the pope and all the hierarchy as guilty of simony, and therefore among those without grace. Anthony Kenny writes:

> It was not Wyclif's assault on the Papacy which led to his final breach with the teaching authority of the Church. It was when he turned to the sacrament of the Eucharist, and attacked the theologians' explanation of its nature, that he began to stand out in clear view as a heretic. When he denounced the Popes and questioned the validity of Papal claims he could find sympathisers even among the higher clergy; when he called for the disendowment of the Church, many laymen and begging friars found his words congenial; but when he renounced the

doctrine of transubstantiation, friars, noblemen and bishops all turned against him, and the university which had sheltered him offered him a home no longer.[24]

It was his writings on the Eucharist after 1380, some of them published versions of the lecture course he gave in Oxford (which led to his expulsion from the university) that brought the whole house down about his ears, and, to confuse the metaphor, unwittingly entangled him in the Peasants' Revolt. He wrote in his last theses against all the Church hierarchy, particularly the cardinals and friars. Wyclif was not condemned by name, nor was he ever excommunicated, as his principal supporter in Oxford, Nicholas of Hereford, was.

In the summer of 1382, Wyclif was attacked in a sermon preached at St Mary's, Oxford, and his followers were for the first time denounced as 'Lollards' – a loose and suitably meaningless term of abuse ('mutterers') current in the Low Countries for Bible students, and thus heretics. Controversy followed the sermon. Wyclif's teachings were declared heretical. He retired to his Lutterworth rectory, and continued to write voluminously – 'some 57 Latin works were written between 1380 and December 1384'.[25] He died at Lutterworth on the last day of 1384. He was buried there, and the church contains memorials to him. In 1428, after his posthumous condemnation by the Church at the Council of Constance, in 1425, his bones were dug up and burned, and the remains thrown in a stream.

Outside England, Wyclif was widely known. Hus in Bohemia preached doctrines similar to Wyclif's. The mother of Richard II's queen, Anne, was Elizabeth of Prague, and relations between the universities of Oxford and Prague (founded by her father) were close. As Wyclif's manuscripts were destroyed in Oxford, Czech scholars recopied those that they already had, so that most of Wyclif's works survive there. In 1415, at the same Council of Constance, Hus, in violation of a safe conduct, was tried, condemned and burned. His followers continued their fight, and can be seen to make a direct link to Luther a century later.

It seems unlikely that Wyclif himself, pen in hand, translated any of 'his' Bible. But that the manuscripts were the work of men close to him, influenced by him, inspired by his teaching and preaching, there can be no doubt. It is the same with the second most extensively preserved Wycliffite English text (again surviving in spite of systematic destruction of such material), the thirty-one fine manuscripts which contain a complete cycle of 294 anonymous sermons. These present a comprehensive view of Wyclif's views, theological, ecclesiastical, social and political, but are not by Wyclif.[26]

'POOR PREACHERS'

It used to be said that from Oxford Wyclif personally sent out his friends
and followers, many of them Oxford scholars like himself, as travelling
'poor preachers': their simplicity of doctrine and attacks on the wealthy
and unholy Church, it was asserted, spread rapidly to many areas of
England. The problem here is lack of evidence. In 1382, 'a preaching expedition in the Winchester diocese undertaken by Nicholas Hereford, John
Aston, Robert Alington and Laurence Bedman, with other unnamed followers, provides certain evidence of concern to spread Wyclif's views
before his death'. Later chroniclers refer to 'later, and more popular preaching, references which can be borne out by material in the episcopal
registers'.[27] This evidence has to be greatly and imaginatively extrapolated
to make a picture of evangelism from Oxford throughout England. There
was romantic appeal, for writers much later, in the notion of the dozens
of 'poor preachers' sent out by 'Doctor Evangelicus' himself, like the
Apostles sent from Christ in Luke 9 (paralleled in Matthew 10 and Mark
6) 'for to preche the kyngdom of God . . . No thing take ye in the weie,
nether yerde [staff], ne scrippe [bag], nether breed, ne money, and nethir
haue ye twey cootis', as the Later Wyclif Version (see below) has it.[28] The
idea also solved the problem of 'the passage from Wyclif's Latin writings,
designed for and circulated in a university environment, to the ordinary
Lollard of the fifteenth century, whose only language was English'.[29] Late
twentieth-century tendencies to try to detach Lollardy from Wyclif, and
indeed to diminish Lollardy altogether as a fifteenth-century force,
have used the earlier removal from the picture of the large numbers of
itinerant 'poor preachers' as proof.

   In her 'A Lollard Compilation and Wycliffite Thought', Anne Hudson
has provided a solution to the problem of transmission which fits available evidence, also deepening understanding of the intellectual grip that
the Lollard movement could have, throughout the country.[30] She begins
by noting that the questions which in the first half of the fifteenth century
formed the basis for investigation of Lollardy were set out in episcopal
documents from Worcester, and from Bath and Wells; all concerning
matters traceable to Wyclif's own writings, they 'involve terminology that
he had made notorious, and ideas that he had rendered suspect'.[31] She
points to neglected sources of transmission; as well as persons, books. A
large number of manuscripts (eighteen in England, more in Bohemia) have
survived which are roughly a compilation of theological notes, in alphabetical order – an 'ambitious [. . .] compilation that, in its longest form,
would extend in print to about a thousand pages'. The books go under
the title of *Floretum* or *Rosarium Theologie*, and are in three forms of varied

length, sharing material. The topics include biblical figures, moral and theological vices and virtues, and ecclesiastical theory and practice.[32] Noticeable is the care throughout to give a multiplicity of full and exact
references: more striking still are the large number of exact references to
the work of 'D.E.' or 'Doctor Evangelicus'. The collections seem to date
from the twelve years after Wyclif's death, when it was still possible to
handle Wycliffite material without danger. That eighteen in Latin and one
in Middle English survived in England, in spite of the wholesale destruction of Lollard books in the fifteenth century, might suggest that they were
widespread. It seems that in these handbooks of Wycliffite thought,
including materials for sermons, for use far from the university, we have
a means of evangelising that before was described as limited to 'wandering preachers'. This is not the place to pursue the history of Lollardy,
except to note that in 1988 Professor Hudson presented important corrections to what had been stated for several decades. Previous standard dismissals, based on readings of ecclesiastical records and chronicles, both
without exception hostile to Lollardy, denied it any force at all after the
1430s. These accounts did not fit, she found, with the evidence from the
Lollard texts themselves, which had not been considered. Such twentieth-
century ignoring of texts is surprising, as opponents at the time insisted
that the heretics had been vociferous in publishing their creed far and
wide in books, pamphlets and broadsheets.[33]

After Wyclif's death in 1384, and the 1401 Act *De heretico comburendo*
handing the punishment of heretics to the state for burning, Lollardy
spread widely from Oxford. In 1407, Archbishop Arundel called a Provincial Council at Oxford, the seat of the heresy, aiming to control
preachers, books and the universities. There in 1409 were adopted a
number of Constitutions (ratified later at St Paul's in London). In Article
7 it was forbidden to

> translate any text of Holy Scripture into the English or other language,
> by way of a book, pamphlet or tract, and that no book, pamphlet or
> tract of this kind be read, either recently composed at the time of the
> said John Wyclif, or since then, or that in future may be composed,
> in part or in whole, publicly or privily, under pain of the greater
> excommunication . . .[34]

until approved by a diocesan or a provincial council, which is not known
to have happened. This ban was used as a means of searching out heretics
well over a hundred years later: Arundel's Constitutions remained in force
until 1529.[35] At Convocation on 17 March 1411, a list was presented of
267 heresies and errors extracted from specific books by Wyclif: an Oxford
bonfire burned his books at Carfax in the presence of the University

Chancellor. Another bonfire, in January 1413, burned Wyclif's works at St Paul's.

The consistent success of Lollardy between 1381 and 1413 among Lollard gentry then expanded far from Oxford because of the persistent hostility of Arundel, particularly in that university. The persecution found its targets in many ways, with possession of vernacular Scripture high on the list.[36] Possession of books and an interest in education in English were two suspicious factors; the latter including a Lollard plan for fifteen new universities in England, to be financed from disendowment of the clergy.[37] The sect was 'suborned, even perhaps hijacked', as Professor Hudson puts it, 'into support for Sir John Oldcastle's revolt of 1414': after that 'indiscretion', it was a fugitive, even an exile, but had a revival in the 1490s, and handed on its life to the new reformers, Tyndale, Barnes, Frith and others from the 1520s.[38]

That last handing on of the baton, taken as read by earlier historians, was denied from the 1960s, when Wyclif was derided and Lollardy (which was said to have had no connection) was 'seen as an incoherent and inchoate assembly of eccentrics, mostly of little education, expressing views which have economic rather than academic roots'.[39] That comment does not mention the Wycliffite Bible, which on investigation would have been found to have very little to say about economics – but then, it would have been a pity to let reading the largest number of manuscripts of the period spoil a theory. Thus, from the 1960s until the end of the twentieth century, the accepted view was either that Tyndale, Barnes, Frith, Roy and others were entirely continental in their influences;[40] or, worse, that there was no kind of challenge to the Church in England at all until Henry VIII and Edward VI started destroying the beautiful national religion.[41]

Parallels of idea and language among heretics of the 1520s and 1530s, and earlier Lollards;[42] the persistence of the Wyclif Bibles; and the story of the two men from Steeple Bumpstead, recorded by Strype, all show an ease of transmission of dissent. In the late 1520s, these men journeyed from Essex to London, and were persuaded to trade in their Wycliffite scriptures for a Tyndale New Testament.[43]

THE WYCLIF BIBLES

The British Library has over forty of the surviving Bible manuscripts from the late fourteenth or early fifteenth centuries; the Bodleian Library in Oxford has almost the same number. The libraries of many Oxford and Cambridge colleges have a single copy. (The prominence of Oxford in the story of these manuscripts is not surprising.) The libraries of some

English cathedrals have a copy: in Manchester the John Rylands Library has fourteen.

Studying these manuscripts reveals that all but a very few are clearly related, and that those that are so related fall into two groups (the handful that are not related will be considered later). That all the related manuscripts have the same origin, in the early reform movement associated with the name of Wyclif, has long been accepted.[44]

The separation into two groups has little to do with the differences of appearance. Some are large, wonderfully decorated and beautifully written complete Bibles, in one or two volumes. Examples of these are the British Library's MSS Egerton 617 and 618 (fig. 6), which probably belonged to Thomas of Woodstock, Duke of Gloucester; or MS 1 C viii, which once belonged to Henry VI; or, in Oxford, Bodley MS 277 and Bodley Fairfax MS 2. At another end of the scale are small volumes containing only the New Testament or even a single book – one not always expected: though the BL Harley MS 984 has only the Gospel of Matthew, Bodley's Douce MS 36 has only the Apocryphal Tobit. Some are everyday books decorated very simply with coloured rules, written in a rough hand.

The two groups into which all the related Bible manuscripts fall are determined by the text. The differences are greater than those of linguistic detail. England was still many centuries from attempts to standardise spelling. No one dialect was common throughout the country. Local forms of grammar, and vocabulary, bring many variations. In these Bibles,

> present participles may end in *and, -ande, -end, -ind, inde, -ing, -inge, -yng, -ynge;* 'their' may be *her, here, ther, their,* or *thair;* 'them' may be *hem, ham, hom, them, tham, theim, thaim.* 'Eye' may be spelled as *ei&e, e&e, i&e, y&e, eighe, eigh, eghe, ehe, ei, ee,* 'flesh' as *fleisch, fleish, flesch, flesh, flehs, flessh* and so on [. . . ;] one will have *clepe* where another has *call,* or *clothed* where another has *clad* [. . .]. [T]here may be mistakes, omissions, alterations and repetitions.[45]

The manuscripts differ in something more than these details: the translation can be seen to fall into two groups according to method, affecting constructions and word order. One group is much larger than the other. The Gospel of Matthew (including its presence in complete Bibles or New Testaments), has about a hundred in the larger group, eighteen in the smaller. Significantly, one or two copies of this Gospel seem to be mixed (see p. 81 below). The Psalms, when alone, have thirty in the larger group, eight in the smaller.

The division was observed and clarified early in Victoria's reign by the two scholars upon whose work we still depend, the Reverend Josiah Forshall and Sir Frederic Madden. Their splendid edition in four large volumes has never been superseded. Published by Oxford University Press in 1850, it is all we have, and it remains just adequate. Forshall and Madden print the whole Bible, with the Old Testament Apocrypha separate as those books were placed by Jerome (and from the Apocryphal New Testament the rare Epistle to the Laodiceans); all the Prologues there were; excellent introductory material of their own; and comprehensive textual variants on each of their 3,221 large pages. Forshall and Madden worked on the edition for twenty-two years. They travelled great distances from the British Museum to libraries and to private houses. They describe 170 manuscripts. They examined and collated, letter by letter, 150 of them.

It is a source of scholarly shame that no one has yet produced an up-to-date, definitive edition of the Wyclif Bible, one of the greatest Christian treasures, using all the modern bibliographical technology. In 1850, Forshall and Madden thanked the Delegates of Oxford University Press for their funding, and noted that 'They have also to express their acknowledgements to the Royal Society of Literature, who at the outset of the design, zealously, though ineffectually, exerted their influence to promote its success.'[46] It must not be thought that, being Victorian, the climate in which they worked was of general encouragement of the task: their word 'ineffectually' says a great deal. They conclude their long Preface with the hope that 'their labours . . . [will] remove some portion of the disgrace which has long been attached to the English nation, for the con-tinued neglect of its earliest versions of holy Scripture'.[47] 'Disgrace' is a strong word; yet it is perhaps not strong enough for today's neglect. Furthermore, it has taken a Norwegian scholar, Conrad Lindberg, to prepare and publish the only properly edited, introduced and annotated sections of the Wyclif Bible ever made: to his labours everyone is indebted. He has published, in admirably scholarly editions, among other Wyclif Bible material, the whole of MS Bodley 959.

Forshall and Madden printed a basic text of the two groups in parallel columns, the one from the smaller group on the left, assembled from four good manuscripts, the one on the right from one manuscript.[48] (A full apparatus of textual variants is given at the foot of every page.) To give some idea of the detectable differences, I give here Isaiah 2:1–3 from single, and different, manuscripts in a more recent, partly modernised, form, but borrowing the Forshall and Madden principle of left and right, and beginning with the Vulgate (which they do not give).[49]

Verbum, quod vidit Isaias, filius Amos, super Iuda & Jerusalem. Et erit in nouissimis diebus praeparatus mons domus Domini in vertice montium, & eleuabitur super colles, & fluent ad eum omnes gentes. Et ibunt populi multi, & dicent: Venite & ascendamus ar montem Domini,

& ad domum Dei Iacob, & docebit nos vias suas, & ambulabimus in semitis eius: quia de Sion exibit lex, & verbum Domini de Ierusalem.

The word that Ysay saw&, the sone of Amos, upon Iudam and Jerusalem. And ther schal ben in the in the last daies beforn maad redy the mount of the hous of the Lord in the cop of mounteynys, and it shal be rerid out upon hillis, and ther schuln flowe to it alle gentilis, and ther schul gon many peplis and seyn, 'Cummeth, stey we up to the mount of the Lord and to the hous of God of Jacob, and he schal techen us his weyes, and we schul gon in his stijes *or pathes.*' For fro Syon schal gon out the lawe, and the word of the Lord fro Jerusalem.

(British Library, Add. MS 15580)

The word which Ysaie, the sone of Amos, si& on Iuda and Iierusalem. And in the last daies the hil of the hows of the Lord schal me maad redy in the cop of hillis, and schall ne reisid above litle hillis, and alle hethene men schulen flowe to him, and many puplis schulen go and schulen seie, 'Come &e! stie we to the hil of the Lord, and to the hous of God of Jacob, and he schal teche us hise weies, and we schulen go in the paths of him.' Forwhi the lawe schal go out of Sion, and the word of the Lord fro Ierusalem.

(Corpus Christi College, Oxford, M 20)

The left-hand version is clearly more literal: the Latin order of words is retained, as in 'the last daies beforn maad redy', or 'and ther schuln flowe to it alle gentilis', or 'fro Syon schal gon out the lawe'. The right-hand version feels more English at these points.

Throughout the left-hand version in Forshall and Madden, many kinds of device of Latin are dressed in English as they stand, so that (as quite often happens with this group) the English sometimes cannot be understood at all without looking up the Latin (which Forshall and Madden do not give). Though still owing a lot to the Latin, the right-hand version is more understandable as English, and even idiomatic. Two factors may allow us to be decisive about what we have. There are far more copies of the right-hand version, showing that it was more popular. And no scribe was ever going to turn an idiomatic version into an unidiomatic version (though that dogmatic statement may turn out to have to be qualified). We can therefore agree with Forshall and Madden that the left-hand column, representing the smaller group, is an earlier version. Until the 1980s, the two versions were always known as 'Wyclif' and 'Purvey', on the grounds that Wyclif commissioned, and probably wrote part of, the first, which turned out to be less than perfect; and then got John Purvey, his secretary, to put the whole thing into better English. Recent doubts about any connection that Purvey had with Wyclif before his last days at Lutterworth, or with Bible translation, have led to his very proper dismissal from this scene.[50] Scholars now refer to either 'EV' for Early Versions or 'LV' for Later Versions.

The Early Versions, 1380–1384

We must for ever be grateful for the pioneer labours – huge, we should always concede – of the dedicated clergyman and knight: but the effect of 'Forshall and Madden' has been to solidify the Wyclif Bible into Block A and Block B. What they, obviously unwittingly, concealed, was that there could have been a more continuous process of retranslation, revision and improvement than their separation suggests. Their textual apparatus, remarkable as it is, does not allow a picture of manuscript succession, which could be labelled EV^1, EV^2, EV^3 and so on. Such revision is not always present in all the texts: study of the earlier manuscripts containing only the Psalms, for example, suggests 'that they form a close and compact group'; 'the text they contain is authoritative'.[51] Yet probing manuscripts can reveal an interesting fluidity, with implications for the greater activities of Lollards, and the organic life of Lollardy.

Let us consider three Old Testament manuscripts of the earlier version, two in Oxford and one in Cambridge. The Bodleian's MS 959, the most literal of all the manuscripts, ends abruptly after two words what we know as verse 20 of Baruch chapter 3. (Though in the Apocrypha in most later printed Bibles, and thus well towards the end of Old Testament material, Baruch is here between Lamentations and Ezekiel, following the Vulgate: so there were still to be done the books of Ezekiel, Daniel, all the minor prophets and the two books of Maccabees, not to mention all the New Testament.) The break comes 'at the end of the second column of the page, just where the scribe would have to wait for his ink to dry before he turned over'.[52] Bodleian Douce MS 369 ends at precisely the same word, though this time the break, in the second column on the page, is about a third of the way down. At this point in Douce 369 another hand, contemporary with the text, has added the words 'Explicit translacionem Nicholay de herford'. This is important in apparently giving rare information about a translator, someone in Wyclif's Oxford circle. A similar note in the Cambridge manuscript (University Library, MS Ee.1.10), in English, appears at the same place, though there is no break: 'Here endith the translacioun of N, and now begynneth the translacioun of J and of othere men.' Not only do these notes give us names to attach to two manuscripts, and thus to all in their later family of texts: they tell us that the work of translation of the early version had been done by several scholars – 'N', 'J' and 'othere men'. Going back to Bodley's MS 959, we find that, separate from the work of translation, the scribing, the writing-out, had been done by five different people. Each of these uses a different dialect. The text is freely corrected, sometimes by the scribe himself, sometimes in erasures, deletions and marginal additions by different hands. The first translator shows serious errors, like rendering the Latin *animo* 'yeer', as if it were *anno*. That, and others like it, could have been because the Vulgate text he was using was faulty: the *animo/anno* mistranslation, at Joshua 9:2, would not show up as nonsense. His grasp of Latin grammar was not absolute. Because of a lack of consistency, we cannot attribute all this to the mind of Nicholas of Hereford. We really do not know how the work of translation was organised. What is clear, however, is that this manuscript, Bodley MS 959, is a draft at an earlier stage than the four manuscripts which make up Forshall and Madden's left-hand column.

Cambridge MS Ee.1.10 just considered, though covering the whole Old and New Testaments, is not a reproduction of all of every book. For a reason not known, from Chronicles to Maccabees, thirty-two books by Jerome's reckoning, it gives only a selection of one or more verses from every chapter, always including the first. The verses given, moreover, can show a greater freedom of expression than in the rest of the manuscript, and the parallel manuscripts from Oxford. This suggests that they are evidence of a stage of transition from left hand to right hand, from EV to LV. It also threatens to drop us into a marsh, as quite large parts of the two supposed 'Nicholas of Hereford' manuscripts are not the same.

This may not matter. The important point is what we might call The Dislodging of the Blocks, the destruction of that Berlin Wall which has kept two sides apart. We have had Wyclif A and Wyclif B, in Darwinian development B being later and obviously better. But some manuscripts have mixed texts, possibly suggesting a preference for the earlier. The British Library's Cotton MS Claudius has a part of Luke's Gospel and the very brief Epistle to Philemon in the earlier version, and the rest in the later. A manuscript in Cambridge (Magdalene College, MS L.5.19) has John's Gospel in the later version, and the rest of the New Testament in the earlier. A complete Bible in Lambeth Palace (MS Lambeth 25) has the Pentateuch in the earlier version, the rest in the later. Study of Forshall and Madden's careful notes on the 170 manuscripts then available shows that such mixing was not uncommon. Even phrases from a later version could appear in an earlier. The earlier texts can be constantly on the move, as it were: the reader can follow changes happening. A clumsy English Latinism can be emended. To take an example at random from Christ

Church, Oxford, MS 145, Matthew 6:23, *ipse tenebrae quantae erunt*, appearing as 'tho derknesses hou grete shul thei be?', in all other earlier manuscripts as, 'how grete shulen thilke [the ilke/tho ilke/tho] derknessis be?' English glosses of difficult Latin words, written within the text itself and underlined, can be watched as they change through different glosses of the same word in other manuscripts until a 'final' reading is reached; that is, the one more frequently reproduced. A new, and un–absolute, doctrine appears: that in these Bibles, even within the earlier version alone, the processes of translation and revision were constantly on the move.[53] We should expect no other from the Spirit of God.

It is hard to imagine why any English reader would prefer even a short passage of the earlier version, and on Darwinian principles it makes no sense. A solution to the problem, and one matching Wyclif's doctrine, was proposed by the scholar of Lollard Bibles, Margaret Deanesly, in 1951. In her influential lecture 'The Significance of the Lollard Bible', she suggested that the earlier version was made in accordance with Wyclif's conception of the Bible as the codification of God's law, something that ought to take the place of contemporary canon law as the basis of Church order and authority.

> In the formulation of law verbal accuracy is of the utmost importance. While men of learning could still use the Latin Bible as their law-book, the less learned clerics and the lay leaders of John of Gaunt's anti-clerical party would have at their disposal a strictly literal rendering of that law-book. Besides, if recourse were had to the standard glosses or commentaries on the biblical text, in which each individual word was annotated, the relevance of these glosses to the English translation would be more apparent if the translation corresponded to the Vulgate word for word.[54]

We are drawn back to the note in the Cambridge MS Ee.1.10 about 'J and othere men'. Suggestions about who J might have been include two Johns, Trevisa and Purvey. Trevisa is considered below. Purvey has been discounted (see note 50): 'and othere men' leads nowhere, except to the sense of several hands at the work.

I have left until now the most striking change of all: that considering only the earlier version, the techniques of translation before Baruch 3:20 differ from those after. Forshall and Madden decided that the Old Testament before Baruch 3 was translated by Nicholas of Hereford: everything after was translated 'not improbably by Wyclif himself'.[55] How much was done, and in what way, by Nicholas is not clear. That Wyclif took over from Baruch 3 is unlikely, as at that time he was unwell, and busy with

other things. Whether any translating at all was done by Wyclif is not
known: there is no convincing evidence. It remains unlikely.

Later, twentieth-century, work finds that the earlier version

> started as glosses with northern forms, went through a redaction in
> Herefordshire and Suffolk dialects, and was then copied with varying
> degrees of translation into a central Midlands dialect by five separate
> scribes working from materials that were in the western form up to
> Judges 7:13 but in the East Anglian form thereafter.[56]

In all the 250 texts, we have only two names: two mentions of Nicholas
of Hereford, and one of 'J'. While understanding an assumption of scholarship, however, compared with the act of the doing, and the doing well,
we find that it matters very little who did the work. The silence, indeed
secrecy, may show us an essential fact, that these Bibles were made in an
atmosphere of danger, even fear. In that light, we can only admire the
determination to take on such large work, and to make the Scriptures
available to everyone who could read or hear.

The Later Version, probably 1388

This, 'LV', however and by whomever it was made, has by a long way the
greater number of surviving copies. That Forshall and Madden could base
their entire right-hand column, the whole Bible, on one manuscript, the
British Library's large folio Old Royal 1.C.8, 'written probably before
1420',[57] though collating it with thirty-four others, tells us that even when
the first copies of it were made probably soon after 1384, the process of
revision was regarded as over. Strikingly, those revisions were more
numerous in the section of the early versions up to Baruch 3, that said
to have been made by Nicholas of Hereford.

Now in the LV the Latin constructions have been replaced – though by
no means completely – by something resembling native idiom. The Vulgate
vocabulary remains, however, especially in difficult words. It might help
in understanding if part of a significant passage in Paul's epistles, the
opening of the eighth chapter of Romans (as recently put into modern
spelling, though without other changes), is quoted here:

> Therefore now no thing of condemnation is to them that be in Christ
> Jesus which wander not after the flesh. For the law of the spirit of life
> in Christ Jesus hath delivered me from the law of sin and of death. For
> that was unpossible to the law in what thing it was sick by flesh God
> sent his son into the likeness of flesh of sin and of sin damned sin in

flesh; that the justifying of the law were fulfilled in us that go not after
the flesh but after the Spirit. For they that be after the flesh savour tho
things that be of the flesh. But they that be after the spirit feel tho
things that be of the spirit. For the prudence of flesh is death; but the
prudence of spirit is life and peace. For the wisdom of the flesh is
enemy to God; forsooth it is not subject to the law of God, sothly
neither it may. Forsoth they that been in flesh moun not please to
God.[58]

This language resembles the tone of a clever modern student from abroad
on his first visit to London, confident that his voluble English will be
understood. The drift is just about clear (we can be certain that he will
get off the number 24 bus at the right place), but one wants to keep
telling him 'we don't say it quite like that', as 'in what thing it was sick
by flesh', where LV closely follows the Vulgate's *in quo infirmabatur per
carnem*. The last two lines in the passage now sound close to gibberish.
Sometimes for the original Greek LV is wrong: 'prudence of flesh' will
not do for the Greek φρόνημα τῆς σαρκὸς (*phronēma tēs sarkos*), which
has the sense of 'earthly minded' rather than a sort of bodily sagacity
suggested by the Latin *prudentia carnis*. The primary meaning of late
Middle English 'prudence', as the *OED* supports, has not changed. One
manuscript, the British Library's Harleian 5017, has a marginal note at this
point, among other things glossing 'prudence of flesh': 'by which a man
can slyly get and pursue fleshly goods', referring to a comment by Nicolas
of Lyra.

Additional matter

A glance at a list of the manuscripts reveals variation in what else came
with the text, almost always wholly in English. A few manuscripts of the
later version have, before Genesis, an English translation of the epistle of
Jerome to Paulinus, with Jerome's epistle to Desiderius in some of them.
Many manuscripts, earlier and later, have prologues to individual books,
and before Isaiah a prologue on the prophets. All of these Forshall and
Madden print, even if they appear in only one manuscript. A number of
both earlier and later manuscripts have tables of epistles and gospels for
church use, summaries[59] and one (BL, Royal 17.B.i) has a concordance.
Later version manuscripts may begin with a long General Prologue, until
now thought, wrongly, to be by John Purvey, in which, *inter alia*, an
evaluative account of Old Testament history occupies many pages, and
some account is given of some of the principles of translation in use. In
this, the writer sometimes speaks of himself in the third person singular;

early in the final chapter he refers to 'divers fellows and helpers', suggesting a corporate work. He distinguishes four stages of the work:

> first, the effort to establish a reliable Latin text; second, a study of the Latin text alongside the *Glossa Ordinaria*, and commentaries, especially that of Lyre; thirdly, attempts to elucidate textual difficulties, particularly those of syntax and vocabulary; fourthly, the translation and then its correction.[60]

What a careful reader receives from this final, and full, chapter is a sense of the fluidity of the entire process. The writer is not standing back to look at a completed work, but commenting on the process of creation and revision as it goes on, and, as Anne Hudson remarks, 'even though the writer acknowledges the existence of *manie good felawis and kunninge* [skilful] at this [revision] stage of the operation, the time that it must have taken is daunting'.[61]

Three major biblical commentaries from this period, in Wycliffite directions, also survive: on the four Gospels (the *Glossed Gospels*) with a long commentary based on the *Catena aurea* of Aquinas; several versions of a commentary on the Psalms (all in English); and a Latin commentary on the Apocalypse.[62]

THE IMPACT OF WYCLIF'S BIBLES

Writers on the English Bible have noticed that phrases from the later version are familiar, because they appear in KJV. At Matthew 25:21, KJV's admired words towards the end of the Parable of the Talents, 'enter thou into the joy of thy lord', have been traced in origin to Coverdale's 1535 revision of Tyndale's 1526 New Testament. That they appear at that point in the later Wyclif has been seized as evidence that Coverdale 'lifted this magnificent rendering straight from the Wycliffe Bible'.[63] Tyndale, in both his earlier, 1526, and later, 1534, translations has 'enter in into thy master's joy'. The Greek at that point has εἴσελθε εἰς τὴν χαρὰν τοῦ κυρίου σου (*eiselthe eis tēn charan tou kuriou sou*). The Vulgate has *Intra in gaudium domini tui*. Tyndale is more exact to both. Coverdale's is a fine phrase, and it is hard to think that it is coincidence that it is first in Wyclif, though as 'Enter thou in to joy of thy lord'. Part of the work on the Wyclif Bibles waiting to be done is a thorough analysis of such apparent borrowings.

Whether or not the first translator from the Greek into English, William Tyndale, had a Wyclif LV beside him as he worked is an open question. Comparing passages in Wyclif and Tyndale from anywhere in the New Testament is to find the same effect: that the Wyclif LV text again and

again has the same words as Tyndale, but preceded and followed by words
and phrases so different as to be nearly incomprehensible. (In the following comparisons, to be consistent, I shall give both Tyndale 1526 and Wyclif
LV in their original spellings.) In Matthew's Gospel 5:4, in the Beatitudes,
Tyndale has the familiar 'Blessed are they that morne, for they shalbe comforted'. Wyclif LV has 'Blessed ben thei that mornen, for they schulen be
coumfortid'. In the following verse, however, where Tyndale has 'Blessed
are the meke: for they shall inheret the erth', Wyclif LV has 'Blessed ben
mylde men, for they schulen welde the erthe'. Chapter 7 of Matthew in
Tyndale begins 'Iudge not lest ye be iudged': Wyclif LV has 'Nile ye deme,
that ye be not demed', and goes on 'for in what doom ye demen, ye
schulen be demed'. Wyclif LV has in Matthew 5 'Ye ben salt of the erth',
and a sentence or two later 'So schyne your light before men, that thei
see yore good werkis, and glorifie your fadir that is in heavenes' – phrases
familiar to many not only in KJV from Tyndale, who does seem there to
be aware of Wyclif LV, but from the Book of Common Prayer. Yet Wyclif
LV at 1 Corinthians 14:29 has 'Prophetis tweine or threi seie, and other
wiseli deme', and we have to turn to Tyndale to find the sense: 'Lett the
prophetes speake two at once, or thre at once, and let other judge.' The
subject-matter is odd, that of speaking in tongues: but the Tyndale
sentence immediately conveys its message to modern eyes and ears. It is
not only a matter of vocabulary, though that had changed in the 150
years between Wyclif and Tyndale: the rhythmic structure of the sentence
is different.

In Wyclif LV, chapter 22 of Luke's Gospel opens with 'And the halidai
of the therf looves that is seide pask nyed.' Wyclif LV here follows the
Latin order precisely, suggesting to modern ears, with the strange vocabulary as well, some kind of pidgin. Tyndale has: 'The feast of swete breed
drue nye whych is called ester.' (It was the Geneva translators in 1557 who
stopped following Luther's 'sweet bread' to give 'unleavened bread', followed by KJV in 1611, which also changed 'Easter' to 'the Passover'. It is
a mark of the un-English Latinity of the Rheims New Testament in 1582
that it here has 'And the festival day of the Azymes approached, which is
called Pasche.')

A passage in the second chapter of Paul's letter to the Colossians in
Wyclif LV is:

And whanne ye weren deed in giltis, and in the prepucie of your fleisch,
he quikenyde togidere you with hym: foryiving to you alle giltis, doynge
awey that writing of decre that was ayens us, that was contrary to us;
and he took away that from the mydill, pitching it on the cros; and he

spuylide principatis and poweris, and led out tristili, opynli ouercominge hem in hym silf.[64]

In Paul's thought, related to Jewish religion, some important work of Christ is going on there, but at the best, reading it is like driving while trying to look through a muddy windscreen. Here is Tyndale in 1526:

> And hath with hym quyckened you also which were deed in synne and in the uncircumcision of youre flesshe, and hath forgeven us oure trespasses, and hath put out the obligacion that was agaynst us, made in the lawe written, and thatt hath he taken out of the waye, and hath fastened it on his crosse, and hath spoyled rule and power, and hath made a shewe of them openly, and hath triumphed over them in his awne persone.[65]

Here the windscreen wipers are at least allowing the driver to see the road. Tyndale's light revision of that in 1534, principally in the order of the first phrases, went on into KJV in 1611: those revisers changed 'hath put out' to 'blotting out', and 'fastened it' to 'nailing it', and enlarged Tyndale's later change of 'obligation' to 'handwriting' – explained in Tyndale's 1534 marginal note as referring to law – to produce 'the handwriting of ordinances'.

Through KJV, Tyndale is responsible for the worldwide circulation of the phrase at Matthew 5:13, 'the salt of the earth', often credited to him as creator.[66] As observed above, however, Wyclif has it. He was not the first. Chaucer's vile Summoner, recorded, as one might say, a little before Wyclif LV, quotes it: 'Ye been the salt of the erthe and the savour'.[67] Four hundred years before that, in the glossing to the Anglo-Saxon Lindisfarne Gospels at that point in Matthew, is 'Ye sint salt eorðes'. This can be used to approach two matters: the second, raised at longer range in chapter 9 below, is that if 'salt of the earth' is what the Greek and Latin have (which they do: ἅλας τῆς γῆς, *halas tēs gēs*; *sal terrae*), can there be any other way of putting them into English? Is there not truth in the accusation that Tyndale's genius has been exaggerated, and that all he did was turn the Greek into English? I shall return to that. (The short answers are yes, no and no.) The first question, for this present chapter, is the more important. How did such a phrase come to Tyndale? Did he have a Wyclif New Testament open on his desk? That the similarities of Wyclif and Tyndale can be at the same time both compellingly present and totally absent points both ways. He was bound to differ in many places; he was, after all, translating the Greek, not the Vulgate's Latin. Perhaps some future comprehensive, detailed analysis of the New Testaments would show a pattern:

that at the points where the Vulgate differs from the Greek, which it does quite often, there Tyndale is unlike Wyclif. This would not take into account changes in language over 150 years, nor Tyndale's genius with the phrasing of spoken English, not scholastic Latin English.

No educated and religiously alert young man brought up in 'God's Gloucestershire' in the late fifteenth and early sixteenth centuries could fail to have heard, and most likely read, a Wyclif Bible. A hostile contemporary apparently recorded that 'a man could not meet two people on the road, but one of them was a disciple of Wyckliffe'.[68] Erasmus's Greek New Testament was published while Tyndale was at Oxford: whether he read to his Magdalen contemporaries, as Foxe records,[69] from that book, in Latin and Greek; or whether it was in his own English, from Erasmus, translating as he went; or whether, in Wyclif's Oxford he read from one of the many copies in the university, we do not know. This last is very possible.

In addition to the excellent recent scholarship of Professor Anne Hudson, a good deal of work remains to be done on the impact of Wyclif's translations on English life. That they were effective among the itinerant Lollard preachers we may take for granted; that those who heard it then were stirred we may also understand. The change would be startling enough from Genesis 1's *Fiat lux, et lux erat,* even to Wyclif EV's 'Be made light: and made is light', never mind Wyclif LV's 'Light be made: and light was made'. Powerful would be the change from *Sic enim Deus dilexit mundum, ut Filium suum unigenitum daret, ut omnis qui credit in eum non pereat, sed habeat vitam aeternam* (John 3:16) to Wyclif LV's 'For God louede so the world, that he &af his oon bigetun sone, that ech man that bileueth in him perische not, but haue euerlastynge lijf'; or from *Surge, tolle grabatum tuum et ambula* (Mark 2:9) to 'Ryse, take thi bed, and walke'. It would be strange if these phrases, and hundreds of others, indeed whole passages, were not lodged in many people's memories. There may very well have been a considerable pool of phrases and passages from Wyclif's Bibles in common life.

We may come at this a different way. Tyndale's first attempt at printing an English New Testament from Greek was begun in Cologne in 1525, and abandoned near the end of the first Gospel when the city authorities raided the printing shop. Sheets survived, and circulated in England, being the first printed 'Lutheran' tracts to arrive there. Tyndale had written for the edition a Prologue, which also circulated in England on its own (before being reissued by Tyndale later). These fourteen pages are an expansion of and alteration to, Luther's *Vorrhede* to his first, 1522, New Testament in German from the Greek. There is in them a curious effect. When Tyndale has left Luther's *Vorrhede* and is writing on his own, he makes whole passages out of Scripture, usually from the Epistles of Paul and John. The strong effect is of someone quoting Scripture from memory. Occasionally there is an exact parallel with Wyclif LV, but most of the time there is no relation to any other version, including his own translation that he is now introducing. If Tyndale wrote these solid paragraphs of argument by quoting Scripture in an English version from memory – then memory of what?

A large amount of research is waiting to be done here. We may for the moment postulate that one effect of solid preaching from Wyclif's Bibles, before the standardisation that came with printed Bibles, was the creation of just such a common pool of English Bible phrases and passages in people's memories. Here, to approach the end of this chapter is the last part of Romans 8 in Wyclif LV, with modernised spelling. Beyond the natural common ground of a Greek original controlling the Latin, and thus the English, we may feel that some phrases did, by whatever means, influence Tyndale. He may have had a manuscript by him: or such phrases, from the heart of the epistle which is itself the very heart of Christian theology, may have been in common use.

> What then shall we say to these things? If God for us, who is against us? The which also spared not his own son, but for us all betook him, how also gave he not to us all things with him? Who shall accuse against the chosen men of God? It is God that justifieth, who is it that condemneth? It is Jesus Christ that was dead, yea, the which rose again, the which is on the right half of God, and the which prayeth for us.
>
> Who then shall depart us fro the charity of Christ? Tribulation, or anguish, or hunger, or nakedness, or persecution, or peril, or sword? As it is written, For we be slain all day for thee: we be guessed [reckoned] as sheep of slaughter. But in all these things we overcome, for him that loved us. But I am certain, that neither death, neither life, neither angels, neither principalities, neither virtues, neither present things, neither things to coming, neither strength, neither height, neither deepness, neither none other creature may depart us fro the charity of God that is in Christ Jesu our Lord.[70]

In 1969, Henry Hargreaves wrote:

> The nobleman's fine copies were meant for, and doubtless remained unused upon, his library shelves; but smaller and cheaper copies were intended for common use among the lower classes. Reading them together in small groups, as the evidence at trials shows that they did, they were in danger of prosecution and even death, but read them they did, and the small and secret Bible-readings and meetings that they

conducted proved a fertile breeding-ground for that Puritanism or nonconformity that has never since died out. The Bible which permeated the mind of later generations shows no direct descent from the Wycliffite versions; at most a few phrases from the later version, particularly of the Psalms, seemed to have found their way into the Tudor translations, and Tyndale's return to the original languages meant that translations based on the intermediate Latin of the Vulgate would soon be out of date. But in their insistence upon the immediacy of 'Goddis law' for every man and their efforts to present it to him in an accurate and understandable form, the Wycliffite translators showed themselves to be the true precursors of the English Protestant tradition.[71]

Anne Hudson's final remark to her chapter on 'Lollard Biblical Scholarship' (1988) is:

> the success of Wycliffite preoccupation with the Bible is seen in the biblical texture of many of their writings [. . .] as well as in the constancy with which adherents to the sect read, studied, and suffered for their copies of scripture.[72]

It is sad that twentieth-century historical assessment of the significance of Wyclif and the Lollards often begins from the position that both his importance and his influence were greatly exaggerated in the sixteenth and nineteenth centuries. A Roman Catholic scholar wrote to me privately to correct an error of mine, asserting that 'Wyclif was by no means the first' to translate the Bible into English. There were 'at least fifty' English versions before him. No evidence was brought in support of that statement: nor can there be; but it is a persistent myth, I have found, among even educated Catholics. Attention by historians to ecclesiastical records of the Lollards, the examination of this person or that, especially after Arundel's Constitutions of 1409, is bound to deliver reductionism. The greatest achievement of Lollardy was its books, a great many of which in England were burned: knowledge of what has survived in Bohemia is now rare, producing today a wide desert of sweeping ignorance. The heart of Lollardy was its English Bible, only now at the start of the twenty-first century beginning to be understood in some quarters as the massive, careful, complex, always developing achievement that it was. Twentieth-century historians have, one hopes unwittingly, distorted: the Bible has usually been kept out of the picture. One can blame them for dismissing the content of the Bible as irrelevant; but blame must be softened in this case, while the greatest manuscript body in English letters is still kept untouched, largely unedited and only limitedly accessible.

APPENDIX: THE ENIGMA OF JOHN TREVISA

John Wyclif was not the remote and rather pitiable figure, lost in his Oxford world of pointless scholasticism and ineffectual heresy, that his later enemies have portrayed. Quite apart from the power of his great number of Latin writings; from the wide spread of his ideas, not just in England; from the official opposition that he provoked, particularly from Archbishop Arundel; and from the great number of Bibles in English that came directly from his initiatives, Wyclif had power at the courts of Edward III and Richard II, and he knew the great and the good.

John Trevisa he must surely have known at Oxford, though proof of direct link is lacking. Both men were at The Queen's College: Trevisa was a Fellow from 1369 to *c.* 1379; he rented a room there from 1382 or 3 to 1386 or 7, and again from 1394. In the earlier years his lodging there coincided with Wyclif, who rented a room from 1374 to 1375 and from 1380 to 1381, and 'possibly for some of the years between'.[73] Nicholas of Hereford was also admitted to Queen's as a Fellow in 1369. Trevisa shared Oxford experiences, particularly a notable expulsion from Queen's, with another Fellow, William Middelworth; all three, Hereford, Middelworth and Trevisa, were ordained priests by Simon Sudbury, Bishop of London, on 8 June 1370. Hereford was 'Wyclif's closest and arguably most radical disciple'.[74]

Trevisa, a Cornishman as might be guessed from the 'Tre-' of his name, was born in 1342, and after Oxford served as chaplain to Thomas, Lord Berkeley, whose ancient castle stands by the River Severn in Gloucestershire, clearly visible from Tyndale's probable birthplace on the Cotswold slopes at North Nibley. As Vicar of Berkeley, he died in 1402.

Trevisa was a translator into English, most famously of Ranulph Higden's *Polychronicon*, written between 1327 and 1352. Recently described as 'Wyclif's favourite history book',[75] *Polychronicon* is a universal history, which, like the *Cursor mundi,* divides it into the seven ages of the world, all with a strong base in the Bible, beginning with Genesis. In this it differs from Geoffrey of Monmouth and the expanded *Brut* chronicle, which starts with Aeneas and Troy. Trevisa translated Higden with vigour, adding his own notes and comments: he objected to some of the monk Ranulph's assumptions. Trevisa also translated Bartholomeus's *De Proprietatibus Rerum* and at least four other books as well. He prefaced his *Polychronicon* with two statements in which the theory of translation is discussed.

In Berkeley Castle, just below the ceiling of the Morning Room, which was formerly the Chapel, are inscriptions in Norman French, the most legible being from Revelation 8:13, *un egle volant.*[76] These have long been

said to be by Trevisa, but the scholar David C. Fowler believes that, since
they are not in English, they were made by a predecessor, perhaps David
of Melksham, who was vicar around 1349–74. By Trevisa's time, say 1385,
the shift of language from French to English was marked.

Did Trevisa, as is often stated, translate the Bible? The blunt answer is
that nobody knows for certain. A good deal of circumstantial evidence
points in that direction, but proof is still lacking. As we saw in the previous chapter, with the exception of two, all the 250 manuscripts of the
Wyclif Bible have no name attached. The absence of any surviving attribution to Trevisa, however, is not sinister, in view of the official disapproval even before 1408.

In 1482 William Caxton printed Trevisa's translation of the *Polychronicon*: in the 'Prohemye' (preface) he explained that Trevisa had translated it,
together with 'the byble and Bartylmew *de Proprietatibus Rerum*' at the
request of Lord Berkeley.[77] After Caxton's remark, the statement appears
repeatedly in connection with Trevisa's name. Indeed, it so appears in Miles
Smith's long preface to the KJV in 1611:

> Much about that time, even in our King *Richard* the second's days, *John
> Trevisa* translated them [the Gospels] into *English*, and many *English*
> Bibles in written hand are yet to be seen with divers [various]; trans-
> lated, as it is very probable, in that age.[78]

It might help if we sharpen the questions: did Trevisa make an independent translation of some or all of the Bible, now lost? Or was he one of
the Oxford scholars who translated 'Wyclif EV'? Could he even be the 'J'
of Cambridge MS Ee.1.10? An answer to the last question will probably
never be found. Tackling the second question, however, does produce some
interesting pointers. Some time after the arrival of a new Provost of The
Queen's College in Oxford in 1376, his election was disputed, and in the
controversy that followed some of the fellows were expelled, including
Trevisa and Middelworth. They carried away with them various things,
including books, and stored them 'in diverse places in the town'.[79] (Wyclif
and Hereford are not mentioned in the dispute because they were not
Fellows, but simply renting rooms.) On 13 May 1378, an indenture was
drawn up in the presence of the Sheriff of Oxford listing the twenty-four
books that had been taken by Trevisa and others. They include, as well as
a Latin text of Higden's *Polychronicon*, a Latin text of the Bible, a Latin
grammar and dictionary, a Concordance to the Bible, and commentaries
on five books of the Bible, two by Nicholas of Lyra. Those could be said
to be a toolkit for turning the Latin Bible into English. Nicholas of Lyra
was a favourite commentator among Wycliffites: Trevisa in his acknowledged translations can be seen referring to him.

It is tempting to see that group at Queen's in the mid-1370s, Hereford, Middelworth, Trevisa and even possibly Wyclif himself, undertaking the translation of the Bible into English. In 1377, Wyclif was already a marked man, and by the end of 1378 had received two charges of heresy. The expulsion of the other three may not have been quite for the cause it seemed, a dispute about the weight of northern bias in the election in the college (which still draws more of its undergraduates from the north of England). Antony Wood, the gossipy Oxford historian who wrote in the 1690s, said of that expulsion: 'whether upon account of heresy or election of a Provost I know not'.[80]

As noted earlier, prefixed to Trevisa's translation of his *Polychronicon* were remarks about the theory of translation. More specifically, the preface entitled 'Dialogue between a Lord and a Clerk upon Translation' puts in the mouth of that Lord a vigorous defence of the Bible in English, including an accurate summary of Anglo-Saxon Bible translating, and mentioning Alfred and Caedmon.

> Also the holy man Bede translated St John's Gospel out of Latin into English. And thou wotest where the Apocalypse is written in the walls and roof of a chapel, both in Latin and in French. Also the gospel, and prophecy, and the right faith of holy church must be taught and preached to English men that can no Latin. Then the gospel, and prophecy, and the right faith of holy church must be told them in English, and that is not done but by English translation, for such English preaching is very translation, and such English preaching is good and needful; then English translation is good and needful.[81]

The need to find clinching evidence of Trevisa as translator of the Bible is now strong: that is to say, Trevisa not as the maker of an independent version, but as one of the Oxford Wycliffite translators.

Caxton was right about the other Trevisa translations he mentioned: why should he not have been right about 'the Bible'? – especially as he shows familiarity with a Wyclif Bible. In his *Chronicles of England*, Caxton remarked:

> who that fleeth fro the face of drede he shall fall in to the diche. And he that wendeth hym oute of the diche he shall be hold[en] & teide with a grenne.[82]

This is from Isaiah 24:18, part of a passage about 'fear, and the pit, and the snare' – if you run from the cause of fear you will fall into a pit, and if you get out of the pit you will be taken in a snare. It is not neatly enough expressed for a general proverb. As Caxton has it, his words are strikingly like Wyclif EV:

He that shall flee from the face of drede shall falle in to the dich and he that taketh himself out of the dich shal be holden with the grene.[83]

The scholar Caxton seems to have been aware of a Wyclif Bible. There is no good reason to doubt his remark about Trevisa, who had died only twenty years before he (Caxton) was born.

Seventy years after Caxton, John Bale in the 1550s, making, in two complementary forms, as full an account as he could of English writers, stated that John Trevisa translated the Bible, both Old and New Testaments, into English. Bale quoted the *incipit* (opening words) of the copy he was consulting: 'Ego Ioannes Treuisa, sacerdos. . . .'[84]

In 1587, Raphael Holinshed, in his *Chronicles*, repeated the statement that Trevisa translated 'the Byble and diuerse other treatises'. He might, of course, simply have been repeating what he saw in Caxton and Bale: but he added three new items, all accurate – that Trevisa was Cornish, that he was a secular priest, and that he was Vicar of Berkeley.[85] Holinshed had an independent source.

In 1662, the admirable Thomas Fuller, in his *History of the Worthies of England*, wrote:

> Some much admire [that] he [Trevisa] would enter on this work [of translating the Bible], so lately performed [. . .] by John Wycliffe [. . .]. Secondly, the time betwixt Wycliffe and Trevisa was the crisis of the English tongue, which began to be improved in fifty, more than in three hundred years formerly. Many coarse words (to say no worse) used before are refined by Trevisa, whose translation is as much better than Wickliffe's, as worse than Tyndal's.[86]

Now Fuller clearly knew Wyclif Bibles well enough to see that there were two distinct versions. The earlier he attributed to Wyclif himself. He ascribed to Trevisa, as that passage shows, the later improved version, Wyclif LV.

To recapitulate: until Daniel Waterton in 1729 merely guessed, as he himself wrote, and 'pitched upon' the unlikely Purvey as the author of Wyclif LV, without giving evidence,[87] and, for reasons unknown, Forshall and Madden accepted this in their great edition of 1850, everyone who gave a name to a Bible from Wyclif's time – that is, everyone up to 1729 – ascribed the work of translation to John Trevisa. Further, to put it no higher, both Trevisa's times and places in Oxford coincided with those of Wyclif and Nicholas Hereford, the latter the only named translator in a manuscript Bible.

Can we take the matter further? Probably. Trevisa wrote about the value of doing Bible translation work again and better.

Clerks know well enough that no sinful man doth so well that he ne might do better, and ne make so good translation that it ne might be better. Therefore Origen made two translations, and Jerome translated thrice the Psalter. I desire not the translation of those the best that might be, for that were an idle desire for any man that is now alive, but I would have a skilful translation, that might be known and understood.

These are the words of a writer who is improving a Bible translation (like Origen and Jerome). They occur in that preface to Trevisa's translation of the *Polychronicon*, the 'Dialogue between a Lord and a Clerk upon Translation', mentioned above, where the subject is giving an English Bible to the people.[88] Trevisa finished his *Polychronicon* on 18 April 1387. The best date for Wyclif LV's completion is 1388. That the words sound like those of someone at the coalface adds to the likelihood of Trevisa being engaged in making Wyclif LV. A recent brief analysis of the 'Dialogue' has shown that when Trevisa summarises the Bible there, as he does in an account of the Creation, he repeatedly falls into exact quotation from the as-yet-uncirculating Wyclif LV.[89]

But, though some likelihood points to Trevisa as having a probable hand in Oxford in Wyclif EV, and after Wyclif's banishment from Oxford and death in Lutterworth, being the reviser of Wyclif LV at Berkeley, the hard evidence is still lacking, and we have to revert to the blunt answer to the question, which is that we do not know.

Chapter 6

BEFORE AND AFTER WYCLIF: THE FOURTEENTH AND FIFTEENTH CENTURIES

WRITING IN ENGLISH IN THE fifteenth century, though often religious, was dependent on liturgy and showed small awareness of the Bible. (Caxton and his *Golden Legend* are considered below.) That was in spite of the wide spread of Wycliffite Bibles in English – and as an unknown number were destroyed, it is unlikely to be known exactly how wide that spread was. There were indigenous cultural achievements, like the growth of High Perpendicular church architecture or polyphonic music (to Latin texts), but all were church based. It has been said that 'the Lollard Bible was a huge success, . . . the only game in town . . . camouflaged . . . as safe reading matter'.[1] But in the long story of the whole Bible or complete New Testament in English and their lively offspring, covering well over 600 years, the 120 years from Chaucer to Tyndale are among the most barren.[2]

It is necessary to track back a little and look at what was happening in the literature of the land late in the fourteenth century, and in the generation before Wyclif. In London the English language had most rapidly evolved into a plasticity capable of being worked by the highest craftsmen, and Chaucer above all.

CHAUCER AND RICHNESS

Geoffrey Chaucer and John Wyclif had friends in common. Chaucer, about twenty years younger, was not an Oxford man, but he was a familiar figure at the courts of Edward III and Richard II, and, like Wyclif, he had John of Gaunt as a patron.

At first very French in his literary influences, from about 1372 Chaucer became increasingly Italian in interest and achievement. The extended characterisation and psychological insights of his superb long poem *Troilus and Criseide* (1380–86), loosely based on Italian sources, suggests a fore-runner of the novel, not to appear as a fully fledged genre for three more centuries. In the *Canterbury Tales*, written between 1387 and 1400, Chaucer's warmth, humour, control of dialogue and character, narrative skills, social and personal realism, poetic brilliance and philosophical understanding make him a delight, still. Though he was neither philosopher nor theologian, he certainly knew what he was writing about when he touched the subjects. He was not another Wyclif, except that in writing for the English in English rather than the French of the court, he shared Wyclif's deepest effect of all, that of bringing the greatest texts to the people in their own language.

Chaucer was not a Wycliffite. He attacked monks and friars with force, but not, as Wyclif had done, the ideals they stood for. In the *Canterbury Tales* the Host smells 'a Lollere in the wind',[3] provoking contempt from the Shipman for someone who will sow discord from glossing the Gospels, but the Host is wrong about the Parson: a Lollard would not have joined the pilgrimage. The fifty-line description of the Parson in the General Prologue is, however, positive and admiring. Beginning 'A good man was ther of religoun', it ends:

> A better preest I trowe that nowher noon ys.
> He waited after no pompe and reverence,
> Ne maked him a spiced conscience,
> But Cristes loore and his apostles twelve
> He taughte; but first he folwed it hymselve.[4]

Moreover, Anne Hudson noted that Chaucer had caught the Wycliffite vocabulary around the figure of the Parson. The later accrual to the *Canterbury Tales* of the Wycliffite 'Plowman's Tale', though not by Chaucer, was not out of keeping. When one notices what the Parson is *not* praised for, especially administration of the Mass and hearing confessions, Chaucer's sympathy with Wyclif looks clearer. 'Had Wyclif wished to versify his own ideals, he could not have wished to alter any of this,' she wrote.[5] Chaucer was biting in his parallel condemnation of the Monk, Friar, Summoner and Pardoner, and mockery of the Prioress.

Chaucer dedicated his *Troilus*, in which there is a central discussion of predestination (Wyclif's subject a decade earlier) to his friend – and Wyclif's – Ralph Strode. Predestination is riotously dealt with in 'The Nun's Priest's Tale', just as Wyclif's topic of 'discernment of authorities' appears in the mouth of the Wife of Bath.

These appearances give some indication of a freedom of intellectual life for educated Londoners, though only up to the statute *De heretico comburendo* in 1401 and Arundel's Constitutions of 1409. Chaucer's writing is

full of the Bible. He refers and quotes in English. It is his appalling
Pardoner who extorts money from his poor English congregations under
the Latin text *Radix malorum est Cupiditas*, preaching only, as he admits,
out of his own covetousness.[6] A full study of the English Bible in Chaucer
has yet to be made: it may be expected to show, probably more in the
later works, that he made assumptions about his readers' Bible knowledge
in English. The 'Pardoner's Tale' itself opens with a flurry of attacks on
debauchery and lust using ancient allusions. Beginning with a reference
to 'holy writ' (which is Ephesians 5), it goes on to Lot and his daughters
(from Genesis 19), a quotation from Seneca, Herod demanding John the
Baptist's head (from Matthew 14 and Mark 6), Adam gluttonously eating
the fruit (from Genesis 3), direct quotation from the Apocrypha (though
not so designated in the Latin; Ecclesiasticus 37), two direct quotations
from Paul (from 1 Corinthians 6 and Philippians 3), and unattributed references to 1 Timothy 5, Proverbs 20, Judges 13 and Numbers 6, all in the
first hundred lines. Near the end of this sequence, a dozen lines are about
cooks labouring to turn raw stuff into something that can satisfy the belly's
'lecherous talent', and suggest mockery not of the sacrament but of the
Church's doctrine of transubstantiation, on which the authority of the
priest depended, a bow in the direction of the Eucharistic controversy
pressed forward by Wyclif. There is even, it is said, direct reference to a
Wycliffite joke about the faithful forbidding friars to enter their cellars
lest the wine be transubstantiated into nothing.[7]

What is clear is that these lines were to be read (and heard: a manuscript illustration shows Chaucer reading to Richard II and his court) with
alert knowledge of the Bible, and preparedness to enjoy various levels of
oblique humour. The direct quotations from Paul, which Chaucer was perfectly capable of putting from Latin into English in verse to suit his
speaker, are – allowing for adjustment for metre – close to Wyclif. The
Pardoner says ' "Mete unto wombe, and wombe eek unto mete, / Shall
God destroyen bothe," as Paulus saith.' Wyclif LV has 'Mete to the wombe,
and the wombe to metis; and God schal distruye bothe this and that.'[8] Of
course, a phrase like 'mete to the wombe' has a proverbial ring: but that
argument cuts both ways. The Wycliffite translators might have picked up
a form of words already well known. It is also possible that they put into
circulation a biblical saying which, because it could be so widely applied,
became immediately popular.

The Pardoner's second direct quotation from Paul is equally interesting
in what it might tell us.

> 'There walketh manye of which yow toold have I –
> I seye it now wepyng, with pitous voys –

> That they been enemys of Cristes croys,
> Of whiche the ende is deeth, wombe is hir god!'

Wyclif LV has 'For many walken, whiche Y haue seid ofte to you, but now Y wepinge seie, the enemys of Cristis cros, whose end *is* deth, whos god is the wombe.'[9] It has to be remembered that, apart from possible individual renderings of the Latin into English in local sermons, the LV's rendering would be the first time these words had been read or heard in English. The point is not only that they are there, but that they would be familiar, and familiar enough to enable the readers and hearers to enjoy the extra edge of the gluttonous Pardoner's use. A modern – perhaps musical – joke about 'the rest is silence' would not work properly unless everyone knew *Hamlet*.

'The Bible was the most studied book in the middle ages' is the opening sentence of Beryl Smalley's classic *The Study of the Bible in the Middle Ages* (1941). She begins her second paragraph, 'Yet this is probably the most neglected aspect of medieval thought'; she did not set out to do more than 'clear the ground' for some future, and almost impossible, history of biblical commentary and interpretation from the eighth century to the fourteenth in Northern Europe.[10] The material is indeed enormous and elusive, still almost completely unprinted and unedited. The unique component in scriptural interpretation amid the medieval work 'in law, in government, theology, philosophy, art, even in science disguised as alchemy' was the intercourse with Jewish scholarship.[11] Yet, wonderfully grand as all this was, it was all in Latin (and Hebrew). The ordinary English person, the man on the Clapham *equus*, as we might put it, was untouched. As Smalley wrote:

> Most of the laity's ideas of Scripture must have reached them at second hand from the clerks:
>
> > Now you talk to me again of Lot and his wife, whom I have never seen or known, nor their city, nor have we been in one time. But I have heard say that an angel commanded them to leave the city where they had dwelt, and not to look back, and because the woman looked back she was changed into a statue of salt. But to me it was never commanded that I should not look back.
>
> This rare letter, which was sent about 1314 from a lay baron to an ecclesiastic, shows the illiterate layman struggling to answer clerical arguments; he recognises his disadvantage.[12]

We have just observed Chaucer's Pardoner, some time shortly after 1380, in 100 lines peck-pecking at a dozen Bible ideas from Genesis, Judges,

Numbers, Proverbs, Ecclesiasticus, the Gospels and Paul's Epistles, and all
– in spite of his sermon's Latin text – *in English*.

Obviously, Chaucer was neither Tyndale nor a seventeenth-century
Cromwellian. He did not make his writing out of Scripture only. Yet
the presence of a passage like that by the Pardoner, or allusions by the
Nun's Priest or the Wife of Bath (both with a fine irreverence), or the
Merchant more solemnly evoking Jacob, Judith, Abigail, Esther and so on,
and much else throughout the Complete Works, imply something new, a
general Bible knowledge among his audience. True, the man on the
Clapham *equus*, not to crack the wind of the poor horse, did not ride
with the pilgrims to Canterbury. Those were all, after their fashion, professional people. Tyndale's 'boy that driveth the plough' as a reader of
Scripture was a century and a half ahead. (Chaucer admired his Plowman,
the poor Parson's brother, but gets this labourer out of the way in thirteen lines to make way for the colourful rogues: he does not give him a
tale.[13]) The point, however, stands. In England, the Bible had begun to
leave the distant realm of the Latin scholars. In Chaucer, it did so in
remarkable verse, which had, with him, suddenly achieved a poetic
maturity which could match the French of Chrétien de Troyes or the
Italian of Dante.

The London English of Chaucer became the norm for literature. He
can properly be credited with establishing that. The Oxford English of
Wyclif was similar enough not to cause problems to Londoners. Further
from London and the East Midlands, what was written could have been
puzzling, as regional variations were strong: nevertheless, it is possible to
see the first outlines of a coming national literature, in Gower, Hoccleve,
Lydgate and Malory above all, in ballads and chronicles – but all of it
secular.

One major poet of Chaucer's time was religious.

WILLIAM LANGLAND

Chaucer's *Canterbury Tales* came twice from Caxton's press in Westminster
after 1476, and once each from the London presses of Richard Pynson
and Wynkyn de Worde. Langland, whose popular *Piers Plowman* was also
written during and after Wyclif's lifetime, a work that still survives in fifty
or sixty manuscripts, was not printed until 1550, when it came from the
reforming press of Robert Crowley. This visionary, semi-allegorical, poem,
vividly full of people and places, was loved by English Protestant readers
in the sixteenth century and long after. Chaucer was the greater writer,

and one does not begrudge the wealthy buyers of his printed works their delight. Yet Langland also spoke for England in English, and was a poet of a very English kind, writing Middle English in an ancient Old English alliterative form, the last significant work of that kind. Though Langland at least began writing, it seems, in London, his two principal versions, each of over seven thousand lines, do not show the luxury of London courts and French or Italian influences. Langland's poem begins 'And on a May morning, on Malvern hills'. All three versions are his dreamer-narrator's search for true Christianity, the spiritual welfare of the ordinary English people faced with the corruption found in society, in the clergy and in the mendicant orders. He quotes from or refers to a Bible (in Latin) frequently, particularly the Psalms, but not the fashionable commentators or patristic writers. He gives dramatic weight to the unbiblical Seven Deadly Sins, central to Roman Catholic theology. His two constant themes are the condemnation of the Church and the search for an inner spirituality, through Piers the Plowman, presented as a type of Christ. Beyond Langland, the figure of the Plowman was used widely in writings of many kinds to embody a Christ-like truth, in opposition to ecclesiastical corruptedness. The abundance of surviving manuscripts of Langland's poem suggests great interest, as with the Wyclif Bibles, which probably in the fifteenth century had many of the same readers.[14]

RICHARD ROLLE

Not long before Wyclif, England had religious writers who were developing in English expression of that inner spiritual life which was at one with the later European movement of reform within the Church specifically known as the *Devotio moderna*. This was the time in England of Richard Rolle, of the *Cloud of Unknowing* and of Julian of Norwich. Richard Rolle of Hampole (near Doncaster in Yorkshire) left Oxford in about 1320 to become a recluse and seek the closest knowledge of God, which he knew could come only from reading the Scriptures and by being apart from the factions in all branches of professional life. He wrote a great deal in English as well as Latin (most of it still unpublished) and was widely imitated. His prose translation of the Latin Psalms with commentary, all in English, circulated throughout the land. It was made a good half century before Wyclif's, about 1327.[15] Though it has a northern English flavour (Psalm 23 (24) has 'for he abouen the sees grundid it: and graid it abouen floden'), it is the first complete Psalter in an English that is recognisable today. Rolle occasionally added or paraphrased, but only when he felt explanation was needed. In his Prologue to the Psalms, he wrote:

> In this worke i seke na straunge ynglis, bot lyghtest and comonest. and swilk [such] that is mast lyke til the latyn. [that is, his Vulgate original text]: so that thai that knaws nought latyn by the ynglis may com til mony latyn wordis. In the translacioun i folow the lettere als mykyll [much] as i may. And thare [where] i fynd na propire ynglis i folow the wit [sense] of the worde, so that thai that sall red it thaim thare nought dred errynge [need not fear being led astray].[16]

Here is the opening of Rolle's Psalm 22 (23):

> Lord gouerns me and nathynge sall me want:
>   in sted of pasture thare he me sett.
> On the watere of rehetynge [reviving] forth he me broght:
>   my saule he turnyd.
> He led me on in the stretis of rightwisnes: for his name.

David Norton writes:

> Thus the only real precedent for the translators of the Wyclif Bible, a precedent approved by the Church, was a literal interlinear guide to the Latin. Rolle was treating a limited part of the Bible in a limited way, opening the literal meaning of the words to his audience but not returning the meaning of the Psalms to a literal level. The presence of the gloss, which was largely a translation of earlier, orthodox works, ensured this. Rather than presenting an English Psalter to the people, he was presenting them with the Latin Psalter as understood by the Church. Further, it was not the largely illiterate masses to whom Rolle was presenting this work, but a small number of illiterate people who could afford the substantial cost of a manuscript or were in a position to copy it for themselves.[17]

MYSTERY PLAYS

The early fifteenth century is the period of the maturity of the great cycles of biblical plays. Surviving manuscripts show that, even by the late fourteenth century, forty-eight plays were regularly being staged at York, twenty-four at Chester, and, not long after, thirty-two plays in the Towneley cycle and forty-two plays at Coventry. All were different, with emphasis on particular stories. Other towns, it seems, had plays, of which the documentation has not survived. That these were high civic events demanding great expense of money and time there is no doubt. In their own different ways, they all tell, with some non-biblical additions (like the Assumption and Coronation of the Virgin), the biblical story from Creation to Doomsday, concentrating on the Fall of Man and Redemption through the Incarnation. The preparation for performance of each section was given to a defined part of the city's life, especially the craft guilds (also called 'mysteries', hence the title, 'Mystery Plays'), so that, for example, the Guild of Shipwrights put on a play of Noah, the Vintners did the Marriage at Cana, the Bakers were responsible for the Last Supper and the Butchers for the Crucifixion. Each section might be performed on a pageant cart, which was wheeled round the city to stop at certain 'stations': the medieval routes are known for York and Chester.[18]

It is likely that these spectacular dramas, which could absorb the energies of most of a city, began, long before, on a smaller scale inside the church buildings, written and prepared by the clergy at first as rather spare dramatic illustration of specific parts of the year's liturgy. They must have seemed to the onlookers as if the stained-glass pictures had come to life. The cycles of plays to be performed outside, however, have reached us in altogether grander forms: God speaks, at some length: Lucifer and the angels fall; Adam and Eve, in 'naked' attire, are seduced by the wily serpent; shepherds and kings crowd the manger; rough soldiers enjoy crucifying Christ; Christ harrows hell; all mankind is judged. Costumes, for example for the Magi or the High Priests, were very expensive. The former windows-come-to-life have an altogether larger scale, fixed to the time of the Corpus Christi processions in June or July. The difference is paralleled, perhaps, by that between a brief cartoon for television and an animated adventure-fantasy for the wide-screen cinema. In the Chester cycle the Cooks provided, for the Harrowing of Hell, 'the various bubbling cauldrons, huge spits and burning coals necessary to evoke the torturous, fiery underworld'.[19]

The language of all the plays, though sometimes Latin, is generally Late Middle English, needing only the lightest modernisation to be understood in the twenty-first century, especially when spoken with strong gestures and staging. It is the Vulgate's Latin independently rendered, always using the patristic interpretations of Christian history. Not only does there seem to be no trace of Wyclif: that absence is forceful. These plays are the Latin Bible, with the Church's additions, given to the people through the Church. Wyclif was a heretic.

With its long paragraphs of lightly rhyming verse, the English can sound stilted, ponderous (and even, dare one say, boring: heard on a cold wet evening in a dripping garden in front of an ancient damp wall, God can be felt to drone on, somewhat). It can also rise to heart-stopping moments

of feeling, as when the cruel soldiers in the York Passion play leave Jesus
on the cross with the words: 'Let him hang there still, / And make faces
at the moon.'

This is particularly true of the six Wakefield plays in the Towneley cycle.
These, as in the other cycles but more powerfully, are skilfully interwoven with the sort of material found in Latin sermons of the time, with
Christian legends, and as well, proverbs, folktales and other secular material, here often comic and always up to date. These six plays show the
hand of a master in liveliness of language, gesture and action.[20] In the
Wakefield *Processus Noe cum filiis*, Noah's wife, a newcomer to the Genesis
story except in the passing phrase 'and his wife', though omitted from the
title of the play, has the second biggest presence. She has taken on the
Termagant role of the ancient Uxor figure. She is given an elaborated,
rich and active part, volubly refusing to 'stir one foot' to enter the ark,
setting herself down on a hill to spin even when everyone else is on board,
until Noah comes out again and beats her: she groans that she may not
survive their fight – but she does go aboard, and shares the wonders of
the experience.[21]

There has been nothing in England quite like these plays since the last
recorded performance of the Coventry cycle in 1580. They are commonly
said to have been actively suppressed under Elizabeth, and certainly the
non-biblical plays, like those on the Assumption or Coronation of Mary,
were removed. It is more likely that, though there was observable official
interest in curtailing 'popish' references, national taste simply changed: two
hundred years is a long time for such an occasion-bound art form to
remain vital, and a new popular drama was rapidly emerging in the developing London theatres. Late twentieth-century revivals (in York regularly
since 1951) are to be commended; but they cannot repeat the occasions
when the entire city shared the most vivid spiritual life.

Secunda Pastorum, in the Wakefield cycle, the Second Shepherd's play,
continues to enchant. The farce of Mak the sheep-stealer (abetted by his
wife) hiding their booty in a cradle, and, found out, being tossed in a
blanket by the shepherds, elides most wonderfully into the Nativity, the
angels off-stage singing *Gloria in excelsis*. The three shepherds offer the
Christ Child cherries, a bird and a ball. The Second Shepherd says:

> A bird have I brought
> To my bairn.
> Hail, little tiny mop!
> Of our creed thou art crop [head];
> I would drink in thy cup [chalice],
> Little day-star [morning-star].[22]

RELIGIOUS LYRICS

That assurance of feeling is everywhere in the religious and secular lyrics in English from these centuries, and most outstandingly in the religious ones. These may sometimes belong to a vernacular and popular religious tradition surfacing in various places, including the mystery plays.[23] They commonly accompanied, as is now known, Latin sermons.

Songs that were sung and danced to before the thirteenth century, and there must have been many, have not survived. The best that can be hoped for is 'stray verses copied in manuscripts with whose contents they have little or no connexion. And the themes of these early lyrics are for the most part religious or didactic.'[24] One survivor is miraculous enough for us to lament the larger loss: in MS Harley 978 in the British Library, a monks' commonplace book from Reading Abbey made in about 1240, the only entry not in Latin or French, is the sophisticated four-part round 'Sumer is Icumen in', copied there with the still-well-known music.[25]

In the hundreds of English lyrics known before the end of the fifteenth century, 'For every secular lyric there are three or four religious.'[26] The religious are all devotional, as this, taking one example of very many, from John Grimestone's commonplace book of 1372, printed in the twentieth century as *Dialogue between Jesus and the B.V. at the Cross*, beginning:

> *Ihesus*
> Maiden & moder, cum & se,
> i child is nailed to a tre;
> hand & fot he may nouth go,
> his body is wonden al is wo.[27]

Two matters call for development, though not here. One is the important work by Siegfried Wenzel showing that most of the surviving lyrics from these centuries were part of sermon material of the time.[28] The second is to note that, attractive as so many of them are, like the mystery plays, they are biblical only in the sense that they touch on a dozen or so Bible stories. Wyclif's complete Scriptures are another world.

SERMONS

The complete Scriptures are another world, moreover, in classic analyses of preaching in these two centuries. In that made by G. R. Owst in his *Literature and Pulpit in Medieval England* (1933), where he ignores the 'Wycliffite sermons', he shows some reference to the Nativity and Passion, as could be expected, and the appearance of Adam or Noah, but all as part of the liturgical, not biblical, tradition. Dr Owst's detailed book does not even have 'Bible' in the index, and 'Scripture' only as one reference to 'Scripture, Holy, four senses of'.

MURDOCH NISBET

One direct derivative of Wyclif LV was the earliest Bible in Scots. It was made by an ordinary farmer, Murdoch Nisbet of Hardhill in Ayrshire, a district which was a centre of Lollardy.[29] He had a Wyclif New Testament, possession of which could have led to severe punishment. About 1520, recognising that the language of it was dated, and was in any case alien, he made his own Scots version. This he did, laboriously with many revisions and corrections, reading his manuscript secretly in a vault that he dug below his farm – remarkable in that the land there is notably wet.[30] The Nisbets, like all the tough Ayrshire hillmen, had a passion for the Scriptures. His precious manuscript was carefully treasured by his descendants, and survived even the most vicious persecution of its Covenanting owners by the Scottish government forces in the later seventeenth century. The final Nisbet owner had nothing left of his inheritance except this New Testament. His widow gave it for safekeeping to a young Edinburgh advocate with Ayrshire connections, Alexander Boswell. He became Lord Auchinleck and the father of James Boswell, the biographer of Dr Johnson. The book was sold, but found again in an Edinburgh bookshop by James Boswell, and it remained at Auchinleck until 1893, when it was sold to the British Museum: it is now in the British Library. In his *Journal of a Tour to the Hebrides* James Boswell describes the near-impossibility of communication between his father and his mentor 'the auld dominie' (Johnson) one wet November day at Auchinleck in November 1773.[31] In the library, Murdoch Nisbet's manuscript, which might have intrigued Johnson, went unnoticed.[32]

Scots, the language of Robert Burns, did not survive (it has of course no connection with the Gaelic of the Highlands and Islands), but the story of Nisbet's making his New Testament is a demonstration of the passionate dedication of communities to Wycliffite Bible translations. Here are a few verses from Nisbet in the Scottish Text Society's edition of 1901–5, Matthew 4:18–19, which appear to differ little from Wyclif LV. In fact, there would have been large differences in pronunciation:

And Jesus walkit beside the see of Galilee and saw twa brethire, Symon that is callit Petir, and Andrew his bruthir, castand nettis into thwe see:

for thai war fischaris. And he said to tham, Cum ye aftir me, and I sal mak you to be made fisharis of men.[33]

WILLIAM CAXTON

William Caxton was a wealthy Low Countries mercer, that is, a dealer in fine textile fabrics such as silk. A successful businessman in Bruges, he set up a printing press there – the first to make books in English – and in 1476 transferred it to Westminster. He remained a merchant and businessman, though becoming as well as a printer, editor and translator, a diplomatic negotiator and a bookseller, and what in later times would be called a publisher. This is not the place to examine his rather skewed reputation as a literary figure.[34]

Two matters about the printing of the Bible are essential. The first can be approached by way of the assertion, still commonly made by enemies of vernacular Bibles, that the housewife in her cottage had no need of a Bible in English, as she had sermons, plays and the *Golden Legend*.[35] Sermons, even if they were in the vernacular, would give little that was biblical. She might have had to travel far (an impossibility) to have seen the plays, which would have been amazingly vivid to her, but giving only short bursts, as it might be said, from the whole Bible. Caxton's *Golden Legend*, so often adduced, is his version in English of the *Legenda aurea*, the thirteenth-century Latin compilation of 'lives of the martyrs, virgins and apostles, apocryphal stories, and episodes from the life of Christ'.[36] This document rapidly grew, and an English translation known as the *Gilte Legende* was made in 1438 and included the lives of many English saints.[37] Caxton's version in 1483 expanded the Latin book from a French as well as the English translation, and added lives of 'Adam, Noah, Abraham, Isaac, Esau, Joseph, Moses, Joshua, Samuel, Saul, David, Solomon, Rehoboam, Job, Tobit, and Judith; and [. . .] a small commentary of the Ten Commandments linked with the life of Moses'.[38]

That seems an advance. Job, for example, did not appear in the plays or lyrics. Yet this is not the Job of the Bible:

> the narrative section of the Vulgate account has been translated, but the middle section of the biblical book in which Job discusses his misfortunes with his three friends is dismissed in a couple of sentences.[39]

That is to say, out of the forty-two chapters of Job, thirty-nine are missing. Caxton makes up for such excision by expansions.

Thus the story of Adam and Eve follows the outline found in Genesis, but it includes apocryphal tales like the quest for the oil of life by Seth and individual details from the works of Bede, Methodius, Josephus and Strabo.[40]

In the *Golden Legend*, amid nearly two hundred saints' imaginary lives, the Bible scraps are lost in a sea of fiction.

The second question to be asked is even sharper. Why did not Caxton, with his business eye for what sold very well, print a Bible? Following Gutenberg in Mainz around 1456, there were ten complete Latin Bibles or Psalters printed in Europe before Caxton's *Golden Legend* in 1483. Bulky though the task of setting up a Bible was, it was not beyond Caxton, who had already printed Higden's *Polychronicon*. More to the point, in Europe before 1483 there were eight Bibles or Psalters printed not in Latin but in German; five New Testaments or Psalters in French; and three (the Old Testament, most of the New Testament, and a Psalter) in Dutch.[41] (These were directly from the Vulgate.) Why did not Caxton print Wyclif's Bible in English?

An answer personal to him is that he was a man of piety, entirely wedded to the life and traditions of the Church, to which the whole Bible was of little importance. A larger answer, with the widest implications, is that it was not permitted in England.

A CENTURY OF REPRESSION

From 1401 and the Act of Parliament *De heretico comburendo* until the 1530s and Henry VIII's break with Rome, writing in England, and most especially that suggesting religious protest or an English Bible, was under the severest censorship in the country's history. Among modern opponents of Protestantism, it is fashionable to call Oliver Cromwell 'England's only dictator': that is a foolish nickname. His generally benign and very English Protectorate lasted a mere five years, 1653–8, during which period of tolerance at home Britain had religious freedoms: for example, Jews were allowed back into the country for the first time since 1290. In contrast, the fifteenth-century iron grip in which Britain was held, made by Archbishop Thomas Arundel's Constitutions of Oxford in 1409, lasted for well over a hundred years, and came ultimately from Rome.

Though before 1400 there was a national literature in sight, and particularly new possibilities could arise after Chaucer, it is true to say that a promised light went out. Where, outside Scotland's Dunbar and Henryson, were Chaucer's successors? The dimming in England soon after

1400 had specific historical causes, the chief being national disruption in the great political instability which broke surface in the Wars of the Roses, and the resulting absence of such patronage as had been effective before 1400, especially in the court of Richard II. One prime cause, however, the effect of *De heretico comburendo* and of Arundel's Constitutions of 1409, has only begun to be acknowledged.

The imposition of a new and severe Church orthodoxy in 1409 was so successful as to make much of the former liberty of religious thought or high creativity impossible. Indeed, had he written after 1409, his anti-clericalism would have led Chaucer himself to be investigated as a heretic. The new severe orthodoxy was, in a great part, caused by the circulation of Wyclif's Bibles.

Vernacular religious writing ceased, or was driven into hiding. Even the possession of a religious vernacular text was enough for evidence of heresy – worse, the secular authorities entrusted with hunting heretics made even the possession of a work in English, however secular, such evidence. It was, as Nicholas Watson put it:

> a situation in which all but the most pragmatic religious writing could be seen, by the early fifteenth century, as dangerous: a perception that led inexorably to a by and large successful attempt to inhibit the further composition of most kinds of vernacular theology.[42]

Arundel's Constitutions, primarily against Lollardy and Wyclif, had implications, Watson continues,

> for the whole intellectual life of fifteenth-century England [. . . ;] the legislation as a whole constitutes one of the most draconian pieces of censorship in English history, going far beyond its ostensible aim of destroying the Lollard heresy and effectively attempting to curtail all sorts of theological thinking and writing in the vernacular.[43]

Articles 6, and 9 to 11

> impose limits on the discussion of theological questions in the schools, provide for a monthly inquiry (no less) into the views of every student at the university, and forbid the study not simply of Wyclif's books but of all recent texts that have not been approved unanimously by a panel of twelve theologians appointed by the archbishop. Less detailed but as stringent are a set of articles, (1–5, 8) [. . . which . . .] affirm the illegality of preaching without a license (to be granted only after examination of the preacher's orthodoxy); forbid preachers to discuss the sins of the clergy or the sacraments in their sermons [. . . ,] extend this ban

to cover schoolmasters and other teachers, and, finally, forbid all argument over matters of faith outside universities.[44]

What had been defined in previous centuries as a minimum necessary for
the laity to know if they were to be saved 'has been redefined as the
maximum they may hear, read, or even discuss'.[45] Even severer restrictions
were imposed on writing: 'Article 7 forbids anybody to make any written
translation of a text of Scripture into English or even to own a copy,
without diocesan permission, or any such translation made since Wyclif's
time'.[46] Anne Hudson has shown that this applied even to single verses.
Furthermore: ' "the expression of ideas gained from Latin books and
expressed in [written] English" could be taken, as a result of this article
and the Constitutions as a whole, as "*ipso facto* evidence of heresy" '.[47]

The Constitutions still had a prominent active place in Thomas More's
Dialogue concerning Heresies, written in the 1520s. Nicholas Watson has
shown two effects: the stopping-up of the vernacular stream of theology
which had flowed in the decades before 1410, 'as innovative as that in any
vernacular';[48] and the shrinking of the circulation of texts. Texts were read:
but they were from previous ages. Just as Caxton in 1483 printed in
English not Langland or a Wyclif Bible but the *Legenda aurea*, Watson has
drawn attention to the power of the debates on translation in Oxford
leading up to the Constitutions: the capacity of the English language was
rejected; the lower classes were refused texts; limitations were imposed on
what it was 'necessary' to know; and the role of the clergy as guardians
of truth and controllers of its communication was emphasised.[49] At root
is alarm about 'the steady "leaking" of biblical material into English
through the fourteenth century, from Rolle's *English Psalter* to *Book to a
Mother*, *The Lyfe of Soule*, the text edited as *Fourteenth-Century Biblical
Versions*, and others'.[50]

Controlled by Rome, what was orthodox Christianity in the English
Church from 1409 until the 1530s was unique in Northern Europe in its
narrowness and terrifying restrictions. Even in 1536, Tyndale, who broke
the barriers and gave the Greek New Testament to the people in printed
English, had, as well as his books, to be burned.

Part 2

AFTER PRINTING

Chapter 7

THE GREEK NEW TESTAMENT OF ERASMUS, 1516 AND AFTER

ERASMUS DISCOVERS LORENZO VALLA

The claim can be maintained that the penetration of mind, body of writing and devotion of heart of one scholar, just within Church orthodoxy, in the last years of the fifteenth century and the first of the sixteenth, changed Northern Europe for ever. From Desiderius Erasmus came a printed Greek New Testament which, swiftly translated into most European vernaculars, was a chief cause of the Continent-wide flood that should properly be called the Reformation.

In the 1480s, Erasmus, a young monk in the Dutch monastery of Steyn, was 'being formed in the most austere and most puritanical traditions of the last great spiritual movement of the middle ages'[1] – that is, the *Devotio moderna*. First propagated some decades before in response to the German mystic Thomas à Kempis, the probable author of *The Imitation of Christ* (first circulated about 1418), at the monastery of Windesheim in Germany, this movement of spiritual enlightenment had spread to religious houses, including Steyn. Anti-intellectual, and formed as a reaction to decadent Scholasticism, at its heart was a meditation on the Gospel, encouraging an inward depth that had effects both moral and psychological.

Erasmus's earliest surviving letters, however, written only a few years after his time at Steyn, reveal him 'as an enthusiastic and slightly intoxicated disciple of Italian humanism'.[2] This shift to a mental Italy was not – or not only – a rebellious late-adolescent separation from the monastic life in which he had been brought up. Everything that had been given to him by the *Devotio moderna* he took with him, making it more and more personal through the rest of his life.

Yet he fell in love with secular Italy and the ancient world. All his realism and growing awareness of the fullness of humanity, all his sense of the possibility of life's experience, grew as he understood that the new Italians were showing him something 'bold and disturbing', contrasting with what was 'worn out or dead in medieval religiosity'. The new Italian books offered instead 'a humanity eager for self-expression and full of self-confidence'.[3] In his new Italian citizenship, as it were, the spiritual ideals of the *Devotio moderna* stayed with him, and leavened the whole.[4] From the pairing grew his response to Lorenzo Valla's gift of Bible understanding – nothing less than the sudden rediscovery of the New Testament.

Lorenzo Valla (1407–57), pioneering theoretician of the new Italian humanism, both in its philological base and as *miles Christianus* ('soldier of Christ'), wrote at Rome towards the end of his life his *Adnotationes in Novum Testamentum*. Erasmus read Valla. At eighteen, he made a summary of Valla's famous *Elegantiae*. At about the same time he probably first discovered Valla's equally well-known *De voluptate*. Early in 1504, Valla was for Erasmus, as for many, simply an exciting model of literary humanism. Later that year Erasmus, then in the Premonstratensian monastery at Louvain, apparently by chance opened the pages of Valla's *Adnotationes*. It is not too fanciful to suggest that the opening of that book on his desk in the Abbey of Park in Heverlee on that day, was, in the world of Bible studies, the moment of the break from the medieval to the modern. Erasmus at once began to set out for himself his life's work, which would be on the Bible. He had found in the Italians, and now greatly developed for himself, a new exegesis based on scientific philology. That was remarkable enough. What made it unique was that he suffused it still with the spirituality of the *Devotio moderna*.

TOWARDS ERASMUS'S GREEK NEW TESTAMENT, 1516

Medieval attempts at biblical exegesis through philology, such as they were, had been confined to the Old Testament. 'Western exegetes of the middle ages could easily find some rabbi willing to initiate them into Hebrew and rabbinic exegesis.'[5] Moreover, the commentaries of the Fathers had suggested that all the work had been done. In the Middle Ages, the suggestion that the Greek of the New Testament existed, and offered problems, was barely visible.

As unwitting preparation for that moment in the library in Louvain late in 1504, Erasmus had already discovered Jerome. He had gone on to study Origen's *Hexapla*. In Paris in 1497, he had begun to make for himself a tentative scheme for biblical studies. Soon after, while staying at Magdalen College, Oxford, and particularly in conversations with John Colet, Dean of St Paul's, he found his faith strengthened, and rejoiced in a new spiritual freedom from the narrow religious tradition throughout Northern Europe.[6] Then, influenced by Colet's interest, but even more by the instrument of scholarship which Valla had given him, Erasmus wrote his commentary on the Epistle to the Romans. He had caused Valla's *Adnotationes* to be reprinted in 1505. During his second stay in England, in Cambridge as the second Lady Margaret's Professor of Divinty, a tenure begun in 1509, and again influenced by his friends among the London humanists, including Thomas More, he confirmed the programme of his life's work. In 1506 he had published his own new Latin version of the Gospels and Epistles. This, based on a Greek manuscript shown to him at St Paul's by Colet, was a start. Enriching Valla's philological criticism with his own inheritance of spiritual and evangelical understanding, Erasmus had begun publicly to renew biblical studies. That he understood that this programme had to be led by a critical edition of the Greek New Testament is clear. (Some portion of the Hebrew Scriptures had been available in print, in a number of editions, since 1477, and the whole Hebrew Scriptures since 1488: Johannes Reuchlin's widely used introduction to the study of Hebrew, *De rudimentis hebraicis* was published in 1506.)

Erasmus stayed in Venice with Aldus Manutius, the greatest printer of humanist texts in Europe, in 1508: this gave him the chance to develop his knowledge of the Greek Fathers: Chrysostom, Basil, and, always his greatest influence, Origen. Slowly he was elaborating his view of exegesis, in which 'philological study of the text prepares the way for a meditation drawing together all that he found most sure in the spiritual exegesis of the Fathers, especially of Origen's school'.[7] His larger design, formed by 1508–9, was

> to reform the Church from within by a renewal of biblical theology, based on philological study of the New Testament text, and supported by a knowledge of patristics, itself renewed by the same methods. The final object was to nourish that chiefly moral and spiritual reform already quite clearly conceived in the *Enchiridion militis Christiani*, published at Antwerp in February 1504.[8]

In all this his central drive was towards expounding his understanding of the *philosophia Christi*.[9] He advanced on four fronts. First, he tried to establish a sound Greek New Testament text and print it with critical commentary and notes. This he did, in 1516 (see below). Second, he wanted to edit and print equally sound editions of those Fathers who were great biblical commentators. Third, at the point where the first two met, he proposed further editions and commentaries of the greatest biblical texts: his four books of commentaries on the Epistle to the Romans in 1502 took final form in a paraphrase of all the epistles in 1523 and 1524. In 1523 he also published his paraphrase of Matthew, dedicated to Charles V; paraphrases of John, Luke and Mark had followed by 1524. (Erasmus did not touch Revelation.) It was these paraphrases, in English translations by various hands, which were later to be placed in every parish church in England, to be freely available alongside the Great Bible of 1539. He published commentaries on Psalms 2, 3, 4 and 85, and on the Lord's Prayer. His fourth front was to expand his Preface to his Greek New Testament into a treatise of methodology, the *Ratio seu methodus compendio perveniendi ad veram theologiam*, which both summed up and fed back into the other biblical work.

All this he did. The importance was not simply in the works themselves, though that was very high. It was even more that the greatest and most famous scholar in all Europe, the author of *The Praise of Folly, The Enchiridion, De copia* and *Adagia* (to whom More's *Utopia* was dedicated), was, as one might put it, 'doing' the Bible. He was undercutting the texts of the Fathers, including some that, to his dismay, he had discovered to be fakes. Not only was he focusing on biblical theology: he was editing the New Testament in Greek.

THE PRINTED NEW TESTAMENT IN GREEK

After a journey up the Rhine in 1514, fêted wherever he went, Erasmus arrived in Basle. He walked into the printing shop of Johannes Froben with a letter from himself to Froben. He said he was an intimate friend of the great humanist, Erasmus, who, he (Erasmus) explained, had entrusted him (the friend of Erasmus) with the business of publishing his books. He then proceeded to take over the shop. Froben, horrified, took a while to realise the joke; but they became good friends. Froben was well-meaning, honest and an excellent printer. Erasmus stayed two years in Basle, and with Froben produced a dozen new works, including a new edition of the *Adagia*, of which the four-thousandth adage was the first statement leading to widely read works by Erasmus attacking war.

In February 1516, the *Novum instrumentum* came from Froben's press, the first edition of Erasmus's Latin translation of the Greek New Testament. Alongside the Latin was the Greek original. About half the volume – over three hundred pages – was given to annotations to the Greek text, and elucidation of errors in the Vulgate. Here were also strong attacks on ecclesiastical abuse. Of the three prefaces, revised from time to time, the first recommended diligent study of the New Testament, and asserted the heretical point that no layman should be denied access to Scripture in his own language. The second explained something of his philological methods. The third, entitled *Apologia*, explained his desire to improve on the Vulgate by strictly following the Greek originals.

The work was dedicated to Pope Leo X, and appeared by privilege of Emperor Maximilian. The text of the *privilegium* [. . .] also advocated the reading of the New Testament, and added that this might prompt the pope 'to make Christians once more acquainted with their Holy Scriptures, even with the teachings of their Master.' Lest the sarcasm be missed, the title-page carried an allegorical drawing of *Envy Defeated*.[10]

Erasmus's full and wordy title-page (fig. 7) says nothing about the Greek, as if that were incidental, part of a ruse to deflect the pope's opposition: Pope Leo X admired and supported Erasmus, and wrote of his admiration for the *Novum instrumentum*, pronouncing it 'a magnificent undertaking'.[11] Erasmus's Latin translation was strong meat enough. He rejected official Vulgate readings, like the *verbum* (for *sermo*) in *In principio verbum erat* at the opening of St John's Gospel. In all, Erasmus made about four hundred changes to the Vulgate, every one defended in his notes. It was the first new Latin translation for almost a thousand years, and the Latin is fresh and vibrant. A modern writer has named it the 'humanist dawn', as opposed to the Vulgate's 'mediaeval dusk'.[12] Another writer described Erasmus's first Preface:

> a remarkable, passionate prefatory piece. He called it *Paraclesis* – a Greek word meaning a summons or exhortation. It was [. . .] an exhortation precisely to the universal mastery of [. . .] God's self-revelation [. . .] as it was completed in Christ, the Word of God incarnate, the fullness of wisdom, discovered in scripture and appropriated as the rule of life.[13]

It is his clearest exposition of the urgent need to find and follow 'the philosophy of Christ' through reading Scripture, and it became very widely known. The last paragraph of Tyndale's Preface to his *Obedience of a Christian Man* (1528) urges his readers to read the Scriptures for themselves: 'A thousand reasons more might be made (as thou mayest see in *Paraclesis* Erasmi).'[14]

One passage of Erasmus's *Paraclesis* is especially relevant to this study:

> Christ wishes his mysteries to be published as widely as possible. I would wish all women to read the gospel and the epistles of St Paul, and I wish that they were translated into all languages of all Christian people, that they might be read and known, not merely by the Scotch and the Irish, but even by the Turks and the Saracens. I wish that the husbandman might sing parts of them at his plow, that the weaver may warble them at his shuttle, that the traveller may with their narratives beguile the weariness of the way.[15]

It was, however, the Greek that was vital. By modern textual standards Erasmus's Greek text is poor. Despite assistance from two scholars, one of whom was the saintly Ioannes Oecolampadius, an expert in Hebrew who later became the aide of the Swiss reformer Zwingli, and though Erasmus could do concentrated work at great speed for twelve or fourteen hours a day, the modern science of textual editing had not been born, and he necessarily floundered. Though he had travelled to find manuscripts (and Cuthbert Tunstall, Bishop of London, found him one that he looked at in London), the ten he used were not good, and he made the mistake of rejecting the best in favour of what he believed were superior and 'very ancient', but which we now know were mediocre copies from the fourteenth and fifteenth centuries. Not finding the last verses of Revelation in any Greek manuscript, he put them into Greek himself from the Vulgate's Latin.

Erasmus produced four more editions of his New Testament, in 1519, 1522, 1527 and 1535. Originally omitting 'the Johannine Comma', that is the passage in 1 John 5:7–8 relating to the 'Three Witnesses in Heaven', he noted that if he should see a good enough manuscript including it, he would include it. Sure enough, one was sent to him, a copy of the Leicester Codex, it seems maliciously prepared to deceive him, and he included it in his third edition, of 1522, to his later regret (the story is told in more detail below, p. 169).

After his death in 1536, further editions of Erasmus's Greek New Testament were printed by others in the next decades; by Beza in Geneva and, importantly, by Robert Estienne, or Stephanus, in Paris. Stephanus's third edition, in 1550, was reprinted for the Elzevir edition in Leiden in 1633, from Erasmus with a little revision, and was there announced on the title-page as the *Textus Receptus*. That 'Received Text' was made the basis of all Greek New Testament translation work, with small exceptions, until the 1880s. In other words, all the earliest translations, by Luther, Tyndale and others, were from a form which had become standard in the Eastern church during the later Middle Ages. After Erasmus, from about 1550, Western textual scholars, as will be seen, laboured to collect material for the revision of that text, most significantly achieved in the work of Westcott and Hort published in 1881. (Nevertheless, from the late twentieth century in some influential Christian circles in North America, any revision of the *Textus Receptus* is regarded as heresy: like the King James Version, which was ultimately based on it, the *Textus Receptus* is said by some to be the given Word of God, perfect and absolute.)

★   ★   ★

THE COMPLUTENSIAN POLYGLOT

Around 1500, the Spanish scholar Cardinal Francisco Ximénes de Cisneros founded – and paid for – the first trilingual university in Spain, devoted to the three ancient biblical languages, Hebrew, Greek and Latin. He assembled scholars at Alcalá de Henares (*Complutum* in Latin). By July 1517, they had made and set up in print a set of six remarkable large volumes.[16] These give the Hebrew, Greek and Latin of the Bible (including the Septuagint Greek for the Old Testament) in parallel columns, with numerous aids to study. The Pentateuch volume includes the Targum of Onkelos, the Aramaic version, known to Jerome and to Renaissance scholars as the Chaldean version, with a Latin translation. The Greek has an interlinear Latin translation. The Hebrew words are keyed to the Latin of the Vulgate, printed down the centre of the page, and a column of the relevant Hebrew roots. The sixth volume has dictionaries and grammars. The New Testament Greek text is based on a few manuscripts of unknown origin.[17] It shows slight awareness of editorial problems – in the Greek New Testament to print, or not, what is in the Greek manuscripts but not in the Vulgate, as for example the last words of the Lord's Prayer in Matthew 6:13 (the answer was 'not'). The pages are beautifully printed, and the whole enterprise is magnificent. Though by July 1517 all the volumes were in print, and though Leo x had written a letter commending the work, Cardinal Ximénes died in that November, and there seem to have been problems with an official *imprimatur*. The printed sheets were not assembled and issued in the six volumes until 1522. Six hundred were published.

By that time, Erasmus's printed Greek text had been in circulation for six years, in three editions; it was the basis of Luther's 1522 German New Testament, and New Testaments in French, Dutch, Danish and Swedish; and Tyndale's work of English translation from 1525. Erasmus's *Novum instrumentum*, in its considerably lower cost, greater availablity (3,300 copies of the first two editions were print[18]), challenging Latin and large annotation, not to mention the fine *Paraclesis* and, above all, the Greek text, not perfect but as near as was then reasonably possible, was the real motor of the European vernacular New Testament translations. Even so, it is striking that as Luther came into print with his 'September Testament', there were two generally sound versions of the Greek New Testament in print.

Chapter 8

THE REFORMATION IN ENGLAND

A BIBLE–BASED POPULAR REFORMATION

I need to make clear the massive impact of the English Bible after Tyndale's first complete New Testament in English in 1526. One way, of several, is to calculate the numbers of new editions of Bibles, or parts, in English. This can be done using the three standard catalogues cited at the head of the chronology (p. 843 below).

The figures must be put into a frame. It is said by opponents of the reformers' English Bible that Mother Church in her wisdom would, as Eamon Duffy wrote, 'sooner or later' have provided her children with an English New Testament 'without the doctrinal uncertainty and conflict which in fact ensued'. Duffy exemplified this with reference to a very popular Harmony, the *Mirror of the Blessed Life of Our Lord Jesus Christ*, translated by Nicholas Love from the thirteenth-century Latin of (it was said) St Bonaventura, and first printed by Caxton in 1484. Love's 'expanded Gospel harmony', his *Mirror* (a book which has in fact very little to do with the New Testament[1]) 'went a long way towards satisfying lay eagerness for knowledge of the Gospels'.[2] It is true that between 1484 and 1622 there were ten new editions of this fanciful little volume. But *RSTC* records a mere two after 1530: one in 1606 and a different translation in 1622, both printed abroad (and see below, pp. 161–2).

From 1525 and Tyndale's 'Cologne fragment', up to 1640 when *RSTC* closes, that catalogue gives, to fresh printed editions of the Bible or parts of it, in English, forty-five dense double-column pages, from page 86 to page 131, averaging forty entries a page. These pages show a total of well over fifteen hundred entries for the Bible, or parts of it, in English (of which over six hundred are of metrical Psalms). An average print-run may be taken as two thousand copies per edition, of Bibles and New Testaments, occasional individual Bible books and some selections. (For further estimation of print-runs, see below, pp. 804n.24.) English New Testaments would have much larger runs: the few selections from Scripture would have smaller runs. Taking the fifteen hundred *RSTC* entries, and multiplying by the probable print-runs, we find that in that period of 115 years, from 1525 to 1640, printed English Bibles and parts numbered, at a modest estimate, over two million. This was for a population of just below, and then just over, six million. No other *RSTC* heading produces figures approaching anywhere near these.

These were Bibles to be read at home or in local gatherings of enquiring Christians. They were also to be read aloud to the people in church, clearly and comprehensibly, in the services of the new Church of England – as they still are. The New Testament was to be read right through, aloud, clearly and in English, to the people, three times in the year (later twice, as now), the Old Testament once a year, and the Psalms, said or sung, every month.

To write about English life between 1525 and 1640 and take no account at all of such enormous popular demand as these totals demonstrate is surely to be perverse. Yet it is not only commonly done: it has been the norm.

The revolution in religion represented here must not be mistaken. A pre-Reformation mass was conducted at the distant altar by the priest, murmuring in Latin with his back to the people. In a post-Reformation service the minister faced his congregation and addressed them in English. It was the difference between a scarcely heard, mumbled *Petite, et dabitur vobis; querite, et invenietis; pulsate, et aperietur vobis,* and the ringing 'Ask and it shall be given you; seek and ye shall find; knock and it shall be opened unto you' (Matthew 7). Everyone used an English service-book made of copious quotation from the Bible in English. These were services into which were inserted the two or three 'lessons' read aloud from Scripture in English, spoken from a lectern close to the worshippers. In the course of the services, sermons, given from pulpits usually even closer to the people, were expositions of Scripture in English.

The avoidance of these things in accounts of the period has been a mystery.

REVISIONIST DENIAL

In the decades before 2000, the orthodoxies of Reformation study changed drastically, in two main directions. On the one hand, Catholic revisionist historians, who dominated the field, represented as something new what was in fact an older dogma, that of 'Catholic continuity' in Britain.[3] In this it is asserted that the political gestures made by the Tudor courts, national and local, which propelled what had become known as the sixteenth-century English Reformation, for a long time barely touched the English population – a population that remained essentially, and over-whelmingly, Roman Catholic. Evidence was drawn from churchwardens' accounts and wills, and a large assumption was made about 'the alleged religious conservatism of many nominal Protestants'.[4]

In the late twentieth century, in lecture halls and classrooms, gone was the old comfortable history whereby 'the English Reformation' meant that by the will of God through the people England became God's Protestant nation in the three decades from 1529 to 1559. Influential writers main-tained that in spite of political bullying led by some figures at the courts of Henry VIII and Edward VI, at the level of popular conviction nothing very much changed. Evidence was produced of a thriving, healthy ortho-dox Catholicism, with little trace of anti-clericalism, right up to Henry's break with Rome in 1533–4. Students of Early Modern History world-wide were taught that the English Reformation was a failure.[5] The revi-sionists claimed that it was only possible to write about a number of attempted reformations (the lower case was part of their larger case) in England, none of them successful.

All this was in the face of several strong, but for a while unarticulated, objections to what were wholly political analyses: that hostility to the Roman Church had been a force in the land from even before Wyclif in the 1380s; that the true effect of the new print culture, and the universi-ties, and national thinking and reading generally, were ignored, as was the new and increasingly unfettered theology; that the evidence was locally selective; that churchwardens' accounts in remoter Catholic districts were, by their very nature, going to demonstrate resistance to change; that no account was given of the very real sufferings of the people, not least as a result of the effect of the 1401 statute *De haeretic comburendo* by which the merest accusation of heresy, however unfounded, could lead to being pub-licly burned alive. Above all, the revisionists were failing to answer Patrick Collinson's pertinent question: 'How did one of the most Catholic coun-tries become one of the least?'[6] Moreover, they were failing to ask why England remained so for ever after, so that, for example, the English Wars of Religion in the seventeenth century were fought between Protestant and Protestant.

It was also in the face of all the evidence that in the second half of the sixteenth century the religious practices of the nation, as well as the enormous bulk of the literature, were officially, aggressively, and massively, Protestant. After Gregory XIII excommunicated and 'deposed' Queen Elizabeth in 1570, there were in England smuggled-in Catholic seminar-ians, Jesuit priests in hiding, and some well-attended masses in barns and some great houses in the north-west and elsewhere. But the Protestant Books of Common Prayer were in daily use in every one of the over nine thousand parish churches in England and Wales from 1549: the Thirty-Nine Articles, printed in every copy, were out-and-out Protestant, even Calvinist: the Books of Homilies to be preached in every pulpit were totally Protestant.

THE WIDER REFORMATION

Historians travelled in another, perhaps less polemic, direction, drawn by the opening of the records of sixteenth-century Eastern Europe, partly from the new access to documents enabled by electronics, and partly by the results of sheer hard work with local collections never read before (as for example in the town libraries of France[7]). Understanding of religious events in the sixteenth century throughout Europe as far east as Transylvania has much increased. Travellers in this second direction notice that Wittenberg is nearly four times closer to Prague than it is to London; and Prague was the first European city to lead the resistance to the Catholic Church. In mainstream sixteenth-century history as taught in Britain and America, those eastern territories were unconsidered, or plain inaccessible: the Cold War alignment separated East and West, in a way strange to the sixteenth century.[8] The eastern countries were profoundly affected by the Protestant Reformation and the rapid and forceful attacks under the Counter-Reformation. That the sixteenth- and early seventeenth-century religious history of such a large part of Reformation Europe is in many aspects still untreated is even more important than countering the wearying reiterations about English Protestant failure. There will in the east be discoveries that will change the whole picture of Europe – and far beyond, for America was heavily settled from this region.

The Reformation horizon is now far wider, and the sky much bigger, than has often been assumed.[9] The peculiarly English Reformation had a long pre-history, and an even longer reach forward, even to 1800.[10] It is carrying things absurdly too far to pretend that, because some people in Lancashire held secret masses, the English Reformation never really happened, and that worshippers in the packed parish churches all over Anglican England could in the twentieth century be discovered to have remained Roman Catholic all along.[11] To quote Peter Lake:

> While [some Catholics] met in barns and private households, the godly inherited the public space of the parish church. And where the altars had been effectively stripped, that was now a public space that proclaimed, at a number of levels, the alteration of religion. The prominently displayed royal coat of arms aside, wall paintings had been

whitewashed over, the Ten Commandments and the odd scriptural
verses replacing them. The altar was now a communion table; the rood
loft with its doom images as well as the images of saints had been
removed. The liturgy was in English, not Latin; the mass had been
replaced with a communion service. No trace of the cult of the saints
or the notion of Purgatory – such central features of the religious system
described by Eamon Duffy – was left in either the service book or the
outward ceremonial face of the Church. Again, whatever else this was,
it was not continuity.[12]

It is certainly in order not to characterise the European Reformation
neatly, whether by reference to Luther's Ninety-Five Theses in 1517; to
the Diet of Worms in 1521; to the Hapsburg succession to the throne of
Bohemia in 1526; to Henry VIII's break with Rome in 1533–4; to the
Netherlands *annus mirabilis*, 1566. Was it, as European historians explain,
theological rather than, as it is said to be in England, political? Did it
follow or cause a sudden social and cultural change? Was it simply about
religious practice? How far was destructiveness creative? Were a handful
of charismatic men the true cause, or did the people spontaneously rise
up? – and if so, why?

In writing the history of the time, it can no longer be held that, given
the tottering, entirely corrupt Roman Church described in older Protestant histories, reform from outside was inevitable. Late twentieth-century
writers, however, tended to go too far the other way, ignoring the real
evidences of corruption described from the ground, with passion, by
William Tyndale or Simon Fish, not to mention Chaucer or Langland.
Chaucer's Summoner or Pardoner, full officials of the Church, were, *tout
court*, corrupt. Nor should we accept a picture, however movingly drawn,
of universal parishes of saintly and contented Catholic peasants rejoicing
in their lowly place, all over England, happily worshipping their saints and
preparing for Purgatory (an imaginary place only three centuries old[13]),
and then shocked by the destruction caused by Protestant guerrillas. We
should see the early sixteenth-century Church in Europe as a bureaucratic
institution which was a massive, successful, complex, deeply rooted multiple organism at work, centrally disturbed, locally various right across
Europe, differing even from village to village, harbouring both great piety
and great social evils, with, in its rare intellectual ventures, a grand and
confused relation to Renaissance humanism, and very little relation at all
to the *ekklesia* of the New Testament.

Finding a reason for what happened across the Continent, and in
England for what Diarmaid MacCulloch described as the 'howling success'
in making England into a Protestant nation by the early seventeenth

century, has puzzled many professional historians.[14] It is strange to watch the refusal of such historians even to begin to consider without hilarity the possible importance of vernacular Bibles and the sixteenth-century impact of their contents. Yet whatever it was that happened, it can be understood that the effects of what can in shorthand be called the English Reformation were also massive, successful, complex, deeply rooted and multiple, various across Europe, vital for the future of America, close to the New Testament, and only to be swept out of sight by perversity.

PROTESTANT BELIEF

It needs to be made clear at this point what the Protestant Reformation was in terms of belief – that it was not some sort of watered-down version of the real thing, rather as Americans think of Canada. Protestantism is not Catholic Christianity gone wrong. Though there was – and is – elasticity and overlap in versions of both sets of belief,[15] Protestantism as it emerged in the sixteenth century was radically, 180 degrees different from Catholicism. The Protestant attacks on Purgatory and the cults of the saints, on confession in the ear, on a celibate priesthood, on seven, rather than two, New Testament sacraments, were not some sort of nibbling at the edges of Church practice. The destruction of those traditions, and many more, came out of a burning core of radical New Testament belief. Far from being on the fringes of the real thing, Protestantism claimed, passionately, to be itself the real thing, the New Testament real thing. From this, thanks to the increasing deviations caused by the powers of the bishops of Rome down the centuries, the Catholic Church had departed. Almost the only thing in common was some belief in the redemption of the world by Our Lord Jesus Christ, as the Protestant Book of Common Prayer has it: yet even on that, William Tyndale noted in his *Obedience of a Christian Man* in 1528 that the pope's Church sold for money what Christ gave freely.[16]

ENERGY AND CULTURAL ENRICHMENT

The energies released were colossal. New states were built. Exceptionally fierce and bloody wars were fought. Martin Luther wrote a book a fortnight every year for thirty years (the modern Weimarer Ausgabe of Luther has nearly a hundred large volumes). The scholars at Calvin's new university in Geneva edited, translated and printed finely a great range of biblical, theological, and secular classical texts. In spite of the shift from

Latin into vernaculars, the book trade was beyond recognition enlarged and internationalised. At the other end of the scale, family life was transformed for very many, especially for women. The possibilities of intellectual freedom began to seem endless. Cultural life was newly energised.

This last is a point of importance. Among the number of ways in which Eamon Duffy's celebrated *The Stripping of the Altars* (1992) can be shown to distort – extrapolating some East Anglian parishes to the whole of Britain; making the Reformation appear as a quite unheralded bolt from the blue; ignoring the powerful intellectual life of the time; omitting the English Bible, and so on – his account of smashings and strippings has had its effect, so that in the year 2000 it was generally understood that in the cultural life of Britain the Reformation was a disaster. Not so. Protestant sacred art in early sixteenth-century Europe developed from Dürer and the Cranachs in Germany to Holbein in England, and, refreshingly, a good deal else artistic, even in Reformed circles.[17] In the intermingling of national and confessional influences in music, it can be shown that 'the reformation made an important contribution to the broadening of musical experience', especially in the extraordinary effect of Psalm-singing.[18] Architecture was grander and more interesting than is usually suggested.[19] It is possible, though unfashionable, to explore as new territory the subject of the Reformation and popular culture, and even the Reformation *as* popular culture.[20] Above all, as will be made clearer in the following chapters, liberation from the threat of charges of heresy allowed the new powers of imagination and inventiveness that were grasped by the poets. The unique, and remarkably rapid, flowering of an English literature after 1550, with, by 1600, hundreds of fine writers including the supreme William Shakespeare, happened in a European country which, in half a century, had become 'one of the least' Catholic.

ENGLISH BIBLES

It also happened in a country with a unique series of printed vernacular Bibles. There were ten new English versions of the Bible or New Testament between Tyndale's first New Testament in 1526 and the famous King James, or Authorised, Version of 1611, and all were influential. Of course, in Germany and France, and in the Netherlands above all, there were important printed vernacular Bible translations, as there were in Scandinavia and even Italy. Yet the printed English Bibles of the sixteenth century should hold a special place in the history not only of England, but of the whole world.

PROTESTANTISM AND THE BIBLE

Luther's Ninety-Five Theses, triggered by the scandal of the sale of indulgences, were presented in 1517. He was excommunicated in 1521. Five years after his theses, his 'September Testament', the first New Testament in German from the Greek, was published in 1522, and had a huge national sale, and wide effects across Europe. From the beginning, the Reformation was powered by the Bible: Luther's *Sola fide* ('By faith alone') and *Sola gratia* ('By grace alone') came from *Sola Scriptura* ('From the Scriptures alone').

Reformers working newly with the Bible, in whatever country, were all concerned with seven matters. First, the confirmation of the canon of Scripture; what books did, and what did not, belong to the complete Bible. Outside the Apocrypha, the fourteen books set aside by Jerome as being in the Greek Septuagint but not in the original Hebrew, and kept apart in Reformation Bibles, some two dozen other books needed consideration, like the Epistle of Aristea or the Book of Jubilees. There was anxiety about the Song of Solomon within the established canon. Outside the New Testament, there were again some two dozen works, like the Gospel of Nicodemus, the Epistle to the Laodiceans or the Epistle of Barnabas to be judged. After Luther, there was concern about the Epistle of James, and there was at first nervousness generally about Revelation. But all reformers without exception printed the whole canon as they inherited it and nothing more. Second, there had to be the establishment of the text in Hebrew and Greek, partly very well done in the Reformation period. Third, attention had to be given to the question of the inspiration of the Bible; especially as it was felt to be challenged by the obvious discrepancies, so that New Testament citations of the Old Testament can be wrong, and the four Gospels can be harmonised only with difficulty. Inspiration, it seemed, did not mean inerrancy. In the Prologue to his first, 1522, translation of the New Testament, Luther asked himself which were the true and noblest books of the New Testament, and answered:

> St John's Gospel and his first Epistle, St Paul's Epistles, especially Romans, Galatians and Ephesians, and the first epistle of Peter. In these works you will find little about the deeds and miracles of Christ, but you will find a masterly description of the way in which faith in Christ overcomes sin, death, hell, and gives life, justification and blessedness.[21]

Fourth were questions of exegesis, especially 'all the hard places', as they were known. Previous interpretation had been in a single mouth, that of a pope, or unanimous church councils. To validate and interpret Scripture,

Luther appealed to the Spirit. Zwingli agreed, but insisted on adding competence in Hebrew, Greek and Latin. Calvin, a little later, agreed with
both, but added common sense.[22] The great change was from the automatic exegesis developed from Origen, that every item of Scripture had
four senses: literal; allegorical, speaking to some belief; tropological, dealing with morals; and anagogical, referring the words to the Last Things,
the Christian hope. Thus, to use the standard illustration: Jerusalem was,
literally, the city the Jews lived in; allegorically it was the Church; tropo-
logically it was the human soul; and anagogically, the Heavenly City. In
the Middle Ages it was generally agreed that the literal came first. The
reformers did not deny allegory, not least because the Apostle Paul uses it
in Galatians 4:22–31. What was new was the abandonment of that automatic ancient woodenness, into the release of being able to interpret the
New Testament afresh in every generation.

The fifth matter implied in Luther's *Sola Scriptura* was the translation
of the whole Bible into vernacular languages. The opposition to this has
retreated, but can still be felt. The sixth concern, the circulation of well-
printed Bibles in the local language as widely as possible, has never ceased
since 1522: it is work that still continues; as a new millennium begins, the
Bible or a New Testament is available in half the world's six thousand languages. Finally comes the reformers' concern for the circulation of aids to
the study of the Bible, in prefaces, marginal and other notes, concordances,
illustrations, Psalms and hymns for congregational singing – and in the
course of preaching.

DISAPPEARANCE

These English Bibles have disappeared from the sight of scholars of Early
Modern History. Sometimes there might be mention of the name of
Tyndale in a list of Cambridge reformers (though the Oxford man Tyndale
was not in Cambridge); or an occasional remark might declare that the
Geneva Bible failed, because the notes were objectionably Calvinist (both
statements are untrue); or a nod might be given in the direction of the
King James Bible of 1611, and the strange genius of its makers. It has been
quite common to write major textbooks about the English Reformation
period without mentioning the English Bible at all. There has been an air
of constraint; a very recent feeling that the field which used to be called
The English Reformation had been invaded and made to grow different
crops – privatised and fenced off as Early Modern History plc, with whole
acres out of bounds. Thus many historians writing about England from
1530 to 1600 have made it all top-down, and said little about the popular

movements of religious reform in England, the existence of which revisionists had taught everyone to deny. Excellent writing, as it might be about Calvinism and the second wave of the Reformation, might usefully analyse the theological tensions of the second half of the sixteenth century in Britain, and put interesting and sympathetic weight on Foxe's *Acts and Monuments* ('*Foxe's Book of Martyrs*'), and yet say nothing at all about the successive Geneva Bibles, which carried far more weight even than Foxe. To the knowledgeable, reading such history was like looking at Stalinist photographs from Moscow in the 1950s: something that had formerly been present had been airbrushed out.

For the English Bible was formidably present. The ten new translations or heavy revisions of the English Bible did not happen to Ovid or Plutarch – or Augustine. The need to keep retranslating or revising came partly from developing understanding of the Greek and Hebrew originals: it also came from demand. To take one illustration: in Shakespeare's fairly short lifetime, from 1564 to 1616, there were three *different* editions of the Rheims New Testament, first printed in 1582. The Bishops' Bible had first appeared in 1568: before Shakespeare died there were forty *different* editions of it. After 1611 and the first edition of KJV, even in the five years before Shakespeare died, there were twenty-six *different* editions of it. In Shakespeare's lifetime alone, there were printed of the Geneva Bible 142 *different* editions – not just reprintings: different editions – in three parallel basic states.[23] That makes a total of 211 English Bibles or New Testaments freshly edited and produced in the fifty-two years in which Shakespeare was alive. It is just possible to estimate print-runs.[24] A modest figure is 2,000 each. That is probably too low: in the three years between 1517 and 1520 Luther's thirty publications 'probably sold well over 300,000 copies':[25] his 1522 'September Testament' was the world's first bestseller; in spite of its fine binding and paper, well-laid-out text and illustrations, and high price, five thousand copies were sold in the first weeks.[26] Luther's printer, Hans Lufft of Wittenberg, retired in 1572 having printed 'almost 100,000 Bibles in Luther's translation'.[27] England had far more Bibles than Germany. In Shakespeare's time, German new editions, always of Luther, amounted to seven.

Estimating 2,000 printed for each English Bible in Shakespeare's lifetime makes 422,00 Bibles bought, just under half a million, just while Shakespeare was alive, out of a population of about six million. Geneva Bibles in particular gripped the nation. They were the Bibles of English poets and prose writers until well into the seventeenth century, Latinist Milton included. The analogy with airbrushing is particularly apt here. Even in modern accounts of sixteenth-century English Bibles, never mind cultural, literary or religious history, Geneva Bibles are often either dismissed in a sentence or omitted. Or they are noted but waved away as 'unacceptably Calvinist', an intention to stigmatise which misses with both barrels (as will be seen in the opening of chapter 17 below), dating from Victorian High Church writers. Figures for Protestant catechisms (Bible-based), of which the total numbers of editions in the sixteenth century alone are colossal, as they are for the metrical Psalms, by Sternhold and Hopkins (or the Scottish Psalms from 1567, always widespread in England) of which there were 274 *different* editions before 1616. Nor do these figures take into account the hearing of the Bible as read in the services in the Book of Common Prayer. As already noted, the New Testament was to be read through three times every year (later, as now, twice), most of the Old Testament once, and all the Psalms every month, as ever since. The airbrushed blank in the picture begins to beggar belief.

ENGLISH REFORMATION ESSENTIALS

A reminder of three further essentials about the English Protestant Reformation is called for. First, in the British islands the Protestant mind thought, wrote and spoke in English. Overwhelmingly the printed matter of all kinds was in English. Latin remained, and there were, for example, Latin plays, 150 of them between 1550 and 1650 performed in Oxford and Cambridge – and Latin poems and prose works: but the early and later reformers powerfully cultivated the mother tongue for Scripture and preaching. England then quite suddenly had an English literature, full, bursting at the seams and overflowing. It need not have been like that. John Skelton, a court poet who knew things, rubbished English in the early 1500s. Erasmus, in five visits to England between 1499 and 1517, two of them long (one a two-year stint in a chair in Cambridge) neither wrote (nor it seems, spoke) a word of English. Thomas More would not have his *Utopia*, printed in Louvain in 1516, published in English lest it be mauled by the common people, and it had to wait until 1557, twenty-two years after his death. Yet before the end of that century, there began a flowering of English writing hardly again surpassed.

Second, Protestantism was an intellectual movement in English, powered by university men, dependent on free discussion at all levels, and on reading *or hearing books read* – a still under-noticed factor. It was distantly related to humanism. It was a release from an Aristotelian world of scholastic speculation. Enormous and demanding books were increasingly bought in many thousands, and read, and heard and thought about. Translations of classical and modern works poured off the presses.

There was a strong element of belonging to a European movement of reform, but people aware of a new and alert English Protestant nationalism freshly studied national history. They did that in huge volumes, Protestant huge volumes. Found in many homes, Raphael Holinshed's *Chronicles* absorbed Edward Hall's, a Protestant account of England's recent upheavals, clearly based on Bible typology. Foxe's *Acts and Monuments* gave the English a new Protestant history from a long time before the Reformation.

Scholars have observed that the writings of the Latin and Greek Church Fathers were increasingly popular in Elizabeth's reign, as shown by the appearance of volumes in libraries.[28] In the ever-increasing flood of printed material from the ancients, however, that was not surprising – and they were all in Latin. Not often mentioned has been the presence of Protestant volumes in English in so many households. Foxe's *Acts and Monuments*, in its two final states published in 1563 (one thick folio volume) and 1570 (two thick folio volumes of over two thousand double-column pages), all very large and expensive, sold, between 1563 and 1616, twenty-eight thousand copies unabridged, and thousands more abridged. A significant number were publicly available, chained in churches: many more were read aloud in lectures and sermons. Off the coast of Mexico, Drake read it to his Spanish prisoners. The most knowledgeable of the early twenty-first-century Foxe scholars, Dr Thomas Freeman, reports that these big volumes were greatly treasured by households, and 'rather uniquely, among early modern English books, this was a book which women were encouraged to read, which did seem popular with them'.[29] Foxe, in his later editions, telling the story of Christian faith from the beginning, prints a large number of documents of all kinds, an invaluable resource. Moreover, his martyrologies express a national grief. One of the sorrows of reading Early Modern English History is in watching the culling of the best minds. Laments for a handful of Jesuits executed bloodily in Shakespeare's lifetime (and far-fetched claims that Shakespeare can be seen to express secret sympathy with them) have to be set in the context of the many hundreds of Lollards and Protestants burned alive not long before; in the popularity of Foxe, these deaths were always fresh in Elizabethan and Jacobean minds. (The Jesuit Robert Parsons claimed in 1580 that only Catholics were made to pay the price:[30] his memory was shorter than the English nation's.)

Third is the sense of liberty, the release of being able to say things without a charge of heresy. Elizabeth had censors, though their role has been exaggerated:[31] these looked out for sedition rather than heresy. There was, as the century advanced, a new inventiveness, a release of imagination into words – English words – which gives the lie to the notion of cultural disaster. The liberated mind and spirit ventured largely. The Latin plays were staged in a few Oxbridge halls before the dons and sometimes a bored and reluctant monarch. The English plays were performed in state-of-the-art theatres, afternoon after afternoon, for thousands of ordinary people.

In that liberty there were disagreements between Protestant and Protestant, but Protestants did not burn Protestants alive. Too much has been made of the factionalism. Sixteenth-century Protestants disagreed. American historians have been alert to these conflicts for understandable reasons: the American eastern seaboard in the seventeenth century is a monument to them. In many – in most – concerns, and for many – most – of them, Protestants in the British Isles were facing the same way, and enjoying the new freedoms to speak out what they understood the Bible to tell them.

Protestantism was biblical. After the 1530s, Bibles in English were everywhere, the whole Bible, well printed, and, by government command, intended to be open for reading in all 9,000 parish churches (with, also in every parish church, Erasmus's *Paraphrases of the New Testament*, in English, open alongside for guidance, a matter rarely mentioned in history books). Bibles were read aloud in churches and other gatherings: even under Queen Mary, large assemblies to read, hear and study the Bible in major cities like London and Bristol were left untouched.[32]

A PUZZLE

Calling to mind again those figures noticed above, that for Germany's few different editions of vernacular Bibles between 1565 and 1616, England had 211, the silence of historians about the extent of the presence of an English Bible, and its content, is puzzling. Some of it must come from a timidity in examining the volumes. A senior scholar of the period states that the Geneva Bibles had no pictures, which shows that he had not opened a copy.[33] Timidity may extend to embarrassment: an American writer on Shakespeare and the Bible suggests nervousness among his colleagues lest they be considered Bible-thumpers.[34] Some reluctance is sectarian: though there is good Catholic Bible scholarship, Bible reading since the Council of Trent has been too Protestant a thing for Catholics to do; and there have always been writers who deny any value in English versions at all, the Vulgate still being said to be sufficient. Whatever the reason, the loss to understanding the English Reformation is great.

Chapter 9

WILLIAM TYNDALE, ?1494–1536

THE BIBLE TRANSLATIONS OF WILLIAM TYNDALE in the 1520s and 1530s are the reason why, reading the English New Testament, and thus in English-speaking churches, we do not say at Matthew 6:11,

> We should be obliged for Your attention in providing our nutritional needs and for so organising distribution that our daily intake of cereal filler be not in short supply,

but 'Give us this day our daily bread.' The first passage was written in the 1940s as a parody:[1] but the point is that the language of civil servants in London just after the Second World War is both dated and datable, whereas Tyndale's sentence in the Lord's Prayer is timeless. The simplicity of those seven words, in Saxon vocabulary and syntax, matching the original *koiné* (common) Greek, has continued since 1526 in almost all English Bible translations, in the twentieth century made in their scores, with only occasionally the substitution of 'today' for 'this day'. So it is with hundreds of the memorable phrases of English-speaking New Testament Christianity: 'Blessed are the poor in spirit' (Matthew 5:3); 'I am the good shepherd' (John 10:14); 'Fight the good fight of faith' (1 Timothy 6:12); and many, many more.

Tyndale's gift, not only to English-speaking New Testament Christianity, but to language and literature, secular as well as religious, came from a unique ability as a translator. He had the technical skills of fluent and accurate Greek, Hebrew, Latin and German (and other languages) and the machinery of recent dictionaries and grammars. He had a complete understanding of the complex art of rhetoric. His twin achievements as a translator, still admired, were accuracy and clarity, the latter allowing him variety of expression. Feeling himself free not to use the same English word every time for the same word in the Hebrew or Greek (a method labelled in the late twentieth century 'formal correspondence'), he made his own meaning-for-meaning translations (lately labelled 'dynamic equivalence'). Tyndale's simplicity, for example in narrative, where he is always superb (as in the Passion narratives in all the Gospels), comes also from a carefully judged flexibility. Hebrew vocabulary can be suggestive in multiple ways: the equivalence that is possible in English makes it better to translate Hebrew than any other language, certainly than Latin, as Tyndale pointed out in his *Obedience* – 'the properties of the Hebrew tongue agreeth a thousand times more with the English than with the Latin'.[2]

Tyndale would have commented that such things matter far less than the truth that 'the Scripture is a light and sheweth us the true way, both what to do and where to hope'.[3] Nevertheless, it is clear that his exceptional gift was to use the direction of spoken English: to catch in his written prose, in the 1520s and 1530s, just those qualities of the emerging language that would endure for centuries.

In Germany in 1526, William Tyndale translated the New Testament into English from the original Greek for the first time. His pocket-size printed volumes were smuggled into Britain. Although they were forbidden, they were eagerly bought.

In 1526 Tyndale opened the whole English New Testament to the people.

Since 1526, there have been, of the whole Bible or New Testament alone, made from Hebrew and Greek into English, in the UK and USA, about nine hundred fresh translations. In addition, since 1526 there have been, of existing whole Bible or New Testament translations in the UK or the USA, some three thousand new editions.[4] The statistics of print-runs are either long vanished or carefully guarded. It is impossible to calculate the number of English Bibles of all kinds printed and in circulation around the world since 1526. One simply thinks of a number, any number, and goes on adding noughts.

THE SIGNIFICANCE OF THE PRINTED BIBLE IN BRITAIN

The story of the Tudor Bibles used to be told as sacred history. Christopher Anderson in 1845, incredulous at the lack of any account that would answer the questions of 'any child to his Parent', set new pious histories in motion when at the beginning of his two long volumes he wrote of 'the distinct tokens of a superintending Providence to be observed and adored' in the 'singular conveyance of the heavenly treasure to our shores'.[5] By contrast, England's new imperialist ambitions under the Tudors could be made to depend on verses, or margins, in a commonly read Old Testament. Solid late twentieth-century scholarly history saw the English Bible as 'the foundation of monarchical authority . . . the text-book of morality and social subordination' – the words are Christopher Hill's in

1993.[6] As seen in the previous chapter, the last twist in the twentieth-century British historians' tale has been denial. Catholic writers of English history revived the older dogma of dominant Catholic continuity in England, asserting that there was in fact no English Reformation to speak of at all, except the political work of a few high-powered destroyers, the people's Reformation being clearly 'a failure' – that insistent, and widely repeated, word is Christopher Haigh's in 1993.[7] Thus the English Bible, far from being the source of either Protestant sanctity or nationalist supremacy, was really non-existent, a few volumes, it was implied, being simply wished on the reluctant nation by a faction at the Tudor courts.

Historians paint the covers of the Bible to taste – 'heavenly treasure', nationalist and imperialist lever, or unwanted official publication. The new printed Tudor English Bible has been simply an object with which to prop up an argument. Much has been learned from Anderson, Hill, Haigh and scores of other wise and hard-working writers. Yet few recent historians seem to have opened the book itself. For evidence of Henry VIII's wish in 1539 to use the English Bible as a political instrument of his absolute power, one need look no further than the title-page of the Great Bible (see pp. 205–7 below). Historians are right to describe that. Not every parish bought that Bible in 1539 as commanded: the injunction from above could be scorned. Yet it is necessary to look beyond the title-page, into the content of the Word of God.[8]

Parishes, however, did buy it, and it was read. By 1539, the English Bible was seeping into the English way of life. It can be calculated that before 1539 almost fifty thousand copies of Tyndale's and Coverdale's New Testaments had been printed abroad and in London for sale in England.[9] Even allowing for losses in transit, or by seizure, and for not all being sold (in fact, an unlikely supposition, given the demand), that is still a large number of individual men and women buying the Word of God in English. In 1537 or 1538, Thomas Swynnerton noted in his handbook of rhetoric (not a religious tract): 'Every man hath a Testament in his hand.'[10] This buying was not at the political whim of the king, nor in order to give the new nation a solid unified ground, but because many people loved it. It told them about God's love for them in Christ Jesus. True, we have no statistics for loving readership: Swynnerton added 'wold to God in his harte'; but 'conversions' are not the point here. The point is the scale of an influence. Turning the pages and looking beyond the title is what has been missing. In the great Christian tradition of the Word and the Church, in the centuries before the 1520s, the Word had almost disappeared. Christian men and women were hungry to have it fully back again.

The world of English speakers (then an unregarded minority, but soon to encompass the globe) in 1526 turned a corner. Through Tyndale's learning and bravery, English readers had access ever after to the whole Word of God in their language. Now taken for granted for nearly five hundred years, that access was bought in the early sixteenth century in blood and ashes. (As Tyndale was first translating and printing his New Testament in Worms, a young man in Norwich was burned alive for the crime of owning a piece of paper on which was written the Lord's Prayer in English.[11])

Not only did Tyndale's solitary work of Bible translation decide, in the words of Bishop Westcott in 1868, 'that our Bible should be popular and not literary, speaking in a simple dialect, and that so by its simplicity it should be endowed with permanence':[12] Tyndale clarified the English language. Since the early eighteenth century, the greatest praise has been heaped on the language of the King James Bible (the 'Authorised Version'), made in 1611. Yet over four-fifths of the New Testament of that version is simply Tyndale's work of eighty years before.[13] In 1611, one of the last years of Shakespeare's writing life, the English language was at a peak. It surprises nobody that the Bible from that time has immortal glory. Yet it should surprise everyone. The work of Tyndale that was taken over in 1611 was done three generations before, when the English language was a poor thing indeed, almost dead at the bottom of the pond. In 1526, a few local documents were beginning to be expressed in English. The language of government, the professions and religion was Latin: the new humanist Latin was a fine vehicle for any thoughts above the mundane. What English prose there was tried for an ornamented and heavily subordinated wandering line in vocabulary that was partly Saxon, heavily Norman-French, and strongly Latinised – see for example Lord Berners's Preface to his translation (1523–5) of Froissart's *Chronicle*.[14] True, in beautiful hand-illuminated missals there were exquisite moments in a lucid English distilled from late medieval books of devotion: but their use was strictly monastic, and rare.

Tyndale, in his Bible translations – including all the historical books, printed after his death – made for the Bible not only a strong direct short prose line, with Saxon vocabulary in a basic Saxon subject-verb-object syntax, but also showed a range of English styles which, coming out of the 1530s, astonishes the knowledgeable reader. No one else was writing English like this in the 1530s. In the Pentateuch, where his aims were as always clarity and the best accuracy that can be achieved, he can match the varieties of the Hebrew, from the strange, spare, stark effects of the Abraham and Isaac story in Genesis 22 to the *novella* style of the long narrative of Joseph at the end of Genesis. The high drama of the Exodus from Egypt and the thunder on Sinai as Moses receives the Commandments Tyndale makes vividly distinct from the often baffling details of the Tabernacle furnishings in Exodus or Deuteronomy, or the tribal lists or ritual laws of Numbers and Leviticus. After Deuteronomy, however, in the eight historical books, as the Hebrew becomes less basic, more colourful and emotionally elaborated (and more difficult), Tyndale can again, while still aiming for clarity, match style for style.

Take as example the sustained grief of King David's lament for Absalom in 2 Samuel 18:

> And behold Chusi came and said: tidings my lord the king, the Lord hath quit thee this day out of the hands of all that rose against thee. And David said, is the lad Absalom safe? And Chusi answered: the enemies of my Lord the King and all that rise against thee, to have thee, be as thy lad is. And the king was moved and went up to a chamber over the gate and wept. And as he went thus he said: my son Absalom, my son, my son, my son Absalom, would to God I had died for thee, Absalom, my son, my son.

Recent readers of Tyndale's Bible translations comment on how modern they feel. At 2 Chronicles 21:18, after telling of the terrible troubles facing Jehoram, Tyndale has 'And after all that, the Lord smote him in his bowels with an incurable disease.' In Romans 5:2, Paul in Tyndale says 'we have a way in through faith' (KJV, 'access by faith'), and in Philippians 3:1, 'it is a sure thing' (KJV, 'it is safe'). At 2 Corinthians 2:17, Paul in Tyndale writes of those 'which chop and change with the word of God' (KJV, 'corrupt': Tyndale gets close to a cognate sailing metaphor in the Greek) and in 2 Kings 4:28, instead of the almost standard phrasing of the question of the Sunamite woman to Elisha, 'Do not deceive me', Tyndale finds the true meaning of the Hebrew with 'thou shouldest not bring me in a fool's paradise'.

Stroke after stroke in Tyndale is English, not Latin as, at the end of Matthew 6, 'For the day present hath ever enough of his own trouble', not 'Sufficient unto the day is the evil thereof'. Paul's 'hymn to love' in 1 Corinthians 13 is just that: 'If I have not love, it profiteth me nothing. [. . .] So abideth faith, hope, and love: but the greatest of these is love.' The word 'love' there angered Thomas More. The Church's word in 1 Corinthians 13 was the Latin *caritas*, charity. Tyndale was translating the Greek ἀγάπη (*agapē*), love.

It is important to stress this. Tyndale understood the real source of power in the English language, which is a plain Saxon base in vocabulary and syntax, *within which*, not on top of which as decoration, great suggestibility is possible. Shakespeare also understood this, as in Hamlet's 'This fell sergeant, death, / Is strict in his arrest.' Good English syntax, which is Saxon syntax, is logical in its subject–verb–object formation ('dog bites man' again). Verbs are at the centre of verbal power in both senses. So, in Tyndale, Jesus says not as it might be, albeit absurdly, in Latinate English, 'The elevation of thy recliner and perambulation imperative is', but 'Take up thy bed and walk'. Saxon words are short. So too are Saxon sentences, in which short phrases are joined by 'and'.

The educated eighteenth-century adoration of all things Latin brought with it that culture's distinction between high and low words. High words like 'virtue', 'piety', 'inspiration' or 'imperial destiny' belong to epic, to aristocracy, to the triumphant history of the nation. Low words like 'gruel' or 'trousers' are the mark of low people, uneducated peasants, both things and people that are nasty, brutish and short. Epic cannot use such words. Seventeenth- and eighteenth-century Bible translators tried to lift the Bible back to the highest, Latin, register: something so holy could absolutely not use vulgar words. Tyndale wanted none of that exclusiveness. The Gospel is for everyone. Jesus said 'Follow me', not 'Be consecutive'. His parables are about lost sheep and lost coins, leaven in breadmaking, sowing seed or working in vineyards. The clarity of Tyndale's new non-Latin English can be savoured in all the Gospels: 'Let not your hearts be troubled. Believe in God and believe in me' (John 14:1). God became man, low experiences and all. The central figure in the Gospels is not entirely Our Lord and Saviour, pictured as a still icon with an elaborate, aureate fixed halo. The Gospel accounts of Jesus in rough Greek are also about him being shunned by the religious for sitting and eating with whores and layabouts.

Tyndale was faithful to the rough everyday Greek, translating in English only a notch above ordinary speech. In the following passage, from Matthew 26, describing an extraordinary spiritual experience, out of 149 words only five are Latinist ('disciples', 'agony', 'possible', 'temptation' and 'spirit'). Note, too, how many are monosyllables.

Then went Jesus with them unto a place which is called Gethsemane, and said unto the disciples, sit ye here, while I go and pray yonder. And he took with him Peter, and the two sons of Zebedee, and began to wax sorrowful and to be in an agony. Then said Jesus unto them: my soul is heavy even unto the death. Tarry ye here and watch with me. And he went a little apart, and fell flat on his face, and prayed saying: O my father, if it be possible, let this cup pass from me: nevertheless, not as I will, but as thou wilt. And he came unto the disciples, and found them asleep, and said to Peter what, could ye not watch with me one hour? Watch and pray, that ye fall not into temptation. The spirit is willing, but the flesh is weak.

The KJV revisers left that almost as it was. They lost the almost palpable weight of 'my soul is heavy even unto the death', removing the article from 'death' and changing 'my soul is heavy' to 'my soul is exceeding sorrowful'. The strength of Tyndale's monosyllables, as in 'let this cup pass from me' or 'not as I will, but as thou wilt' goes with his Saxon syntax: 'And he came unto the disciples, and found them asleep'; he does not use Latinist dependent clauses or participles, as it might be 'When he came', or 'Coming [. . .] and finding them [. . .]'. King James's revisers took out the word 'flat' from 'on his face', thus losing the full force of the Greek ἔπεσεν (*epesen*), and adding the unnecessary intensifier 'indeed' to 'The spirit is willing', something which, as so often with their work, fractionally distances the phrase.

Tyndale's plain style is clear in his translating of Jesus' parables, even in tiny details. In Luke 16, in the Parable of Dives and Lazarus, he has:

The rich man also died, and was buried. And being in hell in torments, he lift up his eyes and saw Abraham afar off, and Lazarus in his bosom, and he cried and said: Father Abraham, have mercy on me, and send Lazarus that he may dip the tip of his finger in water, and cool my tongue: for I am tormented in this flame.

The three small high 'i' sounds, in 'dip', 'tip' and 'finger' make a contrast of scale with the heavy Latin 'tormented'. Some of Tyndale's skill is seen in the familar Christmas story in Luke 2. The words are crafted for being spoken aloud, and they are most often heard as part of a service of carols and readings. The shepherds in the fields, amazed at the angels, set off for Bethlehem. 'And they came with haste, and found Mary and Joseph, and the babe laid in a manger.' It is simple, clear, and especially memorable because of the placing of the 'a' sounds on either side of the central 'Mary': 'and they came with haste' and 'the babe laid in a manger'. Shortly after, 'And all that heard it, wondered at those things which were told them of the shepherds. But Mary kept all those sayings, and pondered them in her heart.' The Greek, at Mary's 'pondered', is συνβάλλουσα (*sunballousa*), which means thrown together. The Vulgate had *conferens*, brought together. Tyndale's word is his own. Not only is it beautifully placed to chime with the earlier 'wondered', making a rhythmically unforgettable sentence – 'all that heard it, wondered [. . .] Mary [. . .] pondered': Tyndale also knew what it is for a woman to ponder something in her heart.

WILLIAM TYNDALE

Early Years

He was born in Gloucestershire, probably in 1494, and probably in one of the villages near Dursley (possibly Stinchcombe). Landowners, wool merchants and administrators, the prosperous family was related to the Tyndales of Northamptonshire, Essex and Norfolk, and may have, long before, originated near the Tyne in Northumberland, as the name might suggest.

The Tyndales were well connected. (It is a neglected fact that William-the-translator was more elevated in his family line than any of his adversaries in England – certainly than Tunstall, Wolsey, Stokesley and More.) Recent work on the Tyndales of Gloucestershire and their close connections with the fourteenth-century Tyndales of Northampton and Norfolk produced the following comment by a genealogist in the family: 'That there had been many profitable marriages by the Tyndales is signified by the number of women espoused [who] were daughters and heirs of knights, or their nieces.'[15] One of the ladies in the royal train of Richard II's Queen Anne, a niece to the King of Bohemia, married Sir William Tyndale; their son, also Sir William Tyndale, at the vacancy of Bohemia's throne, was invited to become the Bohemian king. Three generations later, about 1590, Dr Umphrey Tyndall (President of Queens' College, Cambridge, Dean of Ely and Chancellor of Lichfield) received the same invitation. The good dean also declined, declaring 'That he had rather be Queen Elizabeth's subject than a foreign Prince'.[16]

William had two elder brothers, Richard and Edward. The latter was a considerable figure in the county; his relationship to William is confirmed by a letter from Stokesley, then Bishop of London, in 1533.[17] A younger brother, John, was also in the wool trade. William as a child may have learned his good Latin at Lady Berkeley's Grammar School at Wotton-under-Edge, three miles south-east of Stinchcombe. The first record of him, probably when he was eighteen, from which his likely year of birth may be deduced, is the University of Oxford records, which show him as William Hychyns (a family name) taking BA as a member of Magdalen Hall on 4 July 1512.[18] He was licensed MA on 26 June 1515, and created MA on 2 July 1515, a degree which permitted him for the first time to read theology. That this official study did not include Scripture appalled him.[19] Foxe records that Tyndale 'read privily to certain students and fellows of Magdalen College some parcel of divinity, instructing them in the knowledge and truth of the scriptures'.[20] Erasmus, whose Oxford home some years before had been Magdalen College, and who until recently had been Lady Margaret's Professor of Divinity at Cambridge, published in March 1516 in Basle the *Novum instrumentum*, his Latin translation of the New Testament, with the original Greek alongside. It is more than likely that it was from this influential volume that Tyndale led those private studies. Foxe states that Tyndale went on to Cambridge, but no records support this.[21]

Gloucestershire again

Tyndale went back to Gloucestershire, at an unknown date. He became tutor to the children of Sir John and Lady Walsh at Little Sodbury Manor, a dozen miles south of the district of his birth. Sir John, a county squire of importance, who had been at court with the young Henry VIII (he was later twice High Sheriff) had recently handed over the position of Crown Steward for the Berkeley estate to Edward Tyndale. Lady Walsh came from the Poyntz family, which closely had been connected to the Tudor court since the 1470s; Anne Walsh's nephew Nicholas, their neighbour, was close to King Henry and Queen Anne. Tyndale's duties at Little Sodbury cannot have been heavy. It is probable that he used his time to study, and even begin to translate into English, Erasmus's Greek New Testament. For the Walshes he translated Erasmus's *Enchiridion militis christiani* into English, a book which drew them more to the reformed position, a topic of debate in the house. It is likely that this translation is lost, and is not the version printed by Wynkyn de Worde in London in 1533, revised in 1534.

At some point, Tyndale was ordained priest. He appears to have been in demand in the area as a preacher (at St Mary's Green in Bristol, for example), not surprising when we put together his New Testament theology and the strong commitment to Lollardy in the county. The emphasis on Scripture for the people, and the hostility to the corruptions in the Church were common to many (including Erasmus); but that Tyndale was particularly influenced by Lollard doctrines lacks evidence. Tyndale was accused of heresy, and brought before the bishop's chancellor. Several accounts of this stormy meeting survive. One is from Tyndale himself, in the Prologue to his Genesis of 1530, where he recalled that the chancellor 'threatened me grievously, and reviled me, and rated me as though I had been a dog'.[22] Another is in Foxe, where he is recording the narrative of the local man Richard Webb.[23] Even Thomas More had heard enough to misreport it.[24] After all the shouting, nothing happened.

Richard Webb also recalled that Tyndale went to visit 'an old doctor, that had been archchancellor to a bishop' living nearby. This man, identified as William Latimer by Mozley (though inconclusively, as Latimer had not held such a post),[25] warned Tyndale that 'the pope is the very antichrist', and that if he continued to preach the Scriptures 'it will cost you your life'.[26] Tyndale's most famous Gloucestershire encounter, again as told by Richard Webb in Foxe, was with 'a learned man', who said 'we were better without God's law than the pope's':

> Maister Tyndall hearing that, answered him, I defy the Pope and all his laws, and said, if God spare my life ere many years, I will cause a boy that driveth the plough, shall know more of the Scripture than thou dost.[27]

London

Tyndale, already with the vocation to print the New Testament in English, and needing permission, hoped to be supported by Cuthbert Tunstall, the Bishop of London. Tunstall had been highly praised by Erasmus, with whom he worked in the Low Countries on the second edition of his Greek New Testament, lending him a Greek manuscript and consulting others. He had been at Oxford with Colet, Linacre and More (who singles him out for praise at the opening of his *Utopia*), and was known throughout Europe as a mathematician and classicist. Tyndale, probably arriving in London in the spring of 1523, had a letter of introduction from Sir John Walsh to Sir Henry Guildford, Henry VIII's Controller and Master of the Horse, and he himself wrote to an old friend in Tunstall's service, William Hebilthwayte. All to no end: Tunstall replied, as Tyndale wrote, 'his house was full. [. . .] I [. . .] understood at the last [. . .] that there was no room in my lord of London's palace to translate the new testament.'[28] To show his skill in Greek, Tyndale had taken with him his translation of an oration of Isocrates (which has not survived), the first recorded in English: this suggests that both Tyndale's Greek, and his understanding of classical rhetoric, were excellent. He was later praised by the German scholar Hermann Buschius for his mastery of eight languages: Hebrew, Greek, Latin, Italian, Spanish, English and French, as well as German, which he seems to have been speaking when he met him.[29]

Tunstall, in the summer of 1523, was occupied in Parliament, the first for eight years: though he snubbed Tyndale, it is observable that he did not persecute him. Tyndale stayed in London for almost a year. Foxe records him preaching in St Dunstan's-in-the-West in Fleet Street. His sermons have not survived. St Dunstan's apparently had connections with the growing reform movement, with the Poyntz family and with merchants in the cloth trade, particularly Humphrey Monmouth, who took

Tyndale into his house, where he 'studied most part of the day and of the night, at his book'.[30] Tyndale, by now realising that 'to translate the New Testament [. . .] there was no place in all England',[31] left for Germany, probably in April 1524; the London merchants who supported him at this time included Monmouth, who was therefore in serious trouble in May 1528.[32]

Cologne, 1525

Tyndale is next recorded in Cologne in 1525, seeing through the press of Peter Quentell his English translation of the New Testament. His enemies later accused him of being with 'the arch-heretic Luther', which has led to speculation that he went to Wittenberg, for which there is no evidence, though it was not unknown for the English reformers on the Continent, like John Rogers, to go there, or meet Luther, like John Frith. Mozley's ingenious suggestions about Tyndale's two visits to Hamburg, and matriculation at Wittenberg, are not persuasive.[33] Tyndale had as his assistant, possibly instead of Miles Coverdale, the Observant friar William Roy, and he may have been joined by John Frith. Peter Quentell was, like his father, an eminent printer, accepting serious work from any source. For Tyndale and Roy he had in print a long Prologue and almost the whole of Matthew's Gospel, when the work was stopped. He was also printing books by the strongly anti-Lutheran 'Cochlaeus' (John Dobneck), who learned from the printers, 'after he had warmed them with wine [. . .] the secret by which England was to be brought over to the side of Luther'.[34] He reported this to the authorities. The print-shop was raided, but Tyndale and Roy escaped up the Rhine to Worms. Dobneck said that this 'Lutheran New Testament', with an intended print-run of three, or six, thousand[35] had 'got as far as the letter K', the signature which would have taken the work well into Mark. What we now have is everything up to the middle of Matthew 22, and sheets of this (or more) began to circulate in England, being the first printed Lutheran documents in the country. A single set of finished sheets to Matthew 22, bound in the nineteenth century, is in the British Library (fig. 8).[36]

The description 'Lutheran New Testament' is accurate. In appearance, the pages are a smaller quarto in the style of Luther's first, 1522, 'September Testament', in layout, type, and frequency and placing of marginal notes. Two-thirds of these ninety comments are from Luther, and all are entirely expository. The text shows signs of Luther's influence in occasional word order and vocabulary. The Prologue is Luther's, a little cut and then expanded by Tyndale to twice the length. Tyndale's opening, and manner, is gentler than Luther's. This 'Cologne Fragment' is valued most, however, for being almost the whole of the first Gospel translated from the original Greek, printed in English for the first time. The words of Jesus that have chimed down the centuries appear here first – 'Ask and it shall be given you: Seek and ye shall find: Knock and it shall be opened unto you' (Matthew 7:7); 'Enter in at the strait gate: for wide is the gate and broad is the way that leadeth to destruction' (7:13); and many thought to be proverbial, like 'the burden and heat of the day' (20:12).

The 1526 Worms New Testament

Tyndale and Roy arrived, probably late in 1525, in the safe Lutheran city of Worms, and the small printer Peter Schoeffer undertook an English New Testament, the first ever made, completed in 1526. This is very different from the Lutheran Cologne fragment. It is in octavo (pocket-size, like all Tyndale's books printed in his lifetime) and without Prologue or marginal notes, or attribution to him. This 'bare text' had impact enough (fig. 9). Smuggled down the Rhine and into English and Scottish ports in bales of cloth, copies circulated quickly. For the first time, the whole New Testament, faithfully translated from the Greek, could be read by anyone. That this immediately alarmed the English authorities is amply testified. Tunstall himself sent out in October 1526 a prohibition of the book – 'in the english tongue that pestiferous and moste pernicious poyson dispersed throughout all our dioces of London in great number'.[37] He warned the booksellers. As a grand gesture, he arranged for the burning of Tyndale's New Testaments at St Paul's on 27 October 1526, and himself preached the sermon on the occasion, claiming to have found two thousand errors in them, unsurprising in that Tyndale was not translating from the Latin, but an interesting comment on the position in which the Greek scholar Tunstall found himself. Tyndale later noted that the Church was so devoted to the search for heresy in what he wrote that, though previously they ignored Scripture, now they examined his translation so closely that they would announce to the ignorant people that it was heresy if he failed to dot an i.[38]

In considerable numbers, and to inferior standards, copies were being issued by a printer in Antwerp. Sir John Hackett, English ambassador and Wolsey's agent in the Low Countries, recorded over some months his attempts to hunt down copies there.[39] Tunstall's chaplain wrote of 'many hundreth' burned, 'both heir & beyonde the see'.[40] William Warham, Archbishop of Canterbury, wrote in May 1527 to all his bishops asking them to share the cost of buying up copies in order to burn them. Extant is the reply by the Bishop of Norwich, Richard Nix, 14 June 1527, sending ten marks, offering more, and congratulating the archbishop on doing 'a gracious and a blessed deed' in burning the Testaments, for which God will highly reward him.[41] In November 1527, the arrest by Wolsey of the gentle Cambridge scholar Thomas Bilney heralded an onslaught against the English New Testaments. Records of depositions by the many people arrested in the next year give us a profile of the first readers of Tyndale's translation.

What had been hidden in Latin for many centuries (and for much of that time confined to monasteries) was now suddenly and for the first time available to everybody. Though Christian people in Britain were certainly aware of the great events of the Christian calendar – Advent, Christmas, Lent, Easter, Whitsuntide – many of the words of Jesus in the Gospels, and almost all the writings of St Paul, were unknown to the common man or woman. It is true that the Church allowed to circulate certain Harmonies of the Gospels, in considerable numbers after the coming of printing: but these contained little of the Gospels, and a great deal of modern material. To have the four Gospels, complete and accurate to the Greek originals, was a revelation to the ordinary British Christian. To have as well the complete letters of St Paul was revolutionary. Paul's Epistle to the Romans, in particular, spells out the heart of Christian theology, with its strong emphasis on justification by faith. Though the Church authorities tried to prevent the spreading of Tyndale's Testaments, they did not succeed, in spite of public burnings. There are records from most parts of the country of groups of people meeting to read and hear the Word, so newly arrived. Puzzlement about how the English became so quickly 'Protestant' (the word was not used in the modern sense until the 1550s) can be solved by considering the arrival of the whole of Paul's Epistles in print and in English.

A story told by Edward Hall in his chronicle of 1548 has been much repeated. Cuthbert Tunstall, happening to be in Antwerp, arranged with an English merchant there, Augustine Packington, to go to Tyndale to offer to buy his stock of New Testaments with Tunstall's money. Though Tyndale knew they were being bought to be burned by the bishop, he agreed: 'And so went forward the bargain, the bishop had the books, Packington had the thanks, and Tyndale had the money.'[42] It may well have happened: but not to Tyndale, who would never have agreed to sell New Testaments for public burning. It is more likely to have been a transaction with the Antwerp 'pirate' printer of Tyndale, Christopher Van Endhoven.[43]

This 1526 Worms New Testament is rightly a treasure of English-speaking culture, for its mastery of both the Greek and English languages. Quite apart from the theological impact of these pages, many English phrases have gone into common use, like 'the powers that be' (Romans 13:1). Of Schoeffer's original print-run, only one complete copy survives, discovered in the Stuttgart Landesbibliothek in 1996 (fig. 1). The British Library's fine copy, for two hundred years in Bristol Baptist College, lacks a title-page. St Paul's Cathedral Library's copy lacks the title-page and seventy leaves. There are no more. The volumes live on, of course, in English New Testaments ever since; almost all of them, even now, reflect Tyndale, many very closely.

After seeing the New Testament into print, Tyndale and Roy parted, to Tyndale's relief. He later wrote (in the Prologue to *The Parable of the Wicked Mammon*[44]) of Roy's slipperiness. While in Worms, Tyndale gave to Peter Schoeffer a small book to print, *A Compendious Introduction, Prologue or Preface unto the Epistle of Paul to the Romans*, of which one copy survives, in the Bodleian Library. This, based loosely on Luther's *Vorrhede* to Romans in all his German New Testaments, was the second printed reformed tract circulating in England. It is Luther's exposition of Paul's doctrine of justification by faith alone. It was expanded in Tyndale's 1534 revision of his New Testament.

The Parable of the Wicked Mammon *and* The Obedience of a Christian Man

Tyndale's movements for some years after 1526 are unrecorded, but that all his work from 1528 was published in Antwerp implies that he was living in or near that thriving port, which had strong trade connections with England and many good printers. His first two Antwerp books were from the print-shop of 'Hans Luft of Marlborow', a pseudonym of one of the biggest Antwerp printers, Martin de Keyser or Martin l'Empereur.[45] The real Hans Luft, in Wittenberg, was Luther's prosperous printer, so de Keyser's choice of name was suggestive.

On 8 May 1528, Tyndale's *The Parable of the Wicked Mammon* was published, in his customary small octavo. It soon appeared in the records of the much-sharpened interrogations in England which it provoked, and was officially banned as heretical on 24 May 1530.[46] Following a sermon by Luther, Tyndale develops his exposition of the parable in Luke 16, known since as that of the Unjust Steward, to show the New Testament teaching that though good works are important, they come naturally only from true faith, as fruit comes from the tree. Over-emphasis on works leads only to superstition. Lacking a title-page, the book's first four leaves are a Prologue, 'William Tyndale otherwise called hychins to the reader', a declaration, as he explains, to dissociate himself from the superficial and showy William Roy.

Tyndale's most influential book outside his Bible translations, *The Obedience of a Christian Man*, came five months later, on 2 October 1528.

Enemies were asserting that the reformers throughout Europe were encouraging sedition and teaching treason. Tyndale wrote to declare for the first time the two fundamental principles of the English reformers: the supreme authority of Scripture in the Church, and the supreme authority of the king in the state. The first sentence of his book (after a blessing) is 'Let it not make thee despair neither yet discourage thee O reader, that it is forbidden thee in pain of life and goods or that it is made breaking of the King's peace or treason unto His Highness to read the word of thy soul's health.'[47]

'In pain of life and goods' and 'treason' are now scarcely comprehensible applied to the reading of the Bible in English (and those pains uniquely happened in England). Tyndale makes many pages of his book out of Scripture, and he is scalding about the corruptions and superstitions in the Church. His arguments are carefully developed, and his experiences of ordinary life are wide-ranging. Contrasted with the New Testament Church and faith, he describes the sufferings of the people at the hands, especially, of monks and friars, though the whole intrusive hierarchy, as he sees it, from the pope down, is guilty of 'selling for money what God in Christ promiseth freely'.[48]

Tyndale was a master of English prose: his attacks (for example on the follies of the rival metaphysical schools of theology[49]) make exhilarating reading, and his sympathy with the existential human condition can be moving. Like *Mammon*, the *Obedience* was widely read and immediately banned (the bishops found and published fifty-four articles of heresy in them[50]) and appears in records of interrogations of humble people. At the other extreme, Strype records a story taken from Foxe's papers, of Anne Boleyn showing a copy to her royal husband-to-be, who delighted in it and declared that 'this is a book for me and all kings to read'.[51]

The Pentateuch

In Europe, rabbinical schools flourished, and knowledge of Hebrew was growing. Tyndale learned Hebrew: perhaps in Worms, the main centre of Jewish learning in Germany. Hebrew was almost unknown in England; two scholars in Cambridge who knew Hebrew were neither concerned to translate.

In January 1530, again from 'Hans Luft of Marlborow', copies of *The First Book of Moses called Genesis*, with a prologue headed 'W.T. to the Reader', appeared in Britain. The five books of the Pentateuch could be bought singly or together. Each has a prologue: Exodus, Leviticus and Deuteronomy are in roman type; unusual words are explained after

Genesis, Exodus and Deuteronomy. The Prologue to Genesis, 'showing the use of the Scripture', begins strikingly:

> Though a man had a precious jewel and a rich, yet if he wist not the value thereof nor wherefore it served, he were neither the better nor richer of a straw. Even so though we read the scripture and babble of it never so much, yet if we know not the use of it, and wherefore it was given, and what is therein to be sought, it profiteth us nothing at all. It is not enough therefore to read and talk of it only, but we must also desire God day and night instantly to open our eyes, and to make us understand and feel wherefore the scripture was given, that we may apply the medicine of the scripture, every man to his own sores, unless that we intend to be idle disputers, and brawlers about vain words, ever gnawing upon the bitter bark without and never attaining unto the sweet pith within, and persecuting one another for defending of lewd imaginations and fantasies of our own invention.[52]

'Understand and feel' are the two words with which Tyndale most frequently expresses the response to Scripture: as well as opposing barren scholastic metaphysics, they go a long way to summarise his principles of translation. Scripture is also 'medicine', and at the root of his reception of New Testament Christianity is his grasp that the point of the 'promises' (a favourite word) is healing now, not a far-off compensation for sufferings, after death.

The original Hebrew text of the Pentateuch (or of anything) was in English for the first time. Instead of *Fiat lux, et facta est lux*, Tyndale gave 'Let there be light, and there was light', and the name of God as Jehovah. Tyndale's Hebrew was good. He used, but did not depend on, Luther's Pentateuch of 1523. Tyndale's Genesis has six marginal notes, to Luther's seventy-two. A passage in his *Obedience* declares Tyndale's experience of how well Hebrew went into English.[53] His aim was always to be clear, achieved even when the Hebrew is difficult. His skill with poetry shows what we have lost in not having his Psalms, Job and the Prophets. Of Tyndale's 132 notes in the Pentateuch, a dozen are of one word only. Two dozen mention the pope, for example 'The pope's bull slayeth more than Aaron's calf' at Exodus 32. Most are expository. Tyndale was outstanding in matching varieties of English to the differences in the Hebrew, between the tragi-comedy of the Fall in Genesis 3 and the long novel-like narrative of Joseph and his brothers at the end of that book.

A few lines of Foxe's last, 1576, version of *Acts and Monuments*, tell of Tyndale shipwrecked on the way to Hamburg, losing everything except his life. All his work on the Pentateuch perished. He summoned Coverdale to help him, and in Hamburg translated afresh, living in the house of Margaret Van Emmerson at a time of plague. Foxe is attractively specific, and the story has been widely noticed, but there are too many things against it for modern acceptance. Though Tyndale is at his most autobiographical in the Prologue to Genesis, he does not refer to it. No records of the time mention these momentous events. With his Jonah-like rescue from the sea to disseminate the Word, the story may have a trace of Tyndale's translation of that prophet from the Hebrew, printed at about this time with a long prologue, informative about his ideas on translation. A single copy survives in the British Library.

Tyndale and More, and The Practice of Prelates

In 1528, Sir Thomas More, already a seasoned antagonist of Luther in Latin, was permitted by Cuthbert Tunstall, Bishop of London, to read heretical books in English in order to attack Tyndale. More was determined to crush heretics if need be by fire. In June 1529 appeared More's *Dialogue Concerning Heresies*, in the third book of which Tyndale's New Testament is demolished as heresy, and Tyndale himself vilified as worse than Luther. At bottom, More asserts that Tyndale's offence has been to give the people Paul in English, and to translate key words in their Greek meanings as 'senior', 'congregation', 'love' and 'repent', instead of the Church's 'priest', 'church', 'charity' and 'do penance'.

Tyndale, to whom the attack was unexpected, replied vigorously, even page by page, in his *An Answer unto sir Thomas More's Dialogue* of 1531, at shorter length. His authority is the New Testament. He condemns the Church, so absolutely defended by More, for having perverted Scripture, and for the many corruptions of his day (on which More, he notes, was silent).

More answered Tyndale's answer with his enormous *Confutation of Tyndale's Answer*, almost two thousand heavy pages, of which the first three books were published early in 1532, and a year later the remaining six: all but the fifth book (against Robert Barnes) attack Tyndale. Huge as it is, running to half a million words, it was never finished. Even More's devotees, including his contemporary biographer and admirer Nicholas Harpsfield, and his modern editors, agree that More is, to put it mildly, disordered.[54] Tyndale is intemperately pilloried on almost every page ('a hell-hound in the kennel of the devil', 'discharging a filthy foam of blasphemies out of his brutish beastly mouth'). More's longest work in English does his reputation no favour. Tyndale made no further reply, but More was still attacking Tyndale in his *Apology*, and his *Debellation of Salem and Bizance*, both in 1533.

In 1530, Tyndale published, once again from 'Marborch' (i.e. 'Hans Luft of Marlborow'), his short *The Practice of Prelates*. The pope's conspiracy, as the old image had it, is the ivy strangling the nation's tree. 'Practice' carries also its older meaning, of trickery. Tyndale's attacks on the Roman hierarchy are trenchant in their rhythms, building to a sustained onslaught on the deviousness of 'Wolfsee' (Wolsey). In *Practice* there are few marginal notes: as usual, many were added in editions after his death. In the last pages, Tyndale argues learnedly against King Henry's divorce of Catherine, to the king's reported anger, leading to the removal of those pages in later editions.

New Testament expositions

In about 1530, Tyndale expanded his Prologue to the 1525 Cologne Fragment to make a small, short, book, *A Pathway to the Holy Scripture*, as a guide to the New Testament to be read alongside his unannotated 1526 Worms volume. *Pathway* expounds the central doctrines of Paul in Romans. In September 1531, he published *An Exposition upon the First Epistle of John*. This is a section-by-section unfolding of John, with the decorum of a quieter tone, even in its demands for righteous love. Tyndale does, however, expound John's 'Little children, beware of images', with extended mockery of the worship of saints and their statues. Early in 1533 came his *Exposition upon the V, VI, VII Chapters of Matthew* (that is, the Sermon on the Mount), in which Tyndale contrasts the words of Christ in restoring the true meaning of God's commandments – works resulting from faith – with many corrupt practices of the Church. Unpublished in Tyndale's lifetime, and first printed in 1548, was *A brief declaration of the sacraments*, in which Tyndale argues that it is the inner faith of the communicant which makes the sacrament of the Lord's Supper, a doctrine which More furiously denied, for which John Frith died, and which for four hundred and fifty years has been a central doctrine of the Church of England. (The book, *The Supper of the Lord*, also the subject of a powerful attack by More, was not, as he thought it, by Tyndale.) Also unpublished in Tyndale's lifetime, the manuscript bound with Frith's tract on the subject, was Tyndale's essay on the *cause célèbre* of the will of William Tracy, in which he trusted to be saved by the merits of Christ and not by works, saints or masses. All those printed works came from Martin de Keyser in Antwerp, as himself.

Tyndale was visited secretly in 1531 by Thomas Cromwell's emissary, Stephen Vaughan, who was Henry VIII's factor in the Netherlands. The king, it seems, had got over his anger at *Practice*, and had been persuaded that the country would be safer if Tyndale were in England and at court. In January 1531, Vaughan succeeded in getting a letter to Tyndale, offering, on the king's authority, a safe-conduct and other sureties. Tyndale, with some justification suspecting a trap, refused. As he knew, the situation in England was darkening. One evening in April 1531, Vaughan met Tyndale in a field outside Antwerp, and afterwards wrote to Cromwell a long account of their conversation. Tyndale declared his strong loyalty to the king: he lived in constant poverty and danger to bring the New Testament to the king's subjects: did he fear them more than the clergy, against whom he, Tyndale, wrote to protect the king (citing Wolsey)? Vaughan met Tyndale again in May. Tyndale movingly sent his promise that if the king would grant his people a bare text (of the Scriptures, in their language), as even the emperor and other Christian princes had done, whoever made it, then he would write no more and submit himself at the feet of his royal majesty. A third meeting had the same result. Vaughan wrote twice again to Cromwell on Tyndale's behalf, with no effect. Power at court was shifting. The next emissary sent, Sir Thomas Elyot, a friend of More, went not to persuade but to arrest Tyndale.

Tyndale's 1534 New Testament

The Antwerp printing house of Van Endhoven had published, by 1534, four reissues of Tyndale's 1526 Worms New Testament, in various small sizes, including 16mo. These printings say a good deal about the demand in Britain. In 1534, the widow of Christopher Van Endhoven (who had died in London, imprisoned for printing and shipping English Bibles) asked an English scholar living in Antwerp, George Joye, to oversee another edition, as the Flemish typesetters were not doing well. This he did. He also took the opportunity to make silent alterations to Tyndale's work. In particular, he altered Tyndale's English word 'resurrection', to make it 'the life after this life' and variations. Not to put his name to the changes was bad enough, but in 1533 the Resurrection was the subject of debate among the English reformers.

Tyndale was already preparing his own revision of his 1526 New Testament, which was published in 1534. It shows his maturer thought, and skill, and in many ways improves on the 1526 version. He wrote for it a long Prologue about translation, explaining among other things the importance of appreciating the Hebrew influence on New Testament Greek, something not widely understood before. He also wrote a second Prologue, 'W.T. yet once more unto the Christian reader', in which he strongly attacked George Joye for his impertinence. Tyndale defends his own translation, and adds that Joye is free to come up with his own ideas, as long as he puts his own name to them.

This handsome small volume of 1534, well printed by de Keyser, is the English New Testament as it went forward into other sixteenth-century versions. Eighty-three per cent of the King James ('Authorised') Version New Testament is directly from Tyndale in 1534 (see p. 805, n.13 below). There are now marginal cross-references and notes, many only a single word, and acting as location-finders rather than as exposition, though Tyndale clarifies and explains New Testament life and doctrine in longer notes. Revelation has twenty-two woodcuts, disturbing visualisations of the baffling text. Then follow fifteen pages containing forty Old Testament passages in English, those that were read on certain days in the services at Salisbury Cathedral, which 'Sarum use' became a basis of the Book of Common Prayer.[55] Each New Testament book, except Acts and Revelation, has a prologue. Those to the main Pauline Epistles are important, and that to Romans is especially so: it is Tyndale again translating Luther's own *Vorrhede*, as in his 1526 *A compendious introduction* and *A Pathway*, but now adapting more freely. More copies of this translation have survived. One, in the British Library, was owned by Queen Anne Boleyn, with her royal name on the fore-edges. A revised version of this New Testament, with minor changes, was made by Tyndale in 1535; it is known as the 'GH' edition.[56] Tyndale had made slight revisions to his translation of Genesis, in a reprint of 1534. By the spring of 1535 he had certainly finished translating the historical books of the Old Testament, Joshua to 2 Chronicles, in manuscript. Parts of these books present unusual difficulties, as for example in the 'Song of Deborah', incorporated in Judges 5, one of the oldest documents known, where the Hebrew text is corrupt and problematic: in translating it, Tyndale comes out well. His accuracy to the Hebrew in the range of tones that he can command through all these books is noteworthy.

Tyndale and Frith

John Frith had most probably known Tyndale in England, had, with his wife and family, been with him in the Low Countries, at least, and perhaps also in Germany. Foxe prints two letters from Tyndale to him in the Tower in 1531, both characteristically made of Scripture. The first exhorts him to courage in the likelihood of his coming martyrdom. The second, addressed to Frith under the name of 'Jacob', advises that in writing on 'Christ's body in the sacrament', dependence on the phrases of Scripture would be his wisest policy; and giving him news, including assurance of his wife's support. Frith wrote of Tyndale that 'for his learning and judgement in scripture, he were more worthy to be promoted than all the bishops in England': he commended his 'faithful, clear, innocent heart'.[57]

Arrest and imprisonment

Tyndale had spoken to Stephen Vaughan in 1531 of his poverty, exile, absence from friends, hunger, thirst, cold, and 'the great danger wherewith I am everywhere encompassed' – all, and more, endured because he 'hoped with my labours to do honour to God'.[58] He was relatively safe living with Thomas Poyntz and his wife in the English House in Antwerp, where John Rogers had been chaplain to the English merchants since late 1534. Poyntz was related to Lady Walsh of Little Sodbury. Tyndale could reasonably look forward to completing his translation of the Old Testament. In the spring of 1535, however, a debauched and villainous young Englishman wanting money, Henry Phillips, insinuated himself into the English House and Tyndale's trust, pretending interest in the work of Bible translation, and borrowing money from him. Phillips had gambled away money entrusted to him by his father to give to someone in London, and, full of self-pity, had fled abroad. He promised someone in authority, it is not known whom (suspicion falls on Stokesley), that he could betray Tyndale, Barnes and Joye, for cash. On the morning of 21 May 1531, having arranged for the imperial officers to be ready, Phillips tricked Tyndale into leaving the English House. In the alley he was seized. The officers later said 'that they pitied to see his simplicity when they took him'.[59] Tyndale was taken at once to the procurer-general, who immediately raided Poyntz's house and took away all Tyndale's property, including his books and papers. The Old Testament historical books in English were safely somewhere else, probably with Rogers. We cannot know what further translations were removed and destroyed. Tyndale was taken to the castle of Vilvorde, outside Brussels, where he was incarcerated for the next sixteen months.

The English merchants at Antwerp, outraged at the abuse of their corporate diplomatic privilege, wrote at once to the court at Brussels and to the English government. Their ire was so well known that Phillips, as is the way with bullies, was greatly afraid: not only that the English merchants would lie in wait for him, but because the letters he had sent to England about the arrest of Tyndale included remarks, intended to gain favour at the emperor's court, that were insulting to King Henry. If they were seen by Cromwell, they would lead to his own swift arrest and death. The endeavours of the English merchants faded; the English court lost opportunities. Thomas Poyntz remained active, however. His attempts in Antwerp failing, he wrote to his brother John at the English court, saying that he believed that the king, who never had 'a truer hearted subject to his grace' than Tyndale, had written to Brussels for Tyndale's release, but did not know that his letters had been blocked, probably by Phillips. In any case, the highest political forces were against release. The Holy Roman Emperor, Charles v, at his court in Brussels, was in no mood to assist an English king who had just divorced his aunt.

'The king's grace', Poyntz wrote, 'should have of him at this day as high a treasure as of any one man living . . . there be not many perfecter men this day living, as knows God'.[60] Cromwell meanwhile had written to two leading privy councillors in Brabant. The letters, and the attempts by Poyntz to get results from them, made a tangled skein of contacts and journeys. In the end it seemed that Poyntz had succeeded. He was told at Brussels that Tyndale would be released to him.

Phillips saw his money threatened if Tyndale, in England, talked to Cromwell, or even to the king. So he denounced Poyntz as a fellow heretic of Tyndale. Poyntz was arrested, placed in house arrest, and subjected to a three-month interrogation on more than a hundred articles. The inquisitors always arrived with Phillips at the door. Poyntz, suddenly alert to his danger, escaped and fled to England. His wife refused to join him. His business was in ruins. He lived a further twenty-six years, too poor to benefit from the inheritance of the ancestral manor in Essex. (Phillips lived until 1542, travelling with increasing desperation the length of Europe, denounced by all who came to know him as a perpetual thief and traitor.)

Inquisition

Tyndale meanwhile had been subjected to long examination by the procurer-general. This man, Pierre Dufief, a magistrate of evil reputation, was widely known in the Low Countries for his cruelty. His zeal for hunting down heretics was fuelled by the fact that he was given a proportion of the confiscated property of his victims, and a large fee. Dufief had arranged for Tyndale's English works to be translated into, or at least summarised in, Latin, probably by Phillips.

Tyndale's crime was heresy, being a Lutheran. To his enemies he was the greatest English catch, and his downfall, it was believed, would remove heresy from England, and give glory to his captors. He was tried by seventeen commissioners, led by three chief accusers, at their head the greatest heresy-hunter in Europe, Jacobus Latomus, from the new Catholic University of Leuven/Louvain, a long-time opponent of Erasmus as well as Luther. Tyndale, declining an offer of his own notary and procurer, conducted his own defence, which was not from legal manoeuvering but from scripture. Latomus wrote a detailed record, which shows him precise, and indeed courteous, as to a great scholar. This account was published in three books in 1550, six years after his (Latomus's) death. In that he tells us that

Tyndale wrote his defence in a book on *Sola fides justificat apud Deum*, 'faith alone justifies before God'. Tyndale's apparently frequent phrase, *Clavis intelligentiae salutaris sacrae scripturae,* 'the key to the understanding of scripture as salvation', may supply an alternative title.

Latomus was not trying to discover whether Tyndale was a heretic, or save him from the flames. Those had been determined long before. Latomus was trying to bring Tyndale back to orthodoxy, for the sake of his soul, before he was burned. He could not avoid reproducing a good deal of what Tyndale wrote. As a result, it has been possible to reconstruct Tyndale's 'last, lost' book in detail.[61] It appears all of a piece with everything else he published, in its logical development, clarity and, above all, absolute dependence on, and great knowledge of, Scripture, especially Paul.

One autograph document from these months has survived in the archives of the Council of Brabant. Neatly written in Latin, on one small sheet of paper, and signed 'W. Tindalus', it tells us a great deal. As the first winter approached in 1535, Tyndale wrote, most probably to the Marquis of Bergen-op-Zoom (one of the councillors to whom Cromwell had written), asking him to 'request the commissary' – the procurer-general, Dufief – to let him have some of his own warmer clothing which Dufief had confiscated; what he had was worn out, and he was suffering from a perpetual cold and catarrh. 'And I ask to be allowed to have a lamp in the evening; it is indeed wearisome sitting alone in the dark.' Most urgently he asked to be permitted to have 'the Hebrew Bible, Hebrew grammar, and Hebrew dictionary [i.e. Reuchlin in German] that I may pass the time in that study'.[62] There is no evidence that any of his requests were met. Tyndale was in the prison-cell for sixteen months. The notion that Tyndale spent that time in translating the historical books of the Old Testament takes no account of the physical limitations of his cell and the mechanics of translating, nor of the absolute unlikelihood of his being allowed to continue such heretical labours, especially not in view of the professional hatred felt for him by Dufief. Foxe, however, reported that while Tyndale was in prison, he 'converted his keeper, the keeper's daughter, and others of his household'; others reported that 'if he were not a good Christian man, they could not tell whom to trust'. According to both Foxe and Hall, the procurer-general himself, Dufief no less, wrote that Tyndale was 'homo doctus, pius et bonus, that is to say, learned, godly, and good'.[63]

Two things, among others, are moving about Tyndale's last sixteen months in that cell in Vilvoorde. The first is that from the moment when Henry Phillips led him out to his arrest by the emperor's soldiers, until his last breath, five hundred days later, Tyndale would hear and speak no

English. His jailers would know no English – nobody did who was not English. Church officials and his accusers would automatically speak Latin. For the supreme master of spoken English not to hear any English for so long must have been a severe deprivation.

The second is equally painful. Tyndale had given the English people two New Testaments and a Pentateuch in pocket-sized English books. He had left in manuscript in the English House in Antwerp his English translation of the fourteen Old Testament historical books, printed after his death. He had heard seven years before that most of his 1526 New Testament volumes had been burned and denounced by Erasmus's friend, Cuthbert Tunstall. The new Bishop of London, John Stokesley, was far harsher, and had restarted the policy of burning heretics, not just their books.

Even before his arrest he would not have had any guarantee that his work was getting through. A heavy curtain hung before him, through which he could see little or nothing. English-speaking Christians look back with rejoicing at the miracle of the English Bible. Every one of the thousands of English versions round the world goes back to Tyndale's fundamental work in Worms and Antwerp. His was a dazzling achievement. Of its success he knew nothing. He worked in faith, the existential faith which is the business of getting up and doing it. As he noted in the Prologue to *The Obedience of a Christian Man*, faith in the God of the Bible is huge in its effects.

Martyrdom

The cold machinery of the law could not be stopped. Tyndale was condemned as a heretic early in August 1536, and probably the same day suffered the public, and ceremonial, degradation from the priesthood: the record of payments to Dufief shows the cost of arranging the elaborate ritual. A greater assembly was summoned for a morning early in October (traditionally the 6th) when in an open space a stake, brushwood and logs were prepared. Tyndale was brought out. A chain was placed round his neck. He gave the cry that Foxe records, 'Lord, open the King of England's eyes'.[64] Tyndale was not burned alive: as a mark of his distinction as a scholar, he was strangled first, and then his body was burned.

Cromwell's agent John Hutton wrote to him from Brabant on 13 December 1536: 'They speak much of the patient sufferance of Master Tyndale at the time of his execution.' In 1550, Roger Ascham, tutor to Princess Elizabeth, rode through Vilvorde. He noted: 'At the town's end is a notable solemn place of execution, where worthy William Tyndale was unworthily put to death.'[65]

John Rogers assembled all Tyndale's biblical translations, and a complete English Bible was printed by Matthew Crom in Antwerp, for the publishers Richard Grafton and Edward Whitchurch. At the foot of the title-page are the words 'Set forth with the King's most gracious licence'. Since the name of Tyndale the heretic could not appear, Rogers used the names of two disciples, Thomas and Matthew, and 1,500 copies of 'Matthew's Bible' were imported into England and soon sold out. Thus within months of Tyndale's martyrdom, a complete English Bible, two-thirds of it Tyndale's work, and licensed by Henry VIII, was circulating in Britain. (For an account of this handsome well-printed folio, see chapter 12 below.) Tyndale's work was handed on into successive versions in the sixteenth century, notably the three Geneva versions of 1560, 1576 and 1599. King James's revisers, working between 1607 and 1611, though they made changes, went back to Tyndale afresh.

THE LEGACY OF TYNDALE

Tyndale was in the vanguard of the popular English Reformation. His books, especially *Wicked Mammon, Obedience* and his expositions of Romans, gathered to a head the widespread revulsion at the corruptions and superstitions of the Church as it then was, all of which are clearly described. Scripture had to be the base for these judgements, and it was spelled out with clarity and excellent scholarship, from the original languages. From the great release that justification by faith brings to the sinner, Tyndale showed, always in the language of the New Testament, that central to a Christian's life were not curious rituals and practices, but the promises of God. He was passionate in his wish that Britain could be a Christian state under a Christian prince, free from the intrusions of a totally alien system stemming from the bishop of Rome. Tyndale was a true revolutionary in his political as well as his theological thinking. His courage was great. In opposing the Roman Church he was confronting the greatest power in the western world.

The great change that came over England from 1526, the ability of every ordinary man, woman and child to read and hear the whole New Testament in English, accurately rendered, was Tyndale's work, and its importance cannot be over-emphasised. The Vulgate was incomprehensible to the ploughboy and most of his familiars throughout the land. What the priests let the people know was a fraction of the whole Bible. Now all four Gospels, for example, could be read in their entirety, and the whole of Paul. There is no shortage of evidence of the gatherings of people of all ages, all over the country, to read and hear these English Scriptures – and reading meant, so often, reading aloud.[66]

Tyndale as the first translator of Hebrew into English stands up well to informed scrutiny.[67] His understanding of New Testament theology, and how it related to the Old Testament, pointed forward. He left Luther behind. His fresh appraisals from the Greek effectively liberated New Testament theology in English, allowing the possibility of reinterpretation in every generation, as had clearly happened in the life of the early Church, and could, and did, happen again in Britain and America. In the last hundred years, Tyndale has been judged supreme in accuracy and in aesthetics. Understanding is growing, however, that what a translator like Tyndale believed he was doing went more importantly into other courts. To change the metaphor: lurking in the Scripture landscape of his time lay the monsters of ideology, authority and power. It is the 'interplay of political, spiritual, epistemological, and rhetorical authorities that marks early modern arguments over vernacular scripture'.[68] 'Authority' meaning only 'credibility' was no longer enough.[69] The English Reformation gave new political power, causing urgent debate about what that was and who had the right to wield it. To Henry VIII, in his proclamation of 22 June 1530, prohibiting the use of translations, Tyndale had produced 'pestiferous English books, printed in other regions . . . to pervert . . . the people . . . to stir and incense them to sedition . . .'.[70] Refuting that common charge two years before, Tyndale in his *Obedience* based his claim of the political role of vernacular Scripture on its evident power to maintain God's proper ordering of things, and that the Christian life means obedience to the king not the pope. His point is repeatedly made: Rome is afraid of Scripture, which will pull down papal authority. So the Bible in English is not only a source of doctrine, a text for exegesis. It is itself an agent of the greatest change in national as well as personal life.

Tyndale's gift to the English language is unmeasurable. He translated into a register just above common speech, allied in its clarity to proverbs. It is a language which still speaks directly to the heart. His rhetorical aims were always accuracy and clarity.[74] King James's revisers adopted his style, and his words, for a good deal of their version. At a time when European scholars and professionals communicated in Latin, Tyndale insisted on being understood by ordinary people. He preferred a simple Saxon syntax of subject-verb-object. His vocabulary is predominantly Saxon, and often monosyllabic.[71] An Oxford scholar, he was always rhetorically alert. He gave the Bible-reading nation an English plain style. It is a basis for the great Elizabethan writers, and, as will be seen, there is truth in the remark 'without Tyndale, no Shakespeare'. It is not fanciful to see a chief agent of the energising of the language in the sixteenth century the constant reading of the Bible in English, of which Tyndale was the great maker.

As a means of summing up Tyndale's strengths, here is the last part of Luke 15, the Parable of the Prodigal Son, from his 1534 New Testament.

And he said: a certain man had two sons, and the younger of them said to his father: father, give me my part of the goods that to me belongeth. And he divided unto them his substance. And not long after, the younger son gathered all that he had together, and took his journey into a far country, and there he wasted his goods with riotous living. And when he had spent all that he had, there rose a great dearth throughout all the same land, and he began to lack. And he went and clave to a citizen of that same country, which sent him to his field, to keep his swine. And he would fain have filled his belly with the cods that the swine ate: and no man gave him.

Then he came to himself and said: how many hired servants at my father's, have bread enough, and I die for hunger. I will arise, and go to my father and will say unto him: father, I have sinned against heaven and before thee, and am no more worthy to be called thy son; make me as one of thy hired servants. And he arose and went to his father. And when he was yet a great way off, his father saw him and had compassion, and ran and fell on his neck, and kissed him. And the son said unto him: father, I have sinned against heaven, and in thy sight, and am no more worthy to be called thy son. But his father said to his servants: bring forth the best garment and put it on him, and put a ring on his hand, and shoes on his feet. And bring hither that fatted calf, and kill him, and let us eat and be merry: for this my son was dead, and is alive again, he was lost, and is now found. And they began to be merry.

The elder brother was in the field, and when he came and drew night to the house, he heard minstrelsy and dancing, and called one of his servants, and asked what those things meant. And he said unto him: thy brother is come, and thy father had killed the fatted calf, because he hath received him safe and sound. And he was angry, and would not go in. Then came his father out, and entreated him. He answered and said to his father: Lo, these many years have I done thee service, neither brake at any time thy commandment, and yet gavest thou me never so much as a kid to make merry with my lovers: but as soon as this thy son was come, which hath devoured thy goods with harlots, thou hast for his pleasure killed the fatted calf. And he said unto him: Son, thou wast ever with me, and all that I have, is thine: it was meet that we should make merry and be glad: for this thy brother was dead, and is alive again: and was lost, and is found.

Chapter 10

AFTER TYNDALE

A NEW LANDSCAPE

The corner that English readers turned in the 1530s, stepping into direct access to the whole Bible, did not lead to one or two curious Bible effects, a few odd dark lanes, a couple of twisted alleys. On the contrary: turning that corner was suddenly to be faced with a vast, rich sunlit territory, a land flowing with the milk and honey of new images and metaphors, and the rediscovered ancient monuments of God-given religious, political and social revelation.

In the Early Modern period, the revolution, and its permanence – the words are not too strong – in both native religion and in the language of ordinary expressiveness, would not have happened without the proper making, from the original documents, of the whole Bible in English; work begun, and two-thirds completed, by Tyndale. It is true that, within the broad spectrum that was the Catholic Church in Europe in the early 1500s, there were those humanists, like Erasmus and More, who were allowed to express criticism of the Latin Bible. Erasmus even argued, as we saw, for some of the Bible to be in the vernacular, so that the ploughboy in the fields, and even women, could sing it.

Thomas More, conscious in June 1529 of the demand for a Bible in English, claimed to be heart and soul in favour of the vernacular Scripture. By such, only bad men will be harmed. Even if a hundred heretics be hurt, if one good and devout layman be benefited by the reading, that will be good. But the scheme he proposed is in flat contradiction to this. He suggests in his *Dialogue concerning Heresies* that the Church might satisfy the demand by having certain biblical books, or parts of books, translated into English by the most carefully screened and acceptable scholars. Such a manuscript might then possibly be loaned by a bishop to a specially chosen wise man in a community, who would use it at his discretion, and surrender it to the bishop again when asked, so that it was always in that bishop's control. Each bishop, More advised, should buy a stock of such English Bibles to serve his own diocese. All he need spend is ten pounds or twenty marks. Each bishop would then lend these out to the people. The whole book would go only to a good and safe man. Others would have the parts suited to their capacities: maybe the Synoptic Gospels, but not St John; St Paul's Epistle to the Ephesians, but not to the Romans. Many would get nothing at all. When the borrower died, the bishop would reclaim the book. This proposal is a measure of More's fear of the Bible entire. As a scheme, its impracticality must have been so obvious to Sir Thomas that one may suspect an ironic game. R. W. Chambers calls More's argument that the Bible should be translated into the English tongue 'a noble one'; as it is, More's proposal is ridiculous.[1]

Generally, the Church in the earliest decades of the century observed, and fostered, the popularity of Harmonies of the Gospels in English. The wide readership of these has recently been taken as evidence that no 'outside' translations of Scriptures, with their built-in heresy of being from the Greek and Hebrew instead of the Latin, need ever have been made.

The evil of the 'heretics' was that they bypassed the Latin, disobeying the Church. Second, they provided the whole Bible, all sixty-six books, complete and entire, with no omissions or additions, according to the best texts of the Greek and Hebrew originals. Thus anyone at all, man, woman or child, who could either read or be within earshot of someone reading, could receive this highly sacred, defended, dangerous and difficult (and properly Latin) text with no one in the hierarchical authority to interpret and guide. The resulting free-for-all of interpretation was bound to be an inferno of souls lost, a present hell of heretics destroying Christian heritage, and seething sedition. If only they had stayed with Nicholas Love and his *Mirror*, which was all they needed.

Two things are wrong with this. First, Love's popular *Life of Jesus* is no doubt excellent piety, but, as briefly noted on p. 120 above, it has little connection with the New Testament. True, the Harmony does give some very slight outline of the life of Christ: but Jesus' ministry of teaching and healing is omitted. To turn up the Sermon on the Mount (Matthew 5, 6 and 7) in Love's *Mirror*, for example, is to find the statement: 'he made them a long sermon full of fruit.' And that is all. Instead is Augustine, the importance of poverty, and the Fathers on the *Pater Noster*, with a few phrases from that prayer given in English as the pages pass. The whole of the fourth Gospel is absent. The book is not long, but it is padded out with long meditations by and about the Blessed Virgin Mary, who has the overwhelming presence. Although half the book is on the Crucifixion, the Gospels' narrative is only just visible, overtaken by the Virgin Mary's long accounts of her own suffering at that event. And so on. (It may need pointing out that such passages are not part of the New Testament.) Perhaps this book did, as has been suggested, empower women at the time.[2] But the harsh fact is that from 1526, when the first complete New Testament printed in English from the Greek arrived in Britain, the printing of Nicholas Love's *Mirror* stopped abruptly.[3]

The scholar 'heretics', in giving to everyone the whole Bible, from Genesis 1 to Revelation 22, allowed the biblical principle of its self-interpretation to operate. To the Christian, each Testament comments on the other. The Old Testament looks forward to the coming of Christ: the incarnation recorded in the New Testament fulfils the Old, particularly the Prophets. There are difficulties, it is true, and passages are disturbing even to modern, open, well-evolved minds, as well as the 'dark places' referred to, for example, by the Geneva translators on their title-page in 1560. Worse, as with Shakespeare, readers can find in the volume whatever it is they are looking for. The Bard is found cryptographically announcing that he was really Francis Bacon, or someone even less likely. The Hebrew Scriptures have been read as a code, foretelling selected events in the late twentieth-century history of the USA. What happened in the founding churches of New Testament times was that interpretation was made together, under the guidance of the Holy Spirit. By the time of Tyndale, difficulties had been greatly exaggerated. As anyone knows who has heard an entire Gospel read aloud, it is both challenging and simple to follow. As a way to salvation, which is the New Testament understanding of Scripture, the Bible is joyfully clear.

The vastness of the landscape began to be mapped by the fresh translations of the Bible into English between 1526 and 1611, as explored below. The topography also shows remarkable effects in language and literature, also touched on. When we understand not only individuals reading, but households hearing the Scriptures read aloud, we find we are in the presence of a large cultural phenomenon. 'Whether the Bible was read silently by individuals, read aloud to the assembled family in the privacy of the home, or read in church, Bible reading was present at every moment of existence.'[4]

The sixteenth-century figures are grand enough. Later totals beggar belief. In Britain in the eighteenth and nineteenth centuries, the records show over twelve hundred different Bible editions, largely of KJV.[5] It ceases to be possible to calculate numbers printed, now running into millions. In America, from the first printing of a Bible in 1777 until 1850, there were over fourteen hundred different editions of English Bibles – thirty-four in 1850 alone – almost all of them KJV.[6] For thirty years after 1850, the American Bible, by then an essential item in the furnishing of the American home, was in editions and numbers, a phenomenon beyond calculation. No one knows, or will ever know, how many Bibles the new presses across America, developed by then for newspapers and cheap books, were turning out. As in Britain, new translations appeared in the twentieth century; a fat catalogue of Bibles issued by an American publisher in 2001 is overwhelming in the choices offered.

CONTINUED OPPOSITION IN THE SIXTEENTH CENTURY

In the *Times Literary Supplement* of 4 June 1925, the quatercentenary of Tyndale's Cologne Fragment, a contributor who was spectacularly ill-informed generally about Tyndale announced that the English bishops of Tyndale's time were considering the making of their own English Bible. Tyndale, the writer said, was 'pushing at an open door . . . ; he acted while his betters were deliberating'. Quite apart from the comedy of the phrase 'his betters', the last thing that the martyred Tyndale thought he was doing was 'pushing at an open door'. Nor would the phrase ring true for all those from 1526 who were haled before the bishops for reading an English New Testament, thrown into jail and, not infrequently, burned alive. This was being done to English Bible readers, not only by diehard conservatives who maintained that the original Bible language was Latin and who hated Erasmus, but by the leaders of the new learning, friends of Erasmus: Bishop Tunstall, who twice burned Tyndale's Testaments; Archbishop Warham, who bought them up and burned them, and in 1530, with Fisher's support, sent the mild Thomas Hitton to the stake. Thomas More, Erasmus's closest English friend, gave years of his time and gallons of ink to attacking Tyndale, and wished that more New Testament readers had gone to the fire.

Those men attacked Tyndale's New Testament because to them it was full of 'error'. So, were Tyndale's 'betters' deliberating on their own English New Testament? Let us look first at Henry VIII's Preface, written about the end of 1526, to the English edition of his famous letter against Luther (the one which earned him from the pope the title of *Fidei Defensor* ('Defender of the Faith', still held by British monarchs, with 'F.D.' still on all British coins). The king denounced Luther because he 'fell in device with one or two lewd persons born in this our realm [Tyndale and Roy] for the translating of the New Testament into English'. He says that by the counsel of his prelates he means to burn the book (Tyndale's Testament) and sharply punish its readers. If, he tells his subjects, they will not 'descant upon scripture, nor trust too much your own comments and interpretations', but in all doubtful points follow the advice of their pastoral fathers of the soul, then well-learned men will be encouraged to translate into English 'many good things and virtuous'. He goes on to attack the 'false and erroneous translations corrupted' by 'evil disposed persons'. He announces that 'good men and well-learned may be percase in time coming the bolder . . .' The result will be a New Testament 'truly and faithfully translated, substantially viewed and corrected, by sufficient authority to put in your hands'. The key word here is the obsolete adverb 'percase'. It means 'perchance', or something hypothetical, a tantalisingly distant hope for would-be Bible readers. If the people will be good and become more submissive, the great and the good 'may be percase in time coming the bolder' to give them an authorised New Testament. So much for urgency.[7]

Henry would have written this – if he wrote it at all – after consultation. It tallies near enough with what Thomas More expounded in his *Dialogue* against Tyndale. A year after More wrote that book, the question of making an official English Bible was discussed at length at an assembly of divines convened by the king. Tunstall, Gardiner and Latimer were joined by More, and Archbishop Warham presided. On 24 May 1530, Warham put out a Public Instrument in the name of his colleagues, explaining that the people felt that it was the king's duty to have the Scripture translated into English, and so the king had asked these men to assist him. The Archbishop reassures readers that they had all debated the matter fully and with the greatest freedom. The arguments on each side had been stated. But finally it appeared that the people had no right to demand the vernacular Scripture; it is not necessary for Christian men to have it: because it could work only harm, the king and prelates do well in refusing it. The temper of the people might change for the better, however, [that is, they might become more submissive] so the king has made a promise in presence of the divines. He

> did there openly say and protest that he would cause the New Testament to be by learned men faithfully and purely translated into the English tongue, to the intent that he might have it in his hands ready to be given to his people.[8]

This would be as soon as he could do so without fear of its misuse. In a royal proclamation a month later, the king's undertaking to make a new translation has dwindled. Now he says that if his people would abandon Tyndale's versions and all erroneous and heretic opinions:

> His highness intendeth to provide that the Holy Scripture shall be by great learned and catholic persons translated into the English tongue, if it shall then seem to his grace convenient so to be.[9]

Nothing in fact happened. On 1 December 1530 Latimer wrote to the king:

Other men have showed your Grace their minds, how necessary it is to have the scripture in English. The which thing also your Grace hath promised by your last proclamation: the which promise I pray God that your gracious Highness may shortly perform, even today, before tomorrow. Nor let not the wickedness of these worldly-wise men detain you from your Godly purpose and promise.[10]

In June 1530, Henry made a proclamation 'with the advice of his honourable council' damning erroneous books and heresies, and 'prohibiting the having of holy scripture, translated into the vulgar tongues of English, French or Duche [German] . . .'. In it are named five books, by Tyndale, Simon Fish and John Frith. Tyndale's are *Wicked Mammon* and *Obedience*, though the 'holy scripture' is his as well, of course.[11]

In the following summer, 1531, Stephen Vaughan, in his conversations with Tyndale just outside Antwerp, reported that Tyndale promised that he would immediately cease all his controversial writings, and come over to England to kneel at the royal feet, if the king would license an English Bible, by whomever translated, and as a bare text only.[12] Nearly two years later, this challenge was repeated by John Frith, writing on behalf of Tyndale and himself. The king made no reply.[13] In December 1534 Chapuys reported that fifteen English New Testaments had been burned by the order of the lord chancellor, Audely. There was no motion of any kind towards an English Bible, either from Henry or the bishops.

CRANMER'S PROJECTED BISHOPS' BIBLE, 1534

When Thomas Cranmer became Archbishop of Canterbury on 30 March 1533, a fresh attempt was made. The Convocation of Canterbury in their sessions of autumn 1534, in both Houses, gave a great deal of attention to the matter of heresy and to the English books which were flooding in from overseas. On 19 December, the Upper House resolved that the Archbishop should approach the king and beg him to order first, that all owners of suspected books should exhibit them within three months to persons appointed for the purpose. Cranmer was also to ask the king to order that: 'The Holy Scripture should be translated into the vulgar English tongue, by certain good and learned men, to be nominated by his Majesty, and should be delivered to the people for their instruction.' A third request was intended to curb the presumption of laymen to dispute on faith or Scripture.[14]

What happened next we learn obliquely from a manuscript, formerly possessed by John Foxe, in the hand of Cranmer's secretary Ralph Morice.

The writer is describing the wit of Thomas Lowney, then Chaplain to the Archbishop, and formerly Chaplain of Wolsey's college at Oxford, where he had been imprisoned in 1528 on suspicion of heresy, with, among others, John Frith. The writer explains how Bishop Stokesley had replied to Cranmer on the matter of the translation of the New Testament. It seems that it had been divided into nine or ten parts, and these parts sent to 'The best learned Bishops and other learned men' for their 'Perfect correction thereof', to be sent back to Lambeth by a certain day.

> It chanced that the Acts of the Apostles were sent to bishop Stokesley to oversee and correct, then Bishop of London. When the day came, every man had sent to Lambeth their parts correct: only Stokesley's portion wanted. My lord of Canterbury wrote to the Bishop letters for his part, requiring to deliver them unto the bringer thereof, his secretary. Bishop Stokesly being at Fulham received the letters, unto the which he made this answer: I marvel what my lord of Canterbury meaneth that thus abuseth the people in giving them liberty to read the scriptures, which doth nothing else but infect them with heresies. I have bestowed never an hour upon my portion, nor never will. And therefore my lord shall have his book again, for I will never be guilty to bring the simple people into error.
>
> My lord of Canterbury's servant took the book, and brought the same to Lambeth unto my lord, declaring my lord of London's answer. When my lord had perceived that the Bishop had done nothing therein, I marvel, quod my lord of Canterbury, that my lord of London is so froward, that he will not do as other men do. Mr Lowney stood by, hearing my lord speak so much of the Bishop's untowardness, said:
>
> I can tell your grace why my lord of London will not bestow any labour or pain this way. Your Grace knoweth well (quod Lowney) that his portion is a piece of New Testament. And then he being persuaded that Christ had bequeathed him nothing in his testament thought it mere madness to bestow any labour or pain where no gain was to be gotten. And besides this, it is the Acts of the Apostles, which were simple poor fellows, and therefore my lord of London disdained to have to do with any of their acts.[15]

Thomas Cranmer and others laughed, but such a reply told him that the project was doomed. The Bishop of Winchester, Stephen Gardiner, wrote to Cromwell on 10 June 1535 that he had just completed his portion, the Gospels of Luke and John.[16] We do not know what had happened to any other sections of the New Testament, and we notice that there is no reference at all to the Old Testament. What Cranmer had asked his colleagues to do was to revise and 'correct' Tyndale. We know that Gardiner was very hostile to the idea of an English Bible. His later attempts to 'improve' the Great Bible in 1542 show how ruthless his work must have been on Tyndale's Gospels.[17] Cranmer's excellent intentions had been defeated: he wrote to Cromwell in 1537 praising Matthew's Bible and begging that the king might license it 'until such time that we bishops shall set forth a better translation, which I think will not be til a day after doomsday'.[18]

JOYE AND ROY

Meanwhile, George Joye was himself translating some Old Testament books from Latin into English, and had printed part of Genesis in a large format. Tyndale's letter to Frith, written from Antwerp towards the end of May 1533, states that he had sent two leaves

> to the King and another to the new Queen [Anne, . . .] that he might so go through all the bible. Out of that is sprung the noise of the new bible: and out of that is the great seeking for English books at all printers and book binders in Antwerp, and for an English Priest that should print.[19]

Nothing came of this. Exactly a year later, in May 1534, Joye published with Martin de Keyser his own translation of Jeremiah and Lamentations. Joye had previously printed his *Primer*, the first in English, in Antwerp: it had contained thirty Psalms in English.[20] Medieval manuscript primers were popular small books of devotions in Latin, for laymen. In January 1530, Joye had produced a version of the Psalms, with de Keyser, and, in 1531, of Isaiah. These versions were not from the Hebrew, but from the Latin versions prepared by Bucer or Zwingli. Joye also translated Proverbs and Ecclesiastes.[21] Just over two decades later, in 1545, he produced a very long exposition of Daniel, which even his biographers call 'by all odds Joye's longest and most tiresome book'.[22] Joye's general method was to stay close to his main authority (usually Zwingli) but to introduce variations from the Vulgate and elsewhere. He was not trying for any literal accuracy, and he liked to fill out the text with words and ideas of his own. His trick of coining compounds is taken from the German translators: he may have anticipated Coverdale with 'saving health' (they were both being printed by de Keyser) and we also owe to him the word 'backslide'. These have survived, but his inventions of 'backfall' or 'flockfeeder' have not.[23]

Joye did not break new ground. He made no fresh work from the Hebrew. Early on he showed a certain gift with trenchant English. Yet he was an innovator in that all the books he translated into English had not been touched by Tyndale. Since they were all printed before Coverdale finished his 1535 complete Bible, Coverdale himself presumably made use of them. It is difficult to imagine that the two men did not know each other, as both were working for Martin de Keyser at the same time, at least in 1534. A matter of some delicacy arises here. If Coverdale really was acting as proof-corrector for de Keyser at that time (see chapter 11 below), he very likely saw Joye's little books through the press. It is thus the more surprising that he makes so little use of them himself. Common phrases can be attributed to common sources, such as Zwingli. Work remains to be done relating Coverdale's finished work on these books and Joye's attempts.[24] The available evidence suggests that, had Joye been able to translate into English an entire Bible, it would have been inadequate. Yet God moves in a mysterious way. Joye's translations certainly filled a gap, and there are moments in them which have merit. John Bale described him as *fidelis ac robustus veritati assertor* ('a loyal and vigorous advocate of the truth').[25] Whatever his personal faults, Joye did endure two long and difficult exiles for his religion.

Tyndale's helper William Roy parted from him in the spring of 1526, and left for Strasbourg. Here he translated from the Latin a theological tract originally written in German, *A Brief Dialogue between a Christian Father and His Stubborn Son*, with a preface dated 31 August 1527. The Preface is of considerable interest in that he comments on his work with Tyndale, entirely in the light of its importance and the hostility it produced. Roy is defensive about accusations that as his father was a Jew, he will be in some way inadequate – he denies both charges. He goes on: 'whose cruel tyranny foxy cavillation and resistance have more inflamed my heart and couraged my mind to go about the translation of holy scripture, in so much that I have already partly translated certain books of the Old Testament, the which, with the help of God ere long shall be brought to light'.[26] Roy was writing this book in order that plain folk may know 'how to demean themselves in the profound mysteries and great judgements of God, contained in the Old Testament and Prophets'. He asks his readers to pray for help that he may translate the whole Old Testament, 'whereby ye of England may also know and hear the voice of your true shepherd, walk in his way, follow the truth, and finally obtain everlasting life. Amen'.

Whether Roy had indeed translated any of the Old Testament is unknown. Certainly he never printed even a single short Old Testament book. There is no evidence of any knowledge of Hebrew in Roy, so he was presumably thinking of translating from a Latin version, to which might be added the Septuagint; Tyndale would have made use of Roy's Greek. Tyndale tells us that he did not think highly of Roy's capacity to finish things: he noted on the first page of his *Mammon* that, in Strasbourg, Roy 'professeth wonderful faculties and maketh boast of no small things'; and in that Prologue 'he promiseth more a great deal than I fear me he will ever pay'.[27]

It may be that there was a general lack of trustworthiness in Roy. When in 1516 Erasmus was preparing the first printed edition of the Greek New Testament, he found no Greek manuscript that included the 'Johannine comma', the verse in the Vulgate about the 'three that bear record in heaven' (1 John 5:7), a most significant crux. He wrote that if he ever found a Greek manuscript containing the verse, he would insert it in later editions. He was soon sent such a manuscript, and he did include it (to his later regret). The manuscript he received, the Montfort Codex, was a new copy, made between 1519 and 1522, of the Leicester Codex used by Erasmus, owned by the Franciscan House at Cambridge, and now made with the aim of showing Erasmus to be in multiple error. Among changes to the Leicester original was the inclusion of the disputed verse.

It thus appeared in all translations dependent on that Greek text (which became the *Textus Receptus*, long revered), including the 1611 King James Bible. The first owner of the Montfort was a friar Froye, who was probably the copyist. In 1887, James Rendell Harris argued that this name is probably 'fratis Roye'.[28] William Roy, Cambridge Franciscan, could have been devious enough to make this forgery. The matter has to remain in question.

CONTINUED OPPOSITION

Official opposition to the Bible in English flickered on and off, at various strengths, expressed in declarations attempting to control either the translations, or their notes. Henry VIII's proclamation of 16 November 1538 tried to prohibit the import of 'naughty printed books' from abroad, and the use, on English books printed at home, of '*Cum privilegio regali*, without adding *ad imprimendum solum*'.[29] No one was to import 'any books of divine scripture in the English tongue, with any annotations in the margin' unless they had been examined first.[30]

In 1543, 'Parliament proscribed all translations bearing the name of Tyndale, and required that the notes in all other copies should be removed or obliterated'.[31] There exists in the Bible Society's collection a copy of Matthew's 1537 Bible in which the prologues and notes throughout the volume have been inked over to obliterate them, apparently in response to this edict.[32]

At the same time it was enacted that no women (except noble or gentle women), no artificers, apprentices, journeymen, serving-men, husband-men, or labourers, should read to themselves or to others, publicly or privately, any part of the Bible under pain of imprisonment. Three years later (1546) the king repeated the prohibition against Tyndale's books with many others [. . .]. Thus the Great Bible alone remained unforbidden.[33]

It seems that no one was imprisoned; but there was a great burning of earlier New Testaments, and whole Bibles. 'But in the midst of this reaction Henry died (Jan. 28, 1547). The accession of Edward restored the reforming party to power.'[34] At the young king's coronation, he is said to have insisted that in preference to the three swords presented to him as signs of his three kingdoms, the Bible should be presented: '"That book", added he, "is the Sword of the Spirit, and to be preferred before these swords . . .".'[35]

THOMAS MORE AS BIBLE TRANSLATOR

The fiercest opposition to the 'heretical' makers of freely available English Bibles had been from Sir Thomas More. It is striking, then, to see that scattered throughout his voluminous, and largely polemic, writings are short passages of the Vulgate translated into English.[36] In most of them, the Latin quotation comes first, as being obviously (to More) the true biblical text. Thus in *A Dialogue of Comfort*, in the course of a section about Christ's prayers during his Passion, he writes:

> For proof whereof they [great learned men] lay in these words the authority of Saint Paul, *Cristus humiliauit semet ipsum factus obediens usque ad mortem mortem autem crucis* [. . . ; Philippians 2:8, going on to verse 11]. Christ hath humbled himself, and become obedient unto the death, and that unto the death of the cross, for which thing God hath also exalted him, and given him a name which is above all names, that in the name of Jesus every knee be bowed both of the celestial creatures and the terrestrial and of the infernal too, and that every tongue shall confess that our Lord Jesus Christ is in the glory of god his father.[37]

This is in many ways familiar. Tyndale in 1526 had: 'He humbled himself and became obedient unto the death, even the death of the cross. Where-fore God hath exalted him, and given him a name above all names, that in the name of Jesus should every knee bow . . .' More's Latinate 'celestial creatures . . . terrestrial . . . infernal' are unlike Tyndale's 'things in heaven, and things in earth, and things under earth'. More follows the Vulgate, *in gloria est dei patris* in his last phrase, whereas Tyndale's 'unto the praise of God the Father' is closer to the Greek.

Elsewhere, and more commonly, More simply paraphrases and Englishes the Latin. In the same work, *A Dialogue of Comfort*, a quotation from 1 Corinthians 2:9, *Nec oculis vidit, ne auris audiuit, nec in cor hominis ascendit, que preparuit deus diligentibus se*, is followed by:

> For surely for the state of this world, the Joys of heaven are by mans mouth unspeakable, to mans ears not audible, to mens hearts uncogitable, so farforth excell they all that ever men have heard of, all that ever men can speak of, and all that ever any man can by natural possibility think on.[38]

The expansion, even to volubility, is typical; and he still has not reached the last five Latin words. (Tyndale there has: 'The eye hath not seen, and the ear hath not heard, neither have entered into the heart of man, the things which God hath prepared for them that love him.')

In More's *A Treatise upon the Passion* there is a Latin quotation, from John 13:2–17 (Jesus washing the feet of the disciples), followed by the same passage in More's English.[39] This is Tyndalian in its straightforward economy and directness, but just occasionally awkward ('that likewise as I have done to you, so should you do too' – the repetition of the similar sound in the last seven words can sound like an owl). Several sentences are almost word–for–word Tyndale:

> Jesus knowing that his father had given him all things in to his hands, and that he was come from God and goeth to God [. . . ,] Jesus answered and said unto him, what I do thou knowest not now, but thou shalt know after. Peter saith unto him: Thou shalt never wash my feet. Jesus answered unto him: If I wash thee not thou shalt have no part with me.

Towards the end, More makes Jesus say 'Verily verily I say unto you . . .'. That is Tyndale's invention (Wyclif LV had 'truly, truly') and his formula, throughout John's Gospel, went right through into KJV and far beyond, only Rheims having instead 'Amen, amen'.

More's closeness to Tyndale is enough to argue for dependence, though this has not been stated before. After all, More had the Bishop of London's permission to read Tyndale. Work remains to be done in tracking all More's Bible quotations in English and comparing them with Tyndale. A first examination suggests that More (translating always from the Vulgate) worked in two ways: either making his own short phrase, as in James 4:7 and 1 Peter 5:9 'Stand stiff against the devil'[40], but often expanding and paraphrasing; and direct, and silent, borrowing from Tyndale. A senior More scholar recently wished 'that More had made his own English translation of Erasmus's Greek New Testament instead of writing polemical works'.[41] More's Greek was excellent: his Englishing, it seems, at least on half the evidence, might have been lively. How different the decades following could have been.

The opening pages of More's *A Treatise upon the Passion* have many quotations from Genesis 1 and 3, from the Latin; these are less translations than long, and entertaining, fantasias on the words.[42] There are as well a host of shorter phrases throughout the fifteen large volumes of the *Complete Works*. The longest passage, found in *The Answer to a Poisoned Book*, is of John 6:41–66. It varies very little from Tyndale.[43] It is said that More translated from the Latin, 'so, as in the Wyclif versions, there is a greater use of participles'.[44] Latin word order occasionally jars. More prefers 'descended' to Tyndale's 'came down' – the Latin influence again, though later Wyclif has 'came down'. But often the changes are tiny: to Tyndale's 'He that eateth this bread shall live ever', More adds 'for' before 'ever' (v. 58); to Tyndale's last sentence, 'From that time many of his disciples went back, and walked no more with him', More simply adds 'now' before 'walked' (v. 66).

Sir Thomas More does his reputation no favours in his dealings with those he regards as heretics; close to home, men were reported as flogged, tortured and killed: further off, Luther, Tyndale and others were venomously attacked. Yet, while vicious about half a dozen words in Tyndale's New Testament ('congregation', 'love', 'repent', 'senior' and so on), More clearly respected Tyndale's skill as a translator and power with English. More recognised that English is a proper language. That Tyndale invented an English language in which to translate the Bible it would be impossible for More to acknowledge, yet his imitation was, surprisingly, the sincerest flattery.

Chapter 11

COVERDALE'S BIBLE, 1535

IN ENGLAND, AFTER THE ARRIVAL and eager reception of Tyndale's 1526 New Testament, in various editions amounting to many thousands of copies, the mood was changing. Many people were reading the New Testament in English. Foxe later reprinted from this time *A Compendious old Treatise, showing how that we ought to have the Scripture English*, probably to be dated 1531. After giving many historical examples of the Scriptures being naturally in the mother tongue, it concludes:

> Of these foresaid authorities it is proved lawful, that both men and women lawfully may read and write God's law in their mother-tongue, and they that forfend this, they show themselves ... the very disciples of Antichrist ... in stopping and perverting of God's law. ...[1]

The conservative bishops were seriously alarmed. Not only was heresy abroad, and spreading. Not only was a properly ordered and united nation, which should be naturally under their control, being threatened by a small gang of organised, professional malcontents – plotting outside England, using the very latest technology, and obviously, as the age-old argument always has it, funded from abroad, in this case Wittenberg. Worse, the very idea of national Church was about to be undermined. As Stephen Gardiner put it in 1546, 'each one man [that is, with an English Bible] to be a church alone'.[2] Worst of all, as Tunstall is said to have remarked, 'They will see what we do.'

The pressure from below was unmistakable. Thomas More, relentless enemy of reform of any kind, took on board at least the notion of the Scriptures in something other than Latin. Richard Nix, Bishop of Norwich, complained of those who read the New Testaments in English, 'if they continue any time I think they shall undo us all'.[3]

Nothing ever came of Cranmer's project, begun in 1533, for a Bishops' Bible. The bishops claimed to be too busy. In 1542, Richard Grafton noted in a letter to Cromwell that 'it is now seven years, since the Bishops promised to translate, and set forth the Bible, and as yet they have no leisure'.[4] Cranmer in 1537 urged Cromwell towards the licensing of Matthew's Bible until, as quoted above, 'such time as we bishops shall set forth a better translation, which I think will not be til a day after doomsday'.[5]

THE FIRST COMPLETE PRINTED BIBLE IN ENGLISH

Miles Coverdale's great distinction, working abroad, was, first of all, to have translated and printed for the first time, in 1535, a complete English Bible. This handsome folio, containing the Old and New Testaments and the Apocrypha, with its two columns of angular text well placed on the page, light marginal annotation and 158 illustrations, has to be greatly valued. It rightly stands at the head of the different complete Bible versions in English in the sixteenth and early seventeenth centuries, and all those that came thereafter until the year 2000. It demands the fullest attention.

Further, it was the second half of the Old Testament in 'Coverdale' which made up 'Thomas Matthew's' complete Bible of 1537, the twenty-five books that Tyndale did not reach before his execution. It was this that carried forward the stream of the English Bible, into the Great Bible of 1539, from there to the various Geneva versions, and the Bishops' Bible, and thus to the King James Bible. This was, and was not, a fine thing.

Quite extensive passages of the poetic books and prophets in KJV are, to put it mildly, difficult to follow ('Woe to the land shadowing with wings . . . that sendeth ambassadors by the sea, even in vessels of bulrushes upon the waters, saying Go . . . to a nation scattered and peeled, to a people terrible from their beginning thereto . . .', Isaiah 18:1,2). At the same time, passages from those same poetic books and prophets can catch a reader's breath with beauty ('when the morning stars sang together, and all the sons of God shouted for joy', Job 38:7). Both passages in KJV came directly from Coverdale.

Third, the Great Bible itself (the only English Bible that was ever authorised) was Coverdale's work, revising his own version with both more attention to Tyndale, and a faint but observable direction back towards the Latin.

THE TITLE

Coverdale's 1535 Bible is a big, weighty folio, impressively and elaborately printed in Black Letter. It announces itself as follows (modernised spelling):

Biblia / The Bible: that is, the holy Scripture of the Old and New Testament, faithfully and truly translated out of Douche and Latin into English, MCXXXV. S. Paul. II Tessa.III. Pray for us, that the word of God may have free passage & be glorified./S.Paul. Coloss.III. Let the word of Christ dwell in you plenteously in all wisdom, &c./Josue.l. Let not the Book of this law depart out of thy mouth, but exercise thy self therein day and night.

Though in size far from being a book for the pocket like all Tyndale's, and though his translation did not set a new standard of English prose as Tyndale's did, Coverdale showed the nation what an English Bible might look like. As King Henry VIII broke decisively from Rome, declaring himself 'the only supreme head on earth of the Church of England',[6] here was a well-printed, complete Bible, having both Testaments in full, and the Apocrypha, with some marginal notes and references, and, after the first edition, preliminary pages of advice and help.

The title-page to Coverdale's Bible is by Hans Holbein the Younger. It is a statement not even so much of being 'BIBLIA' in English for the first time, as of the new iconic position of King Henry VIII (fig. 10). He whom, only a little more than a decade before, Pope Leo X had named 'Defender of the Faith', is now shown as a powerful Reformation monarch. No doubt Thomas Cromwell had sponsored the Holbein image,

> even though the king himself rejected change in the official theology and hierarchical structure of church government . . . as a publicly available means of validating Henry's claim to govern without clerical intercession as the sole intermediary between temporal society and the divine order.[7]

The compartments and emblazoned texts tell the story from Adam to Christ, the king himself wielding 'the sword of the Spirit' and the Book 'which is the Word of God' (Ephesians 6:17), flanked by David and Paul, symbolising revelation before and after Christ. On either side of the title, each compartment balances Old and New Testaments: Moses receives, and Esdras preaches, the Law; Christ sends out the Apostles, who then preach the new law at Pentecost – and the keys they carry undermine papal claims of sole right to St Peter's keys. The vertical axis links the Name of God at the top and the monarch below, King Henry's direct line of spiritual authority.[8]

What propelled Coverdale to do the work is not known. Perhaps he knew even before 1534 that the new Archbishop, Cranmer, was hoping to set in motion a project for an authorised English translation; Coverdale could have heard of it from Cromwell. Perhaps he understood the reality of the danger to Tyndale, and feared that he might not finish. Perhaps, with the same understanding, knowing from Cromwell the power of the emperor, and just what offence King Henry was causing him by divorcing Catherine (and Cromwell had had a difficult audience with the emperor on that very matter), Cromwell encouraged Coverdale to do it. There is a tradition that the Secretary gave him financial support.

Coverdale's translation work, in the words of A. S. Herbert, 'does not rank beside Tyndale's'.[9] This is because Coverdale knew neither Hebrew nor Greek. Although his first title-page declares it to be 'faithfully translated into English', it is only in the later editions that it is stated '. . . faithfully and truly translated out of Douche [that is, German] and Latin'; and not until the Dedication to the King beginning the eight preliminary leaves in those later printings, that we find Coverdale noting that 'I have purely and faithfully translated this out of five sundry interpreters.' In the Prologue that follows, 'Miles Coverdale Unto the Christian Reader', he elaborates a little: 'And to help me herein, I have had sundry translations, not only in Latin, but also of the Douche interpreters: whom (because of their singular gifts and special diligence in the Bible) I have been the more glad to follow for the most part.'

The 'five sundry interpreters' turn out to have been the Swiss-German version of the whole Bible made by Zwingli and Leo Juda, printed at Zurich between 1524 and 1529, a version emphasising grace and flow of phrase rather than exactness to the original; the rather curious and over-literal Latin version of the Old Testament made by Sanctes Pagninus, first published in 1528; Luther's German Bible, completed in 1532; the Vulgate; and Tyndale for the New Testament and half the Old.

EARLIER LIFE

Miles Coverdale was born in York in 1488, and was ordained priest in Norwich in 1514. He became an Augustinian friar and went to the house of his order in Cambridge, where he was greatly influenced by the new prior, Robert Barnes, who 'caused the house shortly to flourish with good letters' – Terence, Plautus and Cicero are named.[10] Barnes was increasingly drawn to the movement for religious reform, and 'read openly in the house Paul's Epistles'.[11] He was converted 'wholly unto Christ'. The first sermon in which Barnes followed the Scripture and Luther, given on Christmas Eve 1525, led to his immediate arrest as a heretic. Coverdale was at his side, and, in London, helped to prepare his defence before Wolsey.

Back in Cambridge, Coverdale took his degree. The English historian John Bale, twenty years later, recalled Coverdale at this time. The sketch can stand as an epigraph for all his life:

> Under the mastership of Robert Barnes he drank in good learning with a burning thirst. He was a young man of friendly and upright nature and very gentle spirit, and when the church of England revived, he was one of the first to make a pure profession of Christ . . . ; he gave himself wholly, to propagating the truth of Jesus Christ's gospel and manifesting his glory. . . . The spirit of God . . . is in some a vehement wind, overturning mountains and rocks, but in him it is a still small voice comforting wavering hearts. His style is charming and gentle, flowing limpidly along: it moves and instructs and delights.[12]

Some time before 1527 Coverdale probably met Thomas Cromwell. In a letter to him, 'from the Augustin's this May-day', Coverdale wrote that he had begun to taste of holy Scriptures, but that he required books to help him to a knowledge of the doctors. He desired nothing but books, and would be guided by Cromwell as to his conduct and in the instruction of others.[13] The fact that an Augustinian friar in the late 1520s could find it noteworthy that he was reading the Bible is one thing to observe: another is some shift, even in a few years, in the universities' idea of theology. As noted above, Tyndale in his *Obedience of a Christian Man* of 1528 is scathing about Oxford in his own time a decade before, where theology was Aristotle and fashionable theory, with not a glimpse of even a word of Scripture. Now Miles Coverdale as a friar in Cambridge 'has begun to taste of holy scriptures'.

Coverdale continued to move towards reform. By Lent 1528 he had left the Augustinians and, 'going in the habit of a secular priest',[14] he preached in Essex against transubstantiation, the worship of images and confession to the ear. These were dangerous views, and being, as John Hooker put it, in danger that 'he should above all others be burned',[15] towards the end of 1528 he fled overseas.

His movements in the seven years of this first exile, 1528–35, are uncertain. It is possible that Coverdale was meant in Tyndale's account in his *Parable of the Wicked Mammon* (1528) of the making of his first English translation of the New Testament three years before:

> While I abode a faithful companion, which now hath taken another voyage upon him, to preach Christ where I suppose he was never yet preached (God, which put in his heart thither to go, send his spirit with him, comfort him, and bring his purpose to good effect) . . .[16]

William Roy offered his help instead, and was not wholly satisfactory.[17] The words '. . . another voyage . . . to preach Christ where . . . he was never yet preached . . .' and so on come to a modern reader with tones of courageous missionary work in primitive jungles, yet it seems to refer to Essex. Though the identification with Tyndale's hoped-for helper is seductive, it can be no more than speculation.

Foxe in *Acts and Monuments* has Coverdale in Hamburg for most of 1529, invited by Tyndale to help him retranslate the Pentateuch. The two men worked, Foxe writes, 'on the whole five books of Moses, from Easter till December, in the house of a worshipful widow, Mistress Margaret Van Emmersen, AD 1529; a great sweating sickness being at the same time'.[18] Foxe is attractively specific. Perhaps Coverdale was indeed there; yet the story Foxe tells has too much against it. It is only a few lines in his last, 1576, version of *Acts and Monuments*. There, Tyndale suddenly sails from Antwerp to Hamburg to print his Pentateuch, and loses everything in a shipwreck on the coast of Holland. He proceeds to Hamburg and meets Coverdale there by appointment, and sets about remaking his entire Pentateuch. For Tyndale to have gone to Hamburg makes no sense. Antwerp, where Protestantism first took root in the Low Countries, in 1529 had many fine printers with established trade with Britain. Among them was the dependable Martin de Keyser, who had already printed Tyndale's *Mammon* and *Obedience*. De Keyser would go on to print his other books, including his revised New Testament in 1534. Tyndale had no reason to commit to an unknown printer in Hamburg the first translation ever made from Hebrew into English, his next most precious work after his 1526 New Testament. Coverdale, an educated Christian, was no doubt enriching company for Tyndale; and like Tyndale he had an admirable ear for the rhythms of English. But he knew neither Hebrew nor Greek and would have been of small use for work on the Pentateuch. Comparison of Tyndale and Coverdale translating those five Old Testament books shows the distance in method between the two men, and the unlikelihood of collaboration.

The shipwreck story is certainly dramatic. The most significant point against it, however, is that, though the Prologue to that very Pentateuch is where Tyndale tells us most about himself, he makes no mention of it at all. Nor does Coverdale. Nor does anyone else at the time. Foxe first has it in his last version: perhaps his steady bent in successive editions of his *Acts* to align events in the life of Tyndale, 'the Apostle to the English', with the biblical book of Acts, in which the climactic event is Paul's near-calamitous shipwreck, helped him to feel free to elaborate, in the ancient tradition of writing the lives of saints.[19]

COVERDALE IN ANTWERP

Where Coverdale made his translation, and where his first, and most important, edition was printed has been a mystery. A. S. Herbert sums up: 'It has long been assumed that this was the work of Christopher Froschover of Zurich but the evidence appears to be strongly in favour of E. Cervicornus (Hirtzhorn) and J. Soter (Heil) of Cologne or Marburg.'[20]

Now, we know that Coverdale spent some time in the first half of the 1530s with at least one printer of English books in Antwerp: he is recorded as having corrected proof. Tyndale lived in Antwerp from about 1528 to August 1535: his printer, Martin de Keyser (who was also 'Hans Luft of Marlborow', as noted in the previous chapter) was only one in that city full of busy printers (one street alone contained over sixty print-shops) who made good books in English to be shipped to English and Scottish ports. Antwerp was where fine Bibles in Dutch and French were being made. Antwerp was where John Rogers made his Matthew's Bible, published in 1537 (see chapter 12 below). Moreover, records show that the expenses of Coverdale's English Bible were, at least partly, met by a merchant in Antwerp who had trade links with England, Jacob van Meteren, whose daughter married John Rogers.[21] Coverdale himself seems to allude to that arrangement with van Meteren in his Dedication, 'as the holy ghost moved other men to do the cost hereof', and his Prologue, where he states that he was 'instantly required' to do the work, because he grieved that 'other nations should be more plenteously provided for with the scripture in their mother tongue than we'.[22] These words would apply also to joint help, and an imperative, from England.

Antwerp would be a natural place for the printing of Coverdale's English Bible. Recent work by the Belgian scholar Guido Latré of the Catholic University of Leuven has shown, almost beyond doubt, that Coverdale's English Bible of 1535 was indeed printed in Antwerp. Not only was it printed there: it was made by Martin de Keyser himself. In the light of increasing knowledge of Antwerp from the 1530s as the continental centre of the making of fine vernacular Bibles, this makes sense.

The brief record of Jacob van Meteren's life concludes:

He knew how to distinguish light from darkness, and showed his zeal more especially in bearing the cost of the translation and printing of the English Bible at Antwerp, using for this purpose the services of a learned student named Miles Coverdale, to the great advancement of the kingdom of Jesus Christ in England.[23]

Though he gave no authorities, in 1868 a German scholar, J. P. Gelpert, claimed that Coverdale worked as a 'corrector' (proofreader) with Martin de Keyser in Antwerp. That is not at all unlikely. Native English readers would have been scarce in the city, and in demand for the lively book trade with Britain. It is known that in 1534 and 1535 Coverdale was in Antwerp. Foxe writes that in 1534 John Rogers joined Tyndale and Coverdale there.[24] Independent confirmation may be found in George Joye's tale of how in Antwerp in February 1535 he scorned Tyndale 'and his two disciples that gaped so long for their master's morsel' of Bible translation.[25] Joye, as usual, had a bone to pick – indeed, an axe to grind – and he was smarting under Tyndale's quite justified public rebuke of him for silently altering his 1534 New Testament.[26] He suggests that the two 'disciples' were waiting for Tyndale's work. Coverdale was himself translating the whole Bible: Joye, supporting Foxe, usefully locates him in Antwerp. John Rogers, chaplain to the English House in Antwerp, after Tyndale's execution printed the work of Tyndale and Coverdale to make his 1537 Matthew's Bible (see chapter 12 below): he may have begun some time before Tyndale's arrest, envisioning with him a complete Tyndale Bible with some fresh annotation. Joye gives an impression of Tyndale helping both men, which has not been the usual picture.

The printing of this whole Bible in English was, Coverdale states, finished on 4 October 1535. He gave the people of Britain what so many wanted; a printed English whole Bible. All the reformers, across Europe, insisted that the Scriptures should be taken whole, not in measured droplets. Printing a complete Bible was – and still is – a large undertaking, but it was something that Antwerp printers were accustomed to do. Coverdale's Bible was printed in London, by James Nicholson in Southwark, remarkably soon, in 1537, in both folio and quarto size. Both printings were firsts: the first folio complete Bible printed in England, and the first quarto complete Bible printed in England.[27] Moreover, Coverdale's Bible, in its London printings, opened the eight preliminary leaves of the folio with a Dedication 'Unto the most victorious Prince and our most gracious sovereign Lord, king Henry the eighth . . .' – a dedication to the king, not yet a licence by him. The dedication is made less than twelve months from Tyndale's reported prayer at his death to open the King of England's eyes. A complete Bible in English, in two sizes, was openly printed in London, and dedicated to the king. There is more. The quarto edition, which though still printed in 1537, has to be assumed followed the folio, now has at the foot of the title 'Set forth with the king's most gracious licence'.

It has been pointed out that Cromwell licensed a New Testament drawn out of Coverdale's Bible, printed by James Nicolson four times, all in late

1537 or early 1538. It was printed in 1538 in Antwerp, once by William Montanus and four times by Matthew Crom. 'Thus in a three-year span this NT dominated the market, being printed nine times, by three different printers. It is, however, a virtual unknown in the history of the English Bible.'[28] (I add that these printings increase considerably the tally of English New Testaments circulating in Britain.)

> Coverdale added a number of textual aids to his NT, many of which he lifted from other sources, including Luther's 1536 German Bible and Tyndale's GH NT of 1535. These include Luther's prologue, the lengthy Romans preface from Tyndale, chapter summaries, marginal cross-references, and numerous glosses on the text.[29]

COVERDALE'S TRANSLATION

In telling phrases, C. S. Lewis remarked that among the great scholar-translators of the sixteenth century Coverdale 'shows like a rowing-boat among battleships. This gave him a kind of freedom . . . to select and combine by taste. Fortunately his taste was admirable.'[30] Imitating the Swiss and German Bibles Coverdale coined many compounds, some of which survived, like 'winebibber' at Proverbs 23:20; or did not, like 'unoutspeakable' at Romans 8:26; or should have done, like 'wintercool' at Proverbs 25:13. He has favourite forms, like 'tender mercies', 'lovingkindness' and the excellent 'saving health', all his coinages. His love of variation he defended in his Prologue to the reader as part of his pleasure in a variety of translations.

He followed Tyndale in keeping firmly to 'congregation', 'elder', 'love' and other central New Testament terms for which he had been so attacked, though he used 'penance' for 'repentance' occasionally, pointing out that the former should mean the turning of the whole being to God. His skill with synonyms was most helpful in the poetic and prophetic books of the second half of the Old Testament, where it is most needed: his grasp of the parallelism of Hebrew poetry produced many good passages. His is Isaiah 55:6 as it appears only slightly altered in KJV: 'Seek ye the Lord while he may be found, call upon him while he is nigh'; or, similarly, Psalm 137:1, 'By the waters of Babylon we sat down and wept when we remembered Sion'; and countless more. Unforgettably in Judges 5, Deborah 'brought forth butter in a lordly dish'.

It is instructive to observe Coverdale making his Psalms, with both Hebrew parallelism and congregational singing in mind. The Church of England at worship sang or said Coverdale every day for over four hundred

years, and it is not only singing Anglicans who regret the change from
Coverdale's

> Why do the heathen so furiously rage together: and why do the people
> imagine a vain thing?

to a modern

> Why are the nations in turmoil? Why do the peoples hatch their futile
> plots? (Psalm 2).[31]

Coverdale's Psalms are naturally musical. 'Naturally' does not mean by accident or mindless inspiration: they were crafted to be singable. Many people
cannot read those words of Coverdale in the second psalm without
hearing in their heads Handel's bass aria from *Messiah*. By contrast, the
modern spitting 't' sounds of 'hatch . . . futile . . . plots' feel unfortunate
(and probably defy being set to music, even by a master like Handel) after
the softer running 'n's of 'imagine a vain thing'. For all the spitting,
however, hatching futile plots makes stronger modern sense than imagining vain things.

Coverdale's

> The heavens declare the glory of God: and the firmament sheweth his
> handiwork.

becomes in that modern version

> The heavens tell out the glory of God, heaven's vault makes known his
> handiwork. (Psalm 19).

Both 'hatch their futile plots' and 'heaven's vault makes known', though
more understandable, are difficult mouthfuls. Psalms are poems which were
written to be sung, and are best so translated. Coverdale understood the
clarity produced by alternation of strong and light stresses, as in 'the
firm′ament show′eth his hand′iwork'. The four successive strong stresses
of 'heav′en's vault′ makes′ known″' do not make a congregation sing well.
It is not just familiarity that makes so fluid Coverdale's Psalm 63:

> O God, thou art my God: early will I seek thee.
> My soul thirsteth for thee, my flesh also longeth for thee: in a barren
> and dry land where no water is.

The modern version is bald:

> > God, you are my God; I seek you eagerly
> > with a heart that thirsts for you
> > and a body wasted with longing for you,
> > like a dry land, parched and devoid of water.

Something admirable there has been lost, to produce indeed a verbal 'dry land, parched . . .'. Modern jolting of square carriage-wheels is in Psalm 115: after Coverdale's flowing 'Not unto us, O Lord, not unto us . . .' in that modern version is 'Not to us, Lord, not to us . . .'.

Some of Coverdale's translations have been found 'quaint'. At Isaiah 5:27, for KJV's elevated, careful 'None shall be weary nor stumble among them; none shall slumber nor sleep', Coverdale has 'No one faint nor feeble among them, no not a sluggish nor sleepery person.' The 'certain man' at 1 Kings 22:34, who drew a bow at a venture, and in KJV 'smote the king of Israel between the joints of the harness', in Coverdale, 'shot the King of Israel between the maw and the lungs'. At Jeremiah 8:22, in KJV the haunting question 'Is there no balm in Gilead?' is in Coverdale the statement 'For there is no more Treacle at Galaad.' Psalm 91 has long been loved as the heart of the last office before sleep, Compline, and the phrases in KJV at verse 6, 'Thou shalt not be afraid of the terror by night; nor for the arrow that flieth by day . . .' hit home to the earliest settlers on the coasts of America, fearful of hidden Indians. Coverdale has 'Thou shalt not need to be afraid for any bugs by night', causing our fathers merriment, especially at the presence of a such a low word as 'bugs' in the Bible, making them name this 1535 Bible 'The Bug Bible' (or 'The Treacle Bible', treacle being equally low). But 'bug' was in the sense, surviving in 'bugbear', of a source of persistent dread: Wyclif LV has the splendid 'Of an arrow flying in the day, of a goblin going in darknesses'.

Coverdale's names for some of the Prophets and Writings are now unfamiliar, though not to those who know Wyclif. So for example Obadiah is Abdy, Zephaniah is Sophony, and the Song of Solomon is Salamaan's Balettes. These are simple accidents in the whirligig of time. Essential for evaluating Coverdale's Bible is appreciation of the sense he could show of English words and phrasing, sometimes equal to Tyndale's, and occasionally surpassing him. The five-talent man at the conclusion of Jesus' parable in Matthew 25 is praised, and bidden, instead of Tyndale's 'enter into thy master's joy', with Coverdale's 'enter thou in to the joy of thy lord'. Coverdale reintroduced the familiar 'the pride of life' at 1 John 2:16, for Tyndale's 'the pride of goods' (Wyclif LV has 'the pride of life', following the Vulgate's *superbia vitae*. (Since the Greek so clearly says 'life' (βίου, *biou*), one wonders where Tyndale's 'goods' came from.) At Matthew 21:42, Tyndale's 'The stone which the builders refused, the same is set in the principal part of the corner' Coverdale changes to 'is become the head-stone in the corner' – *caput anguli* in the Vulgate, 'the head of the corner' in Wyclif LV, Geneva, Rheims and KJV. Coverdale took Tyndale's 'similitudes' back to Wyclif's 'parables' at Matthew 13:13 and elsewhere: revising for the Great Bible he changed back to 'similitudes', which was taken over by the Geneva New Testament in 1557. KJV's 'parables' probably came again from Rheims, 1582 (the Vulgate has *parabolis*). Similarly, Coverdale at Matthew 16:23 takes Tyndale's 'not godly things, but worldly things' back to Wyclif's 'not the things that be of God: but the things that be of men'; that is closer to the Greek and the Vulgate, and was followed thereafter into KJV.

Coverdale, wanting his readers to understand, can be bold. Tyndale's 'the treasury' at Matthew 27:6 depends on our understanding that the Greek word κορβαν (*korban*) is a Hebrew word meaning specifically the treasury belonging to the Temple. Coverdale, changing it to 'God's chest', which at first feels clumsy, is good for the context, which is the suicide of Judas and 'the price of blood'. The reverse can apply. At verse 62 in the same chapter, Tyndale's 'good friday' is technically wrong but absolutely clear: Coverdale's 'the day of preparing' is hard to fix. Similarly, it is not easy to understand why Coverdale changed Tyndale at Romans 8:28, 'we know that all things work for the best unto them that love God', to which he reverted in the Great Bible, which went on to Geneva, and which is the basis of KJV ('good' rather than 'the best'), to 'But sure we are, that all things serve for the best unto them that love of God': he certainly did not take it from Luther or the Vulgate.

Coverdale can make long paraphrases (as in Ecclesiasticus 44) which in the end are too diffuse to clarify the matter. This device he is said to have borrowed from the Zurich Bible.[32] Sometimes his dependences served him well. At 1 John 3:17 Tyndale had 'shutteth up his compassion from him', coping satisfactory with the Greek σπλάγχνα (*splagxna*), literally the 'innards' (Wyclif LV has 'entrails'). The Rheims New Testament of 1582 gave 'shut his bowels from him', which is not nice. KJV noted Rheims but stumbled, trying to solve the problem by having both: 'shutteth up his bowels of compassion'. Coverdale, untroubled by the Greek problem, followed Luther to give 'shutteth up his heart'.

At Romans 8:35, Coverdale modernises Tyndale's '. . . other hunger? other nakedness? . . .' to '. . . or hunger? or nakedness? . . .'. Coverdale starts that list, instead of Tyndale's Latinist 'shall tribulation?', which went right through to KJV, with the simple, and piercing, 'Trouble?' To Coverdale we owe 'Seek the Lord while he may be found, call upon him while he is nigh' (Isaiah 55:6), changed by KJV only in the addition of 'ye' after each verb. Coverdale's Psalms are considered in more detail in discussion of the Great Bible, in the next chapter, but Psalm 102:25–7 merits quotation here:

> Thou, Lord, in the beginning hast laid the foundations of the earth, and the heavens are the works of thy hand.
> They shall perish, but thou shalt endure: they all shall wax old, as

doth a garment, and as a vesture shalt thou change them, and they shall be changed.

But thou art the same, and thy years shall not fail.

Where Coverdale is undoubtedly weak is in passages in the Prophets and Writings where his sources let him down, most noticeable perhaps in what one might call the 'Christological' verses of Second Isaiah, chapters 40–55. He also goes badly wrong in the first six chapters of Job. For some parts of his Old Testament after 2 Chronicles, Coverdale could have had several English models. The chief might have been Wyclif, whom he does not mention. Whether or not he used a Wyclif manuscript, or parts, can now be judged only from searching out unique parallels of style: frequent similarities of vocabulary arise from both using the Vulgate (see 170 above). It is to be recalled that Martin de Keyser had printed George Joye's Psalms from Bucer's Latin version in 1530. If Coverdale did work for de Keyser as a 'corrector' in 1534 and 1535, when he was preparing his Bible for the press, he could hardly have avoided this. De Keyser had also printed Joye's Isaiah in 1531, Jeremiah and Lamentations in 1534 and probably his Proverbs and Ecclesiastes in the same year. It is difficult to judge whether Coverdale in those books shows any indebtedness to Joye.[33]

THE BOOK

This first English complete Bible is most attractive to have on the desk, its production values being lifted by the clear page layout, steady decoration and frequent illustrations. The volume opens well, and this, with the summaries at the head of each book, invites the reader. This is in contrast to most early Bibles in German. The freshness of Luther's German Bibles came from their being new not only in that they were from the original Hebrew and Greek, but as cultural objects, well made and with splendid pictures by Cranach and others. Before Luther, there had been in German, from the first in 1466, eighteen from the Vulgate: they could all best be described as solid blocks of heavily printed paper, with no relief, and often no obvious indicators on any page of which chapter of which book a reader might be on (fig. 21). The print-shops of Antwerp did very much better, in several directions.

And now Coverdale's Bible, in English, was complete, and pleasing, and with over 150 pictures. At Genesis 1, the reader is immediately brought in: at 'In the beginning . . .', above a large decorated 'I' at the first word, there are two rows of three panels each, showing the six days of Creation, each a fine dramatic composition (fig. 11). Soon, a crowned Satan tempts Eve, Cain graphically kills Abel. Most of the pictures are in the Old

Testament. At Judges 6, Gideon weeds out his army; behind him is a cameo of him laying out the fleece. Most sixteenth-century reformed, and thus vernacular, Bibles, in whatever language, had a picture of David seeing Bathsheba bathing (2 Samuel 11). Here the space is classically laid out, in the balance and proportion, and perspective, of the buildings. Women, however, are scarce: Eve, Bathsheba and no one else. Holofernes' head is on a pole at a city gate: there is no triumphant Judith holding his severed head: no Ruth amid the alien corn; no Mary Magdalene; not even an apocalyptic Whore of Babylon. The men dominate, and do things – Absalom in 2 Samuel 18 is on a fleeing animal with its ears back, getting his hair caught in a tree in front of his pursuer, who is on a horse with his ears cocked. Such vivid woodcuts came from other Antwerp printers, or further afield, logistics which tended to control the subject matter. Each of the four 'Parts' of the Old Testament has its own decorated contents page: that to the Prophets has a striking picture, upper left, of a moated town, Flemish in style. Battle-scenes, giving a snapshot of contemporary action, are used again and again – in the Pentateuch, in the Books of the Kings, and then in the Apocryphal military histories, the two Books of Maccabees, many times. In all the pictures, drama rather than clarification is dominant.

By contrast with the problems of knowing where you are in the first, fifteenth-century, German Bibles from the Vulgate, mentioned above, Coverdale's chapter headings as well as book titles are repeated at the top of each page. The prefatory summaries to each book, chapter by chapter, are effective: as a random example, that to the Acts of the Apostles contains a typically elegant Coverdale chapter summary, to Acts 27: 'Paul's shipping toward Rome, Julius the captain entreateth Paul courteously, at the last they suffer shipwreck.'

The margins hold occasional clusters of cross-references. Marginal commentary notes are not frequent, but are always illuminatory (or not: in 1 Kings 7, 'uncertain measure of liquor'). At Matthew 23, 'proselyte: a novice or convert': tactfully, at Romans 3:28, 'Some read: by faith only'. As that note shows, the function of these marginal notes is the opposite of polemic. Miles Coverdale was a self-effacing, gentle scholar with a powerful understanding of pastoral needs, and most of his notes can be seen to be aimed to fulfil them.

THE APOCRYPHA INCLUDED

In this first English printed Bible, Coverdale's inclusion of the books of the Apocrypha as a block between the Old Testament and the New should be noted. These fourteen (or fifteen) books of the Jewish Scriptures are scattered throughout the Writings (after the Law and the Prophets) in the Septuagint (Greek) version of the Old Testament. Accepted by Greek-speaking Jews in Alexandria, where the Septuagint was made, but not by Palestine Jews and later rabbinic authorities; kept in circulation by Christians in the first four centuries, for whom the Greek Old Testament was standard; and printed in all early English Bibles and most later editions until 1804 (when the British and Foreign Bible Society, followed by the American Bible Society in 1827, omitted them) and not infrequently included today, they make a vivid, even kaleidoscopic, scatter of late Jewish writings. There are some historical narratives: the Books of Maccabees recount late Jewish military campaigns for independence; some alternative portions of canonical books; some fiction, like the stories of Susanna, of Judith and of Bel and the Dragon – the oriental romance of Tobit remains engaging; some Wisdom books (of which the Wisdom of Solomon is important as attempting to unite Hebrew and Greek theologies); and a little poetry. If the Letter of Jeremiah is counted as chapter 6 of Baruch, there are fourteen books. The apocalyptic work known as 2 Esdras was never in the Septuagint, being written after the New Testament, and survives only in Latin. Similarly the brief Prayer of Manasseh was not part of the original Septuagint.

Jerome, in making the basis of what became the Vulgate, followed the Septuagint in locating these books, but explained that as portions of Scripture they were useful but not strictly canonical. He gave to them the title 'apocrypha', meaning 'hidden'; whatever he felt it meant, it was intended to be pejorative. The Roman Catholic view, officially determined at the Council of Trent, also placed these books within the Old Testament, declaring that, though 'deuterocanonical', they were on the same footing as the Old Testament. Martin Luther in 1534 took Jerome a step further in lowering their status, and first assembled them together after the Old Testament. In 1535, Olivétan's first French Protestant Bible followed Luther, and so did Coverdale.

Coverdale introduced his Apocrypha with some care: it should be remembered that having the books together was new. He wrote, in part (and the passage gives a fine sense of Coverdale the craftsman of English at work):

These books (good reader) which are called Apocrypha, are not judged among the doctors to be of like reputation with the other scripture, as you may perceive by St Jerome in 'Epistola ad Paulinium.' And the chief cause thereof is this: there be many places in them, that seem to be repugnant unto the open and manifest truth in other books of the Bible.

Nevertheless I have not gathered them together to the intent that I would have then despised, or little set by, or that I should think them false, for I am not able to prove it: Yea, I doubt not verily, if they were equally conferred with the other open scripture (time, place and circumstances in all things considered) they should neither seem contrary, not be untruly and perversely alleged. Truth it is: a man's face can not be seen so well in a water, as in a fair glass: neither can it be shewed so clearly in a water that is stirred or moved, as in still water. These and many other dark places of scripture have been sore stirred and mixed with blind and covetous opinions of men, and have cast such a mist afore the eyes of the simple, that as long as they be not conferred with the other places of scripture, they shall not seem otherwise to be understood, than as covetousness expounds them. But who so ever thou be that readest scripture, let the holy ghost be thy teacher, and let one text expound another unto thee: as for such dreams, visions, and dark sentences as be hid from thy understanding, commit them unto God, and make no articles of them: but let the plain text be thy guide, and the spirit of God (which is the author thereof) shall lead thee in all truth.[34]

When we consider how much the reformers objected to the Church's comparatively recent doctrine of Purgatory, for example, as being unscriptural, we can see how tactful that passage is. According to modern understanding, Purgatory was invented in the late twelfth century, as already noted, gathering together some earlier hints from later Fathers. Unknown to the New Testament, or to Christians for a thousand years, the doctrine hangs on some Latin words in the Apocryphal book of 2 Maccabees.[35]

COVERDALE'S PASTORAL AIMS IN ANNOTATING

Coverdale writes in his dedicatory epistle to his first Bible in 1535,

I have neither wrested nor altered so much as one word for the maintenance of any manner of sect.

A few pages later, he sets out his intention.

Go to now, most dear reader, and sit thee down at the Lord's feet and read his words, and . . . take them into thine heart, and let thy talking and communication be of them when thou sittest in thy house, or goest by the way, when thou liest down and when thou risest up . . . in whom [God] if thou put thy trust, and be an unfeigned reader or hearer of his word with thy heart, thou shalt find sweetness therein and spy wondrous things to thy understanding, to the avoiding of all seditious sects, to the abhorring of thy old sinful life, and to the establishing of thy godly conversation.[36]

Martin Holt Dotterweich has pointed out Coverdale's new annotations in his 1537 New Testament. He notes that

While Tyndale and Rogers [in 'Matthew's Bible'] especially have been accused of writing polemical notes, a reading of their margins displays few such annotations; rather, the notes consist primarily of lexical explanation or comparison of a difficult passage to others which explain it, albeit with an identifiably Protestant slant. The same is entirely true of Coverdale . . . [who] took about half his notes from Luther's 1536 Bible, usually translating them straight into English. . . . The other half are difficult to identify, and many probably come from Coverdale's own hand as he attempted to anticipate the points over which his readers might stumble.[37]

This is important. Coverdale, good minister as he was, had a clear aim both to make the text clear, and to encourage his readers, to 'edify' in Paul's sense of building the faith of members of a congregation. Reading his annotations is to understand how well he understood his flock and how they would approach the text. The Protestant authority was not a *magisterium* in Rome: the reformers' right to instruct readers through these Bible margins came from expertise in the original languages and in the analogy of faith.

Coverdale's work of glory remains his Psalter. His translations of the Psalms, slightly modified in 1539 for the Great Bible, went from there into the first service-book of the new Church of England in 1549, the Book of Common Prayer – and stayed there in all Anglican churches worldwide, until the 1960s. 'I will lift up mine eyes unto the hills from whence cometh my help' (Psalm 121) is his, as is 'Whither shall I go from thy spirit? or whither shall I flee from thy presence . . .' in Psalm 139. At the start of the second millennium, the old 'BCP' is not quite forgotten: cathedral and college choirs who 'Make a joyful noise unto the Lord' (Psalm 98, and others) are singing Coverdale's words – as are congregations who still note that the Lord hath let the runagates continue in scarceness (a phrase modernly retranslated as 'rebels must remain in the scorching desert').[38] I shall say more about these psalms in later chapters.

Chapter 12

'MATTHEW'S BIBLE', 1537

TYNDALE WAS STRANGLED AND BURNED ON 6 October 1536. In the sixteen months after his arrest and removal from Antwerp to Brussels, it is not known what had happened to his manuscript translation of Joshua to 2 Chronicles. The papers would be bulky. Somehow on Tyndale's arrest they survived Pierre Dufief's (illegal) raid on the English House to seize all his property. The most likely person to have rescued and hidden them is the chaplain to the English House, John Rogers. He was the man who made sure that they were printed, in what became the most influential of all the early printed English Bibles, 'Matthew's Bible'.

Tyndale may have left other manuscript translations from the Hebrew: next in order after 2 Chronicles would have come books of later Jewish history, Ezra, Nehemiah and Esther. It is hard to think that with his excellent Hebrew he did not look ahead, after the tedious Esther, to the great poem of Job, and then the 150 Psalms. If such manuscript translations of great poetry existed, even traces of them are unlikely now ever to be discovered. That is a matter for grief. We know from the 'Song of Moses' that appears at Exodus 15, as well as from the second chapter of Jonah, that he understood Hebrew poetry and translated it very well. Half the Old Testament, almost all prose, is all there is from his Hebrew work, the first translation into English.

Immediately on Tyndale's arrest, the procurer-general, Pierre Dufief, a man much feared by his enemies, confiscated all Tyndale's property. Tyndale had no earthly rights whatever. He was a heretic, and the destruction of his property, and the burning of his body, were means to purify the Church and perhaps benefit his soul in Purgatory. The letter that Tyndale wrote in prison states that he did not take his work with him: he asked for his Hebrew dictionary and grammar.[1] It is wholly unlikely that his requests were granted, especially those which would enable him to continue the very work of heresy for which he was being punished. The romantic Victorian picture of Tyndale translating the Scriptures while sitting at a rather splendid table in a spacious room in Vilvoorde Castle, divine sunlight playing around his head, is just that – a romantic picture.

His cramped, straw-filled cell would lack any facility for such work. We know from study of what he published that, like all good translators, he used any helps he could find – from the Latin and German versions at the least, as well as the Septuagint: it is unthinking piety which has him dispensing with all these helps and in an ecstasy of inspiration, simply writing it all down as God dictated.[2]

JOHN ROGERS

Having taken his BA at Pembroke Hall, Cambridge, in 1526, Rogers became rector of a London parish. In the latter part of 1534 he moved to Antwerp to become chaplain to the merchants and others who lived there together. He was moving in Reforming circles, and in 1536 or 1537 he married a Flemish woman who was a kinswoman of Jacob van Meteren. The latter had been the sponsor behind the printing of Miles Coverdale's English Bible of 1535. Rogers's wife was described by John Foxe 'more richly endowed with virtue and soberness of life, than with worldly treasures'.[3] Rogers stayed for six years in Antwerp. He then left for Wittenberg, where he matriculated on 25 November 1540. He came into close contact with Lutheran scholars, particularly Philip Melanchthon. He then became one of four superintendents of the Lutheran church in the Dietmarsh region far in the north-west of Germany. Backed by Melanchthon, he accepted the challenge of becoming pastor at Meldorf in that region. The district was hardly sophisticated: while preaching in that town in 1524, Henry of Zutphen had been lynched by a mob whose murderousness had been exacerbated by alcohol provided for the purpose by local monks. Communication by a native German, never mind by an Englishman, would have been difficult, as regional accents were extreme. Melanchthon in a letter of support for Rogers noted that pronunciation would be a real problem, to be solved only by time. Melanchton's letter gives an attractive picture of Rogers:

> a learned man . . . gifted with great ability, which he sets off with a noble character . . . he will be careful to live in concord with his colleagues . . . his integrity, trustworthiness and constancy in every duty make him worthy of the love and support of all good men.[4]

Rogers remained in Meldorf for four and a half years, until the spring of 1548. A year before he left, he was the leader in an initiative by local clergy to try to reduce the number of murders in the region. The people were alarmed because of confusion about self-defence, and because murderers were being allowed to buy their way out of the death penalty. The ministers threatened to stop preaching and administering the sacraments unless the secular authorities enforced the imperial laws against wilful murder: Rogers, in the only letter of his that survives, written from Meldorf, sides with those who think that only those who deliberately murder deserve death. The matter is affecting in view of the manner of his own death.

In January 1547 Edward VI came to the English throne, and Rogers set about returning home. He left Meldorf, to the evident grief of his people, probably in the spring of 1548. By August he was living in London in the house of the Reforming merchant and publisher Edward Whitchurch. He translated a number of books by Melanchton, including *Weighing of the interim*, that 'interim' referring to the emperor's edict of 15 May 1548 bidding Protestants conform to Catholic practices. He was given a number of successive London livings, of increasing influence, and, admired by Ridley, was appointed lecturer in divinity in St Paul's Cathedral. He preached, we are told, powerfully and boldly against the misuse of abbey lands by Northumberland and his party. In April 1552, his wife and those children born in Germany were naturalised as English.

Immediately on the accession of Mary in 1553, Rogers was in trouble. A number of illegal measures were used to silence and then to imprison him, at first by house arrest. On 27 January 1554 he was sent to Newgate. Since his stipend had been, again illegally, stopped, his wife and ten children were in desperate need. Parliament in November 1554 made alterations to the law, allowing the illegally held reforming prisoners to be executed. With the others, Rogers's trial, before Stephen Gardiner and the council, began on 22 January 1555. Rogers defended himself ably, but seven days later he was condemned as a heretic. Six days after that, on 4 February, he was degraded from the priesthood by Bonner, in preparation for execution. Foxe gives details. John Rogers's urgent pleas that he might speak a few words with his wife before his burning were rejected. He was taken to Smithfield to the fire, saying as he went the psalm 'Miserere'. As he went, spectators cried out to him to play the man. To strengthen him against the ordeal, his wife was there with their eleven children, one, whom he had never seen before, at the breast. As he stood at the stake, his pardon was brought should he recant, but he refused. He exhorted the people to stand firm in the faith which he had taught them. When the fire took hold of his body, 'he, as one feeling no smart, washed his hands in the flame, as though it had been in cold water': lifting up his hands to heaven he did not move them again until they were consumed in the devouring fire.[5] He was the first of almost three hundred martyrs under Queen Mary.

In 1535 and 1536, Rogers, friend of Tyndale, was an ideal person to take the translator's work further. He was a graduate with an undoubted flair for languages: one would give a great deal for a moment or two of his preaching in Meldorf in the strong regional dialect. It may have been his sympathy for reform which took him to Antwerp in 1534: indeed, he could hardly have gone to Antwerp not knowing the name of Tyndale. As a later Wittenberg graduate and friend of Melanchthon it is likely that he was already a scholar of the Greek New Testament. In the volume we shall presently consider we can see his grasp of Hebrew and Aramaic, versions of the Old Testament in Greek and Latin, and his use of recent European work on the Scriptures as well as knowledge of the Fathers. His understanding of the religious needs of ordinary people, of the plough-boys of the Dietmarsh region, was one with his later power as a London preacher: he was the first under Queen Mary to be put to silence.

'THOMAS MATTHEW'S BIBLE'

To this steadfast and courageous reformed pastor and preacher the English-speaking Christian world owes a debt of particular gratitude. Working with, apparently, the printer Matthew Crom in Antwerp, John Rogers put together in 1537 a handsome thick folio, well printed in clear black letter in double columns. This contained, for the first time as part of a large complete Bible, all Tyndale's printed Bible translations: that is, the 1534 New Testament and the Pentateuch, the 'Five Books of Moses': they were given almost unchanged. For the first time, moreover, there appeared an English translation of the nine historical books ending at 2 Chronicles made from the Hebrew. That this was the work of Tyndale is now beyond doubt.[6] Tyndale's vulnerable manuscript pages had safely arrived in print.

For the parts of the Bible that Tyndale did not live to reach (or, just possibly, finish), Rogers printed Coverdale. So the high poetry from Job to Malachi, half the Old Testament, twenty-two books of poems and prophecy, and thirteen of the fourteen books of the Apocrypha, Rogers gives in a version, albeit made by a dedicated and learned man, who could sometimes be splendid in his formulations as we saw above, but who knew neither Hebrew nor Greek, Miles Coverdale.

Tyndale's name was heretical. Rogers's volume could not be called 'Tyndale's Bible'. For no certain reason, the title-page states:

> The Bible, which is all the holy Scripture: in which are contained the Old and New Testament truly and purely translated into English by Thomas Matthew.

The likelihood is that the name was chosen because it combines the names of two disciples. There is little weight in the suggestion that a real Thomas

Matthew, a Lutheran fishmonger of Colchester, who might just possibly have been in Antwerp in 1536 and 1537, made this scholarly tome. In any case John Rogers was later described by the Privy Council as 'Rogers alias Matthew'.[7] Perhaps a whiff of the Essex fishmonger among the Antwerp printers put the name in mind.

So in 1537, the London reforming merchants Richard Grafton and Edward Whitchurch underwrote an edition of 1,500 copies which were shipped to England. Richard Grafton was the son of a Shrewsbury skinner whose own father, Adam Grafton, had been a chaplain at court to Edward v and then to Prince Arthur Tudor. This man raised his grandson Richard, apprenticing him to the prominent Cheapside grocer John Blagge, who had among his customers aristocrats and courtiers, including the then still obscure Thomas Cranmer and Wolsey's chief agent, Thomas Cromwell. Richard Grafton was admitted Freeman of the Company of Grocers in 1534. He met and befriended a member of the Haberdashers' Company, Edward Whitchurch. It was Grafton who sent to – now Archbishop – Cranmer a copy of Matthew's Bible. Cranmer on 4 August 1537 wrote to Thomas Cromwell – now King Henry VIII's Vicegerent for ecclesiastical affairs – a letter accompanying this copy, saying '. . . as for the translation, so far as I have read thereof I like it better than any other translation heretofore made.' The Archbishop asked the Vicegerent to show the book to the king, in the hope that he would allow it to go forth to the people, without any danger from any act, ordinance or proclamation.[8]

Cromwell had been able to ensure not just the dedication of this English Bible to the king, as had happened with Coverdale's version, but a licence. The dedication is given in the preliminary leaves, beginning 'To the most noble and gracious Prince King Henry the eight' and ending 'Your grace's faithful and true subject Thomas Matthew'. The very title ends with the words 'Set forth with the King's most gracious licence'.

Cromwell, having showed the new book to the king, began proceedings for setting up an English Bible in every parish church. Cranmer had warned him in the letter he sent with the copy that those who favoured the book would suffer 'some snubs, many slanders, lies and reproaches',[9] because of supposed heretical notes. The chief objection was because it was a Bible in English for everyone to read.

Henry licensed it for distribution at once,

prompting Grafton to send six copies to Cromwell as gift. But Cromwell insisted on paying for the copies, sending £10 to Grafton together with a note saying no favour was required on account of the licence.[10]

Cromwell then encouraged bishops to order copies for their churches. He did more. Early in 1538 he required local Justices of the Peace to make sure that the parish priests were preaching the Word of God, and recommending the people to have an English Bible.[11] Both Archbishops, of Canterbury and York, and at least one other bishop, ordered every beneficed priest to have at least a Latin-English New Testament and to read a chapter a day in it. Demand was high. The first English/Latin diglot New Testament was in 1538, with Tyndale's English and Erasmus's Latin. There were three editions of Coverdale's slightly more Vulgate-based New Testament, with the Vulgate alongside, in 1538.

Less than twelve months before, Tyndale's dying words outside Brussels had been 'Lord, open the King of England's eyes.' Now the king was licensing a complete Bible in English. The ironies are truly tragic. Had Tyndale escaped arrest; had Henry Phillips, the Judas who betrayed him at the English House, not also succeeded in blocking all the English court's attempts to release him; had Tyndale lived for a few more months until the king changed his mind, and even welcomed him home – then we would have had in our English Bibles for ever after as a base text the poetry of the Psalms and the Song of Songs, of Job, the Isaiahs, Jeremiah, Lamentations, Ezekiel, and so much else, a version first made by a master both of Hebrew – and of Hebrew poetry – and of English.

Cromwell found that there were simply not enough copies available. He wanted to place one in every parish church in the land, of which there were almost 9,000. As will be seen in the next chapter, Cromwell succeeded, using an adapted, and especially printed, version of 'Matthew's'. We do not know whether Cranmer knew that the bulk of this admired volume was the work of Tyndale: Cromwell certainly did.[12] Neither would say so, even if both knew – for one of several remarkable features of 'Matthew's Bible' is the occurrence of five very heavily ornamented initials, each taking up a good part of a page. In the preliminary leaves, a page of exhortation 'to the study of the holy Scripture gathered out of the Bible' ends with the flourished initials IR, for John Rogers. The dedication to the king includes the similar initials HR, for Henricus Rex. Before Isaiah is an engraving and two pairs of such initials, RG and EW, for Richard Grafton and Edward Whitchurch. On the last page of the Old Testament, before the Apocrypha, are the elaborated initials WT (fig. 13). The code would be easily broken, but it would allow a discreet screen for officials to hide behind when faced with the body of conservative bishops (including Stephen Gardiner of Winchester) for whom any departure from the Scripture's 'original' Latin remained heresy.

THE FRONTISPIECE

Of the other special features, one deserves more than a note. It is commonly passed about among writers on this period, who have not been able to look at copies of what they discuss, that early printed English Bibles lack illustration. Not only is that generally wrong: in some cases it is spectacularly misleading. The whole-page frontispiece to 'Matthew's Bible', apparently taken from a woodcut used in a Dutch Bible of 1533, shows in remarkable splendour Adam and Eve marvelling at Paradise before the Fall (fig. 12). Unclothed and unashamed, they look with wonder at all the beasts and birds, close and far off, amid the luxuriant landscape of plants and lakes and hills. Benign and not dominant, the Creator watches the scene. Eve laughs at the antics of a monkey in a nearby tree. This is the world, the artist suggests, as it was intended to be. There is no trace of a serpent, nor of figleaves. In view of the usual ripely fierce iconography of the Fall, with the Tree doubling as Cross, with the large apple handed by a defensive Eve to her man, with the coiling serpent with a human face, or the weeping Eve supported by a tight-lipped Adam as they are driven out, this picture is wonderfully positive. Not everything in the Bible, it might suggest, is about sin. Some of it might be about an original and God-created delight.

ROGERS AS BIBLICAL SCHOLAR

He was careful to keep Tyndale's text, following the 'GH' printing of his 1534 New Testament. Coverdale, in translating the Apocrypha, had omitted the short Prayer of Manasseh, so Rogers supplied his own translation. In the sections wholly taken over from Coverdale, however, Rogers felt himself free to make many and considerable changes. He used for Job and Isaiah the commentaries of Oecolampadius. For Job, he even translated afresh the opening chapters, which Coverdale had not done well.[13] Hebrew poetry, though often beautiful, is also often difficult to render. Increased knowledge down the centuries changes the readings drastically. John Rogers's Hebrew restored some coherence to the opening of Job. (Some more correct readings may be regretted: at Job 19:20, the sixteenth-century 'I am escaped with the skin of my teeth' becomes in 1989 'I gnaw my underlip with my teeth', a surrender to better philology with sad effect.)

Coverdale ignored French sources. Rogers took as a basis for his twenty leaves of preliminary matter the French Bibles of Lefèvre (1530, 1534; both printed in Antwerp by Martin de Keyser) and Olivétan (1535). From these texts, and from his own knowledge, he greatly expanded the marginal notes in both the Old and New Testaments. In reproducing Tyndale's Pentateuch he omitted three or four of the original marginal comments against the pope, and inserted his own notes from Pellican's Latin commentary. Tyndale's historical books lacked marginal notes, so Rogers supplied them from the French Bibles, from which source he added to Tyndale's New Testament notes, so that the whole volume has over two thousand marginal notes, not including cross-references.

This was pioneer work in Protestant glossing in English. The Latin Bible had been glossed for centuries. The patristic comments which appeared in the *Glossa Ordinaria*, for example, had been in Bible manuscripts since the twelfth century. The additions by Nicholas of Lyra had been circulating in print from the 1470s. Tyndale offered King Henry a 'bare text', like that of his 1526 Worms New Testament. His Pentateuch has few marginal notes. The first ideal of clearing away the scholastic encroachments gave way quickly to recognition that ordinary people needed a great deal of help. Marginal notes – as seen in Tyndale's own 1534 New Testament – were not for promoting scholastic arguments for readers who were patristic specialists, but for helping the ploughboy. Aristotle did not belong in the margins of Scripture, as Tyndale noted at Deuteronomy 4:2.[14] John Rogers needs more recognition for his contribution to marginal elucidation. Like Tyndale, his scholarship was at the ploughboy's disposal. He was able to refer the reader to the 'Chaldee', the Aramaic version of the Old Testament, commonly called the Targum, and to the Greek Septuagint version, to elucidate Hebrew obscurities. He also took from the French versions chapter summaries throughout the whole Bible. Remembered by few now, sometimes only for his reading of the Hebrew 'hallelujah' as 'Praise the Everlasting', John Rogers, though neglected today, was a modern biblical scholar.

Chapter 13

THE GREAT BIBLE, 1539

COVERDALE IN LONDON

Miles Coverdale returned TO England from his first exile towards the end of 1535. Probably in that year he saw through a London press 'in the shop of J. Rastell' his *Goostly Psalmes and Spirituall Songs drawen out of the Holy Scripture*, printed with the music. These were English versions of German hymns which were already widespread there. They made the first printed English collection of the metrical forms of the Psalms which quickly came to dominate English, and American, Protestant congregational worship. Even today, that old form is not quite dead: a favourite at church weddings, especially when sung to the Scottish tune 'Crimond', is the twenty-third Psalm, beginning:

> The Lord's my shepherd, I'll not want,
>   He makes me down to lie
> In pastures green. He leadeth me
>   The quiet waters by.

That is not by Coverdale, but from a later Scottish collection. Coverdale, however, introduced the German technique into English. His book appeared a dozen years before Thomas Sternhold's first volume of nineteen metrical Psalms was published in 1549, the forerunner of the 'Sternhold and Hopkins' complete Psalmody which, as well as a Scottish version, was printed and bought in very large numbers indeed for over three hundred years (see chapter 18 below). Coverdale in England also anticipated by three decades the great French outpouring of metrical Psalms, a powerful weapon in the swift French Protestant Reformation.

Nine of Coverdale's twenty-four hymns, with two canticles (that is, biblical songs used in worship) and eight of the fourteen Psalms, closely follow Luther's hymnal from Wittenberg. Coverdale wrote in his Preface that he wanted to supply 'goodly songs' to be sung by 'minstrels . . . our young men that have the gift of singing . . . and our women singing at the [spinning] wheels', instead of 'hey nonny nonny, hey troly loly, and such like phantasies'.[1] More significantly, he wanted to prepare the way for a reformed service-book, parallel to continental practices.[2]

Also in 1535, Thomas Gibson published a *Concordance to the New Testament*, based on Tyndale but showing knowledge of Coverdale's 1535 Bible: it was said to be by Coverdale, as was *A faithful and true prognostication upon the year MCCCCCxxxvi* [1536]. *A spiritual almanack* followed, and in 1537 his translation from the German of the short *Message of the emperor and of the bishop of Rome* was printed by James Nicolson of Southwark. The point to note is that Coverdale's properly high reputation as Bible translator should not obscure his importance as an active reformer, steadily bringing to the English public some key German texts. His publications of all kinds number nearly forty.

Yet James Nicolson of Southwark's most important work by far was the printing in 1537 of the first complete Bibles in England, the folio and quarto of Coverdale's Bible, the latter as we saw licensed by the king. Obtaining that licence would have been the work of Thomas Cromwell, now the king's vicegerent for ecclesiastical affairs, to whom Miles Coverdale had first written while still an Augustinian friar at Cambridge in about 1528.[3] In 1536, Cromwell had started proceedings to fulfil his ambition to place an open English Bible in every parish church in the land.[4] Clearly he knew what Coverdale had done. His difficulties were first that James Nicolson's print-run seems to have been small.[5] Second, Coverdale had not translated from the original languages, and thus could not be thought sufficiently scholarly to fulfil the king's promise in 1530 that 'learned men' would 'faithfully and purely' translate the New Testament into English.

Then, on 4 August 1537, Archbishop Cranmer sent to Cromwell the copy that he had just received from Richard Grafton of John Rogers's 'Matthew's Bible', with the note that he liked it 'better than any other translation heretofore made'.[6] Cromwell knew it already, because that version, too, had the king's licence, a semi-official way for Henry VIII to get closer to his promise. Knowing of Cranmer's approval, Cromwell seized on Matthew's as the best way of getting sound Bibles into churches. In this version the king could approve the solid scholarship: Tyndale's, though nobody could say so. Some distribution began. Sympathetic bishops were already forcefully commanding their clergy to get and read the Scriptures. Latimer for one was complaining that his local clergy were being slow:[7] but there was an immediate dearth of copies. Only one thousand five hundred were printed, and there were almost nine thousand parishes.

Reprinting Matthew's on a large scale would risk the chance of hostility from those who remembered how Tyndale had rendered the Greek for what they thought of as 'church', 'priest' and 'do penance', and who recognised the initials 'WT' when they saw them.

'MATTHEW'S' TO BE REVISED

Cromwell solved the problem by initiating, with Cranmer's encouragement, a revision of 'Matthew's Bible'. It was to be a very large and unmissable folio in every church, prominent and easy to read either alone or to a crowd. Grafton and Whitchurch were to publish it. The printing was to be done on the presses of François Regnault in Paris, superior to any in England: they had supplied all English service-books from 1519 to 1534, and there was nothing unusual in such cross-Channel arrangements. The best printing, by some way, was still outside England. The revision of the text would be minimal, but most of the marginal notes would be removed – partly because they do not belong in a volume intended to be read aloud in a church, and not only during services: but partly also because Cromwell, to succeed, needed to keep hostility low. Conservative bishops were perpetually suspicious of reformers' annotations, though easy investigation shows that almost all of them are simple exposition or explanation.

The revising was to be done by Miles Coverdale.[8] This was an inspired choice. True, he lacked Hebrew and Greek: but two-thirds of 'Matthew's' was Tyndale, who was reliable. Coverdale was obviously a good Latinist. Tweaking the Bible, especially the non-Tyndale half of the Old Testament, back towards a 'Latin original' would calm the most reactionary critics, those who still maintained that Hebrew and Greek were subversive interlopers. Moreover, Coverdale's skill with English spoken rhythms would ensure that the Bible in English sounded well in stone churches.

Coverdale went to Paris. Work began. In May 1538 printing was started. Coverdale and the English overseers at the press reported that they were pleased with progress. On 23 June, they sent Cromwell some finished sheets, with an explanation of the principles of translating and editing being used. Richard Grafton, who was there, then complained to Cromwell of the inhibiting and hostile interference by the English ambassador to France. This was the Bishop of Winchester, Stephen Gardiner, no less, a man always hostile to reform as it showed itself in an English Bible. Grafton also reported that costs were outrunning provision.[9] Cromwell sent 600 marks of his own. He convinced the king that he should recall Gardiner. Bonner was nominated Bishop of London and the new ambassador. He was encouraging, and kept Cromwell informed of the good progress of the great project.[10] On 12 September 1538, Grafton and

Coverdale wrote to Cromwell that the work would soon be finished.[11] The English community in Paris under Coverdale was showing solidarity.[12] Cromwell issued his famous Second Injunctions, requiring that 'a Bible of the largest volume' in English be set up in every parish by Christmas 1538.[13] So confident was Cromwell that in his manuscript draft he altered Christmas to All Saints' Day (30 November) bringing forward the requirement by a month.[14]

Then things began to go seriously wrong. In Paris one of the English team was accused of heresy. Bonner reported that some of the English bishops were working with the French court to halt the printing.[15] In London the king altered the terms of the royal warrant, unfavourably.[16] The cause of what was obviously a harmonised attack on the English printing is not known. Coverdale wrote from Paris on 13 December 1538 that some of the 2,500 finished copies had been confiscated by the Inquisition.[17] The work was stopped.[18] What had been printed was seized for burning. Grafton reported

> Not only the same bible being xxv c in number were seized and made confiscate, but also the printer, merchants and correctors with great jeopardy of their lives escaped.[19]

Grafton and Whitchurch, with the other members of the English team, fled to London. There seems to have been direct pressure on the French Inquisitor General from the Vatican, whence came on 24 December 1538 a papal Instruction that Bibles corruptly translated into English were either to be burned or prevented from being printed. This order of Paul III, in Italian, was given to a nuncio in Scotland.[20] The politics were intricate. The cause might not have been purely a conservative attempt in Catholic Europe to halt reform, nor even a desire by some English bishops to thwart Cromwell.

DERRING-DO ON THE HIGH SEAS

To understand the chess game of religious politics, a historian needs first to go back a year and pick up a tale of naval adventures. On the same day, 4 August 1537, that Cranmer sent to Cromwell a copy of Matthew's Bible, it happened that three German merchantmen were raided in the English Channel by three French ships. The French suspected the Germans of carrying contraband: they had orders to prevent such goods reaching any port that was under Spanish allegiance. The German captain, Hans Luben, on the leading merchantman, the *George* out of Hamburg, signalled that he had no contraband and was heading for Hagen in Holland. The

French captain, Pierre Beaucourt, needed action: he sailed under letters of marque and reprisal issued to the brother of the Constable of France, the Sieur de Rochepot. Beaucourt ignored Hans Luben's signal and opened fire on the *George*. Luben himself and every one of his small crew were injured. With a favourable wind, the other German ships fled. Luben surrendered to Beaucourt, who killed the seriously wounded Germans and put Luben and the remaining five adrift in a small boat, intending that they would not survive. Beaucourt put a crew on the *George* which, escorted by the other ships, was towed as a prize towards France.

They never arrived. They were caught in a storm and separated. The French ship towing the *George* was itself set upon by English ships out of Newcastle, and both were taken after some time as captives into Whitby. Beaucourt had escaped, meanwhile, to friendly Scotland. Hearing that his prize lay at Whitby, he went to recover it. He claimed it before Thomas Howard, Duke of Norfolk, Lord Admiral of England. Confusion followed. The Duke mistook the *George* for another ship brought down from Hull: and he found a stay placed on his order from an unexpected quarter. Defying all odds, Luben and his men had been blown to safety on an English shore, and had told how savagely they had been treated by the French. With Hansa backing, Luben secured the arrest of Beaucourt and the stay of the award of the prize to him.

The French claimed that their prize, carrying contraband, was lawful. The Germans denied the contraband, and brought a strong legal case. Cromwell angered the Duke of Norfolk (already his enemy) by appointing an English commission of lawyer-bishops and others to determine the case. On 2 February 1538, sitting at Westminster, this commission refused a French demand for trial in a French court, infuriating the French even more by ruling not only that the case would be tried in England at a place to be chosen by the Germans, but that the captured goods must revert to the consigners. The Duke of Norfolk felt himself to have been humiliated, and did not forget. The French had been defeated on all fronts, and they, too, did not forget.

To return to the problems with the English Bible being printed in Paris:

Immediately on the seizure of the sheets in Paris and the flight of the English team, Cromwell met with Castillon [the French ambassador in London]. He thoroughly briefed the ambassador on the Bible project, mentioning his own investment of 600 marks in the undertaking while broadly hinting that immediate delivery of the sheets might ease the way toward a settlement of other matters then at issue between England and France.[21]

Castillon reported to the Constable of France – who, according to the Imperial Ambassador at the English court, Chapuys, had been the mover of the seizure of the Bible printing in the first place. Cromwell meanwhile, in a letter from Bonner dated 1 January, heard that Francis 1 had promised to return the books. In February Bonner received from the Constable his reluctant willingness to overlook the heresy and the bureaucratic errors – 'the royal licence had been given on the wrong form' – and be rid of the type, printers and even the paper, so that the book could be completed in England.[22] This willingness did not extend to what had been printed.[23] Grafton and Whitchurch returned to Paris, to look for the printed sheets. Foxe tells a story[24] that a corrupt French official had sold everything seized, four vats full of unbound printed sheets, for his own profit. The buyer was a Paris haberdasher, who wanted them 'to lap hats in.' Grafton and Whitchurch found that the Inquisition had burned some of the bound copies, and not all the unbound. They returned to England with the unused paper, the type, the salvaged unbound Bibles, and the French craftsmen. Those rescued sheets were of the Old Testament as far as Job (just over halfway through), and the New Testament as far as 1 Peter (nine-tenths complete).[25] Early in April 1539, fresh printing began in the Grey Friars in London, then in Cromwell's hands.[26] Three thousand copies of this Great Bible were ready, mixing Paris and London printings, by the end of April, as stated at the end of the bound copies.

None was sold until November 1539. Cromwell's hold on power was becoming slippery, but the delay seems more to have been because he was negotiating for the almost 2,500 sets of unbound copies still in the hands of the Inquisitor General. The French, aware of the English need for the Bibles, mounted a new effort to get the prize of the captured German merchant ship, the *George*, to be awarded to the Constable's brother. It seemed to be the moment for trading, ship for Bibles, but it could not be done openly. There followed, behind smiles of friendliness mixed with posturings of outraged honour, a long war of nerves. The exact details are not fully known, but Grafton went again to Paris early in November 1539, and the strong likelihood is that he came back 'with the balance of the Paris printing'.[27] Cromwell could not meet the demand created by the injunctions until he had the Paris copies in his control, nor could he risk repetition of the failure to supply the parishes in 1536. With the copies shipped from France, on top of the first Grey Friars printing, and a second printing of three thousand copies in March or April 1540, the great Injunctions were fulfilled.[28] Cromwell was raised to the peerage, as Earl of Essex. Yet even as he succeeded, his permanent enemies, the Duke of Norfolk and Stephen Gardiner, Bishop of Winchester, were moving against him in Parliament, leading the consideration of the Act for Uniformity in Opinion, the Six Articles. Only weeks after his Bibles began to be set up in parishes, on 10 June 1540, the new Earl of Essex was arrested at the Council Table on charges of heresy and treason. The articles of his accusation were dominated by items charging him with introducing and maintaining dangerous heresies, including Lutheran and Anabaptist doctrines.[29] The embarrassing failure of all that was left of his attempt to secure imperial or French allies against the papal bull of Henry's excommunication, in the king's disastrous marriage to Anne of Cleves sixth moths before, 6 January 1540, had not helped – and now in the royal eye was Catherine Howard, niece of the Duke of Norfolk. One indictment against Cromwell was that he conspired to deny justice to the Constable's brother, Rochepot, and other Frenchmen, because he hoped to convert part of the prize to his own use. He vigorously denied this in a letter of 24 July, writing that if it could be proved to the contrary, then 'I am not such as God shall and may help'.[30] In that letter he pointed out that among those who knew it was untrue were the Duke of Norfolk and at least three bishops, Gardiner, Tunstall and Bonner. What they knew, of course, was that he probably *had* used the prize 'to his own use' in the sense that he seems to have negotiated with the French in order to place a Bible in every parish church in England. He was executed, without trial, on 28 July.

THE GREAT BIBLE

The popular name for this volume, the Great Bible, is perhaps justified by the page size of 337 by 235 mm (roughly 14 by 9 inches). Coverdale's 1535 Bible measures 278 by 186 mm (roughly 11 by 7 inches), but 'Matthew's' 1537 Bible is 302 by 215 mm (roughly 12 by 9 inches). By comparison with some nineteenth-century American Bibles, the book, though large, is not huge. Cromwell had ordered the setting up of 'the holy bible of the largest volume', which certainly identifies it; the popular name may have come from this.

This Bible's distinction is three-fold. First, it was the only Bible ever to be 'authorised' in Britain. (The Bible that from the late eighteenth century until recently was universally known as the 'Authorised Version', that of 1611, now more frequently known by its American name, the 'King James Version', was never authorised. Passionate believers in its royal authority are soothed by the unlikely suggestion that a document of authorisation has been lost.) Second, only thirteen years after Tyndale's first and smuggled-in 1526 English New Testament, it brought the English Bible to the people in a massive way. In most of the parishes, its arrival, and contents, must have been surprising. Third, though Coverdale's revision was generally in a more Latin direction, the parishioners' encounter with the Bible was still with the greatness of Tyndale.

THE GREAT BIBLE TITLE-PAGE

The full, crowded, title-page, from the school of Holbein, is famous (fig. 19). At the top, forced to crouch under the top border by the bulk of King Henry VIII, is a head-and-shoulders God, blessing the moment in history. Through complex rolling scrolls from his mouth, he quotes from his own Word in Isaiah 55:11 and Acts 13:22; that is, in the Great Bible:

> [Like as rain and snow] . . . so the word also that out of my mouth cometh shall not turn again void, but shall accomplish my will, and prosper in the thing whereto I sent it.

And, from Acts, using Paul's first recorded sermon, at Antioch, where he explained that Jesus is the Christ, God declares that in King Henry, like David the son of Jesse as king, he has found 'a man after mine own heart, which shall fulfil all my will'.

Surprisingly, for the title-page of a book announcing itself so strongly in the central panel as 'The Bible in English', God speaks these extracts in Latin. Indeed, all but two of the many scrolled utterances from all kinds of people in the design are in Latin. The very English Bible being handed out in his royal largesse to every rank by King Henry is the *Verbum Dei*. One could argue, with some force, that these citations do not affect the content of the volume; that the Vulgate was the familiar version, and, assuming that what was inside the covers was going to seem strange to many people, the Latin of the tags shows some attempt not to frighten the horses. On the other side, one could also argue, expanding the case from that use of Latin, that the whole title-page, though the dominant King Henry is so expansively in control, represents royal nervousness. The frontispiece to 'Matthew's' Bible of two years before shows God's natural order going enjoyably about its business, *natura naturans*, including our father and mother as equals under God. This Great Bible title-page shows the severity of God's social – and thus political – order as King Henry is passing it down, imposing it even harshly. The Latin might be taken to be saying that no newfangled Scriptures in English, with possibly alarming relations to the 'new' interloping Hebrew and Greek displacing that Latin, however much the title of the volume might bow in those directions ('truly translated after the verity of the Hebrew and Greek texts') were going to disrupt God's, which meant Henry's, kingdom. This title-page is a picture of the king's world: at the top, God has difficulty getting in; at the bottom, distressingly available from the centre, is Newgate Prison.[31]

King Henry hands the *Verbum Dei*, which is not very big, to Archbishop Cranmer on his right and Vicegerent Cromwell on his left. Lest these two powerful men miss the point and become uppish, the largest wording after the central title itself, and more of a panel than a scroll, comes from the king. He quotes at them Daniel 6:26 in Latin; the moment where Darius, King of the Persians says, 'my commandment is, that in all dominions of my kingdom that men fear and stand in awe of Daniel's God': as an assertion of royal authority it is blinding. Cranmer is personally addressed by a scroll giving 1 Timothy 4:11, in Latin; 'Such things command and preach': the biblical context is of the maintenance of social order, and the archbishop is bidden 'command' before preach'; he is to have no doubt of his function in the state. Cromwell's words are from Deuteronomy 1:16 in Latin, 'judge righteously between every man'; though Moses' historic charge is admirable, in this place it is again a piece of state scaffolding.

So far, so good. Cranmer and Cromwell have stood humbly beside and slightly below the king, bareheaded and receptive, their mitre and cap set aside. Now, in the borders beside the central title-panel, they appear again in their full state functions, wearing their headgear of office, and this time facing outward. At their feet, in wreaths, are their respective coats of arms. Each passes a still smaller *Verbum Dei* further down the chain, Cranmer to a priest, with the command to 'Feed ye Christ's flock', 1 Peter 5:2; Cromwell to a nobleman, ordered to 'Eschew evil, and do good', Psalm 34:14. The chain of power is clear.

Below is a rabble. The dominant forces in the whole picture are, in the top third (or just over) King Henry the Eighth, and in the bottom third (or just over) a confusing mass of overdressed people. They are fairly undifferentiated except that one or two are women. They are none of them doing anything except looking faintly pleased. They are certainly not reading from, or even touching, a Bible in English. *Verbum Dei has* stopped in its descent midway in the page, at the priest and the nobleman. True, the priest below the archbishop is preaching to them, apparently *extempore*, as no Bible is visible. What he is telling them is not of the saving love of God in Christ Jesus, in their own vernacular language, but the Latin of 1 Timothy 2:1–2, where Paul exhorts that 'first of all, supplications, prayers, intercessions, and giving of thanks, be made for all men; for kings, and for all that are in authority . . .'. Only two figures in all the crowd are attending to him. Here is the symbol of Henry's fear. The crush of common people may be pleased to hear of the Bible in English, but they are so uncontrollable – not even listening to the sermon – that they must absolutely not handle it. All they exist for, something they do in the woodcut with vigour, is praise the king in Latin: all but two of the interwoven speech-scrolls from the people of England say *Vivat Rex* (the two saying *God Save the King* are possibly children). And balancing the very open pulpit on the left is a shut-in and roofed shape on the right, the prison (Newgate) to which they will go if they don't (praise the king in Latin). The people inside the barred windows are silent, and the prison, unlike the pulpit, has no *Vivat Rex* on the wall. It has been said that the prison is for those who do not accept the Bible in English as well as 'the royal supremacy it apparently speaks'.[32] In view of the indifference of the rabble to anything except uttering their *Vivat Rex*, one may deduce that it is the latter alone that keeps them out of jail.

King Henry is once again, and more firmly, to be seen as both Moses and as King David, Israel's ideal ruler.[33] The close identification of Old Testament figures, particularly kings, with the contemporary world of rulers, was made by reformers throughout Europe, expressed either in support for them or in opposition to them. Particularly in Britain, the monarch could be seen to be doing the work of the Lord in his acts of destroying the power of giant enemies. John Bale, the reforming polemicist, wrote, among other influential works, plays for Thomas Cromwell: his *King John*, written some time in the later 1530s, is important. It is about that English King John who in the early thirteenth century defied the pope. It draws on medieval traditions of using characters with names like Dissimulation or Private Wealth or Sedition to attack corruption by 'the whole heap of adders of Antichrist's generation'; but Bale also drew portraits of the king, of Stephen Langton and Cardinal Pandulphus which look forward to the history plays of Shakespeare and Marlowe. Unlike Shakespeare's King John, however, Bale's king is an idealised Christian hero battling with the immense power of the pope. Bale cited David and Goliath: 'A strong David at the voice of verity great Goliath the pope he strake down.'[34] David's victory with stone and sling was not due to his personal qualities. The stirring story in 1 Samuel 17 tells of the unknown 'stripling' who was not in the least afraid of the giant Goliath's bragging.

> Thou comest to me with a sword, and with a spear, and with a shield; but I come to thee in the name of the Lord of hosts . . . whom thou hast defied. This day will the Lord deliver me into mine hand . . . for the battle is the Lord's, and he will give you into our hands.

At nearly fifty, the obese King Henry VIII in 1539 could not, even in the wildest flattery, be described as a stripling: but it suited the reformers very well to have him as David, not only felling the Philistine giant pope with one simple stone, the Word of God; but as a ruler greatly loved, who had the potential also to be greatly used by God. Bale towards the end of his play takes sentences from Tyndale's *Obedience*.[35] In that treatise Tyndale declared (his words apparently approved by King Henry himself) that kings should be obeyed provided that they themselves obeyed God. Further, they had a duty to read the Scriptures so that they could defeat the usurpation of authority by bishops and clergy. George Joye, exiled like Tyndale in Antwerp, the translator of certain Old Testament books (from Latin), went further, saying that kings should learn the biblical law and teach their subjects to do the same, especially in appointing the godly and learned to teach them.[36]

David was the outstanding ruler, warrior and organiser in Israel's history. His great gift to the new nation was the founding of the sanctuary of Zion, with all that that brought. He established Jerusalem as the capital for ever: his disappointment at not being chosen by God to be the builder of the Temple (the work of his son Solomon) was assuaged by the promise that God would establish the house (lineage) of David for ever (2 Samuel 7:12 and 16).

King Henry as David is bringing a new start to national life, giving 'everyone' the Word of God, establishing England as the sanctuary of Zion in its freedom from the pope and the absolute accessibility of the *Verbum Dei* to everyone — at least in theory. (That David was not perfect, demonstrated by his adulterous affair with the married Bathsheba as much as by his having her husband killed, made a parallel that was noticed: John Bale called Anne Boleyn's sister, with whom Henry had an affair, Bathsheba.)

After Cromwell's fall in 1540, his arms were removed from the title-page, leaving simply a circular white space – perhaps a comment from ambivalence of feeling about him.

TEXT

In the text, Coverdale revised not his own 1535 Bible, but 'Matthew's'. In the Old Testament, he left Tyndale's Pentateuch and historical books more or less alone. Revising his own poetic and prophetic books, he was able to make use of the most recent work of Germany's leading Hebraist, Sebastian Münster, whose new translation of the Hebrew Scriptures into Latin had been printed in 1535. It is far superior to Pagninus's odd Latinizing, which Coverdale had originally used. The Psalms from his original 1535 version he also left more or less alone.[37]

The second edition, in 1540, had a Preface by the Archbishop, Thomas Cranmer, causing this Bible to be sometimes named, from the early nineteenth century, 'Cranmer's Bible'. He commended the widespread reading of the Bible (presumably aloud in church, considering the bulk of the book; his Preface reads well aloud). He appealed to the authority of the ancient fathers Chrysostom and Gregory of Nazianzus, supporting his plea that the Bible was the sufficient rule of faith and life:

> Here may all manner of persons: men, women; young, old; learned, unlearned; rich, poor; priests, laymen; lords, ladies; officers, tenants, and mean men; virgins, wives, widows; lawyers, merchants, artificers, husbandmen, and all manner of persons, of what estate or condition soever they be; may in THIS BOOK learn all things, what they ought to believe, what they ought to do, and what they should not do, as well concerning Almighty God, as also concerning themselves, and all others.[38]

In the fourth and sixth editions, of November 1540 and November 1541, the central panel of the title now had a new inscription, defining this as 'The Bible in English as the largest and greatest volume', and praising the 'supreme head of this his church', which is not the Lord Jesus Christ but 'our most redouted Prince and sovereign Lord King Henry the VIII'. This Bible is to be 'used in every church', by royal command. It has been overseen by two bishops, of Durham and Rochester. 'Durham' was that very Cuthbert Tunstall who denied Tyndale and burned his New Testaments fourteen years before. The need to obey the king came before his scruples about Tyndale; he was now giving his high authority to promulgate his work, as he would well know.

COVERDALE'S FURTHER LIFE

While the printing of the Great Bible was being finished in London, Coverdale was in Newbury. From there he reported to Cromwell about breaches in the king's laws against papism, sought out churches in the district where the honour of Becket was still maintained, and prepared to make a bonfire of any primers and other church books which had not been altered to match the king's proceedings.[39] He had, in 1538, published his Diglot of the New Testament: the Latin was Erasmus's text from his *Novum instrumentum*, the English adapted from his own 1535 translation, but tending more towards the Vulgate. The book, several times reprinted, had a complex history.

The conservatives led by Stephen Gardiner, Bishop of Winchester, rapidly began to recover their power and oppose Cromwell. On 28 June 1539, the Act of Six Articles, which ended official tolerance of reform, became law. Coverdale, like many others, soon fled overseas again.

Second exile, 1540–1547

Before leaving England Coverdale had married Elizabeth Macheson, a Scotswoman of noble family. Her sister Agnes married John Macalpine or McAlpine: all three had come to England as religious exiles from Scotland. Macalpine became canon of Salisbury in July 1538. When Coverdale, with his wife, left England they apparently went straight to Strasbourg, where they were welcomed by the wife of Calvin, who had escaped dissension by moving to that city. John Macalpine and his wife went via Bremen to Wittenberg, where he became Doctor of Divinity. There Philip Melanchthon gave him the name of Maccabaeus (presumably a cognomen for him as an independence-fighter, but perhaps also a joke on his Scottish name, as MacCabaeus). On the invitation of the King of Denmark, Macalpine became Professor of Divinity at Copenhagen, and presently one of the translators of the Danish Bible of 1550. Both 'Maccabaeus' and the King of Denmark will appear later in Coverdale's history.

On 28 July 1540, Robert Barnes was burned alive at Smithfield. Two days later, and without trial, Thomas Cromwell was sent to the block on Tower Hill. The English exiles could not consider return for some time. Coverdale remained in Strasbourg for about three years. He translated books from Latin and German – two were by Bullinger – and wrote an important defence of his martyred friend Barnes. This, the theologically gritty *Confutation of that treatise which one J. Standish made . . .* , joining his revulsion at the death of Barnes to that of Bale, Joye and others in print, is his most significant reforming statement outside his Bible prefaces. He received from Tübingen the degree of Doctor of Divinity at this time, and visited Denmark. He wrote a tract describing the order of the Lord's Supper as he had seen it in Denmark, which was later burned with others at Paul's Cross. While in Strasbourg, Coverdale made an important friendship with Conrad Hubert, Martin Bucer's secretary, who was also preacher at the church of St Thomas. Hubert was a native of a small town forty miles north of Strasbourg, Bergzabern, and on his recommendation Coverdale became in September 1543 assistant minister of Bergzabern and headmaster of the town school, a post he held for five years.

Doctor Coverdale was thankfully welcomed by his predecessor, Nicolaus Thomae, whose illness had undermined his competence. On 22 April 1544, Thomae wrote to Hubert that the new headmaster was 'a man of singular piety and incomparable diligence, a watchful and scrupulous performer of every duty of religion. Alleluia.' Other letters from Thomae before his death[40] in the summmer of 1546 give glimpses of Coverdale. He is now apparently learning Hebrew with admirable diligence. He is shocked at Luther's violent attack late in 1544 on the sacramental views

of fellow-reformers, including Zwingli and Oecolampadius. He gives
amused advice over the dilemma of an aged and widowed ministerial colleague about marrying a young girl. Twenty-one letters to Hubert from
Coverdale himself have survived, giving news of the school and its pupils,
some of whom have gone on to Strasbourg. His duties as assistant minister give him insights into the state of the Church: catechizing is producing good results, but heretical teaching is increasing. He is described
by a correspondent to Bullinger in April 1545 as 'well loved and honoured
by all the ministers of the word and the other learned men of this
region'.[41] He had continued to publish translations of German tracts, and
in that year, his fifty-eighth, he produced *The defence of a certayne poore
christen man.*

In England, meanwhile, as he noted, blasphemous tongues did not cease
to rail on him and to slander him even to the king as a maker of revolution.[42] In the proclamation of 8 July 1546 all his books were condemned,
and about a dozen of them, including his Bible, were burned at Paul's
Cross on 26 September 1546 by Bonner as Bishop of London. King Henry
died on 27 January 1547.

Bishop of Exeter, 1551–1553

Though Henry's successor Edward loved reform, Coverdale stayed for a
further year in Germany, apparently awaiting a summons to return home.
From Frankfurt on 26 March 1548 he wrote to Calvin that he was returning home by invitation after an exile of eight years. He enclosed with the
letter his own Latin and German translations of the new English order of
communion. In London on 24 June he preached the festival sermon for
the Merchant Taylors at St Martin's Outwich. He soon became almoner
to Katherine Parr, now re-married, and worked on her project of the
English translation of Erasmus's paraphrases (see below). He preached the
sermon at her funeral in September 1548 at Sudely Castle in Gloucestershire. In October he was at Windsor Castle as royal chaplain, and probably being consulted with bishops and divines by Cranmer about the
making of the first Book of Common Prayer. From there, writing also on
behalf of Cranmer, he invited Paul Fagius of Strasbourg to England to
escape rising persecution in Germany. He preached at Paul's Cross on the
second Sunday in Lent 1549, again on Low Sunday, and again on Whit
Monday, the day after the 'handselling' (first using) of the English Prayer
Book, when the aldermen assembled on foot in their scarlet robes.[43]

On that day, however, 10 June 1549, events began in the West Country
that were to affect Coverdale greatly. Rebellion broke out in Devon and
Cornwall against the new English Prayer Book. Lord Russell was sent to

put it down. Coverdale went with him as preacher. A later writer recalled that 'none of the clergy were ready to risk life with Russell's expedition but old Father Coverdale'.[44] On the field at Woodbury Windmill, Coverdale preached 'and caused general thanksgiving to be made unto God'.[45] The rebellion was put down by the end of August, but Coverdale stayed on for several months, helping to pacify the people. He was doing the work that properly belonged to the bishop of Exeter: but that prelate, John Vesey, now eighty-six years old, had not stirred from Sutton Cold-field in Warwickshire, his birthplace, for some time before, and had left the diocese to look after itself. That Coverdale was virtual bishop was recognised by Latimer, who in a Lenten sermon in 1550 was insistent that though Vesey bore the title, Coverdale did the work.[46] In a letter to Bullinger of 1 June 1550, Peter Martyr (in England to help Cranmer with the revision of the Prayer Book) described Coverdale as 'a good man who in former years acted as parish minister in Germany' who now 'labours greatly in Devon in preaching and explaining the Scriptures'. He proph-esied that Coverdale would become bishop of Exeter.[47]

Coverdale was active in various offices, particularly that of preacher. Just before Easter 1551 he spent some time with Peter Martyr at Magdalen College, Oxford, attending his lectures on the Epistle to the Romans, and preaching to the people: Peter Martyr called him 'an active preacher, and one that has well served the cause of the gospel'.[48] Coverdale was in demand. In the winter of 1550/51 he preached funeral sermons for Sir James Welford at Little St Bartholomew's and for Lord Wentworth at Westminster Abbey. He was a member of the commission appointed in January 1551 to deal with Anabaptism and other heresy. He sat as judge at the trial of George van Parris of Mainz, an Anabaptist denounced for Arian views: he knew no English, so Coverdale acted as interpreter. Van Parris was burned alive in April 1551.

On 14 August 1551, John Vesey was ejected from his see and Coverdale nominated in his place. Vesey had drained the finances, and the new bishop inherited large debts. Coverdale was poor. He had returned from Germany *pauper in hoc mundo*, as John Bale put it in 1548.[49] He could not raise the £500 due as firstfruits: the Crown, on the plea of Cranmer, remitted it. The wider debts incurred by Vesey were written off, and the whole see was reassessed for the future at less than a third of its former valuation. Coverdale, vested in surplice and cope, was consecrated at Croydon on 30 August 1551, and enthroned on 11 September. A curiosity is that on the day before his enthronement he and his wife were given permanent permission to eat flesh and milk in Lent and other fast days, with not more than five or six guests, despite the act of Parliament that ordained abstinence.[50]

Coverdale was regular in attendance at the House of Lords, and he sat on the commission appointed on 12 February 1552 to reform the canon law. His chief labour, however, was in his diocese. In his *Description of the City of Exeter*, John Hooker, then in his household, gives an account of how he 'most worthily did perform the office committed unto him':

> he preached continually upon every holy day, and did read most commonly twice in the week in some one church or other within this city. He was, after the rate of his livings, a great keeper of hospitality, very sober in diet, godly in life, friendly to the godly, liberal to the poor, and courteous to all men, void of pride, full of humility, abhorring covetousness, and an enemy to all wickedness and wicked men, whose companies he shunned, and whom he would in no wise shroud [shelter] or have in his house and company. His wife a most sober, chaste and godly matron: his house and household another church, in which was exercised all godliness and virtue. No one person being in his house which did not from time to time give an account of his faith and religion, and also did live accordingly . . . Yet the common people, whose old bottles would receive no new wine, could not brook nor digest him, for no other cause but because he was a preacher of the gospel, an enemy to papistry, and a married man.[51]

Hooker reports that Coverdale was the victim of false suggestions, open railings, false libels and secret backbitings. At Totnes and at Bodmin there were apparently attempts to poison him. His enemies the Archdeacon of Barnstaple, John Pollard, and the Vicar of Ipplepen, Walter Hele, were forced by him to recant in the cathedral.[52]

At this time (16 August 1549) the second volume of Erasmus's important and popular *Paraphrases on the New Testament* in English was published. Working with Leonard Cox and John Olde, Coverdale's share was almost certainly Romans, Corinthians, Galatians and a preface, and he edited the whole book.[53] England was twenty years behind Germany, and seven behind France, in translating the *Paraphrases*. About this time he edited a corrected edition of the Lollard tract, *Wiclif's Wicket*. In 1550, Coverdale published a version of Werdmüller's *Precious Pearl*, made at the request and expense of the Duke of Somerset, and very popular. That year saw a new edition of his 1525 Bible, printed by Froschover in Zurich.

On 6 July 1553, King Edward died. On Queen Mary's accession, Coverdale found himself summoned almost immediately to appear before the Privy Council. There he was ordered, on 1 September 1553, 'to attend until the lords' pleasures be further known'.[54] This seems to have meant house arrest in Exeter. In November 1553 and April 1554 both Peter Martyr and the king of Denmark refer to him as having been a prisoner.

On 18 September, Coverdale was ejected and Vesey, now ninety and still in Warwickshire, was reinstated.

Third exile, 1553–1559

Coverdale was in danger. John Hooker records the certainty of his enemies in Devon that he, above all bishops, would be burned. He saw clearly how vulnerable he was, but stated that, in spite of rumours that he would recant, he was 'steadfastly determined never to return unto Egypt, never to kiss the calf . . . never to refuse or recant the word of life . . . for the corn that the Lord hath appointed for his own barn shall be safe enough, and kept full well by the help of him that is owner thereof'.[55]

He wrote an answer to a sermon given at Paul's Cross by Dr Weston which contained the famous words 'you have the word and we have the sword'.[55] He added his name to a statement of belief by twelve of his brethren, prisoners. Meanwhile, the king of Denmark, at the request of Coverdale's brother-in-law 'Maccabaeus' in Copenhagen, wrote to Queen Mary on 25 April 1554 requesting Coverdale's release on the grounds that he had committed no crime: he was imprisoned only through the troubles of the time. If his presence in England is undesirable, adds the king, he, and his, will be welcome in Denmark. Queen Mary's reply, which has not survived, assures her fellow monarch that the only cause of Coverdale's detention was a debt which he owed to the Crown, and there was no need for anxiety on any other account. The king replied on 24 September 1554. He is full of pleasure at her gracious answer, and that his fears were groundless, and he has comforted the grief of 'Maccabaeus' and his wife. He raises one further small point: the debt was due from Coverdale as bishop of Exeter: but Coverdale is no longer bishop of Exeter. What he received from the see was very small. If there are small faults in the accounts, the king is sure that the queen will overlook them. He greatly looks forward to welcoming Coverdale to Denmark and hearing from his own lips the story of the royal clemency.

Queen Mary did not reply for five months. On 18 February she wrote to the king that she would permit Coverdale to go to Denmark, 'though he is not yet quit of the debt of money which he is bound by law to pay to our treasury'. On the next day, 19 February, the Privy Council issued a passport permitting Coverdale 'to pass from hence towards Denmark with two of his servants, his bags and baggages'.[56] Since none of those phrases can, it is hoped, refer to Mrs Coverdale, we must assume that her presence was taken for granted. It is probable that there were children. The party arrived in Denmark, and no doubt the king's wish was fulfilled to hear from Coverdale's own lips the story of exactly how clement his

queen had been – even to the pursuit of debts which her treasury's creative accounting had landed on his shoulders, for moneys belonging to
periods when Coverdale was not bishop. Foxe is undoubtedly right: debt
was merely 'a colourable excuse for shifting off the matter'[57]. Fellow
bishops who conformed and put away their wives found similar debts
cancelled.

The Coverdales did not stay long in Denmark; probably only a few
weeks. The University of Copenhagen honoured him with a present of
wine and claret. The king apparently offered him a benefice, but, not
knowing the language, Coverdale refused. He set off for Wesel, where he
served as chaplain to a small community of English people for three or
four months. Then an invitation came from the magistrates at Bergzaben,
approved by the prince, for him to resume his old work. Coverdale
accepted, and by way of Frankfurt, he arrived on 20 September 1555. He
stayed for two years. Nothing is known of this second period in the town.
He arrived aged sixty-eight and left at seventy.

In the summer of 1557 he moved to Aarau. The English community at
Wesel had been banished for theological reasons, and made its way slowly
to Switzerland, arriving at Aarau on 11 August 1557. Coverdale joined
them. In contemporary documents he is described as born at York, having
a wife and two children, and lodging in the Frauenkloster. Then a little
over a year later he received leave, on 24 October 1558, to settle in Geneva.

Queen Mary died on 17 November 1558. Coverdale did not hasten
home. It is most likely that he had gone to Geneva to work on the English
Bible. Whittingham's New Testament had appeared there in 1557, and the
whole Geneva Bible would be published in April 1560. Though his
Hebrew, and, apparently now, Greek, could not match the local scholars'
skills, he would no doubt have special things to offer as one who nearly
two dozen years before had translated the whole Bible singlehanded, the
only Englishman to have done so: and then revised it under royal authority for successive editions of the Great Bible. A life of Whittingham written
about 1603 states that 'the learned that were at Geneva, as Bishop
Coverdale . . . did undertake the translation of the Geneva Bible'.[58]
Writing later from London on 22 February 1560, to William Cole at
Geneva, Coverdale shows a lively interest in the progress of the work.[59]

On 29 November 1558 he stood godfather to John Knox's son. On 16
December he became an elder of the English church in Geneva. In that
month he joined in the reconciling letter sent by the leaders of that church
to the other English churches on the Continent.[60] He seems to have set
off for England in August 1559. On the way a piece of his luggage went
astray. In London, he and his family were able to lodge with the Duchess
of Suffolk, whom he had known at Wesel; he was now apparently

appointed as preacher and tutor to her children. His letter to William
Cole at Geneva, as well as reporting the arrival of the missing trunk in
December (thanks to a friend in Antwerp), describes the duchess as having
'like us, the greatest abhorrence of the ceremonies', that is, the increasing
use of vestments.[61]

London, 1559–1569

Coverdale did not resume the bishopric of Exeter, though John Hooker
wrote that he was 'appoynted agayne bishop of Exeter, but he refused it
and contented himself to be a preacher of the gospel'.[62] His reasons are
unknown, but several can be guessed. At seventy-two he may have felt
unwilling to take on not only the strenuous life of a bishop if the work
was done well, but the sorting-out of the acute problems in the see. It
had no money. Nor had Coverdale. Once again he had returned from
exile penniless. Dislike of the vestments may have been a reason. Offici-
ating with three other bishops (though technically he was not a bishop)
at the ceremony of the consecration of Archbishop Matthew Parker in the
chapel of Lambeth Palace on 17 December 1559, Coverdale wore a black
gown, though his colleagues were vested in copes.

Not far short of five years after his return to England, in January 1564,
Coverdale accepted from Grindal, Bishop of London, the living of St
Magnus Martyr by London Bridge. He was too poor to pay the firstfruits,
and they were forgiven him by the queen. In Grindal's letter to Cecil
praying for this concession, he pointed out that since his bishopric had
been taken from him, Coverdale had neither pension nor annuity.[63] He
had in the meantime been an active preacher. On 12 November 1559 he
preached at Paul's Cross, and again on 28 April 1560, before the mayor,
aldermen and a great audience. Late in 1563, for a funeral sermon at St
Olave's, Southwark, he received forty shillings. In 1560 he had published
his last work, *Certain most Godly, Fruitful and Comfortable Letters of such True
Saintes and Holye Martyrs as in the Late Bloodye Persecution gave their Lives*,
which remains a valuable source of information. In July 1562 he gave
another funeral sermon, in St Alphage's, Cripplegate, where twelve clerks
sang the service for the widow of a doctor of physic. In 1563 he fell victim
to plague, but recovered. At Cambridge that year he was installed Doctor
of Divinity, by incorporation from Tübingen.[64] In April 1564, he acted
for the Cambridge vice-chancellor in conferring the same degree on
Grindal, who had incidentally done a good deal to try to get a post for
Coverdale: every offer had been declined. Grindal wrote to Cecil propos-
ing 'father Coverdale' for the vacant see of Llandaff.

Surely it is not well that he, *qui ante nos omnes fuit in Christo*, should be now in his age without stay of living. O cannot herein excuse us bishops. Somewhat I have to say for myself: for I have offered him divers things, which he thought not meet for him.[65]

It does not appear that Llandaff was ever offered to him.

Elizabeth Coverdale died in early September 1565, and was buried in St Michael, Paternoster Royal, on 8 September. He married his second wife, Katherine, on 7 April 1566 at the same church. He resigned from St Magnus in the summer of 1566, after two and a half years. A case can be made for his leaving the living on Puritan grounds, as in March of that year Archbishop Parker had caused great consternation among many clergy by his edicts prescribing what was to be worn, and his summons of the London clergy to Lambeth to ask for their compliance. Coverdale excused himself from attending. He could not travel, he said, and there were other reasons. No doubt the reasons were those appearing in the letters sent by him and others to the divines of Geneva and Zurich, declaring the distress of the faithful in England and asking for guidance in this day of perplexity.[66]

As long as his strength permitted (he was now nearly eighty) he preached in London, with a keen following in Puritan circles, though since he was apparently becoming fearful for his safety they could not always find out where he would preach next. In the winter of 1567–8 he preached a course of eleven sermons in Holy Trinity in the Minories. From January 1568 he and his second wife had lived in a house belonging to the Merchant Taylors in the parish of St Benet Fink in Broad Street ward. In January 1569 he gave his last sermon, at a regular service he was attending at St Magnus, when it was found that there was no preacher. John Hooker described what happened.

> . . . certain men of the parish came unto him, and earnestly entreated that considering the multitude was great, and that it was pity they should be disappointed of their expectation, that it would please him to take the place for that time. But he excused his age and the infirmities thereof, and that his memory failed him, his voice scarce to be heard, and he not able to do it, that they would hold him excused. Nevertheless such were their importunate requests that, would he nould he, he must and did yield unto their requests: and between two men he was carried up into the pulpit, where God did with his spirit so strengthen him, that he made his last and the best and the most godly sermon that ever he did in all his life. And very shortly after he died, being very honourably buried with the presence of the duchess of

Suffolk, the earl of Bedford, and many others, honourable and worshipful personages.[67]

Coverdale died on 20 January 1569, and was buried in the chancel of St Bartholomew by the Exchange, under the communion table. The marble stone and brass inscription were destroyed in the Great Fire of 1666. Surviving copies show Latin elegiacs to the effect that he was of singular uprightness and lived for eighty-one years. St Bartholomew's church was in 1840 pulled down to make room for the Royal Exchange. Coverdale's remains were removed to the Wren church of St Magnus Martyr, where they now lie, with a tablet on the east wall, close to the altar, amid T. S. Eliot's 'inexplicable splendour of Ionian white and gold'. He left no will. On 23 January letters of administration were granted to his wife Katherine. It appears that he has no living descendants.

Miles Coverdale was a man who, all his life, was loved for that 'singular uprightness'. He was always in demand as a preacher of the Gospel. He was an assiduous bishop. He pressed forward with great work in the face of the complexities and adversities produced by official policies. His gift to posterity has been from his scholarship as a translator, from his steadily developing sense of English rhythms, spoken and sung: and in his incalculable shaping of the nation's moral and religious sense through the reading aloud in every parish from his 'bible of the largest size'.

Coverdale made clear that his aim was always better understanding. He saw that, because languages were not the same, being literal in translation brought problems. He wrote about this in the preface to the book where it was most plain to see, in his Latin-English diglot (1538).

> Because I am loath to swerve from the text, I so temper my pen, that, if thou wilt, thou mayest make plain construction of [the Latin] by the English that standeth on the other side. This is done now for thee that art not exactly learned in the Latin tongue and wouldest fain understand it.[68]

To make sure that he was clear, and the text neither wrested nor perverted, in that diglot he expanded phrases in square brackets. For example, Luke 6:49, 'But who so heareth and doth [them] not'; John 14:19, 'For I live, and ye shall live [also]'; Romans 11:11, 'But by their fall is health [happened] unto the heathen'.[69] He tried to do the same for the Great Bible, but the annotations that he intended were not printed.[70]

COVERDALE AS REVISER

Coverdale's brief had been effectively to revise 'Matthew's' so that, being more acceptable to all the bishops, it could be put in every parish church.

When we compare his Great Bible with 'Matthew's' where 'Matthew's' is straight Tyndale, however, we find little change. The Old Testament from Genesis 1 to the end of 2 Chronicles in this Great Bible, put out as a vehicle for the power of King Henry VIII, overseen by Cuthbert Tunstall himself, is just that, straight Tyndale, with very small changes. I illustrate, quite at random, from Deuteronomy 32:10. In this poem is being described God's power in his people's history. 'Matthew's' in 1537 had 'He found him in a desert land, in a void ground and a roaring wilderness' (the last two words making a wonderfully suggestive phrase). That is what Tyndale had in his 1530 Pentateuch. Coverdale's own translation, in his Bible of 1535, had been 'He found him in the wilderness, even in the dry desert, where he roared.' Revising for the Great Bible, Coverdale merely added an 'in' to 'Matthew's': 'He found him in a desert land, in a void ground, and in a roaring wilderness.'

Where Coverdale did not have Tyndale before him, from Ezra to Malachi and in the Apocrypha, he was a great deal less even, sometimes printing himself from 1535, sometimes changing for the better, sometimes for the worse. He left his Psalms more or less alone: there were changes, but the Prayer Book continued to use his 1535 version. In the New Testament he could again rely on Tyndale, which he did with insight and skill.

TAVERNER AND CHEKE

In 1539 there appeared a complete new English translation of the whole Bible by Richard Taverner, a scholar of Greek and Hebrew who held high offices in the land. His name does not appear in the list of acceptable earlier translators given to King James's scholars, and that may be why he has so readily been brushed aside, following Westcott's sniffy dismissal of him as one who 'exercised no influence', and who was 'alien'.[71] Both judgements, though they appear to have been massively influential, are odd, making one wonder whether Westcott's dislike had some hidden basis. Fortunately, he is being brought back into view.[72] (A problem of access remains, in that there is no published facsimile.) Taverner's aims were compression and vividness, in which he succeeded. He has been misrepresented, even by Darlow, Moule and Herbert, as merely revising Tyndale and Coverdale in 'Matthew's' Bible, whereas he was effectively starting again. Why Westcott found 'alien' and of 'no influence' the translator who restored to us the word 'parable', (for Tyndale's 'similitude') and others, one cannot imagine. Taverner's Bible went through eight further editions up to 1551.

'Parable', however, appeared as 'biword' in an experimental translation of the Gospel of Matthew (with a little of Mark) using words only of pure Saxon ancestry (and thus in the opposite direction to Stephen Gardiner; see see below p. 228) written in 1550 by Sir John Cheke, formerly Professor of Greek at Cambridge, and tutor to Edward VI. His aims were to try to remove difficult words of Greek and Latin origin, and to try to fit spelling to pronunciation. Occasionally he coined unusual forms: for 'proselyte' he gave 'freshman', for 'resurrection', 'uprising' or 'gainrising'. An 'apostle' is a 'frosent', the 'high priest' is the 'hed bishop'. 'Lunatic' is 'moond', and 'wise men' are 'wizards'. A 'centurion' is a 'hundreder'. 'Foreigners' are 'Welschmen'.[73] Here, curious as it is, is indeed a version which had no influence.

Chapter 14

TOWARDS THE REIGN OF EDWARD VI, 1547–1553

AFTER THE PUBLICATION OF THE Great Bible in 1539 and its minor revisions, and the new translation by Taverner also in 1539, there were many editions and reprintings of English Bibles, especially of Tyndale. There was, however, no new work on translation of the Bible into English for eighteen years, until 1557, when a new English New Testament was published in Geneva, with fresh, though light, annotation. Three years later it was incorporated into a new complete Bible. That Geneva Bible of 1560 (with later revisions in 1576 and 1599) was the most significant book in English for the following hundred years – a large claim, but one that will be found to be justified, not only for Britain, but, from towards the end of the sixteenth century, in the creeks and coastal plains of America. The Geneva Bible was at the heart of the founding of those colonies, as will be seen, in a greater way than even KJV. For many decades, 'Geneva' was the source book for public and personal lives in Britain, and a motor that drove revolution. The events in Geneva which produced that English Bible in 1560 will be made easier to understand by consideration of some part of what happened in the church in England in the thirty years before, especially in the short reign of Edward VI.

DIRECTIONS THAT REFORM SHOULD TAKE, C. 1528

Tyndale can be seen to have been thinking ahead to a peculiarly English Reformation, one that in the end was only partly fulfilled by Elizabeth's Anglican Settlement. He wrote in his *Obedience of a Christian Man* (1528) about church government. On strictly New Testament grounds, he approved a monarch as a ruler to be obeyed, provided that that monarch obeyed God as declared in Scripture. A main section of his book is 'The obedience of subjects unto Kings, princes and rulers', and it is, as is usual with Tyndale, full of the New Testament. The section opens with most of Romans chapter 13, in his own 1526 translation –

Let every soul submit himself unto the authority of the higher powers. For there is no power but of God. The powers that be, are ordained of God . . .

(The familiar phrase, 'the powers that be', was his making.)

Evil rulers must not be resisted: they are 'the rod and scourge where-with God chastiseth us'.[1]

A central section of the book then turns the matter through 180 degrees, expounding 'The duty of kings and of the judges and officers'. Kings should remember that

the people are God's, and not theirs: yea, are Christ's inheritance and possession, bought with his blood. The most despised person in the realm is the king's brother and fellow-member with him in the kingdom of God and of Christ.[2]

(The significance of kings in the thought of Tyndale and other reformers will be discussed later in this chapter.) Essential in all Tyndale's writing is the power of Scripture, which has to be in the mother tongue, as a standard against which to judge all human activity (for we are all part of God's creation) and to demonstrate the truth of God as an active force.

That is the context for what Tyndale and all reformers of the time saw as the hindering, indeed blasphemous, claims to power made by an intru-sive hierarchical organisation, the papal church. This encouraged supersti-tion, kept the Bible from the people, and above all laid down practices which had become wholly corrupt. As A. G. Dickens put it with ironic understatement, 'In both Testaments one might frequently encounter prophets announcing the good tidings, but one could sense singularly little of the medieval or Renaissance papacy.'[3] It is the general blasphemy that especially stings Tyndale. He gives a quotation from the profession of a novice of the Observants, who, in answer to his promising to keep the rules of St Francis, is told by the father, 'And I promise you again ever-lasting life.' Tyndale comments, 'If eternal life be due unto the pilled [bald] traditions of lousy friars, where is the testament become that God made unto us in Christ's blood?'[4] Three times in his *Obedience* he notes that the pope's 'spirituality . . . sell thee for money that which God in Christ promiseth freely'.[5]

Vivid anti-clerical writing was not new in Europe. It had been espe-cially strong in England in the decades before Arundel's Constitutions of 1409 – Wyclif, Chaucer and Langland come first to mind. It sprang to life again in the years when Tyndale wrote. Simon Fish's short *Supplication of Beggars* (1529) is still lively and powerful: Foxe reprints the whole of it,[6] and reports that it was enjoyed by Henry VIII, to whom it is addressed.

Christopher St Germain's book, *Treatise concernynge the Division between the Spiritualitie and Temporalitie*, printed in about 1532, was widely known. Tyndale's chief target was what he called 'the belly brotherhood' of monks and friars, a brotherhood that was increasing daily.[7]

It is noticeable that in all his frequently intemperate attacks on Tyndale, Sir Thomas More never once defended the 'spirituality'. In the Preface to the little book that was his only answer to More's outpourings, Tyndale wrote:

> Judge whether it be possible that any good should come out of their dumb ceremonies and sacraments into thy soul. Judge their penance, pilgrimages, pardons, purgatory, praying to posts, dumb blessings, dumb absolutions, their dumb pattering, and howling, their dumb strange holy gestures, with all their dumb disguisings, their satisfactions and justifyings.[8]

'Dumb', of course, because in Latin.

As other European reformers did, Tyndale identified the figure of an 'antichrist' referred to in the first Epistle of John, 2:1 ('even now there are many antichrists come already' as he translates it) with the most corrupt practices as instructed by the pope. He lays about him with exhilarating force against the money-demands of the multitude of clergy – his observation of the great increase in their numbers is supported by modern calculations, their being a hundred thousand in orders in England, of which ten thousand were monks or friars, in a population of two and a half million.[9] At the highest level, the new readers of the New Testament found a contrast between the simple poverty of Jesus and his disciples and the greed of the already enormously wealthy papal church, not only architecturally in Rome, but in the English monasteries. At the local level, a growing scandal was the priest's right of mortuary, whereby for attending a death he could claim the most valuable item in the household.

> If a poor man die and leave his wife and half a dozen young children and but one cow to find them, that they will have for a mortuary merciless: let come of wife and children what will.[10]

Every parish, however poor, was responsible for the provision of whatever was said to be required.

> None shall receive the body of Christ at easter, be he never so poor a beggar or ever so young a lad or maid, but they must pay somewhat for it. Then mortuaries for forgotten tithes, as they say . . . They will forget nothing. No man shall die in their debt: or if any man do, he shall pay it when he is dead. They will lose nothing. Why? It is God's:

it is not theirs. It is St Hubert's rents, St Alban's lands, St Edmond's right, St Peter's patrimony, say they, and none of ours. Item: if a man die in another man's parish, besides that he must pay at home a mortuary for forgotten tithes, he must pay there also the best that he there hath: whether it be an horse of twenty pound, or how good soever he be: either [or] a chain of gold or an hundred marks or five hundred pounds if it so chance. It is much, verily, for so little painstaking in confession, and in ministering the sacraments. Then beadrolls. Item chrysome [baptism], churchings, banns, weddings, offering at weddings, offering at buryings, offering to images, offering of wax and lights, which come to their vantage . . . The hallowing, or rather conjuring, of churches, chapels, altars, super-altars, chalice, vestments, and bells. Then book, bell, candlestick, organs, chalice, vestments, copes, altar-cloths, surplices, towels, basins, ewers, ship [for holding incense], censer, and all manner ornament, must be found them freely: they will not give a mite thereunto. Last of all, what swarm of begging friars are there! The parson sheareth, the vicar shaveth, the parish priest polleth, the friar scrapeth, and the pardoner pareth: we lack but a butcher to pull off the skin.[11]

Tyndale is scathing about superstition replacing faith, even in performance of the mass.

If any of them happen to swallow his spittle, or any of the water wherewith he washeth his mouth, ere he go to mass: or touch the sacrament with his nose: or if the ass [i.e. the priest] forget to breathe on him [i.e. the bread or chalice], or happen to handle it with any of his fingers which are not anointed, or say *Alleluia* instead of *Laus tibi Domine* or *Ite missa est* instead of *Benedicamus Domino* or pour too much wine in the chalice, or read the gospel without light, or make not his crosses aright, how trembleth he! How feareth he! What an horrible sin is committed! I cry God mercy, saith he, and you my ghostly father. But to hold an whore, or another man's wife, to buy a benefice, to set one realm at variance with another, and to cause twenty thousand men to die on a day, is but a trifle and a pastime with them.[12]

Tyndale's proleptic support of Archbishop Cranmer's modest and unified Prayer Book in English twenty years later, in 1549, can be identified in his attacks on the prolixity, the Latin and the superstition in the services of his time. William Tyndale and Thomas Cranmer had many things in common. Both were high scholars: Cranmer had been a Fellow of Jesus College, Cambridge, while Erasmus was in that university teaching Greek. Both men had far-reaching minds and sympathies across many borders. Both men welcomed fellow workers from whatever distance. Both were masters of English prose. Both were dedicated to the restoration of New

Testament Christianity, and both were killed for it.

Cranmer, like Tyndale, had the ability to know an entire field as a scholar but to get to the very heart of the matter with simple directness. Cranmer's liturgical studies led him to reduce the number of responds and antiphons quite drastically, and to throw out from the daily service altogether the long-traditional readings from lives of the saints and the Offices of the Blessed Virgin Mary, putting in their place, in Mattins, Evensong and Communion, readings in English from the whole New Testament three times a year, and all the Old Testament once a year. That was a Tyndalian thing to do, and of course Tyndale, though he could not be named, had largely provided those Bible translations. Equally Tyndalian was Cranmer's total shift from a religion in Latin to Christianity in English. Here is Tyndale:

> What then saith the pope? What care I for Paul? I command by virtue of obedience to read the gospel in Latin. Let them not pray but in Latin, no, not their *Pater noster*. If any be sick, go also and say them a gospel, and all in Latin . . . It is verily as good to preach it to swine as to men if thou preach it in a tongue they understand not. How shall I be thankful to Christ for his kindness? How shall I believe the truth and promises which God hath sworn, while thou tellest them unto me in a tongue which I understand not?[13]

At the heart of the attacks by all reformers was the contrast between the faith that they felt was so clearly stated in the New Testament in Gospels, Acts and the Epistles, intended for all to read, and that immense system of hierarchies, legal apparatus, superstitious beliefs and, above all, practices, which had grown up many centuries later, based largely on what they saw as the greatest fraud of all. This was the claim that all those things had been given secretly by Jesus to Peter, never written down. These 'unwritten verities' were automatically claimed as standard authorities. For example, John Fisher, that Bishop of Rochester attacked by Tyndale in his *Obedience*, in his own sermon against Luther observes in passing 'Those blessed apostles left unto us also many things by mouth, which is not written in the bible . . .'; and he interprets a phrase of Paul in 2 Thessalonians commending his instruction by sermons and letters (given in Latin) as 'Here ye may see by express scripture of St Paul that we be bound to believe many more things than be written and put in the bible.'[14] Among others, Thomas Cranmer, when Archbishop of Canterbury, wrote *A Confutation of Unwritten Verities, both by the Holy Scriptures and most Ancient Authors*.[15]

The evolution over about twelve hundred years, from the fourth century, of such universal, all-powerful systems, certainly made a religion: but, said the reformers, it was not the Christianity of the New Testament.

The attraction for Tyndale, as for all reformers, lay in the English Church being simply a New Testament congregation of believers, lightly organised by the local Christians themselves, sitting together with an English Bible.

Tyndale, speaking from the New Testament, makes justly high demands of bishops.

> To preach God's word is too much for half a man: and to minister a temporal kingdom is too much for half a man also. Either other requireth an whole man. One therefore cannot well do both. He that avengeth himself on every trifle is not meet to preach the patience of Christ . . . He that is overwhelmed with all manner riches and doth but seek more daily is not meet to preach poverty. . . .[16]

Three years after his death, in 1539, the Act of Six Articles temporarily reinstated what Tyndale wanted abolished: masses for the dead, and the whole fabrication of Purgatory; the Church's seven, not the New Testament's two, sacraments;[17] compulsory confession of the ear; communion for lay persons in only one kind (if in either); and compulsorily celibate priests. He writes well about the need, as well as the New Testament command, for a married clergy.

> He must have a wife for two causes. One, that it may thereby be known who is meet for the room. He is unapt for so chargeable an office, which had never household to rule. Another cause is that chastity is an exceeding seldom gift, and unchastity exceeding perilous for that degree [position], inasmuch as the people look as well unto the living as unto the preaching, and are hurt at once if the living disagree, and fall from the faith, and believe not the word.[18]

There is on record the shock felt by the first readers of Tyndale's New Testament on reading that Jesus' disciples were married.[19]

UNDOING REFORMS

Even while the greater monasteries were being dissolved, and the Great Bible was being placed in every parish church, what could be seen as the first official undoing of reform came in 1539. Cromwell's more reforming Ten Articles of 1536 had been followed by the more reactionary *Bishops' Book* of 1537, printed in great numbers, also called *The Institution of a Christian Man*,[20] expounding, as well as 'the seven sacraments', the Ten Commandments, the Lord's Prayer and the Ave Maria, the conservative doctrines of justification and Purgatory and the importance of the pope.

The passing by Parliament in 1539 of the Act of Six Articles, however, supported by Henry VIII, was a more weighty counter-move back to Rome. On the continent of Europe at this time the foundation of the Society of Jesus (the Jesuits), dedicated to supporting the pope against heresy, indicated a general direction within the Catholic Church. The Six Articles enforced – on pain of death – transubstantiation, communion in one kind, clerical celibacy, monastic vows, private masses and aural confession. A victory for the reactionary bishops and lords, the intention was to begin a suppression of the reforms that had been introduced. Not all bishops agreed. Latimer resigned his see. Cranmer sent away his wife. Power was shifting. The more powerful *King's Book*, or *Necessary Doctrine and Erudition for any Christian Man* of 1543, was supported by Parliament, 'for the advancement of true religion and for the abolishment of the contrary', making it a crime for any unlicensed person to read or expound the Bible publicly to others, and to limit to the upper classes, by law, even the private reading of the Bible.[21] It proscribed 'the crafty, false and untrue translation of Tyndale', and required that the notes in all copies should be removed or obliterated (fig. 14).[22]

In the eight years in which the Act was in force, 1539–47, the Six Articles caused only six martyrdoms[23] – six too many in a civilised realm, but few compared with the almost three hundred in the five years under Mary. The Act of Six Articles was, however, among other things, a blow to the German Lutherans, who had increasingly looked to Henry to lead a united Protestant Europe. Archbishop Cranmer, with Cuthbert Tunstall and other bishops, had entertained three German delegates at Lambeth Palace for a year. They had found agreement in doctrine, but the Lutherans stood firm against continued 'abuses' of practice. The Six Articles sealed the separation.[24]

In 1536 Henry's second wife, Anne Boleyn, after a long courtship, three years of marriage, two miscarriages and the birth of their daughter Elizabeth, had been beheaded on very dubious charges of adultery and incest. Henry's third marriage, to Jane Seymour, was brief: she died giving birth to Henry's only male heir, the future Edward VI, in 1537. Opposition to Henry's political activities, both in his private and national life, and to Cromwell's destruction of the monasteries, caused the scattered rebellious uprisings, in the north of England, mainly in Yorkshire, for a few months from October 1536, later known as 'The Pilgrimage of Grace'. Cromwell organised Henry's disastrous fourth marriage, to the Lutheran aristocrat Anne of Cleves, 'sight unseen' as the modern phrase has it. Henry's dislike of her from the moment she appeared, and the sham of marriage made in January 1540, allowed Cromwell's enemies the lever they needed. Cromwell was arrested in January 1540, held without charge and swiftly beheaded on 28 July 1540, the day Henry married his fifth wife, the young (and slippery) Catherine Howard.

Conservative anxiety about Bibles in English focused on control. The king's proclamation of 6 May 1541, setting up 'the Bible of the largest and greatest volume, to be had in every church', referred to his support for Cromwell's earlier Injunctions for the same, which included admonition to avoid 'contention [and] altercation'.[25] An undated draft for a royal proclamation at about this time, promoting the reading of the Bible, specifically commands that 'any doubt . . . touching the sense and meaning' should not be given 'too much to your own mind, fantasies and opinions', nor 'open reasoning in your open Taverns or Alehouses', avoiding 'all contentions in such Alehouses and other places', but instead recourse should be had to 'such learned men as be or shall be authorised to preach and declare the same': the aim is 'discreet quietness and sober moderation' – that is, unquestioning obedience.[26]

That some 'learned men' may not have been much use in the edifying of a Bible reader 'himself his wife and family' may be demonstrated by the attempt begun in 1542 to revise and correct the Great Bible into conformity with the Vulgate, made by conservatives in the body of bishops.[27] This came to nothing. The king decided that the work should be done by the two universities, Oxford and Cambridge, which meant that it was never heard of again. Most interesting, however, is a clue about how such a revision might have turned out. The powerful Bishop of Winchester, Stephen Gardiner,

> publicly read the Latin words in the Sacred Volume which he desired for their germane and native meaning and for the majesty of their matter might be retained as far as possible in their own nature or be turned into English speech as closely as possible.[28]

Gardiner wanted the heavenly voice at Jesus' baptism to say 'This is my dilect son in whom complacui.'[29] He gave a list of 132 words to be retained if possible. One or two of them might not have caused too much unhappiness, like 'Martyr' or 'Presbyter' or 'Synagogue' – one does have to assume that Gardiner did not know the New Testament in Greek – but 'Commilito', 'Lites', 'Panis propositionis', 'Didragma', 'Ejicere', 'Increpari', 'Zizania' and over a hundred like them have no place in a Bible designed to be understood by ordinary households in English.[30]

In 1543, Parliament passed an Act 'for the advancement of true religion and for the abolishment of the contrary', which banned 'the crafty, false and untrue translation of Tyndale'. Following the King's Book it required the obliteration of notes, now by law (fig. 14).[31] The Act made it a crime for any unlicensed person to read or expound the Bible publicly to others, forbidding even the private reading of the Bible by the lower classes. In 1546, Henry issued a proclamation that 'no man or woman, of what estate, condition or degree, was . . . to receive, have, take, or keep, Tyndale's or Coverdale's New Testament'.[32] In London large quantities of Tyndale's and Coverdale's New, and Old, Testaments were collected and burned at St Paul's Cross, under the initiative of Edmund Bonner, Bishop of London. This ban, when 'the Great Bible maintained its prominent position in every parish church in the Land' was, in the words of F. F. Bruce, 'a monumental piece of absurdity'.[33] There were, in fact, no formal prosecutions at all under either the Act or the Proclamation, though there is a little evidence of attention to people reading the Bible.

KING EDWARD VI

King Henry died in January 1547. The Six Articles were repealed by an early Parliament in the reign of his successor, the nine-year-old Edward VI. By 1549, the reformed Church settlement had established an English liturgy in the first Book of Common Prayer. In theological confession and in church polity, England was well on the way to the Elizabethan settlement. The availability of English Bibles multiplied remarkably (see below). Edward's reign, however, has not always fared well among historians. Diarmaid MacCulloch wrote in 1999:

> A negative image of Edwardian religion has prevailed since the early nineteenth century, the result of disapproval from both Roman Catholics and (within the Church of England itself) Anglo-Catholics. The distinguished Anglo-Catholic church historian Bishop Walter Frere would speak for many when in 1910 he contemplated the six years after 1547 and dismissed them as 'the lowest depths to which the English church has ever sunk' . . . [recent historians] have echoed that dismissal . . . as an unmitigated disaster imposed by alien forces, wrecking not just the beauty of the parish church but also the intricate and orderly structure of village life and the financial system which sustained it . . .[35]

In 1957 another prominent Anglo-Catholic, Fr Humphrey Whistler (like Frere, a member of the Community of the Resurrection) produced an engaging little pamphlet on the Reformation which was intended as an exercise in ecumenism between Roman Catholics and Anglicans, picking up the pieces of misunderstanding from the sixteenth century . . . In this we hear one solution to the problem of the

Edwardian Reformation: simply to deny it any part in the Church of England story . . . Fr Whistler was completely silent on the first half-century of the English Reformation.[36]

Father Whistler wrote bad history. Yet denial – by means of neglect – is still active. Edward was 'a talented member of a talented family . . . the boy's own writings . . . cry out for detailed study',[37] study which has yet to take place. Edward has been dismissed as 'a bright, pathetic . . . manipulated [lad]'.[38] There are many analyses of the intense politics around and made by him; of some of the theological issues debated; of the programmes of removal (sometimes temporary) and destruction revealed in churchwardens' accounts; of the men, and a few women, who controlled events, or were caught up in them.[39] The emphasis is largely on destruction. Edward, it is observed, was given the name of an Old Testament king, Josiah (also a boy), the destroyer of the religion as it had been. Nobody, it seems, even among fine broad-spectrum scholars who regret the distortions of Bishop Frere and Father Whistler, has noted two things: first, in the full Old Testament story, what motivated Josiah; secondly, how widespread was detailed knowledge of the Bible, making the identification far richer than a nickname.

OLD TESTAMENT KINGS

To quote Diarmaid MacCulloch again:

> The rebuilt Church [under Edward] was evangelical in essence. The assignment for evangelicals was a treasure hunt for the *evangelion*, the good news to be found in the New Testament. . . . Yet spokesmen for the Edwardian revolution were also drawn to the Old Testament, where they could view other kingdoms battling against great odds to hear the message of God. Henry VIII had already enjoyed posing as one or other of the two great success stories in Israelite politics, David and Solomon. However, in the turbulence of his son's revolution, other kings of Israel and Judah entered the stage, because they were more urgently scripted to act as a warning or encouragement.[40]

That is helpful: but it does not go far enough. What was being made was a new understanding of the religion of a nation. A strong example will show something of this.

High among evil models among Old Testament kings was Ahab, who is in 1 Kings 17–22. An able and powerful king, to the Hebrew writers he was 'wicked Ahab' with his queen 'wicked Jezebel' (the epithets are in the chapter headings in Matthew's Bible, at 1 Kings 16). This was because he had introduced as an additional god in Israel the Phoenician Baal, to please his wife, who was the daughter of the Phoenician king, the high priest of Baal.

The Hebrew writers do not show Jezebel in full roundedness: they simply tell incidents as illustrations of her powerful character.[41] Her intention, in execution ruthless and extreme like all she did, was probably positive: she hoped that the Phoenician worship would bring with it the more advanced Phoenician civilisation.

Sole champion of the Lord against the royal house was the prophet Elijah. At a confrontation of epic power, Elijah challenged her royal – and apparently all-powerful – control, and the nation's worship of Baal. Tyndale's translation, in Matthew's Bible, and the first in English from the Hebrew, catches the high language (Tyndale uses the Greek name Eliah, from the Septuagint).

> And Ahab went against Eliah. And when Ahab saw Eliah, he said unto him: art thou he that troubleth Israel? And he said: it is not I that trouble Israel, but thou and thy father's house, in that ye have forsaken the commandments of the Lord and hast followed Baal.[42]

The prophet demands the assembly of 'all Israel' on Mount Carmel 'and the prophets of Baal four hundred and fifty, and the prophets of the groves four hundred, which eat of Jezebel's table'.

> And Eliah came unto all the people and said: why halt ye between two opinions? If the Lord be very God, follow him: or if Baal be he, follow him. And the people answered him not one word.

(No other writer in English in the 1530s could command that high tone, the lofty, ringing style belonging to epic. Tyndale's 'halt . . . between two opinions' is striking, and the source of the phrase common thereafter, with 'halt' suggesting 'waver', or vacillate', or 'remain in doubt'. Both Wyclif versions have a form of 'How long halt ye in two parties?' 'Halt' in Tyndale's time primarily meant 'walk with a limp', but the word already contained the sense of ceasing an activity: apparently not long afterwards, it overlapped with the notion of 'stop'. (*OED, v.*[1]. 2; and *sb.*[1], *v*,[2].) Tyndale carried forward not only the people's uncertainty, but an element of inactivity: the people are stuck, wavering on the fence. The two Jerusalem Bibles (1966, 1985) have ' "How long", he said, "do you mean to hobble first on one leg and then on the other?" ', undoubtedly philologically correct, but rather lacking epic force. Equally worth attention are Tyndale's three final thumps of 'not one word'. The phrase demands, in reading aloud, a fractional pause after 'him', before the three heavy stresses. The

Wyclifs have 'not to him a word' and 'not a word to him'. Starting with Geneva (1560), and taken through into KJV, is 'The people answered him not a word', making at the end a light anapaest which weakens the drama. Tyndale understood the artistic decorum of a banging silence.)

The prophet proposes a test. Each side, for Baal or the Lord, will sacrifice an ox on a specially built altar. 'And then the god that answereth by fire, he is the very God.'

> And all the people said: it is well spoken . . . the prophets of Baal . . . took an ox and dressed it, and called on the name of Baal from morning to noon saying: O Baal hear us. But there was no voice nor answer. And they leapt about the altar that they had made. And at noon Eliah mocked them and said: call loud (for he is a god: but he is talking, or occupied, or in the way, or haply he sleepeth) that he may awake. And they cried loud, and cut themselves, as their manner was, with knives and lances, till the blood flowed on them. And when midday was passed, they prophesied until it was time to offer. But there was neither voice nor answer nor any that regarded them.

Elijah then mended his altar with 'twelve stones according to the number of the twelve tribes of the sons of Jacob', and

> made a gutter round about the altar, able to receive two pecks of corn . . . and said, fill four pitchers with water and pour it on the sacrifice and on the wood. And he said: do so again. And they did so again. Then he said: do it the third time. And they did so the third time. And the water ran round about the altar, and the gutter was full of water also.

Elijah prayed, ending,

> Hear me O Lord, hear me, that this people may know, that thou Lord art the God, and that thou hast turned their hearts backward. And there fell fire from the Lord and consumed the sacrifice and the wood and the stones and the dust, and licked up the water that was in the gutter. And when all the people saw that, they fell on their faces and said: the Lord he is God, the Lord he is God.

Such direct intervention was the very stuff of Bibles for the reformers, the immediate presence of the Lord in all his power – and that is not the end of the story. Elijah's following prayer and what came from 'a little cloud out of the sea, like the palm of a man's hand' had similar force. Certainly the late medieval church offered snapshots of the great figures, and a figure of Elijah as the greatest of the prophets would be known, if only from cathedral statuary. After 1537, however, magnificent Old Testament stories, telling of the immediate power of the Lord, were newly heard in full, in English, when so shortly before, such Hebrew-into-English was both impossible and strictly forbidden. Such a narrative as Elijah on Mount Carmel had nothing to do with a religion of making long pilgrimages to offer goods or wealth at the shrines of saints; nor of infrequent, and costly, attendance at intricate rituals in an unknown language: nor of the powers of the local priest, monk or friar to interfere in the intimate life of every household. The Old Testament heroes and villains are larger than life, told with relish directly from the Hebrew, in vigorous English. Elijah in all his godly conviction is a long way from churchwardens' accounts: and church-wardens' accounts by their very nature will always be interpreted in the direction of negativity.

Roman Catholic and Anglo-Catholic historians have made a popular picture of effective, even cosy, English parish life in late medieval times, before the 'brutal' Reformation.[43] They do not mention the heavy repres-sions, the drain on every household's money, the corrupt intrusions: that the people suffered has not recently been so keenly suggested.[44] Bible stories like that of God's power in Elijah showed that his challenges to 'wicked Ahab' were not for the priests but for the people. After the fire descended, 'Then said Eliah unto them, lay hands on the prophets of Baal, let not one of them escape.' The story, though compelling, was not taken too literally. Edwardian reformers were accused of many things, often wrongly: but not of the killing of priests *en masse* or even individually. Diarmaid MacCulloch notes that 'it was remarkable that no Catholic opponents of the regime suffered execution; Henry's murderous religious ecumenism was out of fashion between 1547 and 1553'.[45]

Other prophets around Ahab and Jezebel were subservient to the crown: Elijah alone protested against the importation of a foreign religion, which was how the reformers saw the effect of Rome on England. Having roused the anger of Jezebel, the prophet fled into the wilderness, where he 'sat down under a juniper tree, and desired for his soul that he might die' (1 Kings 19). Nourished by an angel, he went 'in the strength of that meat forty days and forty nights', and on 'Horeb, the mount of God', he hid in a cave. In a justly famous passage (again, Tyndale rendering Hebrew for the first time) he was made to understand another religious truth:

And then the word of the Lord came to him and said what doest thou here Elijah? And he answered: I have been thorough angry for the Lord God of host's sake. For the children of Israel have forsaken thy covenant, and have broken down thine altars and slain the prophets with the sword, and I only am left, and they seek my soul to have it too. And he said come out and stand before the Lord. And behold, the Lord went by and a mighty strong wind that rent the mountains and brake the rocks before him. But the Lord was not in the wind. And after the wind came an earthquake. But the Lord was not in the earthquake. And after the earthquake, came fire: but the Lord was not in the fire. And after the fire, came a small still voice. And when Eliah heard it, he covered his face with his mantle, and went out and stood in the mouth of the cave. And see, there came a voice unto him and said: what doest thou here Eliah? And he answered: I was jealous for the Lord God of host's sake: because the children of Israel have forsaken thy appointment and have cast down thine altars and slain thy prophets with the sword, and I only am left, and they seek my soul to have it.[46]

The Lord instructed him to take the offensive.

Clear enough in those narratives is Elijah as man of God alone, for the people, against a false religious establishment. Yet he came to stand even more for the rights of ordinary people against tyranny. In 1 Kings 21, two chapters after the account of the prophet alone on mount Horeb, it is told how King Ahab wanted to extend his property around the palace, to make a herb garden. A neighbour's vineyard was in the way. Ahab offered the neighbour, Naboth, either a better exchange, or money. Naboth refused: 'the Lord forbid that from me, that I should give the inheritance of my fathers unto thee.' Ahab sulked. He 'laid him down upon his bed and turned away his face and would eat no meat'. Jezebel, finding him, had no truck with such feebleness. She had Naboth arrested on false charges of blasphemy and treason, and stoned to death. Ahab, told that Naboth was dead, got up from his bed and went to take possession of the vineyard. He was met by Elijah, sent by the Lord. Ahab blustered: 'hast thou found me thine enemy at any time?'

And he said yea, because thou art utterly given to work wickedness in the sight of the Lord. Behold, I will bring evil upon thee, and make clean riddance of thee, and will destroy unto Ahab all that pisseth against the wall . . . [and] dogs shall eat Jezebel . . . For there was none at all like Ahab, that was so utterly given to work wickedness in the sight of the Lord, and that because Jezebel his wife pricked him forward.[47]

Dogs did indeed eat Jezebel. When men 'came to bury her, they found no more of her, than the skull and the two feet and the two hands'.[48]

The Old Testament Books of Samuel and Kings ('The four Books of the Kings', or 'of the Kingdoms'), recount the works of kings who did evil followed by kings who did good, all 'in the sight of the Lord'. To the men and women of Edward's reign, Old Testament history was telling British history. From Tyndale in Matthew's Bible, English Bibles first gave (from the Septuagint) the now-familiar order of those books of history, placing after Samuel and Kings the two books of Chronicles and Ezra and Nehemiah. 'Chronicles' is technically one book, a late reworking of the whole narrative from the opening of Genesis to the end of 2 Kings, with additions, slanted towards Judah and the origins of the rituals of the Temple, placed at the very end of the Hebrew Scriptures.

The tick-tock of bad rulers and good in the Old Testament histories became the structure of the writing of Protestant history, first most strikingly in Edward Hall's large chronicle published in 1558, covering the period from 1399 to 1548, *The Union of the Two noble and Illustre Families of Lancaster and York.* The alternation is declared throughout the text. His list of contents has eight entries:

i. The unquiet time of King Henry the Fourth.
ii. The victorious acts of King Henry the v.
iii. The troublesome season of King Henry the vi.
iv. The prosperous reign of King Edward the iiii.
v. The pitiful life of King Edward the v.
vi. The tragical doings of King Richard the iii.
vii. The politic governance of King Henry the vii.
viii. The triumphant reign of King Henry the viii.

Hall's book became wholly absorbed into Holinshed's much fuller *Chronicles of England, Scotland, and Ireland* in 1577, revised and enlarged in 1587. Reading Holinshed, whose volumes lay in many Elizabethan households alongside an English Bible and Foxe's *Acts and Monuments*, was how Protestant Britain learned its own history. Shakespeare, for example, in his own rewriting of English history, helped himself to Holinshed's material, sometimes taking words directly.[49]

MONARCHS AND 'THE TWO REGIMENTS'

The place of a monarch under God was of special importance to English reformers. With the power of Scripture, the corruptions and distortions of the intruding papacy, and the reclaiming of New Testament faith and practices, it is one of the recurring topics in, for example, Tyndale's *Obedience* (1528), a book which opens with passionate pages about evidence in Scripture of the power of God to do the unexpected with nations in crisis. It is strongly present in his *Practice of Prelates* (1530) and *Exposition of Matthew V, VI, VII* (1533), and in Simon Fish's *Supplication of Beggars* (1529). It is implicit in the work of John Frith and Robert Barnes. It is the subject of John Bale's *King John* (probably late 1530s).

In writing the *Obedience*, Tyndale had thought through the New Testament position on 'the powers that be', arriving at what modern political historians see as a paradox. On the one hand, he is said to see, following Luther, the Christian life as implying the separation of the two 'regiments', the spiritual and the temporal, each enclosed in its own separate engagements. On the other hand, *Obedience* has been said to be 'the first thorough-going apologia of Caesaro-papism',[50] a particularly ugly compound word standing for royal supremacy – a prince with absolute control of a nation's religion; what later came to be called, more generally, Erastianism. It has been taken as obvious in the later twentieth century that Tyndale knew, and completely followed, Luther's position of separation: and at the same time he has been automatically taken as expounding the opposite, even to crediting him with attachment to the divine right of kings.[51]

Reading fully the many pages that Tyndale wrote (as opposed to using reach-me-down one-sentence quotations), reveals a position that, even more paradoxically, both enlarges the paradox and dissolves it. His strongest statement about the separation of spiritual and temporal government is in his *Exposition* of the Sermon on the Mount, *Matthew V, VI, VII*. This should not be surprising: the Sermon assembles Jesus' teaching on existential issues, still found to be at the cutting edge of moral dilemmas, but with a dimension that is more than merely moral. In Tyndale's striking opening phrase, those chapters are 'wherein Christ . . . diggeth again the wells of Abraham . . . stopped and filled up with the earth of . . . false expositions.'[52] On an early page of that Prologue, Tyndale observes 'that the clergy have so ruffled the temporal and spiritual regiment together, and made thereof such confusion, that no man can know the one from the other'.[53] Tyndale sees that an acute problem arises with Christ's command 'That ye resist not evil: but whosoever shall smite thee on thy right cheek, turn to him the other also' (Matthew 5:39), one of a group of five admonitions by Jesus countering, and at the same time greatly extending, the Old Testament's 'An eye for an eye and a tooth for a tooth', a statute originally intended to limit rather than encourage revenge. The problem for Christians is, in view of Christ's command not to resist evil and not to inflict violence, whether that disbars them from all secular rule, since secular rule employs force and violence. Not so, says Tyndale.

> I say nay, in the first state, where thou art a person for thyself alone . . . There thou must love . . . yea, and suffer all things (as Christ did) to make peace . . . But in the worldly state, where thou art no private man, but a person in respect of other [people], thou not only mayest, but also must, and art bound under pain of damnation to execute thine office . . . and so punish, and even slay, evil doers.[54]

In 1520, Martin Luther had written sixteen pages *On the Liberty of a Christian Man*. The first sentence became a rallying-call to his supporters: 'A Christian Man is a free lord over everything and subject to no one.' The second sentence, however, is 'A Christian man is an obedient servant in everything and subject to everyone.' So far, so Lutheran. The spiritual and the temporal are parallel aspects of the Christian world, and not as in the medieval church (and under Calvin) with the temporal subordinated. Tyndale, however, was his own man.[55] A Tyndale scholar recently wrote, 'The spiritual regiment is the kingdom of Christ, and in every way the rule of Christ is different from the rule of kings in the temporal regiment.'[56] Tyndale wrote 'Christ's kingdom is altogether spiritual; and the bearing of rule in it is clean contrary unto the bearing of rule temporally.'[57]

> The kingdom of God is contrary. For the Spirit that bringeth them thither maketh them willing, and giveth them lust unto the law of God, and love compelleth them to work, and love maketh every man's good, and all that he can do, common unto the neighbour's need. And as every man is strong in that kingdom, so love compelleth him to take the weak by the hand, and to help him, and to take him that cannot go upon his shoulders and bear him. And so to do service unto the weaker is to bear rule in that kingdom.[58]

'For Tyndale, the separation of the two regiments is not at all as clear cut as it was for Luther, for God is king over both the spiritual and temporal. . . . Every action of a Christian is done in both the temporal and the spiritual regiment(s) and we cannot separate them into two watertight compartments.'[59] God is king over all. His Word in Scripture, the only authority, demands obedience from kings and rulers. God is king of the temporal regiment because it is an ordinance of his own creation, in which we all live, meaning that everyone has a special relation to God. As long as there were people on earth they needed to be governed, Tyndale wrote, and it was 'for their sakes also he [the Father] hath ordained rulers, both spiritual and temporal . . .'.[60] The king's power was hedged 'with his responsibility to God, and the fact that those he governed were his brothers and sisters through God's creation'.[61]

The heart of the matter, in Tyndale's thought, is the king's obedience to God's Word, in Scripture. Indeed, that can be taken as a distillation of all his political writing. Like other reformers, he is 'restoring lost authority to kings by preaching from holy writ'.[62] The Christian commonwealth that he outlined, especially in his *Obedience*, has rarely been visible since he wrote in 1528: but there can be glimpsed a little more of the importance of certain Old Testament kings for the English reformers. As Tyndale wrote, 'As it went with their kings and rulers, so shall it be with ours. As it was with their common people, so shall it be with ours.'[63] Out of several, the prime example of an Old Testament king obedient to Scripture was Josiah. To him was brought Scripture newly declared, and he obeyed it to the letter. The result in the short term was sharp purification of the nation's religion, involving destruction of the old ways. In the long term the result was the remaking of the religion of a newly spiritually ener-gised nation, even while in exile in Babylon. The religion formed there, on the basis of the Scripture to which Josiah was obedient, has produced magnificent literature, music, philosophy and theology, and survives until today.

There will be seen to be parallels in England.

EDWARD VI AS JOSIAH

Josiah pleased the Lord. The boy-king Edward was seen as the boy-king Josiah. This was not empty flattery to the nine-year-old son of Henry VIII on the throne. Edward, like Josiah, had a burning and growing zeal for the Lord, and was influenced by one powerful, and, to him, God-given circumstance. Twentieth-century concentration on the political cat's cradle made by the eminences around him must not be allowed to obscure his genuine piety. His identification with Josiah, however, is rooted in more than simple parallels in age and reforming devotion to the Lord. The key to it is the restoration of an old book, originally given by God, but long buried out of sight.

Josiah, who lived two and a half centuries after Ahab, is the subject of 2 Kings 22 and 23 (and 2 Chronicles 34 and 35). The central verses of his story, as translated by Tyndale, are:

> Josiah was eight years old when he began to reign . . . And he did that seemed right in the sight of the Lord, and walked in all the ways of David his father [i.e. ancestor] . . . And the eighteenth year of his reign . . . [he arranged money] to repair the house [i.e. of the Lord] . . . And Helkiah the priest said to Saphan the scribe: I have found the book of the law in the temple of the Lord . . . And Saphan read it before the king.
>
> And the king as soon as he had heard the words of the book of the law, he rent his clothes and commanded Helkiah the priest and Ahikam the son of Saphan and Achobor the son of Michaiah, and Saphan the scribe, and Asahiah a servant of the king's, saying: go ye and seek of the Lord for me and the people and for all Juda, concerning the words of the book that is found. For it is a great wrath of the Lord that is kindled upon us, that our fathers have not hearkened unto the words of this

book, to do in all points as it is written therein.[64]

(The discovery of the book is marked in Matthew's Bible margin with two pointing hands: there are few such pointers in the historical books.)

Enquiry of 'Oldah the prophetess wife of Selum . . .' who is living in Jerusalem elicits her double interpretation. First (also a passage marked with a pointing hand) the Lord will punish his errant people who have angered him 'with all the works of their hands' (Matthew's margin has 'That is, with their images'.) Second, the king, because he has responded strongly and positively, will be favoured by the Lord.

The young king commanded a great gathering of officials,

> and all the people both small and great. And he read in the ears of them all the words of the book of the covenant, which was found in the house of the Lord. And the king stood by a pillar and made a covenant before the Lord that they should walk after the Lord, and keep his commandments and his witnesses and his ordinances with all their hearts and with all their souls, and made good the words of the said appointment that were written in the foresaid book.[65]

The heading of this chapter in Matthew's begins '*Josiah readeth Deuteronomy before the People*'. It is now accepted that what was found was the law code of Deuteronomy, chapters 5 to 28 of the book in the Bible.

The rest of the story of young Josiah, to the end of the 23rd chapter of 2 Kings, does tell of the thorough destruction of all the idolatrous objects – 'vessels . . . the groves . . . the hill altars' – and the removal of the 'Camarites' (possibly referring to their robes: Matthew's Bible calls them 'black monks of Baal') and others. After the wasting of a grove outside Jerusalem, and the casting 'of the dust thereof upon the graves of the people of the country, Matthew's marginal note comments, 'This did he to the detestation of them that had worshipped them in their life time.'[66] Sometimes Tyndale's phrasing pleases, even though the subject is abhorrent: the sentence 'And he brake down the cells of the male whores that were in the house of the Lord', Tyndale ends 'where the women wove little houses for the grove'.[67] Sometimes it is cryptic: he 'put down the horses that the kings of Israel had given to the sun at the entering of the house of the Lord, in the chamber of Nathanmelech the chamberlain which was of Paruarim, and burnt the chariots of the sun with fire'.[68] Through all the strangeness of language and activity, the need for drastic purifying of religion can be seen: 'And he defiled Topheth also . . . because no man should offer his son or his daughter in fire to Moloch.'[69] Josiah's purification is summed up, '[he] brake the images and cut down the groves and filled the places with the bones of men.'

The chapter continues with the account of a new keeping of the feast of the Passover with fresh solemnity, before telling of the young king's pointless death in battle at Megiddo, to the grief of all Israel, as described in Zechariah 12:9–14, and particularly 2 Chronicles 35:24–5. (Megiddo became 'Armageddon', a place of some great spiritual conflict, at Revelation 16:16.)

Josiah swept away centuries of religious corruption, above all the adulteration of the worship of the Lord by sacrifices to Canaanite gods at all the 'high places'. These corruptions, even in Jerusalem itself, are confirmed in the words of the greatest of the Hebrew writing prophets, the contemporary Jeremiah. The muddle of the text as we have it still allows in chapters 2 to 6 a sight of many kinds of abhorrent heathen worship. Denunciation of the unreformed evils are paralleled by the opening chapters, also in textual confusion, of the prophecies called Zephaniah.

Though it was not immediately visible, Josiah's achievement was a turning point in Israel's history, something entirely driven by the recovery of purer Scriptures, which he and his fellow reformers then gave to the nation as the written law book on which was based a new religious system. Both the book and the system went with the nation into exile. There, in new purity, the book and the practices generated the basis of the future Hebrew religion, including the new presentation of all the written Scriptures.

The attraction of identifying King Edward with King Josiah is now clearer. Destruction – of the intrusive, imported, foreign-based religion – was only part of the programme. More important was the future founding of national worship and life on a book, a divine revelation newly available. Understanding his motivation from the now widely shared English Bible makes a difference to our understanding of King Edward.

JOSIAH'S ENRICHING EFFECTS

A standard history of the reign of Edward VI makes no mention of the Bible at all.[70] Some historians have made a slight, aloof bow in its direction: amid the throng of political grandees, it is made to stand like an unwelcome relative glimpsed at the far end of the room. One writer about King Edward noted that in the mid-sixteenth century, hearing the Prayer Book 'in the household from infancy . . . was second only to hearing the Bible . . . [as an] influence in shaping the English language'.[71] That is true enough. Yet the matter is so much larger than literary style. The key to the time is the rapid growth of experience of the Bible as a base for a new religious covenant.

Refreshingly, Margaret Aston in her books *England's Iconoclasts, 1: Laws Against Images* (1988) and *The King's Bedpost* (1993) – the latter decoding for modern readers a famous, and puzzling, group portrait of figures around Edward (fig. 16) – shows some of the significance, and the wide spread, of the use of Old Testament kings in European Reformation documents. And in courts: Henry VIII and Philip II were elaborately drawn as Solomon, and Francis I and Henry VIII as David. As she remarks, 'kings read *Kings* and pondered and perhaps acted accordingly'.[72] A little later, the Elizabethan *Books of Homilies* will commend the good kings of Juda: Asa, his son Jehoshaphat, Hezekiah and Josiah: all names that today need scholarly notes, but then would be automatically understood. Professor Aston shows the young Edward translating into French, in his best writing, passages from the Books of Kings, and adding his own comments. He gives words from 2 Kings 18, in the Great Bible version, and adds 'How those who do not worship the images are in eternal memory after their death, as Hezekiah and Josiah were and are' (fig. 17).[73]

Margaret Aston tells in a few words the biblical story of Josiah with its three elements: first, the reading of the discovered book of law; second, the making of the new covenant; and third, the destruction of the false religious objects and priests. She shows that in illustrations from Bibles in Europe, the first two are emphasised. They notably lack what she calls 'the purifying bonfire'.[74] One of these, from the Frankfurt Bible of 1534, is used as the illustration at the head of '4 Kings 23' (2 Kings 23) in Coverdale's 1535 Bible. It shows the young king hearing the reading of the new law, and nothing else about Josiah (fig. 15).

The reverence for the rediscovered law led to Josiah's commands to destroy, and Edward presided over ruthless 'purifying', by bonfire and hammer. What needs new emphasis, however, is that Josiah's true significance was in the making of the new covenant and the re-establishing of national religious life. As he and all Bible readers would know well, in Hebrew history these two new elements not only held the nation together in the Exile to Babylon which followed Josiah after so few years: it was the soil in which grew a Jewish identity. This, through the laws of diet, ceremony and conduct, would then survive for 2,500 years until today. It was also the source of a great new literature. Ezekiel was the prophet in Babylon. An unnamed 'Priestly Writer' gathered the traditions of the past and shaped them with a view to a future religious ideal, preserved in the 'Holiness Code'. This is principally what is now Leviticus 17–26, new religious and moral instruction summed up in Leviticus 19:18, 'thou shalt love thy neighbour as thyself'. In its larger version, as 'the Priestly Code', this permeates the whole Pentateuch as it is now, and more. Some of the finest Psalms belong to this period of Exile. Psalm 137 begins, as Coverdale first

put it, 'By the waters of Babylon we sat down and wept.' Moreover, in
the Exile emerged one of the world's great poets, eloquently proclaiming
that nations were in the hand of the Lord, the God of Heaven. It was the
Lord's will that the captives should return to rebuild Jerusalem on a new
religious basis. This prophet-poet profoundly altered understanding of the
revelation of God: instead of the earlier bullying divinity of land-grabbing
tribes (as in the Books of Joshua or Judges) there was now revealed its
opposite, God as the Suffering Servant. The name of this poet of genius
is unknown. His writings are preserved in good order in Isaiah chapters
40 to 55: he is prosaically known as 'Second Isaiah'.

Here is the opening of Isaiah 53, from KJV:

> Who hath believed our report? and to whom is the arm of the Lord
> revealed? For he shall grow up before him as a tender plant, and as a
> root out of a dry ground: he hath no form nor comeliness; and when
> we shall see him, there is no beauty that we should desire him. He is
> despised and rejected of men; a man of sorrows, and acquainted with
> grief; and we hid as it were our faces from him; he was despised, and
> we esteemed him not. Surely he hath borne our griefs, and carried our
> sorrows; yet we did esteem him stricken, smitten of God, and afflicted.
> But he was wounded for our transgressions, he was bruised for our iniq-
> uities; the chastisement of our peace was upon him; and with his stripes
> we are healed. All we like sheep have gone astray; we have turned every
> one to his own way; and the Lord hath laid on him the iniquity of
> us all.

In so far as he saw himself, and was seen as, Josiah, Edward's policy was
to make a core religion of the service of God built from the newly
revealed book, the whole of the Bible in English. He was aware of the
vulnerability of his reform movement, and that his unhappy and reactionary sister would be on the throne if anything happened to him. He
might, or might not, have foreseen the English exile under Mary. It may
never be known, either, whether he had any inkling of a future literature
in English, including fine poets, in the Protestant country he began to
consolidate. For the Edward-as-Josiah parallel is striking in this – so far
unremarked – quality, that out of the reforms he founded there soon came
a great literature.[75]

Roman Catholic and Anglo-Catholic writers led the mourning after
the destruction of the great monasteries under Henry VIII, and of the
richly embellished parish images under Edward VI. The Reformation, they
aver, was a cultural disaster. Everyone must regret the demolition of magnificent abbey buildings, and the scattering to wind and flames of priceless Latin manuscripts from their libraries. The other side of that coin,

however, is not mentioned – the grip that the monasteries had on national wealth, and their great number; the enormous fraud in the veneration of relics, like the 'blood of Christ' at Hailes Abbey; the repression that the supposedly contented people suffered, partly manipulated through fear of Purgatory.

The Reformation was 'a cultural disaster' only for that English life that was controlled from, and funded to, Rome, and for the fixing of experience to the papal past. As outlined in chapter 8 above, the Reformation in fact brought with it a new flood of 'culture', in music, painting, architecture, philosophy, language study, high scholarship, what came to be called the sciences, and above all in literature in English. The remains of Glastonbury Abbey or Fountains Abbey are melancholy to some people who visit them (though not to all). The work of Spenser, Shakespeare, Milton, and a hundred more writers of the time and long after has stirred the hearts and minds of much of the world for four centuries.

In the sixteenth century there were two chief elements in the new religious geology that released the flood of, in particular, highly inventive writing. First was the fact that in a Protestant country, as England has been since 1558, and still is, anything at all can be said – or thought – without a charge of heresy. An allegation of heresy, freely used, would before the 1530s have led to punishment of the most severe kind, ultimate total destruction in this life and the next, the wiping-out of the very existence on earth of the heretic. Thomas More hoped to burn heresy out of the land: the intention returned under Queen Mary. True, even in Protestant England under Elizabeth, there was *political* censorship, applied very variably (and with, it is now understood, its effects in Shakespeare's time exaggerated by late twentieth-century scholars).[76] That is very different from the repression of all independent thought of any kind, under the threat of being branded a heretic, as intended by *De heretico comburendo* of 1401 and the Constitutions of Oxford of 1409, still in force in the 1530s.

The second new element was the provision, easily accessible, of a model of a Plain Style in English, something that will be developed in the following chapter.

ENGLISH MONARCHS AS OLD TESTAMENT KINGS

As Margaret Aston has shown, Edward vi was not the first (nor, indeed, the last) to be entwined, iconically, with an Old Testament king. Henry viii was Moses (not, of course, a king) on the title-pages of the Bibles of 1535 (Coverdale, who praised Henry with that name elsewhere[77]) and 1539 ('Great'), as was seen above. In a private document widely circulated,

Henry VIII was 'Moses' to Catherine Parr, his last wife.[78] The name picks
up a common Reformation identification with the man who led his
people out of slavery, to Pharaoh and to the pope.[79]

English monarchs, right up to the 1660s, were commonly seen as David,
especially James I and Charles II, and most especially Henry VIII. They
were not so identified by themselves.[80] David was the king who united
the northern state of Israel and the southern state of Judah. The appropriateness to James VI and I is more obvious, but Henry united church
and state. He appears in iconography as David the Psalm-maker, with rich
suggestiveness about the fineness of his spiritual life as a favoured one of
the Lord.[81] The problem, however, was always David's principal flaw, his
committing adultery with Bathsheba and having her husband killed. The
response to dark spots in the parallel picture in Henry VIII's life was, in
the court, thoroughly Old Testament, the Penitential Psalms being used to
express the appropriate feelings.[82]

King Edward VI could not so easily be David: if he were not Josiah, he
was better as Solomon.[83] There are two larger matters here, points more
significant than straight iconography. First, what is striking about the use
of Old Testament figures in the reign of Edward VI is that there are so
many of them. David, Solomon and Josiah were united in Edward: but so
were Jehoshaphat, Hezekiah, Jehu and Antiochus, for specific reasons.
Moreover, John Bale, according to a late twentieth-century scholar, citing
2 Samuel 16, the cursing of David by Bahurim on the orders of God,

> did not think kings should be seen as immune to the criticism of their
> subjects, at least not the godly ones . . . allusions are made to Henry
> VII's ideological heritage with a whole series of bad kings from the Old
> Testament . . . part of the false church of Antichrist: 'with such holy
> counsellors . . . nowadays were Ioram, Achab, Ochosias, Ioachim,
> Zedekiah and other kings more of Israel and Juda deceived and brought
> into the great indignation of God.' Writers and preachers expected the
> king and their other readers to go back to the Bible and read about
> the exemplars they mentioned.[84]

Not so. There writes a late twentieth-century scholar. No one hearing the
sermon would need to rush back home and hunt for a Bible and then
turn the pages looking with difficulty for the reference. Bibles were taken
to sermons. More, Bibles were known, completely and in detail, in a
manner beyond anything such modern historians dream. (The present
writer's father, a Nonconformist minister, always began his sermons – two
on Sundays, one mid-week – with the words 'You will find my text . . .',
confident that his listeners had Bibles in their hands, as congregations
would have done for the previous four hundred years.) The Old Testament kings were organic to the reign of Edward VI.

ENGLISH BIBLES

In the twenty-one years between Tyndale's first Testament in 1526 and Edward's accession in January 1547, there had been sixty-four editions (that is, different editions, not counting fresh printings) of a whole English Bible or New Testament.[85] (In the same period, there had been no English print-ings of the Latin Bible, though there had been twenty-two across Europe.[86]) As a figure for English Bibles printed, mostly in England, over two decades, it is impressive, particularly considering the periods of renewed repression latterly under Henry VIII. To put it in economic terms, it speaks of the confidence of printers in a large buying public. Figures for print-runs are not now obtainable; for Bibles, an average of two thou-sand each would probably be acceptable, even modest, giving a rough total of about a hundred and twenty thousand volumes bought.[87] To put it in religious terms, it represents a fair proportion of a population of two and a half million reading the Word of God, and uncountably more hearing it read.

After Edward's succession, merely in his short six-year reign, however, from 1547 to 1553, the number of English editions of the whole Bible or New Testament printed was forty. That is an average of between six and seven a year. Again, these figures take no account of straight reprints: they are all identifiably different editions. (In this time, again, there were no Latin Bibles printed in England: there were four abroad.) This great expan-sion in the production of English Bibles in the six years under Edward has not been prominent in the writing of Early Modern History. It has, indeed, been quite removed from the picture.

Seventeen of the forty are of Tyndale's New Testament, always in pocket, or, at most, quarto, size. Two of those are diglots, with Tyndale's English alongside Erasmus's Latin, volumes sometimes said to have been for the use of priests. Nine are of the whole Great Bible, showing a remarkable demand considering its size and cost. Four are versions of Matthew's Bible, two are of Coverdale's, five are part-versions of Taverner's – interestingly, the second of those was the Apocrypha with some new translations. One new edition, of 1549, was Coverdale's revision of Tyndale's New Testament, the slight changes carefully marked.[88] Two are Great Bible New Testaments printed with Erasmus's paraphrases.[89]

One of the Edwardian editions, of Psalms, marks, probably in 1549, the first appearance of a little book which, with larger contents, was to have colossal influence on British and American religious life, matched only by the New Testament. Modestly entitled *Certain Psalms, chosen out of the Psalter . . .'* by Thomas Sternhold, this book is the first, with nineteen Psalms, of what was to become the phenomenal 'Sternhold and Hopkins', all the Psalms arranged metrically for congregational singing (see chapter

18 below). The neglect of metrical Psalms and their three hundred years of essential part in English and Scottish life is one of the surprises of the writing of national history.

Using the same, still probably over-modest, figure of an average print-run of two thousand yields a total printed, in Edward's reign, of some eighty thousand English Bibles, all in six years. About half were complete Bibles: just under half were fresh editions of Tyndale's New Testaments. The growth of the Bible in English, in Britain and especially, later, in America, was rooted in the reign of the young 'Josiah' – as was the people's singing of the Psalms in English, a religious experience that reforming Josiah himself would have recognised.

THE ENGLISH REFORMATION NOT A 'FAILURE'

Trying to explain the announced 'failure' of the English Reformation, historians at the end of the twentieth century have used different criteria. Raw figures for absences from parish services in Edward's reign are presented, ignoring the equal, or greater, absences under Queen Mary. As a method, trying to take the pulse of the Edwardian English patient in that way involves ignoring too many other variables, including local variations between London and different counties.[90] More interestingly, it has been found that at the leading edge in the parishes reforming preachers themselves were admitting failure, declaring that, to put it crudely, not enough people were being converted. Moreover, the preaching itself was boring – the historians can make this judgement having read some printed sermons of the time (though that the sermons of Latimer, for example, even on the modern printed page, could ever be described as boring defies belief). A Protestant trope in Reformation England (as later in America) was the 'Hosead' or 'Jeremiad', attacks like those made by the prophets Hosea or Jeremiah on the lumpen people for not waking up and embracing their religion fervently. Such hyperbolic Protestant 'complaint' writing has always been common. There is plenty of evidence of preachers finding dullness in the parishes, or attacking the people for preferring popular music and football – substitute circuses, and that complaint can be seen to go back to the fifth century.

Care must be taken to stay in the historical context, which is bound to challenge judgement. The writing by English preachers about the people's indifference to their preaching can, in fact, be lively: they are 'like the smith's dog, who can lie under the hammer's noise, and the sparks flying, and yet fast asleep'.[91] The very vividness of that phrase opens a chink of light. What can be seen is that attending a sermon in a Protestant congregation could be a dramatic experience. The mass performed in Latin had been distant drama, with its gestures, processions and tableaux. Church attendance was now all changed. Because some readers centuries later declare themselves bored, it does not mean that the original occasions were boring. It could have been dramatic for people of all kinds to go as a body to take active part in a church service in English; where everything was close at hand; and particularly to take communion together in both kinds (fig. 18), the New Testament tradition still relatively new again in Europe, with English words; and to hear a long sermon, a speech of carefully crafted plain English delivered from only a few feet away. Such experience in English parish life, repeated in the almost nine thousand parishes throughout the land, has obvious relation to the later, albeit much heightened, experience of the London theatres.[92]

In the Calendar of State Papers there is a record of the impressions of English life made by the imperial ambassador Van der Delft and his secretary. These two witnesses, naturally unsympathetic to reform, tell how, from the beginning of Edward's reign in 1547, they had been unwillingly but repeatedly impressed by the strong impact of the English Reformation on 'the common people', who had turned against traditional religion. They give the cause as dramatic preaching.[93] What has survived of that preaching shows the strongest biblical content, as well as style.

Chapter 15

AN ENGLISH PLAIN STYLE,
AND BIBLE READING

'IN THE BEGINNING WAS THE WORD': but how does God speak? Oracularly, as at pagan Greek Delphi? Commandingly, as to Moses on Mount Sinai? Figuratively, as in the Book of Revelation? Threateningly, as through some Hebrew Prophets? Or simply and plainly, as in the sayings, and particularly the parables, of Jesus? As Peter Auksi wrote in 1995, 'clarity in religious discourse has an aura of moral virtue'.[1]

The English language, when Tyndale began to write, was a poor thing, spoken only by a few in an island off the shelf of Europe, a language unknown in Europe. Now, at the start of the second millennium, when English is spoken by almost two billion people, it is hard to think that in 1500 it was as irrelevant to life in Europe as today Scots Gaelic is to the city of London. By the 1520s English was becoming used for wills and churchwardens' accounts. The Latin of the professions, a particularly barbarous Latin, of the law, medicine, education, the church, was just beginning to yield a little to English. The idea of any great work in English would have seemed incomprehensible, and of an epic in English, madness. By the last decades of the century, not only had the classical epics, Virgil and Ovid, and later even Homer, begun to appear in English, but only fifty years after Tyndale the first epic in modern English began to be published, Spenser's *Faerie Queene*. The idea of the whole Word of God printed in English seemed, as well as dangerous, ridiculous, but soon after the mid-century the whole Bible in English was in many, probably most, households, and read and heard and learned by heart, known in detail even by those who could not read. (How many were illiterate is not known. It is to be noted that Thomas More claimed that two-thirds of English people could read.[2] Since he was opposing an English Bible, his figure may be an exaggeration.)

In Britain, something switched the power-lines of written thought and expression from Latin, or from Latinist confusion, into clear English, understandable throughout the land. I argue here that the switch was thrown by the dominance of the English Bible, and of Tyndale's forms in particular.

In William Tyndale's time England was alone in Europe in not having had for two generations printed Bibles in the vernacular. There had been such in German since 1466, in France since 1474, Italy in 1471, Catalan in 1478, Czech in 1475, Dutch in 1477, and Spanish and Portuguese before 1500. All those were from the Latin, of course, not the original Greek and Hebrew. They were eagerly bought, as observation of the numbers of editions shows: by the time of Luther's ground-breaking 1522 German New Testament from the Greek, there had been twelve separate editions of translations of the Bible in the vernacular in Germany.

Before 1526, England alone in Europe did not have printed vernacular Bibles, which is why, when Europe by 1500 had one thousand printers, most known by name, England had three – Caxton, de Worde and Pynson. The Constitutions of Oxford of 1407–9, forbidding the making or owning of an English translation of the Bible, were still in force. Enough is known, however, from references to the Wyclif, ('Lollard'), manuscript translations, to give a glimpse of a national hunger to know what the whole Bible said, beyond the great central stories of Noah's Ark, Abraham and Isaac, the Crucifixion and Resurrection of Jesus, and Pentecost. Those great stories had been reproduced in paintings, in sculpture, in stained glass, and in plays. But it is difficult to write a popular play about the Epistle to the Romans.

The whole Bible in the vernacular from the original Greek and Hebrew was in the 1520s and 1530s the root of, the heart of, the life-blood of (it is hard to find a powerful enough metaphor) the revolution in Europe, from Luther's 1517 Theses and 1522 German New Testament. The history of the Reformation in each country of northern Europe is striking, but especially in England. Henry VIII divorced Catherine in 1532, and was excommunicated in 1533. Something was happening internationally, nationally, locally, to which knowledge of the whole Bible seemed central. By the 1530s, English printing was picking up a little: but for three decades printers in Antwerp had been profiting from a big English market for books of all kinds. I labour this point slightly because I want to establish the breadth and depth of the effect of Tyndale's Bible translations. The widespread hunger was not for the *Aeneid* or the *Iliad*, or as it might be lives of saints, but the very Word of God.

Statistically, there is a difficulty here. The birth of Anne Boleyn's daughter Elizabeth is well and widely recorded. The process of the dissolution of a monastery is known in detail. But the meeting of a handful of people in a room to read the English Bible is not recorded – indeed, could not be. Secondary evidence suggests that it was a widespread, even massive, new development in the British Isles, from Henry VIII's time. It makes a hidden history of the kingdom.

Instead of hearing *Fiat lux, et lux erat*, or reading Wyclif's 'Be made light, and made was light', people heard and read 'Let there be light, and there was light.' As was noted above, instead of hearing, far off in the church building, *Petite, et dabitur vobis; quaerite, et invenietis; pulsate, at aperietur vobis*, they could have, in their hand by the hearth, 'Ask, and it shall be given you: seek, and ye shall find: knock, and it shall be opened unto you.' Moreover, what they were given was at the highest standard of scholarship. Tyndale got to the heart of the Hebrew language. In the story in 2 Kings 4, the Sunamite couple were given a son against all likelihood, promised them by the prophet Elisha. When the woman went to Elisha to tell him that the beloved and longed-for son had suddenly died, modern and ancient versions make her say something like, 'did I not say that thou shouldest not deceive me?' But the Hebrew doesn't quite say that. There is in the Hebrew an element of wishfulness. So Tyndale has her say, 'did I not say, that thou shouldest not bring me in a fool's paradise?'

Tyndale's vivid English prose, though now so familiar, was unusual in the 1520s and 1530s. When his first New Testament versions were made in 1525 and 1526, the norm for the higher works, if in English at all (and Thomas More would not allow *Utopia* in English), was Latin in a syntax of dependences and many-syllabled, lofty vocabulary. Here is Lord Berners in 1523 introducing his translation of Froissart's *Chronicle*:

> Thus, when I advertised and remembered the manifold commodities of history, how beneficial it is mortal folk, and else how laudable and meritorious a deed it is to write histories . . . [he turned to Froissart] which I judged commodious, necessary, and profitable to be had in English.[3]

Seventy years later, Shakespeare mocked such writing in *Love's Labour's Lost*, where his schoolmaster Holofernes says 'in the posterior of the day', and his curate Nathaniel requests the players to 'abrogate scurrility'.[4]

To think of the Bible as a religious book belonging only to the religious controversies of the time is unhelpful. Religion was not then a separate file to be called up, but the whole of life and death. In other words, any English style found for the Bible was going to be influential. Tyndale found, uniquely, a language register which made a 'plain style' for long after, more influential for all their power than Luther's for Germany or Lefèvre's for France. And even for those who were not especially Bible students, the phrases of Tyndale's Bible entered their minds at services, Sunday after Sunday, year after year, as the lectern and pulpit now dominated all British churches.

A 'plain style', particularly a Christian plain style, feels very easy: that is part of its craft. It seems to avoid all 'colours' of rhetoric, to quote Chaucer's Franklin, and use only 'such colours as growen in the mede [meadow]'.[5] Downright call-a-spade-a-spade directness feels more open and honest, even more moral. In fact, of course, Chaucer's Franklin is teasing. He uses plenty of devices. The making of a plain style involves as much conscious art as any. It is a style in which to present difficult paradoxes as something self-evident, not to be doubted. George Herbert in the 1640s wrote, in two short poems strikingly entitled 'Jordan' (the river-boundary making a title recognising a divide of rhetorical alternatives, the decorative and the plain), 'Shepherds are honest people, let them sing . . . Who plainly say My God, my King' and 'There is in love a sweetness ready penn'd, / Copy out only that, and save expense.'[6] But that metaphysical poet was a master of rhetorical devices. 'Simple style too depends on rhetoric.'[7] For the New Testament Greek of Jesus' sayings, particularly the parables, a 'virtuous' plain simplicity seems right: finite verbs, few participles, subject–verb–object order, few dependent clauses, parataxis (a simple train of complete sentences joined by 'and'), Saxon vocabulary, mostly monosyllables. From Tyndale's Luke 16:

> And it fortuned that the beggar died, and was carried by the angels into Abraham's bosom. The rich man also died, and was buried. And being in hell in torments, he lift up his eyes and saw Abraham afar off, and Lazarus in his bosom, and he cried and said: Father Abraham, have mercy on me, and send Lazarus that he may dip the tip of his finger in water, and cool my tongue: for I am tormented in this flame.[8]

The three small high 'i' sounds – 'dip . . . tip . . . finger' – help a good deal with the contrast of scale in the request. Wyclif had had at that point 'depe the end of his finger'. Tyndale, just before that passage, has 'the dogs came and licked his sores': the later Wyclif had 'the houndis came and lickiden his bilis'. It is not only Tyndale's monosyllables, but the darker chime of 'dogs' and 'sores' which shows something of his rhetorical skill.

But the parables are often spiritually more subtle than the label 'plain and simple' would suggest. Tyndale made the Gospels clear. That clarity, however, only revealed strangeness, and especially within the parables. The woman found her lost groat, but what 'joy is made in the presence of the angels of God' means is both clear and strange.[9] Even the translation of a parable needs to be able to catch some elusive senses, as George Herbert has it, 'at two removes'.[10] The words 'The kingdom of heaven is like a grain of mustard-seed' (Matthew 13:31; Mark 4:31; Luke 13:19) are awkward to think of in any other vocabulary. There is, however, both difficulty and subtlety in the making of them. The difficulty is in the metaphysics of the idea: behind the first clear meaning, of growth, lies – what, exactly? The subtlety was Tyndale's, getting two tiny objects for the one idea in Greek κόκκῳ σινάπεως (*kokkōi sinapeōs*, 'a berry of mustard') with both 'grain' and 'seed'. (The later Wyclif version had 'a corn of seveney'.) Similarly, the sentence from the Christmas story in Luke 2, 'And they came with haste, and found Mary and Joseph, and the babe laid in a manger' which is Tyndale's, conceals at least one trick of its memorability, which is to build round the 'a' sound of 'Mary' in the middle of the sentence more 'a's on either side – 'and *they came with haste* and found . . . *the babe laid in a manger*'.

Tyndale's biblical plain style, itself the product of keen rhetorical craft, did two things in the century after he wrote. First, it established a form of prose for what can only be called un-courtly writers, the mass of ordinary men and women with something important to say, people far removed from the Neoplatonic courtly poets and romancers of the last years of Elizabeth. Now forgotten, they were just as important – not least because that prose led ultimately to the novel, in Defoe in the early 1700s. Second, it established a form for the widest public: if something had to be communicated, then this was the way to do it. Not for nothing were two important early treatises on rhetoric in English, by Secretary of State Thomas Wilson (1553) and, after Erasmus, by Richard Sherry (1550), produced in the reign of Edward VI.[11] English could well not have gone down the road away from Latin as vigorously as it did. Latin remained always alongside, trying to seduce the language back – succeeding from the time of Samuel Johnson in the later eighteenth century, and sometimes before. The strength and firmness of that English highway is due to the English Bible, which is due to Tyndale.

But though that plain style does well for Tyndale's Gospels, what about Paul's Epistles? Paul was a learned and prolific user of rhetorical schemes and tropes – indeed, he is rich in them to the point of abandon. His antitheses, particularly of flesh and spirit, his driving rhythms, his rapid-fire parataxis, his building of climaxes, a Pharisaic Hebrew mind steeped in the Scriptures encountering Hellenism, and writing common, *koiné* Greek, on the absolute frontiers of theology – this sounds at first a funny way to write a plain style. And yet, strangely, the effect of Paul's writing is to create a plain and simple presence – as Peter Auksi put it, 'the early medium of Christian communication was the warmly personal epistle'.[12] The rediscovery of Paul was the driving force of the Reformation, as the people of Europe had Paul in their own tongues. (A fine book by John Coolidge of Berkeley in 1970, *The Pauline Renaissance*, has not, to my knowledge, been followed up.)

A useful illustration of the effect of Paul's stylistic artistry, as translated into English (ultimately by Tyndale), comes at the time of the Restoration in 1660, when the new Royal Society made a sub-committee to devise an English style which would plainly and simply convey to fellow-scientists and ordinary people the results of their (ultimately Bacon-inspired) new empirical science. The committee succeeded admirably, as is well known. Here is Robert Boyle in 1665. Listen to the Saxon words and order, the parataxis, the short units, of the best plain style:

> We took a new pewter bottle, capable to contain, as we guessed, about half a pint of water, and having filled it top full with that liquor, we screwed on the stopple, and exposed it during a very frosty night to the cold air, and the next morning the water appeared to have burst the bottle, though its matter was metalline; and though purposely for this trial we had chosen it quite new, the crack appeared in the very substance of the pewter. This experiment we repeated.[13]

That might have been Tyndale. Independently, Hobbes was writing the same way – and defending his style;[14] and Addison continually defined a mode of writing:

> It was said of Socrates that he brought Philosophy down from Heaven, to inhabit among men; and I shall be ambitious to have it said of me, that I have brought Philosophy out of Closets and Libraries, Schools and Colleges, to dwell in Clubs and Assemblies, at Tea-tables and in Coffee-houses.[15]

Samuel Johnson concluded his account of Addison's life with the sentence:

> Whoever wishes to attain an English style, familiar but not coarse, and elegant but not ostentatious, must give his days and nights to the volumes of Addison.[16]

This was not intended as praise. The sting is in the opening 'Whoever', which did not include Samuel Johnson. He wanted heavily Latinized vocabulary, in order to be less involved with the reader. Nevertheless, he was right about Addison, whose style was a child of the Royal Society's sub-committee.

That came ultimately from an interesting man called John Wilkins, one of the forces behind the founding of the Royal Society and that sub-committee. Wilkins, a gifted mathematician and a sort of gentle Vicar of Bray, was most famous for a book setting out a scheme for a universal language in 1668. His first – anonymous – books were about whether the moon was habitable, suggesting a means of getting to it. While he was chaplain to, among others, Charles I's nephew in 1645 in London, he actively promoted weekly meetings of the scientifically curious – Robert Boyle's 'Invisible College'. He was on the Parliamentary side in the Civil War and he helped Cromwell: he married Cromwell's widowed sister. But as Master of Wadham College, Oxford, after the Restoration he showed lenience and tolerance to Cavalier sons. He made Wadham the leading college in the university, and had as undergraduates Christopher Wren and Thomas Sprat. The London scientifically curious came to Wadham to continue the weekly meetings in his lodgings, and it was from these that the Royal Society was founded, in 1662, with Wilkins as first Secretary. He then became Master of Trinity College, Cambridge. He was made Bishop of Chester in 1668, and was always a man of some influence.

He wrote in 1646 a short and often-reprinted handbook on preaching, *Ecclesiastes or a Discourse concerning the Gift of Preaching, as it falls under the rules of Art*. Language, he wrote,

> must be plain and natural, not being darkened with the affectations of Scolastical harshness or Rhetorical flourishes. Obscurity in the discourse is an argument of ignorance in the mind. The greatest learning is to be seen in the greatest plainness. The more clearly we understand anything ourselves, the more easily can we expound it to others. When the notion itself is good, the best way to set it off, is in the most obvious plain expression. St Paul does often glory in this.[17]

St Paul as plain: that clinches the understanding that Tyndale's New Testament translation soaked in to the making of a plain style, so that he even appears as controlling the crafting of the Royal Society's new, and splendidly clear, scientific prose of the 1660s and thereafter, until the nineteenth and twentieth centuries when Germanic-American obfuscation took over.

THREE INFLUENTIAL PLAIN STYLISTS

The nation which from the 1530s read the English Bible so widely and so deeply took to itself a plain style of the greatest value. Roger Ascham was widely read at the time. He was tutor to Princess Elizabeth. He wrote a book about educational principles, *The Schoolmaster* (1563). He also wrote a little book called *Toxophilus* (1545), about the art of archery. It tells all that is needed to know about bows, and arrows, and marks, and the direction of the wind, and so on. He gives the feel of the bow in the hand and the wind on the cheek, the eye sighting down the arrow. This passage, of plain style at its best, is, as always, commenting on the observation needed for the making of a craft – like writing.

> Take heed also when you shoot near the sea coast although you be two or three miles from the sea; for there diligent marking shall espy in the most clear day wonderful changing. The same is to be considered likewise by a riverside, especially if it ebb and flow, where he that taketh diligent heed of the tide and weather, shall lightly take away all that he shooteth for.[18]

Ascham has something to say in the clearest English; the first twenty words are eighteen Saxon monosyllables plus 'also' and 'although'.

The second example is the first volume of the English translation of Erasmus's *Paraphrases of the New Testament*, commanded by the king, Edward VI to be made accessible in all churches alongside the Great Bible. Erasmus wrote a good Latin: his influence on literary values in England was wholly positive. The English translations of the *Paraphrases*, in two volumes, are good: it was the first, the Gospels and Acts volume, that was to be in churches, and these were made by Edmond Allen, Miles Coverdale, Thomas Key, John Olde and Nicholas Udall. (What the title-page does not say is that Erasmus on the opening of the Gospel of John was translated by Princess Mary, so soon to be the Catholic queen.) The paraphrase on Luke is translated by Udall (who, rather than Tyndale, may be the translator of Erasmus's *Enchiridion*[19]). First, a verse of Luke 6:

> Blessed shall ye be when men hate you, and thrust you out of their company, and rail on you: and abhor your name as an evil thing for the Son of Man's sake.

That is Tyndale except that in the Great Bible, which Udall is quoting, Coverdale changed 'are ye' to 'shall ye be' and added 'on you' to 'rail'. Here is Udall:

> The most part of the people do call such men happy and fortunate, unto whom the people showeth tokens of high favour, and likewise them that are advanced to honours: and such through glorious titles are much renowned. But ye on my word and warrantise, shall be blessed, when men shall have you in derision; when they shall cast you out of their companies as persons to be detested and abhorred: when they shall speak many sore words of reproach and villainy against you for my sake . . .[20]

Here we can watch Udall opening up and simplifying Latinisms – 'The most part of the people' for Erasmus's *Vulgari*; 'are much renowned' for *celebrantur*, 'as persons to be detested' for *execrabilis*, and so on. There are at first sight more Latin-based dependent clauses of 'when', but they are in fact a form of parataxis. The couplings of the train seem only a little more complex because the hooks are slightly fancier. At root, the word order is Saxon.

The third example of mid-century plain style is from the first of the twenty-one *Homilies* in two books, 1547 and 1563, which were appointed to be preached on Sundays in every parish. If the rhythms seem familiar, they recall the Book of Common Prayer, for this is by Cranmer himself. Cranmer said of his writing 'my chief study be to speak so plainly that all men may understand . . . my words be so plain, that the least child in the town may understand them'.[21] This is the second sentence of the first Homily, entitled 'A fruitful exhortation to the reading and knowledge of holy Scripture':

> Therefore as many as be desirous to enter into the right and perfect way unto God, must apply their minds to know holy Scripture, without the which, they can neither sufficiently know God and his will, neither their office and duty. And as drink is pleasant to them that be dry, and meat to them that be hungry: so is the reading, hearing, searching, and studying of holy Scripture, to them that be desirous to know God or themselves, and to do his will.[22]

This passage has a forward drive which gets straight on, without dependences. It is, like Tyndale, grounded in the everyday world of meat and drink, as Cranmer wanted Scripture to be.

INFLUENCES ON TYNDALE

The Gospels are carefully constructed. Early in all three Synoptic Gospels we meet a paralytic released. Mark begins with a run of healing miracles, showing Jesus the releaser. The Greek verbs for those releases are caught by Tyndale:

> the unclean spirit tare him, and cried with a loud voice, and came out of him . . . the fever forsook her . . . he cast out many devils . . . the leprosy departed from him . . . he arose, and took up the bed, and went forth . . .

and so on. The confirmation of the continued healing power in the risen and ascended Christ after Pentecost is in the healing of the man lame from his mother's womb, a miracle of special interest to Luke the physician in what happened to someone crippled from birth.

> And immediately his feet and anklebones received strength. And he sprang, stood, and also walked, and entered with them into the Temple, walking and leaping and lauding God (Acts 3).[23]

Tyndale's 'sprang' and 'leaping' suggest that something more than just remarkable happened to those unused anklebones.

Tyndale's verbs there, and his general rhetorical awareness, are beginning to be seen as the result of technical craft. A book first in print in 1999, Thomas Swynnerton's manuscript *The Tropes and Figures of Scripture*: it was dedicated to Thomas Cromwell probably in 1537–8, but clearly intended for a larger audience. His sixth chapter ends, 'Every man hath a Testament in his hand, wolde to God in his heart.' In 1537 that Testament had to be Tyndale's. Swynnerton tells the reader to look further into the writing of 'Master William Tyndale'.[24] It is the first book of rhetoric in English, a dozen years before Sherry and Wilson, and it is all about Tyndale's Bible translations as models.

David Norton wrote: 'Sir Thomas More's jibe [. . .] that "all England list now to go to school with Tyndale to learn English" has turned out true: more of our English is ultimately learnt from Tyndale than from any other writer of English prose, and many erstwhile illiterates did indeed "go to school with Tyndale" and his successors.' Norton illustrates this with the story of young William Maldon of Chelmsford and the Sunday gatherings of 'poor men' to hear read to them 'that glad and sweet tidings of the gospel'. That led to young William learning to read, and buying, and treasuring, a New Testament – for which his father beat him and nearly killed him.[25]

What were Tyndale's models? West Country speech may be one: Tyndale was a Gloucestershire man. William Langland's *Piers Plowman* was written in the 1380s just a few miles north of Tyndale's home in Gloucestershire, still by the River Severn. Though England's first printer of note, Caxton, printed edition after edition of Chaucer for his courtly readership, no one printed Langland, in his country speech, until Robert Crowley, a man of some importance as printer and writer, produced an edition in 1550. Work has still to be done on Tyndale's Gloucestershire forms – fourteen have been found in Genesis, including Abraham saying to the men he left behind, taking Isaac, 'Bide here [*yurr*] with the ass'.[26] This register of country speech overlaps with proverbs, of which Tyndale is acutely aware ('Judge not that ye be not judged', Matthew 7). Proverbs, slightly heightened everyday speech, give a useful sense of authority as well as memorability.[27] Also possibly influential were some fourteenth- and fifteenth-century devotional tracts, though those tend to be not enough aware of 'the scrubby byways of common lore',[28] essential for Tyndale.

MAGDALEN COLLEGE VULGARIA

There is a further likely influence which has not been noticed. Tyndale made his own that curiously effective register, of short phrases just above the level of common speech. Tyndale was for ten years at Magdalen Hall, then effectively inside Magdalen College, just at the time that in Magdalen School experiments were being made in teaching grammar in English and not Latin. (They did not last, as Lyly's Latin Grammar was imposed on all schools from about 1520.) Those particular teaching books have survived, however, in the *Vulgaria* from Magdalen. Teaching children Latin by means of sentences about common life, in the vernacular English or 'vulgar' (hence *Vulgaria*), had a history older than Magdalen School. Nevertheless, the Magdalen *Vulgaria* are special in several ways.[29] Tyndale's register is a delicate thing of fine tuning: stylistically neither too low nor too high.

The first such teaching book in several ways was John Anwykyll's *Vulgari Terentii*: Anwykyll was the first Master of Magdalen School. He used Terence, with Cicero, as the model for spoken, as well as written, Latin. Terence was thought to be useful because his comedies are set in streets, with street dialogue. Anwykyll's selection of short English phrases from Terence, printed in Oxford (not very well) is hard to find, being rarely attached to his more famous all-Latin *Compendium* of grammar: it has thirty-one leaves, that is, sixty-two pages, with about ten sentences in English on each; each of the six hundred English sentences is followed by Terence's Latin, not attributed to plays, and in no particular order.[30]

The phrases, as Huckleberry Finn said of *Pilgrim's Progress*, are interesting but tough:

There is no thing better nor more laudable than to subdue the desires of the flesh.

I had lever die.

I fear me lest my father bear heavily that yesterday I come not to him.

Would to god thou lovest me as I do thee.

The condition or disposition of women is when a man will they will not, And when a man will not then they desire most.

For though I am worthy this rebuke it was not thy part to do it.

I trow I labour in vain.

Thou singest always one song.

Thinkest thou so evil done or so unworthy that thy son a young man have one leman [mistress] and thou hast two wives and art nothing ashamed.[31]

Terence gave authority, and Anwykyll's was the first of any Terence in English by forty years: the first complete Terence in English was not until 1598, over a hundred years later. His phrases, however, do not, on the whole, sing to us. Anwykyll's book was modestly reprinted.

John Stanbridge, having been Usher at Magdalen, succeeded Anwykyll as Master of the School from 1488. With his similar works, his *Vulgaria*, written probably about 1501, was very frequently reprinted, with possibly over a hundred editions of various titles in thirty years.[32] His English phrases speak more about schoolboy life:

I will wrestle with thee.

I pray thee tell me when the carriers come.

Be the day never so long at last cometh evensong.

Thou speakest many words to me but nothing to the purpose.

I am at my wit's end.

It is out of my wind.

Here be many pretty maids.

Lift up both thy hands to god.

His face is marvellously changed.

I bring thee good tidings.[33]

There are also utterances about language. Before you put it into Latin, this is what you say in English, with short, punchy, Saxon forms, with Saxon vocabulary – 'How fares thou?' This is probably not how schoolboys talked in reality – 'He hath ordained a staff for his own head.'[34] It is classroom language in its best clothes: but Stanbridge's sentences do tend suddenly to resonate.

Robert Whittinton was a pupil of Stanbridge. His *Vulgaria* are a little late for Tyndale's stay at Magdalen, not being printed before 1519: Tyndale's MA was 1515. His books apparently went through 181 editions by 1530.[35] He set off a grammarians' war on the issue of whether imitation or grammatical rules should come first. His English phrases tend to be heavy:

He is a great ravener, specially if he come there as be good dishes.[36]

After Whittinton, the window of opportunity of learning Latin through English closed again, for William Lyly's famous grammar became the official school book by law, and remained so for a century. It was entirely in Latin. For a couple of decades, however, those little Magdalen books did change something. For one thing, at the height of their use in the School, it seems that Erasmus was staying for some months only yards away at the College.[37] His interest in new ways of teaching was always acute, as can be seen from, among much else, his 1511 *De ratione studii* and 1512 *De Copia*. His 1519 *Colloquia* took over in schools in England from the *Vulgaria* because of their better Latin. Erasmus made the books and the models that were to transform the creative powers of English schoolboys over three generations, so that in 1977 Emrys Jones could write, 'without Erasmus, no Shakespeare'.[38] Work remains to be done on precisely what Erasmus did in those months on the Magdalen site. It is hard to think of him as not grasping what was going on in the Magdalen *Vulgaria*.

Two of the *Vulgaria* have survived in manuscript. One is in the British Library's Rose manuscripts.[39] The sentences here are in longer paragraphs, and lack the arresting power of the others. Again the likely dates, 1512–14, or 1522–7, make them too late for our purpose. In bulk, the biggest collection of *Vulgaria* sentences was not at Magdalen, but the book produced privately for Eton College by William Horman. Though this is again late for our purpose (not before 1519), the sentences in it point up the delicacy of the register of the best of the Magdalen books, Stanbridge and one in the British Library; Arundel MS. Horman's fat book is full of detail, but curiously awkward in English expression, and sometimes trivial in subject:

> If the lap of the ear wax red there is somewhat amiss.
> The monk stole away in an uplandish man's weed.
> He became a baker's servant.

Not trivial at all is:

> My father by three wives hath had nineteen children.

Or

> I had wened my son had been utterly lost and gone for ever.

Finally, a sentence which, though powerful, especially for schoolboys, is clumsy English:

> When a woman beginneth to travail against deliverance: it should ease her to keep her breath stiff.[40]

John Holt had been Usher at Magdalen in 1494, and his popular *Lac Puerorum* ('*Milk for Babes*'), though probably written at Lambeth School in 1505, undoubtedly came out of his Magdalen School experience. It is a Latin grammar in English, rather than a *Vulgaria*.[41]

If there is a writer of the time able to be compared with Tyndale it is only Thomas More, though neither the bulk of his writing in English nor his range in English is in any way equal, and he can write tediously badly. R. W. Chambers in a famous essay 'The Continuity of English prose from Alfred to More and his school' found the distinguishing characteristics of More's English prose 'its dramatic quality, its humour, its colloquial ease, its clarity and firmness of structure'.[42] Chambers found that Tyndale and More 'both write the same English', though he gave no sense of the powerful national impact of Tyndale – indeed, he hoped he could give that importance to More. More's English works were not available until the collected edition of 1557. Chambers wrote, a little desperately, that even though they were never reprinted, they must have had some influence.[43] But in 1956 William Nelson of Columbia University edited the anonymous Magdalen *Vulgaria* in the Arundel MS. This is by far the most interesting. It dates from 1501. It is full of Magdalen details, and the manuscript has accompanying Latin letters which mention or were written by Magdalen School teachers. Nelson speculates that more important to Thomas More than the fourteenth- and fifteenth-century devotional tracts, which, with all his great knowledge of English prose, was all Chambers could suggest as possible models,[44] were the Magdalen *Vulgaria*, especially the Arundel one. (Nelson also makes a strong case for More, almost certainly in Oxford before 1500, being probably the author of parts for a Magdalen School play, as mentioned in a letter in that Arundel MS. What Nelson does not notice is that one of the most celebrated of the Magdalen School grammars, Holt's *Lac Puerorum*, has opening and closing verses by More.)

Are we close to a model for William Tyndale's Bible style? No one in his senses would argue that the Word of God is best translated into the language of small boys – Stanbridge has 'Turd in thy teeth' and 'Wipe thy nose' and 'Thou stinkest' (though in Tyndale's John 11, Martha says of her four-days-dead brother Lazarus, 'by this time he stinketh'). Tyndale's power to give to Britain through the spread of his Bible translations a plain style of the greatest importance can perhaps be traced to his absorption, as a boy, of the register of English for translation that he needed. Only Magdalen could have given him that, and he was there at the right time. Those short Saxon units, that so-characteristic trick of the sentence in two halves, are there for him, in the right register, just above normal speech, especially in the Arundel *Vulgaria*. Nelson (who does not mention Tyndale) describes the Arundel *Vulgaria* as language 'that literate folk would wish to speak in early Tudor times'. Exactly.

Here is a passage from the Arundel MS in Nelson's edition. The form, the vocabulary, the sentence lengths, syntax and rhythms, might bring to mind Tyndale's epistles of Paul or parables.

Service is none heritage [i.e., one cannot rely on hired employees as upon one's family] and that we see daily, for an the master like not his servant, or the servant his master, they must depart. Furthermore, we see but few successors cherish such servants as were great with their predecessors. Therefore, my friend, take heed to thyself while thou hast a master and mayest do much with him, that thou mayest have where-with to live when he is gone. I say not this for nought, for I know myself many a praty man that was well at ease but late agon in a good service, masterless, able to bear the king's standard, as would serve full fain without wages for meat, drink and cloth. These be ashamed to beg because they were well at ease so late days. They dare not steal for fear of hanging. Tell me how shall they live? They can no handicraft, they cannot skill of husbandry, they think it a foul shame to foul their hands.[45]

It is an English unusual for the time, that has something to say; that can make both the short Saxon strokes needed for the parables ('They be ashamed to beg') and the rhetorical weight for Paul – 'Therefore my friend take heed to thyself while thou hast a master' comes within range of Tyndale's passage in Ephesians 5, 'Take heed therefore that ye walk cir-cumspectly: not as fools: but as wise, redeeming the time . . .' This *Vulgaria* is not a source for Tyndale's Bible: it may be the beginning of a model. When Tyndale tells the Joseph story, for example in Genesis 43, he writes

When Joseph came home, they brought the present into the house to him, which they had in their hands, and fell flat on the ground before him. And he welcomed them courteously saying: is your father that old man that ye told me of, in good health? and is he yet alive?[46]

This is not what is thought of as 'biblical' English: it belongs to the social novel, and could be Defoe.

How Tyndale found a register for the Word of God in English, and what the important consequences were, need to be to explored further. Tyndale's translations spoke to the people in the recognisable voice of the people in a register only a little raised. That was a difficult thing to do.

Here is Tyndale in his 1534, New Testament, from Romans 8.

Therefore brethren we are now debtors, not to the flesh, to live after the flesh. For if ye live after the flesh, ye must die. But if ye mortify the deeds of the body, by the help of the spirit, ye shall live. For as many as are led by the spirit of God: they are the sons of God. For ye have received not the spirit of bondage to fear any more, but ye have received the spirit of adoption whereby we cry Abba father. The same spirit certifieth our spirit that we are the sons of God. If we be sons, we are also heirs, the heirs I mean of God, and heirs annexed with Christ: if so be that we suffer together, that we may be glorified together.[47]

St Paul, a Hebrew writing in Greek in sentences that tumble over one another, demands above all clarity in translation. Again, Tyndale makes short units, Saxon vocabulary and phrases, and, with his excellent ear for rhythm, unforgettable cadences. 'For as many as are led by the spirit of God; they are the sons of God.' The KJV translators left this passage almost entirely as they found it. They changed Tyndale's 'received not the spirit of bondage to fear any more', which is clear, and final, to 'For ye have not received the spirit of bondage again to fear', which is, as so often, cloudy. They should have good marks for changing Tyndale's 'the heirs I mean of God, and heirs annexed with Christ' to 'heirs of God, and joint-heirs with Christ'.

I shall say more in a later chapter (23) about the plain style as influencing poets and dramatists, as one of the registers available to Shakespeare, a fine subject for study. Here I take two examples, which have to be teasingly brief. Shakespeare knows the value of polysyllabic Latin: Macbeth looks at his bloody hand and says it will 'the multitudinous seas incarnadine': but then he suddenly switches to 'making the green one red'. Falstaff is capable of elaborate syntactical structures and Latinist forms, especially to slip out of responsibility: 'Thou shalt find me tractable to any honest reason. Thou seest I am pacified still.' But when he wants suddenly to turn our hearts over, Shakespeare does not make Falstaff say, as would befit a Latin-educated knight, before the battle of Shrewsbury, 'The advent of the imminent confrontation elevates my apprehensions', but 'I would 'twere bed-time, Hal, and all well.'[48]

Tyndale gave us our Bible language. No sets of words in English have ever been so deeply considered by so many good minds in our nation for so long, and then carried so far in space and time through the KJV.

QUEEN MARY

No Bibles were printed in England between 1553 and 1558, in the reign of Queen Mary. Cardinal Pole, brought in from Rome as Archbishop of Canterbury, advised the queen that the law *De heretico comburendo* should be revived. In those five years about 300 men and women were burned alive. The first was Tyndale's friend and maker of Matthew's Bible, John Rogers, who suffered at Smithfield on 4 February 1555

> with heroic fortitude. Even Catholic opponents said so. The godly who had gathered wept and prayed God to give him courage to bear the

pain and not to recant. Rogers's ashes were collected, a martyr's relics, and some seeing birds fly over as he expired thought this a sign of the Holy Ghost.[49]

The cull included Hugh Latimer and Nicholas Ridley, outside Balliol College, Oxford, and on the same spot the deposed Archbishop of Canterbury, Thomas Cranmer.

About eight hundred men and women fled into exile in Germany and Switzerland, a migration significantly including Bible scholars. Forcing a national return to Roman Catholicism, and the pope's authority, under a childless queen, was bound to be difficult. Pole, who had not lived in England for 34 years, could not begin to understand the national mood. Though there was an understandable drift to conform, the burnings reinforced hostility, as making martyrs always does. The Cardinal saw through Roman eyes, which did not mean that he brushed aside the vernacular Bible: an early programme of his had included a new English translation of the New Testament. But (in the words of Eamon Duffy quoted above, p. xx), the true Catholic way [was] the spirit of the *parvuli*, the 'little ones' of Christ, for whom penitence, not knowledge, was the true and only way to salvation.[50] By 1553, England had at last caught up with most other European countries: the printed Bible in the vernacular had solidly arrived. Moreover, in these islands, now ahead of most other countries, English Bibles had been royally sanctioned. That does not mean that from mid-century the country was painted a uniform colour. Evidence can be found of parishes refusing to buy the Great Bible, or of complaints from the pulpits, familiar down the centuries, that 'young people these days' did not know their Bibles.

BIBLE READING

Richard Tracy, in his *A Supplication to our most Sovereign Lord King Henry the Eighth* in 1544, argued that it was only through suppressing vernacular Scripture that the Roman Church had ever been able to stand.[51] Before Queen Mary, the English Bible had seeped into many parts of national life. Demonstrations of this can be made, even in Mary's reign. The Bibles made under Edward, and the literature, were still there, and being increasingly read even by the supposedly unlettered, though officially forbidden. To go back seven years, to that period after 1543 when Parliament had passed the Act forbidding Bible reading among the lower classes, a Gloucestershire man named Robert Williams bought a copy of a humanist book in English, Thomas Langley's *Abridgement of Polydore Vergil*, first published in 1546. Vergil's 'notable work', as the title-page has it, contained 'the devisers and first finders out as well of arts, . . . civil ordinances, as of rites, & ceremonies, in the church'.[52] It is a difficult book. Robert Williams was a shepherd. He wrote in it:

> At Oxforde the yere 1546 browt down to Seynbury by John Darbye pryse 14d when I kepe Mr Letymers shype I bout thys boke when the testament was obberagatyd that shepe herdys myght not red hit I prey God amende that blyndnes. Wryt by Robert Wyllyams keppynge shepe uppon Senvury hill 1546.[53]

A. W. Pollard prints, apparently from the Foxe papers, the story of William Maldon of Newington.[54] When he was a young man, in the reign of Henry VIII,

> divers poor men of the town of Chelmsford in the county of Essex where my father dwelt and I born and with him brought up, the said poor men bought the New Testament of Jesus Christ and on Sundays did sit reading in lower end of church, and many would flock about them to hear their reading, then I came among the said readers to hear their reading of that glad and sweet tidings of the gospel, then my father seeing this that I listened unto them every Sunday, then came he and sought me among them, and brought me away from the hearing of them, and would have me say the Latin matins with him, the which grieved me very much, and thus did he fetch me away divers times, then I see I could not be in rest, then thought I, I will learn to read English, and then I will have the New Testament and read thereon myself, and then I had learned of an English primer as far as patris sapientia and then on Sundays I plied my English primer, the Maytide following I and my father's apprentice Thomas Jeffary laid our money together, and bought the New Testament in English, and hid it in our bedstraw and so exercised it at convenient times.

Arguments with his mother led to beatings by his father, during which William did not weep ('I rejoiced that I was beaten for Christ's sake') which so angered his father that he tried to hang him, and he was only rescued by his mother and brother. 'I think six days after my neck grieved me with the pulling of the halter.'[55]

Reading the New Testament brought public as well as private hostility: at Enfield in Middlesex a reader, warned off by the constable, had been opposed by the parson, who thought the English New Testament 'the book of Arthur Cobler . . . a green learning that wil fade away'.[56]

William Maldon learned to read English for, and through, Tyndale's New Testament. He was not alone in England. The question of how literate the nation was, for example in Mary's reign, is difficult. Twenty years before, Thomas More, in the course of arguing against a translation of the Bible into English, foresaw confusion and dissension if it were widely available, as in every town and parish there were only four out of every ten who could not read.[57] Perhaps Sir Thomas, as remarked above, exaggerated to make his point, but his fear seems genuine. Tyndale wrote for 'the boy that driveth the plough'. The bulk of Edwardian Bible-printing suggests a healthy rate of literacy, as does the steady growth, year by year, of books of all kinds published in English, with only a slight check to that growth under Mary.[58] But we are dealing here with more than the ability to read 'The Nut Brown Maid' for oneself. To quote Guglielmo Cavallo and Roger Chartier,

> A direct, unmediated relationship between the faithful and the sacred Word made knowledge of the Bible a fundamental spiritual experience, and it raised Bible reading to the level of a model for all other possible forms of reading. Whether the Bible was read silently by individuals, read aloud to the assembled family in the privacy of the home, or read in church, Bible reading was present at every moment of existence. It defined a relationship with writing that was invested with an extraordinary intensity.[59]

As Tyndale translated Hebrews 4:12,

> the word of God is quick [alive], and mighty in operation, and sharper than any two-edged sword: and entereth through, even unto the dividing asunder of the soul and the spirit, and of the joints and the mary [marrow]: and judgeth the thoughts and intents of the heart: neither is there any creature invisible in the sight of it.[60]

A good deal is known about assemblies, small and large, for the reading of the Bible together, in the mid- and later sixteenth century, though it has to be said that the very small ones, in someone's house, have generally only broken the surface of historical record through persecution: the numbers of unrecorded parlour readings across England must be significant. Some of the large assemblies for Bible reading, in cities, were not only large, but were powerful enough locally to be left alone by the bishops under Pole. B. R. White has recorded information about two of them left untouched, in London and in Bristol.[61]

What went on in such gatherings can be illustrated from a later account in a letter. Here is a Lord's Day:

> We begin with a prayer; after, read some one or two chapters of the Bible, give the sense thereof, and confer upon the same: that done, we lay aside our books, and after a solemn prayer made by the first speaker,

he propoundeth some text out of the Scripture, and prophesieth out of the same by the space of one hour or three quarters of an hour. After him standeth up a second speaker . . . [he is followed similarly by] the third, the fourth, the fifth, etc. as the time will give leave. Then the first speaker concludeth with prayer as he began with prayer, with an exhortation to contribution to the poor, which collection being made, is also concluded with prayer. This morning exercise beginneth at eight of the clock and continueth until twelve of the clock. The like course and exercise is observed in the afternoon from two of the clock unto five or six of the clock. Last of all the business of the government of our church is handled.[62]

Tyndale had passed on what he understood from the New Testament – a gathered church, a congregation led by elders and, instead of priests or even presbyters, ministers; the New Testament affirming, in Luther's phrase, the priesthood of all believers. An early marginal note in Tyndale's abandoned Cologne New Testament of 1525 has, against Matthew 16 'Thou art Peter, and upon this rock I will build my congregation', the explanation that the rock is the faith, not Peter, adding 'Then is every Christian man and woman Peter', a truth more shocking than Luther's 'priesthood of all believers'. Central to such Bible-controlled gatherings was their overriding concern, a passionate desire to recover the inner life of New Testament Christianity. They understood something called a conditional covenant, a 'mutualist' position, which was taken wholly, and uniquely, from Tyndale.[63]

Out of these numerous, and often now invisible, Separatist groups, some dating back to Queen Mary's reign, came at the end of the century the denominations called Congregationalists, and Baptists – the latter quite free of influence, it has been definitively shown, from continental Anabaptists.[64] Those original English Baptists have grown to be worldwide, making, it is said, the largest Protestant denomination; in various forms (not always to everyone acceptable) they now dominate much of American religious life. That was true of America from the very beginning. In 1648, Governor William Bradford of New Plymouth, leader of that North American settlement, and one of the Pilgrim Fathers, found that generations were growing up with hazy knowledge of their origins. He wrote an account which refers specifically to their development from Bible-studying, Separatist, proto-Baptist, congregations in England in the 1590s, and even a London conventicle in Queen Mary's day. B. R. White concluded his study of Separatism with the words:

> . . . the Separatist tradition developed the inner core of a species of churchmanship which, powerful and flexible as it was, provided the

characteristic organization not only of the sectaries of the Great Rebellion, but also much of New England Protestantism, and ultimately, that of the United States.[65]

I must be careful. It is one thing to claim, correctly, that Tyndale was the creator of the very influential Bible language. Or that the scholarly phrase 'without Erasmus, no Shakespeare' might well extend to 'without Tyndale, no Shakespeare'. It is quite another to claim that Tyndale caused the United States of America.

But there is a grain of truth there. Certainly Tyndale anticipated the Church of England, and can be seen to stand at the head of the first and peculiarly English Reformation. I am sure he anticipated even more the still unregarded second wave, producing in the light of God's Word a cherished and English individualism which spread worldwide.

BIBLE REFERENCES BY INDIVIDUALS

Awareness of the individual reading of, and knowledge of, the English Bible may come by way of an emerging understanding of the value of Scripture citations in the less acknowledged writings of the 1530s and 1540s, in recent research by Dr Alec Ryrie.[66] As he observes, 'The Reformation was perceived by those who made it, and those who were made by it, as an intellectual event. . . . Protestantism was led from the universities, from the very top of the intellectual food chain.'[67] That high intellectual ground drew towards it newly liberated lay men and women. There is a sense of ordinary people bewildered and disorientated by the loosening of their normal moorings, but finding that it can also be possible to enjoy the liberty of reaching upwards, to new thoughts, and new scholarship, without the oppression of what it is forbidden to think or do, and without the fear of a heresy trial. As Alec Ryrie wrote, the early Reformers 'wanted a nation of Bible-readers; they wanted all England to be a university, in which the ploughmen and the milkmaids sang Scripture as they worked'.[68]

That did not happen, just as the publication of Tyndale's New Testament in 1526 did not sweep the Roman Church away. Instead, a Protestant culture slowly became embedded. It had the Bible at its core. The English reformers did maintain the authority of the Bible and control of its interpretation – never more so than in the making and effect of the Geneva Bible.

Having read 'virtually every piece of English-language printed evangelical material from the period 1539–46 and a fair selection of the more interesting MSS from that period as well',[69] Ryrie has collected from that material a mass of biblical passages, not as passing or marginal references, but 'as the mainstay of other than a stock argument' as well as in unusual settings.[70] He directs attention to Richard Taverner's set of postils (notes or commentaries on the Gospel or Epistle of the day) frequently issued in the 1540s, a 'semi-official' set.[71] An anonymous set of postils printed by Richard Grafton in 1543, Ryrie finds 'the most interesting and certainly the most radical set'. The seven postils on Romans alone, he shows, reveal a freedom of approach, the lectionary, for example, being 'an excuse for Biblical exposition rather than a master', and producing fresh interpretations. 'The author of Grafton's collection went so far as to take his Biblical texts, not from the authorised Great Bible, but from Tyndale's thoroughly illegal 1534 New Testament.'[72] The same is true, on Romans, of half a dozen other writers: and 'too numerous to mention' on Romans 13, showing 'shifting ideas about obedience in the two decades after Tyndale's *Obedience*'. Again, taking only passages in the two letters of Paul to the Corinthians, Ryrie found a dozen controversialists in the 1530s and 1540s prepared to venture into interpretations that were not sanctioned by the Church. In 1539, Richard Busshe, parish clerk of Hastings, was so disturbed by reading 1 Corinthians 9:5, a reference to Peter and other apostles having wives, that he wanted the New Testament burned as heresy. Accused, he defended himself by writing that compulsory clerical celibacy showed that the Bible was pernicious and heretical.[73] The point of all these – and more have been found referring to the Gospels (except Mark) and Acts – is not their silver trumpet calls to battle for the Lord, but their sheer ordinariness: they were issues, yes, of great significance and feeling (and Richard Busshe was not alone in his shocking realisation of the implications of the Apostles being married) but issues that were privately felt, not even part of an evangelical manifesto. In an ocean of new New Testament reading, these references, being only what have survived, must be the tips of quite large icebergs. Thoroughly to stir the metaphor, all the little front-parlour Bible-reading groups in their small way laid down, like coral, massive reefs – on which, apart from the royal politicking, Queen Mary's attempts to restore Roman Christianity foundered. The so-condescended-to *parvuli* (see above, p. xx) now had both knowledge and power. Dr Ryrie's work led him to observe that the most striking fact about early use of the printed English Bible is its heterogeneity. People were not simply drawing on a small reserve of stock passages and prefabricated arguments. Their use of biblical material is eclectic and idiosyncratic, and can only indicate a great series of individual encounters with Scripture.

There can be found, in John Foxe and elsewhere, accounts of the thoroughness of the Bible knowledge of often the humblest men and women: men and women who often could not read. Rawlins White was a Cardiff fisherman burned in 1555. He was illiterate, but in Edward vi's reign he yearned to study the Bible. He sent one of his children to school to learn to read English (an indication that his native tongue was Welsh). The boy would read a portion of the Bible to his father every night, after supper. White would commit this to memory, so successfully that, as Foxe reports, when someone made a Scripture reference he could cite the book, the leaf and the very sentence. Similarly, John Maundrel, who was burned in Salisbury in Mary's reign, carried a Tyndale New Testament everywhere, though he could not read. When he met anyone that could read, his book was always ready. He could recite by heart most places of the New Testament. Joan Waste was a blind woman in Derby who earned her living making hose and sleeves. She saved her money and though she could not read, bought a New Testament, and had it read to her a chapter at a time. This she memorized, so that she could recite many chapters of the New Testament without the book. She was burned in 1558. A Mrs Prest, burned in Exeter, also in 1558, was illiterate, but caused Sir Walter Raleigh's mother to comment that Mrs Prest's Scripture knowledge was even greater than hers, though she could not read.[74]

Two important elements in the reading groups, again often revealed only in accounts of their punishments, too often death by hanging or burning, were, first, that women had equal status with men, and second that this kind of Protestantism was a youth movement. A long additional section in A. G. Dickens's 1989 revision of his *The English Reformation* gives some of the increasing evidence. His description of apprentices and even schoolboys dying for their faith is hard reading. He ends those pages:

> These stories of rebellious youth have hitherto received less attention than they deserve. They illustrate the vitality of the early Reformation with greater force than does that more familiar image of elderly bishops witnessing to their faith at the stake in Oxford and elsewhere.[75]

BIBLE READING AND NATIONAL RESURGENCE

Those who rarely read a Bible might scornfully consider the idea of whole Sundays given to communal Bible-reading and prayer as utterly boring. It cannot have been so. First, those readers were responding to a text that was sometimes difficult and more often exhilarating: something that did more than make sudden sense of life – it opened doors in the mind and spirit. Second, the effect was the opposite of depressing.

I take an illustration from mid-twentieth-century history, a hidden national enterprise in a desperate phase of war.[76] By 1942, almost the entire resources of continental Europe were in the hands of Germany, and Japan had wiped out the western colonial presence in Asia in a couple of months. Democracy appeared to have had its day. Yet out of the flames of destruction, and the bodies of fifty-five million European and Asian people, a new world order was built from 1945. Many of the victories had been narrow or scarcely believable. The Battle of the Atlantic had been almost lost. The terrible siege of Stalingrad ended with a nearly incredible reversing of the unbeatable German army. Behind that latter success lay the fact that, though Hitler rapidly ranged into the industrial heartland of the Soviet Union to make it his, just ahead of the swiftly advancing German army the Russians under extraordinary conditions dismantled their war factories and reconstructed them a thousand miles further east, where they produced the tanks and planes which, in the huge surprise counter-attack at Stalingrad, flung the Germans back (finally to Berlin).[77] That astonishing removal of the factories and workers by rail, so that from shut-down near Moscow, as it might be, production swiftly began again in Siberia, overcoming unbelievable chaos and difficulties, was not only the result of central and local planning. It touched a Russian nerve. The Russian people were united in that miracle, the removal of 1,523 iron, steel and engineering plants to distant safety, by appeal to men and women – especially women – for the survival of Mother Russia. That emotion – hidden from Hitler and his generals – had the immense national driving power that was needed. Decisive also was the simple, formulaic construction of these tanks and planes, which not only helped in making them in the overwhelming numbers needed for the surprise counter-attack, but also allowed them to be repaired quickly on the spot.[78]

The illustration may be overblown. In 1526 England did not change in a few weeks: but the point here is a large national shift, one still under-reported, especially about the part played by women, away from the national repression of Christian resources, while the Bible was still allowed only in Latin, to a dominant energy to restore things again, to end the siege of the vernacular Bible, to claim the nation for God newly revealed. Historians of the sixteenth century know a good deal about the men, and a few women, who controlled England and Scotland from the 1530s onwards: but not much has yet been told about the thousands of ordinary men and women with their Bibles and day-long study.

The driving force there was release: the release that the New Testament can bring to a heart, mind and soul, from reading Paul and believing; from hearing the Gospels and believing – so many of Jesus' miracles are about release. Just as in Russia a complicated state-of-the-art German tank with a minor defect sufficient to make it unusable had to be sent back over hundreds of miles to be repaired, while the extremely basic Russian tank could be mended on the battlefield, so the full panoply of holy objects in a church building, or the limited instruction of a priest, was not needed for the effective story in the Gospels to be understood.

A further illustration, from Tudor schoolrooms, might help to clarify how easily modern misjudgement can happen. A glimpse of a pupil's curriculum, say in a small town in the English Midlands in the early 1570s, can nowadays produce cries of horror. Everything was in Latin, with perhaps some Greek. Attendance at 'petty school' began at the age of five, with a move to Grammar School at eight: the title was correct – Latin grammar was learned, by rote. The hours were long, 7 to 11 in the morning, 1 in the afternoon until 6 or 7 in the evening, each working day throughout the year. The pastimes were few, and the ushers (schoolmasters) were pedants, when not also cruel. The Elizabethan picture is compounded by Victorian portraits of schoolmasters, like Dickens's Doctor Blimber, at whose academy Paul Dombey's spirit was crushed.[79] Shakespeare himself, knowing the Grammar School at Stratford-upon-Avon, seems to fix the picture:

> . . . the whining school-boy, with his satchel
> And shining morning face, creeping like snail
> Unwillingly to school.[80]

Yet a pupil at Stratford-upon-Avon Grammar School in the 1570s received there as good an education as any grammar-school boy in England, being taught by well-paid Oxford men, and in that fact was better educated than his peers at Eton College. Such a pupil was the beneficiary of the process of educational reform, initiated by Erasmus early in the century, which can be traced in the foundation of many excellent grammar schools in the sixteenth century in towns and cities throughout the land, a reform which led to the great flowering of talent in the decades that followed.[81] Paul Dombey's sufferings have had a wide readership. They have been more influential than a true understanding of conditions when Shakespeare was a pupil. Further, the whining schoolboy does not have to be autobiographically decisive. It is fiction; an image by Jaques in a speech in *As You Like It* needed to fill in a few moments of plot business (Orlando going off to fetch Adam), a speech full of stock notions: the Seven Ages of Man were a well-worn literary convention, and to it Jaques adds his own characteristic, and rather insufferable, loftiness. Jaques makes each age unpleasant (the infant is 'mewling and puking' rather than adorably smiling). School did not have to be appalling. There are other schoolmasters in Shakespeare. Holofernes in *Love's Labour's Lost* is ridiculed for his pedantry: but he is neither unbelievable nor indeed, unfamiliar. Moreover, he is given a moment of true moral courage when he rebukes his supposed betters for their bullying, protesting firmly to the lordly young gentlemen 'This is not generous, not gentle, not humble.'[82] Jokes in *The Merry Wives of Windsor* are more at the expense of the interfering Mistress Quickly than the Welsh schoolmaster, Sir Hugh Evans. These are things created by Shakespeare. We cannot take any passages in his plays and poems as personal confessions from his private biography. In Shakespeare's schooling, however hard modern tourists find the benches, however boring modern people might find the curriculum, on the page were passages of Ovid, Virgil, Horace and Juvenal. Not only were all these and more never forgotten by him: they grew in importance in his adult life, particularly Ovid. Ovid is deeply entwined in the excitement of Shakespeare's growing creativity, and one can watch a flowering of Ovidian effects, bringing much else in the making of drama, throughout the two decades of his writing life. For Shakespeare, the poetry of Ovid, begun to be loved at school, was always alive and always growing.[83]

Mid-century Bible reading in its thoroughness can be seen to have had even greater creative effects.

THE ARRIVAL OF ENGLISH

Some time between 1502 and 1505, the English poet and courtier John Skelton wrote of the English language:

> Our naturall tong is rude,
> And hard to be enneude [revived]
> With pullyshed terms lusty;
> Our language is so rusty,
> So cankered and so full
> Of frowardes [awkward words], and so dull,
> That if I wolde apply
> To wryte ornatly,
> I wot not where to fynd
> Termes to serve my mynde.[84]

Skelton's own quirky English poems, though they can have force and charm, are a linguistic muddle, being English with Norman-French vocabulary and Latin forms and insertions. Skelton has no notion that the future would be with a confident, clear, aesthetically beautiful English language. Skelton died in 1529. In the later 1520s and early 1530s Tyndale wrote a new kind of English: both a language for the Bible, which he invented, and a polemic prose of real power. At the back of his 1526 New Testament are two and a half pages 'To the Reader', in which he says he has done his best: but 'consider that I had no man to counterfeit . . . Count it as a thing not having his full shape, but as it were born afore his time, even as a thing begun rather than finished.' He has drawn in many influences 'as far as God gave me the gift of knowledge'.[85] He is aware of the future not only of the translation, but of the language.

There are only a dozen years between Tyndale's martyrdom for heresy in 1536 and Thomas Cranmer's work on the Prayer Book. In his library at Lambeth, Cranmer set himself to learn how others had done it. He studied liturgical examples from all over Europe, before chairing the meetings at Windsor and Chertsey which produced the first Book of Common Prayer of 1549. Cranmer's greatest gift to the nation, even beyond the making of the first complete Prayer Books, must surely be the phrasing of the collects and other prayers he wrote for it. Like many reformers in his ability to take in a whole continent of scholarship, and like Tyndale in particular, he could rework his learning in English of lapidary beauty, memorably speaking directly to the heart. For Tyndale's 'But Mary kept all those sayings, and pondered them in her heart' or 'Ask and it shall be given you; seek and ye shall find, knock and it shall be opened unto you' or 'For this thy brother was dead and is alive again, was lost and is found' can be quoted Cranmer's collect for the twenty-first Sunday after Trinity:

> Grant we beseech thee, merciful Lord, to thy faithful people, pardon and peace: that they may be cleansed from all their sins, and serve thee with a quiet mind: through Jesus Christ our Lord.

That is Cranmer's translation of the fourth-century Gelasian Sacramentary. Or that for the fourth Sunday after Easter:

> O almighty God, who alone canst order the unruly wills and affections of sinful men: Grant unto thy people, that they may love the thing which thou commandest, and desire that which thou dost promise: that so, among the sundry and manifold changes of the world, our hearts may surely there be fixed, where true joys are to be found: through Jesus Christ our Lord.

The rhythmic construction of those sentences is compelling. The ground is Anglo-Saxon monosyllables, with the Late Middle English prose tradition of short sentences for meditation – the same English stream fed both Tyndale and Cranmer – 'that they may be cleansed from all their sins, and serve thee with a quiet mind' – finely decorated in the second collect with three polysyllables (affections, commandest, manifold), the first two from Latin. These are conscious rhetorical devices whereby the great mysteries of our faith are so simply and memorably expressed. Such devices were greatly used by Tyndale. Cranmer has Tyndale's skill in making a Saxon cadence close with a firm consonant ('with a quiet mind', 'true joys are to be found').

Chapter 16

THE GENEVA NEW TESTAMENT, 1557

AFTER THE GREAT BIBLE OF 1539, the next newly prepared English New Testament was printed in Geneva in June 1557. It marked both a great contrast to the Great Bible, and – though at first it might not seem so today – a long stride forward.

For one thing, it is small, an octavo for the hand or pocket (roughly the size of a Prayer Book in a church pew) as editions of the New Testament had been since Tyndale's and Coverdale's over twenty years before.[1] That made a contrast to Henry VIII's original huge folio Great Bible, or Matthew's before that: but the contrast was not only in the pleasing small size.

It is also handsome. For the first time,[2] an English Bible text was printed not in heavy 'Gothic' Black Letter in northern Europe by printers in Antwerp or London, but in Switzerland, by Conrad Badius, the son of the master-printer of Paris, in a clean, clear Roman, a French style also influenced by Italian printers trained in the more refined humanist manner. Its pages are uncluttered, the text ruled off with red lines, with wide margins at the sides, top and bottom, giving an attractive sense of space. The paper shows signs of having been carefully selected: some surviving copies remain unusually fresh; one of the two copies in the Bodleian Library, Oxford, and the copy in Lambeth Palace Library,[3] have paper of still remarkable whiteness, as no doubt do others. The neat notes, an average of two per page, are in the outer margins in roman, with occasional references in italic on inside margins. The thickest cluster of marginal notes accompanies the opening chapters of Matthew's Gospel. Some pages, even of the Epistle to the Romans, have no notes at all. Also for the first time in an English Bible, while the traditional markers A, B, C, and so on are retained in the margins, the text is divided into numbered verses, following the Greek New Testament by Stephanus made in Geneva in 1551, ultimately from Pagninus's edition of the Vulgate made at Lyon in 1527, though – also for the first time in this 1557 New Testament – each verse starts a fresh line with its number, whether it is the beginning of a new sentence or not.[4] This again was new, for the first time outside Latin or Greek. Again for the first time in an English Bible, words not in the Greek, thought to be necessary additions for English clarity, are in italic.

The title-page is another contrast to that of the Great Bible (fig. 20). Instead of announcing its authority by declaring it to be the result of 'the diligent study of diverse excellent learned men, expert in the . . . tongues', it states:

> The New Testament of our Lord Jesus Christ. Conferred diligently with the Greek, and best approved translations. With the arguments, as well before the chapters, as for every Book and Epistle, also diversities of readings, and most profitable annotations of all hard places: whereunto is added a copious Table.

In other words, critical study is invited. Further, the title-page does not announce absolute royal power, as in the Great Bible, in the later Bishops' Bibles, and in the first KJV with massive constructions that block the entrance of the reader. It will be noticed that there are no names, unlike the central panel of KJV, where King James and Robert Barker are prominent. Here, inviting the reader in, is a small, simple engraving in the middle of the page. It is in the manner of an emblem, showing Time leading Truth up out of a cavern. Eyes used to sixteenth- and seventeenth-century Bible title-pages being architecturally organised for essential weight, with pillars and statues, or a heavy iconography of divine and royal supremacy, might find this bizarre; but for printers making an English New Testament in the 1550s, it spoke strongly. This can be demonstrated. That very device was the inspiration for a pageant held in Cheapside at the celebration of Elizabeth's succession. On 14 February 1558, the queen proceeded to a place between two hills where there had been contrived a cave with a door and a lock. At her approach an old man, scythe in hand, and 'having wings artificially made', was seen to come forth. He was leading

> a person of lesser stature than himself, which was finely and well apparelled, all clad in white silk, and directly over her head was set her name and title in Latin and English, *Temporis filia*, the Daughter of Time. Which two so appointed went forward toward the South-side of the pageant. And on her breast was written her proper name, which was *Veritas*, Truth, who held a book in her hand upon which was written *verbum veritas*, the word of Truth.

After a recitation by a small child 'he reached the book to the Queen, who thereupon kissed it, held it aloft for all to see', and so 'laid it upon her breast, with great thanks to the City therefor' . . . the Queen said that 'she would often read over that book.'[5] One might have difficulty thinking of the slightly built queen clutching a massive folio or thick quarto and at the same time retaining her dignity. It is easy to contemplate that little 1557 New Testament volume as it was being 'laid . . . upon her breast'.[6]

The year 1557 and the city of Geneva were both the time and the place for a new English translation. For twenty years, revisions of Olivetan's French New Testament had been published in Geneva, revised by Calvin and Genevan ministers, the latest in 1556.[7] Italian exiles there printed a revised Italian New Testament in 1555, on the way to a whole Bible.[8] A revised New Testament in Spanish was printed there in 1556.[9] (A more detailed account of these appears below.) The last new English Bible had been made, in England, eighteen years before, and that was Coverdale's revision of his work four years before that, nearly a quarter of a century distant.

THE FIRST GENEVA TRANSLATORS

Two months after Queen Mary's coronation on 19 July 1553, William Cecil, formerly Secretary of State (as he would be again, famously, under Elizabeth) began to put into operation a plan for the migration of British Protestants to the Continent. This was supported by English merchants, out of Protestant belief but also with an eye to future trade.[10] The great movement of Protestants to the Continent in January and February 1554 happened before the most serious persecution got under way: the first burning, of John Rogers, maker of Matthew's Bible, took place on 4 February 1555. In the eighteen months before that martyrdom, the migration had been carefully organised.[11]

To settle in one of the continental Cities of Refuge, the migrants had to be religious refugees, that is, they had to be, in the modern phrase, asylum seekers, fleeing persecution. As in order to get in they had to declare that they had been persecuted for religion's sake, it has been said that 'little by little [they] began to believe the myth that they themselves had created', something apparently only revealed as a myth four hundred years later, in 1986.[12] In fact, it is hard to defend that notion of the exiles subscribing only to a myth. The dangers in England were real; the restrictions of Protestants began within a few days of Mary's accession. Before Mary died in November 1558 about three hundred Protestants had been burned alive in England.

In 1555, Calvin had welcomed into Geneva what one might call second-stage English refugees, that is the groups formerly under John Knox in Frankfurt, who had quarrelled with the original settlers there over the need for Anglicanism to reform further, in the direction of the supreme authority being vested in the congregation, as in Geneva under Calvin. The forty-six English who moved to Geneva were given their own place of worship, to be shared with the Italians, and on 15 November 1555 held their first service in their own language according to the rites of the Geneva Reformed Church. One of them was William Whittingham.

The work of preparation of this New Testament was anonymous. So was the Preface, which was less customary: evidence points to it being the single-handed work of William Whittingham, an English gentleman and Oxford scholar. He had been at Brasenose College, then became a Fellow of All Souls, and was finally at Christ Church, from which college he was given leave of absence in 1550 to pursue languages and civil law at Orleans and Paris, and in German universities.[13] In 1552 he visited Calvin in Geneva. He returned to England briefly, but on Mary's accession, he went back to settle in Geneva. It is sometimes said that he married Calvin's wife's sister.[14] He published an edition of Bishop Ridley's Brief Declaration of the Lord's Supper in 1555 and 1556, in 1557 with his own Latin translation.[15] He wrote a Preface for Christopher Goodman's *How Superior Powers ought to be Obeyed* (1558).[16] (Later, in Elizabeth's reign, and after military service under the Earl of Warwick, he became Dean of Durham; he died in June 1579.)

A manuscript *Life* of Whittingham in the Bodleian Library in Oxford tells of a group of 'learned men' in Geneva meeting to 'peruse' the existing English versions of the New Testament[17] (thus making, as David Alexander pointed out, the first such revising committee in English Bible history.[18] The 'learned men' mentioned were indeed learned: Miles Coverdale; Christopher Goodman, another Oxford man, from Brasenose, and then Christ Church, who had become Lady Margaret Professor of Divinity; Anthony Gilbey; Thomas Sampson, from Oxford and Cambridge, who went on to be Dean of Christ Church, Oxford – he had most recently been close to the Hebrew scholar Immanuel Tremellius at Cambridge and Strasbourg; Dr William Cole; and William Whittingham himself. They were possibly joined in committee by John Knox, and certainly later for the whole Bible by William Kette (or Kethe), John Baron, John Pullain, John Bodley and W. Williams.[19] Knox had been chosen as minister from its first day by the English-speaking congregation at Geneva, but did not arrive there until September 1556. He left for Scotland in 1557, but returned early in 1558, finally departing in January 1559, having received the freedom of the city of Geneva.

If William Tyndale had survived, and gone to Geneva as a Marian exile in 1553 at the age of fifty-nine – not an impossibility – he would have found a city humming with Bible activity. In many ways he would have been a happy man. Even more than in Antwerp, in his day the northern centre of translating and printing Scripture, he would have found areas of the city life of Geneva given to scholarship and fine printing. (It is estimated that between 1550 and 1600 some 2,500 titles were printed in Geneva.[20]) Much more, he would have found a new university at the heart of the work: the Academy of Geneva was formally inaugurated on 5 June 1555, with Theodore de Bèze, or Beza, as its first rector. Antwerp, too, had had a newish university nearby, the Catholic University of Leuven, founded in 1425: from there in the mid-1530s the attack on the English reformers was co-ordinated, focusing the Europe-wide condemnation of the Lutheran heresy, examining Tyndale and condemning him to death. Twenty years later, Geneva had its new Reformed university, with new fields of knowledge and study. It became rapidly famous for scholarly enterprise, which included the establishment of good texts of classical writers of all kinds – Virgil, Cicero, even Catullus – and translating them, as well as the Scriptures, into French, Italian and Spanish. Tyndale would have been content to be a senior engineer in that powerhouse.

How much the 'learned men' who were in Geneva contributed to the New Testament (as opposed to the whole Bible that followed) is unclear: there has been persistence in the statement, certainly implied in the Preface, that one man, Whittingham, did it all alone. Not only does the 1557 New Testament itself, however, say nothing about that: the writer of the manuscript *Life* does not mention that he translated the New Testament. It seems a large item to omit. Perhaps assumption of a large share by Whittingham is safest.

PREFATORY MATTER BY CALVIN AND WHITTINGHAM

Not only is the whole work anonymous: how much Calvin associated himself with this New Testament, if he did at all, is also unclear. He apparently wrote an eight-page introductory Epistle declaring with good Epistle-to-the-Romans force 'that Christ is the end of the Law', an important endorsement of this new work. Yet this Epistle Dedicatory is a translation of a piece written twenty years before, and his second published work, Calvin's Preface (in Latin) to the New Testament in Olivetan's Bible of 1535, the first French Protestant Bible (Olivetan was Calvin's cousin).[21] The 1557 English translation of Calvin is well written, indeed lively, and has the distinction of introducing two words into the English language: one of them, 'goodhap', meaning good fortune (*OED* cites this location as first use) did not survive: the other 'bourgeois' (which *OED* does not cite before 1654), certainly did.[22] In the Epistle, Calvin traces the continuing providence of God from the Fall of man to his redemption through Christ Jesus. God has given two testimonies: of nature – 'everywhere, in all places, and in all things, he hath displayed in his ensigns, yea, so clearly blazed his arms, that there was no such idiot which could pretend ignorance in not knowing so sovereign a lord'; and the testimony of the Law and the Prophets established an awareness in men of the confirmation of the Old Covenant in the New through Christ.[23]

The unsigned three-page address, probably by Whittingham, 'To the Reader Mercy and peace through Christ our Saviour', echoes Tyndale's *Obedience of a Christian Man* in its awareness of opposition to the Bible, and of Jesus' Parable of the Sower at Matthew 13, Mark 4 and Luke 8. It continues:

> For this cause we see that in the Church of Christ there are three kinds of men: some are malicious despisers of the word, and graces of God, who turn all things into poison, and a farther hardening of their hearts: others do not openly resist and contemn the Gospel, because they are stroken as it were in a trance with the majesty thereof, yet either they quarrel and cavil, or else deride and mock at whatsoever thing is done for the advancement of the same. The third sort are the simple lambs, which partly are already in the fold of Christ, and so hear willingly their Shepherd's voice, and partly wandering astray by ignorance, tarry the time till the Shepherd find them and bring them unto his flock. To this kind of people, in this translation I chiefly had respect, as moved with zeal, counselled by the godly, and drawn by occasion, both of the place where God hath appointed us to dwell, and also of the store of heavenly learning and judgement, which so aboundeth in this city of Geneva, that justly it may be called the patron and mirror of true religion and godliness.[24]

The writer goes on to explain briefly his care with the Greek and with English phrasing, the division into verses, and the italic insertions. He explains that he has signalled variant Greek readings, especially the ones which make significant changes:

> Moreover, the diverse readings according to diverse Greek copies, which stand but in one word, may be known by this note ", and if the books do alter in the sentence then it is noted with this star ★ . . .

There are nine of these occurrences. Thus, the sentence making Acts 14:7 in Tyndale, 'And there they preached the gospel', has become in '1557', 'preaching the Gospel', with, now added to it from some Greek manuscripts, the words 'In so much that all the people were moved at the doctrine. So both Paul and Barnabas remained at Lystra.'

This is important. It was not the first time in an English New Testament that those additional words had appeared (they are not in any Greek edition by Erasmus, and not in KJV, but they were given in the text in italics in the Great Bible). It was, however, the first time that they had been so clearly marked as an alternative Greek reading, in type in the margin as clear as the main text. Their principal source is that essential Codex which Beza acquired in 1562, which he later gave to the Library of the University of Cambridge where it still is. It had been the property of the Bishop of Clermont in Auvergne: he took it with him to the Council of Trent because at John 21:22 it has a reading (then considered unique, now standard: KJV's 'If I will that he tarry till I come') from which, bizarrely, he argued 'that celibacy had dominical sanction'.[25] The pious bishop had an unintended effect, however. Friends of the Parisian printer and editor, Robert Estienne (Stephanus), sent him from Italy a list of the manuscript's more important variant readings, and more than 350 of these he incorporated in the margins of his first printed Greek New Testament in 1550, basically from Erasmus, but the first with critical apparatus, along with variant readings from fourteen other manuscripts and from the Complutensian Polyglot. (Though only Codex Bezae had any authority, the rest being only late versions of the standard Byzantine text, a reprint of this Stephanus edition first used, on its title-page, the words 'Textus Receptus', with effects that will be shown, in later chapters, to be troublesome in the nineteenth and twentieth centuries.) In about 1550, Robert Estienne sought refuge in Geneva, and no doubt facilitated use of his knowledge by the makers of vernacular Testaments.

On his annotations, Whittingham (if he was the author) risks a boast:

> I have endeavoured so to profit all [help everyone] thereby, that both the learned and others might be holpen: for to my knowledge I have omitted nothing unexpounded, whereby he that is exercised in the Scriptures of God, might justly complain of hardness . . .[26]

Indeed, so comprehensive has he been, that readers have no need of 'the Commentaries'. He is rightly proud of his 'arguments', the summaries of the contents at the head of each book, or of the four Gospels together, made 'with plainness and brevity'[27] to be understood and remembered, which 'may serve instead of a Commentary to the Reader'.[28] The idea of such summaries was not new: Coverdale in 1535 had a page of 'The first book of Moses, called Genesis what this book containeth', though only that page: Matthew's Bible had in the preliminary leaves two large pages of 'The sum and content of all the holy Scripture . . .'. What was in this 1557 volume was fresh. Here are two 'Arguments': the first, that to Romans, could be considered to be summarising the core of New

Testament theology, and is given here in full. The second is more randomly chosen, one of the short-chapter 'Arguments', that to Colossians 2. It is, incidentally, quite incorrect to say that none of the 'Arguments' in the 1557 New Testament was ever reprinted – they were all reproduced in the 1560 Geneva Bible, and in some Geneva Bibles afterwards.

The Argument of the Epistle to the Romans.
   The great miracle of God is declared toward man in Christ Jesus: whose righteousness is made ours through faith. For when man by reason of his own corruption could not fulfil the Law: yea committed most abominably, both against the Law of God and nature: the infinite bounty of God, mindful of his promise made to his servant Abraham, the father of all believers, ordained that man's salvation should only stand in the perfect obedience of his Son: so that not only the Circumcised Jews, but also the uncircumcised Gentiles should be saved by faith in him: even as Abraham before he was Circumcised, was counted just only through faith: and yet afterward received Circumcision, as a seal or badge of the same righteousness by faith. And to the intent, that none should think that the covenant which God made to him, and his posterity, was not performed: either because the Jews received not Christ (which was the blessed seed) or else believed not that he was the true redeemer, because he did not only, or at least more notably prefer the Jews: the examples of Ismael and Esau declare, that all are not Abraham's posterity, which come of Abraham according to the flesh: but also the very strangers and Gentiles grafted in by faith, are made heirs of the promise. The cause thereof is the only will of God: forasmuch as of his free mercy, he electeth some to be saved, and of his just judgement rejecteth others to be damned, as appeareth by the testimonies of the Scriptures. Yet to the intent that the Jews should not be too much beaten down, nor the Gentiles too much puffed up: the example of Elias proveth, that God hath yet his elect even of the natural posterity of Abraham, though it appeareth not to man's eye: and for that preferment that the Gentiles have, it proceedeth of the liberal mercy of God, which he at length will stretch toward the Jews again, and so gather the whole Israel (which is his Church) of them both. This groundwork of faith and doctrine laid, instruction of Christian manners follow: teaching every man to walk in roundness of conscience in his vocation, with all patience and humbleness: reverencing, and obeying the magistrate, exercising charity; putting off the old man, and putting on Christ: bearing with the weak, and loving one another according to Christ's example. Finally S Paul after his commendations to the brethren

exhorteth them to unity, fleeing false preachers and flatterers, and so concludeth with a prayer.

Suspicious readers who cry 'Calvin' every time they see the word 'elect' are not reading their Paul very carefully. Calvin tackled head-on the difficult argument about God's foreknowledge, basically a secular Greek concept, which New Testament writers linked with God's destiny for Israel: but Calvin found it in Paul (Romans 8:29, 11:2, Galatians 3:8) and in words attributed to Peter (Acts 2:23, 1 Peter 1:2). No one could accuse KJV of being 'unacceptably Calvinist', the root of attacks on Geneva Bibles: yet KJV's 1 Peter 1:2 has 'Elect according to the foreknowledge of God the Father', and there are eleven Pauline occurrences of 'elect' or 'election' in KJV, beginning with Romans 8:33, 'Who shall lay anything to the charge of God's elect?'[29]

The 'Argument' to Colossians 2 explains Paul's method:

> Having protested his good will towards them, he admonisheth them not to turn back from Christ to the service of Angels or any other invention, or else ceremonies of the Law, which have finished their office, and are ended in Christ.

All the chapter 'Arguments' were carried forward into the 1560 Bible, but rewritten thereafter.

Reading this New Testament, the 'simple lambs' are to be engaged in private study. For the first time they have between covers not only a good text in English, but, intentionally, everything they could need for interpretation. For example, against Matthew 5:3, 'Blessed are the poor in spirit', the note, to 'poor', is 'That feel themselves void of all righteousness that they may only seek it in Christ.' Against Matthew 16:18, 'Upon this rock I will build my congregation' is, keyed to 'this rock', 'Upon that faith whereby thou hast confessed and acknowledged me: for it is grounded upon an infallible truth.' (Perhaps unsurprisingly, the Catholic Rheims New Testament (1582) has at this point two and a half pages given to small-print annotation, headed 'Of Peter's Primacy'.)

The 'lambs' are to attend closely not only to paragraphs, Tyndale's 'process, order and meaning' of the text, but to verses. The system of location by chapter and verse now makes those verses easily able to be called, as it were, to support a legal case. Moreover, a modern opinion has to be reversed. Faced with the solid weight of passages in the thick Gothic letters of a Great Bible, for example, or the KJV as it first, and for a long time, massively appeared, a modern reader feels in the presence of something not ordinary, to be approached with a special mind and heart; but also prevented, intimidated, shouted at, even bullied. The roman pages of the 1557 Geneva New Testament are a relief, feeling comfortable to absorb. In 1557, however, roman type for the ordinary reader would seem strange, even difficult. A whole New Testament in roman would need unusual concentration – which was the idea.

THE 1557 NEW TESTAMENT TEXT

The New Testament text, though aware of Coverdale's work on the Great Bible, goes back behind that to follow Tyndale in 1534, usually thought to be in a version printed in London by Richard Jugge in 1548. Influential for the first time was Theodore Beza's Latin New Testament published in Geneva the year before, in 1556.

Two qualities make this New Testament forward-looking. The first is the effect of a fresh mind working on a better – if only slightly better – original text, unhindered in carrying forward Tyndale's work of translating from the Greek. The second was the effect of drawing in, without visibly overloading, all the new biblical scholarship current in Geneva in several languages, so that 'with its elaborate apparatus of arguments, notes and tables, it forms the first critical edition of the New Testament in English'.[30]

Samuel Bagster's 1841 *English Hexapla* gives the 1557 New Testament text entire, but without any additional matter. Bagster's choice of this text over the New Testament from the complete 1560 Geneva Bible has been regarded as odd: but his decision was sound, for so much that was later standard (not only in KJV, for example) first appeared in 1557. Here is one of the shortest of Jesus' parables, at Luke 15:8–10, in modernised spelling. I give it first in Tyndale of 1534:

> Either what woman having ten groats, if she lose one, doth not light a candle, and sweep the house, and seek diligently, till she find it? And when she hath found it she calleth her lovers and her neighbours saying: Rejoice with me, for I have found the groat which I had lost. Likewise I say unto you, joy is made in the presence of the angels of God over one sinner that repenteth.[31]

In '1557':

> 8. Either what woman having ten pieces of silver, if she lose one, doth not light a candle, and sweep the house, and seek diligently till she find it?
> 9. And when she hath found it, she calleth her friends, and her

neighbours, saying, Rejoice with me, for I have found the piece which I had lost.

    10. Likewise I say unto you, joy is made in the presence of the Angels of God, over one sinner that converteth.

The dependence on Tyndale is clear: but so are the changes, from 'ten groats' to 'ten pieces of silver', and from 'her lovers' to 'her friends' (the older 'lovers' did not have the sexual sense in Tyndale). Though the Rheims New Testament of 1582, on which it has so often been said that the KJV revisers heavily relied, restored 'groats', KJV itself gave 'pieces of silver' from '1557'. The later Wyclif had had 'besauntis', that is, 'bezants', gold coins current in Europe. KJV followed Tyndale's 'sinner that repenteth' rather than '1557''s 'sinner that converteth', strikingly not taking Rheims 'sinner that doth penance'. The latter's use of the Vulgate's *uno peccatore poenitentiam agite* followed Wyclif's 'one sinful man doing penance', which is contrary to the Greek ἑνὶ ἁμαρτολῷ μετανοοῦντι (*heni hamartoloi metanoounti*).

    Different features of '1557' may be seen in comparing Tyndale in another short parable, from Luke 18:1–5, first in Tyndale:

And he put forth a similitude unto them, signifying that men ought always to pray, and not to be weary saying: There was a judge in a certain city, which feared not God neither regarded man. And there was a certain widow in the same city, which came unto him saying: avenge me of mine adversary. And he would not for a while. But afterward he said unto himself: though I fear not God, nor care for man, yet because this widow troubleth me, I will avenge her lest at the last she come and hag on me.[32]

In '1557':

And he put forth a similitude also unto them, *to this end* that they ought always to pray, and not to wax faint.

    2. Saying, There was a Judge in a certain city, which feared not God, neither reverenced man.

    3. And there was a certain widow in the same city, which came unto him saying, Do me justice against mine adversary.

    4. And he would not for a *long* time: but afterward he said with himself, Though I fear not God, nor reverence man.

    5. Yet because this widow troubleth me, I will do her right, lest at the last she come and make me weary *with her importunity*.

KJV kept the first italics, *to this end*, but not the others, going back to Tyndale's 'a while'. Tyndale's 'hag' did not survive, though it is recorded in *OED* (Hag, *v.*[2].3.), 'to fatigue, tire out, "fag"', first from 1674 (ignoring

Tyndale here) and in use until 1854. The '*importunity*' of '1557' gave the parable its later title, 'The importunate widow': the Latin word is neither in the Vulgate, which has *sugillet me*, figuratively 'taunt' (literally 'beat black and blue') nor Wyclif, which has 'condemn me'.

It should be made clear that though additional phrases like 'weary with her importunity' expand the Greek ὑποπιάζη (*hupopiadzē*), 'afflict, vex' (also literally 'beat black and blue'), it was usually '1557''s marking with italics, not the giving of additional words, which was new. Thus where, to take one example out of hundreds, '1557' has at Romans 10:30, '*I mean* the righteousness which *cometh* of faith', Tyndale had had 'I mean the righteousness which cometh of faith'.

Here, to conclude this all-too-brief discussion of the Geneva New Testament as it first appeared, distinct from that in the later complete Bible, are two passages, with the notes and references. To help to catch the tone of human warmth in this book, the lack of what one might call doctrinal bullying, both are Luke's accounts of young people. The first is from Luke 2:

40 And the child grew, & waxed strong in spirit, and was filled with wisdom, and the grace of God was with him.

41 And his father and mother went to Jerusalem every year ★at the feast of Easter.

42 And when he was twelve years old, they went up to Jerusalem after the custom of the feast.

43 And when the feast was ended, as they returned home, the child Jesus bode still in Jerusalem, unknowing to Joseph and his mother.

44 For they supposed he had been in the company, and therefore went a day's journey, and sought him among the kinsfolk, and acquaintance.

45 And when they found him not, they turned back to Jerusalem, and sought him.

46 And it fortuned after three days, that they found him in the temple, sitting in the midst of the "doctors, both hearing them and posing them.

47 And all that heard him, marvelled at his understanding, and answers.

48 And when they saw him, they were astonied: and his mother said unto him, Son, why hast thou thus dealt with us? Behold thy father and I have sought thee with heavy hearts.

49 Then said he unto them, How is it that ye sought me? ʰWist ye not that I must go about my father's business?

50   But they ⁱunderstood not the words that he spake to them.

51   And he went with them, & and came to Nazaret: and was obedient to them: and his mother kept all these sayings in her heart.

52   And Jesus increased in wisdom and stature, and in favour with God and man.

In the inner margin, at *, are '*Exod.12.c. Levi.23.a. Deut.26.a.*' and at "'*or, learned men.*' In the outer margin, are, at ʰ 'Our duty to God, is to be preferred, before father and mother' and, at ⁱ 'For his vocation was not yet manifestly known.'

The passage is clearly taken from Tyndale in 1534, with ten small changes. The biggest are that verse 43 begins, in Tyndale, 'And when they had fulfilled the days'. In verse 47, everyone marvels 'at his wit'. At verses 51 and 52, 'his mother kept all these things in her heart' and Jesus increased 'in wisdom and stature'. The only marginal note is 'Christ is found disputing in the temple.'

In Acts 20, Luke describes Paul and his companions returning to Asia from Macedonia and Greece:

6   And we sailed away from ᵃPhilippi, even after the days of sweet bread, and came unto them to Troas, in five days, where we abode seven days.

7   And ᵇthe first day after the Sabbath, the disciples being come together for to ᶜbreak bread, Paul preached unto them, ready to depart on the morrow, and continued the preaching unto midnight.

8   And there were many lights in an upper chamber, where we were gathered together.

9   And there sat in a window, a certain young "man named Eutychus fallen into a deep sleep, and as Paul was long preaching, he falling down for sleep, fell from the third loft downward, and was taken up dead.

10   But Paul descended, and *lay on him, and embraced him, saying, Make nothing ado, for his life is in him.

11   So when Paul was come up again, and had broken bread, and eaten, he communed sufficiently, even till the dawning, and so departed.

12   And they brought the boy alive, and were not a little comforted.

The inner margin has "ᶜ*to celebrate the Lord's Supper. Cha 2.g.*', *or, boy.* and * *1. Kin.17.d, 2 Kin.4.f.* The outer margin, "ᵃHe remained there these days because he had better opportunities to teach: also the abolishing of the law was not yet known.' 'ᵇWhich we call Sunday. Of this place and also of the 1.Cor.16.a. we gather that the Christians used to have their solemn

assemblies this day, laying aside the ceremony of the Jewish sabbath.'
('Loft' is 'floor or story' *OED sb.* 5 giving first use to Tyndale at this verse
in 1526.)

Again, there are a dozen small changes from Tyndale, who had in verse
6 'Easter holy days'; in 7 'On the morrow after the sabbath'; in 9, 'Paul
declared, he was the more overcome with sleep' and in 11, 'and communed
a long while'. The Geneva Bible of 1560 similarly made nine changes, in
6 now reading 'unleavened bread'; in 9, 'he overcome with sleep, fell down
from the third loft' and in 11, '*Paul*... a long while till the dawning of
the day *and* so he departed'. And again, the dependence of KJV is clear.

INNOVATION AND SOPHISTICATION

What is not visible to readers in later ages is what is new in the presentation. First, the title-page. In England, the fashion for emblems had not
begun. These, which reached their peak after the late 1560s in England
in collections (Geffrey Whitney's *A Choice of Emblems* in 1586 is a good
example), were still valued, and had influence, a century later. They were
a form which put together on a page a small drawing of symbolic complexity with lines of verse on the same subject. Their religious use was
two-fold; either in the complex and intricate designs favoured among
intellectuals in the Counter-Reformation, or in the popular Protestant
simple form.[33] The genre is classical: it came back into fashion in Italy in
the 1500s. Sometimes between the drawing and the verses was a couplet
motto which summed up the subject with proverbial force. The picture
and the words were at the same time both obvious and enigmatic.
Puzzling them out, and meditating on the relation between the drawing
and the verses, gave pleasure and at the same time conveyed essential and
quite complex truths. For example, an emblem in an anonymous English
collection of 1612 shows Learning, holding a book and the wise serpent
and plodding along the path that leads to the City of Wisdom, being
offered a crown by Time.[34]

What William Whittingham the translator and Conrad Badius the
printer put on their title-page was a new emblem on a classical proverbial subject, that time restores truth. (The saying is also in Matthew 10:6,
'There is nothing covered, that shall not be revealed; and hid, that shall
not be known', and its parallel in Luke 12:1–2.) The iconography in the
drawing is traditional: Time has his scythe, hourglass, wings, forelock and
satyr's legs.[35] That the smaller figure is female was also traditional – Truth
is the daughter of Time.

What has never to my knowledge been remarked before is that this drawing with verses on the 1557 title-page is the first-ever printed English emblem.[36] It predates the first emblem collection by some time. A private manuscript collection, known to few, can be dated *c*.1565. The first printed English collection was made by Whitney in 1586, almost thirty years later. In other words, the 1557 title-page would have been regarded as very sophisticated – not only in using an emblem, but in it being this of 'Time trieth truth', the classical 'Tempus-Veritas' idea central to High Renaissance images and pageantry.

Second, the very fine paper making, the clean layout on the page, and the printing in a clear, small roman type would also have been regarded as very sophisticated (fig. 22). So would the division into numbered verses. All this is so familiar that it takes real imagination to understand its importance. Black letter had been called 'the people's letter'. Though not intended for private readership, the big official Bibles, the Great Bible, the Bishops' Bible and KJV were all printed in that heavy Gothic black letter, as were Tyndale (apart from three books of the Pentateuch), Coverdale and Matthews, all in whatever size. Whittingham and Badius, in the delicacy and clarity of their small pages, were also doing something which would have needed unusual concentration. Further, that they understood that the numbering of verses (for the first time outside Latin) would seem very advanced is shown by their index at the back, 'The Table of the New Testament', where for every entry they give the chapter and then, before the verse-number, the familiar old-fashioned letter, as in 'Rom 3.c.24'.

'1557' IN EUROPE – AND ENGLAND

This New Testament was immediately popular among English speakers on the continent of Europe, and in England, and did much to satisfy a hunger for up-to-date New Testament work in English, known to be being done in Geneva under Calvin. There is interesting evidence that '1557's were imported into England even during the reign of Mary. Foxe records the presence of one in London almost as a matter of course. In 1558, a priest named William Living was interrogated because he was found to have a scientific book, of astronomy (causing the beadle to blame him, as being a conjurer, for the queen's sickness) and then accused by Bishop Bonner's chancellor of being 'a schismatic and a traitor' because he prayed in English. Living reported that, on his way to the coalhouse and the stocks, he was robbed by an underling 'of my purse, my girdle, and my Psalter, and a New Testament of Geneva'.[37]

It is a pity that there is today no facsimile or modern edition of this sweet book, the New Testament of 1557. Seeing Tyndale's work, done two dozen years before, and now intelligently edited, and before it was scrupulously revised for the full Geneva Bible, is a necessary but neglected part of English Bible history. The aids to study, including the marginal notes, tell a good deal about the theological climate of enquiry. As the writer of the Preface noted, both advanced scholars and the simple and unlearned can benefit from all his apparatus. The 'arguments' standing at the head of the Epistles, in brevity, clarity and accuracy were not bettered until those by J. B. Phillips in his *Letters to Young Churches* in 1947 (and it will be noted in chapter 39, p. 744, that C. S. Lewis wished that those had been available to him when he first became interested in the Christian faith). One can imagine a twenty-first-century reader putting down this 1557 Geneva New Testament after having carefully read both text and notes, and asking with surprise, 'But where is the dreaded Calvinism one is told to expect on every page? Where are all those unacceptable attacks on the Catholic Church?' They are not there.[38] Watching the drift of the scholarly annotations is challenging to everything that is usually said about Geneva Bibles. Three-quarters of the marginal notes are purely explanatory rather than doctrinal: the latter are almost entirely scriptural.

Chapter 17

THE GENEVA BIBLE, 1560

THIS COMPACT VOLUME, in size 'a moderate quarto',[1] with its excellent text generally in roman type, the numbered verses set out in two columns, had in addition what amounted to an encyclopedia of Bible information. It was very popular and successful indeed. It was a masterpiece of Renaissance scholarship and printing, and Reformation Bible thoroughness.[2] Having been the people's Bible in the later sixteenth and early seventeenth centuries, it was driven out by political and commercial interests from 1611, and forced out of the public view from 1660. It was made an object of horror by the Victorian High Church, which invented for it a myth of unacceptably total and aggressive Calvinist colouring, not easy to refute as copies were scarce. That invention is still kept alive,[3] as is the notion that Geneva Bibles were popularly disliked before 1600, for which there is no evidence. The value of this remarkable volume in all its wealth, and all its editions, and all its influence, was reduced to a single schoolchild snigger by referring to it – as eighteenth-century booksellers did – only as 'The Breeches Bible', because in Genesis 3 Adam and Eve are given 'breeches' (as in Wyclif and Caxton's *Golden Legend*, incidentally) instead of the KJV's 'aprons'.[4]

THE WORK OF THE GENEVA ACADEMY

The Academy of Geneva under Beza was based on the model established at Strasbourg. The aim was the specialised one of educating men, in large numbers: a learned ministry was always the goal of the reformers, in whatever country. The academy began with 162 students, but five years later, in 1560, it had 1,500.[5] The educational ideal was much broader than studying theology. The Strasbourg Academy had nine faculties, Geneva many more: the academics there became what would now be called 'European leaders in a centre of excellence with best practice in teaching and research right across the humanities'. In the last decades of the sixteenth century Geneva became for many distinguished Englishmen a necessary place in which to study. Beza's scholars were the 'specialist experts' in the 'humane' work of editing ancient texts. The first texts that Calvin edited were classical, and his love for, and knowledge of, the Greek and Roman writers, were profound. The weightiest work, however, was the making of vernacular Bibles from the best Hebrew and Greek texts.

The Geneva revision of Olivétan's French New Testament in 1556, mentioned above as an influence on the 1557 English New Testament, was only one of the French Bibles revised in Geneva. The first printed Bibles in French, amounting to six, all from the Vulgate, and all containing non-biblical matter or glosses, or simply paraphrase, were from the late fifteenth and early sixteenth centuries. In the 1520s, Jacques le Fèvre d'Étaples prepared in Paris a revision and fresh translation of the whole Bible in French, the New Testament appearing in 1523 in Paris. The whole Bible was printed in Antwerp in 1530, by Martin Lempereur, or Merten de Keyser, Tyndale's printer. Le Fèvre's outspoken marginal notes to his New Testament caused offence to the Catholic authorities, and in 1546 it was put on the Index, and many copies were destroyed.[6] A new edition of his whole Bible in 1534, also from de Keyser, though still from the Latin, was, as was seen above, an influence on John Rogers in preparing Matthew's Bible in 1537.

The first French version made with reference to the Hebrew and Greek was that by Olivétan, printed in Switzerland, in Neuchâtel, in 1535. Though Olivétan seems to have had le Fèvre's Bible open beside him, his was a fresh translation from the Hebrew, and from the fourth edition of Erasmus's *Novum Testamentum* (as it was now entitled), 1527. Like Coverdale and Rogers, he printed the Apocrypha as a separate section, though following le Fèvre from the Latin. In the New Testament he was the first to print in smaller type words not represented in the Greek. Though it seems that Calvin had no hand in the preparation, he contributed that Latin Preface which William Whittingham translated into English twenty years later. This Olivétan 'noble folio Bible'[7] also greatly influenced Rogers in making Matthew's Bible, particularly in the borrowing of the Preface to the Apocrypha, and the concordance.

From Geneva also came Estienne and Badius's edition of the Vulgate in 1555: the Old Testament in the Vulgate in 1556–7, and the New Testament in translations by the two most noted Greek scholars, Claude Baduel and Beza.[8] Until the end of 1560, and alongside three reissues of Le Fèvre and one oddity (see below), Olivetan's French Bible was revised and reprinted at least eight times; it is certain that Calvin worked on some of them. All these were printed in Geneva, and the versions from early on became known as the 'French Geneva Version'.[9] (Independently,

Sébastien Châteillon, or Castellio, printed in Basle in 1555 his 'vulgar' French translation, aiming to be intelligible to the common people. Though it was denounced harshly by Calvin as the work of Satan – largely, apparently, because Castellio was 'not one of us'[10] – it now cries out for further study as something original and alive: it is said that its expressions 'are sometimes undignified', which in the twenty-first century does not signal disapproval.[11] Castellio will reappear in chapter 34 below.)

During the next fifteen years, while the English Geneva Bible continued to be printed only in Geneva (in 1560, 1560 New Testament only, 1562 and 1570) – no London printing was permitted by the English bishops, an embargo breached only when the Archbishop of Canterbury, Matthew Parker, died in 1575, as will appear – there were a further eight editions of the French Geneva Version, nineteen more before 1700, and a further dozen in the eighteenth century, with a major revision, effectively the last, in 1805.[12] The story of Bibles in Italian is roughly the same: printed Bibles from 1471, from the Latin; the first full revision and correction with reference to the Hebrew and Greek prepared and printed in Geneva in 1562; and after that five of the seven Italian Bibles before 1665 coming from Geneva. In Spain it is likely that Spanish-language printed Bibles were completely destroyed by the Inquisition, leaving no trace.[13] The Spanish history remains parallel: though the first translations from the original languages were not made in Geneva, a significant reprint of the translation by J. Perez of the New Testament was printed there in 1556. The numbers of Geneva editions in Spanish, which include separate translations of Romans and 1 Corinthians, are understandably smaller; but Geneva copies were smuggled into Spain with great courage.[14] None of these volumes was produced in isolation, and it is possible to trace the migration of illustrative woodcuts, for example, or type, from Bibles in one language to another.[15]

(It is again worth remarking how constant is the pattern throughout the larger continent of Europe, of Bibles in a vernacular being first printed in the fifteenth century, from the Latin, and then remade in the sixteenth century from the Hebrew and Greek – in every country, that is, except one. In Germany, France, all the Low Countries, the Slavonic countries, Switzerland, Italy and Spain including the Catalan-speaking areas, there were printed vernacular Bibles some decades before Erasmus's *Novum instrumentum* of 1516, and in Germany and France, fifty years before. The exception was England.)

The scholar-printers in Geneva – Robert Estienne, Conrad Badius, Jean Crespin, Jean Girard, Nichlas Barbier, Thomas Courteau, Jean Rivery – made twenty-two French Bibles.[16] This was the context in which there appeared in April 1560 the first English Geneva Bible.

GENEVA PRINTING IN ENGLISH

Two at least of the English exiles were printers. One of them, Rowland Hall, an original member of the Stationers' Company in London, set up his press in Geneva in 1558. One of the ministers of the English Church at Geneva was the Hebrew scholar Anthony Gilbey. Another scholar was Thomas Sampson. William Whittingham, New Testament translator, was there. Miles Coverdale received permission to settle in Geneva in October 1588. The 'simple lambs' on the Continent and in England, so helped by Whittingham's New Testament, surely needed a complete Bible on the same model. It was begun a few months after the 1557 New Testament was published, and continued, we are told, 'for the space of two years and more day and night'.[17]

So the first Geneva Bible was made, printed by Hall at his Geneva press in April 1560. The costs of the making were borne by the English congregation generally, and by one member, the wealthy merchant John Bodley, whose son Thomas would later found the Bodleian Library at Oxford. Though Queen Mary had died on 17 November 1558, and all over the Continent exiles (said to number 800 in total during Mary's reign) returned to Protestant England under Good Queen Bess, some of the men who made the Geneva Bible remained there until it was completed in April 1560[18] – probably Whittingham, Gilbey and Sampson, and probably Cole, Kethe and Baron. An early copy was presented to Queen Elizabeth.

This remarkable volume, 'the first great achievement in Elizabeth's reign',[19] printed in London and in Edinburgh after 1575, and always in large quantities, became at once the Bible of the English people. It remained so, through 140 editions – editions, not simple reprintings – before 1644. As will be seen in later chapters (20 and 22), the New Testament was revised by Laurence Tomson in 1576, and new notes by 'Junius' replaced those to Revelation in 1599. In 1610, fifty years after the first making, all three versions were in full printing flood, 120 editions of all sizes having been made. It seemed that nothing would stop them. The translators working for King James after 1604, in aiming 'to make a good one, better' were referring to the Geneva Bible, and in the KJV long Preface, 'The Translators to the Reader', they quoted Scripture almost always from there. But politics ruled. Even the inception, in January 1604, of the 1611 KJV was a political act by reactionary bishops against Geneva Bibles. As will be seen, the large printing of that 'King James' version in 1611, in spite of its immediate unpopularity, was organised in order to push out the Geneva Bibles. Ugly and inaccurate quarto editions of the Geneva Bible, all falsely dated 1599, were printed in Amsterdam, and possibly elsewhere in the Low Countries, up to 1640, and smuggled into England and Scotland against Establishment wishes. The last with full text and notes in England was printed in 1644. Between 1642 and 1715, eight editions of KJV were published with Geneva notes, seven of them in folio, and two of them in one year (1679), statistics which tell their own story.

What arrived in April 1560, and was rapidly developed, was the first complete study guide to the Bible in English, intended to illuminate at every point.

The influence of the Geneva Bible is incalculable. Before the London printings, it was freely available in England in large enough numbers to stir Archbishop Parker into initiating his rival Bishops' Bible in 1568. For over fifty years it was sometimes second to that in Anglican pulpits and on Anglican lecterns. Even so, a study of more than fifty sermons by bishops between 1611 and 1630, including Andrewes, the chief of the KJV revisers, and Laud, the enemy of all things evangelical, shows that in twenty-seven sermons the preacher took his text from the Geneva version, and only in five from the Bishops'.[20] Of the remaining twenty-odd, only about half quote from KJV, and half seem to have made their own version.[21]

The Geneva Bible was, however, the Bible of the English and the Scots at home, and in local reading groups and 'prophesyings'. In Scotland, the Edinburgh 'Bassandyne Bible' of 1579, the first Bible printed in Scotland, a straight reprint of the first Geneva Bible in folio, made in 1561, was ordered to be in each parish kirk. It was dedicated to 'Prince James' – so much for his reported claim at the Hampton Court Conference in 1604 that he had only recently been shown a copy (see below, p. 433).

> [A Scottish] Act of Parliament, passed soon after the publication of the Bible, made it mandatory that every householder worth 300 marks of yearly rent and every yeoman and burgess worth £500 in stock should have a Bible and a Psalm Book, in the vulgar tongue, in their homes, under a penalty of ten pounds; and there is evidence that this act was enforced.[22]

Early in the seventeenth century the Geneva Bible was taken back to Europe, to Amsterdam and the other Netherlands Separatist centres, and from there to America, where, as successive waves of colonists landed, it flourished mightily. It was the Bible of the Elizabethan and Jacobean poets and prose writers, including Shakespeare. If Othello does say that the exemplar who 'threw the great pearl away' was 'the base Judean' as the Folio text has it, and not 'the base Indian', then he took the phrase, with many more, from the Geneva Bible.[23]

The Geneva Old Testament

Two things immediately strike a reader who opens any page of most
Geneva Bibles produced in Geneva or London over almost a hundred
years: the clarity of the roman type in its little numbered paragraphs, that
is, the verses; and the fullness of the surrounding matter. Headings crown
each page, italic summaries are at the head of each chapter, and inner and
outer margins have notes, in small roman or italic, all keyed to the text
by small letters or signs. These invitations to study are at their thickest in
the books of the Prophets, the Psalms, and all the New Testament. There
is never any doubt where one is in the Scriptures. This is a contrast to,
for example, the first German or Dutch printed Bibles from the Latin a
century before, which are solid bricks of printed paper, opening to solid
walls of almost undifferentiated text (see fig. 21). Because of this help with
location, new and special kinds of movement are being set up. One could
not dream that any part of the Dutch Bible of 1477 in that illustration
might cross-refer to any other part, for any reason. The margins of a
Geneva Bible, however, take reference further than ever before. In Genesis
6 and 7, for example, the reader is invited to consider Noah in relation
to verses in 1 and 2 Peter, in Hebrews, in Matthew and Luke. Scripture
speaks within itself: the Word of God is one. The cross-reference to the
well-known eleventh chapter of Hebrews lifts Noah from a primitive tale
to a model 'of righteousness by faith' (Hebrews 11:7), as he was 'warned
of God of the things which were as yet not seen, moved with reverence'
(KJV has 'fear'). Further, as signalled by double marks in the text, the
margin gives alternative meanings for the Hebrew, often a literal meaning.
Genesis 6:13 in Geneva's text reads: 'And God said unto Noah, An end of
all flesh is come before me: for the earth is filled with cruelty through
them . . .'. By means of the margin, this might read, 'And God said unto
Noah: I will destroy mankind, for the earth is filled with oppression and
wickedness from the face of them . . .'. The reader is thus invited to a
further movement, this time of meaning, from text to margin and back
again. A Geneva page is a long way from – indeed, the polar opposite of
– the Bible as Latin mantra, to be used in superstitious ignorance: from
head to foot it takes the reader away from the occult text, from the affectation of what is hidden, and deep into the pleasures of the text and
engagement with the means of salvation.

The triumph of the Geneva Old Testament text (and Apocrypha) can
be shown in detail to be based on Coverdale's revisions in the Great Bible,
but now with corrections from the Hebrew and Septuagint, freshly compared with Leo Juda's Latin version made in Zurich in 1543, and other
helps – Geneva was rich in resources – particularly Olivetan's frequently

revised French Bible, from the 1559 revision of which the 'Arguments' before Job and Psalms were directly translated. The Geneva translators' aim, successfully achieved, was to reproduce what the original says from Genesis to Malachi. This triumph could here be illustrated at great length, causing, no doubt, even greater tedium. It is, one hopes, sufficient to quote some readings, some of which went on into KJV. It is more important to note that, like the misguided Bishops' Bible translators, the KJV translators' denial of marginal notes removed at a stroke that essential element of understanding Hebrew, the openness to engagement, the in-and-out movement between literal sense and meaning, the many kinds of explanations, which the Geneva annotators so constantly used. Often the best that King James's workers could do was to lift 'the literal Hebrew phrase from Geneva's margin into its own text'.[24] Gerald Hammond writes:

> These notes [in the Geneva Old Testament margins], constantly explaining and interpreting, have a significant effect upon the nature of the translation. Because the translators could always use them to clear up ambiguities, explain obscurities, and fill in ellipses, it meant that the actual translation could afford to retain, to a great degree, the ambiguities, obscurities, and ellipses of the original. While the margin is specific and discursive, the text can stand as an evocatively simple rendering of the Hebrew images and metaphors.[25]

Hammond's fifty pages of examination of the Geneva translators at work with the Hebrew remain the best introduction to the subject.[26]

For what has often been overlooked is that the Geneva scholars translated the poetic and prophetic books of the Old Testament into English from Hebrew for the first time. Working from Genesis to 2 Chronicles, they had, behind Coverdale's two versions, the translations of Tyndale directly from Hebrew. But Coverdale thereafter, from Job to Malachi, half the Old Testament, did not translate from Hebrew.

The gain in the sense of Hebrew idiom in English is startling. In the place of Coverdale's Great Bible rendering of the opening of Ecclesiastes 12 –

> Remember thy maker in thy youth, or ever days of adversity come, and or the years draw nigh, when thou shalt say: I have not pleasure in them . . .

– is Geneva's

> Remember now thy Creator in the days of thy youth, whiles the evil days come not, nor the years approach, wherein thou shalt say, I have no pleasure in them . . .

A running commentary on the Hebrew poetic idiom is provided by the marginal notes, twenty of them in the eight verses up to 'Vanity of vanities, saith the Preacher, all is vanity' in verse 8. (Coverdale's Great Bible had 'All is but vanity, saith the Preacher, all is but plain vanity', which, as is usual with Coverdale, is good English idiom – but not Hebrew.) The first five notes are attached as follows:

> Whiles the sun is not dark, nor the light, nor the moon, nor the stars, nor the ªclouds return after the rain:
>
> When the ᵇkeepers of the house shall tremble, and the ᶜstrong men shall bow themselves, and the ᵈgrinders shall cease, because they are few, and they wax dark that ᵉlook out by the windows.
>
> a Before thou come to a continual miserie: for when the clouds remain after the rain, man's grief is increased.
>
> b The hands, which keep the body.
>
> c The legs.
>
> d The teeth.
>
> e The eyes.

In the Geneva Old Testament there are more notes in the poetic and prophetic books than in the narrative histories and laws. Here the Geneva translators show two advantages. First, the sheer strangeness of Hebrew poetry needs interpretative help if it is to mean anything in English, and they have felt free to use whatever kind of comment is best. Sometimes the literal meaning is in the text, and metaphor is in the margin, and sometimes the other way round – but in both cases the strategy is made clear. Sometimes they use straight glossing: at Isaiah 40:6, 'All flesh *is* grass, and all the ᵏgrace thereof *is* as the flower of the field', they note 'k Meaning all man's wisdom and natural powers, James 1:10, 1 Peter 1:24.' The verse in James is 'Again he that is rich [let him rejoice] in that he is made low: for as the flower of the grass shall he vanish away.'; and that in 1 Peter, '24 For all flesh *is* as grass, and all the glory of man *is* as the flower of grass. The grass withereth, and the flower falleth away, 25 But the word of the Lord endureth for ever.' The latter phrase picks up the words two verses later in the Isaiah chapter. It was, and is, a famous passage, much quoted: but the points should not be lost, that for the Geneva translators Scripture is a vast network of related phrases, particularly connecting the Testaments, and this is wholly right, the New Testament alertness to the Old being rich in every chapter. The KJV panels deserve commendation in their frequent preservation of Geneva's richness of internal Scriptural reference. (The Geneva translators did not, of course, invent cross-referring; but they developed it.) This makes it all the more depressing that the KJV panels so dogmatically dropped all the Geneva notes. Their margin alongside the first eight verses of Ecclesiastes 12, for example, contains, apart from two references, only the thin and unhelpful 'Or, the grinders fail, because they grind little'.

The other advantage for their poetic and prophetic books that the Geneva translators took was the division into verses. Paragraphs suited Tyndale's excellent understanding of Hebrew narrative drive. Hebrew poetry works differently. Consider the opening of Job chapter 38, approaching the climax of that unique poem:

> Then answered the Lord unto Job out of the whirlwind, and said,
>
> 2 Who is this that darkeneth the counsel by words without knowledge?
>
> 3 Gird up now thy loins like a man: I will demand of thee, & declare thou unto me.
>
> 4 Where wast thou when I laid the foundations of the earth? declare, if thou hast understanding,
>
> 5 Who hath laid the measures thereof, if thou knowest, or who hath stretched the line over it:
>
> 6 Whereupon are the foundations thereof set: or who laid the cornerstone thereof:
>
> 7 When the stars of the morning praised *me* together, and all the children of God rejoiced.

The complex and cumulative imagery, and above all the parallelisms, are more than weakened if this is printed as a paragraph. Moreover, this is God taking breath, as it were, to go on about his Creation for four long chapters, a total of 126 splendid verses. The immediate establishment of a rhythmic base is essential. The KJV panels understood this, and took over the first six verses unchanged, apart from changing 'set' in verse 6 to 'fastened'. What they did change, however, in verse 7, produced pure magic: 'When the morning stars sang together, and all the sons of God shouted for joy?' The Geneva margin notes their own version of the latter phrase, 'the Children of God', 'Meaning, the Angels'. Throughout Job, the Geneva margins are full and overflowing to occupy the foot of most pages; the KJV margins are almost empty, in each column, as they are throughout the entire volume, with only a few literal readings and references. Here in Job 38:1–7 KJV has nothing but two cross-references and four Hebraisms, none of them in Geneva, and none revolutionary, though 'foundations . . . fastened' does produce '*Heb. sockets . . . made to sink*'.

Geneva's Psalms

The Geneva version of the Psalms needs a separate note. All the Geneva churches, in whatever language, used Psalms intensely for congregational worship, and solutions to problems of translation, and marginal notes, would be unusually available. In Geneva, there had been, we now know, two independent Psalters in English before the whole Bible was printed in 1560. In 1956, Dr David Alexander found in the Bodleian Library a small English prose Psalter, not previously recorded, printed, as he showed, by Badius in Geneva.[27] It has close parallels to the 1560 version, and it is of interest in showing dependence on the French Bible, and on Calvin's *Commentary on the Psalms* of 1557. It also shows the influence of an edition, printed in Geneva in 1556, of Sternhold and Hopkins's metrical Psalms. (Sternhold and Hopkins will be the main subject of the following chapter.) The volume discovered by Dr Alexander is not the same as a small edition of the Psalms, revised from the above and now exactly parallel to the Psalms in the 1560 Bible, which was printed by Rowland Hall in Geneva, 10 February 1559, to honour Queen Elizabeth on her accession.[28]

In other words, the Psalms were special. From 1570, editions of Geneva Bibles could, and usually did, contain at the back the full metrical Psalter of Sternhold and Hopkins: and at the front, from 1579, the whole Book of Common Prayer, including the Psalms in Coverdale's version from the Great Bible at the front.[29] So, from later in Elizabeth's reign, a Geneva volume contained the Psalms in three versions, of which the first and the last were for congregational use. There is additional interest in the Geneva base of English psalmody, as a number of metrical Psalms in Sternhold and Hopkins were made by William Whittingham.

The 1560 Geneva New Testament text

The text of the 1560 New Testament was a careful revision, no doubt by Whittingham himself, of that prepared by him in 1557, now with slightly more attention to Beza's Latin text of 1556, but still closely following Tyndale. It is also said to show dependence on Coverdale's Diglots of 1538.[30] To illustrate the level of revision, the chief changes in 1560 to the passage from Luke 2 (see above on pp. 286–7) are; 41, 'his parents went . . . of the Passover'; 43, 'And had finished the days *thereof* . . . remained . . . and Joseph knew not nor his mother'; 46, 'And it came to pass three days after'; 49, 'Knew ye not . . .'. For this passage, the 1560 New Testament keeps all the 1557 notes, merely reducing the first references to that from Deuteronomy. That the KJV panel kept closely to the 1560 Geneva can be seen at once: effectively the only change is the new phrase in verse 46, 'asking them questions'.

This text, with only minor changes in 1576, remained constant, and was the main stream which carried Tyndale forward, to King James's translators and far beyond. It is one of the curiosities of the writing of history that this slightly updated form of the Tyndale New Testament, central to English-speaking life since early April 1560, has been almost completely ignored as a cultural influence.

Tables and concordances

The numbering of verses allowed accuracy in location. From the first, 1560, edition, and right through until the mid-seventeenth century, there were Tables at the back of the volume, the title of the first neatly illuminating for us how new the system was: 'A brief Table of the interpretation of the proper names which are chiefly found in the Old Testament, where the first number signifieth the Chapter, the second the Verse.' Thus the six pages begin '*Aron*, or *Aharon*, a teacher, Exod.4.14.'. One of the reasons given in the heading to this table is that not knowing the true meaning of Old Testament names has led to the godly, out of ignorance, giving infants, instead of names 'that should ever have some godly advertisements in them . . . the signs and badges of idolatry and heathenish impiety.' Alternative versions of the names are conveniently given in the margin, as 'Henoch, taught or dedicate. Gen.5.18.' has in the margin 'Enoch': or 'Bathseba, the seventh daughter, or the daughter of an oath, 2 Sam.11.3. Bethsabe.'

The second regular table, filling fifteen pages 'after the order of the Alphabet' in three columns, is 'of the principal things that are contained in the Bible', as, taken at random, 'Not an Hair of them shall perish, that suffer for Christ, Luke 21.18. Our Hairs be numbered, Matth.10.30. Christ the Heir of all things. Heb.1.1.'

Later editions of Geneva Bibles usually had two 'right profitable and fruitful Concordances' at the end of the volume, after those tables, 'The first containing the interpretation of the Hebrew, Caldean, Greek and Latin words, and names . . . And the second comprehending all other such principal words and matters . . .'; these, running to nearly two hundred pages, took up about one-sixth of the whole volume. Sample entries are 'God is Almighty Genesis 17.1 and 35.11', or 'Organs invented by whom Gen.4.21' or 'By Faith the spirit is received, Gal.3.2.' In many editions, Sternhold and Hopkins's metrical Canticles, followed by the Psalms, all with music, then followed. The first edition, and others, had a historical table 'from Paul's conversion, showing the time of his peregrination, & of his Epistles written to the Churches'.

Additional matter

Almost every chapter begins with a brief summary, numbered to verses, longer in the New Testament. Each Old Testament begins with a quite extensive précis, 'The Argument'. (It is not explained why Whittingham's fine New Testament 'Arguments' were dropped.) Titles run across the top of every page, and summaries of every column. Books begin with an ornamental letter. There are maps, one at the beginning large, across a double page, and full of detail, followed, or enclosed, by a two-page 'Description of CANAAN and the bordering Countries'. The map presumes close and lengthy attention. Some pages later a half-page map of a large area north of the Gulf, with a long note, explains 'The Situation of the Garden of Eden'. Before the New Testament is a map of the Holy Land. In Exodus and elsewhere, where what is being described is particularly baffling, like the fittings of the Tabernacle or the clothing of the priests, woodcut illustrations are inset. At the beginning of 1 Kings, there are effectively five pages of pictures of, or relating to, the Temple. In 1560, the first edition had twenty-six engravings. In other words, the commonly repeated observation, that there are no illustrations in Geneva Bibles, is not true.

The preliminary matter in later editions can fill many pages, including thirty-two pages of charts of the genealogies of the patriarchs. Many editions begin with the full Book of Common Prayer, giving, as standard, all the Psalms in Coverdale's translation. (So, between the covers, the complete Psalms are given three times: at the front, as Coverdale made them, in the Prayer Book; in the middle, as the Geneva translators made them; and at the end, as Sternhold and Hopkins made them.)

The first edition begins with an Epistle to the Queen, and an address, 'To our beloved in the Lord the brethren of England, Scotland, Ireland &c', both dated 'From Geneva. 10. April 1560'. The address is an expanded version of Whittingham's to his New Testament.[31] Later editions added a two-page address 'To the Christian Reader', a poem and a prayer, and a full-page scheme of 'How to take profit in reading of the Holy Scripture'.

The 1560 Epistle to the Queen

This begins: 'To the most virtuous and noble Queen Elizabeth, Queen of England, France, and Ireland, &c. Your humble subjects of the English Church at Geneva wish grace and peace from God the Father through Christ Jesus our Lord.'

The most suitable epithet for what follows in this four-page address is 'bracing'. It is made of Scripture references, particularly Old Testament history, most especially the work of rebuilding Jerusalem. The Queen is reminded 'how much greater charge God hath laid upon you in making you a builder of his spiritual Temple.' (ii^r) She is to be Josiah in destroying idols: 'the Lord gave him good success and blessed him wonderfully, so long as he made God's word his line and rule to follow, and enterprised nothing before he had enquired at the mouth of the Lord.'(ii^v) She is told that she must earnestly crave wisdom of the Lord. Two things, her Geneva subjects warn her, are necessary:

> first, a lively and steadfast faith in Christ Jesus: next, that our faith ring forth good fruits: . . . For the eyes of all that fear God in all places behold your countries as an example to all that believe, and the prayers of all the godly at all times are directed to God for the preservation of your majesty. For considering God's wonderful mercies towards you at all seasons, who hath pulled you out of the mouths of the lions, and how that from your youth you have been brought up in the holy Scriptures, the hope of all men is so increased, that they can not but look that God should bring to pass some wonderful work by your grace to the universal comfort of his church . . . Therefore even above strength you must show yourself strong and bold on God's matters. . . . (iii^v)

ILLUSTRATIONS

'There were no pictures in the Geneva Bible' writes no less a scholar of the sixteenth century than Patrick Collinson,[32] revealing that even Homer nods, and showing how pervasive is myth. Professor Collinson is far from alone in that observation.

The 1560 Geneva Bible has 33 illustrations, most of which went forward into most following editions: some later editions varied this (fig. 24).[33] Two of these are title-page emblems, and five are maps, four of them being spread over two pages. The rest are to illuminate details in the Tabernacle or Temple or of the visions of Ezekiel, again one being spread over two pages. The intention is edification rather than titillation: unlike other Bibles of the time (and later), there are no jolly pictures of a half-clad Potiphar's wife reaching out to hold a fleeing Joseph, of David watching Bathsheba bathing, or a naked Susannah being spied on by lascivious elders[34] (see figs 34 and 35).

Between 1568 and the last printed, in 1715 (a KJV with Geneva notes), it was precisely the Geneva Bible which carried the tradition forward – Tyndale's Pentateuch has pictures, and his 1534 New Testament has a heavily illustrated Revelation. Continental Bibles were often lavishly illustrated. What historians should have noted is that there are no illustrations in the 1611 KJV, nor the 1610 Douai Bible. The Reformation interest in pictures in Bibles became pushed to one side into the making of Children's Bibles.[35]

THE GENEVA BIBLE NOTES

Apart from the Apocrypha (between the Testaments, and always printed, in spite of what is often said) the margins of every Geneva Bible page are full of notes. Those to Genesis, for example, or the Psalms, or Isaiah, or the Gospels, or Acts, or all the Pauline Epistles, often run on largely at the foot of the pages as well: in Romans, they leave room of only half a page or less of the text. These notes are of many kinds. Occasionally in the Old Testament there are variant translations, as, at random, Ezekiel 45:1, 'upon the four //corners', in the margin '//*Or, court*'. The text at Genesis 4.21 has 'Iubal, who was the father of all that play on the harp and //organs', and in the margin,'//*Or*, flutes and pipes'. Sometimes, because of the nature of Hebrew, these variant translations can be startling. At Judges 6.11, 'Gideon pressed wheat by the winepress // to hide it from the Midianties', there is the alternative, '//*Or, to prepare his flight*'. Modern scholarship prefers the former. Regular marginal notes, especially in the New Testament, give cross-references. About three-quarters of the notes to the Old Testament, and half to the New, are simple definition. (There are ten or so pages in the Apocrypha with completely empty margins, and about a dozen more with only one reference.) Those that are doctrinal notes are scriptural, and not particularly 'Calvinist'. That was to change, but not greatly, with Junius's commentary on Revelation added in 1599, which has anti-papal accounts of history, following John Bale's *Image of the Both Churches*.

Three 'Calvinist' notes, at John 6:37 and 63, and 1 Corinthians 11:24, call for comment, though a better name than 'Calvinist' might be 'biblical'. Annotating the text 'All that the Father giveth me, shall come to me: and him that cometh to me, I cast not away' is:

> The gift of faith proceedeth from the free election of the Father in Christ, after which followeth necessarily everlasting life: Therefore faith in Christ Jesus is a sure witness of our election, and therefore of our glorification, which is to come.

The text of John 6:63 reads, 'It is the Spirit that quickeneth: the flesh profiteth nothing: the words that I speak unto you, are Spirit and life.' The annotation is

The flesh of Christ doth therefore quicken us, because he that is man, is God: which mystery is only comprehended by faith, which is the gift of God, proper only to the elect.

The Corinthians passage simply illuminates the reception of the Lord's Supper as Paul declared it, noting that that is a 'true form', with clear definition of the part played by 'Pastors' and by 'flock'. It is the marginal note, to 1 Corinthians 11:24, that deserves quotation in full:

> We must take a true form of keeping the Lord's Supper, out of the institution of it, the parts whereof are these, touching the Pastors, to show forth the Lord's death, by preaching his word: to bless the bread and the wine by calling upon the name of God, and together with prayers to declare the institution thereof, and finally to deliver the bread broken to be eaten, and the cup received to be drunk with thanksgiving. And touching the flock, that every man examine himself, that is to say, to prove both his knowledge, and also his faith and repentance: to show forth the Lord's death, that is, in the true faith to yield unto his word and institution: and last of all, to take bread at the minister's hand, and to eat it, and to drink the wine, and give God thanks: This was Paul the Apostle's manner of ministering.

There is nothing there that is not the manner according to the Book of Common Prayer, being the central Anglican form (for which John Frith was tortured and martyred in 1533) ever since.

Throughout the 1560 Geneva Bible the margins make what can best be described as a running commentary on the whole Bible.[36]

It has been a commonplace among historians that the Geneva Bible had to be replaced in 1611, or was later absolutely to be rejected, because of the 'unacceptable Calvinism' of its notes. Nineteenth- and twentieth-century rejection of the 'objectionable Calvinism' ignored the Elizabethan theological context, when Elizabeth's court read Calvin; when the nation followed Calvin in much of its theology (as in the Book of Common Prayer, particularly the Thirty-Nine Articles), its philosophy and literature, as did Sidney, Spenser and Shakespeare – *Hamlet* demands Calvin's help in understanding the play.[37] It is important to recognise two things: that in sixteenth-century England Calvin's emphasis on the word, living Christian lives with the emphasis on the Word, was a contributor to the liberation of poetry, and particularly the flowering of drama; and that Calvin was not a 'Calvinist', as will be observed below. Many of the fiercer doctrines were later developments. What happened in apartheid South Africa, in social deeds originating in the beliefs of the Dutch

Reformed Church, should not be laid at the door of the Calvin of the *Institutes*. Under Elizabeth, the works of John Calvin were much printed and bought. A translator of his sermons, Arthur Golding, first gave the world Ovid's complete *Metamorphoses* in English verse (plundered by Shakespeare) in Calvin's colours.[38]

Ignorance of the period making the Geneva Bible 'unacceptable' because it is 'Calvinist', though deplorable, is one thing: distorting the Geneva Bible itself is quite another. That the Geneva marginal notes are 'bitter' and 'regrettable' is plain wrong.

The severest test has been the thirty-six-page analysis by Dr David Alexander, under the heading 'The doctrine of the [Geneva] marginal notes'. His opening paragraph states that

> recent commentators have been unable to find these notes oppressively sectarian or tendentious. To be sure, they represent a particular outlook and there can be no mistaking their puritanism; yet the notes which teach points of theology held in Calvinism or which bewray a puritanical disposition of mind in their authors cannot be fairly said to represent more than a small fraction of the total number. More notes, by far, are concerned to enable the reader more easily and perfectly to understand some of the complexities and obscurities of the word of God.[39]

(Those who dismiss the Geneva notes do not seem to observe Gregory Martin's twenty-five pages of anti-Protestant vitriol, his Preface to his Rheims New Testament of 1582, passages of which make readers of any theological hue squirm with discomfort. To give an example, here is Gregory Martin on Bible translations:

> But the case now is more lamentable: for the Protestants and such as S. Paul calleth *ambulantes in astutia, walking in deceitfulness* (2 Cor 4), have so abused the people and many other in the world, not unwise, that by their false translations they have instead of God's Law and Testament, & for Christ's written will and word, given them their own wicked writing and phantasies, most shamefully . . . [and so on for 150 more words] being indeed through such sacreligious teaching, made the Devil's word.[40]

In Geneva Bibles there is nothing like that, calling the Word of God in vernaculars 'the Devil's word'. Junius's attacks in the notes to Revelation in some Geneva Bibles in 1599 and after are specifically on popes in history, rather than, as here, destruction of the very roots of faith in the Word, poisoning the wells. The Geneva moderation is deemed 'unacceptable': the Rheims venom is, apparently, 'acceptable'.)

To return to the Geneva notes themselves; they are provided for every book in the Bible, though thinly in the Apocrypha.[41] Frequently they are 'aphoristic and hortatory',[42] as that to Genesis 50:15, where Joseph's brothers fear reprisals: 'An evil conscience is never fully at rest'; or to Psalm 19, 'The heavens declare the glory of God', where the third verse, 'There is no speech nor language, where their voice is not heard' has the note 'The heavens are a schoolmaster to all nations, be they never so barbarous.'

The notes work most of the time to increase the reader's understanding of the text. Such explanations are far too frequent even to summarise here, running into hundreds of examples, including technical details of Hebrew rituals or history, or of difficult words. As well as insight, for example showing that for Noah, the dove's olive leaf 'was the sign that the waters were much diminished, for the olives grow not on the high mountains' (Genesis 8:11), they often show a certain charm, as that to Psalm 126:4, 'Nothing can be more comfortable than rivers to them that dwell in the hot countries of the south', or to 1 Kings 15:23, where the elderly King Asa's diseased feet produce the comment 'He had the gout, and put his trust rather in physicians than in the Lord.' Charm can extend to bizarreness: 'Galatians' are glossed at 1 Maccabees 7:2 as 'Or, Frenchmen', and Obadiah 20 has the note 'By the Canaanites the Jews mean the Dutchmen, and by Zarephath, France, and by Sepharad, Spain.'

The Geneva translators' knowledge of Hebrew and Aramaic is often shown, including the difficulty of rendering niceties of Hebrew. As a small example, at Ruth 4:1, where Boaz calls out twice to a passing kinsman, the note has, 'The Hebrews here use two words which have no proper signification, but serve to note a certain person: as we say 'ho, sirrah, or ho, such one.' The translators show knowledge of neighbouring languages: Persian – Artaxerxes means 'an excellent warrior' (Ezra 4:7); Aramaic – as noting that Abba is Syrian for 'father' (Mark 14:36), and elsewhere, though they tend to use 'Syrian' and 'Chaldee' indiscriminately. They refer to the Septuagint (e.g. Numbers 25:8) and to Hebrew commentators, particularly Kimshi (Exodus 38:8). What they strikingly do not do, unlike the Rheims New Testament of 1582, and the Douai Old Testament of 1610, is perpetually (or at all) refer to the Church Fathers for commentary. Certainly these church-based Roman Catholic English versions give solid annotation (unlike KJV): but first of all the Rheims and Douai commentators illuminate what the Church has said about any matter.

CALVIN NOT A 'CALVINIST'

It is important to step aside for a while, before coming back to the theology of the Geneva notes, to consider Calvin and his influence in 1560. It would be surprising if, made in Calvin's city of Geneva, there was no Calvinism in the full 1560 English Geneva Bible. David Alexander begins his main section, 'The Theology of the Notes', with the words, 'Quite simply, it may be said that the theological system taught by the notes is that of Calvinism.' (He notes that the fuller *Institutes* were not published until September 1599, but that the earlier *Institutio*, setting out the basic understanding, dated from 1536.[43]) What has to be pointed out here, however, is that in the Geneva Bible the Calvinism is not a prison, but a door which opens.[44] Later Calvinists, in Northern Europe and in North America, propagated harsh and narrowing developments, extending Calvin's mentor, Augustine, and it must be right to shrink from their excesses. Yet looked at from Scotland, Holland or New England a century and more later, Calvin is hardly 'a Calvinist'. For one thing, his joyful wide reading and scholarship in the pagan classical writers and contemporary theological opponents is the opposite of many later 'Calvinists'. 'Calvin made a sound classical education the foundation of the curriculum in his Genevan Academy.'[45] For another, the mild and studious Calvin was prodded into political action, even to the tragic martyrdom of Servetus, by more fiery reformers in Geneva like William Farel, or even Martin Bucer.[46] Calvin was, before all else, a student of the Bible: he was then called to 'teaching, preaching, political controversy, religious leadership on an international scale'.[47] His great debt to Luther he always acknowledged, but it was 'a long, persistent working of an extraordinary religious mind upon a devoted but critical follower of the next generation whose temperament, training, and social background were worlds removed from his own'.[48] Significant there are the words 'the next generation', thirty years before. Luther in Germany, and Tyndale in Britain, had allowed a return to the earliest Christian experience of reinterpreting the New Testament in every generation, which is what happened in the congregations of the first centuries, and was then shut down by the Church. Calvin in his own very different time and context was opening up the Bible anew. The root, the very heart, the essence – whatever metaphor one chooses – of his 'system' was, above all else, opening the New Testament to scholars and to the people to expound what was written in its core. Calvin's work was sorely needed. It still is. Like Luther, like Tyndale, like – in the twentieth century – Karl Barth, Calvin's door was the Epistle to the Romans.[49] In the middle of the twentieth century, Barth revolutionised theology by properly attending to what the New Testament wrote about God. Calvin in his time did the same.

God is sovereign. That is Calvin's central principle. The 'system' which follows from that has less inexorable logic than has often been imagined. It is an open system, 'faithful to all the paradoxes of biblical thought and Christian experience'.[50] This sovereign God is active, in the individual and in history. The fine-spun abstractions of scholastics, and the philosophers before them, were useless for better living in this world.[51] The proper inheritance was from the rhetoricians, engaged in presenting truth in usable forms – one thinks of Tyndale translating as his demonstration the chief Greek rhetorician, Isocrates. 'Faith is a busy, active thing. It changes society and builds the Kingdom. Faith must result in action.'[52]

So the Bible is not just to be 'read in churches', as the title-page of KJV has it. It is to be actively studied on the page, as something liable to cause change, to be useful, especially if it is illuminated by helps to understanding the revelation of the nature of God, through prefaces and marginal notes. The later vilification of marginal notes, especially by the politicians controlling King James in the early 1600s, was from fear of the working of this sovereign God in places outside the fence of what was narrowly understood as the only apostolic Christianity. The notes they knew were in the Geneva Bibles: they had to be wiped out. Writers in later ages, looking for a term of abuse, called them 'Calvinist'. They meant their readers to recoil in horror, but what they wrote was truer than they imagined.

THE THEOLOGY OF THE 1560 GENEVA NOTES

This can be approached by way of the 1560 title-page (fig. 23). Here again is an emblem, a sort of grown-up cousin of the earlier 1557 emblem, now of the parting of the Red Sea to allow believers into the Promised Land. Three surrounding Bible quotations act as mottoes: from Exodus 14:13, Psalm 34:39 and Exodus 14:14. All are about the power of God. Like the earlier one, it invites the reader in: this time the horizon is limitless – with the pillar of fire and smoke above as guide. The unarmed Israelites are setting off pursued by heavily armed Egyptians, who threateningly fill the foreground: yet God, says the complete emblem, is powerful (and see the quotation from Tyndale at the end of this chapter).

Striking are the words that make the third block of lettering, above the emblem:

> With most profitable annotations upon all the hard places, and other things of great importance as may appear in the Epistle to the Reader.

The marginal notes in the complete 1560 Geneva English Bible are here summarised with representative examples.[53] Their theology begins, as already noted, with the sovereignty of God, the Creator, as the Geneva notes strongly teach (Genesis 2:2; Job 1:6). Man's incapacity causes his confusion about God, who is not changeable (Genesis 6:6; Psalm 106:45). Man's highest duty is to praise God (Psalm 145:4) – as the Westminster Shorter Catechism put it, 'Man's chief end is to glorify God, and to enjoy him forever' (Psalm 9:1; Psalm 100:1).

At the other extreme is the wickedness and depravity of man (Psalm 53:1), which has infected all mankind (Ezra 9:6) into disobedience of God and enmity towards him (Deuteronomy 1:41) even among the saints (2 Samuel 11:15). What good is in man comes from God (1 Kings 8:58; Daniel 2:22). Man, however, in the mercy of God (1 Samuel 21:2), does have hope in the election to salvation (John 17:6; 1 Peter 1:2), dependent not on good works or merit but entirely on God's free mercy (Matthew 25:35; Romans 9:15), resulting in faith and everlasting life (John 6:37), and the ability to praise God (Revelation 14:3).

The reprobate 'perish through their own default' (Luke 2:34; Psalm 147:20; Psalm 109:7). The mercy of God belongs only to Israel, to the Church (Psalm 130:7), that the glory of God may be the more set forth (Exodus 11:9; Ezekiel 10:23). It is God's appointment (Deuteronomy 3:6). Election does not exempt man from wounds (Psalm 38:2; Genesis 44:16; Revelation 9:5; Exodus 2:23; 1 Samuel 30:6,8; Psalm 115:4; Exodus 2:8; Mark 13:22).

A detailed system can be observed in these notes of the nature of God's Word, both Old (prefiguring Christ) and New Testaments. There is a systematic declaration of doctrines of the Church and Sacraments, and Church government and practices. The notes teach certain points about the Christian life, particularly the obedience to magistrates and 'the powers that be' that echoes Tyndale in his *Obedience of a Christian Man* of 1528, though the notes tend to be pessimistic about the true Christian integrity of such powers.

The plain living and high thinking later associated with the word 'puritan' is taught in a number of notes, though not to an extreme. Wine 'doth comfort the heart' (Proverbs 31:7), but drunkenness is 'an horrible thing' (Genesis 9:21). Women, in excessive ways, can distract men (Ezekiel 13:10): the note to 1 Timothy 2:9, 'all pomp and wantonness is condemned which women use in trimming their heads', is preceded by a list which perhaps betrays unwitting enthusiasm: 'to plat, to crisp, to broid, to fold, to bush, to hurl, or to lay it curiously'. Song, and dancing, should not be a cloak to cover wantonness.

THE LATER HISTORY OF THE GENEVA BIBLE

Some of the influence of the Geneva Bible is well described by David Alexander – on later versions such as the Bishops' Bible, the Rheims New

Testament and KJV; on 'prophesyings' and sermons (even including a sermon by Geneva's political enemy, Richard Bancroft); on contemporary books of theology; and on the New England settlers.[54]

In histories written since the mid-nineteenth century, with some rare exceptions, the Geneva Bible has generally been treated briefly, if mentioned at all, and condemned. A complete list of such dismissals and omissions would be a long, sad and depressing revelation of ignorance or bias. The 'unacceptable Calvinism' of its 'bitter' notes led to its 'failure': it was too shockingly Calvinist for the British, who wisely rejected it.

The condemnation parallel to the 'unacceptable Calvinism', that Geneva Bibles were commonly disliked, lacks all evidence (the words of a few bishops busy making their own rival version up to 1568 hardly count). On the contrary, the overwhelming evidence is of overwhelming popularity at every level of British life. David Alexander wrote:

> If the number of editions is taken to be an index of the popularity and influence of the Geneva Bible, one may safely say that it enjoyed great influence. . . . By virtue of its scholarship, it was utilized to a great extent by the Bishops in their version, and through them, by the revisers of the Authorized version. Its users were to be found among Anglican divines, Presbyterians, and Separatists.[55]

In 1868, Bishop Westcott observed of the Geneva marginal commentary, 'if slightly tinged with Calvinistic doctrine, [it is] on the whole neither unjust nor illiberal', an observation retained in W. A. Wright's revision of 1905.

And what of the 'failure'? In 1610, when it was fifty years old, it was, as remarked above, in three versions, apparently unstoppable. It had already had 120 different editions – editions, not reprintings. It went through 140 editions all told, in under a century. (Examination of the figures for editions in Shakespeare's lifetime alone, as on p. 129 above, show the opposite of 'failure'.) It was the Bible of the poets, politicians and preachers (even anti-'puritan' preachers like Laud) as following chapters will show.

Distortion began with the report of King James's seemingly hostile remarks at his Hampton Court Conference in 1604. On that occasion there was apparently agreed denunciation of the badness of the Geneva Bibles. Closer observation reveals the heavy bias of the official reporter, Richard Barlow, for the Archbishop (see below, chapter 25, pp 432–5). Already noted has been the Victorian reduction of this masterpiece of Renaissance and Reformation scholarship to a snigger in the term 'Breeches Bible', still current. Victorian hostility to this version can be further shown.

It is said, no doubt libellously, that in the far west of England, in St Ives in Cornwall, directions used to be given to Talland House where lived

'Virginia Woolf, wife of the famous novelist'. In that house lived also Virginia Woolf's father, Sir Leslie Stephen, whose multi-volume *Dictionary of National Biography*, became, with the *Oxford English Dictionary*, the eighth and ninth wonders of the world. The father of the famous novelist, however, is not without blame for similar prejudice. Some of the biographical essays in Sir Leslie's *DNB* revealed, to put it mildly, marked bias: two of the worst entries, not previously noted, are those by 'Miss Bradley' about the Marian exiles who made the Geneva Bible. Christopher Goodman is 'said to have become Lady Margaret Professor of Divinity'. ('*Said* to have become?' That is like saying 'Mary Tudor is said to have become Queen of England'.) The 'violence' of his 'very acrimonious tracts . . . was generally disapproved' – a remark quite unsupported. On his commentary on Amos, 'so bitter was the feeling' that Goodman 'did not dare to return' – for this extraordinary statement, no evidence is given: her case is weakened by the absence of any record of any such commentary, by Goodman or anyone else. There is no mention of all his work on the Geneva Bible. It does get ten words in her entry on Anthony Gilbey, described as 'one of the most acrimonious and illiberal writers . . .' of 'two original works of bitter invective'. 'Bitter' is also used of Thomas Sampson, though there, as in the entries for William Cole and William Kethe, the Geneva Bible is ignored. This is all in the supposedly standard reference work, *DNB*. (The hostility in these short entries should be contrasted with the admiring reverence in every sentence of the long essay on Gregory Martin.)

Readers in later ages need not feel smug, however. Hostility towards the Geneva Bible persists. It is possible to accumulate pages of references to books (and broadcasts) in which what has become the standard negative description is stated, or in which the Geneva Bible and its massive popularity have been omitted. Here, to avoid tedium, are but two random examples from the later twentieth century. A useful survey published in 1992, dealing thoroughly under the heading of 'Reformation-era English translations', with Wyclif, Tyndale, Coverdale, Matthew's, the Great Bible, KJV and so on, even discussing the fragments from William Roy, and official failed attempts, makes absolutely no mention whatsoever of any Geneva Bible.[56] The few lines about the Geneva Bible in a popular history of the English Bible published in 1996 conclude with the remark, 'Its notes and commentary, for all their scholarliness, were peppered with barbs and ill will.'[57] 'Peppered' is simply untrue. In the 1560 Geneva Bible, most of the notes are elucidatory. In the Old Testament such elucidation is thickest in Job, Psalms and the major prophets. For the first forty years, there were, in the whole Bible and Apocrypha before Revelation, ten notes referring to (not always attacking) the Roman Catholic Church.

'Tablets and Agnus Deis' are condemned in Genesis 35:4. Papists are called idolaters in 2 Kings 17:33. At Isaiah 44:15, 'the Papists make their cake god and the rest of their idols'. At Jeremiah 44:17:

> It seemeth that the Papists gathered of this place their *Salve Regina*, and *Regina caeli laetare*, calling the virgin Mary Queen of Heaven, and so of the blessed virgin and mother of a Saviour Christ made an idol: for here the Prophet condemneth this idolatry.

It is worth noting that all the reformers, including Tyndale, wrote warmly about the Virgin Mary. What they objected to in the Roman Catholic Church was her inclusion in the cults of the worship of saints.

At Revelation 16:2, the Geneva 1560 note is:

> This was like the sixth plague of Egypt, which was sores and boils or pocks: and this reigneth commonly among Canons, monks, friars, nuns, priests, and such filthy vermin which bear the mark of the beast.

Those nasty words make the strongest and least defensible anti-Roman remark in the 1560 Geneva Bible. Far from representing a tendency, in such strength they are alone: and significantly, they are on Revelation.[58] All sixteen pages of that book are thick with marginal notes. Papal references – there are not many – begin with chapter 9, and not all are hostile: as, at 9:2, a simple reference to the keys in his heraldic arms, with, from there to the end, perhaps a dozen references to Antichrist, unlocated. The notes also distinguish between the historical Roman Empire and the current papal empire. The second half of chapter 9 identifies the figures represented as 'the Pope's clergy' in detail. The note to 11:8 links 'the whole jurisdiction of the Pope' with Sodom. The 'unclean spirits like frogs' of 16:13 are

> a strong number of the great devil the Pope's ambassadors, which are ever crying and croaking like frogs and come out of Antichrist's mouth, because they should speak nothing but lies and use all manner of crafty deceit to maintain their rich Euphrates against the true Christians.

There are a score of other, much slighter, references, some no more than putting against 'beast' in 13:1, 'Here is the description of the Roman empire.'

As was noted of the whole volume, David Alexander wrote that 'recent commentators have been unable to find these notes oppressively sectarian or tendentious' (above, p. 306). One marginal note (not in Junius's annotations), to Revelation 9:3, is, however, always quoted to damn the whole Geneva enterprise. When the fifth Angel has opened 'the bottomless pit', out of the smoke come locusts. The 1560 Geneva margin has:

> Locusts are false teachers, heretics, and worldly subtle Prelates, with
> Monks, Friars, Cardinals, Patriarchs, Archbishops, Doctors, Bachelors,
> and Masters which forsake Christ to maintain false doctrine.

This has been singled out and repeated as if it were characteristic of the
whole Geneva Bible. It can be just that, of course: as David Alexander
remarked,

> in one sense this note exemplifies the aim and purpose of the notes:
> to eradicate all false doctrine and to implant in English-speaking Chris-
> tians a deeper knowledge of the defence against it – the Word of God.[59]

Yet in its formulation it is too easily misunderstood. Just as one has rather
wearily to point out that at 1 Timothy 6:10 Paul did not say anything so
foolish as 'Money is the root of all evil', but 'The love of money . . .'; so
here one has to note that the titles in the list are not condemned. It would
be casuistry to argue that all 'Patriarchs, Archbishops, Doctors, Bachelors,
and Masters', are locusts. Many of them have been saintly, as the writers
of the note knew. In view of the great number of scholarly explanations
in all the previous pages of the Geneva Bible, it would be absurd to
condemn an educated clergy ('Doctors, Bachelors, and Masters'). No: those
condemned are those qualified by the final defining clause, 'which forsake
Christ to maintain false doctrine'. Prejudice is not happy with such necessary distinctions, however, preferring to shout 'Pigs!' and throw stones.
Thus the Geneva Bible is dismissed.

HEBREW INTO ENGLISH FOR THE FIRST TIME

Most significant is the most sophisticated element of all in the 1560 complete Bible. Here in the second half of the Old Testament is the translation into English of the twenty-five books after the end of 2 Chronicles
for the first time directly with reference to the Hebrew.

How this important fact has been allowed to be obscured is an enigma.
The Geneva translators used the Hebraist Tyndale closely for the first half
of the Old Testament. Throughout, they had an eye to Coverdale in his
own 1535 Bible, as transmitted also through Matthew's Bible of 1537, and
the revision of it that he made into Henry VIII's Great Bible. But Coverdale
knew no Hebrew. Attempts to challenge his own statement and show that
he did, all fail, and quickly. The books from Ezra to Malachi were translated from the Hebrew into English by no one else before 1560.

Christopher Goodman, Anthony Gilbey and their colleagues were first.
They were, it is now clear, exceptional Hebrew scholars. They were the

first to use at first hand the Hebrew commentary of David Kimshi, followed in those readings in many places in KJV.[60] They had also a remarkable, almost Tyndalian, grasp of English; the knowledge to use available helps in at least five languages (Aramaic, Latin, Greek, German and French); and the ability to work fast. Why are they not better known?

A translation of Hebrew poetry demands marginal notes. The impression given by the authorities who insisted that they be absent (from the Great Bible, the Bishops' Bible and KJV) is that they are political and 'bitter', and *only* political and 'bitter'. This judgement is passed down, still, from writer to modern writer, obviously without any of them having studied even a page.

A faithful translation of Hebrew poetry deals in ellipses and ambiguities, and downright obscurities. The margins can make plain, and can also open up. There can be – and in the Geneva Bible there is – a continual and fruitful dialogue between text and margins. The KJV's occasional printing of the literal sense of a Hebrew metaphor is not adequate. Stripping away Geneva's marginal notes to the Prophets can produce in a reader of KJV a nearly total lack of understanding, something often close to gibberish, though one has not been encouraged to say so.

An example of purely factual help, entirely as KJV fell open at random, is Hosea 12:11.

> *Is there* iniquity in Gilead? surely they are vanity: they sacrifice bullocks in Gilgal; yea, their altars *are* as heaps in the furrows of the fields.

Read out at Morning Prayer, those words might not convey very much. The Geneva text is identical, except that it italicises only the second *are*, and gives the final word as 'field'. Whereas, however, the margin of KJV has cross-references to 4:15 and 9:15, which are simply to the presence of 'Gilgal' in the text, the Geneva margin has:

> The people thought that no man durst have spoken against Gilead, that holy place, and yet the Prophet sayeth, that all their religion was but vanity.

The twenty-five poetic and prophetic books are for the most part in Hebrew which is difficult to very difficult. Even so, half a century later, the work of Goodman and Gilbey and the others was good enough to be taken forward into KJV, when King James's revisers were not following the inferior Bishops' Bible. Four entire centuries later, their work was good enough to be the basis of quite a number of modern versions.

Enough has been said, it is hoped, perhaps barely to suggest the wonderful richness of Geneva's Old Testament. Britain was truly blessed in the men who made it. They make a notable contrast with the experience of

KJV. The first two and a quarter pages of KJV are to modern eyes almost unbearably oleaginous flattery of 'The Most High and Mighty Prince James, by the Grace of God, King of Great Britain, France and Ireland, Defender of the Faith, Etc', extending even to naming him 'Author of the work'. As has been seen, such oil and butter were lacking from the dedication of the Geneva Bible to Queen Elizabeth. Thus, ever after, the name of that odd fellow James lives on everyone's lips, as the 1611 version has carried his name, particularly in America, where he is often raised to an impossible sainthood. The makers of the 1560 Geneva Bible remain out of sight, in the shadows. It is not even certain how many, or who, they were. They were clearly fine Hebrew scholars. There seem to have been not many of them, perhaps no more than two or three Hebraists. Their sense of ministry, of what 'the lambs' needed, and in what kind of English, was strong. They did all their work in three years.

ISAIAH 40 AS AN EXAMPLE

There is space here for only one further illustration of their excellence. Isaiah chapter 40 is the beginning of the words of an unknown prophet, a poet and man of genius, whose name or details are not known, except that he was with the people in captivity in Babylon. From the position of his writing, chapters 40–55 in Isaiah, he is named most prosaically 'Second Isaiah', or 'Deutero-Isaiah'. What follows here is the Geneva Bible rendering of the first eleven verses of Isaiah 40 and then some of the remaining twenty in the chapter, with a selection of the marginal notes. Tyndale did not live to translate any of the poetic books – Job, Psalms or the Prophets (except Jonah). The last time these verses had appeared in English had been in Miles Coverdale's revision for the Great Bible of 1539 of his Bible of 1535, made from five contemporary versions. This was the first time that these words had been in English direct from the Hebrew. Moreover, Coverdale had written in long paragraphs. The Geneva translators both numbered the verses and separated them out, so that Hebrew poetry in English is immediately visible, and even audible. Moreover again, it is English poetry that these undeclared translators, working in a room in a house somewhere in Geneva, achieved. 'The crooked shall be straight, and the rough places plain' is not only accurate to the Hebrew: it is fine English, in rhythm, and in the increasing chime of the parallel words 'crooked – rough'/ 'shall . . . straight'/ 'places plain'. Not for nothing did Handel's librettist, the gifted Jennens, working with these words as they had been taken over almost exactly into KJV, understand how well the verses would go with music, nor Handel fail to set them, in *Messiah*, so that many people cannot hear them without also hearing tenor solo, choir and orchestra. But the point is the musical poetry, and that it is here in the Geneva Bible in English for the first time, and for the first time, directly from the Hebrew.

Comfort ye, comfort ye my people, will your God say.

2 Speak ye comfortably to Jerusalem, and cry unto her, that her warfare is accomplished, that her iniquity is pardoned: for she hath received of the Lord's hand double for all her sins.

3 A voice crieth in the wilderness, Prepare ye the way of the Lord: make straight in the desert a path for our God.

4 Every valley shall be exalted, and every mountain and hill shall be made low: and the crooked shall be straight, and the rough places plain.

5 And the glory of the Lord shall be revealed, and all flesh shall see it together: for the mouth of the Lord hath spoken it.

6 A voice said, Cry. And he said, What shall I cry? All flesh is grass, and all the grace thereof is as the flower of the field.

7 The grass withereth, the flower fadeth, because the Spirit of the Lord bloweth upon it: surely the people is grass.

8 The grass withereth, the flower fadeth: but the word of our God shall stand for ever.

9 O Zion, that bringest good tidings, get thee up into the high mountain: O Jerusalem, that bringeth good tidings, lift up thy voice with strength: lift it up, be not afraid: say unto the cities of Judah, Behold, your God. . . .

11 He shall feed his flock like a shepherd: he shall gather the lambs with his arm, and carry them in his bosom, and shall guide them with young. . . .

18 To whom will ye liken God? Or what similitude will ye set upon him? . . .

22 He sitteth upon the circle of the earth, and the inhabitants thereof are as grasshoppers, he stretcheth out the heavens as a curtain, and spreadeth them out as a tent to dwell in.

23 He bringeth the princes to nothing, and maketh the judges of the earth, as vanity. . . .

26 Lift up your eyes on high, and behold who hath created these things, and bringeth out their armies by number, and calleth them all by names? by the greatness of his power and mighty strength nothing faileth.

27 Why sayest thou, O Jacob, and speakest, O Israel, My way is hid from the Lord, and my judgement is passed over my God?

28 Knowest thou not? or hast thou not heard, that the everlasting

God, the Lord hath created the ends of the earth? he neither fainteth, nor is weary: there is no searching of his understanding.

29 But he giveth strength unto him that fainteth, and unto him that hath no strength, he increaseth power.

30 Even the young men shall faint, and be weary, and the young men shall stumble and fall.

31 But they that wait upon the Lord, shall renew their strength: they shall lift up the wings as the eagles: they shall run, and not be weary, and they shall walk, and not faint.

The first marginal note, to 'Comfort ye', is

> This is a consolation for the Church, assuring them that they shall be never destitute of Prophets, whereby he exhorteth the true ministers of God that then were, and those also that should come after him, to comfort the poor and afflicted, and to assure them of their deliverance both of body and soul.

Five notes later, to 'Prepare ye the way of the Lord', is:

> Meaning Cyrus and Darius which should deliver Gods people out of captivity, and make them a ready way to Jerusalem: and this was fully accomplished, when John the Baptist brought tidings of Jesus Christ's coming who was the true deliverer of his Church from sin and Satan, Matthew 3.3.

Two notes later, to 'All flesh shall see it together', is:

> This miracle shall be so great, that it shall be known through all the world.

The final note to the chapter, out of 32 notes in all, against 'Even the young men shall faint', is

> They that trust in their own virtue, & do not acknowledge that all cometh of God.

What the chapter is about is the power of God, the sovereignty of God, the impossibility of 'figuring' the scale of him, as the heading to the Geneva page has it, and yet his concern for his people cosmically, strategically and personally. This is the point of the Hebrew now in English. This is the point of the Geneva Bible.

Gerald Hammond, the wisest writer on the Geneva Old Testament, observed of it that it was so good that it might reasonably have stood as the definitive English version, as the KJV was destined to do for three hundred years.[61] There is indeed something shocking about the Geneva

English Bible. It is not its Calvinism, which in the theology of the supremacy of the sovereignty of God is its glory; nor its supposed failure, which is a lie; but from 1611 the systematic destruction of it for political, and above all, crude commercial, reasons (see below, chapter 26, esp. p. 458).

It could never, however, be destroyed. Now, apart from some copies in private hands or specialist libraries, it exists with the full notes for twenty-first-century readers only in two modern facsimiles (of the 1560 and 1602 editions) both also generally confined to libraries, and the first of them long out of print.[62] But it is still alive. So much of it went, flatly against King James's wishes, into KJV, a story still untold. It affected our greatest writers, Shakespeare and Milton. It lit the beacon of liberty in the English seventeenth century. Its notes were even added to seventeenth- and eighteenth-century KJVs. The Geneva Bible was 'killed': but it is alive.

Tyndale, on an early page in his *Obedience of a Christian Man*, wrote about the power of God. He explained how the enemies of Christ had the power to arrest Christ, to put him on trial and condemn him to death, with the whole might of Roman and Jewish law, and crucify him.

> Finally when they had done all they could and that they thought sufficient, and when Christ was in the heart of the earth and so many bills and poleaxes about him, to keep him down, and when it was past man's help: then holp God. When man could not bring him again, God's truth fetched him again.[63]

Chapter 18

REFORMATION PSALMS

THE BOOK OF PSALMS

The Book of Psalms is so called from the Greek word for instrumental music, ψαλμόι (*psalmoi*), which means, by extension, the words accompanying that music. They have been used in Jewish worship from the earliest times, and were at once taken over into Christian services.

From antiquity, the 150 Psalms have been divided into five books. Many have acquired titles over the centuries: and tradition has ascribed most of them to personal invention by King David, without any foundation. They divide roughly into various kinds: songs of praise, as 103–104 (both beginning in KJV 'Bless the Lord, O my soul . . .') or of thanksgiving as 100; individual laments, beginning with a cry for help, famously, 22, 'My God, my God, why hast thou forsaken me?', which the Gospel writers record Christ crying aloud on the cross (Matthew 27:46, Mark 15:34): most of those express also the certainty that the Lord has heard prayer, which may show that this form of psalm was for use in worship. There are other classifications, but the first importance of the Psalms lies in their expression of the theology and worship of the people of Israel over many centuries. Christians quickly made them central in public worship; but they have also treasured them as personal prayers from a wide span of human experience – the soul in many states feels the intimate presence of God.

The Book of Psalms was the basis for the liturgy of the medieval church, in Latin of course. In the mass, there was no act of importance without a psalm to accompany it: the whole Psalter would be sung, in the Quire Offices at stated hours, once a week. There is a long tradition of Old and Middle English Psalters. The 150 Psalms have been one of the greatest influences on English lyric poetry down the centuries, particularly from early in the sixteenth century, when they first began to be sung, said and heard in English. Their appeal was in many cases through their honesty, sometimes appearing as anger as in Psalm 5, the peremptory 'Answer me when I call'. Though the ascription to King David is very unlikely, it is not foolish, and one may understand the power of it. In the

Books of Samuel and Kings, David is glamorous but also very human, presented as a charismatic leader, his many weaknesses as well as his strengths not hidden. He lusted for power, for women and for life, and had many contrary feelings about his role as king and his desire to serve his God and his nation. He was a man who knew worship, of success and skilled warfare as well as of Yahweh. So many feelings are in the Psalms, often reduced to an essence of need, fear or joy, that they have been thought to belong to David: more importantly since their making they have been loved by readers and hearers, whether kings or shepherds (or, as in David's case, both). The Bible is full of people joined only in the need to do the will of God. Often confused, some of them are far from admirable, being weak, or adulterers, or cowards, or murderers, or betrayers. Though they have a lofty aim, the Psalms reflect humanity in its grubbiness as well as its exaltation.

The characteristic parallel statement of Hebrew poetry is especially visible in the Psalms ('The earth is the Lord's and the fulness thereof / The sea and all that therein is'). It has led to antiphonal singing, as in later centuries in Christian cathedrals where the first statement, the 'verse', came from one side of the chancel and the second, the 'response' is answered from the other. The reformers, particularly inspired by the German hymn-singing of the followers of Luther, took the Psalms into their services, to be sung by everyone, rather than by having a special choir, or one person, sing them on behalf of the worshippers, who merely joined in an 'Amen'.

Plainsong was purely melodic, with no time-measures or bars, a flexibility to fit the words, all very fine for a monastery, or cathedral choir. There were – and are – problems in getting congregations to sing, together, the uneven lines. The solution lay in translating them into short metrical stanzas, which, to a simple and regular tune, could then be sung by everybody. Just as the Bible itself was from the early sixteenth century across Europe in the common language of the people, so the Psalms became the songs of the people. The devout and faithful Christian could now be in the presence of his or her Maker and Deliverer without the intervention of a priest, so it is not surprising that such Psalm-singing became a badge of the struggle for religious liberty. Even German Psalters at first tended not to include the whole 150 Psalms. The French Psalter, largely made by Theodore Beza in Geneva and Clemont Marot at the French court, became a powerful weapon in the fight for Protestant liberty and belief. In mid-century, Protestantism swept France at great speed, and it was often the people singing Psalms which paved the way for Protestant conversions and Bible-reading. Marot's 'sanctes chansonettes' became fashionable, particularly in and around the court, and the first edition of ten thousand copies soon sold out. Everyone who was anyone needed to be found singing these Psalms to ballad tunes of the times. The Church authorities, alarmed, responded with pagan ditties set to the same tunes. The Marot–Beza Psalter of 1562 remains in use to this day in the Protestant Church of France, its 110 metres and 125 tunes using every device to avoid monotony.

STERNHOLD AND HOPKINS

In Britain the two great collections of metrical Psalms, those by Thomas Sternhold and John Hopkins and, two centuries later, by Nahum Tate and Nicholas Brady, had an influence extending beyond Europe to America.[1] Miles Coverdale had adapted German Lutheran hymns and tunes in his *Goostly Psalms* of 1539, a volume then immediately suppressed by Henry VIII. These were straight translations from Luther, who had prepared a short selection of the Psalms for congregational singing by his followers, within an older German tradition. Coverdale did little more than put Luther's German into English metre: but a new tradition was by this established in England. Coverdale can have had no idea of the extent to which this modest volume would establish such a great part of Protestant worship in Britain – and later, America – for two hundred years and more. Thomas Sternhold published nineteen Psalms in 1549: he was appointed by King Henry VIII himself to his court, for his Psalm-singing. That year Robert Crowley published some Psalms with music for four voices, and forty-four metrical Psalms by John Hopkins were added to Sternhold's. In 1556, an edition with both together was published in Geneva, the first English book printed there, and in 1561 the great London Protestant printer John Day's career began with an edition of Sternhold and Hopkins with tunes, and an 'Introduction to learn to sing'. The following year, 1562, he published a 'Sternhold and Hopkins' with all 150 Psalms. Though many others wrote metrical Psalms for congregations, it was 'Sternhold and Hopkins' which dominated metrical singing in Britain for many centuries. By 1852, there had been over a thousand separate editions.[2]

Under Elizabeth, only John Day held the licence to print Sternhold and Hopkins. His 1567 edition is introduced by 'An Extract of the Queen's Majesty's gracious Privilege and Licence'. In his volume he offers *The Psalms of David in English Meter, with notes* [i.e., music], *the ABC with the little catechism . . . so that no such book . . . be repugnant to the Holy Scripture or the laws and order of our realm*.[3] Day then prints 'A Treatise made by Athanasius the Great . . . how . . . ye may use the Psalms . . .'. He sets out this classic fourth-century exposition in ninety-four single-sentence paragraphs, explaining which Psalms to turn to for what 'effect of the mind'.

Athanasius goes through many existential situations. For example, 'If thou shalt need of prayer for them which withstand thee and compass thy soul about sing the seventeenth Psalm, and 86, 89 and 142 Psalm'. To this, Day added a further twenty-eight situations 'Not comprehended in the former Table of Athanasius'. These include the following splendid curiosity: 'If thou wouldst have Christ to come conquer and beat down Sirians, Idumeans, Ammonites, Papists, Antichristians, Nullicidians, Neutrals, and ingratious Pelagians, use the 68 Psalm' (beginning 'Let God arise, let his enemies be scattered').

Day's collection proper – all are in metrical form – begins with the Veni Creator and the Venite exultemus; then the Te Deum, the Song of the Three Children, the Benedictus, the Magnificat, the Nunc Dimittis, the Creed of Athanasius (after 1639 called 'Quicunque Vult'), the Lamentation of a Sinner, the Humble Suit of a Sinner, the Lord's Prayer, the Ten Commandments, and only then the 150 Psalms. At the end of the volume are two exhortations to praise, before morning prayer and evening prayer; twelve Articles of the Christian faith; and various prayers, complaints and lamentations, the whole volume finishing with prose prayers, some of them over two pages long.

In addition to the huge number of independent editions of Sternhold and Hopkins, a statistic which tells its own story about English Protestant worship from early in Elizabeth's reign, these metrical Psalms were printed in some form at the back of every Geneva Bible after 1560, and most editions of the Book of Common Prayer. Thus 'Sternhold and Hopkins' is universal and automatic in Protestant worship, certainly until 1640 in America and the arrival of the Bay Psalm Book; until 1650 in Scotland (with two hundred editions of the Church of Scotland metrical Psalms right up to 1940[4]); and until 1696 in England when the versions by Tate and Brady began to be used. Even so, to mention metrical Psalms from early Elizabethan times until very recently has meant 'Sternhold and Hopkins' alone (fig. 25). These figures do not include prose versions of the Psalms (as in Geneva Bibles, the Book of Common Prayer and KJV), of which, outside those volumes, there were about six hundred separate editions up to the 1970s: prose Psalms were also regularly printed in the margins of Sternhold and Hopkins.

ARE STERNHOLD AND HOPKINS ANY GOOD?

A simple test might be the 23rd Psalm. Oddly, two versions are printed, with the command 'Sing this as the 21.Psalm' that is to the tune printed at the head of Psalm 21. The head-note reads 'David having tried God's manifold mercies divers ways, gathereth assurance that God will continue his goodness forever.'

> The Lord is only my support,
>   And he that doth me feed,
> How can I then want anything,
>   Whereof I stand in need?
> 2 He doth me fold in coasts most safe,
>   The tender grass fast by,
> And after drives me to the streams,
>   Which run most pleasantly.
>
> 3 And when I feel myself near lost,
>   Then doth he me home take:
> Conducting me in his right paths,
>   Even for his own name sake.
> 4 And though I were even at deaths door,
>   Yet would I fear non ill:
> For with thy rod and shepherd's crook,
>   I am comforted still.
>
> 5 Though hast my table deckt,
>   In despite of my foe,
> Though hast my head with balm refreshed,
>   My cup doth overflow.
> 6 And finally while breath doth last,
>   Thy grace shall me defend:
> And in the house of God will I,
>   My life forever spend.

Uniquely, at this point an alternative version by Thomas Sternhold is printed.

> My shepherd is the living Lord,
>   Nothing therefore I need,
> In pastures fair with waters calm,
>   He set me for to feed.
> 2 He did convert and glad my soul,
>   And brought my mind in frame:
> To walk in paths of righteousness,
>   For his most holy name.
>
> 3 Yea though I walk in vale of death,
>   Yet will I fear none ill:
> Thy rod, thy staff doth comfort me,

And thou art with me still.
4 And in the presence of my foes,
    My table though hast spread:
Though shalt, oh Lord fulfill my cup,
    And eke anoint my head.

5 Through all my life thy favour is,
    So frankly showed to me,
That in thy house forever more,
    My dwelling place shall be.

It is hard to read these without judging them against the later Scottish version ('The Lord's my shepherd, I'll not want, / he makes me down to lie . . .') which, with its tune 'Crimond', has been well loved for so long. Though it may be felt that of the two printed, Sternhold's version is better poetry, the criterion always has to be, rather than any genius there might be within the poetry on the page, what makes for good congregational singing. Here short lines and rhymes are essential, and if the word order gets twisted for the sake of a rhyme, the singers in church are unlikely to be particularly troubled.

Here, as another example, is the beginning of Psalm 91.

He that within the secret place
    Of God most high doth dwell,
In shadow of the mightiest grace,
    At rest shall keep him well.
2 Thou art my hope and my strong hold,
    I to the Lord will say,
My God is he, in him will I
    My whole affiance stay.

3 He shall defend thee from the snare,
    The which the hunter laid,
And from the deadly plague and care,
    Whereof thou art afraid.
4 And with his wings will cover thee
    And keep thee safely there,
His faith and truth thy sense shall be,
    As sure as shield and spear.

5 So that thou shalt not need I say,
    To fear or be affright,
Of all the shafts that fly by day,
    Nor terrors of the night.

6 Nor of the plague that privily
  Doth walk in dark so fast,
Nor yet of that which doth destroy,
  And at noone days doth waste . . .

And so on. Modern readers who love Miles Coverdale's prose Psalms in
the Book of Common Prayer may lament the loss of his 'Whoso dwelleth
under the defence of the most High: shall abide under the shadow of the
Almighty. . . . Thou shalt not be afraid for any terror by night: nor for
the arrow that flieth by day . . .'; or, even more, KJV's 'He that dwelleth
in the secret place of the most High shall abide under the shadow of the
Almighty . . . Thou shalt not be afraid for the terror by night; nor for the
arrow that flieth by day . . .' Those few who know and love the Geneva
versions may regret the loss of 'He will cover thee under his wings, and
thou shalt be sure under his feathers . . .'

Psalm 137 was especially loved as a poem of protest, the refusal under
God by captives to give what was precious to them for entertainment or
interest. Coverdale begins with the well-known

By the waters of Babylon, we sat down and wept: when we remembered thee, oh Sion.
    2 As for our harps, we hanged them up: upon the trees that are
therein.
    3 For they that led us away captive required of us then a song, and
melody in our heaviness: Sing us one of the songs of Sion
    4 How shall we sing the Lord's song: in a strange land?
    5 If I forget thee, oh Jerusalem: let my right hand forget her cunning.
    6 If I do not remember thee, let my tongue cleave to the roof of
my mouth: yea, if I prefer not Jerusalem in my mirth.

Here is Sternhold and Hopkins:

When as we sat in Babylon,
  The rivers round about,
And in rememberance of Sion,
  The tears of grief burst out.
2 We hanged our Harps and Instruments,
  The willow trees upon:
For in that place men for their use
  Had planted many one.

3 Then they to whom we prisoners were,
  Said to us hauntingly:
Now let us hear your Hebrew songs,

And pleasant melody.
4 Alas said we, who can once frame
  His sorrowful heart to sing
The praises of the living God,
  Thus under a strange King?

5 But yet if I Jerusalem
  Out of my heart let slide:
Then let my fingers quite forget
  The warbling Harp to guide.
6 And let my tongue within my mouth
  Be tied forever fast,
If that I joy, before I see
  Thy full deliverance past.

This is barely adequate. The powerful images of refusal in the original Hebrew – of the deliberate setting aside of the harps, and the hope that the body would not even function – are smothered by the need to keep the rhymes and metre moving. One might have thought that this communal experience of religious separation under oppression would produce something a little more energised. Certainly the French version by Clemont Marot, one of the Psalms that took his country by storm, has real power. It is notable how in Sternhold and Hopkins a blanket of words seems so often to smother the fires. Perhaps the best of Sternhold and Hopkins is Psalm 100, to be sung to the tune, still well known, that even then was the 'Old Hundredth', a name that harks right back to the singing of Psalms in Geneva. What follows below, though best known from Sternhold and Hopkins, is the 'Old Version' from Geneva, as it became known after 1696, to distinguish it from the New Version by Nicholas Brady and Nahum Tate made in that year. That is a measure of its popularity. Furthermore, it dominated the singing of metrical Psalms in England and Scotland for almost a century and a half, even though the Psalter had been translated into metrical forms by Archbishop Matthew Parker, Sir Philip Sidney and King James I: and parts of the Psalter were translated by Francis Bacon, John Milton, George Herbert, Richard Crashaw, Henry Vaughan and others.

All people that on earth do dwell,
  Sing to the Lord with cheerful voice,
Him serve with fear, his praise forth tell,
  Come ye before him and rejoice.

2 The Lord ye know is God indeed,
  Without our aid he did us make:

> We are his flock, he doth us feed,
>   And for his sheep he doth us take.
>
> 3 Oh enter then his gates with praise,
>   Approach with joy his courts unto:
> Praise, Laud and bless his name always,
>   For it is seemly so to do.
>
> 4 For why the Lord our God is good,
>   His mercy is forever sure,
> His truth at all times firmly stood,
>   And shall from age to age endure.

This succeeds because of the avoidance of inversions, simple statements, clear rhymes and the dominance of monosyllables. Reading the whole of Sterndale and Hopkins, it is easy to find verses to mock. Comparing these verses for congregational singing with the great outpouring of love-lyrics at the end of the century and in the next – and indeed always present thereafter – so confident and so accomplished, can distort our judgement. If we did not know who wrote it, how would we judge the following, from Psalm 3?

> 6 I will not be afraid
>   Though legions round be laid,
>   Which all against me gather:
> 7 I say no more but this:
>   Up lord now time it is:
>   Help me my God and Father.

That was written in 1585 by Sir Philip Sidney.[5]

PRINTING PSALMS

Probably in April 1578, Robert Barker in London published 'The Book of the Psalms of David, with other books of the Holy Scriptures thereto annexed'. This, from the Geneva version, looked forward to Barker's publication two years later of 'The third part of the Bible, containing five excellent books'. Both were in 16mo, and indicate a need for the biblical Psalms in verse as a separate book.

There had been since 1530 prose versions of the Psalter in English, that being the date of George Joye's translation from Martin Bucer, which was followed by Joye's Psalter again translated, this time from Zwingli. In 1535, Miles Coverdale translated from the Latin of Johannes Campensis his paraphrase of all the Psalms and Ecclesiastes. These versions were reprinted, with additions of prayers and the litany. In 1548, the Psalms from the Great Bible were printed, a version that appeared six times before 1552, even while Coverdale's version was reprinted. It is clear from these details that the demand for the Psalms, in prose, was great. It is an output that would be repeated, with other prose versions until the end of the century, about forty in all, with another thirty before 1640.

The printing of copies of various kinds of metrical versions was so massive as almost to defy description. From Sternhold's nineteen Psalms in 1549 and the addition of the remaining Psalms from Hopkins and others in 1562, until 1640, the number of clearly identifiable separate editions amounts to 559 (see chart, fig. 28).[6] The Stationers' Company became responsible for a good deal of the printing after 1604, taking over from London monopolies. Later there were imports from Amsterdam, and, among many others, in 1609 the printing house of Jaggard, the printer of Shakespeare's First Folio in 1623.

This huge number, averaging over five editions a year (and still taking no account of print-runs) reveals a great deal about the vitality of Protestant congregational life all across England – and this does not include comparable figures for the printing of the Book of Common Prayer, and of Geneva Bibles, with Sternhold and Hopkins at the back.

These figures are only for England. From 1567 different versions began to be made and printed in Scotland, and those only in metre amount to thirty before 1640. Furthermore, to the better known complete Psalters by Parker, Sidney, and King James, mentioned above, must be added the metrical versions by Robert Crowley, Sir Thomas Wyatt, W. Hunnis, F. Seagar, H. Dod, G. Wither, F. Rous and Henry Ainsworth – the last an important metrical version by a fine Hebraist, leader of the Separatists in Amsterdam, whose version became important in America.

Some of the more personal metrical versions of the Psalms will be considered presently. Standing back to take in the statistics of printing, just how big was the production of metrical Psalms reveals a phenomenon in English and Scottish life. The excellent versions of certain Psalms by Sidney and others have attracted attention, rightly. What has not been enough noticed is the poetic liberty brought by translating the Word of God into English, a freedom newly permitted: English poets had discovered that poetry was not immoral (because it was 'feigning'), but that God himself spoke poetry. Far more importantly, the entire nations of England and Scotland were singing Psalms in English (and Scots) on at least every Sunday, and generally more often. Not all of Sternhold and Hopkins is good. Some may be considered bad. Nevertheless, the constant reiteration of godly poems must have had a creative effect. In both countries, the 'mute inglorious Miltons' of Thomas Gray's poem may not have been so mute, though one may assume a lack of glory. There may be much poetry to be discovered in manuscripts overlooked. Some of this may be poor, but it will show bulk. The problem has been that eighteenth-century critics have distorted our judgement. Because Sternhold and Hopkins were doing quite different things from what eighteenth-century poets thought should be done, they were discredited as inferior or beyond even that pale. Those critics started from poetic positions so far from early congregations with their hearty singing that they now seem driven only by prejudice. It is worth pausing to consider the colour-filters through which metrical psalms have been viewed – and damned.

LATER CRITICAL CONDEMNATION

Thomas Warton was Poet Laureate from 1785 to his death in 1790. He had been Professor of Poetry, and later of History, in the University of Oxford. In his celebrated *The History of English Poetry* of 1781 he wrote, with detailed analysis, a seven-page attack on Sternhold and Hopkins, in which the words 'barbarism of style' were on the milder side. What Sternhold and Hopkins wrote was 'obsolete and contemptible . . . an absolute travesty'. It was

> a translation entirely destitute of elegance, spirit, and propriety . . . I presume I am communicating no very new criticism when I observe, that in every part of this translation we are disgusted with a languor of versification and a want of common prosody . . . To the disgrace of sacred music, sacred poetry, and our established worship, these psalms still continue to be sung in the Church of England. . . . It is certain, had they been more poetically translated, they would not have been acceptable to the common people. . . .' though they may have administered spiritual consolation to the manufacturer and mechanic . . .[7]

Nearly forty years later, in 1819, Thomas Campbell wrote:

> In the reign of Edward VI the effects of the Reformation became visible in our poetry, by blending religious with poetical enthusiasm, or rather by substituting the one for the other. The national Muse became puritanical, and was not improved by change. Then flourished Sternhold and Hopkins, who, with the best intentions and the worst taste, degraded the spirit of Hebrew psalmody by flat and homely phraseology; and mistaking vulgarity for simplicity, turned into bathos what they found sublime. Such was the love of versifying holy writ at that

period, that the Acts of the Apostles were rhymed, and set to music by Christopher Tye.[8]

Seen from a meeting house in 1580 by the Thames, or in 1620 in Edinburgh, these judgements would have seemed incomprehensible. Their lack of grasp of what the poems were made for, and their snobbery, can astonish: yet in the year 2000, ignorance has descended even further into the abyss. In superiority of knowledge and judgement such a massive part of English and Scottish life of the time is not even noticed. Moreover, the full story of the writing of English hymns remains to be told. Many of the great ones, by Isaac Watts or Charles Wesley or John Newton, are in that very 'common metre' which is so English, and a gift to the nation from all that singing in just such verses in Sternhold and Hopkins. True, those early psalms have nothing that can match 'When I survey the wondrous cross' or 'How sweet the name of Jesus sounds': but the structures were already in place for Watts and Newton. In ignoring the size of the phenomenon that was Sternhold and Hopkins, a vital piece of British popular history has been wiped out. What is more, Psalm-singing was free.

POETIC PSALMS

In the sixteenth and early seventeenth centuries, every significant English poet translated at least one Psalm, and sometimes several. Thus we have Psalms from Sidney, Spenser, Drayton, Jonson, Milton, Herbert, Vaughan and so on. Every significant poet, that is, except Shakespeare. He was above all a playwright, but his lyric poems do not include a single Psalm. It is intriguing, however, that his sonnet-sequence has 150 poems, the only sequence of the time (and there were many) with that total. That that figure would call to mind the Psalms is shown by the fact that many of the Scottish Psalm books had the simple title 'The CL Psalms'. It would be absurd to try to match any sonnet by Shakespeare with its equivalently numbered Psalm, and even more ridiculous to try to relate the introverted crystallisation of mood that a sonnet represents to the wide display of public and private emotions in the Psalms. Lacking any further clues, a coincidence must be observed, with the nagging feeling that there must be more to it, somehow.[9]

The first English lyric poet to attempt the Psalms in English was Sir Thomas Wyatt. He translated Psalm 37, and then the seven Penitential Psalms (numbers 6, 32, 38, 51, 102, 130 and 143), probably in 1540, on his return to his home in Kent after service abroad. Wyatt was an experimenter with lyric form, and with Henry Howard, Earl of Surrey, the first to try to bring Italian forms into recognisably modern English. Since a good deal of the Italian tradition followed Petrarch, with his anguish of love unrequited by a cold mistress, there would seem to be little overlap with the vocabulary, forms and themes of the Psalms. A further difficulty was that the clarity and precision of Italian forms, helped in rhyme schemes by the purity of the vowels, did not go well into English. When this is linked with the attempts to use many kinds of metre, with lines both very long and very short, we should find ourselves more sympathetic to the labours of Sternhold and Hopkins. Nevertheless, the very exercise liberated Wyatt into trying new methods and schemes. Almost all Wyatt's poems are imagined to be accompanied by music, sung to a lute, and in one way this chimed deeply with experience of the Psalms. Though Wyatt can write poems that are little more than ditties for music, in the tradition of the song books found in the courts of Henry VII and Henry VIII, he can make the music felt in the Psalms work for him with some profundity, beyond the skills of the late-medieval versifiers like Hawes and Barclay.

Wyatt's Psalms were not intended for public singing, and they were accompanied, and illuminated, by poems by him which commented on the imagined experience of their writing, also reflecting on the experience of reading and translating. His Penitential Psalms are not distinguished. Psalm 51 for example, at the heart of the penitential experience, begins:

> Rew on me, lord, for thy goodness and grace,
>   That of thy nature art so bountiful,
>   For that goodness that in the world doth brace
> Repugnant natures in quiet wonderful . . .[10]

This is not compelling. On the other hand the sixth Penitential Psalm, Psalm 130, begins:

> From depth of sin and from a deep despair,
> From depth of death from depth of heart's sorrow,
> From this deep cave, of darkness deep repair,
>
> To thee have I called, O Lord, to be my borrow.
> Thou in my voice, O Lord, perceive and hear
> My heart, my hope, my plaint, my overthrow,
>
> My will to rise; and let by grant appear
> That to my voice thine ears do well entend.
> No place so far that to thee is not near,
>
> No depth so deep that though ne mayst extend
> Thine ear thereto.[11]

('Borrow' in the fourth line means pledge or security.) This gives an appearance of technical as well as personal struggle, but there are in it some flashes where the verse rises towards poetry, as at the sixth line.

SIR PHILIP SIDNEY

Sidney worked on his Psalms in October 1585, in the hope that his new versions would be sung in the parish church at Penshurst, or in his own family chapel. The example of friends may also have suggested to him the value of simple Psalms in English for the religious education of his children: his daughter Elizabeth, his only child, had been born that month. There is strong family feeling. 'The Sister of that Incomparable Sidney', as she signed herself, Mary Herbert, Countess of Pembroke, wrote a moving obituary poem, 'To the Angel Spirit', which prefaces the first printed edition of his Psalms in 1823. In it she suggests that only her brother's wounding and death (in 1586) had brought an end to work on the Psalms, which thus emerge, as Katherine Duncan-Jones put it, not as 'an early work that he never got round to finishing, but a "front-line" composition, left like its author, maimed, sick and bleeding'.[12]

That Sidney was aiming at congregational worship, in a mode very unlike the personal lyricism, for example, of his *Astrophil and Stella* or his sonnets, makes clearer the real difficulties faced by anyone undertaking the Psalms in metre. Thus, verse 9 of Psalm 19 appears as:

> Of him the Feare doth cleaness beare
> And so endures forever,
> His judgments be self verity,
> They are unrighteous never.[13]

If, in a decade when so many wrote so well, the great Sidney himself was in this kind of difficulty, we may have more sympathy with Thomas Sternhold and John Hopkins forty years before. In the forty-two Psalms he set, Sidney was courageous in his experiments in metre and verse form, and that bold variety should be admired. Conditioned by Sternhold and Hopkins, however, and by the Scottish versions, with their solid understanding of what worshippers can sing together, we may feel that his Psalm 23 is too precious in form:

> 1 The lord the lord my shepheard is,
> And so can never I
> Tast misery.
> 2 He rests me in green pastures his.
> By waters still and sweet
> He guides my feet.

3 He me revives, leads me the way
   Which righteousness doth take,
        For his name's sake.
4 Yea tho I should thro vallys stray
   Of death's dark shade I will
        No wit feare ill.

By contrast, Psalm 24 goes for length of line:

1 The earth is God's, and what the Globe of earth containeth,
   And all who in that Globe do dwell;
2 For by his power the land upon the Ocean raigneth,
   Through him the floods to their beds fell.
3 Who shall climb to the hill which God's own hill is named,
   Who stall stand in his holy place?
4 He that hath hurtless hands, whose inward heart is framed
   All pureness ever to embrace . . .

More is happening here than attempts either to provide words for congregational singing, or to educate his little daughter. Sidney is himself involved, as poet, as human being – and indeed as soldier. In an important long letter to Walsingham, the Queen's Secretary, on the 24th March 1586, meditating on his lack of success in the Netherlands as a military leader, he is full of religious thoughts, seeing the conflict as a foreshadowing of Armageddon, and acknowledging his dependence ultimately, not on military strength, but on God, as in Psalm 20.[14] He quotes his own version:

   Now in mee knowledg sayes
That God from fall his own Anoynted stayes.
      From heavnly holy land
      I know that He heares Thee,
Yet heares with powers and helps of helpfull hand.

   Let trust of some men be
In chariots arm'd, Others in chivalry;
      But let all our conceit
      Upon God's holy name,
Who is our Lord, with due remembrance wayte . . .

Sidney was translating throughout from the Latin text. He makes a collection that is interesting, as poetry, but leaves a modern reader longing for the prose versions. In KJV, those verses are:

6 Now know I that the Lord saveth his anointed, he will hear him from his holy heaven with the saving strength of his right hand.

7 Some trust in chariots, and some in horses: but we will remember the name of the Lord our God.

The second verse in Coverdale, and in the Geneva Bible, is identical.

Though he was always a powerfully religious man, ending his days a greatly respected Dean of St Paul's Cathedral, John Donne did not himself directly translate any of the Psalms. He translated *The Lamentations of Jeremy, for the most part according to Tremelius*, and a significant number of his lyrics are steeped in Christian experience. He did, however, write 'Upon the translation of the Psalms by Sir Philip Sidney, and the Countess of Pembroke his sister'. Donne clearly responded to Sidney's work here, and his sister's fine poem, as if the Psalms were the work of both of them – 'A Brother and a Sister, made by thee / the organ, where thou art the harmony'. According to Donne, Mary Herbert did translate at least one Psalm, parallel to her brother's: that is Psalm 97, which begins in KJV 'The lord reigneth; let the earth rejoice; let the multitude of Isles be glad thereof'.

AUGUSTAN PSALMS

To show what became of the endeavour of putting Psalms into verse in the early eighteenth century, here is part of Psalm 91 as translated in 1710 by Alexander Pope.

> He who beneath thy shelt'ring wing resides,
> Whom thy hand leads, and whom thy glory guides
> To Heav'n familiar his bold vows shall send,
> And fearless say to God – thou art my friend!

This is barely recognisable as KJV's moving

He that dwelleth in the secret place of the most High shall abide under the shadow of the Almighty.

2 I will say of the LORD, He is my refuge and my fortress: my God; in him will I trust.

The famous phrases 'He shall cover thee with his feathers, and under his wings shalt thou trust . . . Thou shalt not be afraid for the terror by night; nor for the arrow that flieth by day' appear in Pope as:

> 'Tis Thou shalt save him from insidious wrongs,
> And the sharp arrows of censorious tongues.
> When gath'ring tempests swell the raging main,
> When thunder roars, and lightning blasts the plain,

> Amidst the wrack of nature undismay'd,
> Safe shall he lie, and hope beneath thy shade.
> By day no perils shall the just afright,
> No dismal dreams of groaning ghosts by night.
> His God shall guard him in the fighting field,
> And o'er his breast extend his saving shield:
> The whistling darts shall turn their points away,
> And fires around him innocently play.[15]

Clearly a long way from any notion of congregational singing, this is an instructive paraphrase. Here is the eighteenth-century Man of Reason meditating at leisure on his privilege in being just that. Gone is the urgency of the need for God in the original Psalm, so well suggested by 'The terror by night'. Now 'dismal dreams' and 'groaning ghosts' are domesticated, and no more than the standard apparatus of the conventional Man of Feeling.

Pope's heroic couplets with their supremely clever naturalness seem a long way from the Hebrew Psalms – and even further from the Gospels. One cannot imagine, in Matthew 4, the devil quoting this Psalm: instead of 'He shall give his angels charge over thee, to keep thee in all thy ways. They shall bear thee up in their hands, lest thou dash thy foot against a stone', Pope has:

> I see protecting Miriads round thee fly,
> And all the bright Militia of the sky.
> These in thy dangers timely aid shall bring,
> Raise in their arms, and waft thee on their wings.
> These shall perform th'almighty orders given,
> Direct each step, and smooth the path to Heaven.[16]

Alexander Pope was all his life a devout Catholic, and later engaged in the attack on the Enlightenment notions of Deism. One would think neither position was true here.

A FINAL QUESTION

Who wrote this version of the last Psalm, 150, and when?

> O Praise Jah; Praise God in his sanctity:
> Praise him, in the firmament of his strongness.
> O praise him, in his actions-mighty:
> Praise him, in multitude of his greatness.

O praise him, with the sound of the trumpet-shrill:
Praise him, with Harp and Psalterion.
O praise him, with the Flute and Timbrel:
Praise him, with Virginals and Organon.

O praise him, with the Cymbals sounding clear:
Praise him, with Cymbals that loud-sounding play:
Praise Jah let ev'rything that breath doth-bear:
O glorify-with-praise th'eternal Jah.

That was clearly by someone who knew the Hebrew well, and how to get Hebrew accurately into English, and much more than that, with a knack for getting English to sound like Hebrew. Was it Ezra Pound, in a fit of scholarly accuracy? But Pound knew no Hebrew. Emily Dickinson didn't know Hebrew either. It sounds quite like both, and certainly this poet had a strong effect, albeit sometimes negative, on American life, as will be seen in chapter 30 below.

That psalm came from *The Book of Psalms, Englished both in Prose and Metre*, printed by Giles Thorp at Amsterdam in 1612. The maker was Henry Ainsworth (the spelling above was very slightly modernised).[17] Ainsworth produced prose and metrical versions for his Separatist congregation at Amsterdam, shortly before others there set off in a leaky ship called the *Mayflower*. Ainsworth can be a shaky poet in English, but his Hebrew was very good, as it so often has been among Dissenters down the centuries. For the Psalms, Ainsworth's Anglo-Hebrew did not conquer the world in the way that Coverdale did in prose, and Sternhold and Hopkins did in verse: but he deserves a good deal more study in the field of getting the Hebrew Bible into English, and especially the peculiar art of getting the result singable by a lot of people together. Whatever else, Ainsworth's Psalms are Hebraic in being theologically tough. They live in another world from the late-twentieth-century notion in popular entertainment that a religious experience is singing into a microphone, very slowly, the words 'day by day'.

Chapter 19

THE BISHOPS' BIBLE, 1568

IN THE 1530S, AND FOR SOME TIME AFTER, Cambridge became a centre of preaching. The controversial and popular (and still extremely readable) Hugh Latimer was made Bishop of Worcester from 1535, but resigned in protest at the Six Articles. Imprisoned under Henry VIII, he was released by Edward VI in 1547. He preached a series of sermons before the king, including in 1548 his famous *On the Plough*, where ploughing is preaching, the duty of all bishops; 'for the preaching of the word of God unto the people is called meat: scripture calleth it meat; not strawberries, that come but once a year, and tarry not long, but are soon gone' – Latimer's words became proverbial for non-resident clergy.[1] Arrested under Mary I, he and Ridley were convicted of heresy, and on 16 October 1554 ('one of the blackest days in English history'[2]) burned outside Balliol College in Oxford, Latimer saying as the flames took hold, 'Be of good cheer, master Ridley, and play the man. We shall this day light such a candle, by God's grace, in England, as I trust shall never be put out.'[3]

A Cambridge friend of Hugh Latimer, though lacking his spiritual fires, was Matthew Parker. He was licensed to preach in 1533, and became Anne Boleyn's chaplain in 1535. In 1544 he was made Master of Corpus Christi College, Cambridge, and Dean of Lincoln in 1552. He supported Lady Jane Grey 1553, and then lived in hiding until Mary I died in 1558. Elizabeth I made him Archbishop of Canterbury in December 1559. He revived Convocation and through it published the Thirty-Nine Articles. He was soon embroiled in his own Vestiarian Controversy, becoming increasingly anti-Puritan. He died in 1575. His library remains a glory of Corpus Christi, Cambridge.

He was renowned for his antiquarian learning: his catalogue of British 'antiquities' of 1572 and 1574[4] marks the revival of interest in Anglo-Saxon in these islands. He is even more well known for having successfully encouraged his fellow bishops to do what Cranmer failed to do twenty years before, and make their own Bible translation. Archbishop Parker approved of the Geneva Bible, particularly for reading at home. Queen Elizabeth had granted John Bodley an exclusive patent to print it for seven years, provided it be 'so ordered in the edition thereof as may seem expedient' to the bishops of Canterbury and London: Parker and Grindal recommended a renewal of Bodley's licence in 1565, but no more Geneva Bibles were printed in England until 1575.

A letter to Queen Elizabeth's Secretary, William Cecil, from Richard Cox, Bishop of Ely, survives, dated 19 January 1561. In part of this he presses for consideration of 'the translation of the Bible to be committed to mete [suitable] men and to be viewed over and amended'. He complains of frustration, having previously 'called upon it in both my masters' times'. Now, 'god be praised, ye have men able to do it thoroughly'. He is writing to Cecil 'because God hath appointed you a special instrument in the furtherance of his heavenly truth, under so gracious a sovereign'.[5]

The Archbishop successfully revived Cranmer's plan of parcelling the whole Bible among bishops selected in the hope of their scholarly adequacy, to produce a complete revision that, being carefully orthodox, could be acceptable to the authorities of the new Church of England. The letters of invitation have not survived, though from Parker's list over a dozen bishops who worked on the project, including himself, are known.[6] Strype, in his *Life of Parker*,[7] prints brief extracts of letters to him from five of the bishops engaged in the work: these tell little except that they were nervous about avoiding errors, including in the printing, 'that the adversaries can have no occasion to quarrel with it', as Strype records the Bishop of Worcester putting it. The latter's task had been the Books of Kings and Chronicles; he added that 'the common translation' [the Great Bible] 'followed Munster too much, who doubtless was a very negligent man in his doings, and often swerved very much from the Hebrew.'[8] The same bishop flattered Parker about the necessity of his work, commenting that the Bibles they had 'be not only false printed, but also give great offence to many, by reason of the depravity in reading'. The words 'offence' and 'depravity' should be taken as textual rather than political: the Great Bible has obvious weaknesses in its Hebrew translation, increasingly shown up by the use of Geneva. Similarly, the Bishop of Rochester, who was given the Psalms, felt able to be bold in his work of correction. 'As at the first Psalm, at the beginning, I turn the preterperfect tense in to the present tense: because the sense is too harsh in the preterperfect tense.'[9] That is no great thing: as Tyndale remarked in the first lines of the Prologue to his 1534 New Testament, in Hebrew 'the preterperfect tense and present tense is oft both one'.[10] The first Psalm begins in the present tense in the Vulgate and Luther, to name but two. The good bishop continues,

Where in the New Testament one piece of a Psalm is reported, I translate it in the Psalms according to the translation thereof in the New

Testament, for the avoiding of the offence that may rise to the people upon divers [different] translations.[11]

This, even to put it kindly, is folly. The 'offence' is imaginary. Moreover, did the bishop not know that quotations from the Psalms in the New Testament Psalms were not from Hebrew but from the Septuagint's Greek? In printing the Psalms, wrenching them away from the Hebrew – and only in certain places, which also happen to be especially significant – is a mad way to work.

A letter to Cecil dated 26 November 1566 has survived, from Archbishop Parker, by which time he is far advanced in the work. Commenting that he has 'distributed the bible in parts to diverse men' he writes to ask Cecil to join the team of revisers as 'one of the builders of this good work in Christ's church . . . I am desirous if you could spend so much leisure either morning or evening: we had one epistle of S. Paul or Peter, or James of [for] your perusing.'[12]

The bishops were remarkably speedy. Parker wrote again to Cecil on 22 September 1568 telling him that the work was done and printed. It awaited only 'some ornaments', which were the engraved title-page (attributed to Francis Hogenberg, 'bearing in the centre a rather pleasing portrait of the Queen'[13]) and large portraits of Leicester and Burghley (Cecil) (fig. 26).[14] All the names in Parker's final list of translators are of bishops or, for seven books, three cathedral officers (one prebend and two deans); and one contributing bishop, Llandaff, is missing – he finished Revelation for the Bishop of Lincoln.[15] Cecil does not appear: probably in inviting him the archbishop was oiling government wheels for final royal acceptance. Parker hoped to raise the level of responsibility by having each part of the work attributed, so in the printed volumes initials appear, not consistently, above or below the text. They generally support his list. There is, however, no mention in the list of the Psalms, nor of the Bishop of Rochester. The Psalms as printed are over the initials 'T.B.', identified by Aldis Wright as one of Parker's own chaplains, Thomas Bickley, afterwards Bishop of Chichester.[16] Probably not all the bishops did all the work attributed to them: having those around them who actually did know Hebrew or Greek, they could have perpetually found themselves too busy. Parker referred to the work having been done by 'my brethren the Bishops, with certain other learned men'.[17] The bishops of Norwich and Chichester were given the Apocrypha, and seem to have done very little, as the resulting volume prints the Great Bible version, taken from the Latin, unchanged.

Parker wrote again to Cecil on 5 October, with a bound copy for the Queen. He asked that she might license it, to be the only one commended for public reading in churches, 'to draw to one uniformity'.[18] That would be no great cost to most parishes, he wrote, and the sales would relieve the printer 'for his great charges sustained'. Choirs could continue to use the Great Bible Psalter, in that Bible's second edition of 1572, which had already established itself (was 'much multiplied') in the liturgies; if they wanted to change to the Bishops', they could. Further, Parker pleads that 'Jug only may have the preferment' of this version, 'for if any other should lurch[19] him to steal from him these copies [copyrights], he were a great loser in this first doing'.[20] In other words, please could the London printer Richard Jugge be officially guaranteed the monopoly. The excuse is that without it, he would lose his initial capital investment. It must be said that Jugge had made a handsome, if expensive, volume.

Officially, the work was done episcopally. It was also done quickly. Sadly, it was not done well.

The problem was three-fold. First was the lack of a great enough motivation. Tyndale's shining, overarching cause was bringing the Word to the ploughboy and the king and all in between, even at the cost of his life. Tyndale's scholarship, and his rhetorical craft, had to be of the very highest. The ploughboy deserved no less, for his soul's health depended on his understanding, read on the page for himself, or heard, of God's free promises. Coverdale shared the great cause in two great works, and with John Rogers put the Word in place for royal licence, if not exactly blessing.

From the first, the bishops had strongly opposed an English Bible. A Bishop of London, Tunstall, snubbed Tyndale: his successor, Stokesley, was the probable instigator of the translator's arrest and death. A Bishop of Norwich, Richard Nix, implored the help of King Henry VIII in 1530 in stamping out the New Testament in English. Tyndale understood the bishops well. In several places in his *Obedience of a Christian Man* he set out the New Testament qualities expected of such an 'overseer', (ἐπίσκοπος, *episkopos*), and observed one reality in sixteenth-century England as recorded in the everyday language of the people.[21]

Now Matthew Parker, who liked the Geneva Bible, was aware both of the unforeseen success of it, and of his brethren's alarm that the Great Bible was being deserted even for public reading in churches for a translation (Geneva) which, as Parker put it in his letter to the queen, 'had not been laboured in your realm' (which results in them 'having inspersed divers prejudicial notes which might have been also well spared').[22] This, aimed at the Geneva exiles, was a cheap shot. It raised the familiar Establishment bogey of things true to England being corrupted by foreigners: it simply bypassed the fact that the translations on which everyone depended had been made abroad – that, the work of Tyndale had been

done in Cologne, Worms and Antwerp; of Rogers, in Antwerp; and of
Coverdale originally in Antwerp; all by Englishmen. The Great Bible itself
had been made in Paris. It also disguises the real trouble, which is that the
English labourers in Geneva had done such a good job that the faults in
the Great Bible were increasingly visible. Matthew Parker proposed, and
completed, the Bishops' Bible as a means of blocking the advance of
Geneva into churches. It was not an aim to make the heart sing.

Nor to make the language sing. The second problem was that the
bishops, and above all Parker himself, scholar though he was, could not
write even reasonably pleasing English. One grieves for the absence of
Hugh Latimer for the whole enterprise; he could not write a dull English
sentence, and would have put some tunes into his colleagues' pens. Sentences in letters from the bishops quoted by Strype drop easily into Latin:
so Parker himself ends his letter to the queen – a letter about the 'Treasure', the 'Jewel' that is the Bible in English – with this wearisomely
tangled sentence, and its incongruous conclusion:

> I have been bold in the furniture with few words to express the incom-
> parable value of the Treasure among many things good profitable and
> beautiful, ye have in possession, yet this only necessary, whereof so to
> think, and so to believe, maketh your Majesty blessed, not only here in
> this your governance, but it shall advance your majesty to attain at the
> last the bliss everlasting, which after a long prosperous reign over us,
> Almighty God send you, as certainly he will, for cherishing that Jewel
> which he loveth best, of which is pronounced that Quomodocumque
> coelum et terra transibunt verbum tamen domini manebit in eternum.[23]

(It is both bizarre, and telling, that the archbishop, commending the
'Treasure', the 'Jewel,' of the Bible in English to his queen, climaxes his
words with his versions of Matthew 24:35, Mark 13:31 and Luke 21:33 –
in KJV, 'Heaven and earth shall pass away: but my words shall not pass
away' – in the Vulgate's Latin.)

The intention was to replace Geneva with something better. Examining
what they believed they were doing, but failed to do, shows the third
problem: that their Hebrew and Greek were not good enough. When they
made changes they were simply botching what already existed. Archbishop
Parker's stated aim was lofty, both in his proper regard for the excellence of
the only Bible ever royally authorised in Britain, the Great Bible, and in his
intention to remove its occasional faults. In his letter to the queen he wrote:

> Among divers observations which have been regarded in this recogni-
> tion one was, not to make it vary much from that translation which
> was commonly used by Public order, except where either the verity of

the Hebrew and Greek moved alteration, or where the text was by some negligence mutilated from the original.[24]

(In that sentence one can feel Parker thinking in Latin, an undertow pulling the English back, especially in the conclusion, 'negligence mutilated from the original'.) He sent to Cecil a copy of the 'Observations respected' by his brethren in the work. First was 'to follow the Common English Translation used in the churches and not to recede from it but where it varieth manifestly from the Hebrew or Greek original'. Second, to divide the text into 'sections and divisions' as Pagninus does, and 'for the verity of Hebrew to follow the said Pagninus and Munster specially, and generally others learned in the tongues'. Third, 'to make no bitter notes upon any text', nor 'to set down any determination in places of controversy' – a recipe for national blandness, as if the Bible were a document that could not stand argument. Worse follows: they are to mark unedifying bits which are not to be read in public. Genealogies are mentioned, but nothing is said otherwise about what is unedifying: the opening is as wide as a church door. Again, at their own instigation the bishops are to sanitise Old Testament words offending through 'lightness or obscenity'. Which words? Someone might be offended by 'the blessed word Mesopotamia', as later legend has it. Though the Archbishop received the finished revisions, and obviously had general oversight, there is no mention anywhere of editorial control, of this or of anything, beyond the 'Observations' as sent to Cecil.

Parker himself did more than any other reviser. He worked on Genesis and Exodus, Matthew and Mark, and, the toughest assignment, all the epistles of Paul except 1 Corinthians, but including Hebrews. In the extensive preliminary material (twenty-six leaves) he prepared the one-page 'sum of the whole Scripture'; the eleven-page Tables of Christ's line; the two-page Arguments of the Scriptures; other tables and calendars; and the reprinting, in Black Letter, of Cranmer's Preface to the second Great Bible, 1540. He himself wrote a six-page Preface to the whole Bible, and a one-page Preface to the New Testament on the verso of the separate title. Working with the experienced Richard Jugge, he made a large volume (it is an inch taller than the Great Bible), lavish in its ornaments in initial letters, fresh title-pages with portraits, 124 distinct woodblock illustrations, and four maps, three of them taken from the 1560 Geneva Bible.

The marginal notes, much less frequent than in Geneva, are Protestant. In exerting themselves to abstain from 'bitter notes', however, they habitually deteriorate into ineptitude (a sentence of which the Latinity would no doubt have pleased Matthew Parker). Those words, 'bitter notes', must mean remarks against the pope and his practices, which many later writers, never having studied copies of these Bibles, have taken from this and other comments, and have quite wrongly assumed to be thick on the page of Geneva Bibles. Parker himself took over Geneva notes (not all) in the Pauline epistles. One note, to Psalm 45:9, caught the eye of T. H. Darlow and H. F. Moule in making their *Historical Catalogue of Printed Bibles* in 1903. They called it 'curious'. Geneva Bibles in particular in their notes can produce sudden surprising windows into a larger world: it is strange to see this in Bishops':

> Ophir is thought to be the island in the west coast, of late found by Christopher Columbo: from whence at this day is brought most fine gold.[25]

The Geneva verse numbers are printed here at the side, with the old division-letters, A, B, C and so on as well. The pages look lavish. Two tall columns of text, with chapter contents, and marginal notes in Black Letter, are under page headlines and marginal references in roman. Anticipating heavier use, the New Testament was printed on heavier paper. There is no sixteenth-century English Bible quite so rich, even sumptuous, as this first 1568 Bishops' Bible.

Richard Jugge did well out of his monopoly. In the nine years before his death in 1577 he reprinted the Bishops' Bible in various forms, quarto as well as folio, a dozen times. Walsingham then ensured that his royal patent, which meant the monopoly, went to Christopher Barker (whose house held it for nearly a hundred years). Barker reprinted Bishops' twenty times before 1611, and four times after that, the last being in 1616.

The second folio edition of 1572 showed three interesting changes: first, to the New Testament text, which incorporated some scholarly revisions suggested by Giles Lawrence, Professor of Greek at Oxford. The document setting these out has not survived, though some details were printed by Strype in his Life of Parker.[26] Westcott watches him, in Ephesians 4 as an example, intelligently using, or rejecting, the Geneva readings, but also making his own changes. None of these, however, stir the blood. Ephesians 4:7 begins in the Great Bible 'Unto every one of us is given . . .': Lawrence, following Geneva, changed it to 'But unto every one of us is given . . .'. Westcott's remark about Ephesians that 'the reviser who corrected it [i.e. Lawrence] was not deficient in originality and vigorous scholarship' does not at that point, and many similar, make the rafters ring with hearty agreement.[27] Yet such minutiae, especially in the better understanding of Greek particles, and prepositions, make a fine network of greater accuracy over the whole. Lawrence gave us, through their adoption in KJV, 'the middle wall of partition' at Ephesians 2:14, and 'less than the least of all saints' at Ephesians 3:8. All but two of Bishops' Bibles after this follow all these readings.

Second, the Psalter appeared in two versions, printed side by side: first, in Black Letter, *The translation used in common prayer*, from the Great Bible – the version incorporated in the Prayer Book for many centuries; and parallel to it, in roman type, *The translation after the Hebrews*, the rather hopeful title given to the original Bishops' version. Third, there are changes to the placing of the new illustrations, and many of the initial letters show, rather startlingly, scenes from Ovid's *Metamorphoses*: that beginning the Epistle to the Hebrews is in a printing tradition of splendid inappropriateness, showing Leda and the swan.[28]

How does the work of Matthew Parker himself emerge from modern scrutiny? Busy in his two Books of Moses, he can be watched making alterations to about half the verses. They do not appear to be valuable. As Wesctott noted (admitting his own hesitation, as he could not bring himself to study all the Bishops' Old Testament),

> There is but little to recommend the original renderings in the Bishops' Bible in the Old Testament. As a general rule they appear to be arbitrary and at variance with the exact sense of the Hebrew text.[29]

The Bishops' New Testament work draws a little more commendation, Parker having remained closer to Geneva. Perhaps it was the haste to print, to do something political about the encroaching Geneva, that prevented Parker taking more care over every part, and particularly the Old Testament prophets. That the important 'Suffering Servant' passage in Isaiah 54 could go to press as it was, with, to take an example at random, verse 8 beginning, 'He was had away from prison: his cause not heard and without judgement. Whose generation yet who may number?' suggests something unfinished. Or was Parker deaf to any kind of skill with words? The second verse of Psalm 19 is the clumsy 'A day occasioneth talk thereof unto a day: and a night teacheth knowledge unto a night.' The Hebraist Hugh Broughton (possibly the best in Britain at the end of the sixteenth century) remarked of it: 'Our Bishops' Bible might well give place to the Alkoran, pestered with lies.'[30] The opening of Psalm 23 in Geneva, memorable today for it being taken over almost verbatim into KJV, is

> The Lord *is* my shepherd, I shall not want.
> He maketh me to rest in green pasture, *and* leadeth me by the still waters.

In the Bishops' this has been padded out to:

God is my shepherd, therefore I can lack nothing: He will cause me to
repose myself in pasture full of grass, and he will lead me unto calm
waters.

As the literary scholar and Hebraist Gerald Hammond remarks, 'Words
and more words is the great belief of this translator, born, no doubt, out
of his belief in what constitutes good English style.'[31] After giving more
examples of the Bishops' flatulent enlargement of the English, and mis-
representation of the Hebrew, Professor Hammond writes:

> For the most part the Bishops' Bible is either a lazy and ill-informed
> collection of what had gone before, or, in its orginal parts, the work of
> third-rate scholars and second-rate writers. In no way could it hold
> comparison with the Geneva Bible.[32]

The Bishops' New Testament did one or two things reasonably. The Old
Testament was uniformly bad. Queen Elizabeth did not do what her Archbishop requested, and acknowledge the Bishops' Bible as the standard
English church text. This may have been from rooted policy, to avoid
favour in any direction. It may have also been that it was not good enough.
The Bishops' Bible was always a lavish production, as a piece of book
making, even in smaller size. There were fourteen editions up to Parker's
death in 1575, and a further twenty-two to 1611. Even so, there is an air
of hesitancy. Parker asked if the Queen could license it for the only one
to be read in churches in order 'to draw to one uniformity'; but, hardly
a Hugh Latimer-style call with new religious concern, he asked this largely
in order to recompense the printer. The province of Canterbury in 1571
laid down that every archbishop and bishop was to have the book in his
own house, and

> deans were to see that it was bought and placed in their cathedrals in
> order that vicars, minor canons, the servants of the church, strangers
> and wayfarers might read and hear it, and were also to buy it for their
> own households . . . churchwardens are enjoined to see that a copy of
> the new edition is placed in every church . . .

with the damning proviso, 'if it can be done conveniently'.[33]
    The list of fourteen editions before Parker's death conceals an interest-
ing insight. Though he and the Bishop of London, Grindal, as mentioned
above, had recommended that John Bodley's exclusive privilege for printing the Geneva Bible for another twelve years be extended from 1565,
even though the bishops were putting out a new Bible for church use,
on the grounds that diversity is healthy, Parker and Grindal carefully kept
a proviso of their approval in fact, which they withheld. No Geneva Bibles

were printed in England in the ten years until Parker's death in May 1575 (when they instantly began being printed again in volume) allowing the Bishops' a clear run at the field. A. W. Pollard wrote:

> It is impossible, therefore, to avoid the conviction that to the very end of his life Parker used his control over the Stationers' Company to prevent the Geneva version being printed in England, and also to secure for Jugge the monopoly of printing the Bishops' Bible . . . It seems certain that the Archbishop cared little for providing Bibles for private reading. He saw and met the need of suitable editions for the service of the church, but . . . he did not 'trust the people' with cheap editions of the Bible, and his lack of confidence sealed the fate of the Bishops' Bible.[34]

Perhaps this would not have mattered too much for readings in church while everyone had a Geneva at home. But the aim over the next fifty years was, for political reasons, to oppose Geneva, even as it grew in force and influence, and eventually to kill it outright. This aim was successful. The replacement from 1611 of the remarkable, accurate, informative, forward-looking Geneva even at the time of its greatest growth and power, with the backward-looking, increasingly Latinist, often baldly unhelpful KJV is one of the tragedies of our culture – the exact reverse of what has been said for so long. One must regret that King James in 1605 gave each member of his panels of revisers this Bishops' Bible (in the second, 1572 folio edition, with small New Testament revisions) as their base text.

Chapter 20

LAURENCE TOMSON
AND THE REVISION OF
THE GENEVA NEW TESTAMENT, 1576

REVELATION

The last book in the Bible, and the last to be written, towards the end of the first century, is the Apocalypse. Its title is a Greek word meaning uncovering, revealing: so the book is Revelation. What exactly is being uncovered is not easy to work out, and over the centuries before the Reformation, interest came and went. The book is in a late Jewish tradition, like the Book of Daniel or the thirteenth chapter of Mark's Gospel. Its remarkable language, some familiar from later Hebrew prophecy, is of special divine messages and angels, with imagery of jewels, trumpets and writings, all on a cosmic scale. Its message seems to include comfort for Christians who are suffering persecution at some historical moment, with the promise of a quite new reign of God that is about to come.

The Church had always been uneasy about that book, often doubting whether it was authentic enough (as one of a group of Christian apocalypses from the first and second centuries) to be included in the New Testament canon. In the centuries before the Reformation, sometimes a closer relation between ideas of prophecy and history led to it being understood by sectarian groups (Hussites, some Wycliffites) as meshing closely with the revelation of the Church of Rome as their persecutor, comforted by the promise of a completely new beginning under God's plan for them.

On the whole, however, no one in the later Middle Ages did more than think of it as a puzzling moral allegory. Luther at first dismissed it; Calvin declined to comment on it. Erasmus's position was of doubting its authenticity. Acts and Revelation are the only books in Tyndale's 1534 New Testament without prologues, and, though he prints vivid woodcuts, his marginal notes to Revelation are so minimal as effectively not to exist.

In 1534, for his first complete German Bible, Luther revised his Preface to the Apocalypse, and his views of it. He was prepared to see its prophecies as grounded in history, referring to specific events in the Church before Constantine. He then came to feel that the prophecies could be seen as referring to his own time. The positions were complicated by increasing understanding of the word 'Antichrist' to refer to the pope, and one or more specific popes. The word does not occur in Revelation, but appears four times in the short Epistles of John (1 John 2:18,22; 4:3; 2 John 7) meaning a spiritual enemy. Tyndale, in both 1526 and 1534, translated it as 'antichrist' with a lower-case 'a', and made no comment. Elsewhere in his writing, even before Luther he was eager to see Antichrist, now with an upper case A, as the pope, backed by the systems of the Church, though he was not specific to a historical period, and he was not interested in ideas of an imminent end to world history. 'Antichrist', he wrote, typically, 'is not an outward thing'.[1]

Understanding of the Apocalypse in England changed in the 1540s with the publication of a book, probably in 1545, by John Bale, later Bishop of Ossory in Ireland, entitled *The Image of Both Churches*.[2] Ten years before, Bale had been employed by Thomas Cromwell. For Cromwell's household he wrote Protestant plays, the most famous of which, *King John*, included, as noted above, dramatising some paragraphs of Tyndale's *The Obedience of a Christian Man* of 1528.[3] That play was an influence on Shakespeare's *King John*. When Cromwell fell in 1540, Bale went into exile in Europe: he returned having, among other things, absorbed continental thinking about the Apocalypse. He had a great influence on English thought. *The Image of Both Churches* is a commentary on Revelation. The two churches are those of the spirit and the flesh, the latter seen specifically as the Roman church under the pope, developing the contrast between Jesus in his humble poverty and the pope in his enormous wealth. English reformers continued to understand Revelation, and 'antichrist', as meaning primarily spiritual things, a guide to doctrine: the central problem for reformers presented by a book such as Revelation was that of distinguishing between true and false images.[4] There came in from the Continent through Bale, however, a new understanding as well, now charting periods of suffering and persecution in history, and of the apparent fulfilment of the prophecies of Revelation, becoming more specific as the centuries pass, and pointing towards a future consummation. Bale's central section told of English martyrs from the beginnings of Lollardy until the 1540s.

When John Bale came back from exile in 1547, he took lodgings in London. Sharing the house was John Foxe, who became a lifelong friend. One can easily see the Apocalyptic roots of Foxe's great and developing work, begun when both men were exiles at the time of Queen Mary. The first, 1563, version of Foxe's *Acts and Monuments* in English (it had been started in Strasbourg in Latin) began the story in the year AD 1000. That was the year in which he, following Bale, had found that the Book of Revelation had announced as the year Satan was loosed from the pit, proved by 'the coming in of Mahomet', and when Sylvester II was Pope.

Biblical prophecies and English history intertwined to produce a large literature, in English, written in England, which was ignored for many centuries, indeed until the late twentieth century. 'Ignored' is correct. The standard view in histories of English literature was that the period before the publication in 1579 of Spenser's *The Shepherd's Calendar* was a 'dark age' of Tudor literature. True, Spenser's collection of poems was important; but it has been quite wrong to treat it as a new dawn, heralding the golden day after the darkness of the Reformation had snuffed out the Renaissance in England. The Protestant reformers, it was earlier said, supplanted courtly love poetry with prosaic metrical Psalms. C. S. Lewis did not help by labelling the half-century before Spenser and Sidney the 'Drab Age'.[5] Lewis seemed deaf to, or eager to ignore, a great deal of English writing between Tyndale and Spenser. 'Drab' could mean 'workaday' as in working-clothes: but there is no doubt that the principal meaning has always been dull, boringly ordinary (even, for the noun, of course, low and 'common', as in *Macbeth*'s witches' 'ditch-delivered of a drab'). There was an explosion of English writing and publication of all kinds, in the years after Edward VI came to the throne in 1547. Already by 1548 John Bale was able to sum up a mass of British literature (admittedly, going back eight hundred years to Bede) in his *Illustrium maioris Britanniae scriptorum, summarium.*[6] This literature still needs exploration, particularly in the sixteenth- and seventeenth-century work by women writers and Dissenters, and the heavy dependence on English Bibles, and, after 1560, on the Geneva Bible.[7]

The triumph of this Bible can be seen in its frequent use by so many Elizabethan and Jacobean writers, including Shakespeare, to whom I shall return. Like our English language, the Geneva Bible laid a French influence over a Germanic base. Tyndale was to some extent a Lutheran, though progressively less. The Geneva translators were necessarily Calvinist – though in no way to offend most Elizabethan eyes. Their New Testament marginal notes, it might be said, were so far from being controversial as to be – God save the mark! – boring. That changed abruptly with Laurence Tomson of Magdalen College, Oxford.

LAURENCE TOMSON[8]

Born in Northamptonshire in 1539, he entered Magdalen as a demy in either 1553 or 1556. He was BA in 1559, MA in 1564. Already a Fellow from 1559, he was Bursar of Magdalen from January to May of 1565, when he was given leave to travel abroad for study until December, leave which was extended until July 1567. It is not known for certain where he went, though he certainly accompanied Sir Thomas Hoby on his embassy to France in 1566. He resigned his Magdalen Fellowship in 1569. Thereafter, Tomson's name is frequent in State Papers both Domestic and Foreign. He seems to have become expert in matters French and Scottish. In 1579, for example, while working for Walsingham, he intercepted letters from a papal agent to Mary Queen of Scots which among other things detailed the arrangements for invasion of England, with the aim of putting Mary on the throne, depriving Elizabeth both of her throne and her life. Tomson was by then sufficiently cosmopolitan to be able to be of real use to Walsingham. One can also see his political involvement in the Presbyterian cause. He seems to have been close to the unknown author, or authors, of the Marprelate Tracts written in 1588 and 1589, the seven satirical anti-Establishment pamphlets which so entertained Elizabethan readers with their wit.[9]

Tomson was MP for Weymouth and Melcome Regis, and then for Downton, with heavy Parliamentary involvements. Possibly never quite at the centre, he was nevertheless active at home as well as abroad. The President of Magdalen all this time, from 1561 to his death in 1589, was Laurence Humphrey. Humphrey is well known as a reformed and reforming President: in the domestic Magdalen controversies over vestments and ornaments, and over expulsions and appointments, in those three decades, Laurence Tomson was consulted, as a Fellow and ex-Fellow who kept closely in touch, for his voice of wisdom. Sane and wise letters have survived which show a man treated with respect and affection. His later neglect by Magdalen may be associated with the vocabulary of the Magdalen records, listing Fellows as 'on the Church side' or 'of the Puritan faction'. Tomson died in 1608. Anthony à Wood prints his epitaph, which states that he travelled in Sweden, Russia, Denmark, Germany, Italy and France; was conversant with twelve languages; was famous for his knowledge of theology, of both civil and municipal law, and of all the more refined literature; was distinguished for his public lectures on the Hebrew language at Geneva; and well known for an accurate translation of the New Testament.[10] Extravagant though this is (and it is not all), it is none of it unlikely. There is to date a lack of hard evidence about many of his travels, but it seems likely that he was in Geneva in 1565, a date to be kept in mind. No correspondence between Beza and Tomson has survived, and Beza does not mention Tomson, but since Beza knew most of the leading English scholars personally, it is difficult to imagine that they did not meet.

TOMSON'S GENEVA NEW TESTAMENT REVISION

That meeting is especially likely in view of Tomson's revision of the Geneva English New Testament, based on Beza's important Latin edition of 1565, which also incorporated his (Beza's) latest edition of the Greek New Testament. The notes to the English 1557 and 1560 Geneva versions were completely replaced, and there are many small changes to the text in the light of Beza's Latin, and Greek, readings. Tomson's new edition was published in 1576, and then incorporated into the standard Geneva Bible from 1587, so that from that date on, all Geneva Bibles are either 'Geneva' or, for about half the editions, 'Geneva-Tomson' (and that is not the end of the story).[11] Though some work has been done on the influence of the Geneva Bible on writers like Shakespeare, and as until recently the only facsimile available has been of the 1560 edition, the real interest of Shakespeare in a later Geneva Bible has been obscured. He would have found much to stimulate him, even delight him, in the margins of Tomson's New Testament. Tomson directly translated Beza's short notes, and printed them in his New Testament, as they were in Beza's, in neat small roman. But he also printed in italics in his margins other notes, of his own making, more frequent and longer, which are often appealing. Indeed, a browse through the italic notes of a Geneva-Tomson can sometimes even enchant.

First, he faithfully translates Beza's roman, and the additional italic, notes. At Romans 12:11, 'fervent in spirit, serving the Lord', Beza's better Greek text had added the last three words (they are not in Tyndale). The edition of Beza he is using was that prepared by L'Oiseleur, as he states on his title-page, and L'Oiseleur had put together the notes from Beza and from Joachim Camerarius. L'Oiseleur had here *Recte haec clausula addita, quae distinguit officia Christiana ab officiis Philosophicis.* Tomson in his italics dutifully translates 'This piece is well put in, for it maketh difference between Christian doctrine and Philosophical duties.' Faithful enough, but with some flair for what comes over in English.

Or at Matthew 21:7, a notorious difficulty, where the English text (Tyndale, faithful to the Greek) has 'And brought the ass and the colt, and put on them their clothes, and set him thereon', producing an unhappy picture of the would-be triumphant Jesus trying to ride two animals of different sizes at once. L'Oiseleur has *vestimenta, non assinam,* and Tomson has in his italics 'Upon their garments, not upon the ass and the colt'.

(The 1560 Geneva had not made it clearer with 'He rid on the foal and the dam went by.')

At Luke 20:47, the English text (Tyndale's) has 'which devour widows' houses'. L'Oiseleur has *Metonymia.i.Bona atque rem.* Tomson's italics are 'This is spoken by the figure Metonymy, houses for the goods and substance'.

There is a certain pleasing freedom about what Tomson is doing. Consider Jesus' 'pearls before swine' remark at Matthew 7:6. The 1560 Geneva margin has here: 'Declare not the Gospel to the wicked contemners of God whom thou seest left to themselves forsaken.' That is neither original nor interesting. Beza's 1565 Latin text says the same, in Latin. Tomson faithfully translates it afresh, and prints it in small roman. But then in italic he has

> A pearl hath his name among the Grecians, for the orient brightness that is in it, and a pearl was in ancient time in great estimation among the Latins: for a pearl that Cleopatra had, was valued at 250,000 crowns: and the word is now borrowed from that, to signify the most precious heavenly doctrine.

That is fine. 'His name among the Grecians' is good enough, but the phrase 'for the orient brightness that is in it' sings with suggestion, and indeed beauty, as appropriate for the Grecians. The Latins characteristically put a money-value on it, though the amount is fabulous. It may be unexpected to find in what has popularly been understood a Geneva Bible to be (thick, black, dour, utterly Calvinist to the point of revulsion) gossip about Cleopatra. L'Oiseleur's Latin started Tomson off, with

> *Margarites dicitur Graecis a nitore splendente, Latinis unio. In summo fuit olim pretio, nam unio Cleopatrae aestima fuit ducentis quinquaginto millibus coronatorum . . .*

but *nitore splendente* means 'shining brightness'. Tomson's 'orient' is an English word long associated with exceptionally brilliant pearls, as well as primarily the East. It is well used.

In Mark 15, at the story of the Gadarene swine, where neither the 1560 Geneva nor Beza has any note at all, Tomson has, in italics,

> Strabo in the 16th book saith that in Gadaris there is a standing pool of very naughty water, which if beasts taste so, they shed their hair, nails or hooves and horns.

Even allowing for a shift in meaning of 'naughty' from 'of naught', that is still good; for *stagnum aquae pessimae* 'a standing pool of very naughty water' makes a good sound as well as communicating more strongly.

Laurence Tomson had some gift for English expressiveness. No one has yet begun to explore his marginal notes, especially the L'Oiseleur italics, and especially with a view to their suggestiveness. It is a study that should be made, for Geneva-Tomsons were widely used from 1576 onward, well into the following century, and certainly by Shakespeare. Many of the almost one thousand biblical references in Shakespeare come from the Geneva text.[12] Geneva has, at Jeremiah 13:23, instead of the well-known KJV 'Can the Ethiopian change his skin, or the leopard his spots?', the words 'Can the black Moor change his skin?': immediately *Othello* comes into view. It is likely that Shakespeare used a Geneva-Tomson.

On Colossians 1:16, a difficult verse about all things created, where Geneva 1560 has no note at all, Tomson's italics has:

> He setteth forth the Angels with glorious names, that by the comparison of most excellent spirits, we may understand how far passing the excellency of Christ is, in whom only we have to content ourselves, and let go all Angels.

Tomson is indeed a man with a gift for phrases: where L'Oiseleur's Latin is *Angelis nobis est acquiescendum*, the succinctness of Tomson's 'and let go all Angels' is excellent. Like Tyndale, Tomson is determined to be clear. For Matthew 5:13, he has 'And so are fools in the latin tongue called saltless, as you would say, men that have no salt, or savour and taste in them.'

One can watch Tomson breaking out on his own. On Matthew 5:8. 'blessed are the pure in heart', he leaves L'Oiseleur far behind, with

> Fitly is this word Pure, joined with the heart, for as a bright and shining resemblance or image may be seen plainly in a clear and pure looking glass, even so doth the face (as it were) of the everlasting God, shine forth and clearly appear in a pure heart.

In the preliminary matter, called by Tomson 'The printer to the diligent reader', he explains (this is not in 1560) how to use the notes in relation to the text in admirable plain style:

> Lastly, the notes which go by the order of the letters of the alphabet placed in the text, with the like answering them in the margin [these are the italicised notes; the roman ones from Beza are numbered] serve to expound and lighten the dark words and phrases immediately following them.

It is reassuring to be addressed in such plain style, and something like enthusiasm comes through.

Theologically, Tomson's notes are more filled out, but they clearly come from the same stable as the 1557 and 1560 Geneva New Testaments: as the notes in roman type follow Beza, that is to be expected. The italic notes, Tomson's own, vary in length from a single word to half a column – as, for example, at Luke 7:39, on Christ's forgiveness of the woman, 'which was a sinner', who brought ointment: Tomson makes the point that, summarised, this is not a proof text for the merit of works. In Paul's Epistles Tomson can be watched expanding Beza – the mixture in small-print annotation can take up nearly half the page in Romans 8 and 9, for example. At Romans 3:24, 'And [all] are justified freely by his grace, through the redemption that is in Christ Jesus,' from Beza comes the following, keyed to the words 'freely':

> An argument to prove this conclusion, that we are justified by faith without works, taken from the end of justification. The end of justification is the glory of God alone: therefore we are justified by faith without works: for if we were justified either by our own works only, or partly by faith, and partly by works, the glory of this justification should not be wholly given to God.

The next note is Tomson's, keyed to verse 27, 'By what Law of works?'

> *By what doctrine? now the doctrine of works hath this condition joined with it, if thou doest: and the doctrine of faith hath this condition, if thou believest.*

David Alexander observes that 'Tomson's analysis of the doctrine [of free election] consumes nearly half of the entire page at Rom 9.'[13] True enough: but the notes are all in small roman type, and thus from Beza, with hardly a phrase from Tomson himself. Alexander's valuable seventh chapter, 'The doctrine of the [Geneva] marginal notes',[14] shows where 'Tomson' (as opposed to Laurence Tomson being original) differs from the New Testaments of 1557 or 1560. The honest note to 'Angels' at 1 Corinthians 11:10, 'What this meaneth, I do not yet understand', is in 'Tomson', from Beza. The notes to 'Tomson' are strongest on the doctrines of the Church and the Sacraments. At Luke 5:27, the call of the publican, Levi, a Beza note is 'The Church is a company of sinners through the grace of Christ repentant, which banquet with him, to the great offence of the proud and envious worldlings.' The annotations on the matters of the Church show their origins in the Geneva congregations, with special attention to the tough qualities needed in a minister, unwavering of purpose and looking for 'all manner of reproaches' (at John 16:1); to the primitive Church using laying-on of hands (Acts 6:6); and, just before (Acts 6:3), the qualities of deacons, 'of their learning and manners of life'. The Sacraments are 'signs' at Luke 22:5, and at John 6:48, 'The true use of Sacraments is to ascend from them to the thing itself, that is to Christ.' Ceremonies have a radically new character since the coming of Christ: 'charity is the rule of all ceremonies' (Luke 6:6).

Tomson's Geneva is packed with notes, in roman and in italic, running across the bottom of the page in most of Paul's epistles. With some curiosity, one turns to Revelation – to meet a blank. Tomson, in this book alone, has hardly any notes at all. Turning to Beza, we find that on Revelation he has none whatsoever. It is the same shock that comes from going through Erasmus's *Paraphrases of the New Testament* with considerable enjoyment, and coming to the end of the Epistle to the Hebrews (the last New Testament book but one in Erasmus's order) and turning the page and finding it is the end of the book. Erasmus did not write about Revelation.

Now, the 1560 Geneva Bible begins its full annotation of Revelation with a 350-word Preface generally suggesting that it is about the overthrow of Antichrist, and then in the margin making occasional heavy swipes at the pope – any pope. Thus at Revelation 9:1, where the fifth angel blew and 'I saw a star fall from heaven unto the earth. And to him was given the key of the bottomless pit', 1560 has in the margin 'This authority chiefly is committed to the pope, in sign whereof he beareth the keys in his arms' (that is, heraldic arms). Tomson has (one of only two notes in the entire chapter) 'By the bottomless pit, he means the deepest darkness of hell.' That is not informative. Tomson's Preface to Revelation is at first sight encouragingly long, about fifteen hundred words: but it is all an essay defending the canonicity of Revelation, and no more.

What has happened? Tomson is following his sources: and one feels the nervousness about the Apocalypse. Tomson was a moderate man – a Fellow of Magdalen. He was not going to get caught up in the stuff from John Bale in his *Image of Both Churches* of thirty years before and continuing powerful. At this point (Rev. 9:1) in the *Image*, Bale paraphrases Revelation, having given Tyndale's text,

> They [that is, the Church authorities] slew King Edward [Edward the Second], poisoned King John and famished King Richard the Second. By their own history, they burned Sir Roger Acton Knight, Sir John Oldcastle the Lord Cobham, and Sir Reginald Pecock Bishop of Chichester they imprisoned to death, besides an infinite number of poor simple souls, no lawful cause known . . .[15]

This is prophecy with a bite, English history making the words of the Book of Revelation come true.

Though it is not true, as some Shakespeare scholars tell each other, that John Bale wrote the margins in the Geneva Bible,[16] the 1560 Geneva New Testament and Bale do have in common a view of history fulfilling prophecy, a view closely tied with the national history of the British (supported by the popularity of Foxe's *Acts and Monuments*). Though in its final form Foxe's huge book begins with the Apostles and goes on to England in the 1580s, it does not present England as 'the elect nation', as an influential book has made out.[17] Nevertheless, English history and the Apocalyptic divine plan came to be very closely linked, as is shown by Book One of Spenser's *Faerie Queene* (1590). The subject of this vast and beautiful unfinished poem is the spiritual, moral, emotional and social life of man (see chapter 23 below). The first book, 'Of Holiness', removes that virtue from abstraction and gives to its hero the Red Cross Knight physical, emotional and intellectual experiences. It is, for all Spenser's great learning, a rich and grounded existentialism. The narrative and thematic centres of Book One – to some extent of the whole poem – are in Cantos 8 and 11. In the first, The Red Cross Knight fights and slays the Giant Orgoglio, watched and supported by Una, 'the royal Virgin' (both Elizabeth 1 and the One English Church), and he strips Duessa to reveal her ugliness – the double-dealing Roman Church, the glorious outer garments concealing foulness. In the fight with Orgoglio, the individual sinner is rescued by heavenly grace: the unfaithful man is brought from spiritual whoredom: Elizabeth the First rescues England from captivity to the Church of Rome: and – in a similar fight with the Dragon in Canto 11 – the tree and the well which rescue the Red Cross Knight are both the Tree of Eden and the well of Christ's doctrine. English religious history is in the largest divine frame, and the Book of Revelation, pointing forward as well as back, is a main source.

Something else happened. Some of John Bale's historical ideas were incorporated into the revised notes of the last edition of Matthew's Bible in 1551. The *Paraphrase* on Revelation that Erasmus omitted to write was supplied in 1549 by Leo Juda, and Englished by Edward Allen in later editions of volume two of the *Paraphrases*. These, in précis form, got into the brief notes at the end of each chapter of Revelation in Matthew's, then into the notes of Richard Jugge's revised edition of Tyndale in 1552 (Jugge was the Queen's Printer, with a sharply defended monopoly). The message carried forward, with Foxe's work, is that the times are so hideous that they must be the biblical end.

Laurence Tomson's restraint is remarkable, given so strong a reformers' reading of the times. His caution, however, left a vacuum which had to be filled. What happened next happened well within Tomson's lifetime, could not have happened without his knowledge, and might well have had his co-operation. The story will continue in chapter 22 below.

Chapter 21

THE RHEIMS NEW TESTAMENT, 1582

LACKING EASILY ACCESSIBLE PRIESTS, English Catholics in the last years of Elizabeth's reign needed books, particularly of devotion. They were provided, in English, in not-inconsiderable numbers: between 1570 and 1601 about seventy titles, of meditations, hagiographies, books of prayer and catechisms.[1] It can be argued that the polemical literature from the Catholic exiles and recusants, particularly writings by Robert Persons, William Allen, Henry Garnett, Edmund Campion and Robert Southwell, in its liveliness and wit influenced the characteristic English literary (and especially dramatic) style: Harvey, Nashe and Greene acknowledged as much. Richard Steele in his *Tatler* number 230 in late 1710, a periodical which had become the arbiter of taste, commended the style of Robert Persons.[2]

A special need was for an English vernacular Bible which was acceptable to Catholics, as, of what had been so far produced, none was. Such a volume would give priests, Jesuits secretly in England, and their flocks, some hope of correcting the heretics around them who knew their English Bibles inside out. It would also act as a prophylactic against the reading of the heretical versions.

The English Roman Catholic College at Rheims (part of the University of Douai founded by Philip II of Spain in 1562) worked on a New Testament, first printed in 1582, and the whole Bible on their return to Douai, in 1610. This Rheims New Testament stood not quite outside the English tradition, by now a great one, of Protestant Bibles made from the original Greek and Hebrew, in an English which, thanks largely to 'the heretic' Tyndale, was accurate but stood close to common speech.

Gregory Martin began his Catholic version in 1578. From 'on or about March 16', he translated into English – from the Vulgate – two chapters a day. They were then reviewed by William, (afterwards Cardinal) Allen, the first President of the college, and Richard Bristow. Allen has been described as 'best known as an active participator in the political intrigues of his day. He was created a Cardinal by Pope Sixtus V in 1587, and was promised the appointment of Legate with the mission of reconciling

England to the pope, in case the Spanish Armada should prove successful.'[3] The work took four years.[4] In his long Preface, Martin explains his principles. The appearance of an English Bible, required by circumstances, does not imply that Scripture must be available in the mother tongue. He translates from the Vulgate, which possesses ecclesiastical authority and is the least partial text, 'truer than the vulgar Greek itself'. He follows the Vulgate precisely, making the Latin into an English which reflects it, even at the risk of causing difficulty.

The title-page reads:

The New testament of Jesus Christ, translated faithfully into English, out of the authentical Latin, according to the best corrected copies of the same, diligently compared with the Greek and other editions in divers languages: With Arguments of books and chapters, Annotations, and other necessary helps, for the better understanding of the text, and specially for the discovery of the Corruptions of divers late translations, and for clearing the Controversies in religion, of these days.

There follows, still on the title-page, a quotation from Psalm 118 in Latin, translated as 'Give me understanding'; followed by a Latin quotation from 'S.Aug.tract.2.in Epist.Ioan'.

Omnia quae leguntur . . . That is, All things that are read in holy Scriptures, we must hear with great attention, to our instruction and salvation: but those things specially must be commended to memory, which make most against Heretics: whose deceits cease not to circumvent and beguile all the weaker sort and the more negligent persons.

WHO SHOULD READ

On the verso of the title-page, at the foot, after 'The Censure and Approbation', is another quotation from St Augustine, 'lib.l.c.3. de Serm. Do. in monte . . .', translated as

We must come to the understanding of Scripture through poverty of spirit: where a man must show himself meek-minded, lest by stubborn contentions, he become incapable and unapt to be taught [*indocilis reddatur*].

In looking for poverty of spirit, meekness and docility, this volume has the opposite intention of the Geneva Bible.

A closer look at this Preface reveals, even where he is not translating, the Latin base of Father Martin's English. Writers of prefaces in the

sixteenth century usually allowed themselves a more relaxed approach;
where needed, developing ideas at some length. Gregory Martin's sentences are very long, full of Latin subordination:

> Which translation we do not for all that publish, upon erroneous
> opinion of necessity, that the holy Scriptures should always be in our
> mother tongue, or that they ought, or were ordained by God, to be
> read indifferently of all, or could be easily understood of everyone that
> readeth or heareth them in a known language: or that they were not
> often through man's malice or infirmity, pernicious and much hurtful
> to many: or that we generally and absolutely deemed it more conve-
> nient in it self, & more agreeable to God's word and honour or edifi-
> cation of the faithful, to have them turned into vulgar tongues, than
> to be kept & studied only in the ecclesiastical learned languages: not
> for these nor any such like causes do we translate this sacred book, but
> upon special consideration of the present time, state, and condition of
> our country, unto which, diverse things are either necessary, or prof-
> itable or medicinable now, that otherwise in the peace of the Church
> were neither much requisite, nor perchance wholly tolerable . . .

Two further passages merit quotation, even at length:

> [holy Church and the governors] have neither of old nor of late, ever
> wholly condemned all vulgar versions of Scripture, nor have at any time
> generally forbidden the faithful to read the same . . .

What comes next, in long sentences, is difficult to follow, but the gist
seems to have its heart at

> the provincial Constitutions of Thomas Arundel Archbishop of Canter-
> bury, in a council holden at Oxford . . . where strait [narrow] provision
> was made, that no heretical version set forth by Wyclif, or his adher-
> ents, should be suffered, nor any other in or after his time be published
> to be permitted to be read, being not approved and allowed by the
> Diocesan before . . .[5]

The key seems to be in the word 'provincial'. Later,

> . . . we must not imagine that in the primitive Church, either every one
> that understood the learned tongues wherein the Scriptures were
> written, or other languages into which they were translated, might
> without reprehension, read, reason, dispute, turn and toss the Scriptures:
> or that our forefathers suffered every school-master, scholar, or Gram-
> marian that had a little Greek or Latin, straight to take in hand the holy
> Testament: or that the translated Bible into the vulgar tongues were in
> the hands of every husbandman, artificer, prentice, boys, girls, mistress,

maid, man: that they were for table talk, for ale benches, for boats and barges, and for every profane person and company. No, in these better times men were neither so ill, nor so curious of themselves, so to abuse the blessed book of Christ: neither was there any such easy means before printing was invented, to disperse the copies into the hands of every man, as there now is.

They were then in Libraries, Monasteries, Colleges, Churches, in Bishops, Priests, and some other devout principal Lay men's houses and hands: who used them with fear and reverence, and specially such parts as pertained to good life and manners, not meddling, but in pulpit and schools (and that moderately too) with the hard and high mysteries and places of greater difficulty. The poor ploughman, could then in labouring the ground, sing the hymns and psalms whether in known or unknown languages, as they had heard them in the holy Church, though they could neither read nor know the sense, meaning and mysteries of the Same.[6]

WHY THE VULGATE IS THE TRUE ORIGINAL

On this, Martin writes at some length.

. . . We translate the old vulgar Latin text, not the common Greek text, for these causes (he gives ten).

1. It is so ancient, that it was used in the Church of God above 1300 years ago, as appeareth by the fathers of those times.[7]

He commends Jerome and Augustine and the ancient fathers, and reminds readers that 'The holy Council of Trent . . . hath declared and defined this only of all other Latin translations, to be authentical'. There follow a number of paragraphs in which he maintains that the Latin Vulgate 'Followeth the Greek far more exactly than the Protestant's translations', with two illustrations, and one from Beza in which he commended one reading. A following paragraph can be summed up in its marginal note, 'All the rest misliked of the Sectaries themselves, each reprehending another.' This section ends with number 10. 'It is not only better than all other Latin translations, but than the Greek text it self in those places where they disagree.'

A LATINATE ENGLISH

Gregory Martin takes some pages to explain why his often curious English phrases will soon be in common use. He defends 'The Pasche, the feast of Azymes, the bread of Proposition'. The gorge rises at 'Azymes' (for 'Unleavened Bread'), but logically Martin is making reasonable points: if 'Hosanna, Raka, Belial, and such like be yet untranslated in the English Bibles, why may not we say Corbana, and Parascev' not to mention 'Proselyte' but not 'Neophyte' . . . and if

> Phylacteries be allowed for English Mat.23, we hope that Didragmes also Prepuce Paraclete, and such like will easily grow to be current and familiar. . . Moreover, we presume not in hard places to mollify the speeches or phrases, but religiously keep them word for word, and point for point, for fear of missing, or restraining the sense of the holy Ghost to our phantasy.[8]

Though this Rheims New Testament was not often reprinted, and appeared to have little effect on English culture before 1611, the fact that King James's translators made use of it meant that some of Martin's Latinate words did get into the language, and not only 'Paraclete', but 'acquisition', 'advent', 'calumniate', 'resuscitate', and even 'character', 'evangelise', and 'victims'.

TEXT

The translation does sometimes follow the Vulgate closely. The result has often not survived as English, as in the notorious 1 Corinthians 5:7, 'that you may be a new paste as you are Azymes', or in Ephesians 3:6 'concorporat and comparticipant', or in 2 Peter 2:13 'conquinations and spots, flowing in delicacies'. Less prominent, but also baffling without the Latin, are: Hebrews 13:16, 'Beneficence and communication do not forget: for with such hosts God is promerited'; Romans 6:13, 'Exhibit yourselves to God as of dead men, alive'; Romans 9:28, 'For, consummating a word, and abridging it in equitie: because a word abridged shall our Lord make upon the earth', and many more.[9] However much Gregory Martin pleads in his Preface, keeping such Latin English, without the Latin being known, simply obfuscates.

Gregory Martin scrupulously defends his method, but nowhere does he mention that he is dependent on the earlier English versions, with almost continuing heavy borrowing from Tyndale, from Coverdale's 1538 Diglot, and from Geneva. The opening of the Parable of the Prodigal Son at Luke 15:11–13 will suggest the position:

> And he said, A certain man had two sons: and the younger of them said to his father, Father, give me the portion of substance that

belongeth to me. And he divided unto them the substance. And not many days after the younger son gathering all his things together went from home into a far country: and there he wasted his substance living riotously . . .

This is 80 per cent Tyndale: 'portion' came from Geneva; the first 'substance', in Tyndale, Geneva and KJV 'goods', is the Latin *substantia*, used by Martin here three times for the two distinct Greek words οὐσία (*ousia*, substance, property) for the son's things, and βίος (*bios*, living, livelihood) for what the father gives. 'Not many days' is both the Latin *non post multos dies*, and the Greek μετ' οὐ πολλὰς ἡμέρας (*met ou pollas hēmeras*), which Tyndale had paraphrased to 'not long after', followed by the Great Bible and Geneva: KJV followed the Latin, 'not many days'. Martin is alone in 'all his things' (Latin, *omnibus*), where Tyndale's more thorough 'all that he had' from the Greek intensive of 'everything', ἅπαντα (*hapanta*) went forward through Great and Geneva, weakened in KJV to 'all'. Martin is also alone in 'went from home' rather than Tyndale's 'took his journey' (Great, Geneva and KJV); there the one Greek word ἀπεδήμησεν (*apedēmēsen*) has the sense of going abroad; the Latin in three words, *pergere profectus est*, intensifies the sense of travel. Martin's phrase does not reach out far enough.

The parable ends (vv. 31–2)

Son, thou art always with me, and all my things are thine. But it behoved us to make merry and be glad, because this thy brother was dead, and is revived, was lost, and is found.

Again, 80 per cent Tyndale, with Martin's changes not going forward to KJV. (The change of tense from 'was' to 'art' came from Geneva.)

A comparison of the Rheims New Testament with Tyndale shows widespread striking similarities of phrase, paralleled in Geneva. To take a random, brief, example, in Romans 1:8–10. Here is Tyndale:

First verily I thank my God through Jesus Christ for you all, because your faith is published throughout all the world. For God is my witness, whom I serve with my spirit in the gospel of his son, that without ceasing I make mention of you always in my prayers, beseeching that at one time or another, a prosperous journey (by the will of God) might fortune me, to come unto you.

(Verse 9, the sentence 'For . . . prayers', is KJV exactly: the rest is clearly dependent.) Here is Gregory Martin:

First I give thanks to my God through JESUS CHRIST for all of you, because your faith is renouned in the whole world. For God is my witness, whom I serve in my Spirit in the Gospel of his Son, that without intermission I make a mention of you always in my prayers, beseeching, if by any means I may some time at the length have a prosperous journey by the will of God, to come unto you.

It would be tedious to take more examples. The point is, it is hoped, sufficiently made: that Gregory Martin's declaration of a Latin base, though correct in some vocabulary and phrasing, conceals very large silent dependence on the earlier translators, Tyndale and those in Geneva – the very 'heretics' that he so denounces as leading the flock to the Devil. Tyndale in particular gave him 'chapter after chapter', as Carleton noted, following Westcott, who also noted the dependence on Geneva.[10] Martin is also more dependent on the Greek text than he declares. He gives Greek readings in the margins of most pages: something admirable, for reasons of accuracy; sometimes less so 'For advantage of the Catholic cause'.[11] The most significant dependence on the Greek original receives no mention: that is, the weight to be given to a definite article, for which, lacking articles, the Latin was no help.

James Carleton's analysis, in the minutest details, is thorough to the point of exhaustion. Two important points should be made. First, he is more hesitant than the density of his analysis makes appear. Second, though he points to Tyndale and Geneva in his introduction, he does not point out that he is indeed dealing with minutiae, and that the great sweep of this translation is from Tyndale. A reader's sight is baffled, so that it is not only impossible to see the wood for the trees – the grand forested landscape is invisible.

NOTES

The look of a Rheims New Testament page is good. One pleasing feature is the placing of the notes in a clear type at the foot. This can give a needed sense of breathing space, though a page can feel over-full and cluttered. What is in the notes, is, however, on the whole less helpful. Many of Martin's annotations have a characteristic flavour:

> Matt.4:6, *it is written*) Heretics allege Scriptures, as here the Devil doeth, in the false sense: the Church useth them, as Christ doth, in the true sense, & to confute their falsehood.

Tyndale had at this point only the reference to what is 'written', that is, 'Psalm 91.*c*.', sharpened in Geneva to 'Psalm 91:11'.

Matt.27:46, *Why hast thou forsaken me?*) beware of the detestable blasphemy of Calvin and the Calvinists, who thinking not the bodily death of Christ sufficient, say, that he was also here so forsaken and abandoned of his Father.

Again, Tyndale gave only the reference, 'Psalm 22.*a*'. Geneva did the same, adding, against 'forsaken',

To wit, in this misery: And this crying out is proper to his humanity, which notwithstanding was void of sin, but yet it felt the wrath of God, which is due to our sins.

Rheims has:

Mark 12:17, *To God*) These men were very circumspect and wary to do all duties to Caesar, but of their duty to God they had no regard. So Heretics, to flatter temporal Princes, and by them to uphold their heresies, do not only inculcate men's duty to the Prince. Dissembling that which is due to God: But also give to the Prince more than due, and take from God his right and duty. But Christ allowing Caesar his right, warneth them also of their duty toward God. And that is what Catholics inculcate, obey God, do as he commandeth, serve him first, and then the Prince.

Tyndale had no note there. Geneva simply cross-refers to 'Romans 13.7'. Rheims has:

John 10:1, *Climbeth another way*) Whosoever taketh upon him to preach without lawful sending, to minister sacraments, and is not Canonically ordered of a true Catholic Bishop, or what other Spiritual Pastor so ever, and cometh not in by lawful election and hold Church's ordinance to that dignity, but breaketh in against order by force or favour of men, and by human laws, he is a thief and a murderer, so in came Arius, Calvin, Luther, and all heretics. And all that succeed them in room and doctrine. And generally everyone that descendeth not by Lawful succession in the known ordinary line of Catholic Bishops and Pastors that have ever been in all Countries since their conversion.

Tyndale's note is 'Door', simply locating the passage. Geneva gives more:

Seeing that by Christ only we have access to the Father, there are neither other true shepherds, than those which come to Christ themselves and bring other thither also, neither is any to be thought the true shepherd, but that which is gathered to Christ.

Again, it would become tedious to give more of the Rheims notes in this vein, though there are many of them. The point is, it is hoped, once again sufficiently made: that though the Geneva Bibles have been abused for their 'bitter' notes, that unhappy epithet is more properly applied to those by Gregory Martin in his Rheims New Testament; something not commonly stated, if at all.

WILLIAM FULKE

Scholars in England were quick to reply.[12] William Fulke, Master of Pembroke College, Cambridge, and prolific Protestant polemicist, produced in 1583 a defence of the English versions, dedicated to the queen, attacking, and reprinting, Gregory Martin's *A Discovery of the Manifold Corruptions of the Holy Scriptures by the Heretics, 1582*,[13] and including in places a line-by-line, word-by-word refutation of the Rheims New Testament in parallel with the Bishops'. His *A Defence of the Sincere and True Translations of the Holy Scriptures into the English Tongue, against G. Martin. Whereunto is added a brief Confutation of Cavils, by Diverse Papists in their English Pamphlets, against the Writings of W. Fulke*[14] and the resulting controversy, is said to have brought the Rheims version to the notice of King James's translators, leading them to adopt many of its readings.[15] The Rheims New Testament was not in the list of translations they were recommended to study: yet Fulke's large handsome folio first printed by Robert Barker in 1589 must have been irresistible to many of those scholars. Fulke presented, attractively, in parallel columns, the Bishops' version and Gregory Martin's Rheims version, with a reprint of his point-by-point attack on Martin's Preface. Fulke's title, in full, is:

> The Text of the New Testament of Jesus Christ, translated out of the vulgar Latin by the papists of the traiterous Seminary at Rheims. With Arguments of Books, Chapters, and Annotations, pretending to discover the corruptions of divers translations, and to clear the controversies of these days. [In those latter phrases Fulke quotes Martin's title-page.] Whereunto is added the Translation out of the Original Greek, commonly used in the Church of England. With A Confutation of all such Arguments, Glosses, and Annotations, as Contain Manifest impiety, of heresy, treason and slander, against the Catholic Church [that is, the worldwide, not the Roman] of God, and the true teachers thereof, or the Translations used in the Church of England: Both by authority of the holy Scriptures, and by the testimony of the ancient fathers.[16]

Darlow, Moule and Herbert comment:

> This 'counterblast' to Martin, by printing the Rheims Testament in full,
> side by side with the Bishops' version, secured for the former a pub-
> licity which it would not otherwise have obtained, and was indirectly
> responsible for the marked influence which Rheims exerted in the Bible
> of 1611.[17]

That may be so. Perhaps without Fulke's parallel Testaments, the Rheims
version would have been ignored as, eventually, was Taverner's of 1539 –
which, incidentally, had three times the number of editions that Rheims
achieved. Yet Martin was found to be both too stinging and too devious
to be ignored. Answer was demanded to his untruths and distortions (for
example, that the Greek New Testament was corrupt, and the Latin was
definitive) and to his relentless savagery against the New Testaments in
English from Tyndale onwards, even though, as on his first page, in his
second (characteristically confusing) sentence, he claims that he does
not wholly object to the vernacular translations of the time, though the
existing ones were 'often through mans malice or infirmity pernicious
and much hurtful to many'.

Whether Fulke guaranteed the presence of Rheims in KJV is a more
open question. The standard, and exhaustive, study is that by Carleton.[18]
He appears to have shown great dependence by King James's workers on
their choice of vocabulary and phrase; but his vision was limited.

THE PREFACE TO THE RHEIMS NEW TESTAMENT

To sum up this is one of the extraordinary documents in the history of
Bible translating. There is nothing like it anywhere else. Large parts of the
twenty-six pages are written in bile. To find a way through the maze
of Latinate clauses is hard enough, without the way being made so
unpleasant. As well as playing the deafening music of a whole brass band
of self-righteousness in his constant assertion of the correctness of the
Church and the Fathers, Martin harps on one string, of his detestation of
Reformation scholars, particularly Beza, until the eyes and ears protest.

Though William Fulke did his best, it is impossible to argue with
Martin, who will appear to win every time because he is starting from a
different place. Martin wrote in his Preface '. . . Penance, Doing Penance,
Chalice, Priest, Deacon, Traditions, altar, host, and the like (which we
exactly keep as Catholic terms) proceed even from the very words of
Scripture.' He is being disingenuous. His ground is always that the Latin
tradition of the Church comes first, and if 'the Heretics' say that a Greek

reading is different, then the Greek reading is wrong. Certainly, the Church made the Vulgate. But there can be no question that the first Christian documents were written in Greek, which must have priority.

In 1963, S. L. Greenslade, whose account of English translations in the sixteenth and early seventeenth century in the third and final volume of *The Cambridge History of the Bible* has remained definitive ever since, wrote:

> If ever a vernacular Bible was combative and tendentious, this was – in its Vulgate basis, the version itself, the marginal notes, the lengthy annotations.[19]

Greenslade, though he did not mention the Preface, did not exaggerate. Mercifully, the Rheims New Testament had little effect.

Chapter 22

'GENEVA-TOMSON-JUNIUS', 1599

BETWEEN 1560 AND 1611 THERE WERE SIXTY-FOUR separate editions of the 1560 Geneva Bible or New Testament. Between 1576 and 1611 there were fifty-six editions of Geneva Bibles or New Testaments only, all with Tomson's revisions. Editions of Geneva-Tomson Bibles from 1599 stay faithful to Tomson,[1] except that many have completely new, and very full, notes on Revelation, reprinting a book by 'Junius'. Where, in Tomson's revision, the annotation to the short Epistle of James is fuller than to the whole of Revelation, now Junius's notes to Revelation break all records, squeezing the text into a corner, and being twice as full as for a page, for example, of Romans.

This commentary is itself as rich and full as anything in any Geneva Bible, with summaries, paraphrases, doctrinal comments, historical notes, philological explanations and variants, cross-references and an advanced system of typology from Old Testament figures. The structure of the twenty-two chapters of Revelation, individually and together, is always made clear, which makes it especially approachable – this is here, the next stage is there. It is rhetorically alert, assuming that the reader understands rhetorical terms: synecdoche, metaphor, metonymy, enallage. The comments on the earlier chapters are powerfully Christological, which is theologically reassuring.

Junius's book, *A Brief and Learned Commentary*, written in Latin in 1592, and published in English in 1596,[2] is in two states, and it is the shorter one that is printed from 1599 on, in 'Geneva-Tomson-Junius' Bibles, and New Testaments from 1602. For some reason, this – probably the most influential commentary on Revelation ever in English – has been ignored.[3]

Facing the first page of Revelation in a typical Geneva-Tomson-Junius Bible is 'The Order of the Time whereunto the contents of this book are to be referred', with 'the years of Christ' down the left column. Here is now Revelation firmly in the details of Christian history: '1300, Boniface celebrateth the Iubile'; '1301, About this time was a great earthquake, which overthrew many houses in Rome. Prophecy ceaseth for three years and a half . . .', and so on.

At 14:6, on the Angel with the Everlasting Gospel, Junius writes:

This Angel is a type or figure of the good and faithful servants of God, whom God especially from that time of Boniface the Eighth hath raised up to the publishing of the gospel of Christ, both by preaching and writing. So God first, near unto the time of the same Boniface, used Peter Cassiodorus an Italian: after Arnold de Villa Nova, a Frenchman, then Occam, Dante, Petrarch, after that Johannes de rupa casa, a Frenchman: after again, John Wicklife an Englishman, and so continually one or another unto the restoring of the truth, and enlarging of his church.

ANTI-PAPAL NOTES

Condemnation of the Geneva Bible has suggested that the greatest exception must be taken to Junius's annotations to Revelation and their wholesale attacks on Roman Catholicism. To read all these copious notes carefully, however, is, as one might put it, a revelation. The weight of biblical knowledge and insight; the sympathetic attempts to understand what St John means in each Act of his visual and aural drama; the strong theology of Christ's work of redemption, and the nature of his Church are all expounded with a power that matches the words of the text. Surprisingly, there is a tone of sanity: Junius will not countenance any recent wild expositions of 'the number of the beast: for it is the number of a man, and his number is six hundred threescore and six' (13:18). The mystery in the number, he writes, is its consummation in absolute power, seen, for example, in 'that cruel beast [Pope] Boniface the eight';

Here therefore is the number of the beast, who powereth from himself all his parts, and bringeth them all back again unto himself by his discipline in most wise and cunning manner.

Boniface is not 'the beast': that is the assumption by 'this beast of Rome . . . which of a civil Empire is made an Ecclesiastical hierarchy', of 'divine honours, and divine authority so far, as he is believed to be above the Scriptures', as the note to 13:12 has it.

Clarification of Junius's writing against Rome is important. In significant places, his words are less insulting. Whereas the 1560 Geneva had at Revelation 16:2 the intemperate words 'filthy vermin' for members of holy orders, Junius has at that point, also with reference to the sixth plague, Exodus 9:9:

But it doth signify a spiritual ulcer, and that torture or butchery of conscience seared with an hot iron which accuseth the ungodly within and
both by truth of the word (the light whereof God hath now so long
shewed forth) and by bitterness stirred up and forceth out the sword
of God's wrath.

Junius uses the word 'Catholic' fairly frequently, but always as the Creed
does, to mean the Church of God worldwide, and not as that part overseen by the Bishop of Rome.[4] Second, he uses the name 'Antichrist' no
more than seven times, and never linked to anything specific, but standing for all kinds of enemy of Christ.[5] Junius does attack popes. In the
course of relating the text to Christian history, he comments on four
popes: Gregory VII, Gregory IX, Boniface VIII and Sixtus IV. The two
Gregories are in the notes to 9:4, and Gregory VII again briefly at 20:1.
Gregory VII receives abut 150 words of condemnation for his putting down
of the Emperor Henry IV, and setting 'all Christendom on fire'.

The papal historian Eamon Duffy notes of Gregory VII, that he 'seemed
a dangerous revolutionary, and a zealot determined to concede nothing
. . . Gregory's pontificate represents the highest point of papal aspiration
to dominion over the secular world.'[6] I give here the complete section in
Junius, keyed to 9:6, about Gregory VII:

Now this space [before 'that public and unpunished licence of killing'
heralded by the sixth Angel in verse 13] is to be accounted from the
end of that thousand years mentioned in Chap.20. 3. and that is from
the Popedom of that Gregory the 7. a most monstrous Necromancer,
who before was called *Hildebrandus Senensis*: for this man being made
altogether of impiety and wickedness, as a slave of the devil, whom he
served, was the most wicked firebrand of the world: he excommuni-
cate the emperor *Henry* the fourth: went about by all manner of
treachery to set up and put down Empires and kingdoms as liked
himself: and doubted not to set Rudolph the Swedon over the Empire
instead of *Henry* before named, sending unto him a crown, with this
verse annexed unto it: *Petra dedit Petro, Petrus diadema Rodolpho*: that is,
the Rock to Peter gave the Crown, and Peter Rodolph doth renown.
Finally, he so finely bestirred himself in his affairs, as he miserably set
all Christendom on fire, & conveyed over unto his successors the
burning brand of the same: who enraged with like ambition, never
ceased to nourish that flame, and to kindle it more and more: whereby
Cities, common weals, and whole kingdoms set together by the ears
amongst themselves by most expert cut-throats, came to ruin, while
they miserably wounded one another.

There is one other reference to that pope, keyed to 20:3, 'till the thousand years were fulfilled'. It is, in full:

> The thousandth year falls precisely upon the times of that wicked Hildebrand, who was called Gregory the seventh, a most damnable Necromancer and sorcerer, who Satan used as an instrument when he was loosed out of bounds, thenceforth to annoy the Saints of God with most cruel persecutions, and the whole world with dissensions, and most bloody wars: as Benno the Cardinal reporteth at large.

On Gregory IX, Junius has fewer, but more damning, words. The passage continues immediately from the above at 9:4, 'wounded one another':

> This term of an hundred and fifty years, taketh end in the time of Gregory the 9 or *Hugolinus Anagniensis* (as he was before called) who caused to be compiled by one *Raimond* his Chaplain & confessor, the body of Decretals, and by sufferance of the Kings and Princes, to be published in the Christian world, and established for a law: For by his sleight at length the Popes arrogated unto themselves licence to kill whom they would, while others were unawares: and without fear established a butchery out of the many wicked Canons of the Decretals, which the trumpet of the fifth Angel had expressly forbidden, and had hindered until this time. The effects of these bloody actions are declared upon the sixth verse: that the miserable world languishing in so great calamities, should willingly run together unto death, and prefer the same before life, by reason of the grievousness of the miseries that oppressed them.

('The sixth verse', 9:6, reads: 'Therefore in those days shall men seek death, and shall not find it, and shall desire to die, and death shall flee from them.')

Junius is recounting history.[7] His briefer comments on 'Boniface the eight' are at chapter 11. Keyed to the second verse is:

> ... the end of these years precisely falleth into the Popedom of Boniface the eight, who a little before the end of the year of Christ, a thousand two hundred and ninety four, entered the Popedom of Rome, in the feast of Saint Lucie (as *Bergomensis sayeth*) having put in prison his predecessor *Coelestinus*, whom by fraud, undercover of Oracle he deceived: for which cause, that was well said of him, *Intravit ut vulpes, regnavit ut leo, mortuus est ut canis*. That is, he entered like a fox, reigned like a lion and died like a dog.

At 11:7, Junius writes:

> That beast is the Roman Empire, made long ago of civil, Ecclesiastical: the chief head whereof was then Boniface the eight, as I said before,

who lifted up himself in so great arrogancy (saith the author of the *Fasciculus temporum*) that he called himself, Lord of the whole world, as well in temporal causes, as in spiritual: There is an extant of that matter, written by the same Boniface, most arrogantly, shall I say, or most wickedly, *Ca. Unam sanctam, extra de maioritate & obedientia*. And in the sixth of the Decretals (which is from the same author) many things are found of the same argument.

At 11:11, Junius calls him 'that wicked Boniface'. At 13:18, as noted above, Junius does not find 'that cruel beast, Boniface' related to 'the number of the beast'. His name is mentioned at 14:1 and 14:6, simply in regard to the time, the latter reference being that to Wyclif and others.

Duffy writes of the usurping Boniface, who kept his predecessor 'a prisoner in miserably cramped conditions until his death at the age of ninety', that he 'is a mysterious man, proud, ambitious, fierce'. Duffy is interesting about the inrush of pilgrims and a great deal of money on the promise of ' "full and copious pardon" to all who visited St Peter and the Lateran after confessing their sins'. The Jubilee Pilgrimage of 1300 instituted by him drew, it is said, at any one time 200,000 pilgrims. Ruthless in 'enriching his relatives at the expense of the Church', he was hated by Dante, 'who placed him upside down in a subterranean furnace in hell'.[8]

Sixtus IV is mentioned in passing by Junius in a very long note on Revelation 13:1, to 'and on his head the name of blasphemy', a note partly about the self-exaltation of 'the Popes of Rome' to take unto themselves the very name of God, as illustrated by the pageant at the first entry into Rome of 'Sixtus the fourth'. Duffy points out that the lavishness of Sixtus included a coronation tiara which 'alone cost 100,000 ducats, more than a third of the papacy's annual income'. This man, who commissioned his own Sistine Chapel in the Vatican, lavishly decorated, was, as the papacy maintained, in the spiritual and temporal spheres, in Duffy's words, 'like Christ, supreme in both'.[9] With Sixtus's huge wealth and self-advertisement thought of as Christ-like, it is no wonder that Junius keyed the account of him to the word 'blasphemy'.

THE FULLNESS OF THE MATTER

It has been necessary to have concentrated on Junius's words on four popes, and given the entire material (lines which are a small fraction of the whole large commentary) in order to fix the matter of Geneva Bibles being 'anti-papal.' Certainly those passages are just that. It is, however, all the rest (about thirty thousand words) that is truly significant, the work

of illumination, verse by verse, and word by word, of this obliquely edifying and disturbing last part of Scripture.

I take, as a final example, Junius's notes to the first words of the last
chapter, 22:1, 'And he shewed me a pure river of water of life, clear as
crystal, proceeding out of the throne of God, and of the Lamb.'

> Here is absolved and finished the description of the celestial Church
> (as I shewed before, Chap. 21:12) by the effects in 5 verses, and then
> the book is concluded in the rest of the chapter. The effects proceed-
> ing from God, who dwelleth in the Church, are these: the everlasting
> grace of God, in this verse, the eternal living of the godly, as Chap. 2:7,
> the eternal fruits which the godly bring forth unto God, themselves
> and others, verse 2, ['the tree of life . . . and the leaves of the tree served
> to heal the nations with'] freedom and immunity from all evil, God
> himself taking pleasure in his servants, and they likewise in their God,
> verse 3. The beholding and the sight of God, and sealing of the faith-
> ful from all eternity, verse 4, the light of God and an everlasting
> kingdom and glory, verse 5.

It will be noticed that here and almost entirely throughout this commentary, Scripture is illuminated as being about God and his people, a
dark part of that history being the *Realpolitik* and gigantic wealth of certain
popes.

A special quality of Junius on Revelation in these Geneva margins is
the released imagination – to read the text with Junius in parallel is to
walk up and down in a remarkable mind, in which the Scriptures of both
Old and New Testaments, the older and newer history of Christianity,
the liturgy of the Temple and the magic of numbers, the elements of
nature and a liberated, cosmic, sense of human history are woven into an
extraordinary revelation of the final consummation of all things. The
whole commentary ends, '. . . in Christ Jesus our Lord, until his coming
to judgement. Come Lord Jesus and do it. Amen, again Amen'.

All the important details of this commentary, affecting Shakespeare and
Milton, to mention no others, still need proper study. Hold *King Lear* close
to Junius's Revelation, and the play glows with sudden response. In that
play, quotations and references to the biblical text abound. Near the end
of Act Five, at the final entrance of King Lear with his daughter Cordelia
dead in his arms, the exchange between Kent and Edgar, 'Is this the
promis'd end? / or image of that horror?' (v. 3.263–4), sums up not only
the apocalyptic themes throughout the drama, but a national mood in the
early years of James's reign.[10] The imagery in *King Lear* of cracking
thunder, or catastrophic earthquakes, the eclipse of sun and moon, the
wheel of fire, the lake of darkness, the sulphurous pit, the wrathful dragon,

the prince of darkness, the black angel, even the monsters of the deep, and much else, are steeped in Revelation. That is, the text. Junius's commentary points to the end of Christian time, to a consummation, which is an idea deep inside *King Lear, Macbeth* and *Antony and Cleopatra*, inside Shakespeare's tragic understanding, though it is not, of course, fixed by him to a time in a calendar.[11]

The arrival of such a commentary in 1599 in a good deal of national consciousness as the century turned and Queen Elizabeth was slowly dying, just before that great outburst of Shakespeare's highest tragic and Apocalyptic writing, should surely be more noticed. Finding Junius on Revelation at the conclusion of the Bible must have been as startling to some as would be finding that a modern Bible has printed at the end T. S. Eliot's *The Waste Land*.

The makers of the Bible that is Geneva-Tomson-Junius used everything concrete they could lay their hands on to illuminate Scripture, that enormous volume, for the reader – clear roman and italic typefaces of all sizes, many systems of annotation, maps, diagrams, woodcuts, music (with the automatic inclusion of Sternhold and Hopkins), prologues, summaries, tables, running heads, numbered verses, cross-references, large concordances (sometimes several), all to express revealed and paradoxical truths from the creation of the world to its end. The point of the Geneva Bibles is to help understanding and faith. It is no surprise that the life of Geneva Bibles coincided with the very highest flourishing of literature in English life from 1560 to 1660, that extraordinary uprush of Elizabethan, Jacobean and Caroline drama, poetry and prose.

Who was Franciscus Junius? François du Jon, a French Protestant theologian, son-in-law of the great Hebraist Immanuel Tremellius, whose Latin version of the Old and New Testaments, published in 1579, was the basic Latin text for some generations of European Protestants (and influenced Milton). Du Jon was known for his eirenical intervention in a church dispute in Amsterdam; but he was most famous for his book on Revelation. How famous is easily demonstrated in Oxford. If – and it is a pleasant thing to do – one sits to work in the Upper Reading Room of the Bodleian Library, looking at the big arch below the tower (and facing north) one finds, directly facing, eight of the many painted medallion heads. These ancient murals are of two hundred worthies round the whole room, from Aesop to Ovid, from Copernicus to Cranmer, from Augustine to Duns Scotus, Plato to Petrarch. In that special place on the arch together are the great worthies of the Reformation: from the left, Luther and Erasmus, ending on the right with Beza. Flanking Rainolds in the centre are on the left, Laurence Humphrey, and on the right, Franciscus Junius.

Chapter 23

EXPLORERS OF THE REVELATION: SPENSER AND SHAKESPEARE

EDMUND SPENSER WAS CONSIDERED BY his contemporaries in the 1580s and 1590s to be the greatest English poet, valued in later ages, by Milton himself, for example. 'Epithalamium' is one of the most beautiful love-poems in the language, celebrating his midsummer marriage in southern Ireland in 1594. He was a skilled lyricist and sonneteer, to rank with Shakespeare and Sidney.

Spenser's great unfinished allegory *The Faerie Queene* (only six books and a fragment, out of the proposed twelve, were published) makes the first high English epic, with only Milton's *Paradise Lost* greater. In it, Spenser set out to show, in an original stanzaic form and high language, Aristotle's 'twelve moral virtues' as understood through the British narratives of late medieval and Renaissance romance.

The eighteenth-century Augustan writers admired Spenser's colourful imagery and narrative splendour. *The Faerie Queene* was to them a supreme poem of the imagination, though distasteful in allegory and form. Spenser was supremely important to the English Romantic writers as 'the poets' poet' of dreams, beauty and sensuous appeal. He was the immediate model for Keats, first showing him early in his youth those 'Charm'd magic casements, opening on the foam / Of perilous seas, in faery lands forlorn'.[1] Wordsworth, in Book III of *The Prelude*, recalled at Cambridge reading 'Sweet Spenser, moving through his clouded heaven / With the moon's beauty and the moon's soft pace, / I call'd him Brother, Englishman and Friend'.[2] Now *The Faerie Queene* is less read. The advocacy of C. S. Lewis in the mid-twentieth century, strong on both sides of the Atlantic, showing Spenser to be both fiercely didactic and movingly appealing, has faded, sadly. Spenser, second only to Shakespeare as the poet of that time, like him has much to teach about how to live, morally and spiritually, and about the high shapes of art. Even enthusiasts among twentieth-century academic appreciators, however, found one part of Spenser's mind so strange, even distasteful, as to be something from which commentary had to save him. It is always acknowledged that his models were of many kinds: he combined classical and Christian humanist culture, from Aristotle to Ariosto. His Christian dependence not only on humanism but, as a Calvinist, on the English Bible, however, has been something, it seems, hardly to be mentioned. This is to misrepresent.

Spenser was at Cambridge in the early 1570s, a period when there was great interest in that University in making a new English poetry. After university, he went into the service of the Bishop of Rochester, who had been Master of Pembroke, Spenser's college. From there he moved to the service of the powerful Earl of Leicester, making friends with the earl's nephew Sir Philip Sidney. In 1579 he published twelve eclogues, admired by Sidney, under the title *The Shepherd's Calendar*. In 1580, he became secretary to Lord Grey de Wilton, the Lord Deputy of Ireland. In that country Spenser spent most of the rest of his life, though publishing much fine poetry as a courtier in London. He attracted criticism, not only from Sidney, for his experiments with what Sidney called 'an old rustic language'.[3] In 1580 he published Books I to III of *The Faerie Queene*. Books IV to VI followed in 1595, with a second edition of I to III: the printer was Richard Field, a Stratford man known to Shakespeare.

On Spenser's death in January 1599, the Earl of Essex paid for his funeral in Westminster Abbey, where he was buried near Chaucer: the poets of the age threw elegies into his grave. Queen Elizabeth herself ordered a monument to him, which never materialised. The Countess of Dorset provided one for the Abbey in 1620: though this mistook the dates of birth and death, it did name him 'The Prince of Poets in his Time'. This monument was restored in marble in 1778, with the dates corrected. It may be seen today in Poets' Corner.

In the last decades of Elizabeth's reign, the great men that Spenser knew shared a sense of high enterprise, of discovery of the world and adventure in it. Spenser had that spirit, making high claims for the function of English poetry. He wrote at a time of daunting religious problems, and he can be seen to be occupied not only with the complexities of the formal Elizabethan Settlement, but also with the difficulties produced by dissent from both sides, Protestant and Catholic. Protestants criticised the Church of England, but, more, found the Church of Rome to be deviant and heretical. That national Catholic problem, moreover, involved national security. Formidable Jesuit missionaries, trained to persist till death, began to arrive from Douai in the late 1570s, dedicated to undermining the recently excommunicated queen. Any Protestant writer of the time felt free to attack what was understood as a Catholic threat.

Critics of *The Shepherd's Calendar* have been squeamish in understanding that Spenser was a fully Protestant writer. Three of the twelve eclogues,

'May', 'July' and 'September', deal with religious matters. Spenser's speakers are subtle, and the movement within each poem, and within the whole volume, is complex, but even so the parallel between Spenser's position and that of most Protestant writers of the time is powerful.[4] Commentators have laboured to show a non-existent religious 'balance' in *The Calendar*, and even to 'rescue' Spenser from the Calvinism of the time.[5] This is to assume, from a distorted later perspective, that Calvinism in Elizabeth's court was some sort of reprehensible aberration, and not a norm. Modern historical studies have focused on the conflicts about theories of church government, and certainly from 1570 those issues were both strong and public. More out of sight, however, have been the more central Protestant concerns for an educated, preaching ministry; for further reformation of the Church of England in the light of the Scriptures; and a hatred of episcopal pomp and wealth, with particularly fervent opposition to Roman Catholicism. Spenser can be shown to share the militant Protestantism of the high-born circle in which he moved, particularly of the Earl of Leicester, Lord Grey de Wilton and Sir Philip Sidney. It is hard to read the parable of the Wolf in the 'May' eclogue without seeing that the victim, the young kid, is, as the gloss by Spenser's Cambridge friend 'E. K.' explains 'The simple sort of the faithful and true Christians', deceived by the popish fox.[6] In all three ecclesiastical eclogues, the speakers on both sides are given engaging characteristics. As the dialogues unfold, the flaws in one speaker's argument are steadily exposed. Because Spenser has used the genre of pastoral dialogue, it does not follow that the final effect has to be of ambivalence. 'May', 'July' and 'September' are Protestant in their impetus. They are part of an effect made by the whole of the *Calendar*, relating the work of the poet to that of the pastor. As Spenser concludes the *Calendar*, his purpose has been 'To teach the ruder shepherd how to feed his sheep / And from the falsers fraud his folded flock to keep.'[7]

Spenser's deepest concerns can be seen at their best in 'the great slow swing' of his mind in *The Faerie Queene*.[8] Richly feeding into his poetry more than two thousand years of literature and thought, he was also consciously trying to make a new poetry for England, looking back to the greatness of Chaucer two hundred years before. He wanted poetry to be wholly accessible to the 'vulgar': he did not write in Latin (at all – in this, among the major poets, he was joined only by Shakespeare). He studied how French poetry resolved one Renaissance problem in making national languages capable of carrying the highest subjects. In this respect, of course, he was working parallel to the recent translators of classical authors, and especially the Bible, from the original languages into the vernaculars.

SPENSER AND PROTESTANT UNDERSTANDING
OF THE BIBLE

Though commentators have been unable to avoid Christian significances in *The Faerie Queene*, these have often been seen in terms of recent religious history and doctrine rather than an understanding of particularly Protestant doctrines from the Bible. An example is the passage in Book I Canto II in which the Redcross Knight fights his climactic battle against the dragon, receiving strength from the Well of Life and the Tree of Life (specifically, I. xi. 30) to kill that Devil. These have been taken as standing for the two sacraments of the Church of England, baptism and the eucharist.[9] In Spenser's 'continued allegory and dark conceit', as he expressed his purpose in his prefatory letter to Sir Walter Raleigh, these are present here, but that identification is too schematic. Both the Well and the Tree stand also for the power of Christ in his Person, best interpreted by Revelation 22:1–2, where the 'river of water of life' is not only the sacrament of baptism but the doctrine of Christ:

> For unto life the dead it could restore,
>   And guilt of sinful crimes clean wash away,
>   Those that with sickness were infected sore,
>   It could recure, and aged long decay
>   Renew, as one were borne that very day. (IX.30)

The Book of Revelation was known to all Bible-reading Protestant Christians, with commentaries and annotations. (These, especially those in the Geneva Bibles available to Spenser, lacked the later seedy assumptions of secular as well as religious cosmic significance adduced from that book which have made modern minds avoid it – as examples, it is said that announced there, in code, are the date and time of the last great victory [at 'Armageddon'] for Christian capitalism, or the date and time of the Second Coming of Jesus Christ.) For Spenser, the Well has healing properties far beyond the once-for-all washing of baptism (and in any case we must assume that the Redcross Knight was baptised long before). It has also been said that the Redcross Knight, rising early on the third day to slay the dragon, becomes Christ himself:[10] when seen in the light of the New Testament, this does not make sense. Spenser's point is that the true Christian life is lived in imitation of Christ, not identification with him. The Redcross Knight, for Spenser's epic to work, has to remain human.

A second Protestant characteristic is that his writing, however rich in significance, is never esoteric. The power of Spenser's poems to explicate themselves is striking. His 'continued allegory' should be taken only to the extent that Scripture-readers understood allegory. The Bible contains allegories, of a self-explanatory sort – that is how the early churches could accommodate the Song of Songs. Paul himself in Galatians 4:21–6 commends an Old Testament story as to be taken allegorically. But to write anything which baffles the common reader without access to explanations in the rarefied heights of unusual learning is foreign to Protestant writers. One glory of *The Faerie Queene* is that it is understandable. Allegory, there, is not hiding truths. Spenser wrote at a time when this question was current: Sir John Harrington, for example, pressed an esoteric poetic theory; Sidney the reverse. That *The Faerie Queene* was not read esoterically is shown by a little book by Sir Kenelm Digby, published in 1643 and entitled *Observations on the 22nd Stanza in the 9th Canto of the 2nd Book of Spenser's Faerie Queene*. Digby tackles that one stanza simply because it alone does not fit with Spenser's normal method in this enormous allegory, where he (Digby) notes that Spenser 'doth himself declare his own conceptions in such sort as they are obvious to any ordinary capacity'.[11] Similarly the very frequently used images from the Book of Revelation, not only in Book I, are clear in their sense to any reader familiar with that book and its elucidation in the margins of Geneva Bibles. Spenser's remarkable learning draws on a range of literature, history, philosophy, mythography and iconography, as well as biblical commentaries and religious books. Yet all this becomes transmuted into the narratives of recognisable human beings in romance – all the senses in that highly charged genre become imaginatively available.

To approach a third Protestant characteristic one may take as examples the enemies of the Redcross Knight in the first half of Book I. There is no mystery. Two are papists and two are adherents of Mahomet: though they differ, their nature is clear. The followers of Mahomet (Sansfoy and Sansjoy) attack the Redcross Knight physically. They are familiar figures from medieval romance and Italian romantic epic (Sir Beves killed fifty on a single day[12]). The two papists, Archimago and Duessa, however, work differently, by means of fraudulent 'Shewes'. Here is the alarm felt by Protestants about the seductiveness of Catholic casuistry. In these 'shewes' are created or promoted ambiguous spectacles with which the inexperienced knight has to contend: a 'lowly Hermitage' (i.34) and a 'goodly Lady' (ii.13), 'two goodly trees' (ii.28), a 'goodly building, bravely garnished' (iv.2). 'Goodly', of course, is equivocal for Spenser: the Redcross Knight is to blame not for being deceived, but for his persistence in error after 'warning signals have clearly indicated that the phenomenon on hand ought to be rejected . . . after each adventure his mind is more clouded and his heart more tainted by the nature of the experience he has passed through'.[13] So Archimago's hermitage at first seems to offer a true pastoral simplicity of life, and neither Una nor the Redcross Knight can discern its true meaning. There is, however, no difficulty for the reader, as Spenser guides the response.

One of the characteristics of the Spenserian stanza, with its interlocking rhyme scheme and final longer line, is to allow, often within a single stanza, a characteristic movement from something necessarily complex, physical, moral or psychological to final words which make explicit a meaning which the reader has been discovering. In Book 1 Canto 1 stanza 35, Una and the Redcross Knight, in some distress, have (to the reader's pleasure) arrived at a welcoming house dedicated to humble contentment. The first words of the stanza are 'arrived there', which is gratifying: by the ninth line the reader is alarmed.

> Arrived there, the little house they fill,
>   Ne look for entertainment, where none was:
>   Rest is their feast, and all things at their will;
>   The noblest mind the best contentment has.
>   With fair discourse the evening so they passed:
>   For that old man of pleasing words had store,
>   And well could file his tongue as smooth as glass;
>   He told of Saints and Popes, and evermore
> He strowed an *Ave-Mary* after and before.

This stanza prepares for the discovery that the hypocritical hermit is a sorcerer who deals in 'mighty charms, to trouble sleepy minds' (1.i.36) – a sorcery which Protestant writers claimed belonged to papist clergy.[14]

That Spenser was writing at a time of cultural difficulties is clear. In a way that extended Sidney, he was trying to reconcile the richnesses of pagan and medieval culture, with which literature in English was so newly blessed in the new outpouring of printed material, with the special divine insights of Christianity, and especially Protestant Christianity. Spenser is said to have experienced disillusion with Protestant values, a movement which can be detected, it is claimed, in the addition of the two hymns, of heavenly and celestial beauty, to the previously written two of earthly or natural love and beauty, which are entirely Petrarchan and Neoplatonic. In the dedication of these *Foure Hymnes* (1596), to the Puritan Countesses of Cumberland and Warwick, Spenser suggests that the first two were too pagan, even 'poison', in their 'strong passion'. He begins the second pair of poems by repudiating those earlier follies. According to Fulke Greville, Sidney wanted to destroy *Arcadia* for the same reason.[15] The striking parallel is with Milton who, in *Paradise Regained*, added a fourth temptation to the New Testament's three, in which Christ was tempted to study pagan wisdom. The two, however, divine and pagan, do not have to be absolutes, and there is a large difference of scale between Spenser's youthful ecstasies and the authority of Christ in the wilderness. The criterion, for Protestant writers, is first and always the Bible, which accommodates to religious purposes a good deal of secular writing (the Song of Songs and Esther to look no further). Spenser the epic poet explores large areas of moral, emotional and social experience. The whole of *The Faerie Queene*, as it remains, is built 'in a way which allows neither the protagonist nor the readers to forget the continuing reality of the spiritual realm which is the source and the destiny of moral virtue'.[16]

SIXTEENTH-CENTURY LIBERATION

To Protestants, language itself was liberated, the Word of God being always creatively active. A good deal of the explosion of magnificent poetry in the time of Spenser and Shakespeare can be put down not so much to the latest Italian fashions, as Sidney commended in his seminal *Apology for Poetry* in the 1580s, but the firm understanding that, in spite of Plato, poetry was on God's side after all, because God himself wrote poetry, as the Bible had newly shown. Freshly inventing thoughts, forms, styles and even words, was part of a poet being, as Sidney pointed out, a 'maker'[17] and, as the Bible also showed, could be both unfettered and endless. Hamlet, his mind racing with suggestion, is not threatened with a charge of heresy.

A strong feature of the later sixteenth century was the first arrival in English of the great classical texts. One of the half-dozen most significant of these, Ovid's *Metamorphoses*, arrived first complete in English in 1563–7, translated into jogging verse by Arthur Golding. A long introductory Book by Golding himself sets out to show how biblical Ovid is. Golding was more famous at the time as the translator of a dozen major works by Calvin, including volumes of sermons. Ovid's epic arrives in English as a Calvinist work. Golding's Ovid certainly influenced Shakespeare all his life (though he read the original, of course): a long passage, VII.263–89, makes most of Prospero's speech at *The Tempest* 5.1.33–57.

SHAKESPEARE

It is vital to allow Shakespeare a mind that is open.[18] The seventeenth and eighteenth centuries denied him any learning at all: he was a sport, a child of nature rather than of art. Some sort of Divine Being opened a flap in his head and poured it all in: Shakespeare, they passionately maintained, did not read books. Observers in the nineteenth century found he knew the Bible, and then wrote pious books about Shakespeare's biblical knowledge. At the start of the twenty-first century he is allowed to be both learned and thoughtful. His sources are indeed manifold: classical writers, especially Ovid and Plutarch, frequently in the original (including better Greek, as well as Latin, than Ben Jonson could bring himself to allow), and English versions. He used modern French and Italian works, not always translated. He read books on law, medicine, folklore, alchemy, astrology, natural history and much, much else. The English *Chronicles* of Hall and Holinshed gave him plots. Previous and contemporary English writers, especially Chaucer, Marlowe and Lodge influenced him greatly.

We cannot go to the other extreme and make him a universal genius. There were areas he did not address. He was not interested in the contemporary London scene of sexual transaction and its literature, as Jonson and Middleton were: nor in dramatising Old Testament stories, as quite a number of his contemporaries did; nor did he join the majority of his fellow sonneteers in Englishing some of the Psalms. Nevertheless, multiplicity, of sources, interests – and of levels of reading – should be recognised. Shakespeare knew the Bible with an understanding that is in most ways strange to us. It can be seen most obviously in his many quotations, often from places that are unfamiliar.[19] In *The Merchant of Venice*, 1.3, he makes Shylock, in his first scene, recount a strange incident in the story of Laban from Genesis 30. To tell a story from the Hebrew Scriptures is a natural thing for a Jew to do. Shakespeare expects his audience not only to know it, but to ask themselves why Shylock is telling it there. Shakespeare uses Bible references movingly, as Richard II refers to Judas's greeting to Christ (*Richard II*, 4.1.169–71): comically, as Benedick says he would not marry Beatrice though she were endowed with all that Adam had left to him before he transgressed (*Much Ado About Nothing* 2.1.235–6); and indirectly, as Bottom, waking from his dream in *A Midsummer Night's Dream* 4.1.209–12, misquotes St Paul to describe it – 'The eye of man hath not heard . . .'. More interestingly, Shakespeare makes assumptions about the biblical understanding of his ordinary hearers and readers that allow him to follow New Testament thought into one of its sixteenth-century developments, the encapsulation of New Testament theology, particularly that of Paul, which became known as Calvinism. Both *Julius Caesar* and *Hamlet*, written close together in 1599 and 1600, are in part Calvinist plays.[20] English translations of Calvin's works were almost beyond comparison the most frequent in Europe. William Perkins's Calvinist sermons in Cambridge between 1592 and 1602 were immensely popular: his Calvinist *Golden Chain* was reprinted twelve times between 1591 and 1600. (Work remains to be done on the causes of national ignorance of Calvin in the past three or four hundred years, and the effects of that on the understanding of English and early American literature.[21])

In the second scene of the second Act of *Measure for Measure*, Isabella retorts to the Deputy's Draconian 'Your brother is forfeit of the law', with:

> Alas! Alas!
> Why, all the souls that were were forfeit once:
> And He that might the vantage best have took
> Found out the remedy. (72–5)

Her evocation of the biblical account of the blameless life of Christ, and his work of the redemption of the world in his death, as Christians believe, is at that moment in the play subtly resonant. Isabella takes her theology further:

> How would you be
> If He, which is the top of judgement, should
> But judge you as you are ? O, think on that;
> And mercy then will breathe within your lips
> Like man new made. (75–9)

Her main nouns and verbs are biblical, especially 'souls', 'judge', 'judgement' and 'mercy'. The whole play, however, hangs on more than a pointed biblical reference. In its working-out of the themes not only of justice and mercy, but also of law and love, of grace, remedy and redemption, it is very close to – indeed, only intelligible in the light of – Paul in the Epistles to the Romans and to the Galatians. Shakespeare was not writing theology: he was a poet and maker of dramas. But he seemed to expect his audience to understand the larger world he is in, and that setting his play in contemporary Vienna allows him to make characters who can reflect the human and divine responsibilities that Paul thrusts at us, and make such characters change and grow.

There are many aspects of Shakespeare's poems and plays which can be seen to reflect not simply a Bible knowledge shared with his audience, but the way in which unique elements in, especially, the New Testament, affect his dramatic writing. His uniquely New Testament understanding of the true union in marriage needs exploration. The biblical nature of his historical patterning, with its political implications, goes beyond, to share strategies of many of the poets of the time to preserve, politically as well as religiously, a degree of independence.[22] This is vital. Shakespeare does his unique things for his own poetic and dramatic reasons. Yet in choosing to write, and to rewrite, English history, he cannot help being in a Protestant stream of providential national historiography. Hall, Grafton, Holinshed and Foxe, to name but four, Protestant rewriters all, were doing that, and they were only the higher end of the culture. In the second half of the century, a strong tradition of anonymous chronicle writing, often in doggerel, used the voice of the people to give historical examples, much as Tyndale does at a more dignified level in *The Practice of Prelates*: most of it is apocalyptic in direction, following John Bale.[23]

There is space here to mention only one further matter. In her book, *Shakespeare's Theory of Drama* (1996), Pauline Kiernan discovers a sort of Shakespearean *Defence of Drama* by finding that Shakespeare rejected the mimetic aesthetic of Sidney and his late Renaissance humanist peers.[24] Shakespeare, she finds, did something quite different, valuing instead something she notes as 'presence', the living human body on stage, with its necessarily intensely subjective set of responses. Also in 1996, Deborah Shuger, remarking how Shakespeare's religion has been wrongly seen as defending a conservative social order, noted that in fact he gives dramatic life to 'poor and common speech', the self, as she puts it, as suffering subject: 'Lear's pedigree does not fundamentally alter the fact that he is a powerless and hurt old man tormented by rage, guilt and thankless children . . . the displacing of social discourses of suffering and poverty on to psychological representations' is a legacy peculiarly of Protestant subjectivity.[25]

William Tyndale is relevant here. Always subjective in his responses to the work of the Gospel, in all his writing that is not biblical translation (particularly his *Wicked Mammon* and his *Obedience of a Christian Man*) he allows nothing to stand between the suffering soul and God – and that suffering is often metaphorised by him as either deep poverty or great illness, from both of which the gospel releases the ordinary man or woman or child, he insists, with glorious new and energetic liberty. Secondly, Tyndale translated the Bible for the ploughboy, as he famously remarked, that poor, underprivileged, physically suffering creature. One cannot argue that Shakespeare had read Tyndale's books: but, thirdly, he *had* read Tyndale's translation of the four Gospels. Naseeb Shaheen has shown that they are easily Shakespeare's most-referred-to biblical books, and whether he read Geneva Bibles (the evidence points that way) or the Bishops' Bible, he was still largely reading Tyndale.

One core of the Gospels is the removal of the religious rituals of exclusion: Jesus shocked the righteous by sitting down for meals with moral outcasts. His bodily presence, as a Messiah, someone with the greatest spiritual power who heals and teaches now, and not in some future, was with fishermen and prostitutes and publicans. As Jesus says so often, the Kingdom of God is now. Any over-ritualised religion since the dawn of time can make its priests say that yes, we know, it's rotten, and hard luck, but just do as we say, keep at the ritual, stick it out, give us your money

and you'll end up with the angels in heaven for evermore. The Gospels
do not say this. There is a future; but the world of the Kingdom of God,
as in so many of the parables, is now, even more than then. The finding
of the lost sheep is now. The Prodigal Son returns now. The four Gospels
are full of hard sayings, and the modern scholarly teasing-out of the relation between them as texts has been described as one of the most difficult subjects in the humanities.[26] Yet at the same time they are blazingly
simple, being full of people, usually poor and suffering people, in the presence of an extraordinary teacher and healer. In the healing is the sudden
dramatic conflict between humanity wrong (diseased, ill, deformed) and
humanity right. Here is Pauline Kiernan's 'presence'; what, as Deborah
Shuger pointed out, William Perkins called 'a person of mine own self,
under Christ'.[27] Tyndale brought to English readers the strength of the
inward, spiritual regiment, presence localised not only in the temporal and
secular (that idea originates in Luther) but in the spiritual and subjective,
psychologically represented, taken into a body on the stage. The *mimesis*
of the later humanists, Sidney and the rest pointed to some ethical value
of art. Shakespeare, by contrast, is full of people, quite newly. This came
to him from fifty years of increasing subjectivity, through a Protestant fact,
everyone knowing the Bible in English, especially the Gospels.

Recent commentators express surprise about how new this was. Harold
Bloom, in his introduction to his *Shakespeare: The Invention of the Human*,
writes, 'In Shakespeare, characters develop rather than unfold, and they
develop because they re-conceive themselves . . . [as in] no other writer.'[28]
Shakespeare's theory of drama is of bodily presence, as Pauline Kiernan
shows. That body is in interior, human, conflict. Of Edgar's bedlam beggar
and Lear's nakedness in the storm Deborah Shuger writes:

> Such characters acquire their psychological depth by assimilating the
> ancient Christian discourses of social injustice to the structures of the
> psyche . . . within the tragic protagonist, enabling a fundamentally new
> presentation of the self. . . . Before Lear, kings did not hallucinate or
> run around half-naked with flowers in their hair, weeping over their
> unkind children.[29]

The phrase 'ancient Christian discourses of social injustice' could be
focused on four narratives fully available to all English people, the Gospels.

It has for a long time been noticed that Hamlet's language borrows
heavily from popular speech, his images being 'drawn from the most
common aspects of everyday life . . . which ally him to the lower-class
figures of the Moralities'.[30] Shakespeare had no need to walk to Coventry to see the mystery plays in order to meet ordinary people ('lower-class
figures' in that unfortunate phrase) in dramatic conflict. He could find

those everyday images, heavily pregnant with apparently infinite meaning, at home, in the Gospels. Riches of material from the ancient world, the European Renaissance and recent history were borne to Shakespeare on a great tidal wave. But the great shifting of tectonic plates in Europe which produced the Protestant *tsunami* (far greater than a 'tidal wave') that flooded Europe to such depth gave him, through the Bible in English, a Kingdom of Heaven which is immediate; bodily presence on stage. Here is a parable:

> What woman having ten groats, if she lose one, doth not light a candle, and sweep the house, and seek diligently, till she find it? And when she hath found it she calleth her lovers and her neighbours saying: Rejoice with me, for I have found the groat which I had lost.[31]

What could be simpler? Words have changed: 'groats' has gone, and 'lovers' has become entirely sexual: yet Jesus' story is not only clear; it also goes far beyond rational analysis. Luke tells it in the context of the Pharisees murmuring because Jesus is with 'sinners', and eats with them. The story is not, or not only, about moral outcasts. It is more fully about losing and finding again, an experience that can make one weep, like finding oneself unexpectedly at home again. Jesus uses it to parallel 'joy in the presence of the angels of God', and what *that* means cannot surely be put into rational words at all.

In Hamlet's last desperate seconds, he is fighting for time to tell vital things to the obtuse – and thus suddenly betraying – Horatio:

> Had I but time – as this fell sergeant Death
> Is strict in his arrest – O, I could tell you –
> But let it be. (5.2.328–30)

Shakespeare expresses what might be said given less than a minute to live (unlike Ben Jonson, who expresses what Ben Jonson might say). In that simple language, Hamlet's range of emotion and thought, and the sense of a vast revelation of what it would – will – be like to die, are beyond anything expected. The extraordinary image of the fell sergeant strictly arresting suggests guilt, and martyrdom, and horror, and inevitability, and an arresting being who is both outside and inside the dying body, all in the end of someone's life on earth. Shakespeare is close to Tyndale in that sense of simple words bringing in a new kingdom of possibilities – 'This thy brother was dead, and is alive again; was lost, and is found': or 'Now abideth faith, hope and love, even these three: but the chief of these is love.'

Harold Bloom gets this wrong. He rightly says that only the Bible matches Shakespeare, but he finds that 'what the Bible and Shakespeare have in common is rather less than most people suppose . . . only a certain universalism'.[32] Not so. What Shakespeare and the Bible have in common is that language, at the highest moments, of elemental simplicity, from the Gospels. It is suffering and poverty that are interiorised by Shakespeare. In the Gospels it is 'one sick of the palsy' (whose friends, so dense is the crowd, break open the roof of the house and let him down) to whom Jesus says, 'son, thy sins are forgiven thee.' Shakespeare met suffering people, registered in the ordinary language of the people, in the texts of the Gospels in English, ultimately Tyndale's English. He interiorised their suffering, and put them on the stage.

Chapter 24

THE ENGLISH BIBLE IN AMERICA:
FROM THE BEGINNINGS TO 1640

THE BEGINNINGS

On 13 July 1584, two small English ships, chartered by (though not including) Sir Walter Raleigh, made a landfall at what is now the Outer Banks off North Carolina. That desolate and windswept hundred-and-fifty-mile strip of high sand dunes protects from the Atlantic Ocean the inlets and bays of the inner coast. Such sheltered water was what Sir Walter's men were looking for, as a base from which to attack Spanish ships. They understood that they were also pathfinders for future British settlement.

They were awed by what they found. Across the water inside the Banks, on what was later named Roanoke Island, they saw what they described as unbelievable natural fullness: the land was 'very sandie, and lowe towards the water's side, but so full of grapes as the very beating and surge of the Sea overflowed them' – the words of one of the party, Arthur Barlowe, written with an eye to making it appealing at home. 'I thinke in all the world the like abundance is not to be founde.'[1] At that first encounter, 'having discharged our harquebuz-shot, such a flocke of Cranes (the most part white) arose under us, with such a cry redoubled by many echoes, as if an armie of men had showted all together.'[2]

But there was no army of men. There was nobody at all. The new land seemed empty of humans. On the third day a few Indians appeared, Powhatans, 'gentle, loving and faithful' people. Soon those natives gave a special feast for the brightly clad European visitors, who took the native compliment 'Wind gan con' ('What nice clothes you are wearing'), for the name of the region. After a short stay, the English party sailed away, taking two of the natives with them back to England, to help to tell Raleigh and others what awaited them. Queen Elizabeth, the Virgin Queen, allowed Sir Walter to rename as 'Virginia' this alluring, luscious body of land, inviting conquest. (Perhaps he did so only partly after his Queen: in an essay in the collection *In the American Grain* of 1925, William

Carlos Williams wrote of Raleigh 'plunging his lust into the body of a new world'.)

Under a year later, on 9 April 1585, a second expedition, under Sir Richard Grenville and again sponsored by Raleigh, set out from England, this time with seven ships and five hundred men. These were mostly soldiers, with some gentlemen and merchants. Over a hundred of the men intended to settle. There were no women or children. They took the two Powhatan Indians back to America. To our everlasting benefit, the artist among them, John White, and the scientist, Thomas Hariot, recorded with wonder the rich life around Roanoke.

At home in England in the summer of 1585, Raleigh could feel pleasure that in taking Virginia he was wresting part of a New World from the Spanish, especially as there was (incorrect) talk of silver mines. The openings for political and commercial wealth were announced as the finding of a new Eden. The promises of a Paradise were passed around the City of London in Bible phrases, like Richard Hakluyt's 'the promised land flowing with milk and honey'.[3] In Virginia itself, however, the very real serpent in that Eden, not officially mentioned, was the opposite: sheer lack of food. The English fought the Indians for it. Paradise was abandoned for lack of sustenance. The would-be colonisers had quickly turned those 'gentle, loving and faithful' Indians into violent enemies. All the English were taken off by Sir Francis Drake and his fleet of two dozen ships sailing north past the Outer Banks in 1586. After a few weeks, Sir Richard Grenville, passing the spot to offer supplies, found it deserted but left fifteen of his own men.

Two years later, in 1588, Raleigh sent out three more ships. John White the artist returned as the new Governor of Virginia. He found no trace of Grenville's fifteen men. He established a community on Roanoke, this time with women and children. He rejoiced that in August his daughter Eleanor Dare gave birth to a baby girl, the first English child born in America, christened Virginia. There was little else to be glad about. Food was still desperately short. The Indians killed an Englishman while he was fishing for crabs. Again serious fighting followed. A chief was killed. Leaving his family only a month after his granddaughter had been born, Governor White returned to England for supplies, now to include arms. But England had little to spare for a handful of settlers three thousand miles away. The now-thunderous threat from Spain was just over the horizon. In 1588 the Armada came and was beaten.

In August 1590 White returned to America to relieve the Roanoke colony. He anchored off the island in the shallow waters of what is now Pamlico Sound. He saw no sign of any life. A sailor blew a trumpet.

Nothing happened. They all sang English Psalms and songs. No one took up the familiar tunes. The forest was silent. They landed, to find that the settlement had disappeared. The cabins and the palisade were overgrown. With others, three chests that were Governor White's personal belongings left for his return had been ransacked. His books had been ripped apart and left to moulder. To this day, in spite of an industry of speculation and books 'solving the problem', no one knows what had happened. On a tree were found three carved letters, 'CRO', and on a doorpost 'CROATOAN', the name of an island further south, where there had possibly been friendly natives. What that carving was intended to signify is unknown. Twenty years later, the colonists in Jamestown to the north were told that the Roanoke settlers had been assimilated with Indian tribes. If, as seems likely, the men were killed in Indian attacks, the surviving women and children could have lived on in native villages.[4] Sir Walter's personal enterprise for those three years had cost lives. True, it had yielded valuable experience and information. But when, in March 1602, Raleigh sent out a search for survivors, there was as yet no colony.

ENGLISH BIBLES REACH AMERICA

Thomas Hariot was the scientfic observer. His informative account was modestly entitled *A Brief and True Report of the New Found Land of Virginia*, printed in London in 1588. A second edition of 1590, translated into French, Latin and German, with engravings of John White's drawings, sold all over Europe. Hariot slips from scientific thoroughness at several points. He does not explain the true economic situation: rumours of silver and precious stones overshadow the realities of agriculture. He gives no account of how the hostilities with the Indians arose – especially, how their chief was killed. Indeed, his description of that chief joining in the settlers' Psalm-singing is probably politically misleading. The picture, however, of the religious life of the visitors is important. No doubt in London in those decades the eyes of speculators gleamed with greed, and the tongues of sailors told tales of storms and starvation. But whatever words were spoken in the committee rooms and taverns of London, the religious mission was put first in what was circulating in print. The official London literature was Bible based.

Though there are no lists of the books, it has to be a certainty that there were Bibles in English among the possessions of the voyagers. The would-be colonists were from a Protestant land and Bible-reading homes. English Bibles – more specifically, Geneva Bibles – used as part of daily life arrived in America, (though perhaps not for the very first time on American soil) on Raleigh's ships. Such a strong suggestiveness has three strands.

First, the documents of the time record the understood purpose of such voyages as including, high on the list, the conversion of the pagan inhabitants to Christianity: a large motive in the quest was automatically declared to be a religious one. The title-page of a book printed in London in 1583 begins: *A report of the voyage and successe thereof, attempted in the yeere of our Lord 1583 by sir Humfrey Gilbert knight, intended to discover and to plant Christian inhabitants in place convenient.* An early sentence in that book speaks of sowing the seed of Christian religion among those pagans, 'which must be the chief intent of such as shall make any attempt that way: or else whatsoever is builded upon other foundation shall never obtain happy success nor continuance'.[5] Six years earlier, Dionyse Settle's *A True Reporte of the Laste* [i.e. second] *Voyage made into the West and Northwest Regions, &c. 1577: Worthily atchieued by Capteine Frobisher* noted 'that by our Christian studie and endeuour, those barbarous, people trained up in Paganisme, and infidelitie might be reduced to the knowledge of true religion, and the hope of salvation in Christ our Redeemer'.[6] In that work, English settlers, which almost always means Protestant settlers, had the Bible as their chief instrument.[7]

Second, voyages were presented as automatically religious in another sense. The enterprise by Frobisher just mentioned began on Monday morning, 27 May 1577: on board 'we received all the Communion by the Minister of Gravesend, and prepared us all good Christians towards God'.[8] Not only would few voyages from England have been undertaken without such a Protestant communion: regular services of prayer, Psalm-singing and Bible-reading, usually daily and often twice daily, were so much part of the lives of Elizabethan seamen that they were worth mention only if there was a special reason – like the start of a momentous voyage, or a safe landing on a remote shore. Frobisher, arrived at Jackman's Sound:

> after the ship rode at anker, our generall, with such company as could well be spared from the ships, in marching order entred the lande, having special care by exhortations, that at our entrance thereinto, wee should all with one voyce, kneeling upon our knee, chiefly thanke God for our safe arrival.[9]

Hakluyt's *Discourse* of 1583 has a note in chapter 21 of things to be taken, including

> one or two preachers for the voyadge, that God may be honoured, the people instructed, mutinies the better avoided, and obedience the better

used, that the voyadge may have better successe. That the voyadge be furnished with Bibles and with Bookes of service.[10]

That a function of preachers was to help with discipline may be thought significant. The point here is not to denigrate or idealise preachers and their Bibles, but simply to note their presence.

The account of Martin Frobisher's third voyage in 1578 includes:

> Master Wolfall on *Winter's Furnace* preached a godly sermon, which being ended, he celebrated also a Communion upon the land . . . the celebration of the divine mystery was the first sign, seal and confirmation of Christ's name, death and passion ever known in these quarters. The said M. Wolfall made sermons, and celebrated Communion at sundry other times, in severall and sundry ships, because the whole company could never meet together at any one place.[11]

Third, incidents come to the surface in documents of this time which are revealing of a whole way of life. Thus in chapter 2 of Hakluyt's *Discourse* of 1583 is a description of the dangers faced by English sailors and traders

> in all the King of Spayne his domynions, where our men are dryven to flinge their bibles and prayer bookes into the sea, and to forsweare and renounce their relligion and conscience, and consequently their obedience to her Majesty.[12]

To trade with Spain, Hakluyt notes, ships' masters have to swear to the Spanish king 'to bring no manner of bookes but suche as are allowed by our Catholicke Churche of Rome'. He describes Spanish boarders searching the seamen's chests for books.[13] The point is further driven home by an incident in Hakluyt's *Collection of Voyages*: a ship, the *Tobie*, was wrecked off Morocco in 1593. Clinging to the rigging, the sailors sang the twelfth Psalm, 'Help Lord, for good and godly men'. Sadly, before they had finished four verses, most of the men drowned. Protestant English seamen (as, no doubt, French and Dutch and German) knew the Psalms by heart.

The lure of limitless silver and abundant fertility was obviously strong, with the hope of reward for personally pleasing the queen. Yet these voyages of settlement in the 1580s and after were conducted as part of lives that were as naturally religious as breathing the air. The people of England did not cease to be religious when the monasteries were dissolved in 1539, and altars were turned into communion tables.[14] Throughout the sixteenth century in England, there are constant reiterations of the experience of life being experience of religion, with no separation of the two. Sir Walter Raleigh, and Sir Francis Drake and others, were sea-borne adventurers out to seize the incredible riches being transported back to

Spain.[15] They did this to enrich themselves. They also sailed in such dangerous seas strategically, to attack the fringes of Spanish power. Cutting off the inflowing wealth of the Mediterranean Catholic empire was both a religious imperative and a patriotic pursuit; it was also enterprising and profitable. Raleigh and Drake were patriots. Both were privateers (pirates with government support), religious privateers, Protestant religious privateers. Bible-reading and psalm-singing were part of daily life on board.

That the English Bibles were being taken into a world of opportunity was to be one part of a story seen to have itself a Bible base. The new world was promoted in Europe as naturally abundant, a second biblical Eden. America would soon provide the means for the establishment of what were lived as truly biblical 'congregations', groups of believers with Bibles and acts of worship but no subscription to the massive, complex hierarchy and system of either an English, or papal, church. It would become a God-given chance to start again, to remake the primitive first-century, New Testament, churches of the Acts of the Apostles, long before there were popes or archbishops.

Another part of the story, however, not often then publicly told, was of harshly immediate reality. There were dreadful hardships in an unknown, and thus unpredictable, climate, where pioneer ignorance about crops could make food scarce and colonies could be wiped out by disease. The indigenous tribes of Indians had natural objections to ignorant and arrogant strangers arriving from nowhere and simply marking off and taking over their land and their livelihoods, and even slaughtering them at whim.[16]

DESOLATION

Had the courtier Sir Walter Raleigh himself stood on the Outer Banks in 1584, perhaps with an elegant, finely printed English Bible in his hand, he might have felt he was standing on the moon. The organised civilisations of Europe were far away. People across the continent of Europe, in northern Italy, Spain, Portugal, France, 'Austria' (as it became), western Germany, the Low Countries, England, Wales and Scotland could not always understand one anothers' languages (though common roots made them relatively easy to learn, and for the educated, Latin was everywhere): but they lived together in ancient, cultured cities. Among so many beautiful things, fine Bibles had been made in Venice, Cologne, Paris, Antwerp, Geneva and London. The Bible was the one universal book, in most countries by then eagerly read. In Europe, outside the cities, the people lived in even more ancient and long-cultivated countrysides, thick with thousands of years of tillage. True, there was darkness to the east: the infidel Turks had conquered Hungary and pressed on Vienna. 'Muscovy' was a shadow in the distance, and like the Scandinavian countries good for not much more than trade. Yet even the colder northern cities of Europe like Paris, Antwerp and London had leisure, learning and craft, and manners of high sophistication. Soon, in London, Shakespeare would consummate the power of the English language, and Bacon would found modern scientific method.

The New World was an absolute contrast. There were Mexican-Spanish cities of some splendour far to the south, but this 'Virginian' American coast had windy, empty sandbanks, unpeopled inlets, and behind them vast forests and swamps. What humans there were had impenetrable languages and customs, and too-accurate arrows dealing sudden death from the dark woods. To the west behind the coast, and far to the north and south, were apparently endless miles of the same: inlets, rivers, forests, swamps and hills. Insistent European fantasies peopled them with grotesque shapes living fearfully amid supernatural terrors: Caliban was about the best one could hope for. Yes, there was abundance in many places – lakes and rivers full of fish, vast plains full of buffalo – but the immediate skills needed to find and exploit them were for a long time lacking. Those early communities clung desperately to a bleak edge. In 1526, a Spanish settlement in what would later become Virginia suffered a cold winter, mutiny, a slave revolt and Indian attacks: only 150 men of the original 600 survived.[17] 'During the fierce winter of 1604–5 the entire American empire of France consisted of one miserable colony which lay freezing and half-dead with scurvy on the little island of Saint Croix in Passamaquoddy Bay.'[18] In 1608, on Champlain's third voyage to Canada (out of eleven), all but eight men perished in the first Canadian winter.[19] Already noted has been the total disappearance in 1590 of the first English colony on Roanoke Island, with nothing left except some letters carved on a tree.

What follows here is a brief history of the first settlement of North America, to give some structure to the accounts of the English Bible among those pioneers.

INDIGENOUS PEOPLE AND OTHERS

The 'Indians' had been on the continent first, of course, tens of thousands of years before the European settlements. Mankind crossed a land bridge from north-east Asia and spread southwards, diversifying richly as they went into all the Americas. By 900 BC they had reached the southern tip of South America, and inhabited the Caribbean. Some of them lived in cultures equal to those in Europe at the time. In all, when Columbus arrived, between one and two million lived in what is now the USA:[20] some historians suggest ten to twelve million.[21] Since then, they have been all but wiped out, by imported diseases as much as by gunpowder and steel. 'What happened after 1492 in Meso-America and North-America was a demographic disaster with no known parallel in world history.'[22]

From the east, the Atlantic side, the Vikings had been first. Four to five hundred years before Columbus, they had touched land eight hundred miles to the north of what became Virginia, at the tip of what became Newfoundland. They came in the eleventh and twelfth centuries AD; from there they may have pushed a little south along the coast in exploration.[23] The great distances across the sea, as well as increased ice in the North Atlantic, led to the abandonment of direct contact, though knowledge remained.

Far to the south, the Spanish led as serious colonisers, in warmer waters, thanks to an Italian sailor from Portugal sponsored by the Spanish court. This man, Christopher Columbus, sailing west in 1492, had not, as many expected, fallen off the edge beyond the Canary Isles. That the world was round was still far from being generally understood, but leaving harbour and sailing westward, as many had done before him on the practical assumption that the waters covered a globe, Columbus sighted land in the moonlight in the early hours of 12 October 1492. The next day, for King Ferdinand and Queen Isabella of Spain, Columbus took possession of the island he named San Salvador ('Holy Saviour') in what became the Bahamas. Convinced he was in Asia, he called the natives 'Indians'. Seven months later, in May 1493, Pope Alexander VI (Rodrigo Borgia) issued two bulls, *Inter Caetera* I and II, granting to Spain every future discovery on the Atlantic rim of North and South America. (He gave to Portugal all the riches of the East.) Early in the 1500s, Spanish or Portuguese explorers charted thousands of miles of American coast, South, Central and North. In 1513, Balboa saw the Pacific. Between 1519 and 1521, the Spanish conquered Mexico, and carried away great treasures: these had serious effects on the economies of Europe. By 1530, the land as far north as what was later named Nova Scotia was being described. By the middle of the century, always drawn on by mythical gold, Spain had penetrated further vast territories, including what became Louisiana, Arkansas and Texas, and, 1,200 miles further west, even looking down into the Grand Canyon. The Spanish base was Florida, named by Columbus's friend Juan Ponce de Léon at the first sighting of the American mainland in 1513: it was at Easter-time when, incidentally, flowers were richly blooming.[24] ('La Florida' was a name given later to the whole Atlantic coastline from that peninsula north.) Spanish and Portuguese explorers who had amazingly survived by 'hairbreadth scapes' the horrors of storms, massacres and torture arrived back in Europe full of rosy stories of wealth and opportunity. In 1526, a brief Spanish colony had been planted near what would become Jamestown nearly a hundred years later. By mid-century, Spain was master of the whole of South America except Brazil, and North America from Florida to California. In 1558–61, 1,500 people left Spain to try to establish the first colony in the New World. In 1565, the first permanent colony was indeed settled, at St Augustine in Florida. By 1600, the Spanish had founded about two hundred cities and towns throughout the Americas, with universities at Mexico City and Lima, Peru. They printed books and built cathedrals. It is said that by 1600 the Americas had received about 240,000 people from Spain.[25] Though obviously benefiting from scientific advances – in observation, in navigation, in shipbuilding, and in the making and printing of maps – the settlers attempting to found New Spain still rigidly imposed the medieval church, in absolute union with the state. By 1650, Spanish Jesuits and Franciscans were, or had been, active as missionaries at the heart of the two great continents of the Americas, and up the Pacific coast: by then some settlements on the northern borders of New Spain were deep in what became the United States.

Independent voyagers crossed the Atlantic early in the sixteenth century, but France was next as coloniser. French fishermen, it seems, had continually visited the shoals of cod off the North American coast from the 1480s – a precious find for protein-starved, fish-on-Fridays-eating Catholic Europe. Jacques Cartier explored the St Lawrence in 1534 and 1541. The first serious French settlements were made by Huguenots hoping to begin to live freely as Protestant Frenchmen: in May 1562 they established themselves in Port Royal, in what became South Carolina, and in 1564, at the mouth of the St John's River in Florida. That colony was soon after massacred by the Spanish, an atrocity avenged three years later. Thereafter, France had little spare energy for colonising until the interest in Canada led to Champlain founding Quebec in 1608. After 1627, Richelieu and his successors continued a policy of rather ragged colonisation in the further north. The fur trade was prosperous: beaver fur was especially precious.

The map of the Americas was slowly being coloured by New Spain and New France – and New Netherland and New Sweden. The newly independent Reformed Dutch seized territories from the Spanish and Portuguese in South America (as well as in the Far East). They had sent out an English navigator, Henry Hudson, to find routes to the (East) Indies. In 1609, he sailed up the river that bears his name, and soon established fur trade with the Iroquois. The Dutch West India Company was founded in 1621: within three years it had placed colonists on Manhattan Island and on the Delaware, and soon there were Dutch communities growing on Long Island, Staten Island and what became New Jersey. Encouraged by the Dutch, Swedish merchants (and some from Finland) founded New Sweden in 1638 in what became Wilmington, Delaware.

THE ENGLISH

The English exploration of America began with that merchant of Venice, Giovanni Cabota, known in Bristol as John Cabot. He was employed by Henry VII in 1498 to find a northerly route to the East Indies. His much-publicised voyages began to settle the confusion in Europe about what was America and what was Asia. His son Sebastian's maps of a supposed North-West Passage in the 1550s became important in later English searches. Under Elizabeth I, men from Bristol found new fishing grounds in the western Atlantic. The larger aim of the merchant-explorers by sea was usually to get to the fabled wealth of the East without the nearly impossible costs of overland routes through Europe, the Near East and India. Seeking the elusive sea-routes, the North-East Passage (north of Russia) or North-West Passage (north of Canada) took appalling tolls in money, time and lives. Gradually the eastern American seaboard itself became attractive as worth settlement. That land could offer staging-posts to the ultimate East, which could perhaps then be reached via the south through those terrible Straits which Magellan alone had survived, or via the arctic north through that still-sought North-West Passage. Better still, the English began to realise that they could keep their loot from the Spanish on that side of the dangerous Atlantic. The allure of trading settlements on the eastern American seaboard matured into plans for full-scale colonisation, boosted by the perpetual failure of settlements in Ireland, and the greater promise across the Atlantic than over the English Channel – a quarter of English emigrants had gone to the Continent.[26] Even before Raleigh's ships found Roanoke, Sir Humphrey Gilbert, half-brother to Raleigh, had in passing established the first small English colony in North America on 5 August 1583, at what was later called St John's, Newfoundland. That spot, already long used by visiting English fishermen, became a tiny settlement, which never quite disappeared.

Disaster on voyages was never far away. On 9 September 1583, a heavy storm off the Azores struck Gilbert's two ships. Sir Humphrey was seen sitting in the stern of the tiny *Squirrel* with a book in his hand, and was heard to call out 'We are as near to Heaven by sea as by land.' The *Squirrel* sank at midnight with all hands. Nevertheless, the official mood in England in those later Elizabethan years is dramatically illustrated by the circulation of Gilbert's own printed account of an attempt to get to China by the North-West Passage, his *A Discourse of a Discovery for a New Passage to Cataia* (1576). Richard Hakluyt in 1582 published the first of his descriptions of pioneer explorers, *Divers voyages touching the discovery of America*. Hakluyt's manuscript *Discourse Concerning Western Planting* of 1583 was a blueprint for the notion of a Virginia settlement, on economic and religious grounds: employment and wealth would be there, and the English should carry the glorious Gospel to the simple natives by planting colonies before it was too late – before Catholic 'superstition' pre-empted the territory. Hakluyt's widely read three-volume *Principal Navigations* (1589–1600) had the same powerful message against the spread of Catholicism and the menace from Spain – it first appeared only months after the defeat of the Armada.[27] The colonising English under Elizabeth now felt free to outflank the territorial claims of the Pope and of Spain (which had recently conquered Portugal) using as authority the older charter given to Cabot by the queen's grandfather, Henry VII. On 25 March 1584, a patent was issued to Sir Walter Raleigh to find a suitable American site. He sent the two ships whose arrival began this chapter.

That freedom was the beginning of a development in which, over the next century and a half, the English would show the three essential factors which gave them domination. Being islanders, they knew the sea, and how to maintain supplies. Being sailors, they could carry large numbers to work the new land. Having adaptable skills, they developed that most important operation of all, tillage. Unlike the Spanish, they came to understand that the wealth of North America had to be worked for. Success came when they abandoned the lure of bullion and took to planting.

RELIGIOUS CONFLICTS, AND HARDSHIPS

The six European nations that originally made rival claims for colonial possessions in the New World all founded local missions of their established churches. Though five of those (the Spanish, Portugese, French, Dutch and Swedish) eventually gave up claims to the territories that later became part of the United States or Canada, their established churches remained: so, and in the end more importantly, did the congregations of Dissenters. In the history of the Bible in America, they are all significant. The eventual extraordinary triumph of the English Bible has to be seen as a strong and important element even from the earliest life on the continent. It was only part, however, of a wide spectrum of conflicting religious traditions from Europe. The sharpest differences were matters of faith, between the Protestants (the majority) and the Catholics (the most powerful). The horror felt by Catholics at ruthless Protestant evangelising was matched by the Protestant mission to save the savages from the superstitions and tyrannies of the papacy. From the beginning, every Spanish settlers' ship brought priests. Though the territories were vast and the challenges for evangelism in the common name of Christ were seemingly almost unlimited, the religious story of all the settlements was usually of internal unrest, quarrels, and further separations. And all were on top of the very greatest hardships.

In 1605 and 1606, an exploratory expedition by George Weymouth under the auspices of the Earl of Southampton and his Roman Catholic son-in-law visited Montrachet off the Maine coast, ostensibly to establish a colony for English Catholics. On 13 May 1607, a group of 144 English men set out on what became a twenty-week voyage from Devon in the *Susan Constant*, the *Godspeed* and the *Delivery*. Their voyage was the product of a joint stock company, the London Virginia Company. Late in the previous century, the English merchants' newly available risk capital and new global enterprise had contributed to the founding of the Muscovy Company, the Levant Company, the Orient Company, the English East India Company, the Cathay (China) Company, the Guinea Company, the Eastland Company and above all the two Virginia Companies, one in London and one in Plymouth. The establishment of the latter had been prompted by the printed account of the Weymouth voyages. They had acquired Raleigh's title to Virginia.

Out of the 144 on the three English ships in 1607, only 105 survived the journey. They landed on a peninsula in Chesapeake Bay, some hundred miles north of the coastal Roanoke. They moved up a river which they named the James after their king. The site was unhealthy but easily defensible against presumed Spanish attacks. They sent out exploring parties, began building fortifications, and repulsed an attack by Indians. They called their settlement Jamestown. The sharpest of their number, Captain John Smith, in his *A True Relation*, forcefully pointed out that missionary work was an overlay:

> we did admire how it was possible such wise men could so torment themselves and us with such strange absurdities and impossibilities, making Religion their colour, when all their aim was nothing but present profit, as most plainly appeared, by sending us so many Refiners, Gold-smiths, Jewellers, Lapidaries, Stone-cutters, Tabacco-pipe-makers, Imbroiderers, Perfumers, Silkemen, with all their appurtenances, but materialls, and all these had great summes out of the common stocke.[28]

Motives were intertwined. As well as greed for mined silver and gold (John Smith's 'but materialls' suggests that the immigrant gold- and silver-smiths and so on were to live off the local wealth), the evangelism was also partly a cover for a wished-for life of God-ordained ease in the new Eden. King James's charter granting the patent was insistent, nevertheless, that his intention was 'propagating of Christian religion to such people as yet live in darkness and miserable ignorance of the true knowledge and worship of God'.[29]

Five weeks after the landing, their leader, Captain Newport, sailed to England again, leaving them to their own resources. These, according to the wilder fantasies at large in London at the time, were phenomenal. The words of Seagull in *Eastward Ho!*, the play by Marston, Chapman and Jonson written and performed in 1605, mock, and at the same time encapsulate, the local beliefs (the 'gull' in his name implies someone over-credulous, 'gull'ible, as well as a sea-creature).

> A whole country of English is there, man, bred of those that were left there in '79. They have married with the Indians, and make 'em bring forth as beautiful faces as any we have in England; and therefore the Indians are so in love with 'em, that all the treasure they have, they lay at their feet.

Seagull paraphrases and elaborates Book II of Thomas More's *Utopia*, where gold and pearls (here 'rubies and diamonds') are of mundanely common use. Asked if it is a pleasant country, he explains:

> As ever the sun shined on, temperate and full of all sorts of excellent viands: wild boar is as common there as our tamest bacon is here; venison, as mutton.[30]

The hand of God in the American ventures began to be made more visible: 'the colonizing of Virginia . . . was an act in the economy of redemption, a special and supernatural summons, a maneuver which the wisdom of God had made inevitable from the beginning of time and was now carrying to its foreordained completion.'[31] News reached Europe, for example, in 1609, of a more than usually fearful storm which had wrecked, on the islands of Bermuda, the *Sea Venture*, the ship taking Sir Thomas Gates to be Acting-Governor of the new colony at Jamestown. Printed accounts were read in London with wonder and excitement, telling of how the voyagers not only survived on that mysterious shore, but lived well. Eventually, out of the wreck, they made a new, smaller boat, the *Deliverance*, in which they sailed on to Jamestown, to the astonishment of the colonists there who had long given them up for lost. The reports, and all concerned, made it clear that the whole experience was evidence that Almighty God had a hand in the Jamestown plantation. In 1611, Shakespeare, himself through several friends connected to the Virginia Company, out of that afternoon of shipwreck and survival made a fine play, *The Tempest*. Both wreck and preservation were seen as due to supernatural intervention: high European magic, but ultimately the work of Providence, as the accounts made clear.[32] In Shakespeare's marvellous stage-world, the inhabitants are not only friendly – they can be magically co-operative and divinely eloquent. Shakespeare makes the native Caliban offer to show even the lowest of the survivors 'every fertile inch o' th' island . . . the best springs . . . berries . . . fish . . . crabs . . .' and even special delicacies like 'young scamels from the rock' (whatever they are).[33] In reality 'base Indians' were observed by the earliest Virginia settlers to communicate only in impenetrable strains: but here Caliban is given lines equal in beauty to any from the most nobly born speakers in all Shakespeare:

> Be not afeard. The isle is full of noises,
> Sounds, and sweet airs, that give delight, and hurt not.
>   . . . and then, in dreaming,
> The clouds methought would open and show riches
> Ready to drop upon me, that, when I wak'd,
> I cried to dream again.[34]

Returning to England from Jamestown in the summer of 1607, Captain Newport can have shared none of the fantasies. Instead of a settlers' life of ease and even luxury, with wealth collected for them by timid Indians, the inscrutable Providence had given the Jamestown colonisers a mosquito-infested wilderness where they were trying to survive near-tropical heat and humidity, mortal diseases, several serious mutinies, and the probablity of slaughter by the natives. What fertility the land had they lost at first through planting too late: they then lost all their corn to the rats that had come with the ships. They were slow to learn how to catch game. Supply lines from England were unbearably long and vulnerable to Spanish attack. The supplies when they came were inadequate. The settlers were saved by the many skills of the unconventional and often hated Captain John Smith, whose realism about building houses and growing food on the spot countered the London dreams of searching for gold and finding the Pacific.

In spite of Smith, at the end of the first year, 1609, only thirty-two men had survived out of the 144 who sailed and the 105 who landed. Yet as William Crashaw said of the Virginia settlement, in a sermon, published in 1610, preached in London *before the right honorable Lord La Warre, Lord Governor and Captain General of Virginia*, 'If ever the hand of God appeared in action of man, it was here most evident: for when man had forsaken this business, God took it in hand.'[35]

   Crashaw did not know the half of it. Immediately after the sermon, Lord De La Warre departed for America. In Virginia, the disillusioned Jamestown survivors had already left, and were sailing home down the James River. They met this very Lord De La Warre, their new Governor, sailing up it, with sufficient replacements in his fleet. 'Had they left one day before, or had De La Warre arrived one day later, all would have been lost and savages would have stalked through the empty and rotting wharves of Jamestown.'[36] In 1611, women and children arrived. By 1616, though some 1,600 colonists had been sent from England, only 350 were still alive. Two hundred had returned to England.[37] In 1617, a new Deputy Governor found 'but five or six houses'.[38] By 1618, the population had grown by immigration to just under a thousand; yet in 1623, despite the arrival of at least four thousand more, the population still numbered only twelve hundred.

   Hardships and disasters in the Promised Land were what their Bibles expounded. Some of them had 'belied the Lord', saying 'neither shall evil come upon us; neither shall we see sword nor famine'. But God said:

> Lo, I will bring a nation upon you from far . . . saith the Lord: it is a mighty nation, it is an ancient nation, a nation whose language thou knowest not, neither understandest what they say. Their quiver is an open sepulchre, they are all mighty men. And they shall eat up thine harvest, and thy bread, which thy sons and thy daughters should eat: they shall eat up thy flocks and thy herds: they shall eat up thy vines and thy fig trees: they shall impoverish thy fenced cities, wherein thou trustedst, with the sword. Nevertheless in those days, saith the Lord, I will not make a full end with you.
>
> Jeremiah 5:14–18 (KJV)

'Ravaged by Indian massacres, pestilence, misgovernment, sloth, avarice, disorderliness and neglect, the Jamestown settlement all but expired.'[39] The Lord did not make 'a full end', and the whole Virginia experiment survived, eventually to become the largest English settlement until the Revolution. Its persistence was originally thanks to Captain John Smith: its later influence was due to two percipiences from the wayward Sir Edwin Sandys in London. From 1618 he briefly headed the quarrelsome Virginia Company. By 1640, Virginia, already the largest English colony, with a population of ten thousand, had, through a massive trade in cheap tobacco, a high level of individual independence. (Tobacco exhausted the soil after seven years, a cause of the later moves ever westward.) Sandys, though he did much that was perverse, had ensured that Virginia gave to America two precious inheritances: the right of each settler to own land, for their heirs for ever; and a General Assembly (which very rapidly learned maturity) ensuring government through a machinery of consent. Both of these put Virginian traditions at the heart of America's future.

BOOKS AND BIBLES IN THE EARLY AMERICAN YEARS

In 1584 Sir Walter Raleigh claimed 'Virginia' for his queen. A dozen years before that, in the early 1570s, a Spanish Jesuit mission from Florida had been established north of Roanoke. That mission did not last. It makes an interesting model of how not to do it. It failed because of Jesuit missionary inexperience, conflicts with the Spanish military governor of La Florida, and the unwillingness of the local natives to accept wholesale cultural change – a trinity of causes which would soon be repeated in various ways again and again in the Protestant north. Natives plundered a Spanish settlement, 'ripping up their books and scattering them to the winds'.[40] It is not known what these books were. But it has for some time been known that there had been printing on the American continent a long time before the importation and setting up of 'the first American printing press' in Cambridge, Massachusetts, in 1640. Books impressed the aboriginal inhabitants.[41] There were movable-type presses south of the Rio Grande before and just after 1500: details of who those earliest printers were and where they worked are difficult to come by. They printed notarial forms, official decrees, devotional tracts for hanging on the wall, and doctoral theses, as well as small books. Surviving sheets show good woodcut borders, initials and illustrations. All these date apparently from the 1560s. A Henrico Martin working in 1600 'was the tenth person to practice the printing arts in Mexico in the sixteenth century'.[42] Books printed in Mexico a little later included a small quarto against smoking, another on epidemiology, and larger works on science, navigation and shipbuilding. One surviving woodcut is especially intriguing. The border of Fray Alonso de Veracruz's *Dialectica resolutio cum textu Aristotelis* of 1554 is a direct copy, apparently, of one in the English *Book of Common Prayer* of 1549 printed by Whitchurch.[43] How did an Anglican Prayer Book get to Catholic, Spanish-speaking Mexico within five years of its publication? There is clearly a story waiting to be told.

In those nearly eighty colonial years, between the earliest British colonisers and American printing from 1640, what books had they? In 1583, what had Sir Humphrey Gilbert been reading in the stern of the *Squirrel*, hours before all hands were lost? What books were carried in the immigrants' ships, for use in the brave New World? In Shakespeare's story of *The Tempest*, the usurped Duke Prospero had been cast away, twelve years before, with 'volumes that / I prize above my kingdom'.[44] The island that he reached, in imagination on the route between Naples and Carthage as well as in the Bermudas, was more in touch with the ancient world of Mediterranean learning than was Roanoke across the north Atlantic. Yet the gentlemen, at least, among the first American colonists in the 1580s would not have travelled to what was intended to be a permanent home so lightly as not to have had books with them. It is unthinkable that either John White the artist or Thomas Hariot the scientist did not have small libraries with them – and the destruction of books in John White's chests has been noted. The likelihood that there were Bibles in English inside those few small houses of the settlers is not only because Bibles in those years before and after 1600 were so commonly owned at home. The greater point is that the Bibles can be seen to have been read and believed, and understood to refer to daily experience. The Bible starts with Eden: and the notion of the New World, 'a new heaven and a new earth' is the promise at the very end, in Revelation 21. Even more biblical than settling in a Promised Land was the gospel opportunity to remake Christ's church. Thus in Andrew Marvell's haunting poem *Bermudas*, written a little later in the seventeenth century, are the lines:

> He lands us on a grassy Stage,
> Safe from the Storms, and Prelat's rage . . .
>
> he cast (of which we rather boast)
> The Gospel Pearl upon our Coast.
> And in these Rocks for us did frame
> A Temple, where to sound his Name.[45]

The rebuilding of the primitive church could properly be undertaken. The local churches in the Acts of the Apostles had faced hardships enough, after all, including shipwreck. From such biblical self-consciousness on the American eastern seaboard the interest moves to the opposite coast.

DRAKE IN CALIFORNIA

The distinction of being the first to have an English Bible on American soil may fall to the west coast, to an unknown place on the American Pacific shore, perhaps in what later became California. The history of that west coast is Spanish, though Juan Rodriguez Cabrillo, who discovered the southern California coast, landing at San Diego on 28 September 1542, was Portuguese. Two centuries later the Spanish Franciscan missionary Padre Junipero Serra started his San Diego mission, on 16 July 1769, and began founding to the north the chain of twenty-one missions up the coast which gave California its Spanish heritage of architecture and names, and Catholicism. Long before those Catholic missions, however, that coast was visited by the famous, brave and unruly English Protestant seaman, Francis Drake, who may have taken English Bibles ashore in 1579. Deeply embedded in mythical history, Sir Francis, knighted by Queen Elizabeth for his exploits, has been for centuries an English Protestant national hero, thrilling schoolchildren with his dash and daring and his extraordinary voyage round the world. Not only did he finish his game of bowls on Plymouth Hoe when the invading Armada was dangerously close; he then sailed out in his little *Revenge* and defeated the monster. The latest revisionist historian has set out to destroy all that. Instead of the great and gracious Christian seaman of the enduring English stories, we are now given, by Harry Kelsey, a Francis Drake who was a self-serving thief and robber, an evil, ruthless sociopath, an incompetent commander who just managed to circumnavigate the globe.[46] Though (like every other naval warrior of the time, on whatever side, a point not made by such writers) Drake did dreadful things, he has now become a man quite impossible to like in any way at all.

Revisionism tends to be silent about Drake's faith, dismissing his religious position, if mentioning it at all, as no more than expediency.[47] Most West of England and Midlands people of the era – including, of course the only-slightly-later Pilgrim Fathers – were thoroughly Protestant, and thus Bible-based. Sailors from Devon and Cornwall hated the Spanish Inquisition for its cruelty, with good reason. The pope's granting of the New World to Spain was found outrageous. Drake was, as were Catholics and Protestants alike, driven by ideological as well as patriotic passion.[48] On Drake's ships, as on those of his older cousin John Hawkins, attendance at twice-daily service, Protestant in content, was compulsory for all.[49] Drake's Bible Protestantism was likely to have been educated: his sea companion for some years previously, Thomas Doughty (apparently the object of an appalling atrocity by the autocratic Drake) was a gentleman scholar knowing Greek and Hebrew.[50] Drake, it seems, read to his foreign prisoners the Psalms in English and passages from John Foxe's *Acts and Monuments*.[51]

Drake had set out from England in the *Pelican* on 13 December 1577, with four other ships, to do several anti-Spanish things. Officially he was opening up English trade in unknown regions west of Tierra del Fuego: privately, for the queen, he was then to sail north up the west coast of South America to attack Spanish bullion ships and continue to frighten the Spanish as (their name for him) 'The Dragon'. After Drake's ships had passed through those much-feared Straits of Magellan, the first Englishmen to do so, further calamity struck and the *Golden Hind* (as Drake had renamed the *Pelican* just before entering the Straits) sailed on alone. He harried unsuspecting Spanish vessels, and took gold, silver and jewels into the creaking *Golden Hind*. This new voyage eventually, and famously, took him round the world.

Until the publication of Kelsey's book in 1998, Drake's own account of his voyage elaborated in *The World Encompassed* of 1628, extending reports in Hakluyt and elsewhere, and widely read at the time, had been accepted.[52] Drake was said to have sailed up the Californian coast, experiencing unseasonal cold and dense fog. As the land still set solidly north and west, Drake then realised that there was going to be no way to the east: an easy North-West Passage (over the top of Canada, as one might put it) did not exist. In icy conditions, at around 48 degrees latitude, roughly level with Seattle, he turned round. Sailing down the coast again, on 17 June 1579 he anchored in 'a convenient and fit harbour', as he noted. Though today six places claim the spot (Bodega Bay, Tomales Bay, Drake's Estero, Drake's Bay, Bolinas Lagoon and San Francisco Bay), Kelsey finds the whole northern voyage and visit to California impossible: the given latitudes are false, apparently part of a conspiracy to deceive the Spanish and everyone else, though to what end in 1628 Kelsey does not explain.[53] The claimed non-existence of that northern voyage now takes with it, as it is driven out of history, the story of the month-long landing, and the famous encounter with the adoring Indians.

It is just possible that revisionism is too hasty. To show what has been lost, I give here the story as Drake and others told it, and as it was inserted into Hakluyt. There will be found to be a moral. Drake's company spent thirty-six days ashore, pitched tents, built a small stockade, unloaded the ship and set about a complete overhaul of the laden *Golden Hind*. The Coast Miwok Indians were greatly curious, and friendly: unlike the natives further south, they had never seen Europeans before (their welcome had not been corrupted by hatred arising from the cruelty of the Catholic Spanish). Drake claimed the territory for Queen Elizabeth, naming it, after its white cliffs, 'New Albion' (just as the Romans had called England, seen across the Channel, 'Albion', the White Land). The ceremony involved putting up a brass plate, an inset silver sixpence giving the queen's head.[54] Partly because of their strangeness, and partly because of 'our general's . . . natural and accustomed humanity',[55] and because he 'liberally bestowed on them necessary things to cover their nakedness', his men, pious Protestants, laboured with the unease of being worshipped as gods. The third day of the landing, they witnessed a hideous and bloody native rite of mutilations, at the spectacular arrival of a massive native who was their King. Their general, that is, Drake, 'horrified and unable to stop them, ordered the whole [ship's] company to prayers, and all lifted their eyes and hands to Heaven to show where God was'. To strengthen that information, they read some chapters of the Bible and sang Psalms, with remarkable effect: the natives sat around attentively, 'and observing the end of every pause, with one voice cried "Oh!", greatly rejoicing in the Exercises.'[56] Thirty-three days later, before Drake and his men left, the natives were very pressing, so Drake's company fell to prayers and singing of Psalms, whereby the natives were allured immediately to forget their folly and leave their sacrifice unconsumed. As the *Golden Hind* sailed away, the massed ranks on the cliffs watched until it was out of sight.[57] (Drake then crossed the Pacific, later encountering some navigational difficulties. At one point they met a European ship which made off, 'stoutly refusing to have any dealings with Lutherans'.)

'This story of a California landing is entirely fictitious,' writes Kelsey, on grounds of anthropology, linguistics and navigation: though he unquestioningly accepts unpublished propaganda from the Spanish Inquisition above everything else, we have, he asserts, merely to take his word as a cartographer (a harbour so far north being a funny place from which to set off to cross the Pacific).[58] But let us for a moment be ridiculously fanciful and look at the story with its European Protestant audience in mind. Drake and his men, we are told, read to those natives 'some chapters of the Bible', with great efffect. What is striking in the tale is the belief that the Bible read in English, to inhabitants of a remote land where English had never been heard before and was not understood, would be effective. With that belief goes the conviction that they responded, and in the correct directions of awe, challenge, satisfaction and illumination. The report of that Pacific coast 'experience' is important. It is the first time outside Britain that the English Bible was presented as an instrument of miraculous social engineering. America's own first encounter with an English Bible, on quite the opposite coast to what is usually thought, and fully five years before Raleigh's ships touched Roanoke, is offered in these contemporary written texts as a blessed one.

ENGLISH BIBLES ON THE EAST COAST

On the east coast, settlers had not only brought in Bibles, in English, and read them, but had tried to live by what they read. That was what Protestants did. There are always possibilities of radical misunderstanding about the Bible: that it is a book full of lovely words and stories that can be read as one gracious addition to an already comfortable life, or that it is laughably irrelevant to proper history. This is not what Tyndale and many others died for. The pioneering men and women who tried to cling to life at Roanoke and Jamestown were Bible people. They could hardly be anything else, coming from Jacobean England. (That this is a surprising thing to stress is part of the wider fact; that recent books of American history of the colonial period do not have 'Bible' in the index.)[59] The Bible the settlers brought with them, even some years after the King James Bible was first issued in 1611, was far more likely to have been a version of the 1599 annotated Geneva Bible than, to coin a phrase, the marginally challenged Bishops'. The settlers had arrived in New Canaan, a place that might still, in spite of hardships, be yet seen to flow with milk and honey. In the decades ahead, and long after 1624, when the colony ceased to be under Virginia Company control and became royally owned, the territorial and trade expansions, the sufferings from disease and attacks, the internal dissensions and rebellions, could be, and were, seen in biblical terms. 'The new land was redemption even as it was also riches', as Perry Miller put it.[60] Further north, 'a gentle woman of the Bay Colony' found it 'far better than . . . reports'.

> I have fancied the eyes of the writers were so fixed on their old English chimney tops, that the smoke put them out. The air of the country is sharp, the rocks many, the trees innumerable, the grass little, the winter cold, the summer hot, the gnats in summer biting, the wolves at midnight howling &c. Look upon it as it hath the means of grace, and, if you please, you may call it Canaan.[61]

MAYFLOWER

Between 1606 and 1620, the Plymouth end of the Virginia Company made half a dozen attempts to explore or settle the American coast further north; none was of lasting significance. In September 1620, however, a company sailed from Plymouth which was, in the end, to make the greatest permanent mark on America's later sense of itself as a nation. Included among the 101 passengers were about forty English men, women and children who had been in Leiden in Holland. A dozen years before, they had left the English Midlands to find, successfully, if impecuniously, religious freedom in Holland; but they needed firmer security for their lives as well as their liberty, and hoped to find it in the New World. They were Separatists, self-governing English Christians who from the time of Henry VIII and Edward VI had felt that the English Reformation had not gone far enough: the English Church had gone only halfway back to the ideal, the primitive church of the Apostles. Across England from the 1540s, local Separatist congregations, wholly given to study of the Bible, were many, large and powerful: as noted above, one in London was strong enough to be left alone even under Queen Mary and Cardinal Pole. The Separatists' story in England (pp.267-8 above) remains to be understood. The group who went to Leiden in 1607 and 1608 from the village of Scrooby in Northamptonshire were a tiny fragment of a large countrywide English Separatist tradition which was by then nearly a century old, with congregations in London, in other towns and some villages, strongest in the Midlands.[62]

Members of that English congregation in Leiden (only one of several in Holland) faced severe difficulties for a decade. They were aware of opportunities across the Atlantic. Admiral Coligny, the French Protestant leader, as was well known in Europe, had established a colony in Florida as early as 1560, though it had been wiped out by the Spaniards. The Dutch at that time were themselves beginning to look to America: soon their colony, New Amsterdam on Manhattan Island, would be bought from Indians for a few trifles, a transaction generally described in the USA as 'the best real-estate deal in history'. Captain John Smith had been busy exploring and mapping the North Atlantic coast and naming the region New England. His writings told of fortunes to be made from fishing. On this trade the English Leiden group would have to rely, as they did not have financial backing from a wealthy company of London merchants, though they were approved by the London Virginia Company for the making of an independent plantation. Sir Edwin Sandys had a family connection with them. King James, no less, hearing that the little group proposed to live by fishing, remarked that ' "twas the apostles" own calling'.[63]

Organisation of the expedition was fraught, and clumsy. Prospects were bad. Earlier, most of an English Separatist congregation in Amsterdam had set off for America, and all had been lost at sea. After further serious awkwardnesses – including their surely foolish refusal of Captain John Smith's offer to go with them – they sailed from Plymouth on 16 September 1620 on the *Mayflower*. There were 149 persons on board (too many for that small ship) of whom about thirty-five could reasonably be described as Pilgrims.

It was a relatively safe voyage. Only five died. Inadequate and bad food and overcrowding weakened most on board, however, shortly with wider consequences. Their landfall at daybreak on 9 November was at the tip of Cape Cod, just outside the London Virginia Company's jurisdiction. To strengthen their position ahead of their eventual landing, in the cabin of the *Mayflower* they did what any Separatist congregation of the time would have done, and drew up a covenant of social policy, to govern behaviour and frame 'just and equal laws'. An impression is sometimes given that English Separatism was invented so that the USA could happen, making this handful of English settlers from Scrooby, and then from Leiden, unique – part of an American history that must be in every way special.[64] They were so only in the sense that from humble backgrounds, usually without the guidance of ministers of their congregations, they crossed the Atlantic to find freedom. As noted above, there were in the sixteenth century countless Separatist congregations in England: in 1608, the Amsterdam congregation had substantial members, the Leiden one even more. There were others in Holland. But at the same time the *Mayflower* Compact, though undistinguished in its Separatist context, was still new when set against the political organisation of Stuart England. There, off the coast of America, the compact of government only by the consent of the people was the first step towards the organisation of 'the greatest compact of all, the Constitution of the United States'.[65]

They landed in December 1620 in what John Smith had already named Plymouth Harbour (not on The Rock, which was named early in the eighteenth century: as it was inconveniently far up Plymouth beach, 'it had to be moved down to the water's edge to satisfy visitors' notions of how history ought to happen'[66]). The chance occurrences of a mild winter, quiet Indians (weakened by disease), and a helpful native who spoke English, helped them to establish themselves, but, even so, in their first winter half the crew, half the passengers and all but four of the married women died. The following autumn, in 1621, they celebrated a successful harvest. (In the 1930s, memory of this was made into the national event of Thanksgiving: this was a twentieth-century attempt to fix the ascendancy of the northern United States by the strongest force, a historical commemoration which was also religious.) Ten years later, in 1631, the colony was still small and struggling, with a population of only 550, compared with Virginia's 5,000.[67] Some of the survivors, and newcomers, moved on to found new settlements nearby. One, at Mount Wollaston in 1623, was colourfully run by a cheerful independent, Thomas Morton, who successfully traded and fraternised with the Indians, throwing parties for the native women around his maypole on 'Merrymount', and mocking the Bible-bound pilgrims. His account of it all is properly famous.[68] The shocked pilgrims had him forcibly expelled in 1628.

More and more men and women went to America from England. New developments, and wider expansions from the settlement at Plymouth, began to appear to the north in New Hampshire and Maine. After a pathfinding fishing post had been established in 1623 on the Massachusetts coast, nearly 1,000 passengers and crew set out from Plymouth in

1630 in 11 ships, with 240 cows and 60 horses and a royal charter of the
new Massachusetts Bay Company. They founded Boston and other towns.
They flourished, to become 'Plymouth's large and overbearing neighbour
to the north'.[69] In the decade from 1630, some 20,000 settlers emigrated
from England, a 'Great Migration' to the West Indies as well as America.
They went because in England their common land was being enclosed
and there was monetary inflation. Shifting and rapidly growing popula-
tions in certain areas, on limited amounts of land, made emigration not
just attractive but the only way to survive with dignity: large numbers of
English poor hoped for good wages and 'a house and garden plot'.[70] They
went across the Atlantic because the earlier Elizabethan attempts at full-
scale plantation in Ireland had failed: Ireland as a new Canaan teemed
with insoluble problems.[71] Moreover, a generation of propaganda had done
its work. They went to America because they had heard that it was a Paradise of fertility, awaiting only the honest labour of a new Adam's delving.
There was hope of active trade; solid London citizens in recent times
had found their venture-capital repaid a thousand-fold as what Shakespeare
called their 'wealthy Andrews' docked in the Port of London – or so the
story had it. They more pressingly went, however, to find religious liberty
and escape increasing persecution. Land-hunger, the hope of new business
and the increasing incompetence and remoteness of the Stuart monarchy
were all cause enough for the massive emigration. Yet the religious urge
was strongest. God's work could be done only outside England.

    This last reason was the particular cause of the fresh settlements strung
along the coast in Massachusetts Bay. Though there were some Separatists
among them, the new colonists, arriving in increasing numbers ten years
after the pilgrims, were 'Puritans', refugees from the growing intolerance
in England under King Charles 1 and William Laud, the powerful and
bigoted reactionary Bishop of London, made Archbishop of Canterbury
in 1633. 'Puritan' is a tricky enough word at home in England. It is abroad
that it becomes weaselly. It must be held down and properly disciplined
if it is going to be any use in dealing with New England settlers. Those
must be differentiated again from American successors. (A good account
is given by Sydney Ahlstrom, with special emphasis on the spectrum of
Puritan understandings.[72])

AMERICAN PURITANS

A Puritan had felt the call to godliness of life from personal experience
of Christ as known in the New Testament. Even at the humbler levels,
this godliness went with intellectual vigour, the opposite of superstition.

The 'purer' New Testament example of congregational life inevitably clashed with established traditions of institution or practice (for example, in liturgies, ceremonies and vestments), especially when a root in individual experience led to the liberation of theology, as the New Testament implies; God made his covenant with each human heart. Though that 'purity' of doctrine was collectively guarded with some ferocity, the result of personal conviction in Puritan lives was usually the opposite of grimness and repression – joy in the Lord, energy, fulfilled marriages producing many children. (H. L. Mencken's often-quoted naughty-schoolboy essay on Puritan morality, in his *Prejudices* (reprinted in 1927) should be understood as an ignorant, indeed malicious, squib.)

The new Puritan settlements in America were well run. These particular colonists were industrious, already reasonably prosperous, and knew what they were about. Many were well educated. They quickly established a settled and civilised territory which could keep its distinction as it expanded. They knew before they landed that they were appointed to the work under God, and that remained their understanding. The fact of having followed the will of God and landed from England was, at least in the earliest days, sufficient evidence of being a 'visible saint' and thus able to be a church member. Demonstration of experience of God's saving grace, especially in some extraordinary personal manner, became the mark of the true Christian, able to belong to this church or that, and thus to be in a position of some control in a roughly democratic system.

The Puritan churches, though technically still part of the Church of England, were largely congregationalist in spirit and organisation. In contrast to what had been left behind in England, the local government was godly. Eventually, and inevitably, equality more and more became a secular principle of political life. The clear ideals of the godly, so firmly based in Scripture, were products – indeed they could be called flowerings – of the Reformation in England, characteristically institutionalised. The very origins of the United States of America lie directly in that Reformation, not least in the official welcoming of diversity. The self-governing churches of the New Testament in the first century were all different in local culture across the eastern Mediterranean, in sharpest contrast to the much later monolithic Catholic Church. The new American communities born of the Reformation could in the end co-exist with those of very different backgrounds – from elsewhere in Europe, for example. (A form of coexistence with people from Africa was for a long time shameful. Worse, even that was not possible with 'Indians'.[73])

The prime Puritan church was at Salem. An early pastor there, Roger Williams, was banished for increasingly left-wing political views, like buying the land from the Indians rather than seizing it at gunpoint, and for arguing for even more complete separation of church and state, even greater liberty of conscience, and strengthening the role of women. He founded successful settlements to the south on Rhode Island in 1636. There he was joined for a while by the most celebrated of the radicals, the prophetess Anne Hutchinson, banished from Boston in 1638: in 1643 she and all her family except one daughter were murdered by Indians.

Theologically, the most significant controversy, which erupted in 1636–8 within the Bible-controlled settlements of the Massachusetts Bay Colony, which meant everybody, was about the biblical interpretation of 'sanctification': that is, how godly conduct related to justification. Could visibly good works be a guarantee of justification? Heaven forbid. The theological differences became almost invisble to the naked eye, but that did not stop the heats of months of contention and the imprisonment, trial and expulsion of Mrs Hutchinson, technically, for lying. Inside the muddle and hot tempers, however, what was being argued for, and what, happily for good government, triumphed, was the rejection of licence, of licentiousness, of the 'antinomian' effects of 'enthusiasm'. Deeper laid but even more far-reaching, was the reinforcement of the Scriptures as the foundation of New England beliefs.

In mid-century, as well as Rhode Island, the New England Confederation united developing communities in Connecticut, New Haven, New Hampshire and Maine. Already visible is the American experience of diversity, even under the apparently narrow banner of 'Puritanism'. These settlements, though often turbulent in their local politics, were united against particular enemies – supposedly unorthodox Christians (the early treatment of immigrant Quakers was shocking) and the hostile, organised local indigenous tribes: some decades later, united under Philip, a Wampanoag chief, they struggled in 'King Philip's War' (1675–6), which cost the English much money and damage, and about 600 dead, and cost the Indians loss of power for ever, and about 3,000 dead. Further north in Canada, and west around the Mississippi, the Roman Catholic French were serious rivals. To the south, the Dutch established New Netherland, especially around what was later New York, presently taking over New Sweden on the Delaware, and then themselves surrendering to the English. Further south still, Spain kept Florida as a strategic garrison. Over twenty languages could be heard on or near the island of Manhattan: a 'cultural religious pluralism which in some ways anticipated the experience of the future American nation'.[74] Before the mid-seventeenth century, however, the region of Maryland had been settled under a new principle of toleration for English Roman Catholics, though Protestants outnumbered them. By the end of the century, the colonies that had been founded on one man's special religious purpose included – as well as Roger Williams's 'Baptist' colony on Rhode Island – Lord Baltimore's Maryland and William Penn's most successful Quaker Pennsylvania. Further south still, the Carolinas and Georgia were colonised, their names continuing to root English monarchs on American soil. The French settled in the far south, Louisiana.

Immigration from Europe became massive: forty million, it is said, between 1607 and 1914.[75] But North America is vast, with more than seven million square miles: there is still, even now, a lot of room. It is a shock to realise that even around 1650 some of the celebrated townships had fewer than a dozen buildings, and Naumkeag (later known as Salem) was founded with twenty souls.[76] The need for the firm, even harsh, grip of pioneers remained. The story of the European settlements is of success and of failure. The details are of quarrels, disputes, trials, splits, expulsions and secessions, not to speak of wars against the Indians, with treacheries and massacres by both sides. A century of English colonisation had managed to produce only a few tiny outposts in a thousand miles of coastal plain. Yet prosperity followed successful trade, and all the time one can watch the steady expansion of the control of the eastern seaboard of the continent by the English.

And all of those eastern seaboard people, Separatists and Puritans, royalists and republicans, tobacco-growers and fishermen, explorers and traders, schoolteachers and preachers, had Bibles – English Bibles, brought from England, either part of their travelling baggage or sent on later. These people quoted their English Bibles in their civil arguments and church sermons, in solemn religious disputes and in letters home. Like the earlier Virginians, they were admonished to live Bible lives. The stream of English Bibles in America, first seen as the small springs of those brought by Raleigh and Drake half a century before, rose to its first full flood in the mid-seventeenth century, even though the American *printing* of Bibles was still more than a hundred years away. We get the Bible in America wrong if we do not begin with the large numbers of imports of Bibles from England. The earliest American experience was to a measurable extent biblical.

John Winthrop famously announced to the first Massachusetts Bay settlers, 'we must consider that we shall be as a City upon a Hill', suggesting Jesus' words at Matthew 5:14 on the visibility of his followers. As the decades passed, and individual enterprise and international trade boomed, secular considerations led to greater toleration. This was the end of the very earliest visions of an exclusive New England covenant with God. The colonies there of Massachusetts, Connecticut, New Haven and New Hampshire were the places where Puritanism flowered most fully, and the godly New England character remained admirable in American life over many centuries, not least for the life of the mind: Harvard College was founded as early as 1636.

Yes, of course, what brought the English to America was economics, the threat to native social environments. The effects of the new capitalism are visible, the rise of democracy, the growth of individualism. Yet, with a microscope, inside these modern, sweeping, academic analyses can be seen people moving about, men and women stirred by the new Reformation valuation of the present life under God: something each of them received through being able to hold a Bible in the hand – people reading Paul. In the older medieval religion, the highest calling was to leave the world and be a monk or nun. Now the highest spiritual calling was to know God while being a working man or woman, getting the hands dirty in trade and family life. This meant, among other things, obeying his commands to preach the Gospel in all the world. The root, fount, seed, nucleus, motor – the rich metaphors get near it – of this new release was the Bible, read and learned by heart, referred to and quoted, loved and obeyed. Oddly, this is not said: historians tell us that the settlers lived with a 'world-historical' experiment,[77] but they do not say that this comes largely from the Bible. It may well be that because the Bible has been, most recently, irrelevant to the writing of history, its pages are simply not known.

The five-volume *A History of the Book in America*, published in 2000, has, on the opening page (of over six hundred) in volume one, a remark by the editor, David D. Hall about 'readers who, in the strange setting of the New World, welcomed such familiar texts as the almanac, the catechism, and the Bible'.[78] They brought Bibles with them, or sought to import them. Even in the specialised scholarly world of studying the book trade and book ownership in early colonial America, calculating how many Bibles there were, or analysing which versions predominated, is at the moment impossible. Attempts at addressing proportions of influence (against, for example, other popular books) are distorted by the special nature of the Bible, which was 'living speech, the spoken Word of God'.[79] It was to be spoken and heard, learned by heart and recited, read repeatedly. Evidence from inventories and wills shows a clear pattern of references to 'Bibles and other books' in both categories.[80]

What does emerge clearly is evidence of a felt shortage of Bibles. The Virginia Company wrote in August 1623: 'By this Ship the Hopewell, you shall receive three great Bibles [that is, lectern folios], two Common prayer books . . . being the gift of an unknown person for the use of those Churches that most need them.'[81] Later in the century, the Bishop of London in 1683 'arranged for a shipment of 39 copies . . . to be distributed to parishes in need'.[82] The seal of the Massachusetts Bay Company, depicted an Indian uttering the 'Macedonian plea' to St Paul of Acts 16:9, 'Come over and help us.'

COLONISING: A BIBLE THING

In 1622, John Donne, Dean of St Paul's, celebrated preacher and (as yet privately) poet, addressed the stockholders of the Virginia Company:

> You shall have made this Island, which is but as the Suburbs of the old world, a Bridge, a Gallery to the new; to join all to that world that shall never grow old, the Kingdom of Heaven. You shall add persons to this Kingdom, and to the Kingdom of heaven, and add names to the Books of our Chronicles, and to the Book of Life.[83]

Donne is magnificent. He was only one of a host of less gifted preachers in English pulpits at the time, greatly heeded, saying the same thing, though not so eloquently. Colonising is a Bible thing. Donne sees it, punningly, adding names to the biblical Books of Chronicles, as well as to English history.

From the beginning, fifty or so years before, most documents about the need for settlement in America express that need in religious terms. Thus Richard Hakluyt's *Discourse of Western Planting* (1583), after describing the heathen of North America quotes and enlarges Paul in Romans 10:

> whosoever shall call on the name of the lord shall be saved . . . how shall they preach except they be sent . . . but by whom should these preachers be sent? By them no doubt which have taken upon them the protection and defence of the Christian faith. Now the Kings and Queens of England have the name of Defenders of the Faith. By which title I think they are not only charged to maintain and patronise the faith of Christ, but also to inlarge and advance the same. Neither ought this to be their last work, but rather the principal and chief of all others, according to the commandment of our Saviour, Christ, Matthew 6, First seek the kingdom of God and the righteousness thereof, and all other things shall be ministered unto you.[84]

In chapter 20, entitled 'A brief collection of certain reasons to enduce her Majesty . . . to take in hand the Western voyage and the planting there' Hakluyt's point sixteen is 'we shall by planting there enlarge the glory of the gospel, and from England plant sincere religion, and provide a safe and a sure place to receive people from all parts of the world that are forced to flee for the truth of God's word.'[85] These two arguments, that the heathen must receive the Gospel, and that communities with religious freedom can be established, can be found in most of the material urging colonisation in the West.

Referring to that man of Macedonia who came to Paul in a night vision in Acts 16, asking for him to go there and help (which led to Paul's first work in Europe), Hakluyt wrote:

> Even so we, whiles we have sought to go into other countries (I would I might say to preach the gospel), God by the frustrating of our actions seemeth to forbid us to follow those courses, and the people of America cry out unto us, their next neighbours, to come and help them, and bring unto them the glad tidings of the Gospel.

It would be something of great value to find, from the earliest settlers, a mass of surviving written documents identifying, among other things, their biblical cast of mind. Lacking such an archive, one is dependent on the articulate leaders of the expeditions, whose religious colonising might always be open to suspicion in some degree. While a modern hostile reader might be cynical about the religious aims of men like Hakluyt, what one can observe, however, is his difference from his Spanish predecessors.

Christopher Colombus, no less, in his letter about the island of Hispaniola dated 15 February 1493 concludes:

> Since thus our redeemer has given to our most illustrious King and Queen . . . this victory in so high a matter, Christendom should take gladness therein and make great festivals, and give solemn thanks to the Holy Trinity for the great exhaltation they shall have by the conversion of so many peoples to our Holy Faith; and next for the temporal benefit which will bring hither refreshment and profit not only to Spain, [but] to all Christians.[86]

There is a triumphalism here, and the expression of the capture of entire nations at a stroke. One notes that the function of the Redeemer is to give victory to the Spanish king and queen. By contrast, the tone of the first documents from England is directed towards the native peoples and their need, particularly for the Gospel.

A Report of the Voyage and Success thereof, attempted . . . 1583, by Sir. H. Gilbert, knight . . . to discover and to plant Christian inhabitants in place convenient . . . written by M. Edward Haies, Gentleman (1583) has the following:

> It behooveth every man of great calling, in whom is any instinct of inclination unto this attempt, to examine his own motions: which if the same proceed of ambition or avarice, he may assure himself it cometh not of God, and therefore can not have confidence of God's protection and assistance against the violence (else irresistible) both of sea, and infi-

nite perils upon the land; whom God yet may use and instrument to further his cause and glory in some way, but not to build upon so bad a foundation.[87]

Haies continues, to note 'the prophecy of Christ' about 'his word preached throughout the world', with reference to 'the carriage of his word into those very mighty and vast countries'. Gilbert's own 'true report' begins with poems, including, from Arthur Hawkins

> If we religious be, let's rig our ships with speed
> And carry Christ to these poor souls that stand in need . . .
> For what is done for God, doth find reward full large.[88]

Gilbert's second chapter contains two pages full of biblical illustration of God's authority to 'plant, possess, and subdue' the new world.

> We read in the Old Testament, how that after Noe's flood was ceased, restoration of mankind began . . . God chose out of the multitude a peculiar people to himself . . . at last attaining to the land they were encountered with great numbers of strong people and mighty Kings. Notwithstanding, Iosua their leader . . .[89]

These pages are full of marginal notes to the books of Joshua and Judges. In his sixth chapter, Gilbert writes:

> First and chiefly, in respect of the most happy and gladsome tidings of the most glorious Gospel of our Saviour Jesus Christ, whereby they may be brought from falsehood to truth, from darkness to light, from the highway of death to the path of life, from superstitious idolatry to sincere Christianity, from the devil to Christ, from Hell to Heaven . . . the Gospel must be freely preached . . . we may say with S. Paul: *if we have sown unto you heavenly things do you think it much that we should reap your carnal things* [i.e. 1 Cor. 9:11].[90]

Later he writes:

> since by Christian duty we stand bound chiefly to further all such acts as do tend to the increasing the true flock of Christ, by reducing into the right way those lost sheep which are yet astray . . . Be of good cheer therefore, for he that can not err hath said: *That before the end of the world, his word shall be preached to all nations* [i.e. Matt. 24:14].[91]

It is worth emphasising here not only the primarily religious motives being displayed, but that they are very much Bible-based rather than (as the Spanish were) Church-based. There has to be a point where scepticism ceases, when the essence of the Bible, that is the healing power of

God's own Word and his command to take it to all nations, is what is paramount. These words are coming from a Protestant, Bible-based nation under Elizabeth. Thomas Hariot's *Brief and True Report* of 1588 includes the following:

> Many times and in every town where I came, according as I was able, I made declaration of the contents of the bible, that therein was set forth the true and only God, and his mighty works, that therein was contained the true doctrine of salvation through Christ, with many particularities of miracles and chief points of religion . . . and although I told them the book materially and of itself was not of any such virtue, as I thought they did conceive, but only the doctrine therein contained; yet would many be glad to touch it, to embrace it, to kiss it, to hold it to their breasts and heads, and stroke over all their body with it, to show their hungry desire of that knowledge which was spoken of.[92]

Hariot notes that 'people would be glad many times to be with us at our prayers, and many times call upon us . . . to pray and sing psalms.'

Of course, it can all be taken as propaganda. Under the cover of these highest sentiments, there would, as everyone knew, be plenty of opportunity for 'material ambitions of empire, profit, tobacco, and real estate'.[93] It has been easy to be derisive with hindsight. Yet, when Perry Miller came to examine the documents of the earliest settlers themselves, he found three elements were common to most of them. First, Virginia produced strong evidences of mercantile adventure, but also, second, and interestingly, a literature. This presents a great theme, whereby the daily lives of the settlers were felt to be part of a large cosmic process, a sense of destiny which still governs American thought. But Miller found himself aware of a third factor, unfashionable to consider when he wrote in the 1950s, and still so. The literature

> exhibits a set of principles for guiding not a mercantile investment but a medieval pilgrimage. Whatever were the calculations of the city, the cosmos expounded in the Virginia pamphlets is one where the principal human concern is neither the rate of interest nor the discovery of gold, but the will of God . . . Planters and promoters present themselves as only secondarily merchants and exploiters, only secondarily Englishmen; in their own conception of themselves they are first and foremost Christians, and above all militant Protestants.[94]

Being Protestant, these men and women thought in biblical terms.

Certainly in all the settlements there were predominant difficulties, including in Virginia the hash that the Virginia Company in England could make of everything. Captain John Smith wrote: 'we did admire how it was possible such wise men could so torment themselves and us with such strange absurdities and impossibilities: making Religion their colour, when all their aim was nothing but present profit.'[95] Even so, after studying all the literature there is from this time, no one could be blind to the power that religion had in the lives of the settlers. Even John Smith, while asserting that only wealth would entice men to America, remarked that though he had lived for thirty-seven years amid wars, pestilence and famine and now had nothing but his pains for his reward, still he had

> much reason both privately and publicly to acknowledge it and give God thanks, whose omnipotent power only delivered me to do the utmost of my best to make his name known in those remoter parts of the world, and his loving mercy to such a miserable sinner.[96]

When Lord De La Warre arrived at Jamestown in 1610, just in time to rescue the departing colony, his first act – even before his commission was read – was to hear a sermon. When Sir Thomas Dale landed next year he also immediately repaired to the church for a sermon: and early seventeenth-century sermons were biblical utterances, and, like so many Reformation documents, made of Scripture. Dale wrote to a friend in London that he was engaged in a 'religious Warfare' (Ephesians 6) with no thought of reward 'but from him in whose vineyard I labour [Matthew 20], whose church with greedy appetite I desire to erect' (biblical words all). Underneath expressions which are the conventions of the time, personal conviction comes through. All the literature of this Virginia enterprise is eloquent; 'most of it [was] propaganda, much of dubious accuracy, a large part merely rhetoric': even so, it 'gave expression to to a kind of averageness of the age that is worth serious study'.[97]

WILLIAM BRADFORD, JOHN WINTHROP, JOHN COTTON

The Bible consciousness of these three early leaders will conclude this chapter.

The name of William Bradford (1590–1657) rates barely a mention in Richard Middleton's 1996, and standard, *Colonial America: A History, 1585–1776*. Yet as the leader and far-sighted Governor of the Plymouth settlement for over thirty years, Bradford was important. As the chronicler of its first quarter-century of life, in his history *Of Plymouth Plantation*, begun in 1630 and completed in 1651, he is an essential witness, and often the only source of facts on which all historians depend.[98]

Born a Yorkshireman, Bradford joined the Separatists as a boy, then going with them from Scrooby to Leiden, where he was already a leader

at the age of sixteen. He was first elected Governor in the year following the landing from *Mayflower*, 1621. In 1627 he led the moves for the
assumption of the original merchant-venturers' investment, assuring a
sound financial future for the settlement, which, though kept separate, did
under him co-operate with the New England Confederation.

Bradford's story is biblical in scope and reference, beginning with God's
work in history, and Satan's attacks. Dramatic events have an Old Testament flavour and reference. A profane young man dies horribly halfway
across the Atlantic, the work of 'the just hand of God'.[99] A horrid case of
bestiality is punished by slaughter of the beasts and the young offender,
acting on Leviticus 20, quoted several times.[100] Present from time to time
are the least acceptable parts of the books of Joshua and Judges. Details
of the avenging of Indian attacks by a massacre of Pequots, luridly
desribed, are horrific not only in the atrocity but in the sense of divine
approval:

> . . . and those that first entered found sharp resistance from the enimie,
> who both shott at and grapled with them; others rane into their howses,
> and brought out fire, and sett them on fire, which soone tooke in their
> matts, and standing close togeather, with the wind, all was quickly on
> a flame, and therby more were burnt to death than otherwise slain; it
> burnte their bow strings and made them unservisable. Those that
> escaped the fire were slaine with the sword, some hewed to pieces,
> others runne throw with their rapiers, so as they were quickly dis-
> patchte, and very few escaped. It was conceived they thus destroyed
> about 400 at this time. It was a fearful sight to see them thus frying in
> the fyer, and the streams of blood quenching the same, and horrible
> was the stincke and sente sacrifice, and they gave the prays thereof to
> God, who had wrought it so wonderfuly for them, thus to inclose their
> enimise in their hands, and give then so speedy a victory over so proud
> and insulting an enimie.[101]

One recalls with greater bleakness Richard Hakluyt's remark in his 1585
Pamphlet for the Virginia Enterprise, under 'Inducements to the liking of the
Voyage . . . The ends of the voyage are these. 1. To plant Christian religion, 2. To Traficke, 3. To conquer. . . . To plant Christian religion without
conquest, will bee hard.'[102]

At the other end of the scale is the incident in Winthrop's *Journal* about
Thomas Willett in 1639, after an Indian attack at Kennebeck:

> . . . some Indians coming into the house [the Plymouth trading house],
> Mr Willet, the master of the house, being reading in the Bible, his coun-
> tenance was more solemn than at any other times, so as he did not look

cheerfully upon them, as he was wont to do; whereupon they went out and told their fellows, that their purpose was discovered . . . that they knew it by Mr Willet's countenance, and that he had discovered it by a book he was reading. Whereupon they gave over their design.[103]

Here is a passage from Bradford's history *Of Plymouth Plantation*. It is part of his description of the *Mayflower's* company first setting foot on American soil in late December 1620. He has paused in his narrative to 'stand half amazed' at their condition. After 'a sea of troubles' before they left, and having 'passed the vast ocean . . . they had now no friends to welcome them, nor inns to entertain or refresh their weather-beaten bodies, no houses or much less towns to repair to, to seek for succour'. In Scripture, he notes, the shipwrecked Paul and his company were shown by the barbarians no small kindness: but here 'these savage barbarians . . . were readier to fill their sides full of arrows'. He continues

And for the season it was winter, and they that know the winters of that country know them to be sharp and violent, and subject to cruel and fierce storms, dangerous to travel to known places, much more to search an unknown coast. Besides, what could they see but a hideous and desolate wilderness, full of wild beasts and wild men? And what multitudes there might be of them they knew not. Neither could they, as it were, go up to the top of Pisgah.[104]

Their ship's master urgently needed a better harbour, and threatened to abandon them.

What could now sustain them but the Spirit of God and His grace? May not and ought not the children of these fathers rightly say: 'Our fathers were Englishmen, which came over this great ocean, and were ready to perish in this wilderness; but they cried unto the Lord, and He heard their voice and looked on their adversity,' etc. 'Let them therefore praise the Lord, because He is good: and His mercies endure forever. Yea, let them which have been redeemed of the Lord, show how he has delivered them from the hand of the oppressor. When they wandered in the desert wilderness out of the way, and found no city to dwell in, both hungry, and thirsty, their soul was overwhelmed in them. Let them confess before the Lord his loving kindness, and his wonderful works before the sons of men.'[105]

The scriptural location is not in any way signalled. Everyone would know that it was largely Psalm 107, known as 'the settlers' psalm'. All the phrases are Scripture quotations.

John Cotton of Emmanuel College, Cambridge, became a leading figure in the Massachusetts Bay Colony, known for his biblical knowledge. In

May 1636, 'Mr Peter, preaching at Boston made an earnest request to the Church, that they would spare their teacher, Mr Cotton, for a time that he might go through the Bible, and raise marginal notes upon all the knotty places of the Scriptures.' Before he left England in 1633, Cotton published in 1630 *God's Promise to his Plantation*, in which he develops the idea of 'Planting' as divinely intended. His text is '2 Sam. 7.10. Moreover I will appoint a place for my people Israel, and I will plant them, that they may dwell in a place of their own, and move no more.' All his arguments are interlaced with Bible references and quotations, which come in almost every short paragraph. For example:

> 2. He would give his people a nail, and a place in his Tabernable, Isay. 56.5. And that is to give us part in Christ; for so the Temple typified. So then he plants us when he gives us root in Christ.
>
> Thirdly, When he giveth us to grow up in him as Calves in the stall. Mal. 4.2,3.
>
> Fourthly, & to bring forth much fruit, Joh. 15.1,2.
>
> Fifthly, and to continue and abide in the state of grace.
> This is to plant us in his holy Sanctuary, he not rooting us up.[106]

The dedicated Governor of Massachusetts Bay for almost two decades was the Oxford lawyer John Winthrop – twenty-nine when first appointed. It was his decision, for example, to establish the seat of government on the Shawmut peninsula, which became Boston.

His papers contain many examples of letters to him which show an automatic reference to Scripture. I have space for only a few.

One Thomas James, an ordinary settler, protesting about some treatment that he had received, around 1639 wrote to John Winthrop a letter full of biblical allusion and reference, ending:

> that I may obtain so much as equity and natural justice requireth which Job that president and pattern of equity 29 Job 15 and 12 and 31 Job 13 granted to his bond slaves . . . I hope Sir, one day it will be no grief to you 1 Sam 25.31 etc. The lord Jesus preserve you blameless to that day amen. So prayeth your Humble Servant in all duty in Christ Thomas James.[107]

J. Luxford wrote to John Winthrop in 1639, about the tangled dealings at his farm at Concord, a letter containing many biblical references: for example, 'The Lord help me my fears were never greater, lest my repentence should be Ahabs, or Pharoahs that would do anything.'[108]

Emmanuel Downing wrote to John Winthrop also in 1639 'Job was raised to a full estate in this way by his friends, so I conceive tis a duty and debt the country stands in to free you, and being a way of God you may with Comfort accept it.'[109]

In the same year Lord Say and Seal wrote to Winthrop about an attempt to persuade New Englanders to join his settlement in the Caribbean. His letter is full of biblical example and reference, in the line of 'you desire me to consider the 4 of Nehemiah 1.2.3.4.5 wherein the example of Sanballat and Tobiah are set before me to fright me.'[110]

Quite often, the Bible is not quoted directly, but simply made reference to, as in the letter from Richard Salstonstall and others to Winthrop in 1643 about their desire not to get involved in a dispute with the French, which simply notes 'we conceive the speech of the prophet to Jehoshaphat, 2 Chron. 19.2 and of Solomon Proverbs 26.17 not only discharge but strongly prohibit us.'[111] Winthrop's reply, *c.* 21 July 1643 does the same, inserting 'Prov. 3.27 . . . Exod. 23.4 . . . Deut. 20.10', and 'The fear of man bringeth a snare; but he that trusteth in the Lord shall be safe. Prov. 29.24' – the last sentence in that long document.[112]

Of especial interest is a remark by Francis Kerby in London to Winthrop in New England in 1631 in which he says: 'We hope that God will make Sweden an instrument for the fall of the Antichrist. I find noted in the margin by the Geneva translators Revel: 17.16 that divers nations as the Goths, vandals and Hungarians . . . shall rise up to destroy the whore.'[113]

This evidence of the regular use of the Geneva Bible can be supported by many documents from the colonies. There is no doubt that for a long time, even after 1611, Geneva in one form or another was actively used. Quite often, however, it is difficult to decide from which version a quotation has come, and there seems to have been a tradition of free variation, which, as in the 1520s and 1530s, would argue an oral tradition of Bible knowledge.

Discussing the religious background of the nation which declared independence in 1776, Sydney Ahlstrom remarks of the European settlers that a very high percentage of all the German, Swiss, French, Dutch and Scottish people bore the 'stamp of Geneva' in some broader sense. Though this is a loose generalisation, it still points in the direction of an accepted use of Geneva Bibles as a matter of course. The larger point must always remain that the Puritans in particular always turned first to the Scriptures, 'for the ordering of personal life, the regulation of society, and the structuring of the Church'.[114] The Scriptures even in obscurer parts of the Old Testament, provided explicit directives regarding Church order. The fact that a young Cambridge graduate like John Cotton, or an upright administrator like John Winthrop, thought and expressed themselves, and indeed acted, entirely through the Scriptures, makes its own point. High on the list of necessities for New England life was a learned ministry (Harvard College was founded, as already noted, as early as 1636), which means that these constant references to the Bible, with minds moving easily in and out of the Scriptures in all existential situations, were not the parrot-like repetitions of a few favourite texts, but came from as scholarly an understanding of the heart of both Testaments as could be found anywhere. (The contents of the libraries of leading American thinkers in the late seventeenth century will be considered in chapter 31 below.) A dedicated polemicist like Roger Williams, the breakaway founder of Providence and the Rhode Island settlement, would be expected to be an intense biblicist, to the exclusion not only of the Christian Fathers, but also of other Protestant theologians. Issues of interpreting the Bible were the whole point of his argument. It is a different matter when an ordinary farmer, concerned about an issue of his land, writes a letter to the Governor that is steeped in the Scriptures. It is a reasonable assumption that it represents a natural outcrop of the land that was America in 1639.

Chapter 25

THE KING JAMES VERSION, 1611

THE KING JAMES VERSION, the 'Authorised Version', first printed in 1611, is greatly cherished. For generations, Christians and lovers of fine English have read the Bible only in this version. They have felt that its words spoke to them in a particular way, in public or in private. On great occasions, phrases from this Bible – 'the eternal God is thy refuge, and underneath are the everlasting arms'[1] – have brought whole nations together in shared feeling. In the intensity of solitary grief, words from this book – 'Let not your heart be troubled'[2] – have eased breaking hearts. The cadences of the twenty-third Psalm have been taken deep into memories:

> The Lord is my shepherd; I shall not want. He maketh me to lie down in green pastures: he leadeth me beside the still waters . . . Yea, though I walk through the valley of the shadow of death, I will fear no evil: for thou art with me; thy rod and thy staff they comfort me . . .

High and low, rich and poor have understood that Christmas properly begins with 'And there were in the same country shepherds abiding in the fields, keeping watch over their flock by night,' and Easter with 'And they found the stone rolled away from the sepulchre.'[3] The very essence of what Christians believe has been for centuries in the words of that version: 'For since by man came death, by man came also the resurrection of the dead. For as in Adam all die, even so in Christ shall all be made alive.'[4]

On a historical scale, the sheer longevity of this version is a phenomenon, without parallel. English translations come and go, some with strong effect: but 'King James' is still the bestselling book in the world. Geographically, its spread has been global for hundreds of years: wherever in the world there are English readers, there are copies. In the story of the earth we live on, its influence cannot be calculated. Its words have been found to have a unique quality, of being able both to lift up a dedicated soul higher than had been thought, and to reach even below the lowest depths of human experience.

In that ability it is God revealed, of course. A religion is a revelation or it is nothing. The King James Version, so praised since the eighteenth century for being wonderful literature, is that, certainly, but properly something different. It is the Word of God in English – not exclusively, as it is only a translation of original texts that are difficult in places: yet as fine a piece of that work as we shall find. Sometimes the translation is wrong, or clumsy, or baffling. KJV's readings of the base texts are in hundreds of places now superseded by greater knowledge, or just better texts. Its older English can confuse the tongue.[5] In particulars, it is not perfect. But the great love it has received is justified by its mastery of the craft of the declaration of an incarnate God, who is at the same time sharing both ordinary life, and astoundingly strange.

For some Christians, KJV has endured for almost four hundred years as the most accurate translation there can be: to criticise it in any way is to blaspheme. Anyone who has spent a lifetime with this Bible, even a scholar knowing the Greek and Hebrew originals, can find sympathy with that view. But many Christians cannot share it. To call it the most accurate translation there can be is to make a limit, one that was not even set all those centuries ago (the translators' aim was simply 'to make a good one better')[6] and to indulge in a myth. One of the intentions of this chapter is to clear away misconceptions which impede a proper study of this remarkable publication.

From the start we need to be clear about five things.

First, contrary to what some people believe, this translation was not made personally by King James I. That king, who reigned over Great Britain from 1603 to 1625, prided himself on his biblical scholarship, and as a young man and a good Protestant Scot had made his own metrical versions of thirty of the Psalms, and of the Book of Revelation. But he had nothing at all to do with the work of this translation, beyond approving the idea, keeping a distant eye on the committees of scholars,[7] and receiving a two-page sugary Dedication.

Second, that monarch was certainly not 'Saint James', and to refer to 'the Saint James Bible', as some people do, is to be curiously confused. Three men in the New Testament whom we call St James – one of the Twelve disciples, the brother of Jesus, and the St James who wrote the New Testament epistle (possibly Jesus' brother) – are of course in no way associated with the British King James of nearly sixteen hundred years later, who, though in his very eccentric way a quite good man, was no saint.

Third, contrary to what has been confidently asserted since the early 1800s in Britain, this version was never authorised. 'The Authorised Version' was a title popularly given to it quite late in its history. Though there is evidence of some earlier usage, *OED*, noting that only the Great

Bible of 1540 and the Bishops' Bible after 1572 bore on their titles 'authorised and appointed', gives the first appearance of the phrase, 'What is called our authorized version', as 1824.[8]

Fourth, and also contrary to what has been confidently asserted for several centuries, this version was not universally loved from the moment it appeared. Far from it. As a publication in the seventeenth century it was undoubtedly successful: it was heavily used, and it rapidly saw off its chief rival, the three Geneva Bibles, to become the standard British (and American) Bible. But that success was at first for political and commercial reasons, and largely a result of in-fighting between London printers (see chapter 26, below). For its first 150 years, the KJV received a barrage of criticism. In 1659, for example, a London clergyman and scholar, Dr Robert Gell, published an 800-page treatise denouncing it, 'discussing its faults in detail, counting among them a denial of Christ's authority'.[9]

Fifth – and to be writing this is to be treading on some very sensitive toes – in the stream of hundreds of fresh English translations of the Bible made from 1526 until today, this version has no claim to be considered, as the phrase is, 'inerrant': that is, the pure, and only, Word of God revealed to the world. (This tenet will be considered below in chapter 38.)

(I could add a sixth confusion, characterised by the apparently not apocryphal utterance from Texas denouncing a new translation: 'if the English of the Saint James Bible was good enough for Jesus, it is good enough for me.')

Each of these deviations will be considered: but I need to make clear, firmly and at once, that the qualities and history of the KJV are far more interesting than those five (or six) dogmatic statements aver – though *why* those things are said can be of special concern.

The language of KJV is beautiful. Right through the sixty-six books of the Bible, from 'They heard the voice of the Lord God walking in the garden in the cool of the day' (Genesis 3) to 'God shall wipe away all tears from their eyes' (Revelation 7 and 21), phrases of lapidary beauty have been deeply admired: 'My days are swifter than a weaver's shuttle' (Job 7); 'How art thou fallen from heaven, O Lucifer, son of the morning?' (Isaiah 14); 'The shadow of a great rock in a weary land' (Isaiah 32); 'Ask, and it shall be given you; seek, and you shall find; knock, and it shall be opened unto you' (Matthew 7); 'In him we live and move and have our being' (Acts 17); 'The unsearchable riches of Christ' (Ephesians 2); 'Fight the good fight of faith; lay hold on eternal life' (1 Timothy 6); 'Looking unto Jesus, the author and finisher of our faith' (Hebrews 12); 'Behold, I stand at the door and knock' (Revelation 3).

Phrases from the KJV are so familiar that they are often thought to be proverbial wisdom: 'Am I my brother's keeper?' (Genesis 4); 'Escaped with the skin of my teeth' (Job 19); 'Saying peace, peace, when there is no peace'

(Jeremiah 6); 'They have sown the wind, and they shall reap the whirl-
wind' (Hosea 8); 'The signs of the times' (Matthew 16); 'Fell among thieves'
(Luke 10); 'Scales fell from his eyes' (Acts 9); 'Full of good works' (Acts
9); 'A law unto themselves' (Romans 2); 'Wages of sin' (Romans 6); 'The
powers that be' (Romans 13); 'All things to all men' (1 Corinthians 9);
'Filthy lucre' (1 Timothy 3); 'Let brotherly love continue' (Hebrews 13);
'The patience of Job' (James 5); 'Perfect love casteth out fear' (1 John 4).
If such are not proverbs, it has been thought, then they must surely be
from Shakespeare.

All the quotations so far in this chapter are indeed splendid phrases:
yet, without exception, all of them came to KJV from the Geneva versions, and almost all of those directly from Tyndale. One of the first things
to do in studying the making of KJV is to recognise the nature of its particular dependence upon its predecessors. This is unexpected at a time
when royal politics were strongly against the Geneva versions, and Tyndale
was still publicly unmentionable as a heretic. By those who know little
history, the creation of KJV has often been considered miraculous, being
among other things the only time a work of genius has been produced
by a committee. First on any list of 'miracles' associated with KJV is its
heavy and often verbatim dependence on Tyndale.[10] Not only does
Tyndale-the-heretic come through so cleanly: it is remarkable that, 1611
being a time when the English language was powerful and flexible,
Tyndale's work is so good when it was all done eighty years before, when
the English language was uncertain and restricted.

Not that King James's revisers did not themselves have many good
moments. Even following Tyndale closely, they made admirable changes.
The addition of the word 'little' to Tyndale's phrase 'Suffer the children
to come unto me', as in Mark 10:14, is one of them. With help from
Coverdale and Geneva, delicately sharpening Tyndale's (Matthew 22:14)
'For many are called and few be chosen' to make 'For many are called,
but few are chosen' is another. Yet another is in Romans 8:31, this time
with help from the Vulgate, shading Tyndale's 'If God be on our side: who
can be against us?' to 'If God be for us . . . ?' There is a multitude of such
fine, subtle changes.

On the other hand, there is a greater multitude of meddling for the
worse as will appear below. Adding 'indeed' to Tyndale's 'The spirit is
willing but the flesh is weak' at Matthew 26:41, a change taken from
Rheims, was not good: it adds a touch of distance and formality into Jesus'
direct words to his fearful disciples. Directness is what was lost by turning
into Latin (directly from Rheims, itself directly from the Vulgate) the last
sentence of Matthew 6, so that Tyndale's punchy 'For the day present hath

ever enough of his own trouble' became the more lofty 'Sufficient unto the day is the evil thereof.' Among the worst of many is the loss of character, so present in the Hebrew, in making the serpent in Genesis 3 say to the reluctant Eve not, with Tyndale's instant dismissive ridicule, 'Tush ye shall not die,' but the prissy, considered, 'Ye shall not surely die.'

Moreover, it must also be said, however unpopularly, that quite large tracts of the Old Testament prophecies in KJV are unintelligible. To take only one example, at random as KJV fell open, Micah 1:11: 'Pass ye away, thou inhabitant of Saphir, having thy shame naked: the inhabitant of Zanaan came not forth in the mourning of Bethezel; he shall receive of you his standing.' (One is reminded of the young Robert Browning courting Elizabeth Barrett, and being asked by her what some of his lines meant: he replied, 'Madam, when I wrote those lines, only two beings knew what they meant – God and Robert Browning. Now only God knows.' REB (1989) clarifies the sense: 'Take to the road, you that dwell in Saphir! / Have not the people of Zaanan gone out/ in shame from their city? / Beth-ezel is a place of lamentation; / she can lend you support no longer'.)

For, in its making, KJV was saddled with two disadvantages. First, for political reasons, its base English text had not to be a Geneva version; and, second, there had to be little annotation. Thus was thrown away for readers much of the textual scholarship and all the exegetical commentary richly available. (Geneva made that final phrase in Micah 1:11 '*the enemie* shall receive of you for his standing', with an explanatory note that it means that they will pay for the delay of their enemy, who will not depart until he has overcome. The Hebrew is not easy to follow, and modern understanding is different: but Geneva makes some sense.) Each divine working on the new version received for the base text his own copy of a folio Bishops' Bible – disastrously for the Hebrew poetry. In that version, there had to be strictly no marginal annotation.

To these matters I shall come.

HAMPTON COURT, JANUARY 1604

The world's biggest bestseller had a most off-hand origin. It was initiated from a remark in the last minute of a two-day conference called by King James about something else. Following that royal nod, nothing much seemed to happen for several years. There was no 'noise of the new Bible' at all.

After a six-week triumphal progress from Edinburgh, the new King James I arrived in London early in May 1603. Though well used to a new

Protestant form of government in Scotland, he found his Edinburgh
Presbyterianism did not, at significant points, match the broad Anglican
Church that Elizabeth had bequeathed to him. He called a two-day
meeting of senior clergy in January 1604, to be held at his magnificent
palace of Hampton Court. Tensions in the Elizabethan Church of
England – especially, it was put to him, those caused by the Puritans –
threatened to take away from his Jacobeanly united England and Scotland
any pretence of national religious stability. The conference was presided
over by James himself, who was no mean theologian, and shrewdly alert
to the matters in hand. It was a failure. Indeed, it could hardly have been
otherwise, being, it seems, set by the senior bishops to squash rather
than attend to the anxieties of the less moderate in the Puritan party.[11]
The Puritans were allowed only four representatives to face eighteen
adversaries, led by the archbishop of Canterbury and the bishop of
London supported by seven other bishops, seven deans and two doctors.
Patrick Collinson wrote, 'Late in the afternoon of 16 January, 1604, a
well-informed fly on the wall would have concluded that the puritans
had lost their duel with the bishops game, set and match.'[12] The failure of
the conference had long effects. One was the flight of some groups to
Holland – from whence in 1620 a number sailed in the *Mayflower* to
America.

At Hampton Court, on that last day, and in the last minutes of the afternoon, the leader of the Puritan party, Dr John Reynolds, President of
Corpus Christi College, Oxford, apparently as an afterthought in a discussion of catechisms and the use of the Bible in the Book of Common
Prayer (some parts of which the Puritans opposed) spoke. I give here at
some length the account of what happened written by William Barlow,
his semi-official *Summe and Substance of the Conference*.[13] This is the chief
source for these moments of verbal exchange between Reynolds and the
king, and two things need noting. First, in one important point it differs
from the account given by the chairman of the revisers himself in the
'Translators to the Reader' preface to the finished KJV: and second,
Barlow's account is, again in the words of Patrick Collinson, 'a skilfully
tendentious piece of propaganda, commissioned by [Archbishop] Whitgift
[an opponent of the Puritans], flattering to the king, supportive of the
bishops (whose ranks Barlow was about to join) and damaging to the
credibility of the puritan delegation'.[14] It is, however, the fullest we have,
and it might perhaps give some flavour not only of what took place, but
of the bias in the reporting.

> After that, he [Reynolds] moved his Majesty, that there might be a new
> *translation* of the *Bible*, because those that were allowed in the reigns of

Henry the eight, and *Edward* the sixth, were corrupt and not answerable to the truth of the Original. For example, first, *Galatians*, 4, 25, the Greek word συνστοιχεῖ (*sunstoichei*) is not well translated, as now it is, *Bordreth*, neither expressing the force of the word, nor the Apostle's sense, nor the situation of the place.

To comment in midstream: whether Reynolds omitted to mention the Bishops' Bible as not cognate to the Book of Common Prayer, or as an insult, or whether Barlow is being, indeed, tendentious in his reporting in the way of making Reynolds appear by the omission to be antagonising the bishops, we cannot now know. Secondly, though the Greek word was indeed so mistranslated in the Great Bible, one must feel sure that that trivial point, and the two which followed, were not the best that the Bible scholar Reynolds could do. Was this selective omission? Were words put in his mouth? To continue with Barlow:

> Secondly, *Psalm*, 105,28, *they were not obedient*; the Original being, *They were not Disobedient.*
>
> Thirdly, *Psalm, 106*, verse 30. Then stood up *Phinees* and *prayed*, the Hebrew hath *Executed judgement*. To which motion, there was, at the present, no gainsaying, the objections being trivial and old, and already, in print, often answered; only, my Lord of *London* well added, that if every man's humour should be followed, there would be no end of translating. Whereupon his Highness wished that some special pains should be taken in that behalf for one uniform translation (professing that he could never yet, see a Bible well translated in English; but the worst of all, his Majesty thought the Geneva to be) . . .

Again to comment. *Did* James say that? He is about to appear to be even more dismissive of Geneva Bibles, in a remark that suggests that he knew of them only because one was 'given him by an English Lady', a deliberately sexist and demeaning remark all round. Yet as a scholarly, curious and theologically minded young Scottish king at the age of thirteen, he had in 1579 been presented with, as dedicated to him as '*the richt excellent richt heigh and michtie prince James the Sext King of Scottis* . . .', the first Bible printed in Scotland (in Edinburgh), a Geneva version. Since that date, 1579, and up to January 1604, twenty-five years, no fewer than ninety-two different editions of the Geneva Bible had been published (editions, not just reprintings) – to say he had not seen one would be like a modern man saying he had never seen a telephone directory.

> . . . and this was to be done by the best learned in both the Universities, after them to be reviewed by the Bishops, and the chief learned of the Church: from them to be presented to the *Privy-Council*; and lastly

to be ratified by his *Royal authority*; and so his whole Church to be bound unto it, and none other . . .

Once again: is this anti-Puritan, anti-Geneva ('and none other') insistence the speech of James, or of Barlow? James was a moderate Protestant who had been a successful king of Presbyterian Scotland for many years, a keen and learned follower of ecclesiastical affairs whose general policy was mediation. One must be suspicious.

> . . . Marry, withal, he gave this caveat (upon a word cast out by my Lord of London [the ruthlessly orthodox anti-Puritan Richard Bancroft] that no marginal note should be added, having found in them which are annexed to the *Geneva* translation (which he saw in a Bible given him by an English Lady) some notes very partial, untrue, seditious, and savouring too much of dangerous, and traitorous conceits. As for example, *Exod.* 1.19, where the marginal note alloweth *disobedience to Kings*. And 2. *Chron.* 15,16, the note taxeth Asa for deposing his mother, *only*, and *not killing* her . . .

The Geneva marginal note in Exodus comments on the refusal of the Hebrew midwives to obey the King of Egypt and kill the Hebrew male babies: when called to account, the two midwives tell the king that the Hebrew women are so lively that the babies are born before they can get there. The note is: 'Their disobedience herein was lawful, but their dissembling evil.' In 2 Chronicles 15:16, Asa, having deposed Maachah his mother for idolatry, destroyed the idol. The Geneva note in full is:

> Or grandmother: and herein he showed that he lacked zeal: for she ought to have died both by the covenant, as v.13, and by the law of God: but he gave place to foolish pity, and would also seem after a sort to falsify the law.

King James's mother Mary, deposed as Queen of the Scots when he was two years old, was beheaded in 1587, when James was twenty-one, at the command of Queen Elizabeth, for plotting insistent treachery. Her execution was never far from his mind. He bruised easily. When, in 1596, the second part of Spenser's *Faerie Queene*, Books IV to VI, was published, James wanted the poet to be tried and punished, for something in Book V, Canto ix, 'some dishonourable effects . . . against himself and his mother deceased'.[15]

Barlow concludes that 'all the rest with a grave and judicious advice' led to the king remarking that

> if these be the greatest matters you be grieved with, I need not have been troubled with such importunities and complaints . . . some other

more private course might have been taken for your satisfaction, and withal, looking upon the Lords, he shook his head, smiling.[16]

Barlow makes the king rebuke the Puritans with a knowing wink to the bishops. That the Puritans had real cause for complaint appears in the course of the eleven-page Preface to the finished work, 'The Translators to the Reader'. Miles Smith, final editor of the whole enterprise, wrote:

> For the very historical truth is, that upon the importunate petitions of the Puritans at his Majesty's coming to this crown, the conference at *Hampton Court* having been appointed for hearing their complaints, when by force of reason they were put from all other grounds, they had recourse at the last to this shift, that they could not with good conscience subscribe to the Communion book, since it maintained the Bible as it was there translated, which was, as they said, a most corrupted translation.[17]

Smith's '. . . when by force of reason they were put from all other grounds . . .' does not tally with Barlow's kingly dismissal. Smith continues, however,

> And though this was judged to be but a very poor and empty shift, yet even hereupon did his Majesty begin to bethink himself of the good that might ensue by a new translation, and presently after gave order for this translation which is now presented unto thee.[18]

The proposal, unexpected in the making, was perhaps a useful one. The original Geneva Bible, the last successful new translation from the original languages into English, had been made nearly fifty years before. Further revisions to Geneva had been largely, though not exclusively, to the New Testament annotations. The Hebrew work in the Bishops' Bible of 1568 was a botch, and was understood to be so. The Rheims New Testament of 1582 had been basically from the Latin, was distinctly odd in places, and was not widely used. Since the original Geneva work, there had been great advances in understanding Hebrew.

> The excellent continental scholars Fagius, Tremellius and Chevalier had been brought over to teach Hebrew at Cambridge, the early diction- aries and grammars upon which Tyndale and his successors depended had been revised or superseded, and there was more knowledge of the cognate languages Aramaic and Syriac. Increasing familiarity with Jewish commentaries on the Old Testament was an important factor in Bible study and translation. Kimshi, whose Hebrew is straightforward, was widely and directly known, the more difficult Rashi and Ibn Ezra at least at second hand through the commentaries of Mercier.[19]

For the New Testament, there had been new understanding of Greek, as well as slight movement toward the science of evaluating texts. The English language was changing quickly. Perhaps a new, wholesale revision of the Geneva versions in the best modern English, if universally used because authorised by his Majesty, might go some way to heal the growing dissensions in the Church of England about church practices. The chance was missed. Church politics muddied the stream. The work, undertaken without enthusiasm, limped forward, dragging with it the fetters of the poorest previous English version, the Bishops' Bible. Yet the hand of God must be seen: some fine work was done; and Tyndale's New Testament and the Geneva Old Testament, in spite of official impediments, did shine through.

THE COMPANIES

By 30 June 1604, Richard Bancroft, the Bishop of London, was able to write that his Majesty had approved the list of fifty-four translators, and wished 'all possible speed'. From that time no official record has survived to clarify the division of the work: we are dependent on a number of lists, 'the most trustworthy' being that printed in the fourth edition of Bishop Burnet's *History of the Reformation* of 1715.[20] There were to be six companies, two each in Oxford, Cambridge and Westminster. One Westminster panel undertook the Old Testament as far as the end of 2 Kings; the other, the New Testament epistles. One Cambridge panel worked 'From the First of the *Chronicles*, with the rest of the Story, and the *Hagiographi,* viz. *Job, Psalms, Proverbs, Canticles,* Ecclesiastes': the other, 'The Prayer of *Manasses* and the rest of the *Apocrypha*'. One Oxford panel took the 'four, or greater prophets', Lamentations, and the 'twelve lesser Prophets': the other, the Gospels, Acts and Revelation.[21]

The best accounts list forty-seven rather than fifty-four scholars. One or two of these men are now hardly known (the mysterious 'Dr Ravens' is 'apparently an error'): but the offices held are impressive. Most of the forty-seven are Fellows of Oxbridge colleges, a dozen being Heads. The Regius Professors of Hebrew and Greek in both universities are present.[22] A. W. Pollard noted, 'The choice of revisers seems to have been determined solely by their fitness, and both parties in the Church were represented by some of their best men.'[23]

A few names need attention. The head of the Westminster panel in Burnet's list is 'Mr. Dean of *Westminster*': this was Lancelot Andrewes, Fellow, and, from 1589, Master of Pembroke Hall, Cambridge. His preaching in St Paul's Cathedral in London brought him to the attention of

Queen Elizabeth, who offered him two bishoprics, which he refused. Master of fifteen languages, he was in his many published sermons, and private devotions (*Preces Privatae*, not printed until 1648), a high-flown stylist and a shaping influence on Anglican theology (both qualities praised by T. S. Eliot in his 1928 essay in his *For Lancelot Andrewes*). King James made him Bishop of Chichester in 1605, then of Ely in 1609, and latterly of Winchester in 1619. His brother Roger, also a Fellow of Pembroke Hall, and Master of Jesus College, Cambridge, was on the Cambridge Old Testament panel. Dr John Reynolds, President of Corpus Christi, leader of the Puritans at Hampton Court, was on the Oxford Old Testament panel. Appointed as Dean of Chester and Fellow and Dean of Trinity Hall, Cambridge, now on the Westminster New Testament panel as Bishop of Rochester, was that William Barlow who reported on Hampton Court. John Boys, Fellow of Clare Hall, Cambridge, will soon appear here at length, through the happy chance of the survival of his notes made at meetings of translators: as will Miles Smith of Brasenose Oxford, Prebendary of Hereford Cathedral and, from 1612, Bishop of Gloucester, because he was one of the two final revisers of the whole Bible just before it went to press, and author of the excellent Preface, 'The Translators to the Reader' (see below, pp. 775–93).

There was a sprinkling of bishops, three only in 1607, five to be made. Bancroft had learned the oblique lessons from Cranmer and Parker about their peers' inadequacy, and perhaps knew (as Miles Smith certainly did, as he quoted it in the Preface) the direct statement of Gregory of Nazianzus in about AD 381, that 'he had not seen any profit to come by any synod or meeting of the Clergy, but rather the contrary'.[24] The omission of the scholar Andrew Willet has never been explained: his many and important books of biblical work were constantly in print.[25] To those who know the world of oriental scholarship at the time, the striking omission is of Hugh Broughton. The six dense columns given to his publications in *RSTC* – limited to his works in English – are headed by a despairing note about the complexities of dealing with his output bibliographically, adding 'Matters are further complicated by Broughton's combative spirit, his abrupt and opaque style, and his continual harping upon a few related [biblical] topics.'[26] He could write wonderful English prose as unrestrained and glowing as that of Thomas Nashe or Robert Greene; and, most importantly, he was expert in Hebrew, possibly the best in Europe in 1607. But restraint was not in him. He was noisy and eccentric. At Oxbridge high tables, he would have been the one who passed the port the wrong way, or drank it all himself. (Robert Greene, whom he resembles, though 'Master of Arts of both universities', would have been discreetly stopped by the butler at the door.) His omission was going to be a source of embarrassment and worse to the makers of KJV after 1611, as his criticisms were both accurate and unforgettable – one of the mildest is that he told the Old Testament panels that they had often put the wrong reading in the text and the right reading in the margin, an error fatal for a work designed to be read aloud.

PROGRESS

By 31 July 1604, Bancroft could send a circular to the other bishops, enclosing a letter from the king of the 22nd, saying that 'certain learned men of the number of four and fifty' had been appointed, and further appealing for financial aid: since some of the appointees had no, or very poor, 'ecclesiastical preferment', Bancroft asked to be notified of vacancies of 'parsonages or prebends' to the value of twenty pounds at least (in 2001, about £2,400[27]), so that he could use them for 'the learned men' – *in absentia*, of course.[28] A second circular asked each bishop for donations outright. A. W. Pollard comments: 'The response to the first of these circulars seems to have been very slight; that to the second *nil.*'[29] King James kept a distance from such goings-on, 'being unable to remedy this "in any convenient time"'.[30]

Nothing public then happened for some years: the next Convocation ignored the matter, which appeared from that omission to have been dropped. Yet it is clear that at least a few of the scholars began work, without apparently any sense of pressure, before the year was out. In November 1604, Lancelot Andrewes, Director of the first Westminster company, wrote to Mr Hartwell, secretary to the Society of Antiquaries, 'But that this afternoon is our translation time, and most of our company is negligent, I would have seen you; but no translation shall hinder me, if once I may understand I shall commit no error in coming.'[31] The work, though begun, has a low priority. Some scholars were getting into position in 1605. It has commonly been said that work did not begin until 1607. This follows Westcott's 1868 calculation backwards from the 'twice seven times seventy two [1,008] days and more' the translators said that the work had taken:[32] but Westcott's arithmetic assumed that they did nothing else, even on Sundays.

Ward Allen in 1977 more convincingly showed that the companies had met by late August 1604, at least at Cambridge, as there they received for perusal 'a certain learned epistle of Mr Broughton's': indeed, the evidence is of the first stage of the work being finished by the companies by 1607, and their whole work by the autumn of 1608.[33]

Gilbert Burnet also printed a document of great value, the list of the fifteen *Rules to be observed in the Translation of the Bible* given to each of the companies by Bancroft.[34] Rules 2 and 5 specify not altering names or chapter divisions: 8 to 12 set out the managing of group decisions and appeals to experts and interested parties. Rules 13 and 15 explain who is to be in charge, and arrangements for calling in 'three or four of the most Ancient and Grave Divines' – that cuts out Broughton – for dealing with textual precedents not solvable by following rule 4, which prescribed, in cases of words with 'divers Significations', following 'the most of the Ancient Fathers', where appropriate. Of special interest are the remaining five, as follows:

1. The ordinary Bible read in the Church, commonly called the *Bishops Bible*, to be followed, and as little altered as the Truth of the original will permit.

3. The old Ecclesiastical Words to be kept, *viz.* the Word *Church* not to be translated *Congregation &c.*

6. No Marginal Notes at all to be affixed, but only for the Explanation of the *Hebrew* or *Greek* Words, which cannot without some circumlocution, so briefly and fitly be express'd in the Text.

7. Such Quotations of Places to be marginally set down as shall serve for the Reference of one Scripture to another.

Each of these constraints is what one might expect. Rule 14, however, does, unexpectedly, set the workers free.

14. These translations to be used when they agree better with the Text than the Bishops: *Tindoll's, Matthews, Coverdale's, Whitchurch's, Geneva.*

It used to be said (by C. C. Butterworth, for example, in 1971[35]) that there is 'not the slightest evidence' that some, or all, of these rules were ever followed. Again it is to Ward Allen that we are indebted for the evidence of meticulous carrying out of instructions.[36] Allen summed up his analysis of Lambeth MS.98, with the words, 'The annotated Bishops' Bible, MS.98, Bois's notes, and scattered remarks about the work of King James's translators lead to the conclusion that these translators worked according to their instructions.'[37] In the 124 weeks from November 1604 to May 1607, the Westminster company not only prepared 121 chapters, but circulated them from company to company as instructed. Ward Allen demonstrates that Lambeth Ms. 98 was prepared for the late stage critical review of the New Testament Epistles, in agreement with rule 10. (He shows that of the 6,261 revisions of the Bishops' Bible, 3,287 were made on the basis of this document.[38])

Allen gives, from the notes of John Bois of discussions of 453 places in the Epistles, a vivid picture of a company at work:

> We know from Bois that the members of the meeting engaged in arguments, which were sometimes violent, consulted dictionaries, pored over and discussed current and antique theologians, traced textual variations, studied classical authors to settle questions of diction, thought about style, composed in places original readings. We know . . . that the meeting deliberated over questions which were so difficult that the translators themselves had reached a deadlock over correct answers. In the light of this, thirty-two discussions . . . provided a full day's work.[39]

They disobeyed rule 14 in one important particular. Bancroft's list did not mention the Rheims translation. Bancroft's silence should be taken seriously. It may be true, that, thanks to Fulke's unintended help, as Ward Allen put it, 'the Rheims New Testament furnished to the Synoptic Gospels and Epistles in the A.V. as many revised readings as any other single version.'[40] On the other hand, the coincidence of readings in Rheims and Wyclif could suggest the greater influence of working from the 'common version', the Latin Vulgate. Allen's careful remark refers to occasional details. The base of KJV was always not Bishops', but Geneva, 'the good one' to be made 'better', and, underlying Geneva, the vocabulary, phrasing and rhythms of Tyndale.

REVISION, NOT FRESH TRANSLATION

The instructions given were firm. Since Hampton Court, the enterprise had changed, for reasons that are not known. Instead of a new translation, the six companies, two in Oxford, two in Cambridge, and two in Westminster, were to make a revision, but of the Bishops' Bible. That revision, rather than translation afresh, was agreed is regrettable, but understandable: the monarch wanted results. The whole Bible, with the Apocrypha, contains eighty books, many of them long: an eighteenth-century purveyor of curiosities calculated that, without the Apocrypha, KJV has 773,692 words (and 3,566,480 letters).[41] To use a common base text would have several advantages.

Stepping back to the Bishops' Bible had, however, three great disadvantages, all arising from the direction of greater Latinity. The Bible has a rich variety of styles, unique within one set of covers, from the Hebrew and Greek of its originals. Hebrew poetry has a small vocabulary, but can vary from epic and primitive ballad-of-victory to congregational worship, private religious meditation, proverbial declaration, erotic lyricism, or the vivid intensity of Hebrew prophecy, itself again continually various. Hebrew prose, even within one such book as Genesis, can vary from the surreal to the everyday. Again, though the Greek of the New Testament is the *koiné*, the ordinary language of transaction throughout the eastern Mediterranean at the time (only Luke 1:1–4 is in classical Greek), there are great differences between the Greek of the four Gospels, and between them and the Hebrew mind of Paul writing in philosophical, theological Greek, to say nothing of the special effects of the Epistle to the Hebrews, or Revelation. A good translation gives some sense of these differences. Bending the English towards Latin can lead to a flattening, with everything near to the same sonorous level. The bedroom sensuality of the Song of Songs can come out sounding too similar to the noisy public worship of Psalm 150; and Paul can sound musty and old-fashioned, rather than a mind exploring the frontiers of spiritual, and physical, experience. A fair judgement of KJV is that it can show just that, a flattening. There is a recognisable KJV tone, from Genesis 1:1, 'In the beginning' to Revelation 22:21, 'Amen'. It is sonorous, orotund, high-sounding, a general style that makes it difficult to stoop to the commonplace. Thus KJV's Jacob 'lay with' Leah at Genesis 30:16, where Tyndale has the still-common 'slept with'. Thus in the Gospels, to the socially important, but vertically challenged, Zaccheus, who has climbed a tree to see him, Jesus cannot say playfully, as in the Greek, 'Zacche, come down at once' (Tyndale has 'Zache, at once come down') but in KJV the formal 'Zaccheus, make haste and come down' (Luke 19:5).

One perpetual argument for modern retranslation of the Bible is that KJV is archaic. No one now uses verbal forms like these:[42]

> For he that speaketh in an unknown tongue speaketh not unto men, but unto God: for no man understandeth him; howbeit in the spirit he speaketh mysteries. But he that prophesieth speaketh unto men to edification, and exhortation, and comfort (1 Corinthians 14:2,3).

That is true – though it does not mean that the words cannot now be understood. KJV was born archaic: it was intended as a step back. The Bishops' Bible of 1568 was not only itself out of date: it was a reworking of the second Great Bible, of 1540. The reasons for making KJV look back were three-fold: first, it was intended to reset the standard of the solid middle-of-the-road Anglican establishment, historically built since King Henry handed down the *Verbum Dei*. Second, Latinity, rather than contemporary English, was thought to bring with it the great weight of the authority of the past, of what was understood as fifteen hundred years of solid Christian faith, as well as generations of Latin education: and there were those, as there still are today, who refer to the Bible's 'original text' meaning the Latin Vulgate. There is a third, more fundamental, point. The world is divided into those who think that sacred Scripture should always be elevated above the common run – is not, indeed, sacred without some air of religiosity, of being remote from real life, with a whiff of the antiquarian: and on the other side those who say that the point of the Incarnation was that God became man, low experiences and all, and if the Greek is ordinary Greek, then ordinary English words are essential. The first are apt to say '"Judge not" is an admonition with Dominical authority': the second, 'Jesus said . . .'. In the earlier years of the seventeenth century, the weight of high Anglican politics was heavily on the side of increasing, as it was thought, a worshipful distance.

Yet one grieves at the chance missed in 1607. Had it been Geneva Bibles that were given out as the common base of King James's panels' revision, Geneva Bibles in Tomson's revision, with or without the Junius notes to Revelation, then how fine and forward-looking an 'authorised' version we might have had. The Geneva annotations, so often so helpful in pure clarification, could have been revised: it was only bigotry that kept such illumination away. The music of the English text would not have been lost, as Tyndale could have been even more present. The nearly fifty-year-old Old Testament Hebrew work in Geneva could have been brought up to date, and the New Testament could have been clarified beyond Tomson: on the texts there was plenty of contemporary continental work to draw on. The New Testament *Textus Receptus* which the KJV translated was already in Germany shown up for the ridiculous thing it was – and it is notable, in the making of KJV, how firmly the gates were slammed shut on anything from beyond Dover. In a form of what was said above on the Bishops' Bible, the reverse of what has been said since the mid-eighteenth century – the forcible replacement from 1611 of the remarkable, accurate, informative, forward-looking, very popular Geneva Bibles at the time of their greatest dissemination and power, with the backward-gazing, conservative KJV was one of the tragedies of western culture.

PROCEDURES

Robert Barker, who held the patent for printing the Bishops' Bible, provided '40 large churchbibles' for the project,[43] that is, folio Bishops' Bibles; they were most likely unbound, so allowing the translators, and the companies, to exchange pages. John Bois was a member of the Apocrypha panel in Cambridge, and then a member of the final revision committee in Westminster. It was known from the biography by his contemporary Anthony Walker that he – and apparently he alone – took notes of that committee's work, and it was regretted (for example by Pollard in 1911) that his notes had not survived. All that seemed to be left, as Pollard put it, was 'the finished result and a few remarks on it in the preface'.[44] But they had survived, in Oxford, in the Bodleian Library, and some of them were used by Gustavus Paine in his 1959 book about the translators.[45] Moreover, sheets of the working copies of a 1602 Bishops' Bible were found by Ward Allen to have survived, bound, also in the Bodleian Library, catalogued as 'Bibl.Eng.1602.b.i'. These give Old and New Testament annotations, the New Testament notes being confined to the Gospels (only John 17–21; there are five annotations scattered in the Epistles).

Bible scholars the world over must be for ever grateful to Ward Allen for his outstandingly meticulous scholarship in working with the original materials at the Bodleian, and at Lambeth Library, where he found that MS 98 was the working sheets from a late stage in the revision of the New Testament Epistles. Allen, from the late 1960s, has shown, by painstaking, detailed analysis of this work – the Latin and Greek notes of John Bois (which he translates); Lambeth MS 98 on the Epistles; and the Bodleian Bishops' Bible on the Gospels – the quality, the development and the frequency of revisions in the making of the KJV New Testament. At first in his work on Bois in *Translating for King James* (1969), and then in his book on the work on the Epistles (1977) and Gospels (1995), he gave the world the fullest and most fascinating account of what exactly all the notes indicated.[46] For example, it is very clear that 'the Epistles have undergone more revison in the A.V. than have the Gospels'.[47] Allen concluded that Bois's notes were made in the company, making the final manuscript, a conclusion supported by a full examination of his notes on 1 Peter. Gerald Hammond observed that 'By and large Bois reveals that the deviant, the untraditional, and the eccentric were unlikely to sway the committee.'[48]

There were other influences. Miles Smith, in 'The Translators to the Reader', mentioned two new Latin versions, by Arius Montanus printed in the Antwerp Polyglot in 1575,[49] and by Immanuel Tremellius, the preferred Latin text by Protestants, of 1579.[50] Smith also mentioned the Geneva French version of 1587–8, Diodati's Italian version (1607) and the Spanish version (1602) of Cipriano de Valera. The last three were also mentioned by the lawyer and historian John Selden in his *Table Talk*, posthumously published in 1689, where he wrote, clearly about a meeting of the final board of twelve:

The translators in King James's time took an excellent way. That part of the Bible was give to him who was most excellent in such a tongue (as the Apocrypha to Andrew Downs) and then they met together, and one read the translation, the rest holding in their hands some Bible, either of the learned tongues, or French, Spanish, Italian etc. If they found any fault they spoke; if not, he read on.[51]

Ward Allen reviewed 'the steps which the translators followed in preparing their revision'.

> Each translator completed his revision of a chapter week by week, and each company forged a common revision by comparing these private revisions. This revision being completed, a company circulated its work, book by book, among the other companies. From this circulation there resulted revisions, made in the light of objections raised to the work of a company, and an excursus upon any objection which the original company did not agree to. Then the translators circulated their work among the learned men, who were not official translators, and revised their work in view of suggestions from these men. Now the translators had to circulate these revisions among the other companies. Then, they prepared a final text. This final text they submitted to the general meeting in London, which spent nine months compounding disagreements among companies.[52]

Into this process Lambeth MS 98 fits somewhere. 'After MS 98 was prepared, there were some 3,000 changes made in its text before the text became that of the A.V.'[53]

Ward Allen's exact reprinting of MS 98 shows a little of the density of the work.

> Though MS 98 supplies the text of the Epistles in the A.V. as it was when revision was over half completed, the marginal notes in MS 98 represent only a third of the total in the A.V. The majority of these notes were due, then, to questions raised while the text of the Westminster company was in circulation or under the scrutiny of the general meeting.[54]

The process of elucidating 'the difficulty and ambiguity of St Paul's Greek at this point' is illustrated by 2 Corinthians 1:11. Having watched Tyndale's original frame disintegrate after the Great Bible, in Geneva 1560, Allen analyses the source of the verse in Bishops'.

> You also helping [*Bishops' Bible*] together [*Geneva (1560)*] by [*Bishops' Bible*] prayer for us [*Tyndale*], that [*Tyndale*] for the [*Tyndale: arrangement in sentence, Geneva (1557)*] benefits [*Bishops' Bible*] bestowed upon us [*Geneva (1557)*] by the means of many [*Tyndale*] persons [*Great Bible*] thanks may be given of many on our behalfe [*Tyndale*].

'By gathering parts from here and there and by adding their own inventions, the Bishops framed a verse which does not resemble any one of the translations from which it draws parts. King James's translators changed but two words of the Bishops' verse' (Great Bible's 'gift' for 'benefits'; for Tyndale's 'of many', Geneva 1557's 'by many'.) Both changes, from the Westminster company, are in MS 98.[55]

Allen follows the making of the phrase in 1 Timothy 6:6, from Tyndale's 'Godliness is great riches, if a man be content with that he hath', through the changes in the others (via Bishops' 'great lucre') to KJV's final 'But godliness with contentment is great gain'. The Westminster company supplied 'a word which had recently made its way into the English language, contentment'.

> At the general meeting there was proposed a reading which would have turned the sentence towards Tyndale's frame: *But godliness is great gayne in that it bringeth contentment.* While the Greek text admits this English translation, such a translation did not win the minds or ears of the meeting.[56]

(The linguistic alertness of some translators is impressive: Andrew Downes, Bois reveals, successfully introduced the completely new word 'amazement' at 1 Peter 3:6.)

Allen's definitive, word-by-word, work shows that King James's translators were conservative. It was the Bishops' Bible that was the 'good one' that they hoped to make 'better'. The Bishops' did not have, and KJV was not to have, doctrinal notes in the margin, so the choice of translation of a phrase containing complex issues, like Paul's at Romans 8:6, in KJV 'to be carnally minded' was vital. Allen wrote that the doctrinal notes in Geneva in the sixth, seventh and eighth chapters of Romans 'are so explicit that the most careless of readers is put on his guard against dualistic heresies. . . . But there are no doctrinal notes in the A.V. The translation of this text called, then for caution.' Bois's notes show the making of a compromise: so KJV followed the Bishops' and Tyndale in what it printed, but put in the margin a literal rendering of the Greek, '*the minding of the flesh*', in all its ambiguity.[57]

> Individual translators laboured day after day over sheets from the Bishops' Bible. For three years they gathered weekly to compare what they had done. During that three years the Westminster company revised the 121 chapters of the New Testament epistles. They made 4,131 changes, of which 1,344 were readings of their own invention . . . at the rate of twenty-three changes a week, a careful pace when it is borne in mind that most of the changes were not radical. But there was other work to do. Each company read the work of all other companies.

Manuscripts were prepared and sent out . . . returned . . . revised . . . called in. During the year 1609, the Westminster company reviewed the text in the light of revisions suggested by learned men from far and wide. That work completed, the general meeting in London settled the disagreements between the companies, this work requiring nine months.[58]

'THE TRANSLATORS TO THE READER'

It is a pity that the publishers of KJV, from quite early in its history, have always printed after the title-page the two-page Dedication to King James, and omitted Miles Smith's fine eleven-page Preface, 'The Translators to the Reader'. The Dedication is so fulsomely over-flattering to his Majesty as to suggest to a modern eye that it is mockery; but the fact is that most people have long forgotten how to address a sovereign upon whom their welfare, even their lives, might depend. Even so, to suggest that King James was 'the Author of this work' is going a bit far.

The Preface breathes an altogether healthier air. It begins by observing that no worthy undertaking is without the risk of opposition and mis-understanding: meddling with men's religion makes them especially uncomfortable; 'though they find no content in that which they have, ye they cannot abide to hear of altering'.

The Preface intends to show the new version in its historical perspective, and explain both why it was made and how it was done. In all three it succeeds well. Miles Smith enlarges on the qualities of Scripture, 'a pantry filled with fresh food instead of moldy traditions', and then explains why translation is necessary, and historically how it happened in the Septuagint, in Jerome's work, and recently in vernaculars. He notes the points made by, and answers, the translators' adversaries. Two qualities – apart from the instant readability of these pages – stand out. One is the discussion of techniques of translation, including the important one of not pedantically insisting on verbal consistency, as:

> if we translate the Hebrew or Greek word once by *purpose*, never to call it *intent*; if once, *journeying*, never *travelling*; if once *think*, never *suppose*; if once *pain*, never *ache*; if once *joy*, never *gladness*, etc. . . . For has the kingdom of God become words and syllables? Why should we be slaves to them, if we could be free?[59]

The other, so far unexplained, is the surprising one that with few exceptions, when Miles Smith quotes Scripture, which he does constantly, he quotes not from his own new translation, but from Geneva.

This document is important in the history of the English Bible, and indeed in the story of the vernacular Bible in Europe and beyond. It is printed entire as an Appendix to this book.

TYNDALE IN KJV

A. W. Pollard wrote:

> Whether the wonderful felicity of phrasing should be attributed to the dexterity with which, after meanings had been settled and the important words in each passage chosen, either the board of twelve or the two revisers put their touches to the work, or whether, as seems more likely, the rhythm, first called into being in Tyndale and Coverdale, reasserted itself after every change, only gathering strength and melody from the increasing richness of the language, none can tell. All that is certain is that the rhythm and the strength and the melody are there.[60]

(The Chairman of the New Testament panel of one of the most recent translations, *The Revised English Bible* of 1989, published jointly by Oxford and Cambridge University Presses, reported that they would discuss around the table many variations of a phrase, and finally settle on one: this they often then realised was familiar, and found it was Tyndale.[61])

Ward Allen laid to rest the older notion that the revisers paid little heed to the Bishops' Bible by taking most of the New Testament from Tyndale, the Great Bible, and the Genevas. Often, while words and phrases are taken from those three, the syntax is peculiar to Bishops'. At Romans 14:4, for example, though the diction is Tyndale and the others, following the usual Bishops' eclectic use, the KJV's syntax is pure Bishops', producing the awkward inversion 'to his own master he standeth or falleth'. As Allen notes, 'While it is true that the Bishops' Bible contributed few unique translations of words of the A.V., it is equally true that this text supplied, for the most part, the organisation of sentences in A.V.'[62]

It is that which was retrograde. In Rheims, the combination of the hatred of 'the heretics' and the insistence on the primacy of the Vulgate produced something which was so obviously backward-looking that it can be taken or left. The KJV's reliance on Bishops' for word order, for small unnatural inversions and even for syntax that might be thought strangled (not Ward Allen's epithet), is what is largely responsible for KJV's more subtle sense of distance. Gerald Hammond has shown the likelihood of the KJV Old Testament panels making a deliberate choice of unchanging English formulae for the Hebrew, producing so many 'And it came to pass' or 'And it shall come to pass' sentence openings: see for example

KJV's Isaiah 7:21–3; or, more strikingly still, Genesis 38:27–9, the narrative in which Tamar gives birth to twins:

> And it came to pass in the time of her travail, that behold, twins were in her womb.
>
> And it came to pass when she travailed, that *the one* put out his hand, and the midwife took and bound upon his hand a scarlet thread, saying, This came out first.
>
> And it came to pass as he drew back his hand, that behold his brother came out: and she said, How hast thou broken forth? *this* breach *be* upon thee. Therefore his name was called Pharez.

Hammond writes, 'But now look at Tyndale's rendering of the same passage, where, without any such formula, the translator can register more of the rough urgency of the narrative':

> When time was come that she should be delivered, behold, there was two twins in her womb. And as she travailed the one put out his hand, and the midwife took and bound a red thread about it, saying, This will come out first. But he plucked his hand back again, and his brother came out. And she said, Wherefore hast thou rent a rent upon thee? and called him Pharez.[63]

Though in the New Testament, and particularly in the Epistles, King James's revisers made many changes, and though their base was Bishops', the truth is that the ultimate base was Tyndale. A computer-based American study published in 1998 has shown just how much Tyndale is in the KJV New Testament. New Testament scholars Jon Nielson and Royal Skousen observed that previous estimates of Tyndale's contribution to the KJV 'have run from a high of up to 90 per cent (Westcott) to a low of 18 per cent (Butterworth)'.[64] By a statistically accurate and appropriate method of sampling, based on eighteen portions of the Bible, they concluded that for the New Testament Tyndale's contribution is about eighty-three per cent of the text, and in the Old Testament seventy-six per cent. Behind the statistics is that unmeasurable feeling that KJV's rhythm, vocabulary and cadence, which can be so exquisite and so direct, has a root in an essence of the English language. The cause of that is Tyndale's genius.

To conclude this chapter I give two short passages, Mark 4:14–20, and Colossians 2:8–12, in each case first in Tyndale, 1534, and then in KJV. They were chosen at random, the only guide being that they were run-of-the-mill, as it were midstream, passages.

The sower soweth the word. And they that are by the way's side, where the word is sown, are they to whom as soon as they have heard it, Satan cometh immediately, and taketh away the word that was sown in their hearts. And likewise they that are sown on the stony ground, are they: which when they have heard the word, at once receive it with gladness, yet have no roots in themselves, and so endure but a time: and anon as trouble and persecution ariseth for the word's sake, they fall immediately. And they that are sown among the thorns, are such as hear the word: and the care of this world and the deceitfulness of riches and the lusts of other things, enter in and choke the word, and it is made unfruitful. And those that were sown in good ground, are they that hear the word and receive it, and bring forth fruit, some thirty-fold, some sixty-fold, some an hundred-fold.[65]

The sower soweth the word. And these are they by the way side, where the word is sown; but when they have heard, Satan cometh immediately, and taketh away the word that was sown in their hearts. And these are they likewise which are sown on stony ground; who, when they have heard the word, immediately receive it with gladness; And have no root in themselves, and so endure but for a time; afterward, when affliction or persecution ariseth for the word's sake, immediately they are offended. And these are they which are sown among thorns; such as hear the word, And the cares of this world, and the deceitfulness of riches, and the lusts of other things entering in, choke the word, and it becometh unfruitful, And these are they which are sown on good ground; such as hear the word, and receive it, and bring forth fruit, some thirtyfold, some sixty, and some an hundred.

Beware lest any man come and spoil you through philosophy and deceitful vanity, through the traditions of men, and ordinances after the world, and not after Christ. For in him dwelleth all the goodness of the Godhead bodily, and ye are complete in him which is the head of all rule and power, in whom also ye are circumcised with circumcision made without hands, by putting off the sinful body of the flesh, through the circumcision that is in Christ, in that ye are buried with him through baptism, in whom ye are also risen again through faith, that is wrought by the operation of God which raised him from death.[66]

Beware lest any man spoil you through philosophy and vain deceit, after the tradition of men, after the rudiments of the world, and not after Christ. For in him dwelleth all the goodness of the Godhead bodily. And ye are complete in him, which is the head of all principality and power: In whom also ye are circumcised with the circumcision made without hands, in putting off the body of the sins of the flesh by the circumcision of Christ: Buried with him in baptism, wherein also ye are risen with him through the faith of the operation of God, who hath raised him from the dead.

Chapter 26

PRINTING THE KING JAMES BIBLE

As a piece of church furniture, the 1611 folio KJV was handsomely made (fig. 27). It is a large and heavy volume, equal in size to the formidable Bishops' Bible. The type is even bigger black letter. The verses are numbered and separated in two columns, with pages and columns neatly ruled. Like the object itself, the title-page, better designed than for any English Bible before, gives a sense of ordered massivity.

Almost as soon as KJV was off the press, the printing business of Robert Barker, 'The Printer to the King's most excellent Majesty' as the title-page announces, failed. This wealthy man, brought up in a printing family, son of Queen Elizabeth's printer, now holding the patent which gave him the monopoly of printing the Bible – any Bible, whole or in parts – the Book of Common Prayer, all official documents and all Statutes, and a great deal of additional work which came with all that, went bankrupt.[1] The office of King's Printer was taken from him.

It has been speculated that it was because he bore the costs of King James's new Bible himself, and they were crippling. Perhaps this late suggestion was sentimental, implying that because the book was so beautiful he risked personal sacrifice just to be associated. For a hard professional craftsman, a leading member, like his father, of the Stationers' Company, such mismanagement seems so unlikely as to be impossible: printers, before a word is set, have always cast up costs to the nearest sheet and full point; and he above all knew his market. Perhaps he was living above even his very considerable income. Perhaps he had speculated. Perhaps court politicians set out to ruin him. It seems that we shall never know, as almost all biographical details are lacking. All we know is that the business of the printing of KJV throughout the century and beyond became almost at once devious, and at times vicious. The biggest casualties in these printing wars were the Geneva Bibles.

PRINTERS TO THE CROWN

After Gutenberg, printing developed rapidly in Europe: but not in England. Just before 1500 there were in the towns and cities of the Continent about a thousand printers that are known by name, and there were undoubtedly others. England had, effectively, two. Around that date printing in France or Italy could be to a remarkable standard, in both text and illumination. England's two, Wynkyn de Worde, formerly partner, and then successor, to William Caxton, and Richard Pynson, though busy, produced nothing that could compare. Home production of manuscripts flourished, and for printed books in the decades after 1500, the position in England improved a little.[2] Much was imported: printing, some fine, came from France; some less good was done in Germany and the Netherlands for sale in England. The port of Antwerp was alive with printing Bibles in several languages, including English.[3]

Why popular English printing was held back more than on the Continent is a large subject, though it is related to the repression of communication still in force from the Constitutions of Oxford. Caxton had had royal and noble patronage, and Henry VII, had, as well as a Royal Stationer from 1485, a Royal Librarian from 1492, and maintaining a royal arras-maker, painter and glazier, a 'king's printer' from 1504, probably one William Faques, a minor figure who may have doubled as Librarian.[4] De Worde and Pynson shared a powerful and enlightened patron, the King's mother, Lady Margaret Beaufort. Her influence shaped the future relationship between the makers of printed books and the Crown, though until early in the reign of Henry VIII 'printing was just another technique for producing highly-prized luxury items'.[5]

In the development of English printing in and after the reign of Henry VIII the function of a 'king's printer' is not very clear, nor is how it relates to the growing importance of the business of intellectual property rights.[6] The Stationers' Company may have received its Charter in 1557 partly with the intention of registering a personal claim: from that point, rights in copies were supported by entry in the Stationer's Register. Assumptions encouraged by this procedure fed the development of what was later to become author's copyright. From the 1560s, tensions grew as interests overlapped, those of the court and the book trade, or scholarship and commerce.

Two London merchants, Richard Grafton and Edward Whitchurch, both of whom had printing interests, had arranged the printing of Matthew's Bible, with royal licence, in Antwerp in 1537. In 1539 they took over and finished in London the abortive attempts to finish the Great Bible in Paris. From 1538 Tyndale's New Testament, Coverdale's Diglot and

Taverner's Bible were all printed in London, and English Bible production came from an expanding group of printers, including John Foxe's friend and printer John Day, who reissued Matthew's Bible with revised notes in 1549.[7]

The name of Richard Jugge first appears in 1548 with his careful printing of a Tyndale New Testament.[8] In the middle years of Elizabeth's reign, he was Royal Printer: it was he who held the monopoly of printing Archbishop Parker's 1568 Bishops' Bible, to his own personal profit and also to prevent, as Parker clearly intended, any London printing of the 1560 Geneva Bible (a London printing, as noted above, which began immediately on the death of Jugge's protector, the Archbishop, in 1579).

> On Jugge's death in 1577, the office of Royal Printer was granted to Sir Thomas Wilkes who, for a consideration, transferred a portion of it to Christopher Barker, and on the disgrace of Wilkes in 1589, Barker obtained an exclusive patent for himself and his son Robert . . . [who] at the accession of James 1 in 1603 held the office of King's Printer by virtue of the reversionary patent granted by the late Queen to his father Christopher.[9]

Christopher Barker died in 1599. In 1600, Robert Barker printed his first Geneva version – of several – and first Bishops' version (there would be only one more ever made, in 1602 – though there were reprints, all by him).[10] Soon after James's accession, Robert Barker obtained reversions for his elder son, Christopher, and second son, Robert. But by late 1611 Robert senior had gone: 'though nominally recovered for a short period, and carrying on the name of the family till the close of the century, [the office of King's printer] was never really in the hands of those whose names appear in the imprints.'[11]

QUARRELS

From the beginning of printed KJVs the interest in publishing them was high. A Bible offered to a printer unique qualities. The length of that text was precisely known: 774,746 words, allowing for rapid and exact computation of costs in terms of ems, paper orders and employees' time. A Bible is a book for which demand is always high. There is the challenge of making a book without a single misprint, and in many sizes for many situations. Bible printing is highly specialised: in a competitive situation, the shrewd businessman-printer will hope to benefit from the inexperience of competitors.[12]

Robert Barker's name sits solidly in the catalogue as printer of Bibles – about two dozen KJV including, from 1612, smaller editions printed in roman type, both quarto and octavo, and from 1618, duodecimo; half a dozen Geneva, and three Bishops' – until July 1617. From that month until 7 May 1619, the names of Bonham Norton and John Bill either join him or take his place, until John Bill's death in 1630.[13] In 1618, Robert Barker began a suit against Norton and Bill 'for the recovery of a moiety of the office and stock of the King's Printing House'. Norton, 'next to Barker the most important stationer in the city of London',[14] was Master of the Stationer's Company in 1613, 1623 and 1629; in 1612, already a rich man, he received a legacy from his cousin John Norton, like him a Shropshire man. (As was John Bill, who had been apprenticed to John Norton: Bill is celebrated for his work for Sir Thomas Bodley in buying books abroad for the new library at Oxford.) The plot is thickened by the fact that in 1615 Robert Barker's son Christopher had married Bonham Norton's eldest daughter, Sarah. Norton and Bill were made co-partners in trust for the benefit of that Christopher Barker. But, it was said in Robert Barker's suit, Norton and Bill had reneged, and not only not paid into the trust, but concealed the true profits made from printing, trying to get the whole 'office' (that of King's Printer) into their own hands and putting off all other comers. The sum of £3,000 was said to have been concealed by Bonham Norton from Robert, with the connivance of Christopher. With some 'ifs', the office was handed over to the Barker family from Norton and Bill for £6,500. Deeds were signed. They were then destroyed in a fire – or so Norton and Bill claimed, refusing then either to remove from the office or hand over any money. Bonham Norton said that when he agreed to let his daughter marry Christopher he thought Robert was richer than he was. Norton claimed that he and Bill had paid over £5,800 in settling the Barkers' debts, and wanted this to be set off against the purchase money of £6,500. He also claimed that they were not bound to show their profits.

Chancery referred the case for arbitration, but no settlement was arrived at. The Court itself then decreed in May 1619 in favour of Barker, who was obliged to repay his debts. A new agreement in December 1619 was decided upon by the Court, under the terms of which Robert Barker was to pay Norton £11,000 for his moiety of the office, on security of his manor of Sudely. Some time in 1620, Norton ejected Barker from the office, and the imprints changed again to Norton and Bill. 'As a result, all parties reappeared in the Court of Chancery, and the fight between them raged furiously for the next ten years, to the great profit of the lawyers.'[15]

Three observations might be made. First, as a historical note, it does seem that Robert Barker incurred debts when KJV was printed. Second, it is striking how large are the sums of money involved. As the fighting went on the sums increased: in spite of large initial capital costs, the need for a huge quantity of standing type, and for a skilled workforce (who could not combine Bible printing with jobbing), printing Bibles and Prayer Books was every year very profitable. And third, in all this legal squabbling it would be important that costs in the printing house were kept low. What was being fought over was the marketing of a new Bible in which interest was high, one that could, in fact, easily be reprinted. The market would be helped by it being said to be a royal enterprise, in a way that no previous English Bible had been. The tight group of spitting enemies, four men and one woman (Christopher's wife) were the only people allowed to print KJV, and they would be united only in the desire to keep profits as high as they could be, which meant not stopping the Bible presses to set something else.

One revelation in the quarrelling was that Barker had 'very unadvisedly used (for present money) to sell his books . . . before they were half printed'[16] interfering with the market. This, with the complaint that certain stationers demanded money for imperfect copies, shows that instead of waiting for full new editions, Barker was using the presses to print in parts when work was slack, and selling these off. This goes a long way to explain the imperfections discovered in printings of KJV after the first, to which I shall return briefly.

The fighting became total war. Norton was committed to the Fleet Prison in December 1628, in spite of having been chosen for the third time as Master of the Stationers. Norton was supposed to persuade his daughter to get her father-in-law to sell off his lands, which he (Norton) did not do. So Robert could not pay. The whole thing developed into a Star Chamber matter, a trial begun in July 1630. Norton became increasingly wild. He said, for example, that Barker only got the Court of Chancery result in his favour in 1619 by bribing Sir Francis Bacon with £1,000, though this was highly likely. Between 1630 and 1634, John Bill, and Robert's two sons, Christopher and Robert, died. Norton died in April 1635. In 1635 Robert Barker was committed as a debtor to the King's Bench Prison, where he remained for ten years until his death in 1645.

There was more. During the Commonwealth, the King's Printing House was in the hands of the new appointees, Henry Hills and John Field. At the Restoration a Barker claimed the Printing House (as did a Norton) and promptly assigned it to six others, provoking lawsuits. Christopher Barker's name, with others, and the assigns of John Bill, appear until 1680, when the patent ran out and his name disappears. The descendants of John Bill and his partners Hills and Newcomb carried on the business until it was bought from them for a colossal sum early in the eighteenth century by John Baskett.

'THE LONDON PRINTER'

An anonymous and undated tract, one apparently written in mid-1660, gives the view of some of these events, with new information, from the pen of an over-excited 'London printer'. His short but colourful *Lamentation:, or The Press Oppressed, and Overpressed* claims (implying the failure of the Licensing Laws) that there are too many printers, and that they have too much freedom – by which he means the effect of the Commonwealth. Printing, he writes in an extended title, was properly regulated by the Crown

> till the year 1640; when . . . this Trade, Art and Mystery, was prostituted to every vile purpose. both in Church and State . . . he [the author] bitterly inveighs against Christopher Barker, John Bill, Thomas Newcomb, John Field and Henry Hills, as Interlopers, and, under the King's Patent, were the only Instruments of inflaming the People against the King and his friends, &c.[17]

Presently he muses,

> Never was there such an honourable, ingenious, and profitable Mystery and Science in the World so basely intruded upon, and disesteemed, so unworthily subjected to infamy and Disgrace, by being made so common, as Printing hath been since 1640, in the days of our miserable Confusions and Calamities: Neither can it be repaired, or restored to its native Worth and regular Constitution, so long as such horrid Monstrosities and gibbous Excrescences are suffered to remain and tumour in that disorderly and confused Body. . . .

To whom can he be referring? Why, to 'Mr Christopher Barker and Mr John Bill', who, he reveals, have no practical skill in printing at all: they are but titular, and the work was all done by Thomas Newcomb, John Field, and Henry Hill, described as 'Enemies to his most Sacred Majesty'. Relishing every word he writes (and sets up in type), he continues,

> Have they not invaded, and still do intrude upon his Majesty's Royal Privilege, Prerogative, and Pre-eminence; and by the pusillanimous Cowardice, and insignificant Compact of Mr Christopher Barker, and

another of his name, and, not without probable Suspicion, by the Consent and Connivance of Mr John Bill (though he was artificially defeated in his Expectation of Profit) have they not obtained (and now keep in their actual Possession) the Manuscript Copy of the last translation of the Holy Bible in English, attested with the Hands of the Venerable and learned Translators in King James's Time, ever since the sixth of March, 1655; and thereupon, by Colour of an unlawful and forced Entrance in the Stationers Registry, printed and published ever since, for the most Part, in several Editions of Bibles (consisting of great numbers) such egregious Blasphemies and damnable Errata's, as have corrupted the pure Fountain, and rendered God's holy Word contemptible to Multitudes of the people at Home, and *Ludibrium* to all the Adversaries of our Religion?

Why they received 'the Manuscript Copy' on such a specific date is unknown. Did they? Did such a document exist? Barker in 1611 had to set up from *something*, whether a manuscript or a revised Bishops' Bible, and perhaps whatever it was survived, only to perish in the Great Fire. The point 'London Printer' is making is that in spite of having the original, the printers made such a botch of it.

Not wishing to spoil enjoyment of watching such freely and indulgently thrown mud, one has to question the motive. Especially as he goes on in best tabloid style to reveal that Mr Christopher Barker and his family lodge

at the House of that libidinous and professed Adulterer Henry Hills in Aldersgate Street. One that for his Heresy in Religion (being an Anabaptist) and his Luxury [lust] in Conversation (having hypocritically confessed his Fact in print, and been imprisoned for his Adultery with a Taylor's Wife in Blackfriars would scandalize a good Christian . . .

The old Confederacy compacted between Barker, Hills and Field, by the Agitation of Needham, upon their Conversion of the Copy of the Bible, cannot be forgotten; albeit it tend never so much to the Dishonour, Disparagement, and Prejudice of his Majesty's Affairs?

ARCHBISHOP LAUD AND MICHAEL SPARKE

After the last regular printing of the Geneva Bible in 1644, to buy a Bible was to buy a KJV, though eight of those were printed with Geneva notes until 1715. The triumph of KJV was entirely due to the commercial interests of the owners of the monopoly on the text, the King's Printers, with Cambridge University Press, which also, under Field, claimed the right to print the text.

Geneva Bibles continued to be imported from Amsterdam with success: in the commercial battle it was important for the KJV monopoly holders to besmirch their rivals, even though it is apparent that the imports were of better quality, and they were the Bibles with notes. David Norton observes that

> In the trial of the man principally responsible for suppressing the Geneva Bible, Archbishop Laud, there is a report that because the KJB, described as 'the new translation without notes', was 'most vendible', the King's Printer forbore to print Geneva Bibles for private lucre, not by virtue of public restraint, [and so] they were usually imported from beyond the seas.[18]

Norton adds that Laud gives the Geneva Bible's commercial success as one of his reasons for its suppression – this was in 1640 –

> by the numerous coming over of [Geneva] Bibles . . . from Amsterdam, there was a great and just fear conceived that by little and little printing would quite be carried out of the kingdom. . . . And to preserve printing here at home . . . was the cause of stricter looking to those Bibles.[19]

There was high indignation among the Scots in 1633 at the first printing of KJV in Scotland. This was said to have been done in connection with the coronation of Charles I in June of that year, by Robert Young, said to have become King's Printer in Scotland in April for that purpose. The outrage arose from the inclusion of 'abominable pictures': not only were they 'Popish' and 'Romish Images', and the Scots Bibles were being sold with crucifixes – Laud had let it be known that they were to be called 'The [Arch]bishop of Canterbury's Bibles'. In 1646, William Prynne wrote, of Laud:

> He would suffer no English Bibles to be printed or sold with marginal Notes [i.e. the Geneva version] to instruct the people, all such must be seized and burnt . . . but himself gives special approbation for the venting of Bibles with Popish pictures taken out of the very Mass book, to seduce the people to Popery and idolatry.[20]

A London printer, Michael Sparke, printed in 1641 a small quarto tract of four leaves, *Scintilla*, intended in the name of justice to ignite controversy about the prices of KJVs being printed in London and Cambridge by the holders of the monopoly. In order to defeat this monopoly, Sparke imported large quantities of Bibles printed abroad and sold them more cheaply. Robert Barker obtained a warrant to search the ports and seize all the foreign printed Bibles he could find. In retaliation, Sparke brought an action of trespass against those who seized the books, and carried on importing.[21] Sparke's tract is intended to strike a spark (*scintilla*) to start a conflagration. In 1877, Edward Arber commented on it:

> This tract is a remarkable testimony to the never-ending competition in the book trade; to the power of the King's Printers, partly as paten-tees, and partly as capitalists only; to the vast extent (proportionately to other books) of the production of Bibles etc., and school books under the early Stuarts; and, lastly, to their steady rise in price, despite the much larger editions [i.e. print-runs] than formerly, owing in some degree to the increasing wealth of the country, but still more through monopolies and 'rigging the market'.[22]

In 1652, Sparke issued '*A Second Beacon fired by Scintilla . . .*' against the 'extraordinary' trade by 'a strong and secret Papist' in English Bibles con-taining 'Popish' pictures, 'and I fear Popish notes', specially procured in France.[23]

THE COMMONWEALTH

In one sense 'London Printer' was right: Bible printing in the Common-wealth was in chaos, without the security of a royal patent or entry in the Register, and that at a time when there was greater demand for Bibles than ever. Moreover, costs were frightening London printers, and 'in 1644 no printer still in London had any substantial experience of overseeing this most exacting of printing jobs'.[24] Hills and Field did succeed in March 1655 in getting an entry in the Register, thus automatically ruining their rivals.

> The very next day after the entry . . . Hills and Field obtained a warrant for search-and-seizure from Cromwell's commissioners for regulation of the press and set out to seize other publishers' Bible impressions, in vio-lation of their warrant, which was only to search for 'scandalous, and unlicensed books and Pamphlets'.[25]

When one, William Bentley, complained, Hills and Field seized his equip-ment. Bentley suffered. Hills and Field prospered. A Parliamentary com-mittee found errors in Hills and Field's Bibles.[26] Cromwell conferred the monopoly on KJV to Hills and Field in 1656, and Field also became printer to Cambridge University. 'Having a monopoly on the [KJV] text, he had no interest in reviving the Geneva Bible.'[27]

There has been space only to sketch the story, generally a bitter one, of the printing of KJV in the first fifty years of its existence. More work needs to be done on the effect of the quarrels, which were happening on every side; on sales; and the complex relationships of prices, sizes, regional variations, profit margins and convenience. 'The new translation' triumphed because it was commercially manoeuvred to do so, not because it was new. Perhaps enough has been said here to remove the idea of an automatic instant triumph of KJV based entirely on its 'glorious beauty'.

ERRORS

In the first 250 years of KJV's life, there were many errors. In 1884 Dr F. H. A. Scrivener listed about fifteen hundred.[28] The most famous is in the first edition, the variation at Ruth 3:15 that prints, instead of 'he went into the city', the words 'she went into the city'. So consistent are other differences of typography in the series of printings between 1611 and 1614 in Bibles bearing each reading that they are known to bibliographers and collectors as 'He Bibles' and 'She Bibles'. 'She' is now the preferred reading, the 'He Bible' variants being explained by a parallel printing in a separate printing-house, to raise production levels and increase profit margins, the source-text in one house (the 'She Bible' house) having had additional correction at press. Most were minor typographical errors. The most scandalous, possibly deliberate, came from the King's Printers in London, 'Barker and assigns of Bill' in 1631, when the word 'not' was omitted from the seventh Commandment, to read 'Thou shalt commit adultery'. The printers, that is, those who worked the presses, are said to have been fined £300, and the whole impression, popularly called 'The Wicked Bible' was called in, thus ruining Barker. Hardly a copy survives. Other quaint errors have attracted disproportionate attention.[29]

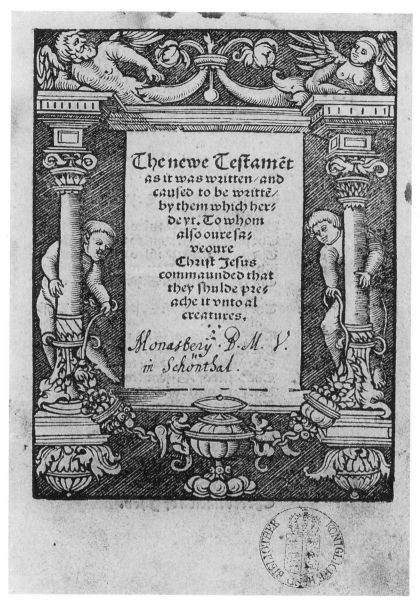

The newe Testamēt
as it was written/and
caused to be writtē/
by them which her=
de yt. To whom
also oure sa=
veoure
Christ Jesus
commaunded that
they shulde pre=
ache it vnto al
creatures.

Monasbery. D. M. V.
in Schöntsal.

1   The title-page of the first complete printed New Testament in English, the translation by William Tyndale made in Worms in 1526. This leaf is in one of the two
copies that have survived: it was discovered in the Bibelsammlung of the
Wurttembergishe Landesbibliothek in Stuttgart in 1996. Tyndale's title reads: 'The
new Testament as it was written, and caused to be written, by them which heard it.
To whom also our saviour Christ Jesus commanded that they should preach it to all
creatures.'

2   Evidence of Christianity in fourth-century Roman Britain. Scratched on the wall of a villa in Corinium (Cirencester) are the words 'ROTAS/OPERA/TENET/AREPO/SATOR'. Translated as 'the sower Arepo holds the wheels carefully', the inscription was felt to be meaningless. In 1926 Felix Grosser arranged the letters into the form of a cross, as shown here, making a Christian cryptogram of a double 'PATERNOSTER', with alpha and omega ('the beginning and the end', Rev. 1:8) before and after each 'Our Father'.

```
        A
        P
        A
        T
        E
        R
A|PATERNOSTER|O
        O
        S
        T
        E
        R
        O
```

3 (below)   Map showing the travels of the Irish *peregrini* ('monks abroad') in the fifth to eighth centuries, and the settlements and monasteries that they founded.

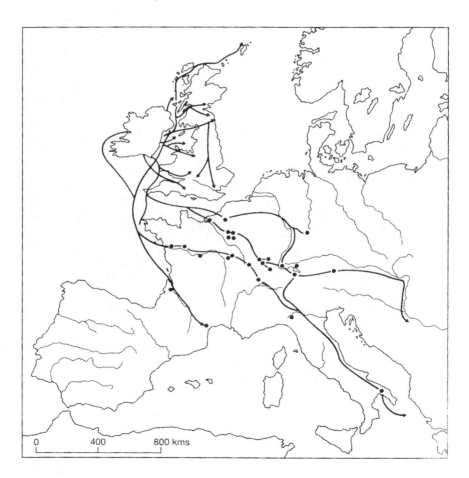

4   The 'Ezra miniature' in the preliminary leaves of the eighth-century manuscript of Jerome's Latin Gospels, the magnificent Codex Amiatinus, made in Northumbria and now in Florence. The picture shows a scribe carefully copying a Bible, in front of one in nine volumes. He is named Ezra. The Hebrew Scriptures had all been destroyed at the time of the Babylonian captivity, and he rewrote them from memory.

5 Part of the eighth-century Ruthwell Cross in Dumfriesshire, Scotland, which presents many biblical scenes. Illustrated here is Christ in Majesty. The borders carry a runic inscription related to the Anglo-Saxon poem *The Dream of the Rood*, based on Matthew 27.

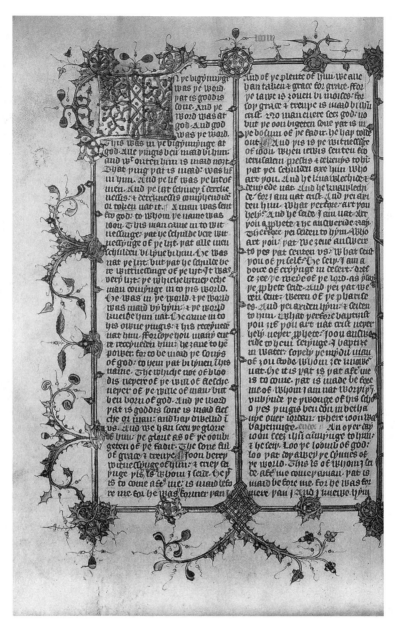

6   The first half of the first chapter of St John's Gospel in a 'Wyclif' (Early Version) Bible manuscript of the 1380s (BL MS Egerton 618). This one, decorated in rich colours, was probably a personal copy belonging to Thomas of Woodstock, Duke of Gloucester. Not many 'Wyclif' Bibles were so magnificent.

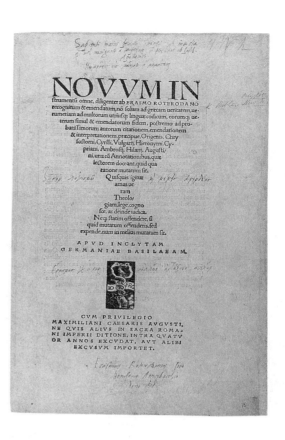

7 The title-page of the first edition of Erasmus's *Novum Instrumentum*, 1516. His influential, and controversial, new Latin translation of the New Testament was intended to challenge the Vulgate, and in its scholarship to be a 'new instrument' of reform. The most effective instrument was in fact the printing, alongside his Latin, of the original Greek New Testament for the first time – a fact not mentioned in the title.

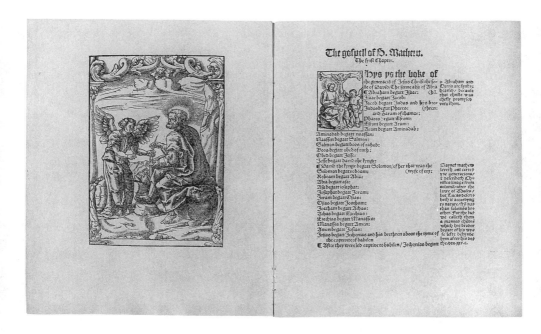

8   The opening of Tyndale's abandoned 1525 'Cologne fragment', his New Testament in English begun with Peter Schoeffer in Cologne, with two representations of St Matthew being helped by an angel. Only up to Matthew 22 was completed before the print-shop was raided. Unlike the successful 1526 New Testament from Worms, and the 1534 Antwerp versions, this Cologne printing was dependent on Luther's 1522 'September Testament' in layout and annotation.

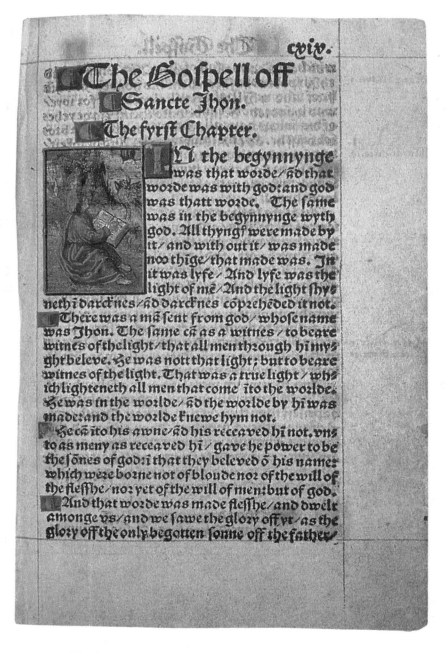

The Gospell off Sancte Jhon.

The fyrst Chapter.

In the begynnynge was that worde/ ād that worde was with god: and god was thatt worde. The same was in the begynnynge wyth god. All thyngſ were made by it/ and with out it/ was made noo thige/ that made was. In it was lyfe/ And lyfe was the light of mē/ And the light ſhyneth i darcknes/ ād darcknes cōprehēded it not.

There was a mā ſent from god/ whoſe name was Jhon. The same cā as a witnes/ to beare witnes of the light/ that all men through hi myght beleve. He was nott that light: but to beare witnes of the light. That was a true light/ whi ich lighteneth all men that come ito the worlde. He was in the worlde/ ād the worlde by hi was made: and the worlde knewe hym not.

He cā ito his awne/ ād his receaved hi not. vnto as meny as receaved hi/ gave he power to be the ſones of god: i that they beleved ō his name: which were borne not of bloude nor of the will of the fleſſhe/ nor yet of the will of men: but of god.

And that worde was made fleſſhe/ and dwelt amonge vs/ and we ſawe the glory off yt/ as the glory off the only begotten ſonne off the father/

9 A page of the first complete New Testament in English from the original Greek, made by William Tyndale, printed in Worms in 1526 and smuggled into Britain. All other English versions are dependent on this 1526 Tyndale version, especially the 1611 'King James' Version. One of the two surviving complete copies is on permanent open display in the Ritblat Gallery of the British Library in London.

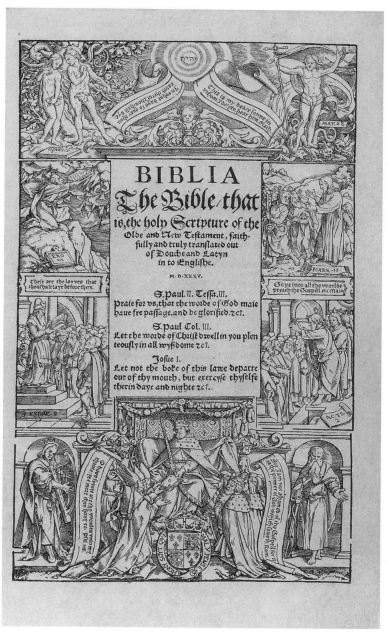

10   The title-page of Coverdale's 1535 Bible, the first complete Bible in English, though 'translated out of Douche [German] and Latin' rather than the original Hebrew and Greek. The design is dominated by the radiant Name of God at the top; at the foot, a modest King Henry VIII distributes 'thy words' and 'the Gospel' to clergy and nobles (a contrast with the title of the 'Great' Bible, 1539)

The first dayes worke. | The seconde dayes worke. | The thirde dayes worke.

The fourth dayes worke. | The fifth dayes worke. | The sixte dayes worke.

The first Chapter.

A

4.Esd.6.d
Eccli.18.a
Iere.10.b
Heb.11.a
Esa.44.c

IN ẏ begyn
nynge God
created hea
uen ⁊ earth:
and ẏ earth
was voyde
and emptie,
and darck-
nes was v-
pon the de-
pe,⁊ ẏ spre-
te of God
moued vpõ
the water.

And God sayde: let there be light,⁊ there
was light. And God sawe the light that it
was good. Then God deuyded ẏ light from
the darcknes,and called the light,Daye:and
the darcknes,Night.Then of the euenynge
and mornynge was made the first daye.

And God sayde: let there be a firmament
betwene the waters, and let it deuyde ẏ wa
ters a sunder.Then God made ẏ firmamẽt,
and parted the waters vnder the firmamẽt,
from the waters aboue the firmament:And
so it came to passe. And God called ẏ firma
ment, Heauen.Then of the euenynge ⁊ mor
nynge was made the seconde daye.

And God sayde:let the waters vnder hea
uen gather thẽ selues vnto one place, ẏ the
drye londe maye appeare . And so it came to
passe.And God called ẏ drye londe, Earth:
and the gatheringe together of waters cal
led he,ẏ See. And God sawe ẏ it was good.

Iob 16.b
Pro.8.c

And God sayde:let ẏ earth bringe forth
grene grasse and herbe, that beareth sede:⁊
frute full trees , that maye beare frute, euery
one after his kynde, hauynge their owne se
de in them selues vpon the earth . And so it
came to passe. And the earth brought forth
grene grasse and herbe, ẏ beareth sede euery
one after his kynde, ⁊ trees bearinge frute, ⁊

B

a

II   The opening page of Coverdale's 1535 Bible translation.

12 The large frontispiece to 'Matthew's' Bible, 1537. It shows Adam and Eve relishing the fullness of Paradise before the Fall, benignly watched over by a discreet Creator. Against the tradition of such iconography, the absence of a serpent is striking.

before the Lorde of hoostes: Therfore maye we saye/that the proude are happie/and that they which deale with vngodlynesse/are sett vp: for they tempte God/and yet escape.

But they that feare God/saye thus one to another: the Lorde consydereth and heareth it. Yee it is before hym a memoryall boke/wryten for soch as feare the Lorde/& remembre his name. And in the daye that I wyll make (sayeth the Lorde of hostes) they shalbe myne awne possessyon: and I wyll fauoure them/lyke as a man fauoureth hys awne sonne/that doth him seruyce. Turne you therfore/and consydre what difference is betwyxte the ryghtuous and vngodly: betwixte him that serueth God/and hym that serueth him not.

For marck/the daye commeth that shall burne as an oue: and all the proude/yee and all soch as do wickednesse/shalbe straw: and the daye that is for to come/shal burne them vp (sayeth þ Lorde of hoostes) so that it shal leaue them nether rote ner braunch.

But vnto you that feare my name/shall þ Sonne of rightuousnesse aryse/& health shalbe vnder his wynges: ye shal go forth/& multiplie as the fat calues. Ye shall treade downe the vngodly: for they shalbe lyke the asshes vnder the soles of youre fete/in the daye that I shall make/sayeth the Lorde of hoostes.

Remembre the lawe of Moses my seruaunt/whych I commytted vnto hym in Oreb for all Israel/wyth the statutes & ordinaunces. Beholde/I will sende you Elias the prophet: before the commynge of þ daye of the greate and fearfull Lorde. He shall turne the hertes of the fathers to their children/& the hertes of the chyldre to their fathers/þ I come not and smyte the earth with curssynge.

¶ The ende of the prophecy of Malachy: and consequently of all the Prophetes.

13   'Matthew's' Bible, 'Set forth with the King's most gracious licence', was distributed to parishes in England in 1537 (a precursor to the official 'Great' Bible of 1539). Though half the Old Testament and all the New Testament were directly Tyndale's work, mention could not be made of his name because he was a 'heretic'. The run of heavily ornaments initials in the volume, however, starting with IR for John Rogers and HR for Henricus Rex, and continuing with the initials for the printers Richard Grafton and Edward Whitchurch, ends, between the Prophets and Apocrypha, with WT, seen here.

14 In 1543, Parliament proscribed all Bibles bearing the name of Tyndale and decreed the removal or obliteration of notes in all other versions. Illustrated here is the end of Tyndale's Prologue to the Epistle to the Romans in his 1534 New Testament, reproduced in 'Matthew's' Bible of 1537 and deleted in obedience to Parliament's order.

15　A sixteenth-century French illustration of the central event in the life of the young King Josiah (in 2 Kings 22) when he hears the newly discovered book of the law (i.e., Deuteronomy). It is noteworthy that no destruction is present in the image, only the reading of words to the king and court. (The king's heavy beard suggests an older man, but is to characterise a monarch.)

16　The dying King Henry VIII points to his successor King Edward VI, the young English Josiah. This cryptic painting, by an unknown artist, depicts a Reformation triumph over both the pope (who has collapsed beneath the Word of the Lord), and idolatry (in the inset, top right, a statue is pulled down). The seated councillors include Archbishop Cranmer.

17   The young King Edward VI wrote out, in his best schoolboy hand, a long list of Old Testament passages against images, translating them from English (the 'Great' Bible) into French as an exercise to give to Protector Somerset. The manuscript is prefaced by pages, of which these are the first, that begin: 'The fervent zeal which I perceive you have for the reformation of idolatry, most dear and beloved uncle, has stirred me as a kind of pastime, while reading Scripture, to note various passages in it which forbid the worship or making of any images . . .' (Trinity College, Cambridge, MS R.7.31)

18   A Victorian photograph of a surviving church interior (at Hailes, Gloucestershire) as it was after the changes under Edward VI. In place of the altar under the east window is a communion table surrounded by benches and spaces for communicants.

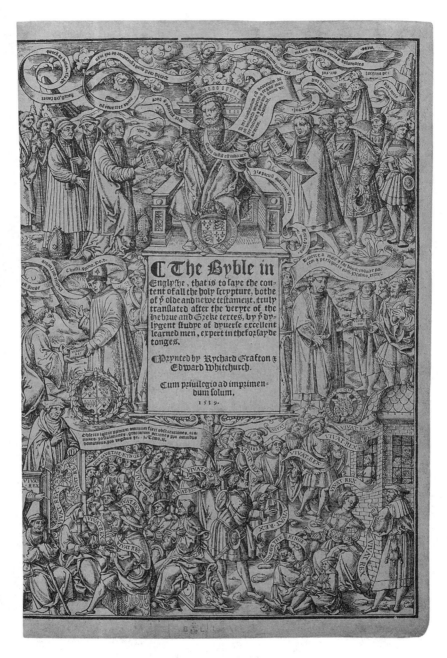

19   The title-page of the 'Great' Bible of 1539, the English version that was to be placed in all parishes in the kingdom. It will be seen that so dominant is King Henry VIII in his authority that God, above him, has to squeeze to get in. Though the king is giving his people a Bible in English, all they can say, without even a glimpse of what is still the 'Verbum Dei', is 'Vivat Rex'.

THE
NEVVE TESTA-
MENT OF OVR LORD IE-
sus Christ.

Conferred diligently with the Greke, and best ap-
proued tranflations.

VVith the arguments, afwel before the chapters, as for euery Boke
& Epiftle, alfo diuerfities of readings, and mofte profitable
annotations of all harde places : wherunto is added a copi-
ous Table.

GOD BY TYME RESTORETH TRVTH

AND MAKETH HER VICTORIOVS.

AT GENEVA
Printed By Conrad Badius.
M.D.LVII.

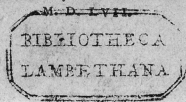
20   Title-page of the 1557 Geneva New Testament, showing the first
printed English emblem.

Trect op te deſen lāde: eñ deſtruect
Ende heliachim elchie ſoen eñ ſobna
die cantellier ende ioabe ſeidē tot rapſaces Wi biddē dattu ons dinē knech
ten ſpreect in ſperſcher talen. wāt wi
verſtaen die tonghe: ende en ſpreect
ons niet aen in ioedſcher talen om dat
tet tvolc hoert: dat optie mure ſittet.
Ende rapſaces antwoerde ende ſeide.
Heeft mi minen here geſonden te di-
nen here ende te di. dat ic deſe redenen
ſpreken ſoude. ende niet tot dien mā-
nen die op die mure ſitten. ſoe dat ſij
mit v luden moeten ete haer mes eñ
drinckē haer orine: Eñ rapſaces ſtōt.
ende riep mit groter ſteminen i ioedſcher talen ende ſeide. Hoert des gro-
ten conincs woerden: die coninc vā aſ
ſprien. Dit ſeit die conic. ezechias en
verleide v niet Want hi en ſal v niet
mogen verloſſen vā mijnre hāt: noch
hi en gheue v ne ghene betruwe optē
here ſegghende. Verloſſende ſal ons
die here beſcrmē: ende deſe ſtat en ſal
niet worden gheleuert in ſconincs hāt
van aſſprien. En wilt ezechiam niet
horen Dit ſeit die coninc van aſſprien
Doet mit mi dat v oerbaerlijc is: eñ
coemt te mi wt. Ende elc eet van ſinē
wijngaerden: ende van ſinen vighebo
mē ende drincket twater van uwer fō
teinen: tot dat ic comē ſal ende v ouer
uoeren ſal in een lant dat uwē lande
ghelijc is in een vruchtelic lant ende
een drachtelic lant in een lant vā wine ende van brode ende van wijngaer
de. in een lant vā olpue ende vā olpe
ende van honighe: ende ghi ſult leuē

ende niet ſteruen. En wilt ezechiam
niet hozen die v bedzieghet ende ſeit.
Die here ſal ons verloſſen. Hebben
der heidenen goden haer lant verloſt
van ſconincs hāt vā aſſprien: Waer
is die god van emath ende arphat:
Waer is die god vā ſepharuaym ana
ende aua: Hebbē ſi ſamarien verloſt
van mijnre hant: Wie ſijn die gode
onder allen gode der werelt die hoer
lantſcap hebben mogen beſcermē vā
mijnre hant: dattie here ſal mogē ihe
ruſalem beſcermen vā mijnre hant:
Eñ tvolc ſweech: eñ en antwoerde hē
niet. Wāt ſi hadden ghebot vanden
conint ontfaen: dat ſi hē niet antwoer
den en ſouden. Eñ helpachim helchie
ſoen die prouoeſt vanden huſe quā eñ
ſobna die cācellier ende ioabe aſaphs
ſoen die ſcriuepne vanden geſten tot
ezechiam met gheſcoerden clederen: eñ
boetſcapten hem rapſatis woerden.

Als die coninc ezechias (Ca. rir
deſe woerden hoerde ſo ſchoer
de hi ſijn clederen. ende toech eñ ſac
tot aen: ende ghinc in ſherē huus: eñ
hij ſant elpachim die prouoeſt vādē
huſe: ende ſobnam die cantellier. ende
die ouders vanden papen mit ſacken
ouerdect tot pſapā dē propheet amos
ſoen. Ende ſeiden. Dit ſeit ezechias.
Deſe dach is die dach van beriſpene
ende van vernope ende van blaſphe-
mien. Die kinder ſijn ghecomen tot-
ten ghebaerne: ende die ghebaren ſal
heeft ne ghene macht. Ofte machſciē
die here dijn god wil hozē al rapſaces
woerden die den coninc van aſſprien

21 A page of the first printed Dutch Bible, from the Latin, 1477. Though beautifully made, for the top end of the market, the volume gives no help at all to the reader. Attentive examination reveals that the right-hand column concludes 2 Kings 18 and begins 2 Kings 19.

the sonne that was lost. By whose examples we are admonished to amende our lyues.

THen resorted vnto him all the publicans, and synners, for to heare him. A The synnere here &c.

2 And the Pharises and Scribes murmured, saying, He receaueth synners, and eateth with them.

3 Then put he forth this similitude to them, saying,

4 * What mã of you hauing an hundred Matth. shepe, if he loose one of them, doth not leaue ninety and nyne in the wyldernesse, and go after that which is lost, vntyl he fynde it?

5 And when he hath founde it, he putteth it on his shoulders with ioye.

6 And assone as he cõmeth home, he calleth together his friendes & neyghbours, B saying vnto them, Reioyse with me, for I haue found my shepe, which was lost.

7 I say vnto you, That likewyse ioye shal be in heauen ouer one sinner that conuerteth, *more* then ouer nynety and nyne a iust persons, which nede no amẽdemẽt of lyfe.

8 Ether what woman hauyng ten pieces of syluer, if she loose one, doth not light a candel, and swepe the house, and seke diligently tyl she fynd it?

9 And whẽ she hath found it, she calleth her friendes, and neyghbours, saying, Reioyce with me, for I haue found the b piece which I had lost.

10 Likewyse I say vnto you, ioye is made in the presence of ỹ Angels of God, ouer one synner that conuerteth.

¶ And

a Which iustifie them selues, and knowe not their own faütes.

b The worde Is drachma, which is some what more in value then fyue pence of olde sterling monye & was equal with a Romain peny.

11 And he sayd, A certain man had two sonnes.

12 And the yonger of them sayd to his father, Father geue me the portion of the C goodes that falleth to me. And he deuided vnto them his substance.

13 So not longe after, when the yonger sonne had gathered all that he had together, he toke his iorney into a farre countrey, and there he waited his goodes with ⸀ryotous liuyng.

14 Now when he had spent all ỹ he had, arose a great dearth throughout all that same land, and he began to lacke.

15 And he went and claue to a citesin of that same countrey: and he sent him to his farme, to feede swyne.

16 And he would faine haue fylled his belly with the huskes that the swyne ate: ⸀and no man gaue to him.

17 Then he came to him self, and sayd, D How many hyred seruantes at my fathers haue bread ynough, and I dye for hunger?

18 I wil arise & go to my father & I wil say vnto him, Father, I haue sinned against ⸀heauen, and before thee.

19 And am no more worthy to be called thy sonne, make me as one of thy hired seruantes.

20 Thẽ he arose and came to his father. & whẽ he was yet a d great way of, his father sawe him, and had compassion, and ran & fel on his necke, and kissed him.

21 And the sonne sayd vnto him, e Father, I haue sinned against heauen, and in thy syght, & am no more worthy to be called thy sonne.

c The Greke worde signifieth so to waste all that a mã reserueth nothing to him self.

⸀For no man had geue ryo him.

⸀That is, agaist God.

⸀Amendement of lyfe.

d God preuẽteth vs & heareth our gronings beforewe crie to him.

e He was touched with the feeling of his synne & therfore was a shamed therof & heauy in hart.

q. iiii.

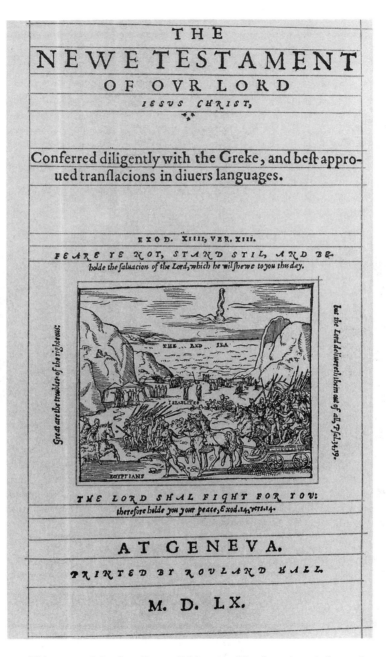

THE
NEWE TESTAMENT
OF OVR LORD
IESVS CHRIST,

Conferred diligently with the Greke, and beſt appro-
ued tranſlacions in diuers languages.

EXOD. XIIII, VER. XIII.

FEARE YE NOT, STAND STIL, AND BE-
holde the ſaluacion of the Lord, which he wil ſhewe to you this day.

Great are the troubles of the righteous:

THE RED SEA

ISRAELITES

EGYPTIANS

but the Lord deliuereth them out of all. Pſal.34.19.

THE LORD SHAL FIGHT FOR YOV:
therefore holde you your peace, Exod.14, vers.14.

AT GENEVA.

PRINTED BY ROVLAND HALL

M. D. LX.

23 Title-page of the first Geneva Bible, 1560. The focus is entirely on the
Scriptures and their promise. This, following the example of Coverdale in
1535, contrasts with the title-pages of the previous 'Great' Bible of 1539, the
following Bishops' Bible of 1568 and the 'King James' Version of 1611, which
make strong political statements about Establishment authority.

n So that the fa-
ciô of the carued
worke might ftil
appeare.

'Or,folding.

32　The two dores alſo were of oliue tree, &
he graued them with grauing of Cherubims and palme trees, and grauen flowres,
and couered thẽ with golde, & layed n thin
golde vpon the Cherubims and vpon the
palme trees.

33　And ſo made he for the dore of the Temple poſtes of oliue tree foure ſquare.

34　But the two dores were of firre tree ' the
two ſides of the one dore were ° round, and
the two ſides of the other dore were roūd:

35　And he graued Cherubims , and palme
trees and carued flowers and couered the

carued worke with golde, finely wrought.

36　¶ And he buylt the ° court within with
three rowes of hewed ſtone, and one rowe
of beames of ceder.

37　In the fourth yeere was the fundation of
the houſe of the Lord laied in the moneth
of Zif :

38　And in the eleuenth yeere in the moneth
of P Bul, (which is the eight moneth) he
finiſhed the houſe with all the furniture
thereof, and in euerie point: ſo was he ſe-
uen yeere in building it.

o Where the
Prieſts were, and
was thus called
in reſpect of the
great court,
which is called
Act. 3. 11 the
porch of Salo-
mon, where the
people vſed to
pray.
p Which con-
teineth part of
October & part
of Nouember.

THE FIRST FIGVRE OF THE KINGS HOVSE IN
THE VVOOD OF LEBANON.

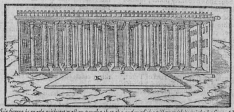

This figure is made without wall or porche, that the order of the pillers within might be ſene. A.B.
The length of an hundreth cubites.B.C. The breadth of fiftie.A.D.The height of thirtie. E.F. G.
H. The foure rowes of pillers. I.The poſtes which ſtayed on the pillers.

THE SECONDE FIGVRE OF THE
SAME HOVSE.

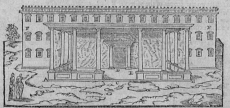

This ſecond figure ſheweth the maner of the houſe without, and the porche thereof which was
fiſtie cubites long. A. B. and thirtie broad. C D.

Chap. 9. 10.
a After he had
built the Tem-
ple.
b For the beau-
tie of the place
and great abun-
dance of ceder
trees that went
to the buylding
thereof, it was
compared to
mount Lebanon
in Syria: this
houſe he vſed in
ſommer for plea
ſure and recrea-
cion.

CHAP. VII.

1　The building of the houſe of Salomon. 15. The excellent workemanſhip of Hiram in the pieces which
he made for the Temple.

1　BVt Salomon was buylding his owne
houſe a thirtene yeeres, and a finiſhed
all his houſe.

2　He buylte alſo an houſe b called the fo-
reſt of Lebanon, an hundreth cubites long,
and fiftie cubites broade,and thirtie cubites hie , vpon foure rowes of ceder pillers
& ceder beames were layed vp6 the pillers.

3　And it was couered aboue with ceder vp6
the beames, that lay on the fourtie & fiue

pillers, fiftene in a rowe.

4　And the windowes were in thre rowes, &
windowe was c againſt windowe in thre
rankes.

5　And all the dores, and the ſide poſtes with
the windowes were foure ſquare , & windowe was ouer againſt windowe in thre
rankes.

6　And he made a porche of pillers fiftie cubites long, and thirtie cubites broade. and
the porche was before d them, euen before
them were thirtie pillers.

7　¶ Thẽ he made a porch e for the throne,
where he iudged, euen a porche of iudgement,

c There were as
many, and like
proportion on
the one ſide as
on the other, and
at euery end e-
uen three in a
rowe one aboue
another.

d before the pil-
lers of the houſe
e For his houſe,
which was at Ie-
ruſalem.

A a.iiii.

25 Title page of the first edition in folio of Sternhold and Hopkins' metrical
Psalms, 1565.

26 Title-page of the Bishops' Bible, 1568, showing the 'rather pleasing' portrait of the queen. The motto, quoting Romans 1:16, says 'I am not ashamed of the gospel of Christ: for it is the power of God unto salvation to everyone that believeth' – impeccable sentiments, but in Latin – bizarre for the introduction to an English translation.

27 Title-page of the 1611 'King James' Version. The main feature is an impenetrable wall, above which the saints Peter and Paul stare at the reader. The intention of solid, and forbidding, authority is unmistakable and should be contrasted with the images of the title-pages of the 1557 Geneva New Testament and 1560 Geneva Bible, which invite the reader in.

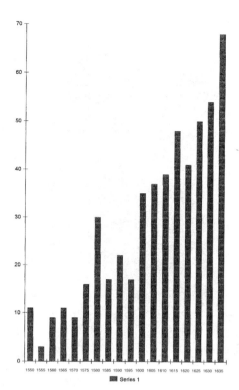

28 Graph showing the numbers of editions of Sternhold and Hopkins' metrical psalms, in five year periods from 1550 to 1640. These large numbers do not include 'S&H' printed in most Books of Common Prayer and all Geneva Bibles.

29 (below) An opening of Daniel Mace's Diglot of 1729, modestly offering a fresh Greek text which was seen to be of some importance to nineteenth-century scholars, and a liberated English translation. The English punctuation attempted to follow the Greek.

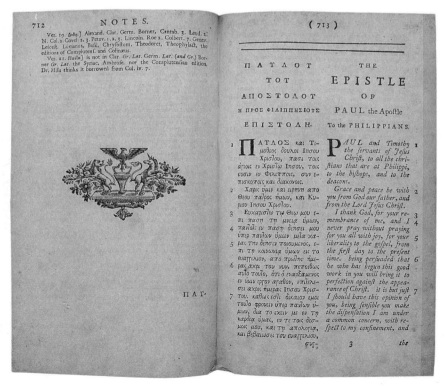

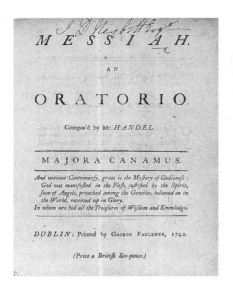

30 Title-page of the word book for
Messiah in Dublin in 1742, showing the
importance of the two-word quotation
from Vergil, 'Majora Canamus', and the
verses from the New Testament,
1 Timothy 3:16 and Colossians 2:3.

31 Susannah Cibber, the London
actress who was a soloist in the first
performance of *Messiah* in Dublin in
1742. Handel is said to have written
that 'He was despised' for her.

32   The Liberty window in Christ Church, Philadelphia, imaginatively constructing a scene of 'The Prayer in the First Congress AD 1774'.

33a and b   Pictures from Isaiah Thomas's 1791 Folio Bible, showing ambivalence in 'biblical' interest in women. In Paradise, while her husband sleeps, a watchful Eve, like a good wife, is alert – but shows a lot of herself in the spotlight. Susanna, rejecting the lustful elders, manages to show them a good deal, and touches them.

34 (*facing page top*)   'The Massacre of the Innocents', from Mathew Carey's Bible of 1801, has erotic display as well as violence.

35 (*facing page bottom*)   Such display has a history. In this small woodcut (5 by 8 cms; here reproduced larger than actual size) at the head of 2 Samuel 11 in the 'Great' Bible, 1539, Bathsheba reveals almost all. In spite of the appearance, it is thought unlikely that she is handing King David's messenger her cell-phone; but bashful she is not.

Pl. 5. Page 536

Herod was exceeding wroth, & sent forth & slew all the children that were in Bethlehem, & in all the coasts thereof, from two years old and under.

Matthew Ch. 2. v. 16.

ℭ The. xj. Chapter.

ℭ The aduoutrye of Dauid wyth Bethsabe the wyfe of Urias. Urias is gylefully slayne.

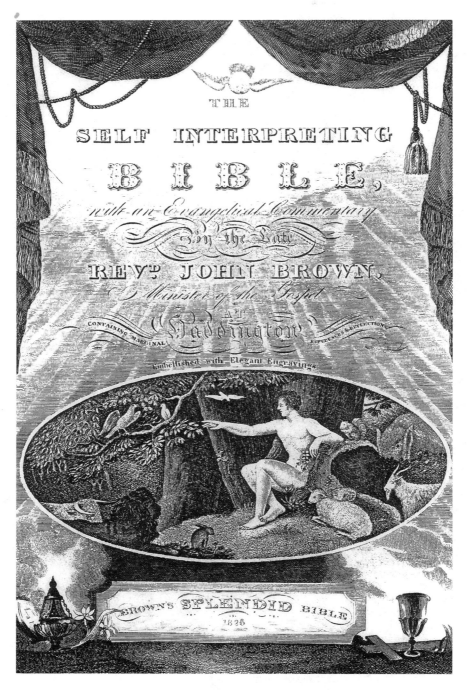

THE

SELF INTERPRETING

BIBLE,

with an Evangelical Commentary

By the Late

REVᴰ JOHN BROWN,

Minister of the Gospel

AT

Paddington.

CONTAINING MARGINAL · REFERENCES & REFLECTIONS

Embellished with Elegant Engravings

BROWN'S SPLENDID BIBLE
1826

36   The title-page of Brown's Splendid Bible, 1826.

38 (*facing page bottom*)   An opening of a nineteenth-century American Hieroglyphick Bible for children, of a kind popular in Europe from the late eighteenth century.

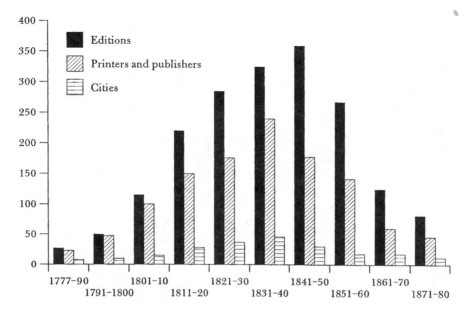

37　Graph showing the production of English Bibles in the United States, 1777–1880.

Thus saith

the　　　　of Bel:

Thou, O　　　set on the

and the

make ready, and shut the

and seal it with
thine own

Bel at Babel, 11.—Thus said the *priests* of Bel : Thou, O
king, set on the *meat*, and the *wine* make ready, and shut the
door, and seal it with thine own *ring*.

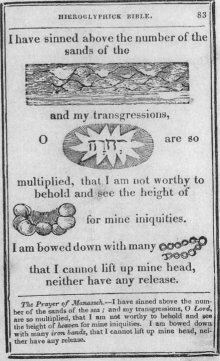

I have sinned above the number of the
sands of the

and my transgressions,

O　　　　　　　are so

multiplied, that I am not worthy to
behold and see the height of

for mine iniquities.

I am bowed down with many

that I cannot lift up mine head,
neither have any release.

The Prayer of Manasseh.—I have sinned above the number of the sands of the *sea ;* and my transgressions, O *Lord*,
are so multiplied, that I am not worthy to behold and see
the height of *heaven* for mine iniquities. I am bowed down
with many *iron bands*, that I cannot lift up mine head, neither have any release.

4 Behold, he that keepeth Israel shall neither slumber nor sleep.

5 The LORD *is* thy keeper: the LORD *is* ᵈthy shade ᵉupon thy right hand.

6 ᶠThe sun shall not smite thee by day, nor the moon by night.

7 The LORD shall preserve thee from all evil: he shall ᵍpreserve thy soul.

8 The LORD shall ʰpreserve thy going out and thy coming in from this time forth, and even for evermore.

PSALM CXXII.

David professeth his joy for the church, 6 and prayeth for the peace thereof.

¶ A Song of degrees of David.

I WAS glad when they said unto me, ᵃLet us go into the house of the LORD.

2 Our feet shall stand within thy gates, O Jerusalem.

3 Jerusalem is builded as a city that is ᵇcompact together:

4 ᶜWhither the tribes go up, the tribes of the LORD, unto ᵈthe testimony of Israel, to give thanks unto the name of the LORD.

5 ᵉFor there †are set thrones of judgment, the thrones of the house of David.

6 ᶠPray for the peace of Jerusalem: they shall prosper that love thee.

7 Peace be within thy walls, *and* prosperity within thy palaces.

8 For my brethren and companions' sakes, I will now say, Peace *be* within thee.

9 Because of the house of the LORD our God I will ᵍseek thy good.

PSALM CXXIII.

1 The godly profess their confidence in God, 3 and pray to be delivered from contempt.

¶ A Song of degrees.

1 UNTO thee ᵃlift I up mine eyes, O thou ᵇthat dwellest in the heavens.

2 Behold, as the eyes of servants *look* unto the hand of their masters, *and* as the eyes of a maiden unto the hand of her mistress; so our eyes *wait* upon the LORD our God, until that he have mercy upon us.

3 Have mercy upon us, O LORD, have mercy

upon us: for we are exceedingly filled with contempt.

4 Our soul is exceedingly filled with the scorning of those that are at ease, *and* with the contempt of the proud.

PSALM CXXIV.

The church blesseth God for a miraculous deliverance.

¶ A Song of degrees of David.

IF *it had not been* the LORD who was on our side, ᵃnow may Israel say;

2 If *it had not been* the LORD who was on our side, when men rose up against us:

3 Then they had ᵇswallowed us up quick, when their wrath was kindled against us:

4 Then the waters had overwhelmed us, the stream had gone over our soul:

5 Then the proud waters had gone over our soul.

6 Blessed *be* the LORD, who hath not given us *as* a prey to their teeth.

7 Our soul is escaped ᶜas a bird out of the snare of the fowlers: the snare is broken, and we are escaped.

8 ᵈOur help *is* in the name of the LORD, ᵉwho made heaven and earth.

PSALM CXXV.

1 The safety of such as trust in God.   4 A prayer for the godly, and against the wicked.

¶ A Song of degrees.

1 THEY that trust in the LORD *shall be* as Mount Zion, *which* cannot be removed, *but* abideth for ever.

2 *As* the mountains *are* round about Jerusalem, so the LORD *is* round about his people from henceforth even for ever.

3 For ᵃthe rod of †the wicked shall not rest upon the lot of the righteous; lest the righteous put forth their hands unto iniquity.

4 Do good, O LORD, unto *those that be* good, and to *them that are* upright in their hearts.

5 As for such as turn aside unto their ᵇcrooked ways, the LORD shall lead them forth with the workers of iniquity: *but* ᶜpeace *shall be* upon Israel.

PSALM CXXVI.

1 The church, celebrating her incredible return out of captivity, 4 prayeth for, and prophesieth the good success thereof.

¶ A Song of degrees.

1 WHEN the LORD †turned again the captivity of Zion, ᵃwe were like them that dream.

Marginal references (centre column):

d Isai. 25, 4.

e Ps. 16, 8, & 109, 31.

f Ps. 91, 5. Isai. 49, 10. Rev. 7, 16.

g Ps. 41, 2, & 97, 10, & 145, 20.

h Deuteron. 28, 6. Prov. 2, 8, & 3, 6.

a Isai. 2, 3. Zech. 8, 21.

b See 2 Sam. 5, 9.

c Exodus 23, 17. Deut. 16, 16.

d Exod. 16, 34.

e Deut. 17, 8. 2 Chron. 19, 8.

† Heb. *do sit.*

f Ps. 51, 18.

g Neh. 2, 10.

a Ps. 121, 1, & 141, 8.

b Ps. 2, 4, & 11, 4, & 115, 3.

a Ps. 129, 1.

b Ps. 56, 1, 2, & 57, 3. Prov. 1, 12.

c Ps. 91, 3. Prov. 6, 5.

d Ps. 121, 2.

e Gen. 1, 1. Ps. 134, 3.

a Prov. 22, 8. Isai. 14, 5.

† Heb. *wickedness.*

b Prov. 2, 15.

c Ps. 128, 6. Gal. 6, 16.

† Heb. *returned the returning of Zion,* Ps. 53, 6, & 85, 1. Hos. 6, 11. Joel 3, 1.

a Acts 12, 9.

40   An illustration by William Blake for his edition of the Book of Job, 1825.

42   Bible reading on HMS *Hyperion*, 1820.

41 *(facing page)*   William Holman Hunt, *The Light of the World* (1851–3). The original is in the chapel of Keble College, Oxford.

43 Thomas James Barker, *The Secret of England's Greatness*, *c.*1863. Queen Victoria, flanked by Prince Albert, is presenting to a 'native' chief a copy of a Bible.

44   A truly American Bible at last. At the White House, 26 September 1952, President Harry Truman is presented with the completed RSV by translation committee chairman Luther A. Weigle and colleagues.

Aren't you worth much more than birds? (6.26)

asks for bread? ¹⁰Or would you give him a snake when he asks for a fish? ¹¹Bad as you are, you know how to give good things to your children. How much more, then, will your Father in heaven give good things to those who ask him!

12 "Do for others what you want them to do for you: this is the meaning of the Law of Moses and of the teachings of the prophets.

The Narrow Gate
(Luke 13.24)

13 "Go in through the narrow gate, because the gate to hell is wide and the road that leads to it is easy, and there are many who travel it. ¹⁴But the gate to life is narrow and the way that leads to it is hard, and there are few people who find it.

A Tree and Its Fruit
(Luke 6.43–44)

15 "Be on your guard against false prophets; they come to you looking like sheep on the outside, but on the inside

they are really like wild wolves. ¹⁶You will know them by what they do. Thorn bushes do not bear grapes, and briars do not bear figs. ¹⁷A healthy tree bears good fruit, but a poor tree bears bad fruit. ¹⁸A healthy tree cannot bear bad fruit, and a poor tree cannot bear good fruit. ¹⁹And any tree that does not bear good fruit is cut down and thrown in the fire. ²⁰So then, you will know the false prophets by what they do.

I Never Knew You
(Luke 13.25–27)

21 "Not everyone who calls me 'Lord, Lord' will enter the Kingdom of heaven, but only those who do what my Father in heaven wants them to do. ²²When Judgement Day comes, many will say to me, 'Lord, Lord! In your name we spoke God's message, by your name we drove out many demons and performed many miracles!' ²³Then I will say to them, 'I never knew you. Get away from me, you wicked people!'

7.12: Lk 6.31　　7.19: Mt 3.10; Lk 3.9　　7.20: Mt 12.33　　7.23: Ps 6.8

Here I am about to starve! (15.17)

of mine was dead, but now he is alive; he was lost, but now he has been found.' And so the feasting began.

25 "In the meantime the elder son was out in the field. On his way back, when he came close to the house, he heard the music and dancing. ²⁶So he called one of the servants and asked him, 'What's going on?' ²⁷Your brother has come back home,' the servant answered, 'and your father has killed the prize calf, because he got him back safe and sound.' ²⁸The elder brother was so angry that he would not go into the house; so his father came out and begged him to come in. ²⁹But he spoke back to his father, 'Look, all these years I have worked for you like a slave, and I have never disobeyed your orders. What have you given me? Not even a goat for me to have a feast with my friends! ³⁰But this son of yours wasted all your property on prostitutes, and when he comes back home, you kill the prize calf for him!' ³¹'My son,' the father answered, 'you are always here with me, and everything I have is yours. ³²But we had to celebrate and be happy, because your brother was dead, but now he is alive; he was lost, but now he has been found.'"

The Shrewd Manager

16 Jesus said to his disciples, "There was once a rich man who had a servant whom he managed his property. The rich man was told that the manager was wasting his master's money, ²so he called him in and said, 'What is this I hear about you? Hand in a complete account of your handling of my property, because you cannot be my manager any longer.' ³The servant said to himself, 'My master is going to dismiss me from my job. What shall I do? I am not strong enough to

dig ditches, and I am ashamed to beg. ⁴Now I know what I will do! Then when my job is gone, I shall have friends who will welcome me in their homes.'

5 "So he called in all the people who were in debt to his master. He asked the first one, 'How much do you owe my master?' ⁶'One hundred barrels of olive-oil,' he answered. 'Here is your account,' the manager told him; 'sit down and write fifty.' ⁷Then he asked another one, 'And you—how much do you owe?' 'A

But now he is alive (15.32)

out and could not pull it back in, because they had caught so many fish.

7 The disciple whom Jesus loved said to Peter, "It is the Lord!" When Peter heard that it was the Lord, he wrapped his outer garment round him (for he had taken his clothes off) and jumped into the water. ⁸The other disciples came to shore in the boat, pulling the net full of fish. They were not very far from land, about a hundred metres away. ⁹When they stepped ashore, they saw a charcoal fire there with fish on it and some bread. ¹⁰Then Jesus said to them, "Bring some of the fish you have just caught."

11 Simon Peter went aboard and dragged the net ashore full of big fish, a hundred and fifty-three in all; even though there were so many, still the net did not tear. ¹²Jesus said to them, "Come and eat." None of the disciples dared ask him, "Who are you?" because they knew it was the Lord. ¹³So Jesus went over, took the bread, and gave it to them; he did the same with the fish.

14 This, then, was the third time Jesus appeared to the disciples after he was raised from death.

Jesus and Peter

15 After they had eaten, Jesus said to

Simon Peter, "Simon son of John, do you love me more than these others do?"

"Yes, Lord," he answered, "you know that I love you."

Jesus said to him, "Take care of my lambs." ¹⁶A second time Jesus said to him, "Simon son of John, do you love me?"

"Yes, Lord," he answered, "you know that I love you."

Jesus said to him, "Take care of my sheep." ¹⁷A third time Jesus said, "Simon son of John, do you love me?"

Peter was sad because Jesus asked him the third time, "Do you love me?" so he said to him, "Lord, you know everything; you know that I love you!"

Jesus said to him, "Take care of my sheep. ¹⁸I am telling you the truth: when you were young, you used to get ready and go anywhere you wanted to; but when you are old, you will stretch out your hands and someone else will bind you and take you where you don't want to go." ¹⁹(In saying this, Jesus was indicating the way in which Peter would die and bring glory to God.) Then Jesus said to him, "Follow me!"

Jesus and the Other Disciple

20 Peter turned round and saw behind

Simon Peter...dragged the net ashore (21.11)

What we see now is like a dim image in a mirror (13.12)

feelings, and thinking were all those of a child,' now that I am a man, I have no more use for childish ways. ¹²What we see now is like a dim image in a mirror; then we shall see face to face. What I know now is only partial; then it will be complete—as complete as God's knowledge of me.

13 Meanwhile these three remain: faith, hope, and love; and the greatest of these is love.

More about Gifts from the Spirit

14 It is love, then, that you should strive for. Set your hearts on spiritual gifts, especially the gift of proclaiming God's message. ²The one who speaks in strange tongues does not speak to others but to God, because no one understands him. He is speaking secret truths by the power of the Spirit. ³But the one who proclaims God's message speaks to people and gives them help, encouragement, and comfort. ⁴The one who speaks in strange tongues helps only himself, but the one who proclaims God's message helps the whole church.

5 I would like all of you to speak in strange tongues; but I would rather that you had the gift of proclaiming God's message. For the person who proclaims God's message is of greater value than

the one who speaks in strange tongues—unless there is someone present who can explain what he says, so that the whole church may be helped. ⁶So when I come to you, my brothers, what use will I be to you if I speak in strange tongues? Not a bit, unless I bring you some revelation from God or some knowledge or some inspired message, or some teaching.

7 Take such lifeless musical instruments as the flute or the harp—how will anyone know the tune that is being played unless the notes are sounded distinctly? ⁸And if the man who plays the bugle does not sound a clear call, who will prepare for battle? ⁹In the same way, how will anyone understand what you are talking about if your message given in strange tongues is not clear? Your words will vanish in the air! ¹⁰There are many different languages in the world, yet none of them is without meaning. ¹¹But if I do not know the language being spoken, the person who uses it will be a foreigner to me and I will be a foreigner to him. ¹²Since you are eager to have the gifts of the Spirit, you must try above everything else to make greater use of those which help to build up the church.

Then we shall see face to face (13.12)

45a–d　A group of some of the five hundred illustrations by Annie Vallotton to the 1976 *Good News Bible*, or *Today's English Version*.

46a and b   The Fall, as told in a comic-book version in the early twenty-first century.

47 A page of Codex Sinaiticus, the fourth-century manuscript of the original Greek of the New Testament. Many earlier Greek manuscripts of parts of the New Testament, some only fragments, have survived: Codex Sinaiticus is the earliest known complete Greek New Testament. It was discovered in the Monastery of St Catherine at the foot of Mount Sinai by Constantine Tischendorf in 1859. Since the late nineteenth century it has been a basis of the firm foundation of the Greek text. Like the Lindisfarne Gospels and Tyndale's 1526 New Testament, it is a jewel on permanent open display in the Ritblat Gallery of the British Library in London (BL ADD MS 43725).

Chapter 27

THE BIBLE IN ENGLAND IN THE SEVENTEENTH CENTURY

IN LATER TUDOR TIMES, and in the seventeenth century, the English Bible was not a special file to be called up when one was feeling religious.

> The Introduction to the 1603 edition of Tomson's Geneva Bible, written by T. Grashop, tells us to remember that the Scriptures contain matter concerning commonwealths and governments, good and evil, prosperity and plagues, peace and war, order and disorder. They cover the common life of all men, rich and poor, industrious and idle. The ideas which divided the two parties in the Civil War, and which divided conservatives from radicals among the victorious parliamentarians, were all found in the Bible.

So wrote Christopher Hill in 1993, in the opening paragraph of the Preface to his *The English Bible and the Seventeenth-Century Revolution*.[1] He continued:

> For most men and women the Bible was their point of reference in all their thinking. . . . The Bible was the source of virtually all ideas; it supplied the idiom in which men and women discussed them. . . . To say that the English Revolution was about religion is tautologous; it took place in the 17th century.[2]

As he noted, 'The Bible was central to all arts, sciences and literature'.[3] The sciences, as they then existed, were declared in relation to what the Bible said; understandable in cosmology and astronomy, more puzzling in relation to astrology or alchemy – or even medicine, though the days of the patriarchs were the days of the giants, and it was observed that the patriarchs lived far longer (and see pp. 11–12 above). The centrality of the Bible is more understandable in the writing of history, so that Raleigh's *History of the World* (1614) was written within the framework of the Mosaic chronology. Writing of the Geneva Bible, Christopher Hill noted:

Among those who used it we may list Sir Walter Ralegh, Sir Philip
Sidney, Thomas Whythorne, Richard Hooker, Henry Vaughan, George
Fox, [Andrew] Marvell: Shakespeare, Massinger, Dryden and Shadwell
(and no doubt many more dramatists) refer to it. Lancelot Andrewes
. . . normally took his texts for sermons from the Geneva version.
Milton and Bunyan cite both the A.V. and Geneva. Milton seems to
have preferred the latter, notably in *Samson Agonistes*; but some of his
amanuenses used the A.V.[4]

The number of Bibles, New Testaments and parts published in England
between 1526 and 1640 was estimated above, in chapter 12, at over two
million. The figure does not mean total readers: for another hundred years,
reading would still usually mean reading aloud, and Bibles would be heard
by a whole household in the parlour, in the open air, in a room in a tavern
or within a church. The English Bible was so present in the lives and
thoughts of the English people in the seventeenth century that in a single
chapter of this book only snapshots can be given. In any case, it is difficult
to imagine a better statement of the complete permeation of English life
by the English Bible than Christopher Hill's book. The first chapter, 'A
Biblical Culture', which is the Introduction, sets the general scene
admirably, with full supporting references. It is pleasing that a historian has
moved studies away from a dogma promulgated in the second half of the
twentieth century, that the key to understanding the events in England
and Scotland between the latter part of Elizabeth's reign and the restoration of Charles II lay in economics. Early in his book, Hill tells the story
of 'the legendary economic historian Jack Fisher' telling 'an importunate
pupil demanding a reading list on 16th and 17th century economic
history' to go away and read the Bible.[6] Economics played an important
part, of course, but, like everything else, they were dyed in the colours of
the Bible, central at every level of thought.

Central, but not always benign. Bible doctrines are radical.[7] The Bible
could be inflammatory in revolution. The Old Testament appears to
advocate extermination and genocide, especially in Joshua and Judges; not
to mention Ezekiel 9:6, 'Destroy utterly the old, *and* the young, and the
maids, and the children, and the women', and Jeremiah 48:10, 'Cursed *be
he* that keepeth back his sword from blood,' as the Geneva Bible has those
verses. The KJV, shorn of notes, does not explain, as Geneva does, that the
slayers in Ezekiel are angels, nor that Jeremiah is reporting Middle Eastern
politics. That might not have mattered: fanaticicism could always find its
avatar. The New Testament is socially radical: 'God is no respecter of
persons' (Romans 2:11), 'if any would not work, neither should he eat' (2
Thessalonians 3:10) – to which remark a Geneva-Tomson note has 'What

shall we do then with those idle bellied monks, and sacrificing Priests? A Monk (saith Socrates, book 8 of his Tripartite history) which worketh not with hands, is like a thief.' The mid-century fantasies of the imminence of Christ's Second Coming (expected in the 1650s), drawn out of the apocalyptic books of Daniel and Revelation, had something to do with the extreme measure of executing the King in 1649. As a source of slogans, the prestige of the Bible sank, insofar as it was associated with political extremity and latter-day confusion, and with failing to foretell the times correctly: King Jesus did not arrive in 1650 to take over.

Mercifully, Christian political fundamentalists were not a majority. There was some cooling, but, outside the court, no national divorce from Scripture, no communal shaking off and moving on into a new relationship with the secular. The godly did not disappear, though after 1660 they did not form the government. Non-biblical Renaissance ideas flourished throughout the century, and grew – biblical influence was never intellectually absolute: yet the Bible springs still flowed, as will be seen. Biblical politics remained a real threat to the monarchy for some decades after the Restoration. Nonconformist congregations flourished and grew in spite of the harsh conditions. The idea of silencing an opponent simply by saying 'The Bible says so' had never been a reality: the flexibility of interpretation was always one of the elements in the near-universal ascendancy of the Bible, which was not much reduced after 1600.

BIBLICAL BALLADS AND POETIC PARAPHRASES

From the 1580s, for a hundred years, the greatness of English literature was built on many foundations, laid in Italy, Spain and France, and on the newly arrived classical Greek and Roman texts. In the successful endeavour to make a literature that led all Europe, a very large, possibly the largest, area of influence was the English Bible. There is space here to do no more than point towards one or two of the literary parts of the territory – generally less known, at the start of the twenty-first century, than the far side of the moon.

In the 107 years between the first Geneva Bible and the first edition of *Paradise Lost* in 1667, particularly over the four decades from about 1580, a shoal of lesser writers published on biblical subjects. The obvious intention was to be biblical *and above all* English. They made their rough and often not very good poems out of the Geneva Bible in various experimental, and sometimes unfortunate, forms; but they were part of the great work of making poetry in English – and prose, we must not forget: those supreme speakers of prose, Shakespeare's Rosalind, Benedick, Falstaff and

Hamlet, created in the same years, 1598–1600, speak a flexible, expressive day-to-day English prose such as had never been heard before, a direct descendant of Tyndale's Bible translations of sixty years before.

Up to 1600, in the new extension of the range of English verse there are obviously major poets to be considered – Edmund Spenser, Philip Sidney, Samuel Daniel and Michael Drayton above all. The separate subject of the Englishing of the Psalms, a major influence on English lyric poetry will be further considered below.[8] I will not lift up my eyes to such hills for the moment, but look briefly at the lowlier mounds and humps of lesser, but more popular, everyday verse – the rise and fall of this genre matching the rise and fall of the Geneva Bible's greatest use.[9]

Consider popular ballads on biblical stories in the late sixteenth and early seventeenth centuries. They were, among other subjects, on David and Bathsheba, Samson, Jephthah – and Hamlet quotes just such a 'pious chanson' in Act 3, scene 2 – Solomon, Job, Jonah, Tobias, Esau's birthright, the fall of Jerusalem, Doomsday and the Resurrection; many were on episodes from the life of Christ.[10] The impact of the Geneva Bible here has yet to be explored: and their decline as a form matches the decline of Geneva as an influence. Exactly parallel is the sophisticated genre of madrigals and lute songs on biblical themes by nearly all English composers of the time, and in just under a third of collections by Byrd and Ravenscroft, which peaks during the period. John Milton's father set texts from the Geneva Bible to polyphonic tunes.[11]

Sidney and Spenser paraphrased the Bible. So did many, many more: poets usually now out of sight, who published such verse paraphrases with success. The way was made open for them by the prose paraphrases which, in the Geneva Bibles, open every book of the Old Testament. These 'arguments', sometimes (as for Isaiah) half a folio page in length, were not in the Bishops' Bible of 1568, and certainly not in AV in 1611. Of course poets read the whole Bible, and did not necessarily need those paraphrases: I believe, however, that verbal connections can be demonstrated, though the detailed comparisons remain to be done. At the highest point of the genre are poetic paraphrases by a later Earl of Surrey, by Henry Lok, John Hall, William Kethe, Thomas Drant, William Forrest, William Hunnis, John Merbecke, Thomas Hudson, William Habington, Thomas Fuller, Sir William Alexander, George Sandys, William Knivett, Henry King, John Weever, Thomas Wilson, Clement Cotton, John Taylor and many more. Some names are familiar from other contexts – Kethe from Geneva, Sandys with the Virginia Company, and so on. The prolific John Taylor, 'the Water Poet', made rhyming paraphrases of the Old, and then the New, Testaments, which, published in 1614, made a cheap and amazingly popular volume known, from its handy pocket size, as 'the Thumb Bible'.[12] It was constantly reprinted in Britain and America for two hundred years, and even translated into French. Good poets like John Donne, George Wither and Francis Quarles paraphrased Lamentations: Quarles went on to paraphrase Jonah, Esther, Job, Jeremiah, the Song of Songs, the story of Samson, and Ecclesiastes. Michael Drayton's first publication was his poem *The Harmonie of the Church* (1594), paraphrasing Bible stories. 'Thomas Middleton served his apprenticeship with *The Wisdom of Solomon Paraphrased* in 1597 before going on to write the plays for which we remember him.'[13] As late as 1627 he published *God's Parliament House: Or, The Marriage of the Old and New Testaments*.

Biblical verse paraphrases of this kind merge into attempts at a biblical epic. In the twenty-first century it is difficult to value these. Not only is the Bible not central: writing an epic poem is no longer considered to be the most admirable thing that a human being can do. It is no longer considered at all. Worthwhile ambitions are establishing world peace, finding a cure for mortal diseases or feeding the globe's hungry masses. These all rank high, above working with children and animals and world travel: writing an epic poem is not even on the list. It was not always so. An epic is a long poem giving to a great nation the story of its foundation, in the most elevated language. The making of it was the mark of the arrival of that national greatness, accompanied by the achievement, by a national poet, of a developed poetic language that could be recognised as high speech. The supreme example was the high style of Virgil's *Aeneid*, written in 30–19 BC. This epic told of the feats of Aeneas during his journey from the fires of Troy, across the Mediterranean, to establish Rome.

The Hexameral epics of the seventeenth century, that is, on the Hexamera, the six days of Creation, were based on the French of Du Bartas, but firmly Englished. Sylvester, Quarles, Wither and Henry More all produced biblical epics, from which grew Cowley's *Davideis*. The cousins of the playwright John Fletcher, Giles and his brother Phineas, each wrote a biblical epic. Milton (of whom more below) topped an English tradition, though it cannot be said that the epics before him were high poetry.

A small and curious genre was of 'character' writing, with perhaps two excellent writers, John Earle and Sir Thomas Overbury, and a hinterland of lesser figures. The aim is to encapsulate a type of person in a brief 200-word essay, as, for example, John Earle's 'An old College Butler', or 'A mere dull Physician' in his *Microcosmographie* of 1628. The form fed Bunyan very obviously (see below) and looks forward to the novel. Though based firmly on the Greek writer Theophrastus of 371–287 BC, the genre owes something to the Wisdom Books of the Apocrypha and Old Testament in the Geneva Bibles, and probably a good deal to the Gospels.

The point of all these references is the imaginary graph showing the same shape for the rise and fall of certain English, mostly poetic, genres and the influence of the Geneva Bibles. The largeness of that presence inspired a large poetic output.

THE 'METAPHYSICAL' POETS

Consider, again, two poems, this time by a great poet indeed, probably written about 1630:

> *The Bunch of Grapes*
> Joy, I did lock thee up; but some bad man
>   Hath let thee out again:
> And now, me thinks, I am where I began
>   Sev'n years ago: one vogue and vein,
>   One air of thoughts usurps my brain.
> I did towards Canaan draw; but now I am
> Brought back to the Red sea, the sea of shame.
>
> For as the Jews of old by Gods command
>   Travell'd, and saw no town;
> So now each Christian hath his journey spann'd:
>
>   Their story pens and sets us down.
>   A single deed is small renown.
> Gods works are wide, and let in future time;
> His ancient justice overflows our crimes.
>
> Then have we too our guardian fires and clouds;
>   Our Scripture-dew drops fast;
> We have our sands and serpents, tents and shrouds;
>   Alas! our murmurings come not last.
>   But where's the cluster? where's the taste
> Of mine inheritance? Lord, if I must borrow,
> Let me as well take up their joy, as sorrow.
>
> But can he want the grape, who hath the wine?
>   I have their fruit and more.
> Blessed be God, who prosper'd *Noahs* vine,
>   And made it bring forth grapes good store.
>   But much more him I must adore,
> Who of the Laws sour juice sweet wine did make,
> Ev'n God himself being pressed for my sake.

The poem is by George Herbert.[14] It is one of the posthumous collection first published by the printer to the University in Cambridge (where Herbert had been Orator) in 1633 under the title *The Temple. Sacred Poems and Private Ejaculations*. The epigraph on the title-page is 'Psal. 29. *In his Temple doth every man speak of his honour.*' Exploring the implications of a church, the poet in *The Temple* meditates on Christian experience of God.

Twenty-first-century readers can find the poems, though potentially almost infinite in meaning, daunting. The difficulty is only partly in grasping the movement of ideas, within the easy flow of familiar words. Problems come equally from the loss of the whole ground of reference. That the interior conflict recorded in this poem is in relation to something in Scripture is not hard to see. What it is more precisely, beyond Old Testament accounts of wanderings in the wilderness, can be, with the loss of automatic familiarity with the Bible, baffling. With that loss goes most of the poem. In one important way, the poem is irrecoverable.

A footnote can point to the story in Numbers 13. Moses sent spies into Canaan, and they returned with news of a land that 'floweth with milk and honey', in token of which richness they brought back 'a branch with one cluster of grapes, and they bare it upon a bar between two'.[15] This helps with Herbert's poem: but not enough. The 'cluster' is not mentioned until line 19, and then to question its absence. There is, however, more in the story. In spite of the fruit, the spies brought back 'an evil report of the land': not only that 'the people be strong that dwell in the land, and the cities *are* walled and exceeding great', but, worse, it 'is a land that eateth up the inhabitants thereof', because they 'are men of great stature'; worst, they are 'giants, so that we seemed in our sight like grasshoppers.'[16]

This is some help with the sense of the scale of Herbert's conflict. But again, only some. A reader needs to have in mind the whole movement of the desert wanderings, told in three books of the Pentateuch (Exodus, Numbers, Deuteronomy), the 'fires and clouds . . . sands and serpents, tents and shrouds', and particularly the 'murmurings'. A Geneva note points out, of the sending of the spies, that 'the people had required it of Moses, as it is in Deut. 1.22': the poem has that quality of need and demand. Further, a Geneva note against 'that eateth up' at the end of the chapter is: 'The Giants were so cruel, that they spoiled and killed one another, and those that came after them.' The poem begins, emphasised in the first lines, with a quality of devouring loss.

The phrases 'locked thee up' and 'let thee out' in the opening are puzzlingly ambivalent: the first seems too strong and negative. 'Some bad man' is not identified: the most that can be said is that he is in Herbert. The movement of the subject, 'joy', needs careful and subtle following, over a long time. Time frames the poem, reaching from Noah to Canaan, on to the Crucifixion and on again to the poet's taking of communion. The point to be made, however, is that even to begin to savour this bunch of grapes the reader needs more than a learned footnote, valuable though that might be: as the Irishman famously said when giving directions, to get there you shouldn't start from here. The poem expects so much more than a footnote. Even to begin to try to follow what happens to joy in the poet, the reader needs automatic knowledge of the bringing of the grapes from a rich, dangerous land, of all the Old Testament history before that sense of arrival, and of Christian sacraments. For such a reader Herbert wrote, about joy. Such a reader no longer exists. The loss of the Bible has meant the loss, not of an external scaffold of references, but of an internal, automatic understanding of human experience that only poets can match.

The second poem by Herbert is apparently more receivable.[17] Within the exact frame of a Shakespearean sonnet, ten of its lines being perfect iambic pentameters, its words undemandingly familiar, it alternates, and then blends, 'I' and 'Him' with satisfying skill.

> *Redemption*
> Having been tenant long to a rich Lord,
>   Not thriving, I resolved to be bold,
>   And make a suit unto him, to afford
> A new small-rented lease, and cancel th'old.
> In heaven at his manor I him sought:
>   They told me there, that he was lately gone
>   About some land, which he had dearly bought
> Long since on earth, to take possession.
> I straight return'd, and knowing his great birth,
>   Sought him accordingly in great resorts;
>   In cities, theatres, gardens, parks and courts;
> At length I heard a ragged noise and mirth
>   Of thieves and murderers: there I him espied,
>   Who straight, *Your suit is granted*, said, & died.

The intense satisfaction produced by the last line is typical of Herbert. The Lord speaks before he is asked. His gift is made in five chiming words, 'is/granted/said/and/died' made of one anothers' sounds, a technique established by the earlier rhymes ('sought . . . resorts . . . courts'), giving the Lord's words an absolute finality. The allegory of the Gospel story is easy to take, disguising the horror in the final syllables. The tone of those is set by the interweaving of the sounds in the words 'mirth' and 'thieves and murderers', where 'mirth' is made of the first syllables of the other two.

These two poems display the 'strong lines' of what came to be called 'metaphysical' poetry (after a remark by Samuel Johnson), fashionable for some decades after about 1590. Herbert shows off less than Donne, but his lines are indeed strong, and he shares, without the 'look-at-me' display of Donne, the ability to reach right across the universe in two words, what the mystified Johnson called 'the yoking together of heterogenous ideas'. To say that the great 'metaphysical' poems – of Donne and Herbert, Vaughan, Traherne and others – are naturally religious is to misrepresent, as if 'religious' were then a separate category. (Donne, at his most erotic, can be theological.[18])

That yoking together of the whole universe is in the parables of Jesus. The kingdom of heaven is like a grain of mustard seed; the meek shall inherit the earth; a camel can't go through the eye of a needle.[19] On writing in English after 1526, the effect of Jesus' 'strong lines', in few words and Tyndalian simplicity ('neither cast ye your pearls before swine'[20]), has been great. Hamlet, walking the stage in 1600, belongs to his time: 'O God, I could be bounded in a nutshell, and count myself king of infinite space, were it not that I have bad dreams.' Hamlet's own time passed, but the play of *Hamlet* lives vividly on, and is now probably more alive than it has ever been. Shakespeare wrote, indeed consummated, a genre, revenge tragedy, that was popular at the time. But Hamlet is timeless, in part, because of his articulation of those paradoxes ('nutshell: infinite space: bad dreams') that are ultimately biblical, especially the ultimate paradox, the Incarnation itself, Almighty and Infinite God as a baby outcast from a crowded inn at the edge of the Roman Empire.

THE SEVENTEENTH-CENTURY POLITICAL REVOLUTION

The presence of the Bible in the politics of the century is, as with the literature, spread far too widely, and soaked into the land too deeply, for more than the smallest snapshots here. 'Society was in turmoil, and the Bible was expected to find solutions to pressing problems', wrote Christopher Hill,[21] and once again, the classic statement is his *The English Bible and the Seventeenth-Century Revolution* of 1993. All I can do is to shine a small light on a few lesser brush-strokes, some revealing details in corners, which can, I hope, stand for the whole immense picture.

Christopher Hill asked whether the Bible might be the equivalent for the English Revolution of Rousseau for the French Revolution and Marx for the Russian: a source of intellectual stimulus, new ideas critical of existing institutions. He found only 'a rag-bag of quotations which could justify whatever a given individual or group wanted to do'.[22] That is damning, indeed. Yet almost all those Geneva references are to the Old Testament. Work remains to be done on the power in this turbulent time of the Geneva New Testament. In the English civil wars, the battles and engagements of Old Testament history, or the sometimes bloody denunciations or exhortations of the Prophets, can plainly be seen to be relevant. Made less visible, so far, has been the effect of the New Testament theology of Paul, with its grounding in the work of 'edification'; or of the ethical demands proposed in the Gospels. Today the latter are not always seen even in attempts at a Christian commonwealth, when in powerful sections of the Christian world, of all persuasions, ostentatious wealth can be paraded as a sign of Christ's special blessing. 'There are few ideas in whose support a Biblical text cannot be found', noted Hill.[23] True. But the New Testament does have an intellectual core, a central doctrine that can turn the world upside down, as the rioters at Thessalonica, intending to lynch Paul and Silas, put it.[24] For three sabbath days Paul had been preaching in the synagogue there, 'out of the scriptures . . . that Christ must needs have suffered, and risen again from the dead; and that this Jesus, whom I preach unto you, is Christ'.[25] The vast work of tracing the Christological, rather than politically radical, New Testament core through the writings of the seventeenth century would probably be impossible; but one notes its absence.

THE DOUAI-RHEIMS VERSION, 1610

The work begun at Rheims by the Roman Catholic exiles with the publication of Gregory Martin's New Testament in 1582 was completed, after long delay, at Douai in 1610 by the addition of the Old Testament. Once again the title-page correctly states that it has been made 'out of the authentical Latin. Diligently conferred with the Hebrew, Greek, and other editions in divers languages'. The Latin was the authorised recension of the Vulgate published under the authority of Clement VIII in 1592, on which Cardinal Allen had worked. It has been noted that the annotations 'are far less copious than in the New Testament, and also less vehement'.[26] A second edition was published in 1635. There were no more editions for 115 years, until 1750, when it was revised by Richard Challoner, with some success.[27]

The same arguments are produced for the dependence on the Latin – so declared in the Preface, because the Hebrew has been 'foully corrupted by Jews', as the Greek had been 'by heretics', but still in the text often silently dependent on the earlier English versions. In the Psalter, Jerome is followed not from his Hebrew text but his Gallican version from the Septuagint, and as Westcott pointed out, the result of going from Hebrew to Greek to Latin to English is that 'where the Latin itself has already lost the sense, the English baffles understanding' as in Psalm 57:10, 'Before your thorns did understand the old briar: as living so in wrath he swalloweth them.'[28] Unlike the (probably exaggerated) effect of the Rheims New Testament on KJV, the Douai Bible had no effect on the life of the time – except in producing in 1719 a rebellious, and effective, priest in Dublin, as chapter 29 will show.

THE SOLDIERS POCKET BIBLE

On this, a textual clarification is needed. The statement that Cromwell's troops went into battle with a copy of the Geneva Bible in their boots has been regularly repeated, no doubt whimsically, but in defiance of all likelihood. Even very small, at 24mo, like the KJV printed by Field in 1653 (17 × 56mm, roughly four inches by two)[29] the result (and without Geneva notes) is barely legible. Even that is too thick and bulky a lump to have, ridiculously, in an army's footwear: they would indeed end up marching on their stomachs, in a different sense from Napoleon's.

What they had was the Soldiers Pocket Bible, a selection of short passages of Scripture, produced, apparently in some numbers, in 1643.[30] It is an octavo, (136 × 78mm, five and a half inches by three), clearly printed on good paper in largeish type (12 point) on sixteen pages. It is a fraction bigger than a modern passport, and as slim. This could be slipped into clothing and worn next to the heart, and would in no way impede action. The eight leaves contain about 150 short Bible verses, thus:

Matt.10.28 And fear ye not them which kill the body.

The verses are collected under sixteen headings, as *A Soldier must not do wickedly . . . A soldier must be valiant for God's Cause . . . A Soldier must pray before he go to fight. . . .* Nearly all the verses are from the Geneva Bible.

Fifty years later this little book was revised 'for our army in Flanders' with the quotations adjusted to KJV.[31] Two hundred years later a total of 50,000 were issued to the Federal troops in the American Civil War.[32]

The title is worth quoting in full:

The Soldiers Pocket Bible: Containing the most (if not all) those places contained in holy Scripture, which do show the qualifications of his inner man, that is a fit soldier to fight the Lords Battles, both before he fight, in the fight, and after the fight: Which Scriptures are reduced to several heads, and fitly applied to the Soldiers several occasions, and so may supply the want of the whole Bible; which a Soldier cannot conveniently carry about him: And may be also useful for any Christian to meditate upon, now in this miserable time of War. Imprimatur, *Edmund Calamy*. Joshua 18, This Book of the Law shall not depart out of thy mouth, but thou shalt meditate therein day and night, that thou maist observe to do according to all that is written therein, for then thou shalt make thy way prosperous, and have good success.

All but four of the verses are from the Old Testament. The four that are not are: the second, Luke 3:14, 'The soldiers likewise demanded of him [John the Baptist], saying, and what shall we do? And he said unto them, do violence to no man, neither accuse any falsely, and be content with your wages': Ephesians 6:10, 'Be strong in the Lord, and in the power of his might': Matthew 10:28, as above: and Matthew 5:44, 'But I say unto you love your enemies.'(In all these, Geneva and KJV agree.) Three pages towards the back give selections from more connected passages, describing battles in Judges, Joshua and 2 Chronicles, with great slaughter.

CROMWELL, JOHNSTON, VANE

I take here small samples of what can only be called Bible saturation in the minds of three otherwise contrasting mid-seventeenth-century statesmen. The first, Oliver Cromwell, was, obviously, very influentual. The effects of the second, Archibald Johnston, are probably known only to students of Scottish religious history. The third, Sir Henry Vane the Younger, has been in the shadows.

Since his lifetime, Cromwell, the pre-eminent soldier and statesman of the Commonwealth, has received attention from considered, but usually opposite, positions, hostile (often extreme) or supportive. His devotion to the English Bible, however, cannot be contested. Geneva versions and KJV had great influence on his thinking and experience. Two examples will have to be adequate to show the biblical movement of his mind. The first is from his letter to his cousin Elizabeth St John, written in October 1638, asserting his commitment to the cause of God. A few sentences will have to stand for the whole. (Biblical references are added: Cromwell understood that his cousin would recognise them at once.)

Yet to honour my God by declaring what he hath done for my soul, in this I am confident, and I will be so (Psalm 27:3). I find that he giveth springs in a dry and barren wilderness where no water is (Psalm 63:1). I live in Meshek, which they say signifies Prologing; in Kedar, which signifies Blackness (Psalm 120:5): yet the Lord forsaketh me not (Psalm 37:28) . . . The Lord accept me in his Son, and give me to walk in the light . . . as he is the light (John 1:7). He it is that enlighteneth our blackness, our darkness (2 Samuel 22:29), I dare not say, he hideth his face from me. He giveth me light in his light (Psalm 36:1). One beam in a dark place hath exceeding much refreshment in it – blessed be his name for shining upon so dark a heart as mine! (2 Peter 2:19, 2 Corinthians 4:6).You know what my manner of life hath been. Oh, I lived in and loved darkness and hated the light (John 3:19). I was a chief, the chief of sinners (1 Timothy 1:15) . . .

Ten years later, in 1648, from a long letter to a fellow Member of Parliament, in his perplexity after victory in the Second Civil War, the following is typical:

Our rest we expect elsewhere; that will be durable (Hebrews 4:9–11). Care we not for tomorrow, nor for anything (Matthew 6:34).This Scripture has been of great stay to me: read it – Isaiah 8:10, 11, 14 – read all the chapter.

Nine years after that, and towards the end of the Protectorate, on 31 March 1657, the second Protectorate Parliament, purged of the republicans who had ruined the first, presented Cromwell with the 'Humble Petition and Advice'. This offered him the crown as an integral part of a more conservative, civilian constitution, intent to replace the Instrument of Government. For five weeks Cromwell hesitated. His decision was a moment when use of the English Bible determined the course of English history. He was being urged to accept the crown by arguments drawn primarily from law, custom and necessity: for the 'kinglings', Scripture had a distinctly secondary place. The Bible's influence on Cromwell's thought during this critical time, however, may be traced through his speeches to Parliament and to the committee that was appointed to persuade him. Over fifty pages in a selected edition are given to his speeches from these five weeks. They are politically eloquent, without obvious Scripture reference: but they reveal a sense of Scripture running just under the surface, the presence in particular of Paul's letters, as in (at random) 'I am persuaded you would glorify God in it, as much as any one thing you can do.'[33] Some of the strongest expressions of his determination to be guided by the 'Word of God' came to him from key texts persuading him to decline: Romans 14:23 (in Geneva, 'whatsoever is not of faith, is sin') and Joshua 6:26 ('Cursed be the man before the Lord, that riseth up and buildeth this city Jericho: and he shall lay the foundation thereof in his eldest son, & in his youngest son shall he set up the gates of it' – the destroyed 'Jericho' standing for the monarchy.) Also influential was his solicitude for the faithful godly who sent in to him remonstrances saturated in Scripture.

Writing in the late 1630s the Scottish politician Archibald Johnstone of Wariston (the legal mind behind the Scottish National Covenant of 1637–8) shows in his diary how much the Bible shaped his reflections on events, and his role in them. In 1638 he saw two Psalms, together with Nehemiah 9, as showing 'very near parallel between Israel and this church, the only two sworn nations of the Lord': the Psalms are 88, in Geneva beginning, 'O Lord God of my salvation, I cry day *and* night before thee . . .', the Geneva headnote beginnning 'A grievous complaint of the faithful, sore afflicted by sickness, persecutions and adversity, being as it were left of God without any consolation . . .') and Psalm 106, in Geneva beginning 'Praise ye the Lord, because he is good . . .', with the headnote beginning 'The people dispersed under Antiochus, do magnify the goodness of God . . .' In that same year of 1638, Johnstone found in the similar Psalm 107 'a perfect pattern of our cause, as the conclusion is of our duty'. Clearly elaborating Geneva, he quotes with approval 'he poureth contempt upon princes, and causeth them to err in desert places out of the way', concluding with Geneva's last verse (43) 'Who is wise that he may observe these things? for they shall uderstand the lovingkindness of the Lord.' Johnston adopted the biblical practice of making important decisions by casting lots, and resorted in that way to Scripture at crucial moments, encouraging others to do likewise.[34] When, in London twenty years later, in the autumn of 1659, the Army and Parliament quarrelled, he used his position on the Council of State to exhort the factions to reunite, citing several Scriptural injunctions towards concord.

In June 1659, Johnstone noted in his diary that 'Sir Henry Vane debated for the Senate from Scripture, and Henry Neville against it without Scripture.'[35] Sir Henry Vane the Younger was a writer and politician in the Commonwealth period. In 1635 he emigrated to New England, and was an early, and disastrous, Governor of the state of Massachusetts: he returned in 1637, becoming a successful Treasurer of the Navy in 1639. From February 1649 he was a member of the Council of State, with responsibilities for European relations. Milton was secretary to that committee. He broke with Cromwell in 1653 over the dissolution of the Long Parliament. He had a high position in the new pantheon of republican heroes. He had a band of significant admirers, including for many years, as a close friend and colleague, Oliver Cromwell himself – who then had to deal with Vane's apparent threats to the stability of the new Protectorate, and reluctantly order his arrest. No less a man than Richard Baxter gave much time and effort to the task of warning his flock against what he saw as the crypto-Catholic heresies of Vane and the 'Vanists'. When Charles II regained his throne, one of his first decisions was that Vane was too dangerous to be left alive: he pulled all the strings he could to suppress Vane's own testimony at his trial, and before his execution.

Clearly he was a man with personal charisma and, as it turned out, important ideas. Though enemies dismissed his works as incomprehensible or impracticable, his writing does in fact reveal a coherent world view, adapted to the needs of the moment but derived primarily from Scripture. He was unswerving in his dedication to the cause of God, and did all he could to promote peace and reconciliation. He was the most important exponent of the idea of 'godly republicanism', which had considerable later development on both sides of the Atlantic.

Vane's principal works are seven in number, the first three being the most important, taking into account his carefully prepared speech and prayers on the scaffold. His first major work, *Zeal examined*, was a significant contribution to the 1662 debate on liberty of conscience. His sympathies are wide, and his tightly organised argument tackles the restrictive proposals coming from the Independent ministers, demonstrating that the magistrate should not punish even idolaters for false worship. What is striking is his open dependence on Scripture both in his plea for freedom of study and debate (against a hypocritical conformity) and in its solid use of Scripture itself on every page. It is likely that it is this book which inspired Milton's sonnet, ending

> Therefore on thy firm hand Religion leans
> In peace, and reckons thee her eldest son.[36]

His second most significant book, *The retired man's Meditations* (1655), presents Vane's complex world view, derived from his extensive study of the Bible, and especially the New Testament (he quotes the Epistles most frequently). These 'meditations' show Vane wrestling with contemporary problems, especially the issues of self-interest, hypocrisy and apostasy raised by the creation of the Protectorate. Vane arrived at an assurance that he possessed an unique insight into the Bible, which would enable him to reconcile all controversies, theological and political. Like *Zeal*, the pages of these *Meditations* are thick with italic Bible quotations.

It seems clear that, like many people at the time, Vane was most familiar with KJV, but used Geneva Bibles – in discussing 1 Corinthians 13, for example, he always uses Geneva's word 'love' and not KJV's 'charity'; and at Philippians 1:23 he echoes Geneva in expressing his desire to depart and be with Christ 'which is best of all' (KJV has 'which is far better').

Vane's third major work, *A Healing Question* (1656) makes a good example of the new complexities of the political scene in the later 1650s, and the increasing difficulty of using the Bible as a base. Christopher Hill put the matter squarely: 'Twenty years of frenzied discussion had shown that text-swapping and text-distortion solved nothing: agreement was not to be reached even among the godly on what exactly the Bible said and meant.'[37] The full title of Vane's book is *A Healing Question propounded and resolved upon the occasion of the late public and seasonable call to HUMILIATION in order to the Love and Union of the Honest Party, and with a desire to apply Balsam to the wound before it become incurable.* Amid the rising noise of theoretical proposals for getting out of what was becoming a swamp, like those from Marchmont Nedham (for example, *The Excellency of a Free State*, 1656) and James Harrington (for example, *The Commonwealth of Oceana* also 1656), Vane was practical, and hence considered dangerous, his title as well as his contents touching the nerve of Cromwell's policy of 'healing and settling'. Vane, concerned that the army leadership was an unelected government, looked for a new kind of republic, still godly, but recognising responses to the apparent divine withdrawal, beginning with self-denial, humility, confession, repentance and love,

> instead of war and wrath, to cast themselves down before the Lord, who is the father of all . . . who expected to have been served by them with reverence and godly fear, for our God is a consuming fire –[38]

– the last twelve words being a direct quotation from Hebrews 12:28–9. His rhetoric in *A Healing Question* is disconcertingly double, being at the same time the voice of reason and moderation, and of a prophet declaring the fiery word of the Lord. The Scripture-based political exuberance of the 1640s has gone. The Bible as a basis for national English Christian government is too contradictory. Significantly, Vane's punning title means both 'matter' and 'query'. For all his apparent assurance, Vane is revealing a crumbling foundation. Christopher Hill recalled Marx's words, 'Cromwell and the English people had borrowed speech, passions and illusions from the Old Testament . . . When the bourgeois transformation had been accomplished, Locke supplanted Habakkuk.'[39] Locke, a good Protestant Christian, was, like other philosophers and theologians, concerned, as one of his treatises expounds, with *The Reasonableness of Christianity*: he wanted to end citation of 'scattered sentences in Scripture-language, accommodated to our notions and prejudices'.[40] Nevertheless, 'he made computations from Daniel with a view to dating the end of the world'.[41] Isaac Newton spent a great deal of time on millennarian studies, giving his mind, over several decades, to writing a commentary on the Book of Daniel. In other words, the new 'scientific' challenge did not make the Bible go away.

THOMAS HOBBES

Hobbes found reasons to question the coherence of the Bible. At the centre of controversy all his life, he is still, even now, surrounded by enemies. As in his own day, critics find in him nothing but 'Atheism, licentiousness and despotism. Pious opinion has always been against him, and ever since he wrote he has been denounced from the pulpit.'[42] Of all his many works in his long life (born in the year of the Armada, he died in 1679 at ninety-one), it is his *Leviathan* (1651) that attracts the most vilification, from the defenders of liberty, of Englishness, of mankind (and of the Deity Himself, Who might be thought to be able to look after Himself). Since Hobbes argued for the complete subordination of church government to the civil power, all the religious parties were against him. His absolutism offended everybody, logically based on the only certitudes that could be claimed, matters demonstrable like mathematics. Hobbes was denounced as a heretic, and *Leviathan* attacked in Parliament as a blasphemous book. Particularly vociferous denunciation came for his summing up of the claim of any organised spiritual power to political dominion. 'The papacy,' he wrote, 'is no other than the ghost of the deceased Roman Empire, sitting crowned upon the grave thereof.'[43] Hobbes is still denounced: the attacks have not lessened. Yet two things need to be noted: first, that, accused even of blasphemy, he was not arrested and burned; he was allowed to publish, without molestation, further attacks on accepted theology. Second, unlike most of his enemies, he is still read. Absolutism is out of fashion, but the stating of the case has never been better done.

Like Locke, Hobbes wrote in the new clear English prose, the usual medium for new writing of any kind. At the foundation of the Royal Society, the primary body in Europe for scientific research, more than a dozen years before Hobbes's death, the first sub-committee appointed, given the task of designing a simple English prose to record scientific experiments, could look to him. To take an example: here is Hobbes, in part 3 chapter 33 of *Leviathan*, headed 'Of the number, antiquity, scope, authority, and interpreters of the Books of Holy Scripture':

> Who were the original writers of the several Books of Holy Scripture, has not been made evident by any sufficient testimony of other history, which is the only proof of matter of fact; Nor can be, by any arguments of natural reason: for reason serves only to convince the truth, not of fact, but, of consequence. The light therefore that must guide us in this question, must be that which is held out unto us from the books themselves: and this light, though it show us not the writer of every book, yet it is not unuseful to give us knowledge of the time, wherein they were written.[44]

The content and authority of the Bible had to be part of Hobbes's matter. The Bible takes its place with, for example, Greek mythology, in supplying him with illustration, though he finds such ancient material vain and superstitious.[45] He fairly frequently quotes from KJV to support a point. As an example of a subject who was honoured by his sovereign, Hobbes uses Mordecai and quotes (probably from memory) Esther 6:11: 'Thus shall it be done to him that the King will honour.'

Hobbes, however, was a man of his time in that he believed that a right reading of the Bible would tend to support his sometimes unorthodox opinions. Dreams or other supernatural explanations of events he counters with natural ones.[46] He seem to be in opposition to supernatural agency. In part 1 chapter 8, however, he uses the Bible as a weapon in his armoury, in his discussion of the question of madness, by way of his elaboration of what he thinks is meant in the Bible by the word 'spirit'.[47] He points out that we are not to look to the Bible for scientific answers:

> Whether the earth's or sun's motion make the day and night: or whether the exorbitant actions of man, proceed from passion, or from the devil, so we worship him not, it is all one, as to our obedience, and subjection to God Almighty; which is the thing for which the Scripture is written.[48]

Hobbes can help to give a balanced view of later seventeenth-century Bible-reading in England, which is not all saturated by KJV. One of the surprising aspects of *Leviathan*, given that it is full of anti-Catholic arguments, is Hobbes's regular use of the Vulgate. It seems to be in the forefront of his mind. Often he will quote a phrase or word from the Vulgate in passing as if to lend authority to his argument. He has a worrying tendency to treat the Vulgate as if it were the original. Discussing the words in Exodus 19:5, Hobbes says that the best translation of the verse is 'Then ye shall be a peculiar people to me, for all the earth is mine; and ye shall be unto me a sacerdotal kingdom, and unholy nation.' Hobbes takes trouble to analyse the origins of the word 'peculiar', which he finds in the New Testament the best translation of the Greek. He quotes the 'Geneva French' version which, with KJV, has nothing of 'sacerdotal': yet he prefers that word in Exodus, supporting his preference with 1 Peter 2:9, which is 'a royal priesthood' in KJV, but '*sacerdotium regale*' in the Vulgate. Thus we are left with the rather bizarre situation of an unorthodox Protestant preferring the rendering 'sacerdotal kingdom' for a verse the original language of which he cannot understand, simply because it accords with his own views and brings the verse into line with one in the Vulgate New Testament. 'It is strange that someone as gifted in the use of English as Hobbes should want to use such a horrible word as "sacerdotal".[49] To trace the origin of all the biblical citations in *Leviathan* would be daunting indeed: it is calculated that there are 657 of them.[50]

Hobbes gives evidence of considerable thought about the matter of translation of the Bible, which makes him very much a philosopher of his time. He was in advance of all the English translations available to him in that he preferred 'Spirit' to 'Ghost', as in part 3 and chapter 24 he writes.

How we came to translate *spirits*, by the word *ghosts*, which signifieth nothing, neither in heaven, nor earth, but the imaginary inhabitants of man's brain, I examine not: but this I say, the word *spirit* in the text sig-nifieth no such thing; but either properly a real *substance*, or metaphor-ically, some extraordinary *ability* or *affection* of the mind, or of the body.[51]

MILTON AND BUNYAN

Two great English writers in the later seventeenth century, for whom the Bible was paramount, both strictly Noncomformists, had contrasting experience of privilege and education.

John Milton was a Cambridge scholar whose very great learning led him to high originality, significantly expressed in English as well as Latin, and whose great abilities led him to high office in government. He did not touch a poetic form without, as it were, consummating it. His masque *Comus* almost signed off the form; his pastoral 'Lycidas' was the last for nearly a century; his *Samson Agonistes* (an attempt at a Christian-Hebrew-Greek synthesis) was the last regularly performed tragedy by a major poet; his subject and form (minor epic) on an event in the life of Jesus, *Paradise Regained*, were not revisited. He challenged, powerfully, the laws govern-ing human freedoms – of expression and discussion (*Areopagitica*), of divorce, and others. He was much travelled, and a man of power. He wrote the greatest English epic poem, *Paradise Lost*.

John Bunyan, an uneducated tinker (a mender of kettles and pans), barely left the fields of his native Bedfordshire. After a powerful conver-sion, compellingly recounted in his *Grace Abounding to the Chief of Sinners* (the title tells all), his passion for the Gospel led him to preaching the uncompromising heart of the New Testament message. His refusal to be silenced caused a long imprisonment. In Bedford jail he wrote the greatest English Christian prose work outside the Bible, with which it was frequently paired for many centuries and in many countries. *The Pilgrim's Progress* is a narrative of spiritual experience *from this World to the Next*, as the title explains. Its Plain Style is cunningly made to express the worldly, shifting, fashionable ways of the world as well as an iron-strong interior spiritual drama.

John Milton

English Renaissance poets tended to be men of affairs. However apparently remote from daily existence the poetic world they created – a rural Arthurian fantasy of Aristotelian moral chivalry, for example – they moved the wheels of national life. So Spenser helped to govern Ireland: Shakespeare was a successful businessman in commercial theatres.

John Milton, the most prodigiously learned, the most polymathic, and in several respects the most significant, English poet, was deeply involved in the politics of the Civil War and the Commonwealth. He was, from 1649 until his blindness in 1651, Oliver Cromwell's Secretary of Foreign Tongues, a post which gave him access to policy and executive decisions especially in foreign matters. His greatest significance in the history of English letters was his *Paradise Lost*. Classically, a nation was judged by the double achievement of having a powerful myth of its foundation, and having the proper high poetic language in which to tell it. John Skelton, at the court of Henry VIII, would have made much merriment out of the very thought of an English epic. In the generation after Skelton, several books of the *Aeneid* were translated into a rather curious English blank verse, which was a step forward.[52] Belonging to another generation after that, Spenser was on the high path: his *Faerie Queene* most imaginatively began to fulfil the criteria, but was only half done; and for elevation, a distancing language, Spenser, though writing English, had to depend on frequent archaisms, condemned by both Sidney and Jonson: words long outgrown, like the ever-present 'eke' and, in the second line of the poem, 'Y cladd'.

In the middle of the seventeenth century, John Milton reached the summit. *Paradise Lost* is, fully, an epic, in English. Englishness, at home and, over the oceans, settling its colonies, could be celebrated. The English language could now reach the highest, Virgilian, levels. In ten, and then twelve, books (the latter the Virgilian norm), a story could fill itself out to its grandest shape. In Milton's double achievement, England as the cultural centre of Europe had arrived: what had been a fantasy of the unattainable in the 1570s was reality in the 1670s.

Three things are immediately striking. First, in the 1670s, the Bible has not gone away from English life. Second, the subject is even grander than a national history: it is an account of the human condition. Third, the high language, after the classical era comparable only with that of Dante, is an English that heavily uses Latin constructions, like the opening six-line syntactical inversion, and vocabulary, as in 'assert eternal providence'.

Milton took a while to find his subject. He can be watched thinking about a hero for an epic. For some time, among other heroes, he considered King Arthur as a mythical figure already developed enough to stand for the nation. He settled on

> . . . man's first disobedience, and the fruit
> Of that forbidden tree, whose mortal taste
> Brought death into the word, and all our woe,

as

> Things unattempted yet in prose or rhyme.[53]

This is, in the largest way, and obviously, a biblical theme. More subtly, so is the language. Latinisms, with their own strong Bible echoes, are an essential part of Milton's verse; but English can now be used with confidence over a wide spectrum. Indeed, there is a Tyndalian effect of Saxon monosyllables ('and all our woe'), and Saxon phrases ('brought death into the world / With loss of Eden, till one greater man . . . / That shepherd, who first taught the chosen seed, / In the beginning how the heavens and earth / Rose . . . / And chiefly thou . . . that dost prefer . . . / the upright heart and pure . . .'[54])

Milton was a scholar of several cultures, including Hebrew. The Jewish commentators and Christian Fathers gave him the theology of the Fall of Man.[55] He knew the Anglo-Saxon poem, 'The Fall of the Angels' (see above, chapter 3, p. ••). He knew his Vulgate very well, and often quoted it in his prose, and echoed it in his verse. The biggest source, however, was the English Bible. His poem is a glorious poetic elaboration of the short biblical story, in the traditions of the Old and Middle English romances, of far-flung stories made from scraps of the Latin Bible.

> So thoroughly is this elaboration a part of our heritage that we are surprised to discover that Genesis does not say that Satan tempted Eve, does not even mention Satan anywhere in the fifty chapters . . . Nor is there any hint that Paradise was on a mountain.[56]

Milton makes his own imaginative set-pieces, like the council in Hell in the first two Books, the journey of Satan in Book 2, the connubial bliss of Adam and Eve in Paradise in Book 4, the war in Heaven in Book 5, and so on. Now, however, the English Bible is everywhere in his poem. The narratives and dialogue – even the marmoreal expository narratives of Raphael in Books 5 to 8, including the stilted exchanges of the Father with the Son – are written with a pen dipped in the ink of the Tyndalian biblical style; to be fanciful, they are composed in the musical keys of English, painted in the colours of English. Behind KJV and the Geneva Bibles was the Hebrew, in the manner of Tyndale, who is quoted, probably unwittingly (as in 'Let there be light'[57]). Milton was a formidable scholar of patristic exegesis;[58] but Tyndale's Satan as sophisticated man-about-town, serpent-about-Paradise, who chats up Eve, calling her 'Sir', and dismisses the real effects of the Temptation with the airy 'Tush, ye shall not die',[59] is there in the knowing nature of Milton's Satan, though marvellously enriched.

> Wonder not, sovereign mistress, if perhaps
> Thou canst, who art sole wonder, much less arm
> Thy looks, the heaven of mildness, with disdain,
> Displeased that I approach thee thus, and gaze
> Insatiate, I thus single, nor have feared
> Thy awful brow, more awful thus retired.
> Fairest resemblance of thy maker fair,
> Thee all things living gaze on, all things thine
> By gift, and thy celestial beauty adore
> With ravishment beheld . . .[60]

How could a girl resist?

But this charmer is not what he seems. There are things the girl should know. He has been, among other things, a cormorant sitting on the tree of life devising death; before that a voyager through space to Hell's gates, opened for him by Sin and Death, to be directed by Chaos to destroy the clean new world; before that a leader in the debate in Hell about how to annihilate God;[61] and before that

> Him the almighty power
> Hurled headlong flaming from the ethereal sky
> With hideous ruin and combustion down
> To bottomless perdition, there to dwell
> In adamantine chains and penal fire,
> Who durst defy the omnipotent to arms.[62]

The sources of such a passage are many, but include much that is biblical. 'I saw Satan, like lightning, fall down from heaven,' said Jesus (Luke 10:18). That is the Geneva–Tomson reading. It is more vividly immediate than KJV's 'I beheld Satan as lightning fall from heaven'. The Geneva–Tomson margin has: 'Paul placeth the devil and his angels, in the air, at Ephes. 6:12 and he is said to be cast down from thence by force when his power is abolished by the voice of the Gospel.' The Geneva–Tomson notes are also suggestive at 2 Peter 2:4, where 'God spared not the Angels that had sinned, but cast them down into hell . . . into chains of darkness': the Geneva–Tomson notes 'Bound them with darkness as it were with chains' and cross-references to Job 4:18 and the note there about the imperfections of angels. The 'everlasting chains' are parallel in Jude 6.

Milton's epic voice is, obviously, classical in inspiration. His mind is exceptionally alert to Renaissance achievements in various genres and languages. The wider canvas of *Paradise Lost*, however, takes its colours from Revelation and other Apocalypses (Daniel; Mark 13) and a treasury of vivid images and ideas from from the poetic and prophetic books of the Old Testament.

The moment of the Fall is memorably told:

> So saying, her rash hand in evil hour
> Forth reaching to the fruit, she plucked, she ate:
> Earth felt the wound, and nature from her seat
> Sighing through all her works gave signs of woe,
> That all was lost. Back to the thicket slunk
> The guilty serpent . . .[63]

This is a voice that had not been heard before. Not only poetically: the cosmic theology, if one may so express it, is here newly stated in high colour and full drama. The heart of this abundant epic in all its wonderful poetry is Calvin's sovereignty of God, humanity's disobedience and depravity, and the mercy and grace of God in redemption through Christ. Calvin, of course; and Augustine before; and centrally the New Testament; and at the core Paul's Epistles. The triumphant acceptability of Milton's epic disguised its radical face, that rulers and councils betray and deceive: all must be of God.[64]

John Bunyan

As a young man, Bunyan could hardly have been more opposite to John Milton, while remaining English. Milton as a precocious boy was the cultivated and wealthy 'lady of Christ's' (that is, Christ's College, Cambridge). Unhappy Bunyan began two and a half year's service in a local company in the Parliamentary army in the Civil War, at sixteen, in 1644 – or so it is said. The surname was deceptively common in Bedforshire at that time, and, as a Bunyan scholar remarked,

> guesswork builds upon the shifting ands of guesswork, and the building is not helped by the fact that references to the passage of time in *Grace Abounding* are frequent but vague.[65]

It was, in its way, his education: he was impressed by the radical freedom of speech in the New Model Army. Demobilised, he married in the direst rural poverty. His new wife, however, brought with her one possession, a copy of a small book, Arthur Dent's immensely popular *The plain man's path-way to heaven. Wherein every man may clearly see, whether he shall be saved or damned. Set forth dialogue wise* (1601, but with 25 editions to 1640)[66], a book which clearly deeply affected the future writer of *The Pilgrim's Progress*. Scripture, his young wife's influence, and the mercy of Providence, as he recounts in *Grace Abounding*, brought him through a crisis in which his inner spiritual enemies assailed him with voices and blows, and converted him from the foul-mouthed adolescent he had been into an upright, Scripture-loving believer.

Compared with the international scholarship of Milton's mind, an account of Bunyan's life as a rural Nonconformist has little intellectual colour. He lived in Bedfordshire. He became sought after locally as a preacher. He refused to undertake not to preach. A few months after the Restoration of Charles II, a local magistrate jailed him. He was in prison for a total of twelve years. He became pastor of the Bedford Separatist Church. He died in 1688 just as the persecution of Nonconformists was ending.[67]

In prison and elsewhere he wrote, a great deal, almost sixty books.[68] He wrote mostly in prose, but with some fine lyric verse, like the Shepherd Boy's song in the Valley of Humiliation in the Second Part of *The Pilgrim's Progress*, 'He that is down needs fear no fall', or Valiant-for-Truth's song, also in the Second Part, which is loved as a hymn, 'Who would true valour see'.[69] He wrote works of genius.

These books were in an English Protestant tradition.[70] *Grace Abounding* (1666) is spiritual autobiography. Bunyan wrote an English of common speech: the wayfarers in *Pilgrim's Progress* talk to each other quite ordinarily of extraordinary matters, another part of the Protestant tradition, seen first in Tyndale's Gospels.

Tyndale had made the parables of Jesus clear to read and hear. The men and women in them leap from the page with vividness and economy. The parables teach about a spiritual world that is other, the opposite of commonplace, though commonly accessible. So Bunyan's people talk of salvation and sanctification through faith while, for example, knitting at the cottage door in the sun.[71]

Above all, Bunyan's writing is made of Scripture. His men and women talk familiarly of all parts of Scripture in support of what they are saying or doing. Bunyan's writing is made of Scripture in the sense that Scripture is special. Bunyan's own narrative voice is not 'biblical'. It is everyday. His Scripture references stand out like sultanas in a scone. His men and women speak of Scripture together because it is their shared and urgent concern.

The Pilgrim's Progress contains many characters who are bored by Scripture, or mocking of it, or so hostile to it as to gang together in the middle of Vanity Fair, and put to trial, and then burn, the good Faithful. Christian and his fellows take the Bible truths into a real, hostile, world – which can still use the Bible against them. Bunyan was described by a clergyman who was later Bishop of Gloucester as 'a turbulent spirit . . . a natural brute beast' who should be 'taken and destroyed', words from 2 Peter 2:12.[72] In Bunyan's unsophisticated allegory of his Pilgrim's progress, his characters, in their hypocrisy or self-deceit, have names now more familiar from the comedies at the exactly contemporary, but enclosed, court of Charles II. Bunyan was as far away from that as could be thought. His Worldly Wiseman is close in labelling to Congreve's Lady Wishfort. Bunyan's By-Ends has a wife who is 'Lady Faining's daughter'. Bunyan's satirical observation is not for a mocking court, sneering at the unfashionable (and rural), but in the stream of the oldest country folk-narrative, as in the moral anecdotes of medieval preaching. Giant Despair and Apollyon are figures from ancient, and pagan, tales. Like their archetypal ancestors, what they do and say is immediately familiar. Bunyan's Greatheart we hope to have as a friend; his Ignorance we have met in a pub.

Bunyan's story of his Pilgrim, made of KJV, is in the full doctrine of an ordinary Christian's biblical engagement in the warfare between good and evil. Those doctrines were from Calvin, before him from Augustine, and before him from the New Testament. In Christian's journey, Calvinism, not hardened into rigidity and harsh repression, is dynamic, creative, the maker of adventure, particularly the cumulative discovery of truths. That the end of the journey is fulfilment is in the most famous passage, from the conclusion of the Second Part, the death of Mr Valiant-for-Truth, with its quotations from 1 Corinthians 15:55:

> When the day that he must go hence was come many accompanied him to the River side, into which, as he went, he said, '*Death, where is thy sting?*' And as he went down deeper, he said, '*Grave where is thy victory?*' So he passed over, and the trumpets sounded for him on the other side.[73]

That is a justly admired high point. More run-of-the-mill moments abound in discoveries for Christian. Evangelist says, early in the book,

> This Legality therefore is not able to free thee from thy burden. No man was as yet ever rid of his burden by him, no, nor ever is like to be: ye cannot be justified by the works of the law; for by the deeds of the law no man living can be rid of his burden: therefore Mr Worldly-Wiseman is an alien, and Mr Legality a cheat, and for his son Civility, notwithstanding his simpering looks, he is but an hypocrite, and cannot help thee.[74]

The first five lines are a neat summary of the Epistle to the Romans. Bunyan's first readers would know that. Some chapters ago, in commenting on the limited Bible reference of medieval stained glass or drama, it was noted that one cannot make a drama out of the Epistle to the Romans. Bunyan did precisely that.

Chapter 28

THE CONSOLIDATION OF KJV, 1660–1710

THE ELDER SON OF CHARLES I was invited back from exile to become King Charles II. That restoration of the monarchy in May 1660 brought with it a national determination that Britain should never again suffer a civil war. It was successful. In the late eighteenth and early nineteenth centuries England remained stable when across the Channel civil revolution was much in the air. The nation wished now for solid reconstruction. Charles II, as well as personal charm, intelligence and wit, had many personal faults, as was notorious: but, a new quality in the Stuarts, he not only understood, he liked the people over whom he reigned.

Charles returned to London amid such scenes of rejoicing that he is said to have wondered why he had stayed away for so long. Though the 'merry monarch' was officially praised everywhere, he did not return to the same constitutional situation as his father. The monarch still had power, but from this time forward, in a steady and continuous movement away from absolute power, the sovereign was constitutionally more under the sway of Parliament.

Consolidation meant a return to former fixed values. An early Parliament restored the supremacy of the Anglican Church. Action was taken against non-Anglicans, which, as well as Roman Catholics, included Baptists, Congregationalists, Presbyterians, Quakers and other Protestant sects. The new Clarendon Code limited any potential influence these might have: they were silenced by laws requiring them to agree with every word of the Book of Common Prayer, and forbidding them to hold a Government office or attend university. (The latter law was changed only in 1827, at the foundation of University College London, which for the first time allowed Nonconformists, Jews, Roman Catholics – and women – to study for, and receive, degrees.) Between one and two thousand Dissenting ministers were forced out of their posts.

One of the most visible signs of firm Anglican restoration was the re-establishment of the Book of Common Prayer, now set in the form which was alone legal until the late twentieth century. There were introduced in 1662 several hundred alterations, changing obsolete phrases, transferring the source for all the Bible readings, except the Psalms, which remained from Coverdale, to KJV, giving that version more recognition (though according to *OED* it was not determinedly named the 'Authorised Version' until 1824). New directions were given to the minister, and the tendency of the revision can be seen in the change from 'Bishops, pastors and ministers' to 'Bishops, priests and deacons'. New State services, particularly those for remembering 'King Charles the martyr' and the Restoration, joined the revised older service commemorating the Gunpowder Treason of 1605. New collects were introduced. The revision was usually towards elaboration of ritual.

This '1662 Prayer Book' was richly and frequently issued. In the hundred years from 1660, some 350 fresh editions were published, about twenty-five of them with full-page engravings, sometimes lavish. These illustrated Bible events throughout the Church Calendar – the angels appearing to the shepherds, Christ riding into Jerusalem, and so on – followed by pictures of saints. About half the illustrated editions have also, against the appropriate services, an engraving of the wicked Guy Fawkes under the eye of God, on his way to blow up the Houses of Parliament, and pictures of the martyrdom of Charles I and the Restoration of Charles II. In spite of infrequent attempts at further revision of '1662', it remained unchanged for three hundred years. An attempt at revision under William and Mary in 1689 did not succeed. A new Scottish liturgy was accepted by Parliament in 1764, an American Prayer Book in 1789. English reform of '1662' was discussed urgently in the nineteenth century. In 1859 the Gunpowder Treason and Stuart services were dropped. An Irish Prayer Book was accepted in 1877 and the Scottish Prayer Book in 1912.

CONTINUAL REPRINTING OF KJV

It is no surprise to find that the period 1660–1710 was, in terms of English Bibles, a time of continual reprinting of KJV and nothing else. The conformity of these editions is striking. It was also the one long period in British history of the Bible when no new translations were attempted at all. In those fifty years, there were 237 separate editions, all of KJV: in the fifty years before 1660 there had been 369 editions, including other translations.[1] Now the new need for an Augustan universality of truth left no room for original experiment. Not for nothing had Newton's work on gravity, published in 1682, shown an ordered universe, banishing the goblins on earth and the demons in the sky. The Bible had joined the Ancients, Homer, Virgil and Horace especially, as the educated man's reasonable authority.

Though the English Bible had in these years of Restoration, and for some years after, several effects to which I shall come shortly, there are only a few publishing deviations of any interest. Oddities include a reprint, perhaps in 1700, of a New Testament, perhaps first issued in 1659 or 1660, in shorthand.[2] Five of the KJVs of the whole Bible seem to have come from Amsterdam (or at least from abroad); it is informative about Protestant communities abroad that two New Testaments, dated 1700, were printed in Amsterdam in parallel columns of English KJV and Dutch, and English KJV and the French Geneva version.[3] 'Solomon's Proverbs' were twice printed (first in 1666) from KJV, arranged alphabetically, as the title-page put it, 'for help of Memory. With an additional Collection of other scripture-Proverbs out of the Old and New Testament': in English and Latin, this became a school book. Here the Bible is in its school-desk moral-instruction garb, in which unexciting clothing it will remain for nearly a hundred years. It is the opposite pole from a book imparting the agonies of the Crucifixion, or from a religious experience which can turn the world upside down.

In 1672, and again in 1679, there appeared editions of KJV with Geneva Bible notes; the latter being probably the earliest English Bible with dates in the margins, calculated from the Creation, so that Job is dated 2400 and the Nativity 4000. (Not until 1701 was a Bible issued with dates divided either side of the Nativity, being either 'Before Christ' or 'Anno Domini'.) This 1679 edition was also the second printed at Oxford, 'at the theatre' (that is, the new Sheldonian, where Oxford University Press was housed). These Oxford Bibles were sold in London by four booksellers, of whom the most industrious was Thomas Guy. He contracted with the University of Oxford and made out of selling Bibles a personal fortune, enlarged by successful speculation: in 1722, two years before his death, he founded and endowed the famous Hospital in Southwark known by his name.

PLOTS

Between 1665 and 1667, three disasters, beyond the sovereign's control, struck the nation – all three events are described in the *Diaries* of Samuel Pepys. In 1665 bubonic plague returned (for the last time), bringing rapid death to tens of thousands in London alone. Daniel Defoe's *Journal of the Plague Year*, published in 1722, though fiction (Defoe was five or six at the time of the plague) still gives a feeling account of the many ways in which the city had to struggle to survive, with a sense of divine punishment arriving, hovering over, and then leaving, the city. In 1666 a fire at a baker's in Pudding Lane went out of control among the close-packed wooden buildings and, raging for three days, destroyed a large part of the city. It is said that the ground was too hot to walk upon for two weeks afterwards. In 1667, in the Medway in the mouth of the Thames, the Dutch attacked and humiliated the English fleet at home.

Firmly within the sovereign's hands, however, was his religious policy. His support of Catholicism and alliances with the French King Louis xiv (including for both some secret treaties), and attempts to ensure the succession of his militantly Catholic brother James, all roused both Protestant anger and Protestant elaboration of plots against them. At several times in Charles's reign the mood in the country was volatile enough for risings to be about to happen against the Royalists, with civil war a too-familiar danger. The most potentially damaging revolt came from the Protestant Duke of Monmouth, Charles's eldest and favourite illegitimate child (he had at least fourteen: Catherine, his queen, bore no children). A few months after James's succession in 1685, Monmouth landed at Lyme Regis in Dorset and proclaimed himself king.

Militarily, there was little problem. The rising was brutally put down, and Monmouth was executed. Politically, he had had a history of defiance of his father. In the autumn of 1678, anxiety over the succession and the fear of royal methods of maintaining authority were the cause of the successes of the newly named 'Whig' party, supporting Monmouth, and led by the Earl of Shaftesbury. Shaftesbury had originally supported the Crown, and then had become a member of Cromwell's council of state, and had then trimmed his sails so carefully as to become Charles ii's Chancellor of the Exchequer. When the news leaked out of the king's secret Treaty of Dover, in which he promised to restore the Roman Catholic faith to England with the help of French troops and money, Shaftesbury went over to the opposition. A 'Popish Plot' of Jesuit conspiracy was discovered; it brought to the surface all the nation's fears and hatreds. The plot was gradually discredited, but the chief issue in the middle of 1681 became that of Monmouth as heir. Shaftesbury, thought in July 1681 to be the inventor of the plot as a means of promoting Monmouth's claims to the throne, was committed to the Tower on a charge of high treason, his trial set for the end of November. Party feelings ran very high.

ABSALOM AND ACHITOPHEL

The tension was reduced by – and this is a surprising word – laughter. More, it was biblical laughter, surely an oxymoron. Just before Shaftesbury's trial (and release by a packed jury), the poet John Dryden in mid-November 1681 published his *Absalom and Achitophel*. A long mock-epic poem of 1,030 lines in heroic couplets arguing in favour of a legitimate heir to the throne, Charles's brother James in spite of his Catholicism, it ran through at least three London editions in four months.

Dryden's base is his love of steadiness and order, well conveyed in the coffee-house conversational tone inside the regular beat of the couplets. He tells the colourful story, from 2 Samuel 15–19, of the rebellion against David of his son, Absalom, who was fatally advised by the senior courtier Achitophel. The melding of Hebrew and English history through the names of the kings was no new thing: and at the Restoration, many preachers and poets had drawn the parallel between David and Charles, and for a slippery, treasonable senior courtier the name of Achitophel had been used by the opponents of Charles I. Two things, both devastating in effect, were new in Dryden's poem: the grand scale, and the wit. Dryden enriched his parallels between English and Hebrew history into a wonderfully textured large tapestry showing both. The more one knows of the details of English life in the late 1670s and early 1680s, the more one is enchanted to find which characters appear, under such appropriate biblical names. The more one knows the English Bible, the more one finds in Dryden's poem. Not only are Charles and Monmouth and all their associates made to fit the biblical story in such rich detail; far beyond that, and beyond discussion about how politically effective the poem was, Dryden's assumption that readers knew their Bibles so well that they could follow everything in the poem is to modern minds remarkable.

John Dryden, fifty years old in 1681, had by then made his name as a poet (he was the second Poet Laureate), essayist and playwright – making tragedy and comedy, and adaptations (some would say, maulings) of Shakespeare. His brilliance in all he touched roused envious attacks from rivals and the subjects of his satirical thrusts, attacks which included a murderously intended assault (just possibly misdirected) one dark December night in Rose Alley, Covent Garden. For many English poets beside Milton, the dream was again to write an English epic. The best that could be managed was mock-epic, all the high ingredients used with solemn seriousness to cause laughter. The earlier interest in 'character' writing came to a special fruition. The 'heroic', that is, epic, couplet was perfect for this. Iambic pentameters rhyming in pairs allow an admirable economy, and a final rhyming stress which can be loaded with wit. 'Zimri', the Duke of Buckingham, is, among other things,

> Beggar'd by Fools, whom still he found too late:
> He had his jest, and they had his estate.

Just before, he,

> Stiff in Opinions, always in the wrong;
> Was everything by starts, and nothing long:
> But, in the course of one revolving Moon,
> Was Chymist, Fidler, States-Man, and Buffoon.[4]

The surface, cleverly accented to make a speaking voice, has a running wit. Most of the point, however, lies beneath. Buckingham, George Villiers, had been Charles's chief minister, and was now a prominent Whig, working with Shaftesbury. His 'character' is here engaging. The force is felt only if the reader knows about Zimri. His story is told in a few verses of 1 Kings 16. KJV editions of the time have the page-heading 'Zimri's treason'. Zimri seized the throne of Israel by murdering the king Elah 'as he was in Tirzah drinking himself drunk' as KJV has it (Tyndale had 'drinking of strong drink': KJV is excellent). In a short and bloody reign of seven days he wiped out Elah's entire family. His rival Omri (important as the father of Ahab) had popular support, and in a coup seized Tirzah: Zimri committed suicide by burning the palace down over him.

To read Dryden's poem as if it were only darkly amusing, like something by Noël Coward, is quite to miss the savagery. Beneath the pleasure in the match of contemporary and biblical are harsh truths that must be learned. By making him 'Zimri', Dryden is saying that Villiers, if he came out of his lordly dilettantism and settled to anything, could be wildly dangerous. Dryden's first readers would not need, and did not get, explanatory notes. Twenty-first-century readers are rarely so knowledgeable: so, like an animal species on earth, the point has become extinct. Even distinguished Dryden scholars today get Zimri wrong.[5] Zimri would have been known as well as Buckingham, from common Bible knowledge, from sermons, from general references in the air (as people today know who Macbeth is).

Dryden wrote for readers, furthermore, who would not need telling that Zimri had nothing whatever to do with David and Absalom, his story being over a hundred years later in Israel's history: he could assume knowledge of the whole Bible. Expounding all the dozens of general Bible references in the poem, from Adam and Eve to the Acts of the Apostles, quite apart from the twenty or so figures in the Absalom story, makes a long document. It is a tale full of quirky life. For example, Aaron, who was with Moses on Mount Sinai receiving the Commandments, had a son Nadab, who was later consecrated priest, and on that very day perished (for offering 'strange fire', Leviticus 10:1, Numbers 3:4). Line 575 of *Absalom and Achitophel* is

> And canting *Nadab* let Oblivion damn

(a line in which the short 'a' sounds around 'Nadab' are held apart by the four beats in another key, 'Oblivion', a word itself tied with 'b' and 'n' to 'canting', 'Nadab' and 'damn'). Nadab is Lord Howard, formerly a sectarian preacher, said while in the Tower to have taken the sacrament using hot ale and apple-pulp instead of wine: so Dryden completes the couplet

> Who made new porridge for the Paschal Lamb.

'Porridge' is a 'low' word, indecorous for the act of communion with the Passover sacrifice (KJV at Mark 14:12 had 'when they killed the passover', but Tyndale in 1526 had 'when they offered the paschal lamb'). In the poem, Lord Howard's action, on the way to damnation not by a grand heresy trial but by oblivion, is much diminished by the word. Moreover, 'porridge' did not just mean warm oatmeal or a vegetable stew: from the 1640s it had taken the sense of something unsubstantial, a hotchpotch, used by opponents as a nickname for Orders of Service in the Prayer Book. Samuel Pepys on Sunday 24 August 1662 recorded:

> . . . they tell me that there hath been a disturbance in a church in Friday-street: a great many young [people] knotting together and crying out "porridge" often and seditiously in the church; and took the Common Prayer-Book, they say, away: and some say did tear it. But it is a thing which appears to me very ominous.[6]

Dryden's 'porridge' is thick with meaning, damning enough for a sectarian preacher: but we must see what has happened to the two words in KJV associated with Nadab, the mysterious and numinous 'strange fire'; they could have stood for outstanding preaching, but for Howard they are deflated to 'porridge'; and worse, the wholly unexciting 'new porridge'. Dryden was master of the craft of destroying by cool insulting dismissal.

The second Book of Samuel tells how David was made king in Hebron (as Charles had been in Scotland); he captured the fortress town of Jerusalem, and made it his capital. From there he brilliantly united and governed the country, a glamorous and popular king. He had married, when a young man, one of his predecessor Saul's daughters, Michal; she had no children. But David had many concubines, as befitted a great king: while in Hebron, for example, he had six sons by six women (and an unknown number of daughters, which did not count in the history). One of those sons was Absalom.

Dryden's mock-epic skill was unmatched. In telling not of rebellion by angels in Heaven, as Milton had, but of politicians in England, his problem was the avoidance of offence either to the king or his adored son, while sharply correcting both. So his portrait of David is, like that of the biblical narrator, affectionate. In his opening 'character', Dryden's texture suggests the sensuality it is condemning, the caressing of the lines intending to flatter the king into not attending to the criticism. The times before 'Priest-craft' were 'pious'; true for Abraham's Old Testament era, before the Levites, but making a point about Charles's difficulties. The suggestion is of a Golden Age to which Charles properly belongs, rather than the harsh political present, with a great deal contained in the single word 'cursedly':

> In pious times, e'r Priest-craft did begin,
> Before *Polygamy* was made a sin;
> When man, on many, multiplied his kind
> E'r one to one was, cursedly, confined:
> When Nature prompted, and no law deny'd
> Promiscuous use of Concubine and Bride;
> Then *Israel's* Monarch, after Heaven's own heart,
> His vigorous warmth did, variously, impart
> To Wives and Slaves: And, wide as his Command,
> Scatter'd his Maker's Image through the Land.
> *Michal*, of Royal Blood, the Crown did wear,
> A Soil ungratefull to the Tiller's care:
> Not so the rest; for several Mothers bore
> To Godlike *David*, several Sons before.
> But since like slaves his bed they did ascend,
> No true succession could their seed attend.

The admiring tone matches well the praise of David in the biblical history: but Dryden's mock admiration, most delicately done ('his bed they did ascend'), elevates Charles in the wrong sphere, that of bed rather than throne. That also accounts for Monmouth's nature.

> Of all this Numerous Progeny was none
> So Beautifull, so brave as *Absalon*:
> Whether, inspir'd by some diviner Lust,
> His Father got him with a greater Gust;
> Or that his Concious destiny made way
> By manly beauty to Imperiall sway.
> Early in Foreign fields he won Renown,
> With Kings and States ally'd to *Israel's* Crown:
> In Peace the thoughts of War he could remove,
> And seem'd as he were only born for love.[7]

To that last line, suggesting his personal attractiveness as well as the cause of his conception, Monmouth could not object: yet as describing a militant rival to the throne it is damning. Again, a large part of the point is that Dryden's readers would know not only that in revolt Absalom died, but that he died strangely as a result of what was taken to be his vanity. Famous for his charm and beauty, he wore his hair in a new fashion (2 Samuel 14:25–6): fleeing in defeat, he was caught by the hair in the branches of an oak tree and killed (2 Samuel 18:9–14).

BIBLICAL SATIRES

The point of the extent of biblical knowledge among politicians and readers of poems may be elaborated largely: it is sufficient here to show a little of what was present in understanding of the English Bible. For Dryden's, though the best, was by no means the only political satire on biblical themes. The prolific Abraham Cowley, regarded as the foremost poet of his day (he stands first in Samuel Johnson's *Lives of the Poets* of 1781), had published in 1656 his *Davideis, a Sacred Poem on the Troubles of David*, the first four books of an unfinished epic: not a satire, and in clunking unreadable couplets, it still pointed in the right direction. In contrast, Samuel Butler's energetic *Hudibras*, appearing between 1663 and 1678, is certainly a satire, on the 'caterwauling brethren', the 'saints' who helped to overthrow the monarchy; but not directly biblical. It influenced Dryden's *Absalom*, which itself released a swarm of inferior biblical-satirical-mock-epic poems in imitation: some were even occasionally by the poets to whom they were attributed. Grub Street was having a field day, revelling in the rich airs of biblical stories.

One of the most interesting, and least known today, is John Caryll's *Naboth's Vineyard*, published in 1679 – that is, just before Dryden wrote *Absalom*: Dryden not only knew it, but borrowed from it. Caryll was a member of a prominent Roman Catholic family (who appear again in the making of Alexander Pope's *Rape of the Lock* in 1712 and 1714): his poem is 'about' the Popish Plot of 1678. The full title is *Naboth's Vineyard: or, The Innocent Traitor: Copied from the Original of Scripture, in Heroick Verse*. The direction of the story is easy to see – greedy Ahab, wicked Jezebel, the false accusation of treason, the murderous mob – but the identifications are not. Malchus is just about visible as Titus Oates, and Arod is, most damningly in the poem, the Lord Chief Justice; but Ahab and Jezebel are unplaceable, and Naboth is either the whole body of English Catholics, or James, Duke of York. Elijah is Elijah. The couplets can be good:

> Ahab distress'd, bow'd to his Lord and pray'd:
> Ahab victorious, proudly disobey'd. (47–8)

They influenced Dryden, in 'He that commands the judge commands the law' (124) and

> But nature furnish'd him with parts and wit
> For bold attempts and deep intriguing fit. (145–6)

This, much extended and sustained, will become 'the packed sagacity and brazen clangour' of Dryden.[8] Caryll dresses the simple narrative operatically, the speeches being strong arias making one point: the characters speak as if they were in a tragedy by Racine. Whereas for Dryden both the tenor and the vehicle are the English Bible, wittily seen as relevant to everything, even the king's bed, Caryll's poem, except for the outline from 1 Kings 20, is, in fact, unbiblical, and the subject is the single one of the manufacture of political injustice. Interesting as the whole poem is, it makes clear by contrast how deeply permeating is the biblical leaven in Dryden's poem, as he assumes the readers' knowledge right through both Testaments.

WRITING BY NONCONFORMISTS, AND WOMEN

That nothing of any interest happened to the English Bible between the 'glorious AV' of 1611 and the official (and heavy-footed) revision of it in 1881–5 is one of the myths that, in later chapters of this book, will be challenged. Another myth is that everything of any significance that was written between the reigns of Henry VIII and Victoria came from 'the Establishment', from male writers close to the Crown. Understanding that this was not so has grown since the last decades of the twentieth century. That there were outstanding women writers in English in the sixteenth century, whose work has remained not only unedited, but out of print, for four hundred years, would not be guessed from, for example, the relevant volumes in the standard *Oxford History of English Literature*, published from the 1950s. An example of work done later in the twentieth century on educated Tudor women, the volume *Silent But for the Word*, published in 1985,[9] reveals an important point: that educated women were 'permitted' to write, provided that what they wrote had reference to the Bible – commenting on it, or even translating it, as Mary Sidney did her Psalms. Since a great deal still remains out of print, the work of evaluating, and bringing into general knowledge, remains to be done.

Valuable as such a volume is, the impression given is that, with one or two exceptions, women writers were all in the higher reaches of society, the Countess of Pembroke, the Viscountess Falkland (Elizabeth Cary). True enough, these were the women with the leisure as well as the education: but from the mid-sixteenth century the rise of literacy was so rapid, and the sense of a permitted plainness of expression spread so wide, that it will be surprising if the forgotten manuscripts of humbler women with something to say, or even printed books that have escaped the standard bibliographies, are not discovered.[10]

The model might be the second half of the seventeenth century, a time in which it is becoming increasingly known that reading the work of the socially elevated, the Drydens and the Carrylls, was not the only story. More accurately, there was important work which was not related to the court at all, not 'authorised' by demonstrating a shared classical education, and being Anglican and Tory. That Dissenters, and later Nonconformists, wrote, has been incontrovertible for centuries: a look at the two Johns, Milton and Bunyan, shows that. But those two were, it has been understood, anomalies.

The unexpected richness, diversity and sheer value of the books by Dissenters before the political defeats of 1660–2, and Nonconformists' writing (and reading) from 1662, in spite of attempts to silence them, is coming to light. Building on the solid work of Christopher Hill and Geoffrey Nuttall, as examples, has been the scholarship of N. H. Keeble.[11] Richard Baxter's large *corpus* is not unknown, and Edmund Calamy's name might ring a bell: but the scores of other writers have not simply been forgotten – they have been denied, then and later, as being incapable of having any interest whatsoever. Perhaps the presence among them of the name of Daniel Defoe, said to have 500 printed works to his name, might change the viewing-filter a little for some, though not all: his *The Shortest Way with the Dissenters* (1702) is a satirical classic – briefly, they should be shot – which led him to the pillory, heavy fines, and prison. Defoe the Dissenter had, justifiably, a very large popular following indeed. The Augustan Dean Swift's only recognition of him (in 1709) was 'That Fellow in the pillory: I have forgot his name.'

Dissent stayed close to its Bible, and worked on it, as the Augustan mainstream did not. Richard Baxter paraphrased the New Testament in 1684, for which work he was jailed. To take random examples from the less known – indeed, unknown writers: 'R. C.' and 'W. B.'. Richard Crane's, *Lamentation Over Thee O London* (1665) used the biblical book. William Bayly's 1662 *The Life of Enoch again Revived, in which Abels Offering is Accepted and Cain's Mark Known, and He rejected* expects knowledge of the early chapters of Genesis. That both men were Quakers, showing what for later Quakers would be an unusual detail of interest in the Bible, makes its own point.

The towering figure remains Bunyan, whose *Mr Badman* (1680) and *The Holy War* (1682), and as noted above, nearly sixty other books, were printed and read in great numbers.[12] In one important sense, in the popular readership (until after the Second World War) of both parts of *The Pilgrim's Progress*, Bunyan has never been away. Late-twentieth-century attention is beginning to bring him back, as much more than the writer of a couple of 'classics'. With this should come a proper assessment of those Dissenting and Nonconformist writers more than forgotten – spurned.

Chapter 29

THE BIBLE IN ENGLAND AND IRELAND, 1710–1760

In the fifty years between January 1710 and December 1759, some two hundred and twenty different editions of the Bible in English were published. Most of them were straight versions of the complete KJV in various regular sizes, with or without the Apocrypha: but there began to be experiments in fresh translation, or at least paraphrase, into prose rather than verse, to which I shall return. Of the KJVs not printed in London, just over a third came from the University printers in Oxford, and over two dozen from several printers in Edinburgh. Another two dozen, all but three from London, were of the New Testament alone. Two New Testaments, of 1708 and 1715, said, too, to have come from Amsterdam, are KJV with Geneva notes. Only a small fistful of the two hundred editions in those four decades has any interest now.

ROBINSON CRUSOE

That by the eighteenth century KJV had seeped far into the ground of English thought and writing is clear from sampling the catalogues of titles since the Restoration. The production of books in the eighteenth century greatly increased, with printing houses much enlarged, and distribution more efficient.[1] Readers were increasingly from all classes: book buyers were less and less assumed to share an elitist classical education. The books in which the Bible was strongly present were not only on the shelves marked 'Religion'.

Forty years after *Absalom and Achitophel*, a work of quite different genius appeared in 1719, this time written for a far wider public. It still has its wide effect, though in a mutilated form. Central images of Daniel Defoe's *Robinson Crusoe* are in modern mythology. The fiction of ingenious survival, however attractive, is usually just that, a fiction, as all but a scrap of the evidence is that ships revisiting the islands of castaways always found either madmen or bones. The mixture of exotic adventure story and a fable of human endurance has come to us labelled 'Robinson Crusoe'. As is well known, Defoe (at almost 60, incidentally; for the time, surprisingly, an old man's book) used reports of castaways, especially the first-hand account of Alexander Selkirk's five years alone. He also used Bunyan's *Grace Abounding*, and the influence of the tradition of spiritual autobiography is strong. What had once been Odysseus outwitting vengeful gods in epic voyaging is now a man alone on his island, soberly manufacturing a middle-class mercantile enterprise: except that 'soberly' will not do. Crusoe develops considerable spiritual stress. What has been leached out of the mythology of Defoe's book is that it becomes intensely biblical, and not just in that Crusoe is a modern Jonah or Job. Leaving his father, as a kind of Prodigal Son, he became, in his 'far country', aware of his spiritual state, at first torn between total despair and satisfaction at the goodness of Providence, and gradually haunted by his failure to repent of his sins. Among all the items he rescued from the wreck were 'three very good Bibles' – the quantity is pure Defoe: one Bible would have been sufficient, but three adds a curious authenticity – and two or three prayer books. The 'miraculous' growth of the corn he had unwittingly sown, a bout of sickness and a frightening dream of Judgement all set him to thoughts of God's purpose for him. A chance discovery of one of the Bibles (while he was looking for tobacco) and a glance at Psalm 50:15, 'Call upon me in the day of trouble: I will deliver thee, and thou shalt glorify me' leads him to prayer. Five days later:

> *July 4.* In the morning I took the Bible, and, beginning at the New Testament, I began seriously to read it, and imposed upon myself to read awhile every morning and every night . . . [he prays for repentance] when it happen'd providentially the very day that reading the scripture, I came to these words, *He is exalted a Prince and a Saviour, to give repentance, and to give remission.* I threw down the book, and with my heart as well as my hands lifted up to heaven, in a kind of ecstasy of joy, I cry'd out aloud, 'Jesus, thou son of David, Jesus, thou exalted Prince and Saviour, give me repentance!'

He immediately has 'a true Scripture view of hope founded on the encouragement of the Word of God'. Though still acutely troubled ('the anguish of my soul would break out upon me on a sudden . . . like a storm') he begins to 'exercise' himself with 'new thoughts', reads the Word of God daily, and finds revelation in 'I will never leave thee, nor forsake thee' (Hebrews 13:5). From that moment, he finds that he could probably be happier as a penitent even in his 'forsaken, solitary condition' than anywhere else. Still aware of the danger of hypocrisy, in his third and fourth years he reads his Bible three times a day:

> I never open'd the Bible, or shut it, but my very soul within me bless'd God for directing my friend in England, without any order of mine, to pack it up among my goods; and for assisting me afterward to save it out of the wreck of the ship.[2]

Later, his assurance threatened by real dangers of attack, his continual Bible-reading restores his faith: later still, at some length he teaches his man Friday Christian theology, so well that at one point he can strengthen Crusoe's faith.

Inside the splendid narrative structure of Robinson Crusoe's energetic survival for twenty-eight years, two months and nineteen days, still so appealing, and always strong on the page, is a spiritual autobiography, familiar since Bunyan. Inside that form, and forcefully presented, is the personal power of the opened Bible.

BIBLES FROM DUBLIN

The catalogue of Bibles in this period shows that to the familiar locations of Bible printers the newcomer is Dublin. There had been talk of English Bibles printed in Ireland since 1699. A New Testament (probably Rheims) was printed in Dublin in either 1699 or 1698: no copy has survived, and it seems to have been suppressed because of its inaccuracy. Bibles are said to have been printed in Belfast between 1704 and 1714, but no copy has been seen since that time, and it is now doubted that they existed. In 1714, however, there did appear a folio King James Bible printed in Dublin by A. Rhames 'for William Binauld, at the Bible in Eustace-street, and Eliphal Dobson, at the Stationers-Arms in Castle-street', the first Bible of any Irish printing to have survived. In 1722, the King James came in two smaller sizes from A. Rhames in Dublin, 'for J. Hyde, R. Gunne, R. Owen and E. Dobson' – of the smaller, in duodecimo, only a fragment (part of Genesis) remains. A quarto Bible was printed in 1739 'for G. Grierson, Printer to the King's Most Excellent Majesty', his Dublin address being 'at the Kings-Arms and Two-Bibles in Essex Street'.

In 1719, twenty years before that quarto, a remarkable Roman Catholic priest of St Michan's, Dublin, Cornelius Nary (signing himself 'C.N. C.F.P.D.', that is, *Consultissimae Facultatis Parisiensis Doctor*, see p. x above) had hit several nails on the head. He complained that the Catholic Rheims-Douai version was unintelligible. Worse, the only editions available were objectionable, being 'so bulky that they cannot conveniently be carried about for Publick Devotion, and so scarce and so dear, that the Generality of the People neither have, nor can procure them for their private use'.[3] Worst, the bulky two-volume quartos of the Rheims-Douai they were having to use were ancient, none in fact having been printed since the edition from Rouen in 1635 – and that was only the second edition of the original 1610 translation. He had a point: several points, in fact. He provided his own translation of the New Testament from the Vulgate, 'with the original Greek, and divers translations in vulgar languages diligently compared and revised' (the last four words should alert the reader to the strong presence of KJV) which he printed – probably in Dublin – in a convenient and pleasing single volume in octavo. In his Preface he noted:

> We have no Catholic Translation of the Scriptures in the English tongue but the Doway Bible, and the Rheimish Testament, which have been done now more than an hundred years since, the language whereof is so old, the words in many places so obsolete, the Orthography so bad, and the translation so very literal, that in a number of Places it is unintelligible and all over so grating to the Ears of such as are accustomed to speak, in a manner, another language, that most People will not be at the Pains of reading them.[4]

Nary's edition was never reprinted. Those critical remarks about Gregory Martin, though justified, sealed his fate. No doubt, given official backing, it could have been successful. His translation is still solidly Rheims, with a few improvements from KJV (and ultimately Tyndale). His Greek occasionally slips. At Romans 8:28, Tyndale's 'all things work for the best' was standard until KJV picked up the συν- (*sun-*) in συνεργεῖ (*sunergei*) meaning 'work together', and gave us 'all things work together for good'. Rheims there has 'cooperate', which is the Vulgate *cooperantur*; Nary has 'contribute', which is too one-directional for the togetherness of synergy. Similarly, the Vulgate's *sancti* at the end of that verse gave Rheims 'called to be saints', which Nary follows. Tyndale's 'called of purpose' at that point needed what first Geneva, and then KJV, supplied, to make the latter's 'called according to *his* purpose', which is good for the Greek, κατὰ πρόθεσιν κλητοῖς οὖσιν (*kata prothesin klētois ousin*), because κλητοῖς (*klētois*) is 'called out, chosen': 'saints' as a word carries too much extra baggage by 1719. At Luke 15:13 Nary's 'spent his substance in a riotous manner' is not sharp enough: one can have a 'manner' without the real thing, and the Greek hits hard with ἀσώτως (*asōtōs*), 'dissolute beyond being able to be saved'. At Luke 15:16, Nary's changing of Tyndale's 'and no man gave him', and even Rheims's 'and no body gave unto him', to 'but was supplied with none' is not for the better. Nor are the next words, starting verse 17; for Tyndale's 'he came to himself', which became standard, Nary made Rheims's 'returning to himself' worse with 'Then entering into himself': the Vulgate's *In se autem reversus*, on which they depend, does not correctly translate the Greek of εἰς ἑαυτὸν δὲ ἐλθὼν (*eis heautou de elthōn*). There could be many similar examples. The errors are both a pity and unexpected. In his strong Preface, Cornelius Nary C.F.P.D. is sound about the need to get behind the Vulgate and its 'great many ambiguities and obscurities in . . . phrases and particles', to the New Testament 'Greek of the Synagogue'; and about the difficulty of dealing with Greek particles. He notes the Septuagint's peculiarities, following 'Hebrew . . . written in a very concise laconic style, expressing things by halfs, and being very barren in particles and prepositions . . .'. He attacks Rheims and other French versions for inaccuracies: at Matthew 1:20 for 'that which is born in her', when the Greek is 'conceived', and at Luke 11:41 he rebukes the Vulgate (and Rheims) for Jesus teaching that alms must be given of *quod superest*, 'what remains', rather than the Greek τὰ ἐνόντα (*ta enonta*) 'what is within', 'what you have'.

One strength of Nary's version is in its modest marginal notes. There are not many per page. They usefully signal the lessons at weekly masses and festivals, and do a little explaining. Sometimes his notes are what is vulgarly called 'Irish' in the sense of illogical: at Matthew 23:15, Nary goes to some trouble to explain the Greek behind 'prosleyte', in fact getting it wrong, and then adds, 'But the word is now so familiar in our language that it hardly needs an explanation.' Sometimes his clarifications are, it must be said, tendentious. At Revelation 1:20, 'the angels of the seven churches' are explained in the margin as the bishops, 'because they are God's messengers, sent to deliver his will to certain people on earth, as the bishops were sent by Christ's institution as messengers to declare his will to mankind'. No doubt Nary's intention was to be helpful to his parishioners: but whereas Protestant commentators (as Junius in the 1599 Geneva) explain the angels as ministers to the churches ('congregations' to Tyndale), Nary does not say that nowhere in the Gospels did Christ institute bishops. And so on: Cornelius Nary's handy volume has faults. Nevertheless, one must salute him, if only for his good intentions and his remarkable, brave, Preface.

In the following year, 1520, Nary published in Dublin a fine 500-page folio, *A New History of the World up to the Birth of our Lord Jesus Christ . . .* , in which, claiming to reconcile what he wrote with the Hebrew and the Septuagint, he set out to confute 'all the objections and causes of our modern libertarians, deists, atheists and pre-Adamites'.[5] He also wrote a twenty-page pamphlet, *The Case of the Roman Catholics in Ireland*.

DOUAI AGAIN

In spite of his reasonable stance that a new translation was needed because the language had changed in 'more than a hundred years', Nary's work did not succeed. It clearly offended the English College at Douai. There, eleven years later, in 1730, Robert Witham, the President of the English College, printed, apparently at Douai itself, his own translation from the Vulgate, with annotations. An octavo in two volumes, it fulfilled some of Cornelius Nary's challenges. Witham attempted to make something fresh and up to date as well as, like Nary, more portable. He announced that he would show the differences between the Vulgate and the Greek text, examine and disprove false interpretations, and explain in his copious annotations the literal sense of the Latin, according to the ancient Fathers (his New Testament notes were reprinted in a Douai-Rheims version in 1813). He slighted Nary as a translator. Then his own translation was attacked with ferocity by James Serces in a book of 1736, *Popery an enemy to Scripture*. Serces, Vicar of Appleby in Lincolnshire, was chaplain to Lord Harrington, 'one of his Majesty's principal Secretaries of State'. His general point, as a good Anglican, is that the Church of Rome sinks the authority of the Holy Scripture by the 'various falsifications introduced in some versions of the New Testament by Divines of that communion, particularly the last in English, by Dr Witham, Professor of Divinity at Douay'. The second half of the book discusses several recent Catholic translations, concentrating on Witham, and attacks, in detail and at length, the use of 'do penance' for 'repent'; and the word 'pilgrim' at the end of 2 Corinthians 5:6 and elsewhere (Tyndale has there 'as we are at home in the body, we are absent from God'). The Greek ἐκδημοῦμεν (*ekdēmoumen*) certainly has the sense of being away from home, abroad from God: but that is a very different thing from journeying as a pilgrim (the Vulgate has *peregrinamur*), the institutional implications of which Serces attacks – and particularly the baseless use of 'pilgrimage' at Luke 9.53, for Christ's 'face was as though he would go to Jerusalem' (Tyndale). Serces reveals 'passages falsified to support Transubstantiation', and many other things.[6] Witham does not come out well.

NEW TRANSLATIONS

There is a pattern in the making of altogether new translations. They are like city buses. Nothing comes for a long time, and then several arrive together. Almost coinciding with Witham's 1730 attempt, came two new

English translations of the New Testament from French versions, representing opposite theological poles, and two more printings of English New
Testaments ultimately from the Vulgate. I shall deal with those four first,
before addressing in more detail a fifth, a London-printed New Testament
of 1729 which was the most important of those years, and indeed of the
four decades.

First from the French was a quarto volume in 1726: an admirable
attempt at flight which only briefly got off the ground. Announced as *A
New Version of all the Books of the New Testament, with a Literal Commentary
on all Difficult Passages* . . . and other aids, including *a general Preface to all
St Paul's Epistles,* . . . it was *Written originally in French by Messieurs De Beau-
sobre and Lenfant by Order of the King of Prussia.* It was all to be printed in
English in monthly numbers, but only Matthew's Gospel was published,
though that, with its introduction, was often reprinted, even as late as 1819.
The two Frenchmen were Protestants in Berlin, both chaplains to the King
of Prussia; Lenfant was pastor of the French Protestant church in the city.
Their French version, significantly from *l'Original Grec,* was first printed
in Amsterdam in 1718, and often reprinted in Germany and Switzerland.

Second, in 1730, came, in two quarto volumes, *The New Testament . . .
According to the Antient Latin Edition. With Critical Remarks . . . From the
French of Father Simon.* This was by William Webster, who was curate at St
Dunstan's in the West (the local church of reforming Londoners in the
1520s at which Tyndale preached). The French version by Richard Simon
had come out in 1702: Simon was 'a forerunner of modern biblical criticism':[7] his version was attacked by Jacques Benigne, Bishop of Meaux in
his own translation of the Gospels from the Vulgate, and the Greek, not
published until 1855.

In 1731 the first of two New Testaments more directly from the Vulgate
was itself rather remarkable. There had been talk of printing Wyclif's complete Bible for some time – it had been proposed in 1719 – and now there
appeared for the first time in print *The New Testament . . . Translated out of
the Latin Vulgat by John Wiclif . . . about 1378. . . .* It was an unbound folio
of which only 160 copies were issued (at one guinea a set of sheets), but
it was a start. It was reprinted in 1810 with different preliminary matter,
and it was one step to Forshall and Madden's four folio volumes of 1850
which, imperfect as they are, are all we have of the complete Wyclif printed
Bible. The editing in 1731 had been done by John Lewis, for over thirty-
seven years Vicar of Minster, near Ramsgate in Kent. He used only two
manuscripts, both of Wyclif LV. The book begins with Lewis's long
account, making not far off half the volume, *A History of the several Translations of the H. Bible and N. Testament, &c. into English, both in MS. and*

Print, and of the most remarkable Editions of them since the Invention of Print-
ing. This was republished on its own in 1739 and again in 1818. In 1731
it was the first history of the English Bible that had been attempted since
Miles Smith's 'Translators to the Reader' in 1611.

BACK TO DOUAI, AGAIN

Then, seven years later, in 1738, Nary's challenge was again partly taken
up, it seems from Douai, and perhaps with some contribution from Bishop
Challoner, in a new edition of the 1582 Rheims New Testament, the first
since the fourth of 1633. The long title-page is polemic in tone: the ANNO-
TATIONS And other HELPS are

> *For the better understanding the* TEXT, and especially *for the Discovery of*
> *Corruptions in divers late Translations, and for clearing up* RELIGIOUS CON-
> *TROVERSIES of the present Times.* To which are added TABLES of the
> EPISTLES and GOSPELS, CONTROVERSIES, and HERETICAL CORRUPTIONS.

The editors of this, only the fifth edition of the Rheims New Testament,
congratulate themselves on the past effectiveness of the 'TABLE of Heretical Corruptions', arranged under books of the New Testament, here
reprinted from the second, 1600, edition of 'Rheims':

> But as Falsehood is inseparable from Heresy, and None can be fit to
> translate faithfully the Word of God, who have not first the Spirit of
> God in them; they ['the Protestants'] have left many other Passages here
> taken notice of, either totally unalter'd, or not alter'd for the better;
> sometimes even for the worse.

The new editors mark with an asterisk the places in this list and in the
text which the Protestants have 'vouchsafed to amend', with marginal
quotations of such alterations. They further mark the text with a dagger
to show those passages 'as still remain corrupt in the latest edition of the
P. [Protestant] Testament'. There are together about a hundred. The list
condemns Tyndale ('reprinted in 1562'), first at Matthew 16:18, where for
'Church' he translates 'Congregation'. It does, however, commend him for
Gabriel's 'Hail full of grace' to Mary at Luke 1:28, 'the *Ave Mary* being
not then banish'd, as since it is'. At John 13:16 is 'For *Apostle* they translate *messenger:* turning an Ecclesiastical word, into the original and pro-
phane signification.' Objection is stated to 'repent' for 'do penance', 'elder'
for 'priest', and 'love' for 'charity'. At 1 Corinthians 9:13, 'for *Altar* they
translate Temple. . . . thrusting the word *Altar* out of the Scripture, when
they pull'd Altars down in Churches.' At 1 Corinthians 11:2, 'For *tradition,*

they say *ordinance, instruction, institution.*' The list ends with a note that 'The Blessed Confessor Bishop Tonstal noted no less than two thousand corruptions in Tyndale's translation in the New Testament only. By which, as by these few here cited for examples, the indifferent Reader may see, how untruly the English Bibles are commended to the people, for the pure word of God.' It is suggested that the editors included Richard Challoner who went on to make significant revisions of the Rheims New Testament in 1749, and of the whole Bible in 1750 (see below).[8]

DANIEL MACE'S LONDON DIGLOT

The outstanding new translation of this period, which, after the dark, overheated sickrooms of controversy, comes like a refreshing breeze on a sunny day, was made, anonymously, in 1729 by Daniel Mace, a Presbyterian minister and New Testament scholar. Not only did Mace print his own, more colloquial (even racy) English translation: like the pioneering Erasmus before him, he printed alongside his own work the New Testament Greek, the first Greek–English diglot since the last edition of Tyndale with Erasmus in 1550. Like Erasmus, his interest was shared between making a modern acceptable translation and making a good Greek printed text. Unlike Erasmus, however, his textual work anticipated at many points modern critical thinking. And unlike Erasmus, he was reviled. Confused with another man, William Mace, his work was ignored and he himself soon forgotten.

Mace's English translation is original, alive and forward-looking. At Luke 7:40, Jesus is about to challenge Simon the Pharisee's sneering thoughts about 'the woman in that city, which was a sinner' (Tyndale, Geneva and KJV) who has anointed Jesus' feet. To Jesus' 'Simon I have somewhat to say unto thee' the Pharisee replies 'Master say on' (all three versions again). Mace has: 'master, said he. lets hear it.' Unusual elements were too much for his peers. Mace begins paragraphs with an upper case initial, but (as there) all other sentences with lower case. His occasional use of colloquial abbreviations like 'don't' and 'can't' may have been found offensive: they always occur in address, and by very late twentieth-century standards seem quite unremarkable. One certainly hears a contemporary speaker at John 4:35, where Tyndale's, Geneva's and KJV's 'Say not ye: there are yet four months, and then cometh harvest?' is in Mace 'Is it not a common saying, 't'other four months, and then comes harvest?' Like many translators who are also true scholars, Mace can go for an unusual technical word. At Luke 15:16, the Prodigal Son has eaten not KJV's 'husks' but 'carruways', with a footnote (only one of four such comments in Luke, all very brief) explaining 'a wild fruit in Syria called Caruba, by Actuarius, Carroua'. The temptation to patronise Mace has to be stifled quickly: the Greek word κερατίων (*keration*) means the fruit of the locust tree; modern translators choose 'pods' (Tyndale had 'cods'). Again, like all translators he cannot resist paraphrase: the Elder Brother at Luke 15:30 insists to their father in Tyndale, Geneva and KJV that the Prodigal Son has 'devoured thy goods with harlots'; (Rheims, 'devoured his substance with whoores'): in Mace, he has lived 'among a pack of loose creatures'. Though 'the Kingdom of heaven' and 'the Kingdom of God' appear most of the time, there are occasional variations, as at Luke 23:51, 'the Messiah's reign', not really defensible for the Greek τὴν βασιλείαν τοῦ Θεοῦ (*tēn basileian tou Theou*). Just as Tyndale got unwittingly left behind with words that did not last, like 'byss' or 'debite', and most translators since Tyndale lose touch more or less often with a direct form of what people actually say, so Mace defeats modern understanding with Jesus in the Mount of Olives before his arrest at Luke 22:44, sweating 'grumes', and Paul warns the flock in Corinth to beware 'raparees' (1 Corinthians, 6:11; the margin explains 'Kidnappers, who stole men to sell them for slaves'). Both are interesting words, but conveyed little not too long after 1729.[9] In spite of how these oddities appear, Mace is genuinely trying to put the New Testament into modern English. Luke 1:28 is ' "Hail, favorite of heaven, the Lord is with thee, thou happiest of thy sex." Mary was surpriz'd at the voice of such an appearance.' Six verses later, she asks 'what should this be without any intercourse with man?' Two verses on, 'even your cousin Elizabeth, old as she is . . .'. At Luke 2:32, Mace has, 'if you only love those, who love you, where's the obligation?' Luke 8:45–6 is revealing: 'master, the crowd are squeezing and pressing about you, and yet you cry, "who touched me?" but Jesus said, "somebody has touched me: for I know what influence my power has had".' There is the strength and weakness of Mace: the fresh English contemporary tone of Luke's voice, unheard since Tyndale: and the final paraphrased words for the Greek's straight 'I felt that power had gone out from me'. The blind beggar at Luke 18:38 'bawl'd out the louder', which is good for the Greek verbs ἐβόησεν λέγων (*eboēsen legōn*). Here is Luke 12:54–7:

> Then said he to the people, when you see a cloud rise out of the west, you say, it is just going to rain; and so it happens. and when the south wind blows, you say, there will be heat; and so it happens. hypocrites, you can judge of the phenomena of the earth, and of the sky, but why can't you discern the present times? why can't you judge what is proper to be done in your own affairs?

And Luke 16:14–15:

> The Pharisees too, who were noted for avarice, heard all this discourse, and treated him with derision. but he said to them, you pretend to piety before men, which, however they may admire, is an abomination to God, who knows your real temper.

This is the end of Luke 16, the Parable of Dives and Lazarus (in which, just before, Mace has kept, and so surely understood the force of, Tyndale's 'dip-tip-finger' phrase):

> upon which he said, father, I beg of you, that you would send him to my father's family, where I have five brothers, to give them warning, lest they also come to this place of torment. but Abraham replied, they have Moses and the prophets, let them mind them. no, father Abraham, said he, they will not: but if any of the dead went to them, they will certainly repent. Abraham replied, if they disregard Moses and the prophets, they will not believe anyone, though he rose from the dead.

Luther A. Weigle of Yale Divinity School regrets Mace's 'pert colloquial style which was then fashionable'.[10] It is hard to agree. Daniel Mace deserved altogether a better fate. A West Country man probably from Tyndale country in Gloucestershire, he went from a ministry in Somerset to Newbury in 1727.[11] Though the historic congregation there dated from the ejection of 1662, it was by then already shrinking because of Whitefield's preaching in the town: Wesley had established a congregation nearby. The fashion among non-Wesleyan preachers, across the denominational board, was to avoid doctrinal teaching, in a general trend of rationalist Arianism (that is, put crudely, denying Jesus his godhead and place in the Trinity). Local congregations were susceptible to Whitefield's and Wesley's gospel fire, and the founding of new chapels. Mace was minister at Newbury for twenty-six years. In that time the flock dwindled so much that his successor in 1753 made the chapel building smaller and took a reduced salary (£45). Daniel Mace died about Christmas 1753, and was buried near his pulpit, though no memorial remains. That is sad, because his work of textual criticism of the Greek New Testament was new, important, especially in Europe, and far ahead of its time.

THE GREEK TEXT OF THE NEW TESTAMENT

Lying behind KJV was the *Textus Receptus*, essentially Erasmus's text, a name coined more or less by accident in 1633, for the printed Greek New

Testament of which 'the textual basis is essentially a handful of late and haphazardly collected minuscule manuscripts . . . in a dozen passages its reading is supported by no known Greek witness'.[12] In spite of that, it was the basis of most New Testament work until 1881. One of the curiosities of Bible history is the superstition about this text, a rigid religious position now recognised as fundamentalism. So intense has been the loyalty of many Christians to this textual monstrosity that to try to amend it, or even criticise it, has been branded as near-sacrilege – indeed, still is, in some places.[13] Gradually after 1633, however, there developed greater consciousness of variant readings, and the assiduous assembly of them, not to make a new and better text, but to print them as *apparatus criticus* alongside the same old corrupt *Textus Receptus*. The great Polyglot Bible, published in London in six folio volumes in 1655–7, contains in its fifth volume the New Testament in Greek, Latin (the Vulgate and the version by Arius Montanus), Syriac, Ethiopic, Arabic and (for the Gospels) Persian. The Greek text has variants at the foot of the page from the then newly, and royally, acquired Codex Alexandrinus, a core Greek uncial text from the fifth century (on permanent display in the British Library). The sixth volume gives a critical apparatus for fifteen other authorities, and variants from Stephanus's edition of 1550. The editor, Brian Walton, was roundly attacked, but replied promptly and effectively. So far, so good. In the next fifty years, important work was done at Oxford. In 1675, Dr John Fell, Dean of Christ Church and later Bishop of Oxford, issued anonymously a small book which was the first Greek text to be printed at Oxford. Dr Fell claimed to give alongside the standard *Textus Receptus* variants from more than a hundred manuscripts and ancient versions. He failed, however, to give citations for all of them, a weakness that should lead to an echo of Thomas Brown's famous adaptation of the Roman poet Martial addressed to this Dean, 'I do not love thee, Dr Fell . . .', except that we *do* know 'full well' why we do not love him, because of the lack of citations. John Mill, a fellow of Queen's College, Oxford, surveyed the entire textual scene and published in 1707 a learned edition of Stephanus's text of 1550 with massive prolegomena, noting points of discussion on almost half the New Testament. For this he too was attacked. Dr Edward Wells published at Oxford between 1709 and 1719 a Greek Testament. 'Though Wells's edition was largely ignored by his contemporaries, history accords him the honour of being the first to edit a complete New Testament which abandoned the *Textus Receptus* in favour of readings from the more ancient manuscripts.'[14]

The names of Richard Bentley and Cambridge (where he was Master of Trinity College) were for a long while synonymous. By no means a modest man, he had been for four decades known throughout Europe as a fine classical textual scholar. He exposed the letters of the Sicilian tyrant of the sixth century BC, Phalaris, as forgeries. He was well known for critical editions of Horace and Terence, both of whom were widely read. He discovered the use in Homer and elsewhere of the unique Greek consonant which was later called the 'digamma' (because it resembled two capital gammas combined). The English poet Alexander Pope, who translated Homer and modelled his satires on Horace, wrote of him with wit and exasperation, mindful of the long quarrels between Bentley and his enemies, which had been both with his own Fellows at Trinity (settled in 1738), and in the wider world. Pope wrote in 1741 of the River Cam as

> Where Bentley late tempestuous wont to sport
> In troubled waters, but now sleeps in Port.[15]

One earlier quarrel dated from twenty years before, when Conyers Middleton in London attacked Bentley's six-page prospectus of *Proposals for Printing* (1720) a critical edition of the Greek and Latin New Testament. Bentley included as specimens the last chapter of Revelation in Greek and Latin: there he abandoned the *Textus Receptus* in more than forty places, even in the mere twenty-one verses of Revelation 21. (Yet that is less suprising when we recall that Erasmus, the founder of that Greek Text, finding that he lacked a complete Greek manuscript of Revelation and being in a hurry, himself made up the Greek of the last verses.

As a classical textual scholar, Bentley reasoned (perhaps a better word would be 'boasted') that by following the oldest manuscripts both of the Greek original, and of Jerome's Vulgate, he could restore the text of the New Testament as it stood in the fourth century.

> By taking two thousand errors out of the Pope's Vulgate, [Bentley refers to Pope Clement's recension of 1592], and as many out of the Protestant Pope Stephen's [referring to Stephanus's Greek text – i.e. of Erasmus's *Textus Receptus*], I can set out an edition of each in columns, without using any book under nine hundred years old, that shall so exactly agree, word for word, and order for order, that no two tallies, nor two indentures, can agree better.[16]

In spite of over one thousand subscribers, and further new evidence from manuscripts and the Fathers, the volume never appeared, and the subscribers had their money back on Bentley's death.

While Bentley was gathering his material, Daniel Mace's diglot came out, in 1729. The full title is worth observing. *The New Testament in Greek and English. Containing the Original Text Corrected from the Authority of the Most Authentic Manuscripts: and a New Version Form'd agreeably to the Illustrations of the most Learned Commentators and Critics: with Notes and Various*

Readings, and a Copious Alphabetical Index. The Greek text has similar small eccentricities to the English – sentences begin with a capital letter only at the start of a new paragraph, in the Greek as well as the English. The standard Greek mark of interrogation, ';', is dropped in favour of '?'. Smooth breathing marks on initial Greek vowels are omitted – technically, they are not needed, as they do nothing except say that the vowel is not rough (when it is sounded with an initial 'h'), and the absence of a rough breathing does not, strictly, need to be confirmed with a smooth breathing. Accents have also disappeared – again, not vital marks. In these respects, however, the text looks odd, and would put off fastidious Augustan readers. (In another respect it looks unusually beautiful, as Mace's printer, James Roberts, who was Master of the Stationers' Company in 1729–31, has made, apparently for this book alone, a full-bodied, clear, antique Greek type which is a pleasure to read (fig. 29).)

For daring to challenge the precious *Textus Receptus*, even though he supported his principal changes with full explanations, Mace was reviled. Between 1731 and 1732, Leonard Twells, Vicar of St Mary's in Marlborough, issued in London in three parts *A Critical Examination of the late New Testament and Version of the New Testament: wherein the Editor's Corrupt Text, False Version and Fallacious Notes are Detected and Censur'd.* This bilious invective need not detain us – the title says it all – except to note that on the Continent the attackers were even more abusive.[17] As Bruce Metzger summed up, 'But most theologians assumed an ostrich-like pose, and Mace's work was soon all but forgotten.'[18]

PRINTERS AND PRICES

In one particular, the editors of the 1738 Rheims New Testament ignored, even flouted, one of the complaints of Cornelius Nary in Dublin, twenty years before: their new edition of was a very bulky folio. Nary had been right to protest – and, too, at the prices charged for Bibles. Nor was he then alone. Prices were set by the bookseller himself, often unreasonably, especially for Bibles full of errors on cheap paper. Complaints led to a royal order, made at Whitehall on 24 April 1724, to amend such abuses. This gave several strict injunctions to the printers of Bibles, including one that the patent holders must set forth clearly 'on the title-page of each book the exact price at which such book is by them to be sold to the booksellers'. Most eighteenth-century Bibles after 1724 give this price, starting with Baskett's 1725 octavo King James Version, of which the general title-page has at the foot *Price six shillings unbound*.

The name of John Baskett as a Bible printer first appeared on the title-page of an octavo KJV dated 1711, '*London: John Baskett and Assigns of Newcomb and Hills*', a statement which then reappeared regularly; for example, on three duodecimo Bibles dated 1713 and 1714, an octavo of 1715, a quarto of 1716, and so on. Baskett also printed in Oxford. His first work there was apparently a folio Bible of 1715, where he is designated on the title-page *Printer to the King's most Excellent Majesty, and the University*: the New Testament title-page gives London, as does that of a Bible quarto also of 1715, though it seems to have been printed in Oxford. Some years later he printed Bibles in Edinburgh, the first, it seems, a quarto of 1726. He had tried, and failed, to buy out the Edinburgh printers Robert Freebairn and James Watson in 1711. In 1716, however, he received a commission as royal printer, in conjunction with the widow of Andrew Anderson, who had been 'his Majesty's sole, absolute, and only printer' in Scotland since 1675. Anderson's 'heirs and successors' were more productive than he was, up to 1716.

These are the years when the patent to print English Bibles finally left the Barker family. Christopher Barker had in 1577 bought a very extensive patent, and then obtained an exclusive patent from Queen Elizabeth in 1589. The Barkers swamped the market with the new King James Version. The patent remained with them until 1709. It then went to Thomas Newcomb and Henry Hills. John Baskett and some others bought from their executors the remainder of their term, which was thirty years from 1709. Four years later, in 1713, Benjamin Tooke and John Barber became the Queen's Printers, a title to begin after Baskett's term had expired, that is, in 1739. John Baskett then bought from Tooke and Barber their reversionary interest, and was able to renew the patent for a further thirty years, until 1799. In fact, the last thirty years of Baskett's patent were bought by 'Charles Eyre and his heirs' for £10,000, and Eyre took possession in 1769 – a new ownership that will be seen to be important in that year. (Before then, I observe in passing the historic beginning in the 1760s of 'Eyre and . . .' on Bible title-pages. For some innocent readers they are words which for over two hundred years were taken as part of Scripture, like Aaron.[19]) A new patent was granted to George Eyre and others in 1799, which came down to the twentieth-century firm of Eyre & Spottiswoode, which still most acceptably prints Bibles and prayer books, in Andover in Hampshire, UK.

About Bible production in mid-century, three things need saying. First and obviously, a licence to print official Bibles exclusively has always been extremely lucrative, as these buyings and sellings show. Second, though exports continued for many decades, in 1769 no one in England foresaw the coming eventual loss of the American market: from 1777, Bibles were printed in America in increasing, eventually gigantic, numbers, from many presses. Third, through all these changes, the quality of production steadily increased. A good Baskett Bible is a thing of beauty in all its parts. That such a good Bible was so far beyond the pocket of the ordinary man-in-the-field, even after a lifetime of saving, was a factor not properly addressed for a further half century, until the foundation of the Bible Society in March 1804.

In the mid-point of the eighteenth century can be seen the filling-out of the shoots of growths which will change the picture. The challenge to the accuracy of KJV, not only in its Greek base but in the accuracy of English translation, had first appeared in 1701 with the Bishop of Worcester's various 'Lloyd Bibles', tentative attempts at 'improvement' which in fact did nothing except tinker with, and from then set in stone, the dates given for biblical events from Creation. The new dates had already been established by James Ussher, Archbishop of Armagh, in 1650–4. With the arrival of Clarke's Notes in 1683 (New Testament) and 1690 (whole Bible) there came the modest restarting of the 'study Bible' tradition. The most often reprinted, far into the nineteenth century, was the much fuller Nonconformist 'Matthew Henry's Bible', which was first published in 1712. Some delicate plants of fresh translation have appeared. The near-divine exaltation of KJV, which will later have tremendous force, began to happen at the same time as the contrary pull of its dismissal as in need of drastic overhaul.[20]

RICHARD CHALLONER

The re-presentation of the Rheims New Testament in 1738 was overtaken in 1749 by the work of Richard Challoner, reprinted in 1750 and again in 1752, 1764 and 1772. He revised the 1738 edition, with few changes, and still including the Approbations from 1582 and 1600, now dated 1748 and signed by Gulielmus Green and Gulielmus Walton; and, at the end, with the more standard tables of Epistles and Gospels, and chronology, the table of Controversies. His more significant work, however, was the revision of the Douai Old Testament, the translation first made in 1609, and not again reissued since the second edition of 1635. The original aim, and Challoner's, was to 'conform it to the most perfect Latin edition', the authorised recension of the Vulgate by Pope Clement VIII in 1592. Challoner (1691–1781) received his Catholic education at Douai, and held important positions there. In 1740 he was made Bishop of Debra (in Ethiopia) though he did not leave London. Later he was Vicar Apostolic of the London District.

Challoner's Old Testament, apparently first printed in Dublin, was in four smallish volumes (smaller than the average paperback), and his New Testament, also from Dublin, as a separate volume, was the same size, at last officially answering Cornelius Nary's plea in 1719 for Catholic translations of the Bible that his parishioners could carry about. His Old Testament was reprinted in 1763. For English-speaking Roman Catholics, Challoner's work, with some later slight changes, was standard for a further two hundred years, until the adoption of the Jerusalem Bible in 1966.

Challoner's New Testament modifications were in the direction of modernisation and simplification, and indeed, for all the claim that it was a lawful translation of the Latin, he brought it closer to Tyndale from the Greek as preserved in KJV (though it is unlikely that he knew Tyndale's translations directly). As F. F. Bruce wrote in 1961:

> The ecclesiastical terms have been retained: our Lord and His forerunner still call upon their hearers to 'do penance' and Christians are still exhorted to pray for their 'supersubstantial' bread; 'the parasceve of the pasch' (John 19:14) has not yet become Passover Eve. But Christ is now said to have 'emptied himself' in Phil 2:7 instead of 'exinanited himself'; the 'azymes' remain in Acts 12:3 but are changed into 'unleavened bread' in Mark 14:12 and Luke 22:1; the 'scenopegia' of John 7:2 becomes intelligible as the 'feast of tabernacles'.[21]

Challoner and his assistant Francis Blyth (Vicar Provincial of the English Carmelites) were both converts, and that they had been brought up on KJV shows in the ease with which those phrases, and rhythms and cadences, appear. The opening paragraph of the Epistle to the Hebrews no longer begins, as in Rheims, 'Diversely and in many ways in times past God speaking to the fathers in the prophets: last of all in these days . . .' which is the Latin (and Greek) order of words and syntax, but now 'God, who sundry times and in divers manners spoke in times past to the fathers by the prophets, last of all, in these days . . .' which closely echoes KJV, which itself, in the recasting to begin with 'God', exactly follows Tyndale.[22]

Challoner pruned the ample annotations of Douai-Rheims, cutting back their insistent, perpetual attacks on the evil work of 'the heretics', the Protestants and their Bibles. 'Even so,' remarks F. F. Bruce,

> some of the notes that were included in editions early in the nineteenth century were sufficiently forthright in their anti-protestant vigour to cause considerable embarrassment to the Roman Catholic bishops of Ireland during the Catholic Emancipation campaign.[23]

★ ★ ★

MID-EIGHTEENTH-CENTURY DIRECTIONS

Two streams were coming together. One, which has received almost all the modern critical attention, is of learned, argumentative discussion of what should be the best vehicle for transmitting the 'Sacred Text', as it was often called. Scholarly understanding, for example of the nature of Hebrew poetry, following Robert Lowth in 1741 (to whom I shall return) was one reason for increasing calls for the revision of KJV. Another was the increasing availability of scholarly material: Samuel Johnson left in his will three different Greek New Testament editions, 'all my Latin Bibles', and a Polyglot Bible.[24] Yet another was, in view of the modern excellence of English, a general revulsion from the perceived 'barbarity' of the old version. This went strangely with eccentric but important declarations that, to quote Jonathan Swift in 1712, KJV and the Book of Common Prayer 'have proved a kind of standard for language . . .'

> . . . I am persuaded that the translators of the Bible were masters of an English style much fitter for that work than any we see in our present writings, which I take to be the simplicity that runs through the whole.[25]

With that learned, even elite, position went the familiar lofty complaint that no one read the Bible any more. Or they read only small controversial bits: thus Nehemiah Grew (1641–1712) remarked in 1701 'As most people admire the tail of a glow-worm, which is a rare sight, more than they do the sun, which shines upon them every day.'[26] Or Boswell in 1763, having enjoyed a tearful read of 'the history of Joseph and his brethren', noted, 'It is a strange thing that the Bible is so little read.'[27]

The Borders laird James Boswell should have known better. At the popular level, the Bible had never gone away. That is the second stream, still, for understandable reasons, hardly mapped, but flowing strongly throughout Britain. The Lothian farmers described in the 1760s may stand for the nation:

> no book was so familiar to them as the Scriptures; they could almost tell the place of any particular passage, where situated in their own family Bible, without referring to either book, chapter or verse, and where any similar one was situated.[28]

Sterndale and Hopkins were passionately defended as being native against the newfangled, superior versions of Tate and Brady. KJV's national grip remained in the family and school as well as in church. In the 1730s began the first of the long success (multiplied in America) of School Bibles, and

Family Bibles, resuscitating the old, and fine, Geneva tradition, and some-times using Geneva material.

It was still not yet quite time to think of a full-scale revision of KJV: it was still the age of attempts to put sublime passages into fresh verse, as the poet Sir Richard Blackmore had done in rhyme in the course of his *Paraphrase on the Book of Job* (1700), and Dennis had done, without rhyme, with Habbakuk 3:3–10 in 1721.[29] Or to continue with prose paraphrases, like Daniel Whitby in 1703, or William Whiston's *Primitive New Testament* in 1745.

Chapter 30

MORE PSALMS, AND HYMNS

John Winthrop, Governor of the Massachusetts Bay Colony from 1630 to 1649, wrote in his *Journal*:

> [1639. 1st month]. A printing house was begun at Cambridge by one Daye . . . The first thing which was printed was the freeman's oath, the next was an almanack made for New England . . . the next was the Psalms newly turned into metre.[1]

The title-page of that 'first printed book in America', *The Whole Book of Psalms Faithfully Translated into English Metre* of 1640, gives no indications of place of printing, nor of the makers of it. It is a small, chunky book, crudely printed with many mistakes, the verses often sitting crooked on the page, and usually awkwardly laid out in a sea of white space. From a first print-run of 1,700, eleven copies survive. The metrical versions were the work of John Cotton, one of the prolific New England scholars and ministers, and others. Thirty years after the event, Cotton Mather, in his history of the religious life of the early New England settlements (*Magnalia Christi Americana*, printed in London in 1702), gave the earliest account that we have of the making of it.

> About the Year 1639. the *New-English Reformers*, considering that their Churches enjoy'd the other Ordinances of Heaven in their *Scriptural Purity*, were willing that the Ordinance of *The Singing of Psalms*, so should be restored among them, unto a Share in that *Purity*. Tho' they blessed God for the Religious Endeavours of them who translated the *Psalms* into the *Metre* usually annex'd at the End of the Bible, yet they beheld in the Translation so many *Detractions* from, *Additions* to, and *Variations* of, not only the Text, but the very *Sense* of the Psalmist, that it was an Offence unto them. Resolving then upon a New Translation, the chief Divines in the Country, took each of them a Portion to be Translated. Among whom were Mr. *Welds* and Mr *Eliot* of Roxbury, and Mr *Mather* of Dorchester.[2]

Mather explained that revision was immediately called for, and listed the revisers, yet adding 'That the Psalms have never yet seen a *Translation*, that I know of, nearer to the *Hebrew Original.*'

Mather probably wrote in the 1690s, and time had blurred the edges of detail, and washed away necessary information. What he noted is generally true: there *was* dissatisfaction with 'the Psalms . . . usually annex'd at the End of the Bible' (that is, Sternhold and Hopkins): some passages of *The Bay Psalm Book* are indeed closer to the Hebrew than Sternhold and Hopkins. But Mather is misleading. In the first place, he gives an impression that the original work was entirely by Thomas Weld and John Eliot of Roxbury (now a suburb of Boston) and Richard Mather, Cotton's grandfather. As a result, in standard histories these three 'chief Divines of the County' have ever since been given as the authors of *The Bay Psalm Book*. Mather's key words, however, are 'Among whom were . . .'. The strongest likelihood is that the 150 Psalms were first turned into English verse in America by a dozen people, including John Cotton (who most probably wrote the Preface – an earlier draft in his hand-writing has survived[3]), John Wilson, Nathanael Ward, Peter Bulkeley, Thomas Shepard, John Norton and others of the younger founding fathers.[4] It has even been said that several of the Psalms (as yet unidentified) were the work of Francis Quarles, the widely read English poet whose *Emblems* of 1635 were universally popular.[5] A later revision was by Thomas Shepard, Cotton Mather's 'Pastor Evangelicus'.

The 150 Psalms are divided into five books, after the Hebrew, unlike Sternhold and Hopkins, and illuminated by commentaries and by English prose versions.

> . . . there were few ministers, even in the outlying parishes, without their Hebrew grammars, concordances, and the huge folios of the leading Reformers. Theological works formed the largest section of these libraries, and among them were many expositions of the Psalms. The translators of *The Bay Psalm Book* must have examined the commentaries of Calvin, Musculus, Osiander, Rivetus and many others, all of which they possessed.[6]

Standard histories also attribute the Preface, which occupies the first thirteen pages of the volume, to Richard Mather. This is unlikely, in view of the manuscript version in John Cotton's hand, and the close match of the Preface and Cotton's ways of thought. But whoever wrote it, it is interesting in its own right both for what it does, and what it does not, say. It sets out to explain the reasons for the making of the book, and it gives us incidentally a picture of what occupied the minds of the church-going people of Massachusetts not quite ten years after the original settlements.

The Preface does not go over the historic reasons for using Psalms, nor does it mention Athanasius's classic *Treatise* (probably written about AD 360) setting out what Psalms to read in what experiences of life. These statements, so prominent in Sternhold and Hopkins, are taken for granted.

The Preface begins by raising three questions that were then causing discord. First, in church, should only David's Psalms be sung? (That means, should other poems, even those by 'godly men', be barred?) Secondly, if so, how close should such Psalms for singing (that is, metrical) be to the original? Thirdly, who should sing them? – everyone, or 'one man singing alone and the rest joining in silence, and in the close saying amen'? The Preface's scriptural defence of singing by the whole church includes the Hebrew characters, printed in large and almost accurate type, of the phrase usually translated as 'psalms, hymns and spiritual songs'. The argument in defence of metrical singing by everyone, conducted over a dozen pages, calls all the time on the usages of the primitive church. Towards the end, the author directs attention to 'the difficulty of *Ainsworth's* tunes, and the corruptions in our common psalm books', as the previous 'translations of the psalms into metre . . . have rather presented a paraphrase than the words of David translated according to the rule *2 Chron.29.30*.[7] Further,

> their additions to the words, detractions from the words are not seldom and rare, but very frequent and many times needless (which we supposed would not be approved of if the psalm were so translated into prose), and that there variations of the sense, and alterations of the sacred text too frequently, may justly minister matter of offence to them that are able to compare the translation with the text . . . whereupon it hath been generally desired, that as we do enjoy other, so . . . we might enjoy this ordnance also in its natural purity . . .

Explanation follows of their method of dealing with the Hebrew, concluding that if 'the verses are not always so smooth and elegant as some may desire or expect; let them consider that Gods altar needs not our polishings: Ex.20.'[8]

What did these principles produce? Here is *The Bay Psalm Book's* opening of Psalm 23:

> The Lord to me a shepherd is
>   want therefore shall not I
> He in the fields of tender grass
>   doth cause me down to lie:
> To waters calm me gently leads
>   Restore my soul doth he . . .

> because thou art with me, thy rod,
> and staff my comfort are . . .

That is not even passable poetry in English: 'want therefore shall not I' is an unhappy line, even as an inversion for the sake of the rhyme. The first version of Psalm 23 in Sternhold and Hopkins is:

> The Lord is only my support
> and he that doth me feed,
> How then can I want anything,
> whereof I stand in need?

Thomas Sternhold's own version is:

> My shepherd is the living lord,
> nothing therefore I need,
> In pastures fair with waters calm,
> he set me for to feed.

And the much-loved version still sung today to the tune 'Crimond' is the Scottish

> The Lord's my shepherd, I'll not want,
> he makes me down to lie
> In pastures green: he leadeth me
> the quiet waters by.

If the Psalms are to be in English metre, this is surely how to do it (and see above, pp. 323–8 for fuller discussion). Perhaps it is unfair to take aim at *The Bay Psalm Book* from the citadel of such an adored and successful version as that Scottish Psalm 23. Yet *The Bay Psalm Book* does lay itself open.

This is the opening of their Psalm 24:

> The earth Jehovahs is,
> and the fulness of it:
> the habitable world, and they
> that there upon do sit.

Here is the whole of a slightly less familiar Psalm, 127, as set out in *The Bay Psalm Book*:

> A Song of degrees for Solomon.
> If God build not the house, vainly
> who build it do take pain:
> except the Lord the city keep,
> the watchman wakes in vain.

2. I'ts [*sic*] vain for you early to rise,
    watch late, to feed upon
the bread of grief: so he gives sleep
    to his beloved one.
3. Lo, the womb's fruit, it's God's reward
    sons are his heritage.
4. As arrows in a strong man's hand,
    are sons of youthful age.
5. O blessed is the man which hath
    his quiver fill'd with those:
they shall not be asham'd, i'th gate
    when they speak with their foes.

This is brief, correctly for that Psalm: sixteen lines, to Sternhold and Hopkins's thirty. Yet 'Lo, the womb's fruit, it's God's reward' deserves entry in a competition for the worst line in English verse: even remotely adequate poetry the whole Psalm is not.

Worse, even, is the start of *The Bay Psalm Book*'s Psalm 137, on a principle of verse-making, of internal rhymes every fourth beat in the longer lines, clearly well beyond the capacity of the maker:

Because there they that us away
    led in captivity,
Requir'd of us a song, and thus
    askd mirth: us waste who laid,
Sing us among a Sions song
    unto us then they said.

This is nearly gibberish. The last two and half lines (not the end of the Psalm) should probably produce, instead of a pious 'amen', a baffled 'eh?'

Not all the versions follow the 'common metre' of 'eight and six': some, as Bully Bottom did, want to 'make it two more . . . written in eight and eight'.[9] Thus, Psalm 18:

Il'e [*sic*] dearly love thee, Lord, my strength.
The Lord is my rock, and my tower,
and my deliverer, my God,
I'le [*sic*] trust in him, *who is* my power
My shield, and my salvation-horn,
my high-fort; Who is praiseworthy,
I on the Lord will call, so shall
I be kept from mine enemy . . .
me fear'd the floods of ungodly . . .
likewise the heavens he down-bow

and he descended, and there was
under his feet a gloomy cloud. . . .
He from mine enemies-strong, and from
them which me hated did rescue:
For they were mightier than I.
They me prevented in the day
of my cloudy calamity,
but for me was the Lord a stay.

Some of this is hardly verse – or sense – at all.

Not all the translators are stuck with eight and six or eight and eight; some go for fours. Psalm 128 ends:

And shalt view well
thy children then
with their children
peace on Isr'ell.

There is much in the content of *The Bay Psalm Book* that can call out mockery. For all the glory of a Scottish version like 'The Lord's my shepherd', however, or even the earlier 'All people that on earth do dwell', the very form itself, of Psalms intended to be sung in metre, invites a certain ruggedness. It was not *The Bay Psalm Book* that rendered Psalm 148 as

Ye monsters of the bubbling deep,
Your Maker's praises spout.
Up from the sands, ye codlings peep,
And wag your tails about.[10]

And Dorothy L. Sayers quotes with glee a partially remembered eighteenth-century English versification of the story of the ark being carried dry-foot across Jordan in Joshua 3:

The [something] torrent, leaping in the air,
Left the astounded river's bottom bare.[11]

The principles of Hebrew poetry were not yet fully understood in the West in 1640: those translators of Bay Psalms who did their best with the Hebrew still had to struggle with a fairly baffling original form, never mind the difficulty of getting it all into singable short verses in English, to be taken line by line by, or for, a congregation. Though tempting, it is quite wrong to bring to these verses high criteria of what lyric poetry should be, never mind Shakespeare or Milton, or the lofty critical canons of the eighteenth or nineteenth centuries (which, of course, found

Shakespeare himself seriously lacking in many places[12]). It is tempting, and some noble minds have been o'erthrown: see, for example, Moses C. Tyler, who in New York in 1880, wrote, of *The Bay Psalm Book*:

> In turning over these venerable pages, one suffers by sympathy something of the obvious toil of the undaunted men who, in the very teeth of nature, did all this; and whose appalling sincerity must, in our eyes, cover a multitude of such sins, as sentences wrenched about end for end, clauses heaved up and abandoned in chaos, words disembowelled or split quite in two in the middle, and dissonant combinations of sound that are the despair of such poor vocal organs as are granted to human beings. The verses, indeed, seem to have been hammered out on an anvil, by blows from a blacksmith's sledge. Everywhere in the book is manifest the agony it cost the writers to find two words that would rhyme more or less; and so often as this arduous feat is achieved, the poetic athlete appears to pause awhile from sheer exhaustion, panting heavily for breath. Let us now read, for our improvement, a part of the fifty-eighth Psalm:
>
> > The wicked are estranged from
> >   the womb, they goe astray
> > as soone as ever they are borne;
> >   uttering lies are they.
> > Their poyson's like serpents poison:
> >   they like deafe Aspe, her eare
> > that stops. Though Charmer wisely charme,
> >   his voice she will not heare.
> > Within their mouth doe those their teeth
> >   break out, o God most strong,
> > doe thou Jehovah, the great teeth
> >   break of the lions young.
>
> It is pathetic to contemplate the tokens of intellectual anxiety scattered along these pages; the prolonged bafflings, perspiration and discouragement which these good men had to pass through, in order to overcome the material problems presented . . .[13]

This, though fun, is unfair. Professor Tyler does not point out that those verses from that Psalm in KJV are:

> 3 The wicked are estranged from the womb; they go astray as soon as they be born, speaking lies.
>
> 4 Their poison is like the poison of a serpent; they are like the deaf adder that stoppeth her ear;

5 Which will not hearken to the voice of charmers, charming never so wisely. Break their teeth, O God, in their mouth: break out the great teeth of the young lions.[14]

There is no reason not to relish the bad lines: but what should be appraised is the religious energy that made the 'first book printed in America' (that is, north of the Rio Grande) a book of congregational Psalms.

The content can be unhappy: the execution is usually worse. There is no space between successive Psalms. Apostrophes appear back to front and in the wrong place – indeed, punctuation seems to be beyond the typesetter, who does not understand full stops and who splits words of one syllable with a hyphen. The page-heads in roman numerals give the only clue of contents, though there may be several psalms on the page, and what is called at the head of the left page a 'Psalm' is on the right a 'Psalme'. Titles appear at the foot of a page. Lines are not straight. Words are omitted or doubled. A list of Errata gives a mere seven mistakes. The book gives the effect of having been made by someone who had not printed a reasonably full book before, on less than adequate equipment. Both these responses to it are correct.

PRINTING *THE BAY PSALM BOOK*

In London in the summer of 1638, Jose Glover, a well-to-do Dissenting minister, embarked with his family on the *John of London* for America. He had with him his wife, five children, servants of both sexes, furniture and costly utensils – and a press, a quantity of paper, and the necessary equipment for types. There is in the records no mention of any plan of starting up a press, but as Glover seems to have had some financial support in Europe, from 'some Gentlemen of Amsterdam', it is likely that religious printing in America was in mind. With him also was Stephen Day of Cambridge, who had with him his wife, two sons, a stepson and three manservants.[15] Glover was described as a clerk (that is, a clergyman) and Day as a locksmith, which is what he had been at home in Cambridge. Day had already been in Massachusetts once before, active in some business to do with iron. It seems that he did not cross the Atlantic this time as a printer. During the voyage, Glover died. On arrival, his widow acquired a good house in Cambridge, in Market Square. Day and his family had more modest lodgings on Crooked Lane, a few hundred yards away. By 10 December 1638, the transported press was set up in Cambridge, at Harvard College, apparently by Day (he was no relation of John Day, the great printer of Elizabeth's reign). His name does not appear in any books printed at Cambridge. When, however, three years later, in December 1641, the General Court granted him three hundred acres of land, he was named 'the first that set upon printing'.

The first product of the press was a single sheet, 'The Freeman's Oath'. Copies have not survived, though what it said is known. No copies have survived, either, of the second, the *Almanack made for New England* by 'Capt. Peirce', though it is thought to have had eight leaves. Almanacs were considered essential in the life of the colony for details of expected weather and general conditions for crops, so to print locally, rather than import, a small, cheap almanac would have been sensible.

The print-run of 1,700 of the third product, the new *Bay Psalm Book*, meant that more copies were made than could have been bought in the young colony. If the population by 1640 was between 15,000 and 20,000 and, if that meant about 3,500 families, then if all the print-run was sold, every other family must have bought a copy, which seems unlikely. Moreover, the northern half of the Bay colony, 'following the lead of Salem and Newbury . . . was always distrustful of Boston, and refused to accept the new translation for their churches'.[16]

Selling out the edition in the colony would have meant that every single family in the southern part bought a copy, something more than just unlikely. (It is not known what happened. It is probable that a substantial part of the print-run was shipped back to England for sale there: especially as the first revision, in 1647, was printed in London. Indeed, there seem to have been English customers for the New England psalters, in various revisions, for a long time, even 130 years.[17] In the revision of 1651, many of the psalms were rewritten by Henry Dunster, the President of Harvard College. Of the nine revisions and reprintings before 1700, six were in England, either in Cambridge or London.) A second American press was imported, again to Harvard College, in 1658. It was a further sixteen years before the monopoly of the two presses in Cambridge, Massachusetts, was broken, and William Bradford set up the first press in Boston.

In December 1638, when the first press was set up in North America, there were many editions of the Psalms in metre, in England, and being imported into America. Sternhold and Hopkins were at the back of every Bible, which in the twenty years before had seen eighty-eight editions. In the same decades, 1620–1640, there had been six new prose translations, and 130 editions of Sternhold and Hopkins, with twenty-four Scottish versions. The Book of Common Prayer had been through sixty-eight editions, always including the psalter. Since the middle of the sixteenth century there had been a dozen independent metrical versions (by Robert Crowley, for example, or George Wither, or King James 1), though not all of them were complete.

WHY WAS *THE BAY PSALM BOOK* MADE?

So what was it that led John Cotton and the others not only to want yet another set of Psalms, but to give to the raw Stephen Day their new metrical versions to print in such numbers? A start of an answer lies in the dissatisfaction generally felt among 'Puritans' with Sternhold and Hopkins. The great success of that metrical version (which, as noted above, reached six hundred editions by the early nineteenth century) came partly from the advantage of including tunes. The English church encouraged congregational singing in each parish, rather than having the Psalms sung by a special choir, as in the cathedrals. Sternhold and Hopkins was printed as an integral part of most English Bibles as well as the Book of Common Prayer, so that, in its two books in constant use, the English church had the Psalms in both prose and verse. Difficulties began to arise with the strictness of the translation. Sternhold and Hopkins, as was said, had 'conferred with the Hebrew': but they based their verses largely on the Vulgate and on Coverdale. By 1600, knowledge of the Hebrew language had greatly increased since Jerome in the fourth century and since Coverdale's sources in 1535 – and since the psalter of Sternhold and Hopkins was first printed in 1562. Separatists had always intended to make a new metrical psalter. The pastor of the English church at Amsterdam, Henry Ainsworth, was a fine Hebrew scholar, and in 1612, after years of work, he published his new translation of the Psalms, in prose and in metre, with full annotations on the original Hebrew senses – a large quarto, including his work on the Five Books of Moses, of 1,610 pages. He was confident that he did not 'omit the grace of the Hebrew tongue' or use 'such uncouth [strange] phrases as the common reader understandeth not'. He wrote:

> And let not the variety of phrase, or sundry interpretations trouble any, but . . . choose out the best. Behold, the Holy Ghost translateth one Hebrew word, by many Greek, to teach us both the ample wisdom comprised in that mother tongue; and that many words may be used which express the meaning of the text unto our understanding.[18]

He included 'singing notes', some of them taken from Sternhold and Hopkins and some from French and Dutch psalters. Ainsworth wrote that 'Tunes for the psalms I find none set of God; so that each people is to use the most grave, decent and comfortable manner of singing that they know . . .'[19] Naturally, the Pilgrims took with them to America this newer Psalm book, which they had already used in Holland for nearly twenty years. Reprinted several times, it remained in use in Plymouth until the end of the colony as a separate entity in 1691.

The founders of the Bay Colony, on the other hand, had been brought up on Sternhold and Hopkins, already approaching its two-hundredth edition. Like Ainsworth and the Separatists to the south at Plymouth, they had for some time been aware of the corruptions in that psalter, and they wished to enjoy the Lord's ordinance 'in its native purity'; so the ministers decided to make 'a plain and familiar translation'.[20] So *The Bay Psalm Book* was to be an expression of their own Calvinism as congregationalist members of the Church of England. The Sternhold and Hopkins volume was not Calvinist enough.

As their intention was so similar to Henry Ainsworth's, why did they not simply accept his? In Hebrew scholarship Ainsworth was unchallengeable; his verses were no worse than those of Sternhold and Hopkins; and that psalter was in daily use only thirty-odd miles to the south of Cambridge. The Massachusetts divines, however, said that they had no excess of confidence in that book. They said that they found the tunes difficult, which does sound like special pleading. A more central objection was that if the Plymouth Separatists had their own new and satisfactory Psalm book, Ainsworth's, it was even more important that the Bay Puritans should have one of their own. Beneath the rawness of such playground rivalry was the knowledge that to have adopted Ainsworth's version would have merged them with the Separatists. One special significance of 'the first book printed in America' was that it identified and distinguished the Bay Puritans. They needed to emphasise their difference from the Pilgrims. 'Nonconformists they were; but that was not separation.'[21] Their principle, established long before they left England, was non-Separatist congregationalism, and they had to use all the ways they could to define that, and make it understood in America. The arrival of a press in the fall of 1638 seemed to be 'a hint from Providence'.[22]

Thinking of the enormous influence that printing had in the expansion of the later United States, it has to be noteworthy that the first book printed in North America, by the inexperienced Stephen Day, and at the behest not of demagogues but of 'the Chief Divines', was to print not a political broadside, not an account of the topography and conditions, nor statements of religious doctrine, nor even special sermons, but that quite remarkable number, in the circumstances, of copies of a thick book of Psalms in metre. Like metrical psalters throughout Reformation Europe, it was not intended for use only by congregations in church services on the Sabbath. Significant Psalms were easily learned, with distinctive tunes, and were to be sung in daily work; while building houses, or labouring in the fields, or manning ships, or doing daily household tasks. Mockery of the poor 'poetry' of *The Bay Psalm Book* tends to fade when the sung Psalm is understood as a powerful weapon. It was not quite now against enemies, as it had been in Europe since Luther. Psalm 46, 'God is our refuge and strength', had been the national anthem of Protestant Germany.

Yet, in the first years of the American experience, the fight was to ensure unity and counter idleness or despair. Essences of the American dream are still, in the new millennium, concord and hope.

Some mockery should also begin to evaporate when *The Bay Psalm Book* is more carefully read and reveals some metrical Psalms that are more than passable: for example, some lines of Psalm 103, and especially Psalm 107. Here are verses of Psalm 103:

> 5. Who with good things abundantlee
>   doth satisfie thy mouth:
>   So that like as the Eagles bee
>   renewed is thy youth . . .
>
> 19. The Lord hath in the heavens hye
>   established his throne:
>   And over all his Royalty
>   doth bear dominion . . .
>
> 21. All yee that are the Lords armies,
>   & blesse Jehovah *still*:
>   & all yee ministers of his,
>   his pleasure that fulfill.

Or from Psalm 107, on the whole less close to KJV:

> 23. They that goe downe to'th [*sic*] sea in ships:
>   their business there to doo
> 24. in waters great. The Lords work see,
>   it'h [*sic*] deep his wonders too.
> 25. Because that he the stormy winde
>   commandeth to arise:
>   which lifteth up the waves thereof,
> 26. They mount up to the skies:
>   Downe goe they to the depths againe,
>   their soul with ill doth quaile.
> 27. They reele, & stagger, drunkard like,
>   and all their witt doth faile.
> 28. Then did they to Jehovah cry
>   when they were in distress:
>   and thereupon he bringeth them
>   out of their anguishes.
> 29. Hee makes the storme a calme: so that
>   the waves thereof are still . . .

All the Bay colonists had known long ocean voyages. As a description of extended seasickness from personal experience, there is sympathy as well as some literary skill in the vowels of verse 26's 'their soul with ill doth quaile'; (Geneva's Psalms has 'their soul melteth for trouble', and KJV has 'their soul is melted because of trouble'. Sternhold and Hopkins are miles away, with 'their soules consume with paine'.)

The enterprise hoped to stand on its greater faithfulness to the Hebrew, being a stricter translation than that generally found in Sternhold and Hopkins, and in Ainsworth's psalter. In bulk, *The Bay Psalm Book*'s poems match the prose versions of Geneva and the KJV, which argues for greater closeness to the Hebrew. Sternhold and Hopkins need a third more space.

If there was any general reliance on an English version, was it KJV? It has been said that in the writings of the younger men, Richard Mather, John Eliot, Thomas Shepard and John Norton, there is no trace of the older Geneva Bible, but what has been felt to be a natural tendency towards the newer, 1611, version.[23] Geneva is found, however, in Weld's *Answer to W.R.* (1644), in Peter Bulkeley's *The Gospel Covenant* (1646), and John Cotton's *Singing of Psalms*, where lines from Psalm 111 are taken from Geneva.[24] The title-page of the first, 1640, edition has two New Testament quotations, one from Colossians 3 and one from James 5. These are identical with those on the more crowded title-pages of editions of Sternhold and Hopkins. The one from Colossians says (in modernised spelling)

> Let the word of God dwell plenteously in you, in all wisdom, teaching and exhorting one another in psalms, hymns, and spiritual songs, singing to the Lord with grace in your hearts.

That is not from the KJV, and not from a Geneva version. It is a touch free, substituting 'God' for the original Greek's 'Christ' – understandably for a collection of Psalms from the Old Testament. In essence, it is Tyndale, whose 1534 New Testament has at that point: 'Let the word of Christ dwell in you plenteously in all wisdom.' (Tyndale loved the word 'plenteous' and its derivatives, and gave it to the English Old Testaments.) That version continues, 'Teach and exhort your own selves in psalms, and hymns, and spiritual songs' (which is the English original of that phrase). The next title-page phrase, 'singing to the Lord with grace in your hearts', occurs in both psalters, Sternhold and Hopkins and *The Bay Psalm Book*, and nowhere else that has been discovered. Tyndale there has 'which have favour with them singing in your hearts to the Lord', a form of words which comes partly from his political desire to avoid the word 'grace'. Fundamentally, however, the whole phrase is Tyndale's (his 1534 version is identical here with his first, 1526, translation).[25]

The second quotation on *The Bay Psalm Book*'s title-page, from James 5, again identical with that in Sternhold and Hopkins, is

If any be afflicted, let him pray, and if any of you be merry, let him sing psalms.

'Afflicted' in the first phrase was first used by the Geneva translators in their 1557 New Testament. The second part is unmistakably Tyndale in his 1534 version: 'merry' is another good Tyndale word, again given by him to later English Bibles. (Wyclif had tended to use 'make feast'; so that in Luke 15, for the elder brother's phrase in Tyndale, 'that I may make merry with my friends', Wyclif's 'make feast' does not quite have that cheerful uninhibited quality that Tyndale has identified in the original, and expressed in 'merry'.[26])

On the title-page of the first substantial book printed in North America, the fortieth to the eighty-fifth words are effectively Tyndale's. This is going to be an effect to be seen down the years. Whether the founding fathers imported Geneva Bibles or King James Versions, they were still importing much of Tyndale. In the two centuries of the English Bible in America from 1777, the same is true. The most American of all translations, the American Revised Version of 1901 and the American Revised Standard Version of 1952 – the latter among the most globally influential of all modern versions – are still frequently Tyndale, still frequently *verbatim*, as at Ephesians 3:3, 'Your life is hid with Christ in God'.[27]

METRICAL PSALMS IN BRITAIN

The name of Nahum Tate, Poet Laureate from 1692, is customarily blackened as the reviser and 'improver' of Shakespeare for the different tastes of the Restoration theatre. Thus, in his *King Lear* of 1681, the Fool is omitted; the King's youngest daughter Cordelia survives a rape by the Duke of Gloucester's bastard son Edmund, and lives to marry Gloucester's rightful son Edgar; similarly, the King does not die at the end of the play, nor do Gloucester, nor Kent, but all live in peaceful retirement. It is startling to think that it was this *King Lear* which held the stage for 150 years, until 1838 and Macready's return to Shakespeare's text.

Outside the theatre, Tate has, for three centuries, been the subject of lofty sneering, as a comically incompetent 'poetaster' – the word is *DNB*'s. Nahum Tate, however, with Nicholas Brady, issued in 1696 *A New Version of the Psalms*, with instant success. Between that date and the last edition in 1740 there were about 360 separate editions, overtopping Sternhold and

Hopkins in those decades, justifiably, for here was a metrical and syntactical assurance that had been needed. His Psalm 42 begins,[28]

> As pants the hart for cooling streams
> When heated in the chase.

His Psalm 34, a properly loved hymn to this day, begins,

> Through all the changing scenes of life
> In trouble and in joy,
> The praises of my God shall still
> My heart and soul employ . . .
> Fear him, ye saints, and you will then
> Have nothing else to fear.
> Make but His service your delight,
> Your wants shall be His care.

Tate and Brady's *Supplement to the New Version of the Psalms* in 1700 introduced biblical paraphrases, and included the eternally popular carol:

> While shepherds watch'd their flocks by night
> All seated on the ground,
> The Angel of the Lord came down,
> And glory shone around.
>
> 'Fear not', said he, for mighty dread
> Had seized their troubled mind;
> 'Glad tidings of great joy I bring
> To you and all mankind.'

That is, surely (in several senses) how to do it. Tate and Brady can occasionally be said to nod, principally in using useful words as fillers to make up the metre. Their stride forward, however, was great, in the making of Psalms for public use, and not, as in the sixteenth and seventeenth centuries outside Sternhold and Hopkins and the Scots, and *The Bay Psalm Book*, as poems for private meditation. It is a difficult art, or at least, craft. The survival of half a dozen of their Psalms as admired hymns explains their success.

HYMNS

Hymns for congregational singing must be theological or they are mere sentimental songs. There is room in the genre for a range of expression, from the meditational, as,

> How sweet the name of Jesus sounds
> In a believer's ear!
> It soothes his sorrow, heals his wounds,
> And drives away his fear –

to the rousing, as

> Guide me, O, thou great Jehovah,
> Pilgrim through this barren land;
> I am weak, but thou art mighty,
> Hold me with thy powerful hand.

The one essential, after sound Christian theology, is short, simple syntax, something that congregations can grasp in a sung line.

The Anglican tradition in Britain has kept alive the communal singing of the whole Psalter. Services in the older 'Free Church' chapels – the Baptists and Congregationalists from the 1590s (at first Dissenters; after 1662 Nonconformists) with the Methodists from the 1740s – have from the first been events where a long sermon was heard in a frame of the heartiest congregational singing, instead of a written Prayer Book liturgy. Set to memorable tunes, several dozen of these are still, mercifully, in the English Christian bloodstream, as 'Glorious things of thee are spoken, / Zion, city of our God.'

England has been blessed in a tradition of hymn writers of unusual insight and skill.[29] In the eighteenth century John Newton, Isaac Watts, William Cowper, the Wesleys and others gave English worship a quite strenuous activity of Christological expression. A century later, Victorian hymns, like Mrs C. F. Alexander's 'There is a green hill far away' or 'All things bright and beautiful', or John Henry Newman's 'Abide with me', or 'Lead, kindly light', came from a different source, that of a more settled, less theological High Church, liturgical, contemplation. The needs of children to sing hymns with direct simplicity produced in the twentieth century, for worship together, a general tendency downwards, towards childishness, rather than childlikeness, as if the great truths of the New Testament had, for everyone, to be reduced to what could be enjoyed, in rhythm and words, at a mental age of four or below. The effects in the more charismatic worship of the visits to Britain in the 1870s of the American evangelists Dwight L. Moody and his gospel singer Ira David Sankey could – and still can – be felt. In Ira Sankey's first collection of *Sacred Songs and Solos* (1874), twenty-four of the thirty-one songs had 'choruses', simple ditties of a few repeated words, usually infantile rather than theological. A later Sankey chorus, still sung, is devoid of spiritual meaning altogether, consisting of

> I am h-a-p-p-y,
> I am h-a-p-p-y,
> I know I am,
> I'm sure I am,
> I am h-a-p-p-y.

Admittedly, it goes on to two more verses, 'l-o-v-e-d' and 's-a-v-e-d', but these tend to be forgotten when stuck with the so-memorable jingle, impossible to dislodge from the mind. Those revivalists' weak dilution of popular Christianity linked with the techniques of the salesman had the effect, even in the later twentieth century, of ensuring that 'hymns' should be about what was 'relevant', that is, supermarkets and buses.

The strenuous eighteenth-century English hymns one might describe as theologically fully adult. Isaac Watts wrote moral songs for children (affectionately mocked by Lewis Carroll[30]). Watts also wrote, as singable by children as by anyone,

> When I survey the wondrous Cross
> On which the Prince of glory died,
> My richest gain I count but loss
> And pour contempt on all my pride.

Briefly to comment on the first line only: the comprehensive breadth of the word 'survey' prepares for the elevation of 'wondrous', leading to the fullness of the abrupt 'Cross', elaborated in the next line. Children deserve the best, which this is. It is the opposite of condescending. 'Dr Watts's Psalms', published from 1710, and collected in his 1719 *Psalms of David Imitated in the Language of the New Testament* – note his concern with what he called 'the gospel-state'[31] – include

> Before the hills in order stood,
> Or earth received her frame,
> From everlasting Thou art God,
> To endless years the same.

That, from 'Our God, our help in ages past', is a version of the beginning of Psalm 90. Again, the combination of vastness of scale and simplicity of terms is related to human experience. This is 'Our God . . . our help . . . Our hope . . . Our shelter . . . our eternal home.' It is, incidentally, in a later verse Time's sons which are borne away and 'fly forgotten as a dream / Dies at the opening day', that is, minutes, hours and days, not people. Even so, the hymn expresses flesh and blood. In this it is unlike Joseph Addison's 'The spacious firmament on high', sometimes sung as a hymn (rather oddly, the point being only that the hand that made the heavens is Divine): this has its glories, as

> Soon as the evening shades prevail
> The moon takes up the wondrous tale,
> And nightly to the listening Earth
> Repeats the story of her birth –

but it is not salvation history. Unlike John Newton's

> Amazing Grace! How sweet the sound
> That saves a child like me!
> I once was lost but now I'm found
> Was bound, but now I'm free.

or

> And can it be that I should gain
> An interest in the Saviour's blood?
> Died he for me, who cause his pain?
> For me, who Him to death pursued?
> Amazing love! how can it be
> That Thou, my God, shouldst die for me!

CHARLES AND JOHN WESLEY

At Christmas, English-speaking Christians usually sing, or hear:

> Hark! the herald-angels sing
> Glory to the new-born King:
> Peace on earth, and mercy mild,
> God and sinners reconciled.

The original, written by Charles Wesley around 1746, began

> Hark, how all the welkin rings,
> 'Glory to the King of Kings.'

The alteration (it must be agreed, an improvement) was made by the Wesleys' one-time colleague George Whitefield in 1753. The change took the lines further in to the New Testament story. Charles Wesley's gifts as a writer of hymns ensure that his words are still sung: '"Christ, the Lord, is risen today," / Sons of men and angels say', or 'Soldiers of Christ, arise, / And put your armour on.' His extraordinary 'Jesu, Lover of my soul, /

Let me to Thy Bosom fly' is closer to the strongly emotional tone of the message that his brother John preached:

> Other refuge have I none;
> Hangs my helpless soul on Thee . . .
> Cover my defenceless head
> With the shadow of thy wing . . .
> Thou of life the fountain art;
> Freely let me take of Thee;
> Spring Thou up within my heart,
> Rise to all eternity.

It is calculated that Charles Wesley wrote over five thousand hymns. The rapid spread across England and Wales of the Wesleys' message of full-blooded salvation, aiming to allow the power of the Spirit through height-ened emotions to revitalise the dry bones of the Church, was fully a New Testament movement, and acceptance of that book was central. Charles's hymns and John's sermons were the Bible energised into the deepest feel-ings of ordinary people, just as the 'lover' of the hymn above, as the lines unfold, is both parental and erotic. Their younger Oxford companion, George Whitefield, broke from them after all three had returned from America. Whitefield had found his own remarkable skills as a preacher: he had also begun to cherish a more fully fledged Calvinism, greatly suc-cessful in Scotland and Wales, and again in America.

More soberly, John Wesley revised the New Testament text in 1755, with a commentary based on a study of the Greek text and many modifica-tions of KJV – as many as twelve thousand all told.[32] This edition was reprinted in 1760 and 1839, with an abridged version in 1790. Though noteworthy in passing, Wesley's revision did not make a lasting noise in the UK, though it was extremely popular in the USA.

In his short Preface, Wesley stresses that his translation is 'for plain, unlet-tered men, who understand only their mother tongue, and yet reverence and love the word of God, and have a desire to save their souls'. The sen-timent, and the manner, echo Tyndale. Wesley acknowledges that his changes to KJV will be criticised all the same as being too few and too many. His understanding is that 'God speaks not as man, but as God. His thoughts are very deep, and thence his words are of inexhaustible virtue.'

The characteristic mark of his edition is the notes, explained by him as being as short and as plain as possible. He lists some learned sources, but in their intended more modest quantity (not always achieved) and undoubted forceful clarity, the notes are his own. To take one example: at the beginning of Luke 16, Jesus' Parable of the Unjust Steward presents a difficulty in verse 8:

And the lord commended the unjust steward, because he had done wisely; for the children of this world are wiser in their generation than the children of light.

How can Jesus be commending an obvious rogue? Wesley's note is,

8. *And the Lord commended the unjust steward* – Namely, in this respect, because he had used timely precaution; so that though the dishonesty of such a servant be detestable, yet his foresight, care, and contrivance about the interests of this life, deserve our imitation with regard to the more important affairs of another. *The children of this world* – Those who seek no other portion than this world. *Are wiser* – Not absolutely; for they are, one and all, egregious fools; but they are more consistent with themselves; they are truer to their principles; thy more steadily pursue their end; they are wiser *in their generation* (that is, in their own way) *than the children of light* – The children of God, whose light shines on their hearts.

Interest remains in Wesley's New Testament only in that many of its variants were adopted by the English revisers in the 1880s, and also influenced the making of RSV in the 1960s. An 'Anniversary Edition' was published in Philadelphia in 1953 in which Wesley's deviations from KJV were signalled by italics or ellipses in the text. These highlight the shift in this version towards a New Testament for people 'of feeling': thus, in Luke 15:20, 'his father saw him, and his bowels yearned.'

OLNEY HYMNS

The 1779 collection known as *Olney Hymns*, assembled in that small Buckinghamshire town by William Cowper and his religious mentor John Newton, also contains unforgettable, and unforgotten, congregational hymns. The second edition of 1781, with 424 pages of hymns, divides them into three books: the first, with 141 hymns, 'On Texts of Scripture'; the second, with 100 hymns, 'On Occasional Subjects'; and the third, with 107 hymns, 'On the Progress and Changes of the Spiritual Life'. Number xv of Book III, by Cowper, begins, famously,

> God moves in a mysterious way
> His wonders to perform;
> He plants his footsteps in the sea
> And rides upon the storm.

Though also about the Creator, the stanzas end with words which make Addison seem cold:

> Ye fearful saints fresh courage take,
>   The clouds ye so much dread
> Are big with mercy, and shall break
>   In blessings on your head.

Still sung are the seven stanzas of III, xxxvii beginning;

> Begone Unbelief,
> My Saviour is near,
> And for my relief
> Will surely appear:
> By prayer let me wrestle,
> And he will perform,
> With CHRIST in the vessel,
> I smile at the storm.

and the hymns beginning

> Sometimes a light surprises
>   The Christian while he sings;
> It is the LORD who rises
>   With healing in his wings (III, xlvii),

> Glorious things of thee are spoken
> Zion, city of our God (I, lx)

and

> Oh! for a closer walk with God —

All these are made of the Bible.[33] It is more than just assumed that the singers will recognise what Scripture they are singing. (Such universal knowledge, now generally gone, would have prevented a hymn beginning 'When Hagar found the bottle spent' sounding as inappropriate as it does today; or, with what one hopes was unintentional ambiguity, 'Once a woman silent stood'.[34]) The famous 'How sweet the name of Jesus sounds / In a believer's ear' elaborates, as the head-note locates, 'Solomon's Song 1:2'.

Chapter 31

THE BIBLE IN AMERICA TO 1776

INCREASE AND COTTON MATHER

The most influential family in early American religious politics were the Mathers. Increase Mather made a considerable impression in the colonies by his upholding of Puritan orthodoxy. He graduated from Harvard in 1656, and then crossed the Atlantic to receive his A.M. from Trinity College, Dublin, in 1658, returning to become the leading enlightened natural philosopher in the America of his time. In 1688 he appealed to King James II for renewal of the Massachusetts charter, granted, more liberally than he expected, by William III. He famously ministered to the congregation of the Second Church of Boston. In that pulpit he was joined from 1685 by his son Cotton Mather (named after his grandfather, John Cotton). Both men were deeply involved in the Salem witch trials of 1692: Increase was sceptical about the evidences of witchcraft, and stopped the executions. (His son, Cotton, was in this less humane.) His fusion of scientific method and religious belief make him the Thomas Browne of America: he is almost as readable. In his *Essay for the Recording of Remarkable Providences* (1684), part of a study of the laws of nature as analysis of divine reason, he is trying to take scientific observation as evidence of a transcendent Mind. One passage is introduced by the sentence 'It is not Heresy to believe that *Satan* has sometimes a great operation in causing Thunderstorms. I know this is vehemently denied by some. The late Witch Advocates call it Blasphemy.'[1] These pages, as an example, are full of Scripture: Job is here not unexpected: but Mather expounds references to Ephesians 2:2, 2 Thessalonians 2:9, Revelation 13:13, and elsewhere, including a number of Psalms. To modern eyes the arguments seem ingenious: equally striking is the automatic assumption not only that Scripture is the authority, but also that it is intimately known.

Cotton Mather entered Harvard at the age of twelve, moving from medicine to theology. Ordained in 1685, at twenty-three, he ministered to Boston's Second Church for the rest of his life. He died in 1727. He was phenomenally prolific, publishing about 450 works. Like his father, he was engaged on the frontier between empirical scientific observation and religious belief. His *Wonders of the Invisible World* (1693) contributed to the hysteria around the witchcraft trials and the twenty hangings: it comes out in favour of the damning verdicts, but lacking evidence is the assertion that he 'even stood at the foot of the gallows bullying hesitant hangmen into doing "their duty"'.[2] He recommended[3] that those possessed of demons be treated with prayer and fasting rather than hanging.[4] Like all American thinkers of the time, he was very aware of the increasing secularisation of colonial politics. He began to find himself marginalised. He was a Fellow of Harvard from 1690 to 1703. He resigned the Fellowship not only because he was disappointed in his hopes of becoming President, as his father had been from 1685 to 1701, but also because the college became less strictly Congregationalist in its policies.

He was one of the founders of Yale as a rival to Harvard on more orthodox principles. His scientific investigations led him to be the first American elected to the Royal Society in England, in 1713: and to the unpopular campaign in Boston promoting inoculation against smallpox (1721).

Cotton Mather's wide reputation, however, was founded on his best-known book, *Magnalia Christi Americana: or, The Ecclesiastical History of New England* published in 1702.[5] It is a collection of accounts of the great works of God in the foundation of the colonies. The exuberance of the story-telling, and prickly debate about his accuracy,[6] are matched by the wilder peculiarities of the typesetting of many of the pages, where words in capitals and in italics grab the reader's attention with vehemence. To turn the pages of the first edition is to feel oneself browbeaten by Cotton Mather's insistence that colonial life was better before. The great acts of God in the arrival and settlement of the original colonists, all of which he records, have, he insists, been forgotten, and America has become secular.

The early words of the book of the prophet Jeremiah are much in mind:

Thus saith the Lord; I remember thee, the kindness of thy youth, the love of thine espousals, when thou wentest after me in the wilderness, in a land that was not sown. . . .

And I brought you into a plentiful country, to eat the fruit thereof and the goodness thereof; but when ye entered, ye defiled my land, and made mine heritage an abomination. . . .

For my people have committed two evils; they have forsaken me the fountain of living waters, and hewed them out cisterns, broken cisterns, that can hold no water. . . .

Yet I had planted thee a noble vine, wholly a right seed: how then art thou turned into the degenerate plant of a strange vine unto me?

Jeremiah 2:2,7,13,21 (KJV)

Like William Bradford before him, Mather writes his account so that Americans – and particularly young Americans – will understand that their country was founded in the work of God. 'The First Age was the Golden Age: to return to That, will make a Man a Protestant, and I may add, a Puritan.' Mather understands that the spring of colonisation was 'The Word of God'. 'The leader of a people in a wilderness had need be a Moses.'[7] He notes William Bradford remarking that the Separatists should be a 'Society of the faithful, that should keep close unto the written word of God, as the rule of their worship'[8]. He assumes Bible knowledge in the reader at every point.

The campaign of the Mathers to renew the churches and restore the 'Rule of the Saints' was embarrassed by the hysteria about witchcraft and the executions at Salem. Such notorious events (not only at Salem) undermined the trust of secular merchants in the religious government of colonies. Scriptural restrictions, particularly from the Pentateuch, became burdensome when the Great Migration ceased in the middle of the century. American trade needed expansion. The new Massachusetts Charter, and the revision of Church doctrines in the Brattle Street Church of Boston, seemed to break the grip of the older orthodoxy. Cotton Mather had quoted an old aphorism in his *Magnalia*, describing Massachusetts, '*Religio peperit devitias, felia devoravit matrem*: religion brought forth prosperity, and the daughter destroyed the mother.'[9] Cotton Mather, however, with the side of his nature that loved enlightened reason, could look forward, and he saw that expanding and loosening the principles of the older Puritanism was where the future lay. By the time he died in 1727, the first signs of the new life that became the Great Awakening could already have been seen in Connecticut and Massachusetts.

What the larger picture shows, at least until 1721, is the steady decline of interest in the Bible. The leaders of thought are now trying to be Enlightenment rationalists. The merchants have little truck with biblical restrictions. Politicians might still quote or refer to a biblical phrase that suggested that America was 'God's country', and it seems that men and women still had Bibles imported from England in their homes. But by the early 1720s, the intensity of the 'Bible commonwealths' had slackened. (All of this would change when the trickle of commercially driven American-printed Bibles from 1777 became a torrent soon after 1800.)

AMERICAN ESTABLISHMENT AND
RELIGIOUS MULTIPLICITY

The colony at Jamestown was abandoned after a terrible fire in 1699. The Separatist Pilgrim colony based in Plymouth had been swallowed up by

Massachusetts in 1691. Boston itself began to be taken over in importance by Philadelphia. The early evangelical flames became duller embers.

Early in the eighteenth century, New England Congregationalism, Anglicanism in New York and the South, Presbyterianism in New Jersey, Pennsylvania and North Carolina; the Baptists in Rhode Island and Quakers in Pennsylvania and New Jersey – all were established in both senses: they were firmly rooted in the landscape, and they were the established church of their district. Though the colonies were all Christian, and though there were Bibles in the households, church attendance declined, and believers were said to be lethargic. In spite of revulsion at the hysteria in Salem and in spite also of the growing influence of scientific thought, ministers were held in respect locally even if their flocks did not generally come to hear them.

There were two strong elements in New England life. First was the development of the covenant theology that so characterised American Protestant thinking. This originated in England before most of the immigrants arrived. It was an amplification of Calvinism to suggest that the relationship between the elect and God was not just in the passive reception of grace, but in an active covenant, for which the model was Abraham and Jehovah in Genesis 15:18 and 17:2–21. God's grace caused a compact between the two partners. The elect soul obeyed God's will, and God granted him or her salvation. So far so good.

Puritan theology in Europe in the early sixteenth century extended this, inevitably, to the local congregation of saints. As long as the church is understood as the communion of the godly together, then it can follow that they can together be doing God's will, making a 'federal' covenant. The passionate hope in Europe was that this would extend to the nation. It could never be realised. In America, however, things were different. Separatists and Puritans alike made the dangerous crossing in order to establish a land dedicated to the will of God. In this new commonwealth they would draw up treaties in which the terms were 'federal': they promised to obey God's law, and he would reward their obedience. Private devotions as well as public communings underlay the understandings of what the will of God could be presumed to be. Thus far historians agree. What is usually missed out of the picture is that both the private and the public declarations came out of intensive study of the Word of God, as all the writings of the period make clear, though it is rarely said. Evidence that the Great Awakening was a revival of the newly eager study of Scripture can be found in many documents. As one example, Jonathan Parsons, in his account of his experience in 1730 as a minister, records 'An uncommon Attention to the Preaching of the Word . . . I seldom went into a House among my Neighbours, but they had some free Discourse about Religion, always searching after the Meaning of some Texts of Scripture.'[10]

The problem for a Christian society aware of its national covenant with God arises in the question of rewards. How does an elect nation know that it is doing God's will? One obvious answer is in its prosperity, and long before Max Weber, a 'Puritan Ethic' of hard work for good reward was articulated. For example, a popular little book among Puritans in England and America, first published in London in 1657, reprinted in Boston in 1683 and again in 1763, has an allegory of charming ingenuity where after several adventures Labour becomes the friend of Godliness, whereupon he prospers amazingly. So far, so obvious. The real difficulty lay with what might generally be called natural disasters – earthquakes, extremes of weather, long droughts, serious epidemics and accidental fires, to which should be added massacres by Indians. These were understood in Old Testament terms, as demonstrations of the wrath of God. The immediate model of such doom was the 'jeremiad', the calls to repentance in the writing of the prophet Jeremiah. The only thing to do was to admit communal fault, undertake to reform, and pray that God would remember his covenant. The church practice that was so much part of European Protestant life, of holding 'fast days', became an even more powerful element in American Puritan life. What were called fast days were not of total abstinence in the monastic tradition, but simply meant eating only basic foods for sustenance. The chief significance was the denial of pleasure for twenty-four hours, whatever physical form it took. A large number of American fast-day sermons have survived. Their titles speak for them: a selection has to include Mitchell's *Nehemiah on the Wall* (1667), William Stoughton's *New England's True Interests* (1668), Samuel Danforth's *A Brief Recognition of New England's Errand into the Wilderness* (1670), the younger Thomas Shepard's *Eye-Salve* (1672), Urian Oakes's *New England Pleaded With* (1673), William Hubbard's *The Happiness of a People* (1676), Increase Mather's *The Day of Trouble is Near* (1673) and his *A Discourse Concerning the Danger of Apostasy* (1677). All these were justly celebrated, and can stand as landmarks in early American literature: they all say that the New England 'errand' had failed. Such jeremiads came from every pulpit. It was clear that the new nation was in decline. 'What for ordinary nations would constitute virtue and civility was miserable inadequacy in a covenanted folk' commented Perry Miller.[11] In 1673, Urian Oakes wrote.

There is great reason to conceive that many Professors [that is professing Christians] may be grown Sermon-proof, that we had as good preach to the Heavens and Earth, and direct our discourse to the Walls and Seats and Pillars of the meeting house, and say, Hear, O ye Walls, give ear O ye Seats and Pillars, as to many men in these Churches, that are deaf to all that is cried in their ears by the Lords Messengers, and are indeed like rocks in the Sea, not to be stirred and moved by the beating and dashing of these waters of the Sanctuary, or by the strongest gust of rational and affectionate discourse that can blow upon them.[12]

There the New England preacher as conscious Old Testament prophet could hardly be clearer, as in the adaptation of the opening words of the book of the prophet Isaiah: 'Hear, O heavens, and give ear, O earth . . .' (Isaiah 1:2). 'The Lord's Messengers' describes both the prophets Haggai (Haggai 1:13) and particularly Malachi, in a passage famous in Christian typology as a prophecy of the coming of the Messiah:

Behold, I will send my messenger, and he shall prepare the way before me: and the Lord, whom ye seek, shall suddenly come to his temple, even the messenger of the covenant, whom ye delight in: behold, he shall come, saith the Lord of hosts. But who may abide the day of his coming? and who shall stand when he appeareth? for he is like a refiner's fire . . . and he shall purify the sons of Levi . . .

Malachi 3:1–3 (KJV)

Urian Oakes did not speak lightly.

The detailed denunciation of the growing number of sins of the people in all these addresses is equally Old-Testament-prophetic in flavour, though with the coloured vocabulary of the originals, with their 'harlots' and 'whoredoms', rather toned down, possibly to avoid suggestion. In 1676 Increase Mather lamented the growth of swearing, which had gone so far that even children in the streets did it: it was 'naturally associated with the vice of cards or dice and with the vicious habit' – a habit indeed so vicious that I hardly dare name it in print – 'of sleeping at sermons'.[13]

Such fast days and jeremiads assumed that the churches spoke for all the nation, even though barely one-fifth of people were, by now, fully accredited church members. It remained a keen social and theological problem how much the church could speak for everyone. Thus a whirl-wind or flood brought calamity to all, but there were difficulties in getting everyone to the days of lamentation, particularly as more and more individualists were settling at the limits of the frontiers in order to prosper on the virgin land and do what they liked, taking no notice of anyone else – and certainly not the pious church elders several hundred miles away.

One unexpected element in the problem was the sudden drying-up of immigrants, as the Long Parliament from 1640 had forbidden emigration. This was serious for the New Englanders: that parliament discouraged trade with the Americas, and so cut off their complicated imports and exports. For the Virginians, there was no problem, as they had one crop marketable anywhere, that is, tobacco. The New Englanders were forced to re-examine just exactly what God meant by prosperity. Anyone exploring any part of the history of North America finds the story becoming ever more complicated. I have only been telling here of the English settlers, who eventually dominated the scene: but all around and among them were the Dutch, Germans, French, Scandinavians and others. Moreover, though none of the settlements had yet what could be considered a history of Americanness, in the sense that the Europeans at home were always aware of solid tradition over many centuries of Englishness or Germanness, yet even so, American Puritan settlements differed from the European, and from each other. This diversity, even within a few miles, remains a powerful American characteristic.

The men who were leading American thought in the mid-eighteenth century – Jonathan Edwards, Benjamin Franklin, even Cotton Mather – were engaging with the new valuation of science, and the growing effects of the thinking of the Enlightenment. One significant issue was the inoculation against smallpox. Older Puritan belief (amounting to bigotry) had maintained that all such pestilences had to be understood biblically, as sent from God with a meaning of rebuke for backsliding. The counter-movement was empirical. Franklin, for example, successfully led his fellow Americans into the new world of scientific discovery and its proper social benefits. Franklin was an enthusiast for his native Pennsylvania, and his home town of Philadelphia. He wrote passionately for toleration. In Pennsylvania itself a German traveller in 1750 reported:

> Coming to speak of Pennsylvania, that colony possesses great liberties above all other English colonies, inasmuch as all religious sects are tolerated there. We find there Lutherans, Reformed, Catholics, Quakers, Mennonites or Anabaptists, Herrnhuter or Moravian Brethren, Pietists, Seventh Day Baptists, Dunkers, Presbyterians, Newborn, Freemasons, Separatists, Freethinkers, Jews, Mohammedans, pagans, Negroes and Indians. The Evangelicals and Reformed, however, are in the majority. But there are many hundred unbaptized souls there that do not even wish to be baptized.[14]

JONATHAN EDWARDS

Jonathan Edwards dominates the history of east coast Christianity in the middle of the eighteenth century. A village preacher's son with no intellectual legacy, he entered Yale College in 1716, shortly before his thirteenth birthday, and went on to study theology there. As an eighteen-year-old, he preached to a New York City congregation of Scottish Presbyterians for six months, and in May 1724 he became a tutor at Yale. That sounds very grand. But the institution that he joined at thirteen had no building, no settled place, and as yet no name: he lamented the lack of stimulus of great teachers, not to mention great books. He lived with nine other freshmen at one of the three locations, a farmhouse only ten miles from his home village. An alert and perceptive boy, however, he had already learned well not only from his own observations of nature – his scientific essay on flying spiders, which is still read, was probably written at the age of eleven – but from his father's books and the home Bible. He briefly joined the New Haven company of undergraduates in 1716, where he fell on Locke's *Essay Concerning Human Understanding* (1690): from it he learned that 'the true nature of things' could come to him as part of his own experience. In the next thirty years, Edwards's religious pilgrimage, intense to himself and important in the history of American Christianity, was always intended to be in philosophical as well as biblical footwear, wanting to keep his emotions in touch with the ground where others – Whitefield comes to mind – were more dangerously unrestrained.

His ministry to the Congregational church at Northampton, Massachusetts from February 1727, begun at twenty-four and soon alongside his seventeen-year-old bride, was at first assisting his grandfather, Solomon Stoddart (famous from 1662 as the innovator of the Halfway Covenant, allowing parents not fully committed to bring children to baptism, and even to take communion). His preaching was the means of the religious revival in its first, New England, phase known later as the Great Awakening. An extraordinary religious excitement gripped the small town of Northampton, and grew. One Sunday morning in 1733, Edwards, as minister, received into membership a hundred new applicants. In these months, people from all over Massachusetts and Connecticut came to watch and report. On another Sunday morning, however, one of the chief men of the town, an uncle Edwards, cut his throat and died. In that cold light, Northampton woke up, and looked round.

THE GREAT AWAKENING

It is sometimes said that the Great Awakening grew out of the ministry of Jonathan Edwards in Northampton – to his own surprise. During a series of sermons he was giving on justification by faith, he reported that he found himself living in a town that 'never was so full of love, nor so full of joy, nor so full of distress as it has lately been'[15] (distress of course at personal sinfulness). What he was preaching was Scripture – Romans 6 above all. The sudden power of his words was not only (as it was with Whitefield for example) in the emotion of listening en masse, but in the fact that such exposition of Paul could be followed up at home. Historians tend not to point out that one of the reasons for the permanent effect of the Great Awakening was just that sustained home study of the Bible. Whitefield had dramatic effects, no doubt quite often hysterical in nature: characteristically, such a 'revival' could be followed by sudden decline and personal and social unsettlement. Growth happened and persisted because so many people were called back to studying the Scriptures, and finding there, in the highest Protestant tradition, the words of personal salvation.

There had been, increasingly from the earliest days, extensions and re-workings of Calvinism, often ingenious. John Cotton 'sweetened his mouth every night with a morsel from the Institutes'.[16] What began to happen in Northampton, and then quickly elsewhere, can probably be best understood as the congregations suddenly finding the authority from God (one even wants to say 'permission') to take the Word outside. Covenants and jeremiads were both alike matters of communal introspection. Suddenly God seemed to be telling his people to look outward. Though, of course, there had been anxieties about the state of grace of the Indians, conversions had been almost entirely a matter of bringing them in one by one to join the gathered saints. Certainly, the Great Awakening regenerated the churches. But it did much more. An essential understanding of preaching before the 1740s was that it was to the committed: though it proclaimed the evangel, it was not in the modern sense evangelising. After 1750, the legacy of Whitefield and the others remained. Of course, the excitement seemed to peter out quite quickly. Attention became fixed elsewhere as the War for Independence took up everyone's energies. Yet the seeds sown in the 1740s came alive in the harvest of the Second Great Awakening of 1800, especially, as will be seen later, in the great mass meetings on the extreme frontiers, particularly at Cane Ridge in 1801 in Kentucky when 20,000 people assembled in the wilderness with frequent ecstatic results.

What happened in New England in the 1730s, became labelled 'The Great Awakening' much later. That title suggests perhaps more of a unified mass movement than the evidence supports. It is still not fully understood what the causes were of unmistakable revival of Christian feeling. On the one hand, a balanced ground was prepared by the preaching and writing of Jonathan Edwards. On the other hand, there seems evidence of a spontaneous infection from group to group. And on a third hand, note has to be taken of the fierce campaign of George Whitefield, itinerant preacher in 1738 and 1739. He returned from England to New England in 1740.

In 1740 Whitefield brought New England within his orbit, and at every place he visited, the consequences were large and tumultuous. Sailing from Charleston, South Carolina, to Newport, he landed on 14 September 1740, and on the following day (Monday) preached twice in the Anglican church. He recorded in his journal that there was 'Great reason to believe the Word of the Lord had been sharper than a two-edged sword in some of the Hearers souls.' On Tuesday he preached again 'With much Flame, Clearness and Power to still greater Auditories', before moving on to his greatest and most decisive triumph – a solid week of amazing activity at Boston. There were prayers at King's Chapel on Thursday morning; preaching to an auditory in South Church on Friday morning, and to five thousand people on the Common in the afternoon. He preached on Sunday afternoon in the First (Old Brick) Church, and afterward outside to eight thousand who could not gain entrance. On Monday he preached to two large outdoor audiences; on Tuesday at Second Church, Wednesday at Harvard, and on the last day of this visit, he honored the 'Great and Thursday Lecture' at First Church, where Edwards nine years previously had made his Boston debut.[17]

Whitefield's whirlwind six-week tour had had an undeniable effect on American Church life. It had also produced the customary effect of violent controversy, both in dislike of the man ('people wallowed in snow, night and day, for the benefit of his beastly brayings'[18]), and in the polarising of congregations. The situation was not helped by a number of imitators, at least one of them (James Davenport) not wholly sane. It remains true however that evidence can be found of 150 towns in New England affected by this revival, and there is no doubt that a large number of local ministers found their continuing work brought to life. Whitefield had rudely remarked 'The reason why congregations have been so dead, is because dead men preach to them.'[19] Now preaching, praying, personal testifying and devotional reading were all newly alive. The latter is important. There had to be a limit to the number of dramatic conversions, which depended on 'an infinitely large reservoir of susceptible sinners'.[20] Bible-reading, however, could go steadily on, and did. What happened had been the first big event that had united all the colonies: in churches from Maine to North Carolina everyone was reading, attentively, the King James Bible.

The preaching of Whitefield and others, though it attracted people from dozens of miles around, and was eagerly looked forward to wherever the events were announced, also attracted severe hostility. Some of this came from entrenched religious conservatism: a famous 'Testimony' in 1744 came from Harvard College against Whitefield. This builds on the notorious hostility of Alexander Garden, the Bishop of London's Commissary in Charleston, South Carolina. (Whitefield's own account of his confrontation with the Commissary, 14–18 March 1740, does unwittingly arouse in the reader a small touch of sympathy for Bishop Garden.[21]) Established Anglicanism, as well as established intellectualism, could not stomach Whitefield. Garden's attack in two printed sermons, under the general title 'Regeneration, and the Testimony of the Spirit', is presented on scriptural texts, the first of which is Romans 8:16, 'The Spirit itself [GREEK the same Spirit] beareth Witness with our spirit, that we are the Children of GOD.'[22] There was also heated opposition from within the Presbyterian churches to the new young breed of itinerant preachers who, lacking any firm root in a ministerial call to the care of any community, took themselves and their volcanic exuberance into other men's pulpits, quite often without invitation. A modern reader finds sympathy for the opposition to this brashness. A venomous anonymous document 'The Wonderful Wandering Spirit', was published in Philadelphia in February 1741 in Benjamin Franklin's *General Magazine*. The writers make an important point. Whereas we can regularly notice local churches seeking guidance from Bible-study, these cruising Evangelists could be accused of empty hot air. In 'The Wonderful Wandering Spirit' are these words:

> [This Spirit] always sets up for a Preacher of Christ and his truths, but frequently forgets its Errand, quotes little Scripture, and preaches itself and its attainments . . .[23]

A sermon frequently printed in the North, by Josiah Smith in 1740, defending Whitefield, is in the old Reformed tradition of being largely made out of Scripture, in its account of his preaching. Gilbert Tennent, one of the Awakening's leaders, in a sermon on Mark 6:34, several times reprinted, entitled 'the Danger of an Unconverted Ministry', is even more scriptural. Whole pages make a catena of biblical quotations.

Jonathan Edwards himself, however, on 10 September 1741 preached at New Haven a ringing defence of the revival. His sermon was entitled 'The Distinguishing Marks of a Work of the Spirit'. What he tries to do is to claim and contain the human emotions produced by the revival as genuine indications of the operation of God. In this sermon, he began his work of speaking for American Christianity as it was being revealed. Inevitably influenced by the new psychology of John Locke, Edwards tried to give a proper scientific base for the new experiences of outpourings. Edwards uses Scripture to great effect, noting the extreme physical affects [not his word, of course, which tended to be 'Affections']. There is an authority in Edwards's words which reassures even the modern reader of a proper understanding of the Bible. Scriptural references are frequent but gently made, even though he finishes with terrible words.

> And though some are so prudent, as not openly to oppose and reproach this work, yet it is to be feared – at this day when the Lord is going forth so gloriously against his enemies – that many who are silent and inactive, especially ministers, will bring that curse of the angel of the Lord upon themselves, Judg.v.23 'Curse ye Meroz, said the angel of the Lord, curse ye bitterly the inhabitants thereof: because they came not to the help of the Lord, to the help of the Lord against the mighty'.[24]

The 'everyone' reading the Bible began to include non-whites. Eleazar Wheelock educated Indian boys around the Connecticut River, a direct cause of the foundation of Dartmouth College in 1769. One result was the unexpected growth of an educated Indian clergy. Another was the reverse, the almost complete obliteration of native African religion among the slaves, the largest ethnic group in America after the English. Not until 1660 had English tobacco-growers begun to follow the Latin American and Caribbean settlements and use African slaves on a large scale, as opposed to a few respected and indentured African servants. Slave-owners (which meant almost everybody who could afford them) tended to repress original African beliefs. The sheer numbers and forceful presence of the slaves, however, led by a kind of underground osmosis to an effect on American Christianity of importance, as African energies and celebrations brought the Gospel message to refreshing life (see below, chapter 33). The main work of evangelising the slaves did not properly begin until the later eighteenth century; African Christianity, when it did emerge strongly, was vividly biblical. Slaves in the fields did not sing about rival doctrines of transcendence, but about Daniel in the lions' den, Moses rescuing his people, Jonah in the belly of the whale – Bible stories ringing with life.

What is religion and what is 'literature' is at this time difficult to judge. The poetry of Anne Bradstreet is justly admired. She took with her to the Massachusetts Bay colony her knowledge of European literary culture. She was a member of an elite – both her father and her husband were governors of the colony. In 1650 some of her poems were printed in England, with anticipation of heavy prejudice because they were written by a woman. Far from quickly diminishing as a momentary oddity, they have grown with time. Her 'Contemplations' refer naturally, as well as to classical tags, to Bible stories and Bible phrases – 'A bridegroom . . . as a strong man, joys to run a race', which is Psalm 19. Adam and Eve and

Cain and Abel occupy several stanzas. Michael Wigglesworth's 1662 poem *The Day of Doom* was a bestseller in New England – it is in 224 stanzas, but even so it is said that many New Englanders knew it by heart even into the twentieth century. His *God's controversy with New England*, inspired by the 1622 drought, is a slightly less extended jeremiad. Also written in 1662, his *In the time of the great drought* is an attempt to re-invigorate New England with a sense of God's mission. Each section is introduced by a verse of Scripture, which it partly expounds. More interestingly, whole sections of it move in and out of Scripture, and expect the reader to recognise this.

> Oh happiest of days wherein
>   The blind received sight,
> And those that had no eyes before
>   Were made to see the light!
> The wilderness hereat rejoyc't,
>   The woods for joy did sing,
> The valleys and the little hills
>   Thy praises echoing.

That is a mixture of Isaiah 35 and Psalm 65.

The most neglected poet of the period was Edward Taylor. At Harvard with Increase Mather, he was minister in Massachusetts in the town of Westfield for over fifty years. His poems were not known until 1937. His *Sacramental Meditations*, written in the early 1700s, are lyrical expositions of Scripture texts, heavily introspective in the recording of personal affect in the work of God in his soul, and extending the particular skills of George Herbert.

THE GREAT AWAKENING'S BIBLICAL ROOTS

Whether the Great Awakening had any greater significance than a regeneration of church life in New England presents a puzzle. It might seem that it was no more than yet another outburst of theological controversy, such as marked the congregations in that region for well over a hundred years. That the first Great Awakening was a wholly biblical affair needs continual stressing. Otherwise all those earliest experiences only make sense as communal hysteria or fashionable cult. What Whitefield, and the Wesleys, preached was the New Testament, the healing and energising work of the Gospel. Historians are prepared to allow in the story of the Great Awakening that it was a religious experience of some significance.

Yet, even when the religious history is explained over hundreds of pages with many detailed references to sermons, journals, published books and letters, there is visible a curious reluctance even to mention the Bible. A student of the period needs only to turn a few pages of the original documents to see at once that they are full of quotations from and references to the Scriptures. To write American colonial-period history without mention of the Bible is to build a house on sand.

Such Bible-blindness remains puzzling. It can be more than that. The standard 650-page collection of documents on the Great Awakening, published in the American Heritage series in 1967, and edited by two eminent Harvard scholars, Alan Heimert and Perry Miller, is apparently invaluable. Here are fifty-three documents of the time, many of them never before in print; the volume presents a properly kaleidoscopic picture of the Great Awakening's events and personalities. This is excellent – except that Heimert writes in his Editor's Note the following sentence: 'I have also occasionally removed, without notice to the reader . . . what struck me as a superfluity of Scriptural citation.'[25] This, from one of the period's leading scholars, is both a pity, and revealing. A pity, because it instantly destroys a significant amount of the value of the documents. To have had on the pages those scriptural citations would have been a most essential means of following the original thought at its depth. It is revealing, however, in that such a historian can be so cavalier. Heimert silently deletes the scriptural citations only because they struck him as superfluous. So speak the 1960s: more recent historians are little better.

The Yale historian Sydney Ahlstrom, at the end of his magisterial account of the religious history of America wrote:

> The future United States was settled and to a large degree shaped by those who brought with them a very special form of radical Protestantism, which combined a strenuous moral precisionism, a deep commitment to Evangelical experientialism, and a determination to make the state responsible for the support of these moral and religious ideas.[26]

This is sound. Ahlstrom's heavy Latin abstract nouns cannot be faulted. Yet there is one omission. The lives they denominate were founded on the Bible. Not only were the forms of prayer and worship in New England made of words rather than images, in the central stream of European Reform: the very daily lives of those men and women who came in such numbers from England were based on the study of an English Bible in the home. The pattern can be seen in so much Protestant writing: here is Samuel Ward, in a sermon delivered in Ipswich in 1615,

Such as read the Bible by fits upon rainy days, not eating the book with John [Rev. 10: 9–10], but tasting only with the tip of the tongue: such as meditate by snatches, never chewing the cud and digesting their meat, they may happily [haply, i.e. by chance] get a smackering for discourse and table talk; but not enough to keep soul and life together, much less for strength and vigour.[27]

The Great Awakening had obvious English influence through Whitefield: yet one must remember that all over Europe in those middle decades of the eighteenth century there were outbreaks of the flames of emotional enthusiasm and regeneration, notably Catholic and Pietist. Against them, however, stood the massive resistances of the entrenched institutions, particularly the solid power of the Roman Catholic Church, and the not much more inclusive Church of England. The older Protestant communities in Europe held on firmly to their ancient ways, and resisted revival. So, though throughout the eastern states of America there were sharply expressed oppositions to the new enthusiasm, America alone had the freedom from unchanging and unchangeable religious establishments. A further American effect was the social freedom. The educated classes of Europe responded to the satisfactions of mind brought by the Enlightenment. In America, the Jeffersons and Franklins embraced that philosophy with eagerness. But in the American wilderness of Kentucky or Illinois, there was neither established church nor the rationalism of thinkers to hinder the 'hordes of simple, excitable, optimistic people'.[28] Before long revivalism itself could be accused of following empty routines, but even then it was better than what Ralph Waldo Emerson described as 'The corpse-cold Unitarianism of Brattle Street and Harvard College'.[29]

The revivalists of mid-century can be criticised, but they did show the churches responding to the colossal challenge that America offered, especially with the sudden opening up of the West. If those in America made mistakes and did not always know what they were doing, and only slowly developed mature judgments, they did take Bible Christianity across the newly found continent and planted it in a host of settlements. The American cry for saving the West grew in the first decades of the 1800s, and partly accounts, as will be seen below, for the remarkable avalanche of newly printed American Bibles.

New England's Great Awakening was all but over by the early months of 1742.[30] In the South, the Awakening ended the near-monopoly of the Episcopal Church, but in New England, and to a degree in the areas of Philadelphia and New York, the revival made Anglicanism more appealing by contrast.[31] Jonathan Edwards began a series of sermons delivered 1742–3 entitled 'The Religious Affections', in which after the ecstasies of

1740–41, he tried to stabilise the experience of 'New Birth' into a life-time's sanctification, and the fruits by which it was known. Edwards followed this with 'The Visible Union of God's People' a call to united prayer.

Chapter 32

THE ENGLISH BIBLE
AGAINST FASHIONABLE DEISM:
HANDEL AND POPE AS EXAMPLES

DEISM

A freely circulating vernacular Bible allows freely circulating ridicule. There were plenty of scoffers, drunk or sober, for whom a talking ass (Numbers 22) or surviving a burning, fiery furnace seven times hotter (Daniel 3) were the stuff of fairy tales. More – indeed, wholly – rational were the thinkers who, in an age of reason, argued against the Christian revelation. Natural religion identified one universal supreme God to be worshipped by the practice of virtue, achievable as sins were forgiven through repentance without any atoning sacrifice. This position of deism, within the broader intellectual framework of the Enlightenment, encouraged denigration of traditional beliefs, and of Scripture above all. Deist biblical criticism, intending to destroy any basis for Christian belief by ridiculing miracles, for example, did open for discussion some important biblical textual problems – discrepancies, for instance, between Old Testament Hebrew and New Testament Septuagint citations. But the aim was to take out of the picture anything supernatural, from the Resurrection itself (a fraud perpetrated by the disciples) to all miracles, and particularly any idea of fulfilment of prophecy. Revelation was close to insanity.

In the 1720s and 1730s, important English deist works, summing up some decades of anti-biblical writing, were written and widely read, as will be seen below. They were translated into German.

For the moment, however, for illustration of a singularly powerful defence of the Bible, I turn to a German, George Frederic Handel in London in 1741.

HANDEL IN LONDON AND DUBLIN, 1741

On 1 May 1750 Handel's oratorio *Messiah* had a special charity performance in Captain Thomas Coram's Foundling Hospital in London. In the seven years before, there had been eight London performances of *Messiah*, only moderately well received. It was that 1750 charitable occasion at Thomas Coram's that fixed it in Great Britain in an apparently everlasting kingdom of wonder, love and praise. As Charles Burney wrote:

> And from that time to the present, this great work has been heard in all parts of the kingdom with increasing reverence and delight; it has fed the hungry, clothed the naked, fostered the orphan, and enriched succeeding managers of the Oratorios, more than any single production in this or any country.[1]

That was written in 1785. From the middle of the nineteenth century, the development of popular choral singing in Britain carried it forward on a great wave of pleasure and fulfilment. 'Small provincial choirs discovered that Handel's music, designed for professional singers to learn on a couple of rehearsals, could be mastered by amateurs in a couple of months.'[2] It is still performed every year across the world, by grand choruses in metropolitan auditoria, by enthusiastic choirs in village chapels, by dedicated authentic-instrument groups with singers. It is a work of genius, which can easily stand such adoration. For many Christians, *Messiah* is part of the Christian year, often essential at Christmas. Unlike the great Passions of J. S. Bach, or the choral Masses of Haydn, Mozart, Beethoven – or even Brahms, for that matter, though that is different – attractive as they are to perform and hear, this oratorio of Handel has generated a comfortable British folk-history. It is possible for a congregation to say of a rival chapel that this year 'they are late with their *Messiah*'. Happy stories are told in English pubs of unwary tenors failing to count in the great 'Hallelujah' Chorus and adding a *fortissimo* 'Hally – *dammit*'. A legendary London conductor has been gleefully credited with asking a body of altos to sing 'Unto us a son is born' with 'a little more conviction and a little less surprise'. The music is rightly adored.

The libretto, however, is a great deal more interesting, and odd, than is commonly observed. It is a string of English Bible quotations assembled with subtlety and high art. What it is not is a Life of Christ. True, fairly early on 'there were shepherds abiding in the fields', and later 'by His stripes we are healed'. The Bible texts do brush against the outline of the Gospel stories. But the libretto of *Messiah* makes a different, most telling and particular use of KJV, and the Psalms in the Book of Common Prayer, exactly located to its time of writing in 1741. To understand this part of the story of the English Bible, and how here the Gospel drama is 'observed and interpreted, as a matter for contemplation',[3] a little exploration is needed of what brought Handel to such an outpouring, and his work to have had such an impact.

The libretto of *Messiah* arrived at Handel's London house in Brook Street, apparently out of the blue, in June 1741. A letter from Charles Jennens in Leicestershire, dated 10 July, mentions the sending of it. Jennens and Handel had already worked together (among other things, on the biblical oratorio *Saul* in 1738) so there was nothing strange in the dispatch – except that this libretto was different from anything that Jennens had done before, or would do afterwards. In that summer of 1741, Handel was writing a series of Italian love-duets.[4] Such ephemera would please any German court, and it seems that Handel was despondently laying the tracks for his departure from England for good. He was unpopular. Fashionable taste was against him. Thirty years before, in February 1711, he had begun his career in London as a twenty-six-year-old, fresh from musical triumphs in Italy, very successfully presenting his opera *Rinaldo*. As late as the spring of 1738, even while his opera *Serse* was failing, a remarkable statue of him by Roubiliac was unveiled in London's pleasure-garden at Vauxhall.[5] Now, early in 1741, he had conducted his last opera, *Deidamia*, which played to empty houses; in doing that, he gave the last performances of any opera under his own direction. For the new proposed high-profile Italian opera company under the young Lord Middlesex, Handel saw nothing but expensive failure.

His own, great, move into English oratorio had not yet brought him any success. Oratorio had begun in Italy at the beginning of the seventeenth century. The form adapted secular musical theatre, with entertainments in three acts, recitatives accompanied by continuo, and choruses, to the telling of sacred stories without stage movement or costumes. These allowed employment for musicians during Lent when operas were prohibited. Handel heard, and himself composed, oratorios in Italy between 1706 and 1710. His second oratorio was *La Resurrezione* of 1708.

> The libretto deals with the events between the Crucifixion and the Resurrection. The representation of Christ himself as a participating character is avoided: a dialogue between Lucifer and an Angel culminates with the harrowing of hell, and the events of the Resurrection are dramatised through the discovery of the empty tomb and the appearance of the Angel.[6]

Such oblique treatment of the central story is striking in *Messiah*. In England Handel wrote occasional oratorio–like works (*Esther, Deborah, Athalia*), but it was not until the summer of 1738 that he suddenly turned, as will be seen, to full-scale biblical oratorios in *Saul* and *Israel in Egypt* – the former, certainly, and possibly both, on librettos by Charles Jennens. Some time in the summer of 1741, Handel apparently received an invitation from the Lord Lieutenant of Ireland to take part in the coming season of oratorio, and other concerts, in Dublin, on behalf of several local charities. The invitation seems to have been unexpected. William, third Duke of Devonshire, had succeeded as Lord Lieutenant the Duke of Dorset, the father of that young Lord Middlesex who was trying to found a new opera company. What exactly happened is unclear, but in mid-August 1741, Handel turned to Jennens's freshly arrived libretto and completed *Messiah* in twenty-four days (unremarkable, for him) in order to take it to Dublin. We can only speculate why. He was perhaps newly energised by the strangeness, and political timeliness, of the libretto. Possibly he relished a new audience outside London. He could have been stimulated by the charitable causes. That he was not thinking of his normal London theatre orchestra with its oboes and bassoons, but in writing *Messiah*, scoring modestly for strings with basso continuo, and occasional trumpets and drums, suggests he had Dublin in mind. Immediately after finishing *Messiah* on 14 September, however, he at once started writing a large-scale biblical oratorio, *Samson*, based on Milton's re-telling of the Judges story in *Samson Agonistes*. This was for a London orchestra, with additional forces including flutes, horns and trombones. That he began this does suggest that he was thinking of staying in London after all, or at least for the next season. He finished the draft of *Samson* on 19 October,[7] and then set out for Ireland soon after the end of that month, arriving in Dublin on 18 November. There is still a great deal we do not know about Handel's visit to Dublin. Before then, he must have made arrangements – of which we have no records – with the Dublin managements about many details, especially the availability of singers. That is particularly interesting, for both *Messiah* and *Samson* are written for four soloists only; soprano, alto, tenor and bass – fairly standard today, but not used by Handel in either the decade before or the decade after those two oratorios. *Messiah* was first performed at the New Music Hall in Fishamble Street on 13 April 1742 before an audience of seven hundred (one hundred more than the hall officially held), and repeated on 3 June.

ALEXANDER POPE, 1741

Coincidentally, it happened that in the second half of 1741 the greatest English poet of the time, Alexander Pope, was revising his widely read three-book mock-epic *The Dunciad*, a high satire of which the ironic subject is Dulness, in all its enervating and destructive forms – though the poem shines with a brilliance that startled literary England, and still dazzles. (Pope was supreme in the direct line from Dryden and *Absalom and Achitophel*.) *The Dunciad* had first appeared in various forms in the late

1720s, and Pope now, rather surprisingly, turned to it again. He published, in March 1742, a new satire, which he called *The New Dunciad: As it was found in the year 1741*. But even before this reached print, he began revising the whole original poem, and now incorporated his new work as Book IV of a quite new four-book *Dunciad*, published in October 1743. This has marked changes. There is a new 'hero': instead of what he called the 'piddling' Shakespeare scholar Lewis Theobald, Pope now attacks someone he feels to be altogether more sinister, the man-about-London actor, dramatist and (to Pope's disgust), Poet Laureate, Colley Cibber. There is a serious darkening of the tone of the new long poem. What had been in the earlier version a prophecy, in the sense of warning about a possible bad future for England, now became prophecy in the more biblical sense of declaring God's Word about what has already arrived. In the new Book IV is now fulfilled what had been only shadowed before: the arrival of an anti-Messiah, 'the Yawn of Gods'.

In the same later months of 1741, England's leading composer, Handel, and England's finest poet, Pope seem, quite separately, to have been diverted into writing about Messiahs and prophecies fulfilled. True, Handel could merely have been stirred by the arrival of something in the post when he was depressed, and Jennens in turn could have found sudden greatness within his own brand of High Church Anglicanism. Pope, while rummaging in old papers, might have found notions kindling into flame again. He was being encouraged by a new friend, William Warburton, to take himself in hand and begin to think about a properly-edited Complete Works. Those things could have been what happened. It would be intriguing, however, if Jennens's new libretto and Pope's new direction came from a common source, especially if the English Bible were relevant to that source.

There was already a strong link between the two men. They had known each other for many years: Pope and his friends had provided Handel with several librettos, some of them biblical.[8] Pope admired Handel's music. One of the damaging myths about Pope (indeed, a straight lie) is that he had no ear for music.[9] At the beginning of the fresh Book IV of his *Dunciad*, written in the autumn of 1741, Pope mentions Handel, in precise circumstances. In the new work, Dulness mounts her throne in line 17: the first of her subjects to address her, from line 45, is the 'Harlot form' of fashionable Italian opera. With the approval of the Empress (Dulness, of course) the ugly performance drives out the Muses. From line 63, however

'But soon, ah soon Rebellion will commence,
If Music meanly borrows aid from Sense:

> Strong in new Arms, lo! Giant Handel stands . . .
> Arrest him Empress; or you sleep no more' –
> She heard, and drove him to th'Hibernian shore.

Such naming in emphatic reality is unusual in the poem. Rebellion, more-over, is located in new musical strength – not, as the poem makes clear, from the 'soft sliding by' of Italian solos and 'quaint Recitativo', but from loudness and choruses. Handel's bigger, and noisier, orchestras for the oratorios *Saul* and *Israel in Egypt* had not pleased London. *Israel in Egypt*, moreover, using only the English Bible text, not only told the story of the people led out to liberty, politically relevant to 1739, when opposition to the power of the first Prime Minister, Robert Walpole, was increasingly vocal: the oratorio did so almost entirely in choruses, as if it were mod-elling the English nation, which, moved by its Bible, was energising itself to claim freedom. The oratorio failed. Eighteen months before that, Handel had done something quite new. In an anthem for Queen Caroline's funeral in December 1737, *The Ways of Zion do Mourn* (a setting of Lamentations 1:4, and from Job, Psalms and Pauline Epistles, already suggesting *Messiah*) he had made Zion's mourning happen entirely in cho-ruses, instead of in the 'normal' way of recitative, aria and then chorus.

HANDEL AND POPE SETTING MESSIANIC TEXTS

Now, writing *Messiah*, Handel again scored for a high proportion of cho-ruses. This partly helped to solve an artistic problem. The biblical libretto of *Messiah* as he received it lacked dramatic conflict. In all the passages from the Prophets, in the place of opposition is the parallelism on which Hebrew poetry is based. For example, *Messiah* numbers 6 and 7[10] begin (both from Malachi 3):

> But who may abide the day of his coming?
> And who shall stand when he appeareth?

and

> And he shall purify the sons of Levi
> and purge them as gold and silver.

Such parallel thought lacks enough contrast to colour a recitative, or an aria, without the expedient of making changes of key or tempo, which could be repeatedly jolting. A change of tempo may be done once, as in *Messiah* 10, which is the contrasting verses of Isaiah 60:2. The bass recitative has one note per syllable in

> For behold, darkness shall cover the earth,
> and gross darkness the people.

This, though still in recitative, then becomes faster running phrases, with greater range, on 'arise' and 'glory'

> but the Lord shall arise upon thee,
> and his glory shall be seen upon thee.

The music then effectively changes key for the concluding words from the next verse, and back to one note per syllable:

> And the Gentiles shall come to thy light,
> and kings to the brightness of thy rising.

Though attractive here, in accumulation such variation could become grotesque.

Much more movement is possible in the far broader scope of a four- or eight-part chorus, especially if it links and contrasts with a preceding aria. So the minor-key conclusion of 11, the bass aria still from Isaiah 9:2, 'The people that walked in darkness', expands harmonically, and wonderfully, with the start of 12, the fresh and graceful 'chamber'-chorus 'For unto us a child is born' from Isaiah 9:6, beginning with the higher voices; darkness is banished by light. Later, coming after the Recitative 31, 'He was cut off', Isaiah 53:8, and the Air 32, 'But thou didst not leave his soul in hell', Psalm 16:10 adapted, there is magnificence in the joyous, complex choral antiphonies of 33, 'Lift Up Your Heads', Psalm 24:7-10.

In all the versions of *The Dunciad* there is a good deal of singing, which has passages close to music-theatre in the use of recitatives, solo arias and choruses. In *The New Dunciad* of 1741 the sense of oratorio is strong: a greater variety of artistic effect contains a musical quality not heard before, a sense of single voices surrounded by groups. The poet's new oratorio-like achievement coincides oddly with that of Handel.[11] Pope's own interest in the idea of Messiah can be traced back to 1712, when he had written, and published in the *Spectator*, a poem of 108 lines which became widely known, subtitled *A Sacred Eclogue, Compos'd of Several Passages of Isaiah the Prophet. Written in Imitation of Virgil's Pollio*. In illuminating footnotes, Pope elaborates the way Virgil's Fourth Eclogue so startlingly parallels passages in Isaiah 'which foretell the coming of Christ and the felicities attending it' as he notes, including a child born of a virgin who will redeem the world, and the rearrangement of the landscape (parallel to 'Every valley shall be exalted, and every mountain and hill shall be made low', Isaiah 40:4) to welcome the coming god, and pastoral serenity, and much else. Pope embroiders twenty-seven passages from sixteen chapters of Isaiah, interweaving them with references to about a third of Virgil's eclogue. Pope's poem is entitled 'Messiah'. In 1728, Samuel Johnson's tutor at Pembroke College, Oxford, suggested that he (Johnson) translate it into Latin as a Christmas exercise, and the result was frequently reprinted. So popular was Pope's poem, that six other Latin translations of it by lesser writers appeared before the end of the century: and indeed, Pope's 'Messiah' became the libretto of a cantata in 1716 – both libretto and music are said to be irredeemably feeble.[12] Celebrating a conjunction of the birth of Christ and classical pastoralism was a congenial occupation in the eighteenth century.

The word-book for Handel's first *Messiah* performances in Dublin has, ruled off for emphasis across the centre of the title-page, in capital letters only a little smaller than those for MESSIAH, AN ORATORIO, the words MAJORA CANAMUS, without attribution (fig. 30). They are the last words of the first line of Virgil's Fourth Eclogue, meaning 'let us sing of greater things'. Connections between Handel and Pope in the creation of the oratorio *Messiah* will be found later in this chapter to point also towards the particular use of the Bible by both men to assert properly Christian doctrine against the increasing claims of deism.

There are other links between Handel and Pope, some more flimsy than others. Handel's alto soloist in the Dublin performances of *Messiah* was the enchanting but rather scandalous Susannah Cibber, the unhappy wife of Theophilus, Colley Cibber's foolish son (fig. 31). She had arrived in Dublin a fortnight before Handel to act, probably, at the Aungier Street Theatre. It is said that Handel wrote 'He was despised' for her, to famous effect (see below). Even while she was singing of fulfilled Messianic prophecy for Handel, Pope was busy writing satirical fulfilled Messianic prophecy about her father-in-law. Both men knew, and at separate times stayed for long periods with, Ralph Allen at Widcombe, Bath, in the grand new house at Prior Park. Allen was a wealthy benefactor, said to be the 'original' of Squire Allworthy in Fielding's *Tom Jones* of 1749: Fielding mocks Allworthy's neighbour, Squire Western, for his fashionably anti-Handel sentiments.[13] Allen also had wide business and artistic connections, including noblemen who were Handel's patrons, the Duke of Chandos for example. One of Allen's fortunes had been made out of organising a national postal service. He travelled England and Wales, and enjoyed making and keeping a network of friends. Someone who consulted him in 1736 about a new postal service between Chesterfield and Manchester, and took his detailed advice, was the third Duke of Devonshire, he who five years later as Lord Lieutenant of Ireland seems to have caused Handel to travel to Dublin, taking the specially written *Messiah* with him. Ralph Allen had a good library, and an interest in religious speculation. It would be good to think that on his travels Allen met and talked to a Warwickshire man who had estates in six counties, a thinker with a strong, indeed passionate, interest in biblical religion, Charles Jennens. At the moment, we have no evidence. The curious myth – again, indeed, lie – that Jennens was an incompetent booby has now, at least in scholarly circles, been thoroughly exploded.[14] His *Messiah* libretto can be seen to have come from a scholarly mind, one not merely abreast of intellectual, religious, musical and artistic thinking, but considerably ahead. A High Churchman and a nonjuror[15] (and thus debarred from public office), with quietly held but very strong beliefs, Jennens saw Anglican Christianity as both the way forward for his country, and also under serious threat, from the Dissenters to a small extent, from Walpole's administration more, but above all from the force of fashionable deism.

HANDEL AND ANTI–DEISM

The deist attack on Christianity was levelled at a paternal God and a personal redeemer. It discredited the idea of the Jewish nation as necessary to the Divine Plan, and the fulfilment of Old Testament prophecies of the Messiah in the person of Christ. Jennens's library contained enough examples of contemporary books representing in particular the Anglican understanding of the nature and mission of Christ – books citing in significant numbers (in several cases, almost half) the Scripture verses that make up his *Messiah* libretto. There can be no doubt that Jennens saw his compilation of Scripture texts as forcefully attacking deism. The very title is an anti-deist banner.

Now, not only does the libretto, as has often been remarked, lack narrative. It also, one might even say, lacks a Messiah. The figure is not shadowy – there is no hint of doubt – but it is elusive, indirect, oblique. The incarnation, the only detail from the Synoptic Gospels in *Messiah*, is conveyed only pastorally, via the shepherds in numbers 13 to 17, from the 'Pastoral Symphony' and 'There were shepherds abiding in the field' from Luke 2 and then through them the words of the angel. Prominence is given to the prophecy about the City of David in number 15, 'And the angel said unto them' by *omitting* Luke's down-to-earth words about 'the babe, wrapped in swaddling clothes and lying in a manger'. Where are the Gospel accounts of the sufferings of Christ, so dramatically present in the German Passions, of Bach for example? They are, in the ten numbers following 23, entirely contained in a group of quotations from Second Isaiah, Psalms and Lamentations. That sequence, from 23, 'He was despised' (Isaiah 53:3) to 32, 'But thou didst not leave his soul in hell' (Psalm 16:10) does convey the Gospel narratives, to those who know them, by a kind of peripheral vision. So the death, burial, resurrection and ascension of Christ, events which are the very centre of the Christian faith, are most obliquely presented. At the climax of this section, two numbers, 34 and 35, 'Unto which of the angels' and 'Let all the angels', are not only not from the Gospels: they are not from Paul either, but from the anonymous Epistle to the Hebrews, 1:5–6. (It is so oblique that it is like recounting the death of Hamlet only by means of words from *Two Gentlemen of Verona*.) Here in Jennens's libretto, obliquity is at three removes. At the first remove from the Gospel events are the Old Testament prophecies. They are, second, being fulfilled in Christ. Third, that fulfilment is only given to angels. It seems a curious way to present Christ as Messiah: but Jennens has a strong point. He is concerned to present the opposite of deist reason. Here is the sense of mystery in the divine revelation. On that word-book title-page, under the MAJORA CANAMUS noted above, Jennens placed two New Testament quotations (both unattributed, but from 1 Timothy 3:16, and Colossians 2:3):

> And without Controversy, great is the mystery of Godliness: God was manifested in the Flesh, justified by the Spirit, seen of Angels, preached among the Gentiles, believed on in the world, received up in glory.
>
> In whom are hid all the Treasures of Wisdom and Knowledge.

The last religious oratorio-librettos from Jennens that Handel had worked on had been *Saul*, and possibly the germ of *Israel in Egypt*, both multivalent in their relation of narrative to contemporary ideas: but they were nothing like this. And it seems that Handel carried Jennens's obliquity further, even into something like satire, an art form that depends on adding elusiveness to the earthiest of realities ('Or stain her Honour, or her new Brocade'[16]). The *Messiah* choruses represent many attitudes, usually expressing the 'all flesh' that shall 'see it together' as the first chorus (4) puts it from Isaiah 40:5 – all too hinderingly human. Thus, after the ponderous opening of the chorus, 37, from Psalm 68:11 in the Prayer Book, 'The Lord gave the word', the 'great . . . company of the preachers' rush about in self-defeating confusion. (Jennens was at first far from pleased with what Handel had done with his words.[17]) The F major smugness of 'All we like sheep', Isaiah 53:26 (26), comes in the very middle of Passion, between 'stripes' and 'scorn'. Did Handel recognise the comic, even ridiculous, ambiguity of the phrase? We hear the chorus telling each other, while beholding the stripes by which they are healed, how fond they are of sheep.[18] Even the sudden single statement in F minor at the end of that chorus, 'And the Lord hath laid on him the iniquity of us all', has in its relief traces of self-regard. The only C major chorus, 41, an aggressively happy canon, sets the words 'Let us break their bonds asunder' from Psalm 2:3. This is easily taken, by the half-attentive, to be the releasing effect of the Gospel. It is in fact the opposite, the self-congratulatory programme of governments who are 'against the Lord and his anointed' ('the Kings of the earth . . . and the rulers . . .', in the previous verse) for getting rid of what they see as the shackles of religion. Moreover, Handel's most brilliant writing, using the choral voices and orchestra in page after page of the grandest of fugues and richest of developments, comes at the very end of the oratorio, in the latter part of the final number, 53, setting what is usually taken as no more than a sort of liturgical punctuation point, one biblical word only, 'Amen', which means 'so let it be'. One could see this as both playful, and a concluding, elaborate, thick-textured surrender to the mystery of God, and delight in the downfall of deism. True, in its Apocalyptic context (Revelation 5:14) it is richer still: but then again, there it is spoken by four beasts.

POPE AND ANTI-DEISM

Pope wrote *The New Dunciad* after Handel had composed *Messiah* and gone to Dublin. (Jennens did not know about either event until some time later.) Jennens himself makes two back-door entries into Pope's new poem. One is, as we saw above, with Handel taking to 'th'Hibernian shore' something new. The other is through Pope's figure of 'Montalto' in Book IV lines 105–14, the 'decent Knight' and Shakespeare editor who is Sir Thomas Hanmer, Speaker of the House of Commons. Pope's friend Warburton, who was encouraging him, had been in correspondence with Hanmer, a relation of Jennens. Jennens comes artistically closer in three ways to Pope's new *Dunciad* work, with its new oratorio-like techniques, particularly its new coherence, contrasted with the patchwork of opera. The first is that very trick of presenting the central figure by allusion. Dulness in *The New Dunciad*, as has often been noticed, though all-powerful, is most remarkably not there.[19] The Mighty Mother comes to the reader through parodies, of *Paradise Lost* or Virgil, or through extensions of Dryden. As, in Jennens's *Messiah* libretto, the Messiah has virtually no bodily presence, so here Dulness is equally absent. Second, though the figure of 'the Anti-Christ of Wit' in the four-book *Dunciad* is locked on to Cibber, the phrase allows the alert reader to identify a secret ingredient, which is the scheme of an inverse Christian theology worked out in some detail, even in the single publication *The New Dunciad*, and kept elusive to avoid a charge of blasphemy.[20] The announced anti-Messiah is a person of a contrary Trinity. This is high serious satire of a new kind.

The New Dunciad has few named targets: its coherence relates to large groups, and the poem sings with a new poetic imagination about the religious life of the whole nation. For, third, *The New Dunciad*, like Jennens's and Handel's *Messiah*, is an anti-deist work. Pope suffered many attacks: one was the ridiculous charge that he was a deist.[21] Pope makes a crucial passage of *The New Dunciad* an anti-deist statement, lines 437–93 in *The Dunciad* Book IV. Pope wrote comments that are more full than usual, on his anti-deist verses. Here, as his own note has it, the Empress Dulness 'charges the Investigators of Nature to amuse themselves in Trifles, and rest in Second causes, with a total disregard of the First'. She is instantly supported by 'a gloomy Clerk/Sworn foe to Myst'ry', who speaks for those who 'reason downward, till we doubt of God.' Even further inside those thirty lines is another shadowy divinity, another anti-Messiah, called 'some Mechanic Cause', or 'Man', or 'Self', a god 'such as Lucretius drew', like Dulness herself.

His lines 'a gloomy Clerk/Sworn foe to Myst'ry', probably refer to Dr Samuel Clarke, chaplain to Queen Anne from 1706 and friend of Isaac Newton. Clarke's *A Discourse concerning the Connexion of the Prophecies in the Old Testament and the Application of them to Christ* (1725) was not his only book to cause a furore. His earlier *Scripture Doctrine of the Trinity* (1712) brought on him the wrath of the orthodox, even to accusations of Arianism. That fourth-century heresy stated that Jesus Christ is not the eternal son of God become man. He is not 'of one substance with the Father' as the corrective Nicene Creed has it. Instead, to Arius and his followers, he is a spiritual being made by God before the creation of the world, given the name 'Son of God' as a title. Declaring Arius of Alexandria a heretic was the battleground of that most important council in church history, at Nicaea in 325. Accusing eighteenth-century philosophers and theologians of Arianism still had weight. The point of the alarm is that such heresies dismantle the orthodox statements of faith, which had been struggled with and fought over from earliest New Testament times. The eighteenth-century deist attempt to disintegrate Christianity has at its core the destruction of any element of divine revelation, of absolute mystery, in the face of reason. Jesus' miracles do not stand up to reasoned investigation. What does, obviously, is 'natural religion', discoverable by reason alone. Samuel Clarke's *Discourse Concerning the Being and Attributes of God, the Obligations of Natural Religion, and the Truth and Certainty of the Christian Revelation*, given as the 1704–5 Boyle lectures (published 1705–6) drew fire from David Hume. Arguments for a religion of reason were used by the orthodox to defend tradition, and to some extent the Bible. Deists used them to criticise the Bible and attack Christian beliefs, an endeavour that stemmed from John Toland's *Christianity Not Mysterious* of 1696, renourished in 1724, especially by the book by Anthony Collins, *Grounds and Reasons of the Christian Religion*, followed in 1726 by his *Literal Scheme of Prophecy* – one gets the idea. By the time of *New Dunciad* in 1741, about forty deist books had been published in England. They included William Harris's *Practical Discourses* (like Collins's first book, in 1724) *on the Principal Representations of the Messiah through the Old Testament*, Thomas Sherlock's *The Use and Intent of Prophecy* (1725), Richard Kidder's *A Demonstration of the Messias* in (1726) and Matthew Tindal's *Christianity as Old as the Creation* (1730). (Tindal has a special mention in Pope's *Dunciad* Book IV, the only contemporary proper name in the anti-deist passage 437–93. His is the last line, 'Where Tindal dictates, and Silenus snores.')

Central in the debate, as becomes apparent, is the question of the Old Testament, especially prophecy. Were the Jews any more than historical antecedents of Christians? Deist writers were fundamentally ahistorical, wishing their 'natural religion' to have nothing to do with something as statedly divinely regulated as biblical history (though they did open up some historical, and critical, problems in passing, which proved important). They tended to regret the immorality and superstition found in the Old Testament. They suggested that looking more closely at the history of the Jews hindered rather than helped belief in the Bible. As condemned in Samuel Clarke's book first noticed above, Old Testament prophecy as it reappeared in the New Testament was a chief issue because such prophecies could not be said to have been fulfilled in the New Testament without allegory, or mystery. Such fulfilled prophecies went against the deist insistence on Christianity's reasoned truth. In removing revelation, whether expressed in mystery, or miracles, deism also removed altogether personal faith, and a personal religion.

MESSIAH BIBLE–BASED

One begins to see the place, and importance, of Jennens's *Messiah* libretto – and of Handel's music. The very title declares the Jesus of the Gospels, 'born in the City of David a Saviour, which is Christ the Lord', as the fulfilment of the Old Testament hopes and prophecies. Those words of the angel are in *Messiah* 14: apart from the orchestral overture (1), and 'Pastoral Symphony' (13), all the passages before 14 are Old Testament prophecies. From 'Glory to God'(17), which is the chorus of the angels from Luke, to the end of the oratorio, thirty-four more numbers in all, twenty-three are either the words of Old Testament prophecies or of Psalms with prophetic intent. Part 3 of *Messiah* begins, famously, with that single soprano upward reach of haunting beauty, 'I *know* that my Redeemer liveth' (45; from Job 19:25), a statement of personal faith if ever there was one, even if it is now thought not to be a satisfactory translation of Job's Hebrew. Towards the end of that number, the change of musical subject at 'For now is Christ risen from the dead' marks the change to New Testament fulfilment, the words of all *Messiah's* numbers 46–51 being from Paul at the end of that 1 Corinthians chapter, 15, which also supplies the words for all those six numbers, then moving to Romans 8 and Revelation 5 for the last two numbers of the oratorio.

Jennens has sometimes been said to have been less original than might at first appear, as his Bible passages occur in those sequences in various parts of the Book of Common Prayer. He could have found the passages for Part 1 in the Christmas service, and for Part 3 in the burial service. That is so obvious that it hardly needs saying. The Part 2 passages are more scattered, but they are all present somewhere in the Prayer Book at strong liturgical moments. The argument needs to be turned, both upside down and round. Not only does the Prayer Book naturally quote the texts that have been central to Christians since the faith began, so that any searcher after Old and New Testament statements of the Good News is going to arrive at these (as well as others, of course, not present): in that sense Jennens and the Prayer Book coincide in orthodoxy. More importantly, the very fact that these *are*, to state it rather gaudily, jewels of the Prayer Book, underlines Jennens's High Church orthodoxy. The future of the country, he is saying, has to lie in the daily worship in its church, and in the biblical story contained in its liturgical year, wherein is contained all the elements that call out personal faith. The Bible has a hundred thousand times the number of texts here used, and the church fathers a million times more: Jennens could have made a compelling libretto, still called *Messiah*, out of all sorts of great stuff. He chose these, the core of his church's Bible in daily use.

THE NEW *DUNCIAD* BIBLE–BASED

Handel was a Lutheran, for whom the Bible was paramount. Pope was born into a Catholic family, and for him the Bible was not so central. Nevertheless, even a contemporary satire like the original three-book *Dunciad* has behind it a screen of Bible references of some power. When Tibbald, the target of the mockery, is crowned king of dunces, a peculiar bird descends on his head[22] parodying the dove seen by John the Baptist at the baptism of Jesus Christ (Luke 3:22) thus making Tibbald 'not merely king but king of kings', and reminding readers that the power of Pope's feelings about the collapse of culture comes from their being, finally, religious feelings.[23] Tibbald, like Moses (Exodus 24:12) and Jesus (Luke 4:5), is called to a mountain top, to survey the 'boundless Empire'.[24] The new dispensation was foretold in ancient prophecies: 'This, this is He, foretold by ancient rhymes . . .'.[25] Even in the earliest version, the climactic third Book ends with a perversion of Tyndale's Genesis 1, '*Let there be darkness*'.[26]

Pope's late friendship with the learned William Warburton changed a good deal for him. They first met in April 1740, a meeting followed by a week or ten days when Warburton was Pope's welcome guest at Twickenham. Already in 1739 Warburton, though then unknown to him, had endeared himself to Pope through his unsolicited *Vindication* (as it came to be called) of Pope's views in his *Essay on Man* (1733–4). These views were subjected to attacks, not least from a wilfully ignorant Swiss professor of mathematics who had no English. In Warburton's refutation of such misconceptions, and analysis of the *Essay*, he steered understanding of the poem closer to the main stream of Christian belief.[27] Quite where Pope stood in his own religious belief at that time is difficult to see. Under the direct influence of Warburton, however, his last, and greatest, work, *The New Dunciad* of 1741, becoming Book 4 of the whole *Dunciad in Four Books* in 1743, is a different matter.

In the new last Book, though it begins with Milton's 'darkness visible', the Chaos out of which God created all, there are few biblical references; the biblical scale is even grander. The poem now has Colley Cibber as a bigger and more serious enemy, and the tone is less playful. But beyond Cibber as a corrupter of values is a scene larger by far, as the poem is lifted to the level of biblical prophecy. As an Isaiah or Jeremiah showed the effect of deserting the Lord in order to 'bow the knee to Baal' (4:93), so Pope, now far more seriously than the destruction of a mere Colley Cibber, shows what happens to the nation's privileged leaders when 'CHAOS! is restor'd; / Light dies before thy uncreating word . . .' (4:653–4).

William Warburton, by training a lawyer but recently ordained. was Pope's closest friend in the last four years of his life (Pope died on 30 May 1744). The friendship was mutually beneficial. Pope introduced Warburton to his influential friends, to good effect (he married Ralph Allen's niece, and found rapid preferment). Pope's faith was strengthened. To adapt a contemporary remark, it was a friendship 'which made Warburton a bishop and Pope a Christian'.[28]

HANDEL'S BIBLICAL FAITH

To Jennen's biblical libretto, Handel responded eagerly. It was true that he needed public delicacy towards his expected audience. 'Everyone was nervous of New Testament words being further reduced in authority by being sung in a theatre by singers of doubtful reputations among decent folk,' as Hamish Swanston put it.[29] Not only did Jennens's wide canvas of biblical texts contain most of the colours of religious controversy of the previous twenty years: only four days before the first London performance of *Messiah*, at Covent Garden on 23 March 1743, the *Universal Spectator* printed a letter from 'Philalethes' (the Greek means 'lover of the truth'), objecting to it. Calling himself 'a profess'd Lover of *Musick*, and in particular of all Mr. *Handel's Performances*, being *one* of the *few* who never deserted him', 'Philalethes' noted that Handel's *Israel in Egypt* had been offensive in using Scripture.

> An *Oratorio* either is an *Act of Religion*, or it is not; if it is, I ask if the *Playhouse* is a fit *Temple* to perform it in, or a Company of *Players* fit *Ministers* of *God's Word* . . . it seems the *Old Testament* is not to be prophan'd alone, nor *God* by the *Name of Jehovah* only, but the *New* must be join'd with it, and *God* by the most *sacred* the most *merciful Name* of *Messiah* . . . .[30]

Whether 'Philalethes' spoke for many people in London is not known. His denigration of theatre and performers cannot have been pleasing to the town, and his letter produced some answers. Perhaps because of it, the performance was announced not as *Messiah* but as 'A New Sacred Oratorio'. This may indicate unease by the management, but may not have helped to quell controversy.

At issue is the 'politically correct' place for the English Bible. Handel was too good a Lutheran to allow bigotry to hinder the public proclamation of the Word of God. More to the point, his new work consummated his own personal, biblical, faith. By the autumn of 1741 he had emerged, restored, from a disastrous year, 1737. In that year his savings had all gone. He had driven himself very hard throughout Lent, with new works and performances (which also meant many rehearsals, as well as the supplementary concertos at each performance) and proposals for more after Easter. In May he was 'very much indispos'd . . . with a Paraletick Disorder, he having at present no Use of his Right Hand, which, if he don't regain, the Publick will be depriv'd of his fine Compositions' as the *London Evening Post* reported on 14 May 1737. At first given out as rheumatism, what Handel had had, on 13 April, was a stroke. The Earl of Shaftesbury diagnosed it as caused by 'Great fatigue and disappointment', further explaining that 'the Palsy . . . took entirely away, the use of 4 fingers of his right hand; and totally disabled him from Playing: And when the heats of the Summer 1737 came on, the Disorder seemed at times to affect his Understanding.'[31] His friends feared for his mental state. He was persuaded to go to the vapour-baths at Aix-la-Chapelle. When he got there, he at once sat in them three times longer than anyone had ever done, and emerged cured: within a few hours, it was said, he was heard playing the organ in the church, brilliantly. The nuns thought it was all a miracle.[32]

On 7 December of that year, 1737, King George II commissioned from Handel the funeral anthem for his mother Queen Caroline. By the 12th, Handel had completed the entirely choral *The Ways of Zion do Mourn*, mentioned above. For Handel, this was a musical development marking both his recovery and his sense of personal loss: he had known Queen Caroline (at first as Caroline of Ansbach) for much of his life, and she had been good to him, 'engaging him as music master and softening where she could the antagonism shown towards him by her husband and son' [i.e. Georges I and II].[33] Now in this anthem he wanted to avoid operatic displays of grief in chromatic arias; he was expressing national grief, in long choruses. At the same time, those choruses made for him a personal statement in another sense. He was moving a long way from what were so often the over-coloured, over-heated solos and false emotions of Italian opera (Pope's 'Harlot form'). He was gathering together, for new explo- ration, his sense of the narrative that Scripture texts could make. For *Saul* in 1739 Handel had been given a libretto by Jennens which allowed him to make a new imaginative reach into the mind, and society, of that king. Musically, he moved boundaries. Personally, he touched borderlines. In the summer of 1737, he had feared madness. He found the work of compos- ing *Saul* difficult, it being the story of the mad king of Israel (it is in 1 Samuel). The autograph is unusually full of crossings-out and rewritings. He was not composing music for a Greek myth, with precise location of causes. This madness – even when Samuel's ghost Freudianly explains it as originating from the probably repressed memory of a disobedient incident when the young Saul spared God's enemy, Agag, as recorded in 1 Samuel 15:9 – has larger, more unknown, sources. God's world contains mystery. Handel was wrestling with the origins of personal madness. He wanted his audience to consider this, and the effect of derangement on those around.

The causes of insanity had just been questioned by Joseph Butler (shortly to become Bishop of Bristol, and later of Durham) in his book *The Analogy of Religion, Natural and Revealed, to the Constitution and Course of Nature* of 1736. As Clerk of the Closet, Butler had attended Queen Caroline's funeral in Westminster Abbey on 17 December 1737, walking in the procession, with a place in the service.[34] It seems more than likely that he had known Handel for some years before that. Butler's conclu- sions to, for example, the madness problem (on which a Christianity based

on reason must founder) were no secret. They were that both nature and
Christianity were odd: mankind is 'in a very strange state . . . but it is not
Christianity that has put us into this state'.[35] Scripture is not to be read
as any ordinary book. The nature of the Kingdom of God is like ordinary life, with lost coins and mustard seed and wedding feasts. Butler even
takes the story of Balaam (in Numbers 22), a subject of deist derision (as
in Tindal) and finds God, and human life, in its inconsistencies: 'strange as
it may appear', Baalam's condition 'is not altogether an uncommon one'.
Worse, the talking ass itself, a source of deist glee, announces in the story,
Butler says, a divine meaning, however unlikely. He argued for a liberty
to be found in Scriptural narrative.

Butler's book has usually been taken as having demolished the deist
position. It was not quite so.

> He had simply countered the deist description of the world with a
> description of his own . . . he had put together assumptions about an
> Eternal God, an immortal soul, and the kind of world we inhabit, which
> enabled contemporary Christians to move forward. . . .[36]

After the release he had found in writing *Saul*, Handel followed the exploration of the strangeness of the world into other Scripture narratives
set as oratorio. It is in this stream that *Messiah* stands. Between *Saul*
and *Messiah*, however, also in 1739, came *Israel in Egypt*, and commercial
failure. He found himself still uncertain about what the marriage of
Bible story and oratorio would produce. The big choruses in *Israel in Egypt*
make sound-pictures of what recitative has announced, and there is a
grander political sense of a nation coming out of 'thick darkness' into
liberty. But *Israel* is oratorio as anthems, to be listened to and admired,
not as common Christian life to be experienced humanly, and loved, as
Messiah is.

A useful illustration of *Messiah's* triumphant solution of Handel's
artistic, and existential, problems is his choice of Mrs Cibber as alto soloist
in Dublin. Her reputation, and some of her effect, have already been noted;
but there is more to be said. Born Susanna Arne, sister of Dr Thomas Arne
the composer (who wrote the music to 'Rule, Britannia' and set such
Shakespeare songs as 'Where the bee sucks'), she was later to become
famous among London theatre-goers. At this time in Dublin, however, she
had been away from the London stage for the three years 1738–41, escap-
ing the persecutions of her husband, Colley Cibber's dreadful son
Theophilus, whom she had married at nineteen and was now leaving for
good. She had endured a miserable marriage as Theophilus's second wife
for four years, and the death of two children. Now the disreputable
Theophilus had in 1739, as all the world knew, taken her to court for

adultery with young William Sloper, the 'gentleman of fortune' who was her protector and partner for the rest of her life, and the father of three of her children. (In that suit, Theophilus Cibber claimed damages of £5,000. The jury assessed them at £10.[37]) It is likely that she met the great David Garrick as she finally left Dublin in August 1742: she had invited her brother and his wife to Dublin in June for a summer season of concerts, coinciding with Garrick's time there. The Arnes and Garrick were on the packet *Lovely Jane* which left Dublin 23 August: Susanna Cibber, finishing her time in Ireland, was also on board, with William Sloper. Thereafter Susanna's long professional partnership on stage with Garrick as his leading lady delighted London. She was loved for her acting in comedy opposite him, and 'though possessing a fine sense of humour, [she] excelled in tragic heroines and put-down females.'[38] For twenty-five years Garrick was, as she put it, 'my lover upon the stage, and my friend off it'.[39]

One of her strengths on stage was her voice: not its power or range – of which Sheridan said 'she had but a moderate share', and Charles Burney called it 'a thread' – nor even her musicality (Sheridan said that 'many of the Italians must be allowed to exceed her'[40]), but its expressiveness. Burney wrote that 'by a natural pathos, and perfect conception of the words, she often penetrated the heart, when others, with infinitely greater skill, could only reach the ear'.[41] Here is Hamish Swanston:

> What Handel found precisely to his purpose was her 'intelligence of the words', her 'native feeling', 'her powers of expression' . . . She was the singer to make an audience attend to the words, learn what Handel was intending them to feel, share what he was suggesting they should know about themselves as 'human race'. . . . She bore the central line of meaning. . . . He gave her several of the best tunes so that the most significant verses should be impressed upon the minds and hearts of his hearers: the prophecy of a liberator in 'Behold! a virgin shall conceive', the effectiveness of liberation in 'Then shall the eyes of the blind be open'd' and, most movingly, the cost of liberty, 'He was despised and rejected of men'.[42]

That Handel, in point of fact, composed all these with Susanna Cibber in mind is not yet firm, though her name does appear on the autograph manuscript of *Messiah*, written between 22 August and 14 September 1741, against number 9, 'O thou that tellest', which is the air and the chorus that follow the recitative 'Behold!' Tradition has it that he did. Tradition thus preserves an essential truth, that Mrs Cibber's remarkable expressiveness of the human condition was what he wanted. A story from the very first performance, perhaps apocryphal, supports the idea.

One impromptu compliment was offered during the performance itself;
the Rev. Dr Delaney, a friend of Dean Swift (and later to marry
Handel's friend Mrs Pendarves) was so transported by Mrs Cibber's
singing of 'He was despised' that he rose from his seat and exclaimed,
somewhat presumptuously for a divine, 'Woman, for this, be all thy sins
forgiven!'[43]

For the only properly 'sacred' oratorio that Handel wrote, that reach of
Bible words deep into human life was essential. The whole work begins
with the releasing phrases, 'Comfort ye . . .'; 'Iniquity' is 'pardon'd'.

HANDEL'S BIBLICAL OUTPOURING

Starting work on Jennens's manuscript on 22 August, Handel had Part 1
finished by 28 August. He completed Part 2 on 6 September, and Part 3
a week later on 12 September. He spent two more days filling up the
inner parts. The speed of this was more convincingly to do with the coherence of Jennens's libretto than with the legend, sentimentally said only to
apply to the writing of *Messiah*, of Handel being in a divinely wrought
white heat of religious inspiration. During those twenty-four days, he is
claimed to have left untouched the food his servant brought, and to have
found his ink mixed with his tears. He is said to have exclaimed, as he
laid down his pen, 'I did think I did see all Heaven before me, and the
Great God himself.' Well, perhaps: the blots and crossings-out and fresh
starts do suggest pressure, and it is nice to be romantic. He did, however,
a fortnight later, finish the first Act of *Samson*, the biggest of all his oratorios, and the whole thing after a month. Nevertheless, the legends of
the writing of *Messiah* point in the right direction. There was something
personal for Handel in the making of this particular biblical oratorio. He
was finding in a Bible narrative, oblique but clear enough, his own way
forward. It took him from despondently fiddling about with Italian love-
duets and the sleazy thing that Italian opera had sometimes become. His
skill in compressing and adapting the KJV for vocal lines is often praised,
rightly. One can perhaps see Handel the Bible-steeped Lutheran boy and
young man in some changes. For example, in 18, 'Rejoice greatly', the
biblical phrase in KJV is 'he is just, and having salvation', which he made
into 'He is the righteous saviour'. Luther has '*ein Gerechter und ein Helfer*',
'a righteous man and a saviour', and that memory of a phrase well known
to him may have helped.

 Samson, performed in 1743, is based on Milton. It could have been in
Handel's mind that this oratorio might thus, being Milton, be an insur-

ance against attacks on him in London for setting Scripture to music for secular locations. (It is noticeable, incidentally, that in Dublin there had been no suggestion at all that it was in any way improper to perform a sacred work in a secular place: Dean Swift's alleged hostility to lending St Patrick's Cathedral choir does not bear scrutiny). Samson, however, is not just an Old Testament hero. Though here Miltonic, he is firmly in the New Testament as a model of faith: in the well-known list of Hebrews 11, he is next-but-one to David himself. That Samson had been, also, for fourteen hundred years a figure of Christ was in Milton's mind, as well. Setting to the grandest music the story of such a figure, or allegory, or type, or shadow, was another riposte to the deists, who knew not 'seems'. Handel's next step, in setting Congreve's *Semele* in 1744 (from Ovid), feels out of line: except that it is about that most unrational of states, inadequacy, especially in dealing with a god. *Joseph and his Brethren*, also of 1744, composed on a libretto by James Miller, challenges an audience's memory of the story at the end of Genesis. It was popular. *Hercules*, first performed in January 1745, was to a libretto by the anti-deist theologian and encyclopedist Thomas Broughton, allowing Handel to expand and express his understanding of mythic narrative, with an underlying quality of analogy to Scripture.[44] He wrote to the press acknowledging the failure of the 'musical drama', and outlining his financial distress as a result: and at the same time insisting on his serious purpose.

> He had meant . . . to join 'good Sense and significant Words to Musick', for the English language was 'so expressive of the sublimest Sentiments' and perfectly adapted to 'the full and Solemn Kind of Musick'.[45]

He wanted an audience who could attend to the 'Musick' with those 'significant Words': that is, to listen to the myth in the new telling of one part of the story of Hercules. *Belshazzar*, written in the summer of 1744 alongside *Hercules*, and like that, performed early in 1745, was again to a libretto by Jennens. The core is Daniel 5, with historical bits from Ezra and further prophecies from Jeremiah and Isaiah. Daniel and his prophecies had been at the heart of the deist arguments. The summer of 1745 saw Handel ill again, 'a good deal disordered in his head' as Lord Shaftesbury put it.[46] The libretto of *Judas Maccabeus* (1747) was taken from 1 Maccabees 3–9 and 2 Maccabees 8–15, and elsewhere, by the Cambridge scholar Thomas Morell. Its songs of victory and liberty were popular in a London still celebrating the defeat of 'Bonnie Prince Charlie', and Handel recovered his health and his bank balance. *Alexander Balus*, the account following that of Judas in 1 Maccabees, was also written to Morell's libretto in 1747, as was *Joshua*, finished the same year. Its ultimate biblical origins need no explanation, though there is much elaboration of other elements. It is the same with *Solomon* and *Susanna* (both 1749), of which the librettists are unknown. Handel's last two oratorio librettos were again by Morrell. Though *Theodora* (1750) is the story of a martyr under the Diocletian persecutions of Christians around 300, Handel's last oratorio, *Jephtha* (written when he was sixty-seven) returns to the Scriptures, the story of another virgin martyr, told in Judges 11. Both allowed Handel to retell stories of horrific circumstances, and move from deistic determinism to some idea of resurrection. At seventy-four, having been for the previous seven years blind, he died in April 1759, eight days after conducting a performance of *Messiah* at Covent Garden.[47]

Over the years of the deist debates, Handel 'had established that his dramatic story tellings should assist in the development of theological understanding'.[48] He had done more. He had ensured that certain phrases of the English Bible sang their way into the minds of hearers ever after – and, through the minds, into the hearts. For many people, it is impossible to hear in the head, or say aloud, the words 'O thou that tellest good tidings to Zion', or 'Lift up your heads, O ye gates' or 'Behold, I tell you a mystery' without Handel's music. Though Handel has been rebuked for awkwardness of stress, as in '*For* unto us a child is born', and though there is evidence of a good deal of revision of some word-setting, by Handel himself and later editors,[49] many phrases of prophecy, Gospel narratives and New Testament Epistles in the KJV, and Psalms in the Prayer Book, remain for ever wedded to his music. Handel thus takes his place with the great hymn-writers; with this difference: that though 'Guide me, O thou great Jehovah' or 'The Lord's my Shepherd; I'll not want' or 'When I survey the wondrous cross' or 'O God, our help in ages past' stay deeply embedded in English-speaking consciousness, they are lines crafted metrically out of the phrases of the Bible. Handel's words are the thing itself. 'And suddenly, there was with the angel, a multitude of the heavenly host, praising God, and saying, Glory to God . . .' Or, 'Since by man came death, by man came also the resurrection of the dead. For as in Adam all die, even so in Christ shall all be made alive . . . Behold, I tell you a mystery. We shall not all sleep, but we shall all be changed, in a moment, in the twinkling of an eye, at the last trumpet. The trumpet shall sound, and the dead shall be raised incorruptible.' There is a natural music in these King James verses. Handel is responding to his love for the English language, that, as was quoted above, he said was 'so expressive of the sublimest Sentiments' and perfectly adapted to 'the full and solemn Kind of Musick'. It is extremely unlikely that Handel had any notion whatsoever of William Tyndale, whose verbal music is in those verses from 1 Corinthians 15, with the smallest of changes.[50] But like Tyndale (who also began – at least – as a good Lutheran) he can make the Word of God sing its way into the heart.

Generally, the field of the English Bible in eighteenth-century England is a flat one: the outstanding biblical outcrops can at best be described as 'interesting'. Beauty is found in secular lyric:

> Full many a gem of purest ray serene
> The dark unfathom'd caves of ocean bear:
> Full many a flower is born to blush unseen.
> And waste its sweetness on the desert air.[51]

and, surprisingly, in satire –

> Soft o'er the Shrouds Aerial Whispers breathe,
> That seem'd but *Zephyrs* to the Train beneath.
> Some to the Sun their Insect-Wings unfold,
> Waft on the breeze, or sink in Clouds of Gold.
> Transparent Forms, too fine for mortal Sight,
> Their fluid Bodies half dissolv'd in Light.[52]

Handel in *Messiah* made for everyone an unforgettable beauty with English Bible phrases that point to the core of the Christian faith.

JONATHAN SWIFT

As a postscript, I offer speculation about Dean Swift in 1741, it being no longer believed that he ended his life in a devastation of madness. The tragic account of Handel while in Dublin calling on Swift and being admitted to 'behold the Ruins of the greatest Wit that ever lived' comes from Mrs Laetitia Pilkington's *Memoirs* written fourteen years later, and no doubt owes something to time and fancy.[53] We have no other evidence of Handel trying to call on the Dean. In his very last years, Swift suffered a severe affliction, a debilitating pain in the middle ear which at its worst made him deaf, and unapproachable. But his distress was intermittent. In May 1740, a letter from Mrs Whiteway reports his health 'as good as can be expected, free from all the tortures of old age: and his deafness, lately returned, is all the bodily uneasiness he hath to complain of'.[54] Swift can hardly have been unaware of Handel's visit to Dublin. From newspaper reports one gets a vivid sense of the *Messiah* arrangements and performances in the city, an impact heightened because they were for charity.[55] Swift had, many years before, been the leading member of the satirical Scriblerus Club, those Saturday meetings with Arbuthnot, Gay, Parnell and

Pope which began in 1713. They were dedicated to promoting (which meant, of course, writing) the works of the pedant Martinus Scriblerus, an imaginary scholar whose notes were, delightfully, always immensely learned and always wholly wrong – a productive vehicle for satire in an age of learned footnotes. Though the meetings themselves did not survive the political changes after the death of Queen Anne in August 1714, the large satirical plans, the central friendships, and the collaborations, continued. Swift in particular was deeply engaged in the first versions of *The Dunciad*. When Pope took up the poem again in 1741, it had new satirical learned notes by 'Scriblerus'.

The Scriblerians (principally Gay) had provided Handel with the libretto for the beautiful *Acis and Galatea* of 1719, and (principally Pope) for the *Haman and Mordecai* which became *Esther*, Handel's first English (and, one notes, biblical) oratorio. It would be pleasant to think, against popular legend, that Swift, the arch-Scriblerian himself, was fully aware of what was going on in Dublin, even though, at the age of seventy-four, he could not get about. He might even have had a hand in drawing Handel to Dublin, though no evidence has survived. Yet as is apparently well documented, Swift refused to let his Vicars Choral (i.e. choristers) join in Handel's performances. That rather tumultuous refusal, dated 28 January 1742, sounds absolute.

> And whereas it hath been reported, that I gave a licence to certain vicars to assist at a club of fiddlers in Fishamble Street . . . I do hereby annul and vacate the said licence; intreating my said Sub-Dean and Chapter to punish such vicars as shall ever appear there, as songsters, fiddlers, pipers, trumpeters, drummers, drum-majors, or in any sonal quality . . . at the instance some obscure persons unknown. . . .[56]

To those who know Swift's techniques of raillery, however, that tone is familiar. For example, three years before, when he was already ill and seventy-one years old, Swift had written a thank-you letter to young Katherine Richardson, who had made for him as a present half a dozen shirts 'although I never once gave you the least cause of displeasure'.[57] 'A club of fiddlers in Fishamble Street' is a performance of Handel's (Scriblerian) *Esther*. Lists were favourite Swiftian devices. But – 'some obscure persons unknown . . .'? *Handel*? The Lord Lieutenant? In any case, Swift had known about Handel's more recent life from the letters to him from Mrs Pendarves, who in June 1743 married that Patrick Delaney who so praised Susanna Cibber in the first performance of *Messiah*, and Dr Delaney had been, until Swift's debility, a frequent companion. Swift may have had a lapse of memory, but the liveliness of the prose doesn't sound like that. And the cathedral singers did indeed take part, at least in the first four Handel performances.

It would be pleasant to think that the apparently everlasting forces of the biblical *Messiah*, from its beginning, may also link not simply with one (Alexander Pope) but (with Jonathan Swift) two of the most forthright powers of the time.

Chapter 33

THE ENGLISH BIBLE IN AMERICA, 1777 TO THE EARLY NINETEENTH CENTURY

AMERICAN BIBLES IN OVERVIEW

In England in 1777, scholars and clerics were disputing and refining the KJV text after 150 years of careful production. In America, the English Bible was being printed for the first time.

The 1777 Aitken New Testament, though rightly a treasure in American life, is not as an object very remarkable. The whole Bible, which followed four years later, again from the Philadelphia printing house of Robert Aitken, is again not a particularly impressive reissue of KJV. Yet once started, American printers were neither slow nor restricted. By 1800, twenty-three years after their first New Testament, there were in circulation seventy different printings of the Bible, some of them already rich with engravings and notes, from presses in eleven different towns. By 1840, there had been over a thousand, from over forty places. Many of those are wonderful volumes to see, and some were made far from the east coast, in Alabama and Missouri. Twenty years after that, in 1860, when print-runs of other books ran to scores of thousands, and there were thousands of local newspapers, a further 650 different American Bibles had been published, some printed in huge numbers. Presses in north-eastern towns still dominated the work, but Bibles came from printers in many states. That mid-century flood (the subject of a later chapter) abated a little in variety, but for the rest of the nineteenth century American-printed Bibles still came from large presses coast to coast, as they did for the whole of the twentieth. There was another strong surge of Bible printing from the 1970s. Today American Bibles are available from a few big publishers in an almost unbelievable variety of translation and annotation and intention. Most of them are, as in earlier times, of reasonable size, made to be carried, or kept at a personal bedside. Yet that part of the account of the English Bible which is especially American has to be, for the middle decades of the nineteenth century, about an avalanche of giant, heavily bound Family Bibles, all of them KJVs, full of pictures and massive extra matter, sold in colossal numbers right across the States as an essential piece of furniture in the American home. The story of the printing of English Bibles in America has been, after a late start, of amazing success, becoming, in the last years of the twentieth century bewildering excess.

THE FIRST PRINTED BIBLES IN AMERICA

The printing of their own Bibles might be thought of as a political necessity for the men who signed the Declaration of Independence in 1776. They should no longer be bound by the British Crown's copyright on the Scriptures.[1] The blocking of imports during the Revolution was only a temporary check, however, on the regular thousands of copies of KJV arriving in the new United States from England. Here one first encounters three unexpected circumstances that will haunt the story of the Bible in America. First is the reluctance of the first Congresses to have anything to do with such a printing. American legend exalts those devout and holy men, as they are said to have been, and makes them eager to support an American-printed Bible. It was not so. In spite of appeals to Congress, the Bible of its printer, Robert Aitken, was a financial disaster. Second is the solid, near-absolute dependence of this new, adventurous nation on KJV, on the Scriptures in archaic English fixed under a British monarch long before. The Crown copyright, legally enforced, was not the only thing that kept the United States back from printing their own Bibles: even from the time that it was no longer law, there can be detected a reverential need for what must have been felt to be the 'proper' Word of God, the KJV. With that goes a third mystery, to which I shall return: that is the failure of American leaders to challenge KJV as a translation, to encourage local American scholars to work afresh from the Greek and Hebrew to make a truly American Bible for the emerging American nation. One reason among others for the long delay (over 140 years after *The Bay Psalm Book*) in printing complete Bibles in America must not be overlooked. This was the gritty fact that though, by the 1770s, there were some fifty printing shops on the eastern seaboard, none of them was equipped, either financially or mechanically, for an operation requiring as much type, paper and labour as printing a complete Bible. Modern methods of paper making and type can disguise what a big book the Bible is. The book of Genesis alone is about forty-five thousand words, the length of a respectable short novel. Yet even so, it is striking how slow America was to Americanise the Bible.

There have been rumours of the discovery of complete American Bibles printed as early as 1752, though no copy of one of these has ever been seen.[2] Robert Aitken's distinction as the first American Bible maker remains solid.

ROBERT AITKEN

Aitken was born into a Quaker family in Dalkeith, just outside Edinburgh, about 1734. There he had apparently learned bookbinding. He sold books, probably in Paisley, west of Glasgow. At the age of about thirty-five he sailed to America to look into the prospects there. In Philadelphia in 1770 he had some success, with sales of a *Shorter Catechism* and *A Dialogue between Jockey and Maggy, or How to Court a Country Girl*. He returned to Edinburgh to collect his wife and children, and in 1771 he was back in Philadelphia as a bookseller, his stock including School Bibles. His premises were 'opposite the London Coffee House, Front Street' – coffee houses in London had for two centuries been where like minds met, and this one in Philadelphia was where Revolutionary activists gathered. From 1774 Aitken was a printer, and when the first Congress met in Philadelphia the publication of its journals was put in his hands, from January 1776. When, in December 1776, under the threat of a British attack on Philadelphia, Congress removed to Baltimore, a resolution was passed sending 'an Express' to find out where Robert Aitken was, and to get him, if he were willing, with the journals already printed and 'his press and utensils to this place at the public expense'. He decided, however, to remain in Philadelphia. With Richard Baiche, son-in-law of Benjamin Franklin, he had begun, in January 1775, a journal, *The Pennsylvania Magazine*. The editor of this, from February 1775 to May 1776 (it closed two months later) was Thomas Paine, who wrote his radical call for democracy, the pamphlet *Common Sense*, anonymously, that April. Aitken was brave to be so publicly associated with Paine, and there is today a colourful notion that he (Aitken) narrowly escaped arrest by the British and 'imprisonment in a British Prison Hulk in New York Harbour'.[3] Arguing for an immediate declaration of independence, Paine's *Common Sense* is said to have sold 120,000 copies in its first year alone, with a readership five times that: it eventually sold half a million copies.[4] (Though books and pamphlets from American presses were rapidly becoming an essential force in the Revolution, few books had runs of as many as two thousand; and pamphlets were lucky to sell half that.) Thomas Paine also began then his *American Crisis* papers, of which the first, from 1776, famously begins: 'These are the times that try men's souls. The summer soldier and the sunshine patriot will, in this crisis, shrink from the service of their country.' Paine, still nearly two decades before *The Rights of Man* and *The Age of Reason* and their international impact (and his official banishment from Britain, convicted *in absentia* of seditious libel) was in America already having a great effect. The eloquent patriotism of that first *American Crisis* paper, ordered to be read to the Revolutionary troops, was said to be very effective in firming the resolve of waverers, not only in the army. Several things, as well as his association with Paine, make Robert Aitken's credentials as an American patriot printer sound.

Paine's later attacks on the Bible might make him an unfortunate bedfellow for Aitken as American Christian hero, but his earlier writing is more positive.[5]

From Aitken's press had already come, as advertised on the last page of his New Testament, a dozen books: the complete verso page offers a picture of Philadelphia life:

Domestic Medicine; or the Family Physician. Price 15 s.
Essay on the Character, Manners and Genius of Women, in different ages.
    Price 7s. 6
Art of Speaking. Price 10s.
*Croxall's Fables of Aesop, with Plates, containing excellent morals. This is
    absolutely the best book for the English scholar.* Price 10s.
Dr Lowth's English Grammar, with critical Notes. Price 5s.
Ruddiman's Rudiments of the Latin Tongue. Price 5s.
Dilworth's Spelling-book.
*An elegant Octavo Edition of the Journals of Congress, printed from the
    beginning.*
Pennsylvania Magazines, 2 vols. Bound. Price 30s.
Walker's Sermons. Price 2s. 6.
Modern Riding-Master. Price 2s. 6.
Grave, a Poem, by J. Blair. Price 1s. 3.
Lives of the Apostles, with Plates, Price 2s. 6.

This is not all. The final five items, and additional paragraph, are of interest:

Copperplate Copy-books. Price 1s. 3.
Larger and shorter Catechisms.
Battledores and Primers.
Writing Paper by the ream or quire; Pens, Wax and Wafers, &c.
Maccuba Rappee. Price 10s. per bottle.

Books bound as usual.

The highest Price given, at the above Printing-Office, for any quantity of clean Linen Rags.

*** *Please forward them to the Printer hereof: The favour will be gratefully acknowledged, and ready money paid.*

(Rappee is grated tobacco, or a most pungent snuff.)

A striking and helpful picture of Philadelphia interests in 1773 also emerges from *Aitken's General American Register*, printed by Joseph Crukshank in that year. Subtitled 'the Gentleman's and tradesman's complete account book, and calendar', Aitken offers fifty-two double pages ruled for entering receipts of money, followed by astronomical and tide data, and then the Contents:

> Table of the kings and queens of England
> Genealogical list of the royal family of Great Britain
> The number of peers, peeresses in their own right, archbishops and
>   bishops in England, Scotland and Ireland
> Kings of Scotland and the time they began to reign
> Lord Lieutenants of Ireland since the union
> His majesty's consuls abroad for the protection of trade
> Births, marriages and issue of the sovereign princes of Europe
> A concise chronological account of the events in America from the first
>   discovery thereof

and seven more American items, including 'His majesty's order concerning the power of civil government over his forces in America', ending with the only local information, 'Public offices &c. in Pennsylvania', which enters B. Franklin as 'alderman, trustee of school, president of philosophical society', and the Library Company of Philadelphia, numbering four hundred members.

The latter items might be expected: but that patriot Robert Aitken could boost his sales with so much British royal material comes as a surprise. It is perhaps a mark of how sophisticated Philadelphians still thought of themselves as civilised British, and possibly of what little else there was to occupy Philadelphian life than conservative 'ex-pat' European-ness. The requirements for entering the local college, 'this seminary, whose plan is truly catholic' are noted by Aitken: 'for admission into the freshman-class, a student must be able to stand an examination in the Latin Classics, the Greek Testament, and Lucian . . .'. Visible here is a hunger for intellectual roots: Lucian was the second-century Greek rhetorician, satirist and teller of fantastical tales. A similar need seems to have fixed in America the perpetual reprintings of KJV.

Aitken's New Testament, 1777

In July 1777, in the third year of the war, and during the ban on the importation of books, three 'Ministers of the Gospel of Christ in the City of Philadelphia' laid a petition before the 'honourable Continental Congress of the United States of North America', noting that

> . . . in our present circumstances, books in general, and in particular, the holy Scriptures . . . are growing so scarce and dear, that we greatly fear that unless timely care be used to prevent it, we shall not have Bibles for our schools and families, and for the public worship of God in our churches.
>
> We therefore think it our duty to our country and to the churches of Christ to lay this danger before this honourable house, humbly requesting that under your care, and by your encouragement, a copy of the holy Bible may be printed, so as to be sold nearly as cheap as the common Bibles, formerly imported from Britain and Ireland, were sold . . . .[6]

Congress referred it to a committee of three, headed by John Adams, which reported back two months later on 11 September 1777, the day when General Howe's campaign against Philadelphia itself began. The report, recorded in the *Journal of Congress* for 1777–8, is significant.[7] The committee, having consulted local printers, were cautious, and

> are of the opinion that the proper types for printing the Bible are not to be had in this country, and that the paper cannot be procured . . . that to import types for the purpose of setting up an entire edition of the Bible, and to strike off 30,000 copies, with paper, binding, &c., will cost 10,272*l*. 10*s*. 0*d* . . .

Procuring such types and paper would be difficult, and the risk in the act of importing great. However,

> the use of the Bible is so universal and its importance so great . . . that the Committee will recommend that Congress will . . . import 20,000 Bibles from Holland, Scotland, or elsewhere, into the different parts of the States of the Union.

Congress was split, even about such a compromise. Seven states, all northern except Georgia, voted for it: New York, Delaware, Maryland, Virginia and the Carolinas were against. There was dissension and postponement. Robert Aitken saw his chance. In presumably the last months of that year, 1777, he printed at his own expense a small duodecimo KJV New Testament, and entered American history.[8]

In his *Early Bibles of America* (1894), John Wright's word for the 1777 Aitken New Testament that he saw in the Lenox Library, New York, is 'humble'. He is rather kind: a modern observer might find it nondescript. Wright calls it 'but a small duodecimo':[9] it is a little larger than Tyndale's first 1526 New Testament from Worms, though not at all so well made.

The text, in two columns, fills the 353 pages tightly: there are chapter and verse numbers, but no headings. This first American Bible printing is in the tradition of Tyndale's 'bare text'. The title-page, like the contents, is straight KJV, concluding, 'Philadelphia: Printed and sold by R. Aitken, Printer and Bookseller, Front Street. 1777'. At the foot is a decorated motto: under a dove with an olive-branch in its beak, two children support a motto, '*Spectamur agendo*', a contrived quotation from Ovid's *Metamorphoses*, XIII, made to mean not 'Let us be observed [*Spectemur*] in action,' but 'We are observed [*Spectamur*] in action.'[10] The olive-bearing dove speaks for itself; the children are interesting. In the next century, American writers about their new nation would allegorise the republic as a child, sometimes with Wordsworthian idealisation of the infant as both innocent and from birth attuned to the goodness in nature.[11] (Not for nothing were the most famous American heroes in the novels of Mark Twain the streetwise child Tom Sawyer and the rough, innocent boy Huckleberry Finn.)

The only additional Bible matter in the Aitken New Testament is the already-standard 'Order of the Books . . . with their Names, and the Numbers of their Chapters' on the reverse of the title-page. The quality of paper, probably made in Pennsylvania, and type (and setting) is not high. The book was, of course, like all at the time, sold unbound by the bookseller. There is a feeling of shortage of space as if paper were rationed – like a war-time book, which it was, of course. Even so the pages are attractive. Like Tyndale in 1526, Aitken gave the reader a clear bare text of the Word of God for his or her pocket. We do not know exactly how many he sold, but it seems that it was few. Entries in his business records show some sales in the last days of August 1777. There are then no more entries until after the British had left Philadelphia in June 1778. On 18 July 1778 he advertised in the *Pennsylvania Evening Post* a new 'neat' edition of the New Testament just published, and sales reappear in his books.[12] Buyers, as well as Congress, were hesitant to get involved.

AITKEN'S BIBLE, 1781

It was, however, a start. Notices have been found of reprints in 1778, like the one just mentioned, and another in 1779, though no copies have emerged. There were fresh printings of New Testaments by other printers: in Philadelphia, by Francis Bailey; beyond, by Isaac Collins in Trenton, New Jersey; Thomas and John Fleet in Boston; and James Adams in Wilmington, Delaware, all before 1781. In that year, 1781, came the next and more significant event: Robert Aitken petitioned Congress for support and sanction for the printing of a complete Bible. He had been busy, and in spite of the constraints of war he had, at his own considerable financial risk, assembled the materials, and begun printing an entire Bible. His petition, dated 21 January 1781, begins to answer some questions.[13]

> To the Honourable The Congress of the United States of America The Memorial of Robert Aitken of the City of Philadelphia, Printer
>   Humbly sheweth
>   That in every well regulated Government in Christendom The Sacred Books of the Old and New Testament, commonly called the Holy Bible, are printed and published under the Authority of the Sovereign Powers, in order to prevent the fatal confusion that would arise, and the alarming injuries the Christian Faith might suffer from the Spurious and erroneous Editions of Divine Revelation . . .

Aitken writes that he has 'both begun and made considerable progress in a neat edition of the Holy Scriptures for the use of schools. But being cautious of suffering his copy of the Bible to issue forth without the sanction of Congress', he asks that they consider it seriously and have it inspected so that 'it may be published under the Authority of Congress', and sold 'in such manner and form as may best suit the wants and demands of the good people of these States . . .'

The two 'Chaplains of the United States in Congress Assembled' described it as 'expensive work'. So it was. Aitken again petitioned Congress, on 26 January 1782, this time for financial help, with no response. He sought help from the state, to the General Assembly of the Commonwealth of Pennsylvania. On 15 March 1782, they agreed to an interest-free loan of £150 for one year. It is not known whether he took up the offer.

When this Bible appeared in September 1782, the first volume included, after the standard KJV title-page, now with the State arms of Pennsylvania, (so the motto is now 'Virtue, Liberty and Independence') a page and a half of the commendations of Congress, giving Aitken 'applause and encouragement' for his work, and formally on 1 September 1782, asking the two Chaplains ('reverend Doctor White and reverend Mr Duffield') to examine the text. William White was Rector of Christ Church: he established the Protestant Episcopal Church in America, and was first President of the first Bible Society in America, that in Philadelphia. George Duffield was pastor of the Third Presbyterian Church in Philadelphia, and worked to found that denomination in the States. While waiting for the report, Aitken sent to Congress on 9 September 1782 a further 'Memorial', pointing out that his Bible had been 'accomplished in the midst of the Confusion and Distresses of War' and suggesting (it seems, fruitlessly) that Congress buy two hundred copies for each State.[14]

The Chaplains' report, dated 10 September 1782, is also printed in the Bible.

Report.

Gentlemen, Agreeably to your desire, we have paid attention to Mr Robert Aitken's impression of the Holy Scriptures, of the old and new testament. Having selected and examined a variety of passages throughout the work, we are of opinion that it is executed with great accuracy as to the sense, and with as few grammatical and typographical errors as could be expected in an undertaking of such magnitude. Being ourselves witnesses of the demand for the invaluable book, we rejoice in the present prospect of a supply, hoping that it will prove as advantageous as it is honourable to the gentleman, who has exerted himself to furnish it at the evident risk of private fortune . . .

(Signed.)
William White, George Duffield.

The Resolution of Congress, apparently also of 10 September 1782, follows:

Resolved, That the United States in Congress assembled highly approve the pious and laudable undertaking of Mr Aitken, as subservient to the interest of religion as well as an instance of the progress of the arts in this country . . . they recommend this edition of the Bible to the inhabitants of the United States . . .

This is interesting in several ways. Congress approved, without doing more than that. They had other things on their mind: under Benjamin Franklin in Paris that September, formal negotiations were beginning for peace with Britain, and thus independence. Their backing was not only religious: the phrase that is parallel to 'the interest of religion' is 'the progress of the arts in this country'. Why Aitken needed that authority has appeared, plausibly, in his Petition quoted above – sacred Scripture needs to be protected. There is also a faint possibility that he appealed to the new government because the old British tradition of printing English Bibles under the patronage of those in power had been so strong that it felt unthinkingly right. Did it not occur to him, however, that he was free to work independently? Of course, he now had the *imprimatur*, as one might term it, of Congress, valuable for sales and publicity – except that sales did not happen. Congress gave their own printer, it seems, no money, nor any other practical help. There is a sense of a small national duty being grudgingly done.

From Aitken's press, the resulting small fat book (sometimes divided into two volumes) was first issued on 25 September 1782 and 'sold by R. Aitken, at Pope's head, three doors above the Coffee House, in Market Street'. Aitken sent a special copy to John Hanson, President of the Congress, for their use, and as a demonstration of what they were so obliquely supporting. It is again printed from KJV in two columns per page in a clear roman font, sometimes poorly inked. As with the 1777 New Testament, the text fits tightly on the page: one book immediately follows the next. There are no extras at all (except in half a page 'The Names and Order of all the Books'); all the 960 leaves are simply chapters and verses of both Testaments (there is no Apocrypha). Aitken printed, it can be calculated, an astonishing ten thousand copies, of which fifty survive.[15] It seems that he lost a great deal of his own money.

Thus, eleven months after the British surrendered at Yorktown, ending the Revolutionary War, America had its own adequately printed complete English Bible. It had to compete with stocks of better-produced copies of KJV from London, Oxford and Cambridge, which, in spite of shipping costs, could be sold in American shops more cheaply. As with his New Testament, we do not know exactly how many Aitken sold. Again hints suggest that it was not many. There was a feeling of loyal rescue. In May 1783 a Synod of Presbyterians in Philadelphia resolved that its 'committee to purchase Bibles for distribution among the poor purchase Aitken's Bible and no other', as well as generally recommending it. Also in 1783, as the war was ending, Dr John Rodgers, pastor of the First Presbyterian Church in New York, wrote to General Washington suggesting that copies of Aitken's Bible should be presented to each of the soldiers in the army when they were discharged. Washington replied warmly. Congress, he wrote, would have done well in making 'such an important present to the brave fellows who have done so much for the security of their country's rights and establishment' – but the suggestion came too late: Congress had already ordered the discharge of two-thirds of the army. In 1789, Aitken asked Congress for a fourteen-year patent 'exclusively to print the Holy Scriptures'. It was refused. In that memorial to Congress he states that in the publication of his Bible he had lost 'more than three thousand pounds in specie'.[16] He died in 1802.

Other printers in other towns (Trenton, Boston, New York, New Haven) produced New Testaments in the ten years after 1782. They seem to have been, if anything, even more 'humble' than Aitken's. For example, from the press of Joseph Crukshank in Philadelphia in 1789 a surviving copy has poor paper and bad inking. It is not at all to be despised, as a much-used workaday Testament. The pages are still full, and there are now minimal page and chapter headings: a step forward.[17] Quite soon,

American paper mills were producing better paper, and typefounding improved. By 1792, other printers in other states had produced more elaborate versions and founded successful, profitable, Bible-publishing firms. Demand for Bibles rose quickly with the local revivals of piety, especially in the north east; with the firmer establishment in the chief towns of old, and new, denominations; and especially with the fiery spread of evangelism, soon to affect dramatically the western frontiers.

THE UNITED STATES AND THE IRREGULAR ADOPTION OF THE BIBLE

From 1774 to 1789, the Continental-Confederation Congress, to give the full title, was the legislative body that governed the United States, from Philadelphia. The view that it consisted of deeply religious and scholarly men is coloured by later myth-making. One of them, it is true, Charles Thomson, a non-delegate who had been elected Secretary to Congress when it was first organised in 1774, went on to be a notable Bible scholar, making a translation from the Septuagint in 1808, as will be seen below (it is 'Cha. Thomson' whose signature appears at the foot of the Resolution of Congress to support the Aitken Bible). A legend has it that before any work was done, that first national Congress began with prayer. The 'Liberty Window' in Christ Church Philadelphia, after the mid-nineteenth-century painting by Harrison Tompkins Matteson, depicts 'The Prayer in the First Congress AD 1774' (fig. 32). In it, thirty-one devout men kneel or stand in united intercession, led in exalted piety by their first chaplain, the Reverend Jacob Duché. Historically, however, the records show that the prayer was made during the second day, and only happened after considerable bickering and disapproval.[18] What triggered the intercessions, it seems, was a report of the seizure by the British of some cannon and powder, and the rise to arms of the Boston neighbourhood. This was later exaggerated into the belief that the British were bombarding Boston, wasting the city, killing their loved ones. The story goes that as 'forty men' sat stunned at the horror, Chaplain Duché was inspired to walk slowly forward, to take his Bible, and – at that moment especially directed by God – to turn to Psalm 35, 'Plead thou my cause, O Lord . . .' and then pray. These men of different beliefs, strangers to one another that morning, all wept. Or so the legend has it. 'Surely these sacred words had been written for this day, for this company and for this hour.'[19] In truth, not a shot had been fired in Massachusetts. Nobody wept (except possibly an elderly Quaker). Duché was an Anglican clergyman, and that was the Psalm for the day. He was not appointed chaplain until two years later. Soon after, he defected to the British. The Christ Church window's heading is 'The Church and Magna Charta': the top section depicts the role of churchmen in 1215 in compelling King John to sign Magna Carta. Yet in that first Continental Congress of 1774, nothing authorised Congress to be concerned with religion. Indeed, it was seen to be important that if Congress was Christian, it was so in a non-denominational, non-polemical way. So it appointed chaplains for itself and the armed forces, enforcing Christian morality on the troops, promoted missionary work among the Indians and proclaimed days of Thanksgiving: for religion it did no more than that. True, the language of Congressional proclamations could be vaguely religious, praying for example for 'a holy, that so we may be a happy people', and occasionally more specifically Christian in content, as the wish that the nation might 'through the merits and mediation of Jesus Christ . . . obtain [God's] pardon and forgiveness'.[20] But the wrestling with the real problem of the relation of government to religion was left to individual states.

In the summer of 1787, a convention met in Philadelphia, under President Washington, and with the respected eighty-one-year-old Benjamin Franklin among the fifty-five delegates, to debate the widespread feeling that the Republic needed a stronger federal government. After four months' intense work, on 17 September it adopted the Constitution of the United States. This document says nothing about religion, except Article VI, which states that for federal office holders, 'no religious Test shall ever be required as Qualification'. Pressure then arose from two groups: those who wanted Congress to declare a more specific Constitutional position for organised faith, and those who were afraid that that might happen. The result was the adoption, within the Bill of Rights of September 1789, ratified in December 1791, of the First amendment. This, the celebrated 'freedom of speech . . . and to assemble' amendment, begins 'Congress shall make no law respecting an establishment of religion, or prohibiting the free exercise thereof . . .' Under this umbrella, individual states could go their own way: but for the last years of the century that was the general American religious climate.

A careful official neutrality about denominations and even faiths went with a steady proclamation of belief in God's interest in the obvious success of the nation and its people, even to declaring His special relationship, binding Himself to a covenant with America above all. (We recall that 'these sacred words [Psalm 35] had been written for this day, for this company and for this hour'.) Statesmen commended the Bible: in a letter to Thomas Jefferson, John Adams, the second President, called it 'the best book in the World'.[21] The people who influenced public opinion still tended to have biblical first names – as had, as one of their names, the first seventeen presidents until Ulysses S. Grant in 1869.[22] Biblical imagery in public statements was common: for the national seal Franklin in 1776 proposed Moses leading the people to safety through the Red Sea: Jefferson suggested the pillar of cloud and fire. As will be seen below, in Isaiah Thomas's address at the opening of his 1791 Quarto Bible, the great and the good of America officially assumed that the social fabric would be strengthened by the access of everyone to the Scriptures. Public statements, from pulpits or political platforms, drew comfortably on scriptural examples. Exodus 1.8 was almost too easy a text in 1773 for a sermon on the virtues of American independence: 'Now there rose up a new king over Egypt, which knew not Joseph'. The cry of Moses to Pharaoh in Exodus 5, 'Let my people go' could stand for the whole Pentateuch experience being now of American liberation from Britain. (The taking of these words for a much more politically significant movement by black slaves, and later by African-Americans generally, hardly needs pointing out.)

The serious use of the Bible in America paralleled, with a difference, the biblical influence in the English Civil War. An event in the United States could do more than echo a conveniently biblical text – it could fulfil it. Whereas in England, Cromwell's men and women had found divine authority for their theological politics in the margins of the Geneva Old Testament, now the new citizens of the United States could be told that they were the fulfilment of biblical prophecy, of God's story in Scripture. In a published sermon entitled *The United States Elevated to Glory and Honour* given by Ezra Stiles, president of Yale College, in 1783, the words of Deuteronomy 26.19, 'to make thee high above all nations which he hath made . . .' were taken to be allusively prophetic of the 'future prosperity and splendor of the United States'.[23] All the long history of the typological use of the Bible had been gathered into American life by Cotton Mather in his *Magnalia Christi Americana* of 1702.[24] Giving it extra point in the Revolution and ever after were the new developing convictions about the United States, grown out of success, that its cosmic destiny was to be God's special nation.

The Bible had been in the flow of American life from the beginning: Old Testament stories and ideas were deep in the national consciousness.[25] Self-interest, and those increasingly distressing assumptions about the United States as God's elect nation, began to muddy the stream. On the one hand the very national structures themselves, distantly based on biblical notions, took on the sort of reverence accorded to the Bible. On the other, this American biblicism had very little to do with the Gospel, with the redeeming work of Christ in the individual soul – indeed, with the New Testament at all. The new American government showed determination to be ethically secure but religiously, as St Paul put it in a different context, 'all things to all men'. Cloudy Bible words from officials, including frequent appeals to God, did not mean that America was becoming in its deepest heart a Christian nation. The national love affair with the idea of every American owning an American Bible went with the fantasy of the whole point of the Bible being American. Part of that movement was the recorded growth of thousands of American church communities. Quite different, and statistically beyond any record, were all the humble, unsung, genuine personal quests in Christ, spiritual maturings nurtured by a Bible, in a different world from rhetoric about America being God's elect nation.

That was something that Jonathan Edwards had understood. In 1750, in the face of the dispute over church purity in which he was forced out of the Northampton pulpit, he had taken the opportunity to separate a national covenant, an Old Testament doctrine increasingly applied to the American nation, from God's covenant of grace, a fundamentally different, because spiritual, New Testament revelation. The carnally generated

> *external people and family of God . . .* was a type of his spiritual progeny. And the covenant by which they were made a people of God, was a type of the covenant of grace.[26]

'Only a handful', wrote Mark Noll, 'of Edwards's closest followers succeeded in using his theological insights'. Most 'joined their fellow Americans in regarding the nation itself as the antitype of biblical patterns'. Noll gives the example of one of 'the handful', Edwards's closest theological pupil, Joseph Bellamy, a Congregationalist from Connecticut. He

> resisted, even during the alarms of the Revolutionary period, the widespread practice of uniting the types of Scripture with the aspirations of American patriotism and continued to use the Bible to speak of the individual's spiritual needs before God.[27]

So did a few others. Three indeed – Levi Hart of Connecticut in 1775, and Jacob Green of New Jersey of the same time, joined especially by Samuel Hopkins of Newport in 1776 – extended an understanding of the Bible to attack the practice of slavery.[28] This was widely assumed to be sanctioned by the Bible, on the two grounds of the model of Israel, which kept slaves, and the fact that the Bible nowhere explicitly condemns slavery. Congress itself, on 18 October 1774, had pledged to 'totally discontinue the slave trade'.[29] Thomas Paine moved to make Pennsylvania the first to emancipate the slaves. Hopkins brought biblical authority: he used both Testaments to challenge in detail the use of slaves, not least

Matthew 22:39, the injunction to love our neighbours as ourselves. 'For Hopkins, to read the Bible . . . was to find a very different public book than that which many of his contemporaries opened to illuminate the Revolutionary era.'[30]

The slaves themselves were hungry for what Hopkins was saying. Their white masters produced a set of half a dozen texts ('Thou shalt not steal', Exodus 20.15: 'Servants, be obedient to them that are your masters . . . with fear and trembling . . .' Ephesians 6.5). These owners limited the Bible to those texts. The slaves found secret access to complete Bibles through the painful labour of learning to read, or through 'gathering to hear a black preacher – "Stealing away to Jesus", as the spiritual put it'.[31] The result was a knowledge of wonderful stories, told from the pulpit or sung in the fields, and believed with a faith that was both spiritual and social.

> The essence of slave religion cannot be fully grasped without under-standing this Old Testament bias. It is important that Daniel and David and Joshua and Jonah and Moses and Noah, all of whom fill the lines of the spirituals, were delivered in *this* world . . . in ways which struck the imagination of the slaves. . . . 'O my Lord delivered Daniel,' the slaves observed, and responded logically: 'O why not deliver me, too?'[32]

Moses was deliverer. Jesus was fellow sufferer and minister to the oppressed, understood individually as redeemer and socially as breaker of fetters. For slaves, 'deliverance from Egypt, the suffering of the oppressed, and the final Day of the Lord had very little to do with the fate of the United States' (see chapter 38 below).[33]

Mark Noll sums up:

> The image of the United States as a biblical nation . . . is an ironic one. Those who applied the Bible's teachings to the nation's destiny most directly seemed to have understood its message least. Those, on the other hand, for whom the country itself was least important seemed to have understood it best.[34]

THE RAPID COMMERCIAL DEVELOPMENT OF EMBELLISHED KJVS: ISAIAH THOMAS AND HIS FOLIO BIBLE OF 1791

In 1791 Isaiah Thomas of Worcester, Massachusetts, printed the first folio Bible from an American press. It came in two large attractive volumes (occasionally in one) with, at the end of the New Testament, an index, and fifty plates. Thomas's printing is the first of many American folio

Bibles. It is also the first of very many American Bibles to be illustrated by Americans, as all the plates, he announces, were made by four American engravers. Thomas should be here saluted as the forerunner of a splendid, American tradition of assertively American Bible illustration, even if the results were often bizarre.

Isaiah Thomas was the kind of craftsman-scholar with enterprise that American Bible printing, after Aitken, needed. Born in Boston in 1750, (his first name suggesting the biblical climate of the time) he had only a few weeks of indifferent schooling. At the age of six he was apprenticed to a printer. At the age of twenty he founded in Boston the patriot newspaper, the sharply named *Massachusetts Spy*. In 1775 he was one of those who joined Paul Revere, William Dawes and others in alerting the countryside before the fighting at Lexington and Concord. In those actions he took part. He moved his presses to Worcester, resumed the *Spy*, began manufacturing paper, and soon became the leading publisher and bookseller of that time. He had branches in half a dozen towns, including Boston and Baltimore. In Worcester he published magazines, a celebrated almanac, the first dictionary printed in America, music (importing type) and, among much else, more than a hundred children's books. In mid-life, in 1800, he published the first American edition of the Greek New Testament, a small duodecimo of 478 pages. He had the assistance of a classical scholar from Yale, Caleb Alexander. There had been, of course, Greek New Testaments in America for a long time, imported from Europe.[35] There were many more Greek New Testaments printed in America in the following centuries, usually, like Thomas's, the *Textus Receptus* with very minor changes. Nevertheless, his was an important first printing. In 1810 he wrote the standard *History of American Printing* in two volumes, and founded in 1812 the American Antiquarian Society. He was a member of nearly every learned society in America, with honorary degrees from Dartmouth and Allegheny Colleges.

> His printing establishments issued over 900 different books, more than those of Benjamin Franklin, Hugh Gaine, and Mathew Carey, his nearest rivals. Indeed, owing to the excellence of his typographical work and the range and number of his imprints, Franklin called him 'the Baskerville of America'.[36]

With the attention of such a man, American English Bible printing was bound to stride forward. In 1790, he issued prospectuses for the two-volume folio, and for a Large Royal Quarto Bible in one or two volumes. All appeared in 1791, and did indeed cover new ground. He printed in both a KJV text which he had worked hard to make completely correct. He himself collated 'nearly thirty' KJVs of various dates, imported from different printers. He then arranged for his own proof sheets to be supervised by local clergymen and scholars. This is all commendable enough: but he also understood his market. The Quarto has some KJV marginal notes, and twice as many others, and cross-references, and, at the back, indexes and tables and John Brown's concordance. Thomas was making Bibles for different needs: his prospectuses were addressed *To the Reverend Clergy*, *To Christians of Every Denomination*, and *To the Publick at large*. The Apocrypha was standard in both, but could be optional in the Folio, as could be the plates (which varied) and the Concordance in the Quarto. In the Quarto were printed, for the first time in America, blank Family Record pages, a feature of so many lavish editions in the next century. Before the standard KJV 'Address of the Translators' is an account of the making of that King James Version. Most remarkably, Thomas announced unique arrangements for payment. The 'Conditions' in the Quarto prospectus, which include advertising the 'elegant new types' helpful to the eyes of 'the aged and infirm', go on in 'Condition IV' to specify that the cost, '*seven dollars*, although the English Editions of the same size, and of an inferior quality, are sold for eight or nine dollars . . .' can, to make up half, be paid in 'Wheat, Rye, Indian Corn, Butter, or Pork'. Post-Revolutionary Massachusetts is vividly seen.

For citizens of the thirteen United States of America in 1791 to be able to buy such a fine English Bible made locally in an already flourishing American tradition was something of which to be proud. For those citizens to read it was another matter. For it to have influenced the way John and Jane Doe grew spiritually and, in their many unsung thousands, built the new Republic, is something else altogether. We know some personal details of some professional ministers and preachers and revivalists with an interest in success. We can follow the writings of theologians and denominational leaders, often with an axe to grind. Of what Tyndale called the 'little flock' we learn only when quarrels break out, just as hospitals everywhere record only the sick. Yet the extraordinary success story of the printing and selling of the Bible in America, which begins with Isaiah Thomas, must also be of that hidden coral, the private and unsung effect in so many souls of 'I am the way, the truth and the life.'[37]

Thomas's magnificent 1791 folio is still a pleasure to handle, with its fifty expensive copperplate illustrations specially produced by four artists, all New Englanders. It expresses the qualities of enlightened improvement for which many in America were reaching. Such personal betterment was not only an ideal, but an American right – more, it was within everyone's grasp: Thomas's volumes were intended to improve American society, socially, morally and intellectually, to make it 'a more courteous, refined and charitable place'.[38] Refinement was the especial domain of women, as was providing in the home a morally educated place for the nurture of children. The young republic increasingly looked to its women to set the tone, ruling the home. Many of the illustrations in this and later American Bibles have at the centre morally superior women. Of the twelve illustrations of Gospel events in Thomas's folio of 1791, four are specifically about women: 'A Woman healed of a bloody issue'; 'Mary Magdalene', haloed and pensive; 'The Woman of Samaria'; and 'Martha'. The first plate to follow the frontispiece of the whole Bible shows 'Genesis Chap. 2'. Adam sleeps against a bank; standing in a spotlight an alert Eve checks the Garden. Similar whole-page plates show, among others, Susanna theatrically rejecting the elders, 'Queen Esther fainting before King Ahasuerus', a collapsing Eve held by Adam as they are driven from the Garden – so much for her earlier diligent housewifery. These make the point splendidly. The trouble is that they make more points than one. The displaying of the women is ambivalent. The Genesis 2 Eve is shamelessly upright, naked from the hips up, and on show. Susanna, clutching her garment inadequately, as she inadequately defends herself, touches the elders (fig. 33). A vulnerable Queen Esther shows a lot of herself. Mary Magdalene thoughtfully exposes her breasts. Such pictures, though triumphs of New England rococo art, offended the refined. Engraving on copper demands separate leaves, a technicality which helps to give a picture unusual prominence. Developments of this apparent ambivalence, displaying wanton pictures in an American Bible, will be seen again.

Printing these Bibles in Worcester, Massachusetts, Isaiah Thomas also established his own paper mill and book bindery to make volumes better than any in Britain. The tone of national self-congratulation is strong in his address 'To Christians of every Denomination' which opens the Quarto. It begins 'The general state of our Country must afford satisfaction to every benevolent mind'. Prosperity, eminence abroad and confidence at home are all rising. Civil rights, the sciences, the arts and education are all improving, thanks to 'the present spirit of industry and economy, which pervades all classes of men'. For all Christians, however, it must be

> their ardent and united wish, independently of foreign aid, to be supplied with copies of the sacred Scriptures, the foundation of their Religion – a Religion which furnishes motives to the faithful performance of every patriotick, civil and social duty, superior to the temptations of ambition, avarice and social duty; – which opens prospects to the human mind that will be realized when the relation to civil

government shall be dissolved, and which will raise its real disciples to their highest glory and happiness when the monuments of human genius, art and enterprise, shall be lost in the general dissolution of nature.[39]

This is the Bible as national tonic. The same self-congratulation was everywhere at the time. In the mid-1790s, Thomas Jefferson, then a member of George Washington's cabinet, wrote:

> In general, our affairs are proceeding in a train of unparalleled prosperity. This arises from the unbounded confidence reposed in it by the people, their zeal to support it, and their conviction that a solid Union is the best rock of their safety, from the favourable seasons which for some years past have co-operated with a fertile soil and a genial climate to increase the production of agriculture, and from the growth of industry, economy and domestic manufactures; so that I believe I may say with truth, that there is not a nation under the sun enjoying more present prosperity, nor with more in prospect.[40]

The population doubled in the twenty years to 1814, to just over eight million. At the same time, imports doubled and exports trebled.[41] The immense territory of Louisiana was acquired in 1803. All that American citizens had to do was to look around them and see a biblical fulfilment, the United States as God's nation, America as an expanding land flowing with milk and honey.

THE AMERICAN FLOOD BEGINS: ISAAC COLLINS'S BIBLE, 1791

British Bible characteristics continued to arrive in America. The Scottish-born William Young printed in Philadelphia small School Bibles: one was priced at 'five-eighths of a dollar'; another included, for the only time in America, the Scottish metrical Psalms. The special names in early American Bible publishing, however, did American things. A name as important as those of Robert Aitken and Isaiah Thomas is Isaac Collins. His 1791 complete Bible was the first printed in New Jersey, at Trenton, between Philadelphia and New York. It became famous for its accuracy: it was adopted as the standard of correctness by later printers, particularly by Mathew Carey, who dominated the field of American Bibles in the early part of the nineteenth century. Collins's Bible's fame and use as beyond reproach were rather unfair, as he failed to correct the persistent error, found in British KJVs since as early as 1629, of printing 'thy doctrine' at 1 Timothy 4:16 instead of 'the doctrine', a reading which Isaiah

Thomas had got right. (The one-letter mistake sounds small; but if Paul was seen to be authenticating a doctrine peculiar to Timothy, instead of 'the doctrine', that is, Christian teaching as so far understood, then a crack could open through which might pour all sorts of heretical creepy-crawlies.)

Collins was a Quaker from Delaware, born in 1746. Having learned his trade elsewhere, he became at the age of twenty-four, in 1770, printer to the state of New Jersey. Editor and printer of material local to the state (a weekly newspaper, an annual almanac), and books including Baxter's *Saint's Rest*, in 1789 he issued a proposal to publish the Bible for four Spanish dollars if he received three thousand subscriptions. He added later that for the money his subscribers would also get Downame's Concordance, popular in England in the mid-seventeenth century. That had first appeared in 1631 in an edition of Barker's 'Wicked Bible'; it had been regularly reprinted in Britain, and was much fuller than John Brown's, running here to over fifty pages. In 1791 Collins printed five thousand copies, and customers could have the Bible with or without the Apocrypha, and with or without 'Practical Observations on the Old and New Testaments by Reverend Mr Ostervald', described as 'Professor of Divinity and one of the Ministers in the Church at Neufchatel in Switzerland', that is, his *Catechetical discourse* translated in 1704. To twenty-first-century eyes, Mr Ostervald's notes might have been better labelled 'Impractical Observations', as, unpaginated between the Apocrypha and the New Testament, they fill a hundred pages of small print, 'illustrating the chapters, a very few except, in their order, with arguments of the different books'. Collins reports that he has taken them from 'Edward Charles Dilly's Octavo from London, 1774' (originally from Cambridge in 1765[42]). He appeals for information about a shorter version ('not so large and full as this') he has heard of, presumably to lessen the density: but he has given the public the best he knows. The Bible pages have fairly frequent marginal notes, taken verbatim from a KJV. Like Thomas, Collins gives four blank pages for 'Family Record'.

What has arrived on American presses, twenty years from Aitken's first work, is the American Bible embellished for home study. Its American-ness is underlined by a significant substitution, for the first time, by Collins, who prints 'An address To the Reader by Dr Witherspoon' in place of the standard KJV 'Dedication to King James'. Witherspoon begins forthrightly by saying that the usual Dedication 'seems to be wholly unnecessary for the purposes of edification', and then adds rather less than forthrightly that it is 'perhaps on some accounts improper to be continued in an American edition . . .'. The address is a history of the origins of the Bible and its translators, with 'An Account of the Dates or Time of Writing the Books of the New Testament', understandably wrong by modern standards. That Scottish Presbyterian scholar John Witherspoon had arrived in New Jersey in 1768, bringing with him, and particularly to the College of New Jersey (Princeton University), the Scottish philosophy of Common Sense, so greatly influential in the new republic. One of the signatories of the Declaration of Independence, he famously remarked that his new country was not only 'ripe for the measure [that is, independence], but in danger of rotting for the want of it'. For twelve years a Congressman, he coined the term 'Americanism'. Here in Isaac Collins's 1791 Bible was a change of authority indeed, from the obsequious bowing to King James.

BROWN'S SELF-INTERPRETING BIBLE, 1778 AND THEREAFTER

Various printers in Philadelphia and elsewhere produced nearly a dozen other complete Bibles or New Testaments in 1791 and 1792. Hugh Gaine, the first to print a New Testament in New York in 1789, imported from Scotland in 1792 a complete Bible in already-set-up ruby type which he then kept standing – ruby, at five and a half points, is very small: the book is unpleasant. Isaac Collins's bulky complete Bible in quarto is easier on the eyes and includes for the first time in America the dates of composition of the New Testament books, with Matthew's Gospel '6 years from the death of Christ'. He adds: 'N.B. The times of writing the EPISTLE of JAMES and that of JUDE are not so certainly known, but supposed 33 years from the death of Christ.' (Standard modern datings are all very much later, with Matthew as late as AD 120.[43]) In the rush of printers in these years to make money, Bibles came in many shapes, some of them ugly. Those that are over-packed strained to get everything between small covers, usually the result of including the Apocrypha. (Another modern myth is here challenged, that Protestant Bibles did not include those Apocryphal books. The present writer's experience of examining Bibles printed in America throughout the nineteenth century is that in the first half, more of them than not included the Apocrypha.) The two columns on the page sometimes had inadequate space between them, though the tendency to give three- or four-word page headings and chapter headings compensates in clarity.

Printers competed in smallness of Bibles: a complete little Bible from Baltimore in 1812 was printed in diamond, at about four and a half points one of the smallest English types. The book is unreadable. (The copy seen was a wedding present to 'Mr and Mrs Phinehas Eastman': possibly it was simply a bridal ornament, in a long and still surviving tradition, and therefore readability did not matter.) Another in diamond came from Woodward in Philadelphia in 1816. In 1812 a Bible was printed for the first time in Vermont, at Windsor, 'the birthplace of Vermont': and in 1815 in New Hampshire (at Walpole). A 1791 New Testament from Newburyport in Massachusetts, has at the end 'An Alphabetic Etymological Explanation of Many Names of Persons, Places, &c. Which are Mentioned in the New Testament'. Printers were eager to supply this kind of information.

That is something that will be noticed increasingly in the profusion of American Bibles of the nineteenth century. Two hundred years after the 1790s, Bibles are usually very different. To stand in front of shelves of New Testaments in a modern American specialist bookstore is to be overwhelmed by choice of Testaments aimed at markets unrecognisable from those of a century or two before. In some modern Testaments and Bibles the commentaries, annotations, even translations (many of them paraphrases) are often directed in slant. They will be bought, the publishers hope, for personal, even solipsistic, reasons. There are Bibles and Testaments for the various stages of marriage and break-up, for the first year of divorce, for older women, for those suffering business failure, for those in therapy, for everyone looking for a quick fix of Personal Truth. Niche marketing must surely be a slippery slope.

It was not like that as the American nation was formed, where 'Self-Interpreting' meant interpretation for oneself, not interpretation of oneself. Two British Bibles reprinted in America for the first time in 1791 and 1792, and constantly reprinted over the next century because of great demand, were John Wesley's 1755 annotated version and John Brown's famous Self-Interpreting Bible of 1778. John Wesley's New Testament translation with annotations was reprinted over a dozen times, and is still in print in America.[44] John Brown's body of work, his 'Self-Interpreting' KJV with its marginal notes, summaries, 'Paraphrases On The Most Obscure Or Important Parts', analyses and 'Evangelical Reflections' was first printed in Edinburgh: 'it was many times reprinted, and proved almost as popular south as north of Tweed'.[45] It proved most popular of all, however, in the United States, where it was reprinted dozens of times, usually in a form either large or very large, sometimes even elephantine, and last printed as a Bible in (probably) 1896, though its New Testaments continued into the 1920s. It was made American by, among other things, the expansion of its material, its frequent great size as a volume and its increasingly eccentric choice of incidents to be illustrated in new full-page American-made engravings. The 1806 version had twenty-four ornamented plates of dramatic scenes distinctly odd in choice of subject. Illustrating the battle of A-i at Joshua 8:20 (only one of many battles in that

book) the plate is full of fighting bodies and horses in the Cecil B. DeMille
school of biblical illustration. The plate of Joab, King David's nephew and
army captain, stabbing Abner, Saul's cousin and his captain, 'under the fifth
rib' at 2 Samuel 3:27 has, in the ornament at the top of the page, cherubs
acting out the murder, above a tragic mask. Another is the strange assassination of Benhadad by the usurper Hazael (he took 'a thick cloth, and
dipped it in water, and spread it on his face, so that he died') at 2 Kings
8:15. It might be possible to construct an argument of nationalist cunning
in such choices of incident, idealising battles to liberate a Promised
Land, or the dread deeds that surrounded monarchs: or the motive was
sensationalism.

The New York printers of a large folio edition of this Self-
Interpreting Bible, for example, dated 1822, so heavy as to be almost uncar-
ryable, chose to make the frontispiece to the whole Bible, no less, an
engraving of David spying on Bathsheba bathing: a picture for which the
word that comes to mind is 'licentious'. This is a frontispiece to a
complete Bible. How can that disreputable incident with its shabby consequences be thought for a moment to represent the content of God's
saving Word? The book of the Acts of the Apostles in that 1822 edition
is introduced by an engraving, 'after Raphael', of Peter and the sorcerer
struck by blindness – an incident that is not in the Bible at all. Nor is the
original by Raphael; it is an elusive painting by the Spanish painter of the
mid-eighteenth century, Raphael Mengs: the original of this particular
painting has disappeared.)

The original 1792 American 'Self-Interpreting Bible', however, had as
frontispiece something altogether more elevating. It is a crude engraving,
of three classically draped women looking pleased. The chief figure
represents America. Her left elbow touches a column with thirteen names,
headed 'Washington'; her left hand holds a scroll labelled 'Constitution';
her right hand is extended to receive from a kneeling woman an open
copy of the 'Holy Bible'. A third cheerful woman stands alongside, holding
a tall Phrygian cap[46] on a pole, gazing fixedly at 'America's' right
shoulder. It is not in any way great art: but it is mightily significant – not
least in being American, and of three women.

That Bible came from New York. Brown's Self-Interpreting Bible of
1792 was the first complete Bible made in New York, by Hodge and
Campbell, just ahead of Hugh Gaine. Hodge and Campbell printed it in
forty parts over two years, taking over a British method of serialisation in
an American publishing enterprise that was later most successful. It was,
like the Collins Bible, and as others had intended before, published by
subscription: the list of subscribers is headed by 'George Washington, Esq.
President of the United States of America'. It has twenty plates, each

labelled '*Engraved for the American Edition of Brown's Family Bible*'. This great stride in self-confidence in Bible publishing is well illustrated by the title-page of the huge Bible from New York in 1836 (reprinting that of 1826) announcing itself as *The Self Interpreting Bible*, and at the foot, below a medallion of a smiling Adam naked in Paradise (probably a conscious symbol of the new Eden, innocent, fresh America), the additional title *Brown's SPLENDID Bible* (fig. 36). Engravings available were varied: they were often of exposed bodies, as, opposite Genesis 4, 'Adam and Eve weeping over the body of Abel', where little of the three bodies is covered. Perhaps such nakedness was, classically, to express primal innocence, the parallel to the new nation of America being implicit: or perhaps people bought books with pictures of naked bodies in them. The frontispiece shows a Charlton Heston-like Moses pointing to Christ carrying his Cross; on Moses' tablet of stone is inscribed '*UNTO HIM SHALL YE LISTEN* Deut.18.15'. That Old Testament passage foretells 'a Prophet', traditionally taken with reference to Christ: even the sparse marginal notes of the 1611 KJV at that point refer to John 1:45, Acts 3:21 and 7:37. As a frontispiece to the whole Bible, it is irreproachable. (The artist has changed KJV's 'hearken' to 'listen', no doubt on grounds of instant intelligibility.)

Chapter 34

TOWARDS 1769, AND AFTER

MANY EIGHTEENTH-CENTURY TRANSLATIONS

The notion that the eighteenth century was a barren period for Bible translations will not survive investigation. The compilers of DMH list, in the words of Neil Hitchin, 'at least forty-four new English translations of bibles, testaments or individual books between 1700 and 1800'.[1] Moreover, Hitchin continues, 'there were many more translations of biblical texts than these', as shown by the 1991 bibliography by W. Chamberlin. The latter lists, between 1700 and 1800, sixteen complete Bible translations, twenty-eight New Testament translations, five abridged new Bibles, thirty-eight newly translated Bible selections, five of the Pentateuch, eleven of Genesis or parts – and so on through most of the sixty-six individual books. Some of these translations have been lost to modern sight, or were never published, at least in full: but this is not barrenness. Some of the impetus came from a new understanding of the Greek and Hebrew originals: a good deal of it, however, was politics, making points from evangelical or High Church positions. As the weaknesses of KJV became more and more apparent, there was pressure to cause a new translation to be authorised 'that would have enabled the Church to encompass the whole protestant nation again'.[2] The moving forces were shunted into sidings by Archbishop Thomas Secker in the early 1760s.[3] What did happen was the sudden elevation of KJV, in spite of the inadequate repairs to its faults, to semi-divine status, and the worship of 'AV' (as it was in the UK) nicknamed 'Avolatry'.

THE GREEK TEXT OF THE NEW TESTAMENT

Until the middle of the eighteenth century, British scholars had led the way in studies of the New Testament in Greek. German scholars then began to classify and label families of Greek manuscripts, clarifying evaluation of rival sources. Since Daniel Mace's diglot of 1729, there had been a score of new editions of the Greek New Testament on the Continent up to 1777. In that year in Halle in Germany appeared the complete edition of a new Greek text of the New Testament. This was the work of Johann Jakob Griesbach, by then professor at Jena. Each page of this large volume has the Greek in two columns, with a wide margin for the owner's notes. This was the first full challenge to the *Textus Receptus*, and giving room for anyone's further comments and discoveries shows how suddenly open the work of establishing a sound Greek text had become. Griesbach printed his own emendations in smaller type, with the old *Textus Receptus* readings below, noteworthy variants or interpolations being signalled by special signs. At the foot of the page is his critical apparatus.

This important book 'laid the foundations for all subsequent work on the Greek text of the New Testament'.[4] The text Griesbach printed brought – and then attracted – a mass of new evidence unknown to Erasmus and the later developers of the *Textus Receptus*, evidence from freshly studied manuscripts, from New Testament quotations in the Greek Fathers, and from early versions of the New Testament in other languages (Gothic, Armenian, Philoxenian Syriac). Until Westcott and Hort's revolutionary edition of the Greek New Testament in England in 1881, Griesbach's work set the new standard. Not only that: Griesbach laid out his editorial principles,[5] of the greatest value to translators. At the head stands the overriding preference for the shorter reading (with a few careful qualifications). What Griesbach's text means, for example, is that the passage in St John's Gospel, the *pericope de adultera*, in which Jesus has thrust before him a woman 'taken in adultery . . . in the very act', and in which Jesus famously says to her accusing scribes and Pharisees, 'He that is without sin among you, let him first cast a stone at her', and concluding 'Neither do I condemn thee: go, and sin no more' (John 7:53–8:11) is marked in the text as special case, and the problematic authenticity is discussed in the apparatus. The same is true of the 1 John 5 *comma Johanneum*, the disputed expansion of the 'three in heaven'.

The significance of Greisbach's text is not only that it is so obviously not the *Textus Receptus* in many hundreds of places, but that it is so very well supported. In Britain, and even more in America, it was a platform from which to make a serious challenge to the KJV, which was the *Textus Receptus* in English.

Two small volumes, however, had been published in London only the year before, in 1776, which were of a newly edited Greek New Testament breaking much new ground. Here was a considerable, and important, challenge to the *Textus Receptus* made on excellent grounds: it is interesting to question the cause of its lack of influence – probably because it was outshone by Griesbach's new science, but perhaps also because the English mood was again for reverence for the *Textus Receptus* and its God-given

clothing in English, KJV. A pinch of flavouring of disapproval may have
been added by knowledge of what this scholar had already done in
English, to which I shall come.

The editor was Edward Harwood (1729–94), a Nonconformist
minister with an Edinburgh DD, his 1767 doctoral thesis being published
in 1773 as *A New Introduction to the Study and Knowledge of the New
Testament.*[6] The title-page of his 1776 two volumes of Greek is:

> ... The New Testament, collated with the most approved manuscripts;
> with select notes in English, critical and explanatory; and references to
> those Authors who have best illustrated the Sacred Writings. To which
> are added, a catalogue of the principal Editions of the Greek Testament;
> and a List of the most esteemed Commentators and Critics.

Dr Harwood produced an admirably useful edition. For his text of the
Gospels and Acts he followed in the main Codex Bezae: for the Pauline
letters, Claromontanus. He utilised others, chiefly Alexandrinus. He
deserted the *Textus Receptus* up to 70 per cent of the time, and anticipated
the epoch-making nineteenth-century work of Karl Lachmann in 1831.[7]
Unlike Lachmann, however, Harwood did set out to make 'a Text of the
inspired writers ... as near to the original autograph of the Evangelists
and Apostles as any hitherto published in the world'.[8] Edward Harwood's
later fame, however, rested on his New Testament not in good Greek texts
but in literary English.

In 1768, on the eve of the first appearance of the Oxford 'standard'
edition of the King James Version in 1769, a revision which effectively set
in stone the form of the 1611 version, including many errors, for generations to come (though ironically almost all copies of this first folio were
destroyed in a warehouse fire) there appeared (from two publishers in
London, one in the Strand and one in Paternoster Row, and others in
Bristol, Liverpool and Warrington) Edward Harwood's New Testament. It
has always been regarded as at best an amusing curiosity, at worst, folly.
When it came out James Boswell called it a 'ridiculous work', and C. S.
Lewis remarked in 1950 that Harwood was 'no doubt ... by our standards,
an ass'.[9] Harwood's title-page explains:

> A Liberal Translation of the New Testament; being an Attempt to trans-
> late the Sacred Writings with the same Freedom, Spirit, and Elegance,
> With which other English Translations from the Greek Classics have
> lately been executed ... with Select Notes, Critical and Explanatory.

Certainly, it feels a long way from Tyndale's simplicity to find – as has often
been quoted in a tone of mockery – the opening of the Parable of the
Prodigal Son in Luke 15 rendered:

A *Gentleman* of a splendid and opulent fortune had two sons. One day the younger approached his father, and begged him in the most importunate and soothing terms to make a partition of his effects betwixt himself and his elder brother – The indulgent father, overcome by his blandishments, immediately divided all his fortunes betwixt them. A few days after, the younger brother converted all the estates that had been thus assigned him into ready money . . .

This younger brother presently 'left his native soil', and degenerated 'by a course of debauchery, profligacy and very expensive and fashionable amusement and dissipation . . .'; again, a long way from the feeling of Tyndale's 'would fain have filled his belly with the cods that the swine ate' – for which Harwood has 'Here he was so dreadfully tormented with hunger, that he envied even the swine the husks which he saw them greedily devour – and would willingly have allayed with these the dire sensations he felt.'

Of course Edward Harwood knew what he was doing. As he puts it in his Preface, he translates 'for the candid and intelligent Christian', aiming 'to clothe the genuine ideas and doctrines of the Apostles with that perspicuity, in which they themselves would have exhibited them had they . . . [lived] . . . now'.[10] Moreover,

> The reader is desired ever to bear in mind, that this is not a *verbal* translation, but a *liberal* and *diffusive* version of the sacred classics, and is calculated to answer the purpose of an explanatory paraphrase as well as a free and elegant translation.[11]

The Prodigal finds that '. . . reflection, which his vices had kept so long in a profound sleep, now awoke', a sentence which may help us to see what is going on. Similarly, when he comes back 'without clothes, and without shoes and with all the haste, that a body pining with hunger, and exhausted by fatigue could make . . .'; and when his father

> rushed to meet him with swift and impatient steps – folded him in his arms – imprinted 1000 ardent kisses on his lips – the tears straying down his venerable cheeks, and the big passions that struggled in his breast, choking his utterance . . .

we know that we are in the worlds of the contemporary novels of Richardson, and of Fielding, Smollett and Sterne, the parents of the English novel of feeling. Samuel Richardson struck something new, in *Pamela* (1740) and especially *Clarissa Harlowe* (1747); by telling his stories of virtuous and passionate young women in the intimacy and immediacy of letter-writing, Richardson brought to the reader the sensations of the moment in his young women in every sentence. In doing this, he shifted the gears of the ancient form of the romance; in its later European form, it had retained the improbabilities and loose narrative of the classical Greek originals, but had developed the tradition of fine sentiments well expressed, especially by the central women. (Good examples from two centuries before, both extremely popular at the time that they were written, and long after, are Thomas Lodge's *Rosalynde* of 1590, the source of Shakespeare's *As You Like It* of 1599; and Robert Greene's *Pandosto* of 1588, Shakespeare's main source for his *The Winter's Tale* of 1610 – Greene's romance was still being read in the middle of the eighteenth century, and Richardson's exemplary servant-girl, Pamela Andrews herself, reads it.) Richardson's epistolary device developed this by allowing the full flowering of the story and the feelings, while keeping it all believable.

Within the intense short form of the Parable of the Prodigal Son (in the original Greek, just under four hundred words long) Harwood allows, or injects, or expands to, huge, Clarissa-like, feeling. In Luke's Greek, the narrative begins like a fairy tale: 'A certain man had two sons.' (That is Tyndale, who has it exactly – it isn't just 'a man' as the Wyclif LV had it; and Wyclif EV's 'Some man' is actually better than LV – the *tis* in the Greek, Ἄνθρωπός τις (*Anthrōpos tis*), gives the sense of 'someone', 'a certain'.) The parable is even more like a condensed Greek romance, a form which Luke knew.[12] Even Harwood's effect of 'he left his native soil' has folk-tale and romance roots. It remains a parable, of course, unique to the Gospels, and the teaching of Jesus, in its mysterious and extraordinary lucid brevity. Watching Harwood 'diffuse' it is to learn much about his intentions. The overwhelming feelings he elaborates are bewildering and destructive, as they are to Clarissa Harlowe.

The story must give the sense of the rapidity of change. The turning point is given by Tyndale 'Then he came to himself', literal to the Greek: εἰς ἑαυτὸν δὲ ἐλθὼν (*eis heauton de elthōn*) means exactly that. Modern versions usually give 'he came to his senses': but Harwood, though his version of the parable is indeed excessively full of feeling, does not make the change happen through the senses at all. For him, 'he came to himself' implies *reflection*. Harwood's basis, at least, is reason. In his Preface, he

> presumes to assert, that the New Testament itself, if carefully and candidly perused, with a mind open to the reception of truth, will, by all rational and intellectual Christians, be judged to conduce to a more clear and comprehensive knowledge of Christianity than those voluminous critics, paraphrasts, illustrators, and interpreters. . . .[13]

Before we watch Harwood at work in the New Testament generally, we should give more attention to that Preface, which is thoughtful, forceful, revealing and long-winded. He announces that he has three aims – 'Freedom, spirit and elegance'. He will give the true signification and force of the original, while elucidating and explaining it 'upon a new and rational plan'.[14] He is writing something new: 'not a *verbal* translation, but a *liberal* and *diffusive* version of the sacred classics . . .'. To pause on these two epithets: 'liberal' was more precise in 1768 than now – and to some moderns, but not then, more pejorative. Then, its general meaning was 'suitable to persons of superior social status' – as Johnson had defined it a dozen years before in his *Dictionary* (1755), 'becoming [to] a gentleman'. Two years later Burke had written of people 'permitted . . . to emerge out of that low rank into a more liberal condition.'[15] 'Diffusive' is, on the surface, just what it suggests – a word for something widely distributed, or, better, shed abroad bountifully. Harwood intends no restriction on the receiving of his version of the word of God. There was, however, a common use of the word in the seventeenth century, not found after the first decades of the eighteenth but still perhaps able to be in mind, which could be used of a body of people to suggest not only that they all shared something but that what was shared was particular, not universal.[16] Harwood continues:

> . . . calculated to answer the purpose of an explanatory paraphrase as well as a free and elegant translation. Every scholar knows, that the idiom and structure of the *ancient* are so essentially different from the *modern* languages, that a *literal* and servile version of a *Greek* and *Latin* author must necessarily be barbarous and unintelligible.[17]

(This is curious. Harwood was writing in the period in which the English language was at its most Latinate: when the long periods which closely followed Latin syntax and sentence-shape, and the borrowing of Latin words with many syllables to give what was thought to be a classical weight, were intended to rescue English from native barbarity.)

'The method I pursued was this.' That is a paragraph opening redolent of Harwood's time. It is both confessional, and a scientific statement. He wants to share with the reader private experiences which will reach a wide public: in that, he is harking back to Rousseau, who reiterates in his *Confessions* of the 1760s that 'the true object of my confessions', however occupied they may be with his inner life, is to be exact.[18] 'Method' implies a cool analytic approach, a taxonomy, making an organised system based on reason. He continues:

> I *first* carefully perused every chapter to investigate and discover the ONE true meaning of the author with all the accuracy and sagacity I could employ, attending to his reasoning, and to the principles and doctrines

he designed to indicate, ever consulting the best commentators upon
abstruse passages, and constantly imploring the infinite SOURCE of light
and wisdom to illuminate my imperfect understanding.[19]

That last phrase is charming, with its chime of 'i-' prefixes – 'imploring',
'infinite', 'illuminate', 'imperfect'. But Harwood cannot bring himself to
say 'God'. The Deity is indeed 'the infinite SOURCE of light and wisdom',
and the periphrasis is elegant, but there is no sense of a God who is in
his terms the 'immanent unexpected', or in the biblical Suffering Servant.
Harwood's 'infinite SOURCE of light and wisdom' is too refined to have
died on the Cross, having 'suffered under Pontius Pilate'. His is a most
reasonable Deity.

His next stage was to 'transfuse' this discovered 'Original . . .'

through the medium of a liberal and explanatory version . . . to clothe
his ideas in the vest of modern elegance. . . . It is pleasing to observe,
how much our language, within these very few years, hath been refined
and polished, and what infinite improvements it hath lately received.[20]

Harwood names models, recent writers who show of what our language
is capable in 'grace and purity in diction . . . elegance and harmony in
arrangement . . . copiousness and strength in composition'. They are
'Hume, Robertson, Lowth, Lyttleton, Hurd, Melmoth, Johnson and
Hawkesworth' (of whom only David Hume and Samuel Johnson have
survived into modern popular awareness). Such recent 'learned and illus-
trious authors . . . in point of true excellence and sublimity will bear the
severest critical comparison with the politest writers of Greece and Rome'
(and Harwood cites in his text parallel passages from 'the Greek and Latin
classics'): more, (and this is the first small shoot of what will become not
just a mighty tree but a large forest) these men are 'a distinguished honour
and ornament to their country'. To get inside the comparison with Greece
and Rome, and the latter phrase, and to paraphrase: God has given such
elegant language as Harwood can use for his Word to the English nation.
Harwood says he will be stigmatised, he knows, for the enormity of trying
'to diffuse over the sacred page the elegance of modern English', especially as 'length of time and custom' have given 'a venerable sacredness' to
– the phrase is striking – 'the bald and barbarous language of the old vulgar
version'. So much for Tyndale and the KJV, alliteratively 'bald and
barbarous' in that 'vulgar version'. Harwood is doing this work to induce
'persons of a liberal education and polite taste to peruse the sacred
volume', especially 'YOUTH' who don't, to paraphrase again, find the old
Bible any fun, regarding it as 'a volume . . . furnishing a study congenial
only to the gloom of old age, or the melancholy mind of a desponding

visionary'. That last splendid phrase damns religious Bible-readers, who are the last thing Harwood wants. Bible-readers must instead 'admire and love the sacred classics, to understand the duties, doctrines and discoveries of the gospel, and to venerate Christianity as the cause of God, of truth, or virtue, or liberty, and of maturity'.[21]

His model, he announces, is 'Castelio' in Latin. He assumes no difficulty in knowing whom he means as someone who 'hath deserved well of mankind for translating the scriptures in a pure, elegant and diffusive style'.[22] Castellio, known also as Sebastianus Castalio or Sébastien Châteillon, was at one time a friend of Calvin and professor of Greek at Basle from 1553. He was bitterly attacked by Calvin's followers for his theological views. He was denied ordination to the ministry in Geneva: one ground was that he refused to acknowledge the divine inspiration of the Song of Songs.[23] He was especially attacked for his independent Bible translations, in Latin in 1551, in French in 1555, (which included the Song of Songs) and printed both in one volume in 1572. His aim in his French version was to produce a work intelligible to the common people. 'The style,' it has been said, 'is brief, nervous, and often effective, but the expressions chosen are sometimes undignified.'[24] He was censured for his French version by Henri Estienne and by various professors at Geneva. It was vilified in a Preface to the French, 1560, Geneva New Testament in a passage that included the words 'd'advertir tous Chrestiens de se garder d'un tel personnage, comme instrument choisi de Satan pour amuser tous esprits volages & indiscrets . . . se jouer de l'Escriture saincte, & l'exposer en risee . . .' (to warn all Christians to be on their guard against such a person, as an instrument chosen by Satan to amuse all flighty and indiscreet people, to play games with the Scriptures and expose them to ridicule . . .').[25] In spite of this, in time this Bible, with its good illustrations, became valued by French Protestants as 'the first translation truly French and truly modern'.[26] In the Advertisement to his French Bible, Castellio wrote: 'as for the French language, I have mostly considered the common people, and so I have a used a common and simple language, as comprehensible as I could make it.'[27]

Castellio's Latin version, dedicated to Edward VI of England, and annotated, (it went into four editions) tried 'among other things to make the Bible eloquent after the Ciceronian standard'.[28] It did more. In his annotations he was trying to follow Erasmus into clarity through high linguistic skills and the recognition that the spiritual sense and the grammar could not be separated. The Spirit of God, he wrote, dictated the matter and teaches from it; he did not have this Spirit, which is not subject to human arts and devices, and that therefore he confined himself to elucidating what the words plainly meant.[29] Castellio used classical substitutes for familiar

Bible words, so that, for example, for *templum* he gave *fanum*, for *synagoga*, *collegium*, and, strikingly, for *ecclesia, respublica*.[30] In 1582, the Catholic Gregory Martin, in his Preface to the Rheims New Testament, attacked Protestants 'shamefully . . . corrupting' in their 'false' translations.[31] He then said that Calvin and Beza were 'as bad or worse' than the Castellio they attack.[32] Castellio, he wrote, used profane terms 'for foolish affectation of fineness and style', whereas the English Calvinists did so 'for furthering their heresies'.[33]

Harwood partly wants to be provocative, to get people to take notice of the Scriptures: Castellio's French version was condemned as frivolous and thus evil. But Harwood hopes to reach behind the French Protestant controversy of two hundred years before to follow the Latin version far back into a classical world which is beyond 'party, sect and denomination'.[34] He has treated the New Testament text just as if it were 'Plato, Xenophon, Thucydides, Plutarch, or any other Greek writer'.[35] He condemns the sectarian prejudices in commentaries and 'the Royal Bible with notes, the Grand comple Bible, the Grand Imperial Bible!'[36] Again, he shudders away from religiosity and 'the sickly dreams of illiterate Enthusiasts and entranced Visionaries, and . . . the sinister production of dark and melancholy Divines, the bigoted abettors of unintelligible mysteries and unscriptural absurdities'.[37] His foundation is 'the plain dictates of reason and the infallible rule and standard of the divine oracles': that there is some fogginess in the last words does not trouble him. 'The love of truth, *as it is in Jesus* . . . is warm and vigorous in the bosoms of immense numbers of my happy countrymen!'[38]

Harwood can be silly, but he sets a stage for a long drama of experimental, even eccentric rather than revisory English versions of the New Testament in England, far from KJV – something that, surprisingly, did not happen in America until well into the twentieth century. In doing that, he gives one picture of the state of the Christian religion in England in 1768. Since one does not often find such a prospect in a passage so decoratively written (and in a sentence so long), there is value in quoting the last paragraph of his Preface in full.

Since deism, infidelity, and scepticism so much prevail in the present age, since even popery *now* hath its public asserters and advocates; since enthusiasm is continually duping and enslaving the credulous and ignorant, both among the *great* vulgar and the small, and is daily making a more rapid and amazing progress all around us; since *rational* Christianity is, at present, regarded with so much contempt, and even horror, by the generality of the world; and since a love of unintelligible mysteries, and a fondness for gloomy and inexplicable doctrines, have, with the majority, discarded reason and common sense from religion, the author flatters himself the present work will be useful to his country, in which it hath been his study to free the New Testament from those false translations, which, at present, deform it, and render it absolutely unintelligible to all common readers; to purify its sacred streams from those corrupt admixtures, by which it was industriously suited to the false taste of the MONARCH and of the age, in which it was translated; to represent it, as it really is, in itself, a most rational, uniform, amiable, consistent scheme, and to exhibit, before the candid, the unprejudiced, and the intelligent of all parties, the true, original, divine form of Christianity, in its beautiful simplicity, divested of all the meretricious attire with which it hath been loaded, and solely adorned with its native elegance and charms, which need only be contemplated, in order to excite the admiration, transport, and love of every ingenious and virtuous bosom.[39]

The New Testament's 'native elegance and charms' are made to appear by Harwood, good Augustan gentleman that he was, for his fellow after-dinner scholars, the cultured and cultivated, secure in their uniform classical standards. The Incarnation, however, speaks to all human life, the poor and penniless, the homeless and dying, the lonely and terrified, the filthy and diseased, the desperate and the ignorant – one does not have to have a classical education to enter the Kingdom of Heaven.

Harwood's Sermon on the Mount, Matthew 5–7, appears as a mixture of philosophical discourse and elaborate manual of polite behaviour. Tyndale's 'Blessed are the merciful: for they shall obtain mercy' is here 'Happy are those who are truly compassionate and charitable – that benevolence which they express towards their fellow creatures shall be abundantly recompensed to them.' One of the strong understandings that Fielding's mid-century novel *Tom Jones* should produce in a reader is the failure of compassion and charity when mercy is needed. Mercy implies insight, something Tom's guardian, the virtuous Squire Allworthy, totally lacks. He is above all benevolent, and benevolence is a weasel word, as Fielding's story amply shows. Here, for Matthew 5:7, it is in no way accurate for Jesus' two 'mercy' words, οἱ ἐλεήμονες (*hoi elēmones*) and ἐλεηθήσονται (*eleēthēsontai*). The sinner, suffering, and undoubtedly guilty, does not want benevolence, but mercy. Tyndale's 'Blessed are they which hunger and thirst for righteousness' appears as 'Happy are those whose minds are inflamed with a sacred ardour to attain universal virtue – their enlarged and generous desires shall be satisfied.' Hunger and thirst are primary needs, simple and physical: Jesus says nothing about inflamed minds or sacred ardour, both being experiences at a distance from the centrally physical. Indeed, there is something suspiciously over-warm about Harwood's vocabulary in that sentence, with its 'inflamed', 'ardour', 'enlarged', 'generous desires' and 'satisfied', a sequence which has nothing to do with righteousness and a good deal to do with the boudoir.

Mockery has greeted Harwood's rendering of the ten Greek words in Matthew 6 which open the Lord's Prayer, Πάτερ ἡμῶν ὁ ἐν τοῖς οὐρανοῖς / Ἁγιασθήτω τὸ ὄνομά σου (*Pater hemōn ho en tois ouranois / Hagiasthētō to onoma sou*), familiar from Tyndale and KJV's 'Our father which art in heaven, hallowed be thy name.'

> O Thou great governor and parent of universal nature – who manifestest thy glory to the blessed inhabitants of heaven – may all thy rational creatures in all parts of thy boundless dominion be happy in the knowledge of thy existence and providence, and celebrate thy perfections in a manner most worthy thy nature and perfective of their own!

Harwood's opening of 1 Corinthians 13 is: 'Could I speak all the languages of men and of angels, and yet had a heart destitute of benevolence, I am no more than a sounding brass or tinkling cymbal.' Tyndale comes ringing through, except for one word. What is 'love' in Tyndale and the Geneva versions in this celebrated marriage-service chapter, altered in KJV under the influence of the Bishops' Bible to the Vulgate's 'charity', is here, in verse one, and all through the chapter, 'benevolence'. If that word was wrong for the Greek in Matthew 5, it is here so inaccurate for the New Testament ἀγάπη (*agapē*) that one is left wondering whether Harwood has understood the New Testament in Greek at all. 'God so loved the world', as KJV has it at John 3:16, 'that he gave his only begotten Son, that whosoever believeth in him should not perish, but have everlasting life.' 'Loved' there is the verb form of ἠγάπησεν (*ēgapēsen*). Benevolence has nothing to do with it. At its best benevolence can be 'affection in human nature', as Bishop Butler had it in 1726.[40] God's love, on the other hand, is what was demonstrated on the Cross, as Paul at the end of Romans 8 states it, using ἀγάπη (*agapē*). True, Tyndale uses 'benevolence' once, at 1 Corinthians 7:3, 'Let the man give unto the wife due benevolence. Likewise also the wife unto the man.' But the Greek noun there is ὀφειλήν (*opheilēn*), the standard Greek word for 'one's due', or 'a debt', with nothing to do with the love of God.

This chapter, 1 Corinthians 13, conveniently shows a good deal more about Harwood's translating mind. I quote first from Tyndale in 1534:

> Love suffereth long, and is courteous. Love envieth not. Love doth not frowardly, swelleth not, dealeth not dishonestly, seeketh not her own, is not provoked to anger, thinketh not evil, rejoiceth not in iniquity: but

rejoiceth in the truth, suffereth all things, believeth all things, hopeth all things, endureth all things. Though that prophesying fail, or tongues shall cease, or knowledge vanish away, yet love falleth never away.

The problems there are not with mistranslation or paraphrase, but with the slight alteration of language: 'frowardly', meaning 'perversely' (in effect, 'going backward': 'froward' was the opposite of 'toward') went out of use in the later nineteenth century. 'Swelleth' might cause a second or two of thought, though for boastfulness it is vivid. A modern reader ignorant of Latinisms might conceivably have difficulty with 'iniquity'. The archaic 'eth' endings might feel distancing. But Tyndale's 'bald and barbarous . . . vulgar version' (in Harwood's words) is more than just understandable: the 'all things' phrases later in the chapter – 'suffereth . . . believeth . . . hopeth . . . endureth . . .' – are strong and well sinewed. They relate to human love as it is experienced.

Next, a modern view of how the Greek can go will help: here is REB in 1989:

Love is patient and kind. Love envies no one, is never boastful, never conceited, never rude; love is never selfish, never quick to take offence. Love keeps no score of wrongs, takes no pleasure in the sins of others, but delights in the truth. There is nothing love cannot face; there is no limit to its faith, its hope, its endurance.

Love will never come to an end. Prophecies will cease; tongues of ecstasy will fall silent; knowledge will vanish.

Here 'quick to take offence' is sound for the Greek παροξύνεται (*parox-unetai*) with its sense of pricking on, exciting someone. 'Keeps no score of wrongs' is certainly good for the accounting metaphor in the Greek λογίζεται (*logizetai*), though 'wrongs' is possibly too weak for the Greek τὸ κακόν (*to kakon*), which primarily means evil. The paraphrase 'there is nothing love cannot face' inverts, and one might think, loosens the original, πάντα στέγει (*panta stegei*), which means, literally, 'everything bears' or 'all things contains'. 'There is no limit to' is simply imported, turning into fixed English nouns the Greek verbs of active believing, hoping and enduring as continuing processes. Otherwise, the passage speaks relatively clearly and accurately.

Here is Harwood:

Benevolence is unruffled: is benign: Benevolence cherishes no ambitious desires: Benevolence is not ostentatious: is not inflated with insolence.

It preserves a consistent decorum: is not enslaved to sordid interest: is not transported with furious passion; indulges no malevolent design.

It conceives no delight from the perpetuation of wickedness: but is first to applaud truth and virtue.

It throws a veil of candour over all things: is disposed to believe all things: views all things in the most favourable light: supports all things with serene composure.

Benevolence shall continue to shine with undiminished lustre when all prophetic powers shall be no more, when the ability of speaking various languages shall be withdrawn, and when all supernatural endowments shall be annihilated.

This, in its polysyllabic Latinist elevation, is rather admirable – but it has nothing to do with the New Testament. How on earth St Paul's πάντα στέγει (*panta stegei*), with its essential meaning of bearing, or holding, can have anything to do with throwing veils of candour over anything baffles the mind. Far from representing St Paul, Harwood's central passage, from 'It throws a veil . . .' to '. . . serene composure', is Fielding's Squire Allworthy to a T – the upright man whose benevolence maintained for long, crucial years the grossest injustice: the admired benefactor who caused evil in his own house not just to exist, unseen, but to flourish: the well-meaning justice of the peace who caused calamities.

It is all self-regarding. The Man of Culture is not 'patient'; he is smooth, 'unruffled'. He is not 'courteous' (Tyndale), or 'kind' (NEB), (the Greek χρηστεύεται, *chrēsteuetai*, is a verb of being kind or merciful) he is 'benign' – smiling, like sunshine. Tyndale's 'dealeth not dishonestly' (the Greek ἀσχημονεῖ (*aschēmonei*) suggests 'curious practice') has become to Harwood preserving 'a consistent decorum' – within a bowshot of the Greek, but too much stressing the self-conscious virtuous appearance in 'preserving'.

What is gained by changing KJV's 'tongues . . . shall cease' to the rigmarole of 'when the ability of speaking various languages shall be withdrawn' is only length. What is lost by changing Tyndale's (and KJV's) correct 'knowledge' to 'supernatural endowments' is something serious. In the New Testament, γνῶσις (*gnōsis*) is not supernatural, except when the word is used for the heretical notion of salvation by superior knowledge held only by certain initiates, as in 1 Corinthians 8, or 1 Timothy 6:20. St Paul does not mean that here – he means knowing everything there is to know, as Harwood himself had noticed earlier in the chapter, when he translated 'had I accumulated all the knowledge of the sons of men'. His wish to be 'diffuse' is betraying him. Nothing is gained, in the second verse of the chapter, by extending the six Greek words πᾶσαν τὴν πίστιν ὥστε ὄρη μεθιστάναι (*pasan tēn pistin hōste orē methistanai*, 'all faith to move mountains from one place to another') to the twenty-one words 'could I exert such stupendous powers as to remove mountains from their basis, and transfer them at pleasure from place to place' – there is serious distortion, for St Paul is not writing about such 'stupendous powers' as a Renaissance high magician might have, a Prospero steeped in recondite books, but a Christian's faith.

What Edward Harwood was trying to do was to take the New Testament over into the literary world: to evangelise, as it were, the novel of feeling. He writes not only in 'the idiom of Hume and Johnson'[41] (that phrase does not do justice to his refinement of feelings): he tries to write the New Testament in the emotionally generous and expansive world of the secular novelists (and poets) – something at least worth trying.

There is something else that must be said. Twenty-first-century readers may be tempted to feel smug: Harwood feels so obviously wide of the mark, and peculiar. Such emotion is misplaced. He was trying to write the New Testament in a familar world of his time. However, 1 Corinthians 13, in a late twentieth-century translation of the New Testament, begins 'If I speak with human eloquence and angelic ecstasy but don't love'. *Ecstasy?* Nowhere in the passage does the Greek refer to that. It continues, 'I'm nothing but the creaking af a rusty gate.' Paul's, and Tyndale's (and Harwood's, indeed) 'sounding brass and tinkling cymbal' have vanished, their place taken by a banal commonplace from a B-movie soundtrack. Later comes 'When I was an infant at my mother's breast, I gurgled and cooed like any infant. When I grew up, I left those infant ways for good.' Barely recognisable as Paul's 'I spake as a child' passage, this, for the sake of appeal to an immediate visual image, again with sound added, totally abandons the Greek. Worse, it corrupts the sense. Paul is not describing infantile gratification. He is illustrating spiritual growth by a parallel with human mental maturation. These quotations are from a popular 1993 New Testament, *The Message.*[42] The chapter ends,

> We don't yet see things clearly. We're squinting in a fog, peering though a mist. But it won't be long before the weather clears and the sun shines bright! . . . Trust steadily in God, hope unswervingly, love extravagantly. And the best of the three is love.

This is the world of feel-good fiction. Instead of the wonder of Paul's 'being known' by God, 'face to face', is the singalong triteness of the sunshine, seriously inaccurate. The final adverbs are imported into the Greek. Tyndale's (and Paul's) 'faith, hope and love' work both ways, from us to God but even more from God to us. 'Love extravagantly' is a dangerous precept, and, like so much in this volume, is about the bright celebration of the self. Eighteenth-century Harwood has always been mocked for addressing a particular readership. The twenty-first-century particularity of the *Message*-bearers reduces the New Testament to the emotions of television soap operas, mixed with a tone of vacuous uplift, and, though claiming on its half-title to be 'from the original languages', distorts the Greek very seriously indeed. Modern readers have no cause to feel superior.

TOWARDS 1769, AND AFTER

It is clear that the triumph of the KJV, according to writers before the Restoration in 1660, owed nothing whatever to any special merits. It was generally referred to as 'the Bible without notes', and sometimes observed simply to be the third attempt in English history at a royally motivated version. Various phrases used to describe it included 'Of the largest volume', and it does seem that the general view of it was as something quite undistinguished. For a considerable time, older versions continued to be used, including even annotated revisions of the Pentateuch, as well as metrical and prose versions of the Psalms, made between 1616 and 1623 by Henry Ainsworth for his Separatist congregation in Amsterdam, circulating in England apparently without official hindrance. Archbishop Laud, though aiming to suppress the Geneva Bible did not – to us, oddly – insist on KJV.[43]

Though not often with Hugh Broughton's dash and ferocity, attacks on KJV continued, combined with serious attempts at inaugurating a full-scale revision. Ambrose Ussher (brother of James Ussher, the well-known Bishop of Armagh who fixed the dates of Bible events, appearing from 1701) began his own translation to replace KJV about 1620. He finished most of the Bible, and even wrote a dedicatory epistle to James I. His work was never printed, and remains in manuscript in Trinity College, Dublin.

Since the King's Printers held the monopoly of KJV, and were not going to print any rival, no printer had interest in reviving the Geneva Bible. Ideas were concentrated on revising KJV. An official move to do so came early in the Commonwealth, when at the end of a sermon to the House of Commons in 1645, John Lightfoot hoped for a new 'Exact, vigorous, and lively translation'. One of the problems tackled by Parliament during the Commonwealth was that of obvious errors in KJV. Some time during the end of the Long Parliament, in 1652 or 1653, another serious attempt was made to introduce correction and revision, always from the point of the true meaning of the original and its clear expression in English.

In 1659, Robert Gell wrote *An Essay toward the Amendment of the Last English Translation of the Bible: Or a Proof, by many instances that the last translation of the bible may be improved*, in which he seems to accept some value in KJV. The length of the book (some eight hundred detailed pages), seems to suggest that it reflects opinions of some time before. Gell's book was the last of its kind. The question of the value of KJV as adequate (which was shortly to change dramatically) was overtaken by the debate about whether or not the Scriptures were inspired. Already by 1667, there is visible a view of the Bible (which by now firmly means KJV) as not only the saving Word, and, moreover, in itself perfect, but also a divinely given compendium of all knowledge. To quote Richard Baxter in 1667, some men

> feign [the Bible] to be instead of all grammars, logic, philosophy and all other arts and sciences, and to be a perfect particular rule for every ruler, lawyer, physician, mariner, architect, husbandman and tradesman to do his work by.[44]

HEBREW POETRY

By the middle of the eighteenth century, great strides had been made in understanding the principles of Hebrew poetry, entirely from the publication of the lectures by the Oxford Professor of Poetry, Dr Robert Lowth. These, numbering thirty-four, given in Latin, between 1741 and 1750, were under the title *De Sacra Poesi Hebraeorum*, published in English with annotations in 1787. Lowth educated the nation in the full qualities of Hebrew poetry which before then had been hidden. He taught the importance of historical imagination, illuminating most unexpectedly the darker corners of a very wide canvas indeed. One of the matters he approached with some care was the opening up of the Hebrew poetic device of parallelism, for the exposition for which he is now chiefly remembered. At this period, the insistence on high Augustan standards of linguistic scholarship allowed a great deal of discussion about taste and the style of the Bible. By now knowledge and use of KJV were so extensive in Britain that there is a sense in which the Augustans were trying to raise it, for their own comfort, to a more elevated level. This might only be in the area of feeling, as in the attempts of Edward Harwood, to whom should be added Anthony Purver.[45]

By the end of the 1760s, another view was appearing, one that itself became a myth, supported by carefully manufactured other myths. This was the birth of 'Avolatry', the elevation of KJV to such heights of inspiration as to be virtually divine and untouchable. From 1769, effectively, there grew the notion that KJV was peculiarly, divinely, inspired. To bolster the supposition it was announced that this translation had been especially venerated from the moment in 1611 that it appeared.

In 1762, however, a serious attempt had been made in Cambridge to correct the text of KJV by widespread revision: spelling and punctuation were changed, the use of italics was regularised and extended, printers' errors were removed and marginal annotations were increased and greatly enlarged. It was in this much-altered form that the 1611 KJV went forward, but not before the work of Dr F. S. Paris of Sydney Sussex College, Cambridge, had been itself revised by Dr Benjamin Blayney of Hertford College, Oxford, with other corrections and increased marginalia, and repeating most of Dr Paris's errors. Thus the birth of 'Avolatry', in which King James's scholars became almost sanctified in their work, and their Bible near divine, coincided with a general acceptance of two modern versions of that very work which were most strikingly changed from the original.

'SHAKESPEARE! SHAKESPEARE! SHAKESPEARE!'

It so happened that the great London actor David Garrick was moved to organise the first celebration of Shakespeare on any scale, a Shakespeare Festival in the obscure borough of Stratford-upon-Avon. The festival lasted three days in the summer, and was the centre of interest in the entire nation. Everyone who was anybody had to be there. James Boswell attended as an armed Corsican Chief. On a specially built stage in a tent by the Avon, some bits of Shakespeare were performed, though the high points of the festival were other performances, including recitations and grand choruses in praise of the now-immortal Bard.[46] Some heights were certainly reached, but the festival ended in grotesque depths as very heavy rain produced severe flooding and many men and maidens in elaborate fancy dress had to be carried by yokels to dry land. The nation was amused by the discomfort of pretentious people: Stratford-upon-Avon began its centuries of commercial success: Garrick's star shone even brighter; and the chief work had been done – from that time Shakespeare was exalted as beyond criticism. He was God's gift to the world through the English language and the English nation. In other words 'Bardolatry' had begun in 1769. What is again odd is that Garrick was praised for his 'restoration' of Shakespeare, particularly *Hamlet*. This was in spite of the fact that the production of *Hamlet* that he made his own had severe cuts including, incredibly, almost the whole of Act Five.

Thus the Bible and Shakespeare, stock items already in position for the relief of every imaginary castaway on British radio's Desert Island, began their exalted life beyond the level of the merely human at the same time, in the summer of 1769, and in a mutilated state.

KJV FOR THE WORLD

In 1776 Geneva-Tomson-Junius was reprinted 'With most profitable annotations'. Those are now described as being made 'By the Archbishops, Bishops, etc. etc.' (Franciscus Junius would have been surprised by his elevation, though no doubt he would understand himself only as an 'etc.') Geneva thus appeared with Parker's piece introducing his Bishops' Bible, and other introductory matter from those bishops. This Geneva Bible, now without the Apocrypha, was reprinted again in 1778. Otherwise from 1769 until the important year of 1804, the roughly 270 editions of the Bible or parts of it published in Britain were solidly KJV, usually now with elaborate notes. William Pine's, for example, printed in 1774, managed to get into a duodecimo volume the whole of KJV and 'several thousand notes'.[47] John Brown's 'Self-Interpreting Bible', first issued in Edinburgh in 1778, was one of the popular successes, reprinted in Britain but conquering America. The emphasis is on 'Family Bibles', either with enormous annotation for family study, or with characteristics that would amuse children, like 'A Curious Hieroglyphic Bible', first issued in London in 1784, often reprinted there and in Dublin, and exceptionally popular in America. In this, small cuts are used to represent some words in a significant passage of Scripture (fig. 37). After Brown's Self-Interpreting Bible, Thomas Scott's Bible with commentary, originally intended to appear in weekly numbers, was extremely popular in Britain and America from 1792.

Over twenty versions were new attempts at translation, some of which became significant in America. All but about a dozen were strongly Protestant, those that were not being reprints of Challoner, or fresh attempts to get some parts of the Jewish Scriptures into English.

The year 1792 was significant for Protestant Christianity, when the first denominational missionary society was founded. A group of ministers and laymen in Northamptonshire in the English Midlands founded the Baptist Missionary Society. They at once sent the polymath William Carey to India, where he was missionary, linguist, botanist, industrialist, economist, medical humanitarian, printer and maker of the first newspaper to be printed in an oriental language, agriculturalist, astronomer, forest conservationist, crusader for women's rights, public servant, moral and cultural reformer and translator.[48] With the help of Indian nationals, Carey translated the entire Bible into Bengali, Oriya, Hindi, Marathi and Sanskrit. He made partial translations into Punjabi, Pashto, Kashmiri, Telegu and Konkani. He translated smaller parts of the Bible into twenty-three other languages and dialects.[49] This was an English venture, and as a child and young man Carey had been brought up to detailed knowledge of the KJV, though he translated from the original languages. The story of British, and later American, 'overseas missions', of which the Baptist Missionary Society was the pioneer, is too large and complex for more than this brief mention. Like Carey, many men and women did, and still do, magnificent translating, teaching and medical work, in Asia, Africa and South America. At the same time, Dickens's caricature of Mrs Jellyby in *Bleak House* (1853), criminally neglecting her family for the narcissistic romance of being known as one who writes immense numbers of letters every week in aid of the missionary settlement at Borrioboola-Gha, hit a Victorian nerve.

On 7 March 1804, however, the British and Foreign Bible Society had been founded. This enterprise, which grew out of the missionary movement, particularly the then recently founded and inter-church London Missionary Society, and the older Religious Tract Society, had as its aim to multiply and make more cheaply available copies of the Scriptures in the United Kingdom, with more than half an eye on the needs of missionaries. Almost at once, it succeeded. 'Almost', because the original committee wisely waited a year until they could take advantage of the development by the Cambridge University Press of a refinement of the process of stereotyping.

That process of printing had a history going back to about 1700. In 1725, it was made commercially practicable by an Edinburgh goldsmith, William Ged. With support from the Earl of Stanhope, an English printer, Andrew Wilson, had refined Ged's method. The basic process was to take a plaster-of-Paris mould of a page of type, thus avoiding resetting. From that mould, a fresh metal plate could be reproduced as often as needed. Ged, it is said, was defeated by the malice of typesetters anxious for their jobs. Wilson, working for the Earl of Stanhope saw (at the same time as others in Europe), that instead of plaster-of-Paris, papier-mâché was just as efficient, cheaper and lighter.[50]

In September 1804 the committee of the new BFBS ordered large editions of the New Testament and the Bible to be printed from stereotype plates, with a prospect of great increase in cheapness and accuracy. The first stereotype New Testament came out in July 1805, and the whole Bible in 1806, this time with 'printed for the B.F.B.S.' on its title-page for the first time. The American Bible Society was founded in 1816. In both nations, mass Bible printing was both possible and achieved. The BFBS alone could report in 1815 that in its first eleven years it had issued 429,768 copies of the Bible, and 481,340 of the New Testament.[51] Quality was high. Prices were kept low. That not far off one million Bibles and Testaments sold in eleven years – all, of course, KJV, without Apocrypha – speaks of remarkable commercial enterprise, overseas development, local organisation, and demand.

From 1804 to 1850 the picture remains the same as it was from 1769, except that all possible numbers increase: a total of around four hundred new editions, reissues of Bibles with popular commentaries, and so many reprints of standard editions that the editors of the definitive catalogue, Darlow, Moule and Herbert (1968) find it impossible to record them after 1824.[52] Thanks to stereotyping, editions and reprints of Bibles could (as with all kinds of book, magazine and newspaper publication) easily run into numbers that are impossible to follow.

Chapter 35

MATHEW CAREY
AND THE AMERICAN BIBLE FLOOD

MATHEW CAREY

The dashing Irishman who established what became America's largest and most important Bible printing-house in the first quarter of the nineteenth century, Mathew Carey, set out in Philadelphia in 1789 to print a Bible in forty-eight weekly parts. He may have managed a few weeks' issues – the evidence is not clear. The fourth part, assuming a roughly equal division of the whole of Scripture into forty-eight, would have offered the end of Exodus and the first twenty chapters of Leviticus: one could understand that subscribers fell away. Morever, this was not KJV that he was printing. Carey has the distinction of being the first American printer of the Roman Catholic Douai version, a printing completed in 1790. Though Carey had plenty of commercial triumphs with Bibles in the decades to come, two things were against his Douai being a success. The first was the small number of Roman Catholics in the United States at the time – an estimated twenty-five thousand (two-thirds of them in Maryland) out of a population of about five million.[1] The second was something met before, the different position of the Bible in the life of that Church. The American Catholic writer John Gilmary Shea, writing in New York in 1859, noted on the first page of his *A Bibliographical Account of Catholic Bibles, Testaments, and Other Portions of Scripture* that

> In the Catholic Church the Holy Scriptures do not occupy the same position as in the various denominations formed among those who left her bosom in the great schism of the sixteenth century. To the Catholic, the Bible is neither a school-book, a ritual, nor a popular treatise on theology; consequently Bibles are not profusely scattered. For reverential perusal and devout meditation, a comparatively small number of them suffices.[2]

Carey abandoned the serial publishing of the Douai, but not the version itself, and formed the firm of Carey, Stewart and Company in Philadelphia to continue the Douai in volume form, among other things. In September 1790 he sent out appeals addressed 'To the Protestants of the United States', noting that

> Many of the most learned Protestant divines have produced weighty objections to particular passages in the Common Church of England translations of the Scriptures. That there are various important errors in it, is too well known to admit of controversy. The frequent demands for a new translation bear the strongest testimony to the truth of this observation . . .[3]

So, with charming and Irish logic, faced with demands for a new translation, Carey asked people to pay 'Six Spanish Milled Dollars' (in sterling about thirty shillings then: in 1999 money, seventy-one pounds[4]) for a reprint of a version dating from 1582 (New Testament) and 1610 (Old Testament) with revisions in 1764. In spite of his heartfelt remarks about 'that wretched, that contemptible prejudice' and 'bigots of every persuasion' who would find 'a Popish Bible . . . a heinous offence', and the fact that his subscription list did demonstrate 'the rapid advances that America has made in the divine principle of toleration' when, on 1 December 1790, he published the two quarto volumes of 'The Holy Bible, translated from the Latin Bible . . .' (also available in a single volume), a straight reprint of Challoner,[5] in double columns with wide margins, now in type specially cast in Philadelphia, (the quartos being the first in that form printed in America), with a 'Table of References' which begins with 'Absolution' (a word not in the Bible), he seems to have sold fewer than 500 copies.[6] They are now rare collectors' items. Carey soon made his name printing KJVs in two sizes and many styles, but twenty-one years after his first attempt, in 1811, he managed to raise a surprising 500 subscribers, as listed, for a more successful and pleasing reprint of his Douai, most from Philadelphia. (Addressing a Catholic audience, a footnote to Matthew 3:2, 'Repent', explains 'from the Latin and Greek' that it means not just repentance but 'penitential exercises'.)

Carey, born in Dublin in January 1760, had begun his working life on a Dublin newspaper, as a journalist so full of zeal to expose the injustices of the British in persecuting Irish Catholics that he had to flee to France. There, Irish charm was joined with Irish luck, as he met, and was befriended by, both Benjamin Franklin (in whose printing house at Passy he worked for a time) and the Marquis de Lafayette. He returned to Ireland and journalism. The English government jailed him for a month for his violent anti-British writing in his *Volunteer's Journal*. Released, and still only twenty-four (and facing a libel suit) he escaped to America disguised as a woman (he was clearly a lad of spirit). He landed in

Philadelphia on 1 November 1784, to wait until the proceeds of the sale of his Dublin newspaper could arrive. Lafayette, then in the town, heard that he had arrived, asked to see him, supported his plans to found a newspaper, and the next morning sent him 400 dollars. With this he established the *Pennsylvania Herald*, which began on 25 January 1785. (Years later, Carey, a successful man, returned the money to the Marquis and 'consigned to him an invoice of tobacco'.[7]) In 1786 the *Herald* was replaced by the monthly *Columbian Magazine*, and alongside it the equally influential monthly *The American Museum*, in which the first article in January 1787 was a new piece by the eighty-one-year-old Benjamin Franklin, 'A Consolation for America'. From his publishing house he re-issued Paine's *Common Sense* and other pamphlets and patriotic studies, including one, much reprinted and translated, on the yellow fever epidemic of 1793; and several satires imitating Samuel Butler's highly successful 1663 anti-Cromwellian poem *Hudibras* in form and content, one of which led to a duel. In 1801 he became the first president of the newly organised American Company of Booksellers. The publishing firm he founded, under successive names, still flourishes.

In the end, Carey issued two more Rheims-Douai Bibles in 1805, (both from Grierson's 1791 Dublin edition prepared by 'Dr Troy'): the second was reprinted in 1811 and 1816. Much more significant was his first KJV in 1801, printed for him in Philadelphia by Joseph Charless in a quarto with a great deal of extra matter and nine historical engravings. This was the first of over sixty KJVs in duodecimo and quarto from Carey in the next twenty years: as well as in size they differ in accompanying material. This first, 1801, Carey Bible has a great deal of extra matter. At the beginning, after 'Subscribers' Names', is a two-page 'Preface by Mathew Carey'. After the Old Testament, the Apocrypha is set in smaller type, with an ornamented 'This Bible is the Property of . . .' blank page before it. 'Family Record' blank pages come twice, before and after the New Testament. At the end, after 'Errata', come

> An Index to the Holy Bible; A Table of Offices; Tables of Scripture Measures; Tables of Proper Names; Table of Time [that is, dates from Creation]; A Clergyman's Address to Married Persons at the Altar; The Old and New Testaments Dissected; Portrait of an Apostolic Preacher, from Cowper; A Table of Kindred and Affinity: and [a description of] Judea, Palestine or the Holy Land.

'The Tables' list over two thousand 'Proper Names', followed by a brief chronological catalogue of apostles and their successors, and 'who founded and presided over the Five Grand Apostolic Churches' [Antioch, Rome, Jerusalem, Byzantium and Alexandria]. The 'Clergyman's Address' includes the injunction 'a wife should not only love her husband, but on every occasion, show him all the attention in her power.' The hundred-line quotation from Book Two of William Cowper's domestic epic *The Task* (1785)[8] briefly exalts the true preacher, 'In doctrine uncorrupt; in language plain / And plain in manner; decent, solemn, chaste . . .', in contrast to the ordained creatures who were pedant, or fop, or thespian, or sensationalist or entertainer. Sometimes included in Carey's Bibles were trivia to lure the feeble-minded: 'the middle verse is the 8th of Psalm 128 . . . the word AND occurs in the Old Testament 35,543 times . . . the 21st verse, ch.7, of Ezra, has all the letters of the alphabet . . .'.[9] What Carey offered was variable. The title-page announces a 'Map of Palestine', which was not always included, though fold-out maps appeared in some reprints. Plates (at first woodblocks, as cheaper) could be omitted or varied – as they were, greatly, over the next decades. Additional material came and went.

Carey knew his markets. In 1796 he had hired one Parson Mason Locke Weems to travel the States, sell his books, and drum up subscriptions for his coming folio Bible. Weems was a colourful reporter (it was he who, in his biography of Washington, gave to American history the fiction of young George and the cherry tree). His correspondence with Carey over the years tells a lapel-clutching story of the making of American books. He wrote on 13 August 1800, 'Many things are not worth powder and shot. The Bible is a Galleon! Reserve your ammunition for that.'[10] Writing from New York nine days later, he tells Carey that their plans to publish a new Bible had

> knock'd up just such a dust here among the Printers as would a stone if thrown smack into the center of a Hornet's nest. The whole swarm is out. You hear of nothing now but printing the Bible. Collins is going to print a bible – Swords is going to print a bible – Hopkins is for a Bible – and Durell for Folio! Everything that can raise a type is going to work upon the Bible. You'd take New York to be the very town of Man-Soul, and its printeriest saints on earth.[11]

Two months later, Carey tells Weems he has abandoned the idea of a Bible, partly because Weems, for all his fire, had not yet sent him any money from book sales, and partly because, (biblically like Matthew 27:19, incidentally) his wife felt badly about it: she told Carey that it had 'dangers . . . far beyond the profits'.[12] Weems pleads for Bibles: they will make them both rich. Carey still wants his money from sales. On 4 March 1801, the inauguration of Thomas Jefferson as President (for the first time in Washington, the new capital) suggested to Carey that his money problems would be eased by government contracts, and he went ahead with his quarto KJV, in hope.

Variety of content, with tables, indexes, commentaries, plates (maps and scenes) and their differently available positions was not all that the public might get in Carey's quarto KJVs. Quality of paper and binding could be chosen, sharply affecting the price. Carey's advertisement of 1816 announced Bibles available from $3.75 for one printed on coarse paper without Apocrypha or plates, to one with Apocrypha, a Concordance, 100 plates and other additions, bound in Morocco gilt with gilt edges, for $20. Before that, he had faced problems of pricing. Here is Weems on the difficulties of selling Carey's 1791 quarto:

> 'What do you have for your Bible?' says the Man to whom I make a leg [i.e, bow] with Book and hat; *Only six dollars Sir.* 'Hoot, hoot' quoth he, 'why Isaac Collins gives us a Bible for 4!!' 'But please to observe, Sir, the style in which this is done: Mr Carey has made on this – here, sir, you see is a fine map on Copper plate of the holy land; here, Sir, is Nazareth where Christ was born, here is Cana of Galilee, where he wrought his first miracle, *here* is a view of the country immortaliz'd by his travels, labours, &c.&c.&c. . . .'. 'All this is clever, yes, 'tis clever enough indeed, but I w'dn't give a fig the more for all that, for it only sarves to make the Children spoil the book, however the Isaac Collins ax'd but 4 dolls for his'n, here's five dolls for your'n.'[13]

Others, reported Weems, would have 'but one *bible*, as one *Wife*, in their life time . . . and to have *that* one of the best sort.'[14]

Carey solved the problem of pricing with his usual boldness. He was the first American printer to grasp the value of standing type. In 1804, he adopted Isaac Collins's text from 1791, supposed to be the most accurate, and kept this quarto Bible standing, so that all subsequent Carey quartos have the same 1,046 pages of text, and with additional material 1,080 pages, thus avoiding costs of typesetting and proofreading. This 1804 'Carey-Collins' has, with ten maps and twenty historical engravings, other new inclusions, as 'A Concise View of the Evidences of the Christian Religion by J. Fletcher' and 'A Table of Passages in the Old Testament quoted by Christ and His Apostles in the New Testament' – the latter a scholarly tool of real value. A Carey Bible from 1818 had maps, some pull-out, and nearly a hundred engravings, often of strange subjects, with a tendency to funny animals – the curious ram of Daniel 8:3 is only one example. This edition also has as frontispiece 'A Scheme exhibiting the Time of the Births and Deaths of the Patriarchs'. Carey, as noted, knew his market better than most; that fact makes this, as frontispiece no less, most odd. In Carey Bibles the choice of paper was extended to choice of binding – to the vexation of Weems: 'The Binders! The Binders! The Binders! Never did a Wild

Asse's Colt so tremble at thought of a Lion as I do at thought of the Binders / Stain'd with paste, the fly leaves look wretchedly patch'd . . .'[15]

Weems told Carey in February 1802 to make certain that his 'Bible contains more Curious things than were ever seen in any other bible . . . Good engravings are a luxury, a feast to the Soul . . . The fame of them goes abroad and the Bible sells with Rapidity'.[16] By 1816, a Carey Bible could have seventy illustrations and maps: by 1818, as noted above, a hundred. They were not only 'a feast to the Soul'. Some were rum, like the peculiar animals just observed. Moreover, Carey went on to produce illustrated Bibles which took the business of pictures beyond proper limits. Many were irreproachable. Some were not, being more than wanton, like Isaiah Thomas's, but positively carnal. Carey's women are not always in tranquil garden scenes. The Slaughter of the Innocents in a Carey Bible is a mass atrocity of assault on near-naked women and babes. Worse, to the point of the reader's absolute disbelief, is the plate in this Bible of the Prodigal Son, an innocent and moving parable. In the upper right-hand corner of Carey's illustration is a drawing of a screaming, bare-breasted woman being molested. Even those with only a sketchy knowledge of Jesus' parables must be outraged by that imposition (fig. 34). The heavier paper for the plates and their frequent clustering in such a volume make them easy to find: the domestic Bible becomes a collection, in the modern phrase, to be enjoyed 'in the comfort and privacy of your own home', of unwholesome pictures. These were books where a near-naked Bathsheba centre-stage being ogled by a handsome young king in the wings could carry more weight than the empty tomb of Christ (and see fig. 36).

Such variety of Bibles in more than sixty different editions, issued over more than twenty years – an output quite unknown in Britain or Europe at the time – made Mathew Carey a household name, but not the greatest fortune: his distribution costs, often across five hundred miles, were high. (Weems gives a powerful picture of travelling on horseback on abominable roads with books, samples and subscription lists, to visit wealthy citizens, courthouses and meetings, and then trying to make sure the books eventually arrived in the right place, undamaged, to be handled by local storekeepers whose incompetence lost their business.) Nevertheless, Carey's production of Bibles established him as a major influence on American life. And here, once again in a study of English Bibles in America, is another phenomenon. Mathew Carey's output of fine Bibles was the most significant thing about him as an American figure. In modern encyclopedia entries about him, though we are invariably told of his two almost pointless Hudibrastic poems, his making of Bibles is not mentioned.[17]

FLOTSAM AND JETSAM OF AMERICAN BIBLE PUBLISHING FROM 1777

In telling the story, we have concentrated on New Testaments and Bibles, printed for commerce in growing numbers. We should mention the small biblical objects floating around those great galleons, the tiny books like T. Ellwood's *Life of David* from J. Crukshank in Philadelphia in 1785, several times reprinted, as was the equally small *Life of Joseph, the Son of Israel* by John Macgowan, finally from Windsor, Vermont: or, just as little, *Beauties of the Bible* by Ezra Sampson, from Boston in 1804. Every year saw some of these appear, beginning with *The New Testament Commands* from Haverhill, Massachusetts, in 1777. Such minute curiosities became a characteristic of American pious publishing for over a century, oddities like *Small rain upon the tender herb* from the Philadelphia American Sunday School Committee in 1835, giving 'A Scripture Quotation for Every Day of the Year', the whole bound book being postage-stamp size. Of the same kind, size, and time, were *Daily Food*, and *Dew Drops*, and many others of equal banality. The great Family Bibles of America had, nearby, these little trinkets, as it might be a few petals of slim, sweetly decorated pocket books with one uplifting ornamented text on each of the few pages. (There is not space here to deal properly with the rising tide of pamphlets and tracts from printers in every state, usually written from private biblical obsessions, often announcing the fulfilment of the wilder prophecies, and all too commonly hardly sane.) In 1815 a New York printer, S. Wood & Sons, first printed a children's small *Hieroglyphic Bible*, the picture-puzzle form from Europe which was always popular in the United States (fig. 37).

While stressing the almost total, apparently rigid, dominance of the English KJV, I should also bring forward the steady printing in America of parts of the Bible, or related matter, in other languages. This happened from as early as 1763, when a Prayer Book in Mohawk was produced in Bethlehem, Pennsylvania. (John Eliot's Indian Bible of a hundred years before was printed in London, of course.) From time to time parts of the Bible were printed again in Mohawk and other Indian languages (Seneca, 1819; Choctaw, 1827 and 1831; Cherokee, 1829 and 1833; Chippewa, 1831, and so on). Spanish and French Bibles were printed from time to time.

CHRISTOPHER SAUER'S GERMAN BIBLE AND KJV

The strongest rivals to English Bibles were those in German, and it would give a wrong impression not to include in the story the year-by-year printing in America of Bibles, Testaments and Psalters in German. The whole German Bible was first printed in Pennsylvania by Christopher

Sauer. He had arrived in America in 1724 at the age of thirty-one. In 1738 he acquired a printing press and began serving the large Pennsylvania German immigrant community. He produced religious and political broadsides, ever-necessary almanacs, an eight-hundred-page hymnal (the immigrants were all members of Protestant sects, either Lutheran or evolved from that denomination, and their worship was full of hymns), and a newspaper. He appealed for subscriptions for a German Bible. A type founder in Frankfurt sent to him, as a gift, sufficient type, and in 1743 he printed Luther's Bible translation, which thus became the first Bible printed in America. The Sauer family, and others, went on to produce German Bibles in great numbers: the American Bible Society itself printed in 1847 a German Bible, and many more after that.

The German presence was strong in colonial America, and after the Revolution. Large settlements in Pennsylvania, which had received about one hundred thousand Germans in the 1720s and after, alarmed Benjamin Franklin, for one, who foresaw an explosion of 'Palatine boors' who 'establish their language and manners, to the exclusion of ours'.[18] By the 1760s, one-third of Pennsylvania's population was of German origin. Germans made successful immigrants, and Pennsylvania prospered. The 'nativist' American objection did not usually last beyond the first generation of immigrants: German-Americans were eager to assimilate.

There has been for some time an intriguing legend about the German language in America, the mention of which can stop dinner-party chatter in a sentence. This states that there was 'during revolutionary days or immediately after', a convention held in the colonies, followed by full discussion in Congress, to decide what the national language would be, and English won, over German, by only one vote. The notion is still widespread in Germany, and seems ineradicable there. It probably came from two historical events. In 1794, the German-speaking citizens of Virginia submitted a petition about the possibility of printing an official German version of Union laws in addition to the English version: the petition was eventually denied by the full Congress, and there is some evidence that the Speaker of the House, himself a German-American, cast the decisive vote. The issue rumbled on for some decades. In 1837 there was discussion in Pennsylvania about the desirability of teaching the German language in some schools. Jürgen Eichhoff is definitive:

> If discussions such as those in Virginia and Pennsylvania gave rise to the legend, it should be emphasised that there never was a proposal to substitute the German language for English in the United States. All proposals were aimed at allowing German in addition to English, and then only locally or in narrowly limited areas.[19]

German Bibles no doubt helped to keep the German language alive in America. The English KJV lived alongside a German neighbour. They did not speak to each other. Well-printed German Bibles in America in great numbers for two and half centuries have not had the slightest effect on the Bible in English in America, as far as can be discovered, even though German solutions to problems of Greek text and vernacular translation could have been helpful – as Tyndale in the 1520s and 1530s knew well enough. Once again, KJV seemed to be unassailable. It is, bizarrely, as if God had said that in America His Word had always to be in the version of early British imperialism.

'SCOTT'S BIBLE' FROM 1804, AND THOMAS JEFFERSON

One of several new Philadelphia Bible printers, William W. Woodward (who had printed Solomon's Song[20]), reissued between 1804 and 1809, in four (or five) quarto volumes, for the first time in the United States, the popular annotated KJV known in Britain as Scott's Bible.[21] Woodward, in his second printing of volume I, after a revision by Thomas Scott made in 1809, includes a 'Recommendation' signed by 'six respectable Ministers of the Gospel in Philadelphia'. That 'respectable' is alarming. Does it stand for 'college trained and church based', as opposed to revivalist preachers? Or could it even be a social epithet? If so, one longs to meet 'six disreputable Ministers', a body that surely includes Jesus' disciples. Two of those respectable men went on to found the Philadelphia Bible Society in 1808, the first such society in America.

The additional material in these volumes of 'Scott' is vast. An edition of 1812 has, at the end of the fifth volume, 365 pages of Concordance in triple columns. Long chapter summaries take up a lot of room, and there are dense references in both margins of every page. Also on every page, at the foot, is a great deal of commentary in small print – on some verses (for example, Exodus 20:13, 'Thou shalt not kill') crowding out all but four words of Bible text. A 'Scott', though a challenge to the eyes, is no worse in that respect than the Book of Revelation in a Geneva-Tomson-Junius quarto. It came across the Atlantic already highly respected. It is said that between 1808 and 1819, in the United States, 25,250 copies were sold.[22] Sir James Stephen, the evangelical humanitarian who reformed the British Civil Service and colonial systems in the 1840s (and was grandfather of Virginia Woolf) called the commentary in an English edition of Scott 'the greatest theological performance of our age and country'.[23]

Thomas Jefferson had, and used, a 'Scott': his volumes, unsurprisingly, are still in the Library of Congress. Jefferson, the third President of the

United States, a lawyer and philosopher, the statesman behind the rights enshrined in the First Amendment, a man of intellect who in retirement founded the University of Virginia, a figure of the Enlightenment, is not generally understood to have been too interested in the Bible. Forty years before he was president, in 1760, he had a religious crisis. Instead of the Anglican creed he inherited, he had embraced a vaguely defined natural religion. He later refused to answer questions about his religious beliefs, even when in the 1800 presidential elections they became an issue: he was described as an irreligious enemy of Christianity. His lifelong belief was in the need for freedom of thought, and the primacy of morality over dogma in religious affairs. Yet in 1803 he wrote, privately, a 'Syllabus . . . of the Merit of the Doctrines of Jesus', in 1804 its successor, 'The Philosophy of Jesus', followed, some years later, by 'The Life and Morals of Jesus'.[24] In these, all in his private manuscript, he is seen to be demythologising the Christian faith. He finds Christianity, 'when purged of corruptions . . . preferable to any other religion but also one of the strongest unifying forces in a republican society'.[25] The (reconstructed) 'Philosophy of Jesus' is a scissors-and-paste compilation from New Testament KJVs published in 1791 and 1799 to make a harmony of the Gospels. Fixing his accounts of Jesus in two columns, Jefferson cut out of the Nativity stories, for example, the shepherds, the angels and the wise men. The Passion narrative is severely truncated: it all ends with John 19:30, 'and [Jesus] gave up the ghost'. 'The Philosophy of Jesus' is in English. 'The Life and Morals of Jesus', though made by the same method, is altogether fuller, and side by side on the page are Greek, Latin, French and English. Jefferson's aim was to offer a code of morals, shorn of superstition and dogma. He explains that these 'doctrines of Jesus are simple and tend all to the happiness of man'. He told Charles Thomson, Secretary to Congress and a Bible scholar (see below) that 'A more beautiful or precious morsel of ethics I have never seen'. He denounces the villainous, or plain stupid, additions by the four Gospel writers, and particularly the writing of 'the first corruptor of the doctrines of Jesus, Paul . . .', finding the genuine sayings of Jesus 'as easily distinguished as diamonds in a dunghill'.[26] The 'pure principles' Jesus taught have been rescued from the 'artificial vestments in which they have been muffled by priests'. This time the manuscript ends with the great stone rolled to the door of the sepulchre at Matthew 27:60. In these private compilations, made out of the Bible in a literal way, Jefferson demonstrates reverence for Jesus as a great moral reformer, and builds the constituent elements of what emerges as his own Christian faith, even including hope for a life after death.[27]

*　*　*

THE SECOND GREAT AWAKENING

As the century turned, more presses in Philadelphia and beyond issued New Testaments: they came from Lancaster and Elizabethtown (Pennsylvania), Boston and Brookfield (Massachusetts), Exeter (New Hampshire) and New Haven. More New York printers made Bibles. By the end of 1810, in thirty-three years since the first Aitken New Testament, nearly two hundred different New Testaments and Bibles had been printed in the United States. Two linked factors of American life were at work. After a hesitant start, New England felt a second Great Awakening, at first from 1797, propelled four years later by developments at Yale. This long-effective revival was marked by calm. Ezra Stiles (that later president of Yale who declared that the Bible was itself fulfilled in America, see above, p. 592), had characterised the first Great Awakening as the time when 'multitudes were seriously, soberly, and solemnly out of their wits'.[28] Such emotional effects and excesses were not now shown. Preaching the plain Gospel truths in those New England churches led to congregations sitting '"with deep solemnity depicted in their countenances" . . . the fruits of conversion . . . renewed spiritual seriousness and reformation of morals'.[29] Out of Yale as the century turned came a new generation of 'New Divinity' men, trained theologians who became ministers in Connecticut and the Connecticut River valley, in touch with the Calvinism of their older predecessors, but newly reformed as keen followers of the ideas of Jonathan Edwards, prepared like him – like William Tyndale, like John Calvin and like Karl Barth – to wrestle with the body of Pauline theology while ministering to a nation whose interests were elsewhere, 'preoccupied by issues of government, law, trade, war and nation-building – not theology'.[30]

BFBS AND ABS

The second factor was the growth, out of this new revival, of American Christian voluntary associations, usually across the denominations. Missionary societies were formed to evangelise the West, and lands overseas. Moral reform societies flourished to fight the demon drink and close down taverns (as John Adams attempted in his native Braintree, Massachusetts). Societies to foster Christian knowledge by education and publication imitated English models – American Sunday Schools began in Philadelphia in 1808. The New England Tract Society, founded in 1814, became in 1823 the American Tract Society, by which time 'it had already printed 777,000 tracts and was publishing a bi-monthly magazine, a Christian almanac, and a series of children's books'.[31]

Particularly strong was the expansion of local Bible Societies, members of different denominations working together to increase literacy generally, and supply cheap Bibles to read. These were developments of the Puritan beliefs that God's Word taught both the way to individual salvation and the way to harmony on earth, and thus prosperity. Before long there were Bible Societies in several states, groups of dedicated men and women, volunteers who bought Bibles at cost, for neighbourhood sale. Such local Bible Societies could, before long, realistically aim to place a copy of the Scriptures in the hands of every citizen.

> The Monroe County (New York) Bible Society illustrated the thoroughness with which such groups could work by giving a Bible to each of the county's 1200 households that an 1824 census had shown to be without the Scriptures.[32]

The American Bible Society, co-ordinating thirty-four local Societies, was founded in New York in 1816, only a dozen years after the formation of the British and Foreign Bible Society in London in 1804. The aim of both societies was the same, to make Bibles 'without note or comment'[33] readily and cheaply available, on the largest possible scale. Both set out to be strictly non-sectarian, within the frame of Protestantism. The American Bible Society ran into difficulties of alleged bias after some years, leading to a secession: but it was very successful indeed in fulfilling its large intention in the expanding nation. ABS arranged the printing and distribution, before 1850, of almost sixty different forms of KJV, in numbers that, for the time, can only be called gigantic. Thus, in the year 1829 alone, the American Bible Society printed 360,000 English Bibles. The usual print-run for a book was about 2,000 copies. In 1845, ABS printed 417,350; in 1848, 760,900. By the 1860s, it printed over a million Bibles a year.[34]

In 1809 type had been imported from a Glasgow foundry by the firm of Hudson & Goodwin of Hartford, Connecticut at the heavy expense, it was claimed, of 6,000 crowns (well over £40,000 in 1999 currency) to make the first edition of what was known as the 'School Bible'. Many copies of this small 'School Bible', were bought for sixty cents each by at least seven widely located Bible Societies, from Albany in New York to Charleston in South Carolina, for distribution. It was a KJV with minimal extra material, printed on paper described as 'the best . . . in this country'. Stereotyping (that is, making plates for printing as often as needed from permanent moulds) was the secret, as it had been just before in Britain. It solved several problems. The American Bible Society officers were alert to new methods of printing, and the adoption of stereotyping immediately it arrived in the USA in 1812, for a small-print volume by 'the Bible

Society of Philadelphia', was well ahead of all their printing competitors. The main rivals to ABS, the impressive firm of Harper and Brothers, took until 1830 to use it. (That first stereotyped American Bible was supported by the British and Foreign Bible Society, who gave a large donation and sent the plates – which were then admitted by the United States government free of duty.[35]) Not only did stereotyping mean that type did not have to be reset, an expensive procedure for a Bible: stereotype plates of a whole Bible could easily take the place of a room-full of costly standing type. Another attraction was that, in theory at least, being smaller and much lighter, stereotype plates could be sent across the States to outlying Societies. Further, the American Bible Society was one of the first publishers to use power presses, greatly multiplying output. By 1829, the Society's printer, Daniel Fanshaw in New York, was operating sixteen Treadwell steam-powered presses exclusively for ABS Bibles.[36] That year, as just noted, the Society printed 360,000 English Bibles. Further still, the Society soon abandoned the earliest practice of selling its Bibles in unbound sheets. That, a common procedure in book production, allowed the owner to have the book bound with extra material: though the Apocrypha or commentaries or concordances were hardly objectionable, they went against the dogma of 'without note or comment'. So the American Bible Society became one of the first American publishers to sell books already bound – and in-house binding, alongside the printing, was more efficient, keeping costs low. The Society's first Bibles, printed in 1816, were small, duodecimos in two columns without margins, with short chapter headings and a couple of pages of tables, and that was all. Simply bound, and cheap at sixty-four cents, they stood as a model for the hundreds of later editions.[37] A medium-sized ABS edition of 1818, from New York, announcing itself as the third, is a fine book; the paper quality is high, page headings are the only additions to the text, which itself sits pleasingly on the page, and the binding is excellent. It marks a sharp improvement in the quality of American personal Bibles, and remains a book to treasure. A pocket ABS Bible from 1826, also from New York, nicely bound, is at a similar high standard: though the type is small, being six-point nonpareil, the text is not difficult to read. A stereotyped, very small ABS Bible of 1829 from Hartford, Connecticut, is beautifully made. With these, as with all their output, ABS had made some effort.

At the start, the society had a ready-made distribution system: local societies and auxiliaries. But, being volunteer groups, they were not often efficient. From the 1840s, the ABS began to employ its own agents across America, engaged, among other duties, in door-to-door visiting. One of several attacks on the society came from objection to its apparent monopoly of Bible-making and selling. In the 1840s it could easily undersell other publishers and booksellers: it was hard to beat a New Testament for six cents (or the whole Bible for forty-five). These volumes were small and austere. A fashion gradually moved in the opposite direction, towards even more enormous, varied, heavily annotated and lavishly illustrated Bibles than had yet been seen. Yet the plain American Bible Society Bibles kept on coming throughout the century, in their millions. In the thirty-four years between Aitken's first American Bible and the formation of the ABS that spring, some 300 different New Testaments and complete Bibles had been printed in America, some elaborate, made by printers and editors who became great names.

In the spring of 1829 the American Bible Society announced that it intended to provide a Bible to every household in the United States within two years. Developments in publishing techniques had by then, the Society reckoned, made it possible to reach a population of twelve million. They fell short, far short. But even to have distributed half a million Bibles between 1829 and 1831, as they did, was an astonishing feat.[38] The American Bible Society became the biggest Bible publisher by far. Of the 1,415 separate American Bibles published by 1850, a large number came from the ABS. Its text established itself as a sort of standard. Other publishers announced their versions as 'conformable to the Standard Edition of the American Bible Society'.[39]

That very firmness, or rigidity, led to attacks on ABS. They came from leaders of sects who saw their view excluded. The concern of the Baptists was that the KJV translated the Greek verb βαπτίζω (*baptizō*) as 'baptise', which through centuries of Church practice had come to mean sprinkling the new-born rather than, as among the earliest Christians recorded in the New Testament, immersion of believers. In the 1830s the Baptists wanted the American Bible Society to use the word 'immerse' for βαπτίζω in all their Bibles. Refusal led to breakaway. The Society's own corresponding secretary, the Reverend Spencer Cone, resigned in 1836 to form the Baptists' own organization, the American and Foreign Bible Society, which saw itself as God's instrument 'in multiplying copies of pure versions of the scriptures, and of counteracting the effects of corrupt and mutilated translations'[40] – by which is meant KJV. In 1850, that former teacher, actor, journalist, secretary and Baptist minister, Spencer Cone, with another Baptist, William Wyckoff, produced their own 'immersion' New Testament, substituting that word wherever 'baptism' occurs. Then their own American and Foreign Bible Society (of which Cone was by that time President) refused to consider their offer of a more complete revision of KJV. Cone again resigned, and in the same year, 1850, founded the

American Bible Union, not only to distribute 'immersion' versions, but to make a completely new translation of the Scriptures that would correct the '*twenty-four thousand* errors found in the KJV'.[41] The project was begun, and abandoned in the 1850s through the inadequacy of the scholarship of many in the team of translators.

IMPORTS AND POLYGLOTS

Among the more solid biblical publications reprinted from England were the six volumes of the *Family Expositor: Doddridge's Notes*, printed in Charlestown in 1808, or, in 1814, the quarto fourth edition of *Newcombe's Harmony of the Gospels in Greek* (Andover, Massachusetts, 1814), a solid basis for scholarship. American editions appeared of much-used and loved British Bible versions and commentaries. George Campbell's new translation of the Gospels of 1789 was first printed in America in 1796; as noted, Philip Doddridge's 'Family Expositor' of 1765 arrived in 1807; Adam Clarke's 1810 eight-volume Commentary in 1811, and Matthew Henry's 1712 'Exposition' in 1816.[42]

A thick alluvium of increasingly heavily laden Bible editions continued to be deposited on American soil. W. W. Woodward's Bible from Philadelphia in 1813, in diamond type, at four and a half points the smallest, adds the Scottish metrical Psalms (and, thoughtfully, six blank pages for 'memorandums') to the second volume.

What was wrongly known as 'Archbishop Newcombe's New Translation' supposedly said to have a Unitarian bias, printed in London in 1808, was reprinted once in Boston in 1809. (Unitarianism was a small offshoot of the Reformation, mainly in south-east Europe. Though keen students of the Bible, Unitarians denied the divinity of Christ, and thus the Trinity. Unitarianism became fashionable in the late eighteenth century in Britain and America. It was strong in the eastern states of the US, where its concerns were described as 'the fatherhood of God, the brotherhood of Man, and the neighborhood of Boston'.) In 1810, James Macknight's translation of the Apostolic Epistles, originally from London in 1795, was also reprinted in Boston in six quite large volumes. This version has in its Preface the daunting remark that it was 'the result of unremitting labour of seldom less than eleven hours a day for almost thirty years'. Moreover, Macknight omitted three quarters of the New Testament. Such application seems obsessive. Macknight's work was republished in one volume in 1835 and again in 1845, this time with George Campbell's Gospels from his version published in London 1789, to make one volume.[43]

Isaac Collins's second edition of 1807, (now from New York) proudly announced plates specially engraved for it 'at great price . . . procuring a single plate from each of the first artists of our country', with some from an engraver from London, and talk of a gold medal for the best: all this produced 'a degree of perfection'. Adding to this advertisement the information that one could buy this Bible without plates perhaps rather spoiled the effect. The engravings tend to illustrate personal drama rather than spiritual maturity, as in one showing Elijah raising the widow's son (from 1 Kings 17). The buyer could have variations in plates, Apocrypha and Ostervald's notes. Also in 1807 appeared for the first time in the United States, from yet another new firm (Jonson, Kimber, Conrad) in Philadelphia, what was known as 'Canne's Bible'. This had continued to be reprinted in England and would be for many years in America in various states (including, unhappily, variations in accuracy) and with large additions. First produced in Amsterdam in 1642, it is a folio KJV text with Geneva and Junius notes, the latter said on the original title-page to have been *'placed in due order by I.C.,*(is that John Canne or Isaac Collins?) with the intention of *'shewing the Scriptures to be the best interpreters of Scripture'*. John Canne, who died in 1667, was said to have been 'the leader of the English Brownists in Amsterdam'.[44] An over-full 'Canne's' from New York in 1817 with fussy pages had a frontispiece from Leonardo's *Last Supper*; some of the engravings were 'after' other Renaissance masters – Holbein, Raphael, Rubens. A 'Canne's' of 1822 had fold-out maps; another of 1826 from Philadelphia had five pages in four columns giving in single lines the contents of all the books of the Old and New Testaments. With their constant heavy marginal annotation and much dense extra matter in one solid quarto, 'Canne's' could be hard going.

It must also be said that some printers – of Bibles of all kinds – did bad work. An 1825 small-print Bible from Lunenberg, Massachusetts was on bad paper, had repulsive binding, and could not even get its title-page right, declaring the date as '825'. From Windsor, Vermont in 1816 came an unpleasant piece of printing, with crowded, uneven type, very poor paper, and crude binding. A Boston 1818 stereotyped Bible was in every respect horrid.

By 1820, there are signs of how great the flood of American-made Bibles will be. In the forty-three years between 1777 and that year, four hundred new editions of complete Bibles or New Testaments had been produced, latterly from several dozen north-eastern towns. By the end of 1830, over three hundred more had arrived, many from more central states, making a total of seven hundred and twenty-six different American Bible editions.[45] By the end of 1840, with not far off four hundred more added in those ten years, the total was eleven hundred, printed in over forty American towns. In the next ten years, by 1850, well over three hundred more appeared. The total since 1777 was by then one thousand four hundred and fifteen different American Bibles and New Testaments, all in seventy-five years.

In Britain in those same seventy-five years, 1777 and 1850, there were published just over one-third of the American output, five hundred and fifty different Bibles and New Testaments. Between 1840 and 1850, when America made nearly three hundred and fifty new Bibles and New Testaments, Britain produced thirty-seven. Yet even they are an inadequate account of what was happening. As totals of separate editions, they do not take into account huge print-runs. Nor do they reveal the variations of what, in many Bibles, could be bought within one edition, and great variety of paper and binding.

A popular Bible known in America, rather disgracefully, as the Polyglot Bible, had particularly success in the north-eastern states. This started life well enough in London in 1816 as the English version of a publication, genuinely a *Biblia Polyglotta*, of English, Hebrew, Greek, Latin, French, German, Italian and Spanish Bible texts, four to a page, published by the scholarly Samuel Bagster, and reissued together in one volume in 1831. That English version was frequently reprinted in London. In 1825 Thomas Wardle in Philadelphia printed a quite different version, picking up a few preliminary leaves from Bagster, and like him, printing KJV, but then entirely re-making the centre reference columns, which were now, as the title-page has it

> from those esteemed authors Canne, Browne, Blayney and Scott, and with those from the Latin Vulgate, the French and German Bibles . . . presenting, in a portable pocket volume, a complete library of divinity. Bonus Textaurius est bonus Theologus . . .

(Blayney had revised the Oxford 'standard' edition of KJV in 1769.)

It was published again in 1831 by Key and Meilke in Philadelphia, and then in various sizes in a near-incredible 120 editions, largely in New England, until 1880. It was not a polyglot at all. The title was a trick, to help unscrupulous door-to-door selling.

> It is said that the house of every substantial farmer in the days following the Revolution had three ornaments − a polyglot Bible, a tin reflector and a wooden clock . . . The polyglot Bible 'all in English' (one Yankee peddler is alleged to have sold £16,000 worth of them) is a myth.[46]

There is a general air of things produced for the gullible end of the market. A 'Polyglot' could boast 'a Copious and Original Selection of

References . . . Exhibited in a Manner Hitherto Unattempted . . .', (as announced in the first from Philadelphia in 1831) which can let in irregularities. Indeed, that same 'Polyglot' from Philadelphia has a peculiar engraving before the title-page: it shows a flaming altar inscribed 'To The Unknown God'. The reprint in 1835 substitutes 'Abel's Sacrifice: Gen.4.44-5.' – yet it has as frontispiece to the whole Bible a set piece 'The Destruction of Pharaoh's Host, Ex.14.26-8.' It seems a long way from the ministry of Jesus.

REVIVALS ON THE FRONTIERS

Out of the Great Awakening, late but fiercely burning flames were the gospel revival movements in the backwoods. These were first marked by the arrival of 'camp meetings' at the turn of the century. Versions of these, supported chiefly by Baptists and Methodists, looked on the Cane Ridge Camp Meeting beginning on 6 August 1801 as the inspiration. At a time when the nearest town to Cane Ridge, Lexington, the largest in the state of Kentucky, had a population of barely two thousand, there assembled on Cane Ridge for six days of 'outpouring of the Spirit' a crowd estimated at between ten and twenty-five thousand. No later account, it is said, has done justice to the extraordinary event, not least in demonstrations of emotions and wild body experiences in the vast crowd:

> . . . the milling crowds of hardened frontier farmers, tobacco-chewing, tough-spoken, notoriously profane, famous for their alcoholic thirst; their scarcely demure wives and large broods of children; the rough clearing, the rows of wagons and crude improvised tents with horses staked out behind; the gesticulating speaker on a rude platform, or perhaps simply a preacher holding forth from a fallen tree. At night, when the forest's edge was limned by the flickering light of many campfires, the effect of apparent miracles would be heightened. For men and women accustomed to retiring and rising with the birds, these turbulent nights must have been especially awe-inspiring. And underlying every other conditioning circumstance was the immense loneliness of the frontier farmer's normal life and the exhilaration of participating in so large a social occasion.[47]

The extreme physical effects on men and women, often beyond belief, defied the descriptive powers, and judgement, of observers. Were they miracles? Cynics said 'more souls were begot than saved':[48] nevertheless, the message that Jesus was Lord was powerfully sustained.

> It marks a watershed in American church history . . . The most important fact about Cane Ridge is that it was an unforgettable revival of

revivalism, at a strategic time and a place where it could become both symbol and impetus for the century-long process by which the greater part of American evangelical Protestantism became 'revivalized'.[49]

Those frontier outpourings, continued through much of the century, were very American in the size and length of their meetings, the extremes of experience, and the rapid growth, all across the West, of local churches. The old north-eastern colonial domination of Congregationalists, Presbyterians and Episcopalians was overtaken in the numbers and speed of expansion of these gatherings of Baptists, Methodists and Disciples. Nevertheless, however primitive and rudimentary frontier religion was then, and continued to be, it was still also conservative, indeed European, in its institutions and practices. Its Bible was still KJV. Right into the twenty-first century, American revivalist meetings, and evangelists, sometimes very unorthodox (even reprehensible, in television manifestations) have always revered KJV.

FEW INDIGENOUS AMERICAN TRANSLATIONS

In Britain, most of the Bibles and Testaments printed in the two hundred and seventy years after 1611 were KJVs, amounting to about sixteen hundred different editions. Yet there was always, even from early in the seventeenth century, a healthy resistance to accepting that version. Geneva, Bishops', and Rheims–Douai were republished some ninety times between 1611 and the full official Revision of 1881. Further, in that period there were in Britain frequent original re-workings of the Greek and Hebrew: thirteen new translations of the Bible, or Old Testament alone, and thirty-seven of the New Testament on its own. A dozen of these were reprinted in the United States. Yet though the teaching of Greek and Hebrew in the divinity schools in America was good, and though a cultured man like Charles Thomson could, as will be seen, teach himself Greek effectively in the 1780s, and though pioneer translators like Julia Smith (1876) did remarkable work, in proportion to the vast output of new editions of Bibles in America the number of new translations by Americans is small. Not only that, but right up to the official American Revised Version of 1901, such new versions as there were seem to have made no impact at all on the dominance of KJV in America. It is as if the great monolith that was KJV in the nineteenth century still had to tower over the United States, a monarch that would brook no rival. The more one looks at this, the odder it seems. Why was there no truly American Bible? The constitutional break from Britain made in 1776 was thorough. America then became a full democracy. Indeed, American democracy since then puts

Britain to shame: by contrast with the United States, then and now, the Old Country remains only half democratic; it is still in so many forms of government ruled from the top down, in secrecy, tradition and mystique. Yet the American Founding Fathers seem not only to have been luke-warm about supporting indigenous American Bible printing, but to have failed even to think of making a truly American Bible, though they were building the new United States into at least a nominal Christian country. There could surely have been little difficulty, even in those early years, in assembling an official group of American scholars to make a true American Version from the original Greek and Hebrew, and break for ever one of the subtlest but strongest links to a rejected way of life. In 1776, KJV was already over a century and a half old. The United States was looking forward. Modern 'virtual history' is the study of the 'what ifs' of history (what would have happened if James 1's son Prince Henry had not died? what if John Kennedy had not been assassinated?). One of the challenges to such scholars might be to think through what the effect could have been of such an all-American Bible soon after the Revolution.

CHARLES THOMSON'S TRANSLATION FROM THE SEPTUAGINT, 1808

Great numbers of Bibles crossed the Atlantic to the New World. One wholly American publication, however, a scholarly work of significance, went the other way. Charles Thomson had been Secretary to the Congress of the United States until 1789, and his signature was on the Resolution to support Aitken's 1782 Bible. Romantic stories used to be told about Thomson, though the fact that they involved several ladies was not the real romance: not even that Jane Aitken of Philadelphia, at 'No. 71, North Third Street', Robert's daughter, and the first woman printer in America, was the – excellent – maker of his four remarkable volumes.

Charles Thomson was born in Maghera, Ireland, in 1729. He and his father sailed for America in 1741. His father died at sea. The eleven-year-old boy landed at New Castle, Delaware. He was rescued from destitution by a family there. They wanted to apprentice him to a blacksmith. He ran away.

> On the road he met a kind-hearted lady who offered him a seat in her carriage. She asked him, 'What would you like to be?' His ready reply was, 'A scholar'. His wish was splendidly realized, for she took him under her care and gave him an education.[50]

Having taken his MA, he taught for a while at what became the University of Pennsylvania, and became a successful merchant. His second wife was a sister of Benjamin Harrison of Virginia, one of the signatories of the Declaration of Independence. Though Thomson made many political enemies, he was respected all his life. He spoke for such minorities as Indians, slaves and Quakers. He was chosen by Indians to keep their record of their proceedings at the treaty of Easton in 1757, and the following year was adopted into the Delaware tribe as 'the man who tells the truth'. He held responsible positions close to government, being re-elected Secretary to Congress each year after 1776. He it was who was appointed to announce to George Washington that he had been elected the first President of the United States.

One day in Philadelphia, so the story went, Thomson drifted into a book auction. The auctioneer was offering a volume that he said was 'in outlandish letters'. Thomson bought it for 'a mere trifle'.[51] He found that he had one volume of the Greek Septuagint, as edited by John Pearson (later Bishop of Chester) in 1665, and printed in four volumes (which included the New Testament in Greek) the same year by John Field in Cambridge. Thomson knew no Greek but was curious both to learn the language and find out what he had. He did both. Then, knowing that he had part of a complete Septuagint, and being able to read it, he longed to find the rest. The next part of the story is indeed strange. Two years later, we are told, Thomson happened to pass the same book auction rooms, and went in, and found that the remaining volumes were at that moment being offered for a few pence. He bought them.

Forced out of national life at the age of sixty, ignored and (apparently wrongly) disgraced, in 1789, at the change of administration with the new Congress under the Constitution, Thomson gave his time to the Greek of the two Testaments. Almost twenty years later, the result was *The Holy Bible, Containing the Old and New Covenant, commonly called the Old and New Testament: Translated from the Greek, by Charles Thomson, Late Secretary to the Congress of the United States . . . Printed by Jane Aitken . . . Philadelphia, 1808* in four smart volumes. Here, for the first time anywhere, was an English translation of the Greek Septuagint. The work had been done by a scholar entirely on his own. Not only that, of course: he had worked in Philadelphia, in a town obviously lacking the libraries of an Oxford, Cambridge, London or Geneva. Moreover, it had been done well. In 1881, privileged to work with all the resources they could possibly need in the Jerusalem Chamber of Westminster Abbey, the great scholars working on the KJV to produce the Revised Version consulted Charles Thomson's versions.

It takes a moment to realise that he translated, single-handedly, the whole Bible, the first American to do so. We have also to bear in mind that he had no immediate access to the work of European textual scholars. His New Testament basis was a version of the *Textus Receptus* as printed by Field, who was reprinting Thomas Buck's edition of 1632, which reproduced the first Elzevir edition from Leiden in 1624, which itself reprinted Beza's of 1565. The history of the variants in the text that Thomson used, and their effect on his translation, has yet to be told.[52]

His English New Testament is more than just commendable. The four volumes still give pleasure. For the first time in American Bible printing the text is not in double columns, but across the page, and in paragraphs. Jane Aitken's press work is clean and attractive. To come to these books after the over-fullness developing in rival American productions by 1808 is to be refreshed. There is no additional material or illustration of any kind, except for rare explanatory footnotes. So, for example, at Luke 9:21, at 'the Christ of God', Thomson notes 'The Messiah or the Anointed'. At 1 John 5:6–8 he has a note explaining why he has printed the 'comma', though he denies its authenticity. Translating, Thomson's model was KJV, though he varies that most interestingly. Thomson's Matthew 6 ends 'sufficient for every day is its own trouble'. Did he in some way have access to a Tyndale New Testament? Or was it a case of great minds thinking alike, when they were translating the Greek text and not copying the Latin? A modern reader of Thomson's New Testament responds well to having the Greek text put into English without paraphrase: a lover of the Greek text feels content. This, let us not forget, was the first translation from the Greek into English done outside Europe.

The Old Testament Septuagint translation was made from the Greek apparently without access to the Hebrew original. Here Thomson did not need to be self-conscious about variation, especially of phrases already embedded in the language. His Psalm 23 begins 'The Lord is my shepherd. I shall want nothing. In a verdant pasture he hath fixed my abode. He has led me by gently flowing water and restored my soul.' That does well; 'verdant' is richer than KJV's 'green', and right for the sense of young verdure in the Greek. At the end of 2 Samuel 18:

And as he was going up he thus expressed himself, Oh, my son, Abessalom! Oh! my son! my son Abessalom! O that they had slain me instead of thee – that I had died in thy stead! Oh Abessalom! my son! my son!

Here Thomson varies the Septuagint's raw double 'me instead of thee' phrase by expanding to 'slain me' and 'in thy stead'.

Thomson's Judges 5, that celebrated difficulty, has the advantage of his Septuagint translator's attempt to make sense of the impossible Hebrew. Thus verses 11 and 12 are:

> Make proclamation on the road, on account of them
> Who shout amidst the drawers of water.
> There let them rehearse gracious deliverances.
> Increase, O Lord, gracious deliverances in Israel.
> Then went the people of the Lord down to their cities.
> Awake, Awake. Debbora! Awake, Awake, utter a song.
> Arise, Barak! And lead thy captivity captive, son of Abineem.

Thomson went on to publish a harmony of the Gospels in 1815. He continued to live among his books in his house near Bryn Mawr, just outside Philadelphia, until his death in 1824 at the age of 94. He was a remarkable man, his Bible work still not properly celebrated. A full new biography, the first (and one not wholly positive), reveals more of his complexity. He is shown to have been important in colonial education, culture, business enterprise, resistance movements and revolutionary politics. The fact that he was the first American to translate the whole Bible, and very usefully, is mentioned, but by the by, and that he did it well, not at all. His work is found to have been 'not totally overlooked by nineteenth-century biblical commentators': that he was important to the British Revisers in 1881 is not mentioned.[53] A proper analysis of what should be his real American distinction remains to be done. His Septuagint translation was reissued in London 1904, reprinted in Hove in 1907, and in Colorado in 1954. His New Testament was apparently reprinted in London in 1929.[54]

KNEELAND, CAMPBELL, WEBSTER, DICKINSON, MURDOCK AND OTHERS

Abner Kneeland was an American eccentric – and God be praised for eccentrics – who, true to the breed, invented a new system of spelling. He started his professional life in 1805 as a Congregationalist-and-Universalist minister, though he had doubts about the divine origin of the Scriptures. He was minister of the Lombard Street Universalist Church in Philadelphia, founding Christian magazines with liberal views from 1817 to 1824. He moved to New York, restless but always radical. Back in Boston he lectured frequently on rationalism. In 1831 he expounded pantheistic views in the *Boston Enquirer*, the first rationalist journal in the United States. In the last blasphemy trial in Massachusetts, after four years of dragged-out court hearings, hung juries and appellate courts, he was jailed in 1838 for 'a certain scandalous, impious, obscene, blasphemous and profane libel of and concerning God'. As a contemporary observed, 'Abner was jugged for sixty days; but he will come out as beer from a bottle, all foaming, and will make others foam.'[55] The cause of the indictment had apparently been his pantheistic remarks in an article in the *Boston Enquirer* of 20 December 1833, though his *Review of the Trial, Conviction and Final Imprisonment in the common jail of the county of Suffolk of Abner Kneeland, for the Alleged Crime of Blasphemy, written by himself* (Boston, 1838) is such a breathless and tangled story that it is hard to keep the events clear. In 1839 he went west to 'Salubria' on the Des Moines River in Iowa, to found a rationalist colony, which did not materialise. He died there in 1844.

While a Universalist, Kneeland published in Philadelphia in 1822 a two-volume New Testament, a Greek and English diglot – as the title-page put it,

> the Greek according to Griesbach [that is, for the first time in America not from the *Textus Receptus*]; the English upon the basis of the fourth London edition of the Improved Version with an attempt to further improvement from the translations of Campbell, Wakefield, Scarlett, Macknight, and Thomson.

This cat's-cradle of influences is further tangled by the fact that, in England Archbishop Newcombe's translation had been taken over as the basis of a version by the Unitarian Thomas Belsham, and thus the Archbishop was thought by some to have been Unitarian. It then became even more complicated as others entered the scene. Yet Kneeland's openly sectarian translation has good points. Printing his Greek text alongside his translation is not eccentric at all, and something that goes back to Erasmus himself. Using Griesbach, though done to fit Unitarian dislike of the *Textus Receptus*, was still sound. Griesbach's text had been printed in Cambridge, Massachusetts by William Wells as long before as 1809, to the dismay of conservative Christians: to make available anything other than the *Textus Receptus* was to attack the KJV, which was a translation of it. Griesbach's text had been embraced by the Unitarian movement. Like Griesbach, and in his own English, Kneeland prints the 'comma' at 1 John 5 as a footnote. He bases his English on Belsham (what one might call the Pseudo-Newcombe) but makes his own strong contribution. His Universalist position did not let him think of eternity, especially eternal punishment: so wherever αἰών (*aiōn*) and its cognates appears in the Greek, Kneeland either prints 'for an age' or transliterates. Thus 'eternity' can become in his English 'aionion', with the intended sense of 'for an age' rather than 'for ever'.

Three years later, in 1826, alongside the thirty-two new editions of the KJV Bible or New Testament published in America in that year alone, was a new translation of the New Testament from the Greek by Alexander Campbell. In America, this version sold more than any other rival to the KJV until the official Revision in 1901 and, with some changes, is still in print. Even so, Campbell did not press his version as a substitute for KJV, even among his own followers.

Alexander Campbell was born in Ireland and well educated in Scotland as a divinity student at the University of Glasgow. He arrived in America in 1809 as a Presbyterian minister, but in 1813 he became a Baptist, convinced by his reading of the New Testament that believers' baptism was what was originally intended. In the years around 1820 Campbell, distressed by squabbles among denominations, and sectarian devotion to many different practices and beliefs, preached in the Midwest and South a return to apostolic Christianity. This meant restoring the primitive church as in the New Testament, and understanding the documents there as the only guide: 'where the Scriptures speak, we speak; where the Scriptures are silent, we are silent'.[56] The churches he founded with his brother Thomas and others were at first simply called 'The Christian Church', but became the 'Disciples of Christ'. 'We neither advocate Calvinism, Arminianism, Arianism, Socinianism' [one should hope not: the latter two are ancient heresies], 'Trinitarianism, Unitarianism, Deism, or Sectarianism, but *New Testamentism*'.[57] Growing in numbers faster than any other Protestant group in America at the time, from 22,000 in 1832 to 200,000 in 1860, the Disciples of Christ are today a respected Christian denomination in the world.

Campbell was a good Greek scholar. He recognised the importance of the one-volume translation of the Gospels by another Campbell, George, as published in London in 1818, with the Epistles by Macknight and the Acts and Revelation by Philip Doddridge, all 'Doctors of the Church of Scotland', as his title-page has it.[58] He tried to get it printed in America, and failed. He then worked to make his own improvements, and the result was the 1826 volume from 'Buffaloe, Brook County, Virginia' entitled *The Sacred Writings of the Apostles and Evangelists of Jesus Christ, Commonly Styled the New Testament. . . .* The English text is across the page and in paragraphs, with verse numbers only at paragraph openings. For the first time, there are titled 'sections' instead of chapters. There is a good deal of additional matter in small print, but it is placed before Matthew and after Revelation, to keep the text absolutely clear for the ordinary enquiring Christian reader, except for some interesting footnotes as 'Aids to translation'. Again, Campbell had used Griesbach. His involvement with that Greek text was greater than any yet seen in America. He wanted, certainly in his earlier editions, to make obvious where the English had previously had to rely on what he felt were spurious Greek readings. So these were at first printed in italics, rather confusingly, as were quotations. From the third edition, that of 1832, this demonstration was removed to an appendix. There is a great deal that seems new, even refreshing. But it is mostly 'seems'. The layout as if it were a novel, and curious apellations ('Testimonies', not Gospels) at first distract from the fact that the text has only been fiddled with, not thought afresh. Campbell substitutes 'immerse' or cognates whenever the Greek has versions of βαπτίζω (*baptizō*). He modernises by removing 'eth' from verb forms, so that 'keepeth' becomes 'keeps'. Other changes do not really modernise: at 1 Thessalonians 4:15 he changes the archaic 'prevent' to 'anticipate', which is both too heavy in English for the Greek φθάσωμεν (*phthasōmen*), 'go before', and wrong as a translation. At Luke 11:17, Campbell has

> But he knowing their thoughts, said to them, By intestine broils any kingdom may be desolated . . . Now, if there be intestine broils in the kingdom of Satan, how can that kingdom subsist?

Substituting some ornate Latinate words for common English does not amount to anything of real use, as, also in Luke 11, 'distempered' for 'evil', 'interposing' for 'answering', and writing 'she came from the extremities', and 'vouchers and accessories'.

We are watching from different positions a phenomenon, that American attempts to create a radical new translation of the New Testament lacked nerve. There was something beyond a reverence for the old, established version. It was as if it had to be untouchable. So much of the 1611 KJV could have been felt to be irrelevant to such an innovative nation two centuries later. Hundreds of words and phrases had not only changed their meaning over two hundred years, or become obsolete, but were now subject to quite new contexts. For the American newly genteel, some of the vocabulary, not to mention the grammar, of KJV was unacceptable.

Precisely these points were expressed by no less a scholar than the great American lexicographer Noah Webster who, with the air of a pioneer at last clearing the jungle, in about 1831 set out to make his own revision of the whole Bible. He considered it the most important enterprise of his life. He had made his name as a young man, soon after graduating from Yale in 1778, with his famous *Spelling Book*, which was important beyond calculation in standardising American spellings as different from English. (This book was so widely used that by 1890 it had, in various forms, sold over sixty million copies.) His widely used *Grammar* was published in 1784. By the time he came to his Bible work, he was for the third time a national institution (and is to this day universally celebrated) for *Webster's Dictionary*, so often, like Hope and Crosby, Morocco bound. This, properly *An American Dictionary of the English Language* (in two volumes, 1828) had about 5,000 words not in English dictionaries, many of them Americanisms, and illustrated its definitions from usage by American writers as well as British. It almost immediately became the recognised authority. (In 1840, Webster almost doubled the number of words defined, to 70,000.)

Thus Noah Webster came to the work of revising the Bible for Americans awesomely equipped. He knew both Hebrew and Greek (and, apparently, eighteen other languages). He had been all his life a student of the Bible, and had already studied the Greek New Testament in close relation to the KJV, working on grammatical points. His massive lexicographical work had made him uniquely sensitive to the American language around him. His *The Holy Bible . . . In the Common Version. With Amendments of the Language* by Noah Webster, LL.D, was published in New Haven in 1833. It is extraordinary – for what it doesn't do. Though it would at the very end of the century influence the scholars making the American Revised Version, Webster's Bible is remarkably muted – and, more strangely still, not uncommonly wrong.

His Preface announces his three aims:

1. The substitution of words and phrases now in good use for such as are wholly obsolete, or deemed below the dignity and solemnity of the subject.

2. The correction of errors in grammar.

3. The insertion of euphemisms, words and phrases which are not very offensive to delicacy, in the place of such as cannot with propriety be uttered before a promiscuous audience.[59]

By 'promiscuous' Webster means 'indiscriminately mixed'. More than the word has changed: it is also a characteristic in an audience that we no longer identify.

On the following page, he lists his principal alterations. These may be classified under seven heads.[60] His changes include archaic words: as well as the obvious 'let', changed in his text to 'hinder', and a score of others, Webster includes 'Yea', which is changed to 'even', 'indeed', 'truly', 'verily', 'yes'. He gives about sixty obsolete meanings, including 'fellow', changed to 'man', 'mad' changed to 'insane', and 'trade' changed to 'employment' or 'occupation'. He further includes, as changed in his text, various 'unsuitable popular phrases' like 'creeping thing' (changed to 'creeping animal') and 'safe and sound' (changed to 'in health'). He notes errors in KJV's grammar, like 'improper use of subjunctives', and in translation, like

'Ethiopia' instead of 'Cush', or 'Red Sea' instead of 'Suf'. The last two final heads are taken as 'changes argued for but not made', sometimes appearing as marginal notes to his text, and his fairly substantial list of passages that need euphemising, teasingly ending with an 'etc.' The only two New Testament ones are in John 11:39, 'stinketh' and in Ephesians 5:5, 'whoremonger'.[61] Further, he says in his second paragraph, many words and phrases are 'so offensive, especially to females, as to create a resistance in young persons to attend Bible classes and schools, in which they are required to read passages which cannot be repeated without a blush', and containing words which on other occasions a child could not utter without rebuke. The list of words turns out to begin with 'barren' at Genesis 20:18, 29:31; 'fruitful' at Genesis 30:22; 'odious' at Genesis 34:30; 'offensive in smell' at Exodus 7:18; and 'putrefy' at Exodus 16:24. It is all very innocent of him, as though schoolchildren have not always been streetwise enough to know where to find 'the dirty bits' and giggle over them.

These changes do not seem to be more than froth. Reading that Preface again, one asks 'Is that all that Noah Webster, of all people, can do?' Studying his Bible text carefully draws the reluctant answer 'yes'. Noah Webster's Bible is straight KJV with minute alterations (occasional 'will' for 'shall': 'treated' for 'entreated') and, in the white centre column of the page, a few tiny references or alternatives. His Bible looks like, and sounds like, KJV. Digging more deeply, one finds printing errors ('This this is the heir', Luke 20:14), and curious oddities like his unexplained dislike of the word 'fetch', even to the point (as in 2 Samuel 14:2 and elsewhere) of wrongly changing it to 'bring' (which implies one movement, not the two of 'fetch'). A more bizarre oddity is his failure to address notorious ambiguities like 'occupy'. This word, which occurs ten times in KJV, gradually developed from the mid-fifteenth century a parallel obscene meaning of 'to have to do with sexually'. Shakespeare was well aware of this: in *2 Henry 4*, at 2.4.140, he makes Doll Tearsheet exclaim 'God's light, these villains will make the word [captain] as odious as the word 'occupy'; which was an excellent good word before it was ill sorted.' This vulgar meaning of 'occupy' was strong enough almost to drive the word out of polite use altogether in the seventeenth and eighteenth centuries.[62] How Noah Webster came not to change it we shall never know. At Luke 19:13, the Parable of the Ten Pounds includes 'he called his ten servants . . . and said to them, Occupy till I come'.

Scholar though he was, Webster was, moreover, often whimsically inconsistent as well as careless. Generally, he combined in his great work the lightest of revisions with needless alterations. His Bible was not a success, at least at first. The price fell in three years from $3 in 1833 to $2 in 1836, and then to $1.50.[63] Webster was keenly hurt. His New Testament was republished in 1839, and the whole Bible in 1841, two years before his death. Only as the century advanced did it become a little more of a success.

Noah Webster's great reverence for KJV meant that what he gave to the world was both timid and sometimes unscholarly. It is as if drawing so close to KJV in America had the effect of making even great scholars slightly unhinged. KJV had become the Ark of the Covenant, where even putting out a steadying hand to it to save it from falling could result in what seems to have been instant, fatal electrocution, as in 2 Samuel 6:6–7.

The other single-handed attempts at Bible revision before the middle of the nineteenth century need not detain us long. Rodolphus Dickinson from South Carolina offered in the same year as Noah Webster's Bible, 1833, a 'Minute Revision and Professed Translation' of the New Testament based on Griesbach. For all Dickinson's huffing and puffing (his is the only New Testament with a portrait of the reviser as frontispiece, his manner distinctly condescending) it is nothing but KJV with heavy frills on, a mere substitution of ornate words, so that in Luke 1, when Elizabeth heard the salutation of Mary, 'the embryo was joyfully agitated', and she exclaimed '. . . blessed is your incipient offspring'. Part of the Magnificat in the same chapter appears as 'He has precipitated potentates from their thrones . . . He has satisfied the necessitous with benefits, but the affluent he has dismissed destitute.' Dickinson gives Ephesians 1:3–14, which in KJV is expressed in fifty-four not-difficult words, in 268 words, many complicated. On the second page of 'The History by Luke' is 'And behold, your cousin Elizabeth is also in gestation with a son . . . with her who is reported sterile . . .'; and on page two of 'Apostolic Transactions' is 'this man . . . caused a field to be purchased with the recompense of his iniquity; and falling prostrate, a violent internal spasm ensued, and all his viscera were emitted.'

Nine years after that, and some three hundred new American editions of KJV later, the publisher David Bernard printed in 1842 a KJV 'Carefully Revised and Amended . . . By Several Biblical Scholars'. Who these were is not known for certain, except that the New Testament was by Dr A. C. Kendrick, a Baptist scholar of Greek language and literature, who, like others before him, objecting to the word 'baptise' substituted 'immersion'. Otherwise, uniformity of spelling, correction of grammar and the changing of 'such terms as are indelicate, antiquated or left untranslated' in KJV[64] was the modest aim. Ten years after that, and this time after nearly four hundred new American editions of KJV, a printer in Auburn in 1852 produced a truncated New Testament version by Hezekiah Woodruff in supposedly idiomatic English 'to benefit the rising generation'. It is KJV with twiddly bits. Spencer Cone and William Wyckoff's 'immersion' version had appeared in 1850, a supposedly wholesale revision of KJV by leaders of the breakaway American and Foreign Bible Society, from the Greek, with help from 200 years of commentaries. Though boasting 'Several Hundred Emendations', it is still essentially KJV. The same is even more true of H. T. Anderson's 'immersion' New Testament of 1864. Various editions appeared between 1858 and 1891 of translations by Leicester Ambrose Sawyer, a Presbyterian minister who within eighteen years became a Congregationalist and then a Unitarian and then a Christian Rationalist and finally pastor, from 1850, of The First Catholic Congregational Church (Independent) of Boston, where he published his New Testament based on Tischendorf's Greek. His Preface calls passionately for translation by individuals, not councils ('A council did not make Paradise Lost . . .'[65]). But that individual most peculiarly made new chapter and verse arrangements, so that the three chapters of the Sermon on the Mount are now Matthew 5. He claims in his Preface 'a thoroughly modern style', but has 'give us today our essential bread', and then reprints Tyndale's 1534 opening of John 1 entire – paying tribute to Tyndale.

More interesting by far is the work of the orientalist James Murdock. In 1851 he translated a New Testament from the Syriac version. Published in New York, and reprinted at least six times, this was refreshingly successful. Syriac is a form of Aramaic, the language Jesus spoke, and the Syriac New Testament, dating from the second century, has much from which we can learn. Murdock's literal translation into idiomatic English is still attractive – he uses English (that is, KJV) forms of names in Syriac – and though KJV still haunts the page, the modern reader recognises a different world at last.

KJV STILL DOMINANT

The point stands. I have glanced at ten American solo versions, made between 1823 and 1864. Apart from James Murdock, none of the originators contributed anything of significance. Shared dissatisfaction with KJV led only to tinkering with it, if 'tinkering' will do for Rodolphus Dickinson's efflorescent elaborations. Even the shift to Greek bases other than the *Textus Receptus* did not force a break from KJV. Even the arch-American-linguist, arch-American-lexicographer and arch-American-grammarian Noah Webster gave his readers the language of 1611, much of it already archaic. By 1850, seventy-three years after the small beginning, nearly fifteen hundred separate editions of KJV had been published in America. Why, one has to ask, was this energetic, ebullient, creative new nation so tied to its Scriptures in ancient form?

Part of the answer might lie in that very ebullience. The rising heat of the new can demand a cooler, older, base to which to return. The religious – or perhaps only denominational – career of the Reverend Leicester Ambrose Sawyer in the 1830s and 1840s, just noticed, illustrates a larger national fluidity. Like the effect of the Wesleys in England and Wales a century before, the possibility of unhindered religious enthusiasm leads, among much else, to movements of people who feel released from fetters. It leads to the dividing of denominations, the formation of new sects, the abandoning of one loyalty for another, so that Mr Sawyer, passionate believer in the individual, can be 'Christian Rationalist' and pastor of a Catholic Congregational Church (Independent) in conservative Boston. Denominations were being founded (that pastor's church was 'The First . . .'), then expanding, splitting off, regrouping, pressing west to the forests and to the featureless plains of Iowa like poor Abner Kneeland, to die in his failed rationalist colony. Sects, properly in the first place small groups feeling themselves alienated, grew like the seed in the parable that fell on stony ground, which sprang up too quickly because it had not much earth, and died. The kaleidoscope of American Christian life in the first half of the nineteenth century had new colours constantly added from an explosion of revivalist preaching, with almost infinite possibilities of further revelation and damnation promised. The sudden social mobility in this age of the American common man, the freedom of that common man – and woman – to move great distances on railroads, and to make fortunes in new mills and enterprises, the challenge to almost all traditional ways brought by the new individualisms – perhaps in all this flux the Bible had to be solid, unchangeable, revered, a true Sacred Text that would not admit a single change, and thus it was the monument, the unaltered KJV.

SACRED FURNITURE FOR THE AMERICAN HOME

The small town of Brattleboro on the Connecticut River in Vermont has a special place in the story of American Bibles. Brattleboro is some way from what, early in the nineteenth century, were the only real centres of Bible publishing and distribution, Boston, New York and Philadelphia. In the days of bad roads rural Vermont was effectively further away still. In 1803 a young printer from New Hampshire, William Fessenden, had set up in Brattleboro a printing and newspaper business. It flourished. He married the daughter of a prosperous local businessman, John Holbrook, a shipper of meat and other local products down the river to Connecticut. In 1815 William Fessenden died. John Holbrook, who had been living

in Connecticut, came back to Brattleboro to save the town's chief industry, taking over his son-in-law's publishing business. He immediately
proposed the production of a large illustrated Family Bible, to be financed
by subscription. New York and Boston Bible publishers foretold certain
failure. Holbrook set up a paper mill, 'in itself . . . quite a project in an
area with no machine shop, no iron foundry, nor engine lathe. The iron
castings were brought by horse from Rhode Island.'[66] In 1816 his large
quarto Family Bible came out, with Apocrypha and engravings. It had
been stereotyped in New York, only four years after the American Bible
Society had first used that method. It was a handsome production. Holbrook had succeeded. After ups and downs, the firm in various forms, in
time chiefly the Brattleboro Typographic Company, produced over a dozen
Bible editions of various kinds (including five 'Polyglots'), some important: 'and between 1816 and 1854 forty-two editions of Bibles came from
eight different firms which were in some way connected to John Holbrook.'[67] One of the skills of Holbrook and his Brattleboro successors was
in watching the market. Another, linked with that, was in choosing illustrations and keeping them fresh. An early (whole page) engraving was of
the Tower of Babel, an image which Americans liked, partly because they
were conscious of different European and Indian languages around them,
partly from their growing fascination with the geography and emerging
history of the Middle East, enjoyed for their own sakes and because of
the light they could cast on the Bible. The picture of the Tower itself is
strong. Holbrook's second edition of the 1816 quarto in 1818 has new
additional preliminary matter, and the Tower of Babel has now flanking it
two cuneiform tablets, captioned 'antiquities from Asia brought to New
York in Jan. 1817 by Capt. Henry Austin . . .'. The left tablet is a 'Copy of
the Scriptures in a fragmentary brick . . . at the Tomb of Daniel the
Prophet . . .'. Some later Brattleboro Bibles, like one of 1819, were printed
on distressingly poor paper. The frontispiece to a very small Holbrook and
Fessenden New Testament of 1824 shows 'The Shepherds Glorify God',
which is good; it is labelled 'Matth. 2', which is not.[68]

HARPERS' ILLUMINATED BIBLE

Brattleboro Bibles were, increasingly, illustrated. That was a development
which was particularly American. With that went bulk. Take, for example,
Harper & Brothers' Illuminated Bible, issued between 1843 and 1846 from
New York in fifty-four numbers varying between twenty-five and sixty
pages, at 25 cents each, and, finally in one grand, enormous volume – at

over thirteen pounds almost too heavy to hold (and this was far from the heaviest). A very large Bible was not intended to be carried about, of course. Tyndale's pocket-books for the ploughboy in the fields do not belong here. Such volumes were for the parlour, to be lovingly placed there as something fixed and admired, a piece of holy furniture in the good American home. This Illuminated Bible, the acme of American Bible production of the time, had heavy embossed leather with metal clasps, high-quality paper, the edges of its pages gilded and some printed in colour. Many of those pages, where they contained the Bible, including the Apocrypha, had lavishly decorated initial letters. All were thick with marginal notes and references. Elsewhere were hundreds of pages of chronological and other tables, an index, a concordance and commentaries of great length in small print. Numberless (almost in both senses) pages of Family Record include special slots for the insertion of family portraits. All these are the skillfully produced extension of familiar characteristics. What was new in this Illuminated Bible, indeed, sensational, were the illustrations: more than sixteen hundred of them.

Before that, no American-made Bible had more than a hundred pictures. A hundred is a large number of plates for a Bible. For technical reasons those had usually been bound in, having been printed on separate sheets, where the quality of paper could be appropriate. Harper & Brothers' new printer and engraver, Joseph Alexander Adams, had brought with him the recently invented process of printing pictures known as electrotyping, which allowed presses to handle large print-runs without damaging the plates. By electrolysis the plates were coated with a thin layer of copper, which gave them adequate strength in high-speed, high-pressure machines. That new method meant that pictures could be on the same page as the text. Today that effect is too familiar even to think about. The impact then was extraordinary. The Bible was suddenly a large and fascinating picture book with the Scriptures attached. The Harper brothers advertised their Bible as 'the most splendidly elegant edition of the Sacred Record ever issued'. The title-page announces that the whole thing is 'Embellished with Sixteen Hundred Historical Engravings'. 'Historical' is the key word. Bible – and associated – history is being lavishly pictured, so that the reader is improving the mind, being educated and entertained. Further, many of the engravings are from European 'Old Masters' and thus the reader is getting history *and* culture. Perhaps 'reader' is the wrong word: one is to imagine the American Family sitting in the American Home in the American evenings looking together at all the pictures in the American Bible: television for the 1840s, only better (fig. 38).

The Harper & Brothers' Illuminated Bible is rightly prominent in American printing history, and not just Bible printing history. The intention was tremendous, the execution marvellous. The numbers off the presses were astronomical for the time at 75,000.[69] There was nothing like this in Britain, nor anywhere in Europe, nor anywhere else. Whether it increased the spiritual understanding of Americans is doubtful: one does not need pictures of a synagogue to be touched by Jesus' healing miracles, nor views of the Mount of Olives to take into oneself St John's Gospel. Tyndale had it right: the place of the Word of God is in the pocket, about the person, frequently read and learned by heart: there is an obvious way in which that Word, in Harper & Brothers' great product, is swamped. Paul's Epistle to the Romans is tough theology, not family entertainment. The Illuminated Bible fed a peculiarly American reverence for the Bible as object. Here, suggested Harpers & Brothers, is a finer product than was ever yet seen in America. Great American enterprises – inventing and using new power-presses, using the telegraph to order copies, delivery by wonderful railroads, advertisement in newspapers and periodicals and stores as never seen before, retail in proliferating bookstores – these are all admirable in their way. Yet the effect is to idealise the product when the buyer finally gets it home (possibly with an image of the local church embossed on the leather cover[70]) and into its special place, so that it is revered as a commodity, a bought thing, rather than read with spiritual hunger for the soul's salvation.

Such solid parlour Bibles in so many homes, and the American Bible Society Bibles in so many pockets: the Word preached from King James Version on Sundays in churches and nightly from revivalists' platforms: the sense of that version as an American monument – these things did give the American nation a sense of itself as a Protestant country. The nearly overwhelming arrival of Irish and other immigrants in the 1840s challenged that, even with violence: they were almost all Catholics. Soon, Roman Catholics outnumbered every other denomination in America. The effect of that on the story of the English Bible in America is still to be seen.

Meanwhile, nothing quite like Harper & Brothers' Illuminated Bible happened again. As it was the culmination of a process, so it was imitated. But after it, Bible production in the United States declined – or at least, the number of producers declined. It is impossible to say how many Bibles were printed or in circulation. The American Bible Society produced, for example, in 1877, another of its very small, 24mo Bibles. It makes only one entry in Margaret Hills' catalogue, but by 1929, of this one edition the number of copies ABS had printed was 3,783,940. There is a falling-off, noticeably sharp, of publishers prepared to venture a Bible. In 1843, the year the Illuminated Bible's instalments began, thirty-two other Bibles, including a few New Testaments, were printed by different publishers in

America. In 1880, there seem to have been two (fig. 36).[71] The numbers of publishers pick up again in 1881 and for a while thereafter, with the first appearance in the United States of the English Revised Version.

In this chapter America has been seen to make the KJV its own in seventy years, from a timid beginning to the most powerful impact.

There is one observation to add. Is it any wonder, when as a central commodity in so many American homes has been a revered book of enormous size, that American literature, and particularly the American novel, scarcely stopping to consider, made itself enormous?

Chapter 36

THE NINETEENTH-CENTURY BIBLE IN BRITAIN, AND TWO ARTISTS

BETWEEN 1800 AND 1899, Darlow, Moule and Herbert's catalogue record about 600 new editions of the Bible, or parts of it, in English, printed in various cities in Britain. (American figures for that century, which are greater, appear above and below, in chapters 35 and 38.) Numbers are now too large for more than a brief mention of significant events, and observable trends, in Bible history. Seventeen new Bible editions appeared in one year alone, 1812. Such is the volume of output that even the assiduous Darlow, Moule and Herbert recognise that after 1824 they can only record 'such editions [. . .] as depart from the norm'.[1]

Two British events in the nineteenth century, one at the beginning and one towards the end, colour all the future of the English Bible. The first is the foundation of the British and Foreign Bible Society in 1804[2] (the American Bible Society followed in 1816). The second is the first official revision of KJV, begun in 1870, and issued as the complete Revised Version in 1885 (considered in chapter 37 below). The BFBS, later simply 'The Bible Society' as it is today, was soon the biggest producer of Bibles in English (always KJV without Apocrypha). The story of great success following the adoption by the BFBS of the new process of stereotyping has been mentioned above (p. 622). BFBS was the sender of missionary Bibles across the globe 'from Greenland's icy mountains to India's coral strand' as the popular Victorian hymn had it.

This is not the place to tell the story of the work of translation of the Bible into the hundreds of languages that the missionaries encountered. The story is an ancient one: one recalls the ninth-century translators St Cyril and Methodius, who invented the Glagolitic language and gave the Slavs the Bible in their own language – so successfully that the Pope disowned their work. In America, John Eliot in 1663, working from Massachusetts, printed the first New Testament in Algonquin, and started the movement to give the native Americans the Bible in their own tongues. Early in the nineteenth century Robert Morrison, the first Protestant missionary in China, published a Chinese grammar and dictionary and a translation of the Bible, under the additional difficulty of getting himself taught Chinese – it was forbidden to teach it to foreigners. Most remarkable was William Carey, the Baptist scholar-missionary who in 1793 sailed for India. In 1809 he translated the whole Bible into Bengali, and then the whole or parts of the Bible into twenty-four other Indian languages or dialects. Though many translators were, like Carey, scholars of Greek and Hebrew, translations were commonly made directly from KJV, the influence of which is still felt strongly in, for example, modern-day China and Japan (figs 41, 42). At the start of the twenty-first century, parts of the Bible have been translated into 2,287 of the world's 6,000 languages, and the work continues strongly.[3]

Parallel in development to the growth of the missionary societies, particularly from the British Nonconformists, were the formation of Sunday Schools for children who, employed six days in the week, had only that chance of self-improvement by learning to read. Bible study, through the possession of a Bible, was the heart of Sunday School teaching. As the century passed, however, the universal acceptance of KJV was challenged in three ways: to a slight extent by the continuation of the British tradition of individual re-translating – about forty such endeavours can be found, mostly of single books[4] (not including the occasional reprinting of 'Douai-Rheims'); by the antiquarian interest in pre-KJV translations (the Gothic and Anglo-Saxon versions of the Gospel of Matthew in 1807, and Forshall and Madden's great four-volume Wyclif in 1850); and by the continued growth of European scholarship challenging the accepted Greek New Testament text on which KJV was based. None of the new and eccentric retranslations has survived as being of interest, except for the revised Gospel of John in 1857 'by Five Clergymen', which prepared the way for the Revised Version;[5] and 'The Twentieth Century New Testament' prepared in 1898 by a learned body of some thirty-three men and two women, attempting to put Westcott and Hort's Greek into 'simple, modern English'.[6]

THE BIBLE IN VICTORIAN CULTURE

To try to illustrate the assumption of near-universal knowledge of KJV as an influence in the whole of nineteenth-century culture is obviously impossible. Part of the response to Darwin's *On the Origin of Species by Natural Selection* (1859) was, as everyone knows, an automatic hostility in that it was said to set up opposition between science and the Bible. Yet, as is usual with 'what everyone knows', the matter is more subtle and much more interesting. In an earlier chapter it was noted how much the

Protestant rediscovery of the Bible in the sixteenth and seventeenth centuries energised the growth of modern science (see above, pp. 11–12): the supposed Victorian conflict was only in the area of interpretation of the first chapters of Genesis. Darwin himself referred to the Creator: at the end of the *Origin*, he wrote, 'I believe that animals have descended [. . .] into which life was first breathed by the Creator.'

> The living power of God, in all the forces of Nature, is indispensable as ever. Without that the world stagnates in a moment, as the wide ocean would freeze to motionless ice were the sun to strike no more his rays upon the dancing wave.[7]

At Darwin's death in 1882,

> suddenly his virtues were discovered. Bishops, and deans, and canons, vied with each other in praise of his genius, his achievement, his character, and even his Christian faith [. . .] It was forgotten that he was a heretic and a maker of heretics. It was forgotten that, while he himself strove to disturb the faith of no man, his teachings cut clean against dogma after dogma in the accepted religion of the state.[8]

More characteristic of the complex high talents of the age was Matthew Arnold. His poems make a slimmer volume than those of his great contemporaries Tennyson and Browning, but his ideas were at once practical (in all that he wrote on education, and the craft of criticism) and reflecting what was felt as at least a melancholy experience, his increasing loss of personal faith, shared with his fellows. Nevertheless, even though characterised by his *Forsaken Merman*, he was unable to enter a church, the English Bible remained central. He wrote, among much else, on *St Paul and Protestantism* (1870) and *God and the Bible* (1875). In 1872, fearing (wrongly) that the Bible might be removed from the syllabus of state schools, he published a selection of chapters from Isaiah entitled *The Great Prophecy of Israel's Restoration (Isaiah Chapters 40–66). Arranged and Edited for Young Learners*. This was to show how to introduce children to great literature. The Preface to this is a kind of manifesto for the Bible as literature. This attractive book was followed in 1883 by *Isaiah of Jerusalem in the Authorised English Version with an Introduction, Correction and Notes*. Arnold suggests only three small corrections, is tolerant of 'AV', chary of revision, scornful of recent German textual critics who undermine one's security in the text, and revels in 'the power of the words as they stand':

> The words of the Authorised Version have associations. 'For every battle of the warrior is with confused noise and garments rolled in blood, but this shall be with burning and fuel of fire.' No one of us understands

clearly what this means, and indeed a clear meaning is not to be got out of the words, which are a mistranslation. Yet they delight the ear, and they move us . . .[9]

Above all, Arnold's *Literature and Dogma: An Essay towards a better apprehension of the Bible* (1873) is a plea for the proper centrality of the Bible in national life, restoring it to people who have thrown it away because of their inability to accept metaphysics, prophecy or miracle.

> When our philosophical liberal friends say, that by universal suffrage, public meetings, Church-disestablishment, marrying one's deceased wife's sister, secular schools, industrial development, man can very well live; and that if he studies the writings, say, of Mr Herbert Spencer into the bargain, he will be perfect [. . .] the Bible is become quite old-fashioned and superfluous [. . .] the masses [. . .] are disposed to applaud them to the echo.[10]

All his working life, Arnold knew the needs of those 'masses' well, particularly the children, whom he loved, in the elementary schools he visited as inspector all over the country. (One notes in contrast that the large bibliography of Arnold's contemporary, John Henry, Cardinal Newman, though full of works on the Church Fathers and Catholic doctrine, and his own pilgrimage, shows no trace of any interest whatsoever in the Bible.) In his 'Dover Beach', Arnold's 'Sea of Faith once, too, at the full' may now be felt as 'retreating': but Arnold never lost his understanding of how central in national life the English Bible must be.

English novels of sentiment (a form at its highest from the Brontës between 1847 and 1853) are steeped in the Bible. Even the free-thinking George Eliot (not writing 'Christian' novels), whose first publication was a translation of the German critical work of David Strauss as *The Life of Jesus, Critically Examined* (1846), and her second a translation of Feuerbach's *Essence of Christianity* (1854) could not, for all her radical genius, avoid it. Later Victorian novelists – Thomas Hardy, for example – confidently assumed detailed, and unelaborated, biblical knowledge in making major effects.

The English Romantic poet, William Wordsworth, wrote in 1815, 'The grand store-house of enthusiastic and meditative Imagination . . . is the prophetic and lyrical parts of the holy Scriptures, and the works of Milton, to which I cannot forbear to add those of Spenser.'[11] Again, it is impossible to comment even briefly on the influence of biblical imagery, themes and moral precepts on English Romantic literature, roughly from *Lyrical Ballads* in 1798 to the death of Wordsworth in 1850. Romanticism revolted against the eighteenth-century appeal to universally obvious harmony and balance, a social consensus, 'the general' – which meant the identically classically educated. Instead, the Romantic individual stood up and received a revelation from God himself, or Nature, or social revolution. The heart of that revelation was imagination, now set free and given full weight and authority. For the Augustan writers (roughly 1660 to the late 1780s) imagination had been an unruly distant relative of proper writing or painting: a half-wild animal to be tolerated and used (Dryden had likened it to 'a questing spaniel'). At the very least, it had to be subject to reason – 'Imagination in a man . . . is supposed to participate of reason' (Dryden again).[12]

By contrast, the Romantic poet was prophet, telling the few others who could hear what he alone had received, something essential for everyone, and enduring the scorn of the limited many. The poetic theories of the time are about the imagination. The young Wordsworth and Coleridge walking in the winter of 1797 along the north Somerset coast, discussing the poetic theory which made the astonishing *Lyrical Ballads* of 1798 and its Preface (and being secretly reported to the Government as probably spies for Napoleon) were formulating a theory of the relation of the imagination to the normal unconscious mind which anticipated Freud by one hundred years. These poetic – and painterly – insights are the reason for the passionate self-expression, the cultivation of spontaneity with unrestrained energy, especially in the imagination. Violence, irregularity, the strange, the shocking, the elemental, are fully present. The focus is on the particular not the general, especially the previously disfranchised particulars, like the broken soldiers or tragic ordinary country women of Wordsworth's poems. Artistic authority came not now from universally approved ancient Greece and Rome, but the Middle Ages, the 'Gothic', and especially Shakespeare, suddenly discovered to have said it all. Inspirations varied, but the common teacher was usually Nature: it was as if some people suddenly woke up, and had sight given them for the first time. Union with Nature was almost religious, certainly individual, and often mystical. It was in total contrast to what had dominated before – intellect, especially reason. Not that the great Romantics were not clever: Coleridge's philosophy dominated much thinking, and it is said that he was the last person who had read everything.

The idea of the fragment was useful to the Romantics. Much of Coleridge's poetry is little else, and a good deal of the poetry of Shelley, Byron and Keats is fragmentary. The glimpse that a fragment can give allows a sharing with the poetic and mystic experience of revelation, that sudden sense of being in touch with something God–given and whole, even the idea, however unexpected the momentary vision, of suddenly coming home, or seeing home and being filled with longing for it. In this sense, all the work of William Blake, for example, adds up to something bigger than the sum of what he did: he was one of those rare artists like Shakespeare, or Mozart, who created a total world which is unlike daily life but yet has its own complete reality and coherence.

Whereas the neoclassical English writers of the Augustan age were constrained by the letter of the text, and produced classical English translations – Harwood's Prodigal Son as an English landed gentleman's son – the Romantic writers were suddenly liberated into a quite new relation with the Bible. The Bible was now seen as one source, and probably the best, of visionary illumination in a way which would have seemed to the Augustans quite mad, literally insane, as Blake was said to be. Put crudely, instead of translating the Bible, the Romantics totally reinterpreted it. The chief example of this is Blake, who, with Turner, in originality and influence dominated the Romantic period in the field of Bible illustration. Turner's Bible scenes were of large events in landscapes, as 'The Deluge' (1805): Blake's response was always highly personal, and commonly derided. Nearly two hundred years later, understanding is a little more sympathetic, and attention can be given to his greatest series of engravings, those commissioned to accompany an edition of the Book of Job, quite unlike any kind of biblical commentary or interpretation that had gone before. 'The Old and New Testaments are the Great Code of Art', wrote Blake:[13] to begin to grasp a little of what he meant some sense of what he believed he was doing is needed.

GOD AND WILLIAM BLAKE

William Blake was born in 1757 into a fairly prosperous family in a spacious old house in Soho in London, then not far from open fields. His father encouraged his artistic leanings, and sent him to the best school for young artists. At the age of 14 he was apprenticed to master engraver James Basire for seven years, learning not only the craft of engraving, but Gothic art, and ancient mythologies and legends. He started as a student at the Royal Academy, but could not endure the life studies, which he said deadened the vigour of his imagination, and withdrew. In 1782, at twenty-five, he married. His wife, Catherine, was young and beautiful, the daughter of a market-gardener, and said to be illiterate. They were unusually happily married for forty-five years, though without children. The couple lived next door to William's family home, and were joined by his younger brother Robert. To William's permanent grief, Robert shortly fell ill, and though nursed continually by William, died.[14] William said that at the moment of death 'he had seen the released spirit ascend heavenward, clapping its hands for joy'. Blake continued to communicate for the rest of his life with his brother's spirit, deriving much comfort from their conversations. Blake also communicated freely with angels and characters from the Bible. Emerging here was not only a Romantic free spirit, but one of England's great visionaries.

Visionaries do not make good accountants, and the Blakes lived in poverty as he struggled to make a living from engraving. It was in 1788, at thirty-one, that he first tried to make words and design marry in a single copper plate. One day his brother Robert appeared in a vision and gave explicit directions, which resulted in *Songs of Innocence and Experience* (1794), printed by him, and bound by Catherine. They represented 'the two Contrary States of the Human Soul'. He and Catherine continued to produce these all his life: such integrated illuminated books were for them a means of reform, politically as well as spiritually, in that they put the means of production back into the hands of the craftsman.

In 1792, when he was thirty-nine, William and Catherine moved to Lambeth. The seven years in this house with a private garden were happy and productive, particularly of a great series of colour prints. In 1800 the Blakes moved to a cottage at Felpham in Sussex (now part of Bognor Regis) to be near William Hayley, who had commissioned plates. Blake found nature overwhelmingly beautiful – it was his first time out of London – but interestingly he did not attempt landscapes or nature studies. Instead, the tops of the trees contained his 'daughters of inspiration' who came down to talk with him: and he told an astounded lady at a party all about a fairy's funeral that he had seen in the garden the night before. After three years the Blakes moved back to London in 1803, when Blake was forty-six, living in poverty in South Molton Street, working on plates for his long poems *Milton* (dictated by angels and by Milton himself) and *Jerusalem* – only one copy of the latter was ever illuminated.

In the summer of 1818, when he was sixty-one, his life was changed by the admiration of a group of young painters, particularly John Linnell and Samuel Palmer, who brought something like worship – and money. The Blakes moved to Fountain Court, off the Strand. At sixty-five, Blake was commissioned by Linnell to make the twenty-two magnificent engravings illustrating *The Book of Job*, and a hundred engravings for an edition of Dante.

As a painter and poet he was in the vanguard of English Romanticism. He was thirteen when Wordsworth was born, thirty-eight when Keats was born. He died at seventy in August 1827, when Keats had been dead for six years, and Wordsworth was fifty-seven. William Blake, never at university, was learned in the Bible, in the Western mythologies, in European literature (as noted, Milton was so deeply in him that he dictated poems to him), in the history of sculpture and painting. He knew in detail the texts and commentaries on the Bible and Dante, had studied and absorbed the Near Eastern Gnostic writers of the second century AD and after, for example Marcion; the *Hermetica*, those theological and philosophical writings ascribed to Hermes Trismegistus from the first to the third centuries AD; and the major Alchemists, like Paracelsus. He was familiar with Plato and Plotinus, and Neoplatonic theology, and the various interpretations of myths. He knew the theological system of Emmanuel Swedenborg, powerfully set out about the time Blake was born in the 1750s, based on direct contact with the spiritual world. Many people in Europe at the time found Swedenborg dull and inconsiderable, if not vaporously mad. But Swedenborg influenced, among others, Baudelaire, Balzac, W. B. Yeats – and Blake. From nature came the discovery of innocence of mind as capable of wisdom and revealing truths, whether in children (Jesus' 'babes and sucklings') or untutored minds, or even the apparently unhinged – like Wordsworth's 'Idiot Boy'.

Apparently an awkward, stubborn little man, his poetry and paintings provoked derision among the learned and the great and the good, just as did the early poetry of Wordsworth, and all the poetry of Keats. His poetry and paintings show huge and visible faults and blindnesses. Charles Dickens comes to mind: the faults in his novels are glaring – one thinks of his failure to animate very good people, especially very good women; or the stereotyped idylls to which he banishes his newly married lovers at the ends of his novels, where they sit at a cottage door under rambling roses with one house-trained older person and some miraculously arrived babies. There are in Blake large faults, of drawing, or of impenetrability; but like Dickens – someone equally enthralled by the grotesque – Blake had genius.

He was poet, prose writer, painter, engraver and prophet. His work is all on a miniature scale: the engravings and illuminated pages are measurable in centimetres, and the paintings are small. But the imaginings are grand. Just as William Tyndale gave us the whole New Testament in English in all its enormous significance in little books to slip in a pocket, so all Blake's small books and pictures give a sense of being parts of a colossal vision of the world's histories and geographies, its mythologies and spiritual revelations, fragments of some unfallen world 'among the Rivers of Paradise' – a world of the unhindered energy of spiritual life.[15]

Blake's symbolic world

Blake is at once instantly and dramatically understandable, and totally baffling. The poem known to the world as *Jerusalem*, beginning 'And did those

feet', with the four imperatives, 'Bring me my Bow . . . Arrows . . . Spear
. . . Chariot . . .' and the ringing 'I will not cease from Mental Fight, /
Nor shall my sword sleep in my hand / Till we have built Jerusalem.
. . .' seems to express a sort of religious aspiration, when sung without
thought to Parry's rousing music. The poem prefaces Blake's long vision-
ary and didactic poem *Milton*, and it is a small miracle not of propaganda
for the Christian wing of the Green Party, but of statements of some of
Blake's disturbing system of symbols. An alert singer might just notice that
this city of Jerusalem (as in the poem) has no Divine King, whether King
David or Jehovah, at the heart of it: there are only 'feet', a 'Countenance
Divine' and a 'holy Lamb', on the literal level vague and fragmented.
Further, the famous 'dark Satanic Mills' are nothing whatever to do with
the Industrial Revolution, but are educational systems of logic and reason,
the work of Bacon, Newton and Locke. The four 'Brings' are for specific
mystic and sexual activity: and the whole is a challenge, as the words just
before the verse demonstrate, to the worlds of 'Corporeal War', to fashion
and advertising, to 'a Class of Men whose sole delight is in Destroying',
and 'Greek or Roman Models'.[16]

Blake's output of long visionary poetic works and paintings is immense.
His short lyrics and sketches catch in quite miraculous brevity the essences
of all his thought.[17] They are all, long poems, and short, and the paintings
which are integral to them, the workings-out of systems of symbols. These
symbols are age-old, and were only in the latter part of the twentieth
century seen and partly understood. The greatest series of paintings, almost
the last work he did, illustrate the Book of Job.

To approach those pictures, to educate the palate, I here consider four
works. The poem from *Songs of Experience*, 'The Tyger', was the product
of much labour through three versions. It is impossible to paraphrase – a
good sign of a symbol working well. It begins:

> Tyger, Tyger, burning bright,
> In the forests of the night;
> What immortal hand or eye,
> Could frame thy fearful symmetry?

The poem has a concentration of cosmic distance and depth, within a
single natural frame. Attempts to disentangle all the symbolic filaments do
not result in anything coherent: the poem and painting ask questions, of
which the poem is entirely made. None is answered. Even the illustrations
are inconsistent: they were made throughout Blake's working life, as
demanded. In some the tiger is a ferocious carnivore in lurid colours,
clearly a Tiger of Wrath. In others he is more of a stone lion, or a smiling
pussy-cat. It is in the nature of symbols to move about, for responses to

be different in different moods and at contrasting times, and for the symbol itself to reflect this.

The Tigers of Wrath in Blake are beasts of ferocious revolt as well as animals of predatory instinct which stalk the Child and the Lamb of Innocence. Here the tiger may be revolt in the forests of oppression, or it may be the burning ferocity of lustful energy circumscribed by mortality: or both, probably. So the first stanza, in twenty words only, juxtaposes the timeless immortal distances of forest and night, and measure, the mortal concentration of fixing the tiger's symmetry within a finite frame. The fifth stanza gathers another universe of meaning to the immensity he has already grasped.

> When the stars threw down their spears
> And water'd heaven with their tears:
> Did he smile his work to see?
> Did he who made the Lamb make thee?

'Tyger, tyger' is at one level a poem of creation. Blake has caught infinity within two burning eyes, and eternal action in a single deed.[18] The forests of the night are infinite forests of darkness as expounded in the important and wholly symbolic *The First Book of Urizen*. Urizen is the god-like force of calculation, reason, logic – the killing opposite of imagination, which is fire and true life. Urizen pretends to create, as it were by mathematics. The familiar painting 'The Ancient of Days', which is the frontispiece to *Europe, a Prophecy*, it shows Urizen, the Creator, in the act of defining the material world, which leads to death. The poem *Europe* describes through symbolic characters how man became subject to the laws of repressive religion and morality, and how these brought with them the evils of war, famine and plague.

Blake's symbolic language is difficult, though he worked within a tradition thousands of years old. If there is a single key to it, it is his defence of the prophetic tradition of the Bible against the rationalising of the classical inheritance. At the heart of that experience is the permanent conflict between the spiritual and the material, of which, Blake wrote, the spiritual is the only true reality. Swedenborg taught him the three states of life: the body, that is, life in material form; the mind, a spectral emanation from the body; and the true spiritual emanations. Since the Fall, Blake shows, creation has been divided, allowing one part, the hateful dominion of Reason and Law, 'Urizen', to arrogate to itself the ultimacy which can only be in divine unity. So 'Urizen' *prevents* reunion. Spiritual insight is the same as artistic imagination; the spiritual alone is real, so the imagination alone is real. Blake's attempt to unify design – painting, drawing, words – is one step towards imaginative, and therefore the ultimate and proper spiritual, unity. Blake's imagination throughout his life soared across the oceans that separate the stars; the forests of the night, the mountains and snows and floods, the shores of eternity, vista beyond vista, even beyond imagination. The fire burns in the uplifted hand, thunder and cloud arranged in solemn array against it. The forge and furnace, hammer and chain, make an incomparable integration of symbol and thought.

Description of an illustration from 1805 may help: *The Four and Twenty Elders casting their Crowns before the Divine Throne*, from a set of fifty small commissioned pictures of subjects from the Bible. Revelation 4:2–5:1 says in part:

> And immediately I was in the spirit; and, behold, a throne was set in heaven, and one sat upon the throne . . . and I saw the four and twenty elders sitting clothed in white raiment . . . and before the throne there was a sea of glass like unto crystal: and in the midst of the throne, and round about the throne, were four beasts full of eyes before and behind . . . And I saw in the right hand of him that sat on the throne a book written within and on the back side, sealed with seven seals . . . (KJV).

Blake's whole design is a striking sense of revelation, set about by gently symbolic eyes and faces to present the adoration of 'him that sat on the throne'. This is a spiritual version of even the spirituality of that revelation. All the items are observable, but there is a radiance at the heart which is very alluring. The spiritual world draws us in.

By contrast in visual strength are many paintings based on the Old Testament, especially Genesis, combining horror, power and an expressionist landscape, with unexpected delicacy. Examples are *The Body of Abel found by Adam and Eve; Cain, who was to bury it, fleeing from his Parents*, or *God judging Adam* (which for over a hundred years was thought to be *Elijah in the Fiery Chariot*). This elderly bearded God employs the tyranny of pure reason; the Jehovah of the Old Testament, or the Creator in *Elohim creating Adam*, are to Blake strikingly close to the symbolic figure of 'Urizen' as 'The Ancient of Days', quite without mercy, love or imagination.

In about 1818, Blake wrote the longish poem *The Everlasting Gospel*. The Prologue to that asks, noting the 'Moral Virtue' of Plato and Cicero . . . what then did Christ inculcate? Forgiveness of Sins. This alone is the Gospel, and this is the Life & Immortality brought to light by Jesus.'[19] The poem is against equating Christianity with simply moral virtues which are deadly, crucifying Jesus.

> The Vision of Christ that thou dost see
> Is my Vision's Greatest Enemy [. . .]
> Thine is the friend of All Mankind
> Mine speaks in parables to the Blind [. . .]
> Both read the Bible day & night,
> But thou read'st black where I read white.

At his forgiveness of the woman taken in adultery, Jesus' shocked enemies cried,

> '. . . Crucify this cause of distress,
> 'Who don't keep the secrets of holiness!
> 'All Mental Powers by Diseases we bind,
> 'But he heals the deaf & the dumb and the Blind.
> 'Whom God has afflicted for Secret Ends,
> 'He Comforts & Heals & calls them Friends.'

Blake adds

> I'm sure this Jesus will not do
> Either for Englishman or Jew.[20]

Blake's Jesus is wholly scriptural. For Blake, paramount in Jesus is the mystery of his divine nature. Blake struggled with a language of theology and symbol which had lost all meaning, or which had suffered distortion. Christianity for Blake is on the highest level of metaphysical discernment, equal to what is most profound in other traditions. His Jesus is a revelation of the Divine Presence, and thus is the vital and absolutely challenging presence of Imagination.

Between 1797 and 1800 Blake made thirty-seven tempera paintings, nine of which illustrate the childhood of Christ, themes 'which are rare in Protestant iconography but not uncommon in 16th–17th century Italian Catholic art'.[21] At Felpham, and for the same patron, Thomas Butts, he worked on a series of more than eighty watercolours of biblical subjects, twenty-seven on Old Testament subjects, five from St Paul, twelve from the Apocalypse and the majority on subjects from the Gospels. Blake's Bible paintings, always with figures dominating, and with stylised drapery and a two-dimensional quality, echo medieval book illumination.

Blake's illustrations to Job

Two years before his death, Blake engraved book illustrations which are a different world. In 1825, he was commissioned to produce twenty-two engravings to the Book of Job. In these we get his final word about the nature of God. With its strong characterisation of Job and his three friends, and the supernatural figures, that ancient long poem in the Old Testament about the undeserved suffering of a good man, who will not, as he is advised, 'curse God and die', works like a Greek tragedy, and it dates from about the same time as the *Oedipus* plays of Sophocles. Blake illustrates the poem faithfully. The twenty-two pictures, studied even with only a fraction of Blake's great learning, can, uniquely, open the Bible text for a reader.[22]

The prose opening sets the story of the 'perfect and upright' man Job in the land of Uz (which probably means he was a gentile), and then:

> Now there was a day when the sons of God came to present themselves before the Lord, and Satan came also among them. And the Lord said unto Satan, Whence comest thou? Then Satan answered the Lord, and said, From going to and fro in the earth, and from walking up and down in it. And the Lord said unto Satan, Hast thou considered my servant Job, that there is none like him in the earth, a perfect and an upright man, one that feareth God, and escheweth evil? (1:6–8, KJV).

So Satan is sent to try Job.

Satan (the name in Hebrew means no more than 'adversary') is already suggestive: half angel, half demon, a figure waiting for Blake, like the Everyman quality of Job and his wife, and his family and friends. The story of Job was always important to Blake (he first mentions it in *The Marriage of Heaven and Hell* of about 1793, and the Book of Job is in some ways parallel to Blake's *The Visions of the Daughters of Albion* of the same year). Here in these last engravings Blake follows the story faithfully. What he does with it, inside each engraving, is wholly his own, as he presents the spiritual meaning, against materialism, or what he calls 'Natural Religion'. For Blake, the mind is not, as Locke and his followers had taught, the mere passive recipient of sense impressions, but an active agent, which is capable of immeasurable thought.[23] Put briefly, the God of Blake's Job is the living Person who transcends reason, with a human face. Satan, the adversary, is earthly Selfhood.

The first picture shows Job and his extended family sitting piously and virtuously under a tree, a pastoral idyll, faithful to the biblical setting. That is fine, except that they are all static: piety has no movement. Virtue admits no conflict. Blake has shown the life of the family, viewed from outside, wholly admirable. The upper half of the second picture has energy: 'When the Almighty was yet with me, When my children were about me' (29:5) Here is seen that outer situation of Job in relation to his inner worlds. This is the beginning of Job's Day of Reckoning, the Day mentioned at the foot of the picture:

There was a day when the Sons of God came to present themselves before the Lord & Satan came among them, to present himself before the Lord.

Job is as yet spiritually unawakened: he has not fallen into the power of Satan the Selfhood, who makes his entry – from the evil side, the left – before the enthroned God Within. At the top of the picture is the Angel of the Divine Presence, with an unclouded halo, the living light of the spiritual sun; and above, the Hebrew *Yahweh Elohim*. The face of the Angel of the Divine Presence is Job's face. He is now waking up to the fact that he, like all human beings, is made in the divine image, or imagination. The Angel of the Presence is pointing to a scroll which six angels are unrolling on the highest step of the throne – completing the circle with 'Hast thou considered my servant Job' and so very probably the record of Job's blameless life. The Angel's right foot is forward, right here being the side of mercy. Satan appears with three figures, and together they make what Blake called the four energies of Job's psyche: reason, feeling, sensation and intuition, of which one – 'Urizen' the reasoner – has become Satan. (Blake called the four 'the Zoas', possibly after Ezekiel in the Greek Septuagint, perhaps 1:15.) On either side of Satan are faintly seen Job and his wife. Below, the rigid family group of the first plate has now been disturbed: the sons and daughters have withdrawn, and are questioning. Two angels are showing Job the scroll. Job is pointing to the book in his hand, saying he has obeyed the Law. It is still a pastoral world, with shepherd and shepherdess and sheep-fold gates in the margins. Blake is beginning to move beyond the empirical mind into the mind beyond reason, the prophetic tradition of the Jews.

Two plates of increasing external disaster to Job follow, and the fifth illustration (fig. 39) is like the second, but now the spiritual world, the 'Family Divine', has been silently removing, no longer able to visit Job in his unknown world, and looking down in alarm. 'Then went Satan forth from the presence of the Lord', that is, back into Job's inner world. This engraving shows the transfer of power and energy from the eternal to the temporal world: Satan in the centre is wakeful and active, funnelling, almost squirting, his material and mortal energies on to Job. But the God Within is drowsy, his book closed and the scroll in his left hand relinquished. His halo is now darkening. Below, Job and his wife are desolate, giving coldly in charity (the loaf of bread seems to weigh heavily, like a stone) to a blind beggar and his drooping dog. Job and his wife are descending into the material world, the rocky landscape, matter which is solid and lifeless. In the margin the serpent appears, a symbol of matter because an eater of dust (Gen. 3:14). The quotation from Psalm 104 below, is quoted in Hebrews 1:7. 'Who maketh his Angels Spirits & his Ministers a Flaming Fire'.

Omitting three more of disasters, we come to the first climax of the inner world. 'Then a Spirit passed before my face: the hair of my flesh stood up'. This is from Job 4, the first speech of one of the three friends or 'Comforters', Eliphaz the Temanite, in which he describes a dream – you can see him expounding it with his hand reaching up into the cloud of unconsciousness. In Job 4:12, he says,' Now a thing was secretly brought to me, and mine ear received a little thereof.' This is a breaking-through of a new revelation, which, in what several native races in the world call a Big Dream, can come once or twice in a lifetime.

> In thoughts from the visions of the night, when deep sleep falleth on men,
> Fear came upon me, and trembling, which made all my bones to shake.
> Then a spirit passed before my face; the hair of my flesh stood up:
> It stood still, but I could not discern the form thereof: an image was before mine eyes, there was silence, and I heard a voice, saying,
> Shall mortal man be more just than God? Shall a man be more pure than his maker? (4:13–17, KJV).

The cloud opens to reveal those inner spaces which exist not for the senses but for the imagination; an opening of consciousness, the first opening of Job's spiritual understanding. The standing figure is haloed in the aura of the inner light, a 'deep and dazzling darkness' powerfully communicating Eliphaz's partial understanding and sense of unapprehended meaning, and the elusiveness of a dream. In the margins are leafless trees, branches bending to touch the ground.

Omitting another, of external scorning, we come to *With Dreams upon my Bed thou scarest me and affrightest me with Visions*. Now Job's tribulation reaches an ultimate horror, Satan appearing as the God of This World, assuming the aspect of the Most High. Hell seems to close in on Job. He lies on the couch of death obsessed by the 'reasoning spectre'. The same dream horror Blake had given to Jesus in an earlier painting, *Christ's Ugly Dream*. This false God, 'the very cruel being', appears throughout Blake's work, and is 'Urizen'. Flames are the only marginal decoration. Chief of the texts is 'Satan is transformed into an Angel of Light & his Ministers into Ministers of Righteousness', adapted from 2 Corinthians 11:14. At the foot, from 2 Thessalonians 2:4, 'Who opposeth and exalteth himself above all that is called God or that is worshipped.' Above that are two quotations from Job, his protest, and his famous prophetic vision of the final knowledge of Jesus Christ, 'I know that my Redeemer liveth . . .'

(19:25–7). Blake has changed KJV to read, instead of 'though my reins be consumed within me', 'though consumed by my wrought image', a possible reading of the difficult Hebrew phrase – the idol Selfhood here depicted. He has the cloven hoof, horns, cruel mouth, hard eyes, of 'Selfhood', or empirical ego, which knows no other world than mortality, and so frames laws. This self-sufficient rational mind is 'Urizen', which declares spiritual vision and the Imagination to be 'delusion and fancy', with something to lose,' its own delight'. It is selfish in the familiar sense, as materialism has always to be: the living Imagination is a region of freedom, boundless, eternal, immortal.

There follow, after another 'external' portrayal, two exceptional engravings. The first is *Then the Lord answered Job out of the Whirlwind* (fig. 35). Suddenly Job can see in his internal world the power and majesty of the spirit of God. His amazement and awe are at his 'second birth'. Even the left side is redeemed. The previous picture was the natural man, human Selfhood. This is the spiritual man, human Imagination, with new energy in wind (i.e. spirit) but also a gentle face, taking up from *Songs of Innocence*, 'The Divine Image',

> For Mercy has a human heart,
> Pity a human face,
> And Love, the human form divine,
> And Peace the human dress.

Caught in the whirlwind round the margin are the properly divine Elohim, the seven spirits of God. It is important to recognise that God here for the first time is seeing Job, that recognition from above which is the true beginning of identity, whether from the mother's face to the infant, or God to the emerging person.

The next, *When the morning Stars sang together, & all the Sons of God shouted for joy*, is a picture of the Imagination of God, who for the first time is central, crouched but alert, his right foot of mercy forward, his arms extended, as on the Cross: a rich picture indeed. The words are from chapter 38, given to the Lord answering Job 'out of the whirlwind', about his transcendent powers of creation, a chapter entirely in questions. Verses 4–7 begin the relentless demands with 'Where wast thou when I laid the foundations of the earth?', the moment celebrated in the song of the morning stars and the Sons of God. As Job is reborn in the creative act of the shift of centre, finding God, not the human Selfhood, there, so he, his wife and his three friends now sit 'looking upwards in attitudes of attentive listening as they receive the teaching of the God Within'.[24]

Of the remaining seven, the most significant is the sixteenth, entitled *Thou hast fulfilled the Judgment of the Wicked*. This is a vital stage on the inner journey, showing Satan's final end. Under the title is written, from Luke 10:17–18, 'Even the Devils are Subject to Us thro thy Name. Jesus said unto them, I saw Satan as lightning fall from Heaven.' Satan, now fully darkened, is falling headlong (with echoes of Michelangelo's *Last Judgement* which Blake admired) accompanied by a male and a female figure, which are the 'Selfhoods' of Job and his wife, which had entered with Satan in the second engraving. Job's three friends peek at this with terror: Job and his wife gaze fully on it in penitent meekness. The radiant forms of Job's two guardian cherubim witness the fall of Satan. Satan is enveloped in flame. He, and his dark flames, are arranged to look like a shadow or reflection cast by the enthroned Imagination. Above that are two child-angels weeping, presumably in acts of repentance as they live in the new spiritual world. At the foot is 1 Corinthians. 1:27 'God hath chosen the foolish things of the World to confound the wise. And God hath chosen the Weak things of the World to confound the things that are mighty.' By God's right hand are three child-spirits, another by his left.

Satan is making a dramatic exit from the story of Job. Blake always argued that there is no Satan, only the 'Satanic State' of Selfhood – that is, not dualism, but supreme God, Imagination, and then nothing. Satan entered and set in motion his own sequence of events and experiences, but as Job awoke to his inner world, God – Imagination – triumphed.

The event is followed by 'I have heard thee with the hearing of the Ear but now my Eye Seeth thee'. The words are from the last chapter of Job (42:5), the culmination. God is no longer hearsay, but vision, the God of whose Presence, as the Divine Body of the God Within, Job had in his first state been unconscious. Now he stands before him in human form, blessing Job and his wife. There is no longer any division between Job's inner or outer world, and Job and his wife are now within the sphere of the radiance. The three friends are unable to face the Presence (but curious) and bow themselves turned away in fear. The figure of the God of Job 'in the form of a man' is the Divine Humanity, but does not resemble any representation of Jesus. Blake respects his Old Testament source.

The female angel on the right of that margin, surrounded by words from John's Gospel about the Father's love, is about to wake. There are four more engravings closing the external story in great happiness.

REALISM, AND VICTORIAN ENERGY

Romantic interest in the exotic East was a strand in the growing fashion, towards the middle of the century, for books recording with new accuracy both the places mentioned in Scripture and the traditions found

there. Some of these spilled into lavish editions of the Bible, particularly
in America, where every large page could show, as islands in the columns
of print, half a dozen miniature pictures, of views or customs referred to
in the text. A new realism went with the idea 'that inner truth could be
achieved by historical accuracy',[25] an idea that appealed to both the new
rationalism whereby 'Jesus was a wise man but not a magician',[26] and to
the High Church Tractarians trying with some success to follow Catholic
emancipation in 1829 with the revival of High Church medievalism. Both
movements were important for the Pre-Raphaelite painters, and it is one
of those, Holman Hunt, who will make the second example of biblical
painting in the nineteenth century.

'Victorian' as a term is more than just useful: it is explicit. The useful-
ness is demonstrated by Lionel Lambourne in the first paragraphs of his
Victorian Painting (1999):

> The future Queen Victoria was born in 1819, ascended the throne in
> 1837 and died in 1901. She reigned for 63 years, longer than any pre-
> vious monarch, and gave her name to a great period of English history,
> social life and artistic endeavours. As decorative art terms the words
> *Early*, *Mid*, *High* or *Late* Victorian are readily understood from Kansas
> to Karachi and Canberra to Canada. The convenient brevity of these
> phrases makes them more useful than the cumbersome alternatives of
> 'third quarter of the nineteenth century', or 'during the second Presi-
> dency of Grover Cleveland (1892–6).'[27]

The explicitness of the word, still unpopular in some influential parts of
academia, brings with it the exuberance of Victorian art, its absolute confidence in whatever genre, from narrative to panorama, from portraits to
social realism, and in the high thinking that motivated so much of it.
Certainly at times, and in parts of society, propriety dictated what could
– or rather, what could not – be exhibited. Not always acceptable, for
example, would be a voluptuous painting by William Etty in which a
young woman's clothes were exquisitely delineated, in a heap beside the
pool. Again, sometimes attempts at strong sentiment deteriorated into the
sentimental. Yet the last word that could be applied to Victorian painting
is 'stuffy'. Queen Victoria herself 'in 1853 expressed admiration for
Mulready's drawings of the nude, brushing aside officials who tried to
prevent her seeing them in an exhibition'.[28] In the previous year she had
bought for Albert's birthday Franz Xavier Winterhalter's *Florinda*, a large
and eloquent painting of young women, most of them almost unclothed
and all wonderfully grouped and lit, which she found 'most lovely' and
hung in her sitting-room at Osborne.[29]

The expressive human body, whether nude and unbashful, or clothed and with a speaking presence (as in a Sargent portrait) or multiplied in amused social richness (as in Frith's *Derby Day*) is what is celebrated in any broad exhibition of Victorian art. The prime theorist was John Ruskin, who never attended a life class, but whose enthusiasm for 'minuteness of handling and complete naturalism'[30] influenced artists of all kinds – Etty, who found 'God's most glorious work to be Woman', dedicated himself to painting her 'more finely than had ever been done'.[31]

RUSKIN AWAKENS HUNT

Most Victorian painters took many biblical subjects: it is odd a century and a half later to contemplate exhibitions of advanced modern art in which the Bible is so present. Holman Hunt's progress to understanding solutions to his artistic problems is linked to his attempts to convey spiritual truths through the illumination of verses from the Bible: most famously, then, as now, of Revelation 3:20. 'Behold, I stand at the door and knock: if any man hear my voice, and open the door, I will come into him, and sup with him, and he with me': the original of Hunt's *The Light of the World* (the title is from John 8) hangs in Keble College, Oxford. To this I shall return.

Ruskin was for thirty years the defender of the Pre-Raphaelite Brotherhood. This small group of accomplished painters was founded in 1848 by the ex-Florentine Dante Gabriel Rossetti, originally as a secret society: they signed their paintings at their first exhibition in 1849 only with 'PRB'. The initials, and name, which were soon revealed, stood for a protest against the conventional 'grand manner'. Millais and Holman Hunt defined that as having distorted truth of feeling from the time of the Florentine Raphael (1483–1520). Ruskin, in his doctrine of fidelity to nature and detail, and his skill at exposition of biblical typology, had already awoken Holman Hunt with two paragraphs in the second volume of his *Modern Painters* (1846) on Tintoretto's *The Annunciation* (Luke 1:26–38), one of the series in the Scuola di San Rocco, Venice (1585–7). Ruskin wrote that, startled by the rush of angel wings,

the Virgin sits . . . houseless, under the shelter of a palace vestibule ruined and abandoned, with the noise of the axe and the hammer in her ears, and the tumult of a city round about her desolation. The spectator turns away at first, revolted, from . . . a mass of shattered brick-work, with the plaster mildewed away from it, and the mortar mouldering from its seams . . . nothing more than such a study of scene as Tintoret could but too easily obtain among the ruins of his own Venice, chosen to give a coarse explanation of the calling and the condition of the husband of Mary.

Beyond the merely picturesque, however, 'the whole symmetry' of the picture highlights 'a white stone, four square, the corner-stone of the old edifice, the base of its supporting column'. This, Ruskin suggests, sufficiently explains the typology of the whole.

> The ruined house is the Jewish dispensation; that obscurely arising in the dawning of the sky is the Christian; but the corner-stone of the old building remains, though the builders' tools lie idle beside it, and the stone which the builders refused is become the Headstone of the Corner.[32]

The last words are, of course, from Psalm 118, quoted by Jesus about himself, as 'the Lord's doing', in all three Synoptic Gospels (Matthew 21:42; Mark 12:10; Luke 20:17), an identification picked up by Peter in Acts 4:11, and repeated in 1 Peter 2:7 – in other words, Ruskin's interpretation is fully biblical, and he would be confident that his readers would understand at once.

The impact on Hunt was great. In his *Pre-Raphaelitism and the Pre-Raphaelite Brotherhood* (1905), Hunt recalls telling Millais that Ruskin's descriptions of Venetian painting make you 'see them with your inner sight, and you feel that the men who did them had been appointed by God, like old prophets, to bear a sacred message . . . [Tintoretto's 'Annunciation'] suggests an appropriateness in Joseph's occupation of a carpenter, that at first one did not recognise; he is the new builder!'[33] In that book he tells how he and Ruskin visited the Scuola in 1869 and first stood before the painting. Ruskin had not looked at those pages of *Modern Painters* for many years, and in front of the picture he read the paragraphs aloud. Hunt wrote: 'The words brought back to my mind the little bedroom, twenty-two years since, wherein I sat till the early morning reading the same passage with marvel.'[34] Hunt's direct examination of the painting, he was gratified to find, supported Ruskin's interpretation: 'there could be no doubt that Tintoretto had the purpose to suggest the desolation that had come upon the existing Israelitish Church, and its replacement by a new edifice.'[35]

Hunt's particular combination of realism and an intricate symbolism, a considerable technical achievement, was born of his excitement at imagining Tintoretto's discovery of it in that 'Annunciation' painting. He wrote:

> I thought what happiness Tintoretto must have felt when he had this illuminating thought presented to him, and of his joy in carrying it out

on canvas, and was wondering how few were the men who had pondered over the picture to read it thoroughly, until in fulness of time the decipherer came along and made it clear.[36]

Hunt links that joy with his understanding of what it signifies.

When language was not transcendental enough to complete the meaning of a revelation, symbols were relied upon for heavenly teaching, and familiar images, chosen from the known, were made to mirror the unknown spiritual truth. The forerunners and contemporaries of Tintoretto had consecrated the custom, to which he gave a larger value and more original meaning. How far such symbolism is warranted depends on its unobtrusiveness and its restriction within limits not destroying natural beauty. There is no more reason why the features belonging to a picture should be distorted for the purpose of such imaginative suggestiveness than that the poet's metaphors should spoil his words for ordinary uses of man. Tintoretto's meaning was expressed with no arbitrary or unnatural disturbance of the truth.[37]

Some years later Hunt wrote in a letter to Ruskin that before he had read him, he had been 'a contemptuous unbeliever in any spiritual principle but the development of talent, and Shelley and Lord Byron and Keats were my best modern heroes – all read by the light of materialism – or sensualism.' Ruskin's paragraphs spoke to him with 'the voice of God. I read this in rapture and it sowed some seed of shame.' Indeed, 'All that the Pre-Raphaelite Brotherhood had of Ruskinism came from this reading of mine.'[38]

The Pre-Raphaelites did not have a monopoly of medievalism, and Victorian art, even at its most symbolic, was not by any means only religious. Holman Hunt's biblical paintings, exceptionally popular and some still admired, may stand, however, for a great deal of representation of the Bible in English painting during the long life of Victoria.

TYPOLOGY

Ruskin in *Modern Painters* showed, especially in the earlier volumes, his understanding of biblical typology. Brought up strongly Evangelical, ingrained within him was the typological exposition in the New Testament especially in Paul's Epistles and in the Epistle to the Hebrews – indeed, the latter was seminal, in its typological interpretation of key Old Testament ideas of spiritual exodus, ritual and liturgy.[39] Chapters 8 and 9 of the Epistle to the Hebrews discuss the Old and New Covenants. Hebrews 9:19 has 'For when Moses had spoken every precept to all the people according to the law, he took the blood of calves and of goats, with water, and scarlet wool, and hyssop, and sprinkled both the book, and all the people.' Behind this verse is a network of Old Testament passages on which the typology depends, including Exodus 12 for the first Passover (with hyssop at Exodus 12:22); Exodus 24:6–8; Leviticus 14:4–6, 16–17:11 and chapters 23–32 for the great Day of Atonement; Numbers 19:1–10 for the ritual sacrifice of the 'Red cow without blemish' (Numbers 19:6 for hyssop); Psalm 51:7. Compare also John 19:36–7 with Exodus 12:46, Psalm 34:20, and 1 Corinthians 5:7. Ruskin's Coniston Notebook gives the central series of his sermons, including 10 'The law of sacrifice', 11 'Sacrifices of the old law', and 12 'Sacrificial ceremonies', and from Notebook iv:13 'The annual atonement'.[40]

Ruskin fully understood the sharp distinction between typology and allegory. Though the New Testament does at one point use allegory (in Paul's account of Hagar at Galatians 4:22–31) the allegorical method of interpreting Scripture did not come into Christianity until Origen in the fourth century: it was the subject of strong attack by all the Reformers, on the grounds of the danger of making Scripture mean anything the Church needed it to mean. In allegory, the first term is discardable once the secondary meaning has been understood. In typology, in complete contrast, both poles remain fully alive. Thus Jesus himself makes a typological interpretation of his own death and resurrection by reference to Jonah and the whale. We are thus to see all the content of that prophecy present (including divine intervention, events in nature, and above all the call to preach the Word of God universally) in the interaction of interpretation between the Old Testament prophetic insight and the New Testament fact of death and the Resurrection. For the Reformers, whose Scripture had to be both complete and self-interpreting, typology, thus blessed by Jesus, allowed a place in the life of Christian congregations for even the remotest sections of, for example, the Book of Leviticus, now seen to be a type of ritual sacrifice relating to Christ's Passion.

This Evangelical training lay at the root of Ruskin's earliest thinking, aligned with Carlyle and Coleridge, especially his central understanding that reality was essentially spiritual and a reflection of the Divine principle. Ruskin is able to see aspects of the visible world as 'types' of aspects of the nature of God. He moved on from this point towards full engagement with criticisms of society (culminating in 'Unto this last' of 1860, only fully printed in 1906 but greatly influential).

THE PRE-RAPHAELITES

Ruskin was drawn reluctantly to the support of the Brotherhood – they were harshly criticised – but the poet Coventry Patmore prevailed upon

Ruskin to write to *The Times* in their defence. Ruskin admitted to a 'very uncertain sympathy', fearing High Church, even Roman Catholic leanings: but he was able to find in the painting *Convent Thoughts* (1851), a picture by Charles Collins, associated with the Brotherhood, in spite of the clearly pro-Catholic intention, room for high praise of the painter's depiction of a leaf: he wrote 'I never saw it so thoroughly or so well drawn'. Behind the praise lay his understanding that the leaf and its plants were almost divine prototypes in shape and structure of the work of God in making the natural world. In a similar vein Ruskin was able to interpret geology – not for nothing does the celebrated portrait of him by Millais show him standing thoughtfully on a rock in a Scottish stream. Ruskin's defence was effective and by 1853 Rossetti's brother wrote 'We have emerged from reckless abuse to a position of general and high recognition.'

The Brotherhood's techniques of brilliant colour on a flat white base, of a complete avoidance of theatrical lighting for artificial shadows and an attempt to use medieval aspirations to art with a high spiritual content, drew them to illumination of texts or scenes from the Bible. These paintings were full of careful detail, where the research could have been carried to extreme lengths (as in the case of Hunt working by the shore of the Dead Sea for *The Scapegoat*). They were not illustrations of the kind popular in America which we might call 'Lands and Life in the Time of our Lord'. Controlling the image was a unified and integrated symbolism which responded to observation, thought and meditation over a long period – as with Ruskin's interpretation of *The Annunciation* by Tintoretto.

Holman Hunt was the theoretician of the Brotherhood and his belief (which did not last all his life) that nature was the handiwork of God allowed him to produce extraordinary paintings, not always derided at the time or since: they still do warrant great attention. He successfully drew on typological symbolism for *The Scapegoat*, *The Finding of the Saviour in the Temple*, *The Triumph of the Innocents*, *The Shadow of the Cross* and many more. His *The Light of the World* (fig. 40) was his triumph in combining realism, vision and religious iconography, and all in a way which was immediately accessible, as shown by the painting's continual popularity in Europe and North America ever since it was painted in 1851–3.

Hunt's The Light of the World

The figure of Christ is solid. Hunt wrote to a friend,

> In England as you know spiritual figures are painted as if in vapour [. . . here . . .] it is the Christ that is alive for ever more [. . .] firmly and substantially there waiting for the sleeping soul.[41]

The lighting combines the symbolic and the natural. There is in the natural light of the dawn and the moon a promise of a new day, a new life once the soul awakens to Christ. It is a night scene, as Hunt pointed out, 'lit mainly by the lantern carried by Christ'. He 'had followed metaphorical explanation in the Psalms, "Thy word is a lamp unto my feet, and a light unto my path" [Psalm 119:105], with also the accordant allusions by St Paul to the sleeping soul, "The night is far spent, the day is at hand."[Romans 13:12].'

Hunt wished to use natural symbolic language drawn from reflectiveness rather than iconographic traditions.

> The closed door was the absolutely shut mind, the weeds the cumber of daily neglect, the accumulated hindrances of sloth, the orchard the garden of delectable fruit for the dainty feast of the soul. The music of the still small voice was the summons to the sluggard to awaken and become a zealous labourer under the Divine Master: the bat flitting about only in darkness was a natural symbol of ignorance; the kingly and priestly dress of Christ, the sign of His reign over the body and the soul [. . .][42]

Hunt might have added to the reference to Elijah (1 Kings 19:12), to Proverbs (6:9) and to the Epistle to the Hebrews (*passim*) the force of the parables of Jesus, as in that of the Sower (Matthew 13, Luke 8).

Whereas Blake's Job engravings had to endure imprisonment in scorn for two centuries, Hunt's *The Light of the World* immediately generated, and still does, not only perpetual reproductions, and pilgrimages to see the original in the chapel of Keble College, but, later in the nineteenth century a host of now-forgotten poems.[43] It is a painting in which Hunt achieved something rare, the confident combination of Pre-Raphaelite realism, imaginative vision and true Christian power, in which the biblical typology allows continual revelation of new meaning.

Chapter 37

THE ENGLISH REVISED VERSION, 1870–1885

A TROUBLED START

On Thursday 10 February 1870, Dr Samuel Wilberforce, Bishop of
Winchester, who was presiding, submitted a proposal to the Convocation
of Canterbury:

> That a Committee of both Houses [that is, the Upper and Lower
> Houses of the Church of England's Convocation of the Province of
> Canterbury] be appointed, with power to confer with any Committee
> that may be appointed by the Convocation of the Northern Province
> [that is, in York] to report upon the desirableness of a revision of the
> Authorized Version of the New Testament, whether by marginal notes
> or otherwise, in all those passages where plain and clear errors, whether
> in the Hebrew or Greek text originally adopted by the translators, or
> in the translation made from the same, shall, on due investigation, be
> found to exist.[1]

This, rather odd in its inclusion of Hebrew for the New Testament (just
possibly uncorrected from a larger proposal to include the whole Bible,
but still unfortunate) was apparently a simple, straightforward statement.
The outcome was complicated.

In making the proposal, Bishop Wilberforce said:

> I think it is the clear and bounden duty of the Church, as the putter
> forth to the people of the Word Of God, to use every means within
> her power to see that which she does put forth to the people is the
> very word of God.[2]

He would change only those passages which conveyed a wrong impression, either from the text used or from the changes in language. The public
awareness of the unreliability of the Authorised Version is, he said, a danger.

> I think that the wide-spread conviction of such a state of things among
> our people is one likely to be of the most damaging effect, especially
> upon those who are not critical scholars themselves, but who pick these

matters up from the oft-repeated statements in the public prints [. . .]
I think that instead of avoiding evil by shutting these things up when
they have become thoroughly matters of public knowledge – instead of
avoiding scandal and the danger of shaking the minds of any men, and
making them regard Scripture with less reverence, by altering nothing
and consenting to examine nothing, we do for these weak brethren
raise a stumbling-block which we could remove if with knowledge and
power we moderately and wisely, but determinedly, entered upon the
matter.[3]

The meeting on that day consisted of twelve bishops. The Bishop of
Gloucester and Bristol, C. J. Ellicott, who was to be of great importance
in the enterprise, said that he had scruples about revision, though use
needed to be made of the Codex Sinaiticus, which had been discovered
in 1844. He was aware of important textual errors in AV, for example the
doxology at the end of the Lord's Prayer, and the last verses of Mark,
the latter error having 'historical and even doctrinal importance'.[4] The
Bishop of St David's mentioned three common objections to revision: the
need to wait for further advances in biblical scholarship; the dangers of
creating a division between a 'Church' Bible and a 'Dissenting' Bible
(Dissenters should be invited to take part in revision): and clergy might
be alienated by changes to some of their 'favourite texts', like Haggai 19,
'the desire of all nations' (again an odd remark, it being a prophetic book
assuredly not in the New Testament). The Bishop of Lincoln suggested
that new renderings could be put in the margins, and if in time found to
be sound, might eventually, if officially approved, be read out in churches.
The Bishop of Lichfield proposed asking the British and Foreign Bible
Society for 'the assistance of some of their leading members', as the Society
is a 'highly important and influential organ, to whose decisions [Non-
conformist bodies] will naturally yield assent.'[5]

The following day, Friday 11 February 1870, the Lower House, suggesting fourteen nominees for what was now 'Revision of the Old and
New Testaments', proposed 'that the Convocations of Armagh and Dublin,
as well as the Convocation of York, be communicated with on this important inquiry'.[6] A Canon Selwyn added, 'However much we may differ in
opinion about the Ritualists, we may thank them for bringing this subject
under the notice of the Upper House, for it arose out of the Lectionary
Committee'[7] – a remark interesting both as revealing conflicts, and true
origins of the call for this revision, that a prime concern was the Bible as
read aloud in churches.

There the matter rested for a while.

Since the day it appeared, there had always been felt a need to improve and correct KJV, and expositions – often strongly worded – of both errors and necessary changes had been regularly published. These rose in number and in strength in the first sixty years of the nineteenth century, as the implications of newly found Greek texts (like the Codex Sinaiticus) and new scholarly methods were understood.[8] That there had been in the first half of the nineteenth century a noticeable falling-off of interest in KJV can be demonstrated by the figures for sales from Cambridge University Press. These show a very sharp rise in Bibles and Testaments sold between 1810 and 1850, even to nearly 450,000 in 1840. By 1850 the total had fallen to just over 66,000.[9] As recently as 22 July 1856 a motion had been presented to the House of Commons urging the Crown to appoint a Royal Commission to undertake a major revision of AV. The proposer, Mr James Heywood, MP for North Lancashire, referred to a recent sermon to the Queen on the text 'Be not slothful in business' (Romans 12:11): Mr Heywood said that the verse should actually be translated 'Be not backward in zeal'. He further pressed the point that in the United States a society had been formed to revise the Bible, the American Bible Union. For the government, Sir George Grey replied that the adoption of the Motion would 'tend to unsettle the faith of the great body of the people'. The Motion was withdrawn.[10] The Revd S. C. Malan, Vicar of Broadwindsor, published *A Vindication . . .* , rejoicing over the failure of Mr Heywood's motion.[11] Three years later, in 1859, no less a star than the Baptist preacher C. H. Spurgeon, in his Preface to a book on the English Bible, argued for revision, not replacement of AV: 'it ought to be done, and must be done. The present version is not to be despised, but no candid person can be blind to its faults . . . I love God's Word better than I love King James's pedantic wisdom and foolish kingcraft.'[12]

A good deal of notice had been taken of the volume published in 1857, *The Gospel According to St. John, after the Authorised Version; Newly Compared with the Original Greek and Revised*, by Five Clergymen.[13] The five included C. J. Ellicott, the Bishop of Gloucester and Bristol who would go on to reply to Bishop Wilberforce in Convocation in February 1870, and G. Moberly, later Bishop of Salisbury, who also spoke then – indeed, four of the Five became members of the New Testament Revision Company. They pointed out in their Preface (by Moberly) that such revision had been discussed extensively and for some time past, producing polarised and exaggerated opinion about the extent of AV's mistakes, either representing them as far greater and more considerable than they are, or almost wholly denying their existence.[14] They went on to publish their revisions of Romans and of 1 Corinthians in 1858.

The meeting of the Upper House on Tuesday 3 May 1870 carried the matter further. At that meeting, five resolutions were passed: that revision be undertaken; that it affect margins as well as text; not to make a new translation; to make changes in the style of the existing version; and to appoint their own members to undertake it with help where needed from 'whatever nation or religious body'.[15] Two days later, on Thursday 5 May, the Lower House, receiving the five resolutions, debated the matter at length, confusedly and with heat; the record shows muddle – Archdeacon Ady protested that the House did not know what it was voting on.[16] There was dismay at what was not clear, and real alarm, not only about dreadful outsiders who might be invited to have a hand. A Dr Fraser summed up other fears:

> If into this version we now insert the lancet of critical revision, we shall, unless we act with very great caution, be cutting, or may cut, through the very nerves of faith; we may wound the arteries of the soul, and spill on the ground the life-blood of many souls both amongst ourselves and those Dissenting bodies which have grown up under the shadow of the Establishment; and we may do this without any adequate result.[17]

After high-flying arguments about everything in sight, and beyond, including how unfair it was that the Lower House could nominate only an equal number of participants as the Upper House, the motion was carried by twenty-three to seven.[18]

The general principles on which both companies of revisers were instructed to proceed were: (1) to introduce as few alterations as possible into the text of the Authorised Version, consistently with faithfulness; (2) to limit, as far as possible, the expression of such alterations to the language of the Authorised and earlier English versions; (3) each Company to go twice over the portion to be revised, once provisionally, the second time finally, and on principles of voting as hereinafter is provided; (4) that the text to be adopted be that for which the evidence is decidedly preponderating; and that when the text so adopted differs from that from which the Authorised Version was made, the alteration be indicated in the margin; (5) to make or retain no change in the text on the second final revision by each Company, except two-thirds of those present approve of the same, but on the first revision to decide by simple majorities; (6) in every case of proposed alteration that may have given rise to discussion, to defer the voting thereupon till the next Meeting, whensoever the same shall be required by one-third of those present at the Meeting, such intended vote to be announced in the notice for the next Meeting; (7) to revise the headings of chapters, pages, paragraphs, italics and punctuation; (8) to refer, on the part of each Company, when considered desirable, to Divines, Scholars, and Literary men, whether at home or abroad, for their opinions.[19]

IMMEDIATE PROBLEMS

There were five immediate problems: the first was Wilberforce himself. T. H. Huxley had declared that he would rather be descended from a humble monkey than a man such as Bishop Wilberforce.[20] Newly Bishop of Winchester, Samuel Wilberforce had been Bishop of Oxford for twenty-four years: in 1854 he had founded Cuddesdon Theological College (still influential a century and half later). Well known for his pastoral initiatives and encouragement of the building of churches, he was perhaps less admired as a scholar, as his startling inclusion of 'Hebrew' in revision of the New Testament might show. The Bishop of Gloucester and Bristol, C. J. Ellicott (the leader of the Five Clergymen) wrote in a private letter:

> My only care is to keep him as much out of the chair as can cleverly be done. He has not criticism enough for it, and he gave mortal offence to some during his short tenure of the chair. I received private notice that resignations would be sent in if I did not continue some adjustment.[21]

Ellicott had already written to Wilberforce, as early as 31 May 1870:

> I think I must ask you to give me a position of authority, so as better to negotiate, direct etc., in all details. If you don't mind, then, I will ask you to be general chairman, i.e. of the whole concern and its parts, and I will ask you to constitute me company chairman.[22]

Wilberforce did not attend revision sessions 'owing to the enormous pressure of the work of the Winchester diocese'.[23] He died in 1873.

The second difficulty was that the Convocation of York was not co-operative – Wilberforce had to admit that he had been mistaken. A resolution was adopted by them in which they stated that:

> although blemishes existed in [the text of the Authorised Version] such as had from time to time been pointed out, yet they would deplore any recasting of the text. [They did not] accordingly think it necessary to appoint a Committee to co-operate with the Committee appointed by the Convocation of Canterbury, though favourable to the errors being corrected.[24]

Wilberforce had originally said: 'I speak without committing any breach of confidence when I say that such a plan would meet with the approval of his Grace the president of the Northern Convocation.'[25] The two Joint Committees could then agree on textual and translational revision, pressing for the appointment of a Royal Commission, which could then revise their work. 'If there were a consensus of opinion in the Royal Commission and in the two Houses of Convocation in each of the provinces of England, we should have guarded sufficiently against the danger of rash, immature and unwise changes.'[26]

The Convocation of York felt differently. At the session on 23 February 1870, the Bishop of Carlisle said that he 'could not disguise from himself that there were very great dangers connected with the scheme proposed . . . He would not, on any account, touch the present version.' The Archbishop himself, William Thompson, spoke of one result being a translation greatly altered and modified . . . that would have suffered severely in the process. 'Was the Bible to be laid on the table of the anatomist and subjected to this rude process? [. . .] The Nonconformists deeply valued the authorised version: they had circulated it by millions and millions, and they had contributed some of the most eminent names to this particular branch of study.' He had been surprised by the Southern Convocation, and was 'almost dazzled and dizzy by the rapidity of Church movement in this time. [. . .] He begged for a little breathing time before they sent their beloved Bible to the crucible to be melted down and recast. (Applause).'[27] And so on, and so on. Here is the first powerful statement of opposition: the extreme touchiness of AV's defenders is visible in all the reports of the York discussions. There would be more in this vein.

The third difficulty was over the inclusion of Americans. On 7 July 1870 in the Lower House of the Convocation of Canterbury, Lord Compton moved 'That the joint Committee on Revision may associate with themselves one or more divines of the American Church.'[28] This was carried, but many questioned the motion afterwards, partly on the grounds of practicality and partly of consistency. (The American relationship will be discussed below, and in the following chapter.) Meanwhile, what was revealed was a lurking problem about whether the phrase 'the American Church' could be construed as 'fixing a limit of communion with our own'.[29] Dr Jebb, Canon of Hereford, said, 'I cordially support the spirit of the resolution, but to commit ourselves to any formal recognition of any sects or divisions among Christians is, I think, foreign to our duty as the Convocation of the Church of England.'[30] This ambiguous remark is capable of meaning both ultimate ecumenism, making no distinctions at all between any who confess that Jesus is Lord, impossible in 1870, and a refusal to acknowledge any others than the Church of England. The latter meaning indicates something that was obvious from the earliest Convocation debates, how self-regarding these very senior members of the Church of England were in their thinking. 'Christians' meant themselves. It is true that out of the eventual sixty-five scholars in the two committees, twenty-four were from other denominations,[31] but the point remained: though never so described, this was to be at root another 'Bishops' Bible'. Wilberforce remarked that the Church of England gave the world the Authorised Version; therefore it should 'remove what blemishes exist in that version'.[32] That is fair enough: but, as the whole story of the Revision showed, the Church of England could be bigoted.

Which leads to the fourth, and sensational, difficulty. An Old Testament scholar, the Revd Dr George Vance Smith,[33] had been immediately invited to join the New Testament Committee. He had been invited by a majority of only one and Wilberforce said that had he been present when the vote was taken he would have opposed it. In framing the fifth resolution, it had never occurred to him that it would apply to any member of that body, but rather to 'eminent Hebrew scholars' (he still seemed to think the New Testament was originally in Hebrew). He acknowledged 'so great a distinction between inviting members of the Hebrew faith, the great guardians of the Word of God of old, and one known amongst ourselves as denying one of the Persons of the Godhead . . .'. For Dr Smith was a Unitarian, even a 'Socinian' (that is, a follower of two sixteenth-century Italian theologians who denied the divinity of Christ). There was deep offence. The record shows months of unpleasant bitterness, calling, for example, the co-option of a Unitarian 'a still more objectionable act' than allowing in Non-conformists, a compromise of essential principles, 'and a needless departure from the example of those to whom under God's Providence we owe that most precious inheritance, the Authorised Version of holy scripture'.[34]

Worse, much worse, was to come. Apparently at the suggestion of Professor Westcott,[35] the newly appointed chairman of the New Testament Committee, Bishop Ellicott, invited all the members of that Committee to take Holy Communion in the Chapel of Henry VII in Westminster Abbey on Wednesday 22 June 1870. It was an occasion that moved one of the partakers into verse. Written that day, a sonnet by Edward Bickersteth, Dean of Lichfield, ends

> Do thou impart.
> True wisdom, light celestial. All beside
> Is dark. Light comes if only thou be near.[36]

In fact, it was the dreaded Vance Smith who was near. When it got about that he had shared the communion there was great outrage. At the session of the Lower House on Thursday 7 July, Archdeacon Groome moved 'That the thanks of the house be presented to the Dean of Westminster for granting the use of Henry VII Chapel to the committee for the revision of the Authorised Version of the Bible.' This disingenuous motion was likely, as it was immediately pointed out, to lead to 'considerable debate'. That, in the event, was putting it mildly. Simmering underneath was all the bad feeling about what was becoming 'the Westminster Scandal', now the horrendous mistake of sharing communion with a Unitarian. The Dean of Westminster graciously replied that he wanted no vote of thanks, and bravely added that he had no regrets about what had happened.[37]

Angry letters were written to the press. The *Church Herald* on 6 July 1870 declared,

> That no element of abomination might be wanting [. . .] The communion of 22 June may therefore be taken as a deliberate embodiment of insult and defiance to the whole of Catholic Christendom, and to the ancient faith of the Christian world [. . .] a Presbyterian, Baptist, Independent – these are bad enough; but Socinian![38]

Two days later, on 8 July, the *Church Times* contained the words,

> The invitation of the Dean of Westminster to the heretics and schismatics [. . .] to participate in the Holy Sacrament of the Altar is the deepest insult that has ever been offered to the Church of England [. . .] There can be no possible defence for such an act of desecration as the administration of the Holy Communion to Presbyterians, Baptists and Unitarians.[39]

On 5 July 1870, the Bishop of Rochester presented a petition from the English Church Union to the Upper House at Canterbury (circulated to all Bishops) 'To take such steps as may seem expedient to relieve the Church of England from complicity with a scandal so fraught with possibilities of disaster.'[40] Bishops in the Upper House were quick to say that they were not involved: either they had never received the invitation or they did not know more than two or three of their fellow communicants. The 'Westminster scandal' reverberated for many months. On 15 February 1871 the Bishop of St Asaph said that 'one needs to balance the breach of faith to Vance Smith in removing him from the Committee and the breach of faith to Christ. Therefore he should be removed.'[41] The following day, Dr Jebb referred to it as 'an enormous calamity',[42] and Dr Jelf said that it was 'agitating the Antipodes, and stirring a large portion of the Episcopal Church in the United States, and is felt by every English-speaking race in the world.'[43] To their great credit, the revisers of the New Testament Committee did not remove Vance Smith, who went on to do good work.

The fifth difficulty, however, though it did not emerge immediately, became increasingly important, and is an issue which is still powerful, particularly in America. This concerns the contributions to the New Testament Company made by two members, both leading Greek scholars, B. F. Westcott and F. J. A. Hort. The former was Canon of Peterborough and Regius Professor of Divinity at Cambridge (and from 1890 Bishop of Durham). Hort was Hulsean Professor of Divinity at Cambridge. Their two-volume work, *The New Testament in the Original Greek*, was published in 1881, five days before the appearance of the Revised New Testament. The work for this, 'the most noteworthy critical edition of the Greek Testament ever produced by British scholarship',[44] greatly affected the making of the Revised New Testament. Their clarity of procedure led to establishment of the true inferiority both of what they called the Syrian (also known as the Byzantine) text, of which the *Textus Receptus* was the latest form, and the Alexandrian text, which, with a European Old Latin version, made the basis of the Vulgate; and elucidation of the reliability of Codex Vaticanus and Codex Sinaiticus (fig. 47), which strongly concur, the basis of what was named by them the Neutral text: the latter, with local help from 'Western' texts (e.g. Codex Bezae) make their Greek New Testament.[45]

Among the revisers, disagreement arose between conservatives who were reluctant to see any alteration to KJV and its *Textus Receptus* base, and those who recognised the importance of the scholarship of Westcott and Hort. The conservatives were led by Dr F. H. A. Scrivener. He was a Cambridge scholar who was already taking in hand the necessary revision of KJV. There had been a growing fear that KJV had been corrupted by printers and editors (the last being Blayney in Oxford in 1769) from its first, 'inspired', 1611, printing. Scrivener's achievement was also work in progress while he was a member of the Revising Company, his Cambridge Paragraph Bible of 1873, 'this important and elaborate attempt to publish a trustworthy text of King James' version'.[46] Successfully republished as a popular book in 1884 was his long Introduction, and the five valuable tabular Appendices: the first is a fifty-page 'List of wrong readings of the Bible of 1611 amended in later editions', and the third, a shorter 'List of original readings of the Bible of 1611 examined and arranged'. His last Appendix analyses the work of the makers of KJV in relation to 'Stephens' (the *Textus Receptus*) and 'Beza' (his editions of 1589 and 1598).

The disagreement is something that has increased in force ever since. In spite of a general consensus towards revision, and a recognition of the true science of Westcott and Hort, powerful lobbies in Britain and America with vehemence denounced, and still do denounce, any changes to KJV.

The grounds of the attack have always been three-fold: that KJV is inspired by God and must not be changed in any way; that its Greek base, the *Textus Receptus*, was criminally distorted by Westcott and Hort; and that the glory of the English language was being lost. The last point, still present, is perhaps no longer expressed with the force of Lord Shaftesbury, who wrote in a letter to *The Times* in March 1870,

> I will maintain that a rude and sudden descent from the majestic and touching tones of our wonderful version [KJV, of course], to the then Frenchified and squeaking sentences in modern use, would be an irreparable shock to every English-speaking man who has drunk in the old and generous language with his mother's milk.[47]

Shaftesbury successfully foretold an effect of the Revised Version, the licensing of so many other future attempts.

THE WORK OF REVISION BEGINS: THE NEW TESTAMENT

Work began on Wednesday 22 June 1870. The New Testament Company[48] met first a week later in the historic Jerusalem Chamber in Westminster Abbey, and then for a total of just over 400 days. In the first nine days of the work, they revised only 153 verses.[49] Some members suggested a division into two companies, one for the Gospels, one for the Epistles. The suggestion was abandoned on the grounds that no satisfactory division of people could be devised and that no time would really be saved as the second revision (when the two sub-companies would meet together) would simply re-open all the questions. The KJV's 'division of the NT between two companies is seen by the writer of the preface to the RV NT as being "beyond all doubt the cause of many inconsistencies" (p. vii).'[50] RV must be the outcome of a consensus of all the scholars present.[51] The RV Preface notes among the five classes of scholarly change: those required by a changed reading of the Greek; where the KJV is wrong, or chooses 'the less probable of two possible readings'; corrections of inconsistencies; and subsequent alterations necessitated by these changes.[52] The average pace of the first revision was only thirty-five verses a day: a day was seven hours of revision including a lunch break.[53]

Among many who published on the experience, a member of the New Testament panel, W. G. Humphry, Vicar of St Martin-in-the-Fields, wrote a commentary on the work, the Introduction of which gives valuable notes on progress. In it he says that change was not made for the sake of change or out of pedantry. Tyndale was paraphrased in places:

The few paraphrases which on account of their inaccuracy have been removed in the present revision, we part with regretfully; they are so pithy, so idiomatic, so characteristic of Tyndale.[54]

It will be observed that in the present Revision a return has frequently been made to the very words, and still more often to the sense, of Wycliffe's and the Rhemish versions and, substantially, to the rendering of the Vulgate; and in a considerable number of such passages the Greek Text has been followed which underlies the Vulgate, in preference to that of Stephens [the *Textus Receptus*], on which Tyndale and the Authorised Version are based. These instances, so far as they go – and they go a good way – serve to show that the textual authorities upon which the current Greek text have been amended are in agreement with the Vulgate, and that the Vulgate represents better and older MSS. than those which were known to Erasmus, Beza, or Stephens; in other words, they support the principle adopted by modern critics of preferring the testimony of the few ancient MSS. which are now known, to that of the later but more numerous authorities.[55]

There was considerable opposition to the effect of the Latin Vulgate, which destroyed the importance of the Greek article, and the Greek aorist. The most commonly expressed dislike was to the change in the Lord's Prayer from 'deliver us from evil' to 'deliver us from the evil one'.

One member of the New Testament Company – Edward Bickersteth, he who at the beginning had been inspired to write sonnets – noted that there are 150,000 variants in the text of the Greek New Testament. Only four hundred of these materially affect the sense. Of these four hundred, only about fifty are important. Of these fifty, not one affects any article of faith which is not abundantly sustained by other and undoubted passages.[56]

The sixty-five members of the Old and New Testament companies were continuing in the line of William Tyndale's solitary labour. Edward Bickersteth in another sonnet looked back on 'those peaceful hours' of work by the New Testament Company. They met (for the first time on 30 June 1870) in all for four consecutive days per month, except during August and September, for nearly ten and a half years. A day's work began at 11.00 a.m. and continued, with half an hour off for lunch, until 6.00 p.m. Proceedings began with three collects and the Lord's Prayer, followed by minutes, correspondence and business, and then the work of revision. Discussion of textual emendations came first. Generally Dr Scrivener and Dr Hort would present relevant evidence and arguments, usually on opposite sides. That settled, there came discussion of proposed alterations, and, if necessary, voting. They had made a rule that at the second revision a two-thirds majority was needed for any alteration. The result of this was that the judgement of a bare majority had to be relegated to the margins. Only once did they refer out, when the New Testament Company asked the First Sea Lord about nautical terms in Acts 27.[57]

Dean Bickersteth looked back on 'hearts . . . refreshed with light / Drawn from the fountains of the Infinite'.[58] One can understand what he means: to work with the living text of Scripture is indeed to be in the presence of divine power. Yet he was too bland. There were very considerable differences over the basic Greek text, which produced sharply maintained positions, even to the point of fears of blasphemy. The Bishop of Salisbury, George Moberly, later recalled

> That although both the chief schools of biblical criticism were most ably represented among us, yet inasmuch as it shortly became apparent that the views of one of them [Westcott and Hort] generally carried, on a division, a majority of votes, the chief supporter of the other [Scrivener] refrained from challenging a division in many instances, preferring to wait for the second revision, when the requirement of two-thirds of the company present would necessarily operate in a conservative direction, excluding various changes which would have been carried by a mere majority in the first instance.[59]

Was the Revised New Testament good? After well over a century and many other translations, one imagines a less than ringing reply: 'Yes, possibly, on the whole, in some ways.' The revisers, who had so fully laid out their intentions and procedures in their Preface to the New Testament, in the end made over 36,000 changes,[60] many thought to be unnecessary, like the change in the Lord's Prayer from 'Lead us not . . .' to 'Bring us not . . .'. David Norton remarks that 'The RV was a compromise between the irresistible need to revise and the immovable monument' of the KJV.[61] The revisers could write 'translationese' ('Thy will be done, as in heaven, so on earth') or foolishness ('if thy right hand causeth thee to stumble . . .'). It was 'Cambridge' work, as 'formal equivalence' was later named, that is, translating the original words and nuances as literally as possible, rather than 'Oxford' translating, 'dynamic equivalence', conveying the sense in free and idiomatic English without much regard for the exact wording of the original.[62] In some regards, they made the language even more archaic than KJV, adding such ancient English words as 'howbeit', 'behooved' and a dozen others, newly joining 'haply' to KJV's 'lest' in seventeen places, and newly adding '-ward' to make 'to us-ward' in four places.[63] One scholar estimated that the Revised Version New Testament is more archaic than KJV in at least 549 places.[64] Changing Tyndale, and

KJV, in order to translate the same Greek word with the same English word each time, produced, for example, a jarring four uses of 'straightway' in the four short verses of Mark 1:18–21.[65] Often there seems little point in the changes.[66] There has been a general sense that 'the almost pedantic accuracy and precision which the revisers aimed at' produced 'a schoolmasters' translation'.[67] But they broke the hold of the *Textus Receptus*, and allowed good scholarship to decide a troubling crux or two.[68] For this they were vilified by some at the time, and have been attacked by others, with ferocity, ever since.[69]

As Luther A. Weigle wrote:

> the Revised Version is a milestone in the history of the English Bible. It was the response of sound scholars to the more accurate knowledge of the ancient text and its meaning which was becoming available in the nineteenth century [. . .] In general aim and method, the Revised Version pointed the way for future translators.[70]

The full use of the newly available 'Western' Greek texts, especially the Codices Vaticanus and Sinaiticus, and the technical skills of Westcott and Hort, clarified disputed phrases without obscuring the issues: so at Luke 23:34 the marginal note reads, 'Some ancient authorities omit, "And Jesus said, Father, forgive them; for they know not what they do."' Some much-loved phrases were relegated to the margins, like the angel troubling the water at John 5:4, or the Ethiopian eunuch's declaration of faith at Acts 8:37. The intrusive sentence at the 'Johannine comma', making KJV's 1 John 5:7, 'For there are three that bear record in heaven', was omitted altogether, without marginal note. One can understand the strong feelings that were raised. Yet Westcott was undoubtedly right, that the revisers had 'placed the English reader far more nearly than before in the position of the Greek scholar'.[71]

The Old Testament

The Old Testament Company met in Westminster Chapter Library for ten days every two months (except during August and September), over fourteen years, finishing on 20 June 1884. Modern judgement of their work is a different story. A firm ancient text meant few disputes. Great strides in understanding Hebrew led to a sense that in many places the KJV's muddy windows had been washed with clean water and, especially in the poetic books and the Prophets, it was for the first time in English possible to see sense. An example is the opening of Job 28, where the first eleven verses of KJV sound wonderful but are impossible to follow. They are a description of mining operations, which the revision makes clear.

Printing Hebrew poetry as English poetry was a valuable advance. Only rarely does philology intrude: a crucial phrase in the famous poetic account of old age in Ecclesiastes 12, just before 'or ever the silver cord be loosed or the golden bowl be broken', replaces 'desire shall fail' with 'the caper-berry shall fail', a reading deserving a medal from a Society of Pedants.

Including the Americans

On 7 July 1870 the Lower House of Convocation passed a revised resolution, that 'This house respectfully prays the Upper House that the joint committee appointed for the preparation of a scheme of revision of the authorised version of the Bible be instructed to invite the co-operation of some American divines.' This was then passed unanimously.

It was in fact some time before anything could be done with the Americans. In August 1870, Dr Angus, the Principal of the (Baptist) Regent's Park College, visited New York on behalf of the revisers. He arranged with Dr Philip Schaff, a Presbyterian scholar in New York, that he should select and invite suitable American scholars for the purpose. Not much then happened. Nearly a year later, in October 1871, Dr Schaff visited England: he was invited to be present at one of the meetings of the New Testament company. By December 1871, it was reported that the arrangements for the American work were complete. The American companies, however – most of their number being non-Episcopalians – did not hold their first meeting until 4 October 1872, by which time the Westminster Old Testament committee had been twice through the Pentateuch. The original American Old Testament Company consisted of eleven members. The New Testament Company consisted of fifteen members including Dr Schaff and a Unitarian.[72] They met for work in the Bible House, New York. By that time, the English revisers had been once over the Synoptic Gospels and twice over the Pentateuch. Some British work was sent over to America from time to time, and their criticisms were considered when the English revisers came to the second revision. More American criticisms were taken into account before the very final revision was fixed, in which American amendments or alternative readings were printed as an appendix to the earlier editions of the English Revised Version. The Americans were less tolerant than their English colleagues of traditional usage and archaisms. When the English revisers had put alternatives chosen by a majority that was not two-thirds into the margins, the Americans often wanted to transpose text and margin.

In December 1872 an agreement was reached with the University Presses of Oxford and Cambridge which allowed them exclusive copyright of the finished work. In return the two Presses would not only bear the expenses of production, but together should give £20,000 towards the revisers' expenses. Until then, there had been no talk of remuneration. In 1877 strong claims by the American revisers led to their undertaking to print no separate edition of their own for fourteen years after the appearance of the first English edition. The Oxford and Cambridge presses agreed that all their published copies should contain an appendix setting out the preferences of the American revisers where there had been significant disagreements. After the fourteen years were over, in 1901, the Americans produced their American Revised Version, published by Nelson in New York. It included not only what had appeared in the agreed appendix, but also many more additional alterations, producing bad feeling between the British and American Revisers.

The Apocrypha

In the course of the negotiations up to December 1872 with the Oxford and Cambridge presses, a suggestion was made that the Revised Version should include the Apocrypha. It had always been felt that much had been wrong with the 1611 version of this. An agreement was reached that when the New Testament work was finished, the company should divide itself up into three committees in London, Westminster and Cambridge to work on the six most important Apocryphal books. In the ten years from 1882 these revisions were finished. A small sub-committee of the Old Testament Company, entrusted with the rest of the Apocrypha, began work in July 1884, and continued for about ten years. The American committee did not co-operate in any revision of the Apocrypha.

THE RECEPTION OF THE REVISED VERSION

All through the work of revision, the intense interest shown in many books and articles with wide readership is something to later ages surprising. There was very great international excitement at the publication of the Revised New Testament on 17 May 1881, at a level unbelievable in the world of the second millennium. A copy was presented that day to the Convocation of Canterbury, and to Queen Victoria (the order of presentations is significant).

> The streets around the publishing house in London were blocked from early dawn until late in the afternoon, and there were the same scenes at the great railway termini. A million copies had been called for in

England and America. Within a few days nearly four hundred thousand of the Clarendon Press edition had been sold in New York. Two daily papers in Chicago had the work telegraphed to them, and gave it complete in their columns. In less than a year three million copies had been sold.[73]

Those sales in the UK and the USA were enormous. So was the disappointment. Attacks, soon on the whole revision, were directed on the changes to KJV which were felt to be both far more than expected and unnecessary. The revisers were said to have had no ear for English, which was too often true. Not everyone approved the printing in paragraphs according to sense divisions. The traditional headings of chapters and pages were found to be omitted. The use of italics, which had run riot in successive editions of KJV, was restricted and regularised. Virtually no marginal cross-references were included, immediately felt to be a weakness. The margins now contained brief comments of many kinds, giving notice especially of alternative renderings. The two-thirds rule had meant that some of the most valuable work of the revisers had had to go into the margins.

The revisers had aimed to revise, not to rewrite. Hence they were at once both Jacobean and Victorian, something which was bound to produce unacceptable hybrids. They claimed in their New Testament Preface to have kept as much of KJV as was consistent with 'faithfulness' and clarity. Old Testament characters mentioned in the New Testament were given the more familiar names.

In spite of the original aims of changing little, the final publication showed changes amounting to many thousands, estimated as an average at between two and three per verse for the New Testament. For the Old Testament the average was lower, partly because variations in the original text were fewer, and partly because the Old Testament Company, having learned from the criticism levelled at the New Testament version, became more cautious. For the New Testament, the textual problem was genuinely serious and difficult. Westcott and Hort were internationally respected scholars and their work was immediately recognised to be of the greatest importance. They undoubtedly exercised great influence on the judgement of the New Testament Company: they did not, however, control it, and day by day, their suggestions were countered by the assiduous Dr Scrivener. On the whole, however, Westcott and Hort could be seen to have been on the right lines, and their effect was to give English readers a New Testament closer to the original than any that had been based on the *Textus Receptus*.

After the complete Revised Version was first published (the Old Testament appeared on 19 May 1885) no changes were made to the wording of either text or margins. It was, however, thereafter published in many forms, including several with AV and RV in parallel columns, and later with cross-references in the margin. Each University Press produced editions of the Greek Testament with reference to the revisers' work. It was said that it was unfortunate that cheaper versions of RV had not been issued.

CONTINUED OPPOSITION

It was also said that the Revised Version in all its work represented the labours of a larger and more representative group of scholars than had ever assembled before; this extensiveness did not happen again until the 1950s. Great care had been taken to find the best-qualified scholars, regardless of their church connections. That is not quite what appeared, and it remains noticeable how much the work was dominated, not always to advantage, by senior clerics of the Church of England. Throughout the making and after publication, there was a large flow of literature in relation to the enterprise. Some of this was from members of the various committees defending their procedures.[74] Some was in the nature of passionate attacks on the whole exercise. In 1872, the vicar of St Mary's, Oxford, published a book against Vance Smith having been invited to communion in Westminster Abbey, and even being a reviser: for so long, and longer, did the 'Westminster scandal' rumble on. The same writer, Dr J. W. Burgon, by then Dean of Chichester, published three long and exhilaratingly intolerant articles, republished as a book in 1883 entitled *The Revision Revised*. C. J. Cadoux writes,

> The writer had the effrontery to suggest that these twenty-odd accomplished scholars who for eleven years had devoted their continuous labours without payment to the production of a better English version of the New Testament should receive from the Church 'nothing short of stern and well merited rebuke'.[75]

Cadoux is right. Yet Burgon is by far the liveliest writer of English on the scene. We are back in the territory of Hugh Broughton (see pp. 437–8). After some of the pusillanimous in-fighting of the New Testament Company, Burgon's earthquake, rushing mighty wind and fire come with considerable refreshment, even though the divine Word is the still small voice. He is outrageous, with nothing at all good to say about the whole RV, but always extremely readable.

How it happened that, with so many splendid scholars sitting round their table, they should have produced a Translation which, for the most part, reads like a first-rate school-boys crib – tasteless, unlovely, harsh, unidiomatic; servile without being really faithful – pedantic without being really learned – an unreadable Translation, in short; the result of a vast amount of labour indeed, but of wondrous little skill – how all this has come about it were utterly useless at this time of day to enquire.[76]

Because of his splendid energy, Burgon is thought to have had a quite disproportionate influence on public opinion: Cadoux claims that his writings 'Are supposed to have hindered very considerably the acceptance of the Revised Version by the British public'.[77] This is overdoing it. The chief and uncontrovertible reason for the British public not accepting the Revised Version was that it was not very good. In spite of many formal defences, a storm of criticism followed, some by the ignorant or prejudiced or both, outraged by the loss of favourite phrases or by the replacement of the *Textus Receptus*. Some of it was more scholarly.[78]

In favour of the Revised Version has to be the fact that both companies succeeded in clarifying some obscurities and infelicities in KJV. Cadoux remarks that the Revised Version is 'immeasurably and unquestionably more correct'. David Norton writes that in spite of, even because of RV, KJV's general reputation continued to grow. RV 'has not become a significant work of English literature'.[79]

What Cadoux goes on to say, however, raises an issue which is out of his sight. He writes,

Give what weight you please to the arguments about rhythm, music, dignity, and the devotional value arising from long familiarity and sacred associations; these surely ought not, in the judgement of any educated and responsible Christian, to outweigh considerations of truth and falsehood.[80]

Would that it were so simple.

Chapter 38

THE ENGLISH BIBLE IN AMERICA, 1841–1899

A STRIKING PART OF THE STORY of the English Bible in America is the huge number printed in the second half of the nineteenth century. Between the beginning of 1840 and the end of 1900, 1,053 different editions of the English New Testament or complete Bible were published, as indicated by the standard bibliography. As will be seen, that figure is itself inevitably a large underestimate; but even as the figure stands, it is a lot of Bibles; an average of just over seventeen different editions a year, and well above the parallel figures in Britain.[1]

Those editions were in all sorts of shapes and sizes. They could be bought in extravagant leather or serviceable cloth bindings, with a multitudinous choice of styles (perhaps with the words of Jesus in red, or Old Testament verses starred if they were prophecies fulfilled in the New); or of all kinds of marginal notes, prefatory essays, commentaries, concluding concordances and explanations of terms, 'Tables of Offices and Affinities', metrical Psalms, blank pages for family records, special decorations and (often crudely made) pictures, coloured or not; Bibles in all possible sizes, from what we might call gigantism to a sort of microscopism – the latter sold not entirely as curiosities. In those sixty years, Bibles were printed in many different American cities; still chiefly in Philadelphia and New York (where the names of such Bible publishers still active today, as J. B. Lippincott and A. J. Holman and Co. began to appear).[2]

The names of British publishers – Thomas Nelson and Sons, Oxford University Press or William Collins and Company – appear on title-pages of Bibles in America, but they could by now be from American addresses. Editions of the Bible were still imported from these presses, either complete, or as sheets or plates: but no longer were the States significantly dependent on imports of Bibles from Britain.

It remains noteworthy that of all those Bibles now printed in America, so few were fresh American renderings of the Greek or Hebrew. Of that average of seventeen Bibles each year, in all that time of vigorous expansion, when the flood of people from Europe and their immediate descendents for the first time filled the territories from coast to coast and made across the States such new civilisations, only a handful out of the total of 1,053 were not KJVs, some being Catholic versions, Rheims-Douai or fresh from the Vulgate. The new republic's love affair with the English Bible was with the Word still dressed as an old, monarchical parent of empire. Much of the additional matter, from points of detail like the use of italics to the great bulk of additional matter, still came from British KJVs. It is odd.

Those few brave attempts at Americanisation all failed, either to catch the public interest or to influence later translations; even the great Noah Webster did not do that. What did have large effects as entirely American were not new versions but certain works loosely based on, and sometimes contrary to, the Bible, to be read alongside, or instead of, the Scriptures, for example *The Book of Mormon*. To such things I shall turn later. Meanwhile, and before I consider possible reasons for the continuing and extravagant all-American devotion to KJV, we need to grasp the scale of Bible printing, and Bible selling, in those sixty years.

Commercial publishers do not issue complete lists of printings, and guard information about numbers of copies printed. For those Bibles, it is not possible to calculate how many were bought in the United States. The best that can be done is to make an intelligent guess, and then multiply: whatever is decided will undoubtedly be far too low. So many firms were involved in printing the Bible in the middle and later decades of the nineteenth century that by no means all of them reached the bibliography based on the American Bible Society's holdings: the figure of 1,053 is likely in that respect to be far lower than reality.[3] Using that ABS list, a graph showing numbers of different verions produced in America in the nineteenth century (fig. 37) shows that, with a steady rise before and an apparently rapid falling away after, the peak for Bible production in America came between 1841 and 1850, with over 350 different American editions in those ten years. Yet it was not quite like that.

> By the 1850s, the American Bible Society was regularly printing well over one hundred editions of a bible from a single set of plates. Thus, what looks like a single edition of the Bible in the Hills bibliography was often several hundred printings of that edition, which translates into hundreds of thousands of volumes.[5]

Many noughts should be added to the totals. Further, what looks like a rapid falling off in the second half of the century is an effect of what has just been noticed, that though fewer sets of plates may have been involved, in a smaller number of printing houses, the volume of Bibles printed in each edition probably rose. This would be understandable, parallel to the similar development in both the American Bible Society and the American and Foreign Bible Societies.[6]

We are in the presence of a Bible-buying phenomenon, beyond anything seen anywhere else in the world. In the United States in the second half of the century it went with being able to buy more magazines and books, as the scale of printing and distribution, especially of cheap reading matter, exploded. Yet in America at that time the English Bible was special. The earlier Protestant faith in teaching people to read, meshed with religious beliefs, had made the Bible the most imported book, and then the most printed, most distributed and most read text in North America. Even more than in the eighteenth century, if any book touched the lives of Americans, it was a Bible.[7] A writer in 1817 commented that Americans were a people who 'knew much of their bible' and 'little besides'.[8] Greatly increasing even from 1817, Bible language and stories dominated the world of American print 'creating countless idioms, metaphors, narrative themes and publishing innovations'.[9] That is easy to see, but difficult to grasp in the early twenty-first century. Recent books on America's cultural history have had to take space to explain the importance of the Scriptures in the country's traditions, having first introduced the book to readers who may not have heard of the Bible.[10] As Paul Gutjahr wrote:

> When formerly bibles were regularly read in school classrooms and treated as the Ur-text of all important knowledge, now teachers are forbidden even to display a bible on their desks.[11]

It was a cultural phenomenon, however, with one additional factor, that not every Bible printed was read from cover to cover. In the words of Margaret Hills, bibliographer of the American Bible Society, the Bible 'may be the most published and even the most unread book, but a good proportion of the copies printed, somewhere, sometime, meet a heartfelt need of some man, woman, or child'.[12]

THE BIBLE IN THE SCHOOLS

By 1850, Roman Catholics made the largest denomination in America, a position they have held ever since.[13] The older assumptions, basically rural and Bible-based, that America was pioneering, farm-labouring and Protestant, became rapidly challenged in the middle and later nineteenth century, linked with the huge development of industrial processes and large cities. The greatest change was through immigration.

American history has been largely the story of migrations. That of the hundred years or so between the Battle of Waterloo and the outbreak of the First World War must certainly be reckoned the largest peaceful migration in recorded history; probably the largest of any kind, ever. It is reckoned that some thirty-five million persons entered the United States during that period, not to mention the large numbers who were also moving to such places as Argentina and Australia.[14]

The famous 'melting pot' image may obscure the fact that though these people, from two dozen European, Balkan and Baltic countries, were absorbed into American life, they fiercely retained their ethnic characteristics.[15] This was, in religious matters, of particular importance for the Irish.

Between 1845 and 1848 Ireland suffered its terrible potato famine. A million people died of starvation and disease, a million more emigrated (not only to America, of course; and, from the turn of the next century, into England and Scotland).[16] 'The exodus from Ireland became a desperate, frantic flight . . . By 1850 the census reported 961,719 Irish in the United States, and over 200,000 came in that year alone. In aother decade the figure had risen to 1,611,304.'[17] 'The Roman Catholic Church experienced a phenomenal growth in numbers, reaching 1.75 million by 1850, and doubling this figure in another decade.'[18]

The result, for national religion, was a mesh of acute problems, within Catholicism, and in relations with other Christians. Ten years before, in the summer of 1840, Irish Catholics in Philadelphia had, not entirely unwittingly, provoked a matter of religious politics into full rioting.[19] At issue was the reading of the Bible in schools. Mandatory in the state from 1838, the Bible as textbook was attacked by the Catholic Bishop of Philadelphia, Thomas Kenrick, in a campaign parallel to one in New York. Protestant opponents, joined by patriotic 'nativist' Americans objecting to immigrants generally, put it about that Kenrick wanted to take the KJV out of the schools altogether, which was not true: he wanted the Douai Bible to be read by Catholic children, who would be excused from the Protestant devotions. Politics, some of it reprehensible, kept the fire alight. In the late spring and summer of 1844, Philadelphia became a place of passion, riot – and armed militia. The hot molten core of prejudice on both sides now erupted. 'Although Irish Catholics had initiated the disorder, they quickly were forced on the defensive and received a great deal of punishment.'[20] Catholic houses were burned: large parts of the suburb of Kensington were in flames. The rioting flared again in July as 'ruffians' attacked holiday-makers overnighting from the Independence Day celebrations. Sleeping picnickers were severely beaten. Full riot flared again. Gradually, Philadelphia calmed down, and Bishop Kenrick made no further complaints against Bible reading in the public schools.[21] But the matter was never forgotten, and 'nativists', glossing over their part in it all (burning Catholic churches and homes, for example) always maintained that at the bottom of the conflict were Catholic attempts to exclude the Bible from the schools. It did not help that only a few days after the early July riots, Pope Gregory XVI warned Italian Catholics against the distribution of Protestant Bibles 'in the vulgar tongue' by Bible Societies.[22]

SLAVES

Many American Protestants feared the growing influence of the Roman Catholic Church. American life in the nineteenth century, however, was dominated by the much sharper question of slavery. After 1776, the Northern states abandoned what few slaves they had fairly quickly: New Jersey was the last there to put an end to the practice, in 1804. By federal law of 1808, slaves could no longer be imported from Africa. By then, one inhabitant in five was an Afro-American. By 1860, 'though there were nearly four million slaves, there were nearly twenty-seven million free whites, and only 488,000 free blacks.'[23] The most important event since the Revolution, the Civil War, the War Between the States, of 1861–5, was a war about slaves. It settled some larger issues and left others worse: the romanticising South failed to win independence. After defeat, the whites there had permanent reason to resent the North, or, more strongly, for those still naming themselves Confederates, to hate Yankees.

The war was inevitable, given the limited provinciality of the slave-owners, and the often appalling conditions of the slaves. What had been already bad had become worse, as

> in state after state, manumission was outlawed, and the status of the free black was reduced. In this way the South bound itself anew to slavery and to the proposition that slavery was to be eternal.[24]

Without any political cohesion, or military power, or any social force of any kind, the enslaved Afro-Americans won their case.

> Their essential victory is demonstrated by their religion and by the great music evolved from their plantation work-songs; from the celebration songs . . . and above all from the spirituals, with their message of human sorrow, divine consolation and ultimate joy.[25]

The spirituals, sung to simple rhythms, were often Bible phrases. The writer of one of their earliest appreciations, in 1856, contrasted 'the song-loving Negro and his natural musicianship with the average, anxious

American, who though "favoured above other people on earth" goes to his task "songless and joyless"'.[26] Shortly after, Thomas Wentworth Higginson of Boston, 'the commander of a Negro regiment in the Civil War', who was also a student of Scottish ballads, found himself musically in a similar world to that of the ballads, and observed in the spirituals 'their elements of patience in this world and triumph in the next, Biblical imagery, mystical effect, passionate striving, and the "stimulus to courage and a tie to heaven"'.[27] A modern writer comments on their 'childlike simplicity of thought and strangely consummate artistry of mood which could be paralleled only in the Middle Ages. . . . The spirituals show a remarkable knowledge of the Bible.' They were perhaps 'the only Bible the slaves had'.[28]

> We read in the Bible and we understan'
> That Samson was the strongest man.
> Samson went out at one time
> And killed about a hundred Philistines.
> Delilah fooled Samson, this we know
> Because the Holy Bible tells us so.
> She shaved of his head just as clean as your han'
> And his strength became as any other man.[29]

'Moses' burial, the Hebrews in the fiery furnace, David's flight from Saul and his fight with Goliath, and the slaying of Abel are all told . . . ("Cain hit Abel in de head wid de leg of a table").'[30] Here is the Creation:

> Lord he thought he'd make a man,
> Mixed a little bit o' dirt and san'.
>
> Thought he make a 'oman too,
> Didn't know zacly what to do.
>
> He took a rib from Adam's side,
> And made Miss Eve fo' to be his bride.
>
> Put 'em in a garden rich and fair,
> To' em to eat whatever was there.
>
> Of this tree you must not eat,
> If you do you'll have to skeet.[31]

The Crucifixion is memorably described in 'He Never Said A Mumblin' Word', and, famously, in

> Were you there when they crucified my Lord?
> Were you there when they nailed him to the tree?

Were you there when they pierced him in the side?
Were you there when the sun refused to shine?
Were you there when they laid him in the tomb?

In other spirituals were the lament of Mary, Jesus's burial and his rising from the tomb. New Testament theology was taken personally. So a spiritual is the words of Paul in Romans 7:

O wretched man that I am!
O wretched man that I am!
Who will deliver poor me?
My heart is filled with sadness and pain,
Who will deliver poor me?

The great Old Testament prophecies were sung:

Oh rise, shine, for thy light is a coming.
Oh rise, shine, for thy light is a coming.
My Lord says he's coming by and by.

And the Book of Revelation:

My Lord what a morning!
My Lord what a morning!
My Lord what a morning!
When the stars begin to fall.

You will hear the trumpet sound
To wake the nations underground,
Standing at my God's right hand,
When the stars begin to fall.[32]

It was a crime to teach slaves to read and write, lest they began to get, and disseminate, the wrong ideas, about liberty, dignity, justice and personal fulfilment. But, like their English spiritual forebears, they heard the Bible read. It is startling how wide is the Bible knowledge in the spirituals, the basic materials of which have been described as 'native African rhythms and the King James Version of the Bible'.[33] One might expect 'D'ol ark she landed on de mountain top' or a song like 'My Lord says he's gonneter rain down fire' to include Pharaoh, Gabriel and Moses: or 'Dere's a star in de East on Christmas morn' or 'De angel roll de stone away' at Easter. But in just one short collection are Jacob's ladder, 'brudder Elijah', Ezekiel's wheel, the writing on the wall, Mary and Martha, the Pool of Bethesda ('God's a-gonneter trouble de water'), Pentecost ('Walk in Jerusalem just like John') and the words of Jesus 'I am de way' and 'Feed my sheep' – all taken in to the life of the singers, and retranscribed.

The intensity of the suffering and hope comes out in in 'I thank God I'm free at last', that is, 'Way down yonder in de graveyard walk': the singer will 'meet my Jesus in de middle of de air'.

Thus Bible phrases in the spirituals were more than simply hauntingly memorable: they were the good news of life affirmed and passed on: 'gospel' indeed. I glanced in a previous chapter at the Old Testament base of many slave songs.[34] The hope, however, the goal, the energy was as much from the New Testament, in songs about the Kingdom, taken, though not entirely, in its future senses. Stealing away to Jesus meant some comfort now.

The Bible said to support slavery

Collection of the spirituals has been a comparatively recent thing, having to overcome 'the immemorial stereotype that the Negro in America is nothing more than a beggar at the gate of the nation, waiting to be thrown the crumbs of civilisation' (a phrase itself echoing Luke 16).[35] The spirituals of the slaves were a far truer representation of Scripture than their owners' obdurate assertion that not only did the American Constitution sanction slavery: the Bible commanded it. Leviticus 25:44 was to be taken as gospel: 'Both thy bondmen, and thy bondmaids, which thou shalt have . . .'. This reading, of course, took no regard of the fact that Hebrew slavery was a mild form (not least in allowing freedom after seven years) of that found in Greece or Rome at the time, or, especially, in Assyria or Egypt: not for nothing was the desert nation founded by Moses in escape from Egyptian slavery.

In the New Testament, Paul himself, at the opening of the sixth chapter in his first letter to Timothy, the first of what are called the 'Pastoral' Epistles, was quoted:

1   Let as many servants as are under the yoke count their own masters worthy of all honour, that the name of God and his doctrine be not blasphemed.

2   And they that have believing masters, let them not despise them, because they are brethren; but rather do them service, because they are faithful and beloved, partakers of the benefit. These things teach and exhort.

3   If any man teach otherwise, and consent not to wholesome words, even the words of our Lord Jesus Christ, and to the doctrine which is according to godliness;

4   He is proud, knowing nothing, but doting about questions and strifes of words, whereof cometh envy, strife, railings, evil surmisings,

5 Perverse disputings of men and corrupt minds, and destitute of the truth, supposing that gain is godliness: from such withdraw thyself.

The passage was a gift to the defenders of American slavery. They tended not to read four or five more verses further on:

For the love of money is the root of all evil . . . But thou, O man of God, flee these things; and follow after righteousness, godliness. faith, love, patience, meekness.

So Scripture was found to give authority to the master race, particularly of planters (that is, those who owned more than twenty slaves), who asserted 'the ignorance, shiftlessness and helplessness of blacks – a race so inferior that it needed enslavement . . .'.[36] It is distressing to read the large pro-slavery literature which claims support for the 'peculiar institution' from the Bible. An early work, by Thomas Stringfellow, written in Richmond in 1841, is reasonably mild. In *A Brief Examination of Scripture Testimony on the Institution of Slavery*, Stringfellow states that slavery is 'recognised and sanctified by God himself . . . appears to have received the approval of God'. His arguments are from the Old Testament time of the Patriarchs, that is from Abraham and Isaac to Moses and Aaron, in the Pentateuch. New Testament support for slavery usually came from the fact that it is mute on the subject. Thomas Stringfellow, however, manages to argue that Jesus Christ himself was not silent on slavery: the early verses of the sixth chapter of Paul's first letter to Timothy seem to accept slavery (though Paul is stating that servants should not despise 'believing masters'). The third verse is: 'If any man teach otherwise, and consent not to wholesome words, even the words of our Lord Jesus Christ . . .'. Though the matter at issue is social relations generally, and Jesus' command that believers serve each other, not slavery at all, Stringfellow expounds his discovery of Jesus' implied support of slavery at length.

A long book, of 569 pages, by Revd Josiah Priest, printed in Glasgow, Kentucky in 1852, is entitled simply *Bible Defence of Slavery*. Further down the title-page is the announcement that it is intended to attack 'that system of pseudo-philosophy, or fanaticism, ylcept Modern Abolitionism'. It is all powerful stuff, with sensational accounts of 'negro uprisings' and the bloody atrocities committed on whites, especially women and babies, with some white women reserved for a fate worse than death. The author finds that a well-known verse in chapter 58 of the prophet Isaiah, explaining that the Lord requires his people 'to deal thy bread to the hungry . . . and bring the poor that are cast out to thy house . . . that thou hide not thyself from thine own flesh . . .' (verse 7), on which the abolitionists based an argument, is not about slavery at all. Almost all the book is rant, most of

it revolting. Expounding with some heat the commonly mistaken interpretation of a verse (23:20) in the prophecy of Ezekiel (a book to which
one does not turn for calm spiritual refreshment), Revd Josiah Priest
hammers home the true meaning, which is that 'a Negro man's sexual
member was the same as to elongation and magnitude as the brute called
an ass'.

A slightly later (1862), and even longer, book by M. T. Wheat, also from
Kentucky (Louisville), has as title: *The Progress and Intelligence of Americans:
Collateral Proof of Slavery, from the First to the Eleventh Chapter of Genesis, as
Founded on Organic Law; and from the fact of Christ being a Caucasian, owing
to his peculiar parentage; Progress of Slavery South and West, with free Labour
advancing, through the acquisition of territories; advantages enumerated and
explained.* The book, as meandering as its title, is also unreadable racist rant.
An apparently more balanced book came from the Bishop of Vermont,
John Henry Hopkins. This is high, and learned, polemic: *Scriptural, Ecclesiastical and Historical View of Slavery from the Days of the Patriarch Abraham
to the Nineteenth Century* (New York, 1864). The published work consists
of Hopkins's thirty-eight-page pro-slavery pamphlet, ingenious in argument, followed by a protest against it signed by well over 200 clergy. The
remaining 330 small-print pages, heavily subduing the protesters, give the
standard pro-slavery view, that God had commanded the Patriarchs and
Hebrew people to keep slaves. A pamphlet by the Revd M. J. Raphall, 'a
discourse delivered at the Jewish synagogue, New York, on the Day of the
National Fast, 1861', concludes that though a slave has rights, slavery has
long existed, that slaveholding is no sin, and that slave property is expressly
placed under the protection of the Ten Commandments. The penultimate
paragraph of the anonymous pro-slavery pamphlet, *A Brief Reply to an
Important Question . . . from an Implicit Believer in Holy Scripture*, printed in
London in 1863, begins: 'The one cry of the South is for peace. Is that a
less Christian cry than the Northern shriek for blood and war?'

The Bible against slavery

One of the leaders of the other side, the Revd Dr Charles Elliott, published in Cincinnati in 1850 his full-length *Sinfulness of American Slavery;
proved from its evil sources; its injustice; its wrongs; its contrariety to many scriptural commands, prohibitons and principles, and to the Christian spirit; and from
its evil effects; together with observations on emancipation and the duties of
American citizens in regard to slavery.* On the title-page are the words 'Thou
shalt not steal – Eighth commandment: Exodus 21:16, 1 Timothy 1:9,10.'
(The Exodus verse states 'And he that stealeth a man, and selleth him
. . . he shall surely be put to death.' The 1 Timothy reference is also to

'menstealers'.) At the end of the book are a hundred pages of small print analysing 'the many Scriptural prohibitions . . . commands . . . principles'. These include the prophet Jeremiah, 22:13, 'Woe unto him . . . that useth his neighbour's service without wages . . .'; Luke's Gospel 10:7, 'the labourer is worthy of his hire', also in Paul's first letter to Timothy, 5:18; and Paul's letter to the Colossians, 4:1, 'Masters, give unto your servants that which is just and equal . . .' Not only are the Ten Commandments against slavery: it is contrary to the spirit of Christianity. A long chapter, 7, refreshing after the narrowest outlook of much of pro-slavery writing, gives the 'witness and testimony of many of the wisest and best men the world ever saw, comprising the principal theologians, statesmen, moralists, and philanthropists of Great Britain and the United States': the extracts are from the poems of James Thomson, S. T. Coleridge, John Milton, Alexander Pope, Joseph Addison, Robert Burns, William Cowper, and many more.[37]

Albert Barnes published in Philadelphia in 1846 his detailed *An Enquiry into the Scriptural View of Slavery*. His conclusion, after long and careful scriptural analysis, is that 'the principles laid down by the Saviour and his apostles, are such as are opposed to slavery, and if carried out would secure its universal abolition.'

One can easily find many publications pressing the same point, at greater or lesser length. In volume, the number of publications taking each side, of books or shorter pamphlets, is about equal: there are a large number, throughout the 1840s, 1850s and earlier 1860s. A reader who samples them with modern sensibilities has no doubt that, simply in terms of debate, the abolitionists made the better use of Scripture.

The exploitation of slaves commanded by the Bible

Yet a supposed assurance of God's command to keep submissive slaves was taken as entitlement to inflict daily toil without end on men, women and children; whippings (even to death); the permanent separation of families, as fathers or children were suddenly sold 'down the river' on an economic whim (a cruelty unknown in, for example, the Caribbean); delegation to sadistic overseers; and all the everyday toil of oppression and misery. A West African observer, looking back in 1788 on the horrors of crossing the Atlantic on a slave ship, recalled one later day being sent to the house of a Virginian gentleman to fan him:

> when I came into the room I was very much affrighted by some things I saw, and the more so as I had seen a black woman slave as I came through the house, who was cooking the dinner, and the poor creature

was cruelly loaded with various kinds of iron machines; she had one particularly on her head, which locked her mouth so fast that she could scarcely speak; and could not eat or drink. I was much astonished and shocked at this contrivance, which I afterwards learned was called the iron muzzle. . . .[38]

Pro-slavery campaigners could accuse their enemies of exaggeration, of taking the exception to be the norm. It was argued that – rather as it is said that hunting to a cruel death is good for the fox – slavery was good for the African: he was introduced to civilisation and Christianity. Some Southern planters were, no doubt, humane people. Nevertheless, 'in some states of the South the slave was worked to death, as it was more profitable to the slave holder to use up his slaves quickly'.[39] Not only did pro-slavery campaigners adduce support from Scriptures: 'the ministers and members of orthodox churches in the South held slaves to the number of at least 600,000 . . . The slave-holding South managed to get the Christian Church, on the whole, on its side.'[40] It is startling to find Southern ministers at the front of the debate. For American slavery meant very real abuses. It was evil: 'to treat a man as if he were no man but a beast is theologically false, morally wrong, economically unsound, and politically and socially disastrous.'[41] Sidney Ahlstrom opens Part VI of his massive *A Religious History of the American People*, 'Slavery and Expiation', with these words:

That the united states – the first new nation, the elect nation, the nation with the soul of a church, the great model of western democracy – moved into the nineteenth century with one of the largest and cruelest of slave systems in its midst with full constitutional protection is surely one of the world's greatest ironies.[42]

There are those who find 'ironies' too mild and academic a word.

There were some slaves in the North, treated at times with appalling severity, but only as a luxury for the wealthy few. In the South, slaves were the main part of the economic system. The abolitionist movement grew out of the continued Puritanism of the New England farmers as they settled the Midwest. They did not, on moral, ultimately Christian, grounds, want slave-ownership to spread. There were serious complications as new states were founded: Texas and Missouri in 1845, Kansas and Nebraska in 1854.

Even the changes overtaking the morally upright intellectual leaders in Massachusetts, however, as they discarded traditional Christianity – Harvard was now Unitarian – or moved even further into sub-Wordsworthian worship of Nature with Emerson, could not remove the sense that life in

America was about improvement, making over the world on a new model. Being American, from the beginning, meant striving to be prosperous, and making everything better. Both endeavours were often bound up in a religious conversion, still the heart of spiritual experience for most. Being born again (sometimes repeatedly) awakened the social conscience. There was much to put right, the educated North saw, but slavery in particular was bad – if only as spoiling the view of America as God's country.

America's greatest writers silent on slavery

Putting together two large things reveals a mystery. By 1860 and the start of the Civil War, the great intellectual writers of the North were approaching their peaks. Ralph Waldo Emerson, the friend of Carlyle, Coleridge and Wordsworth, had published half a dozen influential books, and that year, 1860, saw the appearance of his *The Conduct of Life*. The poets Henry Wadsworth Longfellow, Edgar Allen Poe, John Greenleaf Whittier and Walt Whitman had been rightly celebrated for decades, in Europe as well as America. Nathaniel Hawthorne had many books behind him, and *The Scarlet Letter* of 1851 is described, still, as a classic of the Puritan dilemma. Herman Melville had had four successful novels published: though in 1860 he was losing popular ground with *Moby Dick* and above all *Pierre*, he remained a force in America.

The mystery is this. The greatest issue in America up to 1865 was slavery. In 1860 most of the four million African slaves in America were scandalously exploited and deprived. The matter was heating up enough in the two decades before 1860 to erupt into a disastrous secession within the precious republic, and civil war. Yet few of the Northern writers dealt with it, and none with weight. Emerson's friend Wordsworth, in his greatest poem, which we know as *The Prelude* (begun before 1800, published in 1850), had written at length and powerfully about a huge external, political event, the French Revolution, especially his own objective experiences, a young man in France at the time. In contrast, in America, Hawthorne fretted about the clashes that Puritanism made inside his soul. Washington Irving and James Fenimore Cooper wrote about other things. Melville brought the far-off and exotic tropical Pacific close to the eastern American hearth in *Oomoo* and *Typee* and *Mardi*. But there, on the doorstep, were four million daily, existential clashes of white and black, an exoticism of race and suffering that cried for understanding, a gift of a subject for grand novels of the forces of history over vast territory on the scale of *War and Peace*. They did not happen. The great literary artists of the North remained silent. There were some inferior poems from Robert Lowell, Longfellow and William Culler Bryant: Whitman made a remark in 'Song of Myself', and wrote 'Ethiopia Saluting the Colours'. Whittier wrote about it, far from his best – indeed, it is argued that he might have achieved a greater degree of universal recognition as a poet had he not dissipated so much of his time and talent in the anti-slavery cause.[43] Melville touched on it in the short story 'Benito Cereno'. There were five or six anti-slavery novels in the 1830s and 1840s 'too crudely executed to warrant literary considerations'.[44] But the giants were dumb.

Slaves did appear in American fiction, grinning, amusing furniture in the Southern plantation romances, with smiling white teeth in happy black faces. They were there to add a touch of colour to pictures of the social harmony of the plantation idyll, where everyone was in that sacred American institution, the one big happy family. That slaves were people, and had feelings, and that the uniquely American cruelty was the ability of owners to break up families at a whim, was absolutely avoided.[45]

Uncle Tom's Cabin

It was left to a forty-year-old Calvinist Congregationalist minister's daughter and faculty wife in Maine to change everything, until then the writer of only a volume of undistinguished New England short stories. Harriet Beecher Stowe's *Uncle Tom's Cabin* of 1851 'swept the nation like a cyclone':[46] swept not just the literary scene, and not only America. First begun to be serialised in Washington DC in June, 1851, it was in Britain by November of that year: 'one could enter a London bookshop and chose among twenty different editions of the book'. By the end of 1856, 'British sales of the novel totaled a million copies – twice the American sales of the same period.'[47] By 1860, translations, often in several different versions, had appeared, not just in French, German, Spanish, Italian, Swedish and Russian; they were 'in every corner of the globe. Hindus, Wallachians, Finns, Armenians, Javanese, all could read the novel in their native tongues.'[48]

In structure, *Uncle Tom's Cabin* is a domestic sentimental novel, still by far the most readable of all such fiction from earlier nineteenth-century America. The high emotions in the parlour, the narcissistic and neurotic wives, the too-sensitive aesthete, the enchanting little girls, the deathbed scenes, the bullying, coarse men, the desperate journeys, the beautiful young women, the violence to vows and the tragic separations are all here – with one tremendous difference. This 'escapist fiction' is grounded in an appalling reality.

> The novel's sentimentalism continually calls atttention to the monstrous actuality which existed under the very noses of its readers . . . Mrs

Stowe aroused emotions . . . in order to facilitate the moral regeneration of an entire nation. Mrs Stowe was deeply serious – a sentimen-
talist with a vengeance . . .[49]

The inescapable reality was that the slaves' home lives were broken up
for profit. Young children were wrenched away to be sold. Couples were
split, families were disintegrated, decent people were put to lifetimes of
humiliating toil, good men and women were injured and killed, all in the
name of money. Slaves were property.

There are stereotypes in *Uncle Tom's Cabin* – comic and slothful servants,
brutish white men soaked in drink, tear-jerking deaths – but they are
swept aside by the power of people we meet, by 'the shrewdness, the
energy, the truly Balzacian variousness of Mrs Stowe's characterizations'.[50]
The men, women and children, of whatever colour, whether in North or
South, active or suffering, speaking or silent, filling so large a canvas, stay
in the mind. That they, and their often terrible situations, are so believable is one reason for the novel's moral force. Another is that the narrator makes clear that she is telling the truth: she documents the harshnesses
and violence, sometimes with tones of irony. Most significantly, the moral
structure is underpinned by Christian values. These can be too obviously
accompanied by violins for modern taste. Yet at the root of the book is
the understanding that the rock on which personal and national morality
is properly built is the Bible. Chapter xxii, just beyond the mid-point of
the book, which has as its title the biblical 'The grass withereth – the
flower fadeth' (Isaiah 40:8) finishes with a dialogue set off by little Eva's
question to her mother, 'why don't we teach our servants to read?'

> 'What a question, child! People never do.'
> 'Why don't they?' said Eva.
> 'Because it is no use for them to read. It don't help them to work
> any better, and they are not made for anything else.'
> 'But they ought to read the Bible, mamma, to learn God's will.'
> 'O! they can get that read to them all *they* need.'
> 'It seems to me, mamma, the Bible is for everyone to read themselves.
> They need it a great many times when there is nobody to read it.'
> 'Eva, you are an odd child,' said her mother.

Eva's mother tells her that she will have no time to read the Bible to the
servants when she comes to be dressing and going into company.[51]

Tom has a Bible, heavily used, and reads it, with labour. He could not
write: 'the mail for him had no existence, and the gulf of separation was
unbridged . . .' But we 'follow him for a moment, as, pointing to each
word, and pronouncing each half aloud, he reads,

'Let – not – your – heart – be – troubled.   In – my – Father's – house – are – many – mansions. I – go – to – prepare – a – place – for – you.'

Such 'ingots of gold' are 'such sublime words of hope . . . such future reunion'.[52] As the novel advances, and greater evils are committed, Bible quotations increase, appearing as epigraphs to half a dozen chapters, beginning with chapter XXXII, '*The dark places of the earth are full of the habitations of cruelty*' from Psalm 74, and heralding the arrival of Tom and others at Legree's brutal establishment. Bible words are not soft options. Perhaps there is here one clue about the failure of the great writers of the North to engage with slavery as an epic subject. Instead of expositions of the harsher truths of Bible theology, the intellectual fashion of the north east was for Emerson and uplift, and the elevated unworldly gaze of Transcendentalism. Mrs Stowe had been brought up a Calvinist. That is not a theology to shirk analysis of evil. Five years after the publication of *Uncle Tom's Cabin*, the death of her eldest son finally drove her away from Calvinism; but it had done its work. Calvinist divinity is the most New Testament, indeed the most Pauline, of all. Her sarcasm about the support of slavery by the churches is powerful.

> O, Dr. G— preached a splendid sermon . . . The text was 'He hath made everything beautiful in its season;' and he showed how all the orders and distinctions in society came from God, and that it was so appropriate, you know, and beautiful, that some should be high and some low, and that some were born to rule and some to serve, and all that, you know; and he applied it so well to all this ridiculous fuss that is made about slavery, and he proved distinctly that the Bible was on our side . . .[53]

Not only can one feel the cushions on the pews: in its blandness, the text (part of Ecclesiastes 3:11) could hardly be further from the message of the Gospels and Paul (and it is a million miles from Calvin). The application of those words in that Christian pulpit, moreover, is to the last degree perverse.

Harriet Beecher Stowe knew that her readers would take the point. Her subtitle, 'Life Among the Lowly' (originally announced as 'The Man that Was A Thing'), is one reason for the immense readership, as exploited workers across the world found it a parable. Such readers, however, could know not only *Uncle Tom's Cabin* in their own languages, but also by then the whole Bible. Uniquely, Mrs Stowe wrote to an understood response. 'Come unto Me, all ye that labor and are heavy laden, and I will give you rest', Tom reads to the two exhausted, hopeless, downtrodden women in 'the scene of misery and oppression' on his arrival at LeGree's. The immediate effect is the opposite of sentimental. "'I know the Lord an't here,' said the woman.' She goes 'to camp down, and sleep while I ken.' Tom sits in 'fierce conflict . . . the crushing sense of wrong, the foreshadowing of a whole life of future misery, the wreck of all past hopes' challenging his faith. The moment is apparently transformed by pure saccharine, when he dreams of little Eva reading from Isaiah 43:2: 'When thou passest through the waters, I will be with thee . . .' The moment is coloured with doubt. 'Was it a dream? . . . *It is a beautiful belief . . .*'[54]

THE CIVIL WAR AND THE BIBLE

In the Civil War, both sides were able to use the Bible. Abraham Lincoln's flat statement in his second inaugural was 'Both use the same Bible'. And not only the Old Testament. Paul's brief letter to Philemon accompanies the return to him of a runaway slave, Onesimus. In those twenty-five verses Paul does not denounce slavery: rather, he notes that Onesimus will return to being 'profitable' (11) and of 'benefit' (14). (Significantly Paul, ever the rhetorician, plays on the name, as ὀνήσιμος *(onēsimos)* means 'useful, profitable'.) In more theologically weighty moments, Paul stressed the unity of all people in Christ, whether 'bond or free' (1 Corinthians 12:13; Galatians 3:28). Paul's silence on slavery was read as affirmation.

Part of the problem for both sides is the breadth of meaning of the Greek word for slave, δοῦλος *(doulos)*, in the New Testament: it can mean something less pejorative than the English word 'slave' suggests, as in the very opening words of Paul to the Romans, 'Paul, a servant of Jesus Christ . . .'. The more important difficulty for the pro-slavery disputants lay in their shaky moral ground. Their structures were insupportable by any proper reading of the New Testament. Reading the bitter contentions of the time makes this clear.

It becomes clear, however, that though 'Both use the same Bible', and though it is always KJV, that Bible is being used differently. For some ministers and men who use it publicly – unhappily, only a few – it is the source-book of a life of faith in Christ, a fountain of daily spiritual refresh-ment which never fails, a revelation of the Fatherhood of God. For others, as has always happened, it is a book in which even a minister's ingenuity can find authority for bigotry. After hearing a Confederate Presbyterian preacher, a woman wrote, 'What a sermon! . . . A red-hot glow of patri-otism passed through me. . . . There was more exhortation to fight and die, à la Joshua, than meek Christianity.'[55] There is vast evidence of what Mark Noll called such 'prostitution of Scripture'.[56]

Early in the Civil War a Presbyterian teased II Chronicles 6:34–35, King Solomon's prayer for success in battle for Israel, into a biblically worded analysis of the current crisis: 'Eleven tribes [that is, the Confederacy] sought to go forth in peace from the house of political bondage, but the heart of our modern Pharaoh is hardened, that he will not let Israel go.'[57]

Even a cursory knowledge of that original biblical passage shows this as such a distortion as to be almost comic: but the politics made to hang from it were deadly. One of over 400 sermons published after the assassination of Lincoln expounded II Samuel 18:32, in which King David hears of the death in battle of his rebellious son Absalom, concluding that no one 'will be able to separate in thought the murder of the President from [Jefferson] Davis' persistent effort to murder the Union'.[58]

What emerges again is the familiar double interpretation.[59] Scripture is the richest source of useful metaphor with high authority, so that in the South Lincoln was Pharaoh, Jefferson Davis was Moses, and the Yankees in general, Judas.[60] In 1864, a minister could ask his congregation with great feeling, 'were not the victorious Hebrews vastly outnumbered by the Yankees of the desert?'[61] This is reasonable enough. That rhetorical method has been used to rouse hearers and readers for many centuries.

The other use of Scripture, again as seen above, is altogether more insidious. In this, the Bible is fulfilled in America. American people live in God's country as God's people in a unique sense. Even beyond Ezra Stiles's exaltation in 1783 of a prosperous America as foretold in Deuteronomy, seventy years later millennial themes make America the ultimate state in world history. A work published in 1854 has as title *Armageddon: Or The . . . Existence of the United States Foretold in the Bible, Its . . . Expansion into the Millennial Republic, and Its Dominion of the Whole World*.[62] Such fantasisers still exist, generally harmlessly: people who claim to have been selected for abduction into flying saucers by little green men, or that Elvis Presley is still alive, or who believe that the Earl of Oxford wrote the works of Shakespeare. This particular delusion, however, that the Bible foretells America's world dominion, a trumpet sounded constantly in the later nineteenth, and twentieth, centuries, is alarming and found to be dangerous when seen from any of the many nations of the earth that are not America. Reading Scripture typologically, an American tradition brought to its fullness in Cotton Mather's *Magnalia*, turned into reading Scripture to establish a super-patriotic nationalism. That the political rather than theological foundation of this deviation was laid down before and during the Civil War is not suprising. That it had power is a demonstration of how deeply ingrained in American culture was a sense of the importance of the Bible: perhaps no more than a sense, because such folly does not survive any reasonable Bible reading; and because the high colouring depends on only a rough awareness of, particularly, the Old Testament.

Jonathan Edwards's Bible theology showed God's covenant making America the new Israel as a wholly spiritual thing. Some of his followers tried to counter the growing, and obviously tempting, typology of nationalism at the time of the Revolution, and focus attention on what they saw the types as being about, that is, the individual's spiritual life. Some went further, and found the identification of Israel with America to be cancelled by the Bible's injunctions against slavery.

Slaves and sermons

Which brings us back to the slave experience, half a century on. Slaves scorned the whites' preaching from the Bible on only a few self-serving precepts, as 1 Peter 2:18, 'Servants, be subject to your masters with all fear . . .' Such sermons were summed up ' "Serve your masters. Don't steal your master's turkey. Don't steal your master's chickens. Don't steal your master's hogs. Do whatsomever your master tell you to do." Same old thing all de time.'[63] The literature on the slaves' own use of Scripture is now too large to be presented in detail here. What shines through is the vividness of the whole Bible taken as applying to individual slaves, and to the whole slave nation. And here is white American nationalism standing on its head. Instead of the Bible foretelling America's shining cosmic dominance, now the Bible told of escape from the America which was slave-holding Egypt: the Exodus under Moses, a key figure, was the escape into new nationhood from the harshness of purely American slavery.

> Moses had become Jesus, and Jesus, Moses; and with their union the two apects of the slaves' religious quest – collective deliverance as a people and redemption from their terrible personal sufferings – had become one . . .[64]

'In sum, deliverance from Egypt, the suffering of the Saviour, and the final Day of the Lord had very little to do with the fate of the United States.'[65] The slaves made little distinction between the sacred and the secular. Their sermons and songs were what might be called biblically political: the only public life the slaves could have was through their religious, outstandingly biblical, life.

> Preoccupied as they were with the Bible's unfathomable mysteries, with its message of hope for those who despaired, and with its offer of a reality more fundmental than even the scourge of slavery, the slaves'

silence on the fate of the nation as such may have been the most authentically scriptural comment on the national destiny of the entire period.[66]

War

Though the South appeared politically strong, controlling Congress and even the Presidency, the Union was increasingly unstable. Fulfilling the United States' 'Manifest Destiny' to occupy all the land (the phrase, though new, reflected the cruder expansionism of the earliest colonists under God's command as set out in the Old Testament), the occupation of the further West and South, with extremist threats to carry slaves there, caused great unrest in the North and Midwest. All this disturbance was not helped by the huge Irish and German influx, not far short of a million immigrants in the dozen years after 1850, mostly settled in Boston, New York and Philadelphia, and disrupting national equilibrium further. World markets even for King Cotton vacillated, suddenly threatening the slave-dependent rich planters of the Deep South. If in 1858 the anti-slavery North should win the Presidency – which meant Abraham Lincoln, of the new party of Republicans – extremists in the South threatened secession. Lincoln did not win then; but he made a national reputation.

The ridiculously small fuse was lit at Harper's Ferry on the upper Potomac in Virginia, on 16 October 1859. A controversial adventurer named John Brown – variously described as 'Connecticut-born wanderer and Bible-reading son of the Puritans', and 'a half-crazy, horse-stealing fanatic',[67] – already famous for murdering five pro-slavery men in Kansas in 1856, led twenty-one followers and seized the Federal arsenal there. His plan was, with Northern arms and money (which he had quickly established), to unite and arm the slaves so that they could rise against their masters. The twenty-two were captured with insulting ease by Colonel Robert E. Lee of the US army.

After a trial in which he had protested with some dignity that his only desire was to free the slaves, Brown was hanged. Northern revulsion at him and his bloody exploits, and the people's sheer common sense, were ignored: his words had reached the intellectual abolitionists of New England. Wendell Phillips said he had been 'the impersonation of God's order and God's law'. Henry David Thoreau found him 'a saintly martyr'.[68] Thomas Bingham Bishop wrote a meeting-camp song to a catchy tune, 'Gone to be a soldier in the Army of the Lord', the words of which he quickly changed, on hearing of Brown's death, to 'John Brown's body lies a-mouldering in the grave . . .' Such things revealed to the Southern leaders the general intentions of the North, clearly planning to call a revolt of the slaves. Harper's Ferry fired the South. Those states could by then respond with some unity, as a slave-owning body: within the greater patriotism for America, they had manufactured for themselves a passion for a new nation, unified in religion, culture, politics and trade, sentimentally calling itself 'Dixie' (probably meaning everything south of the Mason-Dixon line).

In 1860, Abraham Lincoln became President. At once, South Carolina, Mississippi, Florida, Alabama, Georgia, Louisiana and Texas seceded, making, on 4 February 1861, the Confederated States of America, with their own President, Jefferson Davis.

> These events struck the North with amazement. The Union of the American States was such a profound commitment; the pride in the achievements of the American Revolution was so enormous; the belief in the promises of liberty, equality and property [*sic*?] if America held together was so deep, that it seemed impossible that American citizens could really mean to destroy what the President-elect called 'the last, best hope of Earth.' . . . [But] their new Confederacy . . . had finished with Uncle Sam.[69]

Fighting began in April 1861. Virginia, Arkansas, Tennessee and North Carolina seceded. The Confederacy was now too big for Lincoln's statesmanship, fine though that was proving to be. The issue was still slavery, even if disguised as the Southern states' rights. This is not the place for an account of the disastrous four-year war. There was, on both sides, much bravery and brilliance, and much stupidity and failure. The great battles between large, often barefoot armies, famous for ever in American history, propelled the fine soldiers – Lee, Jackson, Grant, Sherman – into the American pantheon, and caused the most appalling casualties ever seen on American soil. At the decisive battle at Gettysburg, Pennsylvania, 1–3 July 1863, Robert E. Lee's furthest strike into the North, over 45,000 were killed, wounded or missing. On both sides, the fighting was in the name of God:[70] but Abraham Lincoln wondered

> what sins of omission or commission he and his countrymen had committed to deserve this chastening at God's hands . . . The deepest sin, of course, the root of the whole matter, was slavery . . .[71]

By the time the Civil War was entirely over, in July 1865, well over 600,000 soldiers had died. It was disastrous in every other way for the South. Great estates had been ravaged. The chaos had for ever loosened the slave bondage; very many had run away, a significant number to join the Union armies. The hammer blow was Lincoln's brave Emancipation Proclamation of the summer of 1862, which freed them, to their everlasting

gratitude: they were declared completely equal with whites in 1870. One
might see God's hand in the phrase in the Declaration of Independence,
made 'Fourscore and seven years ago', as Lincoln began his brief (under
two minutes) address at the cemetery for the fallen at Gettysburg, 'the
proposition that all men are created equal'. But his assassination on Good
Friday 1865 was surely the work of the Devil, destroying with one evil
act, the murder of a good and great man, what hope America had of any
kind of just, long-term settlement of the peace. That crazed political killing
and the bungling that followed ensured that festering hatreds would
continue for a very long time.

BIBLE DISTRIBUTION

As we saw, those tumultuous decades leading up to the Civil War were
the times when more English Bibles were printed in America than ever
before, and perhaps since. The American Bible Society's bibliography lists
450 different editions from the start of 1850 to the end of 1870: and as
we also noticed, that figure is too low.

Problems of distribution of Bibles make an interesting indicator of what
life was like in America between 1861 and 1866, during 'the War Between
the States'. The American Bible Society, for example, found that it could
not keep in touch with its Southern Auxiliaries because 'communication
between North and South was virtually impossible, both emotionally and
physically'.[72] 'By order of Mayor Brown of Baltimore the Marylanders had
destroyed direct railroad connections and telegraphic communications
with the North [in the spring of 1861].'[73] The paths of trade were virtually closed.[74]

The Confederate States Bible Society was organised in 1862, 'based
upon the foregone conclusion that our country [the South] would achieve
its independence', working 'as confidently as though the world had already
received us into the brotherhood of nations'.[75] It published a Soldiers' Testament for the use of the Confederate Army.[76] There was from the start
a Bible famine: stocks were quickly exhausted, and 'at the outbreak of the
War there was no Bible printing south of the Mason–Dixon line'.[77] Some
Southern states managed to send envoys to England through the Government's strong naval blockade of 3,500 miles of coast, to try to arrange
the importation of Bibles from the British and Foreign Bible Society.
These would parallel the way 'the Confederate States of America looked
to England for warships, rifles, and diplomatic recognition'.[78] The envoys
knew that it would be difficult to get them in, and that the inland route
down from New York was working well: the ABS official overseeing

Southern Bible distribution observed crossly that Southerners 'can get Bibles and Testaments far more readily from New York than from London & with actual permits and help of our own government instead of encountering the hazards of a blockading fleet'.[79] It was more romantic to have adventures. After eight months in Europe, the most celebrated envoy, the disputatious Presbyterian minister Dr Moses D. Hoge, returned to the port of Wilmington, North Carolina, in October 1863, 'his ship under fire as she went through the harbour'.[80] Under the blockade, cargoes including books were lost.

> [The] idea that the Bibles ... from England might cross the Atlantic and enter a Confederate port under a flag of truce had to be abandoned ... Hoge had to have his Bibles and tracts shipped in small installments from time to time as opportunity offered itself. They were crowded aboard different vessels bearing medicines, gunpowder, and other contraband. Some of these shipments were sunk, others captured at sea. Still other consignments met with various misadventures and were destroyed or lost at such places as Havanna. . . .[81]

A copy of the 'special edition of the New Testament' in 12mo, said to have been 'printed in 1863 by the Oxford Press' (though not recorded elsewhere) bears a handwritten note: 'From the cargo of the Anglo-Rebel Blockade Runner *Minna*, captured December 6th, 1863, off Wilmington, by the government Dispatch Ship *Circassian*, Captain W. B. Eaton.'[82] There is clearly a stirring tale of Bible smuggling to be told: the records, however, do not now exist.[83] A letter of thanks to the BFBS from the Confederate States tells of sending the books 'almost exclusively to the soldiers, sometimes two or three thousand to supply a single order ... '.[84] The BFBS had made a free grant of 10,000 Bibles, 50,000 Testaments and 250,000 Gospels and Psalms (it is always striking how large the numbers are, of Bibles promised or distributed). Most were smuggled in. 'But,' as the ABS Secretary wrote, 'what ... are they among so many?'[85]

The correspondence of the period in the archives of the ABS shows that though there was success in sending many thousands of Bibles from the North to Virginia through Maryland, further south there was still a desert. The ABS *Record* for January 1863 noted that in the South 'The churches ... are to a large extent demoralized, and, in some places of the first importance, entirely closed.' The writer quoted a letter from New Orleans: ' "Our clergy, with but one or two exceptions (I mean Protestant), have loaned themselves to strife and blood ... The Methodist ministry left the city ... we are entirely without a pastor in any church here." '[86] In spite of blockades, strained relations, insolences of office, and the destructions of war, Bibles later flowed South in some numbers: 20,000 'to the Confederate Army of the Mississippi Valley . . . For Genl Bragg's Army and for Hospitals within the rebel lines' in Tennessee, 50,000 Bibles or portions were granted, and arrived – and the payment the ABS was offered was in cotton.[87]

The weakest position taken by the ABS in the decades before the war was over Bibles for slaves. Northern abolitionists had pressed for a more aggressive policy, but the society reiterated its position that it left all that as a local matter in the hands of its Southern Auxiliaries. These it claimed to admire, but they were often inadequate or inert: in any case all had resigned by July 1861.[88] Few Bibles were distributed to slaves either before the war or in the first years. Liberated 'Freedmen' after 1862 received Bibles from Northern troops advancing on Southern soil. Few slaves could read. Runaways captured by Federal troops tended not to be returned to their masters, but impounded for use as 'contrabands' (the name stuck). A letter in the ABS archive is from a sergeant in charge of a 'Colony of Contrabands – now numbering nearly 1000 souls'. They

> have prepared a house of worship and are desitute of a Bible for their
> pulpit . . . Though but three or four of the colony can read – yet any
> published matter you feel disposed to send will be read and listened to
> with avidity.[89]

'In the year 1863–4, the Managers [of ABS] reported that 100,000 negroes were in the Union army.' The ABS, probably realistically, granted 18,424 books.[90] By 1865, the ABS's army agent was reporting that 'The Freedmen are rapidly learning to read.' A modern historian notes that 'The former slaves' extraordinary educational appetites stimulated perhaps the most dramatic rise in literacy rates in American history. The Bible was both an important literacy tool for freedmen and a key stimulus in the desire to read.'[91] Even so, ABS agents found 'prevailing racist feelings among many leaders of the local [ABS] auxiliaries'. One agent from the North wrote home from a Galveston hotel, sitting 'in a hot room with a dim light, and surrounded by a large company of bugs and mosquitoes', telling of encountering 'bitter feeling toward the Northern people'. Auxiliaries on the spot could be at best ambiguous and at worst hostile to work among the freedmen: and 'black citizens received minimal opportunities to participate in the Bible cause'.[92]

The 'poor bloody infantry' of all wars, foot-soldiers on both sides, were hungry for New Testaments. The ABS tried to supply them, sending even more urgently to the sick and wounded in the appalling hospitals.

> One copy [of three or four left] was a short time since, eagerly taken
> by a sick soldier at the Circle Hospital, a Vermont boy, whose interest

in perusing the volume was so marked as to attract the notice of those near him. He has since died, holding the book in his hand . . .[93]

Prisoners of war held in the North were revealing.

Of those taken at Antietam and South Mountain, only about one in twenty had a copy of the New Testament, or any part of the Bible. Hundreds of those who did possess them had taken their copies from the knapsacks and pockets of retreating, defeated, wounded or dead Union soldiers. Many of these Testaments contained the presentation label of the New York and other Bible societies pasted on the inside of the cover. . . . A few have refused [the Scriptures]; but these exceptions were either those who could not read, or who were bitter in their remarks and feelings toward our goverment . . . Tens of thousands of these soldiers have been released . . .[94]

Distribution of Bibles among soldiers demands the question 'Do the soldiers ever refuse the Scriptures?' Documented in the ABS archive are many answers in the vein of 'All the reports . . . agree in stating, that none scarcely, except Roman Catholics, refuse the sacred Volume, and that very many of them accept it both cheerfully and gratefully.'[95] The question 'Do our soldiers read the Bible?' produces variations on the answer 'more than ever'.

A historian working 'with the research assistance of ABS staff' calculated that

When the tragic War between the States was at last ended, the records of the American Bible Society in the North showed it had distributed 5,297,832 Bibles and parts thereof to soldiers and *civilians* [our italics], Confederates and Federals.[96]

The statistics of over 500 recipient groups during the years 1861 to 1886 make touching and illuminating reading. In 1861, 'Soldiers – Fortress Monroe, 1,600 Testaments . . . Escaped Slaves at Fortress Monroe, 12 Testaments.' In 1862, 'Cavalry Rgt. at Gettysburg, 20 Bibles, 600 Testaments . . . Sick-Wounded on Steamer "Daniel Webster", 100 Portions . . . Hospital – Harpers Ferry, Va. 100 Bibles, 200 Testaments.' In 1863, 'Louisville Bible Society – for Army of the Cumberland, 29,000 Testaments, 6,000 Portions . . . Vt. Regt. in Fla., 12 Bibles, 3 Testaments.' In 1865, 'US Christian Commission 2,000 Bibles, 53,000 Testaments . . . Colored People, 31 Bibles.' 1866, 'Freedmen, Missouri, 12 Testaments, 50 Portions.'[97]

The Confederate States Bible Society attempted permanence: it failed.[98] In August 1865, in the course of celebrating the Jubilee year of the American Bible Society, the trumpets of which 'are in full harmony with the harps of peace', the ABS prepared a statement, 'The American Bible and the South'.[99] In all, during the war the ABS had sent more than 300,000 Bibles and Testaments 'for gratuitous distribution *among the armies and people of the Southern States'*. There had been delays and failure:

> Since the close of the war a number of boxes have been discovered at Norfolk, Richmond and elsewhere, which . . . will yet be transmitted to the destination among the destitute people of the regions for which they were given – now that the armies have been broken up.

Tens of thousands of prisoners of war had been given Testaments. In the work of reconstruction, an obstacle was, as well as shortage of cash and men, 'a prevailing indisposition to cooperate with any northern organization. This, under the circumstances, is not strange.'

Nevertheless, the Jubilee *Report* notes

> the painful destitution which prevails . . . From Texas to the Border States . . . [there is] great want, accompanied by all the desolation, poverty, and suffering which now reign over that vast territory . . . Our purpose is to supply the entire population of the South, irrespective of colour . . . The war has put the stamp of nationality upon our precious Bible. No other book has been so much in demand, none so thoroughly used in all the opposing armies as 'the New Testament of our Lord and Saviour Jesus Christ' . . . Four millions of freed people, and millions more of the white race – all alike destitute – are pleading for the Bible as their first and greatest spiritual want . . . Providence has plainly ordained that we shall be one people, with one government, one civilisation, one Bible, one Christian faith and destiny.[100]

NOVELISED BIBLES

Bibles printed in America in the second half of the nineteenth century could be enormous.[101] As an object, such a Bible did not entice. When, to make it less forbidding, the whole thing was compressed to quarto size, the fonts now so small that even healthy eyes needed a magnifying glass, then a would-be reader could justifiably feel put off the Word.[102]

What allured Americans, increasingly, were novelised parts of the Bible, especially fictional lives of Christ. They came in pleasing and easy-to-buy volumes, regularly serialised in monthly magazines.[103] Such fiction had been published in Britain from the eighteenth century, and had been popular with church members. America did it bigger. Paul Wright's imaginative expansion of the Gospels *A New and Complete Life of Our Blessed*

Lord and Saviour Jesus Christ, went through fourteen printings from first publication in London in 1785, then in Philadelphia, and finally in New York before 1818.[104] There were many, many others.[105] The sales of Lew Wallace's *Ben-Hur: A Tale of the Christ*, first published by Harper Brothers in New York in 1880, were said to be more than two million, with further translations into many foreign languages. (The book might have had as a strapline on the cover 'Later To Be A Major Motion Picture'. That came in 1959, famously with an enhanced chariot race, and even less of 'the Christ'.)

There were also objections. American Protestants at the start of the century were nervous about fiction. The Bible was enough.

> Alexander Campbell stressed throughout his ministry that to understand the Bible one must imagine oneself 'in Judea, in Rome, or in Corinth, and not in these places in the present day; but . . . nearly two thousand years before we lived at all.' Bible readers 'must mingle with the Jews in their temples and synagogues . . . must visit the temples and altars of the Pagan Gentiles . . . must converse with Epicurean and Stoic philosophers – with Pharisees and Sadducees – with priests and people, that died centuries before . . .'[106]

Just as the blank leaves for family history in the middle of a large Bible allowed the owners to insert themselves, as it were, into the narrative, so the growth of information available in these Bibles about the Holy Land, with 'imaginative reconstructions' of places and events, from the Garden of Eden to Paul preaching in the household of Caesar, encouraged just that – personal imagination. This, rather than faith, was, perhaps insidiously, becoming the key to receiving Scripture. (It has ever since been a characteristically large American response. As the great resources of film and electronics have become available, this American way with imgination about the Bible has grown into new genres of 'comic book' Bibles or animated versions of biblical stories (fig. 46).) The effect was also to bypass the Bible itself. It was more fun to imagine Eden than to wrestle with the theology of Paul's Epistles. The writer of an American Tract Society pamphlet, Tract 515, 'Novel Reading', feared that story-book versions would make the Bible itself seem 'a wearisome book'.[107] As Paul Gutjahr wrote, 'While religious fiction might point readers to the Bible's story, it also gave them an excuse not to read it.'[108] Already mentioned has been Paul Wright's seminal *New and Complete Life* of 1785, giving readers the 'real facts' of Jesus' life in Palestine, seductively elaborating the Gospel accounts with details of historical settings from other, pagan, writers. This was presently got up to look like a folio Bible with ornamented leather bindings, and Isaiah Thomas's copperplate engravings from his 1791 edition, no less, with Thomas's name expunged.[109] His intention was two-fold: to make the biography of Jesus easy, and to allow the reader to match his or her own biography, strictly in moral terms. Once again, a long way from William Tyndale.

Even further from William Tyndale is the most striking Jesus fiction in the first half of the nineteenth century. It is one which had great influence, an effect probably today even greater. Unlike Lew Wallace's best-selling *Ben-Hur: A Tale of the Christ*, set in Palestine and across the eastern Mediterranean, in this new and treasured volume, the moral avatar Jesus himself, after his death and Resurrection in the first century, came to America. He did this because Noah in his ark had been carried away by the flood far from the traditional location of Eden; so far, in fact, that the ark settled in what became the United States; to try to be exact, on a small hill in north-west Missouri. Thus the Protestant typology which had made America, either spiritually or in fertile essence, God's Promised Land, was taken to a new limit. America *is* the Promised Land, where God worked his original work, and where, because of that, his Risen Son had to walk.

The story is confusing. The book tells of two families: one leaves Jerusalem by boat in 600 BC and eventually settles in America. The other does the same, but only after the failure of the Tower of Babel. In America, their heirs fall out and destroy each other: the only survivors are the American Indians. In stating this, this fiction was not new. A number of early nineteenth-century writers had confidently made the American Indians 'the ragged remnant of the once proud inhabitants of the Holy Land, but their mere presence pointed to the cosmically significant role of the United States in this history of the world'.[110] The new, 1830, fiction, is important because it becomes a different New Testament story. Christ visited North America. The book is a

> unique, and stunningly American, life of Christ . . . [who was] not some distant, exotic figure stranded in a remote Middle Eastern location. He was a Messiah who had physically visted the Americas. One did not need to know arcane, historical lore or the geography of Palestine to understand Jesus and his teaching; one could gain such understanding by exploring American history and the American landscape.[111]

This particular fiction was made to look like a Bible, in two ways. From the outside, the size, paper, type and original brown leather binding with gold bars on the spine exactly matched the latest American Bible Society's issues. Inside, the titles of separate parts of the story, the chapter divisions, the two columns of print divided into numbered verses, with references, made it look very much like a Bible. More cunningly still, the language was – still is – a pastiche of KJV. Opening the book at random, at the start of The Book of Mosiah chapter 29, we read

> Now when Mosiah had done this he sent out throughout all the land, among all the people, desiring to know their will concerning who should be their king.
>
> 2 And it came to pass that the voice of the people came, saying: We are desirous that Aaron thy son should be our king and ruler.
>
> 3 Now Aaron had gone up to the land of Nephi, therefore the king could not confer the kingdom upon him . . .

Neither 'Mosiah' nor 'the land of Nephi' appear in the Bible: both are part of the larger fiction. 'The land of Nephi' is, as far as one can tell, Missouri.

There is a further factor. The highest possible claims were made for this writing. Though as imitation KJV it is always long-winded and even tedious, and to any even slightly knowledgeable mind has nothing whatsoever to do with the Bible, it was maintained as a religious book of better authenticity even than the Bible itself. Knowledge of the work of the German scholars had trickled down and been distorted to offer to suggestible people the notion that KJV is mutilated, a version passed down through centuries of inadequate manuscripts and distortions, and thus not to be trusted as the Word of God. In contrast, this new American book was 100 per cent authenticated. Far from being at the mercy of ancient and foreign scribes and copyists, it was divinely revealed, as a complete whole, in America.

What has been described is, of course, *The Book of Mormon*. The exotic history of the Church of Jesus Christ of the Latter-Day Saints, and the global spread of Mormonism, are not part of this study. This book is about the Bible in English, and not about a volume so obviously intended to replace it, however deeply influenced. Modern academic Mormons, who in many fields in science and the humanities command respect in the scholarly world, are increasingly interested in the origins of the English Bible, the making of KJV, and the part played by William Tyndale. Nevertheless, one must contrast *The Book of Mormon*. Its origins were as follows. Joseph Smith was a young man born in poverty and hardship to an unsettled family. Around 1825, on the meagre farm in Palmyra, New York, and now one of a family of eleven, Joseph took to treasure hunting and revivalist religion for comfort and hope. Neither improved his fortunes. When he was fourteen, two angels visited him to tell him that all religious denominations were corrupt, and that God would reveal true religion to him if he would wait. Seven years later, God directed him to gold plates buried in the earth near his home. From these Smith translated the 600 pages of *The Book of Mormon*. The gold plates then disappeared.

The Book of Mormon, before long produced in very great numbers, at first sold slowly. It was, however, influential. Described there, though the narrative was only a small part of the whole, with only a glancing relationship with the New Testament, was a Jesus who was American, for Americans.

The American religious sentimental novel

The Book of Mormon also showed the way forward for an especially American kind of Jesus fiction, the sentimental novel with a religious message. *Uncle Tom's Cabin* was published in 1852. In that same decade before the Civil War, two novels – Susan Warner's *The Wide, Wide World* (1850) and Maria Cummins's *The Lamplighter* (1854) – had equal sales of well over 100,000 copies, figures before then unknown for American fiction. The Jesus who is referred to is an oblique, remote guide. Readers were to find in the central characters of Susan Warner's dozen sentimental novels those elements which were supposed to be the backbone of a 'Christian', and great, nation. These sugary figures flicked a glance at high moral values. That they were part of America's everyday life, being housewives, businessmen, little girls, ministers, farmers and even slaves was thought somehow to reinforce the humanity of Christian teaching. The New Testament was again being prostituted, though more vacuously. Rather different, and commercially even more successful, was Joseph Holt Ingraham's *The Prince of the House of David* of 1855, a sensational full-blown biography of Jesus which sold 180,000 copies before 1858, and remained in print for over a hundred years after that.[112] The story of Jesus' ministry is told in letters to her father from a young Jewish girl, Adina, who happens to be in Palestine during the exact three years. The novel is

> a bold mixture of biblical truth and sensational melodrama . . . stirring subplots centred on treachery, love, friendship, and misplaced religious devotion, as well as a compelling picture of Jesus as God 'veiled in the flesh'.[113]

The hunger of American readers for geographical and historical details on which their imaginations could feed is well satisfied. The subtitle is *Three Years in the Holy City . . . by an Eye-witness, all the Scenes and Wonderful Incidents in the Life of Jesus of Nazareth*. Adina dutifully gives, at length and meticulously, descriptions of the Holy Land and its customs, in order to fix Jesus in his earthly setting, particularly in houses attractively ornamented with Family Bibles, to give a place for his frequently described 'domestic intercourse and friendly companionship'.[114] That phrase of Ingraham's, from his Preface, gives a clue to his commercial success. His novel is aimed at what his women readers could admit to needing from a man, and such a man. Moreover, this Jesus quite remarkably shares what the author identified as their feminine qualities, especially their nervous afflictions. Not for nothing is the narrator a young woman. This Jesus can be pale and interesting. Adina writes that Jesus seemed to her to be 'weary and pale, and . . . seemed to suffer, as from time to time he raised his hand to his temples'.[115] This Jesus, from time to time, had a headache. Bad as such discomfort can be, one protests at such trivialisation of his 'human infirmities' inescapably bestowed on him by his Father 'for the good of men', as Adina puts it on the subject of his headaches.[116] Ingraham misquotes and misappropriates the risen Jesus' words at Luke 24:46, changing them to 'It behooves me to suffer all things', in relation to the headaches. So much for the New Testament's analyses of the darkest depths of human spiritual as well as physical experience, endured by Jesus as the Suffering Servant foretold by Isaiah. With headaches went greater moral sensitivity. A feminised Jesus could be the model for womankind's uplifiting power in the new nation, felt to be urgently needed. Ingraham dedicated his book 'To the Daughters of Israel', that is, 'American women who, like Adina, might be persuaded of Christ's messianic mission':[117] in this case, to civilise their menfolk. (The – at first, anonymous – large-selling novel by Maria Cummins, *The Lamplighter: A Tale* of 1854, mentioned above, consummates the story on the last page with the words, 'The blind girl's prayers are answered; her last, best, work is done; she has cast a ray from her blessed spirit into his darkened soul.' The book ends with supposed 'biblical' words whispered in 'gentliest, holiest accents'.) Paul Gutjahr comments:

> Adina . . . exercises a great deal of moral influence in the book, particularly over the men in her life. . . . Such arguments, laced heavily with bible verses, show that Adina not only has an obvious intelligence and broad knowledge of the Scriptures, but also . . . model arguments for Ingraham's women readers who could identify with Adina's struggle to 'moralize' the men around her.[118]

Ingraham went on to make a good deal of money out of Old Testament fictions, *The Pillar of Fire; or, Israel in Bondage* (New York, 1859) and *The Throne of David* (Philadelphia, 1860).

The genre of biblical fiction in America in the second half of the nineteenth century is coloured strongly by portrayals of Jesus as moral instructor. The exception is the biggest seller of all, *Ben-Hur* (1880), the gigantic sales of which show that Protestant Christian objections to fiction had been overcome. Lew Wallace's subtitle, *A Tale of the Christ*, was a canny cast in the profitable Jesus fiction waters. Set in Bethlehem, Jerusalem, Antioch, Egypt, Rome and elsewhere, it is only obliquely about 'the Christ'. The novel is a wide-screen Technicolour adventure yarn of murder plots, love affairs, powerful male bonding and set pieces, including a sea battle and the famous chariot race. The swashbuckling is ponderous. A visit to the lawless love-grove of Daphne, and Part IV, chapter 12 'A Roman Orgie', are sweetly harmless: Cleopatra, sketched from Shakespeare, is sultry. The narrative is set moving by the colourfully drawn Three Wise Men meeting on their desert way to Bethlehem to visit Mary, admiringly described, and The Birth. 'The wonderful Nazarene' arrives first after five hundred pages, and leaves at once, having healed a noisy crowd of lepers. At Gethsamene, Ben-Hur speaks to Him, offering rescue (a detail omitted by all the Gospels). A crowd of many thousands rushes to Calvary. A sanitised Crucifixion is watched by the main characters, Bathasar, Simonides, Ben-Hur, Esther and 'the two faithful Galileans'. Everything in the book is on the largest scale. Wallace, famously, did his research as only a driven American could do it. He travelled to Washington and trawled all the thousands of relevant holdings in the Library of Congress for weeks to collect evidence of Jewish and Roman life. He could not make his hero a galley slave without giving his readers three pages on the arrangements of a trireme, with additional glosses. His chariot race is technically perfect. No wonder Hollywood made a movie out of it. The great biblical motion-picture epics are remarkable for getting all the historical reconstruction correct, down to different thongs on sandals – and missing the point of the story. (As Bible readers know, King David felt shame and guilt before the Lord, not so much for taking Bathsheba when she was already married, but for arranging for her husband Uriah to be in the forefront of the hottest battle, and so killed (2 Samuel 11). In Hollywood's *David and Bathsheba* (1951), Gregory Peck as King David reaches for a harp, 'authentic' in every detail, and begins 'The Lord is my Shepherd . . .', while Susan Hayward as Bathsheba, with a biblically modest cleavage, gazes at him with adoration – 'For this woman . . . he broke God's own commandment!' In this film David is right to dispose of Bathsheba's husband Uriah, obviously the guilty party in her marriage: in the script she suffers 'mental cruelty' from her husband, something every Californian at the time would recognise as grounds for divorce.) So Wallace missed the point of 'a Tale of the Christ'. His many readers were led to feel that in learning so much about conditions at the time of Jesus they were somehow nurturing their souls. What they were doing was relishing a pagan adventure with Christmas-tree trimmings. *Ben-Hur* was one outcome of the Americans' passion for exact historical and geographical details in their

Bibles. That supposed authenticity allowed the book to be appropriated as a Christian message, even to being used in Sunday Schools. Any supposed Christian message in the book is drowned in the novel reader's natural self-indulgence. There is obviously a place for strong feelings in Christianity. But if the faith is about nothing but exotic large-scale adventures and lurching passions, with occasional sightings of a shadowy figure not even called Jesus, that faith is not worth having. In Europe in the Middle Ages the religious plays in the market-places were both stark and festive: but the audiences for them did not have complete Bibles in their language within comfortable reach, for hard study is needed. *Ben-Hur* showed the way to Christianity as easy American entertainment.

Chapter 39

BIBLE TRANSLATION INTO ENGLISH IN THE TWENTIETH CENTURY

Whereas in America in the second half of the nineteenth century, Bibles printed in uncountable numbers made a spate of KJVs, with a bare dozen of private new versions, in the twentieth century, especially in America, especially since 1945, new translations make the flood. Some were modest affairs, the work of one dedicated scholar, like Moffat, Weymouth, Knox or Phillips in Britain; in America, Goodspeed or Lattimore. Most, later in the century, were grand American productions, the salaried work of big, well-funded comfortable committees with full secretarial support, massive publicity and marketing organisations and claims of gigantic print-runs and sales. It is all a long way from Tyndale, hungry, cold and alone in his Antwerp room.

Like Hollywood movies, many of the later productions were remakes, so that from America came the New King James Version of 1982 (and before that in 1970 'The King James II Version', a curious title indeed); after the Revised Standard Version of 1952, the New Revised Standard Version of 1989; after the Good News Bible in 1976, a completely revised edition (the fourth) in 1994; after the New International Version of 1978, the New International Reader's Version in 1997; and, from Britain, after the Jerusalem Bible in 1966, the New Jerusalem Bible in 1985; and after the New English Bible in 1970, the Revised English Bible in 1989. Those are by no means all. Again in America, the Amplified Bible of 1965 did what it announced, and indicated to most of KJV's words 'additional shades of meaning'. The Living Bible of various dates in the 1960s was an out-and-out paraphrase, not always wise. The Reader's Digest Bible of 1982 got the whole thing down to some hours' reading. The various forms of *The Message* of the 1990s make a feel-good handbook which often grossly mistranslates (see chapter 34 above). Even that is not, again, by any means all. Not only have all these lasted, but all of those just mentioned are, as the new millennium gets underway, in print and in use.

The drive for change comes, even more than from better understanding of the original textual bases (by 1990, less of a consideration), from commercial ambition, from sectarian interests, and from social and linguistic fashions. The Good News Bible (1994) is not alone in adopting 'inclusive language'. Moreover, for some large groups of consumers, the Bible, it seems, must not be found disturbing, whether by calling God (in Jesus' words) 'Father' (which is 'patriarchy'), or, as with *The Message*, jettisoning theology altogether to suggest that it may just be possible that you may not at all times feel totally good about yourself. That is an even longer way from Tyndale.

The bizarre and the reprehensible, many though they are among the more than twelve hundred different Bible translations published since 1945, should not distract from the solid dozen or so of major twentieth-century endeavours. The British Revised Version of 1885, and its American cousin of 1901, did indeed open a door. There are now far too many even to mention. In this necessarily long chapter will be considered, though lamentably briefly, the principal twentieth-century versions. There has been such intense communication across the Atlantic that the American and British contributions can be intermingled.

THE AMERICAN STANDARD VERSION, 1901

Americans were fully drawn into the work on the Revised Version in 1870s London late, and by the British reluctantly. At first they partly took it over and then, in 1901, wholly made it their own.

Against the ten years taken by the British revisers, the Americans met in Bible House, New York, for twenty-nine years. The British and American teams never met, but as was seen above, the American president of the whole project, Dr Philip Schaff, received Dr Joseph Angus in New York in August 1870, and he himself visited the English companies in the Jerusalem Chamber in the summer of 1871, and again in July 1875. There was a good deal of correspondence all the time. The Americans, intentionally or not, were made to feel like colonial cousins.[1] They were told bluntly to get Bishops on to their company.[2]

After the romantic start of the relationship, like a new mistress Philip Schaff had to ask the 'where do I stand?' question; 'whether the Americans are simply *advisers*, or fellow-*revisers* and fellow-*authors* . . . I wish you to consider that we do not claim an *equal* share, but only a *just* and *equitable* share in determining the final text.'[3] Schaff proposed closer co-operation. 'Adopt some members of the American Companies into your Companies', or 'A Conference Committee, at the close of the work, to sit in London (or in New York if you will honor us with your presence and give us the pleasure of showing you a most cordial and liberal hospitality). . .', or simultaneous publication with variations.[4] In the end pusillanimity reigned and the British agreed merely to send the Americans a list for consideration.

The Americans had high hopes. In 1885, Talbot W. Chambers, a member of the American Old Testament Committee, wrote *A Companion to the Revised Old Testament*, a book much admired by Bishop Ellicott. In his Preface, he says of the KJV that that book at first was received by cold indifference by some and with violent opposition by others, yet it survived both. Although universally known as 'the Authorised Version'

> no trace of such authorisation has ever been found in any records of the time, whether civil or ecclesiastical. Neither the crown nor Parliament nor the privy council nor the convocation appear to have given it any public sanction. Yet . . . entirely on its own merits, it quietly superseded all its predecessors and rivals. It is not therefore unreasonable to expect that the present revision will in time noiselessly accomplish the same result, and at length come to be recognised as the Bible of the English-speaking peoples.[5]

'Noiselessly' was not to be, but nor was 'recognised'. The English Revised Version in May 1881 came out to tremendous publicity in the USA, exceeding that in Britain. As touched on above, it generated enough excitement to make the Chicago *Daily Tribune* and the Chicago *Times* print the entire revised New Testament on 22 May 1881, employing 92 typesetters who worked for 12 hours. Three million revised New Testaments were sold in both countries in the first year. As also noted, disappointment set in rapidly. It was kindly said that it could be useful for study. The loss of the KJV 'music' was the chief complaint.

At the end of the British revising process, sharp disagreement had broken out between the US and British revisers. The American committee members pledged not to publish their own version for fourteen years. Then the British publishers, the Oxford and Cambridge University presses, agreed to print in their editions an appendix containing some 300 of the American alterations. This would not do. The American preferences, all thoughtful, ran into thousands. The Americans continued to meet. Thomas Nelson & Sons in New York took over the publishing. Two unauthorised 'American' editions appeared from other publishers, incorporating the 300 appendix variations into the texts. Oxford and Cambridge presses did the same.

The Americans worked on. They disapproved strongly of both the the texts that were printed without their alterations (many of them clarifying

RV's incomprehensible archaisms, for example 'amerced'), and the condescending treatment they were receiving. They decided to go for their own
copyright, and in 1901 Thomas Nelson published the American Standard
Version, incorporating all the thousands of American preferences. In 1919,
the copyright was transferred to the International Council of Religious
Education, which in its turn, after the Second World War, inaugurated a
further revision, which became the popular Revised Standard Version.

What was all the fuss about? There were many changes, certainly.

> The new version had page headings; altered paragraphing, punctuation
> and use of italics; revised marginal readings and renderings and
> cross-references; and changes in the text which the whole American
> Committee had approved, including the use of 'Jehovah' for the
> Tetragrammaton.[6]

Bishop Lee of Delaware, a member of the New Testament Committee,
calculated that in the Epistle to the Hebrews the American Company
made 913 changes: the British Company made 476 of the same changes.
The American Company made 1,781 changes to the Book of Job from
KJV: the British made 1,004.[7] Many of the changes were sensible, removing the British revisers' infelicities, intended or final, in the New
Testament translating the Greek δήναριον (*dēnarion*) as 'denary' instead of
'penny' – giving rise to the point that it would be pronouced 'deanery',
and the jest that the revisers would be said to have 'sold a deanery for a
penny'.[8] The sensible Americans removed many of the British revisers'
additional archaisms, not to mention follies, like 'footstool of his feet' at
Matthew 5:35. The London journal *Athenaeum* of 28 May 1881, wrote:

> Several of the recommendations of the American Committee might
> have been adopted with advantage. The general excellence of the sug-
> gestions of the American Revisers is undoubted, and they ought not to
> have been so often neglected.[9]

The problem lay more with the tone of the British references to the
Americans. The American Appendix printed in the British RV conveyed
'the idea that the printing of the Appendix was a *favor* rather than a right,
and that it contained *all* the work of the American Committee'.[10]
Moreover, the Preface to the British RV's did not state explicitly that
American changes were in fact adopted.[11]

After that late nineteenth-century American revision, first in this
chapter must stand one of the most successful, the American re-working
of it.

★   ★   ★

THE REVISED STANDARD VERSION, 1952

In the first decades of the twentieth century, dissatisfaction with the American revision was justifiably high. The 1901 American Standard Version, ASV, had been made by devoted men with the highest intentions, but they had worked under disadvantages, particularly that of being before the sudden great increase in the availability of older manuscripts and greater knowledge of the ancient languages.[12] Inconsistencies in English renderings, and a persistent attachment to the vocabulary of KJV, ('murrain', 'besom', 'scall'), produced something that was neither fish, flesh nor good red herring.[13] Difficulties produced by archaic vocabulary can be exaggerated. Objections, however, to 'he cast down his rod' instead of 'he threw down his rod', or 'he took to wife' instead of 'he married',[14] are not quite as pedantic as they seem. At issue is not understanding, but tone. ASV was, once again, not the clean new all-American Bible of the future, that ideal which had eluded the republic since Noah Webster.

In 1928, Thomas Nelson's copyright of ASV passed to the (American) International Council of Religious Education. In 1929 that body appointed fifteen scholars to consider the need for further revision. There was immediate conflict between them. Some argued that revision was doubly necessary as both the 1881 and 1901 revisions ought not to have been made. James Moffat wanted ASV further revised, but still in the 'Tyndale-King James' tradition. Edgar Goodspeed wanted a new translation in 'present, colloquial English'.[15] After two years' consideration, the committee recommended a further revision, but work was held up by lack of resources during the Depression. It was resumed in 1937. The New Testament was published in 1946 and the complete Bible in 1952. The Apocrypha was added in 1956.

The intention was to make a Bible 'in English diction which is designed for use in public and private worship', as the 1946 Preface put it. There it is noted that the 1881 and 1901 revisions 'are too obviously "translation English". They are mechanically exact, literal, word-for-word translations [. . .] rather than the order which is natural to English.' The aim was still, however, to preserve 'those qualities which have given the King James Version a supreme place in English literature.' These are the words of Luther A. Weigle, of Yale Divinity School, who became chairman of the thirty-two strong committee, and later the chief defender of the work. The affiliated denominations of the International Council of Religious Education supplied an Advisory Board of fifty representatives with an impressive fairness; included, for example, were both the African Methodist Episcopal Church in Philadelphia and the African Methodist Episcopal Zion Church in Chicago, and four different kinds of Lutheran church.

Specialists were consulted on the history of medicine, English usage, the names of trees and – in the case of Professor G. R. Driver of Oxford – on 'drafts of many of the Old Testament books'.[16]

The result, RSV, was a very great, and very American, success.

> The first printing of the completed Bible produced a million copies; if stacked they would have made a pile twenty-four miles high. More than three thousand religious services, which were attended by an estimated two million people, were held simultaneously across the nation to celebrate the publication.[17]

> It was said to be the largest single order ever placed with a commercial printing house. That first run of nearly 1 million copies required 1,000 tons of paper, 2,000 gallons of ink, 10 tons of type metal, and 140 tons of binder's board. The 23-karat [*sic*] gold leaf used to emboss the title on the cover amounted to two million square inches, enough to pave one mile of residential street.[18]

This was in every way an American affair. Booklets were produced for the more than 3,400 services held on Tuesday evening, 30 September 1952, across the USA, to celebrate the publication. The cover of that from Shenectady, New York, shows a map of the USA, giving the numbers of celebrations in each state, and extending to Canada, Hawaii and the Canal Zone. A press photograph taken four days earlier, on 26 September, shows a broadly smiling Luther Weigle, supported by broadly smiling identical men, presenting at the White House a copy of the new RSV to a near-identical President Harry Truman, who is smiling broadly (fig. 44). The message was of unprecedented, specifically American success. A truly American Bible had at last arrived. In 1962 the exclusive rights to Thomas Nelson & Sons expired, and other publishers began printing, including ABS. By 1990 some fifty-five million copies of RSV had been sold.[19] Not everyone welcomed the new version and certain new readings: from the beginning, well-stimulated and very public outrage, coast to coast (detailed at the end of this chapter) took the committees by surprise.

Luther A. Weigle wrote in the Preface:

> The Revised Standard Version is not a new translation in the language of today. It is not a paraphrase which aims at striking idioms. It is a revision which seeks to preserve all that is best in the English Bible as it has been known and used throughout the years.

The care with the text went with the rule that changes to ASV required a two-thirds majority of the entire committee, not, as with the earlier revisions, two-thirds of those present. Care was also taken to examine the latest findings on the Greek text. RSV brought welcome clarification: for

KJV having Paul 'opening and alleging' that Christ should suffer, at Acts
17:3, in RSV he is 'explaining and proving'. The 'froward' master at 1 Peter
2:18 became 'overbearing'.[20]

It is characteristic that 'Lord' is used rather than 'Jehovah' (or 'Yahweh'),
on the grounds that, as Weigle wrote, they 'do not represent any form of
the name ever used'. Eighty changes were made to the New Testament
for the whole Bible in 1952, to make identical English for parallel passages in identical Greek, changes not in the direction of more modern
English.

The double columns, lack of illustrations or commentary, traditional
title-page and marginal references limited to cross-references or a few
alternative readings all remind readers of KJV: RSV is *the* Bible – as the
title has it, 'Being the Version Set Forth A.D. 1611 [. . .] Revised A.D. 1952'.

In Britain, RSV was immediately accepted, as representing the modern
understanding of Greek and Hebrew texts, not restricted to Elizabethan
and Jacobean English (as the makers of both the Revised Versions had
been) and not a paraphrase for easy reading, or a literal-based study aid.
RSV managed to convey to congregations even in the most formal services in the most ancient British cathedrals the sense of what was happening in the Greek and Hebrew, without jolting them with anything
racy, or taking them abruptly away from the beauty of the familiar KJV.[21]
The appropriate word is 'dignity', standing without holding hands with
its cousin 'pomposity'.

Here is Romans 12:14–17 in RSV:

> Bless those who persecute you: bless and do not curse them. Rejoice
> with those who rejoice, weep with those who weep. Live in harmony
> with one another; do not be haughty, but associate with the lowly; never
> be conceited. Repay no-one evil for evil, but take thought for what is
> noble in the sight of all.

'. . . haughty, but associate with the lowly' is an improvement on KJV's
'Mind not high things, but condescend to men of low estate', with its
room for snobbish misunderstanding about elevated thoughts, social
condescension, and low estate.

In the Old Testament, RSV sets out Hebrew poetry as English poetry,
to great advantage:

> Listen to me, my people,
>   and give ear to me, my nation;
> for a law will go forth from me,
>   and my justice for a light to the peoples.
> (Isaiah 51:4–5).

The parallelism is now obvious, and the tone is accurate. Quite often, KJV is retained entire, as, wisely, for Psalm 23, or hardly changed, as in Psalm 24:

> The earth is the LORD's and the fulness thereof,
>   The world and those who dwell therein;
> For he has founded it upon the seas,
>   And established it upon the rivers.
>
> Who shall ascend the hill of the LORD?
>   And who shall stand in his holy place?
> He who has clean hands, and a pure heart,
>   who does not lift up his soul to what is false,
>   and does not swear deceitfully.

In the last two lines, the present tenses are sound Hebrew, and 'to what is false' is clearer than 'unto vanity'.

In Britain, RSV had several advantages. Individual translations like those made by Moffat or Phillips were always going to feel odd when read out in services conducted with some ceremony, and RSV was close enough to KJV to be used comfortably there. Second, it had some authority, being originally commissioned by an impressive ecumenical body: as the first serious such challenge to KJV and both RVs, it was welcomed. Third, it was understood to be soundly based on good texts, not doctrinally shackled to any readings, recognising that care was needed with everything, and that even Westcott and Hort could be wrong. Moreover, as the Preface pointed out, the great increase in Greek texts, especially the papyri, had shed new light on the meaning of the New Testament Greek text. RSV has generally been in Britain the longest-respected of the twentieth-century versions.

In America, the large success of RSV had interesting effects. Unusually, after publication the committee was kept in being, and received criticisms and comments: in successive printings, small alterations were made.[22] Several larger developments followed. First was, in 1962, *The Oxford Annotated Bible*, RSV with solid introductions and footnotes, the work of two of the most respected American biblical scholars, Herbert G. May of Oberlin, Ohio, and Bruce M. Metzger of Princeton. The notes are low-key. On Isaiah 7:14, they note,

> *Young woman.* Heb. almah, feminine of elem, young man (1. Sam. 17.56; 20.22), the word appears in Gen.24.423, Ex. 2.8, Is.68.25, and elsewhere, where it is translated 'young woman', 'girl', 'maiden'.

In the text, the Isaiah quotation at Matthew 2:23 has 'a virgin', annotated only 'See Is. 7.14.n.'. At Matthew 17:18, 'shall I found my church', the notes are, 'For the view that all the apostles form the foundation of the church', see Eph. 2.20; Rev. 21.14. *Church*, see Gal.1.13.n.', where the note is:

> The *church* is the people of God, whom he has called into fellowship with himself through the redemptive work of Jesus Christ. The word may refer to the total number of believers throughout the world, or to those in one locality, whether gathered for worship or scattered by persecutions.

This volume was expanded in 1977, to add *with the Apocrypha*; the inclusion of 3 and 4 Maccabees and Psalm 151 made this Bible acceptable to Orthodox communions.

A step forward in the same direction had been the production in Britain of a Catholic edition of RSV in 1966 (the same year as the Catholic Jerusalem Bible). This was introduced by Cardinal Heenan, Archbishop of Westminster. He pointed out that in the previous four hundred years, 'Catholics and Protestants have gone their separate ways.' Their mutually suspected translations had been biased, he wrote, 'in the interests of doctrinal presuppositions'. Now:

> the sciences of textual criticism and philology, not to mention others, have made such great advances that the Bible text used by translators is substantially the same for all – Protestants and Catholics alike.

It happens, however, that in places

> considerations of Catholic tradition have favoured a particular rendering or the inclusion of a passage omitted by the RSV translators.[23]

The alterations were apparently listed in full.[24] No changes were listed to the Old Testament text; the only change was apparently the order of the books, the placing (or omission) of some Apocryphal books and the numbering of the Psalms. Even the Messianic phrase at Isaiah 7:14 remained the controversial 'young woman' (instead of KJV's 'virgin', and the Vulgate's *virgo*). In the New Testament text, the disputed ending of Mark's Gospel 16:9–20 was printed, with the shorter alternative in the margin; and the fullest version of the story of the woman taken in adultery, John 7:53–8:11. Omitted in the lists, however, was the silent alteration of RSV's 1 Corinthians 6:9 'sexual perverts' to 'homosexuals' in the Catholic edition of 1966. Also not in the lists was the Catholic revision of the comment on Matthew 17:18.

Other revisions of RSV followed. In 1973, in response to the wish of Lady Priscilla Collins, 'a convert to Catholicism and wife of Scottish publishing magnate Sir William Collins' to see 'a Bible acceptable to

Protestant, Catholic, and Eastern Orthodox Christians';[25] the resulting 'ecumenical edition', from Collins in Glasgow, was a new RSV, with some slight changes. It had little impact.

A complete revision of RSV was undertaken and published in 1990 as the New Revised Standard Version. Prompted by the women's movement, and after consideration over two decades, the RSV committee, chaired first by Herbert May and then by Bruce Metzger, had decided that the frequent readings of 'man' and 'men' were not supported by the original Hebrew and Greek; the archaic second person singular (*thee, thou, thine*) was removed in prayers addressed to God. High hopes for the success of the resulting NRSV were not met: by the 1990s, too many new versions were competing. A weird American extension of the NRSV process, for those who did not think that that text was 'politically correct' enough, produced the Inclusive Version of the New Testament and Psalms in 1995. The editors systematically altered objectionable and oppressive language in NRSV; an observed patriarchy in 'the kingdom of God' was removed, to make 'the dominion of God'. 'The Jews' in the fourth Gospel became 'religious authorities'. Jesus' naming of God as his 'Father' would not do, and became – in defiance of the Greek, and indeed of both understanding and sanity – 'Father-Mother', causing Jesus to say 'I am in the Father-Mother, and the Father-Mother is in me . . .' It was maintained that the resulting incomprehensibility revealed the otherness of God.[26] That is not New Testament Christianity.

J. B. PHILLIPS

J. B. Phillips startled Christians in Britain with the publication in 1947 of his wartime attempt to make the Epistles of Paul hit home, his *Letters to Young Churches*. Here was something that was indeed new. Phillips had succeeded in finding a contemporary idiom which did not instantly become dated, a real achievement. The blessed St Paul was suddenly a real man, the people he was writing to were real people, and the problems they were facing, of morals and management, were real problems. One could watch scales falling from readers' eyes. Phillips once remarked that one of the origins of his work was the effect on a group of his young parishioners when he asked them 'Does God understand radar?' With a characteristically hard-hitting five-page introduction by C. S. Lewis, the book had great success. Lewis concluded with a theologically strong paragraph pointing out the error of a popular view:

A most astonishing misconception has long dominated the modern mind on the subject of St Paul. It is to this effect: that Jesus preached a kindly and simple religion (found in the gospels) and that St Paul afterwards corrupted it into a cruel and complicated religion (found in the epistles). This is really quite untenable. All the most terrifying texts came from the mouth of Our Lord: all the texts on which we can base such warrant as we have for hoping that all men will be saved come from St Paul.[27]

And indeed, one of the significant effects of Phillips's work was the sense of the sudden arrival of Paul – the whole of Paul – in the modern popular understanding of what Christianity was about. Lewis wrote:

the nineteenth-century attack on St Paul was really only a stage in the revolt against Christ . . . Everything [men] disliked in Christianity was therefore attributed to St Paul. It was unfortunate that their case could not impress anyone who had really read the Gospels and the Epistles with attention: but apparently few people had . . .[28]

Phillips changed that, greatly to his credit. In the next decades, many people read the Epistles with attention, astonished to find that Paul was not both stuffy and distantly unpleasant, but spoke to modern dilemmas of belief and behaviour.

C. S. Lewis pointed particularly to the value of the 'abstracts' that Phillips printed before each letter, humbly noting that 'it would have saved me a great deal of labour if this book had come into my hands when I first seriously began to try to discover what Christianity was'.[29] Those 'abstracts' are indeed especially helpful: but one notes Lewis's strategy in not commenting on the quality of the translation.

This is, not surprisingly, variable. One of Phillips's most successful passages is the opening of Romans 12.

With eyes wide open to the mercies of God, I beg you, my brothers, as an act of intelligent worship, to give Him your bodies, as a living sacrifice, consecrated to him and acceptable by him. Don't let the world around you squeeze you into its own mould, but let God re-mould your minds from within, so that you may prove in practice that the Plan of God for you is good, meets all His demands and moves towards the goal of true maturity.

This is excellent. The 'eyes wide open' phrase refers back to previous ideas, and the image of moulding, especially from *within*, odd as it is, is outstandingly better in modern impact than KJV's 'transformed by the renewing of your mind', though both are accurate to the Greek.

Phillips's two drawbacks were occasional paraphrase and occasional verbosity, both inevitable. His strengths were the absolute avoidance of 'translationese', and the quite uncanny power of his modern phrases to leap off the page, as in the same chapter, Romans 12:16–19:

> Live in harmony with each other. Don't become snobbish but take a real interest in ordinary people. Don't become set in your own opinions. Don't pay back a bad turn by a bad turn, to *anyone*. Don't say 'it doesn't matter what people think', but see that your public behaviour is above criticism. As far as your responsibility goes, live at peace with everyone. Never take vengeance into your own hands, my dear friends: stand back and let God punish if he will.

The latter phrase, 'stand back . . .' is exhilaratingly good, and makes sense after KJV's 'but rather give place unto wrath'. Phillips wrote for *The Churchman* in June 1961 a short article, 'The Problems of Making a Contemporary Translation',[30] which explained his 'meaning-for-meaning' policy, and the one enormous obstacle he faced, the adored unintelligibility of KJV. He pointed out that

> From long practice Bible-lovers probably 'translate' as they read. They do not realise that such words as 'let', 'prevent', 'conversation', 'wealth' and many more have completely altered their meaning. Such archaisms as 'much people followed him', 'which of them twain', 'Peter and Barnabas waxed bold', 'straitened in your own bowels' are practically meaningless today.[31]

Observing the twin points that the documents are ancient and must not be mistaken for contemporary writing, and that inspiration must mean elevation of style, he decided to ignore both.

> My reason is simply that after three hundred and fifty years of the Authorized Version, many exciting and challenging truths have been redered impotent by sheer beauty of language as well as by the familiarity of repetition.[32]

The text was well broken into short paragraphs introduced by subheadings, with chapter and verse in the margins only at the start. Phillips followed the great success of these *Letters* with *The Gospels in Modern English* in 1952, using the same layout and principles, with the addition of Revelation making the entire New Testament shortly after.

CORPORATE BIBLES

Whereas in the hundred years before the Second World War the more interesting work had been done by single translators, for example, Julia

Smith in 1876, Ferrar Fenton in 1901, James Moffatt in 1935 and C. K. Ogden in 1949, coming to a climax with J. B. Phillips, and important joint work was only in an edition from ABS, and the various Revised Versions: now, Bibles with widespread and lasting readerships came from committees, which, though generally unable to be quite 'official' in the manner of the intentions behind KJV or the RVs, were made up of senior scholars from many denominations with their approval, latterly in the 1989 REB uniting Protestants and Catholics. This has not been simply because the better understood technical problems are felt to demand more specialists round the table – experts in various kinds of Hebrew and Greek, in palaeography, history, geography, natural history, theology, bibliography, varieties of English usage, and so on.

THE NEW ENGLISH BIBLE

There have been, since the Second World War, five important new translations circulating in Britain. The first was RSV in 1952, followed by The Jerusalem Bible, 1966; Today's English Version, or the Good News Bible, 1976; and the New International Version, complete in 1978. The main Bible event in the world of British Christians after the Second World War was, however, the publication in 1961 of the New English Bible New Testament alone, and in 1970 the whole New English Bible (with some New Testament corrections). Publication of the New Testament was timed for 350 years after KJV, and 80 years after the RV New Testament.

NEB arose from an 'overture' (proposal) received by the General Assembly of the Church of Scotland, in May 1946, from the Presbytery of Stirling and Dunblane, 'that a translation of the Bible be made in the language of the present day'. Soon, invitations were sent to the Protestant denominations and to the British and Scottish Bible Societies. Participants were invited on merit, not denominational attachment. Roman Catholic scholars were invited as observers in 1966. A literary panel was set up.[33]

Word spread within British universities in the late 1940s and 1950s, particularly in Oxford, about the radical nature of the translation work, which was being done afresh from the best available texts. It was said to be deliberately releasing itself from 'Bible English', from the inherited line from Tyndale to RV, and thus no rival to RSV. The general director was the Revd Professor C. H. Dodd of Oxford, the greatest scholar in New Testament studies. The lists of members of the panels show name after name of the most distinguished Bible scholars in the land – half the Old Testament panel were Professor Sir Godfrey Driver, the Revd L. H. Brockington, the Revd Dr N. H. Snaith, the Revd Professor N. W. Porteous and the Revd Professor H. H. Rowley. The Apocrypha and New Testament panels showed similar distinction.

Stories emerged from Old Testament meetings held in the Oriental Institute at Oxford about the chairman Sir Godfrey Driver's enterprise in locating, for baffling Hebrew words, illuminating parallels of vocabulary in languages in neighbouring countries. Observers gave gleeful imitations of his own renderings of the calls of obscurer birds and animals, now for the first time firmly identified, he believed. (A story, not it is said apocryphal, relates to his insistence that the famous and numinously suggestive 'pelican' in KJV's (and the Prayer Book's) Psalm 102:6, 'I am like a pelican of the wilderness: I am like an owl of the desert', with all the patristic history of the image of the Christ-like pelican drawing its own blood to feed its young, was not a pelican at all, but, Driver claimed, a Yellow-bellied Bulbul. It is said that he was greeted with cries of 'Put it in the margin, put it in the margin'. Certainly, philological and ornithological faithfulness can go only so far: as a line, 'I am like a Yellow-bellied Bulbul in the wilderness' may be thought to have lost something, particularly when sung by choristers at Evensong.) That many of the renderings of the Hebrew were new was obvious: but which ones, of the many that did not appear in the standard lexicons, had the full backing of the committees, was not made clear.[34]

From January 1948 to 1970, the multi-denominational Joint Committee overseeing the work met in the Jerusalem Chamber at Westminster Abbey, like their forebears making the RV. This committee considered the results not only of the individual work of scholars as submitted to the panels, but of the attention of the literary advisers. Sometimes NEB does very well. To go back to Romans 12, now to verses 11–15, NEB gets a sense of 'a kind of liturgical formula' – as against Phillips, who produces 'a rambling series of homilies'.[35] Here is Phillips:

> Let us not allow slackness to spoil our work and let us keep the fires of the spirit burning, as we do our work for God. Base your happiness on your hope in Christ. When trials come endure them patiently: steadfastly maintain the habit of prayer. Give freely to fellow-Christians in want, never grudging a meal or a bed to those who need them. And as for those who try to make your life a misery, bless them. Don't curse, bless. Share the happiness of those who are happy, and the sorrow of those who are sad.

That is fine and clear: yet NEB has achieved something finer:

> With unflagging energy, in ardour of spirit, serve the Lord.
> Let hope keep you joyful; in trouble stand firm; persist in prayer.

Contribute to the needs of God's people, and practise hospitality.
Call down blessings on your persecutors – blessings, not curses.
With the joyful be joyful, and mourn with the mourners.

It is absolutely not KJV, nor RV, nor RSV. It is a fresh English voice, and
good for the Greek.

This is something that can be seen everywhere in NEB, and be valued.
On the other hand, there can also be seen everywhere in NEB places
where things went wrong. At Romans 5:2, NEB's 'let us exult in the hope
of the divine splendour that is to be ours', goes on too long and stum-
bles at the end (RSV has 'we rejoice in our hope of sharing the glory of
God'). Spoken aloud, the sounds made in Matthew 12:10, 'Their aim was
to frame a charge against him', are unhappy, and at Esther 6:11 'attired
Mordecai' sounds misleadingly of exhaustion. At Luke 10:40, Mary says to
Jesus of her sister Martha, too casually, 'Tell her to come and lend a hand',
where Tyndale's 'Bid her therefore that she help me' uses the properly
weightier 'help' (in that, KJV follows Tyndale, as do all the main translations). At Psalm 94:20, the sense of KJV's 'Shall the throne of iniquity have
fellowship with thee?' can just about be teased out to give a glimmer of
light; NEB's 'Shall sanctimonious calumny call thee partner?' has gone back
into darkness.

Unlike RSV, NEB New Testament was at first printed in a single
column on the page, with verse numbers in the margins.

> Any system of division into numbered verses is foreign to the spirit of
> this translation, which is intended to convey the meaning in continu-
> ous natural English rather than correspond sentence by sentence with
> the Greek.[36]

The translators' Introduction gives space to the question of the kind of
English to use, and to explaining their principle of what later in America
would be called 'dynamic equivalence', that is to say, translating into
English idiom rather than on a literal word-for-word system; so the
Hebrew phrase 'Blessing I will bless', as in KJV (Gen. 22:17, Heb. 6:14),
becomes in NEB 'I will bless you abundantly'; and the opening words of
the Song of Songs, literally in Hebrew 'let-him-kiss-me with-kisses-of-his-
mouth', retained in KJV as 'Let him kiss me with the kisses of his mouth',
become in NEB 'that he may smother me with kisses' – modern, but not
quite right.[37] At Matthew 25:14 are 'bags of gold' for 'talents' – though the
talents could have been silver.[38]

The makers of NEB were proud of having literary advisers. It would
be interesting to know in some detail not only how much they were able
to do, but how much of what they did survived. There are some out-

standingly good 'hits', which may have come from them. Judges 5, the almost impossibly difficult 'Song of Deborah', is a notorious challenge. At verse 6, there is a sense of serious unease about the situation being described. KJV had 'the highways were unoccupied, and the travellers walked through byways'. RSV kept 'byways'. The Jerusalem Bible and New Jerusalem give 'bypaths'; the New International Version has 'winding paths', and the Good News Bible, 'side roads.' Only NEB has 'devious paths', which is excellent. On the other hand (and that qualification is a phrase any reader of NEB is constantly using), how could literary experts allow a change at the end of Psalm 23 from KJV's expressive phrase, soaked deeply into English-speaking life, 'all the days of my life' to the banal 'my whole life long'? – or, while keeping in essence Coverdale and KJV at verse 2, 'He makes me lie down in green pastures', in verse 4 change Coverdale's and the KJV's phenomenally expressive 'the valley of the shadow of death' to 'a valley dark as death'? NEB accurately and intelligibly keeps the 'troubled hearts' of John 14:1, but then in the next verse introduces something both archaic and unclear with 'many dwelling-places'.

The poet Philip Larkin later recalled that 'he had the honour to serve briefly as a literary adviser to the NEB'. He did not stay long. 'The whole text seemed to me lacking in vitality, rhythm, distinction and above all memorability, and I found myself revising almost every sentence [. . .] after a year they stopped sending me anything, so I presumed I had been weighed in the balance and found wanting.'[39]

In literary Britain in 1962 one could hardly look higher than to T. S. Eliot. He reviewed NEB for the *Daily Telegraph* on 16 December of that year.

We are [. . .] entitled to expect from a panel chosen from among the most distinguished scholars of our day at least a work of dignified mediocrity. When we find that we are offered something far below that modest level, something which astonishes us in its combination of the vulgar, the trivial, and the pedantic, we ask in alarm: 'What is happening to the English language?'[40]

On the other hand, defending themselves, the makers of NEB had found that:

Sober and scholarly assessments were made in great number, and were generally favourable on balance [. . .] Only a few attacks were made, and these were from individuals or small groups, both high-church and conservative Protestant, who were strongly attached to traditional language on religious and literary grounds.[41]

T. S. Eliot's damning words might partly be explained by his own firm 'high-church' adherence; or by his curiously old-fogeyish denial of the nature of the English language to change (the heart of his review) so that the use of NEB in services 'will become an active agent of decadence'.[42] One illustration in his review draws some sympathy: 'Surely others besides myself will take no comfort from being told, as the first beatitude: "How blest are those who know that they are poor."'[43] General praise for the sound scholarship and the pains taken always led to a serious objection: Luther A. Weigle regretted the decision to substitute 'Messiah' for 'Christ' – 'if the early believers were followers of the "Messiah", why call them "Christians"?'[44], a fair point. Also from the RSV camp, Bruce M. Metzger rightly objected to the addition of words not present in the Greek, against the translators' declared intention not 'to encroach on the field of the commentator', so that in John 10 κόσμος (*kosmos*) is twice translated 'godless world'. Though it was elsewhere noted that underneath NEB lies 'a Greek text that is as good as any that can be constructed in existing circumstances', the production of a uniform 'contemporary English' ironed out the differences between the writers.[45]

Later, heavy attacks on NEB came from two quarters. In Britain, full-scale stylistic objections came from Ian Robinson in 1973 ('two consecutive well-written pages could not be found in it'). Gerald Hammond in 1982 objected with searing heat to renderings of Hebrew and to banal English. Both Hammond and Robinson exposed, with some scorn, clumsiness everywhere. In the USA, Jack P. Lewis in 1981 found many inaccuracies of Greek and Hebrew rendering, and inconsistencies, wilful paraphrase, or intrusive commentary disguised as translation, vocabulary that was too British and would not be understood in America.[46] To British readers of Lewis, the piling up of the latter objections, expressed forcibly as a weakness, becomes a little hard to take. (One of the seven paragraphs attacking un-Americanness begins, 'The NEB often uses verbs which are not generally used in America today. Most frequent is "fetched".'[47]) The British translators making a British version had a hard enough task without having to be constrained by things not American, including embarrassment, for example, at the word 'piss'.[48]

The first complete NEB in March 1970 showed acceptance of criticisms leading to changes in the New Testament; for example, the original Matthew 5:48 (in KJV, 'be ye therefore perfect, even as your Father which is in heaven is perfect') was changed from 'You must therefore be all goodness, just as your heavenly Father is all good' to 'There must be no limit to your goodness, as your heavenly Father's goodness knows no bounds.' The earlier New Testament was withdrawn, and the complete NEB was published in many styles. The 1972 complete edition had many additions, as a new note to the Introduction explained, 'designed to help readers understand a little of the background of the Bible'. New in this edition were the useful maps and the many detailed illustrations by Horace Knowles (who also illustrated the Good News Bible); some of these are good, as in the picture of a Jewish marketplace, highlighting the multi-cultural world in which the New Testament was written, acting as fron-tispiece to the New Testament, or the view of Jerusalem separating the Gospels of Luke and John; others are unremarkable, like the drawing of a mattock in 1 Samuel 13.

In 1965 the Church of England had officially authorised NEB, with RSV, as a permissible alternative to KJV for the Epistles and Gospels at Holy Communion. The NEB New Testament was used in other services, and widely in the Free Churches and schools. In spite of the huge sales of RSV, the NEB New Testament had sold remarkably well. The initial estimates of 'a quarter to half a million' were quite wrong: before the com-plete NEB in 1970, the New Testament had sold seven million copies.[49]

A final judgement of NEB is difficult. The 1961 New Testament version of Matthew 5:3 (Tyndale's and KJV's cloudy 'Blessed are the poor in spirit') was 'How blest are those who know that they are poor', which turns cloud into darkness. On the other hand – that phrase again – this was amended in the later revision to 'How blest are those who know their need of God'. That is not a translation of the Greek. but it is an inspired reflec-tion of the sense. The NEB translators could bring freshness and shed light on over-familiar passages, providing a reader has access to the original, or a more literal translation, like RSV. Perhaps the best one can say is that 'the NEB is not a Bible that can stand alone.'[50]

THE JERUSALEM BIBLE

A papal encyclical of 1943 gave permission for the unrestricted use of ancient manuscripts and other material in Bible study and translation. In 1948 the École Biblique in Jerusalem began publishing fascicles of an extensive Bible commentary with introductions to books and copious annotations, the work of about forty scholars, continuously revised. In 1961 these were collected, abbreviated and compressed into *La Bible de Jérusalem*. These were then translated into English, work which was melded into the work of the French scholars. It was soon clear that it was impossible to attach these notes to an existing English Roman Catholic version, so a completely new translation was undertaken, under the editorship of Alexander Jones, and portions parcelled out among a twenty-seven-strong team of translators. A number of scholars defaulted, with two effects:

Alexander Jones personally translated a large number of books; and he
brought in his young nephew, the Oxford Greek scholar Anthony Kenny.
The latter worked so well and quickly that he was promptly given the
prize New Testament task, the Epistle to the Romans. Sir Anthony's interesting accounts of the procedures in his autobiography, *A Path from Rome*
(1985), show, some of them as very strange. Though the translators were
working from Greek and Hebrew, there still had to be some pretence that
they were translating the Vulgate. Having finished with some pride, the
translators then found that what they had done was given – ostensibly to
improve their English style, but perhaps to ensure good Catholic readings
– for heavy revision by a French monk. The English Jerusalem Bible first
came out from the Catholic publishers Darton, Longman & Todd in 1966.

> Matching the distinctive freshness and excitement in churches that
> have largely used the AV for the previous three centuries has been the
> freshness and excitement of those twentieth century translators whose
> church had previously only used the Latin Vulgate or the Douai-Rheims
> English Bible.[51]

The full Jerusalem Bible has introductions to biblical books, extensive
notes and general study aids[52] (severely abridged for the 'Popular edition'
in 1974). The intention was to keep abreast of theological thinking, and
archaeological and textual discoveries. The annotations, notes on historical background and variant readings made it a very useful scholarly tool,
and ahead of other versions. Since 'Vatican Two', the Second Vatican
Council (1962–5), it had been possible to write, for example, about the
different strands in the Pentateuch, from different dates and with different
purposes, known by scholars for over a century as 'J, E, D and P'. That is
done in the introduction and notes: the translators act on the differences,
so that the divine name in 'J', where historically there had been LORD, is
now given as Yahweh. This has not been greeted with enthusiasm. Psalm
23 begins 'Yahweh is my shepherd / I lack nothing', and Psalm 24, 'To
Yahweh belong earth and all it holds'.

What the translators understood to be poetry – in large parts of the
Fourth Gospel, for example – they print as poetry. If a general fault has
been found, it is that there feels to be a certain over-formality: one can
admire and respect, but possibly not love, these words. On the other hand,
the translators score well in notorious passages, as in the complicated
opening of the Epistle to the Hebrews, or Romans 8:18 and following –
which begins 'I think that what we suffer in this life can never be compared to the glory, as yet unrevealed, which is waiting for us.' Also greatly
to be welcomed is the sense of ecumenical breadth, the welcoming of

even the idea of alternative versions. It is no surprise to find that the Catholic/Protestant divide is clearest in the notes to 'Thou art Peter . . .' and to the Sacraments: but even the notes in this Catholic English Bible have come a great distance since the Rheims New Testament in 1582.

After what seems to have been once again the customary tangled start, the Jerusalem Bible was revised by Dom Henry Wansbrough and published in 1985. Wansbrough, a member of the Pontifical Biblical Commission and Master of St Benet's Hall, Oxford, was at the time of the revision at Ampleforth, as a monk and teacher. For one reason and another, he found that he was doing most of the work of revision himself, a task complicated by official, and necessarily deferentially ultra-careful, relation with the French *Bible de Jérusalem* project, not only because of the pretence of basing the work on the Vulgate, but also not to jar French sensibilities – as Wansbrough put it, 'one does not joke about Waterloo to a Frenchman'.[53] His work of revision was heavy. Yahweh remains the divine name, and much has been kept; but progress was made towards some inclusive language, and elements which were narrowly Roman Catholic were removed. The New Jerusalem Bible has gone a long way to improve unpleasant mouthfuls: JB's Mark 13:19, 'For in those days there will be much distress as, until now, has not been equalled since the beginning when God created the world, nor ever will be again' (which may be that French monk's idea of English) is in NJB: 'For in those days there will be great distress unparalleled since God created the world, and such as will never be again.' Tyndale, as Hilary Day has pointed out, at that point had 'For there shall be in those days such tribulation, as was not from the beginning of creatures which God created, unto this time, neither shall be.'[54] Wansbrough is a great admirer of Tyndale as Bible translator, and the influence can be seen.[55]

THE NEW AMERICAN BIBLE, 1970

In 1970, the Catholic Biblical Association of America revised the popular Confraternity New Testament of 1941 – itself a revision of Rheims-Challoner – to make the New American Bible, advertised as the 'first complete American version of Holy Scripture translated directly from the original Hebrew, Aramaic, and Greek',[56] which is, to put it gently, misleading (or to put it more bluntly, wholly untrue – what of RSV?). The translators – claimed in the Preface to be 'some fifty biblical scholars, not all Catholics' – pride themselves on 'good American English . . . It is not as pungent and colorful as the New English Bible. Its translations are not striking but neither are they clumsy.'[57] The latter claim is not justified – 'While they were there the days of her confinement were completed' (Luke 2:6); 'There were shepherds in that locality, living in the fields and keeping night watch by turns over their flocks' (Luke 2:8). When it is not clumsy, it is Tyndale: 'They went [Tyndale, 'came'; the NAB scholars were not alert to Tyndale's memorable vowel-chime] in haste and found Mary and Joseph, and the baby lying in the manger' (Luke 2:16). The Prodigal Son's elder brother tells his father that 'this son of yours returns after having gone through your property with loose women' (Luke 15:30). Luke 16 begins: 'A rich man had a manager who was reported to him for dissipating his property' (Vulgate: *dissipasset bona ipsius*; Tyndale, and KJV, 'had wasted his goods').

The first printing of NAB, with thin type in double columns on poor paper, feels unpleasant. Indeed, not only the NAB Preface gives the impression that the work was done by people who did not actually *like* the Bible. One reads with astonishment the paragraph in the Preface about the ugliness of the Fourth Gospel.

> The Gospel according to John comprises a special case. Absolute fidelity to his technique of reiterated phrasing would result in an assault on the English ear that would be almost unendurable [. . .] the very repetitiousness which the author deliberately employed is at the same time regarded by those who read and speak English to be a serious stylistic defect. Only those familiar with the Greek originals can know what a relentless tattoo Johannine poetry can produce.[58]

Any stick, it seems, will do to beat the Gospel of Love.

THE BIBLE SOCIETY'S
TRANSLATOR'S NEW TESTAMENT, 1973

Though never intended for a wide market, one modern translation of the New Testament deserves special mention. This is the Translator's New Testament, published in 1973 by what was still the British and Foreign Bible Society. More literal than most modern attempts, but still graceful, it was intended for translators in the field, and is equipped with 150 pages of 'Translational Notes' and Glossary, always of especial value for students and expositors of the Greek New Testament. To take one pointed example: Romans 12 contains a verse bringing outstanding problems, given in this version as 'No, if your enemy is hungry, feed him; if he is thirsty, give him something to drink; for by so doing you shall heap coals of fire on his head.' 'Coals of fire' is a quotation from Proverbs 25:22, and Phillips, for example, simply gave the KJV version, indented, headed by 'And these are God's words'. There is logic in this, as the words are, for Paul, already ancient: but Phillips ducks the problem of what the last phrase means: he does not even give a marginal reference. The Translator's New Testament however, signalling a difficulty, and aware of how peculiar the image is, and dangerous to translate literally, directs the reader to a note.

> A quotation from Pr. 25:22. The sense in both contexts is not that of revenge but of kind treatment that will make the enemy feel ashamed of himself [and, presumably, blush]. Although it is uncertain how the metaphor came into being, this interpretation has been emphasized since the time of St Augustine.[59]

THE NEW INTERNATIONAL VERSION, 1978

Limitations of space prevent attention to all the publication of new American translations, there being several a year since 1950 (six in 1961 alone), and to do so would be tedious. Room will be made at the end of this chapter, however, for three largely American phenomena: the heated defence of KJV ignited by blazing hostility to RSV in 1952, (an appropriate epithet) on several grounds, one being the lie that its makers were Communists; the use of the English Bible for reading secret codes of what the Bible has successfully foretold in the past (eccentric but harmless) and foretells in the future (potentially dangerous); and the Bible in comic books and animated videos. No one can tell how many private translations have been made that have never reached print. Manuscript versions may lie in the desk drawers of unknown people who are geniuses, or barely sane: the ease of modern desktop publishing, and of electronic cataloguing, now make such unacquaintance increasingly unlikely. Perhaps we should be grateful. Over twelve hundred already published in forty-five years make a lot to take in. Some of those are a little odd – like the Gospels translated into English by three Jesuits in 1957 from a text in French; or, in 1971, as mentioned, that new revision named the 'King James II Version', a startling new title for abridgement of the 'Saint James' Version.

Three of those from America, the RSV (1956), the New International Version (1978) and the Good News Bible or Today's English Version (1976) have achieved worldwide status. NIV is the Bible used by Evangelicals, to some extent taking the place of KJV – but only to some extent, and in spite of the rise of the passionate defence of KJV.

It is reported that the completed NIV cost $2,500,000, and that before publication day, 27 October 1978, advance sales had reached 1,200,000 copies. Its first printing was the largest ever done for an English Bible. The more than 110 scholars participating in the project represent evangelical scholarship of the United States, Canada, Great Britain, Ireland, Australia, and New Zealand. They also unofficially represent thirty-four different religious groups. An hourly stipend, in addition to travel expenses, was paid to the translators for the time they spent. They were divided into twenty teams with a translator, co-translator, two consultants, and an English stylist assigned to each team.[60]

Hearing of such Olympic-style organisation, one thinks that those teams had better succeed. NIV 'was designed for both young and old, for private study and public reading, ease in reading and comprehension'.[61] There was much fussing over inserted words (in half-square brackets), direct quotations (in quotation marks), capitalisations and paragraphing. Notes, printed with the text, are more extensive than in RSV. In the text, NIV supplements the ancient, standard Masoretic Hebrew text with readings from the Dead Sea Scrolls with caution. In the New Testament, a critically reconstructed Greek text is the base, rather than the *Textus Receptus*. In forty-five cases, *Textus Receptus* readings (thus in KJV) lacking older evidence are relagated to the margin.[62] The Committee on Bible Translation responsible for this version has been notably open to suggestions from readers, often adopted in later editions; its members will consider such revisions at five-year intervals.

A reader familiar with KJV will feel at home with NIV. Here is almost word-for-word KJV in the twenty-third Psalm, 'Even though I walk through the valley of the shadow of death' and most of the rest; 'Hallowed be your name', 'debtors' and 'debts' in the Lord's Prayer in Matthew 6; 'fishers of men' in Mark 1; 'speaking in tongues' in Acts 2, and 'have not love' in 1 Corinthians 13. Theologically, here are 'justification', 'sanctifying' and 'blood'. Here is 'Lord' not 'Yahweh', with extensions ('Sovereign Lord', 'Lord Almighty') sorted out in the notes. Proper names are as in KJV, with occasional notes. Cautious Anglicizing is helpful: the 'teraphim' become 'household gods', 'Syria' becomes 'Aram' and its language 'Aramaic'. Grievously for Tyndale's poetic line ending with 'peacocks', at 1 Kings 10:22 Solomon's ships bring him 'Gold, silver and ivory, and apes and baboons'. Neither Joseph nor Tamar have coats of many colours, but 'ornamented robes'.

The normal difficulty of balancing older reverence of language and racy-sounding modern speech is only partly resolved: 'Three in the afternoon' is at Acts 10:3, but 'sixth hour' and 'ninth hour' at Luke 23:44.

'Pottage' becomes 'stew', 'kinsman' becomes 'relative', 'sojourned' becomes 'stayed'. The Queen of Sheba is 'overwhelmed' by Solomon's sumptuous household at 1 Kings 10:5, instead of other modern versions' 'there was no more spirit in her' – but Tyndale has, simply, 'she was astonished'. The Israelites making bricks without straw at Exodus 5:8 are not to 'reduce the quota': Tyndale has 'lay unto their charge' – which, one wonders, sounds more modern? 'Everyone is looking for you' at Mark 1:37 replaces 'all men seek for thee'. Is that an improvement? At 1 Samuel 14:6, where Tyndale had Jonathan saying to 'the young man that bare his harness: come and let us go over unto the standing of these uncircumcised', NIV has the toe-curling 'Come, let's go over to the outpost of those uncircumcised fellows' (to which the reply should be, but isn't, 'Top hole, old bean, what a wheeze!'). As always in these enterprises, under the cover of 'dynamic equivalence', paraphrase creeps in, and, as so often, is no improvement. Is Jethro's 'Go, and I wish you well' to Moses at Exodus 4:18 really better than (Tyndale's) 'Go in peace'?

NIV looks like a Bible: that is to say, it looks like KJV, with heavy type in two columns. There is a lot of poetry laid out, which means that on many pages, not only in the poetic and prophetic books of the Old Testament, new sentences start new numbered verses, as in KJV. Heavy paragraphing tends to produce the same effect. The large question is whether it was necessary. Even in 1978 the field was crowded. Yes, RSV had notoriously (and correctly) given Isaiah 7:14 as 'young woman' causing the hysterical hostility that will be noticed later. NIV reverts to KJV's 'virgin shall conceive', without any note, though all the American versions from 1901 had an explanatory note. More than often, the 'modern' tone is unhappy: at John 2:4, Jesus says to his mother 'Dear woman, why do you involve me?' which might be a line from a George Bernard Shaw play of the 1890s. (Here the Amplified Bible (1965) shows its ridiculous colours, with '[Dear]' – annotated on the page from 'G. Abbot-Smith, *Manual Greek Lexicon of the New Testament:* "a term of respect and endearment" – ' woman, what is that to you and to Me? [What do we have in common? Leave it to me!].) The Greek is brief, Τί ἐμοὶ καὶ σοί, γύναι; (*Ti emoi kai soi, gunai;*, what to me and to you, woman?)

Hostile commentators with electron microscopes detected in NIV a theological tincture invisible to the naked eye, but in fact there is little in NIV to frighten the horses. Its devoted sectarian use across the world, even to the point, distressingly, of bigotry, must be because true believers are restrained from looking at other versions. To be 'washed in the blood of the Lamb' in some communities one must, if not holding a large floppy-backed KJV, be seen to use NIV. There has surely to be agreement with the reviewer who remarked 'At times it is so close to the RSV – [he might have added, KJV] – that one wonders why all this energy and money should have been spent on another version.'[63]

THE GOOD NEWS BIBLE,
TODAY'S ENGLISH VERSION, 1976

In NIV, John 14:1, that precious verse from Tyndale ('Let not your hearts be troubled. Believe in God and believe in me') appears almost intact: '"Do not let your hearts be troubled. Trust in God, trust also in me."' This is not true of the third enormously successful and continually selling American version of the 1970s, begun in the 1960s, known as the Good News Bible or Today's English Version, finally issued complete in 1976. To the translators', and sponsors', shame John 14:1 appears here as: '"Do not be worried and upset," Jesus told them. "Believe also in God and believe also in me."' The first phrase could not be more wrong, on three grounds. First, the Greek has nothing about worry or upsetness. It is Μὴ ταρασσέσθω ὑμῶν ἡ καρδια (*Mē tarassesthō humōn hē kardia*), five words about not-being-troubled hearts. There is a world of difference between that and what the GNB gives. The second error is in significance. Jesus is beginning to tell his disciples something of the greatest seriousness imaginable, that he is going from them in terrible circumstances but that he also goes 'to prepare a place' for them. Something is already being communicated of almost bottomless spiritual significance, shadowing Jesus' death on the Cross and the true understanding of Heaven. Thirdly, a troubled heart is the stuff of great grief, or the source of vocation, or of spiritual growth. It has nothing to do with being worried or upset, which is local and temporary. Worry is self-absorbed, about paying one's bills, or about other people not doing what we think they should do ('I'm so worried about him: he's seeing that girl again'). Upsetness is even more self-absorbed ('How *could* you? Now I'm upset – I'm so upset I've got to go and lie down.')

This mistranslation is all the more grievous on two further counts: that the aim of GNB was, as the Foreword states, 'to follow the original texts [. . .] in a standard, everyday, natural English', pitched, as the chairman of the committee, Robert G. Bratcher put it, 'at the [American] elementary school reading level'.[64] The 'original text' has most blatantly not been followed at John 14:1, for no discernible reason, for it is surely impossible to believe that even those readers in school would not understand either 'troubled hearts' or the high seriousness of the context. The second count is a sad one. This version, again as the Foreword states, 'has been translated and published by the United Bible Societies', led by ABS, of which Bratcher was a leader.

'Good News for Modern Man: The New Testament in Today's English Version' had first appeared in 1966, later with alterations for a British edition, and frequent substantial revision in successive editions. The Bible Societies are good at such continual revision and repackaging, as well as work that is truly interdenominational, even to there being a Catholic edition of GNB in 1979. The strengths of GNB, described as 'the shifting from traditional theological language to language as common as that used in the newspaper',[65] are also its weaknesses. Ditching 'traditional theological language' can easily slide into ditching theology. Romans 5:1, 'Now that we have been put right with God through faith' does sound at first to be a clarification: but 'put right' is what happens to a faulty machine, and losing 'justified' so arbitrarily, without a note, cancels important theological understanding. Paul's 'justified' is not the same as being 'put right'. Further, 'placing communication with the reader above the pursuit of English literary style'[66] may or may not sound admirable, but it brings with it a uniform flatness, from Genesis 1 to Revelation 22, a tendency to dullness found most seriously in the Psalms. For KJV's (and the Prayer Book's) opening of Psalm 91, 'He that dwelleth in the secret place of the most High shall abide under the shadow of the Almighty. I will say of the Lord . . .', GNB begins 'Whoever goes to the Lord for safety, whoever remains under the protection of the Almighty, can say to him . . .' which is the language of an advertisement for insurance. Job 38:7, in KJV 'When the morning stars sang together, and all the sons of God shouted for joy', a phrase to set the blood coursing, is in GNB the lyric to a sentimental song, 'In the dawn of that day the stars sang together, and the heavenly beings shouted for joy.' Slightly lifted above the flat surface are colloquialisms: David's brother Eliab says to him, in the original GNB, 'You smart aleck, you!', changed later to 'You cheeky brat, you!' In Ecclesiastes 2:8, 'the Philospher' boasts 'I had all the women a man could want.' The 'Unforgiving Servant' at Matthew 18:24 'owed him', in the first GNB editions, 'millions of dollars'.

Director of ABS translations was Eugene Nida, who in 1974, with Charles Taber, published *The Theory and Practice of Translation*.[67] Nida was President of the American Society of Linguistics, and underpinned ABS practice with learned theory; he had written *Towards a Science of Translating* in 1964. He clarified and elaborated the distinction between translating with formal equivalence, whereby the grammatical structure of the orginal is reproduced as much as possible; paraphrase, where the ideas are restated in different language; and dynamic equivalence, 'which attempts to make the same impression on the current reader that the original did on its readers . . . form is sacrificed in the interest of meaning'.[68] The last is the guiding principle of GNB, so 'a land of milk and honey' becomes 'a rich and fertile land' and 'apple of the eye' bcomes 'what is most precious to me'. At 1 Corinthians 16:9. 'a wide door' becomes 'a real opportunity'. Psalm 23's 'Anointed my head with oil' becomes 'welcomed me as an honored guest'. Matthew 6:3's 'Let not your left hand know what your right hand does' becomes 'that your closest friend will not know'. Sometimes (as we saw with John 14:1), paraphrase is inaccurately free: at Ruth 1:1, instead of Tyndale's and KJV's 'In the days when the judges judged', GNB has, in defiance of the Hebrew, 'Long ago, in the days before Israel had a king.' 'Dynamic' is a technical term in the science of linguistics (the phrase later became 'Functional Equivalence'). The application of that cold science to putting the exotic colour and tactile materiality of Hebrew into English kills metaphor. In Psalm 1, it changes KJV's 'nor sitteth in the seat of the scornful' to 'or join those who have no use for God'. It could possibly be mistakenly thought that the Word of God is best expressed in the tones of the *New York Times*: but the Word of God is crammed with both colour and mystery (otherwise it is hardly 'of God'). It is surely unfortunate to lose the sense of otherness in slicing away Hebrew and Greek vividness, like ('mercy seat', Exodus 25:17, now 'lid', or 'the finger of God', Luke 11:20, now 'God's power'[69]). In the context, is 'But Jesus kept quiet' (Matthew 26:63) better than Tyndale's and KJV's 'But Jesus held his peace?' The Greek ἐσιώπα (*esiōpa*) contains the sense of holding something that is secret, something personally valuable that is out of the ken of others, appropriate for Jesus, especially at that moment. 'Kept quiet' has more to do with bodily control, a denial of the immanence. Moreover, is 'held his peace' so impossible to understand? More powerfully, to Anglicize the verb of Jesus' terrible last cry into 'My God, my God, why did you abandon me?' (Matthew 27:46, from Psalm 22:1, where it is also 'abandon') instead of 'forsake', feels like changing for the sake of change; and in the process a large dimension has been lost. There is a crucial diference between 'abandon' and 'forsake': the first is casting away into immediate forgetfulness – an abandoned car; the second contains a wilful emotional tearing away – loss, denial and renunciation, with mutuality still strong. Spenser introduces his Una as a 'Forsaken, woeful, solitary maid', not 'abandoned'.[70] The difference in sound is also crucial. One has only to imagine Christus in J. S. Bach's *St Matthew Passion* trying to sing, instead of the heart-wrenching 'forsaken', 'why hast thou abandoned me?' to catch that.

ABS is rightly proud of the formation of the United Bible Societies' translation work. Nida's teams, originally working with South American languages, included specialists in all the then modern theories of discourse, including cultural anthropologists and experts in audience studies and communication. Where, one asks, was the New Testament theologian? To be fair, in spite of muddying (of 'justified', as we saw) GNB can at times be reassuringly strong in expressing Paul. Romans 8:31–2 is

> In view of all this, what can we say? If God is for us, who can be against us? Certainly not God, who did not even keep back his own Son, but offered him for us all! He gave us his Son – will he not also freely give us all things?

That is fine. Yet in spite of some syntactical loosening, most of these phrases are KJV unaltered, and all three sentences have not only the smell of Tyndale, but his words – 'who can be against us?', 'him for us all', 'give us all things' – phrases which sum up Christian theology.

GNB, like most other twentieth-century Bibles, comes in many forms of its 'bestselling version'. All of them have Introductions to each book, admirably clear and brief, that to Romans (though again ducking 'justification') being a model. Some of them have five hundred illustrations by a Swiss-born artist, Annie Vallotton, not liked by everyone (fig. 45). Later versions showed responses to pressure from scholars and critics, even as many as 'between 700 and 800' changes in the second edition[71] and, from the fourth edition, towards inclusive vocabulary.

Through his scholarship, Eugene Nida's linguistic distinction revitalised ABS Bible translation. For a general impression of what the Bible might generally be saying, GNB successfully fulfils its aim, of being readable by anyone who can read English. Whether that impression would ever be followed by pursuit of a truer study of the deeper riches in the Hebrew and Greek is the question. In the name of fashionable communications-theory, slicing away metaphors in English removes the potential for mystery which is at the heart of what is meant by the Holy.

Well known in North America is an engaging experiment in going beyond J. B. Phillips in putting the Epistles of Paul into modern expression. Clarence Jordan's *Cotton Patch Version of Paul's Epistles* (New York, 1969) is subtitled: *A Colloquial Modern Translation with a Southern Accent, Vigorous and Fervent for the Gospel, Unsparing in Earthiness, Rich in Humour.* It casts incidental light on the problems tackled by Eugene Nida's team of translators. Jordan makes clear in his page or two of introduction what he is after, which is letting Paul be himself 'without artificially clothing him with the image of immaculate sainthood'. He is interested in ideas rather than words, so that 1 Corinthians 8:4, in KJV 'eating meat sacrificed to idols', becomes 'working on Sunday'. Paul in *Cotton Patch* writes letters to the Christians in Washington, Atlanta, the Georgia Convention, and so on.

Jordan is refreshing. On the one hand, he recognises that Paul's writing can be difficult to the point of impossibility.

> But there have been times when I simply could not latch on to either Paul's words or his ideas, and have had to muddle through as best I could. In these instances I have found myself in perfect agreement with Peter, who said that 'our beloved brother Paul, according to the wisdom given unto him, hath written to you . . . some things which are hard to understand', 2 Peter 3:15–16.

On the other, Jordan recognises that language changes. He has fun with the difficulties that could face a Ph.D. student two thousand years hence with the sentence, 'perfectly understandable in the American South in the 1960's', if he wrote to a friend, 'we had Coke and hot dogs for lunch, fish and hush puppies for supper, and then sat around shooting the bull until midnight.' (A spoof editorial suggestion notes the American preoccupation with eating dogs.)

While a long way from the vacuous uplift of, say, *The Message*, Jordan is not aiming for the definitive technical theological words, but, to mix metaphors, hard-hitting illumination. Thus his Romans 5:1 is : 'Since we have been put in the swim with God because of our faithulness, we have a close relationship with him through our Lord Jesus Christ.' Six verses later: 'while we were real sick, in the nick of time Christ died for people who couldn't care less for a loving God.' Two verses after that, 'But God convinces us of *his* love, because *while we were still sinful trash*, Christ gave his life for us.' In the last chapter of Romans, he out-Phillips Phillips, surely to good effect:

> Say hello to Prissy and Adrian, my co-workers in Christ Jesus. They stuck their necks out to save my life. . . . Best wishes to Ansley, so dear to me in the Lord. Greetings to Howard, our Christian co-worker, and my dear Stocky. Regards to Everett, a true Christian. Say hello to the Harris Baker family. Hello, Cousin Helena. Hello to the faithful Nicholson family. . . . Give my love to Austin, Phill, Herb, Perry, Herman and the brothers with them. . . . Give everybody a big hug. All of Christ's churches greet you.

THE REVISED ENGLISH BIBLE

For the first time published by both Oxford and Cambridge University Presses together, the Revised English Bible of 1989 continued where NEB left off, and was the work of some of the same scholars. Sponsoring this

British, wholly new, version (rather than a revision making adjustments to NEB) the Joint Committee of the Churches now included, and involved, the Roman Catholic Church, and, presently, as well as the major Nonconformist churches, the Salvation Army and the Moravian Church. As always, scholarly integrity and total intelligibility were the first aims: but now 'liturgical use' is included.[72] In double columns REB feels much more 'biblical' than NEB. Where NEB had made its standard Hebrew text the 1937 *Biblia Hebraica*, REB used the 1966–7 *Biblia Hebraica Stuttgartensia*.

Rather unfairly, REB has received scant popular attention in North America. The translators' claim, not only to do real work on the original texts, but to aim for a higher level of English (though they do not put it quite like that) deserve praise. They understood the point of the spoken word.[73] To move from GNB to REB is to move, at Luke 13:20–21, from GNB's

> What shall I compare the Kingdom of God with? It is like this. A woman takes some yeast, and mixes it with forty litres of flour until the whole batch of dough rises.

That reads aloud badly: the awkward 'with'; 'takes some yeast' (a mouthful to say, and, for clear hearing, the yeast should come first); and the mock-homespun 'the whole batch of dough'. REB has

> To what shall I compare the kingdom of God? It is like yeast which a woman took and mixed with three measures of flour till all was leavened.

That is not only ecomonical and clear. It is a straight improvement on NEB's 'The kingdom of God, what shall I compare it with?' REB is close in manner to Tyndale, and, in 'which a woman took', identical. The chair of the New Testament translating committee, Dr Morna D. Hooker, the Lady Margaret Professor of Divinity in the University of Cambridge (a chair of which the second holder was Erasmus) has written well about their handling of a number of New Testament theological cruces, in relation to Tyndale.[74] She discusses among other things the Greek 'revealed his Son in me' at Galatians 1:16; – does the Greek verb κατοπρτιζω (*katoptrizō*) at 2 Corinthians 3:18 mean 'seeing' or 'reflecting'? The Greek phrase πιστις Χριστου (*pistis Christou*) might mean Christ's faithfulness, or our faith in him. On Colossians 1:24, over which there has been much modern theological dispute, Paul apparently speaking of making up what is lacking in the sufferings of Christ, Professor Hooker pointed out that 'If only earlier commentators had turned to Tyndale, they would not have got into such a tangle.' Tyndale's text is accurate to the Greek, and he adds a further clarifying note.

It is good to have the problems of translating not in the world of cultural anthropology or advanced theory of linguistics, but Pauline theology. REB consistently reads aloud very well. John 14 begins

> Set your troubled hearts at rest. Trust in God always; trust also in me. There are many dwelling-places in my Father's house; if it were not so I should have told you.

If Tyndale has to be changed, that is the way to do it – and the last ten words are pure Tyndale anyway, apart from 'would' to 'should'. Romans 5 in REB begins:

> Therefore, now that we have been justified through faith, we are at peace with God through our Lord Jesus Christ, who has give us access to that grace in which we now live; and we exult in the hope of the divine glory that is to be ours.

Whereas *The Message* early in Matthew 7 seems to be translating a different book from the New Testament altogether, with 'Don't bargain with God. Be direct. Ask for what you need. This isn't a cat-and-mouse, hide-and-seek game we're in', REB has

> Ask, and you will receive; seek, and you will find; knock, and the door will be opened to you. For everyone who asks receives, those who seek find, and to those who knock, the door will be opened.

That, in all its dignity and clarity, is the Greek in modern English.

THE TOTAL OF NEW TRANSLATIONS IN THE TWENTIETH CENTURY

Over twelve hundred new translations into English of the Bible, or parts of it, were made from the original Hebrew and Greek between 1945 and 1990. Thirty-five were fresh translations of the whole Bible, and eighty were fresh translations of the New Testament alone.[75] These are large figures.

Admittedly, a few of that total were of short biblical books: one each of the minor prophets Malachi and Zephaniah, two of the Epistle to Titus: but in those years all the Psalms, or selections, were retranslated over one hundred and twenty times; the book of Job was retranslated thirty-six times, the Gospel of John thirty-three times, the Epistle to the Romans twenty-six times, and Revelation twenty-three times.

The figures are compiled from Chamberlin, whose catalogue lists 1,268 new translations in that half-century; the British Library catalogue shows a few more. Since the publication of Chamberlin's work in 1991, other translations have appeared. They include *The Message* (1993), *The Promise*, 'a fresh presentation' of the Bible Societies' Contemporary English Version (1995), which began as the *Into the Light New Testament*, now the whole Bible, 'the work of a decade of translation work by more than 100 consultants';[76] or *God's Word of Freedom* (also 1995) from *God's Word to the Nations Bible Society* in Cleveland, Ohio. Such Bibles can now carry a sticker, 'AS SEEN ON TV'. There are others.

Taking in New Testaments as well as whole Bibles, between 1939 and 1997 there were in the UK alone 70 reprintings of KJV. Calculating new translations on the same criteria, and including translations of individual books, one arrives at a figure of fresh translations of the Bible of close on 1,500 in the twentieth century.

'KJV ONLY'

That is not quite the end of the story. In the last decades of the twentieth century there has emerged in the United States of America a phenomenon which should be noted. This is a loudly proclaimed declaration of several entwined beliefs. These go beyond the familiar views of millions of American Christians who prefer KJV to any other version. There are, however, more aggressive 'KJV Only' beliefs.[77] These may be locked in to other rigidly sectarian positions on a dozen issues, so that not to be a heretic in some parts of some Southern states of America a Christian might have to be, as it were, 'a KJV Only Pro-Disney Boycott State Subsidized Schools Against Women in Ministry Dispensational Premillennial Calvinisitic Resurgent Conservative Southern Baptist'; more, it would be heresy to believe all that but to go on, instead of 'KJV Only', to 'Gender Inclusive Modern Versions'.[78]

There are more extreme beliefs still, stating that KJV is the inspired and inerrant Word of God in every letter and syllable, and even, (wrongly), that the KJV translators used better Greek texts than modern translators. At yet further extremes, scholarship and good sense are increasingly left behind. It is said quite widely that both the Greek and the Hebrew texts used by the KJV translators (and only those) had been both inspired and supernaturally preserved. There are in the United States small groups that go beyond even that, claiming

> that the KJV was written in eternity, and that Abraham and Moses and the prophets all read the 1611 KJV, including the New Testament. These individuals believe that Hebrew is actually English. . . . Such groups are, for rather obvious reasons, very small.[79]

This is in spite of the fact that printings of KJV, even from the beginning, have differed from one another.

Eccentric individual positions are usually harmless. Capable of doing damage, however, are the strong assertions that because KJV is the only, and inerrant, Word of God all current Bible retranslations, without exceptions ('NIV, NASB, NKJV, NRSV, NAB, REB, RSV, CEV, TEV, GNB, Living, Phillips, New Jerusalem & New Century'[80]) are not only wrong, but active in a secret conspiracy to deny Christian truth.[81] Thus, modern translators using Greek and Hebrew texts that have occasional different readings from those used by the KJV translators are corrupting God's Word. This slippery slope leads quickly to the persuasion that KJV was especially re-inspired by God in English (and, as is commonly thought, personally translated by the English monarch James I). If the ancient Greek and Hebrew texts are found to differ from KJV, they are wrong and must be altered to fit (a position, incidentally, close to that of Gregory Martin upholding the Catholic Latin Bible against the Greek and Hebrew in his Preface to the 1582 Rheims New Testament). From there it is a short plunge to that conviction that the modern versions using such 'corrupt' texts are parts of 'a massive conspiracy' to destroy God's true revelation of Himself, that found uniquely in KJV. It is a conspiracy, moreover, that finds the work of Antichrist not only in the modern use of certain ancient central Greek manuscripts which have readings which differ from KJV, but even extends, backwards in time, to the making of those ancient Greek manuscripts themselves. Thus Tischendorf's great Codex Sinaiticus, placed by Westcott and Hort as first in rank of all Greek New Testament manuscripts, is damned. Decades after Tischendorf, Sinaiticus is known to be less perfect than was assumed, but it is still of supreme importance. Because Westcott and Hort placed it foremost, displacing the *Textus Receptus*, it is said to be the work of Satan, so that a 'KJV Only' partisan observed that within two years of 'England's national acceptance' of this 'depraved' Codex, 'the city of London was was in smoldering ruins'[82] – this presumably refers to the devastation of the Second World War, from the bombing of British cities throughout the autumn of 1940 to the massive civilian casualties in London in 1941 and 1942, and even in 1945, in the last stages of the war, when Germany was facing defeat, when the pilotless V1 and V2 'revenge weapons' killed nearly 9,000 civilians: for London, terrible events indeed, but hard to fit with Westcott and Hort in 1881.

The chief characteristic of a theory of 'massive conspiracy' is that it can absorb everything in sight, and far beyond normal vision as well. There has to be no regard for accuracy of any kind. Material invented out of fantasy can be presented as revealed fact. Developing their discovery of conspiracies to corrupt God's Word, writers misquote modern versions and give false information about them: as when they say that KJV is the ony Bible that distinguishes between the Hebrew *Adonai* and *JHVH*, using 'Lord' for the former and 'LORD' for the latter, which is obviously untrue. Sound, patient, balanced and detailed scholarship, like that of the customary 'KJV Only' villains, Westcott and Hort, can be misrepresented, twisted and misquoted in the confidence that readers of 'KJV Only' tracts are not going to discover the distortions by consulting Westcott and Hort's originals; partly because they are hard to find, and partly because to read them would be consorting with the enemy.

To call all this a debate is to give it a dignity that it does not warrant. The delusions, the convictions that, as it were, the earth is indeed, after all, flat, and not only the centre of the solar system but also of the universe, make sorry reading. The usual level of discourse is, as James White put it, 'insulting rhetoric'.[83] It can be worse than that. The NIV translation panels have been attacked for 'containing homosexuals'. That is not true.[84] The repeated false assertion brings with it various kinds of poison which should not be present in Christian analyses of Bible translations. Over the borderline of sanity is the announcement that editors of new versions have been found 'in mental institutions, seance parlours, prison cells and court rooms for heresy trials' and five have been struck dumb.[85]

In discussing modern Bibles, it might be thought better to ignore the extreme 'KJV Only' writings as being too unbalanced to have significance. Yet they should be noticed. They are the recent outcroppings of a much older rocky seam in American society.[86] American objections to the English Revised Version in the 1870s were not only to the occasionally distressingly patronising tone used towards them by the British revisers: there were public disgreements about the authority of Scripture, about traditional readings challenged by the latest technical scholarship. Again, in the middle of the twentieth century, in 1952, when in America the new RSV was found to render the traditional Messianic words in Isaiah 7:14, 'a young woman shall conceive' instead of 'Behold, a virgin shall conceive', there was national outcry. In 'the greatest Bible translation controversy in American religious history'[87] the vehemence and broad base of the attacks surprised the makers.[88] Denunciation from all over the United States and from many denominations came not only in books, pamphlets, newspaper articles and radio broadcasts: on the night of 30 November 1952, an independent pastor in North Carolina gave a two-hour oration, in a spectacular open-air ceremony ('every member [of the congregation] received a small American flag'). He then held up a copy of RSV, especially labelled 'FRAUD', tore out the page containing Isaiah 7:14, and set fire to it. A pastor in Ohio apparently burned the whole volume.[89] Burning a Bible was itself denounced, but expressions of 'Christian' hatred flourished. In intemperate tracts, RSV was denounced as – inevitably, given the period, of the 1950s and early 1960s, – 'communist'. Attacks on the 'Red Bible' came to a head when 'the U.S. Air Force Reserve published a countersubversive training manual warning recruits to avoid [. . .] the communist-tainted RSV Bible'.[90]

A national fear of conspiracy did not die at the end of the Cold War, as any observer of Washington politics or rural America at the turn of the millennium could see. The late twentieth-century 'massive conspiracy' promulgated by the 'KJV Only' camp is only one, but it is unfortunate. In 1995 it was noted, alarmingly, that 'Responsibility must be laid at the door of the "KJV Only" camp for the destruction of many Christian churches.'[91]

Such destruction, by splitting apart, must be lamented. Yet what is note-worthy is that in current American life, in what has been described as the 'contemporary Babel'[92] of competing Bible versions, the KJV, usually in less disintegrative ways, is still so strongly present. Dietrich Bonhoeffer observed that American Christianity, uniquely for any nation on earth, has no visible unity: 'no central organization, no common creed, no common cultus, no common church history and no common ethical, social or political princples'.[93] Though between 1952 and 1990 fifty-five million copies of RSV were sold, and other versions could show colossal sales figures, KJV still outstrips all rivals.[94] It may perhaps be that KJV has continued to stand even in a limited way for some form of American Christian unity. The reasons for its dominance are understandable, if not always commendable. What is so surprising is the continual flourishing in the American republic of a monarchical version, frequently beautiful but already archaic in 1611, often erroneous, sometimes unintelligble, but persistently loved as 'our American Bible', or even 'the American Book';[95] the constant strong presence of KJV in five hundred years of American history – still there, still very much alive.

Chapter 40

CONCLUSION

The number of English Bibles printed since 1526 is incalculable – one thinks of a number, and goes on adding noughts. Oxford University Press's annual catalogue for 1930 offers about 2,000 different kinds of KJV or RV: spread over more publishers, modern Bible catalogues in the UK and USA come to roughly similar totals, though the available kinds are usually fancier and fuller, with 'study Bible' notes. Total numbers are more than astronomical. What can be estimated, however, is the number of new translations into English, since 1526 from the original languages. It was seen above that, incuding whole Bibles, New Testaments and some single books like the Psalms, the twentieth century saw about 1,500 new translations from Greek and Hebrew into English. By careful use of DMH, Hills and Chamberlin, from 1526 to 1900 one can find the same figure, about 1,500. So from Tyndale printing his first complete New Testament in Worms, in 1526, to the year 2000, there have been about 3,000 new translations of the Bible into English.

What of the future? An attempted answer must consider several large matters.

LOSS OF EARS

It does not need saying that the world after A.D. 2000 is dominated by visual experiences. Insistent television and advertising gives us continually shifting coloured images, sometimes of high sophistication, which fill our waking hours. At one side of the field, the banality of advertisements for things that people are made to want but do not need makes the brain resist. At the other, views from the Hubble Telescope of distant galaxies, or of Earth from the Space Shuttle, properly produce awed attention. In the middle of the field are heads incessantly talking at us.

Visual Bibles have been made for some years: not just a few fixed-video-camera records of someone reading Scripture, though they do exist, but many animated re-creations of Bible stories, sometimes charming and

helpful, often regrettable. The English Bible is here in new territory altogether. There is no knowing what will follow; whether, for example,
'cartoon' stories about King David and his warriors performed by
American vegetables[1] will lead to full personal experience of Christ
through the Bible is so far unknown: faith may move mountains, but that
seems unlikely – and see figs 45 and 46.

There is here a serious problem. It can be stated as the loss of our ears.
While the visual dominates, aural attention fades. Not only do television
and computer images, by their very speed and impermanence, encourage
inattention to themselves: they rob us of our attention to words. Can we
remember twelve words from last week's television?

In Act 2 of Shakespeare's *Hamlet*, the Prince enthusiastically receives
travelling players to the royal palace at Elsinore. He demands a speech at
once from their leader, First Player. We are to understand that they represent travelling players from a company at the new Globe Theatre in
London, led by a great actor. Hamlet wants to hear again a speech he
heard some years ago, and heard only once: he quotes twelve and a half
lines of it, and clearly could go on with the rest of the speech, and stops
only because he wants to listen to a professional.

Hamlet is not a professional actor; yet he recalls, correctly, a dozen lines
heard once, long before. The point of the scene is in the antique words
and their account of a fallen father, not astonishment at the Prince's feat.
In 1600, it was automatic to remember what was heard, undistracted. As
noted above (p. 270), accounts of men and women interrogated under
Queen Mary in the 1550s include references to detailed Bible knowledge
in the victims, even though they could not read.

William Tyndale and Miles Coverdale translated the Scriptures to be
heard. Absorbed into KJV, their work has endured. Consider the way the
words of KJV sing in Handel's *Messiah*. Consider even more J. S. Bach's
St Matthew Passion, in its English version. Evangelist sings the story, from
KJV, with dramatic interpolations from other figures, including Christ. The
moment of Peter's recognition of his betrayal of Jesus is musically famous
for the moving *melisma* on the words 'wept bitterly'. That is Tyndale's translation, kept down the ages. It is the very end of Matthew 26, in Tyndale
and KJV:

> And Peter remembered the words of Jesus which said unto him: before
> the cock crow, thou shalt deny me thrice: and he went out at the doors
> and wept bitterly.

(KJV omits the Greek of 'at the doors'.)

One would think that there is no other way to translate the passage,
the adverb πικρῶς (*pikrōs*) meaning just that, 'sharply', 'harshly' or 'bitterly'.

The rhythmic extension of the simple English 'wept' into the drawn-out 'bitterly' is superb, whether sung or spoken.

Now, the makers of the Contemporary English Version (1995), in their 'Welcome' on page vi, claim that

> The *Contemporary English Version* has been described as a 'user-friendly' and a 'mission-driven' translation that can be *read aloud* without stumbling, *heard* without misunderstanding, and *listened to* with enjoyment and appreciation, because the style is lucid and lyrical.

These points are important. Serious faults in widely used versions have been the very qualities implicit in the CEV's 'Welcome': that they have been, at a simple level, hard to read aloud, and at a more sophisticated level, they have made hearers wince. One turns to the last words of Matthew 26 in CEV in the confidence that in view of the claims made, Tyndale's power of being clear and transmittable to the ear will have been preserved. Not so. The last sentence is 'Then Peter went out and cried hard.'

What can have happened? 'Crying hard' is what a hungry baby regularly does: there is no content of Peter's shocked, unsearchable personal horror and grief – and it is impossible to imagine a heart-rending musical setting of the words. Can it be that the makers of CEV thought that 'wept' and 'bitterly' would not be understood? Moreover, when spoken aloud, the two stressed monosyllables of 'cried hard', without the descending relief in 'bitterly', do not transmit well – the voice has to press both ugly words unnaturally. Devastating as Peter's experience was, it was not ugly.

The words of KJV, usually Tyndale, sing out in Bach, in Handel (and not only in *Messiah*), and in modern works like Walton's *Belshazzar's Feast* – where the dramatic power of the last word of Daniel 5:30, 'In that night was Belshazzar the king . . . slain' is electrifying. (GNB/TEV has 'That same night Belshazzar the king . . . was killed', and CEV the prosaic 'That same night, the king was killed.' Unsurprisingly, the haunting chorus in Walton's oratorio, to KJV's Psalm 137, 'By the rivers [Walton sets 'waters', effectively] of Babylon, there we sat down, yea, we wept, when we remembered Zion', is in CEV, 'Beside the rivers of Babylon we thought about Jerusalem, and we sat down and cried.')

For all the enormous marketing pressures behind such modern enterprises, the future of English Bibles seems uncertain. Tyndale's English Testaments in the 1530s, with Coverdale's Bible, did, however much writers hostile to the very idea of a popular Reformation ignore them, sweep the country, change the minds of men and women, energise the language, and, at all levels of society, stimulate an imaginative flowering at the end of the

century, unique to England and never lost. It is true to say, 'without
Tyndale, no Shakespeare'.

This, it seems, will not happen again: there could only have been one
Shakespeare. One the one hand, English is now a worldwide, multiple language, still 'English' though in a hundred creoles and dialects. On the
other, whether the national religious convictions of the sixteenth and seventeenth centuries, based so much on English Bibles, could ever happen
again in a world distracted by instant messages and pictures about nothing,
does appear unlikely.

LOSS OF THEOLOGY

An observable loss in the later chapters in this book has been theology.
English Bibles now must, as noted above, speak the language of the *New
York Times*. (A distingushed exception is REB, for which one should be
grateful.) Modern hymns, no longer about the 'wondrous Cross', have to
be about what is supposed to be relevant to the everyday lives of the congregations, that is, again as we saw, buses and supermarkets. Though the
English Bible was a cause of the release of language in the sixteenth
century, and though the growth of a preaching culture then and after (still
neglected by those for whom history is only policy), it was theology that
unlocked the energy. The popular Reformation was people reading Paul,
and Paul is theology. The place of theology has been taken by abstract
theory. Ultimately from French philosophy, and developed in America,
these notions have often in the humanities made the 'text' a dirty word,
and reference to it the cause of superior amusement at such naivety.

Until the 1930s, one usually spoke of the user of a Bible as 'a believer',
of whatever denominational colour. Thereafter, as with western national
economies, the important figure is 'the consumer'. The result, over decades,
has been a tendency to water down, to avoid words or theology that might
disturb.

Perhaps the future of the Bible in English lies in the opposite – proper
rigour, even harshness, an avoidance of meal in the mouth, the embracing of difficulty. Tyndale's Pilate in John 19 'took Jesus and scourged him'
(as in KJV). It is probably true that 'scourge' for a particularly severe and
cruel torture by whipping is not in everyday English, though it survives
as a noun in a context of divine chastisement: but that should not mean
in this particular case that the severity should be reduced even to 'be
beaten with a whip' (CEV). Expressing an appalling infliction of suffering
can stand an uncommon word. Jesus himself is clear-eyed about what it
is to be human under God. He speaks nothing about 'feeling good about

yourself' (as obedient consumers should) but about observed death, poverty, disease, need, the shocking hypocrisy of religious officialdom, spiritual hunger and fulfilment, and the love of his Father.

In Jesus' parable in Luke 18: 9–14, one of the two men, vividly drawn with great economy, stands in the Temple and certainly feels good about himself. In brisk moments a modern reader might even feel that of the two, in the office or town meeting, it is the Pharisee who is preferable. He is a religious orthodox. Though self-important, he is a pillar of the community, a moral man, upright in his dealings, and he has a healthy sense of his own ego-value. The other man's profitable activities as a tax farmer were barely legal – the modern equivalent is perhaps a loan-shark – and in his self-abasing frame of mind he would be depressing company.

Yet Jesus' parable is seen to be slanted against the Pharisee. It is not only that the Pharisee reveals himself to be full of self-conceit, and his sneering 'or as this publican'. It is not just that it would be astonishing if Jesus had, as it were, kicked out the humble publican and told everyone to be like the Pharisee. It is not just that in the Gospels the Pharisees and the other members of the religious establishment despised Jesus because he was a social undesirable, actually sitting down and eating with known prostitutes and villains and the lowest underclass. The slant against the Pharisee comes from something altogether different. The parable is not about the two men at all, but about the nature of God. The Pharisee sees God full on as really like himself, a being both pompous and self-righteous. The Pharisee is already elevated, 'not like other men'. His God is *perhaps* just a notch above him. The Greek, and Tyndale, explain: he 'stood and prayed thus with himself'.

In that temple, the publican, by contrast, meets the full transcendence of God. 'Standing afar off, he would not lift up so much as his eyes unto heaven, but smote upon his breast, saying, God be merciful to me a sinner.' God is too glorious to be looked at. His presence fills a human with a sense of absolute unworthiness but at the same time a longing to be at home with him. There is no bar to that except acknowledgement of the otherness of God, expressed as the sinfulness of the human and the mercy of God. What is wrong with the Pharisees' God as 'super-me' is his glee in his separation from other people. He spells out exactly who are milling around in the dirt at the base of his pedestal far, far below him – 'extortioners, unjust, adulterers'. Just visible squatting there, as it were, is 'this publican'. But, says Jesus, that is where the transcendent God himself now is, squatting on the dirt. Prostitutes and publicans are 'dirty', and Jesus was with them and loved them. There could be no worse 'dirt' than to be tortured and crucified for all mankind. Jesus finishes the parable saying that this man went down to his house 'justified, rather than the other'

(KJV). 'Justified', is the Greek verb δικαιόω (*dikaioō*), as in Paul: not so much 'put right' as 'now in proper relation with God'. Paul wrote of the horror of sin, of separation from God, and, in Tyndale's enduring translation, of now being justified by faith. Tyndale not only led the way from Greek and Hebrew into English: his understanding and expression of New Testament theology was first class: he is now being recognised as a superior theologian to any other figure of his time.

> His consistent theology relied solely on the Scriptures, a covenant theology based on the Fatherhood of God, the blood of Christ, and the work of the Holy Spirit, which does not create the problems raised by Lutheranism and the federal theology of the Swiss Reformers.[2]

These understandings were his motives for translating, and make the material heart of what he did.

THE WORD OF GOD

There is an Italian proverb, *traduttore traditore*, 'the translator is a traitor'. No translation can be perfect: matter will be left out, new shadings brought in. I have been critical of recent attempts to make heavily marketed Bibles which seemed to me to betray rather more than was warranted.

Yet to stand at this point, momentarily at the end of a line since 1526 of so many fresh attempts to make the New Testament in English, calls for rejoicing. For nearly five centuries, the Word of God has gone out unhindered, and souls have received it with blessing. What Tyndale opened has indeed never been shut up.

What Tyndale opened still has unique force. His vocabulary occasionally sounds antique, but often does not. I finish this book with Jesus' words from John 15, in Tyndale:

> As the father hath loved me, even so have I loved you. Continue in my love. If ye shall keep my commandments, ye shall bide in my love, even as I have kept my father's commandments, and bide in his love. These things have I spoken unto you, that my joy might remain in you, and that your joy might be full.[3]

THE TRANSLATORS TO THE READER
THE PREFACE TO THE FIRST,
1611 EDITION OF KJV

Zeale to promote the common good, whether it be by deuising any thing our
selues, or reuising that which hath bene laboured by others,
deserueth certainly much respect and esteeme, but yet
findeth but cold intertainment in the world. It is wel-
commed with suspicion in stead of loue, and with emulation in stead of thankes:
and if there be any hole left for cauill to enter, (and cauill, if it doe not finde a
hole, will make one) it is sure to bee misconstrued, and in danger to be condemned. This will easily be granted by as many as know story, or haue any experience. For, was there euer any thing proiected, that sauoured any way of newnesse
or renewing, but the same endured many a storme of gaine-saying, or opposition? A man would thinke that Ciuilitie, holesome Lawes, learning and eloquence,
Synods, and Church-maintenance, (that we speake of no more things of this
kinde) should be as safe as a Sanctuary, and ‖ out of shot,[1] as they say, that no
man would lift vp the heele, no, nor dogge mooue his tongue against the motion-
ers of them. For by the first, we are distinguished from bruit-beasts led with sen-
sualitie: By the second, we are bridled and restrained from outragious behauiour,
and from doing of iniuries, whether by fraud or by violence: By the third, we
are enabled to informe and reforme others, by the light and feeling that we haue
attained vnto our selues: Briefly, by the fourth being brought together to a parle
face to face, we sooner compose our differences then by writings, which are end-
lesse: And lastly, that the Church be sufficiently prouided for, is so agreeable to
good reason and conscience, that those mothers are holden to be lesse cruell, that
kill their children assoone as they are borne, then those noursing fathers and
mothers (wheresoeuer they be) that withdraw from them who hang vpon their
breasts (and vpon whose breasts againe themselues doe hang to receiue the Spirituall and sincere milke of the word) liuelyhood and support fit for their estates.
Thus it is apparent, that these things which we speake of, are of most necessary
vse, and therefore, that none, either without absurditie can speake against them,
or without note of wickedness can spurne against them.

Yet for all that, the learned know that certaine worthy men[2] haue bene

The best things haue been calumniated.

brought to vntimely death for none other fault, but for seeking to reduce their Countrey-men to good order and discipline: and that in some Common-weales[3] it was made a capitall crime, once to motion the making of a new Law for the abrogating of an old, though the same were most pernicious: And that certaine,[4] which would be counted pillars of the State, and paternes of Vertue and Prudence, could not be brought for a long time to giue way to good Letters and refined speech, but bare themselues as auerse from them, as from rocks or boxes of poison: And fourthly, that hee[5] was no babe, but a great clearke, that gaue foorth (and in writing to remaine to posteritie) in passion peraduenture, but yet he gaue foorth, that hee had not seene any profit to come by any Synode, or meeting of the Clergie, but rather the contrary: And lastly, against Church-maintenance and allowance in such sort, as the Embassadors and messengers of the great King of Kings should be furnished, it is not vnknowen what a fiction or fable (so it is esteemed, and for no better by the reporter himselfe,[6] though superstitious) was deuised; Namely, that at such time as the professours and teachers of Christianitie in the Church of Rome, then a true Church, were liberally endowed, a voyce forsooth was heard from heauen, saying; Now is poison powred down into the Church, & c. Thus not only as oft as we speake, as one saith, but also as oft as we do any thing of note or consequence, we subiect our selues to euery ones censure, and happy is he that is least tossed vpon tongues; for vtterly to escape the snatch of them it is impossible. If any man conceit, that this is the lot and portion of the meaner sort onely, and that Princes are priuiledged by their high estate, he is deceiued. As *the sword deuoureth aswell one as the other*, as it is in *Samuel*;[7] nay as the great Commander charged his souldiers in a certaine battell, to strike at no part of the enemie, but at the face; And as the King of *Syria* commanded his chiefe Captaines *to fight neither with small nor great, saue onely against the King of Israel*:[8] so it is too true, that Enuie striketh most spitefully at the fairest, and at the chiefest. *Dauid* was a worthy Prince, and no man to be compared to him for his first deedes, and yet for as worthy an acte as euer he did (euen for bringing backe the Arke of God in solemnitie) he was scorned and scoffed at by his owne wife.[9] *Solomon* was greater than *Dauid*, though not in vertue, yet in power: and by his power and wisdome he built a Temple to the LORD, such a one as was the glory of the land of Israel, and the wonder of the whole world. But was that his magnificence liked of by all? We doubt of it. Otherwise, why doe they lay it in his sonnes dish, and call vnto him for ‖ easing of the burden,[10] *Make*, say they, *the grieuous seruitude of thy father, and his sore yoke, lighter*.[11] Belike he had charged them with some leuies, and troubled them with some cariages; Hereupon they raise vp a tragedie, and wish in their heart the Temple had neuer bene built. So hard a thing it is to please all, euen when we please God best, and doe seeke to approue our selues to euery ones conscience.

　　If wee will descend to later times, wee shall finde many the like examples of such kind, or rather vnkind acceptance. The first Romane Emperour[12] did neuer doe a more pleasing deed to the learned, nor more profitable to posteritie, for conseruing the record of times in true supputation; then when he corrected

The highest personages haue been calumniated.

the Calender, and ordered the yeere according to the course of the Sunne; and yet this was imputed to him for noueltie, and arrogancie, and procured to him great obloquie. So the first Christened Emperour[13] (at the leastwise that openly professed the faith himselfe, and allowed others to doe the like) for strengthening the Empire at his great charges, and prouiding for the Church, as he did, got for his labour the name *Pupillus*,[14] as who would say, a wastefull Prince, that had neede of a Guardian, or ouerseer. So the best Christened Emperour,[15] for the loue that he bare vnto peace, thereby to enrich both himselfe and his subiects, and because he did not seeke warre but find it, was iudged to be no man at armes,[16] (though in deed he excelled in feates of chiualrie, and shewed so much when he was prouoked) and condemned for giuing himselfe to his ease, and to his pleasure. To be short, the most learned Emperour of former times,[17] (at the least, the greatest politician) what thanks had he for cutting off the superfluities of the lawes, and digesting them into some order and method? This, that he hath been blotted by some to bee an Epitomist, that is, one that extinguished worthy whole volumes, to bring his abridgements into request. This is the measure that hath been rendred to excellent Princes in former times, euen, *Cum bene facerent, malè audire*, For their good deedes to be euill spoken of. Neither is there any likelihood, that enuie and malignitie died, and were buried with the ancient. No, no, the reproofe of *Moses* taketh hold of most ages; *You are risen vp in your fathers stead, an increase of sinfull men.*[18] *What is that that hath been done? that which shall be done: and there is no new thing under the Sunne,*[19] saith the wiseman: and S. *Steuen, As your fathers did, so doe you.*[20] This, and more to this purpose, His Maiestie that now reigneth (and long, and long may he reigne, and his offspring for euer, *Himselfe and children, and childrens children alwayes*[21]) knew full well, according to the singular wisedome giuen vnto him by God, and the rare learning and experience that he hath attained vnto; namely that whosoeuer attempteth any thing for the publike (specially if it pertaine to Religion, and to the opening and clearing of the word of God) the same setteth himselfe vpon a stage to be glouted vpon by euery euil eye, yea, he casteth himselfe headlong vpon pikes, to be gored by euery sharpe tongue. For he that medleth with mens Religion in any part, medleth with their custome, nay, with their freehold; and thouth they finde no content in that which they haue, yet they cannot abide to heare of altering. Notwithstanding his Royall heart was not daunted or discouraged for this or that colour, but stood resolute, *as a statue immoueable, and an anuile not easie to be beaten into plates,*[22] as one sayth; he knew who had chosen him to be a Souldier, or rather a Captaine, and being assured that the course which he intended made much for the glory of God, & the building vp of his Church, he would not suffer it to be broken off for whatsoeuer speaches or practises. It doth certainely belong vnto Kings, yea, it doth specially belong vnto them, to haue care of Religion, yea, to know it aright, yea, to professe it zealously, yea to promote it to the vttermost of their power. This is their glory before all nations which meane well, and this will bring vnto them a farre most excellent weight of glory in the day of the Lord Iesus. For the Scripture

His Maiesties constancie, notwithstanding calumniation, for the suruey of the English translations.

saith not in vaine, *Them that honor me, I will honor*,[23] neither was it a vaine word that *Eusebius* deliuered long agoe, that pietie towards God[24] was the weapon, and the onely weapon that both preserued *Constantines* person, and auenged him of his enemies.[25]

But now what pietie without trueth? what trueth (what sauing trueth) without the word of God? what word of God (whereof we may be sure) without the Scripture? The Scriptures we are commanded to search. Ioh. 5. 39. Esa. 8. 20. They are commended that searched & studied them. Act. 17. 11. and 8. 28, 29. They ar ereproued that were vnskilful in them, or slow to beleeue them. *Mat.* 22. 29. *Luk.* 24. 25. They can make vs wise vnto saluation. 2. *Tim.* 3. 15. If we be ignorant, they will instruct vs; if out of the way, they will bring vs home; if out of order, they will reforme vs, if in heauines, comfort vs; if dull, quicken vs; if colde, inflame vs. *Tolle, lege; Tolle, lege.*[26] Take vp and read, take vp and read the Scriptures, (for vnto them was the direction) it was said vnto S. *Augustine* by a supernaturall voyce. *Whatsoeuar is in the Scriptures, beleeue me*, saith the same S. *Augustine*,[27] *is high and diuine; there is verily trueth, and a doctrine most fit for the refreshing and renewing of mens mindes, and truely so tempered, that euery one may draw from thence that which is sufficient for him, if hee come to draw with a deuout and pious minde, as true Religion requireth.* Thus S. *Augustine.* And S. *Hierome*[28]: *Ana scripturas, & amabitte sapientia & c.* Loue the Scriptures, and wisedome will loue thee. And S. *Cyrill* against *Iulian*;[29] *Euen boyes that are bred up in the Scriptures, become most religious, &c.* But what mention wee three or foure vses of the Scripture, whereas whatsoeuer is to be beleeued or practised, or hoped for, is contained in them? or three or foure sentences of the Fathers, since whosoeuer is worthy the name of a Father, from Christs time downeward, hath likewise written not onely of the riches, but also of the perfection of the Scripture? *I adore the fulnesse of the Scripture*, saith *Tertullian* against *Hermogenes*.[30] And againe, to *Apelles* an Heretike of the like stampe, he saith; *I doe not admit that which thou bringest in* (or concludest) *of thine owne* (head or store, *de tuo*) without Scripture. So Saint *Iustin Martyr*[31] before him; *Wee must know by all meanes*, saith hee, *that it is not lawfull* (or possible) *to learne* (any thing) *of God or of right pietie, saue onely out of the Prophets, who teach vs by diuine inspiration.* So Saint *Basill*[32] after *Tertullian, It is a manifest falling away from the Faith, and a fault of presumption, either to reiect any of those things that are written, or to bring in* (vpon the head of them, ἐπεισάγειν) *any of those things that* are not written. Wee omit to cite to the same effect, S. *Cyrill* B. of *Hierusalem* in his 4. *Cataches.* Saint *Hierome* against *Heluidius*, Saint *Augustine* in his 3. booke against the letters of *Petilian*, and in very many other places of his workes. Also we forbeare to descend to latter Fathers, because wee will not wearie the reader. The Scriptures then being acknowledged to bee so full and so perfect, how can wee excuse our selues of negligence, if we doe not studie them, of curiositie, if we be not content with them? Men talke much of εἰρεσιώνη,[33] how many sweete and goodly things it had hanging on it; of the Philosophers stone, that it turneth copper into gold; of *Cornu-copia*, that it had all things necessary for foode in it; of *Panaces* the herbe,

The praise of the holy Scriptures.

that it was good for all disease; of *Catholicon* the drugge, that it is in stead of all purges; of *Vulcans* armour, that it was an armour of proofe against all thrusts, and all blowes, &c. Well, that which they falsly or vainely attributed to these things for bodily good, wee may iustly and with full measure ascribe vnto the Scripture, for spirituall. It is not onely an armour, but also a whole armorie of weapons, both offensiue, and defensiue; whereby we may saue our selues and put the enemie to flight. It is not an herbe, but a tree, or rather a whole paradise of trees of life, which bring foorth fruit euery moneth, and the fruit thereof is for meate, and the leaues for medicine. It is not a pot of *Manna*, or a cruse of oyle, which were for memorie only, or for a meales meate or two, but as it were a showre of heauenly bread sufficient for a whole host, be it neuer so great; and as it were a whole cellar full of oyle vessels; whereby all our necessities may be prouided for, and our debts discharged. In a word, it is a Panary of holesome foode, against fenowed traditions; a Physions-shop[34] (Saint *Basill* calleth it) of preseruatiues against poisoned heresies; a Pandect of profitable lawes, against rebellious spirits; a treasurie of most costly iewels, against beggarly rudiments; Finally a fountaine of most pure water springing vp vnto euerlasting life. And what maruaile? The originall thereof being from heauen, not from earth; the authour being God, not man; the enditer, the holy spirit, not the wit of the Apostles or Prophets; the Pen-men such as were sanctified from the wombe, and endewed with a principall portion of Gods spirit; the matter, veritie, pietie, puritie, vprightnesse; the forme, Gods word, Gods testimonie, Gods oracles, the word of trueth, the word of saluation, &c. the effects, light of vnderstanding, stablenesse of perswasion, repentance from dead workes, newnesse of life, holinesse, peace, ioy in the holy Ghost; lastly, the end and reward of the studie thereof, fellowship with the Saints, participation of the heauenly nature, fruition of an inheritance immortall, vndefiled, and that neuer shall fade away; Happie is the man that delighteth in the Scripture, and thrise happie that meditateth in it day and night.

But how shall men meditate in that, which they cannot vnderstand? How shall they vnderstand that which is kept close in an vnknowen tongue? as it is written, *Except I know the power of the voyce, I shall be to him that speaketh, a Barbarian, and he that speaketh, shalbe a Barbarian to me.*[35] The Apostle excepteth no tongue; not Hebrewe the ancientest, not Greeke the most copious, not Latine the finest. Nature taught a naturall man to confesse, that all of vs in those tongues which wee doe not vnderstand, are plainely deafe; wee may turne the deafe eare vnto them. The *Scythian* counted the *Athenian*, whom he did not vnderstand, barbarous?[36] so the *Romane* did the *Syrian*, and the *Iew*, (euen S. *Hierome*[37] himselfe calleth the Hebrew tongue barbarous, belike because it was strange to so many) so the Emperour of *Constantinople*[38] calleth the *Latine* tongue, barbarous, though Pope *Nicolas* do storme at it:[39] so the *Iewes* long before *Christ*, called all other nations, *Lognazim*, which is little better then barbarous. Therefore as one complaineth, that alwayes in the Senate of *Rome*, there was one or other that called for an interpreter:[40] so lest the Church be driuen to the like exigent, it is necessary to haue translations in

Translation necessarie.

a readinesse. Translation it is that openeth the window, to let in the light; that breaketh the shell, that we may eat the kernel; that putteth aside the curtaine, that we may looke into the most Holy place; that remooueth the couer of the well, that wee may come by the water, euen as *Iacob* rolled away the stone from the mouth of the well, by which meanes the flocks of *Laban* were watered.[41] Indeede without translation into the vulgar tongue, the vnlearned are but like children at *Iacobs* well (which was deepe) without a bucket or some thing to draw with:[42] or as that person mentioned by *Esay*, to whom when a sealed booke was deliuered, with this motion, *Reade this, I pray thee*, hee was faine to make this answere, *I cannot, for it is sealed*.[43]

The translation of the olde Testament out of the Hebrew into Greeke.

While God would be knowen onely in *Iacob*, and haue his Name great in *Israel*, and in none other place, while the dew lay on *Gideons* fleece onely, and all the earth besides was drie;[44] then for one and the same people, which spake all of them the language of *Canaan*, that is, *Hebrewe*, one and the same originall in *Hebrew* was sufficient. But when the fulnesse of time drew neere, that the Sunne of righteousnesse, the Sonne of God should come into the world, whom God ordeined to be a reconciliation through faith in his blood, not of the *Iew* onely, but also of the *Greeke*, yea, of all them that were scattered abroad; then loe, it pleased the Lord to stirre vp the spirit of a *Greeke* Prince (*Greeke* for descent and language) euen of *Ptolome Philadelph* King of *Egypt*, to procure the translating of the Booke of God out of *Hebrew* into *Greeke*. This is the translation of the *Seuentie* Interpreters, commonly so called, which prepared the way for our Sauiour among the Gentiles by written preaching, as Saint *Iohn* Baptist did among the *Iewes* by vocall. For the *Grecians* being desirous of learning, were not wont to suffer bookes of worth to lye moulding in Kings Libraries, but had many of their seruants, ready scribes, to copie them out, and so they were dispersed and made common. Againe, the *Greeke* tongue was wellknowen and made familiar to most inhabitants in *Asia*, by reason of the conquest that there the *Grecians* had made, as also by the Colonies, which thither they had sent. For the same causes also it was well vnderstood in many places of *Europe*, yea, and of *Affrike* too. Therefore the word of God being set foorth in *Greeke*, becommeth hereby like a candle set vpon a candlesticke, which giueth light to all that are in the house, or like a proclamation sounded foorth in the market place, which most men presently take knowledge of; and therefore that language was fittest to containe the Scriptures, both for the first Preachers of the Gospel to appeale vnto for witnesse, and for the learners also of those times to make search and triall by. It is certaine, that that Translation was not so sound and so perfect, but that it needed in many places correction; and who had bene so sufficient for this worke as the Apostles or Apostolike men? Yet it seemed good to the holy Ghost and to them, to take that which they found, (the same being for the greatest part true and sufficient) rather then by making a new, in that new world and greene age of the Church, to expose themselues to many exceptions and cauillations, as though they made a Translation to serue their owne turne, and therfore bearing witnesse to them-selues, their witnesse not to be regarded. This may be supposed to bee some cause, why the Translation of the *Seuentie* was allowed to passe for currant. Not-withstanding, though it was commended generally, yet it did not fully content the learned, no not of the *Iewes*.[45] For not long after *Christ*, *Aquila* fell in hand with a new Translation, and after him *Theodotion*, and after him *Symmachus*: yea, there was a fift and a sixt edition, the Authours wherof were not knowen. These with the *Seuentie* made vp the *Hexapla*, and were worthily and to great purpose compiled together by *Origen*. Howbeit the Edition of the *Seuentie* went away with the credit, and therefore not onely was placed in the midst by *Origen* (for the worth and excellencie thereof aboue the rest, as *Epiphanius* gathereth) but also was vsed by the *Greeke* fathers for the ground and foundation of their Commentaries.[46] Yea, *Epiphanius* aboue named doeth attribute so much vnto it, that he holdeth the Authours therof not onely for Interpreters, but also for Prophets in some respect: and *Iustinian* the Emperour enioyning the *Iewes* his subiects to vse specially the Translation of the *Seuentie*, rendreth this reason therof, because they were as it were enlightened with propheticall grace.[47] Yet for all that, as the *Egyptians* are said of the Prophet to bee men and not God, and their horses flesh and not spirit:[48] so it is euident, (and Saint *Hierome* affirmeth as much)[49] that the *Seuentie* were Interpreters, they were not Prophets; they did many things well, as learned men; but yet as men they stumbled and fell, one while through ouersight, another while through ignorance, yea, sometimes they may be noted to adde to the Originall, and sometimes to take from it; which made the Apostles to leaue them many times, when they left the *Hebrew*, and to deliuer the sence thereof according to the trueth of the word, as the spirit gaue them vtterance. This may suffice touching the Greeke Translations of the old Testament.

There were also within a few hundreth yeeres after CHRIST, translations many into the Latine tongue: for this tongue also was very fit to conuey the Law and the Gospel by, because in those times very many Countreys

Translation out of Hebrew and Greeke into Latine.

of the West, yea of the South, East and North, spake or vnderstood Latine, being made Prouinces to the *Romanes*.

But now the Latine Translations were too many to be all good, for they were infinite (*Latini Interpretes nullo modo numerari possunt*, saith *S. Augustine*.[50]) Againe they were not out of the *Hebrew* fountaine (wee speake of the *Latine* Translations of the Old Testament) but out of the *Greeke* streame, there-fore the *Greeke* being not altogether cleare, the *Latine* deriued from it must needs be muddie. This moued *S. Hierome* a most learned father, and the best linguist without controuersie, of his age, or of any that went before him, to vndertake the translating of the Old Testament, out of the very fountaines themselues; which hee performed with that euidence of great learning, iudgement, industrie and faithfulnes, that he hath for euer bound the Church vnto him, in a debt of spe-ciall remembrance and thankefulnesse.

Now though the Church were thus furnished with *Greeke* and *Latine* Translations, euen before the faith of CHRIST was generally

The translating of the
Scripture into the
vulgar tongues.

embraced in the Empire: (for the learned know that euen
in *S. Hieroms* time, the Consul of *Rome* and his wife were
both Ethnicks, and about the same time the greatest part of
the Senate also[51]) yet for all that the godly-learned were not content to haue the
Scriptures in the Language which themselues vnderstood, *Greeke* and *Latine*, (as
the good Lepers were not content to fare well themselues, but acquainted their
neighbours with the store that God had sent, that they also might prouide for
themselues[52]) but also for the behoofe and edifying of the vnlearned which
hungred and thirsted after Righteousnesse, and had soules to be saued aswell as
they, they prouided Translations into the vulgar for their Countreymen, insomuch
that most nations vnder heauen did shortly after their conuersion, heare CHRIST
speaking vnto them in their mother tongue, not by the voyce of their Minister
onely, but also by the written word translated. If any doubt hereof, he may be
satisfied by examples enough, if enough wil serue the turne. First *S. Hierome* saith,
Multarum gentiũ linguis Scriptura antè translata, docet falsa esse quæ addita sunt, &c.[53] *i*
*The Scripture being translated before in the languages of many Nations, doth shew that
those things that were added* (by *Lucian* or *Hesychius*) *are false.* So *S. Hierome* in that
place. The same *Hierome* elsewhere affirmeth that he, the time was, had set forth
the translation of the *Seuenty*, *suæ linguæ hominibus.*[54] *i.* for his countreymen of
Dalmatia. Which words not only *Erasmus* doth vnderstand to purport, that *S.*
Hierome translated the Scripture into the *Dalmatian* tongue, but also *Sixtus Senen-*
sis,[55] and *Alphonsus à Castro*[56] (that we speake of no more) men not to be excepted
against by them of *Rome*, doe ingenuously confesse as much. So, *S. Chrysostome*[57]
that liued in *S. Hieromes* time, giueth euidence with him: *The doctrine of* S. *Iohn*
(saith he) *did not in such sort* (as the Philosophers did) *vanish away: but the Syrians,*
Egyptians, Indians, Persians, Ethiopians, and infinite other nations being barbarous people,
translated it into their (mother) *tongue, and haue learned to be* (true) *Philosophers*, he
meaneth Christians. To this may be added *Theodorit*,[58] as next vnto him, both for
antiquitie, and for learning. His wordes be these, *Euery Countrey that is vnder the*
Sunne, is full of these wordes (of the Apostles and Prophets) *and the Hebrew tongue*
(he meaneth the Scriptures in the *Hebrew* tongue) *is turned not onely into the Lan-*
guage of the Grecians, but also of the Romanes, and Egyptians, and Persians, and Indians,
and Armenians, and Scythians, and Sauromatians, and briefly into all the Languages that
any Nation vseth. So he. In like maner, *Vlpilas* is reported by *Paulus Diaconus*[59] and
Isidor[60] (and before them by *Sozomen*[61]) to haue translated the Scriptures into the
Gothicke tongue: *Iohn* Biship of *Siuil* by *Vasseus*,[62] to haue turned them into *Ara-*
bicke, about the yeere of our Lord 717: *Beda* by *Cistertiensis*, to haue turned a great
part of them into *Saxon*: *Efnard* by *Trithemius*, to haue abridged the French Psalter,
as *Beda* had done the *Hebrew*, about the yeere 800: King *Alured* by the said *Cist-*
tertiensis,[63] to haue turned the Psalter into *Saxon*: *Methodius* by *Auentinus*[64] (printed
at *Ingolstad*) to haue turned the Scriptures into ‖ *Sclauonian*: *Valdo*, Bishop of
Frising by *Beatus Rhenanus*, to haue caused about that time, the Gospels to be

translated into *Dutch*-rithme, yet extant in the Library of *Corbinian*: *Valdus*, by diuers to haue turned them himself, or to haue gotten them turned into *French*, about the yeere 1160*: *Charles* the 5. of that name, surnamed *The wise*, to haue caused them to be turned into *French*, about 200. yeeres after *Valdus* his time, of which translation there be many copies yet extant, as witnesseth *Beroaldus*.[65] Much about that time, euen in our King *Richard* the seconds dayes, *Iohn Treuisa* transla-tion them into *English*, and many *English* Bibles in written hand are yet to be seene with diuers, translated as it is very probable, in that age. So the *Syrian* trans-lation of the New Testament is in most learned mens Libraries, of *Widminstadius* his setting forth, and the Psalter in *Arabicke* is with many, of *Augustinus Nebiensis* setting foorth. So *Postel* affirmeth, that in his trauaile he saw the Gospels in the *Ethiopian* tongue; And *Ambrose Thesius* alleageth the Psalter of the *Indians*, which he testifieth to haue bene set forth by *Potken* in *Syrian* characters. So that, to haue the Scriptures in the mother-tongue is not a quaint conceit lately taken vp, either by the Lord *Cromwell* in *England*,[66] or by the Lord *Radeuil* in *Polonie*, or by the Lord *Vngnadius* in the Emperours dominion, but hath bene thought vpon, and put in practise of old, euen from the first times of the conuersion of any Nation; no doubt, because it was esteemed most profitable, to cause faith to grow in mens hearts the sooner, and to make them to be able to say with the words of the Psalme, *As we haue heard, so we haue seene.*[67]

Now the Church of Rome would seeme at the length to beare a motherly affection towards her children, and to allow them the Scriptures in their mother tongue: but indeed it is a gift, not deseruing to be called a gift, an vnprofitable gift:[68] they must first get a Licence in writing before they may vse them, and to get that, they must approue themselues to their Confessor, that is, to be such as are, if not frozen in the dregs, yet sowred with the leauen of their superstition. Howbeit, it seemed too much to *Clement the* 8. that there should be any Licence granted to haue them in the vulgar tongue, and therefore he ouerruleth and frustrateth the grant of *Pius* the fourth.[69]

The vnwillingnes of our chiefe Aduersaries, that the Scriptnres should be diuulged in the mother tougue, &e.

So much are they afraid of the light of the Scripture, (*Lucifugæ Scripturarum*, as *Tertullian* speaketh[70]) that they will not trust the people with it, no not as it is set foorth by their owne sworne men, no not with the Licence of their owne Bishops and Inquisitors. Yea, so vnwilling they are to communicate the Scriptures to the peoples vnderstanding in any sort, that they are not ashamed to confesse, that wee forced them to translate it into English against their wills. This seemeth to argue a bad cause, or a bad conscience, or both. Sure we are, that it is not he that hath good gold, that is afraid to bring it to the touch-stone, but he that hath the counterfeit; neither is it the true man that shunneth the light, but the male-factour, lest his deedes should be reproued: neither is it the plaine dealing Mer-chant that is vnwilling to haue the waights, or the meteyard brought in place, but he that vseth deceit. But we will let them alone for this fault, and returne to translation.

Many mens mouths haue bene open a good while and yet are not stopped

The speaches and
reasons, both of our
brethren, and of our
Aduersaries against this
worke.
with speeches about the Translation so long in hand, or
rather perusals of Translations made before: and aske what
may be the reason, what the necessitie of the employment:
Hath the Church bene deceiued, say they, all this while?
Hath her sweet bread bene mingled with leauen, her
siluer with drosse, her wine with water, her milke with lime? (*Lacte gypsum malè
miscetur*, saith *S. Ireney*,[71]) We hoped that we had bene in the right way, that we
had had the Oracles of God deliuered vnto vs, and that though all the world had
cause to be offended and to complaine, yet that we had none. Hath the nurse
holden out the breast, and nothing but winde in it? Hath the bread bene deliuered by the fathers of the Church, and the same proned to be *lapidosus*, as *Seneca*
speaketh? What is it to handle the word of God deceitfully, if this be not? Thus
certaine brethren. Also the aduersaries of *Iudah* and *Hierusalem*, like *Sanballat* in
Nehemiah, mocke as we heare, both at the worke and workemen, saying; *What
doe these weake Iewes, &c. will they make the stones whole againe out of the heapes of
dust which are burnt? although they build, yet if a foxe goe vp, he shall euen breake downe
their stony wall.*[72] Was their Translation good before? Why doe they now mend it?
Was it not good? Why then was it obtruded to the people? Yea, why did the
Catholicks (meaning Popish *Romanists*) alwayes goe in ieopardie, for refusing to
goe to heare it? Nay, if it must be translated into English, Catholicks are fittest
to doe it. They haue learning, and they know when a thing is well, they can
manum de tabulâ. Wee will answere them both briefly: and the former, being
brethren, thus, with *S. Hierome, Damnamus veteres? Minimè, sed post priorum studia
in domo Domini quod possumus laboramus.*[73] That is, *Doe we condemne the ancient? In
no case: but after the endeuours of them that were before vs, wee take the best paines we
can in the house of God.* As if hee said, Being prouoked by the example of the
learned that liued before my time, I haue thought it my duetie, to assay whether
my talent in the knowledge of the tongues, may be profitable in any measure to
Gods Church, lest I should seeme to haue laboured in them in vaine, and lest I
should be thought to glory in men, (although ancient,) aboue that which was in
them, Thus. *S. Hierome* may be thought to speake.

And to the same effect say wee, that we are so farre off from condemning any
of their labours that traueiled before vs in this kinde, either
in this land or beyond sea, either in King *Henries* time, or
King *Edwards* (if there were any translation, or correction
of a translation in his time) or Queene *Elizabeths* of euer-renowned memorie,
that we acknowledge them to haue beene raised vp of God, for the building
and furnishing of his Church, and that they deserue to be had of vs and of
posteritie in euerlasting remembrance. The Iudgement of *Aristotle* is worthy and
well knowen:[74] *If Timotheus had not bene, we had not had much sweet musicke; but if
Phrynis (Timotheus his master) had not beene, wee had not had Timotheus.* Therefore
blessed be they, and most honoured be their name, that breake the yce, and giueth
onset vpon that which helpeth forward to the sauing of soules. Now what can
bee more auaileable thereto, then to deliuer Gods booke vnto Gods people in a

tongue which they vnderstand? Since of an hidden treasure, and of a fountaine that is sealed, there is no profit, as *Ptolomee Philadelph* wrote to the Rabbins or masters of the Iewes, as witnesseth *Epiphanius:*[75] and as *S. Augustine* saith; *A man had rather be with his dog then with a stranger*[76] (whose tongue is strange vnto him.) Yet for all that, as nothing is begun and perfited at the same time, and the later thoughts are thought to be the wiser: so, if we building vpon their foundation that went before vs, and being holpen by their labours, doe endeuour to make that better which they left so good; no man, we are sure, hath cause to mislike vs; they, we perswade our selues, if they were aliue, would thanke vs. The vintage of *Abiezer*, that strake the stroake: yet the gleaning of grapes of *Ephraim* was not to be despised. See *Iudges* 8. *verse* 2.[77] *Ioash* the king of *Israel* did not satisfie himselfe, till he had smitten the ground three times;[78] and yet hee offended the Prophet, for giuing ouer then. *Aquila*, of whom wee spake before, translated the Bible as carefully, and as skilfully as he could; and yet he thought good to goe ouer it againe, and then it got the credit with the Iewes, to be called καιὰ ἀκρίβειαν, that is, accuratly done, as Saint *Hierome* witnesseth.[79] How many bookes of profane learning haue bene gone ouer againe and againe, by the same translators, by others? Of one and the same booke of *Aristotles* Ethikes, there are extant not so few as sixe or seuen seuerall translations. Now if this cost may bee bestowed vpon the goord, which affordeth vs a little shade, and which to day flourisheth, but to morrow is cut downe; what may we bestow, nay what ought we not to bestow vpon the Vine, the fruite whereof maketh glad the conscience of man, and the stemme whereof abideth for euer? And this is the word of God, which we translate. *What is the chaffe to the wheat, saith the Lord?*[80] *Tanti vitreum, quanti verum margaritum*[81] (saith *Tertullian*,) if a toy of glasse be of that rekoning with vs, how ought wee to value the true pearle? Therefore let no mans eye be euill, because his Maiesties is good; neither let any be grieued, that we haue a Prince that seeketh the increase of the spirituall wealth of Israel (let *Sanballats* and *Tobiahs* doe so, which therefore doe beare their iust reproofe (but let vs rather blesse God from the ground of our heart, for working this religious care in him, to haue the translations of the Bible maturely considered of and examined. For by this meanes it commeth to passe, that whatsoeuer is sound alreadie (and all is sound for substance, in one or other of our editions, and the worst of ours farre better then their autentike vulgar) the same will shine as gold more brightly, being rubbed and polished; also, if any thing be halting, or superfluous, or not so agree-able to the originall, the same may bee corrected, and the trueth set in place. And what can the King command to bee done, that will bring him more true honour then this? and wherein could they that haue beene set a worke, approue their duetie to the King, yea their obedience to God, and loue to his Saints more, then by yeelding their seruice, and all that is within them, for the furnishing of the worke? But besides all this, they were the principall motiues of it, and there-fore ought least to quarrell it: for the very Historicall trueth is, that vpon the importunate petitions of the Puritanes, at his Maiesties comming to this Crowne, the Conference at Hampton Court hauing bene appointed for hearing their complaints: when by force of reason they were put from all other grounds, they had recourse at the last, to this shift, that they could not with good conscience subscribe to the Communion booke, since it maintained the Bible as it was there translated, which was as they said, a most corrupted translation. And although this was iudged to be but a very poore and emptie shift; yet euen hereupon did his Maiestie beginne to bethinke himselfe of the good that might ensue by a new translation, and presently after gaue order for this Translation which is now presented vnto thee. Thus much to satisfie our scrupulous Brethren.

Now to the later we answere; that wee doe not deny, nay wee affirme and auow, that the very meanest translation of the Bible in

An answere to the imputations of our aduersaries.

English, set foorth by men of our profession (for wee haue seene none of theirs of the whole Bible as yet) containeth the word of God, nay, is the word of God. As the Kings Speech which hee vttered in Parliament, being translated into *French, Dutch, Italian* and *Latine,* is still the Kings Speech, though it be not interpreted by euery Translator with the like grace, nor peraduenture so fitly for phrase, nor so expresly for sence, euery where. For it is confessed, that things are to take their denomination of the greater part; and a naturall man could say, *Verùm vbimulta nitent in carmine, non ego paucis offendor maculis, &c.*[82] A man may be counted a vertuous man, though hee haue made many slips in his life, (els, there were none vertuous, for *in many things we offend all*[83]) also a comely man and louely, though hee haue some warts vpon his hand, yea, not onely freakles vpon his face, but also skarres. No cause therefore why the word translated should bee denied to be the word, or forbidden to be currant, notwithstanding that some imperfections and blemishes may be noted in the setting foorth of it. For what euer was perfect vnder the Sunne, where Apostles or Apostolike men, that is, men indued with an extraordinary measure of Gods spirit, and priuiledged with the priuiledge of infallibilitie, had not their hand? The Romanistes therefore in refusing to heare, and daring to burne the Word translated, did no lesse then despite the spirit of grace, from whom originally it proceeded, and whose sense and meaning, as well as mans weakenesse would enable, it did expresse. Iudge by an example or two. *Plutarch* writeth,[84] that after that *Rome* had beene burnt by the *Galles,* they fell soone to builde it againe: but doing it in haste, they did not cast the streets, nor proportion the houses in such comely fashion, as had bene most sightly and conuenient; was *Catiline* therefore an honest man, or a good Patriot, that sought to bring it to a combustion? or *Nero* a good Prince, that did indeed set it on fire? So, by the story of *Ezrah,* and the prophesie of *Haggai* it may be gathered, that the Temple built by *Zerubbabel* after the returne from *Babylon,* was by no meanes to bee compared to the former built by *Solomon* (for they that remembred the former, wept when they considered the later)[85] notwithstanding, might this later either haue bene abhorred and forsaken by the *Iewes,* or prophaned by the *Greekes?* The like wee are to thinke of Translations. The translation of the *Seuentie* dissenteth from the Originall in many places, neither doeth it come neere it, for perspicuitie, grauitie, maiestie; yet which of the Apostles did condemne it?

Condemne it? Nay, they vsed it, (as it is apparent, and as Saint *Hierome* and most learned men doe confesse) which they would not haue done, nor by their example of vsing it, so grace and commend it to the Church, if it had bene vnworthy the appellation and name of the word of God. And whereas they vrge for their second defence of their vilifying and abusing of the *English* Bibles, or some pieces therof, which they meete with, for that heretikes (forsooth) were the Authours of the translations, (heretikes they call vs by the same right that they call themselues Catholikes, both being wrong) wee marueile what diuinitie taught them so. Wee are sure *Tertullian* was of another minde: *Ex personis probamus fidem, an ex fide personas?*[86] Doe we trie mens faith by their persons? we should trie their persons by their faith. Also S. *Augustine* was of an other minde: for he lighting vpon certaine rules made by *Tychonius* a *Donatist*, for the better vnderstanding of the word, was not ashamed to make vse of them, yea, to insert them into his owne booke, with giuing commendation to them so farre foorth as they were worthy to be commended, as is to be seene in S. *Augustines* third booke *De doctrinâ Christianâ.*[87] To be short, *Origen*, and the whole Church of God for certain hundred yeeres, were of an other minde: for they were so farre from treading vnder foote, (much more from burning) the Translation of *Aquila* a Proselite, that is, one that had turned *Iew*; of *Symmachus*, and *Theodotion*, both *Ebionites*, that is, most vile heretikes, that they ioyned them together with the *Hebrew* Originall, and the Translation of the *Seuentie* (as hath bene before signified out of *Epiphanius*) and set them forth openly to be considered of and perused by all. But we weary the vnlearned, who need not know so much, and trouble the learned, who know it already.

Yet before we end, we must answere a third cauill and obiection of theirs against vs, for altering and amending our Translations so oft; wherein truely they deale hardly, and strangely with vs. For to whom euer was it imputed for a fault (by such as were wise) to goe ouer that which hee had done, and to amend it where he saw cause? Saint *Augustine*[88] was not afraide to exhort S. *Hierome* to a *Palinodia* or recantation; the same S. *Augustine*[89] was not ashamed to retractate, we might say reuoke, many things that had passed him, and doth euen glory that he seeth his infirmities.[90] If we will be sonnes of the Trueth, we must consider what it speaketh, and trample vpon our owne credit, yea, and vpon other mens too, if either be any way an hinderance to it. This to the cause: then to the persons we say, that of all men they ought to bee most silent in this case. For what varieties haue they, and what alterations haue they made, not onely of their Seruice bookes, Portesses and Breuiaries, but also of their *Latine* Translation? The Seruice booke supposed to be made by S. *Ambrose* (*Officium Ambrosianum*) was a great while in speciall vse and request: but Pope *Hadrian* calling a Councill[91] with the ayde of *Charles* the Emperour, abolished it, yea, burnt it, and commanded the Seruicebooke of Saint *Gregorie* vniuersally to be vsed. Well, *Officium Gregorianum* gets by this meanes to be in credit, but doeth it continue without change or altering? No, the very *Romane* Seruice was of two fashions, the New fashion, and the Old, (the one vsed in one Church, the other in another) as is to bee seene in *Pamelius* a Romanist, his Preface, before *Micrologus*. The same *Pamelius* reporteth out of *Radulphus de Riuo*, that about the yeere of our Lord, 1277. Pope *Nicolas* the third remoued out of the Churches of *Rome*, the more ancient bookes (of Seruice) and brought into vse the Missals of the Friers Minorites, and commaunded them to bee obserued there; insomuch that about an hundred yeeres after, when the aboue named *Radulphus* happened to be at *Rome*, he found all the bookes to be new, (of the new stampe.) Neither was there this chopping and changing in the more ancient times onely, but also of late: *Pius Quintus* himselfe confesseth, that euery Bishopricke almost had a peculiar kind of seruice, most vnlike to that which others had: which moued him to abolish all other Breuiaries, though neuer so ancient, and priuiledged and published by Bishops in their Dioceses, and to establish and ratifie that onely which was of his owne setting foorth, in the yeere 1568. Now, when the father of their Church, who gladly would heale the soare of the daughter of his people softly and sleightly, and make the best of it, findeth so great fault with them for their oddes and iarring; we hope the children haue no great cause to vaunt of their vniformitie. But the difference that appeareth betweene our Translations, and our often correcting of them, is the thing that wee are specially charged with; let vs see therfore whether they themselues bee without fault this way, (if it be to be counted a fault, to correct) and whether they bee fit men to throw stones at vs: *O tandem maior parcas insane minori:*[92] they that are lesse sound themselues, ought not to obiect infirmities to others. If we should tell them that *Valla, Stapulensis, Erasmus*, and *Viues* found fault with their vulgar Translation, and consequently wished the same to be mended, or a new one to be made, they would answere peraduenture, that we produced their enemies for witnesses against them; albeit, they were in no other sort enemies, then as *S. Paul* was to the *Galatians*,[93] for telling them the trueth: and it were to be wished, that they had dared to tell it them plainlier and oftner. But what will they say to this, that Pope *Leo* the Tenth allowed *Erasmus* Translation of the New Testament, so much different from the vulgar, by his Apostolike Letter & Bull;[94] that the same *Leo* exhorted *Pagnin* to translate the whole Bible, and bare whatsoeuer charges was necessary for the worke? Surely, as the Apostle reasoneth to the *Hebrewes*, that *if the former Law and Testament had bene sufficient, there had beene no need of the latter.* [95] so we may say, that if the olde vulgar had bene at all points allowable, to small purpose had labour and charges bene vndergone, about framing of a new. If they say, it was one Popes priuate opinion, and that he consulted onely himselfe; then wee are able to goe further with them, and to auerre, that more of their chiefe men of all sorts, euen their owne *Trent*-champions *Paiua* & *Vega*, and their owne Inquisitors, *Hieronymus ab Oleastro*, and their own Bishop *Isidorus Clarius*, and their owne Cardinall *Thomas à Vio Caietan*, doe either make new Translations themselues,[96] or follow new ones of other mens making, or note the vulgar Interpretor for halting; none of them feare to dissent from him, nor yet to except against him. And call they this an vniforme tenour of text and iudgement about the text, so many of their Worthies disclaiming the now receiued conceit? Nay, we wil yet come neerer the quicke: doth not their *Paris*-edition differ from the *Louaine*, and *Hentenius* his from them both, and yet all of them allowed by authoritie? Nay, doth not *Sixtus Quintus* confesse, that certaine Catholikes (he meaneth certaine of his owne side) were in such an humor of translating the Scriptures into *Latine*, that Satan taking occasion by them, though they thought of no such matter, did striue what he could, out of so vncertaine and manifold a varietie of Translations, so to mingle all things, that nothing might seeme to be left certaine and firme in them, &c? Nay further, did not the same *Sixtus* ordaine by an inuiolable decree, and that with the counsell and consent of his Cardinals, that the *Latine* edition of the olde and new Testament, which the Councill of *Trent* would haue to be authenticke, is the same without controuersie which he then set forth, being diligently corrected and printed in the Printing-house of *Vatican*? Thus *Sixtus* in his Preface before his Bible. And yet *Clement* the eight his immediate successour, publisheth another edition of the Bible, containing in it infinite differences from that of *Sixtus*, (and many of them waightie and materiall) and yet this must be authentike by all meanes. What is to haue the faith of our glorious Lord IESVS CHRIST with Yea and Nay, if this be not? Againe, what is sweet harmonie and consent, if this be? Therfore, as *Demaratus* of *Corinth* aduised a great King, before he talked of the dissensions among the *Grecians*, to compose his domesticke broiles (for at that time his Queene and his sonne and beire were at deadly fuide with him) so all the while that our aduersaries doe make so many and so various editions themselues, and doe iarre so much about the worth and authoritie of them, they can with no show of equitie challenge vs for changing and correcting.

But it is high time to leaue them, and to shew in briefe what wee proposed to our selues, and what course we held in this our perusall and suruay of the

Bible. Truly (good Christian Reader) wee neuer thought

The purpose of the Translators, with their number, furniture, care, &c.

from the beginning, that we should neede to make a new Translation, nor yet to make of a bad one a good one, (for then the imputation of *Sixtus* had bene true in some sort, that our people had bene fed with gall of Dragons in stead of wine, with whey in stead of milke:) but to make a good one better, or out of many good ones, one principall good one, not iustly to be excepted against; that hath bene our indeauour, that our marke. To that purpose there were many chosen, that were greater in other mens eyes then in their owne, and that sought the truth rather then their own praise. Againe, they came or were thought to come to the worke, not *exercendi causá* (as one saith) but *exercitati*, that is, learned, not to learne: For the chiefe ouerseer and ἐργοδιώκτης vnder his Maiestie, to whom not onely we, but also our whole Church was much bound, knew by his wisedom, which thing also *Nazianzen*[97] taught so long agoe, that it is a preposterous order to teach first and to learne after, yea that τὸ ἐν πιθῳ κεραμίαν μανθάνειν to learne and practise together, is neither commendable for the workeman, nor safe for the worke. Therefore such were thought vpon, as could say modestly with Saint *Hierome*, *Et Hebrœum Sermonem ex parte didicimus, & in Latino penè ab ipsis incunabulis &c. detriti sumus. Both we haue learned the Hebrew tongue in part, and in the Latine wee haue beene exercised almost from our verie cradle.* S. Hierome maketh no mention of the *Greeke* tongue, wherein yet hee did excell, because hee translated not the old Testament out of *Greeke*, but out of *Hebrewe*. And in what sort did these assemble? In the trust of their owne knowledge, or of their sharpenesse of wit, or deepenesse of iudgement, as it were in an arme of flesh? At no hand. They trusted in him that hath the key of *Dauid*, opening and no man shutting; they prayed to the Lord the Father of our Lord, to the effect that S. *Augustine* did; *O let thy Scriptures be my pure delight, let me not be deceiued in them, neither let me deceiue by them.*[98] In this confidence, and with this deuotion did they assemble together; not too many, lest one should trouble another; and yet many, lest many things haply might escape them. If you aske what they had before them, truely it was the *Hebrew* text of the Olde Testament, the *Greeke* of the New. These are the two golden pipes, or rather conduits, where through the oliue branches emptie themselues into the golde. Saint *Augustine* calleth them precedent, or originall tongues;[99] Saint *Hierome*, fountaines.[100] The same Saint *Hierome* affirmeth,[101] and *Gratian* hath not spared to put it into his Decree. That, *as the credit of the olde Bookes* (he meaneth of the Old Testament) *is to be tryed by the Hebrewe Volumes, so of the New by the Greeke tongue*, he meaneth by the originall *Greeke*. If trueth be to be tried by these tongues, then whence should a Translation be made, but out of them? These tongues therefore, the Scriptures wee say in those tongues, wee set before vs to translate, being the tongues wherein God was pleased to speake to his Church by his Prophets and Apostles. Neither did we run ouer the worke with that posting haste that the *Septuagint* did, if that be true which is reported of them, that they finished it in 72 dayes;[102] neither were we barred or hindered from going ouer it againe, hauing once done it, like S. *Hierome*,[103] if that be true which himselfe reporteth, that he could no sooner write any thing, but presently it was caught from him, and published, and he could not haue leaue to mend it: neither, to be short, were we the first that fell in hand with translating the Scripture into English, and consequently destitute of former helpes, as it is written of *Origen*, that hee was the first in a maner, that put his hand to write Commentaries vpon the Scriptures, and therefore no marueile, if he ouershot himselfe many times. None of these things: the worke hath not bene hudled vp in 72. dayes, but hath cost the workemen, as light as it seemeth, the paines of twise seuen times seuentie two dayes and more: matters of such weight and consequence are to bee speeded with maturitie: for in a businesse of moment a man feareth not the blame of conuenient slacknesse.[104] Neither did wee thinke much to consult the Translators or Commentators, *Chaldee, Hebrewe, Syrian, Greeke,* or *Latine*, no nor the *Spanish, French, Italian,* or *Dutch*; neither did we disdaine to reuise that which we had done, and to bring backe to the anuill that which we had hammered: but hauing and vsing as great helpes as were needfull, and fearing no reproch for slownesse, nor coueting praise for expedition, wee haue at the length, through the good hand of the Lord vpon us, brought the worke to that passe that you see.

Some peraduenture would haue no varietie of sences to be set in the margine, lest the authoritie of the Scriptures for deciding of controuersies by that shew of vncertaintie, should somewhat be shaken. But we hold their

Reasons mouing vs to set diuersitie of sences in the margin, where there is great probability for each.

iudgmēt not to be so sound in this point. For though, *what-soeuer things are necessary are manifest*, as S. *Chrysostome* saith,[105] and as S. *Augustine*,[106] *In those things that are plainely set downe in the Scriptures, all such matters are found that concerne Faith, hope, and Charitie.* Yet for all that it cannot be dissembled, that partly to exercise and whet our wits, partly to weane the curious from loathing of them for their euery-where-plainenesse, partly also to stirre vp our deuotion to craue the assistance of Gods spirit by prayer, and lastly, that we might be forward to seeke ayd of our brethren by conference, and neuer scorne those that be not in all respects so complete as they should bee, being to seeke in many things our selues, it hath pleased God in his diuine prouidence, heere and there to scatter wordes and sentences of that difficultie and doubtfulnesse, not in doc-trinall points that concerne saluation, (for in such it hath beene vouched that the Scriptures are plaine) but in matters of lesse moment, that fearefulnesse would better beseeme vs then confidence, and if we will resolue, to resolue vpon mod-estie with S. *Augustine*, (though not in this same case altogether, yet vpon the same ground) *Melius est dubitare de occultis, quam litigare de incertis*,[107] it is better to make doubt of those things which are secret, then to striue about those things that are vncertaine. There be many words in the Scriptures, which be neuer found there but once, (hauing neither brother nor neighbour, as the *Hebrewes* speake) so that we cannot be holpen by conference of places. Againe, there be many rare names of certaine birds, beastes and precious stones, &c. concerning which the *Hebrewes* themselues are so diuided among themselues for iudgement, that they may seeme to haue defined this or that, rather because they would say some-thing, thē because they were sure of that which they said, as S. *Hierome* some-where saith of the *Septuagint*. Now in such a case, doth not a margine do well to admonish the Reader to seeke further, and not to conclude or dogmatize vpon this or that peremptorily? For as it is a fault of incredulitie, to doubt of those things that are euident: so to determine of such things as the Spirit of God hath left (euen in the iudgment of the iudicious) questionable, can be no lesse then presumption. Therefore as S. *Augustine* saith,[108] that varietie of Translations is prof-itable for the finding out of the sense of the Scriptures: so diuersitie of signifi-cation and sense in the margine, where the text is not so cleare, must needes doe good, yea, is necessary, as we are perswaded. We know that *Sixtus Quintus*[109] expresly forbiddeth, that any varietie of readings of their vulgar edition, should be put in the margine, (which though it be not altogether the same thing to that we haue in hand, yet it looketh that way) but we thinke he hath not all of his owne side his fauourers, for this conceit. They that are wise, had rather haue their iudgements as libertie in differences of readings, then to be captiuated to one, when it may be the other. If they were sure that their hie Priest had all lawes shut vp in his brest, as *Paul* the second bragged,[110] and that he were as free from errour by speciall priuiledge, as the Dictators of *Rome* were made by law inuiolable, it were an other matter; then his word were an Oracle, his opinion a decision. But the eyes of the world are now open God be thanked, and haue bene a great while, they find that he is subiect to the same affections and infirmities that others be, that his skin is penetrable,[111] and therefore so much as he prooueth, not as much as he claimeth, they grant and embrace.

An other thing we thinke good to admonish thee of (gentle Reader) that wee haue not tyed our selues to an vniformitie of phrasing, or to an identitie of words, as some peraduenture would wish that we had done, because they obserue, that some learned men some where, haue beene as exact as they could that way. Truly, that we might not varie from the sense of that which we had translated before, if the word signified the same thing in both places[112] (for there bee some words that bee not of the same sense euery where) we were especially carefull, and made a conscience, according to our duetie. But, that we should expresse the same notion in the same particular word; as for example, if we translate the *Hebrew* or *Greeke* word once by *Purpose*, neuer to call it *Intent*; if one where *Iourneying*, neuer *Traueiling*; if one where *Thinke*, neuer *Suppose*; if one where *Paine*, neuer *Ache*; if one where *Ioy*, neuer *Gladnesse*, &c. Thus to minse the matter, wee thought to sauour more of curiositie then wisedome, and that rather it would breed scorne in the Atheist, then bring profite to the godly Reader. For is the kingdome of God become words or syllables? why should wee be in bondage to them if we may be free, vse one precisely when wee may vse another no lesse fit, as commodiously? A godly Father in the Primitiue time shewed himselfe greatly moued,[113] that one of newfanglenes called κράββατον σκίμπους, though the difference be little or none; and another reporteth,[114] that he was much abused for turning *Cucurbita* (to which reading the people had beene vsed) into *Hedera*. Now if this happen in better times, and vpon so small occasions, wee might iustly feare hard censure, if generally wee should make verball and vnnecessary changings. We might also be charged (by scoffers) with some vnequall dealing towards a great number of good English wordes. For as it is written of a certaine great Philosopher, that he should say, that those logs were happie that were made images to be worshipped; for their fellowes, as good as they, lay for blockes behinde the fire : so if wee should say, as it were, vnto certaine words, Stand vp higher, haue a place in the Bible alwayes, and to others of like qualitie, Get ye hence, be banished for euer, wee might be taxed peraduenture with S. *Iames* his words, namely, *To be partiall in our selues and iudges of euill thoughts*. Adde hereunto, that nicenesse in wordes[115] was always counted the next step to trifling,[116] and so was to bee curious about names too:[117] also that we cannot follow a better patterne for elocution then God himselfe; therefore hee vsing diuers words, in his holy writ, and indifferently for one thing in nature: we, if wee will not be superstitious, may vse the same libertie in our English versions out of *Hebrew & Greeke*, for that copie or store that he hath giuen vs. Lastly, wee haue on the one side auoided the scrupulositie of the Puritanes, who leaue the olde Ecclesiasticall words, and betake them to other, as when they put *washing* for *Baptisme*, and *Congregation* in stead of *Church*: as also on the other side we haue shunned the obscuritie of the Papists, in their *Azimes Tunike, Rational, Holocausts, Prœpuce, Pasche*, and a number of such like, whereof their late Translation is full, and that of purpose to darken the sence, that since they must needs translate the Bible, yet by the language thereof, it may bee kept from being vnderstood. But we desire that the Scripture may speake like it selfe, as in the language of *Canaan*, that it may bee vnderstood euen of the very vulgar.

Many other things we might giue thee warning of (gentle Reader) if wee had not exceeded the measure of a Preface alreadie. It remaineth, that we commend thee to God, and to the Spirit of his grace, which is able to build further then we can aske or thinke. Hee remoueth the scales from our eyes, the vaile from our hearts, opening our wits that wee may vnderstand his word, enlarging our hearts, yea correcting our affections, that we may loue it aboue gold and siluer, yea that we may loue it to the end. Ye are brought vnto fountaines of liuing water which yee digged not; doe not cast earth into them with the Philistines.[118] neither preferre broken pits before them with the wicked Iewes.[119] Others haue laboured, and you may enter into their labours; O receiue not so great things in vaine, O despise not so great saluation! Be not like swine to treade vnder foote so precious things, neither yet like dogs to teare and abuse holy things. Say not to our Sauiour with the *Gergesites*, Depart out of our coasts;[120] neither yet with *Esau* sell your birthright for a messe of potage.[121] If light be come into the world, loue not darkenesse more then light; if foode, if clothing be offered, goe not naked, starue not your selues. Remember the aduise of *Nazianzene*,[122] *It is a grieuous thing* (or dangerous) *to neglect a great faire, and to seeke to make markets afterwards*: also the encouragement of S. *Chrysostome*,[123] *It is altogether impossible, that he that is sober (and watchfull) should at any time be neglected*: Lastly, the admonition and menacing of S. *Augustine*.[124] *They that despise Gods will inuiting them, shal feele Gods will taking vengeance of them*. It is a fearefull thing to fall into the hands of the liuing God; but[125] a blessed thing it is, and will bring vs to euerlasting blessednesse in the end, when God speaketh vnto vs, to hearken; when he setteth his word before vs, to reade it; when hee stretcheth out his hand and calleth, to answere, Here am I; here we are to doe thy will, O God. The Lord worke a care and conscience in vs to know him and serue him, that we may be acknowledged of him at the appearing of our Lord Iesus Christ, to whom with the holy Ghost, be all prayse and thankesgiuing. Amen.

Abbreviations

ABS	American Bible Society
ASV	American Standard Version
AV	Authorised Version
BFBS	British and Foreign Bible Society
BS	Bible Society (British)
CEV	Contemporary English Version
CWM	*Complete Works of St Thomas More*
DMH	Darlow, Moule and Herbert
DNB	*Dictionary of National Biography*
F&M	Josiah Forshall and Frederic Madden, eds, *The Holy Bible, Wycliffite Versions*, 4 vols (Oxford, 1850)
FQ	*The Faerie Queene*
GNB	Good News Bible
JB	Jerusalem Bible
KJV	King James Version
LP	*Letters and Papers . . . Henry VIII*
LXX	Septuagint
NAB	New American Bible
NASV	New American Standard Version
NEB	New English Bible
NIRV	New International Readers' Version
NIV	New International Version
NJB	New Jerusalem Bible
NKJV	New King James Version
NRSV	New Revised Standard Version
NT	New Testament
OT	Old Testament
PS	Parker Society
REB	Revised English Bible
RGNB	Revised Good News Bible
RSV	Revised Standard Version
RTEV	Revised Today's English Version
RV	Revised Version
RSTC	Pollard and Redgrave, rev. Jackson, Ferguson and Pantzer, *Short-Title Catalogue . . .* , 1475–1640.
S&H	Sterndale and Hopkins
SP	*State Papers Domestic . . . Henry VIII*
TBT	*The Bible Translator*
TEV	Today's English Version
TNT	*Tyndale's New Testament* (Yale)
TOT	*Tyndale's Old Testament* (Yale)

Notes

PREFACE

1 Serious historians have written large books about the English Reformation with scarcely a mention of the Bible. A prime example is Duffy, 1992; see also the 'Debate' following David Aers's review of that book (*Literature and History,* 3rd ser., III/2, 1994, 90–105), in which Duffy claimed that it 'is a contribution to the history of the Reformation' (ibid., IV/1, 1995, 86–9). The eleven mentions of the English Bible are dismissive; reading the Bible is mentioned six times, as something peculiar. Erasmus is mentioned only twice, as the writer of a prayer for the Church.

2 The definitive study is Shaheen, 1999.

3 Hill, 1993, *passim.*

4 Duffy, 1997, 293.

5 David Lyle Jeffrey, *Dictionary of Biblical Tradition in English Literature* (Grand Rapids, Michigan, 1992). The million words in these nine hundred entries are sharply uneven in value, and there is no index.

6 *OED*, 'Puritan': 'A. *sb.* 1. *Hist.* A member of that party of English Protestants who regarded the reformation of the church under Elizabeth as incomplete, and called for its further "purification" from what they considered to be unscriptural and corrupt forms and ceremonies retained from the unreformed church: subsequently, often applied to any who separated from the established church on points of ritual, polity, or doctrine, held by them to be at variance with "pure" New Testament principles.' The entry goes on to explain the denominational spread of the term beyond the Church of England, summed up by the words, 'In later times, the term has become historical, without any opprobrious connotation.' Further definitions are all to do with scruples of religion, the rider 'or morals' not appearing until late, supported by a quotation from Charlotte Smith, 'Brought up among the strait-laced [. . .] puritans of the United States', dated 1798. See also Collinson, 1983, 8–10.

7 Collinson, 1983.

8 Lamont, 1996, 1.

9 A. C. Grayling, *The Guardian,* G2 (17 May 2001), 8.

10 Leites, 1986, 12.

11 Ibid., 12–13; further examples, *passim,* and sources, 164.

12 Ibid., 16. Leites is fully aware of 'the ethic of mainstream Puritanisms [which] placed severe constraints upon erotic pleasure' (ibid.); but this was not because Puritans thought that sex in itself was bad, but because the pleasures of a life given to amorousness and eroticism 'are, at their fullest, highly passionate and agitated' (ibid.). Leites sets out to examine how 'the prudishness of the late eighteenth and nineteenth centuries, commonly called Puritanism' developed from 'the non-prudish character of seventeenth-century Puritans' (17).

13 Poole, 2000, 14.

14 Ibid., 12, 76, 151.

15 Elucidating Maria's remark is problematic. See Holden, 1954, 40–43. It is just possible that it suggests sexual licence.

The strength of the persistent stereotype of Puritan New Englanders as sour, repressed and joyless 'is due in no small part to the influence of Nathaniel Hawthorne, whose fictional works have cast a powerful spell over many generations of readers. The Puritans who haunt the pages of his novels and short stories are blinkered, judgmental, repressive, and tormented. Characters such as Arthur Dimmesdale [in *The Scarlet Letter*] embody and sustain the image of Puritans as bedeviled by sexual frustration and "the haunting, haunting fear that somewhere, someone may be happy"'. Thus writes Richard Godbeer in his scholarly, judicious and well-documented study, *Sexual Revolution in Early America* (2002 (p. 54). (His quotation is from H. L. Mencken's very influential 1928 squib, quoted in Randall Stewart, *American Literature and Christian Doctrine* (Baton Rouge, 1958), p. 4.) He stresses the unexpectedly rich significance, including the Puritans' eroticization of the spiritual, in their insistence of sexual pleasure in marriage: 'Puritan teachers lauded marital sex as an expression of love and fellowship between husband and wife. [. . .] God had ordained sex between husband and wife in part for purposes of procreation, but "conjugal union" also embodied the love that should unite a married couple. [. . .] Puritans held that both sexes should experience "delight" during sexual intercourse' (Godbeer, 2002, 54–5, 58, 59).

16 Poole, 2000, 4.

17 Basil Hall, 'Puritanism: The Problem of Definition', *Studies in Church History* (1965), 290. For some general recent discussions on the meanings of the word, see B. R. White, 'The Fellowship of Believers: Bunyan and Puritanism', in *John Bunyan: Conventicle and Parnassus. Ten Centenary Essays*, ed. N. H. Keeble (Oxford, 1988), esp. 1–2, 18–19 and notes; Vincent Newey, 'With the Eyes of my Understanding: Bunyan, Experience, and Acts of Interpretation', in Keeble, ed., 189–96, esp. 190. For large (but still severely select) bibliographies, see Poole, 2000, 189–90, and Lamont, 1996, *passim*.

18 Duffy, 1992, 530.

19 See below, p. 67.

20 *TNT*, 3.

CHAPTER 1

1 I owe the observation to Michael Schmidt.

2 Five additional Psalms, 151–5, were known only in Syriac in the Syrian Bible until the Hebrew original of three of them, 151, 154 and 155, turned up among the Dead Sea Scrolls.

3 The phrase in this context is adapted

from a paragraph by Gershom Scholem, in his *Major Trends in Jewish Mysticism* (New York, 1941/1995), 350.

4 I am grateful to Carsten Thiede for help here and in some other places in this chapter.

5 John Buchan, *Sir Walter Scott* (1932), 20.

6 Quoted by Simon Hoggart in the Saturday Review section of *The Guardian* (16 September 2000), 12.

7 Alter and Kermode, 1987, 66. Damrosch's fine chapter, 66–77, sets Leviticus in its fullest religious context. See also Douglas 1969.

8 *John Buchan Journal*, XVIII (Spring 1998), 2.

9 *Verzeichnis der in Deutschen Sprachbereich Erschiedenen Druchs des XVI. Jahrhunderts* (Stuttgart, 1984), I, 2; *Short Title Catalogue of Books printed in France* [. . .] *1400–1700 in the British Museum* (1924, rev. 1960).

10 Harrison, 2001. This scholarly, detailed and significant book moves the subject beyond earlier, and important, linkings of the rise of science with Puritanism, made in England from the 1930s; and from the more searching research, again in England, from the 1970s.

11 Harrison, 2001, 79.

12 Ibid., 96. Harrison's quotation is from Norton, 1993, I, 132, who is citing William Fulke in 1583 citing Lindanus.

13 Tyndale, 1528, ed. Daniell, 2000, 22–3, 208–9.

14 Harrison, 2001, 97.

15 The definitive study of Shakespeare's grammar for over a century has been E. A. Abbott, *A Shakespearian Grammar* (1870). His opening words state that in Elizabethan English, 'almost any part of speech can be used as any other part of speech', 5.

16 DMH, 26.

17 *The Message: The New Testament in Contemporary Language*, ed. Eugene H. Peterson (Colorado Springs, 1998), 19–20.

18 *TNT*, 27.

CHAPTER 2

I am much indebted to my elder son, Christopher Daniell, for help with material in this chapter.

1 One cannot, of course, handle the manuscript. The British Library now has an interactive computer facility, invented by the BL's Clive Izard, which is always available to the visiting public. Known as 'Turning the Pages', it allows one to do just that, turn the virtual pages of parts of priceless and untouchable manuscripts, including the Lindisfarne Gospels.

2 Deirdre O'Sullivan, 'Space, Silence and Shortages on Lindisfarne', in *Image and Power in the Archaeology of Early Medieval Britain: Essays in Honour of Rosemary Cramp*, ed. Helena Hamerow and Arthur MacGregor (Oxford, 2001), 49.

3 Ibid., 46.

4 Ibid., 47.

5 Ibid., 48.

6 Richard Marsden, ' "Ask What I Am Called": The Anglo-Saxons and their Bibles', in Sharpe and Van Kampen, 1998, 151; *Historia Dunelmensis ecclesiae* ll, chs 11–12, in *Symeonis monachi Opera omnia*, ed. T. Arnold, Rolls Series 75 (1882–5), I, 63–8; and *The Church Historians of England*, III, ii, containing *The Historical Works of Symeon of Durham*, trans. J. Stevenson (1855), 660–63.

7 Morrell, 1965, 160–62.

8 Ibid., *c.* 54–60, 132–3.

9 Fowler, 1986, 91.

10 Sparks, in H. Wheeler Robinson, ed., 1940, 100–27.

11 Loewe, in Lampe, ed., 1969, 107.

12 Though the origins of the papacy are lost in the mists of pious invention, Damasus is reckoned the thirty-sixth pope. See Duffy, 1997, *passim.*

13 Loewe, 1940, 102.

14 See Cunliffe, 2001, 564.

15 Thomas, 1981, 42.

16 Ibid., 43.

17 C. F. Mawer, 'Evidence for Christianity in Roman Britain: The Small Finds', *British Archaeological Reports*, (1995), 243.

18 Ibid., 72.

19 J. M. C. Toynbee, 'Christianity in Roman Britain', *Journal of the British Archaeological Association*, 3rd ser., XVI (1953), 2–3.

20 These are conveniently listed in Toynbee, 1953, 2.

21 As, for example, in *Christianity in Britain 300–700*, ed. M. W. Barley and R. P. C. Hanson (Leicester, 1968).

22 Thomas, 1981, 83. Details are given in Williams, 1912, 183–5, 449–50.

23 Gregory of Tours, *Historia Francorum*, iv.16, quoted in Williams, 1912, 185. See also Thomas, 1981, 82.

24 Williams, 1912, 185.

25 Marsden, 1998, 156; see also Michelle P. Brown, 'A New Fragment of a Ninth-Century English Bible', *Anglo-Saxon England*, XVIII (1989), 33–43.

26 Marsden, 1998, 156, 168.

27 The position is neatly explained in C. Daniell, 1991, rev. 1996, 23.

28 Bettenson, ed., 2/1963, 211–2.

29 C. Daniell, 1991, rev. 1996, 24; Richard N. Bailey, 'The Cultural and Social Setting', in Ford, ed., 1988, I, 107–8.

30 Bettenson, 2/1963, 212.

31 C. Daniell, 1991, rev. 1996, 24.

32 Marsden, 1998, 147.

33 Mackie, 1964, rev. and ed. Lenman and Parker, 2/1985, 26. On St John, see the last paragraph of this chapter, p. 43.

34 David N. Dumville, 'The Importation of Mediterranean Manuscripts in Theodore's England', in *Archbishop Theodore: Commemorative Studies on his Life and Influence*, ed. Michael Lapidge (Cambridge, 1995), 100.

35 Paul Meyvaert, 'Bede and the Church Paintings at Wearmouth-Jarrow', *Anglo-Saxon England*, VIII, (1979), 64–7, 74–7.

36 Benedicta Ward, 'Bede and the Psalter' (Jarrow Lecture, 1991), 3–4.

37 Peter Salway, 'The Cultural and Social Setting', in Ford, ed., 1988, I, 47.

38 Marsden, 1998, 149. The story is told in *Willelmi Malmesbiriensis monachi de gestis pontificum anglorum*, ed. N. E. S. A. Hamilton, Rolls Series 52 (1870), v, 377–8.

39 *Boswell's Life of Johnson*, ed. George Birkbeck Hill (1887); rev. and enlarged L. F. Powell (Oxford, 2/1964), v, 334.

40 Isabel Henderson, 'The Arts of Late Celtic Britain (AD 600–900), in Ford, ed., 1988, I, 215.

41 Marsden, 1998, 151, 165.

42 Ibid., 151–3, 165–6.

43 For a spirited defence of the importance of Anglo-Saxon textual studies, as against claims for the supremacy of Irish or Italian texts, see Christopher Verey, 'A Northumbrian Text Family' in Sharpe and Van Kampen, 1998, 105–22.

44 Marsden, 1998, 152.

45 Ibid., 154.

46 Ibid., 155–6.

47 Thomas, 1981, 81; and see Williams, 1912, 453.

48 Bailey, in Ford, ed., 1988, I, 108.

49 George Hardin Brown, *Bede the Educator* (1996), 6.

50 Fowler, 1986, 85.

51 'Bede's works indicate that Northumbrian schools largely depended upon Irish knowledge and methods. We would expect no less. Not only was Northumbria originally evangelized by the Irish, but the stream of communication between the two nations was friendly and constant. Moreover, the mass of Northumbrian scholars received some or all of their formal training in Ireland.' Charles W. Jones, *Bedae Opera de Temporibus* (Cambridge, Mass., 1943), III.

52 See Sarah Larratt Keefer and David R. Burrows, 'Hebrew and the *Hebraicum* in Late Anglo-Saxon England', *Anglo-Saxon England*, XIX (1990), 80; and E. F. Sutcliffe, 'The Venerable Bede's Knowledge of Hebrew', *Biblica*, XVI (1935), 300. There is evidence of knowledge of Hebrew in twelfth-century England: see Beryl Smalley, 'A Commentary on the Hebraica of Herbert of Bosham', *Recherches de théologie ancienne et medieval*, XVIII, (1947), 29–65; and R. Loewe, 'Herbert of Bosham's Commentary on Jerome's Hebrew Psalter', *Biblica*, (1953), 44–77, 159–92, 275–98.

53 Bertram Colgrave and R. A. B. Minors, eds, *Bede's Ecclesiastical History of the English People* (Oxford, 1981). The anonymous *Compendious Old Treatise, showing how that we ought to have the Scripture in English* (1531) notes Bede as having 'translated a great part of the Bible into English, whose originals bene in many abbeys of England' (quoted by John Foxe, *The Acts and Monuments of John Foxe*, ed., rev. and corrected J. Pratt, 8 vols, 4/1877, IV, 673). There is no surviving evidence for this.

54 Given in Ford, ed., 1988, I, 183–4.

55 From *Medieval English Literature (The Oxford Anthology of English Literature)*, ed. J. B. Trapp (New York, 1973), 20.

56 Dumville, in Lapidge, ed., 1995, 113; and see Marsden, 1998, 150; and McGurk, (Paris, 1961), II.

57 F. Louis Bouyer, 'Erasmus in Relation to the Medieval Biblical Tradition', in Lampe, 1969, 492, referring, strikingly, to the young Desiderius's education just before 1500.

58 M. J. Hunter, 'The Gothic Bible', in Lampe, ed., 1969, 340–41. See also *The Gospels: Gothic, Anglo-Saxon, Wycliffe and Tyndale Versions*, with Preface and Notes by Joseph Bosworth (4/1907), i–ix.

59 See especially Hunter, in Lampe, ed., 1969, 338–62.

60 W. B. Lockwood, 'Vernacular Scriptures in Germany and the Low Countries before 1500', in Lampe, ed., 1969, 417.

61 Loewe, in Lampe, ed., 1969, 102–54, esp. 113–14.

CHAPTER 3

For material in this chapter I am indebted to the help of Dr Victoria Thompson.

1 Tyndale, *Obedience*, 2000, 19. The reference has not been identified. Athelstan (reigned AD 925–39) followed the example of his grandfather Alfred in his enthusiasm for learning and the education of the nation. Tyndale may have learned of him from reading the account of English kings written around 1120 by William, the librarian of Malmesbury Abbey, a dozen miles from Tyndale's birthplace.

2 Asser, *Life of King Alfred*, trans. Simon Keynes and Michael Lapidge (Harmmdsworth, 1983) 75, 99–100, 268.

3 For details of manuscripts mentioned in this chapter, see Morrell, 1965, *passim*. See also Tyndale, *Obedience*, 2000, 207. In note 133 of that edition, I remark that the translations mentioned by Tyndale as being 'caused by' Athelstan are 'not identified'. In an unpublished article, Michael Wood has pointed out that John Bale commented on Athelstan's sponsorship of Anglo-Saxon Gospels. In his *Scriptorum illustrium maioris Brytannia* (Basle, 1557–9), in the section on 'Ethelstanus' (226–7), Bale wrote: '*Nam scripturas divinas, teste Malmesburio, uerti fecit in Anglosaxonicum idioma, ex purissimis Hebraeorum fontibus, per quosdam Hebraeos ad Christianismus (ut credere par est) in suo regno conuersos.*' ('According to William of Malmesbury, this king ordered the

translation of the Gospels from the purest founts of the Hebrews by certain Jews resident in his country who had been converted to Christianity for that purpose.') The supposition that the Gospels were translated from Hebrew may show how widespread was ignorance of the original biblical languages. Although that remark by William of Malmesbury in the twelfth century is not known to have survived, Michael Wood observed that the source of Bale's story could be narrowed down. Thomas Tanner, in his *Bibliotheca Britannico-Hibernica* (1748), 267, supplied a precise date for the translating, 930, and in a footnote suggested that Bale got it from John Leland. Leland, in his *Collectanea*, ed. T. Hearne (1772), III, 157, wrote that he saw at Malmesbury Abbey a copy of a versified version of the Gospels made by William. Leland gave the same reference in his *Commentarii de Scriptoribus Britannicis*, ed. A. Hall (Oxford, 1709), 196. No poetry by William has been identified, but it is likely that such a work had in its introduction a mention of earlier versions of the Gospels. Certainly, on the Continent, Hebrew assistants of Carolingian (AD 751–961) scholars are well attested. An important clue to the truth of William's story might be Michael Wood's recognition that Canterbury was the original location of most of those Anglo-Saxon Gospel manuscripts. Athelstan was known as a collector of Gospel books. It could be a reasonable guess that he gave precious manuscripts to Canterbury scribes as the basis of translation into West Saxon. Tanner's date of 930 would fit the known evidence. Such royal patronage would be recorded. I am grateful to Michael Wood for the use of his material here.

4   F&M, II 758–9.

5   Fowler, 1986, 95.

6   J. Wilcox, *Aelfric's Prefaces* (Durham, 1996), 2.

7   Clemoes, in Clemoes, ed., 1959, 245–6.

8   Clemoes, ed., 1997.

9   *Councils and Synods of Great Britain with Other Documents Relating to the English Church*, I/I: *871–1066*, ed. D. Whitelock, M. Brett and C. N. L. Brooke (Oxford, 1981), 484.

10   Bradley, 1982, 9–10.

CHAPTER 4

1   Neatly put as 'The simplest solution is the best.'

2   William Tyndale's mixed horror and scorn that Oxford, and European, theology, even when he was at Magdalen Hall two hundred years later, was still dominated by these theoretical quarrels, and had nothing whatsoever to do with God speaking to the individual heart through Scripture, makes exhilarating reading. See Tyndale, *Obedience*, 2000, 22–3.

3   Deanesly, 1920, 142, 143, 221. A. C. Paues, ed., *A Fourteenth Century English Biblical Version* (Cambridge, 1904), xvii–xxii.

4   George Sampson, *The Concise Cambridge History of English Literature* (Cambridge, 1941), 28.

5   Tyndale, *Obedience*, 2000, 24; Coverdale: see below, Chapter 13, note 1.

6   Original and translation from Fowler, 1986, 128.

7   Ibid., 131.

8   Ibid., 133.

9   Ibid., 133–40 (a detailed account).

10   Karl D. Buelbring, ed., *The Earliest Complete English Prose Psalter* (1891).

11   Printed in H. R. Bramley, *The Psalter and Certain Canticles with a Translation in English by Richard Rolle* (1884). See also Paues, ed., 1904, xxxi–lvi.

12   Fowler, 1986, 146. The forthcoming book by Ralph Hanna of Keble College, Oxford, on fourteenth-century London literature, will include a chapter on 'English Biblical Texts before Lollardy and their Fate'; thanks to the kindness of Dr Hanna, I have been able to see a draft copy. His examination of MS Pepys 2498 (Magdalene College, Cambridge) reveals a unique harmony of the Gospels, a prose Apocalypse with commentary, 'The Early English Prose Psalter' and a unique Bible-based recension of *Ancrene Riwle*. 'From the large manuscript, an interested reader could assemble a substantial, if incomplete – there would be no Acts or Epistles [. . .] – New Testament with authoritative commentary, together with a commented Psalter.'

13   Amply described in Fowler, 1986, 165–93.

CHAPTER 5

1   The statement by Thomas More, made
in defending the Church from the charge of
keeping the Word of God from the people –
that long before the days of Wyclif the whole
Bible had been translated into the English
tongue, and that he had seen such translations
– is still quoted as evidence to show, among
other things, that Tyndale did nothing remarkable. It has never stood up to examination. He
saw Wyclif versions. *CWM* VI, i, 317.
2   Hudson, 1988, 231, n.19.
3   Mozley, 1937, 348–9.
4   Kenny, 1985, 66.
5   Hargreaves, in Lampe, ed., 1969, 388.
6   Ibid. Some attitudes do not change. In
the course of a major public lecture on
Shakespeare, at which I was present, a distinguished Renaissance scholar, who had close
connections with the Vatican, remarked that
the Church condemned the translations of
Scripture into English as blasphemy. That is an
extraordinary word for giving the work and
words of Jesus and Paul to ordinary people
(and see p. 2 above). The lecture was given in
the year 2000.
7   See Geoffrey Shepherd, 'English
Versions of the Scriptures before Wyclif', in
Lampe, ed., 1969, 384.
8   Hargreaves, 1969, 391.
9   Ibid.
10   Ibid., 388.
11   Mozley's attempt (1937, 53) to find
Tyndale's name in code in the Wittenberg
registers is not convincing.
12   See the note in F&M, I, vii. See also
McVeigh's introduction to his translation and
edition Wyclif, 1992; Bruce, 1961; and Kenny,
1985.
13   Bale, 1548, f. 154ᵛ; and 1557–9,
i.450–56.
14   A Bulgarian scholar, Dr Georgi
Vassilev, is working on some influences on
Wyclif's thought from European theology,
particularly Cathar dualism, and evidences of
Wyclif's knowledge of the Greek New
Testament. He may be reached via the Agency
for Bulgarians Abroad, Sofia 1000, 2a Al.
Dondoukov bd. E-mail abal@bulgaria.com.
15   Kenny, 1985, v–vi.
16   Ibid., 107.

17   Clear accounts of Wyclif's philosophy
are given, with admirable clarity and brevity,
by Kenny, *passim*.
18   Ibid., 57.
19   Ibid.
20   Ibid., 63.
21   Ibid., 64–5.
22   Bruce, 1961, 13.
23   Kenny, 1985, 11, 46–7.
24   Ibid., 80; for Kenny's explanation of
the difference between the Real Presence, in
which Wyclif largely believed, and transubstantiation, which he renounced, 80–90.
25   Hudson, 1988, 241, n.72.
26   *English Wycliffite Sermons*, I and III ed.
Anne Hudson, II ed. Pamela Gradon (Oxford,
1983–90).
27   Hudson, 1985, 13. I am much indebted
to this book.
28   F&M, IV, 174–5.
29   Hudson, 1985, 13.
30   Ibid., 13–29. Also helpful about the
dissemination of Lollard thought through
written material is the work of Ralph Hanna,
chapter 4, n. 12 above.
31   Hudson, 1985, 14.
32   Ibid., 14–15.
33   Hudson, 1988, 7.
34   Pollard, ed., 1911, 80–81.
35   Hudson, 1988, 489.
36   Ibid., 120–73; and esp. 175–80, 231.
37   Ibid., 174–5.
38   Ibid., 1–2.
39   Ibid., 61.
40   For example, Clebsch, 1964. Smeeton,
1984, went against that grain, but did not
make a wholly convincing case.
41   See especially Duffy, 1992, *passim*.
42   Smeeton, 1984, *passim*.
43   Strype, 1721/1821, I.ii.54–5; Mozley,
1937.
44   Hargreaves, 1969, 389: 'The consensus
[. . .] challenged only once, in an ill-advised
essay by the late Cardinal Gasquet, whose
conclusions   have   since   been   proved
untenable.'
45   Ibid., 394.
46   F&M, I, xxxviii.
47   Ibid.
48   Ibid., I, xxiv.
49   Hargreaves, 1969, 396–7.
50   Hudson,   1985   ('John   Purvey: A

Reconsideration of the Evidence', 85–110) reviews what little contemporary, and near-contemporary, evidence there is about Purvey. She shows clearly that his involvement in any part of the Bible versions, including the General Prologue, was a nineteenth-century invention. Purvey was not associated with Bible translation even by Bale and Foxe, both always eager to see 'the prohibition of vernacular scriptures as one of the surest marks of the beast upon the Roman church' (102). Forshall and Madden, 1850, I, xxi, on very shaky ground (that of an admitted guess by an eighteenth-century writer, one Waterland, or Waterton), attributed not only the Later Version and other works to Purvey, but the authorship of the General Prologue (and others). This error was followed to such an extent (Deanesly, 1920, 266–7, even added *The Compendious Olde Treatise* to his list of writings) that one used to read of 'Purvey's Principles' of Bible translation.

51 Hargreaves, 1969, 402.

52 Ibid., 400; and 400–7 for material in these paragraphs.

53 Well summarised by Hudson, 1988, 238–40.

54 Deanesly as summarised in Bruce, 1961, 15.

55 F&M, I, xvii.

56 Hudson, 1988, 19, citing M. L. Samuels in C. Lindberg, 'The Manuscripts and Versions of the Wycliffite Bible: A Preliminary Survey', *Studia neophilologica*, XLII (1969), 329–47, esp. 337.

57 F&M, I, xxxiv, xxxix.

58 *The Wycliffe New Testament (1388): An Edition in Modern Spelling [. . .]*, ed. W. R. Cooper (2002), 254–5, lightly revised.

59 Hudson, 1988, 235.

60 Ibid., 243.

61 Ibid., 246.

62 Ibid., 248–68 (for details of all three).

63 Cooper, 2002, xi.

64 F&M, IV, 433.

65 *The New Testament Translated by William Tyndale* (1526); ed. W. R. Cooper (2000), 427.

66 I have so credited him, wrongly, myself, in *TNT*, x, and in Daniell, 1994, I.

67 *The Riverside Chaucer*, ed. Larry D. Benson (Boston, 3/1987), 119: 'The Summoner's Tale', line 2196.

68 Quoted by Anderson, 1845, I, xl. The remark is attributed to 'a Canon of Leicester', who according to Anderson is also the author of the objections quoted above, that what Christ had given to the doctors and clergy was now spread abroad, 'laid more open to the laity, and *even to women* who can read' (his italics) (I, xli).

69 Foxe, 1877, V, 114–15.

70 Lightly revised from Cooper, 2002, 256–7.

71 Hargreaves, 1969, 414–15.

72 Hudson, 1988, 277.

73 Emden, ed., 1957–9, III, 2103.

74 Hudson, 1988, 395.

75 Ibid., 397.

76 My thanks to Kate Jones, guide at Berkeley Castle, for her help.

77 Hudson, 1988, 395.

78 See Appendix, below.

79 Fowler, 1995, 155.

80 Ibid., 158.

81 Ibid., 159.

82 Caxton, 1480, f.128^r.

83 See W. R. Cooper, 'John Trevisa, the Translator of Wycliffe B: A Consideration of the Evidence', forthcoming.

84 Bale, 1557–9, quoted in Fowler, 1995, 85.

85 Holinshed, 1587, II, 509.

86 Thomas Fuller, *The History of the Worthies of England* (1662), quoted in Fowler, 1995, 216.

87 Daniel Waterton, *Works* (1729), X, 361, quoted in Pollard, 1991, 1–2.

88 *Fifteenth Century Prose and Verse*, intro. A. W. Pollard (1903), 207.

89 Cooper, priv. comm.

CHAPTER 6

1 Ralph Hanna; see chapter 4, n. 11, above.

2 I am grateful for the learning and wisdom of Thomas Buhler of Yale University Press in London.

3 The Host's rebuke is because the Parson rebuked the Host for swearing. *The Riverside Chaucer*, ed. Larry D. Benson, 3rd edit. (Boston, 1987), 104: 'The Epilogue of the Man of Law's Tale', line 1173.

4 Ibid., 31–2: 'General Prologue', lines 477–8, 524–8.

5 Hudson, 1988, 391.

6 *Riverside Chaucer*, 195: 'The Pardoner's Prologue', line 433.

7 Ibid., 196–8, lines 483–588, and see pp. 907–8.

8 Ibid., 181: 'The Pardoner's Tale', lines 522–3; F&M, IV, 347.

9 *Riverside Chaucer*, 182, lines 530–3; F&M, IV, 426.

10 Smalley, 1941, ix, xiii. 'Geographically, the book is limited to England, northern France, and the Rhineland, where much the same educational system obtained.' Ibid., xiv.

11 Ibid., x, xii.

12 Ibid., xii–xiv.

13 *Riverside Chaucer*, 'General Prologue', lines 529–41.

14 For helpful notes on the Bible in Chaucer and Langland I am grateful to Dr Joan Bridgman.

15 *The Psalter [. . .] and Certain Canticles [. . .] by Richard Rolle of Hampole*, ed. H. R. Bramley (Oxford, 1884), xv.

16 Ibid., 5.

17 Norton, 2000, 6.

18 For some material here, I am grateful to Dr Orlaith O'Sullivan.

19 O'Sullivan, priv. comm.

20 The fullest account is given by Cawley 1958, xi–xxxviii.

21 Ibid., 14–28.

22 Ibid., 62: *Secunda Pastorum*, lines 722–7 (modernised).

23 Ibid., xxii; 104, n. 10 458 ff.

24 Brown, ed., 1932, xi.

25 Ibid., 168.

26 Robbins, ed., 1952, xvii.

27 Brown, ed., rev. G.V. Smithers, 2/1924, 85.

28 Wenzel, 1986.

29 I am indebted to Mary Clow for details of her research into Nisbet, his New Testament and the story of his family.

30 His descendant, James Nisbet, recorded that he 'being in the same Danger [of being taken and burned], digged and built a Vault in the Bottom of his own House, to which he retired himself, serving GOD, and reading his new Book. Thus he continued, instructing some few that had Access to him, until the Death of King *James* the V.' *A True Relation of the Life and Sufferings of John Nisbet in Hardhill* (1719), 1.

31 James Boswell, *The Journal of a Tour to the Hebrides with Samuel Johnson LLD* (1785); ed. Peter Levi (Harmondsworth, 1984), 394.

32 The failure to connect is all the sadder in view of Johnson's interest, expressed almost three years later in a letter to William Drummond, in a Gaelic Bible for the use of Scots Highlanders. *Letters of Samuel Johnson, LLD*, ed. G. Birkbeck Hill, 2 vols (Oxford, 1892), II, Letter 184, 13 August 1766.

33 *The New Testament in Scots*, ed. Thomas Graves Law, 3 vols (Edinburgh, 1901–5).

34 See the definitive studies by Blake, 1969; 1973; 1976.

35 Christopher Howse in the *Daily Telegraph*, 23 June 2001, A4, reviewing A. McGrath, 2001, used two familiar arguments: first, that there had never been any need of anything but 'the Vulgate (the brilliant work of St Jerome [. . .])'; and that 'An illiterate housewife in the 15th century knew [the Bible] through the homilies of the parish priest, and through Bible stories from the *Golden Legend* and other popular collections.' Quite what those other 'popular collections' were Mr Howse does not explain. Even if they existed, they were unlikely to contain, for example, Paul's Epistles, the foundation of Christian theology, which are not in the *Golden Legend*, either. How 'the illiterate housewife' was supposed to have access to a *Golden Legend* or to understand the Latin of the Vulgate (which, even in the parts which Jerome wrote, was anything but 'brilliant') is never made clear in such remarks, still frequently made. They show a lack of knowledge of the fifteenth century, the *Golden Legend* and the Bible.

36 Blake, 1969, 117.

37 Ibid., 118.

38 Ibid., 118.

39 Ibid., 120.

40 Ibid., 120.

41 Figures from Darlow and Moule, 1903–11, II, i, 298–9, 376–8, 481–4.

42 Nicholas Watson, 'Censorship and Cultural Change in Late-Medieval England: Vernacular Theology, the Oxford Translation Debate, and Arundel's Constitutions of 1409',

Speculum, LXX (1995), 825. I am indebted to this seminal article throughout these paragraphs.

43 Ibid., 826.
44 Ibid., 827.
45 Ibid., 828.
46 Ibid., 828.
47 Ibid., 829.
48 Ibid., 831.
49 Ibid., 840–51.
50 Ibid., 846.

CHAPTER 7

1 Bouyer, in Lampe, ed., 1969, 493.
2 Ibid.
3 Ibid., 495.
4 These matters are further developed with attractive brevity in Harbison, 1956; and at fuller length in McGrath, 1987.
5 Bouyer, 1969, 493.
6 That narrow tradition is vividly demonstrated in Tyndale, *Obedience*, 2000, 19–24.
7 Bouyer, 1969, 496–7.
8 Ibid., 497.
9 See McConica, 1991, 45–62.
10 Faludy, 1980, 157.
11 Ibid., 161.
12 A. Bludau, quoted in ibid., 161.
13 McConica, 1991, 45.
14 Tyndale, *Obedience*, 2000, 25.
15 Quoted in Daniell, 1994, 67.
16 For good brief accounts, see De Hamel, 2001, 221–4, with illustration; and Metzger, 2/1968, 96–8.
17 Metzger, 2/1968, 97–8.
18 Ibid., 100.

CHAPTER 8

1 For a fuller treatment of Love's *Mirror*, see Daniell, 1994, 96–100.
2 Duffy, 1992, 79. See also Chapter 10, note 2, below.
3 See the important introductory article by Tyacke, in Tyacke, ed., 1998, 1–32, esp. 1–3. A clear explication of the long existence of the denial of a popular Reformation, even from 1525, is given by O'Day, 1986. The late twentieth-century senior revisionist historians have been J. J. Scarisbrick for the earlier period, and Christopher Haigh for the later, joined by Eamon Duffy, whose *The Stripping of the Altars: Traditional Religion in England c.1400–c.1580*, 1992 is, in fact, largely about the fifteenth century (see Preface, note 1, above).
4 Tyacke, 1998, 3.
5 Haigh, ed., 1987. The process of late twentieth-century Catholic revisionism may be said to have been adumbrated in his earlier *Reformation and Resistance in Tudor Lancashire* (1975). See also Haigh, 1993.
6 Patrick Collinson, 'Comment on Eamon Duffy's Neale Lecture and the Colloquium', in Tyacke, 1998, 75.
7 See Pettegree in Pettegree, ed., 2000, 1–2. Under his direction the formerly unread French documents are being studied systematically by teams from the St Andrews Reformation Studies Institute.
8 Ibid., 5.
9 For important exposition of older ideas influencing the Reformation understanding of Scripture, see G. R. Evans, *The Language and Logic of the Bible*, 2 vols (Cambridge, 1985), particularly the second volume, *The Road to Reformation*. McGrath, 3/1999, touches on the same matter, especially in chapter 8.
10 Tyacke, 1998, *passim*.
11 Haigh, in three pages at the close of his *English Reformations: Religion, Politics and Society under the Tudors* (1993), 277–9, announces, and gives the evidence for, a popular Reformation ('the ministers were creating a Protestant nation').
12 Peter Lake, 'Religious Identities in Shakespeare's England', in *A Companion to Shakespeare*, ed. David Scott Kastan (Oxford, 1999), 76.
13 Le Goff, trans. A. Goldhammer, 1984. Invented as a place rather than a mere concept in the 1170s in Paris, and redefined in the thirteenth and fifteenth centuries, Purgatory depends not on the words of Jesus, nor on the writings of Paul, nor on the Old Testament, nor even on the teaching of the older Church Fathers, but on a few words in an Apocryphal book, at the end of 2 Maccabees 12. No one could ever claim that 2 Maccabees was in any way a central book of the Christian Bible; it is a mixture of late Jewish military history and priestly controversy.

14   Diarmaid MacCulloch, 'The Impact of the English Reformation', *Historical Journal*, XXXVIII (1995), 152. This statement might be contrasted with Christopher Haigh's remark that '[t]here might have been no Reformation: indeed, there hardly was one' in his 'The English Reformation: A Premature Birth, Difficult Labour and a Sickly Child', *Historical Journal*, XXXIII (1990), 459.

15   Care has to be taken with terminology. To Luther's insistence that the New Testament taught justification by faith, and that works were secondary, the Church responded that they had been preaching justification since Augustine. But the Church's doctrine had always been subtly different: 'justification' was dominated by 'justification by grace', which means faithfully receiving the Church's sacraments. It extends to justification by degrees, a sort of topping-up mechanism, even to their being something called 'more justification'. This is not what the New Testament means, and not what the Reformers meant. See Whale, 1955, 43–80.

16   Tyndale, *Obedience*, 2000, 18, 125, 170.

17   See Pettegree's chapter 'Art', in Pettegree, ed., 2000, 461–90.

18   Francis Higman, 'Music', in ibid., 491–504, esp. 491–2.

19   Andrew Spicer, 'Architecture', in ibid., 505–34.

20   Trevor Johnston, 'The Reformation and Popular Culture', in ibid., 545–60.

21   Quoted by Bainton in Greenslade, ed., 1963, 21.

22   Ibid., 5.

23   Figures from DMH, 1968, supported by Chamberlin, 1991. Some material here was first given as the keynote lecture at the Shakespeare International Conference, The Shakespeare Institute, Stratford-upon-Avon, August 2000, and reprinted in a shortened form in *Shakespeare Survey*, LIV (Cambridge, 2001), 1–12, and quoted here by permission. Always needing clarification is the question of what is a reissue or reprinting and what a fresh edition. The entries in DMH are from observation and record the differences of page size, format (folio, quarto, octavo) and so on which constitute a fresh edition. DMH's notes recording 'Another Edition' have not been included in the totals here.

24   Estimates can be made on the basis of entries in surviving account books recording the day's work of a printer. Print-runs for smaller books tended to be less than those for bigger books, for obvious reasons of the costs of re-setting. A half run would be 650 copies, a full run 1,300. Bibles would have either 1,300 or 2,600.

'In England from 1586 until 1673 edition quantities were limited by decree on behalf of the journeymen compositors to 1,500 copies of ordinary books, or 3,000 copies of books in small type, and of small books such as catechisms [. . .]. It is clear from the complaints of the journeymen that the masters ignored the decree and printed a large edition whenever it suited them to do so.' (Gaskell, 1974, 162.) See also W. W. Greg, *A Companion to Arber* (Oxford, 1967), 37.

25   Dickens, 1966, 51.

26   Steinberg, rev. James Moran, 3/1974, 144.

27   De Hamel, 2001, 237.

28   Sixteenth-century library inventories 'reveal that seventy-two Cambridge scholars selected at random by that most random selector, death, owned 253 copies of the ten principal Greek Fathers': Harold Weatherby, 'The True Saint George', *English Literary Renaissance*, XVII (1987), 123. See also Debora K. Shuger, 'Subversive Fathers and Suffering Subjects: Shakespeare and Christianity', in *Religion, Literature, and Politics in Post-Reformation England, 1540–1688*, ed. Donna B. Hamilton and Richard Strier (Cambridge, 1996), 46–69.

29   T. S. Freeman, ' "The Good Ministrye of Godlye and Vertuouse Women": The Elizabethan Martyrologists and the Female Supporters of the Marian Martyrs', *Journal of British Studies*, XXXIX (2000), 31–2.

30   Lake, 1999, 60.

31   See Richard Dutton, *Mastering the Revels* (Iowa City, 1991); and Gerald M. Pinciss, *Forbidden Matter: Religion in the Drama of Shakespeare and His Contemporaries* (Cranbury, NJ, 2000), 20–21, 113.

32   White, 1971, 2 and *passim*.

33   Collinson, 1982, 236. For the pictures in Geneva Bibles, see p. 303 below.

34   Stephen Marx, *Shakespeare and the Bible* (Oxford, 2000), 2.

CHAPTER 9

1 By Ivor Brown in *Say the Word* (1947), 7.

2 Tyndale, *Obedience*, 2000, 19.

3 Prologue to Genesis, *TOT*, 7.

4 Figures estimated from DMH, 1968 and Hills, 1962.

5 Anderson, 1845, I, vi.

6 Hill, 1993, 5.

7 Haigh, 1993, *passim*.

8 It is striking that at the large Sixteenth-Century Studies Conferences held in America since 1981, attended each year by many hundreds of leading historians and others from around the world, Bibles of any kind have been effectively ignored. Between 1995 and 2001, out of a total of about 2,700 papers given, fewer than half a dozen were about any European Bible, and all were short papers.

9 The figure can be calculated thus: Cochlaeus's (and Spalatin's; see note 35 below) figure of 6,000 for the unfinished 1525 translation may be a guide to the successful print-run in Worms in 1526 (for Cochlaeus's original Latin text, and a translation, see Pollard, ed., 1911, 99–108). Tyndale's own revisions of 1534 and 1535 (DMH 13, 15) may each be over modestly thought of as having 3,000 copies printed (Cochlaeus's other figure), a large run for books of the period, but not for Bibles. There were twelve 'piracies' of Tyndale's New Testaments before the end of 1536, by Antwerp printers (DMH 12, 16, 17, 19, 20, 21, 22, 23, 24, 25, 26,) and in England (DMH 27). Reckoning 2,000 for the 'piracies', the total for Tyndale is 36,000. This excludes the editions of Coverdale's New Testament printed in England (DMH 28, 29, 30, 31, 40, 41, 42, 43), the editions of Coverdale's Diglot (DMH 37, 38, 39) and the one-off 'Tyndale Diglot' (DMH 36), which make another twelve. On the same estimate, this would make a grand total of 48,000 English New Testaments printed, all before 1539.

10 Swynnerton, ed. Rex, 1999, 171.

11 *RSTC*, 15180: *A Treatise Made by John Lambert*, ed. John Bale (1548), 3v.

12 Westcott, 1868, rev. Wright, 3/1905, 158.

13 The true figure is 83 per cent. See John Nielson and Royal Skousen, 'How Much of the King James Bible is William Tyndale's?', *Reformation*, III (1998), 49–74. Note the refutation there of Butterworth's figure of 18 per cent (in his *Literary Lineage of the King James Bible*, 1941) from a double methodological error.

14 Quoted in Chapter 15, below, and see note 3, p. 812.

15 Tony Tyndale, 'Wycliffe, Queen Anne of Bohemia and the Tyndales of Hockwold, Norfolk', *Tyndale Society Journal*, XI (1998), 42.

16 Ibid., 42–3.

17 LP, III, no. 405; VI, no. 82.

18 Emden, ed., 1957–9, 567–9.

19 Tyndale, *Obedience*, 2000, 18–23.

20 Foxe, 1877, V, 114–15.

21 Ibid., V, 115.

22 *TOT*, 4.

23 Foxe, 1563, 514.

24 CWM, VI, i, 424; see also Tyndale, 1531, ed. O'Donnell and Wicks, 2000, 214.

25 Mozley, 1937, 32.

26 Foxe, 1877, V, 116–17.

27 Foxe, 1563, 514; Foxe, 1877, IV, 117.

28 *TOT*, 5.

29 Mozley, 1937, 67.

30 Foxe, 1877, IV, 617–18, 753; Strype, 3 vols, 1721, II, 364.

31 *TOT*, 5.

32 Foxe, 1877, IV, 679; Strype, 1721, II, 364.

33 Mozley, 1937, 48.

34 Pollard, ed., 1911, 107.

35 Ibid., 104. See Mozley, 1937, 67, for Spalatin's 'six thousand'. This 1526 Worms New Testament is now also available in print, ed. W. R. Cooper, 2000.

36 It is not impossible that others may be found.

37 Pollard, 1911, 134.

38 *TOT*, 3.

39 Pollard, 1911, 134–49.

40 Ibid., 125.

41 BL Cotton MS Vitellius IX f.131.

42 Edward Hall, *The Union of the Two Noble and Illustre Families of Lancaster & York* (1548), reprinted as *Hall's Chronicle* (1809), 762–3.

43 I am grateful to Andrew Hope for this information, priv. comm.

44 Tyndale, 1528, in Walter, ed., 1848, 107–8.

45 For identification of this 'Hans Luft', see Guido Latré, 'The 1535 Coverdale Bible and its Antwerp Origin', in O'Sullivan and Herron, eds, 2000, 92.

46 On the interrogations, see Foxe, 1877, IV, 688–92, and V, 32–41; on the ban, ibid., V, 570–7.

47 Tyndale, *Obedience*, 2000, 3.

48 Ibid., 170.

49 Ibid., 22–3.

50 Foxe, 1877, V, 570–82.

51 Strype, 1721, I, 172–4.

52 *TOT*, 7.

53 'The propertuies of the Hebrew tongue agreeth a thousand times more with the English than with the Latin. The manner of speaking is both one, so that in a thousand places thou needest not but to translate it into the English word for word when thou must seek a compass [go round] in the Latin [. . .] so that it have the same grace and sweetness, sense and pure understanding with it in the Latin, as it hath in the Hebrew.' Tyndale, *Obedience*, 2000, 19. The useful similarities of Hebrew and English syntax have not been disputed.

54 *CWM*, VIII, iii, 1260.

55 *DMH*, 15.

56 Ibid.

57 Foxe, 1877, V, 130–4.

58 Daniell, 1994, 213.

59 Foxe, 1877, V, 128.

60 Daniell, 1994, 370.

61 Robert J. Wilkinson, 'Reconstructing Tyndale in Latomus: William Tyndale's Last, Lost Book', *Reformation*, 1 (1996), 252–85, 345–400.

62 Daniell, 1994, 379.

63 Foxe, 1877, V, 127; Hall, 1548, reprinted 1809, 818.

64 Foxe, ibid.

65 Daniell, 1994, 384.

66 The classic story is of 'the poor men' of Chelmsford meeting to hear the New Testament read aloud: Foxe, 1877, VIII, 638–40.

67 Comparison of Tyndale's Pentateuch and historical books with late twentieth-century literal translations into English by Hebrew scholars is revealing, but only of how reliable Tyndale is – not, as might be thought, how wide of the mark. See for example the

incidental quotations in Alter and Kermode, eds, 1987, and Fox, 1995. For example, Tyndale in 1530 has at Genesis 3:2–5: 'And the woman said unto the serpent, of the fruit of the trees in the garden we may eat, but of the fruit of the tree that is in the midst of the garden (said God) see that ye eat not, and see that ye touch it not: lest ye die. Then said the serpent unto the woman: tush ye shall not die: But God doth know, that whensoever ye should eat of it, your eyes should be opened and you should be as God and know both good and evil.'

Everett Fox in 1995 has: 'The woman said to the snake: / From the fruit of the (other) trees in the garden ye may eat, / but from the fruit of the tree that is in the midst of the garden, / God has said: / You are not to eat from it and you are not to touch it, lest you die. / The snake said to the woman: / Die, you will not die! / Rather, God knows / that on the day that you eat from it, your eyes will be opened and you will become like gods, knowing good and evil.'

68 Richard Duerden, 'Equivalence or Power?: Authority and Reformation Bible Translation', in O'Sullivan and Herron, eds, 2000, 15.

69 Ibid., 14.

70 Daniell, 1994, *passim*.

71 Significantly, a recent study of his 135 neologisms shows that half were of 'Germanic' (that is, Saxon) origin, most likely to be understood by the ploughboy. (Jeannette Mitterhofer, unpublished dissertation, *Tyndale's Neologisms in his Bible Translations*, University of Zurich, October 1999; priv. comm.) See also Daniell, 1994, and Robinson, 1998, both *passim*.

CHAPTER 10

1 *CWM*, VI, i, 341; Chambers, 1942, (in which 'Bible' does not appear in the index).

2 Kristina Bross, priv. comm.

3 *RSTC* records nine London printings of Nicholas Love's *Mirror* before 1525; after that year, a revised edition was printed in Douai in 1606, and another translation, also abroad, in 1622 (*RSTC*, 13034). I am grateful to Andrew Hope for drawing my attention to this.

4 Cavallo and Chartier, eds, trans. Cochrane, 1999, 32 and *passim*, esp. 276–8.

5 *DMH.*

6 Hills, 1962.

7 The king's text is given in Mozley, 1953, 32.

8 Ibid., 34.

9 Ibid.

10 Ibid., 35.

11 Pollard, ed., 1911, 163–9.

12 Quoted in Daniell, 1994, 216.

13 Mozley, 1953, 35–6.

14 Ibid., 36.

15 Pollard, 1911, 196–8.

16 I am grateful to Dr Ruth Mayers for her investigation into the possibility that Gardiner's Gospel revisions might have survived, in London or Winchester or elsewhere; nothing was found.

17 Pollard, 1911, 272–5.

18 Mozley, 1953, 39.

19 Pollard, 1911, 174–5.

20 Butterworth and Chester, 1961, 52.

21 Mozley, 1953, 49; DMH, 10.

22 Butterworth and Chester, 1961, 235.

23 Ibid., 54.

24 See the brief treatment in Mozley, 1953, 53, with some examples of Joye at work, 53–9. See also Butterworth and Chester, 1961, 132–4.

25 Butterworth and Chester, 1961, 17.

26 Mozley, 1953, 42.

27 Tyndale, 1528, in Walter, ed., 1848, 38.

28 J. R. Harris, *The Origin of the Leicester Codex* (1887).

29 Pollard, 1911, 241. Pollard pointed out that permission to print should not be made to appear as royal approval.

30 Ibid.

31 Westcott, 1868, rev. Wright, 3/1905, 85.

32 DMH, 19.

33 Wescott, rev. Wright, 3/1905, 87.

34 Ibid., 86.

35 J. Strype, *Ecclesiastical Memorials* (1721), II, 35, on the authority of Bale; and see Westcott, rev. Wright, 3/1905, 86.

36 I am grateful to Anne O'Donnell, S.N.D., for pointing me in the direction of many more of these than I was aware of. She also directed me to two books by Father Germain Marc'hadour: *Thomas More et la Bible: La Place des livres saints* (Paris, 1969); and

The Bible in the Works of Thomas More, 5 vols (Nieuw, 1969–72). See also the analysis in *CWM*, VI, 508–12.

37 *CWM*, XII, 66.

38 Ibid., 309.

39 Ibid., 13, 100–2.

40 *Devout Instructions and Prayers*, ibid., 13, 213.

41 Priv. comm.

42 *CWM*, XIII, 12–18.

43 All twenty-five verses, John 6:41–66, are conveniently printed as an Appendix by Norton, 1993, I 323–7, where they are set out parallel to Tyndale, the Rheims version and KJV.

44 Norton, 1993, 323.

CHAPTER 11

1 Foxe, 1877, IV, 676.

2 Stephen Gardiner, *A declaration of Such True Articles as George Joye hath gone about to confute as false* (1546), sig.L5^r.

3 Pollard, 1911, 160.

4 *SP*, 1830, I, 592.

5 Cranmer, ed. Cox, 1846, II, 344.

6 Hughes and Larkin, eds, 1964, 230–31.

7 King, 1993, 78.

8 Ibid., 79–80.

9 DMH, 1968, 9.

10 Foxe, 1877, V, 415.

11 Ibid.

12 Bale, 1548, 721; translated Mozley, 1953, 3.

13 *LP*, 1880, v.106: *SP*, 1830, i. 383–4.

14 Foxe, 1877, V, 40.

15 Harte, 1926, 16.

16 *Doctrinal Treatises*, ed. H. Walter (Cambridge: PS, 1848) 37.

17 Daniell, 1994, 109.

18 Foxe, 1877, V, 120.

19 Daniell, 1999, 26–8.

20 DMH, 9.

21 Symeon Ruytinck's *Life of Emanuel van Meteren*, reprinted in his *Nederlandtsche Historie* (1614), fo. 672. See also Pollard, 1911, 198–200.

22 Pollard, 1911, 200, 203.

23 Ibid., 200. In a footnote, Pollard notes how this has 'some weight as evidence as to where the Bible of 1535 was printed', but

dismisses it as a 'version' of a 'legend . . . at third hand.' For Coverdale printing in Antwerp, see Guido Latré, 'The 1535 Coverdale Bible and its Antwerp Origin', in O'Sullivan and Herron, eds, 2000.

24 Foxe, 1877, VI, 591.

25 *Joye* (1535), ed. Arber (1882), 22.

26 'William Tyndale yet once more unto the Christian Reader', *TNT*, 13–16.

27 DMH, 32, 33. For Antwerp printers, see Arblaster et al., 2002, *passim*, esp. p. 4.

28 Martin Holt Dotterweich, unpublished paper given to the Tyndale Society Conference, San Diego, 26 February 2000, and here quoted with permission. Cromwell's licence is mentioned in a letter to Cromwell from Coverdale.

29 Ibid.

30 Lewis, 1950, 11.

31 In *REB*.

32 Westcott, 1905, 165.

33 See the lack of conclusion in Butterworth and Chester, 1961, 121–5.

34 DMH, 18.

35 LeGoff (1984).

36 Quoted in Norton, 2000, 30–31.

37 Dotterweich, op. cit.

38 *REB*.

CHAPTER 12

1 See Daniell, 1994, pl. 14 and p. 379.

2 See Robert J. Wilkinson, 'Reconstructing Tyndale in Latomus: William Tyndale's last, lost, book', *Reformation*, 1 (1996), 252–85.

3 Foxe, 1877, V, 840.

4 Mozley, 1953, 122–3.

5 Foxe, 1877, VI, 611–12.

6 For evidence and analysis, see Daniell, 1994, 336–57.

7 Mozley, 1953, 139–40.

8 SP, 1830, I, 561–2. Pollard, 1911, 215.

9 Quoted by A. J. Slavin, 1979, I, 7–8.

10 Ibid., 8; and see his n. 23.

11 Dickens, 1989, 115.

12 E. R. Reigler's unpublished Ph. D. diss., 'Printing, Protestantism and Politics: Thomas Cromwell and religious reform' (University of California, Los Angeles, 1978), demonstrates Cromwell's biblical and other related printing projects to advance a godly reformation.

13 Mozley, 1953, 154. I spent an over-excited hour in the British Library in the last days of 1999, trying to make the discovery of the new century; to show to myself that those chapters of Job were in fact a hitherto lost fragment of translation by Tyndale, in Rogers's possession. I had to acknowledge defeat. Those chapters bear no trace of Tyndale's translating signature.

14 *TOT*, 262.

CHAPTER 13

1 *RSTC*, 1996, 5892. See Norton, 2000, 32–3.

2 Celia Hughes, 'Coverdale's Alter Ego', *Bulletin of the John Rylands University Library of Manchester*, LXV, 1982, 103.

3 See chapter 11 above, n. 13.

4 *LP* XII, ii, 296.

5 See the note at the end of the DMH entry for no. 32, on p. 17.

6 See above, p. 194.

7 L&P, XII, ii, 841–2, p. 296.

8 Ibid., 171.

9 SP, 1830, I, 575–6.

10 Foxe, 1877, V, 410.

11 SP, 1830, I, 588–9.

12 *LP* XIII, ii. 277.

13 D. Wilkins, *Concilia Magnae Britannia et Hiberniae* (1737), III, 815.

14 I am indebted in these pages to Professor A. J. Slavin; not only for his 'The Rochepot Affair' *Sixteenth Century Journal*, X (1979), 3–19 (the reference here is to, 11, n. 36.), but for further details from his unpublished paper, 'Tyndale's Revenge: Henry VIII Gives an English Bible to The People', given at the Tyndale Symposium, The Huntington Library, October 1996; and for private communication.

15 SP, 1830, VII, 61.

16 Ibid., I, 591–2. See also Slavin, 1979, II, nn 38 and 39.

17 BL Harleian MS 604 f. 113 (13 December 1538).

18 BL Cottonian MS Cleopatra E.V.f. 326.

19 Quoted in S. L. Greenslade, ed., *The Coverdale Bible*, 1535, (1975), 151; and Slavin, 1979, 12.

20 Slavin, 1979, 12, n. 43.

21 Ibid., 12, n. 47.

22 Ibid., 13, n. 50.

23 Ibid., 13.

24 Foxe, 1877, V, 411.

25 Greenslade, 1963, 23.

26 C. J. Sisson, 'Grafton and the London Grey Friars', *The Library* 4th ser., XI (1931), 121–49.

27 Slavin, 1979, 16.

28 Ibid., 14–19.

29 The Articles are given in full by Burnet, 1679. The Act is 32 Henry VIII, cap. 62.

30 Quoted in Slavin, 1979, 4.

31 A good account of the title-page, and of the impact of the Great Bible, is given by David Scott Kastan, ' "The Noise of the New Bible": Reform and Reaction in Henrician England', in *Religion and Culture in Renaissance England*, ed. Claire McEachern and Debora Shuger (Cambridge, 1997), 46–68.

32 Ibid, 57.

33 King, 1993, 80–82.

34 *Kynge Johan: A playe in two partes*, ed. J. P. Collier (1838), 43.

35 See Rainer Pineas, 'William Tyndale's Influence on John Bale's Polemical Use of History', *Archiv für Reformationsgeschichte*, LIII (1962), 79–96.

36 George Joye, *Daniel* (1545), Ai^r; Evii^r; Fii^v.

37 The English text of Coverdale's first diglot New Testament (1538) was from the Latin Vulgate, printed alongside. In more closely following the Latin, he was diplomatically trying 'to reassure his timid friends, and to confute his critics' (DMH, p. 21). The prefaces to the three editions in the same year, 1538, are, as David Norton notes, 'the only places where he writes about the principles of translation' (Norton, 2000, 31). Coverdale intended to be 'very scrupulous to go from the vocable of the text' (quoted in Norton, 32) – 'that is, he sought to be as literal as possible' (ibid.).

38 Quoted in Bruce, 1961, 71.

39 Mozley, 1953, 7.

40 George Pearson, ed. *The Remains of Myles Coverdale* (Cambridge: PS, 1846), 503–25.

41 Mozley, 1953, 12.

42 Ibid., 13.

43 Ibid., 14.

44 *A brieff discourse off the Troubles Begonne at Franckford Anno Domini 1554* [*RSTC* 25442, but not written by Whittingham], 232.

45 Mozley, 1953, 15.

46 *The Sermons of Hugh Latimer*, ed. G. E. Corrie (Cambridge: PS, 1844), 272.

47 Mozley, 1953, 15.

48 Ibid., 15.

49 John Bale, *Illustrium maioris Britanniae Scriptorum Summarium* (1548), 141.

50 Mozley, 1953, 16.

51 John Hooker, in R. Holinshed, *Chronicles* (1587), III, 1308; in Harte, ed., 1926; BL Harleian MS 5827 ff. 46 and 72.

52 Ibid.

53 J. K. McConica, *English Humanists and Reformation Politics* (1968) 231–2, 240–49.

54 Mozley, 1953, 17.

55 Ibid., 18.

56 Ibid., 20.

57 Foxe, 1877, VI, 706.

58 Anon., *A brieff discourse*, 3.

59 Mozley, 1953, 23.

60 *A brieff discourse*, 224–5.

61 Mozley, 1953, 23.

62 BL Harleian MS 5827 f. 46–7.

63 E. Grindal, *The Remains of Archbishop Grindal*, ed. W. Nicholson (Cambridge: PS, 1843), 284.

64 Mozley, 1953, 24.

65 Grindal, 1843, 283.

66 *A brieff discourse*, 254.

67 BL Harleian MS 5827 f. 46–7; and Harte, 1926, 16.

68 Quoted in Norton, 2000, 32.

69 Ibid.

70 Ibid.

71 Westcott, 1905, 211.

72 See the useful article, with valuable references, by Vivienne Westbrook, 'Richard Taverner Revising Tyndale', *Reformation*, 2 (1997), 191–205.

73 Published in 1843 in an edition by James Goodwin, DMH, 1847.

CHAPTER 14

1 Tyndale, *Obedience*, 2000, 36, 58.

2 Ibid., 63.

3 Dickens, 1989, 159.

4 Tyndale, *Obedience*, 2000, 84.

5 Ibid., 18, 125, 170.

6 Foxe, 1877, IV, 656–64.

7   Tyndale, 2000, 152–3.

8   *Answer*, PS 9: ed O'Donnell and Wicks, 8. It was on this passage that More commented, 'Judge, good Christian reader, whether it be possible that he [Tyndale] be any better than a beast, out of whose brutish beastly mouth cometh such a filthy foam of blasphemies . . .' *CWM*, VIII, i, 135.

9   Christopher Haigh's estimation, in *English Reformations* (1993), 5–6, for the early 1530s.

10   See Tyndale, *Obedience*, 2000, 93, 187. In 1511 Richard Hunne of London challenged the right, and was murdered in suspicious circumstances: see W. R. Cooper, 'Richard Hunne', *Reformation*, 1 (1996), 221–51.

11   Tyndale, *Obedience*, 2000, 92–4.

12   Ibid., 103–4.

13   Ibid., 90.

14   See ibid., xii–xiii and note.

15   *RSTC*, 1996, 5996.

16   Tyndale, *Obedience*, 2000, 68.

17   That is, in the New Testament, baptism and communion.

18   Tyndale, *Obedience*, 2000, 86–7.

19   For example, Richard Busshe in 1539: see below, p. 269.

20   *RSTC*, 1996, 5163, 5168.

21   *RSTC*, 1996, 5168.

22   In this copy of Matthew's Bible in the Bible Society library at Cambridge all notes, of whatever kind, have been blacked out.

23   Alec Ryrie, 'Persecution, survival and compromise: English protestantism and the state 1539–47' (unpublished M. Litt dissertation, University of St Andrews, 1994), Appendix 1.

24   MacCulloch, 1996, 218–21.

25   Pollard, 1911, 261–2.

26   Ibid., 260.

27   Pollard, 1911, 272–4.

28   Ibid., 274.

29   Bruce, 1961, 79.

30   The complete list is given by Pollard, 1911, 274–5.

31   I am especially grateful to Joe Johnson for providing me with striking evidence of this from his personal collection of Bibles.

32   Quoted in Bruce, 1961, 78–9.

33   Ibid.

34   See Muriel McClendon, *The Quiet Reformation* (Stanford, 1999), 83.

35   MacCulloch, 1999, 105. It remains extraordinary that the 'intricate . . . structure', not to mention the 'financial system' described, are not noted as themselves from 'alien forces', that is, the Bishop of Rome.

36   Ibid., 157–8.

37   Ibid., 20–21.

38   D. E. Hoak, *The King's Council in the Reign of Edward VI* (Cambridge, 1976), 470.

39   See the Bibliography in MacCulloch, 1999, 250–65.

40   Ibid., 14.

41   Jezebel may or may not have been sexually promiscuous, as she is often today described. There is no record. Her 'whoredoms' refer to her ardent worship of the alien gods Baal and Asherah, even from the throne of Israel. The word does not have a sexual connotation.

42   Quotations are from *TOT*, 492–3.

43   Particularly Duffy, 1992, of course.

44   The viciousness of Chaucer's clerical rogues in his *Canterbury Tales* (1380s) is still recognisable in Simon Fish's *Supplication of Beggars* (1529), *RSTC*, 10883.

45   MacCulloch, 1999, 17.

46   *TOT*, 494.

47   *TOT*, 497–8.

48   2 Kings 9; *TOT*, 516.

49   See *Narrative and Dramatic Source of Shakespeare*, ed. Geoffrey Bullough, 8 vols (1960), III & IV, passim.

50   J. J. Scarisbrick, *Henry VIII* (Berkeley, Calif., 1968), 247.

51   Tyndale's political position is summed up, with analysis of scholarship previous to his own, by Thompson, in Baker, ed., 1979. I acknowledge my particular debt to Richard Duerden, for conversations and for three articles on the *Obedience* which are important, not least for their valuable references: 'The Temporal and Spiritual Kingdoms: Tyndale's Doctrine and its Practice', *Reformation*, 1 (1996), 118–28; 'Justice and Justification: King and God in Tyndale's *Obedience of a Christian Man*, in *William Tyndale and the Law*, ed. Anne O'Donnell and John Day (Washington, DC, 1996), 69–80; and 'Equivalence or Power? Authority and Reformation Bible Translation', in *The Bible as Book: The Reformation*, ed. Orlaith O'Sullivan and Ellen Herron (2000), 9–23.

52 Tyndale, *Expositions*, PS, 1849, 3.

53 Ibid., 6.

54 Ibid., 61.

55 I am also indebted, again for conversations as well as for his writings, to the Revd Dr Ralph Werrell.

56 Werrell, 2001, 275.

57 *The Practice of Prelates*, PS, 1849, 49.

58 Ibid., 50.

59 Werrell, 2001, 293–4.

60 *Exposition of Matthew*, PS, 1849, 8.

61 Werrell, 2001, 298; and see *Exposition of Matthew*, 86f.

62 Richard Duerden, in O. O'Sullivan, *op. cit.*, 17; Tyndale, 2000, 103.

63 *TOT*, 11.

64 *TOT*, 535–6.

65 *TOT*, 537.

66 *TOT*, 537.

67 *REB* has 'He also pulled down the quarters of the male prostitutes attached to the house of the Lord, where women wove vestments in honour of Asherah' (2 Kings 23:7).

68 2 Kings 23:11. *REB* has 'He did away with the horses that the kings of Judah had set up in honour of the sun at the entrance to the house of the Lord, beside the room of the eunuch Nathan-melech in the colonnade, and he burnt the chariots of the sun.'

69 *TOT*, 537.

70 Jennifer Loach, *Edward VI*, (1999).

71 MacCulloch, 1999, 12.

72 Aston, Cambridge, 1993, 26.

73 Aston, 1988, 276.

74 Aston, 1993, 38.

75 There is no mention of this point in John N. King's pioneering, and still essential, study of Edwardian literature, *English Reformation Literature: The Tudor Origins of the Protestant Tradition* (Princeton, 1982). He remarks on his first page that 'little work has been done in the early literature of the English Reformation.' This remains sadly true, in spite of his magnificent lead.

76 See the clarification in, for example, Gerald M. Pinciss, *Forbidden Matter: Religion in the Drama of Shakespeare and his Contemporaries* (Newark, 2000), 15 and *passim*.

77 Dedication to the 'second tome' of Erasmus's *Paraphrases on the New Testament*. *RSTC*, 2854. 6.

78 Antonia Fraser, *The Six Wives of Henry VIII* (London, 1992), 380.

79 King, 1993, 83.

80 See King, 1989, 182–266.

81 Developed in detail by King, 1993, 83–5.

82 Ibid., 86.

83 See King, 2001.

84 Bradshaw, 1998, 58; Bale in Bradshaw n. 135; 94.

85 Figures from DMH. This catalogue is always the basis for noting a new edition. The total of sixty-four is made up of sixteen of Tyndale's New Testament; twenty-two of Coverdale's Bible and offshoots; two of Matthew's; three of Taverner's revision of it; fourteen of the Great Bible, and the rest of single Old Testament books by reformers like George Joye.

86 Darlow and Moule, 1911, 2, ii, 923–37.

87 Joye's Psalms, for example, would have had a shorter run: the various Great Bibles very much longer.

88 DMH, 80.

89 DMH, 72, 73.

90 The matter, with useful references, is discussed by MacCulloch, 1999, 105–16: the necessarily negative qualities of churchwardens' accounts are pointed out on 106.

91 J. Rogers, *The Doctrine of Faith* (1634), 97–9; quoted by Duffy, in Tyacke, ed., 1998, 41.

92 It is important not to be seduced by evidence of secret well-attended Catholic masses in the second half of the sixteenth century in barns and Catholic houses, especially in the north-west of England, into denying the transformation of the parish churches. See Peter Lake, 'Religious Identities in Shakespeare's England', in A Companion to Shakespeare, ed. David Scott Kastan (Oxford, 1999) esp. 76. It is also important to recognise that England's unique popular drama later in the sixteenth century, with hundreds of playwrights working for one or another of the six large theatres in Shakespeare's time, would not have happened in a country that was not in a rooted Protestant tradition. See Bryan Crockett ' "Holy Covenage" and the Renaissance Cult of the Ear', Sixteenth Century Journal, xxiv (1993), 47–65, esp. 64.

93 *Calendar of State Papers, Spanish 1547–9*,

ed. P. de Gayangos, G. Mattingly, M. D. S. Hume and R. Taylor (1862–1954), pp. 46, 52, 205, 222, 230, 462–3.

CHAPTER 15

1 Auksi, 1995, 5.

2 *CWM*, IX, 13.

3 Quoted in J. W. Hebel, H. H. Hudson *et al., Tudor Poetry and Prose* (New York, 1953), 560.

4 *Love's Labour's Lost*, 5.1.78. 4.2.50.

5 'The Franklin's Prologue', *Riverside Chaucer*, 163, lines 723–4.

6 *The Works of George Herbert*, ed. F. E. Hutchinson (Oxford, 1978), 56–7, 102–3.

7 M. J. Piret, 'Some Aspects of George Herbert's Rhetorical Art', M. Litt. diss., 1989 (Bodleian MSS M. Litt. c.988), abstract.

8 *TNT*, 118.

9 *TNT*, 116.

10 'Jordan', in Herbert 1978, 56.

11 *RSTC*, 25799, *The Art of Rhetorique*; 22428, *A Treatise of Schemes and Tropes*.

12 Auksi, 1995, 161.

13 Robert Boyle, *New Experiments and Observations touching Cold* (1665), 297.

14 *The English Works of Thomas Hobbes,* ed. W. Molesworth (1832) III, 25.

15 Joseph Addison, *Spectator*, Monday, 12 March 1711: no. 10.

16 Samuel Johnson, *Lives of the English Poets*, ed. G. Birkbeck Hill (Oxford, 1905), II, 150.

17 John Wilkins, *Ecclesiastes* (1646), 72.

18 Roger Ascham, *The Whole Works . . .* ed. J. A. Giles (1865); *Toxophilus, Part Two*, vol. 3, 157.

19 Daniell, 1994, 72.

20 *TNT*, 99. *Erasmus's Paraphrase of the Gospels and Acts* (1548), fol. lxxv.

21 Cranmer, Cox, 1844–6, I, 140, 108.

22 *Certain Sermons or Homilies, appointed to be read in Churches* (1623), 1.

23 *TNT*, 168.

24 Swynnerton, 1999, 170–71.

25 Norton, 2000, 10–11, referring to More, CWM, VIII, 187, and Pollard, 1911, 115.

26 Stella Read, 'Tyndale's Speech', in *The Tyndale Society Journal*, 3 (December 1995), 58–9.

27 Daniell, 1994, 17–18.

28 The excellent phrase is by Michael Piret, in his 'Herbert and Proverbs', *Cambridge Quarterly*, 17, no. 3 (1988), 223.

29 On *Vulgaria* generally see Orme, 1973, 98–100; and more particularly Nelson, 1956, *passim*.

30 John Anwykyll, *Vylgari Terentii*, found in some copies of his *Compendium totius grammaticae* (1483). I used the Bodleian Library copy, shelfmark Inc.e.E2.1483.1(1).

31 Ibid., ff 51, 51v, 55, 55v, 60, 71, 73v.

32 *RSTC*, 1966, 2, 359–63, makes some headway in the difficult task of cataloguing these little books.

33 *The Vulgaria of John Stanbridge and the Vulgaria of Robert Whittinton* ed. Beatrice White, *EETS* vol. 187 (Oxford, 1932), 15, 16, 18, 20, 22, 25, 26, 28, 14, 23.

34 Ibid., 14, 23.

35 See, for all Whittinton's books, *RSTC*, 1966, 2, 454–60.

36 White, *op. cit*, 59.

37 See Hastings Rashdall, *The Universities of Europe in the Middle Ages*, ed. F. M. Powicke and A. B. Emden (Oxford, 1936), vol. 3, 231.

38 Emrys Jones, *The Origins of Shakespeare* (Oxford, 1977), 13.

39 Nicholas Orme, 'An Early-Tudor Oxford Schoolbook', *Renaissance Quarterly* xxxiv, 1, Spring 1981, 11–39.

40 Horman, ed. James, 1926, fols 27v, 288, 135v, 154, 141, 146.

41 *RSTC*, 1966, 13603.7–13606.5.

42 R. W. Chambers, 'The Continuity of English Prose from Alfred to More and his School' in *The Life and Death of Sir Thomas More by Nicholas Harpsfield*, ed. E. V. Hitchcock, *EETS* 186 (Oxford, 1932). The summary of Chambers is by William Nelson in his *A Fifteenth-Century School Book from a Manuscript in the British Museum*, 1956, xxvii.

43 Ibid., liii–lviii and *passim*, cxliii, cxlvii.

44 Ibid. cxlii–xlvii and *passim*.

45 Nelson, Arundel *Vulgaria*, no. 263, 61.

46 *TOT*, 70.

47 *TNT*, 233.

48 *Macbeth* 2.2.62; Falstaff in 1 *Henry* IV, 3.3.171 and 5.1.125.

49 Brigden, 1989, 573.

50 Duffy, 1992, 530.

51 *RSTC*, 1966, 24165, sig. A3ᵛ: referred to by Ryrie, *op. cit*, 3.

52 *RSTC*, 1966, 24654.

53 Quoted in Bruce, 1961, 79.

54 Pollard, 1911, 268–71.

55 269–71; Duffy, 1992, 223, gives the source as J. G. Nicholls, ed., *Narratives of the Days of the Reformation*, Camden Society, LXXVII, 1859, 248–50. Duffy tells the story twice; as evidence of 'contentious' Bible reading (420) and earlier as 'a fascinating story, for it demonstrates not only the use of the primer by the urban middle classes, but the extraordinary fact that the son of a tradesman literate in Latin before he could read English' (222–3). That 'literacy', however, extended only to 'the reciting of Our Lady's Matins' (420). Some might think that 'the extraordinary fact' is that Duffy ignores the communal reading of the New Testament, which is the point of the story.

56 Duffy, 1992, 420.

57 *CWM*, IX, 13.

58 See *RSTC*, 1966, 3, 342–6. A glance at the whole Chronological Index, from 1475–1640, 331–404, shows just how steep became the rising curve of numbers of books printed in Britain.

59 Introduction to Cavallo and Chartier eds; trans. Cochrane, 1999, 32.

60 *TNT*, 350.

61 White, 1971, *passim*.

62 Ibid., 126–7. See also Norton, 2000, 166 for a hostile but revealing account of Bibles being read at meetings.

63 White, 1971, 55.

64 Ibid., 161–4.

65 Ibid., 169.

66 I express here my gratitude to Dr Ryrie of the University of Birmingham not only for sharing with me his research done in 1999 and 2000, but also for doing so with such efficiency and promptness.

67 Alec Ryrie, 'Foolishness to the Greeks: language and control in the early Reformation', unpublished paper (2000), 1. See also Alec Ryrie, *The Gospel and Henry VIII* (Cambridge, 2003), chapters 4 and 5.

68 Ryrie, 2000, 10. See also Alec Ryrie in *The Beginnings of English Protestantism*, ed. Alec Ryrie and Peter Marshall (Cambridge, 2002).

69 Ryrie, priv. comm.

70 Ryrie, 1994, 10.

71 *RSTC*, 2972.7. Only one (imperfect) copy of the Grafton survives, in Cambridge University Library. The Taverner postils are 'semi-official' because they were sponsored by Cromwell; from Taverner's status as clerk of the signet; and because they were frequently reprinted in the 1540s, when evangelical literature was driven overseas.

72 Ryrie, 2000, 4

73 MS PRO E 36 / 120 fol. 8^{r-v} (LP XIV (ii) 301).

74 Foxe 1570, 1726, 2073, 2137, 2251.

75 Dickens, 1989, 338.

76 Richard Overy, *Why the Allies Won* (1995), 180–81.

77 Briefly described in Overy, 1995, 79–80.

78 Overy, 1995, 185, 201–4.

79 Charles Dickens, *Dombey and Son* (1848), chapters 11, 12 and 14.

80 *As You Like It*, 2.7, 145–7.

81 Emrys Jones, *The Origins of Shakespeare* (Oxford, 1977), 9–13.

82 *Love's Labour's Lost*, 5.2,621.

83 Jonathan Bate, *Shakespeare and Ovid* (Oxford, 1993).

84 'Phyllyp Sparowe' in *John Skelton: The Complete English Poems*, ed. by John Scattergood (Harmondsworth, 1983), 91.

85 *The New Testament, Translated by William Tyndale . . . 1526*, ed. W. R. Cooper (London, 2000), 554.

CHAPTER 16

1 There were four octavos of the Great Bible New Testament, in 1540, 1546, 1547 and 1550.

2 For the first time, that is, apart from Exodus, Leviticus and Deuteronomy in Tyndale's 1530 Pentateuch.

3 Bodleian pressmark N.T.Eng.1557.F.2: Lambeth shelfmark ★★E2070.

4 'The Hebrew Old Testament had long been divided into verses, but not chapters; the New Testament into chapters, not verses. The compilation of dictionaries and concordances led inevitably to chapter and verse divisions in both by the 1550s.' (Hammond, 1982, 238).

5 I am grateful to Dr David Alexander for permission to use his unpublished Oxford D. Phil. thesis: [J. D. Alexander], 'The Genevan version of the Bible: Its origin, translation and influence' (1957), Bodleian shelfmark MS.D.Phil.d.1810. This reference is p. 43: see

also John Nichols, *The Progresses and Public Processions of Queen Elizabeth* (1823), l. 35.

6   The scene was still well known half a century later. It was reproduced at the conclusion of Thomas Heywood's 1605 history play, *If You Know Not Me You Know Nobody, with the Building of the Royal Exchange, and the Famous Victory of Queen Elizabeth*, and a year later in the first scene of Thomas Dekker's more crisply titled allegorical history play, *The Whore of Babylon*, 1606.

7   Darlow and Moule, 1903–11, II, i, 882–390.

8   Ibid., nos 5589, 5592.

9   Ibid., no. 8468.

10   The archivist of Holy Trinity Church Geneva, Dyne Steel, opens *A History of the English Church in Geneva* (Geneva, 1986) with an account of the Marian Exiles (1555–1559). See also the standard study, Garrett, 1938, 1966.

11   Steel, 1986, 1.

12   Ibid., 2.

13   See Green, 1871.

14   See DMH, 1968, 61 and Westcott, 1905, 90, n. 1.

15   *RSTC*, 1996, 21046.

16   *RSTC*, 1996, 12020.

17   MS Wood E.4.ff.40–50; see also MS Rawlinson J.folio 7, 207–10.

18   Alexander, 1957, ii.

19   Lloyd E. Berry, ed., *Facsimile of The 1560 Geneva Bible* (Wisconsin, 1969), 8; and Garrett, *op. cit.*, *passim*.

20   Paul Chaix, Alain Dufour and Gustave Moeckli, *Les Livres Imprimés à Genève de 1550 à 1600* (1959).

21   Details of Olivetan in Darlow and Moule (1903–11) II, i, no. 3710.

22   Alexander, 1957, 39.

23   Sigs. [★.ii., and ★iii] quoted in Alexander, *op. cit.*, 38–9.

24   Pollard, 1911, 275–6.

25   See Metzger, 1961–2, 75.

26   Pollard, 1911, 277.

27   Ibid., 278.

28   Ibid., 277.

29   The others are: Romans 9:11; 11:5, 7 (Israel), 28; Colossians 3:12; 1 Thessalonians 1:4; 1 Timothy 5:21 (angels); 2 Timothy 2:10; Titus 1:1.

30   DMH, 1968, 61.

31   *TNT*, 116.

32   *TNT*, 120.

33   See King, 1982, *passim*, and esp. 184–206.

34   The collection is *The Mirror of Majesty* (1612). See Chew, 1962, chapter 2, 'The World of Time'; 18.

35   As in emblem 67 in *The Emblems of Thomas Palmer: Two Hundred Poosees*. Sloane MS 3794, ed. John Manning (New York, 1988), 246 n.

36   I am grateful to Simon McKeown for alerting me to this, and for material on emblems.

37   Foxe, 1877, VIII, 529.

38   Gillian Stickings (priv. comm.) pointed out that the note to Romans 9:15 could be said to be Calvin enlarging Paul: 'As the only will and purpose of God is the chief cause of election and reprobation: so his free mercy in Christ is an inferior cause of salvation, and the hardening of the heart. An inferior cause of damnation.' This was taken over into the 1560 New Testament, as was that to John 6:37, 'God doth regenerate his elect, & causeth them to obey the Gospel.' David Alexander lists another part of the same note: 'faith in Christ Jesus is a sure witness of our election, and therefore of our glorification which is to come.' Alexander also observes John 17:6 in both, where man's election to salvation, in spite of his corruption and iniquity, 'standeth in the good pleasure of God.' The free election of God is noted at Galatians 1:5 and 1 Peter 1:2.

Comments on the Roman Catholic Church are indeed few, and confined to Revelation, which has, apart from simple cross-references and explanatory words on the inside margins, eighty-eight comments in the outside margins, the 'anti-Rome' ones amounting to, at most, six. Thus, to Revelation 2, 'Papists' are listed with 'Anabaptists, Libertines, Arians, &c'. In Romans 12 'Antichrist' is mentioned once, unlocated, as it is in the 'Argument'. Three notes to Revelation 13 mention 'the Romish antichrist . . . devilish doctrine whereby the Romish Antichrist is maintained,' and two more mention 'Antichrist', unlocated, as also in chapter 17. Three references in the rest of Revelation (17:8, 13; 18:13) to 'the Roman empire' suggest 'the whore of Rome'.

CHAPTER 17

1 Westcott, 1905, 93. The page size is 218 mm × 139 mm.

2 The best general account remains the 28 pages of introduction by Lloyd E. Berry to the facsimile of the 1560 Geneva Bible published by the University of Wisconsin Press in 1969. Thorough as he was, Berry remarked how much remained to be done; little has changed since 1969. Lewis Lupton left unfinished at his death in 1995 his twenty-five-volume, lavishly illustrated but curiously produced, *The History of the Geneva Bible* (1968–): though one commends the intention, the title is misleading, as a great deal of pre-Reformation and Reformation English Bible material is described volume by volume, not always accurately.

3 See for example, Pope, 1952.

4 Hammond, 1982, 99, points out that Tyndale's 'aprons' does well for something wrapped around the waist: 'breeches' is a contemporary equivalent for 'something whose primary purpose is to cover the genitalia . . . risking the risibility of the anachronism of Adam and Eve walking around in fig-leaf breeches.'

5 Cameron, 1991, 394–5.

6 Darlow and Moule (1903–11), II, 1, nos 3705 and 3708.

7 Ibid., II, 1, no. 3710, to which the reader is referred for more material.

8 Berry, 1969, 7.

9 Darlow and Moule, 1903–11, vol. II, 1, nos 3711 (New Testament), 3713, 3716 and note, 3718 (New Testament), 3719, 3721, 3722, 3723.

10 The phrase is British Prime Minister Margaret Thatcher's: the parallel of Castellio with Hugh Broughton and his treatment by the exclusive translators producing the 1611 KJV is striking.

11 Darlow and Moule (1903–11), II, 1, no. 3720.

12 Ibid., II, 1, *passim.*

13 John Goldfinch, British Library, priv. comm.

14 See the note at Darlow and Moule (1903–11), II, 3 no. 8468.

15 See, for example, the note to Darlow and Moule (1903–11) II, 2, no. 5592.

16 Berry, 1969, 7. See also Paul Chaix, Alain Dufor and Gustave Moeckli, *Les Livres Imprimés à Genève de 1550 à 1600* (Geneva, 1959).

17 Pollard, 1911, 280.

18 Some evidence from a letter from Miles Coverdale to William Cole: Alexander, 1957, ii, and Mozley, 1953, 316.

19 Hammond, 1982, 89.

20 See Randall T. Davidson, 1881, 436–44.

21 Randall T. Davidson, quoted by Berry, 1969, 19.

22 *Acts and Proceedings of the General Assembly of the Kirk of Scotland*, 1 (Edinburgh, 1840), 443.

23 Richmond Noble, 1935, 90–93. *Othello*, ed. E. A. J. Honigmann (Walton on Thames, 1997), 342–3.

24 Hammond, 1982, 101.

25 Ibid., 106.

26 Ibid., chapters 4 and 5, 89–136.

27 Now in *RSTC* as 2383.6, and DMH as 2331. The Bodleian shelf mark is Arch.A.g.12. See Alexander, 1957, 44.

28 Not in DMH, but *RSTC* as 2384.

29 Contrary to the note by David Norton, 1993, I, 343.

30 Berry, 1969, 10.

31 It is reprinted in Pollard, 1911, 279–83.

32 Patrick Collinson, *The Religion of Protestants* (Oxford, 1982), 236.

33 The 1602 folio edition, for example, has a dozen illustrations in the early chapters of Exodus.

34 See Bottigheimer, 1996, 116ff.

35 Bottigheimer, 1996, *passim.*

36 The phrase is DMH, 61.

37 Alan Sinfield, 'Hamlet's Special Providence', *Shakespeare Survey*, 33, (1980), 89–97.

38 See *RSTC*, 4442 and 18956–62.

39 Alexander, 1957, 171.

40 Rheims NT, 1582, sig. biᵛ.

41 See for the paragraphs that follow Alexander's pioneering study, in chapter VII of his unpublished Oxford University thesis. As access to that work is limited, I summarise in some detail.

42 Alexander, 1957, 172.

43 Ibid., 175 n. 3.

44 I write here independently of David Alexander.

45 Ibid., 145–6. An American Calvinist pastor of my acquaintance refuses on religious grounds to read *Hamlet*, for example, because it is secular.

46 See Harbison, 1956, 142–3.

47 Ibid., 143.

48 Ibid., 137.

49 Calvin's first commentary, 1536. For Barth, see John Webster, *Karl Barth* (2000).

50 Ibid., 156.

51 Ibid., 161–2

52 Ibid., 163.

53 I return here to dependence on David Alexander, 1957.

54 Alexander, 1957, 191–206.

55 Alexander, 1957, 191.

56 R. H. Worth Jr., *Bible Translations: A History through Source Books* (Jefferson, N.C., 1992). In a small-print note 'Breeches Bibles' are mentioned in a collection of 'Singular Renderings': otherwise there is no mention at all.

57 Mary Metzner Tramell and William G. Dawley, *The Reforming Power of the Scriptures* (Boston, Mass.: 1996), 163.

58 The Basle reformer Heinrich Bullinger's *A Hundred Sermons* (Latin, 1557; English, 1561, *RSTC*, 4061, 4062), containing his writing on the Apocalypse, influenced the Geneva exiles, and thus their Bible, and later Elizabethan thought. See K. R. Firth, *The Apocalyptic Tradition in Reformation Britain 1530–1645* (1979), 80; and Bauckham, *Tudor Apocalypse* (1978), 49. The interest in the Apocalypse can be shown by the fact that, counting second editions, there were eighteen published commentaries between 1560 and 1622 (Bauckham, 137).

59 Alexander, 1957, 189–90.

60 Berry, 1969, 11. See Daiches, 1941, 179ff. For their translation methods see Alexander, 1957, 100–75.

61 Hammond, 1982, 137.

62 Berry, 1969; and *The Geneva Bible: The Annotated New Testament, 1602 edition*, ed. by Gerald T. Sheppard (New York, 1989).

63 Tyndale, *Obedience*, 2000, 5.

CHAPTER 18

1 For a general introduction to metrical Psalms, see Henry Alexander Glass, *The Story of the Psalters: A History of the Metrical Versions of Great Britain and America* (1888). For metrical Psalms in English, see Zim and Chamberlin, 1987, 268–84, 344–54. Norton, 2000, 115–39 is particularly clear on the issue of poetic values.

2 See *RSTC*, I, 99–117, for the hundreds of editions up to 1640. The larger figure is based on an estimate of entries in the British Library catalogue.

3 Not in *RSTC*; copy seen in the Henry E. Huntington Library.

4 See Millar Patrick, *Four Centuries of Scottish Psalmody* (Oxford, 1949).

5 *The Poems of Sir Philip Sidney*, ed. William A. Ringler, Jr. (Oxford, 1962), 272.

6 *RSTC*, as n. 1 above.

7 *The History of English Poetry* (1781), III, 172–9.

8 *Specimens of the British Poets; with biographical and critical notices, and an essay on English poetry* (1819), I, 116–17.

9 I confess moments of near insanity when I have spent time trying to match numbered Shakespeare sonnets to Psalms, and then, finding no match (as there cannot be), resorting to the tricks beloved of people trying to find ciphers in Shakespeare, and working backwards, or from the centre outwards, or starting from Shakespeare's (supposed) date of birth, or the defeat of the Armada, or Pearl Harbour, or whatever. That way madness lies, as someone remarked. The celebrated 'proof' that Shakespeare was, after all, 'brought in by King James to add the poetry to his translation', as the persistent American myth has it, is in Psalm 46, where the 46th word from the beginning is 'shake', and the 46th word from the end is 'spear' (but only if you omit 'Selah'). Forty-six is the key, because in 1611 Shakespeare was forty-six, and his birth and death days were (said to be) 23 April, which add up to forty-six, and 'the name "Shakespear" has four vowels and six consonants . . . It follows that, since Shakespeare wrote the Psalms . . .' – what does follow is unexpected – '. . . and Shakespeare was not the real Shakespeare, the Authorized version must show the hidden hand of Francis Bacon.' The quotation is from William F. Friedman and Elizebeth S. Friedman's splendidly sane, and strongly recommended, analysis *The Shakespearean Ciphers examined . . .*

(Cambridge, 1957), 183–4. Those are pages describing even richer looniness; beyond the remarkable prescience in 1611 of the day of his death, and the even more remarkable, nay miraculous, way the Psalm works even in the Great Bible of 1539, 25 years before Shakespeare was born.

10 The *Collected poems of Sir Thomas Wyatt*, ed. Kenneth Muir (1949), 216.

11 *The Poetry of Sir Thomas Wyatt: A Selection and a Study*, by E. M. W. Tilyard (1949), 136.

12 Katherine Duncan-Jones, *Sir Philip Sidney, Courtier Poet* (1991), 277.

13 *Sidney*, ed. Ringler, (1962), 294, 302.

14 Duncan-Jones, *op. cit.*, 287–8.

15 *The Poems of Alexander Pope: A one-volume edition of the Twickenham text*, ed. John Butt (Methuen, 1963), 113.

16 Ibid., 113–14.

17 See Henry Ainsworth, *The Book of Psalmes . . .*, selected, edited and with a Preface by Gordon Jackson (Lincoln, 1999).

CHAPTER 19

1 Six of Latimer's sermons are reprinted in *Hugh Latimer: The Sermons* (Manchester, 2000), and see 35: this famous remark is in Latimer, ed. G. E. Corne, 1844, I, 62 and n.

2 Ibid., x.

3 Foxe, 1877, VII, 550.

4 *RSTC*, 19292: in 1571 Parker oversaw an edition of the Gospels in Anglo-Saxon, parallel with the text of the Bishops' Bible. The Preface is by John Foxe, and includes a sketch of the early work of translating the Scriptures, and the literary work of Bede, King Alfred and others.

5 Pollard, 1911, 287.

6 Pollard, 1911, 295–7.

7 Strype, 1821, 415–7: and see Pollard, 1911, 288–91.

8 Strype, ibid., and Pollard, 1911, 289.

9 Strype, ibid., and Pollard, 1911, 289.

10 TNT, 3.

11 Strype, ibid., and Pollard, 1911, 289–90.

12 Pollard, 1911, 267–8.

13 Ibid., 32.

14 Ibid., 291, 32–3.

15 Ibid., 295–7, 30–31.

16 Ibid., 32.

17 Ibid., 294.

18 Ibid., 293.

19 According to *OED*, 'lurch' as a verb in this secondary, and later sense, means 'To get the start (of a person) so as to prevent him from obtaining a fair share of food, profit, etc.' It was new, and probably colloquial, when Parker wrote. *OED*'s first quotation is from 1530. This from Parker in 1568 is the second.

20 Pollard, 1911, 293–4.

21 Tyndale, *Obedience*, 2000, 157: and 7, 67, 68, 73, 86, 89, 92, 99, 105, 128.

22 Pollard, 1911, 295.

23 Ibid., 295.

24 Ibid., 294.

25 Darlow and Moule (1903–11), V, 70.

26 Strype, 1821, II, 223.

27 Westcott, 1905, 238. Westcott gives fifteen dense pages, 230–44, to the Bishop's Bible. There is useful and balanced analysis of Bishops' Old Testament readings in Partridge, 1973, 86–94.

28 One recalls the thirteen naked ladies surrounding the title to Tyndale, *Obedience*, 2000, 1528.

29 Westcott, 1905, 237.

30 Quoted Partridge, 1973, 88.

31 Hammond, 1982, 141.

32 Ibid., 143.

33 Pollard, 1911, 38.

34 Ibid., 40.

CHAPTER 20

1 *The Parable of the Wicked Mammon* (1528), PS, 42.

2 *RSTC*, 1296.5. There is a useful account of Bale, and of his rescue from centuries of denigration, in King, *English Reformation*, 56–75.

3 R. Pineas, 'William Tyndale's Influence on John Bale's Polemical Use of History', *Archiv für Reformationsgeschichte*, 53, 1962, 79–96.

4 Vividly presented in Spenser's *Faerie Queene*, Book 1, where the Red Cross Knight has difficulty in discriminating between Una and Duessa because of the illusions created by Archimago, the Antichrist figure who is the source of false images.

5 In his widely used *Oxford History of English Literature* volume, *English Literature in*

the Sixteenth century excluding Drama by C. S. Lewis (Oxford, 1954). 'Drab' is the title of the large second section of the book, 157–317, before the 'Golden' period begins with Sidney and Spenser.

6   *RSTC*, 1295.

7   See below, chapter 27.

8   The best account remains that by Irene Backus, in two states: as 'Laurence Tomson (1539–1608) and Elizabethan Puritanism' in *Journal of Ecclesiastical History*, 28 (1977), 17–27; and at greater length in her Appendix, 'Laurence Tomson 1539–1606', to her *The Reformed Roots of the English New Testament* (Pittsburgh, 1980), 173–201.

9   *RSTC*, 17453 to 17465.

10   Anthony à Wood, *Athenae Oxoniensis*, ed. P. Bliss (1895), II, 44.

11   See below, chapter 22.

12   Shaheen, 1999, *passim*.

13   Alexander, 1957, 178, n. 1.

14   *op. cit.*, 171–190.

15   Bale, ?1545, sigsP vii^v–viii^r.

16   See chapter 22, n. 11, below.

17   R. J. Baukham, *Tudor Apocalypse, Sixteenth Century Apocalyptism, Millenarianism and the English Reformation: From John Bale to John Foxe and Thomas Brightman* (Abingdon, 1978), 129–33, 143–6, 175–80; and see Glyn Parry, 'Elect Church or Elect Nation? The Reception of the *Acts and Movements* in *John Foxe: An Historical Perspective* ed. David Loades (Aldershot, 1999), 167–181.

CHAPTER 21

1   See Ceri Sullivan, *Dismembered Retoric: English Recusant Writing 1580–1603* (Madison, 1995), *passim*.

2   *The Tatler*, ed. Donald F. Bond, 3 vols (Oxford, 1987), III.

3   Carleton, 1902, 13.

4   Carleton 1902, 13–18, gives details of the origins and making of the work.

5   Rheims NT, 1582, a ii^v.

6   BL, C.110.d.2, 3–4.

7   Rheims NT, 1582, b iii^r.

8   Ibid., b iii^v.

9   Sketched in Westcott, 1905, 245–55.

10   Carleton, 1902, 20. Westcott, 1905, 254, n. 1.

11   Carleton, 1902, 19, n. 1.

12   See DMH, note to 202.

13   *RSTC*, 17503.

14   *RSTC*, 11430.

15   Carleton, 1902, *passim*.

16   DMH, 202.

17   DMH, 104.

18   Carleton, 1902, 13.

19   Greenslade, 1963, 162.

CHAPTER 22

1   With occasional small variants, as Mark 15:1 from Tomson's 'Deliver Jesus to Galilee' to 1599 'Deliver Jesus to Pilate'; or in the note to John 20:13, from 'Marie spake' to 'Many speak'. My thanks to Gillian Stickings for these.

2   *RSTC*, 7296.

3   Even in the useful work by Kathleen Firth, *The Apocalyptic Tradition in Reformation Britain, 1530–1645* (Oxford, 1979); and *The Apocalypse in English Renaissance Thought and Literature: Patterns, Antecedents and Repercussions*, ed. C. A. Patrides and Joseph Wittreich (Manchester, 1984) where there are two one-word mentions; and Joseph Wittreich's '*Image of that Horror: History, Prophecy and Apocalypse in King Lear* (San Marino, CA, 1984).

4   See the note to Revelation 12:3, where the evil 'great red dragon' has 'seven heads' to 'withstand those seven Churches spoken of, that is, the Catholic Church. . . .'

5   See the notes to 11:1, 14:1, 14:14, 15:1, 16:1 and 16:19 (twice).

6   Duffy, 1997, 97–8.

7   Eamon Duffy (1997) writes: "Gregory IX . . . was committed to stamping out heresy [particularly the Albigensians], and he put the seal on the use of force against error in 1231, when he absorbed into canon law the imperial legislation which decreed the burning of convicted heretics by the secular power. In the same year he instituted the papal Inquisition . . . in the hands of the friars, especially the Dominicans, whose sometimes relentless activities earned them the nickname *Domini canes* – the hounds of the Lord (the pope). The Inquisition . . . was soon active in France, Italy, Germany, the Low Countries and northern Spain, and under its fierce scrutiny

Catharism shrivelled and faded away" (115). Those last five words, with their images of wizened fruit and harmless disappearing, are Duffy's euphemism for the cruel persecution of Cathars under eighteen popes, and the massacre of many thousands of innocent men, women and children – at the very least, 21,000. I am grateful to Michel Roquebert for his clarification of this issue.

8 Duffy, 1997, 119–22.

9 Ibid., 142–4.

10 See Wittreich's essay, 'Image of that horror: The Apocalypse in *King Lear*', in Patrides and Wittreich, *op. cit.*, 174–206; and his expansion of it at book length, *op. cit.*

11 Significantly, it is said that John Bale's modification of millennial ideas at Revelation 20 'became his one significant contribution to the influential notes on Revelation in the Geneva Bible of 1560' (Bauckham, 1978, 218). It is probably a misunderstanding of this remark that has led to the misinformed notion that Bale wrote the Geneva margins.

CHAPTER 23

1 John Keats, 'Ode to a Nightingale', stanza VII.

2 Wordsworth, *The Prelude*, Book III (1805), lines 281–4.

3 Sir Philip Sidney, *An Apology for Poetry* (probably early 1580s), ed. Geoffrey Shepherd (1965), 133.

4 See Hume, 1984, *passim*.

5 Rosamund Tuve, quoted in ibid., 4.

6 Quoted in ibid., 25.

7 *Spenser's Minor Poems* ed. Ernest de Sélincourt (Oxford, 1970), 121, lines 239–40.

8 *Spenser: Selections from the Minor Poems and the Faerie Queene*, chosen and edited by Frank Kermode (Oxford, 1965), 19. This twenty-six-page 'Introduction' is one of the clearest brief accounts of Spenser's mind.

9 Hume, 1984, 105. Spenser quotations are from Spenser's *Faerie Queene*, ed. J. C. Smith, 2 vols (Oxford, 1909).

10 Explicated and challenged by Rosamund Tuve in her *Allegorical Imagery* (Princeton, NJ, 1966), 404.

11 Digby, op. cit., sig. A4. Quoted in Hume, 1984, 183.

12 *The Romance of Sir Beues of Hamtoun* (c. 1300), ed. E. Kölbing, E. E. T. S., Extra Series, xlvi, xlviii, lxv (1885–94), 30. Noted in Hume, 1984, 81 and 190.

13 Hume, 1984, 81.

14 Bale, ?1545 291: quoted in Hume, 1984, 82.

15 See Ronald A. Rebholy, *The Life of Fulke Greville, First Lord Broke* (Oxford, 1921) 75–7.

16 Hume, 1984, 144.

17 Sidney, 1965, 99.

18 The regular revival of an old fashion for maintaining that Shakespeare was a Catholic is based on no external evidence that will stand up. Shakespeare was baptised, married and buried a Protestant, and he lived and worked in a late-Elizabethan and Jacobean cultural world that was overwhelmingly Protestant. To try to draw any facts about his personal beliefs from his poems and plays is not legitimate.

19 See above, Chapter 22, pp. 374–5, and Shaheen, (1999).

20 See *The Arden Shakespeare: Julius Caesar*, ed. David Daniell (1998), 6; and on *Hamlet* see chapter 17, n. 37, above.

21 *The Cambridge Bibliography of English Literature*, ed. F. W. Bateson in five large volumes (1969). The standard reference work, it has three entries under 'Calvin'. Even Francesco Guicciardini, obscure for English literature, has more.

22 Norbrook, 1984, 6.

23 See Betteridge, 1996, 10, 51–79.

24 Kiernan, 1996, 58, 61.

25 Shuger, 1996, 55.

26 Sanders and Davies, 1989, vii.

27 Shuger, 1996, 55–7.

28 Bloom, 1999, xvii.

29 Shuger, 1996, 57.

30 Annabel Patterson, quoted in Shuger, 1996, 57.

31 *TNT*, 116.

32 Bloom, 1999, 3.

CHAPTER 24

1 Barlowe (Boston, 1898), 2.

2 Ibid., 3.

3 Epistle dedicatory to Sir Walter Raleigh

by R. Hakluyt, in *Correspondence of the two Richard Hakluyts* (BL Ac.6172/129), II, Doc 56, p.368 (translation). See Hakluyt, 1935. The seventeen Old Testament occurrences of the phrase begin in Exodus 3, where the Lord promises Moses to bring his people 'out of the hand of the Egyptians . . . unto a good land and a large, unto a land flowing with milk and honey . . .' (v.8).

4 There are scraps of evidence that this is what happened; see Lacey, 1973, 157. For one of many voyages to the wilder shores of speculation, see Lee Miller, *Roanoke: Solving the Mystery of England's Lost Colony* (2000). In this it is claimed that the disappearance of 116 people was the result of a complex conspiracy against Raleigh by the inner circle of Queen Elizabeth's court, in which Burghley, Walsingham, Leicester, Hatton and Essex are suspected.

5 See *RSTC*, 3610. The full title of the book continues: *upon those large and ample countreys extended Northward from the cape of Florida, lying under very temperate Climes, esteemed fertile and rich in Minerals, yet not in the actual possession of any Christian prince, written by M. Edward Haies gentleman and principal actour of the same voyage, who alone continued unto the end, and by Gods speciall assistance returned home with his retinue safe and entire.* In Hakluyt, 1599, 144.

6 *RSTC*, 22265. In Hakluyt, 1599, 34.

7 Hakluyt, 1584, specifies in chapter 21 that 'no man be chosen that is known to be a Papist, for the special inclination they have of favour to the King of Spain'; in the margin, 'A most needful note'. See *Documentary History of the State of Maine. Vol. II containing a Discourse on Western Planting, written in the year 1584 by Richard Hakluyt*, ed. Leonard Wards and Charles Deane (Cambridge, Mass., 1877), p. 167.

8 Hakluyt, 1599, 61.

9 Hakluyt, *op.cit.*, 34. The passage continues '. . . that by our Christian studie and endeauour . . .' as given above.

10 Hakluyt, 1877, 166.

11 Hakluyt, 1599, 91. Like Jackson's Sound, Winter's Furnace is the location of a mine, identified with Newland Island. See *Archeology of the Frobisher Voyages*, ed. William W. Fitzhugh and Jacqueline S. Olin. (Washington D.C.: 1993), 104, 108, 141.

12 Hakluyt, 1877, 13.

13 Ibid., 17.

14 Harry Kelsey begins his study of Drake, 1998, with the 1539 dissolution of the abbey of Tavistock in the time of Francis Drake's grandfather. Kelsey correctly notes 'An entire way of life had come to an end'. He does not observe that in England thereafter almost everyone had a different, and popular, way of religious life, based on the Bible and preaching, which was extraordinarily alive and full of energy. In this Protestantism, with a passionate West Country hatred of Catholicism and Spain, Drake shared. (See also below, n. 46.)

15 Lacey, 1973, 76–7.

16 A brief account of the diversity, richness and destruction of American Indian life is given by Sydney E. Ahlstrom in his *A Religious History of the American People* (New Haven and London, 1972), 100–4.

17 Ahlstrom, 1972, 40.

18 Ibid., 54.

19 Ibid., 56.

20 Garraty, 1998, 11.

21 Brogan, 1990, 8.

22 Morris and Morris, 1996, 3.

23 Any reliable evidence is lacking.

24 Samuel Purchas is specific: 'so called, because it was discovered by the Spaniards on Palm Sunday or as most interpreted Easterday, which they call Pasqua Florida: and not, as Thenet writeth, for the flourishing Verdure thereof': Purchas, 1617, Ch. VII, para 1.

25 Garraty, 1998, 4.

26 Brogan, 1990, 14.

27 Michael Drayton's poem 'You brave heroic minds' ends with praise of Hakluyt's book:

> Thy voyages attend
> Industrious Hackluit,
>   Whose reading shall inflame
>   Men to seek fame
> And much commend
> To after-time thy wit.

Poems, ed. John Buxton (Cambridge, Mass., 1963), I, 123–4.

28 Smith, 1986, III, 272.

29 Nye and Morpurgo, 1955/70, 25.

30 Marston, Chapman and Jonson, *Eastward Ho!* (Manchester, 1979) scene 3, lines 18–42. Wild boar is not found in America.

31   Miller, 1956/64, 111.

32   The storm was the work of 'a greater power than the Spanish monarch, the Caribbean storm-god *Huraca'n . . .*' Barbour, 1969, I, viii.

33   Shakespeare, *The Tempest*, 2.2.38–62.

34   Ibid. 3.2.130–8.

35   William Crashaw, *A Sermon preached in London . . .* (1610) sig. I.2ᵛ

36   Miller, 1956/64, 111.

37   Brogan, 1990, 14.

38   Ibid., 19.

39   Ahlstrom, 1972, 105.

40   Charlotte M. Gradie, 'Spanish Jesuits in Virginia: The Mission That Failed', *The Virginia Magazine of History and Biography*, 96 no. 2, April 1988, 131–56.

41   See James Axtell, 'The Power of Print in the Eastern Woodlands', *The William and Mary Quarterly*, 3rd ser., XLIV no. 2, April 1987, 300–09; and the extract from Drake's *The World Encompass'd* below.

42   Szewczyk, 1989, 71. I am indebted to that book for much in this part of this chapter. See also Lawrence E. Wroth, 'Juan Ortiz, and the Beginnings of Wood Engraving in America' in *The Colophon: A Book-Collectors' Quarterly*, Part 12 (New York, 1932), n.p. Ortiz was a Frenchman working in Mexico as a wood-engraver and maker of metal type. In February 1574 he was tortured by the Inquisition (together with thirty-six Englishmen captured from Sir John Hawkins's fleet) by cord, rack, garotte, and water strangulation, for a heresy of such subtlety that no one else had noticed it: it was contained in four appreciative lines that Ortiz had added at the foot of a print of 'Our Lady of the Rosary'.

43   *RSTC*, 162 67; and Szewczyk, 1989, 60.

44   *The Tempest*, 1.2.167–8.

45   Marvell, 1971, 18.

46   American interest in destroying Drake's reputation goes back at least to the 1920s, especially Henry R. Wagner's *Sir Francis Drake's Voyage Around the World: Its Aims and Achievements* (San Francisco, 1926). Reviewers have pointed out errors and omissions in Kelsey's book: for example, Simon Adams in *The Times Literary Supplement*, 23 October 1988, 20. I find it striking that Kelsey gives unquestioning value to the papers of the Spanish Inquisition (as he correctly states, hitherto ignored) as giving the truth about Drake and his ships. He gives no sense at all that the Inquisition set out to examine their victims with their own reasons to hate Protestants and Drake.

47   See Kelsey, 1998, 16, 29–30, 31, 111.

48   Evidence comes in Kelsey from a Spanish notary of the Inquisition: 'Francis Drake, a firm English protestant. . . .'. Ibid., 22 and 430 n. 43.

49   Kelsey writes of ordinary seamen in Hawkins's ships that 'so firm was their resistance [to the effects of the Reformation] . . . that they usually had to be menaced with a whip and threatened with imprisonment before they would attend religious services' (20). He supports this assertion by reference (p. 429. n.33) to words in two documents from the Spanish Inquisition, the records of the confessions of two captured English seamen. One says that 'a man was sent around with a whip to force men to attend religious services', and the other 'that the punishment for missing religious service was twenty-four hours' imprisonment in the chain locker.' It is curious that Kelsey does not challenge the anti-Protestant bias, nor the fact of single sources, not to mention the possible distortion of information extracted under torture, for which the Inquisition was notorious. In fact, hostile testimony from the Inquisition often suggests that the sailors had an active Protestant faith. For an account of the daily on-board life of Elizabethan seamen, see Cheryl A. Fury, *Tides in the Affairs of Men: the Social History of Elizabethan Seamen, 1580–1603* (Westport, 2002). Her pages 114 to 123 give a detailed picture of the sailors' Protestant religious life: that definitive account disposes of Kelsey's assertion of the necessity of force.

50   Bradford, 1966, 97.

51   Recorded in the examination by the Mexican Inquisition of Gomez Rergifo, captured by Drake on 13 April 1579. See *Sir Francis Drake: An Exhibition to Commemorate Francis Drake's Voyage around the World, 1577–1580, at the British Library* (1977), 43. See also Herbert E. Bolton and Douglas S. Watson, *Drake's Plate of Brass: Evidence of his Visit to California in 1579* (San Francisco, 1937), 5.

52   The complex history of its making is given by a sceptical Kelsey (1998), 177–84.

53 Ibid., 174–91.

54 The story in Hakluyt is in *The third . . .*, 440–2. The memorial was

of our being there, as also of her Maiesties right and title to the same, namely a plate nailed upon a great poste whereuon was ingrauen her Maiesties name, the day and year of our arival there, with a freegiuing up of the Prouince and people into her Maiesties hands, together with her highnes picture and armes, in a piece of sixe pence of current English money under the plate, where under was also written the name of our Generall.

Claims and counter-claims continue to be made for the discovery of this plate: see Bolton and Watson, *op. cit., passim*, and Kelsey, 1998, 188–9 and n. 69.

55 Ernle Bradford wrote, '[Drake] was far in advance of his age in his humanity and compassion. His treatment of Spanish prisoners, his conduct towards Negroes and American Indians and his consideration towards his own sailors mark him as exceptional in his own age, and still worthy of emulation in ours.' Bradford, 1965, Preface. Hakluyt refers to Drake's 'naturall and accustomed humanitie' (v.3, 440–1).

56 *The third . . .*, as given in the 1598 edition. The 1600 edition has 'But we used figures to them of disliking this, and stayed their hands from force, and directed them upwards to the living God, who only they ought to worship', 442.

57 Op.cit, from the 1598 edition. The 1600 has: '. . . yet they could not be long absent from us, but daily frequented our company to the hour of our departure, which departure seemed so grievous unto them, that their joy was turned into sorrow. They entreated us, that being absent we would remember them, and by stealth provided a sacrifice, which we misliked.' 442.

58 Kelsey, 1998, 190.

59 See, for example, Middleton, 1996.

60 Miller, 1956/64, 101.

61 Quoted in Samuel Eliot Morison, *Builders of the Bay Colony* (Oxford, 1930), 42–3.

62 See White, 1971.

63 Brogan, 1990, 35.

64 Even the generally wise Sydney Ahlstrom suggests this, 137.

65 Brogan, 1990, 40. But see Middleton, 1996, 78: 'Traditional accounts have glorified the compact as the beginning of American democracy, but its true intent was the exact opposite: to preserve power and authority in the hands of the few'.

66 Brogan, 1990, 37, n. 13.

67 Ibid., 38.

68 See Thomas Morton, *New English Canaan or New Canaan . . .* (Amsterdam, 1637), Book 3, chap. xiv, 132–3.

69 Ahlstrom, 1972, 139.

70 Quoted in Brogan, 1990, 15.

71 There are schools of both criticism and performance that see Shakespeare's *The Tempest* as drawing on the Elizabethan experience of Ireland: see for example Paul Brown, '"This thing of darkness I acknowledge mine": *The Tempest* and the discourse of colonialism' in *Political Shakespeare: New essays in cultural materialism* ed. Jonathan Dollimore and Alan Sinfield (Manchester, 1985), 55–8. In a BBC Radio 3 production of the play, directed by Sue Wilson, broadcast 10 February 1996, Caliban was a gruff recalcitrant Irish peasant, and Ariel was given to flights of Celtic fancy.

72 Ahlstrom, 1972, 123–34.

73 The Indian commissioner as late as 1872 looked forward to the time when 'the last hostile tribe becomes reduced to the condition of suppliants for charity.' Hugh Brogan, quoting this, adds 'the seal of the Massachusetts Bay Company showed a naked Indian begging for the light of the Gospel in words adapted from the Acts of the Apostles (xvi, 9): "Come over and help us." The Puritans went over and helped themselves.' Brogan, 1990, 67; and see 62–3.

74 Ahlstrom, 1972, 200.

75 Brogan, 1990, 60.

76 The New England town of Lancaster, to take merely one example, had, in 1682, 17–18 families and 100 residents. See Jaffee, 1999, 83.

77 Jehlen and Warner, 1997, 151.

78 David D. Hall, ed., *A History of the Book in America* (Cambridge, 2000), 1.

79 Hall, *op. cit.*, 122.

80 Ibid., 72, 74, 109, 125.

81   Ibid., 66.

82   Ibid.

83   Quoted by Louis B. Wright in Wright, 1943, III. See also Norton, 2000, 150–52, for Donne's eloquence in relation to Scripture.

84   Hakluyt, 1877, 8–9.

85   Ibid.

86   *Select Documents ilustrating the four Voyages of Columbus* (London: The Hakluyt Society, nos LXV and LXX, 1930, 1933), LXV, 18.

87   *A Report.... in Hakluyt's Collection of the Early Voyages, Travels, and Discoveries of the English Nation ...*, new edition (1810), III, 184–5.

88   Gilbert, 1583, sig. S.iii^v.

89   Ibid., sig. C.iv^v.

90   Ibid., sig. F.i^v–ii^r.

91   Ibid., sig. H^r.

92   Hariot, 1931, E4^{r-v}.

93   Miller, 1956/64, 99.

94   Ibid., 101.

95   Smith, 1986, III, 272; quoted above, p. 400.

96   Smith, 1986, 958, 90, 103.

97   Miller, 1956/64, 100. See also Hadfield, 2000.

98   The manuscript disappeared, and was discovered in the library of the Bishop of London. It was published in 1856 by the Massachusetts Historical Society.

99   Bradford, 1968, I, 149.

100   338–9. Bradford, incidentally, in *Plymouth Plantation* (1968) quotes almost entirely from Geneva Bibles.

101   Ibid., 2, 250–51.

102   Hakluyt, 1935, 2, 332.

103   *Journal*, I, 323.

104   Ibid., I. 155–6

105   Ibid., I, 156–8.

106   John Cotton, *God's Promise to his Plantation* (1630), 15.

107   Winthrop, 1929–47, 4, 89–90.

108   Ibid., 126–7.

109   Ibid., 173.

110   Ibid., 264.

111   Ibid., 397–401.

112   Ibid., 405–410.

113   Ibid.

114   Ahlstrom, 1972, 129.

CHAPTER 25

1   Deuteronomy 33:27.

2   John 14:1.

3   Luke 2:8; 24:2.

4   1 Corinthians, 15:21–2.

5   There is an important point here, which one may approach from two sides. It is often said that KJV is 'obscure, confusing, and sometimes even incomprehensible to many younger or poorly educated people' (Carson, 1979, 101–2). Yet on the one hand younger people can often set themselves to learn the great disciplines of medicine or law, where the vocabulary and speech forms are far more thoroughly obscure. The language of theology can be difficult, but not impenetrable. On the other hand, the absolute incomprehensibility of some of KJV's words can be exaggerated. Certainly many verses in the prophetic writings are unintelligible in KJV: that is a result of faulty work, usually in the model, the Bishops' Bible. Yet many odd-sounding words have survived and still lead a vigorous life. This is well shown by Vance, 1999, where such words are explained and, fascinatingly, shown to appear not only in most modern Bible translations (whose justification can be precisely their removal), but also in the most recent newspapers and magazines. (Vance arranges his words alphabetically, and his Table of Contents reads like a good modern poem, 'Ear to Experiment ... Ignominy to Issue ... Napkin to Nurture ... Quarter to Quit ... Unawares to Utter ... Vagabond to Vocation'.)

6   See Appendix, p. 789, below.

7   See the letter from William Eyre to James Ussher in Dublin, 5 December 1608, quoted by Allen, (1969), xvi, 'order taken from the King's Matie, for the work to be finished and printed 'as soon as may be'.

8   The matter is discussed by Pollard, 1911, 58–60. David Norton, 2000, 93, notes Ambrose Usher's referring to 'the authorised Bible' as early as 1620.

9   Erroll F. Rhodes and Liana Lupas, in their edition of Miles Smith, *The Translators to the Reader: The Original Preface of the King James Version of 1611 Revisited* (New York, 1997), 1–2.

10   See note 64 below.

11 See the valuable clarifications by Collinson, 1986, 27–52.

12 Ibid., 44.

13 Reproduced from Pollard, 1911, 46–7.

14 Collinson, 1986, 37.

15 See Goldberg, 1983, 1.

16 Pollard, 1911, 46–7.

17 See below, Appendix, pp. 785–6, for original-spelling transcription.

18 See below, Appendix, p. 786.

19 Greenslade, 1963, 165.

20 Burnett, 1715, Part II. 'A Collection of Records', p. 333 and foll; Pollard, 49.

21 As given in Pollard, 1911, 49–52.

22 See the brief biographies assembled from *DNB* by Pollard, 1911, 49–53; and Bobrick, 2001, 217–37.

23 Pollard, 1911, 53.

24 See Appendix,

25 See *RSTC* 25672–25707.

26 *RSTC*, 170.

27 Bank of England archives: I am grateful to Lucy Davies.

28 Pollard, 1911, 48.

29 Ibid., 48–9. The letters are reprinted 331–4.

30 Ibid., 48.

31 Quoted in Allen, 1977, xii.

32 Appendix, p. 790, below.

33 Allen, 1977, xiv–xvii, xxvii.

34 Given by Pollard, 1911, 53–5.

35 Butterworth, 1941, 212–14.

36 See, first, Allen, 1969, *passim*; and Allen, 1977, (that is, Lambeth MS. 98), xixff.

37 Ibid., lxxxiii.

38 Ibid., xxi.

39 Ibid., xxiv.

40 Ibid., xxv. But see n. 64 below: 'revised readings' certainly; but the base remained Tyndale and Geneva, which exerted the strongest influence.

41 Norton, 1993, II, 50: in the one-volume edition, (2000), 216.

42 But see n. 5 above.

43 Bodleian MS. Don. c. 88, quoted by Allen, 1997, xxvii.

44 Pollard, 1911, 60.

45 Paine, 1959.

46 See n. 37. above; and Allen and Jacobus, 1995: that is, the Gospels notes in the Bodleian Bishops' Bible.

47 Allen, 1977, xxiii.

48 Hammond, 1982, 181.

49 Darlow and Moule, 1903–11, 6163 and 1422.

50 Ibid., 6165.

51 Pollard, 1911, 61.

52 Allen, 1997, xli–xlii.

53 Ibid., lxxx.

54 Ibid., xlviii.

55 Ibid., l.

56 Ibid., lv.

57 Ibid., lxv–lxvi.

58 Ibid., lxxxiii–lxxxiv.

59 See below, Appendix, p. 792.

60 Pollard, 1911, 61.

61 Hooker, 1997, 137.

62 Allen, 1997, xxxiv.

63 Hammond, 1982, 194–5.

64 John Nielson & Royal Skousen, 'How Much of the King James Bible is William Tyndale's?', *Reformation*, 3 (1998), 49–74.

65 *TNT*, 66–7.

66 *TNT*, 296.

CHAPTER 26

1 The definitive account remains Plomer 1990, 353–75. But see also David Mckitterick, *Printing and the Book Trade in Cambridge, 1534–1698*, 2 vols (1992) I, 195–6.

2 Certain kinds of manuscript newsletters – works for private distribution – continued to circulate into the eighteenth century.

3 Latré, 2000, 89–102.

4 Merand Grant Ferguson, 'A Study of English Booktrade Privileges during the Reign of Henry VIII', University of Oxford D. Phil. diss., 2002, 41–5, 62 and notes. She refers to CPR Part I Henry VII p. 2, n. 5, and Edwards and Meale, 1993, 113.

5 Ferguson, 2002, 43–4, 52.

6 Ibid. 48 (Pynson); 147–51, 165, 170–5 (Berthelet); 183–8 (Grafton).

7 DMH, 74.

8 DMH, 69.

9 Plomer, 1909, 353.

10 DMH, 257, 259.

11 Plomer, 1909, 354.

12 See P. M. Handover, *Printing in London from 1476 to Modern Times* (London, 1960), 74. In any case, competition was tightly controlled. Until the end of the eighteenth century, in theory until the Licensing Laws finally expired in 1695, printing of all kinds

was strictly regulated both by the Crown and by the Stationers themselves. It was restricted to London, except for a press each at Oxford, Cambridge and York. The number of printers in the kingdom was to be no more than twenty, with only one journeyman and one apprentice each, except for members of the Stationers' Company's Court, who could have two. In practice, by the end of the century it all became impossible to enforce. I am grateful to Robin Myers, Archivist of the Worshipful Company of Stationers and Newspaper Makers, for help at a number of points in this chapter.

13 McKerrow in DMH p.147.

14 Plomer, 1909, 355.

15 Ibid., 361.

16 Ibid., 362.

17 This and the following quotations from Thomas Osbourne, *The Harleian Miscellany* (1745), III, 277-82.

18 Norton, 2000, 91.

19 Ibid., quoting William Laud, *Works*, 7 vols, (Oxford, 1847-57), IV, 263. Norton, 2000, 89–107, is illuminating on the defeat of Geneva Bibles.

20 William Prynne, *Canterburies Doom* . . . (1646), 109-10, 471, 491, 497, 515. See also Darlow and Moule, 1903–11, I, 171.

21 *DNB*, 'Robert Barker'.

22 Arber, vol. IV, 1877, 35: the tract is reprinted in full in DMH, 182–7.

23 DMH, 167.

24 William M. Baillie, 'Printing Bibles in the Interregnum: *The Case of William Bentley* and *A Short Answer*, Publications of the Bibliographical Society of America, XCI (1997), 65-91.

25 Ibid., 81.

26 Ibid., 82.

27 Norton, 2000, 95. Again, Norton is illuminating on the Commonwealth period, especially attempts at revision of KJV, 94–103.

28 Scrivener, 1884, Appendix A, 147–237.

29 Some two dozen 'curious editions' are listed by Chamberlin, 1991, 12–14.

CHAPTER 27

1 Hill, 1993, vii.

2 Ibid., 34.

3 Ibid., 31.

4 Ibid., 58. As one further example out of many possible, Richard Baxter's reliance on the Bible can be reliably assessed. In Keeble, 1991 (rev. ed. 1994), the Bible makes by far the longest entry, including cited texts right through from Genesis to Revelation, though with the majority from the New Testament. Out of a total of about 150, most (24 entries) are from Revelation.

5 Ibid.; and C. J. Sommerville, 'On the Distribution of Religious and Occult Literature in Seventeenth-Century England', *The Library*, 5th ser., XXIX, (1974).

6 Hill, 1993, 4.

7 See ibid., *passim*, but esp. 72–8.

8 Chapter 30.

9 See King, 1991; and Lewalski, 1979.

10 Some documentation is in Hill, 1993, 338.

11 Hill, 1993, 339, and n. 14. See Lewalski, 2000, 3.

12 *RSTC*, 23810: the Testaments do not have separate entries.

13 See Hill, 1993, 337–49. Biblical verse paraphrases are enumerated in L. B. Wright, *Middle Class Culture in Elizabethan England* (Chapel Hill, 1935), 237–9.

14 Herbert, 1978, 128.

15 Numbers 13:28, 24. Quotations are from Geneva.

16 Ibid., 33, 34.

17 Ibid., 40.

18 John Donne, Elegie XIX, 'To his Mistris going to Bed', esp. l.41 '(Whom their imputed grace will dignifie)', in Donne, 1962, 97.

19 Matthew 5:5 – more unexpectedly, it is the meek, not the poor as is commonly misreported; Matthew 13:31, Mark 4:31, Luke 13:19; Matthew 19:24, Mark 10:25, Luke 18:25.

20 Matthew 7:6.

21 Hill, 1993, 4.

22 Ibid., 188.

23 Ibid., 5.

24 Acts, 17:6. KJV is here better than Geneva. In the previous verse, Geneva's 'vagabonds and wicked fellows' (Tyndale, 'evil men which were vagabonds') is to be preferred to KJV's snobbish 'certain lewd fellows of the baser sort': but Geneva's 'subverted the state of the world', like Tyndale's 'that trouble the world' misses in English the force of particular confusion, in the Greek.

25   Acts 17:1–3, KJV.

26   DMH, 128.

27   DMH, 1089.

28   Westcott, 1905, 252.

29   DMH, 638.

30   DMH, 577.

31   DMH, 830.

32   See DMH, 191.

33   See *Speeches of Oliver Cromwell*, ed. Ivan Roots (1989), 113–67. I am grateful here, and in the following pages, to Dr Ruth Mayers for the use of her unpublished research.

34   Sir Archibald Johnstone of Wariston, *Diary* (Edinburgh, 1911–40), 340–1, 301 and *passim*.

35   Ibid., III, 71, 120.

36   Milton, 1968, 327.

37   Hill, 1993, 421.

38   Vane, 1656, 313.

39   Hill, 1993, 40. While recognising the force of the phrase, Hill points out that 'Habakkuk is not one of the prophets most quoted by Puritans'.

40   Locke, *The Reasonableness of Christianity* (1695), 291–5: Hill, 1993, 426. See Spellman, 1997.

41   Dewhurst, 1963, 204; Hill, 1993, 427.

42   Oakeshott, li. I am grateful to James Stickings for help in these pages.

43   Quoted in George Sampson, *The Concise Cambridge History of English Literature*, (Cambridge, 1941), 391.

44   Hobbes, 1946, 257.

45   Ibid., 73–6.

46   Ibid., 111–13.

47   Ibid., 49.

48   Ibid., 50.

49   James Stickings, priv. comm.

50   Wolfgang Palaver, in *International Hobbes Association Newsletter*, new ser., 10 (November, 1989), 24–31. Herr Palaver calculates that in Hobbes's six major political works there are 1,327 Biblical quotations (Hill, 1993, 20). See also Joshua Mitchell, 'Hobbes: The Dialectic of Renewal and the Politics of Pride' in his *Not by Reason Alone: Religion, History and Identity in Early Modern Political Thoughts* (Chicago, 1993), 46–72.

51   Hobbes, 1946, 259–60.

52   *Certein Bokes of Virgiles Aeneidos turned into English Meter by Henry (Howard) Earle of Surrey* (1557); *RSTC* 24798.

53   *Paradise Lost*, Book 1; 1–3, 16. Quotations are from the edition by Alastair Fowler (1968, 1971). See J. B. Broadbent, *Some Graver Subject: An Essay on 'Paradise Lost'* (1960).

54   1; 3–18. Only 'prefer' is latin.

55   See Williams, 1948, *passim*.

56   Ibid., 4,

57   *Paradise Lost*, Book 7, 243. In *Paradise Regained*, Milton makes Jesus exalt the Scriptures, 'Sion's songs', above the literature and thought of Greece, which Satan recommends (IV, 331–364).

58   Williams, 1948, 114–17.

59   *TOT.*

60   IX:532–41.

61   IV:194–6; II:629–1009; II:1–505.

62   I:44–9.

63   IX:780–5.

64   Milton's 'dearest and best possession', his Bible-based *De Doctrina Christiana*, was unpublishable, even abroad, even in Latin, as 'it shattered the idea of a single Biblical truth acceptable to the rulers of his country.' Hill, *English Revolution*, 6.

65   Roger Sharrock in his edition of *Grace Abounding* (1962), xii–xvii.

66   *RSTC*, 6626–39.

67   For Bunyan in his historical, political, religious and literary setting see Hill, 1988.

68   Hill, 1988, xv–xvii.

69   Bunyan, 1995, 290, 354–5.

70   The comedy of attempts to show some sort of enduring Roman Catholic strain in Bunyan is exemplified by Maurice Hussey finding in the wicket gate in *Pilgrim's Progress* 'evidence of Bunyan's retention of Catholic formulas', a memory of the confessional-box: 'the time Christian spends here can legitimately be interpreted as a reference (perhaps unconscious) to that Catholic sacrament' ('The Humanism of John Bunyan' in *From Donne to Marvell: Volume 3 of The Pelican Guide to English Literature* (Harmondsworth: 1956), 224). Fiddlesticks! That remark could have been written only in ignorance (perhaps unconscious) of the hundred-year-old Dissenting tradition to which Bunyan belonged, and above all of the Bible, of which the incident, like so much in Bunyan, was made (see Matthew 7:7,8; Luke 12:36; Luke 13:24,25 and Ephesians 6:7 among others). Here in unhappily sober statement is what the Catholic

Ronald Knox made into splendid fantasy, showing by spoof 'historical method' the absurd notion that the author of *The Pilgrim's Progress* was a Roman Catholic. It is parallel to his 'proof' by the same methods that the author of *In Memoriam* was really Queen Victoria (both in Ronald Knox, *Essays in Satire*, 1928, 201–22, 223–38). The book also contains his delicious 'Absolute and Abitofhell' (81–90), a parody of Dryden on the vapidness of his Oxford contemporaries in the 1920s:

> When Suave Politeness, tempering bigot Zeal,
> Converted 'I believe' to 'One does feel' (85).

Or

> 'His pregant logic filled their only want,
> Tempering Ezekiel with a dash of Kant (88).

71 *Grace Abounding*, 1962. See, for fuller clarification of Bunyan's rich spiritual and Non-conformist community background, the essays in the excellent *John Bunyan: Conventicle and Parnassus* ed. Keele, 1988.

72 See *Grace Abounding*, ed. R. Sharrock (Oxford, 1962), 127; and n. 138 in Hill, *English Revolution*, 33.

73 Bunyan, 1995, 370–1.

74 Ibid., 54–5.

CHAPTER 28

1 Figures from DMH.

2 Darlow and Moule (1903–11), I, 529, 676.

3 Ibid., II, i., nos 333 and 3777.

4 Dryden, 1961, lines 561–2, 547–50.

5 Dryden, 1961, p. 55, n. 544, where it is simply said that Zimri conspired against Elah, with no explanation of who Elah was or why Zimri was so bloodily dangerous.

6 *The Diary of Samuel Pepys*, ed. Robert Latham and William Matthews (1970), vol. III, 178.

7 Dryden, 1961, 17–26.

8 The phrase is Robert Ireland's: I am indebted to him for providing me with a print-out of this 1679 edition of Caryll.

9 Hannay, 1985.

10 See, for good recent work in this field, essays in Keeble 2001; especially Part Two, 'Radical Voices' 71–123; and Part Three, 'Female Voices', 127–178.

11 By Christopher Hill, particularly *Puritanism and Revolution* (1965); *The World Turned Upside Down* (1972); *Milton and the English Revolution* (1977); *Some Intellectual Consequences of the English Revolution* (1980) and *The Experience of Defeat* (1984). By Geoffrey Nuttall, *Visible Saints: The Congregational Way 1640–1660* (1957); with others, *The Beginnings of Nonconformity* (1964); *Richard Baxter* (1965); *Christianity and Violence* (1972). By N. H. Keeble, particularly *The Literary Culture of Nonconformity in Later Seventeenth-Century England* (1987), in which the Bibliography may stand as a modern introduction.

12 For general publishing figures, see Keeble, 1987, 128–9.

CHAPTER 29

1 See Feather, 1988, 94 and *passim*.

2 Daniel Defoe, *Robinson Crusoe* (Everyman's Library, 1962), 71–2, 84.

3 Quoted in DMH, 246.

4 Ibid., 245–6.

5 Libertarians advocate freedom of the will: Nary's use antedates *OED*'s first record by 69 years. Deists, maintaining religion based only on reason, opposed to the mystery of revelation, will feature in the next chapter. Atheists need no gloss. Pre-Adamites argued for a human race before Adam, the parents of Gentiles, whereas Adam was the source only of the Jews.

6 James Serces, *Popery, an Enemy to Scripture* (1736), 72 and *passim*.

7 Darlow and Moule (1903–11), II, 1. 407.

8 H. Cotton, *Rhemes and Doway* (Oxford, 1855), 47; Pope, 1952, 352ff.

9 'Grume' is a word of the time for a clot of blood, not recorded in *OED* after 1807, when it appeared in lines in the Connecticut poet Joel Barlow's epic about Columbus, *The Columbiad*, Book 5, lines 480–1, 'His blood-stain'd limbs drip carnage as he strides / And taint with gory grume the staggering tides.' A 'Raparee' (properly 'Rapparee') was an Irish bandit: the word had a roughly similar life. Its

later, and rare, application outside Ireland is exemplified by Sir Walter Scott in *The Antiquary* using it for a German.

10   In Greenslade, 1963, 364 – that is all Weigle writes about him in his survey of translations after 1611.

11   Biographical details from *DNB*, and from H. McLachlan, 'An Almost Forgotten Pioneer in New Testament Criticism', *The Hibbert Journal*, XXVII, 1938–9, 617–625.

12   Metzger, 1968, 106.

13   I myself have been publicly reviled for speaking well of Westcott and Hort, the scholarly makers of the pioneering 1881 two-volume *The New Testament in the Original Greek*, not knowing that I could in any way be giving offence to a member of a North American lecture audience in the late 1990s. For her, the *Textus Receptus* was the Word of God.

14   Metzger, 1968, 109.

15   *The Dunciad: Book IV*, 201–2. Bentley loved port, and said of claret, 'It would be Port if it could.' The mock-scholar Martinus Scriblerus noted the obvious, as usual: of this line he wrote, 'now retired into harbour, after the tempests that had long agitated his society' (i.e. Trinity College).

16   Quoted from *Bentleii Critica Sacra* ed. A. A. Ellis (Cambridge, 1862), xv, by Metzger, 110.

17   According to Metzger, 1968, 111–12, they included Pritius, Baumgarten and Masch.

18   Ibid., 112.

19   A personal communication from my late father, minister and New Testament scholar, who had it from a colleague from the West Indies.

20   See Norton, 2000, 197–8, referring to Henry Felton in 1713 and Charles Gildon in 1721.

21   Bruce, 1961, 125.

22   In a fine set of modern studies of Challoner, *Challoner and his Church. A Catholic Bishop in Georgian England* (Cambridge, 1981), there is, rather incredibly, no mention of Bible translation at all. Perhaps it is significant that the volume is edited by Eamon Duffy. For some discussion of Challoner's important Bible work one has to go back to 1909, and E. H. Burton's *The Life and Times of Bishop Challoner (1691–1781)*.

23   Bruce, 1961, 126.

24   Boswell, 1973, 1381; and see Norton, 1993, II, 58.

25   Norton, 1993, II, 40 n. 45.

26   Ibid., II, 32.

27   Ibid., II, 53.

28   Ibid., II, 94.

29   Discussed in ibid., II, chapter 1.

CHAPTER 30

1   Winthrop, 1825–6, 171.

2   Mather, 1702, III, 12, 100, b.

3   Zoltán Haraszti, *The Bay Psalm Book . . . a Facsimile of the first edition of 1640: with a Companion volume, The Enigma of the Bay Psalm Book* (Chicago, 1956), 17, 20–25.

4   Haraszti, *op. cit.*, 33.

5   Ibid., 51–5.

6   Ibid., 38.

7   In Geneva (followed closely by KJV) the verse reads:

Then Hezekiah the King, and the Princes commanded the Levites to praise the Lord with the words of David, and of Asaph the Seer, so they praised with joy, and they bowed themselves, and worshipped.

The Geneva marginal note against 'words' reads: 'With that Psalm whereof mention is made, 1 Chron. 16.8'. That verse comes in the Chronicler's account of the placing of the Ark of the Covenant in the Tabernacle, followed by Asaph the chief Levite's special song, which begins (verse 8) 'Praise the Lord and call upon his name: declare his works among the people.' This is a version of part of Psalm 105, a psalm wholly about, as the Geneva headnote has it,

the singular grace of God, who hath of all the people of the world chosen a peculiar people to himself, and having chosen them, never ceaseth to do them good, even for his promise sake.

The relevance of these Scriptures to the settlers of New Canaan is obvious. The Geneva margin at 1 Chronicles 16:8 comments on 'works': 'Whereof this is the chiefest that he hath chosen himself a Church to call upon his name.'

8 Exodus 20, in which the Ten Commandments are given to Moses, concludes with God's commands to Moses not to make 'gods of silver, nor gods of gold', for the simple 'altar of earth' or unhewn stones.

9 Shakespeare, *A Midsummer Night's Dream*, 3.1.22–4.

10 Quoted in C. S. Nutter and W. F. Tillett, *The Hymns and Hymn Writers of the Church* (New York, 1911), 93.

11 D. L. Sayers, *The Mind of the Maker* (1941), 144; attributed by her to 'some minor eighteenth-century poet, I think.'

12 See, for example, critics quoted in the six volumes of Vickers, 1974–81: note especially the writing of Charlotte Lennox, vol. 4, 110–46.

13 Tyler, 1880, I, 276.

14 The point is made by Haraszti, *op. cit.*

15 See, for this and what immediately follows, Winship 1945, 72–9.

16 Ibid., 34.

17 Ibid., 23.

18 Ainsworth, *Annotations Upon the First Book of Moses . . .* (1616), sig. ★★★.

19 Ibid. See also Ainsworth, *The Book of Psalms: Englished both in Prose and Metre* (Amsterdam, 1612), sig. A.i^iv.

20 *Bay Psalm Book*, Preface.

21 Haraszti, *op. cit.*, 8.

22 Ibid., 10.

23 Ibid., 126, n. 10.

24 Ibid., 128, n. 12.

25 *TNT*, 297.

26 *TNT*, 367.

27 It might be thought that that is the only way to express the Greek. *The Good News Bible* of 1966 (also known as *Today's English Version*) has 'God revealed his secret plan and made it known to me'.

28 Lacking any information, it is assumed that the author was Tate not Brady – or at least 'Tate', a figure of the authors so close as to be indistinguishable. For an excellent commentary on metrical Psalms, see Zim, 1987.

29 See, for wide-ranging discussion, Routley, 1952; and Watson, 1997.

30 Among other parodies, Watts's 'Tis the voice of the sluggard; I heard him complain / "You have wak'd me too soon, I must slumber again"' became in *Alice's Adventures in Wonderland*, 'Tis the voice of the lobster; I

heard him declare / "You have baked me too brown, I must sugar my hair".'

31 See the spirited defence of Watts (who should need no defence) by Davie, 1990, 817–28; and Zim, 1987.

32 Bruce, 1961, 130.

33 The references go far beyond the headnotes to each hymn. To give examples: 'Sometimes a light' echoes a score or so of references to such light in the Psalms, but especially 112:4; 'arise with healing in his wings' is Malachi 4:2, almost the last words in the Old Testament. 'Gorious things . . . is Psalm 87:3; 'Fearful saints' echoes several Psalms, especially 89:7; 'Showers of blessing' is obliquely from Ezekiel 34:26 – and so on.

34 Hagar's 'bottle' is Genesis 21:15; the silent woman faces Jesus.

CHAPTER 31

1 Increase Mather, *Essay for the Recording . . .* (1684), 124.

2 Garraty, 1998, 55.

3 Quoted in *Early American Writing*, ed. Giles Gunn (Harmondsworth, 1994), 260.

4 Ibid., 258.

5 See chapter 30, above, n. 2.

6 See Buell, 1986, 218–24.

7 Gunn, 1994, 266.

8 Ibid., 263.

9 Ahlstrom, 1972, 164.

10 Heimert and Miller, 1967, 37.

11 Miller, 1967, 26.

12 Ibid.

13 Ibid., 27.

14 Quoted in Brogan, 1900, 95.

15 Jonathan Edwards, quoted in Ahlstrom, 1972, 282.

16 Miller, 1967, 61.

17 Ahlstrom, 1972, 284.

18 Ibid., 285.

19 Ibid., 284.

20 Ibid., 287.

21 See Heimert and Miller, 1967, 42–3.

22 Ibid.

23 Ibid., 213.

24 Ibid., lxix.

25 Ahlstrom, 1972, 1090.

26 S. Ward, *A Coal from the Altar* (1615), 57.

27 Miller, 1967, 84.
28 Quoted in ibid., 84.
29 Heimert and Miller, 1967, 257.
30 Ibid., 339.
31 Ibid., 563.

CHAPTER 32

1 Charles Burney, 'Sketch of the Life of Handel', in *An Account of the Musical Performances . . . in Commemoration of Handel* (1785), 27.
2 Burrows, 1991, vii.
3 Ibid., viii.
4 Their music would soon reappear in *Messiah*: 'Nò, di voi non vuo fidarmi' transmuted into the chorus number 12, 'For unto us a child is born', accounting for the unidiomatic word-stress on '*For* . . .'; and 'Quel fior che all'alba ride' became the choruses numbers 7 and 21, 'And he shall purify' and 'His yoke is easy', inappropriate coloraturas and all. See also Hogwood, 1984, 169.
5 The statue is now in the Victoria and Albert Museum, London.
6 Burrows, 1991, 3.
7 Ibid., 13.
8 *Haman and Mordecai* became the never-quite-satisfactorily-finished *Esther*. See Keates, 1985, 84.
9 See Brownell, 1976, 554–570. This is an account of the origins, and the inaccuracy, of the slander: it deserves to be more widely known. A small part of it appears updated and condensed as Appendix A to Brownell's *Alexander Pope and the Arts of Georgian England* (Oxford, 1978).
10 Using the numbering of movements in the Novello edition, ed. Watkins Shaw (vocal score 1959); this adapts Ebenezer Prout's 1902 system, and differs from the Peters and Bärenreiter editions. For clarification, see Burrows, 1991, ix.
11 For details, see my 'Pope's *Dunciad*, Handel's *Messiah*, and Dean Swift', in *The Timeless and the Tem-poral: Writings in honour of John Chalker by friends and colleagues*, ed. Elizabeth Maslen (1993), 134–51. I have here used material from that chapter.
12 See C. H. Kitson, 'Musical "Depreciation"', *Music and Letters*, 12 (April 1931), 184–93.

13 Henry Fielding, *Tom Jones*, Book IV, chapter 5.
14 See Ruth Smith's important studies in Smith, 1989, 161–89; and 1983, 115–33.
15 That is, originally, one of the clergy who would not swear allegiance in 1689 to William and Mary, holding themselves still bound by the oath they had taken to the deposed Catholic king, James II. By mid-eighteenth century, being applied to those who could not accept the legitimacy of the Hanoverian succession, it implied a dilemma for Anglicans, who could not accept, either, the only alternative, the Catholic Stuart heirs. The word signifies not swearing an oath.
16 Alexander Pope, *The Rape of the Lock* (1714), canto 2, line 107.
17 See Landon, 1984, 172–4.
18 I owe this observation to my younger son, Andy Daniell.
19 'From the first, readers of *The New Dunciad* complained of its obscurity.' James Sutherland, ed., *Alexander Pope: The Dunciad*, Twickenham Edition, v (1943), xxxi.
20 See Williams, 1956, chapter vi.
21 See Atkins, 1971–2, 257–78.
22 *The Dunciad Variorum*, 1:243–5.
23 Mack, 1985, 464.
24 *The Dunciad Variorum*, 3:59–60.
25 Quoted by Mack, 1985, 472.
26 Mack, 1985, 464.
27 Ibid., 238–9.
28 Ibid., 733.
29 Swanston, 1990, 93.
30 Ibid., 94–5.
31 Quoted in Hogwood, 1984, 137.
32 Mainwaring, quoted in ibid., 138.
33 Hogwood, 1984, 145.
34 Swanston, 1990, 86.
35 Quoted in ibid., 77.
36 Ibid., 77.
37 Carola Oman, *David Garrick* (1958), 76.
38 George Winchester Stone, Jr. and George M. Kahrl, *David Garrick: A Critical Biography* (Carbondale, IL., 1979), 58.
39 James Boaden, ed., *The Private Correspondence of David Garrick with the Most Celebrated Persons of his Time* (1821), 1.39.
40 Thomas Sheridan, *British Education* (1756); quoted in Robert Manson Myers, *Handel's Messiah: A Touchstone of Taste* (New York, 1948), 100.
41 Burney, 1785, 27.

42 Swanston, 1990, 95.

43 Hogwood, 1984, 176.

44 For a discussion of this, see Swanston, 1990, 106–17.

45 Swanston, 1990, 118.

46 Quoted in Swanston, 1990, 122.

47 That Handel's English Scripture-based oratorios, a form he invented, dominated the choral scene in England and America for many decades, can be seen from the central chapters, IV and V, of Howard E. Smither's *A History of the Oratorio: Volume 3; The Oratorio in the Classical Era* (Chapel Hill and London, 1987).

48 Swanston, 1990, 153: and see 118–54 for a discussion of some theological implications of Handel's later oratorios.

49 See Burrows, 1991, 75–82.

50 Tyndale wrote 'by Adam . . . by Christ', 'and that in a moment', 'at the sound of the last trumpet. For the trumpet shall blow . . .'. Handel's musical cadence 'at the last trumpet' would have pleased Tyndale, and adapts KJV's 'at the last trump'.

51 Thomas Gray, 'Elegy written in a Country Churchyard', stanza 14.

52 Alexander Pope, *The Rape of the Lock*, canto II, 57–62.

53 Quoted in Hogwood, 1984, 177.

54 Herbert Davis, ed., *The Correspondence of Jonathan Swift*, vol. V, (Oxford, 1965), 188.

55 Burrows, 1991, 14–20.

56 Quoted in Landon, 1984, 181.

57 Davis, 1965, V, 87–8.

CHAPTER 33

1 See John Alden, 'The Bible as Printed Word' in Frerichs, 1988, 14.

2 See DMH, 272–3.

3 Robert Dearden, Jr. and Douglas S. Watson, *An original leaf from the Bible of the Revolution and essay concerning it* (San Francisco, 1930), 12.

4 Cmiel, 1990, 50.

5 'The Bible is more 'the word of a demon, than the word of God . . . a history of wickedness that has served to corrupt and brutalize mankind', Paine, ed. Conway, 4 vols, 1894–6, 677; and see Keane, 1995, 389–99. Earlier he had used Scripture to back his arguments against the monarchy, and had

mentioned religion favourably: see Hypatia Bradlaugst Bonner, *Paine's Political Writings . . .* (1909), 15, 19. In the *Epistle to Quakers* he wrote, 'The writer of this is one of those few, who never dishonours religion either by ridiculing or cavilling at any denomination whatsoever. To God and not to man, are all men accountable on the score of religion' (Bonner, 35).

6 Hills, 1968, n.p. [1].

7 See Wright, 1894, 55.

8 Or not: his name does not appear in the index of modern American histories consulted.

9 Wright, 1894, 56.

10 I am grateful to Robert Ireland for this elucidation.

11 As examples, Emerson, Hawthorne and Twain, following Wordsworth, 'Ode on Intimations of Immortality', *passim*.

12 Hills, 1968, n.p. [7].

13 Ibid.

14 Dearden and Watson, *op. cit.*, 21.

15 See Holmgren 'A Pious and laudable Undertaking': The Bible of the Revolution', *American History*, X, 6 (Oct 1975), 12–17.

16 Wright, 1894, 64. Specie is coin as opposed to paper money. The sense is 'real money'.

17 Copy seen in Henry E. Huntington Library. Hills, 1962 (no. 22) gives 'Not Located'.

18 *Journals of the Continental Congress, 1774–1789*, Tuesday, September 6, 1774, 10.00 am.

19 See, for example, 'Good men sometimes differ': World Wide Web, 2000, http://www.reagan.com/.

20 Quoting the Book of Common Prayer.

21 Quoted by Noll, 1982, 40.

22 Ibid., and 53. n. 13.

23 Ibid., 1982, 44. Later writers of fiction make deluded characters find Deuteronomy 28:1–14 'a concise and complete history of the United States . . . from 1607 to 1837' (John D. MacDonald, *Condominium* (1985), 72).

24 See above, p. 540.

25 'The Old Testament is truly so omnipresent in the American culture of 1800 or 1820 that historians have as much difficulty taking cognizance of it as of the air people breathed,' Perry Miller, 'The Garden of Eden and the Deacon's Meadow', *American Heritage*,

December 1955, 54. G. M. Marsden in 'Perry Miller's Rehabilitation of the Puritans: A Critique', in *Church History*, 39 (1970), found that Miller under-estimated Puritan Bible-orientation.

26   *The Works of President Edwards*, ed. E. Williams and E. Parsons, 8 vols (1817), VII, 102.

27   Noll, 1982, 47.

28   Ibid.

29   Morris and Morris, 1996, 94a.

30   Noll, 1982, 48.

31   Ibid., 49.

32   Levine, 1977, 50–51.

33   Noll, 1982, 50.

34   Ibid., 51.

35   Darlow and Moule (1903–11), 11.2, 687.

36   Metzger, 1968, 117.

37   John 14.6.

38   See Gutjahr, 1999, 47.

39   Wright, 1894, 82–3.

40   Quoted in Brogan, 1990, 255.

41   Brogan, 1990, 256.

42   DMH, 1164.

43   There have been recent attempts to bring the writing of that Gospel to a much earlier date, even to within living memory of Christ, on the basis of newly studied papyrus fragments.

44   DMH, 1114; see above, p. 536–7.

45   Note to DMH, 1261.

46   Close-fitting Greek conical cap, resembling that given to a Roman slave on manumission, and used by the French Revolutionists and in the United States as a symbol of liberty.

CHAPTER 34

1   Hitchin, 1999, 67. This essay, pp. 67–92, is valuable.

2   Hitchin, 1999, 92.

3   See ibid., 85–6.

4   Metzger, 1968, 19.

5   See ibid., 120.

6   Harwood, 1773.

7   Metzger, 1968, 116–17.

8   Quoted by Metzger, 1968, 116. n. 3.

9   Boswell, 1963, 333; Lewis, 1950, in *They asked for a Paper* (1962), 44.

10   Harwood, 1773, iii.

11   Ibid., iii–iv.

12   See Loveday Alexander, ' "In Journeyings Often": Voyaging in the Acts of the Apostles and in Greek Romance' in *Luke's Literary Achievement: Collected Essays*, ed. C. M. Tuckett (Sheffield, 1995), 17–49: and R. I. Pervo, *Profit with Delight: The Literary Genre of the Acts of the Apostles* (Philadeplphia, 1987).

13   Harwood, 1773, vii.

14   Ibid., iii.

15   *OED* liberal a.1.

16   *OED* diffusive a.3.

17   Harwood, 1773, iii–iv.

18   Rousseau, *Confessions*, trans. J. M. Cohen (Harmondsworth, 1953), VII, 262.

19   Harwood, 1773, iv.

20   Ibid., iv.

21   Ibid., v.

22   Ibid., v.

23   See Greenslade, 1963, 8–9, and above, p. 293.

24   Darlow and Moule (1903–11), II, i, 389.

25   *La Bible . . .* , Francois Perrin (Geneva, 1563).

26   Greenslade, 1963, 116.

27   Norton, 1993, I, 127n.

28   Ibid., I, 132.

29   See Greenslade, 1963, 83.

30   Which Latin edition Harwood was familiar with we do not know: the fourth, in 1573, has on the NT title-page, and on the last page of the volume, a figure holding a lamp, with the legend *Lucerna pedibus meis verbum tuum*, which is Psalm 119:105.

31   Rheims NT, sig. B1^v.

32   Ibid., sig. B.2^r.

33   Quoted in Norton, 1993, I, 134.

34   Harwood, 1773, vi.

35   Ibid., vi.

36   Ibid., vii.

37   Ibid., vii.

38   Ibid., vii.

39   Ibid., viii.

40   'If there be any affection in human nature, the object and end of which is the good of another, this is itself Benevolence, or the love of another.' 'Sermon on Human Nature', 1726, in *Works*, II, 6.

41   Bruce, 1961, 130.

42   *The Message: The New Testament in Contemporary Language*, Eugene H. Petersen (Colorado Springs, 1993).

43 See David Norton's single-volume revision, *A History of the English Bible as Literature* (2000), 92–104, 242–71.

44 Ibid., 148–9.

45 Ibid., 231–8.

46 For an entertaining and scholarly account of the proceedings see Deelman, 1964. See especially p. 216 for Garrick's words, to musical accompaniment, crowned by the chorus's ecstatic paean to

The lov'd, rever'd, immortal name!
Shakespeare! Shakespeare! Shakespeare!

47 DMH, 1239.

48 See Vishal and Ruth Mangalwadi, 1999, 17–25.

49 Ibid., 134.

50 Steinberg, 1974, 278–9.

51 DMH, 327.

52 DMH, 368.

CHAPTER 35

1 Ahlstrom, 1972, 531.

2 Shea, 1859, 3.

3 Wright, 1894, 70–1.

4 Figures from the Bank of England. In 1770 one Spanish milled dollar was worth four shillings and sevenpence halfpenny. In 1790 what was one pound is in 1999 £51.37. I am grateful to Lucy Davies.

5 See above, pp. 514–15.

6 Hills, 1962, p. 4.

7 Wright, 1894, 69.

8 Extracted from lines 326–480.

9 Thanks to the presence of 'Artaxerxes', 'Ezra' and 'require'.

10 I am grateful to Paul Gutjahr for pointing me to this goldmine – *Mason Locke Weems: Letters*. 3 vols, ed. Emily Ellsworth Ford Skeel (New York, 1929). The quotation here is from 11, 137.

11 Ibid., 139–40. 'Man-Soul' is the city in Bunyan's *Holy War* (1682).

12 Ibid., 143.

13 Ibid., 206.

14 Ibid., 111, 148.

15 Ibid., 251.

16 Ibid., 11. 228.

17 See for example, the entry on Carey in James D. Hart, *The Oxford Companion to American Literature* (1995).

18 Quoted in Middleton, 1996, 394.

19 Jürgen Eichhoff, 'The German Language in America', in *America and the Germans: An Assessment of a Three-hundred-year History*, ed. Frank Trommler and Joseph McVeigh, vol. 1, *Immigration, Language, Ethnicity* (Philadelphia, 1989), 223–40. See also Jürgen Eichhoff, 'Die Deutscher Sprache in Amerika', in Frank Trommler, ed. *Amerika und die Deutschen* (Opladen, 1986), 235–52, esp. 250.

20 Wright, 1894, 324.

21 DMH, 1366.

22 See the quotation in Wright, 1894, 203. It is odd that Wright later remarks of Woodward's venture with 'Scott' that 'it was not a financial success', 324.

23 DMH, 309.

24 This paragraph is heavily dependent on *Jefferson's Extracts from the Gospels: 'The Philosophy of Jesus' and 'The Life and Morals of Jesus'*, ed. Dickinson W. Adams and Ruth W. Lester (Princeton, 1983). See also the references in n. 8 to the Introduction to Hatch and Noll, 1982, 12–13.

25 Adams and Lester, *op. cit.*, 28.

26 Letter to William Short, 13 April, 1820.

27 Adams and Lester, *op. cit.*, 39–41.

28 Quoted by Ahlstrom, 1972, 404.

29 Ibid., 417.

30 Ibid., 414.

31 Ibid., 425.

32 Noll, 'The Image of the United States as a biblical Nation' in Hatch and Noll, 1982, 40.

33 *Annual Reports of the American Bible Society,* vol. 1 (New York, 1838).

34 Gutjahr, 1999, Appendices 2 and 58.

35 Hills, 1962, p. 37.

36 *Annual Reports*, op. cit., 24.

37 Price from Gutjahr, 1999, Appendix 3.

38 ABS, Board of Managers Minutes, 27 March, 1856.

39 For example, Hills, 1962, no. 1450.

40 *First Annual Report of the American and Foreign Bible Society* (1838), 10.

41 William H. Wyckoff and C. A. Buckbee, eds. *Documentary History of the American Bible Union* (New York, 1875–66), vol. 1, 13.

42   See DMH, 1340, 920 and 1577.

43   DMH, 1340.

44   DMH, 195.

45   Figures from Hills, 1962.

46   Quoted in Hills, 1962, p. 112.

47   Ahlstrom, 1972, 433.

48   Ibid. 433.

49   Ibid, 433, 435.

50   Wright, 1894, 117. The story is supported by Schlenther, 1990, 18.

51   Wright, 1894, 113.

52   See, as a start, Darlow and Moule, (1903–11), 11, 603–4, no. 4669. Thomson's manuscripts have survived; see Hills, 1962, p. 27.

53   Schlenther, 1900, 211.

54   Hills, 1962, p. 27: not in DMH.

55   Quoted by Hills, 1962, p. 74.

56   Alexander Campbell, *The Christian System* (1866), 6.

57   Campbell's newspaper, *The Christian Baptist* (1823), vol. 1, 94: quoted by Gutjahr, 1999, 126.

58   See references in Hills, 1962, p. 88 and DMH no. 1759: the 1818 London edition referred to is not in DMH.

59   Webster, *The Holy Bible* . . . (1833), iv.

60   In this and the following paragraph I am indebted to David Norton's 'Noah Webster's 1833 Bible', in *Reformation*, 4 (1999), 197–230, and priv. comm.

61   See Norton, 1993, 11, 242–8.

62   See the note in *OED* after 'occupy' v. 8.

63   Hills, 1962, p. 123.

64   Ibid., p. 169, no doubt quoting a Preface.

65   Webster, 1833, vii.

66   See Hills, 1962, p. 48.

67   Gutjahr, 1999, 83.

68   The shepherds are in Luke 2.

69   Gutjahr, 1999, 93–4.

70   Ibid., 94.

71   Five under '1880' are of uncertain dates: see Hills, 1962, p. 293.

CHAPTER 36

1   DMH, 368.

2   The story is briefly told in DMH, 326–7.

3   Figures from the Bible Society, 2003, and from David Crystal, *Language Death* (Cambridge, 2000), 4.

4   For examples from the first decades, from 1800 to 1833, see DMH nos 1468, 1484, 1505, 1508, 1536, 1566, 1652, 1738, 1765, 1777, 1783 and 1783a, 1784, 1797.

5   DMH, 1914.

6   DMH, 2084. Reissued in 1961 by the Moody Press in Chicago. This translation has received high praise, not least from E. H. Robertson. He had found from years of work in a study group using various translations, that this was 'the most faithful rendering of the Greek in nearly every difficult passage we encountered'; Robertson, 1990, 54.

7   Both quotations from Richard A. Armstrong, 'Charles Darwin: a lecture delivered at Nottingham on 10 December 1882', in *Modern Sermons* (Manchester, 1883), 29, 31–2.

8   Armstrong, *op. cit.*, 24.

9   Matthew Arnold, *Isaiah of Jerusalem in the Authorised English Version with an introduction, corrections and notes* (1883), 2.

10   Arnold, 1873, 311.

11   William Wordsworth, *Poems* (1815), Preface, ed. Stephen Gill (Oxford, 1984) 634.

12   John Dryden, 'A Defence of an Essay of Dramatique Poesie', in *Dryden: Poetry, Prose and Plays*, ed. Douglas Grant (1952), 451.

13   From Blake's annotations surrounding his engravings of 'The Laocoön', in Blake, 1965, 271.

14   It is curious how some English Romanticism seems to take unusual creative energy from almost unbearable loss. The losses of emotional stars in the short life of Keats make an example. In six years of phenomenal artistic growth, Keats lost his mother, his uncle and his brother, and then was forced from his beloved Fanny Brawne, and England.

15   Quoted by Raine, 1970, 8.

16   Preface to *Milton*, in Blake, 1961, 375.

17   I once met a student, the son of a wealthy and famous man, who announced that his favourite poem was Blake's 'The Sick Rose', from *Songs of Experience*. I admired his regard for it, until I found that it was almost the only piece of literature he knew, and that was because it is only thirty-four words long.

18   Gardner, 1954, 123.

19 Blake, 1961, 131.

20 Ibid, 141–2.

21 Kauffmann, 1977, 21.

22 In what follows I am partly dependent on Raine, 1982.

23 Raine, 1982, 13.

24 Ibid, 224.

25 Kauffmann, 1977, 23.

26 Ibid.

27 Lambourne, 1999, 6.

28 Lambourne, 1999, 282.

29 Ibid.

30 David Barrie, in Ruskin, 1987, xli.

31 Lambourne, 1999, 282.

32 Landow, 1979, 2–3.

33 Ibid., 4.

34 Ibid., 6.

35 Ibid.

36 Ibid.

37 Ibid.

38 Ibid.

39 See Finley, 1992, 227–39,

40 Landow, 1979, 9.

41 Ibid., 32.

42 Hunt, 1905, I, 350–1.

43 See Landow, 1979, *passim*; and Richard Glover, 1871.

CHAPTER 37

1 *Chronicle of Convocation 1870*, 74.

2 Ibid., 75.

3 Ibid., 76.

4 Ibid., 82.

5 Ibid., 88.

6 Ibid., 164.

7 Ibid., 165.

8 An account of early seventeenth-century attempts to revise KJV is in Norton, 2000, 94–103. Eighteenth-century calls for revision of KJV and of resistance to them are mentioned in Norton, 2000, 259–62, and in the nineteenth century, mentioning several dozen, in Cadoux, 1940, 235–40. See also Weigle, 1963, 361–82, esp. 368–71.

9 M. M. Black, *Cambridge University Press 1548–1984* (Cambridge, 1984), 147.

10 *Hansard*, 3rd ser., CXLIII (30 June–29 July 1856), 22 July 1856, 1221–6.

11 Cadoux, 1940, 238.

12 C. H. Spurgeon, Preface to H. H. C.

Conant's *History of the English Bible* (1819), x–xi.

13 There was a considerable amount of agreement between this revision and RV.

14 G. Moberly, Preface to *St John's Gospel after the Authorised Version* (1857), ii, iv–viii. The revision was based on the *Textus Receptus*, with occasional changes – forty-six in all, xiii.

15 Bruce, 1961, 136.

16 *Chronicle*, 1870, 361.

17 Ibid., 352. Dr Fraser had clearly been a student of Dickens's Revd Mr Chadband in *Bleak House* (1852–3).

18 *Chronicle*, 1870, 371.

19 *RV* NT, Preface, viii.

20 For Huxley's exact words, as trenchant but more interesting, see Janet Browne, *Charles Darwin: The Power of Place* (2002), 122.

21 Meacham, 1970, 305.

22 Ibid.

23 Reginald W. Wilberforce, *Bishop Wilberforce* (1905), 222. This differs both from the reason apparently given by Gladstone, that Wilberforce refused to work with a 'Socinian', and from Wilberforce's remark in a letter to Gladstone of 22 February 1870: 'I would not give up on translation [?revision] for anything. Nor have I the faintest idea of the Bishop of St David's vision of a fresh, once and for all, version.' Meacham, 1970, 303–4.

24 Westcott, 1905, 321.

25 *Chronicle*, 1870, 78.

26 Ibid.

27 Proceedings in the York Convocation, as reprinted in Vance Smith, *York Letters* (1870), Introductory Statement, 6–8.

28 *Chronicle*, 1870, 562–3.

29 Ibid., 563–4.

30 Ibid., 564.

31 Listed by Newth, 1881, Lecture 9, 113–14. In addition to the 41 C. of E., there were 2 Episcopal Church of Ireland, 1 Episcopal Church of Scotland, 4 Baptists, 3 Congregationalists, 5 Free Church of Scotland, 5 Established Church of Scotland, 1 United Presbyterian, 1 Unitarian and 2 Wesleyan Methodists.

32 *Chronicle*, 1870, 211.

33 Joint author of a revision of the Old Testament, *The Holy Scriptures of the Old Covenant, in a revised translation*, 3 vols (1859–62).

34 Dr Jelf at Convocation Session xxxii, Tuesday 14 February 1871; *Chronicle* 1871, 33.

35 Westcott, 1903, 391.

36 *Sonnets written in the course of the Revision of the Authorised Version of the New Testament A.D. 1870 – A.D. 1880* by Edward Bickersteth D.D. (1881), 23 June 1870.

37 *Chronicle*, 1870, 565.

38 *Chronicle*, 1871, 285.

39 Ibid. It is perhaps worth pointing out that the figures for membership of Nonconformist churches and chapels in 1870 were very high. In many areas in the north, Midlands, west of England, and Wales, the chapels, especially Baptist, Congregationalist and Methodist, were the true centres of the communities, and attendance far outstripped the parish churches.

40 *Chronicle*, 1870, 427.

41 *Chronicle* 1871, 76.

42 Ibid., 189.

43 Ibid., 168.

44 Metzger, 1968, 129.

45 See, for an extended summary, Metzger, 1968, 129–38.

46 Note to DMH, no. 1995.

47 Letter to *The Times*, 5 March 1870.

48 They are listed in Cadoux, 1940, 242–5.

49 Newth, 1881, 120.

50 Norton, 2000, 329.

51 Newth, 1881, 121–2.

52 RV NT Preface, xi.

53 Newth, 1881, 125.

54 Humphry, 1882, xvi.

55 Ibid., xx.

56 Edward Bickersteth, *The Revised Version of the New Testament. A Lecture deleivered in the Chapter House of Lichfield Cathedral on December 30, 1884* (1885), 15.

57 Ellicott, 1901, 32.

58 Bickersteth, *Sonnets*, Christmas 1880.

59 George Moberly, *Charge Delivered to the Clergy and Churchwardens of the Diocese of Salisbury at his Fifth Visitation, held in July and August 1882* (1882), 17–18.

60 Christopher Wordsworth, '*On the Revised Version of the New Testament'. An Address Read at the Lincoln Diocesan Conference (October 21, 1881) by the Bishop of Lincoln* (1881), 6. Bishop Wordsworth had resigned early from the Old Testament company. His passionate

belief in KJV as 'the priceless blessing of a sacred bond of union of eighty million Christians in all parts of the world'(7) is weakened by his adjoining remarks about losing through revision the unity of 'the Anglo-Saxon race'(7).

61 Norton, 2000, 331. His pages on *RV* (327–52), are valuable.

62 Cadoux, 1940, 251; pages 249–54 give a balanced assessment of *The Character of the Achievement*.

63 Weigle, in Greenslade, 1963, 372.

64 Hemphill, 1906, 85.

65 For detailed analysis, see Lightfoot, 1871, 33–194.

66 See Bruce, 1961, 143–4.

67 Bruce, 1961, 142.

68 Ibid., 141. Detailed information on the changes can be found in Westcott, 1897, *passim*, and Lightfoot, 1871.

69 See for example the attack on the RV as 'Apostasy', because of Westcott and Hort, in David W. Cloud, *For Love of the Bible: The Battle for The King James Version and the Received Text from 1800 to Present* (Oak Harbor, WA., 1995), chapter 3.

70 Weigle, in Greenslade, 1963, 372.

71 Westcott, 1897, 4.

72 Details in Westcott, 1897, 328–9.

73 W. J. Heaton, *Should the Revised Version of the Scripture be Further Revised?* (Birmingham, 1905), 1–2.

74 Cadoux, 1940, 257.

75 Ibid., 261.

76 Quoted in Bruce, 1961, 150.

77 Cadoux, 1940, 262.

78 Cadoux gives a useful outline of the controversies, 1940, 259–65. See also Bruce, 1961, 148–52.

79 Norton, 2000, 327.

80 Cadoux, 1940, 266.

CHAPTER 38

1 Figures from Hills, 1962, and DMH.

2 Hills, 1962, nos 1134, 1787.

3 Ibid., *passim*.

4 Gutjahr, 1999, 182.

5 Ibid.

6 Ibid., 182–3.

7 Adapted from Gutjahr, 1999, 1.

8 'Popular Reasons for Studying the Scriptures' in *The Christian Disciple*, VI (1817), 3–6: quoted in Gutjahr, 1999, 1.

9 Gutjahr, 1999, 1.

10 For example, Hirsch, Kett and Trefil, 1988, 1–26; and Bloom, 1987, 56–7.

11 Gutjahr, 1999, 1–2, with reference to Carter, 1993, 11. I know of the disciplining of a Californian teacher for reading to her class, in the third week in December, a sentence from the Christmas story in Luke 2.

12 Hills, 1962, xxvi.

13 Ahlstrom, 1972, 513.

14 Brogan, 1990, 404.

15 Ibid., 404, 416.

16 The point is made by Brogan, 1990, 405.

17 Ahlstrom, 1972, 541.

18 Ahlstrom, 1972, 542.

19 See, for a full account, Lannie and Diethorn, 1968, 44–106.

20 Lannie and Diethorn, 1968, 76.

21 Ibid. 1968, 87.

22 Ibid.

23 Brogan, 1990, 289

24 Ibid., 298.

25 Ibid., 289.

26 'Evangelist' in *Dwight's Journal of Music*, vol. 10, no. 7 (15 November 1856), 51–2: quoted in Burr, 1961, II, 840.

27 In *Atlantic Monthly*, XIX, no. 116 (June 1857), 685–94: Burr, 1961, 840–41.

28 Butcher, 1972, 98–100.

29 Quoted by Butcher, 1972, 100.

30 Ibid., 101.

31 Ibid., 'Skeet' = scoot.

32 Quotations from Thurman, 1947, 26–7, 41, 44. The Bible references are to Revelation 6:13, 9:14, Acts 7:55–6, and elsewhere.

33 Johnson, 1926, 12.

34 See above, chapter 31, p. 550.

35 Johnson, 1926, 18.

36 Brogan, 1990, 296.

37 Charles Elliott, *Sinfulness of American Slavery* . . . (Cincinnati, 1850), 167–243.

38 From *The Interesting Narrative of the Life of Olaudah Equiano, or Gustavas Vassa the African: Written by Himself* (New York, 1791): quoted in *America Through The Eyes of Its People: Primary Sources in American History* (New York, 1997), 36–7.

39 Leonard D. Agate, 'Slavery (Christian)' in *The Encyclopaedia of Religion and Ethics*, ed. James Hastings (1920), XI, 610.

40 Ibid.

41 Agate, *op. cit.*, 611.

42 Ahlstrom, 1972, 635.

43 See Butcher, 1972, 120.

44 Kenneth S. Lynn, introduction to Stowe, 1962, vii.

45 Ibid., viii–ix.

46 Ibid., ix–x.

47 Ibid., xxviii.

48 Ibid., xxviii.

49 Ibid., x.

50 Ibid., xi.

51 Stowe, ibid., 268–9.

52 Ibid., 150.

53 Ibid., 188.

54 Ibid., 357–8.

55 Mary Boykin Chesnut, quoted in Silver, 1964, 54; and quoted in Noll, 1982, 39.

56 Noll, 1982, 42.

57 Ibid., 41–2.

58 Henry A. Nelson, *The Divinely Prepared Ruler, and the Fit End of Treason* (Springfield, IL., 1865), 32: and see Noll, 1982, 42 and 54, n. 28.

59 See above, chapter 31.

60 See Noll, 1982, 44.

61 Joseph Cross, *Camp and Field* (Macon, 1864), quoted in Silver, 1964, 40; and in Noll, 1982, 44.

62 Cited in Bercovitch, 1972, 301; and Noll, 1982, 44.

63 Quoted in Hamilton, 1972, 38–9; and Noll, 1982, 48.

64 Eugene D. Genovese, *Roll, Jordan Roll: The World the Slaves Made* (New York, 1976), 253.

65 Noll, 1982, 50.

66 Ibid., 51.

67 Compare Ahlstrom, 1972, 658, and Brogan, 1990, 314.

68 Both quoted in Brogan, 1990, 318.

69 Ibid., 321, 323.

70 See for example Ahlstrom, 1972, 672.

71 Brogan, 1990, 348.

72 Compagno, 1964, i; I am especially grateful to the American Bible Society for permission to quote from this unpublished MS, and to Dr Liana Lupas of ABS for access to it.

73 David Saville Muzzey, *The United States of America Through the Civil War*, I (New York, 1922), 546–7; quoted in Compagno, 1964, I.

74 Ibid., 3.

75 *First Annual Report* of the CSBS (1863), 31; quoted in Compagno, 1964, 7.

76 Hills, 1962, no. 1763. Wosh, 1994, writes that in 1862 and 1863 the CSBS published 'two editions of the Bible specifically for southern soldiers', 216, though such editions do not appear in Hills.

77 Willoughby, 1944, quoted in Compagno, 1964, 5.

78 Wosh, 1994, 217.

79 Ibid., 217.

80 Campagno, 1964, 6.

81 W. Edwin Hemphill, 'Bibles Through the Blockade', *The Commonwealth* (published by the Virginia Chamber of Commerce), XVI, no. 8, August 1949, 12: quoted by Compagno, 1964, 6.

82 Willoughby, 1994, 29; quoted in Campagno, *op. cit.*, 6.

83 See Compagno, 1964, 7.

84 BFBS *Report* (1864), 248; quoted in Compangno, 1964, 6.

85 Ibid., 8.

86 Ibid., 15.

87 Ibid., 36–8.

88 Wosh, 1994, 201, 212 and *passim*.

89 Quoted in Compagno, 1964, 42.

90 Ibid., 43.

91 Wosh, 1994, 218.

92 Ibid., 224.

93 Letter from Dorothy Lynde Dix, superintendent of women war nurses, quoted in Compagno, 1964, 48.

94 ABS *Record*, 1863, 36–7; quoted in Compagno, 1964, 68.

95 Quoted in Compagno, 1964, 70.

96 Willoughby, 1994, 32; quoted in Compagno, 1964, 103.

97 Tables in Compagno, 1964, 106–16.

98 Wosh, 1994, 216–7.

99 Quoted in Compagno, 1964, 97–8.

100 *American Bible Society Report* (September 1865), 136–8; quoted in Compagno, 1964, 102.

101 For example, those recorded by Hills, 1962, at 1742, or 1929.

102 See Hills, 1962, no. 1618.

103 See Alice L. Birney, *The Literary Lives of Jesus* (New York, 1989).

104 Gutjahr, 1999, 150–51.

105 Birney, *op. cit.*, passim.

106 Quoted in Gutjahr, 1999, 146, from Alexander Campbell, *The Sacred Writings of the Apostles and Evangelists of Jesus Christ Commonly Styled the New Testament*, 2nd edit. (Bethany, VA. 1828), xxxvii.

107 Quoted in Gutjahr, 1999, 147.

108 Ibid.

109 Ibid., 148–51.

110 Ibid., 154.

111 Ibid., 155.

112 Bode, 1949, 146.

113 Gutjahr, 1999, 160–61.

114 Joseph Holt Ingraham, *The Prince of the House of David* (New York. 1855), vi.

115 Ingraham, *op. cit.* 175, 200–02.

116 Ibid., 175–6.

117 Gutjahr, 1999, 163.

118 Ibid., 163–6.

CHAPTER 39

1 See, for example, *Historical Account of the Work of the American Committee of Revision of the Authorized English Version of the Bible. Prepared from the Documents and Correspondence of the Committee*, 1885; and the article there partly quoted from *The Times* (London), 'weekly edition', 20 May 1881, which is remarkably scathing about the US insistence of having an American appendix giving differences from the English RV: '. . . the differences are really of such little moment' that many will wonder 'that the American divines thought it worth while thus to formally record their dissent.' Few Americans agreed.

2 Letter to Bishop Ellicott to Dr Schaff, *Documentary History of the American Committee on Revision. Prepared by order of the Committee for the use of its members* (New York: 1885), 59.

3 Address by Dr Schaff, on behalf of the American Committee, to the British New Testament Committee, in the Jerusalem Chamber, 8 July 1875: *Documentary History*, 90.

4 Op. cit., 91–2.

5 Chambers, 1885, vi

6 Hills, 1962, pp. 331–2.

7 Schaff, 1883, Appendix. Letter from

Professor Mead of Massachusetts to Professor Green of Princeton, quoted in Scaff, 1883, 481.

8   Ibid., 490. The level of humour in the Jerusalem Chamber was not very high.

9   Ibid., note to 491.

10   Ibid., 483–4.

11   A useful list of changes may be found in the Appendix to Hitchcock, 1881.

12   Outlined by Lewis, 1981, 85–96.

13   Ibid., 96–105, esp. 102.

14   Ibid., 104.

15   Weigle, 1950, 99.

16   See *An Introduction to the Revised Standard Version of the Old Testament by Members of the Revision Committee, Luther A. Weigle, Chairman* (1952), 88–92, where the Revision Committees for both Testaments, the Advisory Board, and consultants, are listed.

17   Lewis, 1981, 108.

18   Kerr, 1999, 173.

19   Thuesen, 1999, 152.

20   See Lewis, 1981, 120–27.

21   Weigle recalled that the propounder of an up-to-date reading, defeated in committee, told James Moffatt, who was present and had joined in rejecting it, that he had taken it from *Moffatt's New Testament*. 'Dr Moffatt replied without hesitation: 'That was all right for my translation; but it will not do for this. We are making this translation for use in public worship in the churches.' (*The English New Testament* (1950), 123).

22   Lewis, 1981, 118.

23   The Holy Bible. Revised Standard Version. Containing the Old and New Testaments. Catholic Edition (Walton-on-Thames, 1966), v–vi.

24   Ibid., 254–9.

25   Thuesen, 1999, 152, 199–200.

26   See *The New Testament and Psalms: An Inclusive Version*, ed. Victor Roland Gold et al. (New York, 1995), xii.

27   J. B. Phillips, *Letters to Young Churches: A Translation of the New Testament Epistles* (1947), ix.

28   Phillips, *op. cit.*, x.

29   Phillips, *op. cit.*, ix.

30   Reprinted in *The Bible Translator*, XVI, no. 1. (January 1965), 25–32.

31   Phillips in *TBT*, 26.

32   Phillips in *TBT*, 28.

33   See, for detailed analysis, and bibliography, chapter 6 in Lewis, 1981, 129–64.

34   The subject is well discussed by James Barr, 'After Five years: A Retrospect of Two Major Translations of the Bible, *Heythrop Journal*, 15 (1974), 381–405.

35   See William A. Smalley, 'Phillips and the New English Bible: some comments on style', in *The Bible Translator*, XXI (1970), xxxi. 165–70.

36   Final note, 'Marginal Numbers', to the Introduction. The complete Bible was printed with two columns from 1972, with triple columns in smaller fonts for historical and legal documents, lists of names, genealogies and the like, e.g. Numbers 26–36.

37   Hammond, 1982, 1–2. Hammond is scathing – surely rightly – about the loss there 'of everything which makes the Hebrew so erotically powerful [. . .] in rejecting the alien and introducing the familiar the modern version has ceased to be a translation.' He gives many such examples.

38   The illustrations are not in the 'Introduction'.

39   Philip Larkin, *PN Review*, 13 (1979), 15.

40   Quoted in Nineham, 1965, 96.

41   Hunt, 1970, 27–8: Mr Hunt, on the staff of OUP, was actively involved in the production of NEB.

42   Eliot, in Nineham, 1965, 101.

43   Eliot in Nineham, 1965, 98. The translation was changed for the 1970 complete Bible version to 'How blest are those who know their need of God.'

44   Quoted in Nineham, 1965, 91.

45   Anonymous review in *The Times Educational Supplement*, quoted in Nineham, 1965, 70, 73.

46   Robinson, 1973, 28. Hammond, 1982, *passim*. Lewis, 1981, 129–163.

47   Lewis, 1981, 159.

48   Ibid., 158.

49   Hunt, 1970, 28–9.

50   The phrase is James Stickings's.

51   Hargreaves, 1993, 74. I owe this quotation, and some ideas here, to Dr Hilary Day, her article on the Jerusalem Bibles, and the essay by Dom Henry Wansbrough, 'Editing the Jerusalem Bible', which she commissioned for *The Tyndale Society Journal*, 6 (1997), 34–42.

52 Once again, for details see Lewis, 1981, chapter 8, 199–214.

53 Wansbrough in *Tyndale Society Journal*, 42.

54 *Tyndale Society Journal*, 39.

55 Wansbrough, priv. comm.

56 Chamberlin, 1991, 50.

57 Ibid.

58 NAB, Preface, vi.

59 p.473

60 Lewis, 1981, 294.

61 Ibid.

62 Ibid., 304.

63 Foy E. Wallace, Jr., and D. Evert, both quoted in Lewis, 1981, 328.

64 Lewis, 1981, 263.

65 Ibid., 271.

66 Ibid., 277.

67 Nida and Taber, 1974.

68 Lewis, 1981, 279.

69 Even *The Message* has 'God's finger'.

70 *FQ*, 1.3.3.

71 Lewis, 1981, 268.

72 *REB*, Introduction to the New Testament, iii–iv, and Preface to the whole Bible, viii.

73 *REB*, Preface, viii–ix.

74 Hooker, 1997, 127–42.

75 Figures calculated from Chamberlin.

76 Bible Society leaflet, *Into the Light Bible* (*CEV*).

77 See White, 1995, *passim*.

78 My thanks to the Revd Gregory Patton of Louisville, Kentucky for this list.

79 White, 1995, 6.

80 Quoted in ibid., 96.

81 Ibid., 4, 186.

82 Quoted in Ibid., 49.

83 Ibid., 92. The insults are racy: objecting to an opponent named Stewart Custer, one of the leading 'KJV Only' commandos calls him 'Stewsie-woosie' and 'Stu baby'. An ultimate insult is to call someone '*you Bible-rejecting LIBERAL!!*' (ibid., 111).

84 Ibid., 245–6.

85 An anonymous assertion, given without evidence, quoted by White, ibid., 96, from the back cover of one of the more virulent 'KJV Only' books: there is no indication that this is by the book's author.

86 Thuesen, 1999, 99–102, and esp. chapter 2, 41–66.

87 Ibid., 4.

88 Ibid., 97–9.

89 Ibid., 97.

90 Ibid., 104, on which page is also the diverting story of the Californian radio evangelist who apparently invented as an RSV-supporting opponent 'Professor George Stevenson', who argued that RSV had been prepared so as to be palatable to communists. Though the publishers of RSV, Thomas Nelson, offered a reward of five hundred dollars to anyone who could produce Stevenson, it was never claimed. The radio evangelist died having an adulterous affair with an employee: her husband found them in a motel and shot him dead.

91 White, 1995, v.

92 Thuesen, 1999, 152 and *passim*.

93 From 'Protestantism without Reformation' (1939); quoted in Thuesen, 1999, 67.

94 RSV sold thirty million up to 1974. 'The American Bible Society estimated that in 1969 the KJV still outsold its nearest competitor three-to-one.' Lewis, 1981, 115.

95 At ABS in 1996, the makers of a new version, *The Bible for Today's Family*, were frequently abused by callers for 'destroying the Saint James Bible', which was 'our American heritage', and 'our American Bible' (Dr Liana Lupas at ABS, priv. comm.).

CHAPTER 40

1 I am not making this up.

2 Werrell 2002, abstract; quoted with permission.

3 *TNT*, 156.

APPENDIX

1 ἔξω βέλους.

2 Anacharsis with others.

3 Locri.

4 Cato the elder.

5 Gregory the Diuine.

6 Nauclerus.

7 2 *Sam*. 11. 25.

8 1. *King*. 22. 31.

9 2. *Sam*. 6. 16.

10 σεισάχθειαν.

11 1. *King.* 12. 4.
12 C. Cæsar. Plutarch.
13 Constantine.
14 Aurel. Victor.
15 Theodosius.
16 Zosimus.
17 Iustinian.
18 *Numb.* 32. 14.
19 *Eccles.* 1. 9.
20 *Acts* 7. 51.
21 Αὐτὸς καὶ παῖδες, καὶ παίδων πάντοτε παῖδες.
22 Suidas. ὥσπερ τὶς ἀνδριὰς ἀπερίτρεπτος καὶ ἄκμων ἀνήλατος.
23 1. *Sam.* 2. 30.
24 θεοσέβεια.
25 Eusebius lib. 10. cap. 8.
26 S. August confess. lib. 8 cap. 12.
27 S. August. de utilit. credendi cap. 6.
28 S. Hieronym. ad Demetriad.
29 S. Cyril. 7°. contra Iulianum.
30 Tertul. aduers. Hermo. Tertul de carne Christi.
31 Iustin προτρεπτ. πρὸς ἕλλην. οἷόν τε.
32 S. Basil. περὶ πίστεως. ὑπερηφανίας κατηγορία.
33 Εἰρεσιώνη σῦκα φέρει, καὶ πίονας ἄρτους, καὶ μέλι ἐν κοτύλῃ, καὶ ελαιον, &c. (An oliue bow wrapped about with wooll, wherevpon did hang figs, & bread, and honie in a pot, & oyle.)
34 κοινὸν ἰατρεῖον. S. Basil. in Psal. primum.
35 1. *Cor.* 14.
36 Clem. Alex. 1°. Strom.
37 S. Hieronym. Damaso.
38 Michael, Theophili fil.
39 2. Tom. Concil. ex edit. Petri Crab.
40 Cicero 5°. de finibus.
41 *Gen.* 29, 10.
42 *Ioh.* 4. 11.
43 *Esay* 29. 11.
44 See S. August. lib. 12. contra Faust. c. 32.
45 Epiphan. de mensur. & ponderibus.
46 See S. August 2°. de doctrin. Christian. c. 15°.
47 Nouell. diatax. 146. προφητικῆς ὥσπερ χάριτος τερίλαμψάσης αὐτούς.
48 *Esa.* 31. 3.
49 S. Hieron. de optimo genere interpret.
50 S. Augustin. de doctr. Christ lib. 2. cap

11.
51 S. Hieronym. Marcell. Zosim.
52 2. *King.* 7. 9.
53 S. Hievon. præf. in 4. Euangel.
54 S. Hieron. Sophronio.
55 Six. Sen. lib. 4.
56 Alphon. à Castro lib. 1. ca. 23.
57 S. Chrysost. in Iohan. cap. 1. hom. 1.
58 Theodor. 5. Therapeut.
59 P. Diacon. li. 12.
60 Isidor. in Chron.
61 Goth. Sozom. li. 6. cap. 37.
62 Vaseus in Chron Hispan.
63 Polydor. Virg. 5. histor. Anglorum testatur idem de Aluredo nostro.
64 Auentin. lib. 4. ★Circa annum 900. B. Rhenan. rerum German. lib. 2.
65 Beroald.
66 Thuan.
67 *Psal.* 48. 8.
68 δῶρον ἄδωρον κοὐκ ὀνήσιμον. Sophocles.
69 See the obseruation (set forth by Clemen. his authority) vpon the 4. rule of Pius the 4. his making in the Index, lib. prohib. pag. 15. ver. 5.
70 Tertul. de resur. carnis. *Ioan* 3. 20.
71 S. Iren. 3. lib. cap. 19.
72 *Neh.* 4. 3.
73 S. Hieron. Apolog. aduers. Ruffin.
74 Arist. 2. metaphys. cap. 1.
75 S. Epiphan. loco antè citato.
76 S. Augustin. lib. 19. de ciuit. Dei c. 7.
77 *Iudges* 8. 2.
78 2 *Kings* 13. 18. 19.
79 S. Hieron. in Ezech. cap. 3.
80 *Ierem.* 23. 28.
81 Tertul. ad Martyr. Si tanti vilissimum vitrum, quanti pretiosissimum Margaritum: Hieron. ad Saluin.
82 Horace.
83 *Iames* 3. 2.
84 Plutarch. in Camillo.
85 *Ezrah* 3. 12.
86 Tertul. de præscript. contra hæreses.
87 S. August. 3. de doct. Christ. cap. 30.
88 S. Aug. Epist. 9.
89 S. Aug. lib. Retractat.
90 Video interdum vitia mea, S Aug. Epist. 8.
91 Durand. lib. 5. cap. 2.

92   Horat.
93   Galat. 4. 16.
94   Sixtus Senens.
95   *Heb.* 7. 11. & 8. 7.
96   Sixtus 5. præfat. fixa Biblijs.
97   Naxianzen. εἰς ῥν. ἐπισκ. παρουσ. Idem in Apologet.
98   S. Aug. lib. 11. Confess. cap. 2.
99   S. August. 3. de doctr. c. 3, &c.
100 S. Hieron. ad Suniam & Fretel.
101 S. Hieron. ad Lucinium, Dist. 9 ut veterum.
102 Ioseph. Antiq. lib. 12.
103 S. Hieron. ad Pammac. pro libr. aduers. Iouinian πρωτόπειροι.
104 φιλεῖ γὰρ ὀκνεῖν πράγμ' ἀνὴρ πράσσων μέγα. Sophoc. in Elect.
105 πάντα τὰ ἀναγκαῖα δῆλα. S. Chrysost. in 2. Thess. cap. 2.
106 S. Aug. 2. de doctr. Christ. cap. 9.
107 S. August. li. 8. de Genes. ad liter. cap. 5. ἅπαξ λεγόμενα.
108 S. Aug. 2°. de doctr. Christian. cap. 14.

109 Sixtus. 5. præf. Bibliæ.
110 Plat.in Paulo secundo.
111 ὁμοιοπαθὴς. τρωτός γ' οἱ χρὼς ἐςτί.
112 πολύσημα.
113 *Abed.* Niceph. Calist. lib. 8. cap. 42.
114 S. Hieron. in. 4. Ionæ: See S. Aug. epist: 10.
115 λεπτολογία.
116 ἀδολεσχία.
117 τὸ σπουδάξειν ἐπὶ ὀνόμασι. See Euseb. προπαρασκευ. li. 12. ex Platon.
118 *Gen.* 26. 15.
119 *Ierem.* 2. 13.
120 *Matth.* 8. 34.
121 *Hebr.* 12. 16.
122 Nazianz. περὶ ἁγ. βαπτ. δεινὸν πανήγυριν παρελθεῖν καὶ τηνικαῦτα πραγματείαν ἐπιζητεῖν.
123 S. Chrysost. in epist. ad Rom. Cap. 14. orat. 26. in ἠθικ. ἀμήχανον σφόδρα ἀμήχανον.
124 S. August. ad artic. sibi falsè obiect. Artic. 16.
125 *Heb.* 10. 31.

Chronological List of Bibles in English to Which Reference is Made

The list below is an outline of the principal Bible texts in English discussed in this book. Printed Bibles listed here are a small fraction of the three thousand or so new English versions and fresh editions, for which the standard catalogues are *RSTC* (printed books to 1640), DMH (British Bibles to 1961), Hills, 1962 (American Bibles to 1957) and Chamberlin, 1991 (all Bibles in English to *c.* 1990). Place of publication of printed books is London unless otherwise stated.

c. 657–80   Caedmon's free hymn: parts surviving in a late 9th-century Anglo-Saxon version

c. 698   The Lindisfarne Gospels: Aldred's Anglo-Saxon gloss 946–68

c. 800   The Rushworth Gospels: Farman and Owun gloss into Anglo-Saxon, late 10th century

10th century   Gospels translated into West Saxon

9th to 11th centuries   Lambeth, Royal and Vespasian Psalters (and 11 others) glossed or translated into Anglo-Saxon

?10th century   Proverbs and Ecclesiasticus glossed into Anglo-Saxon

11th century   Aelfric's Anglo-Saxon Heptateuch

Late 10th or early 11th centuries   Judith; Christ I, II and III; Genesis A and B; Daniel; Exodus: Anglo-Saxon poems with some relation to Bible texts

Early 13th century   The *Ormulum*: a poetical version of Gospels and Acts

c. 1250   Genesis and Exodus: a metrical version of parts of the Pentateuch, with many alterations and secular additions

c. 1340   Richard Rolle, Psalter: *The Psalter and Certain Canticles with a Translation in English by Richard Rolle*, ed. H. R. Bramley (Oxford, 1884)

c. 1340   Psalter   *The Earliest Complete English Prose Psalter*, ed. Karl D. Buelbring (1891)

14th century   Psalter: *a Fourteenth Century English Biblical Version*, ed. A. C. Paues (Cambridge, 1904)

1340–50   Translation of the Anglo-Norman Apocalypse

c. 1380   Wyclif Early and Late Versions: *The Holy Bible, containing the Old and New Testaments, with the Apocryphal Books, in the Earliest English Versions made from the Latin Vulgate by John Wycliffe and His Followers*, ed. Josiah Forshall and Frederic Madden, 4 vols (Oxford, 1850)

1388   *The Wycliffe New Testament: An Edition in Modern Spelling* [. . .], ed. W. R. Cooper (2002)

c. 350–1526   *The Gospels: Gothic, Anglo-Saxon, Wycliffe and Tyndale Versions*, with Preface and notes by Joseph Bosworth (4/1907)

1525   William Tyndale, The New Testament (Matthew 1–22) (Cologne); *The Beginning of the New Testament Translated by William Tyndale 1525: Facsimile of the Unique Fragment of the Uncompleted Cologne Edition*, ed. A. W. Pollard (Oxford, 1926)

1526   William Tyndale, *The New Testament as it was written and caused to be written, by them which heard it. To whom also our Saviour Christ Jesus commanded that they should preach it unto all creatures* (Worms): *The Text of the Worms Edition of 1526 in Original Spelling*, ed. W. R. Cooper, with Preface by David Daniell (2000)

1530   William Tyndale, *The First Book of Moses* [The Pentateuch] (Antwerp)

1530   George Joye, *The Psalter of David in English* (Antwerp)

1530   William Tyndale, *The Prophet Jonas* (Antwerp) in *Tyndale's Old Testament: Being the Pentateuch of 1530, Joshua to 2 Chronicles of 1537, and Jonah*, in modern spelling, ed. and with Introduction by David Daniell (New Haven and London, 1992)

1531   George Joye, *The Prophet Isaye* [Isaiah] (Antwerp)

1534   George Joye, *The Proverbs of Solomon [and Ecclesiastes] Newly Translated in English* (Antwerp)

1534   George Joye, *Jeremy the Prophet and Lamentations* (Antwerp)

1534   William Tyndale, *The New Testament, Duly Corrected and Compared* (Antwerp): *Tyndale's New Testament: Translated from the Greek by William Tyndale in 1534*, in modern spelling, ed. and with Introduction by David Daniell (New Haven and London, 1989/1995).

1535   Miles Coverdale, *Biblia. The Bible: that is, the Holy Scripture of the Old and New Testaments, Faithfully Translated into English* (Antwerp): the Coverdale Bible, ed. S. L. Greenslade (1975)

1535   Miles Coverdale, *Ghostly Psalms and Spiritual Songs drawn out of the Holy Scripture*

1537   *The Bible, which is all the Holy Scripture* [. . .] *truly and purely translated into English by Thomas Matthew* (Antwerp): 'Matthew's' Bible

1538   Miles Coverdale, *The New Testament both Latin and English* [. . .] *Faithfully Translated by Miles Coverdale*: 'Coverdale's Diglot'

1538   *The New Testament in English and Latin*: Tyndale and Erasmus Diglot

1539   Richard Taverner, *The Most Sacred Bible* [. . .] *translated into English* [. . .] *by Richard Taverner*

1539   *The Bible in English* [. . .] *Translated* [. . .] *by the Diligent Study of Diverse Excellent Learned Men*: 'Great Bible'

1549   Sir Thomas Wyatt, *Certain Psalms Chosen out of the Psalter of David, called the vii Penitential Psalms, drawn into English Meter*

1549   Thomas Sternhold (with 44 by John Hopkins), *All such Psalms of David* [. . .]

1549   R. Crowley, *The Psalter of David* . . .

c. 1549   Thomas Sternhold, *Certain Psalms chosen out of the Psalter of David, and drawn into English metre*

c. 1550   Sir John Cheke, *The Gospel according to St Matthew, and Part of the First Chapter of [. . .] Mark, Translated into English from the Greek, with Original Notes,* ed. James Godwin (1843)

1557   *The New Testament of Our Lord Jesus Christ. Conferred diligently with the Greek. With the Arguments, [. . .] Diversities of Readings, and most Profitable Annotations of All Hard Places* (Geneva)

1557   The Psalms of David (Geneva)

1559   The Book of Psalms (Geneva)

1560   *The Bible and Holy Scriptures contained in the Old and New Testament. Translated according to the Hebrew and Greek [. . .] With most Profitable Annotations upon All the Hard Places* (Geneva): first Geneva Bible

1562   Thomas Sternhold and John Hopkins and others, *The Whole Book of Psalms, collected into English Metre [. . .]: With Apt Notes to sing them withal*

1567   Thomas Sternhold and John Hopkins, *The Psalms of David in English Meter, with Notes*

1568   *The Holy Bible. Containing the Old Testament and the New* 'Bishops' Bible

1572   *The Holy Bible*: 'Bishops' Bible', second folio edition with corrections by Giles Lawrence

1576   *The New Testament of Our Lord Jesus Christ translated out of Greek by Theodore Beza*: Geneva – Tomson

1579   Thomas Sternhold and John Hopkins, *The Psalms of David in English Meter.* Includes *A Treatise made by Athanasius the Great*

1582   *The New Testament of Jesus Christ, translated faithfully into English, out of the authentical Latin* (Rheims)

1585   Sir Philip Sidney, *The Psalms of David*: in *The Poems of Sir Philip Sidney,* ed. William A. Ringler, Jr. (Oxford, 1962), 270–337; and see 546–52

1599   *The Bible, [. . .] that is [. . .] with [. . .] Annotations*: Geneva-Tomson-Junius

1610   *The Holy Bible Faithfully Translated out of the Authentical Latin. Diligently Conferred with the Hebrew, Greek, and Other Editions in Divers Langauges [. . .] With Arguments [. . .] Annotations [. . .] for Discovery of Corruptions in some Late Translations: and for Clearing Controversies in Religion* (Douai)

1611   *The Holy Bible, containing the Old Testament and the New: Newly Translated out of the Original Tongues: & with the Former Translations diligently Compared and Revised, by his Majesty's Special Commandment. Appointed to be Read in Churches*: KJV

1612   Henry Ainsworth, *The Book of Psalms: Englished both in Prose and Metre* (Amsterdam): selected, ed. and with Preface by Gordon Jackson (Lincoln, 1999)

1613   *The Holy Bible*: KJV 'Great She Bible'

1633   *The Holy Bible* (Edinburgh): first Scottish KJV

1640   *The Whole Book of Psalms faithfully translated into English Metre* (Cambridge, Mass.): The Bay Psalm Book

1642   *The Holy Bible [. . .] With Most Profitable Annotations [. . .] which Notes have never before been set forth with this new translation (Amsterdam)*: first 'Canne's Bible'; KJV with Geneva–Tomson–Junius notes

1643   *The Soldiers Pocket Bible*

1659   Jeremiah Rich, *New Testament in shorthand*

1666   Anon., *Solomon's Proverbs, alphabetically collected [. . .] for help of Memory*

1672   *The Holy Bible [. . .] With Most Profitable Annotations* (Amsterdam): KJV with Geneva notes

1683   New Testament with notes by Samuel Clark

1690   Samuel Clarke, *The Holy Bible [. . .] With Annotations and Parallel Scriptures. To which is Annex'd a Harmony of the Gospels [. . .] And a Table of the Promises in Scripture*: first Bible with Clark's notes

1696   Psalter: Nahum Tate and Nicholas Brady, *A New Version of the Psalms*

1700   *The New Testament [. . .]/Het Niewe Testament* (Amsterdam): parallel texts in English and Dutch

1700   *Le Nouveau Testament [. . .]* The New Testament (Amsterdam): Parallel texts in English and French

1701   *The Holy Bible* (Oxford): first 'Lloyd' Bible

1712   *The Holy Bible*: first 'Baskett' Bible

1710   Alexander Pope, Psalm 91: in *Poems on Several Occasions* (1717); and in *The Poems of Alexander Pope: A One-volume Edition of the Twickenham text*, ed. John Butt (1963), 113–14

1712   *An Exposition of the Prophetical Books of the Old Testament* (with text): First 'Matthew Henry' Bible

1714   *The Holy Bible* (Dublin): first Irish KJV

1719   Cornelius Nary, *The New Testament [. . .] Newly Translated out of the Latin Vulgate and the Original Greek, and Divers Translations in Other Languages Diligently Compared and Revised. Together with Annotations [. . .] and Marginal Notes* (Dublin)

1729   *A New Version of All the Books of the New Testament [. . .] Written Originally in French [. . .] by Order of the King of Prussia*: Matthew's Gospel only

1730   *The New Testament [. . .] According to the Antient Latin Edition [. . .] With Critical Remarks from French translation by Father Simon*

1730   Robert Witham, *Annotations on the New Testament [. . .] by R. W.* (Douai): newly translated from the Vulgate

1731   *The New Testament [. . .] Translated out of the Latin Vulgate by John Wiclif [. . .] about 1378*: first printed Wyclif

1738   *The New Testament [. . .] out of the Authentical Latin* (?Douai): Rheims revised

1729   Daniel Mace, *The New Testament in Greek and English [. . .] from the Authority of the most Authentic Manuscripts*: Diglot

1750   Richard Challoner, *The Holy Bible, translated from the Latin Vulgate [. . .] First Published by the English College at Douai [. . .] Newly Revised and Cor-*

rected, according to the Clementin Edition of the Scriptures. With Annotations for Clearing up the Principal Difficulties of Holy Writ (?Dublin)

1755   John Wesley, *Explanatory Notes on the New Testament With revisions of the text* (i.e. Wesley's Version of the New Testament)

1762   *The Holy Bible* (Cambridge): Paris's 'Cambridge Standard Edition' of KJV

1765   Philip Doddridge, *A New Translation of the New Testament [. . .] Extracted from the Paraphrase of the Late Philip Doddridge, D. D., and Carefully Revised From 'The Family Expositor'*, 1739–56

1768   Edward Harwood, *A Liberal Translation of the New Testament; Being an Attempt to Translate the Sacred Writings with the same Freedom, Spirit, and Elegance, with which Other English Translations from the Greek Classics have lately been executed [. . .] with Select Notes, Critical and Explanatory*

1769   The Holy Bible (Oxford): Blayney's 'Oxford Standard Edition' of KJV

1774   *A Commentary on the Holy Bible: Containing the Whole Sacred Text [. . .] with Notes* (Bristol): notes by Willaim Pine, in 'the smallest type'

1776   *The Holy Bible [. . .] With Most Profitable Annotations [. . .] by the Archbishops, Bishops, etc. etc.*: a reprint of Geneva-Tomson-Junius, 1599

1777   *The New Testament of Our Lord and Saviour Jesus Christ* (Philadelphia): Aitken KJV New Testament; first New Testament printed in America

1778   John Brown, *The Self-Interpreting Bible [. . .] With Explanatory Contents, Parallel Scriptures, Large Notes and Practical Observations* (Edinburgh)

1779   Robert Lowth, Isaiah, *A New Translation, with a Preliminary Dissertation and Notes*

1782   *The Holy Bible, containing the Old Testament and the New* (Philadelphia): Aitken KJV Bible; first complete Bible printed in America

1784   *A Curious Hieroglyphic Bible; Or, Select Passages in the Old and New Testaments, represented with Emblematical Figures*

1789   George Campbell DD, *The Four Gospels, translated from the Greek*

1789   *The New Testament* (New York)

1790   *The Holy Bible* (Philadelphia)

1790   Mathew Carey, *The Holy Bible, translated from the Latin Vulgate [. . .] Doway, Anno 1609. Newly Revised* (Philadelphia)

1791   *The New Testament* (Newburyport, Mass.)

1791   Isaiah Thomas, *The Holy Bible* (Worcester, Mass.): first American folio KJV

1791   Isaac Collins, *The Holy Bible* (Trenton, N.J.): substitutes for the royal Dedication 'Dr John Witherspoon, "To the Reader"'

1792   Revd Thomas Scott, *The Holy Bible [. . .] With Original Notes [. . .] to which are added a Concordance, General Index, and Tables*

1792   *The Holy Bible* (New York): in ruby type

1792   *The Self-Interpreting Bible* (New York)

1795   James Macknight, *A New Literal Translation from the Original Greek, of Apostolic Epistles* (Edinburgh)

1801   *The Holy Bible* (Philadelphia): first Mathew Carey KJV

1804   *The Holy Bible* (Philadelphia): first Mathew Carey KJV in standing type

1804–9   *The Holy Bible* (Philadelphia): first American Scott's Bible

1805   *The Holy Bible, Translated from the Latin Vulgate [. . .] Doway, Anno 1609. Newly Revised* (Mathew Carey, Philadelphia)

1805   *The New Testament* (Cambridge): first stereotyped

1806   *The Holy Bible* (Cambridge): first stereotyped for the BFBS

1807   Samuel Henshall, MA, *The Gothic Gospel of Saint Matthew, from the Codex Argenteus of the Fourth Century, with the Corresponding English, or Saxon, from the Durham Book of the Eighth Century*

1807–8   *The Family Expositor: or, a Paraphrase and Version of the New Testament; with Critical Notes, 6 vols* (Charlestown, Mass.): first American Doddridge

1808   Charles Thomson, *The Holy Bible, Containing the Old and New Covenant [. . .] Translated from the Greek* (Philadelphia)

1808   Newcome, *The New Testament, in an Improved Version, upon the Basis of Archbishop Newcome's New Translation*

1809   *The Holy Bible* (Hartford, Conn.): first 'School Bible'

1812   *The Holy Bible* (Baltimore): in diamond type

1812   *The Holy Bible* (Windsor, Vermont)

1815   *The Holy Bible* (Walpole, New Hampshire)

1816   *The Holy Bible* (Philadelphia): in diamond type

1816   *The English Version of the Polyglott Bible . . .*

1816   *The Holy Bible [. . .] together with the Apocrypha [. . .] J. Holbrook's Stereotype Copy* (Brattleborough, Vermont): first Brattleboro

1818   *The Holy Bible*: 'Third Edition', ABS (New York)

1822   *The Self-Interpreting Bible* (New York)

1823   Abner Kneeland, Η ΚΑΙΝΗ ΔΙΑΘΗΚΗ: *The New Testament in Greek and English*; the Greek according to Griesbach (Philadelphia)

1825   *The Old and New Testaments, having a rich and comprehensive assemblage of half a million parallel and illustrative passages, from those esteemed authors Canne, Browne, Blayney, and Scott* (Philadelphia): first American 'Polyglott' Bible

1826   *The Holy Bible* (New York): first ABS Pocket Bible

1826   Alexander Campbell, *The Sacred Writings of the Apostles and Evangelists of Jesus Christ, Commonly Styled the New Testament* (Buffalo, Virginia)

1833   Noah Webster, LL.D., *The Holy Bible [. . .] In the Common Version. With Amendments of the Language* (New Haven)

1833   Rodolphus Dickinson, *A New and Corrected Version of the New Testament* (Boston)

1836   *The Self-Interpreting Bible* (New York): 'Brown's SPLENDID BIBLE'

1841   Samuel Bagster, *The English Hexapla, exhibiting the Six Important Translations of the New Testament Scriptures*

1842   *The Holy Bible* (Philadelphia): revised by several scholars, including Dr A. C. Kendrick; an 'immersion' version

1843–6   *The Illuminated Bible [. . .] Embellished with Sixteen Hundred Historical Engravings [. . .]* (New York): first Harper's Bible

1850 *The Holy Bible*, ed. Josiah Forshall and Frederic Madden See *c.* 1380 above

1850 *The Commonly Received Version of the New Testament [. . .] With Several Hundred Emendations*, ed. Spencer H. Cone and W. H. Wyckoff (New York and New Orleans): 'immersion' version

1851 James Murdock, DD, *The New Testament, or, The Book of the Holy Gospel of [. . .] Jesus the Messiah: A Literal Translation from the Syriac Peshito Version* (New York)

1852 Woodruff, *An Exposition of the New Testament* (Auburn, NH) in idiomatic English

1857 Five Clergymen, *The Gospel According to St. John [. . .] Newly Compared with the Original Greek and Revised*

1858–61 Leicester Ambrose Sawyer, *The Holy Bible [. . .] Translated and Arranged, with Notes* (Boston)

1864 H. T. Anderson, *The New Testament Translated from the Original Greek* (Cincinnati, OH): an 'immersion' version

1876 Julia Smith, *The Holy Bible [. . .] Translated Literally from the Original Tongues* (Hartford, Conn.)

1877 *The Holy Bible* (New York)

1881 *The New Testament [. . .] Translated out of the Greek: Being the version set forth A.D. 1611 compared with the most ancient authorities and revised A.D. 1881* (Cambridge): *RV*

1883 *Isaiah of Jerusalem in the Authorized English Version*: introduction, corrections and notes by Matthew Arnold

1885 *The Holy Bible [. . .] Revised* (Oxford): *RV*

1895 *The Apocrypha [. . .] Revised A.D. 1894* (Oxford): *RV*

1898 *The Twentieth Century New Testament: A Translation into Modern English, made from the Original Greek* (Chatham and London): Westcott and Hort's text

1901 *The Holy Bible [. . .] Being the Version set forth A.D. 1611 [. . .] Revised A.D. 1881–1885: Newly edited by the American Revision Committee A.D. 1901* ('The American Standard Version') (New York): *ASV*

1901 James Moffatt, *The Historical New Testament [. . .] A New Translation* (Edinburgh)

1903 Richard Francis Weymouth, *The New Testament in Modern Speech: An Idiomatic Translation into Every-day English*, ed. Ernest Hampden-Cook (Frome and London)

1903 Ferrar Fenton, *The Bible in Modern English*

1913 *The New Testament*: second Moffatt

1931 Edgar J, Goodspeed, *The New Testament* (Chicago)

1944 Ronald A. Knox, *The New Testament [. . .] Newly Translated from the Vulgate Latin at the Request of the Lordships, the Archbishops of England and Wales* (London and New York)

1947 J. B. Phillips, *Letters to Young Churches: the Epistles of the New Testament translated into modern English*

1949   Ronald A. Knox, *The Old Testament Newly Translated from the Latin Vulgate: translated at the request of the Cardinal of Westminster*

1949   C. K. Ogden, *The Bible in Basic English* (Cambridge)

1952   J. B. Phillips, *The Gospels in Modern English*

1952   *The Holy Bible. Revised Standard Version [. . .] Being the Version set forth A.D. 1611 [. . .] Revised A.D. 1881–1885. Newly edited by the American Revision Committee A.D. 1901, and revised A.D. 1952* (Toronto, New York and Edinburgh): *RSV*

1955   J. B. Phillips, *The Young Church in Action:* Acts of the Apostles translated into modern English

1955   J. B. Phillips, *The New Testament*

1961   *The New English Bible: The New Testament* (Oxford): *NEBNT*

1962–82   Richard Lattimore, *The New Testament* (New York)

1962–82   Kenneth N. Taylor, *The Living Bible* (Wheaton, Illinois): paraphrase

1965   *Amplified Bible containing the Amplified Old Testament and the Amplified New Testament* (Grand Rapids, MI)

1966   *The Jerusalem Bible* (London and New York): *JB*

1966   *The Revised Standard Version, Catholic Edition* (Walton-on-Thames)

1966   *Today's English Version of the New Testament* (New York) *TEV*

1968   William Barclay, *The New Testament: A New Translation*

1969   Clarence Jordan, *The Cotton Patch Version of Luke and Acts [. . .] A modern Translation with a Southern* [USA] *Accent* (New York)

1969   *The [1560] Geneva Bible: A Facsimile* (Wisconsin): introduction by Lloyd E. Berry

1970   *The New English Bible* (Oxford and Cambridge): *NEB*

1970   *The New American Bible: Translated [. . .] by Members of the Catholic Biblical Association of America* (New York): *NAB*

1971   *King James II Version of the Bible* (Byron Centre, Michigan)

1973   *The Revised Standard Version, Ecumenical Edition* (Glasgow)

1973   *The Translator's New Testament*

1976   *Holy Bible. Today's English Version. Also Good News Bible* (New York): *GNB/TEV*

1978   *The Holy Bible: New International Version* (Grand Rapids, Michigan): *NIV*

1982   *The New King James Bible* (Nashville, Tennessee) *NKJV*

1983   *The Reader's Bible* (Pleasantville, N.Y.)

1985   *The New Jerusalem Bible* (London and New York): *NJB*

1989   *The Geneva Bible: The Annotated New Testament, 1602 Edition* (New York): Facsimile of Geneva-Tomson-Junius, ed. Gerald T. Sheppard

1989   *The Revised English Bible* (Oxford and Cambridge): *REB*

1989   *The New Revised Standard Version: NRSV*

1994   *Holy Bible: Revised Today's English Version. Also Revised Good News Bible* (New York): *RTEV/RGNB*

1990   *The New Revised Standard Version* (New York and Edinburgh): *NRSV*

1993   Eugene H. Peterson, *The Message: The New Testament in Contemporary Language* (Colorado Springs)

1995   Victor Roland Gold et al., eds, *The New Testament and Psalms: An Inclusive Version* (New York)

1995   *The Contemporary English Version* (New York); also as *The Promise* (Nashville, Tennessee): *CEV*

1995   *God's Word of Freedom* (Cleveland, Ohio)

1997   *The Holy Bible: New International Readers' Version* (Grand Rapids, Michigan): *NIRV*

Select Bibliography

Place of publication is London unless otherwise stated.

PRIMARY SOURCES

Aelfric's Prefaces, ed. J. D. Wilcox (Durham, 1996).
Aelfric's Catholic Homilies: The First Series, ed. Peter Clemoes (Oxford, 1997).
Ainsworth, H., *Annotations upon the Five Books of Moses, and the Book of the Psalms* (1622).
Anon, *A Brieff discourse off the Troubles begunne at Franckford Anno Domini 1554*.
Anwykyll, John, *Compendium totius grammaticae* (Oxford, 1483).
Arber, Edward, *Transcript of the Registers of the Stationers' Company*, 5 vols (1887).
Bale, John, *The Image of Both Churches, after the Revelation of St John the Evangelist* (?1545).
——, *Illustrium maioris Britanniae scriptorum [. . .] Summarium* (Ipswich, 1548).
——, *Scriptorum illustrium maioris Brytanniae [. . .] Catalogus* (Basle, 1557–9).
Barbour, Philip L., ed., *The Jamestown Voyages under the First Charter 1606–1609* (Cambridge, 1969).
Barlowe, Arthur, *The First Voyage to Roanoke, 1584* (Boston, 1898).
Bede, the Venerable, *Historia ecclesiastica gentis Anglorum* (c. 731), ed. Bertram Colgrave and R. A. B. Minors as *Bede's Ecclesiastical History of the English People* (Oxford, 1981).
Bedae Opera de Temporibus, ed. Charles W. Jones (Cambridge, Mass., 1943).
Blake, William, *Blake, Poetry and Prose*, ed, David V. Erdman and Harold Bloom (New York, 1965).
——, *Poetry and Prose of William Blake*, ed. Geoffrey Keynes (1927/61).
Boswell, James, *The Ominous Years: 1774–1776*, ed. Charles Ryskamp and Frederick J. Pottle (1963).
——, *Boswell's Life of Johnson*, ed. R. W. Chapman (Oxford, 1973).
Bradford, William, *History of the Plymouth Plantation, 1620–1647* (New York, 1968).
Brereton, John, *A Briefe and True Relation of the Discoverie of the North Part of Virginia* (1602).
Bunyan, John, *The Pilgrim's Progress* (1678–84), ed. Roger Sharrock (Harmondsworth, 1955).
——, *Grace Abounding to the Chief of Sinners* (1666), ed. Roger Sharrock (Oxford, 1962).

Burnet, Gilbert, *The History of the Reformation of the Church of England* (1679, rev. 4/1715).

Cawley, A. C., ed., *The Wakefield Pageants in the Towneley Cycle* (Manchester, 1958).

Caxton, William, [continuation of] R. Higden, *The Description of Britain* (1480).

——, *The Chronicles of England* (1480).

Chaucer, Geoffrey, *The Complete Works*, ed. Larry D. Benson (Boston, 3/1987) (*Riverside Chaucer*).

Chronicle of Convocation 1870, 1871.

Chronicle of Convocation 1871.

Documentary History of the American Bible Union, ed. William H. Wyckoff and C. A. Buckbee (New York, 1875–86).

Documentary History of the American Committee on Revision: Prepared by Order of the Committee for the Use of Its Members (New York, 1885).

Donne, John, *Complete Poetry and Selected Prose*, ed. John Hayward (1962).

Dryden, John, *Absalom and Achitophel* (1681), ed. James Kinsley and Helen Kinsley (Oxford, 1961).

——, *Dryden: Poetry, Prose and Plays*, ed. Douglas Grant (1952).

Early American Writing, ed. Giles Gunn (1994).

Emden, A. B., ed., *A Bibliographical Register of the University of Oxford to A.D. 1500*, 3 vols (Oxford, 1957–9).

Erasmus, Desiderius, *The First Tome or Volume of the Paraphrase of Erasmus upon the New Testament* (1548).

——, *The Second Tome* (1549).

Foxe, John, *The Acts and Monuments* (1563).

——, *The Acts and Monuments* (1570).

——, *The Acts and Monuments of John Foxe* (1563–76), ed., rev. and corrected J. Pratt, with introduction by J. Stoughton, 8 vols (4/1877).

Gilbert, Sir Humphrey, *A True Report . . . M. Haies* (1583).

Hakluyt, R., *The Writings and Correspondence of the Two Richard Hakluyts*, ed. Eva G. R. Taylor, 2 vols (Cambridge, 1935).

——, *The Third and Last Volume of the Voyages, Navigations, Traffiques and Discoveries of the English Nation* (1599).

——, *A Particular Discourse Concerning the Great Necessity and Manifold Commodities that are like to grow to the Realm of England by the Western Discoveries lately Attempted* (1584), ed. Leonard Woods and Charles Deane as *The Discourse on the Western Planting* (Cambridge, Mass., 1877).

Hakluyt's Collection of the early Voyages . . . ed. R. H. Evans, III (1810), 184–5.

Hariot, Thomas, *A Brief and True Report of the New Land of Virginia, 1588: A Facsimile Reproduction of the 1588 Quarto*, with introductory essay by Randolph G. Adams (Ann Arbor, 1931).

Harwood, Edward, *A New Introduction to the Study and Knowledge of the New Testament*, 2 vols (1767, 2/1773).

Herbert, George, *The Works of George Herbert*, ed. F. E. Hutchinson (Oxford, 1978).

Historical Account of the Work of the American Committee of Revision of the Authorized English Version of the Bible: Prepared from the Documents and Correspondence of the Committee (New York, 1885).

Hobbes, Thomas, *Leviathan, or the Matter, Form and Power of a Commonwealth Ecclesiastical and Civil* (1651), ed. Michael Oakeshott (Oxford, 1946).

Holinshed, Raphael, *The Firste (Laste) volume of the Chronicles of England, Scotlande, Irelande, etc.* 3 vols (1597).

Horman, William, *Vulgaria*, ed. M. R. James (Oxford, 1926).

Jefferson, Thomas, *Jefferson's Extracts from the Gospels: 'The Philosophy of Jesus' and 'The Life and Morals of Jesus'*, ed. Dickinson W. Adams and Ruth W. Lester (Princeton, 1983).

Joye, George, *An Apology made by George Joye to satisfy if it may be W. Tyndale* (1535), ed. Edward Arber (Birmingham, 1882).

Latimer, Hugh, *The Sermons of Hugh Latimer*, ed. G. E. Corrie (Cambridge, 1844).

Letters and Papers, Foreign and Domestic, of the Reign of Henry VIII, ed. J. S. Brewer, J. Gairdner, R. H. Brodie et al., 21 vols (1862–1932).

Marvell, Andrew, *Poems and Letters*, ed. H. M. Margoliouth, rev. Pierre Legouis (Oxford, 3/1971).

Mather, Cotton, *Magnalia Christi Americana: Or, the Ecclesiastical History of New-England, from the first in the year 1620, unto the year of Our Lord 1698*, 7 vols (1702).

Milton, John, *Complete Shorter Poems*, ed. John Carey (1968).

——, *Paradise Lost*, ed. Alastair Fowler (1968).

More, Thomas, *The Complete Works of St Thomas More* (New Haven and London, 1964–).

Paine, Thomas, *Collected Works*, ed. M. D. Conway, 4 vols (New York, 1894–6).

Pollard, Alfred W., ed., *Records of the English Bible [. . .] 1525–1611* (Oxford, 1911).

Pope, Alexander, *The Poems of Alexander Pope: A One-Volume Edition of the Twickenham Text*, ed. John Butt (1963).

Purchas, S., *S Purchas, His Pilgrimage* (1617).

Robbins, Russell Hope, ed., *Secular Lyrics of the XlVth and XVth Centuries* (Oxford, 1952).

Ruskin, John, *Modern Painters*, ed. and abridged David Barrie (1987).

Sidney, Philip, *The Poems of Sir Philip Sidney*, ed. William A. Ringler, Jr. (Oxford, 1962).

——, *An Apology for Poetry*, ed. Geoffrey Shepherd (1965).

Smith, John, *A True Relation of such occurrences and accidents of note, as hath hapned in Virginia, since the first planting of that colony*, in *The Complete Works of Captain John Smith*, ed. Philip L. Barbour, 3 vols (Chapel Hill and London, 1986), III.

Smith, Miles, *The Translators to the Reader: The Original Preface of the King James Version of 1611 Revisited*, ed. Erroll F. Rhodes and Liana Lupas (New York, 1997).

Spenser, Edmund, *Selections from the Minor Poems and the Faerie Queene*, ed. Frank Kermode (Oxford, 1965).

State Papers Domestic of the Reign of Henry VIII, 11 vols (1830–52).

Stowe, Harriet Beecher, *Uncle Tom's Cabin: Or, Life among the Lowly*, ed. Kenneth S. Lynn (Cambridge, Mass., 1962).

Strype, J., *Ecclesiastical Memorials: Relating chiefly to Religion, and the Reformation of it. And the Emergencies of the Church of England, under King Henry VIII, King Edward VI, and Queen Mary*, 3 vols (1721).

Swynnerton, Thomas, *A Reformation Rhetoric: Thomas Swynnerton's 'The Tropes and Figures of Scripture'*, ed. Richard Rex (Cambridge, 1999).

Tudor Royal Proclamations, ed. Paul Hughes and James F. Larkin, 3 vols (New Haven and London, 1964–9).

Tyndale, William, *The Obedience of a Christian Man* (Antwerp, 1528), ed. with Introduction by David Daniell (2000).

——, *The Parable of the Wicked Mammon* (Antwerp, 1528), in *Doctrinal Treatises [. . .] by William Tyndale*, ed. Henry Walter (Cambridge, 1848).

——, *The Practice of Prelates* (Antwerp, 1530), ed. Henry Walter (Cambridge, 1849).

——, *An Answer vnto Sir Thomas Mores Dialogue* (Antwerp, 1531), ed. Anne M. O'Donnell, S. N. D., and Jared Wicks, S. J. (Washington, DC, 2000).

——, *An Exposition upon the V, VI, VII Chapters of Matthew* (Antwerp, 1533), ed. Henry Walter (Cambridge, 1849).

Vane, Sir Henry, the Younger, *The Healing Question* (1656).

The Vulgaria of John Stanbridge and the Vulgaria of Robert Whittinton, ed. Beatrice White (Oxford, 1932).

Weems, Mason Locke, *Letters*, ed. Emily Ellsworth Ford Skeel, 3 vols (Published privately, New York, 1929).

Winthrop, John, *A Journal, 1630–1644 . . .* (Hartford, Conn., 1790).

——, *The History of New England*, ed. James Savage (Boston, 1825–6).

——, *Winthrop Papers*, ed. A. B. Forbes, 5 vols (Boston, 1929–47).

Wyatt, Thomas, *The Collected Poems of Sir Thomas Wyatt*, ed. Kenneth Muir (1949).

Wyclif, John, *On Simony*, trans. and ed. Terrence A. McVeigh (New York, 1992).

SECONDARY SOURCES

Aers, David, 'Altars of Power: Reflections on Eamon Duffy's *The Stripping of the Altars: Traditional Religion in England 1400–1589*, in *Literature and History*, 3rd ser., III/2 (1994), 90–105.

Ahlstrom, Sidney E., *A Religious History of the American People* (New Haven and London, 1972).

Alexander, J. D., 'The Genevan Version of the Bible: Its Origin, Translation and Influence' (D. Phil. dissertation, University of Oxford, 1957; Bodleian MS.D.Phil.d.1810).

Allen, Ward, *Translating for King James: Notes Made by a Translator of King James's Bible* (Nashville, Tennessee, 1969).

——, *Translating the New Testament Epistles 1604–1611: A Manuscript from King James's Westminster Company* [Lambeth MS 98] (Nashville, Tennessee, 1977).

——, and Edward C. Jacobus, *The Coming of the King James Gospels: A Collation of the Translators' Work-in-Progress* (Fayetteville, 1995).

Alter, Robert, and Frank Kermode, eds, *The Literary Guide to the Bible* (1987).

Amory, Hugh, and David H. Hall, *The Colonial Book in the Atlantic World: The History of the Book In America* (Cambridge, 2000).

Anderson, Christopher, *Annals of the English Bible*, 2 vols (1845).

Arblaster, Paul, Gergely Juhász and Guido Latré, *Tyndale's Testament* (Turnhout, 2002).

Arnold, Matthew, *Literature and Dogma: An Essay towards a Better Apprehension of the Bible* (1873).

Aston, Margaret, *England's Iconoclasts*, I: *Laws against Images* (Oxford, 1988).

——, *The King's Bedpost: Reformation Iconography and a Tudor Group Portrait* (Cambridge, 1993).

Atkins, G. Douglas, 'Pope and Deism: A New Analysis', *Huntington Library Quarterly*, XXXV (1971–2), 257–78.

Auerbach, Erich, *Mimesis: The Representation of Reality in Western Literature*, trans. Willard R. Trask (Princeton, 1953/74).

Auksi, Peter, *Christian Plain Style: The Evolution of a Spiritual Ideal* (Montreal, 1995).

Backus, Irene, 'Laurence Tomson (1539–1608) and Elizabethan Puritanism', *Journal of Ecclesiastical History*, XXVIII (1977), 17–27.

——, *The Reformed Roots of the English New Testament* (Pittsburgh, 1980).

Bailey, Richard N., in Ford, ed., 1988, I, 100–12.

Barr, James, 'After Five Years: A Retrospect of Two Major Translations of the Bible', *Heythrop Journal*, XV (1974), 381–405.

Bercovitch, Susan, ed., *Typology and Early American Literature* (Amherst, 1972).

Bettenson, Henry, ed., *Documents of the Christian Church* (Oxford, 2/1963).

Betteridge, Thomas, *Histories of the English Reformations 1530–83* (Aldershot, 1996).

Blake, N. F., *Caxton and His World* (1969).

——, *Caxton's Own Prose* (1973).

——, *Caxton: England's First Publisher* (1976).

Bloom, Allan, *The Closing of the American Mind* (1987).

Bloom, Harold, *Shakesepeare: The Invention of the Human* (1999).

Bobrick, Benson, *Wide as the Waters* (New York, 2001).

Bode, Carl, *The Anatomy of Popular Culture* (Westport, Conn., 1949).

Bottigheimer, Ruth B., *The Bible for Children: From the Age of Gutenberg to the Present* (New Haven and London, 1996).

Bouyer, F. Louis, 'Erasmus in Relation to the Medieval Biblical Tradition', in Lampe, ed., 1969, 492–505.

Bradford, Ernle, *Drake* (1966).

Bradley, S. A. J., *Anglo-Saxon Poetry* (1982).

Bradshaw, Christopher, 'Scripture Reference in the Reign of Edward VI' (Ph.D. dissertation, University of St Andrews, 1997).

——, 'David or Josiah? Old Testament Kings as Exemplars in Edwardian Religious Polemic', in *Protestant History and Identity in Sixteenth-Century Europe*, ed. Bruce Gordon (Aldershot, 1996).

Brigden, Susan, *London and the Reformation* (Oxford, 1989).

Brogan, Hugh, *The Penguin History of the United States of America* (1985/90).

Brown, Carleton, ed. *English Lyrics of the XIIIth Century* (Oxford, 1932).

——, *Religious Lyrics of the XIVth Century*, rev. G. V. Smithers (Oxford, 2/1924).

Brownell, Morris R., 'Ears of an Untoward Make', *Musical Quarterly*, LXII (1976), 554–70.

Bruce, F. F., *The English Bible: A History of Translations* (1961).

Buell, Lawrence, *New England Literary Culture: From Revolution through Renaissance* (Cambridge, 1986).

Burr, Nelson R., *A Critical Bibliography of Religion in America*, 2 vols (Princeton, 1961).

Burrows, Donald, *Handel: Messiah* (Cambridge, 1991).

Butcher, Margaret Just, *The Negro in American Culture: Based on Material Left by Alan Locke* (New York, 1972).

Butterworth, Charles C., and Allan G. Chester, *George Joye (1495?–1553)* (Philadelphia, 1961).

——, *The Literary Lineage of the King James Bible* (Philadelphia, 1941).

Cadoux, C. J., 'The Revised Version and After', in Wheeler Robinson, ed., 1940, 235–74.

Cameron, Euan, *The European Reformation* (Oxford, 1991).

Carleton, J. G., *The Part of Rheims in the Making of the English Bible* (Oxford, 1902).

Carson, D. A., *The King James Version Debate* (Grand Rapids, 1979).

Carter, Stephen, *A Culture of Disbelief* (1993).

Cavallo, Guglielmo and Roger Chartier, eds, *A History of Reading in the West*, trans. Lydia G. Cochrane (Cambridge, 1999).

Chamberlin, William J., *Catalogue of English Bible Translations: A Classified Bibliography of Versions and Editions including Books, Parts, and Old and New Testament Apocrypha and Apocryphal Books* (Westport, Conn., 1991).

Chambers, R. W., *Thomas More* (1942).

Chambers, Talbot W., *A Companion to the Revised Old Testament* (New York, 1885).

Chew, Samuel C., *The Pilgrimage of Life* (New Haven and London, 1962).

Clebsch, William A., *England's Earliest Protestants 1520–1535* (New Haven and London, 1964).

Clemoes, Peter, 'The Chronology of Aelfric's Work', in *The Anglo-Saxons: Studies in Some Aspects of Their History and Culture Presented to Bruce Dickins*, ed. Clemoes, (1959), 245–6.

Cmeil, Kenneth, *Democratic Eloquence: The Fight over Popular Speech in Nineteenth-Century America* (New York, 1990).

Collinson, Patrick, *The Religion of Protestants: The Church in English Society 1559–1625* (Oxford, 1982).

——, *English Puritanism* (1983).

——, 'The Jacobean Religious Settlement: The Hampton Court Conference', in *Before the English Civil War: Essays on Early Stuart Politics and Government*, ed. Howard Tomlinson (1986), 27–52.

Cooper, W. R., 'Richard Hunne', *Reformation*, 1 (1996), 221–51.

———, 'John Trevisa, the Translator of Wycliffe B: A Consideration of the Evidence', *Reformation*, forthcoming.

Compagno, Dorothy U., *Distribution of the Scriptures in the U.S.A. 1861–1900*, ABS Historical Essay #14, Part VI-A; *The Civil War* (unpublished, American Bible Society, 1964).

Cowper, William, and John Newton, *Olney Hymns in Three Books* (2/1781).

Cranmer, Thomas, *Writings*, ed. J. E. Cox, 2 vols (Cambridge, 1844–6).

Cunliffe, Barry, *Facing the Ocean: The Atlantic and Its Peoples* (Oxford, 2001).

Daiches, David, *The King James Version* (1941).

Daniell, Christopher, *A Traveller's History of England* (Adlestrop, 1991, rev. 1996).

Daniell, David, *William Tyndale: A Biography* (New Haven and London, 1994).

———, 'Tyndale and Foxe', in *John Foxe: An Historical Perspective*, ed. David Loades (Aldershot, 1999), 15–28.

———, 'Shakespeare and the Protestant Mind', *Shakespeare Survey*, LIV (Cambridge, 2001), 1–12.

Darlow T. H., and Moule, H. F., *Historical Catalogue of the Printed Editions of Holy Scripture in the Library of the British and Foreign Bible Society*, I: *English*; II: *Polyglots and Languages Other than English* (1903–11).

Darlow, T. H., and Moule, H. F., rev. by A. S. Herbert, *Historical Catalogue of the Printed Editions of the English Bible, 1525–1961* (1968).

Davidson, Randall T., 'The Authorisation of the English Bible', *Macmillan's Magazine*, XLIV (1881), 436–44.

Davie, Donald, 'Psalmody as Translation', *Modern Language Review*, LXXXV (1990), 817–28.

Deanesley, Margaret, *The Lollard Bible and Other Medieval Versions* (Cambridge, 1920).

Deelman, Christian, *The Great Shakespeare Jubilee* (1964).

De Hamel, Christopher, *The Book: A History of the Bible* (2001).

Dewhurst, K., *John Locke (1632–1704): Physician and Philosopher* (1963).

Dickens, A. G., *Reformation and Society in Sixteenth-Century Europe* (1966).

———, *The English Reformation* (2/1989).

Douglas, Mary, *Purity and Danger* (1969).

Duerden, Richard, 'The Temporal and Spiritual Kingdoms: Tyndale's Doctrine and Its Practice', *Reformation*, 1 (1996), 118–28.

———, 'Justice and Justification: King and God in Tyndale's *Obedience of a Christian Man*', in *William Tyndale and the Law*, ed. Anne O'Donnell and John Day (Washington, DC, 1996), 69–80.

———, 'Equivalence or Power?: Authority and Reformation Bible Translation', in O'Sullivan and Herron, eds, 2000.

Duffy, Eamon, *The Stripping of the Altars: Traditional Religion in England c.1400–c.1580* (New Haven and London, 1992).

———, *Saints & Sinners: A History of the Popes* (New Haven and London, 1997).

Ellicott, C. J., *Addresses on the Revised Version of Holy Scripture* (1901).

English Wycliffite Sermons, 3 vols: I and III ed. Anne Hudson; II ed. Pamela Gradon (Oxford, 1983–90).

Faludy, George, *Erasmus of Rotterdam* (1980).

Feather, John, *A History of British Publishing* (1988).

Ferguson, Meraud Grant, 'English Printing and the Stationers' Company in the Sixteenth Century' (D.Phil. dissertation, University of Oxford, 2001).

Finley, C. Stephen, *Nature's Covenant: Figures of Landscape in Ruskin* (Philadelphia, 1992).

Ford, Boris, ed., *The Cambridge Guide to the Arts in Britain*, 9 vols (Cambridge, 1988).

Fowler, David C., *The Bible in Early English Literature* (Seattle and London, 1986).

——, *The Life and Times of John Trevisa, Medieval Scholar* (Seattle and London, 1995).

Fox, Everett, *The Five Books of Moses: A New Translation with Introductions, Commentary, and Notes* (New York, 1995).

Freeman, T. S., '"The Good Ministrye of Godlye and Vertuouse Women": The Elizabethan Martyrologists and the Female Supporters of the Marian Martyrs', *Journal of British Studies*, XXXIX (2000), 8–33.

Frerichs, Ernest S., *The Bible and Bibles in America* (1988).

Friedman, William F., and Elizabeth S. Friedman, *The Shakespearean Ciphers Examined* (Cambridge, 1957).

Frye, R. M., *Shakespeare and Christian Doctrine* (Princeton, 1963).

Gardner, Stanley, *Infinity on the Anvil: A Critical Study of Blake's Poetry* (Oxford, 1954).

Garraty, John A., *The American Nation: A History of the United States* (New York, 1968).

Garrett, Christina H., *The Marian Exiles: A Study in the Origins of Elizabethan Puritanism* (Cambridge, 1938, 2/1966).

Gaskell, Philip, *A New Introduction to Bibliography* (Oxford, 1974).

Glover, Richard: *'The Light of the World': or, Holman Hunt's Great Allegorical Picture Translated into Words* (1862/71).

Godbeer, Richard, *Sexual Revolution in Early America* (Baltimore, 2002).

Goldberg, Jonathan, *James I and the Politics of Literature* (Baltimore and London, 1983).

Green, M., *The Life and Death of Mr William Whittingham, Dean of Durham* (1871).

Greenslade, S. L., ed., *The Cambridge History of the Bible: The West from the Reformation to the Present Day* (Cambridge, 1963).

Gutjahr, Paul C., *An American Bible: A History of the Good Book in the United States, 1777–1889* (Stanford, 1999).

Hadfield, Andrew, 'The Revelation and Early English Colonial Ventures', in O'Sullivan and Herron, 2000, 145–56.

Haigh, Christopher, *Reformation and Resistance in Tudor Lancashire* (Cambridge, 1975).

——, ed., *The English Reformation Revised* (Cambridge, 1987).

——, *English Reformations: Religion, Politics and Society under the Tudors* (Oxford, 1993).

Hall, David D., 'Readers and Writers in Early New England' in Amory and Hall, 2000, 117–51.

Hamilton, Charles V., *The Black Preacher in America* (New York, 1972).

Hammond, Gerald, *The Making of the English Bible* (Manchester, 1982).

Hannay, Margaret P., ed., *Silent but for the Word* (Kent, Ohio, 1985).

Harbison, E. Harris, *The Christian Scholar in the Age of Reformation* (New York, 1956).

Hargreaves, Cecil, *A Translator's Freedom: Modern English Bibles and Their Language* (Sheffield, 1993).

Hargreaves, Henry, 'The Wycliffite Versions', in Lampe, ed., 1969, 387–415.

Harrison, Peter, *The Bible, Protestantism, and the Rise of Natural Science* (Cambridge, 2001).

Harte, W. J., ed., *Gleanings from the Commonplace book of John Hooker* (1926).

Hatch, Nathan G., and Mark A. Noll, eds, *The Bible in America: Essays in Cultural History* (New York, 1982).

Heimert, Alan, and Perry Miller, eds, *The Great Awakening: Documents Illustrating the Crisis and Its Consequences* (Indianapolis, 1967).

Hemphill, Samuel, *A History of the Revised Version of the New Testament* (1906).

Hill, Christopher, *A Turbulent, Seditious, and Factious People: John Bunyan and His Church, 1628–1688* (Oxford, 1988).

——, *The English Bible and the Seventeenth-Century Revolution* (1993).

Hills, Margaret T., *The English Bible in America: A Bibliography of Editions of the Bible & the New Testament Published in America 1777–1957* (New York, 1962).

——, 'The First American Bible: An Historical Preface', in *The Holy Bible, As Printed by Robert Aitken and Approved and Recommended by the Congress of the United States in 1782* (New York, 1968).

Hirsch, Mark J., Joseph F. Kett and James Trefil, eds, *The Dictionary of Cultural Literacy* (1988).

Hitchcock, Roswell D., *The New Testament [. . .] with the Readings and Renderings Preferred by the American Revision Committee* (New York, 1881).

Hitchin, Neil W., 'The Politics of English Bible Translation in Georgian Britain', *Royal Historical Society Transactions*, 6th ser., IX (1999), 67–92.

Hogwood, Christopher, *Handel* (1984).

Holden, William P., *Anti-Puritan Satire 1572–1642* (New Haven and London, 1954).

Hooker, Morna D., 'Tyndale's "Heretical" Translation', *Reformation*, II (1997), 127–42.

Hudson, Anne, *Lollards and Their Books* (London and Ronceverte, 1985).

——, *The Premature Reformation: Wycliffite Texts and Lollard History* (Oxford, 1988).

Hughes, Paul and James F. Larkin eds, *Tudor Royal Proclamations*.

Hunt, Geoffrey, *About the New English Bible* (Oxford and Cambridge, 1970).

Hunt, William Holman, *Pre-Raphaelitism and the Pre-Raphaelite Brotherhood* (1905).

Hunter, M. J., 'The Gothic Bible', in Lampe, ed., 1969, 338–62.

Hume, Anthea, *Edmund Spenser: Protestant Poet* (Cambridge, 1984).

Humphry, W. G., *A Commentary on the Revised Version of the New Testament* (1882).

Jaffee, David, *People of the Wachusett: Greater New England in History and Memory, 1630–1860* (Ithaca and London, 1999).

Jehlen, Myra, and Michael Warner, eds, *The English Literatures of America, 1500–1800* (1997).

Johnson, James Weldon, ed., *The Second Book of Negro Spirituals* (New York, 1926).

Kastan, David Scott, ' "The Noise of the New Bible": Reform and Reaction in Henrician England', in *Religion and Culture in Renaissance England*, ed. Claire McEachern and Debora Shuger (Cambridge, 1997), 46–68.

Kauffmann, C. M., *The Bible in British Art, 10th to 20th Centuries* (exhibition catalogue, Victoria and Albert Museum, September 1977).

Keane, John, *Tom Paine* (1995).

Keates, Jonathan, *Handel: The Man and His Music* (1985).

Keeble, N. H., *The Literary Culture of Nonconformity in Later Seventeenth-Century England* (Athens, Georgia, 1987).

——, *A Subject Index to the 'Calendar of the Correspondence of Richard Baxter'*, (Oxford, 1991, rev. enlarged 1994).

——, ed. *The Cambridge Companion to the Writing of the English Revolution* (Cambridge, 2001).

Kelsey, Harry, *Sir Francis Drake: The Queen's Pirate* (New Haven and London, 1998).

Kenny, Anthony, *Wyclif* (Oxford, 1985).

Kerr, John Stevens, *Ancient Texts Alive Today: The Story of the English Bible* (New York, 1999).

Keynes, Geoffrey, ed., *Poetry and Prose of William Blake* (1961).

Kiernan, Pauline, *Shakespeare's Theory of Drama* (Cambridge, 1996).

King, John N., *English Reformation Literature: The Tudor Origins of the Protestant Tradition* (Princeton, 1982).

——, *Tudor Royal Iconography: Literature and Art in the Age of Religious Crisis* (Princeton, 1989).

——, 'Recent Studies in Protestant Poetics', *English Literary Renaissance*, xxi (1991), 283–307.

——, 'Henry viii as David: The King's Image and Reformation Politics', in *Rethinking the Henrician Era: Essays on Early Tudor Texts and Contexts*, ed. Peter C. Herman (Urbana, 1993), 78–92.

——, 'James i and King David: Jacobean Iconography and Its Legacy', in *Royal Subjects: The Writings of James VI and I Reconsidered*, ed. Daniel Fischlin and Mark Fortier (Detroit, 2001).

Lacey, Robert, *Sir Walter Ralegh* (1973).

Lake, Peter, 'Religious Identities in Shakespeare's England', in *A Companion to Shakespeare*, ed. David Scott Kastan (Oxford, 1999), 57–84.

Lambourne, Lionel, *Victorian Painting* (1999).

Lampe, G. W. H., ed., *The Cambridge History of the Bible*, II: *The West from the Fathers to the Reformation* (Cambridge, 1969).

Lamont, William, *Puritanism and Historical Controversy* (1996).

Landon, H. C. Robbins, *Handel and his World* (Boston, 1984).

Landow, George P., *Replete with Meaning: William Holman Hunt and Typological Symbolism* (New Haven and London, 1979).

Lannie, Vincent P., and Bernard C. Diethorn, 'For the Honor and Glory of God: The Philadelphia Bible Riots of 1840', *History of Education Quarterly* (1968), 44–106.

Latré, Guido, 'The 1535 Coverdale Bible and Its Antwerp Origins', in O'Sullivan, and Herron, eds, 2000, 89–102.

Le Goff, Jacques, trans. A. Goldhammer, *The Birth of Purgatory* (1984).

Leites, Edmund, *The Puritan Conscience and Modern Sexuality* (New Haven and London, 1986).

Levine, Lawrence, *Black Culture and Black Consciousess: Afro-American Folk Thought from Slavery to Freedom* (1977).

Lewalksi, Barbara, *Protestant Poetics and the Seventeenth Century Religious Lyric* (Princeton, N.J., 1979).

——, *The Life of John Milton* (Oxford, 2000).

Lewis, C. S., *The Literary Impact of the Authorised Version* (1950).

——, *English Literature in the Sixteenth Century excluding Drama* (Oxford, 1954).

Lewis, Jack, *The English Bible from KJV to NIV: A History and Evaluation* (Grand Rapids, 1981).

Lightfoot, J. B., *On a Fresh Revision of the English New Testament* (1871).

Loewe, Raphael, 'The Medieval History of the Latin Vulgate', in Lampe, ed., 1969, 102–54.

MacCulloch, Diarmaid, 'The Impact of the English Reformation', *Historical Journal*, XXXVIII (1995), 151–4.

——, *Thornas Cranmer* (New Haven and London, 1996).

——, *Tudor Church Militant* (1999).

Mack, Maynard, *Alexander Pope: A Life* (New Haven and London, 1985).

Mackie, J. D., *A History of Scotland* (1964), rev. and ed. Bruce Lenman and Geoffrey Parker (New York, 2/1985).

Mangalwadi, Vishal and Ruth Mangalwadi, *The Legacy of William Carey: A Model for the Transformation of a Culture* (Wheaton, Illinois, 1993/9).

Marsden, G. M., 'Perry Miller's Rehabilitation of the Puritans: A Critique', *Church History*, XXXIX (1970), 91–105.

Marsden, Richard, '"Ask What I Am Called": The Anglo-Saxons and their Bibles', in Sharpe and Van Kampen, eds, 1998, 145–76.

McConica, James, *English Humanists and Reformation Politics* (1968).

——, *Erasmus* (Oxford, 1991).

McGrath, Alister E., *The Intellectual Origins of the European Reformation* (Oxford, 1987).

——, *Reformation Thought: An Introduction* (Oxford, 3/1999).

——, *In the Beginning: The Story of the King James Bible and How it Changed a Nation, a Language, and a Culture* (New York, 2001).

McGurk, Patrick, *Latin Gospel Books from A.D. 400 to A.D. 800* (Paris, 1961).

McLachan, H., 'An Almost Forgotten Pioneer in New Testament Criticism', *Hibbert Journal*, XXVII (1938–9), 617–25.

Meacham, Standish, *Lord Bishop: The Life of Samuel Wilberforce* (Cambridge, Mass., 1970).

Metzger, Bruce M., *The Text of the New Testament: Its Transmission, Corruption, and Restoration* (Oxford, 2/1968).

——, 'The Influence of Codex Bezae upon the Geneva Bible of 1560', *New Testament Studies*, VIII (1961–2), 72–7.

Middleton, Richard, *Colonial America: A History, 1585–1776* (Oxford, 2/1996).

Miller, Perry, 'The Garden of Eden and the Deacon's Meadow', *American Heritage*, VII (December 1955), 60.

——, *Errand into the Wilderness* (New York, 1956/64).

——, *Nature's Nation* (Cambridge, Mass., 1967).

Morrell, Minnie Cate, *A Manual of Old English Biblical Materials* (Knoxville, 1965).

Morris, Jeffrey B., and Richard B. Morris, *Encyclopedia of American History* (New York, 7/1996).

Mozley, J. F., *William Tyndale* (1937).

——, *Coverdale and His Bibles* (1953).

Nelson, William, *A Fifteenth-Century School Book from a Manuscript in the British Museum (MS Arundel 249)* (Oxford, 1956).

Newth, Samuel, *Lectures on Bible Revision* (1881).

Nida, Eugene A., and Charles R. Taber, *The Theory and Practice of Translation* (Leiden, 1974).

Nielson, John, and Royal Skousen, 'How Much of the King James Bible is William Tyndale's?', *Reformation*, III (1998), 49–74.

Nineham, Dennis, ed., *The New English Bible Reviewed* (1965).

Noble, Richmond, *Shakespeare's Biblical Knowledge* (1935).

Noll, Mark A., 'The Image of the United States as a Biblical Nation', in Hatch and Noll, eds, 1982, 39–58.

Norbrook, David, *Poetry and Politics in the English Renaissance* (1984).

Norton, David, *A History of the Bible as Literature*, I: *From Antiquity to 1700*; II: *From 1700 to the Present Day* (Cambridge, 1993); rev. and condensed in one volume as *A History of the English Bible as Literature* (Cambridge, 2000).

——, 'Noah Webster's 1833 Bible', *Reformation*, IV (1999), 197–230.

Nye, R. B., and J. E. Morpurgo, *A History of the United States*, I: *The Birth of the U. S. A.* (1955/70).

O'Day, Rosemary, *The Debate on the English Reformation* (1986).

Orme, Nicholas, *English Schools in the Middle Ages* (1973).

Orlinsky, Harry M., and Robert G. Bratcher, *A History of Bible Translation and the North American Contribution* (Atlanta, 1991).

O'Sullivan, Orlaith, and Ellen N. Herron, eds, *The Bible as Book: The Reformation* (2000).

Paine, Gustavus S., *The Learned Men* (New York, 1959).

Partridge, A. C., *English Biblical Translation* (1973).

Pettegree, Andrew, ed., *The Reformation World* (2000).

——, *Europe in the Sixteenth Century* (Oxford, 2002).

Piret, Michael, 'Herbert and Proverbs', *Cambridge Quarterly*, XVII (1988), 222–43.

Plomer, H. R., 'The King's Printing House under the Stuarts', *The Library*, 2nd ser., II (1909), 353–75.

Pollard, A. W. and G. R. Redgrave, *A Short-Title Catalogue of Books Printed in England, Scotland, & Ireland and of English Books Printed Abroad 1475–1640*, rev. and enlarged, begun by W. A. Jackson and F. S. Ferguson, completed by Katharine A. Pantzer, 3 vols (2/1996).

Poole, Kristen, *Radical Religion from Shakespeare to Milton: Figures of Nonconformity in Early Modern England* (Cambridge, 2000).

Pope, Very Revd Hugh, OP, rev. and amplified Revd Sebastian Bullough, OP, *English Versions of the Bible* (New York and London, 1952).

Raine, Kathleen, *William Blake* (1970).

——, *The Human Face of God: William Blake and the Book of Job* (1982).

Reformation (Oxford and Aldershot, 1996–).

Robertson, E. H., *New Translations of the Bible* (1990).

Robinson, Ian, *The Survival of English* (Cambridge, 1973).

——, *The Establishment of Modern English Prose in the Reformation and the Enlightenment* (Cambridge, 1998).

Robinson, H. Wheeler, ed., *The Bible in Its Ancient and English Versions* (Oxford, 1940).

Routley, Eric, *Hymns and Human Life* (1952).

Ryrie, Alec, 'Persecution, Survival and Compromise: English Protestantism and The State 1539–47' (M. Litt. dissertation, University of St Andrews, 1994).

——, *The Gospel and Henry VIII* (Cambridge, 2003).

Salway, Peter, 'The Cultural and Social Setting', in Ford, ed., 1988, I, 30–48.

Sanders, E. P., and Margaret Davies, *Studying the Synoptic Gospels* (1989).

Scarisbrick, J. J., *Henry VIII* (Berkeley, Calif., 1968).

Schlenther, Boyd Stanley, *Charles Thomson: A Patriot's Pursuit* (Newark, Delaware, 1990).

Scrivener, F. H. A., *The Authorised Version of the English Bible (1611)* (Cambridge, 1884).

Shaheen, Naseeb, *Biblical References in Shakespeare's Plays* (Newark, Delaware, 1999).

Shea, John Gilmary, *A Bibliographical Account of Catholic Bibles, Testaments, and Other Portions of Scripture* (New York, 1859).

Shepherd, Geoffrey, 'English Versions of the Scriptures before Wyclif', in Lampe, ed., 1969, 362–87.

Schaff, Philip, *A Companion to the English Testament and the Greek Version* (1883).

Sharpe, John L. and Kimberly Van Kampen, eds, *The Bible as Book: The Manuscript Tradition* (London and Delaware, 1998).

Shuger, Deborah K., 'Subversive Faiths and Suffering Subjects: Shakespeare and Christianity', in *Religion, Literature and Politics in Post-Reformation England, 1540–1688*, ed. Donna B. Hamilton and Richard Strier (Cambridge, 1996), 46–69.

Silver, James W., *Confederate Morale and Church Propaganda* (Gloucester, Mass., 1964).

Slavin, A. J., 'The Rochepot Affair', *Sixteenth Century Journal*, x (1979), 3–19.

Smalley, Beryl, *The Study of the Bible in the Middle Ages* (Oxford, 1941).

Smeeton, Donald, *Lollard Themes in the Reformation Theology of William Tyndale* (Kirksville, 1984).

Smith, Ruth, 'Intellectual Contexts of Handel's English Oratorios', in *Music in Eighteenth Century England: Essays in Memory of Charles Cudworth*, ed. Christopher Hogwood and Richard Luckett (Cambridge, 1983), 115–33.

——, 'The Achievements of Charles Jennens (1700–1773)', *Music and Letters*, LXX (1989), 161–89.

Sparks, H. F. D., 'The Latin Bible', in H. Wheeler Robinson, ed., 1940, 100–27.

Spellman, W. A., *John Locke* (1997).

Steinberg, S. H., *Five Hundred Years of Printing*, rev. James Moran (Harmondsworth, 3 / 1974).

Strype, John, *The Life and Acts of Matthew Parker* (1711), ed. (Oxford, 1821).

Swanston, Hamish, *Handel* (1990).

Szewczyk, David, *39 Books and Broadsides Printed in America before the Bay Psalm Book*, rev. Cynthia Davies Buffington (Philadelphia, 1989).

The Bible Translator (London and New York, 1950–).

Thomas, Charles, *Christianity in Roman Britain to AD 500* (1981).

Thompson, W. D. J. Cargill, 'The Two Regiments: The Continental Setting of William Tyndale's Political Thought', in *Reform and Reformation: England and the Continent c. 1599–c. 1750*, ed. Derek Baker (Oxford, 1979).

Thuesen, Peter J., *In Discordance with the Scriptures: American Protestant Battles over Translating the Bible* (New York, 1999).

Thurman, Howard, *The Negro Spiritual Speaks of Life and Death: Being the Ingersoll Lecture on the Immortality of Man, 1947* (New York, 1947).

Tyacke, Nicholas, ed., *England's Long Reformation, 1500–1800* (1998).

Tyler, Moses C., *A History of American Literature* (New York, 1980).

Vance, Laurence M., *Archaic Words in the Authorized Version* (Pensecola, 1996/99).

Verey, Christopher, 'A Northumbrian Text Family', in Sharpe and Van Kampen, eds, 1998, 105–22.

Vickers, Brian, *Shakespeare: The Critical Heritage, 1693–1801*, 6 vols (1974–81).

Watson, J. R., *The English Hymn* (Oxford, 1997).

Watson, Nicholas, 'Censorship and Cultural Change in Late-Medieval England: Vernacular Theology, the Oxford Translation Debate, and Arundel's Constitutions of 1409', *Speculum*, LXX (1995), 822–64.

Weigle, Luther A., *The English New Testament: From Tyndale to the Revised Standard Version* (1950).

——, 'English Versions since 1611', in Greenslade, ed., 1963, 361–82.

——, *An Introduction to the Revised Standard Version of the Old Testament by Members of the Revision Committee* (1952).

Wenzel, Siegfried, *Preachers, Poets and the Early English Lyric* (Princeton, NJ, 1986).

Werrell, Ralph, 'The Theology of William Tyndale' (Ph.D. dissertation, University of Hull, 2002).

Westbrook, Vivienne, 'Richard Taverner Revising Tyndale', *Reformation*, II (1997), 191–205.

Westcott, Arthur, *Life and Letters of Brooke Foss Westcott* (1903).

Westcott, B. F., *A General View of the History of the English Bible* (1868), rev. W. A. Wright (3/1905).

——, *Some Lessons of the Revised Version of the New Testament* (1897).

Westcott, B. F. and F. J. A. Hort, *The New Testament in the Original Greek*, 2 vols (Cambridge, 1881).

Whale, J. S., *The Protestant Tradition: An Essay in Interpretation* (Cambridge, 1955).

White, B. R., *The English Separatist Tradition: From the Marian Martyrs to the Pilgrim Fathers* (Oxford, 1971).

White, James R., *The King James Only Controversy: Can You Trust the Modern Translations?* (Minneapolis, 1995).

Wilkinson, Robert J., 'Reconstructung Tyndale in Latomus: William Tyndale's Last, Lost, Book', *Reformation*, I (1996), 252–85, 345–400.

Williams, Arnold, *The Common Expositor: An Account of the Commentaries on Genesis, 1527–1633* (Chapel Hill, 1948).

Williams, Aubrey, *Pope's Dunciad: A Study of Its Meaning* (1956).

Williams, Hugh, *Christianity in Early Britain* (Oxford, 1912).

Willoughby, Harold R., *Soldiers' Bibles through Three Centuries* (Chicago, 1944).

Winship, George Parker, *The Cambridge Press, 1638–1692: A Reexamination of the Evidence concerning the Bay Psalm Book and the Eliot Bible as well as Other Contemporary Books and People* (Philadelphia, 1945).

Wosh, Peter J., *Spreading the Word: The Bible Business in Nineteenth-Century America* (Ithaca, NY, 1994).

Wright, John, *Early Bibles of America: Being a Descriptive Account of Bibles Published in the United States, Mexico and Canada* (New York, 1894).

Wright, Louis B., *Religion and Empire: The Alliance between Piety and Commerce in English Expansions, 1558–1625* (1943).

Zim, Rivkah, *English Metrical Psalms: Poetry as Praise and Prayer* (1987).

Index

Photograph Credits

1, 15: Courtesy of Württembergische
Landesbibliothek, Stuttgart. Photo: Joachim
Siener; 2: J. M. C. Toynbee, 'Christianity in
Roman Britain', *Journal of the British
Archaeological Association*, 3rd series, XVI (1953),
p. 3; 3: Barry Cunliffe, *Facing the Ocean*,
Oxford University Press, 2001, p. 472;
4: reproduced by permission of Biblioteca
Medicea Laurenziana, Firenze. Photo:
MicroFoto; 5: reproduced by permission of
Corpus of Anglo-Saxon Stone Sculpture,
Department of Archaeology, Durham
University. Photo: T. Middlemass; 6, 7, 8, 9, 10,
13, 19, 21, 24, 6, 27, 29, 30, 35, 47: reproduced
by permission of The British Library;
12, 14: reproduced by kind permission of
Dr Joe Johnson, Paxton, Florida;
16, 43: reproduced by permission of the
National Portrait Gallery, London;
17: reproduced by permission of Trinity
College Library, Cambridge; 18: reproduced
by kind permission of The Council for the
Care of Churches); 20, 22: reproduced by

permission of Lambeth Palace Library;
23: Stanley Morison, *La Bible Anglaise de
Geneve*, 1972, p. 63; 25, 36, 38: reproduced by
permission of The Huntington Library,
San Marino, California; 28: copyright David
Daniell; 31: ©Private Collection/Bridgeman
Art Library; 32: reproduced by kind
permission of Christ Church, Philadelphia;
33: courtesy of the Lilly Library, Indiana
University, Bloomington, Indiana;
34: reproduced by permission of Beinecke
Rare Book and Manuscript Library, Yale
University; 39: reproduced by permission of
Iowa State University Library); 40: courtesy
of Tate, London); 41: reproduced by
permission of the Warden and Fellows, Keble
College, Oxford; 42: reproduced by
permission of the National Maritime
Museum, Greenwich; 44: Photo © AP/Wide
World Photos; 45: reproduced by permission
of the American Bible Society; 46: from
Rob Snuggs, *The Comic Book Bible*, Barbour
Publishing, Uhrichville, Ohio, 1995